Handbook of
Health
Administration
and Policy

PUBLIC ADMINISTRATION AND PUBLIC POLICY

A Comprehensive Publication Program

Executive Editor

JACK RABIN
Professor of Public Administration and Public Policy
School of Public Affairs
The Capital College
The Pennsylvania State University—Harrisburg
Middletown, Pennsylvania

ANNALS OF PUBLIC ADMINISTRATION

Handbook of Health Administration and Policy

edited by

Anne Osborne Kilpatrick
James A. Johnson

Medical University of South Carolina
Charleston, South Carolina

MARCEL DEKKER, INC.   NEW YORK · BASEL

Library of Congress Cataloging-in-Publication Data

Handbook of health administration and policy / edited by Anne Osborne
  Kilpatrick, James A. Johnson
      p. cm. – (Public administration and public policy ; 70)
    Includes bibliographical references (p.   ) and index.
    ISBN 0-8247-0221-2
    1. Health services administration—Handbooks, manuals, etc.
  2. Medical policy—Handbooks, manuals, etc. 3. Medical care-
  -Handbooks, manuals, etc.   I. Kilpatrick, Anne Osborne.
  II. Johnson, James A.   III. Series.
  RA427.H29   1998
  362.1'068—dc21

                                                              98-37296
                                                              CIP

This book is printed on acid-free paper.

Headquarters
Marcel Dekker, Inc.
270 Madison Avenue, New York, NY 10016
tel: 212-696-9000; fax: 212-685-4540

Eastern Hemisphere Distribution
Marcel Dekker AG
Hutgasse 4, Postfach 812, CH-4001 Basel, Switzerland
tel: 44-61-261-8482; fax: 44-61-261-8896

World Wide Web
http://www.dekker.com

The publisher offers discounts on this book when ordered in bulk quantities. For more information, write to Special Sales/Professional Marketing at the headquarters address above.

Current printing (last digit):
10 9 8 7 6 5 4 3 2 1

PRINTED IN THE UNITED STATES OF AMERICA

To the memory of Sara Nelle (Sally) Osborne, for her contributions and service as a community leader and "professional volunteer" to the health care of others. Her commitment to making the world better set an example for those who knew her. We hope this book will provide some toward realizing that dream.

FOREWORD

The effective delivery of health care services is a work in progress. I have been both an observer and participant in this process during the second half of the twentieth century and change has been constant and dramatic. We have seen the development of a health care system described as the best in the world and, at the same time, criticized as too costly, inefficient and inadequate in providing care to all citizens.

We have seen government move from a minor participant in health matters to the largest purchaser of health services in our nation. We have witnessed regulation tried as the primary controlling factor for cost and quality and now the apparent shifting of health care into the private sector marketplace.

As we approach the twenty-first century the question as to the social obligation of health care providers is heard repeatedly. The appropriate role for physicians in our evolving delivery system is debated and unresolved. As we seek to minimize variance in the provision of health services both clinically and logistically, we appear to be making wellness our primary emphasis rather than depending on acute, episodic care as our standard for improving the general health status of our people.

In any case, the fact that we must have effective executives and managers to lead us through the maze of continuing change is clear. These individuals will need both natural skills and developed abilities. They will need to understand the changing science of medicine, the principles of public health, the use of computer technology and they will surely need solid values, human insight and a strong social conscience.

This timely handbook on health administration and policy should prove to be a helpful tool for leaders as well as those who join them in working for constant improvement in the way we provide health services to our people.

D. Kirk Oglesby, FACHE
Anderson Area Medical Center
Anderson, South Carolina

ACKNOWLEDGEMENTS

Given the magnitude of an undertaking like this book, there were many people involved. The chapter authors worked hard to assure their material would be timely and relevant to readers across a broad spectrum of the worlds of practice and academia. Additionally, the associate and assistant editors were undaunted by the many challenges of working in that netherworld between us the editors, the authors, and the publisher. The reviewers also had a special role in assuring quality and refinement in each chapter. Our hats are off and our hearts are full with gratitude for the wonderful spirit of hard work and commitment each of these authors, editors, and reviewers brought to this project. We also need to acknowledge the many behind-the-scenes staff people at the Medical University of South Carolina for their quieter but all important role. We have traveled a long road in order to bring this book to you. Our hope now is that you gain as much from reading it as we have in experiencing the journey.

-Anne Osborne Kilpatrick and James A. Johnson

Reviewers also included:

Patricia Alt
Roger Amidon
Charles Austin
Joy Clay
Roslyn Ferrell
Greer Gay
Saundra Glover
David Graber
Mary Ellen Guy
Regina Hall
Stephanie Hill
Patricia Holsclaw
Kathi Kelly
Judith Kirchhoff
Nancy Lawhead

Fran Lee
Michael Levy
Joe Linder
Brian Martin
Michael Matthews
Shawn McMillan
Alysia Olshinski
Bonnie Rogers
Douglas Singh
Genie Stowers
Gary Tencer
Glenda Lee Thompson
Karen Wager
Barry Weisglass

CONTENTS

The Health Care Delivery System

Social, Legal and Ethical Issues

PART II   THE ADMINISTRATION OF HEALTH CARE

Managing Strategy and Change

CONTRIBUTORS

Editors
Anne Osborne Kilpatrick
James A. Johnson

Associate Editors
Regina Hall
Patricia W. Holsclaw
Glenda Lee Thompson

Assistant Editors
Roslyn Ferrell
Kathleen Gesehues

Graphic Designer/Typesetting
Lesley M. White

Contributors
William E. Aaronson, Ph.D., Temple University, Department of Health Administration, School of Business Management, Philadelphia, PA

John R. Adams, Ph.D., Western Carolina University, College of Business, Cullowhee, NC

Patricia M. Alt, Ph.D., Towson State University, Department of Health Science, Towson, MD

Charles J. Austin, Ph.D., Medical University of South Carolina, Department of Health Administration and Policy, Charleston, SC

Edward R. Balotsky, M.B.A., Winthrop University, Department of Management and Marketing, College of Business Administration, Rock Hill, SC

Robert L. Barber, C.M.A., F.H.F.M.A., M.A.P.A., CMPA, Carolinas Hospital Network, Director of Managed Care, Charlotte, NC

Judith T. Barr, Sc.D., Northeastern University, National Education and Research Center for Outcomes Assessment in Health Care, Boston, MA

Thomas J. Barth, Ph.D., University of Memphis, Memphis, TN

Lynn W. Beasley, Newberry County Memorial Hospital, Newberry, SC

Stuart B. Boxerman, D.Sc., Washington University School of Medicine, Health Administration Program, St. Louis, MO

Mark S. Boyd, M.H.A., Ovation Healthcare Research, Highland Park, IL

Suzan D. Boyd, Dr.P.H., M.M., M.S., University of South Carolina, Department of Health Administration and Policy, School of Public Health, Columbia, SC

Thomas E. Brown, M.B.A., Richland Memorial Hospital, Columbia, SC

Roger J. Bulger, M.D., Association of Academic Health Centers, Washington, DC

Ruth Ellen Bulger, Ph.D., Uniformed Services University of the Health Sciences, Office of Research, Bethesda, MD

Leon Burton, M.H.A., Franklin C. Fetter Health Center, Charleston, SC

Roseann Carothers, M.H.A., M.B.A., Care Alliance Medical Services Organization, Department of Network Development, Charleston, SC

Joy A. Clay, Ph.D., University of Memphis, Department of Political Science, Graduate Program in Health Administration, Memphis, TN

Catherine M. Crawford, Ph.D., National Health Information Center, Washington, DC

Ken Czisny, Ph.D., California Lutheran University, School of Business, Thousand Oaks, CA

Rebekah Damazo, R.N., M.S.N., P.H.N., California State University, School of Nursing, Chico, CA

Krishna S. Dhir, Ph.D., Pennsylvania State University at Harrisburg, School of Business Administration, Middletown, PA

Evelyn T. Dravecky, Ph.D., University of California Los Angeles School of Medicine, Los Angeles, CA

Dale S. Duncan, R.N., Anderson Area Medical Center, Clinical Performance Measurement, Anderson, SC

Zakiyyah El'Amin, R.N., M.P.H., Alameda County Department of Public Health, Office of AIDS Administration, Oakland, CA

Gerald Eldridge, Georgia State University, Atlanta, GA

Veronica Elliott, M.P.H., Birch and Davis Associates, Inc., Health Policy Group, Silver Spring, MD

Esther M. Forti, Ph.D., R.N., Medical University of South Carolina, Department of Health Administration and Policy, Charleston, SC

Myron D. Fottler, Ph.D., The University of Alabama at Birmingham, Department of Health Services Administration, School of Health-Related Professions, Birmingham, AL

Bruce J. Fried, Ph.D., University of North Carolina at Chapel Hill, Department of Health Policy and Administration, School of Public Health, Chapel Hill, NC

Leonard H. Friedman, Ph.D., M.P.H., Oregon State University, Department of Public Health, College of Health and Human Performance, Corvallis, OR

Donna L. Gellatly, M.B.A., FHFMA, C.P.A., Financial HealthCare Associates, Palos Hills, IL

Robert T. Golembiewski, Ph.D., University of Georgia, Athens, GA

David R. Graber, Ph.D., Medical University of South Carolina, Department of Health Administration and Policy, Charleston, SC

Howard P. Greenwald, Ph.D., University of Southern California, Sacramento Center, Sacramento, CA

Mary E. Guy, Ph.D., Florida State University, Department of Political Science and Public Affairs, Tallahassee, FL

Kent P. Hill, Memphis VA Medical Center, Memphis, TN

Patricia W. Holsclaw, M.H.A., Medical University of South Carolina, Department of Health Administration and Policy, College of Health Professions, Charleston, SC

Barbara J. Holt, Ph.D., West Virginia University, Center for Aging, School of Medicine, Morgantown, WV

David M. Hunt, M.S.P.H., C.I.H., Medical University of South Carolina, Environmental Health Sciences, Charleston, SC

James A. Johnson, Ph.D., Medical University of South Carolina, Department of Health Administration and Policy, Charleston, SC

Frederick G. Jones, M.D., Anderson Area Medical Center, Anderson, SC

Jacqueline K. Jones, M.H.A., Medical University of South Carolina, Department of Human Resources, Charleston, SC

Lauren Jones, Ph.D., Organizational Learning Group, Mt. Pleasant, SC

Leslie Jones, South Carolina Department of Insurance, Life and Health, Columbia, SC

R. Martin Jones, Ph.D., Medical University of South Carolina, Health Administration and Policy, Charleston, SC

Walter J. Jones, Ph.D., Medical University of South Carolina, Department of Health Administration and Policy, Charleston, SC

Arnold D. Kaluzny, Ph.D., Research University of North Carolina at Chapel Hill, Department of Health Policy and Administration, School of Public Health, Chapel Hill, NC

Thomas W. Kent, Ph.D., Consultant, Charleston, SC

Bruce W. Kieler, Dr.P.H., University of California, Berkeley, CA

Anne Osborne Kilpatrick, D.P.A., Medical University of South Carolina, Department of Health Administration and Policy, Charleston, SC

Judith J. Kirchhoff, Ph.D., Long Island University, School of Business, Public Administration and Information Services, Brooklyn, NY

Yvonne J. Kochanowski, M.B.A., M.P.A., Steel Edge Business Consulting, Placerville, CA

Dale Krane, Ph.D., University of Nebraska at Omaha, Department of Public Administration, Omaha, NE

Rhonda Walker Mack, Ph.D., College of Charleston, School of Business and Economics Charleston, SC

Evelyn P. Mahairas, Ph.D., L.S.W., D.C.S.W., B.C.D., VA Medical Center, Coatesville, PA

Brian C. Martin, Ph.D., East Tennessee State University, Department of Public Health, Johnson City, TN

Toni Marzotto, Ph.D., Towson State University, Department of Health Science and Department of Political Science, Towson, MD

Margaret F. Mastal, Ph.D., R.N., Kaiser Permanente, Clinical Coordinator--Specialties, Springfield, VA

Thomas McIlwain, Ph.D., Medical University of South Carolina, Charleston, SC

Wes McKenna, M.H.A., Care Alliance Medical Services Organization, Charleston, SC

Reagan McLaurin, Ph.D., Western Carolina University, College of Business, Cullowhee, NC

David M. Mirvis, M.D., University of Tennessee Medical School, Memphis, Department of Preventive Medicine, College of Medicine, Memphis, TN

Kenneth H. Mulholland, Jr., M.S., VA Medical Center, Memphis, TN

Larry A. Mullins, M.A., Good Samaritan Hospital, Corvallis, OR

Margaret A. Neale, Ph.D., Stanford University, Graduate School of Business, Stanford, CA

John F. Newman, Ph.D., Georgia State University, Institute of Health Administration, College of Business Administration, Atlanta, GA

Meredith A. Newman, Ph.D., Washington State University, Department of Political Science, Vancouver, WA

Alysia Olshinski, M.H.A., Medical University of South Carolina, Department of Health Administration and Policy, Charleston, SC

Vincent Omachonu, Ph.D., P.E., University of Miami, Department of Industrial Engineering, Coral Gables, FL

Jo Ann Ott, P.A.C., Research Associate, School of Health Administration and Policy, Arizona State University, Tempe, AZ

Jeffrey T. Polzer, Ph.D., University of Texas, Department of Management, Austin, TX

Joanne C. Preston, Ph.D., Pepperdine University, Culver City, CA

Kathleen M. Reding, Ph.D., Western Michigan University, School of Public Affairs and Administration, Kalamazoo, MI

Mary L. Richardson, Ph.D., M.H.A., University of Washington, Graduate Program in Health Services Administration, Seattle, WA

Elliott C. Roberts, Sr., M.H.A., Louisiana State University Medical School, Health Systems Research and Public Health, Baton Rouge, LA

Elaine Rubin, Ph.D., Association of Academic Health Centers, Washington, DC

James V. Salvo, Jr., C.P.A., M.B.A., Medical University of South Carolina, Department of Health Administration and Policy, Charleston, SC

Michel E. Samuels, Dr.P.H., University of South Carolina, Department of Health Administration, School of Public Health, Columbia, SC

Ishak Saporta, Ph.D., Tel Aviv University, Tel Aviv, Israel

Grant T. Savage, Ph.D., Texas Tech University, Graduate Program in Health Organization Management, College of Business Administration, Lubbock, TX

Eugene S. Schneller, Ph.D., Arizona State University, School of Health Administration and Policy, College of Business, Tempe, AZ

Leiyu Shi, Dr.P.H., M.B.A., M.P.A., University of South Carolina, Department of Health Administration, School of Public Health, Columbia, SC

Erin Silva, B.S.W., Medical University of South Carolina, Center for Rural Health Studies, Charleston, SC

John Simmons, M.D., Employees Health Plan, Spartanburg, SC

David Snyder, M.A., Medical University of South Carolina, Department of Health Administration and Policy, Charleston, SC

Carleen Stofkopf, Sc.D., University of South Carolina, Department of Health Administration, School of Public Health, Columbia, SC

Genie N. L. Stowers, Ph.D., San Francisco State University, Public Administration Program, San Francisco, CA

Denise Strong, Ph.D., University of New Orleans, College of Urban and Public Affairs, New Orleans, LA

Rosemary L. Taylor, C.P.A., M.B.A., Texas Tech University Health Sciences Center, Office of Managed Care, Lubbock, TX

Winfield C. Towles, M.D., The Horizon Group, Inc., Mt. Pleasant, SC

J. Larry Tyler, FACHE, FAAHC, FHFMA, Tyler and Company, Atlanta, GA

Mary Ellen Uphoff, M.P.H., R.N., B.S.N., University of Nebraska Medical Center, Omaha, NE

David M. Ward, Ph.D., Medical University of South Carolina, Department of Health Administration and Policy, Charleston, SC

Andrea W. White, M.H.S.A., Ph.D. Candidate, Medical University of South Carolina, Department of Health Administration and Policy, Charleston, SC

Thomas M. Wilson, Ph.D., Auburn University at Montgomery, Air University Graduate Program, Montgomery, AL

M. Elizabeth Woodard, M.H.A., Ph.D. Candidate, University of Alabama at Birmingham, Health Services Program, Birmingham, AL

Handbook of
Health
Administration
and Policy

INTRODUCTION

In an era of major social and cultural change, many challenges compel us to manage health organizations and policy with greater efficiency, effectiveness and value. This period, at the cusp of the millennium, offers opportunities unique in the history of our society. Specifically, the health care leader can participate in the refinement of what many would deem the "best health care system in the world." However, to prepare for an effective role in this exciting time, policy makers, managers and professionals in health services will need new knowledge, tools, skills and particularly new perspectives. The exponential increases in information, technology, and science contribute to the profound need for a commitment to lifelong learning. By making this commitment, the health care leader is better able to do this important work and benefit from its many rewards.

What is in the future of health care? As of this writing, issues which should affect our nation's health policy include the tremendous organizational changes reflected in mergers, networks, and affiliations. There is increasing involvement of funding agencies in the direct provision of services. Policy continues to be shaped by forces and events in the greater society: governmental investigations of the world's largest investor-owned health care corporation; the re-engineering of Medicare and Medicaid; changes in health professions education; professionalization and deprofessionalization of multi-skilled employees; the fragile future of rural and inner-city public hospitals; influences of managed care on provision, funding, configuration of providers and services; and a call from communities for more involvement in improving their health status.

As one of the largest sectors of our economy, health care accounts for about one-fifth of the nation's GNP. Even with increasing scrutiny from all levels of government and the private sector, growth in this arena continues to escalate. Thus, health care administrators are placed in an increasingly influential and challenging role. The enormous scale of the health care system is coupled with an increasingly complex environment containing competition, regulation, technology, advances in medical sciences, changing demographics, and tumultuous diversity in resources. This environment offers the health services administrator a range of challenges and opportunities. However, to be effective the administrator will need a comprehensive understanding of health care policy, health services delivery and organization, and health care management.

This comprehensive text offers a broad view of the three areas described above and is designed to serve as a companion reference for academic texts in health care management, as well as to provide an overview for practitioners and a manual for those involved in health administration. This handbook specifically addresses US health policy and administration. Contributors have compiled chapters which contain additional references for readers and which should extend the information-seeking process for readers.

This handbook should serve as an important resource for administrators, as well as health care managers, executives, policy makers and students. The educational experience of working on a book of this magnitude, in a field which changes with the publication of every day's news, has provided a renewed respect for those who choose to serve in the field of improving health status for all of us. We have included contributions from scholars in the academic arena, as well as leading practitioners developing and implementing policy and practice.

Several significant areas of health policy and practice were deliberately omitted due to rapidly changing knowledge that would preclude a timely and useful inclusion in this handbook. Other publications in this handbook series are forthcoming and will address these and many other policy and administrative issues. Specifically, this handbook does not address in any significant way the following subject areas: compensation, labor relations, and mental health administration. However, there is a significant body of work available elsewhere on these subjects.

What we realized was that this book needed to be completed. Although there will always be more to write, particularly in this field, it was time to move forward and share this work. The reader will find the book is divided into three parts: the Environment of Health Care, the Administration of Health Care, and the Future of Health Care. Each of these sections is divided into chapter clusters that parallel the range of knowledge and expertise needed by students and practitioners. The chapters within each subsection were selected based on the usefulness of the information and the relevant expertise of the contributing authors.

Anne Osborne Kilpatrick
James A. Johnson

1.
U. S. SOCIETY AND ITS HEALTH SERVICES ORGANIZATIONS

Walter J. Jones, *Medical University of South Carolina, Charleston, SC*

John Simmons, *Employees Health Plan, Spartanburg, SC*

For much of the world, the Twentieth Century has brought impressively rapid socioeconomic advances (along with, of course, some unpleasant correlates, such as persistent and occasionally cataclysmic warfare). Within this framework of progress, the exceptional form and scope of development in the United States is commonly accepted and frequently commented upon by historians and social commentators (Bell, 1973). The formation and evolution of the U. S. health care system fits into this pattern of unique social evolution.

Of course, observers certainly differ as to whether or not all of these differences have resulted in "better" or "worse" health care organization and service delivery than is found, for example, in Canada or major Western European nations such as Germany (Rothman, 1993; Reinhardt, 1994). From the standpoint of overall resource availability, technological capabilities, and clinical sophistication, the U. S. health care system is clearly the best in history. On the other hand, it has performance gaps and inefficiencies that make its operational effectiveness uneven at best (Hsiao, 1993).

A broad description of the U. S. system captures some of its complex and contradictory nature. Health care employs more individuals, and is the third largest economic sector in the nation (Mick and Moscovice, 1993; Koch, 1993). Yet there is no overall organizational plan, or budget, for all of these activities. Americans like to think of their health care system as part of the private sector, and have continually rejected efforts to establish national health insurance or a national health service. Yet the proportion of total health care financing that comes from state and local governments is approximately 44%, and rising (Levit et al., 1994). Most U. S. health insurance is generally not really "insurance" as the word is commonly taken, but prepayment for services. As a result, individuals increasingly complain about the cost of care, but usually have no idea of how much any given service actually costs to produce. Until recently, even the producers of many services could not clearly relate their outputs to expenses (Feldstein, 1993).

While the U. S. system is increasingly characterized by the development of national health care provider organizations, most health care regulation is still the responsibility of the states. The states, in turn, heavily rely on the self-regulatory efforts of providers and professionals (Brown, 1994). Americans are generally intensely nationalistic and think of their nation as a world apart from other nations, yet U. S. health care has almost no national uniformity. The U. S. has the finest clinical facilities in the world, and, yet, relying on lavishly funded and educated medical "scientists", experiences huge variations in actual clinical practice patterns and outcomes (Wennberg, 1984; Chassin et al., 1986). More than in almost any other wealthy nation, treatment is highly dependent upon where one lives, one's age, one's income, and, especially, the nature of one's employer (Torrens, 1993). Any generalization about U. S. health services must admit to almost endless exceptions and amendment.

I. U. S. HEALTH SERVICES, PAST AND PRESENT

The U. S. health services system has, historically speaking, gone through three major evolutionary stages. It is fair to say that the current systemwide turbulence and structural flux signals the beginning of a fourth major period of change (Table 1).

Until around 1850, there was little health care anywhere, in the sense that medical practice was not clearly linked to a scientifically-established body of knowledge. The

Table 1 - The Development of U.S. Healthcare, 1700s to the Present

Time Period	1700s-1850	1850-1945	1945-1975	1975-1996
Scientific Development	Low	Rapid Growth	Rapid Growth	Rapid Growth
Service Delivery	Individual Physician	Individual physician, hospital	Individual physicians, group practices, hospitals	Individual physicians, group practices, hospitals, HMOs networks
Delivery Location	Home, "Hospital" (for poor)	Doctor's office, hospitals	Doctor's office, group practices, hospitals	Doctor's office, clinics, hospitals
Development Features	Pre-scientific	Development of clinical sanitation, study of microorganisms, growth of hospitals and academic medical centers	Growth of private (BC-BS) and public (Medicare, Medicaid) insurance	Movement toward network development, cost containment and managed care

best of what passed for health care at that time existed in the larger cities of Europe. Wealthy Americans travelled abroad to get the best care, or engaged the services of the best available physicians in their homes. Only the poor willingly went to hospitals for care since they were rife with infectious diseases and unskilled personnel.

During the next ninety-five years, the world was transformed by the Industrial Revolution. From 1850 until the end of World War II, health care was transformed through the growing application of science. Armed with the discovery of microorganisms by Pasteur and others, health practitioners developed viable practices of sterilization and purification, which dramatically increased the effectiveness of treatment (Ackernecht, 1973). Practical applications of clinical sanitation, developed by such pioneers as Florence Nightingale, meant that hospitals need no longer endanger their patients with infection and pestilence (Ashley, 1976).

Along with those in other nations, U. S. medical facilities and personnel radically improved their operations. The process of industrialization also meant urbanization, so cities such as Boston, New York and Philadelphia grew rapidly. It was correspondingly logical for modern hospitals to expand within these urban areas. The urban general hospital soon became the hub of health services, and more and more patients resided in these hospitals, not at home, when receiving treatment (Starr, 1982). Prodded by the active and expanding American Medical Association, medical schools steadily realigned their curricula to provide students with clinical training that incorporated the latest findings in medical science (Johnson and Jones, 1993).

Inevitably, the most advanced medical schools formed partnerships with nearby urban general hospitals, and created what are now called academic medical centers. In addition to education, these centers, led by Johns Hopkins Medical Center in Baltimore, sponsored active medical research programs (Chesney, 1943). In alliance with urban hospitals and medical associations, city and county administrations dramatically professionalized the discipline of public health. For the first time, the poor were able to obtain at least minimally effective care at newly established public hospitals. Mortality rates fell as cities developed water purification systems, waste treatment plants, and systems for mass vaccination and quarantine to counter epidemic diseases (Rosen, 1958).

A. The Twentieth Century

Medical treatment steadily became more sophisticated, effective and popular. It also got more expensive. This could be handled by out-of-pocket payments by patients while economic conditions generally improved, as they did during the 1890 - 1930 period. When the Great Depression hit in the 1930s, however, many hospitals and doctors faced unpaid bills and bankruptcy. In response, states began to support the development of health insurance programs, jointly paid for by employers and their workers. Led by the state Blue Cross and Blue Shield Associations, more and more medical treatment was paid for by insurance, and out-of-pocket payments began to steadily decline (Roemer, 1978). With readily available funds from a broad and growing enrollee base, physicians and hospitals were able to continuously expand their services without worrying too much about how much it actually cost to produce specific treatments (Stevens, 1989).

The development of the U. S. health care system was also given a tremendous boost by the traditional impetus to medical progress: large scale warfare. Between 1939 and 1945, the United States became the foremost military power in the world, with huge and well-equipped armed forces. An integral part of the modern American military was its effective medical system (Long, 1946). To handle casualties, the military developed a comprehensive system of battlefield treatment that would eventually evolve into what we now recognize as modern emergency medical services. The medic and (in the subsequent Korean and Vietnam conflicts) the "M.A.S.H." unit, with plasma, field surgical centers, helicopters and overland transport, removed the death sentence from most battlefield casualties, and contributed immeasurably to our knowledge of trauma care. To handle longer term care, the nation set up a large system of veterans' hospitals.

At the end of World War II, demobilization included military medical administrators who had gained an aptitude and taste for large scale medical organization. They rapidly rose to the top of hospital administrations, and promoted system expansion so as to have the large facilities they wished for. The nation, flush with military victory and unprecedented economic prosperity, enthusiastically supported the massive increases in health services provision made possible by legislation such as the Hill-Burton Act (U. S. DHEW, 1966). Like the nation, U. S. health care had entered a Golden Era. For the next thirty years in American medicine, all things would seem possible, and enormous achievements would be accepted as routine events (Stevens, 1989). Fueled by increasing government grants, subsidies and tax advantages, health professions education mushroomed in the 1950s and 1960s, led by the medical and nursing schools. Hospitals steadily accumulated more complex and powerful technology. Physicians prospered, in solo and, increasingly, group practice. As subsidiary professionals, nurses and allied health workers also became more abundant and technically proficient.

The 1960s marked the high water mark for American social and governmental activism in the Twentieth Century. In 1965, Congress enacted Medicare and Medicaid, and thereby brought about the largest expansion of access to health care in American history. Medicare provided a nationally standard health insurance package for almost all citizens over 65, and became an intensely popular public initiative (Marmor, 1973). As a combined national and state government program, Medicaid attempted to provide basic health coverage for large categories of citizens who qualified as "poor" under varying definitions (Stevens and Stevens, 1974). Both programs enabled large numbers of Americans to receive critically needed medical services. But they also illustrated the extent to which major public policies could bring about significant unanticipated consequences.

As most economists now recognize, the vast influx of government Medicare and Medicaid money, by powerfully (and intentionally) increasing the demand for medical services, also dramatically (and unintentionally) contributed to the development of health care cost inflation that has bedeviled U. S. health services to this day (Feldstein, 1993; Aaron and Reischauer, 1995). From the mid-Sixties on, cost containment became a steadily larger issue for health service payers and providers. In the 1970s, Presidents Nixon, Ford and Carter also included health services within their general efforts to control economic inflation. Essentially, all of the anti-inflation efforts in the 1970s failed, particularly with respect to health services (Koch, 1993).

By the late 1970s, President Carter was willing to attempt to impose targeted cost controls on hospital services, but his efforts were stymied by his own political weakness, along with strong hospital industry and physician opposition. Federal policymakers increasingly recognized the insustainability of health services inflation, and its resistance to traditional controls. Business executives were increasingly vocal about the growing burden health care costs placed on businesses in increasingly competitive marketplaces (Iglehart, 1982; Davis et al., 1990).

The 1980s brought a major national political shift to the right, with the election of Ronald Reagan as President. In 1983, the nation also saw the beginning of a new strategy at cost containment. With the passage of the Tax Equity and Fiscal Responsibility Act in 1982, and the more sweeping Social Security Amendments of 1983, the Federal Government began to attempt to use its position as the largest purchaser of health services to control its health care costs (Schweiker, 1983). Other large businesses, with equally onerous health insurance costs, took notice, and made efforts, individually and in purchasing alliances, to modify the rate at which costs went up. The state of California shocked its health insurers by establishing an effective system of competitive bidding for MediCal, its Medicaid variant (Johns et al., 1985). Payments for health services were increasingly shifted from a cost-plus to one or another flat-rate or capitated basis, which penalized excessive hospital stays or service utilization. Fee-for-service medicine began a steady decline, as payer resistance to higher costs spread throughout the system.

By the late 1980s, the nation's health services system was clearly in transition into a new era, which would be dominated by what would become known as "managed care." Though the term itself is of recent origin, the basic principles of managed care were in fact developed and refined by the Health Maintenance Organizations (HMOs), which were initially developed in California and other western states to provide comprehensive care to employees of large industries (Brown, 1983). Though the HMOs were steadily growing by the late 1980s, much of the managed care movement involved other health services organizations attempting to build upon the practices that HMOs had developed (Prottas and Handler, 1987).

Managed care (which will be described in greater detail later in this chapter) has several primary characteristics, including capitated reimbursement and the use of various incentives for cost-effective care, such as utilization review and provider accountability for patient health outcomes (Williams and Torrens, 1993a). Traditional Twentieth Century U. S. health care operated under the basic incentive to provide more and more services, with the assumption that insurers would pick up the ultimate bill. Clinical quality mattered; the costs incurred in attaining it did not. The gradually increasing constraints on revenue generation thus shattered the basic dynamic of the system (Starr, 1982). For the first time, U. S. health services organizations had to begin operating with the same concerns for the "bottom line" of revenues and expenses long familiar to economic enterprises in other sectors.

To effectively operate in this system, health providers have been forced into steady institutional consolidation since the 1980s. To meet the cost containment demands of payers, physicians have been forced to affiliate with larger group practices, which have in turn been compelled to develop managed care forms through such entities as Preferred Provider Organizations (PPOs) (Feldstein, 1993). Hospitals have also been forced to restructure. Many small hospitals, especially in rural areas, have been forced to close down by the new system's cost imperatives - leaving some citizens without reliable access to care (Fuchs, 1994). The crown jewels of the old American health services system - the large urban general hospitals - are merging into large metropolitan, regional and even nationwide networks in order to financially survive.

As a result, hospital administrators, whether for-profit, not-for-profit, or even governmental, increasingly employ standard American private sector corporate practices (Stevens, 1989). They diversify services and "downsize" their workforces. In recognition of the high costs of inpatient hospital care, they alter their identities by shifting as much of their business as possible into outpatient care. By the 1990s, the most rapidly growing forms of U. S. health services were home health care, ambulatory services (provided through hospital clinics or, increasingly, satellite centers in suburbs), and - because of the inexorable "graying of America" - long term care (Special Committee on the Aging, 1991).

The 1990s have seen U. S. health services attempt a rapid and characteristically American attempt at self-reinvention. U. S. health providers spent over a century developing an emphasis on technology-intensive inpatient hospital care. In the last decade, the system has hastened to reverse direction - to move out of the hospital, and to limit the application of technology and specialized services to the cost-effective minimum. Its objective of combining cost control with clinical effectiveness is shared by the health systems of all other nations in the Nineties. Yet the methods being employed in this process of reinvention are quite unique.

II. THE MAJOR COMPONENTS OF U. S. HEALTH SERVICES

The American health services system may indeed be a "nonsystem," as suggested by some observers, but that does not make it any less complex. Because of the wealth, size, diversity and heritage of the nation, U. S. health care is provided through a wide range of entities of all sizes and varieties. Some are apparently simple and straightforward, such as the family physician's office. Others are staggeringly complicated, such as the modern academic medical center. They are organized in many different ways, and funded by a blend of public and private sector monies. Some offer general care, while others are extremely specialized. Some offer treatment for the entire population, others target highly specific subgroups.

At the center of U. S. health services, though seldom recognized as such, is the "hidden health system" of personal, family and informal community care (Levin and Idler, 1981). As in most countries, an enormous amount of medical care is provided by oneself, parents, and other acquaintances. Most basic preventive health education is provided through the family. Social observers have noted the connection between family and community disruption, and increases in pathological health behaviors, including drug addiction and violence (Christoffel, 1994). In one major area of health services - long term care - existing service delivery organizations and financing mechanisms would almost immediately collapse without the basic support of family caregiving (Wiener et al., 1994). Though few think of it in this manner, public policies which support and protect family structures profoundly assist the rest of the health services system, in the U. S. as elsewhere.

As cost containment measures increasingly limit the expansion of care financed by public and private insurance, many individuals are beginning to make greater efforts to gain control of their own health care. Following the calls to self-empowerment, and being skeptical of the care prescribed by established medical authorities, a significant number of U. S. citizens are now using "alternative" medical practices and products (Wallis, 1991). Since the safety, efficacy and effectiveness of many of these practices and products have not been substantiated by systematic research, the use of alternative medical practices has engendered political conflict between adherents and government regulators (Wallis, 1991). On the other hand, some practices originally viewed as unscientific and eccentric, such as acupuncture, are now moving into the medical mainstream as ongoing research suggests their effectiveness.

A. Primary Care

At the next level, for most citizens, comes the primary medical caregiver. Traditionally, these individuals have included the family physician and the dentist, operating as solo practitioners or, more recently, as members of group practices. Though its prevalence is somewhat exaggerated in the public's mind, it is true that, for the majority of U. S. citizens, their initial and most frequent contact with the health services system involves meetings with primary medical caregivers (DeLozier and Gagnon, 1991). Most of these encounters involve consultation about frequent and non-emergency conditions, including important physiological events that are not abnormalities or diseases - pregnancy and childbirth.

Because of their historic importance as an place of entry and referral for the health care system, primary caregivers have held an honored (and financially prosperous) place. Most recently, however, there has been a strong trend toward substituting mid-level providers (MLPs) for physician services (Riportella-Muller et al, 1995). With the now-dominant imperative of cost containment, increasing proportions of doctors rely upon auxiliary medical professionals such as Physician Assistants (PAs), Nurse Practitioners (NPs), or Certified Registered Nurse Midwives (CRNMs) for initial screenings and ongoing patient contacts (Pew Health Professions Commission, 1993). Managed care organizations, such as HMOs and large hospital networks, rely upon such substitutions as a matter of course, citing increased cost-effectiveness in care (Dial et al., 1995).

Resistance is a primary response by physicians to current systemwide changes, such as the substitution described above, and managed care network development. The AMA vigorously opposes changes that would result in single payor or national health insurance (with the exception of the plan developed by the AMA itself). Other evidence for this resistance is found in state medical society sponsorship of "any willing provider" laws. And in its last several meetings, the AMA has debated and now supports measures assuring a "point of service option" in insurance plans (American Medical Association, 1995). With the capabilities to diagnose and treat most illnesses today, change is perceived as a threat. It is difficult for many physicians to understand change as a process that can preserve what is good about healthcare and improve access and efficiency at the same time.

Along with resistance to change, we can see a counter trend, with many physicians involved in activities that are attempting to direct change. One has only to review and assess the rapidly growing numbers of physician sponsored delivery models in order to see physician efforts to direct change. Almost all physicians are now

Table 2 - Hospitals–Summary Characteristics, by Type of Service and Control

ITEM	1960	1970	1980	1988	1989	1990	1991	1992	1993	1994
NUMBER:										
All Hospitals	6,876	7,123	6,965	6,780	6,720	6,649	6,634	6,539	6,467	6,374
With 100 Beds or More	2,903	3,488	3,755	3,681	3,650	3,620	3,611	3,572	3,558	3,492
Non-Federal										
Short-term General	6,441	6,715	6,606	6,438	6,380	6,312	6,300	6,214	6,151	6,067
and Special	5,407	5,859	5,904	5,579	5,497	5,420	5,370	5,321	5,289	5,256
Nongov't. Nonprofit	3,291	3,386	3,339	3,242	3,220	3,191	3,175	3,173	3,154	3,139
For Profit	856	769	730	790	769	749	738	723	717	719
State and Local Gov't.	1,260	1,704	1,835	1,501	1,466	1,444	1,429	1,396	1,390	1,371
Long-term General and Special	308	236	157	129	138	131	126	115	117	110
Psychiatric	488	519	534	726	741	757	800	774	741	696
Tuberculosis	238	101	11	4	4	4	4	4	4	5
Federal	435	408	359	342	340	337	334	325	316	307
BEDS (000):										
All Hospitals	1,658	1,616	1,365	1,241	1,226	1,213	1,202	1,178	1,163	1,128
Rate Per 1,000 Population	9.3	7.9	6.0	5.1	5.0	4.9	4.7	4.6	4.5	4.3
Beds Per Hospital	241	227	190	183	182	182	181	180	180	177

Source: The Universal Healthcare Almanac

interested in belonging to at least an IPA and many want to be in a more integrated system. Many physicians are now creating PPO and HMO models with almost total ownership by the physicians. These attempts recognize the changes that are occurring, and physicians in such activities hope to either direct or at least be participants in the changing activity.

B. Hospitals

Most citizens will also have at least occasional contacts with the system through treatment at a hospital. As mentioned earlier, hospitals have seen their formerly dominant position erode with the arrival of managed care. Nevertheless, they are still the primary location for most specialized health care. Most women still give birth at hospitals, and almost all surgical procedures are performed there (American Hospital Association, 1991). There are several major types of hospitals (Table 2). The bulk of hospitals are classified as short-term, providing wide ranges of specialized services while attempting to limit patient length of stay. The most significant long-term facilities are psychiatric hospitals. The bulk of hospitals in the U. S. are not-for-profit, but the proportion of for-profit (investor-owned) hospitals is now beginning to rise along with the growth of national networks. Even not-for-profit facilities have been forced to reconfigure their operations to maintain their competitive viability (Melnick and Zwanziger, 1988).

Because of capitation and prospective payment systems (as well as the improved efficacy of many medical techniques), the average length of stay at a hospital has rapidly declined in the last fifteen years. However, the increased use of ambulatory and home health care has also screened out relatively healthier individuals who would formerly have been inpatients (Williams, 1983). Consequently, the average hospital patient is much poorer health than previously. Their more extreme conditions usually require the intensive employment of complex technology and highly-trained clinicians. Thus, while overall hospital costs have begun to level off, the unit costs of treatment have in fact risen sharply (Feldstein, 1993).

This is a particularly serious problem for the specialized hospitals that are affiliated with academic medical centers. Ironically, the very success of academic medical centers in conducting research into and developing effective treatments for extreme conditions has saddled them with dangerous financial liabilities. The hope of obtaining offsetting revenues from primary care and other outpatient services is now driving these entities into the arms of national care networks (Church, 1995). However, the cost structures of academic medical centers are inevitably higher because of their research and educational functions, and most payers do not wish to subsidize these. As a result, some observers have expressed great concern for the future of these centers in managed care settings (Anderson et al., 1994).

Public hospitals, including those run by the Department of Veterans Affairs, have even more intractible problems. A disproportionate number of their patients suffer from serious and chronic medical problems, and these patients often live in settings which work against effective preventive care and health maintenance (Allison, 1993). In the last thirty years, their strongest financial lifelines have been Medicaid and veterans appropriations in the Federal Government budget. However, recent and proposed future cutbacks in Medicaid threaten to destroy the financial viability of many public hospitals, and the move toward a Federal balanced budget will mean revenue cuts for already stretched VA facilities (Rangel, 1991; Billings et al., 1995). Nonpaying patients (often poor people who cannot qualify for Medicaid) and veterans cannot be legally turned away, and other hospitals have no financial incentive to treat them. Short of national and state policy reforms which provide more revenue, many public hospitals are financially doomed, and closures have risen steadily in the last five years (Andrulis et al., 1996).

C. Ambulatory Care

Historically, most U. S. residents have only infrequently needed medical care beyond the informal, physician and hospital levels. In recent years, though, ambulatory care and home health institutions have taken on much more extensive service delivery responsibilities. As mentioned earlier, cost containment pressures have provided a major incentive to keep treatment out of the hospital, and inpatient hospital treatment is of constantly briefer duration. This means that patients are often discharged "sicker and quicker" (Feldstein, 1993). As the nation's population has aged, the health care system has also been confronted with a greater proportion of chronic conditions that cannot be finally "cured" (Scanlon, 1988). This means that ongoing and followup aftercare and rehabilitation, often in the home, is both more necessary and more frequent. Increasingly sophisticated technology has also permitted ambulatory care professionals to carry out clinical techniques that previously were monopolized by the large hospitals (Henderson, 1992).

Ambulatory care is often provided in the physician's office, or in a hospital clinic. In one sense, ambulatory care is quite traditional; until hospitals established safe and high quality treatment facilities, most preferred health care was ambulatory (Roemer, 1981). Individuals visited a physicians's office, or the physician came to the patient's home with his famous little black bag. What is new is the development of a widening array of other ambulatory care facilities, largely in lieu of hospital care.

Physicians, working out of group practices, are capable of substituting diagnoses and treatments that previously would require hospital facilities. Group practices provide physicians with numerous advantages, including professional management, shared facilities, and improved contracting negotiating ability (the latter of significance in managed care settings). Patients have potential access to a wider range of clinical specialities. On the other hand, physicians have to relinquish some of their traditional professional autonomy to gain these benefits, and patients may feel that their care is more impersonal and bureaucratic (Freeborn and Pope, 1994; Fogarty, 1995).

Outside of the physician's office, there are increasing numbers of clinics specifically devoted to one or more forms of outpatient care. With the advent of the "deinstitutionalization movement" in the 1950's and 1960's, most mental health care moved out of psychiatric hospitals to outpatient clinics, which rely heavily on counseling and psychotropic drugs to stabilize chronic mental conditions such as schizophrenia and depression (Rumer, 1978). There are centers that specialize in "same day surgery," with no overnight stay for patients needing relatively straightforward procedures (Burns, 1984). There are also the oxymoronically-named "minor emergency clinics," which focus on treatment for manageable though potentially serious problems (for example, stepping on a rusty nail, or severely spraining one's ankle). In the public health sector, clinics administered by county, state or specialized national government agencies (such as those serving veterans or Native Americans) provide such services as walk-in prenatal care, vaccinations, pharmaceutical services, and sexually-transmitted disease treatment for little or no cost to the patient (Public Health Foundation, 1990).

D. Home Health

The growth of home health services is even more far-reaching and potentially important. Skilled home health care nurses and allied health professionals can provide monitoring of chronic illnesses, and provide rehabilitation therapy for patient development after a hospital stay. Hospitals increasingly rely on home health care services to complete the caregiving that they can no longer afford to provide in-house (Evashwick, 1987). When combined with the growing ability to continuously monitor patient status at home via telemedicine, home health services, hospitals and physicians now have the theoretical capability to approach the ideal "continuity of care" suggested for treatment of varying and/or chronic medical conditions (Milio, 1996). Much of managed care is based upon the faith that caregiving systems such as these can be made cost-effective (Boland, 1991).

E. Long-term Care

Only a minority of Americans require the services of long-term care institutions. However, because of their cost and rapidly growing demand, the issues of future long-term care finance and administration are critical for the U. S. and all other wealthy nations with aging populations. The fastest growing proportion of the elderly in the U. S. are those over 85 years of age (U. S. Commission on Aging, 1989). A large number of these older seniors have permanently lost one or more crucial motor functions, and/or suffer from growing mental disability. As mentioned earlier, most custodial care for these seniors is provided by family members. However, those who cannot be adequately cared for in a home setting usually need to be moved at least temporarily into a nursing home. More recently, the demand for long term care has risen because of the HIV epidemic. Those individuals in the terminal stages of AIDS (tragically, often only in their twenties or thirties) also often lose physical and mental skills and need custodial and rehabilitative care (O'Connell, 1990).

Nursing homes are extremely expensive, with charges ranging from $30,000 - $60,000 for a year's stay (National Center for Health Statistics, 1991). There also is a significant undersupply of places in nursing homes, with many having long waiting lists for admission (Feldstein, 1993). Finally, there are ongoing quality concerns. U. S. nursing homes have always had wide variations in staff competence and the comfort and safety of facilities, and there are periodic and widely-publicized scandals over the barbaric treatment of helpless and disoriented residents at one or another home (Institute of Medicine, 1986). Governments and long term care professional groups have established, and attempt to maintain, reasonable performance standards, but problems persist (Coleman, 1991).

Since it is projected that there will be millions of additional nursing home places required in the next thirty years, it is unclear how the U. S. will be able to provide adequate long term care for those who need it. Long term care financing is unlike that for any other health service. With high costs, most individuals needing permanent nursing home care are forced to "spend down" their assets (essentially bankrupting themselves) before they can qualify for Medicaid subsidies (Spence and Wiener, 1990). As a result, the fastest growing part of the Medicaid program, which was created to fund care for "the poor," is in fact long term financing for middle-class elderly citizens who have expended most of their assets (Rivlin and Wiener, 1988). As we will see later, this places an additional strain on a Medicaid system that is already in financial crisis.

As with hospital care, one response to these cost problems has been to maximize the amount of long term care that is provided in ambulatory and home settings. Only a minority of the elderly are likely to need long term care for extended periods (Wiener et al., 1994). Unfortunately, these individuals are also less likely to be able to be adequately cared for at home. They are also the most likely seniors to face bankruptcy (usually within two to five years of entering a nursing home or other extended care facility). Ultimately, only a combination of increased public and private insurance (with correspondingly higher taxes and premium payments) may be able to finance the enormous amount of care that will be needed by 2020, when the bulk of the "baby boom" generation will be over sixty-five (Wiener et al., 1994).

F. Mental Health

Mental health care has also been affected by the cost containment imperative. The very definition of mental illness has varied significantly in the U. S. throughout the 20th Century. (For example, homosexuality was classified as a mental disorder by the American Psychiatric Association until the early 1970s; its reclassification only came about after a bruising fight within the Association.) By current reckoning, between 15% - 25% of Americans suffer from at least one mental disorder (DHHS, 1986). Primary care for mental health, however, is not as well developed as that found for "physical" health (even though most mental health problems are related to underlying physical conditions). Until the 1960s, individuals who were recognizably mentally ill were often warehoused in asylums and psychiatric hospitals, with little access to effective care. Two factors changed this picture:

1. From a scientific standpoint, the development of psychopharmacology, in the 1950s and beyond, provided the first significant possibility of large scale outpatient treatment (Levine, 1981). Mentally ill individuals could be stabilized with medication, and function as productive members of society while receiving occasional counseling. This ended the need for large numbers of inpatient psychiatric institutions, and, along with cost considerations, led to the second, organizational, development - deinstitutionalization.
2. The deinstitutionalization movement involved a radical decline in the number of inpatient psychiatric facilities, as well as sharply decreased lengths of stay for those still receiving inpatient treatment. The central assumption of the movement was that most of the mentally ill could be adequately treated through medication and other services provided by community mental health centers (Rumer, 1978).

The current mental health service delivery system resulted from these two developments. However, those envisioning widespread deinstitutionalization did not expect that the same impetus for cost savings that spurred outpatient care would also lead to funding cutbacks for the mental health centers that were essential for providing that care. Such cutbacks left gaping holes in mental health care availability (Richardson, 1993). Social disintegration in the U. S. - family and community dissolution, accompanied by increasing levels of homelessness, violence and drug abuse - also contributed to a steady increase in the numbers of citizens (particularly youth) needing mental health services (Lamb, 1990). All too often, those services were not available. Mental health services feel the acute pressures of inadequate service capabilities and growing service demands, coupled with continually increasing pressures for cost containment. Most recently, there have been efforts to apply managed care principles, with systematic case management, utilization review, and, in some cases, the establishment of capitated payment systems (Borenstein, 1990; Dorwart, 1990).

G. Health Professions

Education institutions, often with highly traditional methods of operation, are now endeavoring to reinvent themselves in order to survive the movement toward managed care and competition. Historical system incentives, as mentioned earlier,

favored the training of physician specialists, with nursing and allied health professionals in decidedly subordinate positions. Academic medical centers, following the standard set by Johns Hopkins at the beginning of the 20th Century, developed curricula
that often focused on technology-intensive treatment of complex and acute infirmities
(Starr, 1982). This in turn socialized medical students into looking at patients as bun-
dles of physiological systems (as opposed to a more holistic approach), and taught
them to rely on technological "fixes" for health problems that were often in fact the
results of human lifestyle decisions (Mechanic, 1986).

Within this system, the most prestigious physicians were in fact not devoted to
patient care, but to basic biomedical research, funded by increasingly generous Federal
revenues from such agencies as the National Institutes of Health (NIH). This in turn
accelerated the pace of technology-driven clinical advances, which led to more specialized physician training, in a never-ending cycle (Gelijns and Rosenberg, 1994).
Nursing and other health professions, within tight limits set by physicians, emulated
the medical specialization model (Aiken, 1982; LeRoy and Ellwood, 1985; Feinberg and
Langner, 1988).

This set of arrangements could only survive with constantly expanding levels of
funding, and a minimum amount of scrutiny from those who provided it (who, in the
case of state universities, included legislators and taxpayers). Medical cost inflation
and governmental budgetary limits, with the subsequent rise of market competition
and managed care, has placed severe pressure on this previously-insulated system
(Epstein, 1995). Medical educators must now train marketable and cost-conscious
practitioners - and learn those habits in conducting their own research and patient
care. Federal and state governments are increasingly forcing academic medical centers
to generate their own revenues, without subsidies and regulatory preferences and protections (Blumenthal and Meyer, 1996). The Nineties have seen constant downsizing
and reengineering efforts, as medical universities streamline their staffs, develop more
cost-effective clinical procedures, and re-engineer themselves to become bottom-line
and customer-conscious enterprises.

This changing environment, at least to date, has relatively favored nursing and
allied health professionals (Havighurst, 1989). It has become cost-effective for health
care providers to substitute other workers for physicians in service provision. The
greatest gains have been made by the so-called "mid-level providers" (MLPs), including Physician Assistants (PAs), Nurse Practitioners (NPs), and Nurse Midwives (NMs).
Often working as managed care "gatekeepers," and with populations historically experiencing access problems (the poor and rural residents, in particular), MLPs have
become hot commodities in health care job markets (Mick et al., 1992; Riportella-
Muller et al., 1995). In contrast, some physician subspecialists (formerly in highly paid
and prestigious positions) have been forced to drastically lower their fees, or retrain
for primary care, to remain employable (Cooper, 1994; Foreman, 1996).

H. Public Health

State and local public health and hospital agencies have faced a wide range of
pressures and new challenges in the 1980s and 1990s. Factors which have increased
public health workloads include the growing HIV / AIDS epidemic, growing teen
pregnancy and single parenthood rates, family and community instability, increases in

crime and violence (particularly among inner-city youth), and growing immigrant populations in both rural and urban areas (Institute of Medicine, 1988). Yet the general public disillusionment with government and the public sector has precluded significant funding increases in most areas (HIV / AIDS being a partial exception). The most visible constituencies of public health agencies, the poor and minority group members, do not have the political power of other pro-health spending groups (like the predominantly white, middle class elderly, in the case of Medicare). Consequently, public health organizations have had to make do with tight funding for some time now (Evans, 1996). Federal support for public health has also been uncertain, since Republican presidents have generally called for a lower national government profile, and less funding (Shonick, 1993).

The nation's public hospitals face a particularly desperate financial situation, with soaring service demands from Medicaid and uninsured populations (Andrulis, 1989). Historically, public hospitals have been able to offset high levels of nonpaying patients by imposing higher charges on those patients with insurance (the source of the infamous $10.00 aspirins and $25.00 bandages). Now, however, cost-containing insurers are increasingly refusing to subsidize the care of nonsubscribers in this manner. State and local governments are also clearly refusing to increase their appropriations to make up for this shortfall (Andrulis et al., 1996). Academic medical centers, which have often been affiliated with public hospitals for research and instructional purposes, are facing their own financial troubles. The result has been a slow-motion collapse of "charity care" institutions, as emergency rooms shut down, and public hospitals downsize or consolidate within larger urban areas (National Association of Public Hospitals, 1993).

The crisis in public health, particularly that faced by public hospitals, is clearly related to the historically problematic relationship between capitalist America and its poorer citizens alluded to earlier in this chapter. It stems directly from the uniquely uncoordinated financial system for U. S. health care, and the growing inadequacies of Medicaid, the insurance program originally intended to pay for the care of the poor - at least, those which might qualify under its complex and varying guidelines.

Other specialized public health systems, such as the those administered by the Department of Veterans Affairs (DVA), and the Bureau of Indian Affairs (BIA), face uncertain futures. Both the DVA and BIA are the products of specific historical and political forces and compromises that have lost much of their original force and rationale. They serve defined client groups, but without a clearly defined future purpose. It is not at all certain that they can fit into the growing environment of managed care networks that will dominate U. S. health care in the coming decades.

Despite the serious and growing concerns about the structure and viability of the system of medical facilities administered by the U. S. Department of Veterans Affairs, veterans health care is still politically popular and an important part of U. S. health services (Torrens, 1993). Public policies have always held that the federal government has the responsibility to provide adequate medical care to veterans (Veterans Administration, 1986). Federal administration has meant guaranteed funding for VA facilities, at least at maintenance levels. However, along with revenue have come program requirements and restrictions (such as the inability of veterans' spouses, children and other dependents to receive care from VA centers) that prevent VA medical centers from effectively joining in the growing regionalization and networking of services

(Mirvis and Kilpatrick, 1995). The VA faces a rapidly rising caseload (the veterans of the Second World War are now senior citizens), with increasingly severe Federal budgetary controls that limit its ability to respond. As a result, it faces increasing marginalization and organizational decline, unless it can somehow redefine its mission, and develop a greater ability to interact with other health service providers.

Many of the same factors facing the VA also confront the BIA, which provides health care for Indians (Native Americans) on the numerous reservations around the U. S. On the whole, Native Americans have the worst health indices of any significant, identifiable ethnic group (National Center for Health Statistics, 1991). Many tribal societies have been devastated by poverty and alcoholism, which in turn has resulted in an emigration of their most vigorous and enterprising members. Some tribes have been able to prosper through the development of specialized industries, or, more controversially, the establishment of gambling facilities on reservation lands. The federal guarantee of assistance to Native American tribes, sanctioned by treaty, is not in question (Randall, 1989). However, many observers have concluded that federal government efforts at service provision, however well-intentioned, have resulted in bureaucratic imperialism and the fostering of tribal dependency. It is not clear what reforms would be most effective, but it is clear that continued efforts will have to be made to provide health services to Native Americans (Indian Health Service, 1986).

I. Governmental Agencies

Governmental regulatory, research and financing agencies play major roles in the U. S. health care system. Since over forty percent of U. S. health financing comes from one level or another of government, federal, state and local policymakers are justifiably concerned about the uses to which the funds are put. At the federal level, the Medicare and Medicaid programs are administered by the Department of Health and Human Services, with funding and oversight from Congressional Senate and House Committees. Similar arrangements hold at the state level, which each state administering Medicaid or its equivalent, as well as various public health and welfare programs (some through local governments). Several federal organizations play notable roles in health policy and administration:

1. The Food and Drug Administration (FDA) is the federal agency mandated to oversee the safety and efficacy of most pharmaceuticals, and a wide range of medical devices. The FDA regulates the introduction of most drugs into American health markets. In its regulatory role, the FDA requires that pharmaceutical and equipment manufacturers conduct lengthy and stringent testing of their products before clearing them for use (Food and Drug Administration, 1977). The FDA also regulates medical advertising, and has the authority to legally challenge and direct the cessation of product advertising that is deemed to be fraudulent or misleading. In this capacity, the agency has historically been plunged into notable political controversies, such as those around products such as saccharin, silicon breast implants, and cigarette additives (Foreman, 1994). (For obvious reasons, the tobacco industry and legislators from tobacco-growing states have worked energetically to keep the FDA from directly regulating tobacco products, particularly cigarettes.)

2. The National Institutes of Health (NIH) are primarily responsible for financing and overseeing advanced medical research, including most clinical trials. NIH funding is much sought after by academic medical center researchers, and this gives NIH the opportunity to significantly affect U. S. medical practices and technologies through providing or withholding funds for development (Bloom and Randolph, 1990). Most "cutting edge" research into new medical areas (such as HIV / AIDS, cancer and cardiovascular disease) is NIH-funded. More broadly, one can look at NIH funding priorities and practices as a significant indicator of, and contributor to, the high technology focus of U. S. health care. Consequently, the agency can both take some credit for major medical innovations, and some blame for a relative lack of concern for research into possibly more cost-effective primary care and health education methodologies (Geljins and Rosenberg, 1994).

3. The Health Care Financing Administration (HCFA) is charged with administering Medicare and the federal components of Medicaid. Its policies thus have an impact on the largest components of U. S. government health spending. Along with the Prospective Payment Assessment Commission (ProPAC), HCFA controls the Medicare prospective payment system, which has dramatically altered service delivery incentives throughout the health care industry. HCFA, with input from other agencies, also assesses whether or not new medical procedures and technologies should be eligible for federal reimbursement, and its decisions are generally followed by state government and private sector payers (Geljins, 1990; Fuchs, 1993). This function has placed HCFA into controversies surrounding the nation's financial support for "cutting edge" technologies in such areas as organ transplantation. Since HCFA is centrally involved with federal reimbursement policies, it is clearly an important part of national cost containment efforts.

4. Through comparatively small, the Agency for Health Care Policy and Research (AHCPR) is important because it funds health services research in such areas as medical outcomes, organization, quality and cost effectiveness. The results, which are placed in the public domain, provide health providers, payers and citizens with potentially valuable information about the impacts of current and new forms of health service delivery (Gaus and Fraser, 1996). In the mid-Nineties, AHCPR became a special target of Congressional Republicans, who argued that its funded research could just as easily be done by private health organizations (Association for Health Services Research, 1995). The agency's supporters argued that the public nature of its research was vitally important, and worth preserving. At least through 1996, AHCPR's supporters prevailed; the agency survived, through its budget was significantly reduced.

5. Workplace safety issues are the special concern of the Occupational Safety and Health Administration (OSHA). OSHA has the responsibility for investigating workplace hazards, and the ability to conduct inspections. If the results of investigations warrant, the agency also has the power to demand changes in, or elimination of, workplace practices that place workers at risk (Foreman, 1994). OSHA efforts have often engendered great hostility from employers, who argue that OHSA guidelines are often nitpicking, inordinately expensive or complex to comply with, or just plain ridiculous (Kelman, 1980). (The requirement by OHSA that agricultural field workers have a defined number of portable toilets per acre is a

famous and frequently-cited example.) Not surprisingly, organized labor groups are strong supporters of OSHA. Though OSHA regulations are frequently criticized, its central mission is not seriously questioned by federal policymakers.

6. The U. S. Public Health Service (PHS) is the primary federal public health organization and works with state and local agencies on a wide range of public health issues. The head of PHS, the U. S. Surgeon General, has occasionally become a high-profile national figure by using the position as a "bully pulpit" to talk about national health concerns. Julius Richmond, Surgeon General in the Carter Administration, crusaded for increased awareness of proper health promotion and disease prevention activities (U. S. Department of Health and Human Services, 1980). In the 1980's, Surgeon General C. Everett Koop publicized the nature of the HIV / AIDS epidemic, and talked frankly and publicly about proper "safe sex" prevention practices (Shilts, 1987). Within PHS, the Centers for Disease Control (CDC) have garnered the most publicity, particularly with their efforts to detect and monitor the spread of epidemic diseases such as HIV / AIDS (Foreman, 1994). With heightened public concerns about new and virulent epidemic agents (not only HIV / AIDS, but Ebola, Lassa and Hanta viruses), CDC's public health role is likely to remain important in the decades to come.

The final major structural feature of current U. S. health care, the growing provider networks, are a consequence of the managed care imperative referred to earlier. Barring radical reform, such as the development of a national health service, large private sector regional and national provider networks will probably be the primary structures for service delivery in the first part of the 21st Century. Many, if not most, of the other structural elements described above will be subsumed within them.

REFERENCES

Aaron, H. J. and Reischauer, R. D. (1995). The Medicare reform debate: What is the next step? *Health Affairs* ,14(4): 8-30.

Ackerknecht, E. H. (1973). *Theraputics From the Primitives to the 20th Century.* Hafner Press, New York, NY.

Aiken, L. (1982). *The impact of federal health policy on nurses. In Nursing in the 1980s: Crises, Opportunities, Challenges.* (L. Aiken, ed.), Lippincott, Philadelphia, PA.

Allison, F. (1993). Public hospitals - Past, present and future. *Perspectives in Biology and Medicine, 36:* 596-610.

American Hospital Association (1991). *Hospital Statistics.* American Hospital Association, Chicago, IL.

American Medical Association (1995). *AMA Delegates Report, 1995.* American Medical Association, Chicago, IL.

Anderson, G., Steinberg, E. and Heyssel, R. (1994). The pivotal role of the academic health center. *Health Affairs, 13*(3): 146-158.

Anderson, O. W. (1989). *The Health Services Continuum in Democratic States.* Health Administration Press, Ann Arbor, MI.

Andrulis, D. P. (1989). *Crisis at the Front Line.* Priority Press Publications, New York, NY.

Andrulis, D. P., Acuff, K. L., Weiss, K. B., and Anderson, R. J. (1996). Public hospitals and health care reform: Choices and challenges. *American Journal of Public Health, 86:* 162-165.

Ashley, J. A. (1976). *Hospitals, Paternalism and the Role of the Nurse.* Teachers College Press, New York, NY.

Association for Health Services Research (1995). *Congress cuts health services research.* HSR Reports (October): 1+.

Bagby, N. S. and Sullivan, S. (1986). *Buying Smart: Business Strategies for Managing Health Care Costs.* American Enterprise Institute, Washington, DC.

Bell, D. (1973). *The Coming of Postindustrial Society.* Basic Books, New York, NY.

Billings, P., Mahairas, E. and Gourley, W. (1995). *The future of the V. A. health system: Point-counterpoint.* Presented at the 123rd Annual Meeting of the American Public Health Association, October 29-November 2, 1995.

Bloom, F. E. and Randolph, R. (1990). *Funding Health Sciences Research: A Strategy to Restore Balance.* National Academy Press, Washington, DC.

Blumenthal, D. and Meyer, G. S. (1996). Academic health centers in a changing environment. *Health Affairs, 15*(2): 200-215.

Boland, P. (1991). *Making Managed Healthcare Work: A Practical Guide to Strategiesand Solutions.* McGraw-Hill Publishers, New York, NY.

Borenstein, D. B. (1990). Managed care: A means of rationing psychiatric treatment. *Hospital and Community Psychiatry, 41*: 1087-1091.

Brown, L. D. (1983). *Politics and Health Care Organization.* Brookings Institution, Washington, DC.

Brown, L. D. (1994). Implementing health reform: What the states face. In *Making Health Reform Work* (J. J. DiIulio, Jr., and R. P. Nathan, eds.), Brookings Institution, Washington, DC: 143-156.

Burns, L. A. (1984). *Ambulatory Surgery: Developing and Managing Successful Programs.* Aspen Systems, Rockville, MD.

Chassin, M. R., Brook, R. H. and Park, R. (1986). Variations in the use of medical and surgical services in the Medicare population. *New England Journal of Medicine, 314*: 285-309.

Chesney, A. M. (1943). *The Johns Hopkins Hospital and the Johns Hopkins School of Medicine, Vols. 1 - 3.* The Johns Hopkins Press, Baltimore, MD.

Church, G. J. (1995). Teaching hospitals in crisis. *Time, 146,(July 17)*: 40-42.

Christoffel, K. K. (1994). Reducing violence: How do we proceed? *American Journal of Public Health, 84*: 539-541.

Coleman, B. (1991). *The Nursing Home Reform Act of 1987: Provisions, Policy, Prospects.* University of Massachusetts Gerontology Institute, Boston, MA.

Cooper, R. A. (1994). Seeking a balanced workforce for the 21st century. *Journal of the American Medical Association, (September 7)*: 680-686.

Davis, K., Anderson, G. F., Rowland, D. and Steinberg, E. P. (1990). *Health Care Cost Containment.* Johns Hopkins University Press, Baltimore, MD.

DeLozier, J. E. and Gagnon, R. O. (1991). *1989 Summary: National Ambulatory Care Survey. Advance Data from Vital and Health Statistics. No. 203.* National Center for Health Statistics, Hyattsville, MD.

Dial, T. H., Palsbo, S. E., Bergsten, C., Gabel, J. R. and Weiner, J. (1995). Clinical staffing in staff- and group-model HMOs. *Health Affairs, 14*(2): 168-191.

Dorwart, R. A. (1990). Managed mental health care: Myths and realities in the 1990s. *Hospital and Community Psychiatry, 34*: 616-622.

Epstein, A. M. (1995). U. S. teaching hospitals in the evolving health care system. *Journal of the American Medical Association, (April 19)*: 1203-1207.

Evans, C. A. (1996). Public health: Vision and reality. *American Journal of Public Health, 86*: 476-479.

Evashwick, C. (1987). Definition of the continuum of care. In *Managing the continuum of care* (C. Evashwick and L. Weiss, eds.). Aspen Publishers, Rockville, MD.

Feinberg, W., and Langner, S. R. (1988). The other face of competition: Nursing's struggle for autonomy. In *Money, Power and Health Care* (E. M. Melhado, W. Feinberg, and H. Swartz, eds.). Health Administration Press, Ann Arbor, MI: 233-262.

Feldstein, P. J. (1993). *Health Care Economics*. Delmar Press, Albany, NY.

Fogarty, W. M. (1995). Private practice: Solo or group. In *Medical Practice in the Current Health Care Environment* (J. C. Edwards, ed.). Johns Hopkins University Press, Baltimore, MD: 87-103.

Food and Drug Administration (1977). *General Considerations for the Clinical Evaluation of Drugs*. U. S. Government Printing Office, Washington, DC.

Foreman, C. H., Jr. (1994). *Plagues, Products and Politics*. Brookings Institution, Washington, DC.

Foreman, S. (1996). Managing the physician workforce: Hands off, the market is working. *Health Affairs, 15*(2): 243-249.

Freeborn, D. K. and Pope, C. R. (1994). *Promise and Performance in Managed Care*. Johns Hopkins University Press, Baltimore, MD.

Fuchs, B. (1994). *Health Care Reform: Managed Competition in Rural Areas*. Congressional Research Service, Washington, DC.

Fuchs, V. R. (1993). *The Future of Health Policy*. Harvard University Press, Cambridge, MA.

Gaus, C. R. and Fraser, I. (1996). Shifting paradigms and the role of research. *Health Affairs, 15*(2): 235-242.

Gelijns, A. (1990). Comparing the development of drugs, devices and clinical procedures. In *Modern Methods of Clinical Investigation* (A. Gelijns, ed.), National Academy Press, Washington, DC: 247-301.

Gelijns, A., and Rosenberg, N. (1994). The dynamics of technological change in medicine. *Health Affairs, 13*(3): 28-46.

Havighurst, C. C. (1989). Practice opportunities for allied health professionals in a deregulated health care industry. *Journal of Allied Health, 18*: 9-32.

Henderson, J. (1992). Surgicenters cut further into market. *Modern Healthcare, (May 18)*: 108-110.

Hsiao, W. C. (1993). Introduction - what nations can learn from one another. *Journal of Health Politics, Policy and Law, 17*(6): 13-636.

Indian Health Service (1986). *A Comprehensive Health Care Program, 1955-1985: Thirty Years of Progress*. U. S. Department of Health and Human Services, Washington, DC.

Iglehart, J. K. (1982). Health care and American business. *New England Journal of Medicine, 306*: 120-124.

Institute of Medicine (1986). *Improving the Quality of Care in Nursing Homes*. National Academy Press, Washington, DC.

Institute of Medicine (1988). *The Future of Public Health, 1988*. National Academy Press, Washington, DC.

Johns, L., Anderson, M. D. and Derzon, R. A. (1985). Selective contracting in California: Experience in the second year. *Inquiry, 22*: 335-347.

Johnson, J. and Jones, W. (1993). *The AMA and Organized Medicine*. Garland Publishing: New York, NY.

Kelman, S. (1980). Occupational Safety and Health Administration. In *The Politics of Regulation* (J. Q. Wilson, ed.), Basic Books, Inc., New York, NY.: 236-266.

Koch, A. L. (1993). Financing health services. In *Introduction to Health Services* (S. J. Williams and P. R. Torrens, eds.), Delmar Publishers, Inc., Albany, NY: 299-331.

Lamb, H. R. (1990). Will we save the homeless mentally ill? *American Journal of Psychiatry, 147*: 649-651.

LeRoy, L., and Ellwood, D. (1985). *Trends in health manpower. Health Affairs, 4*: 77-90.

Levin, L. S., and Idler, E. L. (1981). *The Hidden Health Care System: Mediating Structures and Medicine*. American Enterprise Institute, Washington, DC.

Levine, M. (1981). *The History and Politics of Community Mental Health*. Oxford University, Oxford, UK.

Levit, K. R., Cowan, C. A., Lazenby, H. C., McDonnell, P. A., Sensenig, A. L., Stiller, J. M., and Won, D. K. (1994). National health spending trends, 1960-1993. *Health Affairs, 13*(5): 14-31.

Long, P. H. (1946). Medical progress and medical education during the war. *Journal of the American Medical Association, 130:* 983-990.

Mechanic, D. (1986). *From Advocacy to Allocation.* The Free Press, New York, NY.

Melnick, G. A. and Zwanziger, J. (1988). Hospital behavior under competition and cost containment policies. *Journal of the American Medical Association, 260:* 2669-2775.

Mick, S. S., Morlock, L., Salkever, D. and deLissovoy, G. (1992). Medical, Professional and Other Personnel in Rural Hospitals. *Studies in Rural Health Care,* University of Michigan, Ann Arbor, MI.

Mick, S. S. and Moscovice, I. (1993). Health care professionals. In *Introduction to Health Services* (S. J. Williams and P. R. Torrens, eds.), Delmar Publishers, Inc., Albany, NY: 269-296.

Milio, N. (1996). *Engines of Empowerment.* Health Administration Press, Chicago, IL.

Mirvis, D. M. and Kilpatrick, A. O. (1995). *The future of the VA health care system: Point-counterpoint.* Paper presented at the 123rd Annual Meeting of the American Public Health Association, San Diego, CA, October 29-November 2, 1995.

National Association of Public Hospitals (1993). *Rebuilding America's Urban Health Safety Net.* National Association of Public Hospitals, Washington, DC.

National Center for Health Statistics (1991). *Health, United States, 1990.* U. S. Government Printing Office, Washington, DC.

O'Connell, P. G. (1990). AIDS: A medical rehabilitative perspective. In *Productive Living Strategies for People with AIDS* (J. A. Johnson, ed.), Haworth Press, New York, NY: 19-44.

Pew Health Professions Commission (1993). *Primary Care Workforce 2000: Federal Health Policy Strategies.* Pew Health Professions Commission, San Francisco, CA.

Prottas, J. M. and Handler, E. (1987). The complexities of managed care: Operating a voluntary system. *Journal of Health Politics, Policy and Law, 12:* 253-269.

Public Health Foundation (1990). *Public Health Agencies, 1990.* Public Health Foundation, Washington, DC.

Randall, M. (1989). Government in the U. S.: Managing for policy and political accountability. In *A Future of Consequence* (G. L. Filerman, ed.), Witt Associates, Inc., Oak Brook, IL.: 248-280.

Rangel, C. (1991). A federal response. In *Imminent Peril: Public Health in a Declining Economy* (K. M. Cahill, ed.), Twentieth Century Fund Press, New York, NY: 105-115.

Reinhardt, U. E. (1994). Perspective on the German health care system. *Health Affairs, 13*(4): 22-24.

Richardson, M. (1993). Mental health services. In *Introduction to Health Services, 4th ed.* (S. J. Williams and P. R. Torrens, eds.), Delmar Publishers, Inc., Albany, NY: 219-241.

Riportella-Muller, R., Libby, D. and Kindig, D. (1995). The substitution of physician assistants and nurse practitioners for physician residents in teaching hospitals. *Health Affairs, 14*(2): 181-191.

Rivlin, A. M. and Wiener, J. M. (1988). *Caring for the Disabled Elderly.* Brookings Institution, Washington, DC.

Roemer, M. I. (1978). *Social Medicine: The Advance of Organized Health Services in America.* Springer Press, New York, NY.

Roemer, M. I. (1981). *Ambulatory Health Services in America.* Aspen Systems Corporation, Rockville, MD.

Rosen, G. (1958). *A History of Public Health.* MD Publications, New York, NY.

Rumer, R. (1978). Community mental health centers: Politics and therapy. *Journal of Health Politics, Policy and Law, 3:* 531-558.

Scanlon, W. J. (1988). A perspective on long term care for the elderly. *Health Care Financing Review, Annual Supplement:* 7-16.

Schweiker, R. S. (1983). "Hospital prospective payment for Medicare." Testimony before the U. S. Senate Committee on Finance, Subcommittee on Health. Government Printing Office, Washington, DC.

Shilts, R. (1987). *And the Band Played On.* St. Martin's Press, New York, NY.

Shonick, W. (1993). Public health agencies and services: The partnership network. In *Introduction to Health Services, 4th Ed.* (S. J. Williams and P. R. Torrens, eds.), Delmar Publishers, Inc., Albany, NY: 73-107.

Special Committee on the Aging, U. S. Senate (1991). *Long Term Care: Projected Needs of the Aging Baby Boom Generation.* General Accounting Office, Washington, DC.

Spence, D. A. and Wiener, J. M. (1990). Estimating the extent of Medicaid spend-down in nursing homes. *Journal of Health Politics, Policy and Law,* 15: 607-626.

Starr, P. (1982). *The Transformation of American Medicine.* Basic Books, Inc., New York, NY.

Stevens, R. (1989). *In Sickness and in Wealth.* Basic Books, Inc., New York, NY.

Stevens, R. and Stevens, R. (1974). *Welfare Medicine in America: A Case Study of Medicaid.* The Free Press, New York, NY.

U. S. Commission on Aging (1989). *Projections of the Population of the United States, by Age, Sex and Race.* U. S. Commission on Aging, Washington, DC.

U. S. Department of Health, Education and Welfare (1966). *Hill-Burton Progress Report, July 1, 1947 - June 30, 1966.* Government Printing Office, Washington, DC.

U. S. Department of Health and Human Services (1980). *Promoting Health /Preventing Disease.* U. S. Department of Health and Human Services, Washington, DC.

U. S. Department of Health and Human Services (1986). *Facts and Figures from the Alcohol, Drug Abuse and Mental Health Administration. No. 4.* U. S. Government Printing Office, Washington, DC.

Veterans Administration (1986). *Facts About the Veterans Administration.* V. A. Office of Public and Consumer Affairs, Washington, DC.

Wallis, C. (1991). Why New Age medicine is catching on. *Time, 138 (November 4):* 68-76.

Wennberg, J. E. (1984). Dealing with medical practice variations: A proposal for action. *Health Affairs,* 3: 6-32.

Wiener, J. M., Illston, L. H., and Hanley, R. J. (1994). *Sharing the Burden.* Brookings Institution, Washington, DC.

Williams, S. J. (1983). Ambulatory care: Can hospitals compete? *Hospital and Health Services Administration,* 28: 22-34.

Williams, S. J., and Torrens, P. R. (1993a). Managed care: Restructuring the system. In *Introduction to Health Services* (S. J. Williams and P. R. Torrens, eds.), Delmar Publishers, Inc., Albany, NY: 361-373.

2.
FEDERALISM AND HEALTH CARE

Patricia M. Alt, *Towson State University, Towson, MD*

Toni Marzotto, *Towson State University, Towson, MD*

I. UNLIMITED NEEDS

Health and medicine are basic concerns of American citizens. Conditions once handled by the moral, religious or criminal systems, such as alcoholism, anxiety, over-work, and child abuse, are now classified as sicknesses to be treated by mental- or physical-health professionals (Stone, 1979). Add to this the progress in medical tech-nology, the increase in the length of time people live with chronic conditions, the growth in the proportion of the population over 85, and the shift in insurance coverage and the stage is set for a health care crisis (Jacobs, 1995; Lammers and Leibig, 1990; Leibig, 1992; Ginsburg, 1994).

The U.S. health care system absorbs a huge proportion of national resources. Total spending from all sources in 1993 was $884 billion, a sum that amounted to 14 percent of the Gross Domestic Product (GDP) for that year and an average of $3,300 spent for every man, woman, and child in the nation. That share of GDP has been growing larg-er. In 1965, medical expenditures were only 6.2 percent of GDP; from 1965 to 1993, they grew between 5 and 16 percent every year (USDHHS, 1994). While some authors claim that the proportion of GDP is less significant than the effect of spending it on health rather than other items (opportunity costs), and that the United States is able to spend so much because of excellent worker productivity, most analysts and politicians are concerned (Pauly, 1993; Jacobs, 1993). As Figure 1 illustrates, the United States spends more of its GDP on health care than other developed countries and the gap continues to widen (USDHHS, 1994).

Figure 1 - Comparison of Health Expenditures and Gross Domestic Product for Selected Countries

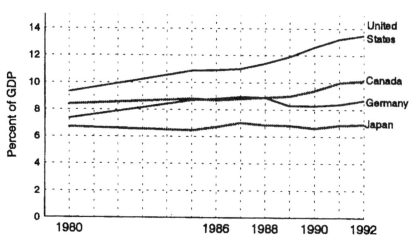

Source: USDHHS, Health, United States 1994, 30.

While the states have long been active players in health care, their role changed in the 1980s and evidence suggests that they will face even more changes in the future (Grogan, 1995; Altman and Morgan, 1993; Bowman and Kearney, 1986; Dodson and Mueller, 1993; Grey, 1994). Changes in the fiscal and philosophical position of the federal government forced states to take a more prominent role in the health care arena (Hebers, 1987; Hanson, 1993; Williamson, 1989). As the perception of fiscal crisis at all governmental levels deepens, both states and the federal government are looking for ways to cut expenditures by changing coverage and/or entitlement, and (where possible) to shift the costs to another level of government or the private sector (Walters, 1994; Vladeck, 1995; USGAO, 1995b).

Although social scientists and politicians of every political stripe agree that the American health care system needs to be reformed, they disagree vehemently on what should be done. The struggle over the composition of the Clinton health reform plan, and its eventual demise, simply exacerbated that situation. It is little wonder, then, that those examining the future roles of states in the evolving system are in equal disarray. There is no denying the variety and complexity of state reforms up through the early 1990s, but will they survive in the face of further federal retrenchment or dissolve into caution and paralysis as the nationwide reform they had anticipated fails to occur? (Sparer, 1995; IHPP, 1995). This chapter examines the changing role and commitment of the states to health care.

II. FEDERALISM: ADVANTAGES AND DISADVANTAGES

States play a vital role in our federal system. Although most people think of Washington, D.C. when they hear the word "government," state and local governments actually provide most of the services that people use (Dye, 1990; Kincaid, 1990; Walker, 1995) Moreover, policies are not simply created by national officials and then routinely implemented by state and local governments in exactly the same form. Rather, state officials make policy and adjust national efforts to match their own particular needs (Boeckelman, 1992; Anton, 1989). For example, the Medicaid program delegates to state officials broad authority to determine who in their state receives coverage, what medical services are covered, and how much providers are paid for delivering care (Adams, 1995; Fossett, 1993; Gold and Felt, 1995). One consequence of this state-based system is wide interstate variation in all phases of health care policy. Here lie both the advantages and disadvantages of federalism.

The federal system is central to government and policy in America. The nation's founders established a federal system for several reasons, one of which was to allay the fears of those who believed that a powerful and distant central government would tyrannize the states and limit their voice in government (Peterson, 1995; Walker, 1995). The promise of a federal system is that subnational autonomy will provide flexibility, innovation, and efficiency by allowing policymakers who are closest to the people to tailor their efforts to local public needs. At the same time, there would be national support for basic governmental services to all citizens, no matter where they live (Bensel, 1984; Derthick, 1992).

The fifty state governments are often characterized as "laboratories of experimentation" (Osborne, 1988) where prospective federal policies may be tried out on a smaller scale and where existing federal programs can be adapted to the conditions and needs of individual states. Because the federal system assigns states important responsibilities for public policies, it is possible for the diversity of opinion within the country to be reflected in different state policies (Peterson, Rabe and Wong, 1986; Peterson, 1995). If citizens in Oregon wish to ration health care (Strosberg, Wiener and Baker, 1992; Neubauer, 1993; Fox and Leichter, 1993), they can vote for politicians who support it, while those in Hawaii can seek to make health care universal (Dick, 1994; Thorne et al., 1995). Of course, in those two examples as in many others, the implementation of the programs requires Federal approval—an ERISA waiver in Hawaii, a Medicaid waiver in Oregon (Thorne et al., 1995).

The disadvantage of federalism is that subnational policymakers might respond only to private, rather than public demands since it is much easier to influence decision-makers in a smaller arena. Thus policies may be skewed in favor of parochial concerns rather than national interests (Anton, 1989). States differ in the resources they can devote (or are willing to devote) to health care services. As a result, state health care financing varies across the country, producing different benefits depending on the state in which a person lives. For example, in 1993 California spent $2,801 for each Medicaid beneficiary while New York spent $7,286 per beneficiary (Sparer, 1995). Client differences as well as state commitment to health care led New York to spend $6.5 billion more than California on half as many people (Sparer, 1995). As Figure 2 illustrates, 1993 Medicaid payments vary by state.

Diversity in policy can also discourage states from providing overly generous services. Many states fear that generous Medicaid benefits will strain their treasuries by attracting poor people from states with lower benefits. Since states are in competition with one another, any state that provides more generous programs that attract more poor people risks becoming a welfare magnet (Bloksberg, 1989; Dodson and Mueller,

Figure 2 - Payment per Medicaid Recipient by State - Fiscal Year 1993

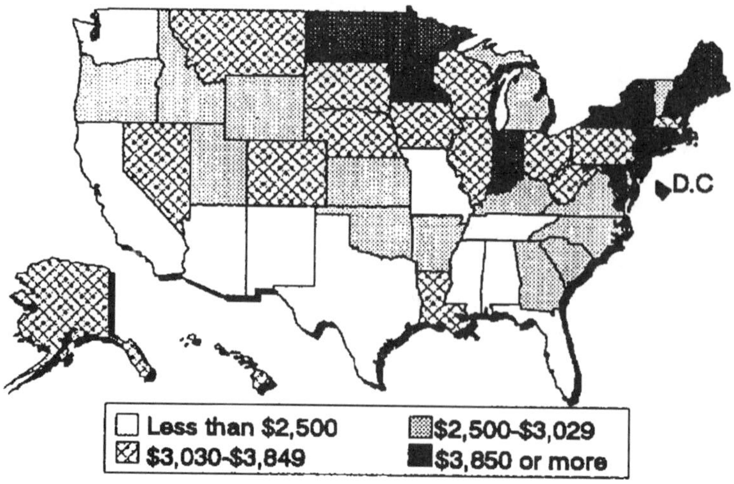

Source: USDHHS, Health, United States 1994, 44.

1993). To avoid becoming a magnet, states often cut benefits, thus inducing a race to the bottom (Peterson, 1995). A national program with uniform benefits, however, provides no incentive for recipients to move to other state. Thus, despite their desire for more program responsibility, the nation's governors in early 1996 proposed that any changes in Medicaid protect them against overly large variations among states (Peirce, 1996).

Fortunately, state responses to policy needs have not displayed the extremes in performance that would validate either the worst fears or the highest hopes of a federal system (Coughlin et al., 1994). State policies are neither totally dominated by internal economic considerations nor completely responsive to public needs. In order to understand the variation in health policy across the states, it is useful to examine various perspectives on federalism and models of state government behavior.

III. FEDERALISM: OLD AND NEW

State responsibilities in health care have increased significantly since 1935 (Morine and Belkin, 1994). This expansion of state policy responsibility did not occur in a vacuum, however. Important changes in state political systems predisposed the states to successfully handle increased authority in health care (Bowman and Kearney, 1986; Conlon, 1988), whether these policies were developed spontaneously by the states or thrust upon them by national political figures (Buerger, 1995). In this section we briefly recap national and state-level political changes that led to the states' increased role in health care.

The cornerstone of the national government's relations with state and local governments is fiscal federalism (Kenyon and Kincaid, 1991; Aaron, 1992), the pattern of spending, taxing, and providing grants in the federal system. State governments can influence the national government through local elections for national office, but the national government has a powerful source of influence over the states — money (Derthick, 1970; Boeckelman, 1992; Bowman and Kearney, 1986). A grant-in-aid is the main instrument the national government uses for both aiding and influencing states and localities.

There are two major types of federal aid for states and localities—formula and project grants (Grey and Eisinger, 1991; Aaron, 1992; Raffel and Raffel, 1994). Formula grants are monies divided among a group of entities such as states, cities, or universities. Formula grants are distributed as their name implies, according to a formula. These formulas vary from grant to grant and may be computed on the basis of population, per capita income, percentage of rural population, or some other factor. States do not apply for a formula grant; a grant's formula determines how much money each will receive. These grants are distributed more or less automatically to states or communities, which have some discretion in deciding how to spend the money (Conlon, 1988; Walker, 1995). The most extensive health-related formula grants are those for Medicaid, AFDC, and child nutrition programs.

The two primary varieties of formula grants are categorical grants and block grants. From 1950 until 1965, categorical grants were increasingly used to encourage state and local public health agencies to move into areas regarded as national priorities (Davis and Schoen, 1978). Due to increases in the number and dollar, categorical grants accounted for 80 percent of all federal aid to state and local governments by 1965 (Shonick, 1993). These grants can be used only for special purposes or categories of state and local spending. They also come with strings attached; virtually every categorical grant comes with rules and requirements about its use. Many states were unhappy with them due to the red tape involved, and because a considerable proportion of them went directly to local governments or other local-level organizations by passing the states (Conlon, 1988; Anton, 1989; Walker, 1995).

Block grants are a second type of formula grant. Block grants are used to support broad programs in areas like community development and social service. In 1966, primarily in response to state government complaints, the decision was made at the national level to move as many programs as possible into block grants, reversing the trend toward increasing numbers of categorical grants (Walker, 1995). Although states prefer block grants, in principle, the dollar amount grew very slowly. One argument for slow growth is that the coalitions supporting block grants are too diffuse to muster the necessary lobbying muscle to force Congress to increase the funding for them (Walker, 1995). A political rule of thumb is that the less specific the program, the harder it is to pry funds out of Congress to increase the size of that program.

Project grants constitute the other major type of grants in which money is given for a very specific purpose, and generally only to a recipient organization which can justify a request for the money (Conlon, 1988; Aaron, 1992). As funding for categorical grants shrank in the late sixties, project grants increased as a way to continue to fund valued activities. Project grants are awarded competitively, with no guarantee that all applicants will receive funds. They are typically reviewed by outside review committees and awarded based on the merit of the proposed project. They are also theoretically time-limited for the most part, serving to demonstrate new approaches to programs before wider formula grants are developed (Swartz and Peck, 1990).

Revenue sharing was yet another response to states' requests for more money with fewer strings. First proposed in the Johnson administration, revenue sharing became a favorite of the Nixon administration (Tallon and Nathan, 1992). In revenue sharing programs, virtually no strings were attached to federal aid payments—they could be used for almost any policy area. Although revenue sharing was a help to many poor states and localities, it never amounted to more than 2 percent of all state and local revenues. In 1987 the program fell victim to the Reagan budgetary axe. (Shonick, 1993; Williamson, 1989).

President Reagan's "New Federalism" program, launched after the 1980 election, was the most far-reaching domestic initiative in twenty-five years (Conlan, 1988; Williamson, 1989). Federal activities under new federalism can be grouped into two general categories. First, the federal government sought to devolve increasing responsibility for most domestic programs to the states (where, it was argued, responsibility for most domestic programs belonged). Returning responsibility to the states was supposed to render policymaking and implementation more efficient, effective and responsive to citizen demands. A good deal of pressure was placed on state governments to accept greater responsibility in several policy areas (USGAO, 1995a; USGAO, 1995b). In fact, it was during this period that the "great swap" was proposed, whereby the federal government proposed that the states take full responsibility for Medicaid programs in return for the federal government taking over the Aid to Families with Dependent Children program (Tallon and Nathan, 1992).

Second, in an effort to shrink domestic expenditures, the federal government slashed its contributions to many of the programs which had been given back to the states (Conlan, 1988: Nathan, 1987). While many researchers have questioned the proposed benefits of Reagan's new federalism, some have argued that new federalism was a guise for an underlying goal of significant policy retrenchment in the areas of health,

Figure 3 - Federal Aid as a Percentage of State/Local Budgets

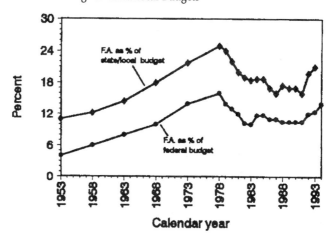

➡ **Series 1:** Federal aid as a percentage of state/local expenditures after transfers.
➡ **Series 2:** Federal aid as a percentage of federal expenditures from own funds.

Source: *Advisory Commission on Intergovernmental Relations, Significant Features of Fiscal Federalism: 1993, vol. 2 (Washington, DC: Advisory Committee on Intergovernmental Relations, 1993).*

social welfare, and environmental protection (Nathan and Doolittle, 1983). For example, as Figure 3 illustrates, federal grants as a percentage of total state expenditures fell from 26 percent in 1978 to just under 18 percent in 1989 (ACIR, 1994).

During this same period, however, the proportion of federal aid to individuals increased significantly. Health costs went from 3 percent of the federal aid dollars to states in 1960 to 37 percent in 1992 (USOMB, 1992). Thus despite an overall decline in federal aid, money for health programs as a percentage of federal aid continues to grow.

Although accurate cost comparisons are dependent on which years are chosen, most statistics reveal that federal aid to state governments increased, especially in the health area. For example, from 1975 to 1993, per capita Federal aid to state and local governments increased by 84 percent (USDHHS, 1995). However, non-Medicaid federal aid per capita only increased by 32.2 percent in that time while Medicaid federal aid per capita jumped by 372 percent (USDHHS, 1995). After a decade in which inflation accounted for most of the increase, there was a sharp increase in federal aid, primarily for Medicaid, beginning in 1989. This occurred due to increases in medical inflation, population increases, greater unemployment and loss of job-related health insurance due to an economic slowdown, and Congressional authorizations to change Medicaid by expanding eligibility, compensating hospitals for care of the poor, and allowing provider contributions to offset the state portion of Medicaid spending (IHPP, 1995; USDHHS, 1995).

Increases in state policy responsibility were not simply a function of Reagan's new federalism. In their roles as regulators of insurance, states explored new ways to ensure wider coverage for their citizens. Although Hawaii was the only state which passed legislation establishing uniform health insurance coverage requirements in 1974 before the Federal ERISA law made that impossible (Chirba-Martin and Brennan, 1994), many other states established their own individual approaches to reform before the Clinton administration's effort in 1993. Even Hawaii had to persist through numerous court challenges until Congress granted them an exemption from ERISA to allow their plan to proceed (Neubauer, 1993; Fox and Leichter, 1993; Crittenden, 1993).

Actually, the ERISA situation is a good example of the difficulties facing state-level reform. Passed in 1974 as an effort to reform the nation's pension system and make employee retirements more secure, the Employee Retirement Income Security Act (ERISA) has had a strong impact on health insurance. The law allows self-insured companies to be exempt from state regulations, preempting those regulations with federal control. However, it imposes virtually no substantive requirements regarding employee benefit plans, and its implementation by the U.S. Labor Department has focused entirely on pension plans (Chirba-Martin and Brennan, 1994). This precluded states from requiring truly universal coverage, since they cannot control the level of benefits provided to the 40 percent of employees in self-insured health plans (Sullivan et al., 1992).

IV. DETERMINANTS OF STATE POLICY VARIATION

As noted earlier, the states play a key role in the policy process. While the federal government often sets general goals and guidelines, individual states have a significant amount of discretion regarding the type and stringency of the program they implement (Boeckelman, 1992). Most of the oversight, implementation, and enforcement of policy takes place at the state level. Some states have used the discretion afforded by federal legislation to go beyond the requirements of federal health statutes (Sparer, 1995). Moreover, states often have significant health programs and responsibilities of their own, separate from those required by the federal government (Jacobson, 1995; Hanson,1994; Leichter, 1992; Leichter, 1993a; Justice, 1988). One consequence of this state-based system is the wide variation in all phases of health care policy. Trying to understand the reasons for and causes of this state-wide variation is the subject of much research. Three models dominate the study of comparative state policy — the economic, the political, and the group theory models. These models apply to all policy areas, but are quite useful in understanding state roles in health.

A. Economic Model

The economic-determinants or affordability model is based on the assumption that wealthier states can afford more services and can innovate with new techniques (Dye, 1990; Nelson, 1994). Although the measures of wealth may vary, state per-capita income is often used as one indicator. Based on this model we would expect to find that wealthier states provide their citizens with more generous health care services than do poorer states. For example, Connecticut was ranked first in personal income per capita in 1990 (US Department of Commerce, 1995); in 1992 it ranked second in per capita expenditures for Medicaid recipients (USDHHS, 1993). For example, in Table 1 we see the relationship of per capita income for the ten wealthiest and ten poorest states and per capita Medicaid and Medicare payments. There is a relationship for some states, but not a uniformly clear-cut one.

The theoretical explanation given for the influence of economic variables is that economic development provides a state with the resources needed to expand public programs (Dye, 1990; Bowman and Kearney, 1986). A related argument is that economic development creates an expanded set of demands to which policy-makers respond (Sharkansky and Hofferbert, 1969). Critics of this model have argued that the affects of income and industrialization on public policy are indirect, mediated through political institutions. Demands are translated into policy through the political system.

B. Political Model

A second theory, based on the political determinants or political culture model, argues that a state's own unique political culture determines public policy (Elazar, 1984). The approach is based on the assumption that political structures and institutions are important factors accounting for policy differences among states. Much of the recent research in comparative state politics has illustrated that political institutions and political conditions in the state do matter in the policy process (Plotnick and Winter, 1995). States with high citizen involvement and professional legislatures are more likely to increase spending for social programs. Conversely, states with a tradition of lower government involvement in social programs will maintain that stance even in the face of federal pressure and incentives to shift, according to this model. This argument suggests that each state has a distinctive political and institutional history, and this legacy can be expected to have fiscal consequences (Peterson, 1995).

Table 1 - Comparison of State per Capita Income with Medicaid and Medicare Payments for the Ten Richest and Ten Poorest States in 1992.

RANKED: TEN RICHEST STATES	RANK: MEDICAID COSTS PER PERSON	RANK: MEDICARE PAYMENTS
Richest: 1 Connecticut	2nd	6th
2 New Jersey	9th	13th
3 New York	1st	8th
4 Massachussets	4th	3rd
5 Maryland	8th	9th
6 Hawaii	31st	33rd
7 Alaska	18th	37th
8 Nevada	12th	11th
9 New Hampshire	3rd	34th
10 Illinois	22nd	18th

RANKED: TEN POOREST STATES	RANK: MEDICAID COSTS PER PERSON	RANK: MEDICARE PAYMENTS
41 Alabama	44th	20th
42 Kentucky	36th	26th
43 South Carolina	33rd	42nd
44 Idaho	19th	49th
45 Louisiana	17th	4th
46 New Mexico	45th	45th
47 Arkansas	29th	25th
48 Utah	34th	47th
49 West Virginia	37th	35th
Poorest: 50 Mississippi	49th	18th

Source: Table compiled from USDHHS, Health, United States Statistical Abstracts of the United States
U.S. Department of Health and Human Services Health Care Financing Administration

States with strong health care programs are more apt to have citizens who are predisposed to government involvement in solving social problems.

The political culture variable has also been measured in terms of partisanship based on the argument that Democrats lend more support to health efforts than do Republicans. When Democrats dominate a state house or legislature, then hypothetically the state has more developed health care programs (Anton, 1989). Alternative measures of political culture use composite measures of citizen's involvement in the decision-making process. This view emphasizes public concern, welfare, and participation. States can be characterized as either moralistic, individualistic (market-oriented), or traditionalistic (status quo-oriented) (Elazar, 1985).

C. Group Model

The group theory or pluralist model is based on the idea that public policy is a product of a competitive compromise among organized (and some unorganized) groups (Oliver and Dowell, 1994). The interest group perspective is based on the expectation that state and local policy-makers are closer to the people but also that certain groups of people utilize that proximity more effectively than others (Bentley, 1967).

The political role of interest groups is especially important at the state level since there is a good deal of evidence that the diversification of organized interests is weaker (Walker, 1995). In many states those groups representing dominant economic interests are by far the most influential. The influence of these groups is particularly strong in regulatory policy (Kettl, 1987), and in less industrialized states where countervailing interests are no match for the dominant industrial concerns. State policy-makers subvert federal intentions because, even if not part of the organized interests themselves, they are part of the existing power arrangement that depends on support from powerful groups for its existence.

Since all groups are not equal in terms of their resources and influence, more dominant groups have the ability to control the political agenda, thus preventing open debate over the full range of policy options. This theory is supported in the health care field where the opposition of providers, insurers, and suppliers effectively tabled recent efforts at national health reform (Bowman and Pagano, 1995; Galston and Tibbetts, 1994). If policy-makers had been united in their position, then interest group opposition might have been thwarted. But given the diversity of the views on health reform, it was easy for opponents to portray the entire effort as flawed.

V. STATE CAPACITY: CAN STATES ACCEPT RESPONSIBILITY?

The performance of a state's political system depends to a great extent on the capacity of its governmental institutions. As the states' responsibility for health programs increases, an important question arises over the ability and competence of the states to administer these programs. Research in the 1950s and 1960s generally concluded that the states were ill suited to accept or carry out an expanded role within the federal system. State governments labored under outmoded constitutions and revenue systems, unrepresentative and unprofessional legislatures, weak governors, and weak and disjointed administrative agencies. State governments were criticized as being racist, incompetent, and unwilling to change and for routinely ignoring their policy responsibilities (Davis and Lester 1989; Sanford 1967). A few researchers, however, claimed that states were unfairly charged with fiscal irresponsibility and administrative incompetence (Elazar, 1974).

The capacity of the states to accept and administer expanding policy authority has increased in the past two decades. According to the ACIR (1985), almost every facet of state government structures and operations has been transformed. Beginning in the late 1960s and continuing through the 1970s, state governments underwent a metamorphosis from which they emerged stronger, smarter, and more willing and able to undertake significant policy responsibility. Reagan's new federalism initiatives prodded the states to continue reforming and improving their governmental institutions through the 1980s (Bowman and Kearney 1986, 1988).

State capacity has been described as "the ability to anticipate and influence change; make informed and intelligent decisions about policy; attract and absorb resources... and evaluate current activities to guide future actions" (Honadale, 1981, p. 578). When discussing the capacity of state governments to accept significant policy responsibilities, however, one has to be specific about what type of "capacity" one is talking about, since capacity is a multi-dimensional concept. Charles Warren (1982) has categorized state abilities in this area as fiscal capacity, managerial capacity, and political capacity. All three forms are necessary if states are to adequately carry out policy responsibilities. Fortunately, these three types of capacity have all improved over the past twenty-five years. In terms of policymaking and implementation, states are more representative, responsible, activist, and professional today than they ever have been (ACIR 1985).

A. Fiscal Capacity

Fiscal Capacity refers to revenue levels, revenue sources and the use states make of these revenue sources. Excluding social security, states spend far more on civilian domestic programs than does the federal government, and this gap has been increasing (Gray and Eisinger 1991). Developing and administering these policies takes money, and states lacking adequate fiscal capacity will find both of these tasks difficult. State governments have been forced to increase their fiscal capacity in the face of reduced aid from the federal government, and they have responded. State governments are using many more revenue sources in the 1990s than they did in the 1960s. Of particular note is the tremendous increase in the use of state personal and corporate income taxes, which by 1990 were responsible for 40 percent of state revenues—nearly double the level in the 1960s (ACIR, 1992).

Increased spending for social programs accompanied this increased utilization of revenue sources. States spent nearly $600 billion in 1990 compared with only $73 billion in 1964 (constant 1987 dollars) (ACIR, 1992). Per capita state spending rose faster than spending at any other level of government, increasing 269 percent in constant dollar terms between 1959 and 1979 (Davis and Lester, 1989). Although recent economic downturns had many states running large general fund deficits, states have been covering these using surpluses in state social insurance funds (IHPP, 1995).

B. Managerial Capacity

Clearly, state fiscal capacity has improved over the past few decades, but what of managerial capacity? Managerial capacity refers to the ability of states to successfully carry out their charges in program design, policy execution and implementation, and the delivery of public services (Warren, 1982). Managerial capacity is closely tied to the capacity of state government institutions. The office of governor has been strengthened throughout the nation. Fewer term limitations and an increased reliance upon professional staffs have created more professional state chief executives (Beyle and Williams, 1972).

Perhaps no institution of state government has been transformed to the degree of state bureaucracies. Administrative reorganizations and constitutional revisions have rationalized bureaucratic structure in many states. State administrators are better educated, more professional, better compensated, and more representative of the general public than their counterparts of just a decade or two ago. This increase in professionalism has led to a higher degree of policy competence among state administrators (Haas and Wright, 1988). One argument has been made that much of the improvement in state bureaucratic capability has resulted from federally required levels of bureaucratic staffing and competence that have accompanied the increased devolution of policy authority to the states. Whatever the cause, the effect is undeniable.

C. Political Capacity

State political capacity is more difficult to define, but it relates to the ability of state governments to "articulate needs, weigh competing demands, establish priorities, and allocate resources" (Warren, 1982, p. 37). From this definition, political capacity appears to overlap the institutional improvements associated with managerial capacity. Political capacity refers to a state's ability to make difficult, necessary, and innovative policy decisions. Skeptics of devolving increased policy responsibility to the states are most concerned about questions of political capacity. Many critics of state capacity openly wonder whether state governments have improved enough to adequately handle their new policy responsibilities (ACIR, 1985). State governments have been increasingly prominent in policy innovations, however, suggesting that some of the worries of these critics may be unfounded.

VI. STATE HEALTH POLICY BEFORE 1965

A. Historical View

In the early days of the Republic, the states had little or no role in health care. Only local governments were involved in the regulation and protection of public health. The federal government monitored the borders and quarantined immigrants if necessary, and it did provide health care to soldiers and those in the merchant marine. In the mid-1800s, professional health departments emerged in big cities, led by local Health Officers. Constitutionally, those individuals were empowered by their states to carry out the state's "police power" to "enact and enforce laws to protect and promote the health, safety, morals, order, peace, comfort, and general welfare of the people" (Shonick, 1993). Typically, big city governments provided garbage and sewer services, furnished safe drinking water and kept rabies, disease-bearing insects, and epidemic diseases under control. The importance of these measures should not be overlooked, as they contributed the principle element to increased life expectancy. Local governments also supported some direct health services, sometimes providing free clinics and immunization for the poor and supporting charity wards in county hospitals (Raffel and Raffel, 1994)

Only slowly did states themselves develop a health function, usually in response to local requests for assistance. Between 1870 and 1910, all the states created a state-level health department of some sort. Most of them had overt linkages with local health departments (Raffel and Raffel, 1994). However, they varied widely in the functions which they performed and in how strongly the state supported local efforts. A 1925 study found that the proportion of local health department funds provided by the states ranged from 48% down to practically nil (Shonick, 1993). Basically, the role of the states was to monitor and encourage the local governments as they carried out their health care functions.

After the passage of the Social Security Act in 1935, the states expanded their involvement in a wide range of public health programs. Expenditures for state health departments grew from $12.9 million in 1930 to $37 million in 1946 (Shonick, 1993). The Mountin Report in 1946 analyzed the effects of ten years of federal grants-in-aid on state and local health programs. It found that the states had increased their program involvement and their personnel significantly during that time, becoming more professionally staffed in all areas of health (Shonick, 1993).

However the prevailing attitude among federal policymakers and social scientists until the 1980s was that state governments could not be trusted to appropriately care for the public's welfare. The growth in state programs was largely due to federal categorical grant programs which delineated how funds were to be spent, the types of personnel which were to be hired, and requirements that states provide matching funds out of their own budgets. As Thompson (1986) pointed out, there were a number of roots for the "dismal view of the states" in health policy. These included concerns about states' commitment to the assurance of equal access to health care for all their citizens, particularly when that access might require redistributive policies (Lowi, 1969). Another major area of worry was over the states' ability to formulate and carry out policies, given their histories of less than adequate professional staffing for government. Yet another concern was the lack of tax progressivity at state and local levels, leading to the likelihood that programs would be disproportionately paid for by those least able to fund them (Thompson, 1986).

B. Expansion of State Roles

In the mid-1960s, the volume and complexity of federal health legislation increased dramatically and expenditures exploded. Medicare and Medical Assistance (Medicaid), the most important programs, were enacted in 1965 after years of debate in Congress over the federal role in providing or insuring medical care. Many legislators had long disputed any federal responsibility in this area, while others had advocated a program of national health care along European lines. A compromise was reached in which social insurance would be extended to cover serious health needs of the aged; this was the birth of Medicare. Almost as an afterthought, Medicaid was added to help the states pay the medical expenses of welfare recipients. Neither program was designed to change the organization or delivery of health care in the U.S. but only to pay some of the bills and increase access to many not adequately served (Raffel and Raffel, 1994).

While states had no role in Medicare, they were to administer Medicaid within broad Federal guidelines, and to provide their proportionate share of its costs (approximately 50 percent to 80 percent nationwide, varying with states' assessed taxing capabilities and with the provisions of the particular sections of the program). Early on, it became apparent that Medicaid was going to cause problems for the states. The federal law required that all states provide five "basic" services: (Shonick, 1993)
- inpatient and outpatient hospital care
- nursing homes
- laboratory services
- x-ray services and
- private physician services.

They were also permitted to add "optional" services, for which the federal government would provide matching funds. States were required to pay hospitals (and later nursing homes) on a cost-related basis, and were forbidden to assign patients to particular providers. As Vladeck (1979) pointed out, the combination of financial accountability without the authority to shape programs for themselves left states in an untenable position, not only with regard to the Medicaid program, but also in other areas of health care funding and regulation such as provider licensure and health planning. The argument that responsibility for payment must be linked with authority for administration and regulation runs through the literature as a counterpoint to that examining the commitment of various levels of government to health care, and to that questioning the appropriate level of government involvement in the field.

By 1986, Thompson was able to show that the levels of disparity among states in capacity, commitment, and progressivity had diminished markedly. However, substantial variation remained as did states' reluctance to expand programs which might commit them to economically difficult promises. In the late '80s, states were becoming more dissimilar in revenue capacity and tax effort, as well. Reagan's New Federalism delegated more responsibility to the states, but also placed more Federal regulation on their behavior. At the same time, limits on taxing and spending (beginning with Proposition 13 in California) were enacted in many states, hindering their ability to make up the fiscal difference in programs caused by Federal cuts in grants.

As grant coverage declined and the ranks of the uninsured grew, Congress acted to require the expansion of Medicaid to the most vulnerable populations, particularly poor pregnant women with incomes up to 133 percent of the Federal Poverty Level (FPL) and their infants up to one year old; children under 6 years old in families with incomes under 133 percent of the FPL; children born after September 30, 1983 in families with incomes below the FPL; and Medicare beneficiaries (aged, blind, and disabled) with incomes below the FPL (USDHHS, 1995). In many states, the maximum level of income for Medicaid eligibility was considerably less than the Federal Poverty Level ($11,522 for a family of three in 1993). These new areas of coverage changed the character of Medicaid which had previously served poor persons in families receiving AFDC cash assistance and the aged, blind, or disabled receiving SSI cash assistance. By making Medicaid eligibility separate from other cash assistance programs, it was allowed to grow even as those programs shrank (USDHHS, 1993). This put additional pressure on states as they had to cover these new categories of Medicaid eligibles even as they were pushing other impoverished citizens out of the welfare rolls.

VII. THE STATES TAKE OVER

During the last few years, several states have passed comprehensive health care reforms. Despite the concentration of media attention on Washington, states have become major players in the health care arena. This is due in large part to concern over rising health care costs. In 1994, health care expenditures (mainly from Medicaid) ate up 18 percent of state budgets, and they will absorb over 25 percent in the mid-1990s. From 1989 to 1993, state spending on Medicaid more than doubled to $55 billion (USDHHS, 1995). As a result of spending more on health care, states are forced to spend less on higher education, roads and other priorities. There was also a sense in the early 1990s that a national package of health care reform was imminent. If a state wanted to shape its own health system, it needed to be in place before the national reform happened (IHPP, 1995). As a result, state efforts to reform health care accelerated in the early 1990s.

However, it soon became clear that health care reform in the U.S. would not be led by the national government. State health reforms have become the leading edge of change in the 1990s and are defining the outlines of the new health care system in the U.S. While the availability of Federal matching funds and new coverage for Medicaid recipients is a central element in the calculations, states are developing unique responses to the health care needs of their citizens. The Intergovernmental Health Policy Project identifies the major categories of these responses under the headings of access to care, managed care, cost containment, and provider availability (IHPP, 1995). These fit with the commonly accepted areas of concern about health care: access, cost, and quality. The solutions to these three problems are widely regarded as being in conflict. Guaranteeing access to health care for all Americans could increase costs and could reduce quality. Some health policy scholars, however, believe that cost control and universal access can only happen together. At the state level, efforts to change access, cost, and quality have hinged on improvements in state capacity and concomitant ambitiousness in policymaking. States have been willing to try new paths, often with federal encouragement.

A. Access to Care

The states have undertaken many methods to improve access to care. Concerns have included the maldistribution of resources in disparate geographical areas and the differential ability of citizens to obtain insurance coverage. States have also been eager to try new approaches to the Medicaid program, tailoring it to their specific populations. In the recent past, health care commissions in forty-two states have produced reports with their recommendations being embodied in a stream of legislative efforts reflecting the national debate on health reform (IHPP,1995). Medical savings accounts and tax incentives for insurance coverage have passed in a minority of states. Forty-three states have some sort of program using public funds or private resources to target expanding coverage to vulnerable populations such as children, indigent, and the uninsured (IHPP, 1995). Some of the central elements in the unadopted Clinton plan have been incorporated as part of various states' packages, as well (Tallon and Nathan, 1992). Efforts to expand access have concentrated on three major areas; universal coverage, insurance market reforms, and Medicaid waivers (IHPP, 1995).

1. Universal Coverage

One approach has been the attempt to establish comprehensive plans for universal coverage. Only Hawaii has managed to implement a mandatory financing scheme, due in part to its plan escaping the pressures of ERISA. In Washington and Minnesota, where sweeping expansions were passed in the early '90s, significant portions of their laws were repealed in 1995, due to federal inaction (Sparer, 1995). Oregon's pay-or-play law will expire in 1996 without an ERISA waiver, which is not expected in the near future (Crittenden, 1995; IHPP, 1995). Massachusetts has established a new commission to explore its employer mandate law before it is implemented, delaying that process yet again. Finally, the Florida Health Security Act was not even considered during the 1995 legislative session (IHPP, 1995). Uncertainty over what Congress will do has stalled most of these programs or slowed them to a crawl, as the states fear being left with expanded programs and reduced federal support. As noted earlier, states do not want to become health care magnets (Peterson, 1995).

2. Insurance Market Reform

Since 1980 the percentage of the population with health insurance coverage declined due to high levels of unemployment and economic changes (Holahan et al., 1995). In 1993, 16.8 percent of the population were not covered by either a public or private health insurance program. While this had only expanded from 15 percent in 1988, the distribution of the uninsured had shifted. Medicaid had been expanded to cover a larger proportion of the poor and near-poor, while employer-sponsored coverage had shrunk for all segments of the population (Holahan et al., 1995). Thus, there had been a shift of responsibility for insurance away from the private sector and toward public programs at the same time that the country seemed to be moving away from expanding government roles.

States' efforts to expand access to care were intimately linked to these shifts in insurance coverage. In the early '90s, most states enacted laws leading to insurance market reforms to enable small businesses and individuals to more easily purchase insurance (IHPP, 1995). States also sought to prohibit discrimination against high risk individuals who were more likely to get sick, and to allow people to change jobs without losing their insurance coverage. Other states have moved to establish purchasing alliances to enable small companies to negotiate as a group with insurance plans and/or providers, thus receiving better rates (IHPP, 1995). While there is tremendous variety in the particulars of these plans, all reflect a common concern that the private insurance market be made more accessible to workers. However, many of the new laws are being tested in court as the insurance industry resists them.

3. Medicaid Waivers

States are able to apply for two types of waiver from Federal regulations on Medicaid. Those under section 1915(b) of the Social Security Act allow them to run their programs somewhat differently than the basic model for operating Medicaid. Waivers under section 1115 of the same Act allows states to change any aspect of the Medicaid program in order to implement statewide research and demonstration projects (Riley, 1995; IHPP, 1995; USDHHS, 1995). The design and use of these waivers has grown rapidly in the early 1990s, with 43 states having 1915(b) waivers as of 1995, five operating under 1115 waivers, six with 1115 waivers approved and beginning to be implemented, and another twenty in various stages of developing them. The thrust of almost all of these waivers has been to develop managed care approaches to Medicaid (Riley, 1995). From January of 1994 to December, 1995, the percentage of Medicaid recipients getting their care from managed care plans jumped from 14 percent to 23 percent, with no end in sight to the trend (IHPP, 1995). However, most of the programs implemented so far apply only to recipients of Aid to Families with

Dependent Children. These individuals (mostly women and children) constitute 75 percent of the enrollees in Medicaid, but account for only about one-fourth of the spending (IHPP, 1995; USDHHS, 1995).

As states seek to expand the waivers to their disabled and elderly populations, they are moving into areas where the value of managed care is less obvious, and where provider interest groups and patient advocacy organizations are more vocal. The National Association of Community Health Centers is suing to stop the implementation of 1115 waivers, claiming that they will siphon off clients from these "providers of last resort" and will leave the poor and disabled without sufficient sources of care (IHPP, 1995). Similar concerns surfaced in the establishment of TennCare, the statewide managed care system in Tennessee. Using twelve insurer groups known as Managed Care Organizations (MCOs), the state shifted 800,000 recipients into managed care, and added 400,000 with no previous insurance (some critics doubt these numbers, claiming they are "double counted" (IHPP, 1995). The issues in Tennessee are echoed nationwide: are there enough primary care providers to adequately serve the clientele? Is it equitable for Medicaid to pay approximately one-third the rate which a provider would be receiving from a private pay patient? How can these MCOs be regulated to ensure fiscal accountability? What level of copayment and deductibles is reasonable for those with incomes above the poverty line? (IHPP, 1995; Thorne et al., 1995).

As states grapple with these issues and wait for federal clarity, they are often slowing the process of reform. States such as Ohio, which has received a federal waiver to implement a statewide OhioCare demonstration, have declined to move forward until the current debate over turning Medicaid into a block grant is resolved. Other states, stung by new limits on payments to hospitals, are maneuvering to expand their programs before any block grant is passed. Illinois, Louisiana, and Florida, for instance, are seeking to enlarge their spending on Medicaid in order to position themselves to be eligible for a larger amount from any block grant which might occur (IHPP, 1995). States which already have waiver programs, such as Hawaii, are tightening client eligibility claiming pressure sluggish economies. There is no doubt that access to care is closely linked to concerns about cost containment at both the federal and state levels.

B. Cost Containment

Reversing a decline in the use of regulation in the early 1980s, states have moved back toward efforts to control the growth of health care costs. One of the most popular means is the use of Certificate of Need (CON) programs. As of 1995, thirty-eight states had some form of CON, regulating the building or expansion of health care facilities or services and/or the purchase of major medical equipment (IHPP, 1995; Raffel and Raffel, 1994). In addition, facility rate-setting continues to exist in New York and Maryland, although New Jersey and Massachusetts have disbanded their systems. Other cost-control mechanisms include physician fee regulation (enacted but not implemented in two states), uniform claims forms (required in thirty-eight states), data collection guidelines in forty-six states, clinical practice guidelines for some conditions (in eleven states), and self-referral restriction in thirty-four states (IHPP, 1995).

All of these endeavors share a common intention of controlling the expansion and complexity of the medical care system. By limiting the supply of hospital beds or specialized procedures, CON laws seek to ensure that care is only provided to those who genuinely need it. Fee regulation and rate-setting aim to limit the amount of "profit" to be made by providers of care, as does the control of self-referral. The development of uniform claims forms, data collection guidelines, and clinical practice guidelines is intended to provide a rational framework for the practice and reimbursement of medicine such that analysis of practice patterns could produce cost-beneficial changes in care. The hope is that establishing a watchdog function over providers (and insurers) will lead to more careful use of resources. Of course, questions inevitably arise regarding the effect of cost control efforts on the quality of care being delivered.

C. Quality of Health Care/Provider Availability

Overlapping with access and cost concerns, particularly in the area of managed care, is the underlying commitment of the states to ensure the quality of care being provided. This can be done by reviewing the actual care received using some set of objective standards, by regulating insurance coverage, or by controlling who is allowed to practice in the first place. Dating back at least to the first licensure laws, and to the public provision of medical and nursing education, the stated commitment to quality has been a stable piece of state involvement in health care (Vladeck, 1979). Some states are even beginning to involve themselves in the assessment of medical technologies as the federal government withdraws from the field (Mendelson, Abramson and Rubin, 1995).

Following the example set by the National Health Service Corps, forty-eight states currently have loan forgiveness programs for medical students who promise to practice in underserved areas or in specialties where there is a shortage of health professionals (IHPP, 1995). Six states actually have quota measures requiring medical schools to produce a certain percentage of primary care providers in their graduating classes. Another way of ensuring provider availability is by having charitable immunity laws protecting doctors who provide free care: those laws now exist in 22 states (IHPP, 1995). All of these efforts seek to improve the supply of basic medical care, particularly since managed care programs rely heavily on primary care practitioners for preventive and first level care.

In the arena of managed care, state legislatures have sought to protect patients and providers through a series of efforts. Thirty-two states have enacted "Any Willing Provider" laws, which require managed care organizations to accept any provider who agrees to abide by their contract. In the majority of cases, however, these provisions apply only to pharmacists. Similarly, "Freedom of Choice" laws allowing managed care enrollees to use the provider of their choice are also primarily aimed at pharmacies. Ten states have passed laws mandating certain practices by managed care organizations (including such items as coverage of bone marrow transplants and 48-hour inpatient care after normal delivery). All states have laws covering the existence of HMOs, and many are currently wrestling with legislation to deal with the existence of Accountable Health Plans, Provider Networks, and the many other quasi-insurance/quasi-provider organizations which are rapidly emerging (IHPP, 1995).

VIII. INTO THE FUTURE

States are capable of tremendous variety in the design and implementation of health policies. While much of their initial growth in this area stemmed from the requirements of federal categorical grants, many states now have a critical mass of policymakers, administrators, providers and advocates who influence their path as much as federal policy. No one simple explanation seems to work in this situation. Economic influences apply, in that downturns in a state's employment situation cause extra pressure on Medicaid and reduce the likelihood of innovative programs. However, wealthier states vary among themselves in the depth and breadth of health coverage they offer to their citizens (see Table 1). Political culture also shapes the situation, with some states having a long history of regulatory approaches to health care delivery (Maryland), while others are more generous in benefits to the poor (New York). Group pressures shape the areas in which a state seeks to improve its health system, also. Nursing home groups are often extremely powerful, for example, in restraining Medicaid cost-control efforts for the elderly and disabled. With major shifts at both the state and federal level in political willingness to provide social programs, the role of the states may well be a measure of the country's continued commitment to its citizens' health.

REFERENCES

Adams, E.K. (1995). Equity in the medicaid program: Changes in the later 1980s. *Health Care Financing Review, 16* (3): 55-74.

Advisory Committee on Intergovernmental Relations (ACIR) (1985). *A Question of State Government Capacity.* Government Printing Office, Washington, DC.

Advisory Committee on Intergovernmental Relations (ACIR) (1992). *Significant Features of Fiscal Federalism.* Government Printing Office, Washington, DC.

Advisory Committee on Intergovernmental Relations (ACIR) (1993). *Significant Features of Fiscal Federalism.* Government Printing Office, Washington, DC.

Altman, D. and Morgan, D. (1993). The Role of State and Local Government in Health. *Health Affairs*: 8-31.

Anton, T. (1989). *American Federalism and Public Policy.* Temple University Press, Philadelphia.

Anderson, G., Chaulk, P., and Fowler, E., (1993). Maryland: A Regulatory Approach to Health Systems Reform. *Health Affairs, 12* (Summer): 40-47.

Aaron, H. J. (1991). *Serious and Unstable Condition: Financing America's Health Care..* The Brookings Institution, Washington, DC.

Barrilleaux, C. and Miller, M. (1992). Decisions Without Consequences: Cost Control and Access in State Medicaid Programs. *Journal of Health Politics, Policy and Law, 17*: 97-118.

Bensel, R. (1984). *Sectionalism and American Political Development: 1880-1980..* University of Wisconsin Press, Madison.

Bentley, A. (1967). *The Process of Government.* Belknap Press of Harvard University Press, Cambridge, MA. Originally published in 1908.

Beyle, T. and Williams, J. (1972). *The American Governor in Behavioral Perspective..* Harper and Row. New York.

Blewett, L.A. (1994). Reforms in Minnesota: Forging the path. *Health Affairs, 13* (Fall): 200-209.

Bloksberg, L.M. (1989). Intergovernmental relations: Change and continuity. *Journal of Aging and Social Policy, 1*: 11-36.

Boeckelman, K. (1992). The influence of states on federal policy adoptions. *Policy Studies Journal, 20* (3): 365-375.

Bovbjerg, R. and Holahan, R., (1982). *Medicaid in the Reagan Era: Federal Policy and State Choices.* Urban Institute, Washington.

Bowman, A. and Kearney, R. (1986). *The Resurgence of the States..* Prentice-Hall, Englewood Cliffs, N.J.

Bowman, A. and Kearney, R. (1988). Dimensions of state government capability. *Western Political Quarterly, 41:* 341-362.

Bowman, A. and Pagano, M. (1995). The state of American federalism, 1993-1994. *Publius: The Journal of Federalism, 24 :* 1-17.

Brown, L.D. (1993). Commissions, clubs, and consensus: Florida reorganizes for health reform. *Health Affairs, 12* (Summer): 7-26.

Budget of the U.S. Government Fiscal Year 1996.. (1995). U.S. Office of Management and Budget, Washington, DC.

Buerger, E. (1995). State health-care reform initiatives. In *The Council of State Governments. The Book of the States, 1994-95.* Lexington, KY.

Brecher, C. (1995). *The Privatization of Public Health Care..* The Twentieth Century Fund, New York, NY.

Cartland, J. and Yudkowsky, B. (1993). State estimates of uninsured children. *Health Affairs, 12* (Spring): 144-151.

Chirba-Martin, M. and Brennan, T. (1994). The critical role of ERISA in state health reform. *Health Affairs, 13* (Spring II): 142-156.

Conlan, T. (1988). *New Federalism: Intergovernmental Reform from Nixon to Reagan.* The Brookings Institution, Washington.

Conlan, T. J. and Beam, D. R. (1992). Federal Mandates: The Record of Reform and Future Prospects. *Intergovernmental Perspective* (Fall): 9-23.

Coughlin, T.A., Ku, L., and Holahan, J. (1994). *Medicaid Since 1980.* Urban Institute Press, Washington.

Coughlin, T.A., Ku, L., Holahan, J., Heslam, D., and Winterbottom, C., (Coughlin et al.) (1994). State Responses to the Medicaid Spending Crisis: 1988 to 1992. *Journal of Health, Politics, Policy and Law, 19*: 837-864.

Council of State Governments. (1995). *The Book of the States, 1994-95.* Lexington, KY.

Crittenden, R.A. (1993). Managed Competition and Premium Caps in Washington State. *Health Affairs, 12* (Summer): 82-88.

Crittenden, R.A. (1995). Rolling back reform in the Pacific Northwest. *Health Affairs, 14* (Summer): 302-305.

Cromwell, J., Adamache, K., Ammering, C., Bartosch, W.J., and Boulis, A. (1995). Equity of the Medicaid Program to the Poor Versus Taxpayers. *Health Care Financing Review, 16* (3): 75-104.

Davis, C. and Lester, J. (1989). Federalism and Environmental Policy. In (Lester, J., Ed.). *Environmental Politics and Policy.* Durham, NC: Duke University Press.

Davis, K. and Schoen, C. (1978). *Health and the War on Poverty: A Ten-Year Appraisal.* Brookings Institution, Washington, DC.

Derthick, M. (1970). *The Influence of Federal Grants.* Joint Center for Urban Studies, Cambridge.

Derthick, M. (1992). Up-to-Date in Kansas City: Reflections on American Federalism. *P.S. Political Science and Politics:* 671-75.

Dick, A.W. (1994). Will employer mandates really work? Another look at Hawaii. *Health Affairs, 13* (Spring): 343-349.

DiIulio, J., Jr. and Nathan, R. (Eds.). (1994). *Making Health Reform Work: A View from the States.* The Brookings Institution, Washington.

Dobson, A., Moran, D., and Young, G. (1992). The Role of Federal Waivers in the Health Policy Process. *Health Affairs, 11* (Winter): 72-94.

Dodson, A. and Mueller, K. (1993). National Health Care Reform: Whither State Governments? *Policy Currents*, 3:: 7-26.

DuNah, R., Harrington, C., Bedney, B., and Carrillo, H. (1995). Variations and Trends in State Nursing Facility Capacity: 1978-93. *Health Care Financing Review*, 17(1): 183-199.

Dye, T.R. (1990). *American Federalism: Competition Among the States*. Lexington Books, Lexington.

Elazar, D. (1974). The New Federalism: Can the States be Trusted? *The Public Interest*, 35: 89-102.

Elazar, D. (1984). *American Federalism: A View from the States* (3rd ed.) Harper and Row, New York, NY.

Feldman, P., Gold, M., and Chu, K. (1994). Enhancing Information for State Health Policy. *Health Affairs*, 13(Summer): 236-250.

Folkemer, D. (1994). *State Use of Home and Community-Based Services for the Aged Under Medicaid: Waiver Programs, Personal Care, Frail Elderly Services and Home Health Services.* Intergovernmental Health Policy Project, Washington, DC.

Fossett, J.W. (1993). Medicaid and Health Reform: The Case of New York. *Health Affairs*, 12 (Fall): 81-94.

Fox, D. and Leichter, H. (1991). Rationing Care in Oregon: The New Accountability. *Health Affairs*, 10 (Summer): 7-27.

Fox, D.M. and Leichter, H.M. (1993). The Ups and Downs of Oregon's Rationing Plan. *Health Affairs*, 12(Summer): 66-70.

Fox, M.H., Weiner, J.P., and Phua, K. (1992). Effect of Medicaid Payment Levels on Access to Obstetrical Care. *Health Affairs*, 11(Winter): 150-161.

Fraser, I , (1995). Rate Regulation as a Policy Tool: Lessons From New York State. *Health Care Financing Review*, 16(3): 151-176.

Fuchs, B. and Hoadley, J. (1987). Reflections from inside the beltway: How Congress and the President grapple with health policy. *P.S. Political Science and Politics*, (Spring): 212-220.

Galston, W. and Tibbetts, G. (1994). Reinventing federalism: The Clinton/Gore Program for a new partnership among the federal, state, local and tribal governments. *Publius: The Journal of Federalism*, 24: 23-48.

Gardner, A. and Neubauer, D. (1995). State report: Hawaii's health quest. *Health Affairs*, 14 (Spring): 300-303.

Ginsburg, E. (1994). *Critical Issues in U.S. Health Reform.* Westview Press, Boulder, CO.

Gold, M. and Felt, S. (1995). Reconciling practice and theory: Challenges in monitoring medic-aid managed-care quality. *Health Care Financing Review*, 16(4): 85-105.

Gold, S.D. (1993). Cadillac or Yugo? *State Legislatures*, 19: 32-36.

Gold, S.D. (1992). One approach to tracking state and local health spending. *Health Affairs*, 11(Winter): 135-144.

Grey, V. and Eisinger, P. (1991). *American States and Cities.* Harper-Collins, New York.

Grey, V. (1994). Federalism and health care. *Political Science and Politics* 27: 15-17.

Grogan, C. (1995). Hope in federalism? What can the states do and what are they likely to do?. *Journal of Health Politics, Policy and Law*, 20: 477-484.

Haas, P. and Wright, D. (1988). The Changing Profile of State Administrators. In Thad Beyle, *State Government.* Congressional Quarterly Press, Washington, DC.

Hall, W. and Griner, P. (1993). Cost-Effective Health Care: The Rochester Experience. *Health Affairs*, 12 (Spring): 58-69.

Hanson, R.L. (1994). Health care reform: Managed competition, and subnational politics. *Publius: The Journal of Federalism*, 24: 49-68.

Hanson, R.L. (1993). Defining a Role for States in a Federal Health Care System. *American Behavioral Scientist*, 36 : 760-781.

Hebers. (1987). The new federalism: Unplanned, innovative and here to stay. *Governing*, 1, 28-37.

Hoadley, J.F. and Cox, D.F. (1994). Measuring State Health Spending: Another Look. *Health Affairs*, 13(Winter): 202-207.

Holahan, J.F. and Cohen, J.W. (1986) *Medicaid: The Trade-off Between Cost Containment and Access for Care.* Urban Institute, Washington.

Holahan, J., Coughlin, T., Ku, L., Lipson, D.J., and Rajan, S., (Holahan et al.,). (1995). Insuring the Poor Through Section 1115 Medicaid Waivers. *Health Affairs, 14*(Spring): 99-216.

Holahan, J., Rowland, D., Feder, J., and Heslam, D. (1993). Explaining the Recent Growth in Medicaid Spending. *Health Affairs, 12*(Fall): 177-193.

Honadale, B. , (1981). A Capacity Building Framework: A Search for Concept and Purpose. *Public Administration Review, 41:* 577-89.

Iglehart, J.K. ed (1993). *Debating Health Care Reform: A Primer from Health Affairs.* Project Hope, Bethesda.

Intergovernmental Health Policy Project, (IHPP) (1994). *State Profiles: Health Care Reform (2nd ed.).* George Washington University, Washington.

Intergovernmental Health Policy Project, (IHPP) (1995). *Fifty State Profiles: Health Care Reform, 1995.* George Washington University, Washington.

Jacobs, L.R. (1995). Politics of America's Supply State: Health Reform and Technology.*Health Affairs, 14*(Summer): 143-157.

Jacobs, L.R., Shapiro, R.Y., and Schulman, E.C. (1993). Medical Care in the United States: An Update. *Public Opinion Quarterly, 57:* 394-427.

Jacobson, P.D. (1995). Washington State Health Services Act: Implementing Comprehensive Health Care Reform. *Health Care Financing Review, 16*(3): 177-196.

Justice, D. (1988). *State long term care reform: Development of Community Care systems in six states.* National Governors' Association, Washington.

Kaiser Commission on the Future of Medicaid. (1995). *Medicaid and Managed Care: Lessons from the Literature.* Kaiser Commission (March), Washington.

Kenyon, D. and Kincaid, J. (1991). *Competition among State and Local Governments: Efficiency and Equity in American Federalism.* Urban Institute, Washington.

Kettl, D.F. (1987) *The Regulation of American Federalism.* Johns Hopkins University Press, Baltimore.

Kincaid, J. (1990). From Cooperative to Coercive Federalism.*The Annals of the American Academy of Political and Social Sciences, 509:* 148-152.

Kinney, E.D. (1995). Malpractice Reform in the 1990s: Past Disappointments, Future Successes? *Journal of Health Politics, Policy and Law, 20:* 99-135.

Kovner, A.R. (1990). *Health Care Delivery in the United States (4th edition).* Springer, New York.

Kronick, R. (1993). Where Should the Buck Stop: Federal and State Responsibilities in Health Care Financing Reform. *Health Affairs, 12*(Supplement): 87-98.

Kunde, J.E. and Stenberg, C.W. (1993). How will the Clinton Era Affect State and Local Government? Some Early Views. *State and Local Government Review, 25:* 207-210.

Ku, L. and Coughlin, T.A. (1995). Medicaid Disproportionate Share and Other Special Financing Programs. *Health Care Financing Review, 16*(3): 27-54.

Lammers, W.W. and Leibig, P.S. (1990). State Health Policies, Federalism and the Elderly. *Publius: The Journal of Federalism, 20:* 131-148.

Leibig, P.S. (1992). Federalism and Aging Policy in the 1980s: Implications for Changing Interest Group Roles in the 1990s. *Journal of Aging and Social Policy, 4:* 17-33.

Leichter, H.M. (1992). *Health Policy Reform in America: Innovations from the States.* M.E. Sharpe, Armonk, NY.

Leichter, H.M. (1993a). Health Care Reform in Vermont: A Work in Progress. *Health Affairs, 12*(Summer): 71-81.

Leichter, H.M. (1993b). Minnesota: The Trip from Acrimony to Accomodation.*Health Affairs, 12*(Summer): 48-58.

Leichter, H.M. (1994). Health Care Reform in Vermont: The Next Chapter.*Health Affairs, 13*(Winter): 78-103.

Levit, K.R., Cowan, C.A., Lazenby, H.C., McDonnell, P.A., Sensenig, A.L., Stiller, J.M., and Won, D.K. (1994). National Health Spending Trends, 1960 - 1993. *Health Affairs, 13*(Winter): 14-31.

Levit, K.R., Lazenby, H.C., Cowan, C.A., and Letsch, S.W. (1993). Health Spending by State: New Estimates for Policy Making. *Health Affairs, 12*(Fall): 7-26.

Levit, K.R., Lazenby, H.C., Cowan, C.A., Won, D.K., Stiller, J.M., Sivarajan, L., and Stewart, M.W. (1995). State Health Expenditure Accounts: Building Blocks for State Health Spending Analysis. *Health Care Financing Review, 17*(1): 201-254.

Lipson, D.J. (1991). An Overview of State Roles in Health Care Policy. In Litman, T.J. and Robins, L.S. *Health Politics and Policy (2nd edition)*. Delmar Publishers, Albany.

Lohr, K.N. and Marquis, M.S.. (1984) *Medicare and Medicaid: Past, Present, and Future.* Rand Corporation, Santa Monica.

Lowi, T.J. (1969). *The End of Liberalism: Ideology, Policy, and the Crisis of Public Authority.* Norton, New York.

Marmor, T.R. (1994). *Understanding Health Care Reform.* Yale University Press, New Haven.

Mashaw, J.L. (1993/94). Taking Federalism Seriously: The Case for State-Led Health Care Reform. *Domestic Affairs*, 1-21.

McCall, N., Rice, T., and Hall, A. (1987). The Effect of State Regulations on the Quality and Sale of Insurance Policies to Medicare Beneficiaries. *Journal of Health Politics, Policy and Law.* 12: 53-76.

McManus. S.A. (1991). Mad About Mandates: The Issue of Who Should Pay for What Resurfaces. *Publius: The Journal of Federalism*, 21: 59-76.

Mechanic, D.M. and Surles, R.C. (1992). Challenges in State Mental Health Policy and Administration. *Health Affairs, 11*(Fall): 34-50.

Mendelson, D.N., Abramson, R.G., and Rubin, R.J. (1995). State Involvement in Medical Technology Assessment. *Health Affairs, 14*(Summer): 83-98.

Milbank Memorial Fund, (1993). *The States That Could Not Wait: Lessons for Health Reform from Florida, Hawaii, Minnesota, Oregon, and Vermont.* Milbank Memorial Fund, New York.

Miller, N.A. (1992). Medicaid 2176 Home and Community-Based Care Waivers: The First Ten Years. *Health Affairs, 11(Winter):* 162-171.

Morgan Q. (1994). *Health Care State Rankings 1994.* Lawrence, KS.

Morone, J.A. and Belkin G.S., eds (1994). *The Politics of Health Care Reform: Lessons from the Past, Prospects for the Future.* Duke University Press, Durham.

National Commission on the State and Local Public Service (1993). *Frustrated Federalism: Rx for State and Local Health Care Reform.* Nelson A. Rockefeller Institute of Government, Albany.

National Governors Association, (1993). *State Progress in Health Care Reform.* National Governor's Association, Washington.

Nathan, R. P. and Doolittle, F. (1983). *The Consequences of the Cuts: The Effects of the Reagan Domestic Program on State and Local Governments.* Princeton Urban and Regional Research Center, Princeton.

Nathan, R. P., et al. (1987). *Reagan and the States.* Princeton University Press, Princeton.

Nelson, H. (1994). *Federalism in Health Care Reform: Views From the States That Could Not Wait.* Milbank Memorial Fund, New York.

Neubauer, D. (1993). Hawaii: A Pioneer in Health System Reform. *Health Affairs, 12*(Summer): 31-39.

Oliver, T.R. and Dowell, E.B. (1994). Interest Groups and Health Reform: Lessons from California. *Health Affairs, 13*(Spring II): 123-141.

Osborne, D.E. (1988). *Laboratories of Democracy: A new breed of governor creates models for national growth.* Harvard Business School Press, Boston.

Osborne, D. (1993). A New Federal Compact: Sorting Out Washington's Proper Role. In Will Marshall and Martin Schram, *Mandate for Change.* Berkeley Books, New York.

Pauly, M.V. (1993). U.S. Health Care Costs: The Untold True Story. *Health Affairs, 12(Fall):* 152-159.

Peirce, N. (1996). Breaking the Log Jam: Governors to the Rescue. *Baltimore Sun (February 14)*: 17A.

Peterson, P.E. (1995). *The Price of Federalism*. The Brookings Institution, Washington.

Peterson, P.E., Rabe, B.G., and Wong, K.K. (1986). *When Federalism Works*. The Brookings Institution, Washington.

Plotnick, R. D. and Winter, R. F. (1985). A Politico-Economic Theory of Income Distribution. *American Political Science Review, 79*: 458-73.

Pollack, D.A., McFarland, B.H., George, R.A., and Angell, R.H. (1994). Prioritization of Mental Health Services in Oregon. *Milbank Quarterly, 72*: 515-550.

Raffel, M.W. and Raffel, N.K., (1994). *The U.S. Health System: Origins and Functions (4th edition)*. Delmar Publishers, Albany.

Riley, T. (1995). State Health Reform and the Role of 1115 Waivers. *Health Care Financing Review, 16*(3): 139-150.

Rivlin, A. M. (1993). *Reviving the American Dream: The Economy, the States, and the Federal Government*. The Brookings Institution, Washington.

Rogal, D.L. and Helms, W.D. (1993). State Models: Tracking States' Efforts to Reform Their Health Systems. *Health Affairs, 12*(Summer): 27-30.

Rotwein, S., Boulmetis, M., Boben, P.J., Fingold, H.I., Hadley, J.P., Rama, K. L., and Van Hoven, D. (1995). Medicaid and State Health Care Reform: Process, Programs, and Policy Options. *Health Care Financing Review, 16*(3): 105-120.

Sabatini, N. (1993). Maryland Health Reform Revisited. *Health Affairs, 12*(Winter): 256.

Sanford, T. (1967). *Storm over the States*. McGraw-Hill, NY.

Sharkansky, I. and Hofferbert, R. (1969). Dimensions of State Politics, Economics, and Public Policy. *American Political Science Review, 63*: 867-879.

Shonick, W. (1993). Public Health Agencies and Services: The Partnership Network, In Williams, S.J. and Torrens, P.R. *Introduction to Health Services (4th edition)*, Delmar Publishers, Albany.

Shortell, S.M. (1992). A Model for State Health Care Reform. *Health Affairs, 11*(Spring): 108-127.

Soumerai, S.B., Ross-Degnan, D., Fortress, E.E., and Abelson, J., A Critical Analysis of Studies of State Drug Reimbursement Policies: Research in Need of Discipline. *Milbank Quarterly, 71*: 217-252.

Sparer, M.S. (1995). Great Expectations: The Limits of State Health Care Reform. *Health Affairs, 14*(Winter): 191-202.

Sparer, M.S. (1993). States in a Reformed Health System: Lessons from Nursing Home Policy. *Health Affairs, 12*(Spring): 7-20.

Stone, D.A. (1979). Diagnosis and the Dole: The Function of Illness in American Politics. *Journal of Health Politics, Policy, and Law 4*: 507-521.

Stone, D.A. (1992). Why the States Can't Solve the Health Care Crisis. *The American Prospect, 9*: 51-60.

Strosberg, M.A., Wiener, J.M. and Baker, R. eds. (1992). *Rationing America's Medical Care: The Oregon Plan and Beyond*. The Brookings Institution, Washington.

Sullivan, C.B., Miller, M., Feldman, R. and Dowd, B. (1992). Employer-Sponsored Health Insurance in 1991. *Health Affairs, 11*(Winter): 172-185.

Swan, J.H., Harrington, C., and Grant, L.A. (1993). State Medicaid Reimbursement for Nursing Homes, 1978-1988. *Health Care Financing Review, 14*(4): 111-131.

Swartz, T. R. and Peck, J. E. (1990). *The Changing Face of Fiscal Federalism*. Sharpe, Armonk, NY.

Tallon, J.R., Jr. and Nathan, R.P. (1992). A Federal/State Partnership for Health System Reform. *Health Affairs, 11*(Winter): 7-16.

Thompson, F.J. (1986). New federalism and health care policy: States and the Old Questions. *Journal of Health Politics, Policy and Law, 11*: 647-669.

Thorne, J.I., Bianchi, B., Bonnyman, G., Greene, C., and Leddy, T. (Thorne et al.,) (1995). State Perspectives on Health Care Reform: Oregon, Hawaii, Tennessee, and Rhode Island. *Health Care Financing Review, 16*(3): 121-138.

Tudor, C.G. (1995). Medicaid Expenditures and State Responses. *Health Care Financing Review, 16*(3): 1-10.

U.S. Department of Commerce, (1995). *Statistical Abstracts of the United States, 1995.* Government Printing Office, Washington.

U.S. Department of Health and Human Services, (USDHHS) (1994). *Health, United States 1994,* DHHS, Washington.

U.S. Department of Health and Human Services, Health Care Financing Administration, Office of Research and Demonstrations, (1995). *Medicare and Medicaid Statistical Supplement, 1995.* Baltimore, Md.

U.S. General Accounting Office, (USGAO) (1994). *Medicaid Long-Term Care: Successful Efforts to Expand Home Services While Limiting Costs (GAO/HEHS-94-167).* Washington.

U.S. General Accounting Office, (USGAO) (1995a). *Medicaid: Restructuring Approaches Leave Many Questions.* (GAO/HEHS-95-103).

U.S. General Accounting Office, (USGAO) (1995b). *Medicaid: Spending Pressures Drive States Toward Program Reinvention.* (GAO/HEHS-95-122).

U.S. General Accounting Office, (USGAO) (1995c). *Medicaid: States Turn to Managed Care to Improve Access to Control Costs.* (GAO/HRD-93-46).

U.S. General Accounting Office, (USGAO) (1995d). *Medicare: Tigher Rules Needed to Curtail Overcharges for Therapy in Nursing Homes.* (GAO/HEHS-95-23).

U.S. Office of Management and Budget (USOMB) (1995). *Budget of the U.S. Government, Fiscal Year 1996.* Government Printing Office, Washington.

Vladeck, B.C. (1979). The design of failure: Health policy and the structure of federalism. *Journal of Health Politics, Policy and Law,* 4: 522-535.

Vladeck, B.C. (1995). Medicaid 1115 Demonstrations: Progress Through Partnership.*Health Affairs,* 14(Spring): 217-220.

Volpp, K.G. and Siegel, B. (1993). New Jersey: Long Term Experience with All-Payer Rate Setting. *Health Affairs,* 12(Summer): 59-65.

Wade, M. and Berg, S. (1995). Causes of Medicaid Expenditure Growth. *Health Care Financing Review,* 16(3): 11-26.

Walker, D.B. (1991). American Federalism from Johnson to Bush. *Publius: The Journal of Federalism,* 21, 105-119.

Walker, D. B. (1995). *The Rebirth of Federalism: Slouching Toward Washington.*, Chatham House, Chatham, NJ.

Walters, J. (1994). Reinventing the Federal System. *Governing,* 7: 49-53.

Warren, C. (1982). State Government's Capacity: Continuing to Improve. *National Civic Review,* 71: 34-39.

Weissert, W.G., Cready, M., and Pawelak, J.E. (1988). The past and future of home and community based long-term care. *Milbank Quarterly, 66:* 309-388.

Wiener, J.M. (1992). Oregon's Plan for Health Care Rationing. *The Brookings Review. (Winter).*

Wiener, J.M. Illston, L.H. and Hanley, R.J. (1994). *Sharing the Burden: Strategies for Public and Private Long-Term Care Insurance.* The Brookings Institution, Washington.

Williamson, R. S. (1989). *Reagan's Federalism: His Efforts to Decentralize Government.* University Press of America, Lanham, MD.

Zimmerman, J. F. (1992). *Contemporary American Federalism: The Growth of National Power.* Praeger, New York.

3.
PROFESSIONAL REGULATION

Denise Strong, *University of New Orleans, New Orleans, LA*

Policies designed to establish the credentials and competence of health professionals significantly affect the nature and quality of health care. Such policies play a major role in determining entry into particular professions, health manpower supply and the quality of practicing professionals. To illustrate, consider the role of training institutions and the institutions that certify and license health professionals. Institutions that train professionals will determine the curriculum, teaching and testing strategies to enable their students to successfully meet practice entry requirements. The standard entry requirements will influence who actually enters the profession. Only those who have access and ability to acquire the knowledge and skills will enter a profession. The standard entry requirement will thus have the effect of limiting the supply of practitioners to which the public will have access.

Furthermore, the ethical and professional standards to which a practitioner must adhere are in part determined by regulatory policies established by regulatory agencies such as state licensing boards. Thus, such policies can determine who remains fit to practice and who should be barred from professional practice. In addition to ethical standards of conduct, policies may be established to determine whether an individual remains competent and stays abreast of new knowledge, technology and other developments in his or her field of practice.

These policies can influence the quality and cost of health care services. Furthermore, health dollars—whether private or public—are directed toward practitioners deemed fit to practice. Consequently, the policies that make such a determination indirectly influence the way health dollars are spent. If, for example, the federal government stipulates that public health programs such as Medicaid must use only

51

licensed practitioners, the policies that determine who can be licensed clearly affect the way public health dollars are spent.

Despite their importance, policies that regulate health professionals are often overlooked in health care policy debates. Debate concerning health care tends to focus on issues such as financing, insurance, access and malpractice, with inadequate attention to the health care practitioners who provide health care services.

This chapter addresses the public policies and institutions that regulate health professionals. The chapter discusses the historical evolution of health professional regulation, the role of professional associations, state and federal government in regulating the health professions, and debates related to the effectiveness of current regulatory strategies.

I. PERENNIAL QUESTIONS

Two sets of questions persist throughout the development of the health professions and the policies designed to regulate them. One set pertains to the process whereby decisions are made about health professionals. These questions include the following:

- Who should decide who gets to practice?
- How should decisions be made about health professionals?
- How should we decide who is competent, who has the knowledge, skills, and characteristics appropriate for professional practice?
- What accountability mechanisms should be established to monitor practice?
- What processes should be used if a practitioner fails to meet his or her professional obligations?

The second set of questions addresses the substantive policy issues such as:

- What education, training and experience should health professionals be expected to have?
- What standards of practice, if any, should health professionals be expected to adhere to?
- What recourse do consumers of health professionals have if they are not satisfied with the treatment they have received?
- What constitutes substandard care?
- What restrictions or limitations, if any, should be imposed on practitioners based on their training, education and/or experience?

These two sets of questions have been addressed throughout the history of the professions in this country. They are also being addressed in the debates over health how to appropriately regulate the health professions. There is no real definitive answer to these questions because the shape of each of the professions is profoundly influenced by social, economic and technological developments. Thus, regulatory strategies will also be shaped by these forces.

The policy environment in which health professional regulation occurs is complex and comprises public and private sector interests, organizations and values. Among these are the payers of health care, consumers, regulators, health care providers—individual and institutional— and the educational institutions that train health care professionals. Relevant economic and technological factors include the pressure by major third party payers to slow the growth of health care expenditures, the growth of managed care and the proliferation of group practice and the increase in the number of allied health practitioners. Changes in the health care delivery system will continue to shape and be shaped by the health professional regulatory system. Consequently, we can expect that pressure will increase on the regulatory system to change as well.

II. DEFINING REGULATION

In broad terms professional regulation refers to external controls over the practice of a particular profession using a range of mechanisms: control by the marketplace, control by members of the profession and professional organizations, and control by government through the use of state police powers. Licensure, certification and registration are some of the mechanisms whereby society determines whether individuals should be allowed to perform certain functions or provide services.

III. TYPES OF REGULATION

Three major forms of government regulation are licensure, certification and registration. Each type of regulation differs in terms of constraints and consequences. Licensure refers to the exclusive right of a particularly defined group to practice an occupation or profession. Licensure defines who may practice, what qualifications are required to engage in that practice, what activities can be included in that practice (Shimberg, 1984). The effect of licensure is to give a monopoly to an individual or to a group who meets specified criteria.

Certification allows use of a title by an individual who meets certain criteria. Certification does not limit who may engage in a particular set of activities; rather, it regulates the title that an individual may use. Certification means that if an individual meets certain educational and experience criteria, that person may use a particular title. Other people may engage in practicing the same activities, but they may not use that title (Shimberg, 1984). Certification may be granted by a government agency or by a private entity.

Registration requires any one wanting to engage in a particular occupation to register with a state designated agency. Registration does not require particular educational or training criteria, only that an individual register with the state before practicing the profession.

Each of these control mechanisms may be found alone or in combination. The terminology used in defining regulation is not clear and consistent. For example, the term "registered nurse" is far more restrictive than the designation would indicate. Registered nurses are actually licensed by state licensing boards. For this reason, the National Society of Professional Engineers suggests a consistent use of credentialing terminology to eliminate confusion:

   a. limit use of term licensure to actions by state government.
   b. limit use of term certification to refer to actions by a profession or
      occupation to establish competency standards; some states use certification to

refer to licensure processes.
  c. some professions use term registration (e.g. registered nurses) as the equiva-
     lent of licensure (Health Professions Regulation-Maine, 1997, p. 14).

IV. EMERGENCE OF REGULATORY STRATEGIES

A profession's efforts to police itself may begin as a voluntary effort by members
of a profession to enhance its image, promote the professional development of its
members, share knowledge and expertise and protect the interests of the profession.
Individuals joining such an organization may agree to adhere to specified standards of
conduct or may profess beliefs in specified professional tenets. For example, in 1840
one of the early health professional associations, the American Society of Dental
Surgeons, stipulated in its Constitution that "Any member of the Society may be
expelled for immoral conduct, malpractice in business or other sufficient cause"
(McCluggage, 1959, p. 58). The Society's rules were limited to those who were organizational members, with no consequences for dentists who were not members. This
type of regulation, also known as collegial regulation, has dominated in the health professions (Friedson, 1983). In fact, a characteristic of a profession is its power and
authority to regulate itself (Friedson, 1983). The voluntary nature of such self-policing
restricts the degree and nature of the control professionals can impose on their peers
and the profession as a whole.

As a result of the limitations of self-policing, the profession may seek the power of
government to provide more extensive regulation than is possible through collegial
regulation. When that happens, controls exerted by members of a profession may be
exerted in tandem with government regulation. Statutes, regulations and court decisions provide the public regulatory framework. Statutes such as practice acts typically
establish broad guidelines for what is allowed and what is prohibited, and regulations
provide the details necessary to implement the guidelines.

Although federal regulation plays a significant role, state governments have been
the major public regulators of health professionals. The regulatory apparatus, therefore, varies by state and by profession. The complexity of health professional regulation is in part due to the decentralized nature of government regulation and the particular nature of each profession's regulatory policies and practices. Generalizations
about health professional regulation may thus be tenuous, but are important if we are
to understand and evaluate relevant public policies.

State licensing boards, theoretically acting on the public's behalf, establish the conditions whereby the public can be assured that health care professionals are competent
to provide health care services. In effect, the licensing boards serve as intermediaries
between the educational institutions that train the professional, the individual practitioner, third-party payers, institutional health care providers (e.g., hospitals, clinics and
nursing homes) and the consumers of health care services.

Professional regulatory entities have two major functions. The first is to determine the extent to which professionals have the knowledge and skills to practice.
Individuals who claim to have health services expertise and who, by virtue of their
expertise, desire the authority or right to engage in provision of health care services,

are required by society to meet specified standards for safe practice. The second is to ensure the standards and conduct of those already in the profession do not endanger the public's health, safety and welfare.

V. LEGAL AND CONSTITUTIONAL FOUNDATIONS OF PROFESSIONAL REGULATION

A major factor in the development of regulatory policies governing health professionals is that they evolved in the context of the constitutional structure of American government. Legal and constitutional issues were reflected in efforts to balance the respective rights of practitioners, consumers and the public. The United States Constitution guarantees citizens the liberty to practice their vocation. Citizens also have the right to equal treatment before the law and due process of law. Consequently, government efforts to control or limit these rights may be subject to challenge through the courts.

One such challenge was the case of Dent v. West Virginia, 1889, in which the constitutionality of the states' power to determine who may practice a profession was established. This case considered whether West Virginia violated the Fourteenth Amendment, by requiring all who wanted to practice medicine in the state to present evidence of their training to a state board of health. The court held that the state may insist upon establishing standards for the practice of medicine because, "The power of the state to provide for the general welfare of its people authorizes it to prescribe all such regulations as in its judgment will secure or tend to secure them against the consequences of ignorance and incapacity, as well as of deception and fraud." (Dent v. West Virginia, 1889). The court articulated a right to practice one's vocation, but also established that there was no absolute right. One's right to practice a vocation was tempered by the state's authority to establish guidelines to protect the public.

The right to practice a profession or occupation is a constitutionally protected right. Consequently, government cannot limit or remove that right without according due process (Mashaw and Merrill, 1985). Among due process rights are the right to be informed of allegations of wrongdoing, to present evidence, confront and cross examine witnesses and a public hearing.

These elements of due process may detract from administrative efficiency but are an important factor in the procedures licensing boards use to discipline or sanction a licensee. Due process requirements as well as rules of evidence may create procedural delays and hinder boards from acting forthrightly to discipline professionals that pose a threat to public safety and welfare. The due process requirements affecting regulatory boards have been criticized as contributing to regulatory board inefficiency. However, such criticisms fail to recognize that administrative agencies are obligated to meet constitutional, as well as statutory, standards of conduct. Board decision-making processes must balance several interests that may conflict — the interests of the public and the interests of individual practitioners.

VI. ROLE OF PROFESSIONALS IN PROFESSIONAL REGULATION

The current model of self regulation is one in which professionals determine standards of care, requirements for entry into the profession and ethical standards. Professionals also control and administer the regulatory bodies, determine violations and appropriate sanctions for violators of professional standards.

Organized professionals have been the driving force behind the emergence of regulatory policies and strategies. Health professional regulation is unlike other areas of public life where muckraking exposés or crises (e.g., an oil spill) generate public interest in government regulation. The early history of health professional regulation illuminates the lead role practitioners played in defining practice boundaries, entry requirements and standards for conduct. Health professionals also have been instrumental in determining the regulatory administrative structures states have established to administer laws and regulations. National and state professional groups have worked closely with state legislators to ensure the enactment of legislation deemed important to the interests of the respective professions.

The perspective of professionals on their regulatory roles can be found illuminated in editorials and articles in professional journals. Generally, professionals argue for their domination in the regulatory process. In medicine, for example, the professional medical journals articulate several themes concerning the responsibility of the professions and the source of weaknesses in the disciplinary system. First, the profession is responsible for maintaining professional standards. Professionals are obligated to protect the public from the "unqualified, unfit and impaired" physician (Galusha, 1989). Second, professional standards and accountability are maintained by several mechanisms: the peer review processes of professional associations and the licensing and disciplinary functions of the state licensing boards (Galusha, 1989). Third, the obligation of professionals to ensure high standards is best fulfilled by professionals acting independently of bureaucratic, state-imposed mandates. Professional autonomy and discretion are considered critical to ensure professional quality and accountability.

VII. FEDERAL ROLE IN HEALTH PROFESSIONAL REGULATION

Although professional regulation has traditionally been a state government function, the increase in federal dollars allocated to health care in the late 1960s brought the matter to Congressional attention. Thus, in 1971, Congress directed the Secretary of Health, Education and Welfare to conduct a study on health professional credentialing to include:

> identifying the major problems associated with licensure, certification, and other qualifications for practice or employment of health personnel...together with summaries of the activities (if any) of Federal agencies, professional organizations, or other instrumentalities directed toward the alleviation of such problems and toward maximizing the proper and efficient utilization of health personnel in meeting the health needs of the Nation (DHEW, Report on Licensure and Related Health Personnel Credentialing, 1971).

The rationale for such a study was that health care had become a national priority, thus, health professional licensure and credentialing could no longer be left exclusively to health professionals and their associations. Public/private cooperation with significant federal input was viewed as the best way to make needed changes in policies and practices. The study concluded that significant reforms were needed to ensure that regulatory policies adequately protected the public's welfare.

The study concluded that changes were needed in both the public and private arenas of regulations, credentialing and accreditation. The study articulated concerns about the proliferation of legislation delineating scopes of practice for newly emergent professions. The concern expressed was that narrowly defined educational and training requirements would conflict with the trend toward broadening the tasks that emergent professions could assume responsibility for. One of the study's recommendations was that states observe a two-year moratorium on new scope-of-practice legislation and that in the interim the states evaluate existing practice acts. States were also urged to be more flexible in defining scopes of practice and in expanding functions delegated to the respective professions. In the area of ensuring competence of practitioners, the report recommended that states and professional associations initiate continuing education programs (U.S. DHEW, 1971).

VIII. STATES' ROLE IN REGULATING HEALTH PROFESSIONALS

Government regulation of professionals in the United States has historically been the province of state governments. Each state develops its own regulatory guidelines and administrative structures. Each state also decides which occupations or professions to regulate, the regulatory scope and the nature of regulation it will impose. Thus, a practitioner's right to practice is, in essence, place-bound. Furthermore, each state's jurisdiction over a practitioner is limited to practice in that state.

The limited jurisdiction of state regulation limits the mobility of practitioners to practice outside the states or states in which they are licensed. It can also limit the ability of states to discipline practitioners who could simply re-locate to another state, apply for a license and resume practice, if they were subject to state disciplinary action. The absence of state coordination and communication around licensure issues facilitated the ability of impaired or incompetent practitioners to continue to practice unimpeded by sanctions of other states.

Regulatory powers are delegated to health professional boards by state legislatures. Enabling statutes enumerate the powers of such boards, the appointment and removal of members and the administrative structures which will support the boards' work. Professional Practice Acts also typically delineate the scope of practice, the professional titles that may be used and that fall within the boards' jurisdiction, the grounds on which practitioners may be disciplined and the types of sanctions boards may impose.

IX. ADMINISTRATIVE DIMENSIONS OF HEALTH PROFESSIONAL REGULATION

In addition to deciding the type of regulation appropriate for a profession, a series of administrative decisions are required to establish the regulatory administrative structure. A policy decision to regulate health professionals raises a host of administrative issues. For example, what administrative structure should be adopted? What oversight mechanisms should be established to ensure legislative oversight of health professional regulatory boards? How will board members be held accountable? The responses to these questions varies greatly by state.

In some states, health professionals are regulated by an executive branch agency headed by a gubernatorial appointee. In other states, each profession is governed by a multi-member commission or a board, appointed by the Governor or the Legislature. Although the administrative structures may vary, the essential regulatory functions are similar:

1. An administrative entity (e.g. a commission or a board), composed of professionals, appointed by a gubernatorial or legislative authority.
2. An administrative entity given delegated powers to oversee the profession.
Some of these powers include the power to:
   a) establish entry requirements into the profession.
   b) determine who has met entry requirements and to waive the requirements or "grandfather" in specified groups of practitioners.
   c) establish the standards of conduct to which professionals must adhere.
   d) sanction professionals who fail to adhere to the established standards.
   e) impose practice restrictions.

These boards were initially typically composed solely of practitioners. In some states, professional associations appointed the board members. In other states, the professional associations recommended candidates to the governor.

X. LICENSURE AND ENTRY REGULATION

Establishing licensure requirements is a significant function in the regulation of health professionals. The types of requirements may include education, training, citizenship and residence. In some instances, licensure requirements appear to have no direct relationship to the knowledge and skills needed to practice the profession safely. So some observers have questioned whether entry requirements represent a valid effort to protect the public or whether they represent an effort to limit entry into the profession. Similar questions have been raised about the extent to which codes of conduct are legitimate efforts to protect the public versus efforts to limit competition or unorthodox, but safe, approaches to health care.

Technological developments that impact professional practice are issues state boards must address as well. For example, the Louisiana State Board of Medicine recently addressed the question of the practice of medicine across state lines. The Board's opinion was that any rendering of a medical judgment by a physician in another state is the unauthorized practice of medicine in Louisiana unless the Board had issued a license (Louisiana State Board of Medical Examiners, December, 1996).

XI. ENFORCING REGULATORY POLICIES GOVERNING HEALTH PROFESSIONALS

When practitioners fail to adhere to regulations and standards of conduct, health professional boards may take disciplinary action. The legal grounds on which a professional can be disciplined vary by state. Derbyshire indicates that in 1961 there were 90 grounds for license revocation across the country. Only nine of these were similar in 30 states and there was no one ground for revocation that was found in all states (Derbyshire, 1983).

The enforcement authority of boards enables them to investigate practitioners for possible violations, determine whether a violation has occurred and to impose penalties. Violations include two broad categories of conduct: 1) Conduct that is directly detrimental to the health, safety and welfare of patients, and 2) Conduct that is considered inappropriate for professionals. Examples of the first category may include: fraud, misrepresentation, negligence in treating a patient, abuse of drugs or alcohol and practicing while ill with a contagious disease. Examples of violations that fall within the second category include failing to display one's license or being convicted of a felony.

Penalties boards are authorized to impose may range from a relatively mild letter of reprimand to a permanent license revocation.

A long standing problem in professional regulation is the reluctance of professionals to report their peers to regulatory authority. This problem has been noted in other professions outside the health field. One response has been to introduce statutes to counteract the reluctance of practitioners to report their colleagues. Mandatory reporting laws require professionals and institutions (e.g., hospitals) who have observed or have knowledge of violations by their peers must report that information to the relevant regulatory board. The enactment of statutes mandating the reporting of violations was necessary to increase reporting of violations by health professionals. As a result, of mandatory reporting laws some observers believe that the rate of disciplinary actions taken by boards has increased (Dolan and Urban, 1983; HHS, Dentists, 1988; HHS, Medical, 1986).

Impaired practitioners laws are also designed to address the problem of substance abusers who provide health care services. Impaired practitioner laws are designed to protect substance abusers from disciplinary action if they voluntarily seek treatment. Such laws are believed to increase the reporting of "problem" practitioners. Presumably, colleagues will be more willing to report colleagues who are substance abusers if they know their colleagues' licenses will not be revoked as a result (Derbyshire, 1976).

XII. REFORMS IN HEALTH PROFESSIONAL REGULATION

Emerging trends in the delivery of health care services will have a significant impact on the way the health professions are regulated. The model of the profession as an autonomous, self-governing occupation is being challenged by economic, political and social counter-forces.

What are these trends and what other changes are being advocated in the regulation of health professionals? One major trend is the emergence of third party payers as active participants in deciding the standard of care for which they will pay. If professional authority to make treatment decisions is shared with other entities such as third party payers, then it may be appropriate that the responsibility for any consequences also be shared.

A second trend is the increased emphasis on consumer choice in recent proposals to reform the health care delivery system. Such concern is in line with pressures by consumer advocacy groups for the health care industry to be more responsive to the concerns of consumers and patients. Consequently, the scrutiny of professional regulation is likely to increase, particularly by those interested in consumer rights.

A third trend relates to malpractice reforms advocated by the health professionals, particularly physicians, and the insurance industry. Arguments to limit liability have given opponents of such reforms an opportunity to highlight what they say is the ineffectiveness of the current system for regulating health professionals.

In addition to the trends highlighting professional regulation is the long standing reforms offered by both critics and defenders of the current system. The more radical of these reforms is that that we eliminate professional regulatory boards. Friedman (1962), for example, has long advocated the abolition of all state regulation of occupations to be replaced by free market regulation. Most reform proposals involve adjustments to the current system. Among the reform proposals are increasing citizen participation, periodic review of statutes and centralized data banks to track practitioners who have been disciplined.

A. Citizen Members

Increased lay participation is a significant development in the evolution of health professional regulation. The addition of citizen members to health professional regulatory boards is one of the many reforms advocated to strengthen the credibility of professional boards. A more radical proposal is that boards dominated by professionals be dismantled and replaced with licensing boards composed of non-professionals. It is argued that such boards would be much more likely to make decisions favorable to the public (Cohen, 1980).

However, there is evidence that there are no dramatic differences in decisions made by boards when citizen members are added. However, even in the absence of significant impact, the broader question of effective citizen participation in government decision making remains. Perceptions of the effectiveness of citizen members may be influenced by the functions of boards to which citizens are appointed. Citizen members may tend to feel more effective in deciding broad policy issues as opposed to deciding how to discipline individual professionals. Citizen members may be more effective in the policy development functions of professional regulatory boards rather than the enforcement functions (Chesney, 1984).

B. Sunset Legislation

Sunset legislation is another reform that purports to curb the power of regulatory boards in establishing a specified lifetime for a board. At the end of that pre-specified time the board would be eliminated unless the legislature specifically renewed the board. Sunset legislation was a reform advocated in the early 1980s in a number of states. Texas, for example, adopted sunset legislation. However, indicators that regulatory agencies with political clout are less likely to be eliminated, may thwart the intent of sunset legislation (Slaughter, 1986).

C. National Practitioner Data Bank

A significant weakness of regulating professionals at the state level has been that practitioners denied the right to practice in one state simply moved to another and continued to practice. Licensing boards have not had sophisticated data bases and often have not communicated administrative actions taken against practitioners to boards in others states or institutions providing health care. Furthermore, hospitals and other health care facilities often were unable to find out if a health professional had any adverse actions taken against his or her license. Finally, actions through malpractice suits and settlements have not generally been available to licensing boards or to institutions hiring practitioners.

In an effort to address the lack of a national, coordinated system, Congress created the National Practitioner Data Bank (NPDB), under the 1986 Health Care Quality Improvement Act. The NPDB became operational in September 1990 and is administered by the United States Public Health Service. Its purpose is to identify health practitioners who have had adverse disciplinary actions taken against them.

Under the provisions of the Health Care Quality Act, Title IV, licensing boards, professional associations, malpractice insurers, hospitals and other health care institutions are required to report disciplinary actions against practitioners to the NPDB. Institutions that employ health practitioners are required to query the NPDB prior to a hiring decision and to routinely make queries about medical staff every two years (Oshel, Croft and Rodak, 1995).

SUMMARY

Disagreement over the value and the ultimate goals of health professional regulation should be expected given the diversity of interests, goals and values that can be found among the respective government agencies, health professional associations, consumer groups and private organizations. The issues are complex and will continue to engender debate as health professional regulation evolves.

The challenge for health regulatory policy is to balance competing and often conflicting values. What is the appropriate balance between containing costs and ensuring quality health care? Administrative efficiency may be a value that could be instrumental in forming public policy on health professional regulation. A competing value would be the protection of due process rights of health professionals.

Professional expertise has been a major criterion for determining who should make policies governing health practitioners. The reasoning seems to be that since health professionals possess knowledge that the lay person lacks, then it is only the professional who is capable of setting standards for practice and of making judgments on practitioners who deviate from appropriate professional practice. Such reasoning places a premium on technical expertise and assumes no other knowledge base or values system is relevant to health professional regulation. The inference is that the standards of the professions should be determined solely by members of the profession. Implicit in such reasoning is the notion that technical expertise drives normative standards. That is, the values and standards to which professionals are expected to adhere, can be determined solely by members of the professions. The values and standards are influenced by professional socialization which tends to emphasize group solidarity (Lewis and Lewis, 1970). Thus the professions' value systems may not support full exploration and analysis of the broad range of issues affected by regulatory decision making.

Despite widespread disagreement about appropriate policies to regulate professionals, it should not be surprising that independent regulatory boards persist despite widespread criticism that they are inefficient and ineffective. The reason they persist is that their functions are not primarily economic. Independent regulatory boards, such as health professional regulatory boards have political and legal functions as well. The use of independent boards composed of professionals is a political strategy to delegate tasks too controversial for existing units of government to handle (McGraw, 1984). The arguments for economic efficiency versus legal due process for the individual reflect a fundamental issue that confronts regulatory boards — how to balance the rights of the individual against the good of the society. Given the pervasive effects of health professional regulation on the nature and quality of health care, a broader public participation on health professional boards and in formulating policies is warranted.

REFERENCES

Akers, R. L. The Professional Association and the Legal Regulation of Practice. *Law and Society Review.*

Chesney, J. D. (1994). Citizen Participation on Regulatory Boards. *Journal of Health Politics, Policy and Law* 9.

Cohen, H. S. (1980). On Professional Power and Conflict of Interest: State Licensing Boards on Trial. *Journal of Health Politics and Law* 5(2): 291-308.

Dent v. West Virginia, 129 U.S. 114, 121-129 (1889).

Derbyshire, R. C. (1974). Medical Ethics and Discipline. *Journal of the American Medical Association 228*: 1.

Derbyshire, R. C. (1983). How Effective is Medical Self-Regulation? *Law and Human Behavior* 7,(2/3): 193-202.

Dolan, A. K. and Urban, N. D. (1983). The Determinants of the Effectiveness of Medical Disciplinary Boards: 1960-1977. *Law and Human Behavior, 7*(2/3): 203-217.

Friedman, M. (1962). *Capitalism and Freedom*. The University of Chicago Press, Chicago.

Friedson, E. (1983). The Reorganization of the Professions by Regulation. *Law and Human Behavior 7*(2/3): 279-290.

Galusha, G. L. (1989 April) Concentrating on the Problem Physician: Perspectives in Medical Discipline. *New York State Journal of Medicine,* 219-221.

Grad, F. P. and Marti, N. (1979). *Physicians' Licensure and Discipline*. Oceana Publications, Inc., Dobbs Ferry, NY.

Illich, I. (1976). *Medical Nemesis: The Expropriation of Health*. Random House, New York.

Lewis, H. R. and Lewis, M. (1970). *The Medical Offenders*. Simon and Schuster, New York.

Mashaw, J. L. and Merrill, R. A. (1985). *Administrative Law: The American Public Law System* (2nd. ed.). West Publishing Co, St. Paul.

McCluggage, R. W. (1959). *A History of the American Dental Association: A Century of Health Service.* American Dental Association, Chicago.

McCraw, T. K. (1984). *Prophets of Regulation.* Belknap Press of Harvard University Press, London.

Oshel, Croft and Rodak, (1995).

Shimberg, B. (1984). The Relationship Among Accreditation, Certification and Licensure. Federation Bulletin. *Federation of State Medical Boards of the U.S.:* 99-116.

Slaughter, C. (1986). Sunset and Occupational Regulation: A Case Study. *Public Administration Review, 46:* 241-245.

U.S. Department of Health and Human Services. (1988). Office of Inspector General. *State Licensure and Discipline of Dentists. August.*

U.S. Department of Health, Education and Welfare. (1971). Report on Licensure and Related Health Personnel Credentialing.Office of Assistant Secretary for Health and scientific Affairs. *DHEW Publication* No. HSM 72-11 U.S. Government Printing Office, Washington.

U.S. Department of Health, Education and Welfare. (1973). Developments in Health Manpower Licensure. *DHEW Publication* No. HRA 74-3101 U.S. Government Printing Office, Washington.

U.S. Department of Health and Human Services. (1986). Office of Inspector General. *Medical Licensure and Discipline: An Overview.* June.

4.

OCCUPATIONAL AND ENVIRONMENTAL ISSUES FACING HEALTH CARE MANAGERS

David M. Hunt, *Medical University of South Carolina, Charleston, SC*

R. Martin Jones, *Medical University of South Carolina, Charleston, SC*

Occupational and environmental regulations and requirements, including legal liabilities for corporate officials, are an ever-present challenge facing health care administrators. Government agencies at the local, state, and federal level impose a myriad of reporting and recordkeeping requirements, inspect the workplace, and enforce laws. Public interest groups bring pressures which may quickly elevate an occupational or environmental issue to prominence. The local community, including employees, residents in the surrounding neighborhood, and the local business community, are increasingly important factors in a manager's ability to run an effective health care business. Media coverage of chemical emissions, reports of employee health concerns, or emergency situations can be an opportunity to demonstrate advanced planning and preparation, or a public relations nightmare.

This chapter addresses some of the key occupational and environmental issues facing health care managers from a regulatory, accreditation, and community expectation perspective. Occupational and environmental issues are described and culminate in a discussion of organization/program issues incorporating the Joint Commission on Accreditation of Healthcare Organization's (JCAHO) "Management of the Environment of Care" standards. The seven JCAHO "management plans" are discussed and suggested as an overarching structure for incorporating Occupational Safety and Health Administration (OSHA) and Environmental Protection Agency (EPA) requirements. (OSHA and JCAHO have entered into a three-year partnership to minimize duplication in compliance activities and to improve management of safety and health issues in health care organizations.) While federal-level requirements are presented, most organizations deal with state and local officials on a regular basis since many state and local requirements originate from federal policies.

Federal and state regulatory oversight is moving away from strict regulatory enforcement of specific limits toward a focus on ensuring that an organization is including employees, the community, and local government in managing issues of concern. Health care organizations must form partnerships with these groups regardless of regulatory requirements, given the current awareness and concerns of the general public for occupational and environmental issues.

The chapter is intended to inform the reader of areas of concern so they may ask questions of specific managers (industrial hygiene, safety, security, or environmental) to determine regulatory compliance and program quality. Health administrators will be affected by these issues and requirements, whether they have functional responsibility for meeting them. The chapter does not deal with all areas of possible liability and is not intended as a reference for professionals responsible for compliance or risk management. To best ensure compliance, skilled professionals in the respective areas of health, environment, and security should manage these programs.

The authors believe health care administrators must embrace the health and safety of employees and community members and be actively concerned for environmental quality. Occupational and environmental issues are as important and necessary business concerns as patient care. The time, effort and resources devoted to occupational/environmental issues will be well spent and rewarding.

I. OCCUPATIONAL CONCERNS

A. History of OSHA

The Occupational Safety and Health Act (OSHAct - Public Law 91-596) was passed by Congress on December 29, 1970. PL 91-596 created the Occupational Safety and Health Administration (OSHA) under the Department of Labor (DOL). OSHA is the federal government agency charged with developing and enforcing safety and health standards in the workplace.

Standards can address specific hazards and have very detailed compliance guidance (e.g., noise); they can specify programmatic requirements (e.g., hazard communication); or, they may simply set an allowable level of exposure (e.g., Permissible Exposure Limits - PELs) and leave it to the employer to achieve compliance. In the absence of a specific standard addressing a hazard, the "general duty clause," which requires employers to maintain a workplace free of "recognized hazards," may be used to issue citations. Standards are established through the rulemaking procedure in which OSHA announces the intent to issue a standard (Advanced Notice of Proposed Rulemaking - ANPR); holds hearings to receive comments from potentially affected organizations/individuals; if justified, issues a proposed rule (Notice of Proposed Rulemaking - NPRM); receives comments again; and, if warranted, issues a final rule. This process is used when new or revised standards are issued and typically takes between two to five years. OSHA must determine, based on substantial evidence in the record, that there is a "significant risk of health impairment under existing conditions" before they proceed with a new standard. OSHA has chosen at times to target specific hazards for "special emphasis enforcement programs" to address the most serious health and safety hazards. In 1997, as a part of its "nursing home initiative,"

OSHA began inspecting nursing homes because of high rates of employee musculoskeletal disorders resulting from patient handling (e.g., transfers, position changes, etc.).

States are encouraged to develop their own programs, known as State Implementation Plans (SIPs), which must be as stringent as federal regulations. Approximately half of the states have opted to develop SIP programs. Therefore, some state-specific regulations may differ from others.

B. OSHA Standards Frequently Cited in the Health Care Setting

OSHA statistics on citations issued and penalties assessed helped to identify occupational issues in the health services sector (Standard Industrial Classification [SIC] Major Group 80). Table 1 presents the ten most frequently cited violations for the period October 1994 through September 1995 and Table 2 presents information on the top five citations against which the highest, total penalties were assessed. The statistics on citations reflect the number of times a problem was found in a health care setting. The penalties ranking is important to show where OSHA officials feel are the most serious problem areas. According to OSHA, the most frequently cited standard and the one with the highest monetary penalty was employee exposure to Bloodborne Pathogens. The second most frequently cited standard in this sector was Hazard Communication. However, the second highest penalty assessed was for violation of the Respiratory Protection standard although it was fifth in frequency. General duty clause citations were issued largely for tuberculosis exposures and ergonomics associated with patient handling, in the absence of specific standards addressing those hazards.

Table 1 - Ten Most Frequently Cited Violations in the Health Care Industry
(Major Group 80 Health Service)

Standard	Number of Violations
Bloodborne Pathogens	843
Hazard Communication	443
Recordkeeping	141
(Log and Summary of Occupational Injuries and Illnesses)	
The Control of Hazardous Energy (Lockout/Tagout)	101
Respiratory Protection	96
Access to Employee Exposure and Medical Records	82
Personal Protective Equipment	81
Medical Services and First Aid	80
Formaldehyde	58
Electrical, Wiring Methods, Components & Equipment	57

Table 2 - Five OSHA Citations With the Highest Penalty Assessed
(Major Group 80 Health Service)

Standard	$ Total Penalty
Bloodborne Pathogens	$572,375.00
Respiratory Protection	$174,320.00
General Duty Clause	$123,040.00
Hazard Communication	$105,339.00
Asbestos	$102,350.00

C. Proposed OSHA Rules

1. Safety and Health Programs

In 1989, OSHA issued non-mandatory guidelines based on the best safety and health management practices observed since the Agency was established. OSHA is expanding this concept in response to the "reinventing government" move and as a part of the effort to change its fundamental mode of operation. In its report entitled "Reinventing Labor Regulations" (OSHA, 1995a), the Department of Labor stated that employers now have "a real choice between a partnership with OSHA and a tradition-al enforcement relationship." OSHA has structured this opportunity around a pro-posed rule "Comprehensive Occupational Safety and Health Programs" (OSHA, 1995b). Based on the reduction in job-related injuries and illnesses, workers' compen-sation costs, and absenteeism recognized by participants in OSHA's "Voluntary Protection Program" (VPP), the Agency has proposed to center its regulatory agenda around worksite-specific safety and health programs. The proposed standard also results from OSHA's experience with its "Maine 200" program which identified approximately 200 companies in Maine with high workers' compensation claims. Companies which cooperated with OSHA's request to develop comprehensive safety and health programs received limited "program inspections" and demonstrated reduc-tions in the indices of safety and health program status.

This proposed rule would encompass at least the following six elements: manage-ment commitment to the program; active employee participation; work site safety analysis of health hazards of all types; prompt elimination or control of those hazards; safety and health training for employees, supervisors, and managers; and regular eval-uation of the effectiveness of the safety and health program. As a compliance/enforce-ment incentive for instituting such safety and health programs, employers who can demonstrate effective and comprehensive programs under this proposed standard would receive penalty reductions for any violations cited.

2. Tuberculosis

Tuberculosis (TB) is a contagious disease caused by the bacterium *Mycobacterium tuberculosis* and is generally acquired by inhaling airborne particles carrying the bacterium. From 1985 through 1992 the number of cases reported rose by 14 percent. In addition to the increase in the number of TB cases reported, strains resistant to traditional drugs have emerged which have a higher mortality associated with them. In determining there to be a "significant risk," OSHA found that as the number of persons who have tuberculosis requiring health care increases, so does occupational exposure. Conditions contributing to transmission include delayed diagnosis, delayed and inadequate isolation, inadequate ventilation in isolation rooms, lapses in TB isolation practices, and lack of adequate respiratory protection.

In 1997 OSHA issued a proposed standard entitled "Occupational Exposure to Tuberculosis." A separate standard from bloodborne pathogens is necessary because the route of disease transmission is different. OSHA's draft overview of a proposed TB standard would apply to work settings where six or more individuals with suspected or confirmed TB are encountered per year.

The proposal would apply to health care facilities such as hospitals, long-term care and hospice facilities, home health care and home-based hospice care, drug treatment facilities, emergency medical services, and laboratories and ventilation systems where *M. tuberculosis* may be encountered. The proposal requires an exposure control plan (similar to the one required by the Bloodborne Pathogens standard) which includes identification of those who have, or may have, occupational exposure to TB at their work setting. Compliance methods require the use of isolation rooms, masking or segregating patients, the use of respiratory protection by health care providers, medical surveillance, and employee information regarding TB.

3. Ergonomics

Ergonomics is the study of man's structure and function and how work-related tasks and work station design impact health. Work-related musculoskeletal disorders are a leading cause of disability in American workplaces and according to the Bureau of Labor Statistics (BLS, 1997a) more than five hundred thousand workers suffer back injuries each year and back injuries account for one of every four workplace injuries. Further, one out of every three dollars spent on workers' compensation claims goes toward musculoskeletal disorders. These disorders arise from prolonged fixed or awkward posture, exertion of force, repetitive movement, vibration, or lifting heavy objects. These stresses are known as "signal risk factors" and in the health-care setting, patient handling is the biggest risk factor. Three out of four low back injuries reportedly occurred while the employee was lifting. Specifically, OSHA has issued citations using the general duty clause for ergonomic violations.

In March of 1995, OSHA issued a draft of its "Prevention of Work-related Musculoskeletal Disorders Standard." In this standard, employers must conduct initial assessments to identify signal risk factors; fix or control risk factors through a "job improvement process" (back belts and wrist supports are not recognized as control mechanisms); train employees in problem jobs on how to recognize and control risk factors and signs and symptoms of injuries; and provide prompt assessment and treatment by a health care provider at no cost to the employee.

4. Violence in the Workplace

According to the Bureau of Labor Statistics (BLS), workplace violence is the number two leading cause of occupational fatalities (after automobile accidents), accounting for 15 percent of the nation's total deaths in 1996. It was the leading cause of death for women on the job in 1996 (BLS, 1997b) and BLS data for 1993 revealed that health care workers have the highest incidence of assault injuries. In March 1996, OSHA issued final guidelines for workplace violence prevention programs specific for health care workers in institutional and community settings. OSHA can use the guidelines as establishing a recognized health hazard and issue citations for non-compliance under the general duty clause.

OSHA identified risk factors in its guidelines and divided them into three categories: environmental; administrative and work practices; and, perpetrator and victim. Environmental risk factors include the prevalence of handguns, the decrease in medical and mental health care for the mentally ill, and the increasing use of hospitals by police and the criminal justice systems for acutely disturbed violent cases. Administrative and work practices contributing as risk factors include staffing patterns such as shortages and reduction of trained, regular staff. Other work practices increasing risk included isolated work with clients in examination or treatment activities, working alone or in remote areas, and working at night. Perpetrators were identified as most often male with widely ranging ages, suffering from mental illness, and with a history of violence. Victims were most often persons in a position of lesser authority such as nurses' aides, who work alone or at night, or work in correctional facilities, drug abuse or mental health clinics, or emergency rooms.

OSHA identified key elements of a workplace safety and security program and developed a checklist to help employers determine if they have a potential or present problem. OSHA's suggestions for program development are extensive and include elements such as a written policy and employee involvement in the safety and security program and decisions affecting worker safety and health. Worksite analysis, hazard prevention and control measures, and post-incident follow-up should be included in the program as well. Workplace violence should be addressed in the institution's security management plan, a part of the JCAHO required Management of the Environment of Care standards.

5. Indoor Air Quality (IAQ)

Most IAQ problems result from building construction techniques employing energy conservation measures by minimizing the infiltration of outside air. Inadequate outside air will result in the increase of indoor air contaminants, both chemical and biological. Unfortunately, IAQ investigations frequently do not identify a cause for reported complaints unless the problem is fairly obvious. An increasing concentration of carbon dioxide as measured over a workday indicates there is a lack of fresh air being introduced into the building. Ventilation problems were found to be the culprit in over fifty percent of IAQ problems (NIOSH, 1987), followed by inside the building contamination sources (17%), and outside contamination sources (11%).

OSHA has published a proposed standard dealing with indoor air quality issues. Indoor air quality problems are manifested in two fairly distinct conditions classified as Sick Building Syndrome (SBS) or Building-related Illness (BRI). SBS is characterized by irritation of the mucous membranes (eyes, nose, or throat), mental fatigue and headache, cough, hoarseness, etc. and is not easily traced to a specific substance, but is perceived as resulting from some unidentified contaminant or combination of contaminants. Legionnaires' disease is typical of BRI in that there are specific medical conditions of a known cause, which can often be documented by physical signs and laboratory findings. Typical BRI illnesses include sensory irritation caused by known agents, respiratory allergies and infections, and signs and symptoms indicative of chemical or biologic substance exposure. Such agents include volatile organic compounds (VOCs), formaldehyde, carbon monoxide, pesticides, or bacteria, viruses, molds, or fungi.

D. The Hazard Communication Standard or "Employee Right To Know"

The Hazard Communication Standard (HCS) addresses all chemical hazards. A health hazard is defined as a chemical for which there is statistically significant evidence that acute or chronic health effects may occur in exposed employees. The HCS requires chemical manufactures or importers to determine the hazards of each product, and communicate this hazard information to customers through labels and material safety data sheets (MSDSs). Employers must then maintain MSDSs accessible to employees for all hazardous substances used in the workplace.

Employers must develop, implement, and maintain at the workplace a written hazard communication program for employees handling or otherwise exposed to health hazards. The absence of a written hazard communication program is the most frequently cited OSHA general industry violation.

E. Bloodborne Pathogens

OSHA regulates contact with blood and body fluids under its Occupational Exposure to Bloodborne Pathogens standard. OSHA determined there was a "significant health risk" as the result of occupational exposure to blood and other potentially infectious materials. Specifically, the standard was designed to eliminate or minimize occupational exposure to Hepatitis B Virus (HBV), Human Immunodeficiency Virus (HIV), and other bloodborne pathogens. Contact with and exposure to blood and body fluids may occur as a result of medical and surgical procedures such as labor and delivery, blood or body fluid collection and analysis, the handling of contaminated waste (e.g., gloves, linens, bandages, protective clothing, etc.), or suctioning airways. Sharps (needles, capillary tubes, slides and cover slips, scalpel blades, etc.) are a very common source of exposure, and needlesticks are one of the most frequently reported injuries among health care workers.

Exposure to bloodborne pathogens is unique in that most occupational health illnesses (versus injuries) arise from cumulative exposure to chemical agents which results in chronic health effects. Bloodborne pathogen exposures either result in infection or they do not. OSHA's approach is that any exposure incident may result in infection and subsequent disease and, therefore, must be prevented. Risk is based upon the virulence of the pathogen, the size of the delivered dose, the route of exposure, and worker resistance (age, physical condition, HBV vaccinations, etc.). Recent information (CDC, 1995), indicates the risk of HIV infection increases with an increase in the amount of blood encountered and the blood source stage of illness, e.g., terminal patients.

OSHA found that exposure can be minimized or eliminated using a combination of engineering and work practice controls, personal protective clothing and equipment, training, medical surveillance, Hepatitis B vaccinations (provided at no cost to the employee based on a finding of exposure potential), and signs and labels. The OSHA standard specifically requires the preparation of a written Exposure Control Plan (ECP) which addresses the elements of an earlier voluntary guideline (CDC, 1989) establishing "universal precautions" to be taken during any potential encounter with bloodborne pathogens. Universal precautions is an infection control approach which assumes that all human blood and certain human body fluids are infectious.

F. Laboratory Safety

In 1990 OSHA instituted the rulemaking procedure for "Occupational Exposure to Toxic Substances in Laboratories." This standard requires employers to ensure that employees are not exposed to hazardous chemicals above established Permissible Exposure Limits (PELs). It also requires the preparation of a written Chemical Hygiene Plan (CHP) which sets forth procedures, equipment, personal protective equipment, and work practices.

The standard was designed to provide for a comprehensive approach for the protection of laboratory workers. It requires development and implementation of work practices and engineering control measures expressly tailored to the individual workplace.

G. Asbestos

Asbestos-containing materials (ACMs) are often found in older hospital facilities in pipe or boiler insulation, sprayed-on fireproofing, or sprayed-on acoustical or other surfacing materials. Exposures can occur when these materials are disturbed during maintenance or renovation activities, or when materials are in poor condition due to aging, damage, or loss of adhesion from getting wet. The OSHA Construction Industry standard takes a presumptive approach requiring that such materials be presumed to contain asbestos if they were installed "no later than 1980." While the OSHA standard does not require a building owner to conduct a comprehensive inspection to identify ACMs (as EPA required of schools), samples of suspect materials must be taken to rebut the required presumption. Virtually all health care facilities built prior to 1980 should have a detailed asbestos management plan.

H. Chemical Agents

Chemical agents are encountered in many locations throughout health care settings. Routes of exposure include inhalation, ingestion, and skin absorption. Effects can range from acute to chronic including death after a long latency period (time between exposure and disease manifestation). Most chemical agents are regulated by OSHA and have either substance-specific standards or established Permissible Exposure Limits (PELs). Common substance specific requirements of OSHA standards include exposure monitoring, medical surveillance, hazard communication, emergency procedures, primary reliance on engineering controls and work practices to reduce exposures, selection and maintenance of personal protective equipment, and recordkeeping.

Guidelines cover the following agents and others:

1. Ethylene Oxide (EtO)
2. Formaldehyde
3. Waste Anesthetic Gases (WAGs)
4. Toluene and Xylene
5. Glutaraldehyde
6. Latex

I. Exposure to Hazardous Drugs

Occupational exposure to pharmaceuticals in the health care setting can occur during the preparation, administration, or disposal of "hazardous drugs" (HDs). Pharmacists, nurses, physicians, and other health care workers may be exposed by inhalation of dusts or aerosols, skin absorption, or ingestion.

In 1994, OSHA revised its Hazard Communication Standard (HCS) with technical clarification regarding hazardous drugs and pharmaceutical agents. The requirements apply to all locations where employees are occupationally exposed to HDs such as hospitals, physicians' offices, and home health care agencies.

Where hazardous drugs are used in the workplace, a written Hazardous Drug Safety and Health Plan should be developed. Such a plan assists in protecting employees from health hazards associated with HDs and keeping exposures as low as reasonably achievable. The ASHP recommends that the plan include standard operating procedures, control measures, employee information and training, and medical consultation and examination.

J. Physical Agents

Physical agents are usually well identified and controlled in the health care setting. Some physical hazards such as lasers and radiation are used in clinical treatments by trained personnel in restricted areas. Others, such as noise and electrical hazards, may be a problem for exposed maintenance personnel.

Electrical Hazards - exposure may occur due to improper maintenance of electrical equipment, abuse, or misunderstanding the equipment and/or its controls. Oxygen-enriched atmospheres and water may contribute to hazardous conditions. Acute health effects include painful shocks, respiratory inhibition, deep burns (electric and thermal), heart rate irregularities, and death.

K. Emerging Issues

While other health hazards identified in this chapter are well recognized, several less well defined work-related illnesses are emerging as areas of potential concern, including:

1. Multiple Chemical Sensitivity (MCS) - a vague illness, questionably organic, causing headaches, eye, ear, nose, and throat irritation, chest pain, fatigue, muscle pain, coughing, nervous problems, etc.
2. Shiftwork Maladaptation - an interruption in the body's "circadian rhythm" or programmed schedule which results in physical ailments.
3. Stress - generalized anxiety, depression, job dissatisfaction, and drug/alcohol abuse brought about by stressful situations such as life-threatening injuries and illnesses, overwork/understaffing, management practices, etc.

Persons responsible for workers' compensation programs should carefully follow the literature as these issues are better defined. Significant liability in terms of publicity and workers' compensation claims may be associated with these issues. Prompt and careful management of employees affected by these conditions is mandatory.

II. ENVIRONMENTAL ISSUES

A. Environmental Protection Agency Background

The U.S. Environmental Protection Agency (EPA) was formally established as an independent agency in the Executive Branch on December 2, 1970. The Agency is charged by Congress to protect the Nation's land, air, and water systems. Under a mandate of national environmental laws, the Agency attempts to strike a balance between human activities and natural systems by identifying, assessing, and managing serious risks to public health and the environment. EPA works with state, county, and municipal governments to carry out its mission. State and local standards may exceed federal standards, but they cannot be less stringent.

EPA administers 11 comprehensive environmental protection laws including the Clean Air Act, the Clean Water Act, the Safe Drinking Water Act, the Comprehensive Environmental Response, Compensation, and Liability Act ("Superfund"), the Resource Conservation and Recovery Act (RCRA), and the Toxic Substances Control Act.

B. Hazardous Wastes

1. The Resource Conservation and Recovery Act

The Resource Conservation and Recovery Act (RCRA), as passed in 1976 and amended in 1984, was the first comprehensive attempt to deal with the problem of solid waste in general, and specifically hazardous waste. RCRA directed EPA to institute a national program to control hazardous wastes from "cradle to grave" to ensure human health and the environment are protected. RCRA defines hazardous wastes and sets standards from generation through storage, transport, treatment, and ultimate disposal. Health care facilities which treat, store, or dispose (TSD facilities) of hazardous wastes must comply with established standards, obtain permits for these activities, and use a recordkeeping or manifest system to track wastes. The RCRA program includes oversight of underground storage tanks for petroleum or such hazardous compounds as benzene. States may assume responsibility for managing RCRA programs subject to EPA approval.

A hazardous waste is a solid waste which because of its quantity, concentration, or physical, chemical, or infectious properties may cause an increase in mortality or result in serious illness, or pose a substantial hazard to human health or the environment when improperly treated, stored, transported, or disposed. Wastes are classified as hazardous on the basis of four characteristics: ignitability; corrosivity; reactivity; and, toxicity.

2. Comprehensive Environmental Response, Compensation and Liability Act

The Comprehensive Environmental Response, Compensation and Liability Act (CERCLA), or "Superfund" was established by Congress in 1980 to deal with the legacy of abandoned waste sites or emergencies created by spills or other releases of hazardous substances. A Trust Fund was set up to provide a source of funds for emergency response and cleanup of these hazardous waste sites, financed mainly by taxes on the chemical and petroleum industries. Additionally, the government can recover the costs of cleanup from persons responsible for the release or improper disposal (dumping). Under the standard of strict joint and several liability, if the costs of a cleanup cannot be divided among potentially responsible partners (PRPs), any party may be held responsible for all the costs.

This law imposes long-term liability on waste generators such as health care institutions. Under CERCLA, the owners and operators of a facility releasing or threatening to release hazardous substances to the environment may be held liable for the damages resulting from a discharge or the cost of actions taken to prevent a discharge. This liability also applies to generators who placed hazardous materials in a disposal site from which there was a release or a threatened release. Generators thus have a continuing liability for wastes which were transported to disposal sites, even permitted disposal sites, should these wastes be discharged to the environment (including leaching to groundwater). Liabilities imposed by CERCLA would therefore argue for waste minimization first, destruction of hazardous and medical wastes wherever possible, and, finally, land disposal.

C. Medical Wastes

While the vast majority of solid wastes generated by hospitals are non-hazardous, the American Hospital Association estimates that approximately 10-12% are potentially infectious. Therefore, "medical waste" management is a critical part of any health care facilities' compliance program. Typical materials classified as medical waste by EPA include cultures and stocks, pathological wastes, human blood and blood products, sharps, animal waste, and isolation waste.

Many states have their own medical waste regulations which may differ significantly. However, generally, health care organizations must determine if a medical waste is a regulated medical waste, and how much regulated medical waste is generated in a calendar month.

D. Air and Water Issues

1. Clean Air Act

The Clean Air Act (CAA) of 1970, along with its 1977 and 1990 Amendments, were written to protect the public health and welfare against the adverse effects of air pollution. The Act sets limits on how much of a given pollutant is permitted in the air and is designed to ensure consistent air quality among states. States must develop state implementation plans (SIPs) to achieve "attainment" of primary standards designed to protect public health. EPA must approve each SIP and may take over enforcement of the CAA if the plan is not as stringent as the federal standards. Hospitals which own or operate incinerators, fossil fuel-fired boilers or generators, or other equipment which emit air pollutants must comply with CAA provisions and keep records such as the date of incineration cycle, length of cycle, and total weight of waste incinerated per cycle.

2. Clean Water Act

The Clean Water Act National Pollutant Discharge Elimination System (CWA NPDES) regulations require local wastewater districts to develop a pretreatment program outlining the authority, procedure, and discharge limits for an enforcement program to be conducted at the local level. Hospitals discharge some wastes into the sewer that are perfectly acceptable to treatment facilities, but problems can arise when chemicals such as solvents or heavy metals are discharged by laboratories, maintenance, or other departments.

E. Emergency Planning and Community Right-To-Know Act (EPCRA)

The Superfund Amendments and Reauthorization Act of 1986 (SARA) was signed into law on October 17, 1986. Title III of SARA is known as the "Emergency Planning and Community Right-To-Know Act of 1986" (EPCRA). EPCRA requires states to establish local chemical emergency preparedness programs and to receive and distribute information on hazardous chemicals present at facilities within local communities. EPCRA has four major components: emergency planning; emergency release notification; community right-to-know reporting; and, toxic chemical release inventory reporting.

EPCRA required governors to designate emergency planning districts within each state to prepare and implement emergency plans. EPCRA requires facilities that produce, use, or store any of the substances on the EPA's List of Extremely Hazardous Substances (EHSs) in quantities above the threshold planning quantity (TPQ) to notify these planning districts.

III. PROGRAM ORGANIZATION ISSUES

A. General Program Suggestions

The organization of an effective health care facility safety and health program begins with an individual, the safety officer, who is responsible for overall program development and implementation. Ideally, that individual should report directly to the chief executive officer (CEO) to ensure there are no intermediate obstacles preventing effective communication of program status or emerging issues and requirements. The CEO must fully support the safety program and understand the potential legal, regulatory, and tort liabilities of non-compliance. The safety officer is supported by a safety department which is staffed by trained and experienced personnel including safety specialists and industrial hygienists. The traditional staffing ratio of one full-time person per 300 - 500 employees may be reduced if safety and health are truly the responsibilities of first-line managers. A qualified individual should oversee the development, implementation, and monitoring of safety plans and an individual should be identified to intervene if conditions pose an immediate threat to life or health. Safety and health performance should be closely monitored and supported by an active safety committee composed of members from various departments throughout the facility. Subcommittees may have areas of responsibility dealing with specific issues, such as Joint Commission on Accreditation of Healthcare Organizations (JCAHO) management plans.

The consolidation of various occupational and environmental responsibilities at a health care facility into a single office responsible "to ensure health" may offer some efficiency and economy of scale. Such responsibilities should include safety, industrial hygiene, security, environmental, employee health, workers' compensation and even wellness and employee assistance programs. Such a department should have the mission to provide a workplace "free from recognized hazards" to ensure regulatory compliance, to reduce occupational injuries/illnesses, to manage workers' compensation costs, and possibly to provide an outside source of income by offering all of these services to industry.

B. Joint Commission on Accreditation of Healthcare Organizations

The Joint Commission on Accreditation of Healthcare Organizations (JCAHO) has recently established its "Management of the Environment of Care" as the new model for health care facility compliance. Management plans are designed to provide a "safe, functional, and effective environment for patients, staff members, and other individuals." Environment of Care (EC) management plans addressing seven standards in the area of occupational and environmental health must be written, implemented, maintained, tested, and inspected. While the standards do not address specific OSHA or EPA regulatory compliance requirements, a program designed to ensure that management plans are effective and implemented will incorporate those regulatory requirements. As mentioned previously, OSHA and JCAHO have entered into a partnership to minimize duplication of compliance activities, and OSHA requirements should be addressed in the EC management plans.

The seven management plans address safety, security, hazardous materials and wastes, emergency preparedness, life safety, medical equipment, and utility systems. The 1997 Hospital Accreditation Standards (HAS) provides a detailed description of the standards' intent, implementation, and evidence of performance.

C. Employee Health Services

Healthcare facilities must make available occupational health services for their employees. These services typically include pre-placement, periodic, episodic, and exit physical examinations. Pre-placement examinations are intended to physically qualify the individual for the intended position to ensure he/she can perform the job safely and effectively without endangering the employee or others, and to document "baseline" conditions. However, the Americans With Disabilities Act (ADA) should be consulted to ensure compliance with its requirements regarding physical examination, disclosure of results, and disability classification.

Exposure to some chemical substances (e.g., asbestos, ethylene oxide, and formaldehyde) above regulated levels requires periodic (usually annual) examinations, and exposure to bloodborne pathogens may require immunization. Some OSHA standards require medical examinations upon an incident which results in an unknown exposure or overexposure. The use of respiratory protection requires medical examination and approval before use. Control of workers' compensation costs involves prompt evaluation, the use of limited work regimes, and follow-up procedures to ensure early return-to-work. Finally, for the employee and employer, it is always wise to conduct exit examinations upon termination.

D. Workers' Compensation

Potential workers' compensation cases of injuries and illnesses which involve lost time must be recorded in the "OSHA Log." The Log is intended to provide information for employers and employees to raise their awareness of the kinds of injuries and illnesses which occur in the workplace and related hazards. Subsequently, employers should identify and correct hazardous workplace conditions. One other use of the Log data is by OSHA compliance officers who, at the beginning of a planned program inspection, review the data to determine where to focus inspection efforts. Finally, the Bureau of Labor Statistics (BLS) uses the information gathered from the Logs in an annual survey to measure the magnitude of occupational injury and illness across the country.

Workers compensation payments are generally the "exclusive remedy" of injured or ill employees, and facilities pay an insurance premium to cover employees. Premiums are based on the industry and facility experience. Demonstration of reduced workers' compensation costs through an active safety and health program can result in lowered premiums. Therefore, early intervention can be financially beneficial and speed patient recovery. Case management involves a coordinated effort among health care providers such as occupational physicians and nurses and safety and industrial hygiene professionals. It involves a prompt examination (within 24 hours) by a primary care provider, follow-up investigation of the circumstances leading to the injury or illness, and early return to work through the use of limited or modified duties. A comprehensive workplace safety and health program, as discussed, may logically be the organizational location of the workers' compensation management effort.

Aggressive case management, also known as multi-disciplinary case management or managed care, has been shown to significantly reduce recordable injuries, the average number of lost days per injury, the rate of new lost-time injury claims, and the average cost per new workers' compensation claim in the health care setting (Mcgrail, 1995).

Further evidence of the ability to control costs was provided by a survey of 650 U.S.-based organizations which showed worker's compensation costs fell 18% in 1994 (Tillinghast, 1995). This was attributed in part to increased use of safety and health programs at work, managed care, less reliance on traditional insurance, and legislative reforms in various states.

Tables 3 and 4 present information on the five most common injuries or illnesses (frequency) and events or exposures which resulted in the most lost time cases (severity) in the health services major group (BLS, 1997a). The BLS report states that nursing homes led all other industries in the rate of injuries due to overexertion. To completely describe the example of a nursing aide who sprains his/her back while lifting a patient, the report identifies the effect as a sprain and/or strain, the back as the body part affected, overexertion as the event, and the patient as the source. This example is used because it is commonly accepted that the highest cost workers' compensation case in the health care setting results from back injuries. Nursing aides and orderlies, responsible for more "bed and body work," experienced more lost time injuries and illnesses than did registered nurses, than did licensed practical nurses. Other sources indicate the most common type of injury resulted from needlesticks (Rowe, 1991).

In 1995, the last year for which records are available, the injury incidence rate stood at 7.5 cases for every 100 full-time workers in private industry, the second yearly decline in a row (BLS, 1997a). By comparison, the major group health services (SIC code 80) had an injury rate which was worse than all of private industry with a total

Table 3 - Five Most Frequent Injuries/Illnesses Which Result in Lost Time
(Health Services Major Group)

Nature of Injury/Illness	Number	Percent
Sprains, strains	120,973	57.9
Bruises, contusions	18,426	8.9
Back pain	10,739	5.1
Fractures	6,757	3.2
Cuts, lacerations, punctures	5,356	2.6

Table 4 - Five Most Frequent Events or Exposures Which Result in Lost Time
(Health Services Major Group)

Event or Exposure	Number	Percent
Overexertion in lifting	55,902	26.7
Contact with object, equipment	26,486	12.7
Fall on same level	25,530	12.2
Exposed to harmful substance	10,530	5.0
Assault, violent act	9,425	4.5

case rate of 8.6 cases per 100 full-time workers. Further, hospitals (SIC code 806) had a worse rate than did the health services sector with an incidence rate of 9.0 per 100 full time employees, and nursing and personal care facilities (SIC code 805) had a rate of 17.8 per 100 full time employees.

SUMMARY

Occupational and environmental issues present a significant challenge to health care managers. However, they can be handled efficiently and effectively in a centrally managed program which controls OSHA and EPA regulatory risk, properly addresses JCAHO requirements, ensures patient and employee health and security, reduces workers' compensation costs, and possibly produces an outside source of revenue. There are emerging work-related issues, such as indoor air quality, that will most likely require more effort and attention on the part of health care administrators than they have historically. Employee illnesses and concerns may not have well identified or agreed upon symptoms or causes. Such instances require a careful approach with a responsive attitude because, if ignored, they will not go away. Early response by professionals who investigate perceived and real problems with medical evaluation and intervention when called for, and management commitment and support are key elements of an effective program. Health care mangers should strive for the equivalent of a 'green industry' by going beyond simple regulatory compliance to consciousness of the organization and its employees, the community, and surrounding environment.

REFERENCES

Bureau of Labor Statistics (March 12, 1997). *Survey of Workplace Injuries and Illnesses, 1995.*
Bureau of Labor Statistics (August 7, 1997). *National Census of Fatal Occupational Injuries, 1996.*
Centers for Disease Control (1995). *MMWR.,* 44 : 929 - 933.
Centers for Disease Control (1989). *Guidelines for Prevention of Transmission of Human Immunodeficiency Virus and Hepatitis B Virus to Health-Care and Public-Safety Workers.*
Dubnoff, S. D. (1996). Comments at ABA Occupational Safety and Health Law Committee Mid-Winter Meeting, as reported in *BNA 25 OSHR,* 1366.
Mcgrail, M.P., Tsai, S.P., and Bernacki, E.J. (1995). *Journal of Occupational and Environmental Medicine, 37:* 1263-1268.
Occupational Safety and Health Administration. (June 15, 1995). *Reinventing Labor Regulations.*
Occupational Safety and Health Administration. (Nov. 28, 1995). *Unified Regulatory Agenda* (60 FR 59503).
Occupational Safety and Health Administration. (July 20, 1995). *Draft Instruction on Uniform Procedures for TB Inspections, Citations Under General Duty Clause.*
Rowe, P. and Giuffre, M. (1991). *AAOHN Journal, 39:* 503-7.
Tillinghast-Towers Perrin and Risk and Insurance Management Society Inc., *1995 Cost of Risk Survey.*

5.

HEALTH CARE FINANCE AT CENTURY'S END: IMPACTS OF COST CONTAINMENT FINANCIAL INCENTIVES

Judith J. Kirchhoff, *Long Island University, Brooklyn, NY*

To say that the medical care industry is in transition during the waning days of the twentieth century is to understate. To say that cost concerns are driving the transition and that cost containment is its goal is to state the obvious. To say that cost containment leads to financing strategies that compel the precise organization, delivery and outcome changes actually occurring in the medical services system of the health care industry is to recognize conventional wisdom of economics: economizing mandates the effort to maximize outputs relative to given inputs. In economics, dimensions of effectiveness, like access and quality, are defined by market logic as firm survival and consumer satisfaction (Kotler, 1987). That is, efficiency subsumes effectiveness.

Cost containment mandates efficiency in delivery of medical services. Efficiency is a relationship between inputs and outputs that minimizes the cost for a unit of output. Efforts to achieve lower costs without affecting the quality of care are efficiency improvements (Eastaugh, 1992). In the medical services industry at century's end, the mandate of efficiency drives a transition from fragmented, independent, unconnected service units to corporate delivery—a managed care system or integrated network offering a continuum of medical care (MacLeod, 1995).

The literature identifies common strategies for achieving cost containment: reducing overutilization of medical care, substituting less costly for more expensive services, reducing service intensity, and earning profits for payers and providers. Since cost containment compels efficiency, these strategies become operating goals (Perrow, 1961).

Medical services can be described as "intensive technologies" (Thompson, 1967). Intensive technologies provide a variety of combined services and are characterized by reciprocal interdependence of activities. Thompson's example of a general hospital can easily be expanded to a community-based example. A patient may require services that cause movement back and forth from physician to diagnostic testing facility to hospital, and within the hospital from admitting to pre-surgery to operating room to recovery to a medical unit and an outpatient setting.

The technology of medical practice itself is defined by Perrow (1967, p. 197) as a "craft" technology. This technology has fairly stable activities, but requires extensive training and experience to perform.

Technologies are partly responsible for the organization and management systems necessary for efficiency. Technologies with activities of reciprocal interdependence are characterized by high need for communication, mutual adjustment among participants, many unscheduled communications and shared responsibility (Thompson, 1967). Reciprocal interdependence causes a high demand for close physical proximity of activities or highly reliable communication links. Management planning should emphasize training and constant evaluation. Writing today, Thompson no doubt would have emphasized the importance of information systems technologies as well. In intensive technologies, poor coordination is equivalent to inefficiency, so organizational strategies are intently focused on coordination (Daft, 1989).

Coordination ties elements of an organization or process together (Daft, 1991). Effective coordination includes the quality of collaboration among participants, the degree to which parties of an organization or process cooperate with other participants to achieve common goals. Coordination creates from disparate parts an integrated whole through communications, task forces, teams, and integrating managers (Daft, 1991). The communications of importance are the financial incentives used to focus medical services managers' attention on efficiency. The complexity in the use of financial incentives derives from the interorganizational nature of the medical services delivery system.

We describe the system of incentives as the flow of money among participants—the revenues and expenditures, or sources and uses of funds (Cleverly, 1992). Sources include revenues and money received for services delivered. Uses of funds are expenditures, payments made to acquire resources necessary to operate, sustain and grow. Revenues are generated from various sources and expended to achieve organizational goals. To achieve cost containment, a participant seeks to fix (and then reduce) amounts expended. Because whatever is expended by one party is revenue to another, expenditure restraint leads to revenue constraints for transactional partners, who in turn must seek cost containment. Thus, in an interorganizational context, cost containment sets up a chain reaction.

The purpose of this chapter is to describe the processes and effects of cost containment strategies by examining financial incentive impact on operating managers. The intent is not to provide new knowledge; rather, it is to facilitate understanding of the changes occurring. The discussion begins with a brief description of the transitions in medical services delivery, followed by the examination of financial incentives and their impacts. The chapter ends with some observations about the potential long-term implications of the impacts for service delivery and quality of care.

I. TRANSITION IN MEDICAL SERVICES DELIVERY

First, we must define some terms. In medical services, two capture the transition from independent, disparate, uncoordinated participants to a coordinated system: managed care and integration. Managed care can be viewed as an integrative manager in coordination. Managed care refers generally to cost containment activities aimed at reducing inappropriate use of medical care by management both of physician behavior and patient utilization of services (MacLeod, 1995).

Integration refers to one process for coordination—linking purchasers, payers, providers and patients through a variety of communication and organization arrangements (Conrad and Dowling, 1994). Integration in medical services includes organization ownership and continuity of care strategies. Ownership arrangements include vertical and horizontal integration (Kongsvedt and Plocher, 1995). Vertical integration combines sequential steps in the medical care process in the same organization, a staff model health maintenance organization (HMO) wherein all medical activities are delivered under the auspices of a single owner. Vertical integration turns market decisions into administrative decisions (Williamson, 1975). Separate organizations can be integrated through contracts and other operating agreements.

Horizontal integration creates more capacity for delivering a single service, usually through mergers in which one organization absorbs another. Columbia/HCA Healthcare Corporation is one example. The increased use of horizontal alliances and sponsorships has accelerated in the last few years as well. Alliances are networks for negotiating with payers, and sponsorships are agreements in which an operating entity retains its independence but allies with others for negotiations, efficiency improvements and sharing of resources.

Organizational integration makes the care process more efficient for the patient. Establishing continuity of care reduces costly duplication of activities; for example, a PCP may refer a patient to a specialist, ordering diagnostic tests completed by diagnostic centers sent to the specialist so the specialist does not separately order the same tests. Following treatment, the specialist sends a copy of the report to the PCP where it can link this care episode to future patient needs. Such efficiencies create a seamless appearance and facilitate a holistic, patient focus. In this way, efficiency contributes to effectiveness, at least in terms of patient satisfaction (Kaplan and Ware, 1995). These implied relationships lead to the view that the overall goal and desired outcome of managed care is quality—competently delivered, appropriate care at reasonable cost (Brown and McCool, 1994).

II. FINANCIAL ENVIRONMENT IN MEDICAL SERVICES

Financing of medical care in the United States can be addressed from the perspectives of revenues and expenditures or sources and uses of funds. Revenues and expenditures can be examined from the perspectives of society, payers, providers or patients, from the perspective of an organization like an HMO or a hospital, or an individual such as a physician or patient.

Viewed from the macro level of society, revenues are total funds paid out of pocket by individuals, collected from premium payments by employers and employees, and appropriated by federal, state and local governments. With respect to premium payments, what once was called health insurance is now referred to as prepaid health care coverage (MacLeod, 1995).

Public sources of funds for medical services include Medicare, Medicaid, coverage for Armed Forces and their dependents, the Veterans Administration (Knickman and Thorpe, 1995). Nearly three-quarters of public funds are federal; the majority of state medical care spending supports Medicaid and care for the mentally ill and mentally retarded.

The term expenditures refers to the same number, the total amount of money spent on medical care (Knickman and Thorpe, 1995). Total funds define the size of the industry and are often represented as a percent of gross national product (GNP) in a given year, accompanied by the expected rise in future years.

Public expenditures prior to the 1967 introduction of Medicare and Medicaid represented a small percentage of total health expenditures (from nine percent in 1929 to 22 percent in 1965), but grew rapidly to about 43 percent of all expenditures in 1991; here it has remained (Knickman and Thorpe, 1995). That percentage also is expected to rise, given the aging of America. Employers, employees and taxpayers, therefore, have joined the battle against rising medical care costs.

Nationally, medical care expenditures are separated by the reporting agency, the Health Care Financing Administration (HCFA), into two categories: (1) research and medical facilities construction and (2) payments for health services and supplies (Knickman and Thorpe, 1995). In the second, expenditures are separated by their shares of total medical care payments. Hospital care ranks first, followed by physician care, nursing facility care, drugs and drug sundries and dental (Knickman and Thorpe, 1995). Additional categories are "other professional services," other health services and administrative expenses. Given the many changes in care settings, one can corresponding changes in these categories (Mezey and Lawrence, 1995).

This macro view of medical care expenditures is static and does not address the specific financial incentives used to contain costs. Cost containment dynamics unfold in the use of financial incentives to push participants to focus on achieving efficiencies. Incentives must be considered in the context of sources and uses.

III. FINANCIAL INCENTIVES IN THE MEDICAL SERVICES SYSTEM

Financial managers describe organizations in terms of both the sources and the uses of funds while operating managers are concerned primarily with uses. Using these categories, we can describe the role of money in the medical care system as it passes from one participant to another; from purchasers to payers, from payers to providers and from patients to providers.

A. Purchaser-Payer Transactions

Since the U.S. medical care system is based upon employer-provided health care coverage, the cycle begins when an employer offers health plan benefit to employees. A benefits package is proposed at a specific premium price by insurers and health plans based on forecasts of medical care utilization derived from demographics and other characteristics of employees and the work situation; this is called experience rating (Knickman and Thorpe, 1995; Wagner, 1995). Health plans provide a financial incentive to employees in offering lower premium rates than indemnity insurers and low co-payments for within-network services. Enrollees pay more for out-of-network care with higher co-payments and deductibles.

The employer offers agreed upon insurance or health plans to employees, employees choose a plan, and employers remit premiums to the insurer or plan. Public payers traditionally operated like indemnity insurers, but recently are urging health plans to enroll Medicare and Medicaid eligible persons with federal and state governments paying the premiums (Zarabozo and LeMasurier, 1995; Herrick, 1995).

Premium dollars, then, represent expenditures to employers and revenues to insurers and health plans, who refer to enrollees as covered lives. Not surprisingly, employers are motivated to keep their expenditures for health care coverage low while health plans seek to increase their revenues. Thus employers seek low premium rates even when this means reducing benefits. For a growing number of employers, expenditure concerns have led to discontinuing coverage altogether, especially in small businesses with few employees or low paid employees.

Health plans seek to increase revenues, but given employers' sensitivity to premium rates, health plans are constrained from increasing their revenues by increasing premium rates as they did when cost was not an issue and the annual rate of increase was slow. Health plans must keep premium rates competitive and low enough to encourage employers to provide health care coverage to their employees. One recent report on the uninsured in New York State notes that about 22 percent of the uninsured work for companies of more than 1,000 employees; even large companies have abandoned health care coverage for their employees ("New York Study," 1997). Employees participate in their health care coverage to the degree that they contribute financially to the employer's expenditures on premiums and in their use of medical care services. In the latter role, they are patients and their relationship is with providers.

Health plans use premiums and other revenues (Ward, 1995) to pay for costs of marketing benefits packages to employers; enrollee covered medical services; managing provider and patient behavior to control utilization and remain profitable; and costs involved in reducing utilization or intensity. The first two functions continue from the fee-for-service system, with the exception that marketing now has been expanded to other customers, including enrollees, health plan direct consumers (Kotler, 1987). The third is a feature of the transition to managed care caused by employers' increased sensitivity to their expenditures for employee health care coverage. The fourth is to increase profitability.

Conventional wisdom says that 15 cents of every medical care dollar is devoted to administrative functions and 85 cents pays providers for services rendered (Dobson and Berghelser, 1993). These figures, however, refer to traditional payer functions of marketing benefit packages and processing claims. The financial impact of additional managed care administrative activities to both payers and is not yet well understood. According to one source ("Managed care revenues," 1996), in 1993, half of all enrollees were in plans that spent less than 11.2 percent of revenues on administration, and another 25 percent were in plans that spent 7.6 percent or less. Large plans spent the lowest percentage of revenues on administrative costs—an average of 9.4 percent of revenues for plans having over 250,000 enrollees—as compared to 16.2 percent for plans with fewer than 20,000 members.

B. Payer-Provider Transactions

The portion of every dollar paid by health plans for costs of enrollee care constitutes expenditures of the health plan and revenue to providers. According to health insurance statistics, 35 percent of enrollees will not have a claim during a typical year, while 5 percent of enrollees will account for over 50 percent of all health expenditures during the same period (Lee and Rogal, 1997).

Health plan expenditures are payments to contract providers or salaries if the health plan is also the provider of services. Currently, an increasing percentage of medical care is provided through contractual arrangements between payers and providers (DeLoitte and Touche, 1996), but the scope of hierarchies also is increasing by vertical and horizontal integration. According to a survey by the American Medical Association, the number of physicians in group practices (horizontal integration) rose 14 percent from 1991 to 1995, to just over a third of all U.S. physicians ("Physician forecast," 1996). While most groups are small (3-4 physicians), nearly one-third of physicians in groups belong to practices containing 100 or more physicians. In addition, the structure of physician groups is shifting from partnerships to professional corporation.

Contracts typically favor payers—capitated rates, discounts, defined case rates for documented service delivery, of which Medicare's diagnostic related groups (DRGs) are perhaps the most familiar (Kongstvedt, 1995). Capitation rates and other payment forms fix expenditures for the health plan and stabilize providers' revenue levels, cash flow, and, to some degree, service volumes (Kralewski et al. 1994; Feldman et al. 1995). Prompt payment of correctly completed claims is also included in the contractual arrangement as an incentive for physicians to become a plan provider. Providers include primary care physicians (PCP's) and specialist physicians, institutions like acute care hospitals, a growing variety of outpatient settings including day surgery centers, urgent care centers, diagnostic centers, pharmacies, therapists and home health organizations.

Capitation provides a per-enrollee, per-month rate for each enrollee registered with the provider. As recently as 1994, just one-third of health plans used capitation rates for physicians services ("Managed care revenues," 1996). By the end of 1996, 92 percent of health plans were using capitation as the form of payment for physicians. Nearly 90 percent of physician practices expect to be capitated within the next two years.

Capitation payments are used for PCP gatekeepers who control access to the rest of the medical care system and for certain specialists (Kongstvedt, 1995). The capitated payment is designed to cover enrollee medical care within the general practitioner's scope of practice. The capitated payment rate is based on health plan estimates of utilization by enrollees of similar demographic and health conditions, but is unrelated to the amount of care delivered to any particular enrollee during the contract period. Payers employ formulas for determining number of enrollees per PCP, number and kinds of specialists, and geographic distribution to minimize travel distances.

According to recent research ("Physician forecast," 1996), the U.S. would need about 37,000 fewer specialist physicians by the year 2,000 if the total population were enrolled in HMOs. The U.S. would also need 6,300 more OB/Gyn and 34,000 more

PCPs including internists, family practitioners, general practitioners and pediatricians and specialists. The greatest increase would be in the South, where demand would rise nearly 30 percent, followed by the West (26 percent), Midwest (25 percent) and the Northeast (7 percent).

The assumption underlying capitation payment is that some enrollees will use more and some less care than is average for all enrollees (Lee and Rogal, 1997). Should the physician have a large number of enrollees who use more than an average numbers of physician visits during a contract period (usually one year), that physician works harder and gets paid less than a physician whose average enrollee uses less care during the year. The incentive, then, is for a physician to have large numbers of enrollees who have few medical needs. For enrollees who visit the physician, the incentive to the physician is to prescribe less treatment. Thus, capitation incentives are the exact opposite of those in a fee-for-service system.

Capitation rates stabilize both expenditures of health plans and revenues of service providers, but not without impact on provider income. For example, a study by the American Medical Association (AMA) found that physician income fell about four percent for the first time since the survey was started in 1982 (CIS, 1996a). Most affected by the declines were hospital-based physicians and certain specialists and subspecialists. Least affected were primary care physicians. Health plans are able to predict their costs from numbers of covered lives and capitated rate providers know what their revenues will be by the number of enrollees among their patients and the capitated rate.

For outside care, the PCP refers patients to within network specialists. The health plan pays specialists on fee-for-service contracts usually characterized by straight percentage, volume discounts, sliding scales or capitated rates. Whatever the payment mechanism, specialists are paid from a pool of funds representing a percentage of the PCP capitation rate. What remains in the fund at the end of the contract period is shared by PCPs as a "bonus" for minimizing referrals to specialists (Kongstvedt, 1995). Diagnostic tests, prescription drugs and hospital stays are carved out of the physician payment system as are certain kinds of care such as mental health services (Anderson and Berlant, 1995). Payments to these providers are negotiated separately by the health plan also using discounts with volume guarantees and case rate payment incentives. Services relating to certain highly technical specialists are likely to remain fee-for-service because their use is infrequent (Kongstvedt, 1995).

Discount, case rate and per diem rate contracts involve negotiations between payers and providers over the amount of the discount from charges (providers' regular price) and assumptions used in setting case rates or global fees. The discount usually depends on the number of covered lives and the expected volume of procedures (Feldman, et al., 1993). The case rate or global fee incorporates assumptions about episode duration (hospital length of stay) and procedures included (Kongstvedt, 1995). For example, the case rate for a normal birth without complications can be determined by the usual pattern of care: a short stay in the hospital, use of a birthing room and nursery, particular diagnostic tests and other per diem services for mother and child. Total number of expected episodes, like the expected number of normal births for total enrollees, is less predictable.

Health plan expenditures for various types of care are estimated from historical utilization data, enrollee demographics and epidemiological data (Lee and Rogal, 1997). Providers assume some of the risk of costs beyond that authorized by the health plan. Even when extraordinary cases warrant additional compensation, the rate is usually discounted from the provider's charges. The health plan, then, has an advantage in negotiating contracts unless the provider also does cost analyses. The purpose for accurate forecasting of costs and utilization is to reduce the risk for providing care beyond that authorized by the health plan and to maintain financial viability. Hospitals are severely affected by the changes. For example, hospitals experienced nearly a 20 percent decrease in average daily census from 1984-1994, along with a 9.2 percent decrease in the number of hospitals and 11.3 percent reduction in number of hospital beds (Milliman and Robertson Inc., 1996).

One should not confuse hospital revenues with profits, however. While utilization is falling, hospital profits are rising (CIS 1996a, 1997). The total margin for hospitals rose to 4.8 percent in 1994, with the expectation of continued increases. Long term care, home health and physician practice management organizations also showed healthy profit margins.

C. Provider-Patient Transactions

In a fee-for-service system, physicians and other providers set prices for services, and patients—frequently through third party payers—pay full fees. Prices in such a system are controlled only to the extent that third party payers (mostly indemnity insurers) limit their payments to usual and customary or reasonable charges (Cleverly, 1992).

Other providers in the fee-for-service system based prices on management's forecasted budgetary needs and assumptions about other variables such as occupancy rate and charity care levels (Cleverly, 1992). Many states have rate-setting laws governing reimbursable expenses for certain categories of patients.

As a result, charges varied by payer, thus shifting costs of care from one payer to another (Cleverly, 1992). During the early years of Medicare and Medicaid, public payers subsidized private patients. As regulations made it more difficult to sustain such subsidies, providers shifted costs more heavily toward private payers, who then effectively subsidized publicly supported patients (Rakich, et al., 1985; Cleverly, 1992); when employers became cost-conscious, private payers shifted payment.

Now that almost three-quarters of U.S. employees with health insurance are enrolled in managed care plans (CIS, 1997), care delivery prices are negotiated. By no means are provider prices uniform. Providers seek to influence prices, but payment incentives change the substance of negotiations, focusing them on number of enrollees, their characteristics and service utilization levels. Once the per member per month (PMPM) capitated rate for physicians is set, for example, the physician's revenue from that payer is capped (Kongstvedt, 1994). Additional revenue for enrollees derives from enrollee co-payments for each visit, which are set by the payer in its contract with enrollees.

In this managed care environment, physician control of revenues depends upon the PCP's decisions about how many health plans to accommodate. For other providers, incentives for increasing treatment volume remain in the case rate and discounted charges payment forms, so the health plan uses organizational strategies to control.

Providers' ability to influence contract negotiations with payers depends on the providers' influence on the market for services. If providers are the only or clearly dominant provider in a market, their influence is greater. If providers join together to negotiate with health plans, they are more influential than if they negotiate individually.

Patients participate in their decision to purchase indemnity health insurance or to enroll in a health plan, usually through their employer; they are restricted to choices authorized by the employer. As an enrollee, the employee may immediately select a PCP from the network or may wait until a health condition requires a physician visit. In either case, the PCP begins collecting the PMPM rate when the enrollee becomes a patient. If the enrollee does not selects a PCP and does not get sick, the only benefit lies in the certainty of assured access. Thus, the payer has no incentive to urge the enrollee to select a PCP. PCPs want enrollees on their patient lists, but hope they do not need services. The financial focus on cost containment places the burden of medical care utilization on the enrollee, who must decide to become a patient to receive the actual benefits of prepaid health care coverage. In addition, the patient has become the consumer actively participating in health care choices (Havighurst, 1991). Financial incentives of managed care cost containment compel participants to respond by achieving efficiencies, by coordinating.

IV. IMPACTS OF FINANCIAL INCENTIVES ON OPERATIONS

Usually, the emphasis on cost containment and resultant shift in medical services from fee-for-service to capitated payments, case rates and discounted charges leads to financial strategies for maximizing revenues and minimizing expenditures. This produces a tension that forces each participant to capture revenues through market power and skillful negotiating while reducing costs through management initiatives. In short, the emphasis shifts from delivering services to managing resources.

A. Incentive Impacts and Employer Responses

Employers respond to their need to contain health care expenditures for their employees in two ways, both organizational: deciding whether to offer health care coverage (or discontinue it) and how to contain expenditures for offered coverage. Some employers discontinue coverage, thus contributing to the increased number of uninsured individuals in the U.S. The face of the uninsured includes employees of companies with over 1,000 employees, contradicting the myth that large employers offer comprehensive benefits. Also among the uninsured are families earning between $15,000 and $25,000 per year ("New York Study," 1997). The percentage of those under age 65 without health insurance rose nearly five percent 1990 to 1995, and the number of uninsured children grew at twice the rate of adults. The 1996 Health Care Portability and Accountability Act is designed in part to reduce the number of uninsured; states are moving to block health plans from disinsuring, but the lack of insuredness is likely to remain a policy problem for the foreseeable future (Brown, 1991).

Employers who offer health care coverage have a number of options to contain expenditures. Larger employers may fund and pay their own health care costs, negotiating directly with providers (Eastaugh, 1992). Others purchase coverage from insurers, health plans or both. In these cases, premium rates are based on covered benefits, demographic analysis, and/or the employer's historical use of medical services (Ward, 1995). Some employers shift more of the premium costs to employees as a method of containing their costs (Eastaugh, 1992).

More benefits have higher premium rates, so expenditures can be reduced by limiting benefits. Higher utilization results in higher premiums. Thus, employers are demanding better information from payers about employee utilization. On average, health care coverage costs more than managed health plan coverage (Eastaugh, 1992). Thus, employers who cannot limit the amount they contribute to premiums may elect not to offer an indemnity plan. By federal law, employers who offer health care coverage must offer a health plan option if it is available (Brecher, 1994). Given assumptions about economies of scale and management control, open health plans cost more than closed plans (Kongstvedt and Plocher, 1995). Therefore, employers may limit employee choice to a single cost-efficient option determined by the employer. Clearly, an employer may contain expenditures by seeking cost-effective combinations.

Employee options are limited by employer decisions about coverage. The employee may seek another employer, buy additional coverage through an outside source, or elect to be covered under a spouse's plan. Such election does not save that employee's contribution to the employer's premium; instead, it triggers coordination of benefits between the two health plans such that the employee's plan is the primary payer and the spouse's plan is the secondary payer. Coordination of benefits revenue is a substantial source of payer revenues (Ward, 1995).

B. Incentive Impacts and Payer and Provider Responses

Health plan responses to employers' cost sensitivity focus both on organizational and service delivery coordination. Health plans perform three key functions. They market benefits packages to employers, process and pay enrollee medical care claims, and manage care using coordination strategies. Marketing and payment include developing products and providing customer service, processing and paying claims, analyzing costs and forecasting utilization to determine revenue needs. The third function (managing care) encompasses a wide range of activities from developing provider networks to delivering medical services (Pine and Kongstvedt, 1995). These activities are necessarily replicated in provider organizations, both to fulfill health plan (and regulator) reporting requirements and to generate strategic management information (Duncan, et al., 1995).

Health plans increasingly turn to automation of claims processing to reduce administrative claims processing costs by eliminating the paper and people involved in these transactions (Duncan, et al., 1995). At the same time, health plans add organization control and accountability infrastructure, and costs, for managed care management. Thus, while automation of claims processing may save administrative costs, new costs are added in the form of coordination activities; therefore, these new costs may cause a net increase in the cost of doing business.

With these changes in health care and periodic audits, the federal government estimates that health care costs will be reduced by ten percent. Audit programs focusing on claims processing, duplication of services, up-coding, insufficient documentation, failure to provide the service and medical necessity already have been instituted. In addition, the government has changed its focus from looking for mistakes to looking for patterns of fraud and schemes to defraud. In essence, they will deploy significant resources to prepare and implement audits and investigations, and negotiate settlements. Likewise, providers will be required to employ equally substantial resources to ensure their compliance with federal laws and regulations.

Health plans' and providers' largest expenditures are for services delivered; both pursue ways to coordinate more efficient service delivery. Health plans and providers employ both organizational and service delivery strategies. Health plans seek to reduce health plan expenditures for service delivery while providers seek to maximize revenues from health plans while lowering their delivery costs. Health plans seek to improve profits by lowering their expenditure risk in selection of members (Rother, 1997) while under risk-adjusted payments, non-capitated providers benefit from providing high revenue services to those who have health care coverage. This particular dynamic raises the concerns about access (Donelan et al. 1997) and costs which initially triggered the 1990's health care reform debate.

One coordinating strategy is to turn market transactions into administrative decisions by creating hierarchical organizations (Williamson, 1975). Hierarchies are formed by bringing functions into the organization that formerly were acquired through contractual relationships. Hierarchical integration can be horizontal or vertical.

Horizontal integration increases an organization's capacity and achieves economies of scale by centralizing some activities. A hospital may acquire other hospitals and establish central purchasing and laundry functions to achieve cost savings. Or a physician may join a group practice in the same specialty or other specialties for the purpose of sharing certain functions and facilities.

Vertical integration occurs when multiple functions in the service delivery chain are combined into a multi-functional organization. An acute care hospital, for instance, may become multi-functional by opening, merging with or acquiring physician practices, opening or acquiring imaging centers and laboratory capability, a nursing facility and home medical services. The strategic goal is to achieve market dominance in a geographic area (Duncan, et al., 1995.)

One such vertical integration strategy emerging from federal legislation to provide incentives for enrolling Medicare eligible individuals in health plans is the Provider Sponsored Organization (PSO). A multi-service integrated delivery system (Peters, 1997), the PSO combines medical services delivery to direct enrollees and through contracts to other health plan members with purchasing, management, marketing and negotiation services for its sponsors. The PSO is sponsored by physicians, hospitals and other healthcare providers licensed or certified to provide a broad range of healthcare services. Thus, the PSO is a network that seeks to combine the scale economies of large size with the strengths of narrowly focused and personalized service delivery. In addition to stimulating the use of varied organizing strategies, financial incentives lead health plans and providers to coordinate service delivery to enrollees through the use of gatekeepers, now a defining feature of all managed care plans. The managed care gatekeeper is the PCP point of entry into the medical care system and, providing services directly, decides when and which specialist is needed.

Concerns about whether plan physicians are proscribed from discussing all treatment options are sources of consumer dissatisfaction with health plans, and dissatisfaction is a major source of disenrollment (Shimshak, et al., 1994). These concerns already have led many states to require direct access to some specialists, emergency rooms, and to explicitly prohibit health plan gag orders (Abbey, 1997; Carneal, 1997). In other strategies, health plans may limit the number of enrollees per physician or the number of physicians in the plan (Kongstvedt, 1995), except in states with "any willing provider laws" (Carneal, 1997, pp. 463-465). PPOs provide physicians (and patients) the greatest amount of choice regarding their relationship with the health plan and closed panel or staff model HMOs the least.

Physicians may respond to the capitated payment environment by limiting the number of enrollees from a particular health plan or by accepting patients from several health plans. They also may join with other physicians in group practices that share expenses and profits or independent practice associations (IPAs) that negotiate contracts with health plans. Physicians can increase personal capacity to deliver services by adding professional staff. Additionally, physicians may become owners of other medical services providers, like laboratories, imaging centers or therapy practices, ownership heavily regulated heavily to limit physicians from profiting through referrals to self-owned ancillary services (Rodwin, 1993; Abbey, 1997).

Another coordinating strategy is development of clinical practice guidelines, which the American College of Physicians defines as a means of providing knowledge developed in the scientific practice of medicine and putting it in a useful format for physicians, patients and others to make judgments about the best use of health care resources (Nash, 1995). Systematically developed clinical practice guidelines for specific clinical conditions differentiate what constitutes clearly appropriate care from clearly inappropriate care and identifies care about which clinical evidence is equivocal and consensus among physicians non-existent (Nash, 1995). Clinical practice guidelines are communications tools likely to evolve into standards of quality that can be used by all participants.

Practice guidelines are rejected by some physicians as "cookbook medicine" (Eastaugh, 1992, p. 108), an effort to eliminate specialists. That may be an exaggerated fear, but practice guidelines are likely to become quality standards (Nash, 1995). At the very least, they become technical standards for evaluating physician technical competence (Rodwin, 1993). One danger is that practice guidelines may substitute for the "prudent professional" standard in establishing legal liability (Pozgar, 1996, p. 46) and stifle physician judgment when complexity requires creative application of medical knowledge.

In the absence of clear indicators of what is appropriate, health plans use more limited information to establish efficiency in the delivery of medical services. They may use encounter data to determine what a typical or average physician does for various clinical conditions. That information can be used to establish criteria for pre-certification or denial of proposed treatments by other participating physicians, thus creating uniform methods for treating specific clinical conditions among a health plan's participating physicians or monitoring the use of resources by physician and group.

A wide variety of performance measures are used to convey health plan service delivery and patient satisfaction levels and outcomes (Siren and Laffel, 1997). Performance information is used by health plans as a marketing tool and by employers and employees as management information to support choices among health plans and benefit packages. Many states mandate health plan distribution of its statistics to ensure that consumers can compare plans (Abbey, 1997).

Standardization actions contribute to cost containment if this movement enables a net reduction in procedures and protocols used to treat specific clinical conditions. Since standardization can be internal to each health plan, it can lead to health modification for cost-cutting purposes. For example, since clinical guidelines are developed from the treatment decisions of many physicians in a system biased toward overtreatment, the average clinical treatments also are biased. Theoretically, then, less treatment will yield appropriate outcomes (not necessarily greater satisfaction) for the patient. Such subtle pressures may contribute to physician complaints about interference in clinical decisions. When complaints are frequent enough and loud enough, a backlash occurs, often resulting in constrictive legislation (Abbey, 1997). Legislation adds costs of compliance to health plan cost structures.

Regarding discount contracts and case rates, while the price per procedure is known, the number of procedures is necessary to predict health plan expenditures and provider revenues. Health plans reduce expenditures by minimizing the volume of services delivered, and health providers need to increase the volume of chargeable procedures to compensate for discounted payments (Cleverly, 1992).

Hospitals, for example, rely on volume of patients to support their high capital investment in plant and equipment. If case rates are the primary form of hospital revenue, the incentive is to increase the volume of patients and shorten the stay for each. They must deliver high reimbursement rate services and capture market share. Integration occurs when large hospitals purchase smaller hospitals to control the inpatient capacity in a geographic area or when hospitals increase the variety of services they offer. Hospitals may become a health plan, contracting with multiple health plans, providing services to affiliated physicians at attractive rates, purchasing physician practices, and aggressively promoting themselves. A hospital also may specialize in procedures with a high rate of financial return or seek additional markets by joining with counterparts in other geographic locations. In the process of expansion, hospitals form holding companies to keep management and accountability for each entity separate and distinct (Pozgar, 1996).

The effects of expansion are increased revenues and decreased costs from economies of scale. Much reallocation of resources occurs, primarily shifts from more intense and expensive services to less intense and less costly services. One reason hospitals expand in these other directions is to ensure that the reallocation of resources does not cause the hospital to lose revenues to other providers. Thus, growth is a survival strategy. Hospitals without the resources to grow are likely to disappear, either ceasing to operate, changing their services, or being acquired by others.

Hospitals and other medical services providers also seek to increase revenues per service delivered with internal strategies. One now prohibited method for increasing revenues per service encounter under discounted fee-for-service payments is to unbundle component procedures, billing for each procedure separately. Another is upcoding, a process of assigning physician narrative descriptions of diseases, injuries or medical procedures to the diagnosis category that pays the most.

Case rate payments incorporating all services within an episode of care are designed to make such practices obsolete. However, questions still arise when multiple entities within a complex service organization participate. This latter situation leads to regulations like the 72-hour rule, which seeks to ensure that all related services are captured in the case rate. Under the Medicare prospective payment system, diagnostic services provided to a beneficiary by the admitting hospital (or by an entity wholly owned or operated by the hospital or another entity under arrangement with the hospital) within 72 hours prior to the day of admission are included in the inpatient DRG payment. HCFA's long standing policy is to consider such non-physician services as part of the inpatient care episode.

A nationwide computer match of inpatient and outpatient services identified over 1.1 million claims valued at $200 million (2-year period 1992 and 1993) for non-physician outpatient services rendered during the 72-hour payment window and by a provider other than the inpatient provider (DHHS, 1997). Most institutions found in non-compliance signed a settlement agreement, implemented additional manual and electronic controls, and paid the amount requested to the Department of Justice and applicable beneficiaries to avoid the minimum $5,000 penalty per case (Sparrow, 1996). In addition to these and similar strategies for increasing revenues, hospitals and other providers seek efficiencies in service delivery activities by analyzing costs and work procedures to identify unnecessary costs and activities. These actions are the substance of the re-engineering and continuous quality improvement (CQI) initiatives sweeping the medical services industry (Shortell, et al., 1995). Re-engineering, TQM and CQI are by definition coordinating strategies. They employ task forces and teams to document work procedures and analyze them for activities that do not add value, thereby streamlining processes to reduce costs and increase productivity. Some outputs of CQI processes are called critical pathways. They chart patient care for the clinical condition during each inpatient day. As the patient moves toward recovery and discharge, the intensity of services diminishes until the patient reaches self-care status and receives little more than meals and documentation of vital signs. Certainly, some patients continue to need attention of skilled personnel. These patients may be transferred to another unit or to an affiliated or hospital-owned long term care center.

The process of analysis and coordination that leads to efficiency is confused by cost-cutting strategies like "downsizing" (Haddock, et. al, 1995). Cutting jobs to cut costs saves money quickly, but undermines cooperation essential to coordination and efficiency. The logic of downsizing is to have fewer people do more work while the logic of quality improvement efficiency is eliminate unnecessary tasks so people can be more productive. Coordination for efficiency enables increased service or activity volume without increasing employment whereas downsizing may negatively affect morale such that productivity is decreased. Thus, we argue, downsizing is neither a goal nor a desirable method for cost containment.

Quality improvement cost containment strategies do result in resource reallocation, however, and change the nature of many jobs. Fewer skills may be needed for some tasks and different skills for others. These realities, and the specific nature of changes in medical services lead to re-deployment of many RNs from medical services in hospitals to utilization review for hospitals and health plans; from inpatient to outpatient care settings, from institutional to home care and from acute care to long term care settings. Thus, cost containment strategies catalyze changes throughout the service delivery system.

C. Incentive Impacts and Patient Responses

Patients are direct consumers of health care, those purchasers who access the system when their health dictates the need for medical care (Long, 1994). The current transition to managed care was preceded by an earlier shift from a medical care system in which individuals paid for routine medical services out of their own pockets and were insured for extraordinary expenses, like hospital care, to a system of prepaid health care in which all medical services are prepaid. In this type of system employees are purchasers of health care coverage; as enrollees they are entitled to covered medical services, and as patients they are consumers of medical services.

Everyone needs medical services. How much one needs is determined by such factors as age, gender, genetics, psychological disposition, lifestyle and environment (Evans and Stoddart, 1994). The process of being a patient in the medical services system begins when a person visits a physician to symptoms. Obviously, the patient's presence is integral to the delivery and consumption of services. What transpires thereafter derives from the physician's diagnosis and the complexities of decisionmaking and production.

Financial incentives affect the patient in choices of PCP and, unless the patient is prepared to pay, in the sources of specialty, hospital, prescription medicine and other types of care. Decisions made within the system affect how that care will be delivered. All of these processes should create patient satisfaction.

Are patients satisfied? Responses to independent surveys (CareData, 1996) suggest that the answer is no. In a mail survey based on responses from 23,000 HMO and POS plan enrollees in 13 markets, 60 percent of HMO members are highly satisfied with their health plans, and 67 percent were highly satisfied with the quality of medical care. Only 52 percent, however, are highly satisfied with the customer service and plan administration. In the fee-for-service system, the average satisfaction rate of patients, measured primarily as satisfaction with their personal physician, was 82 on a scale of 100 (Kaplan and Ware, 1995). If we assume that the personal physician indicator is comparable to the quality indicator in the recent survey, the results suggest that health plans have a long way to go to achieve the average level of patient satisfaction in the previous system. This, coupled with the recognition that the shift to managed care is reducing worker choices because employers who offer health care coverage are limiting the number of plans available to them. According to one survey the percentage of employers offering three or more plans is rapidly declining and almost half of responding employers offer only one plan. A study cited in CIS Technologies (1996c) suggests that enrollee satisfaction will be problematic for health plans. The likely result is that health plans will invest more money in marketing activities to keep their enrollees.

V. IMPLICATIONS FOR THE MEDICAL SERVICES INDUSTRY

The shift to corporate delivery of medical services is driven by cost containment, the tools of which drive many of the changes and catalyze responses of participants. What becomes clear is that increased costs may be caused not by cost containment strategies themselves, but by participant responses to the impacts of these strategies. Thus, cost containment is, in the long run, about increasing costs in the medical services industry.

Where cost containment-driven costs will increase can be discerned from the responses of participants to the impacts of financial incentives. For example, it can be said that the changes in payment incentives to providers has shifted the focus of providers from overtreatment to undertreatment. Providers receive either capitated rates per enrollee or case rates for a bundle of services. That, combined with health plan benefit limits, will suppress utilization for the foreseeable future. Thus, it is not likely that per enrollee or per episode prices or costs will increase. If the number of episodes of care increases, costs will rise, but as a function of increased demand, not price and cost pressures. Given the aging of the U.S. population and the strong correlation between age and use of medical services, demand will rise.

Likewise, cost containment strategies drive consolidation and integration with their attendant economies of scale and organization restructuring such that costs, hence expenditures, are reduced. However, large scale organizations require additional coordination, training and documentation. Health plans have shifted some of the utilization risks to providers, but pre-certification and utilization review activities require significantly more knowledge and energy than claims processing. Indeed, many nurses restructured out of direct care are now employed by health plans for utilization review.

Additionally, purchasers demand information about services delivered to assist in coverage decisions. Enrollees want to know satisfaction levels of other members. Quality monitors seek performance information. Health plans, providers and quality monitors stress the need for performance standards. Federal and state regulators require compliance reporting and conduct detailed audits and investigations to detect and prevent fraud and abuse. These customer demands require documentation, analysis and reporting far beyond that required for claims processing in the fee-for-service system. Not only is the amount of required information increased, but also the competencies needed to prepare the information are increased. Skilled labor is high-priced labor. Finally, the shift to corporate medical services delivery is accompanied by a marketing approach. This requires payers and providers to undertake market research and marketing activities targeted to the needs of all external and internal customers. These are new functions for the industry and represent new costs for the system. Thus, even as the shift toward corporate delivery of health care is containing costs in many aspects of medical services delivery, it also is adding costly requirements. Determining the costs of new requirements and their impacts both on the quality of medical care and on the health status of U.S. citizens is a political, socioeconomic and research agenda for the new century.

REFERENCES

Abbey, F. B. (1997). Health care reform—The road lies with managed care. In Kongsvedt, P.R. (Ed.). *Essentials of managed health care.* (2nd ed., pp. 17-35). Gaithersburg, MD: Aspen.

Abbey, F. B. (1995). Managed care and health care reform—evolution or revolution? In Kongsvedt, P. R. (Ed.). *Essentials of managed health care.* (10-23). Gaithersburg, MD: Aspen.

Anderson, D. F. and Berlant, J. L. (1995). Managed mental health and substance abuse services. In Kongsvedt, P. R. (Ed.). *Essentials of managed health care.* (150-162). Gaithersburg, MD: Aspen.

Brecher, C. (1995). The government's role in health care. In Kovner, A. R. (Ed.). *Jonas's health care delivery in the United States.* (5th ed.,322-347). New York: Springer.

Brown, L. D. (1991). The medically uninsured: problems, policies and politics. In Brown, L. D. (Ed.). Health policy and the disadvantaged. (169-183). Durham, NC: Duke University Press.

Brown, M. and McCool, B. P. (1994). Vertical integration: exploration of a popular strategic concept. In Brown, M. (Ed.). *Managed care, strategies, networks and management.* (41-54). Gaithersburg, MD: Aspen.

Carneal, G. (1997). State regulation of managed care. In Kongstvedt, P. R. (Ed.). *Essentials of managed health care.* (2nd ed., 453-469). Gaithersburg, MD: Aspen.

CIS Technologies. (1996a, September 4). *Newsletter.* On-line to e-mail list. Washington, DC: Author.

CIS Technologies. (1996b, September 18). *Newsletter.* On-line to e-mail list. Washington, DC: Author.

CIS Technologies. (1996c, October 19). *Newsletter.* On-line to e-mail list. Washington, DC: Author.

CIS Technologies. (1997, March 12). *Newsletter.* On-line to e-mail list. Washington, DC: Author.

Cleverly, W. O. (1992). *Essentials of health care finance.* (3rd ed.). Gaithersburg, MD: Aspen.

Conrad, D. A. and Dowling, W. L. (1994). Vertical integration in health services: theory and managerial implications. In Brown, M. (Ed.). *Managed care, strategies, networks and management.* (pp. 27-40). Gaithersburg, MD: Aspen.

Daft, R. L. (1991). Management (2nd ed.). Chicago: Dryden Press.

Daft, R. L. (1989). *Organization theory and design.* (3rd ed.) St. Paul, MN: West Publishing.

DeLoitte and Touche LLP. (1996). Valuation insights, health care industry.

Department of Health and Human Services (DHHS). (1997). Health care financing administration projects. Office of Inspector General Fiscal Year Work Plan.

Dobson, A. and Berghelser, M. (1993). Reducing administrative costs in a pluralistic delivery system through automation. Washington, DC: Lewin VHI.

Donelan, K., Blendon, R. J., Hill, C. A., Hoffman, C., Rowland, D., Frankel, M. and Altman, D. (1997). Whatever happened to the health insurance crisis in the United States? In Lee, P. R. and Estes, C. L. (Eds.). *The Nation's Health.* (5th ed., 283-291). London: Jones and Bartlett Publishers.

Duncan, W. J., Ginter, P. M. and Swayne, L. E. (1995). *Strategic management of health care organizations.* (2nd ed.). Cambridge, MA: Blackwell.

Eastaugh, S. R. (1992). Health economics: efficiency, quality and equity. Westport, CT: Auburn House.

Evans, R. G. and Stoddart, G. L. (1994). Producing health, consuming health care. In Evans, R. G., Barer, M. L. and Marmor, T. R. (Eds.). Why are some people healthy and others not? *The determinants of health of populations.* (27-65) New York: Aldine deGruyter.

Feldman, R., Kralewski, J., Shapiro, J. and Hung-Ching Chan (1995). Contracts between hospitals and health maintenance organizations. In Brown, M. (Ed.). Managed care: strategies, networks and management. (107-120). Gaithersburg, MD: Aspen.

Haddock, C. C., Nosky, C., Fargason, C. A., and Kurz, R. S. (1995, Spring). The impact of CQI on human resources management.*Hospital and health services administration, 40(1).* 138-154.

Havighurst, C. C. (1991). The changing locus of decision making in the health care sector. In Brown, L. D. (Ed.). Health policy in transition, a decade of health politics, policy and law (129-168).

Herrick, R. R. (1995). Medicaid and managed care. In Kongstvedt, P. R., *Essentials of managed health care.* (pp. 234-242). Gaithersburg, MD: Aspen.

Kaplan, S. H. and Ware, J. E. (1995). The patient's role in health care and quality assessment. In Goldfield, N. and Nash, D. B. (Eds.). *Providing Quality Care, Future Challenges.* (2nd ed., 25-58). Ann Arbor: Health Administration Press.

Knickman, J. R. and Thorpe, K. E. (1995). In Kovner, A. R. (Ed.). *Jonas's health care delivery in the United States.* (5th ed., 267-293). New York: Springer.

Kongstvedt, P. R. (1995). Compensation of primary care physicians in open panels. In Kongstvedt, P. R. (Ed.). *Essentials of managed health care.* (76-90). Gaithersburg, MD: Aspen.

Kongstvedt, P. R. (1995). Negotiating and contracting with consultants. In Kongstvedt, P. R. (Ed.). *Essentials of managed health care.* (91-99). Gaithersburg, MD: Aspen.

Kongstvedt, P. R. (1995). Negotiating and contracting with hospitals and institutions. In Kongstvedt, P. R. (Ed.). *Essentials of managed health care.* (100-109). Gaithersburg, MD: Aspen.

Kongstvedt, P. R. (1995). Changing provider behavior in managed care plans. In Kongstvedt, P. R. (Ed.). *Essentials of managed health care.* (110-120). Gaithersburg, MD: Aspen.

Kongsvedt, P. R. and Plocher, D. W. (1995). Integrated health care delivery systems. In Kongstvedt, P. R. (Ed.). *Essentials of managed health care.* (35-49). Gaithersburg, MD: Aspen.

Kotler, P. and Clarke, R. N. (1987). Marketing for health care organizations. Englewood Cliffs, NH: Prentice Hall.

Kovner, A. R. (1995). Introduction. In Kovner, A. R. (Ed.). *Jonas's health care delivery in the United States.* (5th ed., 3-10). New York: Springer.

Kralewski, J. E., Feldman, R., Dowd, B. and Shapiro, J. (1994). Strategies employed by HMOs to achieve hospital discounts: a case study of seven HMOs. In Brown, M. (Ed.). *Managed care: strategies, networks and management.* (91-98). Gaithersburg, MD: Aspen.

Long, M. J. (1994). The medical care system, a conceptual model. Ann Arbor: Health Administration Press.

MacLeod, G. K. (1995). An overview of managed health care. In Kongstvedt, P. R. (Ed.). *Essentials of managed health care.* (1-9). Gaithersburg, MD: Aspen.

"Managed care revenues climb as enrollment soars." (1996, July 12). Managed care outlook, 6.

Mezey, A. P. and Lawrence, R. S. (1995). Ambulatory care. In Kovner, A. R. (Ed.). *Jonas's health care delivery in the United States.* (5th ed., 122-161). New York: Springer.

Milliman and Robertson, Inc. 1996. Fifth annual inter-company rate survey.

Nash, D. B. (1995). Accountability for hospital quality: the role of clinical practice guidelines. In Goldfield, N. and Nash, D. B. (Eds.). *Providing quality care, future challenges.* (2nd ed., 11-24). Ann Arbor: Health Administration Press.

"New York study finds uninsured on the rise." (1997, Feb. 25). The New York Times (A1, B2).

Perrow, C. (1967, April). A framework for the comparative analysis of organizations. *American sociological review 32 (3).* (194-208).

Peters, J. R. (1997). Legal issues in integrated delivery systems. In Kongstvedt, P. R. (Ed.). *Essentials of managed health care. (2nd ed., pp. 506-525).*

"Physician forecast shows maldistribution." (1996, Dec.). *Health strategic management, 7.*

Pine, M. and Kongstvedt, P. R. (1995). Quality management. In Kongstvedt, P. R. (Ed.). Essentials of managed health care. (163-172). Gaithersburg, MD: Aspen.

Pozgar, G. D. (1996). *Legal Aspects of Health Care Administration.* Gaithersburg, MD: Aspen.

Rakich, J. S., Longest, B. B. and Darr, K. (1985). *Managing health services organizations.* (2nd Ed.). Philadelphia: W. B. Saunders Company.

Rodwin, M. A. (1993), *Medicine, Money and Morals.* New York: Oxford University Press.

Rother, J. (1997). Consumer protection in managed care: a third generation approach. In Lee, P. R. and Estes, C. L. (Eds.). *The nation's health.* (5th ed., 349-357). London: Jones and Bartlett Publishers.

Shimshak, D. G.,DeFuria, M. C., DiGiorgio, J. J. and Getson, J. (1994). Controlling disenrollment in health maintenance organizations. In Brown, M. (Ed.). *Managed care, strategies, networks and management.* (231-238). Gaithersburg, MD: Aspen.

Shortell, S. M., Levin, D. Z. O'Brien, J. L., and Hughes, F. X. (1995, Spring). Assessing the evidence on CQI: is the glass half empty or half full? *Hospital and health services administration, 40(1).* 4-24.

Siren, P. B. and Laffel, G. L. (1997). Quality management in managed care. In Kongstvedt, P. R. (Ed.). *Essentials of managed health care.* (2nd ed., 274-298). Gaithersburg, MD: Aspen.

Sparrow, M. (1996). License to steal: why fraud plagues America's health care system. Boulder, CO: Westview Press.

Thompson, J. D. (1967). *Organizations in Action*. New York: McGraw Hill.

Wagner, E. R. (1995). Types of managed care organizations. In Kongstvedt, P. R. (Ed.). *Essentials of managed health care*. (24-34). Gaithersburg, MD: Aspen.

Ward, D. L. (1995). Operational finance and budgeting. In Kongstvedt, P. R. (Ed.). *Essentials of managed health care*. (191-208). Gaithersburg, MD: Aspen.

Williamson, O. E. (1975). *Markets and Hierarchies: Analysis and Antitrust Implications*. New York: The Free Press.

Wolford, G. R., Brown, M. and McCool, B. P. (1994). Getting to go in managed care. In Brown, M. (Ed.). *Managed care: strategies, networks and management*. (3-16). Gaithersburg, MD: Aspen.

Zarabozo, C. and LeMasurier, J. D. (1995). Medicare and managed care. In Kongstvedt, P. R. (Ed.). *Essentials of managed health care*. (209-233). Gaithersburg, MD: Aspen.

6.
PRIVATE INSURANCE OPTIONS

Leslie Jones, *South Carolina Department of Insurance, Life and Health, Columbia, SC*

In 1994, national health care expenditures exceeded $ 949.4 billion, or 13.7% of the gross national product (Levit, et al. 1996). Paying for health care services constitutes, by far, the largest service industry in America. Only manufacturing ranks above it in real dollar volumes. The increasing cost of health care has been the subject of much debate and controversy over the past two decades. Table 1 shows the extent of the growth in both public and private expenditures during the past 45 years.

An important aspect of the cost of health care is the mechanisms which exist for financing this cost. Currently in the United States, several options exist for financing the cost of health care. These options can be broadly classified as private insurance and public financing of health care. Private health insurance is typically provided through an employer sponsored health plan or an individual contract and may be provided on a fee for service basis or through a managed care arrangement. Public financing of health care is generally provided through the Medicare and Medicaid programs.

This chapter will provide an overview of both the public and private options for financing the cost of health care. It will also include an in-depth discussion of both fee for service and managed care arrangements.

I. PRIVATE INSURANCE OPTIONS

Private health insurance began in America in 1850 with the Franklin Health Insurance Company of Massachusetts, but modern health insurance began in 1929 in

Table 1 - National Health Expenditures, United States, Selected Years

Year	Total (Billions)	Per Capita	Percent of GNP
1960	$ 26.9	$ 141	5.1
1970	73.2	341	7.1
1980	247.2	1,052	8.9
1990	697.5	2,688	12.1
1994	949.4	3,510	13.7

Source: Adapted from Levit, K.R., Lazenby, L.S., Stewart, M.W., Braden, B.R., Cowan, C.A., Donham, C.S., Long, A.M., McDonnell, A.L.,, Sensenig, A.L., Stiller, J.M., and Won, D.K. (1996, Fall). National Health Expenditures, 1994. Health Care Financing Review, 17(3), 205.

Texas. It was in that year that a group of teachers made a contract with Baylor Hospital in Dallas, Texas to provide some limited hospital coverage-resulting in the first Blue Cross plan. In 1940, about 12 million people, or about 9% of the total U.S. population, had some kind of medical expense coverage. By 1950, the numbers had grown to nearly 77 million people or 53% of the population. From this modest beginning, the private health insurance industry developed and continues to be an important mechanism for financing the cost of health care in the United States--about one-third of the delivery of all services (Williams and Torrens, 1993). In 1994, health care expenditures from private sector insurance exceeded $ 266.8 billion (Levit, et al.). Private health insurance is typically provided through an employer sponsored health plan, a group health plan, or an individual contract. An employer sponsored health plan may be a group contract which is fully underwritten by an insurance company or a health maintenance organization (HMO), in which case the plan is referred to as a fully-insured arrangement, or the employer may self insure, in which case the plan is self-funded arrangement. Whether the plan is an individual contract or a group contract provided through a fully-insured or self-funded arrangement, the coverage may be provided on a fee for service basis or through a managed care arrangement.

A. Fee For Service

Traditionally, private health insurance was provided by an insurance company on a fee for service basis. Under a traditional fee for service or an indemnity arrangement, the providers of the health care services are paid by the insured individual and the insured individual is reimbursed for actual medical expenses incurred in accordance with the terms of the contract between the individual and the insurance company. These arrangements are generally referred to as medical expense insurance contracts. The most common medical expense insurance contracts are hospital and surgical expense insurance and major medical expense insurance.

B. Hospital and Surgical Expense Insurance

The first medical expense contracts were known as hospital and surgical expense insurance. Hospital and surgical expense insurance contracts may be sold separately or as a package. If the policies are sold as a package, the combined policy is generally referred to as hospital-surgical expense insurance policy.

Hospital expense insurance typically provides reimbursement for expenses incurred for necessary treatment and services performed in a hospital as a result of an accident or sickness. Reimbursement is usually made for some portion of the hospital room and board expense and is based on the actual cost of the room up to some specified maximum amount for a specified number of days. The insurance policy may also provide reimbursement for miscellaneous expenses associated with a hospital confinement (e.g., drugs, laboratory fees, x-rays and use of the operating room) and hospital outpatient services (e.g., x-ray, laboratory and emergency services rendered on an outpatient basis). The reimbursement is usually based on actual charges up to a maximum amount per accident or sickness.

Surgical expense insurance provides reimbursement for physicians' services associated with a surgical procedure, administering anesthesia, or in-hospital medical services. The amount of reimbursement for expenses associated with a surgical procedure will generally be based on the actual cost of the surgery up to some maximum. The maximum amount may be listed in a surgical schedule. The amount of reimbursement may also be based on a percentage (e.g., 80%) of the reasonable charges for the procedure. The definition of reasonable charges may vary, but it will generally reflect the average amount charged for the procedure by physicians in a particular geographic area.

In-hospital medical services are physicians' services rendered to a patient admitted to a hospital for treatment of an accident or sickness where the accident or sickness does not require surgical care. The reimbursement will typically be a specified amount per day up to a maximum number of days during one period of confinement. However, the reimbursement may also be based on a percentage of the reasonable charges.

Hospital and surgical expense insurance policies typically provide first-dollar coverage. This means that the insurance company will begin reimbursing the insured for expenses associated with covered services immediately rather than requiring the insured to pay for an initial amount of the expenses and then reimbursing the insured only for those expenses in excess of that amount.

Although hospital and surgical expense insurance policies provide first dollar coverage, they are typically limited with respect to the amount that the insurance company will reimburse for a covered accident or sickness. As described above, the limits are maximums placed on the number of days for which the benefit is payable and/or the amounts that are payable. If an insured is faced with an extended or catastrophic illness, he or she may find that the coverage provided under a hospital-surgical expense insurance policy is inadequate.

Many hospital-surgical expense policies have been replaced by major medical expense polices. The original major medical policies have been expanded to include some of the benefits of hospital-surgical expense insurance and are referred to as comprehensive medical insurance.

C. Major Medical Expense Insurance

The need for health insurance to cover extended or catastrophic illnesses and a broad spectrum of medical services both in and out of the hospital led to the development of what is widely known as major medical expense insurance. Major medical expense insurance generally covers all hospital, medical, surgical services and supplies necessary to treat an accident or illness. Most policies will only cover those services prescribed by a physician as medically necessary. In addition the policies will typically not pay more than the reasonable and customary charge for a covered medical service or supply. Reasonable and customary charges are generally based on the average charge for the medical supply or service in a particular geographic area. In addition to restricting the reimbursement to reasonable and customary charges, some policies may place an inside limit or specified dollar limit on certain medical services such as hospital room and board and certain surgical procedures.

Major medical expense insurance has three distinct features which essentially define the terms of the contract. These features are the deductible, the coinsurance amount and the maximum policy benefit.

The deductible is the amount of covered medical services and supplies which the insured must pay before benefits are payable under the terms of the major medical expense insurance contract. The deductible is usually a specified dollar amount such as $250, $500, or $1000. Higher deductible amounts may be applied if the major medical policy is used to supplement an underlying hospital-medical expense insurance contract. Major medical expense insurance contracts with lower deductibles (e.g., $250, $500, $1000) are comprehensive major medical expense insurance contracts. The deductible is inversely related to the premium. In other words, the higher the deductible, the lower the premium.

The deductible may be calculated on a per person or a per family basis. If the deductible is calculated on a per person basis, each person covered under the contract must satisfy a separate deductible before benefits are payable. In this case, the deductible is typically deemed to be satisfied if two or three of the family members meet the deductible. If the deductible is calculated on a per family basis, the covered medical expenses incurred by all family members are aggregated. In this case, benefits are payable under the policy once the aggregated amount exceeds the specified deductible limit.

The deductible will typically be specified on a per illness or per benefit period basis. If specified on a per illness basis, the deductible must be satisfied for each separate covered illness before benefits are payable under the policy. If the deductible is specified on a per benefit period basis, the deductible must be satisfied in each benefit period before benefits are payable under the terms of the contract. The benefit period may be based on a calendar year or a specified period of time beginning on the policy anniversary date (e.g., 2 years).

Coinsurance refers to the portion of the covered medical expenses which must be paid by the insurer and that which must be paid by the insured after the deductible has been satisfied. For example, if the coinsurance percentage is 80%, the insurer will pay 80% of the covered expenses after the deductible has been satisfied, and the insured will pay the remaining 20% of the covered expenses. Since the amount of the covered expense will typically be based on reasonable and customary charges, the insured must typically pay for any amounts which he or she has been billed in excess of reasonable and customary charges. The fact that the insured must share in the cost of the medical expense tends to encourage the insured to control medical expenses to the extent possible.

An important caveat should be made at this juncture. If the amount which the insured is billed is less than reasonable and customary charges, the insurer may not base the coinsurance amount payable by the insured on reasonable and customary charges but rather must base the coinsurance amount on the actual amount which the insured has been billed for the service in most states.

The coinsurance percentage may vary by covered service. For example, the coinsurance percentage may be 100% for hospital room and board expenses that fall with the inside limits and 85% of all other covered expenses after the deductible has been satisfied.

The coinsurance amount may also vary depending on the amount of covered expenses incurred in a benefit period. For example, the coinsurance amount may be 80% of covered expenses up to $5000 above the deductible and 100% of covered services in excess of $5000 above the deductible in a benefit period. This feature has the effect of placing an upper limit on the insured's liability in the event of a serious or extended accident or illness. The maximum amount which the insured must pay for both the deductible and coinsurance amounts in a benefit period is commonly referred to as the maximum out of pocket.

The maximum policy benefit defines the maximum amount which the insurer will pay under the terms of the contract. The maximum policy benefit is typically stated on a per illness or a maximum lifetime basis.

If the maximum policy benefit is stated on a per illness basis, the policy will state a maximum dollar amount (e.g., $100,000) which the insurer will pay for each illness or accident. If the maximum policy benefit is stated on a maximum lifetime basis, the policy states a maximum dollar amount which the policy will pay for all illnesses or accidents combined. Typical lifetime maximum policy benefits are $1,000,000 or $2,000,000. However, some policies have unlimited lifetime maximum benefits.

For example, a major medical expense insurance contract has a per individual, per benefit period deductible of $500, an 80% insurer coinsurance percentage for covered expenses up to $5,000 above the deductible in a benefit period, and a 100% insurer coinsurance percentage for covered expenses in excess of $5,000 above the deductible in a benefit period. The maximum policy benefit is based on a lifetime maximum of $1,000,000. The benefit period is defined to be a calendar year.

Suppose an insured individual incurs $6,750 of medical expenses in a calendar year. Further suppose that the reasonable and customary charges for the services received by the insured are $6,000. The insured must pay the first $500 of covered expenses to satisfy the deductible, plus 20% of the next $5000 in covered expenses or $1000. Thus, the maximum out of pocket for the insured is $1,500. It is important to note that the insured will owe an additional $750 for the difference between the amount the insured was actually charged for the services and the reasonable and customary charges for the services. Thus, the total amount the insured must pay for medical expenses incurred in the calendar year is $1,500 plus $750 which equals $2,250.

Medical expense insurance contracts typically contain various limitations and exclusions. Limitations and exclusions define those circumstances in which benefits are not payable or may be limited. Limitations and exclusions are included in medical expense insurance contraction for various reasons. The most common reasons are to avoid duplication of benefits, to exclude or limit the amount payable for procedures which are routine or not medically necessary, to exclude procedures resulting from self-induced injuries, and to protect the insurance company from adverse selection.

Insurance companies typically include limitations and exclusions to avoid duplication of benefits so that the insured does not profit from an accident or illness. Exclusions of this type typically stipulate that benefits will not be paid if the accident or illness is covered by a government agency (e.g., worker's compensation) or another insurance policy. When the insured has more than one insurance policy that will cover the same accident or illness, the insurance contract will typically contain a coordination of benefits provision. This provision stipulates which insurance company has primary responsibility for payment of the claim and which has secondary responsibility and how payments will be made such that the insured will receive all benefits to which he or she is entitled, but not more than 100% of covered expenses.

Examples of provisions designed to exclude or limit the amount payable for procedures which are routine or not medically necessary are exclusions of cosmetic surgery, health examinations or periodic checkups, dental care and treatment, eye examinations and the purchase of eyeglasses, mental and nervous disorders and custodial care. Some important caveats apply to the above statement. Some major medical expense contracts now include first dollar coverage for periodic health examinations up to some maximum amount (e.g., $100). This feature is becoming more prevalent with the focus on health care cost containment and preventive care as a means for achieving this. Dental care and vision care may be provided by a separate insurance policy or may be added to a major medical expense insurance contract for an additional premium. Many states require that insurance companies offer optional coverage for mental and nervous disorders. Custodial care may be provided by a separate policy called a Long Term Care policy.

A common limitation included in medical expense insurance contracts to protect the insurance company from adverse selection is referred to as the "preexisting conditions limitation." This limitation typically excludes coverage for illnesses for which the insured has been diagnosed or received medical treatment for a certain period of time. For example, a preexisting condition may be defined as a condition for which the insured has received medical treatment or advice within twelve months preceding the effective date of the policy. The preexisting condition limitation may exclude that condition for up to twelve months after the effective date of coverage or twelve months without medical care, supplies, or treatment for the condition, whichever comes first.

D. Managed Care

One problem with the traditional fee for service arrangement is the lack of connection between the person paying the bill, the insurance company, and the person receiving the services, the insured. Under this type of arrangement, there is little financial incentive for the insured to control the cost of health care, either by questioning the bill received and/or the procedures performed, since the majority of the burden for financing the services rests with the insurance company. This "disconnect" is one of the reasons suggested for the spiraling health care costs experienced in the United States in the 1970s and 1980s. These spiraling costs and the resulting increase in premiums led insurers to look for effective methods of containing these rising costs. The methods which were subsequently developed to help restrain these costs by providing checks and balances on the delivery of health care are collectively referred to as "managed care."

The term "managed care" has recently become synonymous with health maintenance organization (HMO). These insurance-like organizations first emerged in 1929 when the Ross-Loos Clinic in Los Angeles established the first prepaid group practice organization, although the concept had been in existence since the late 1800s at the Mayo Clinic. Kaiser of California is generally recognized as the founder of the organized health maintenance system with its establishment of coverage for the health needs of workers building the Grand Coulee Dam in 1930 (Williams and Torrens, 1993). Growth of the concept was relatively slow within the U.S. until the 1980s when enrollment began growing as a response to ever increasing costs and escalating premium payments.

One of the first methods adopted to control costs is often referred to as "utilization review." Utilization review involves the use of techniques such as pre-admission screening and in-hospital case management to control the number of unnecessary and inappropriate procedures.

Another method for controlling the cost of health care involves contractual arrangements with providers of health care. These arrangements have evolved over time and may have many forms. Currently, the most common arrangements are preferred provider arrangements (PPAs), health maintenance organizations (HMOs), point of service arrangements (POSs), and provider sponsored organizations (PSOs).

A PPA is an arrangement in which a group of providers contract with insurers or other organizations (e.g., a self-funded employer) to provide medical services to participants for a negotiated fee. The providers agree to accept the negotiated fee as payment in full for services rendered to the participants. An insurer may offer incentives in the form of lower deductibles or higher coinsurance amounts to encourage insured individuals to use the network of preferred providers.

A health maintenance organization (HMO) arranges to provide comprehensive health care services, including hospital, medical, surgical and preventive services, to its members or enrollees for a fixed prepaid fee. The HMO enters into contracts with providers to render these services. The providers may be employed by the health maintenance organization or may contract with the HMO to provide services for a negotiated fee.

An HMO differs from an insurance company in several important areas. First, the enrollees are generally required to use only those providers who have contracted with or who are employed by the HMO, often referred to as "in-network" providers. Exceptions to this rule may be made in the case of an emergency or in the case where a specialist is needed who is not an in-network provider. Second, an enrollee must generally select a primary care physician (PCP) from among the HMO's in-network providers. The PCP is responsible for managing the enrollee's care. Accordingly, an enrollee must typically receive a referral from his or her PCP before seeing a specialist. If a referral is not obtained, the HMO will typically not pay for any services provided by the specialist. Third, HMO providers are usually paid based on the number of enrollees they service, rather than being reimbursed for the services which they provide. Lastly, HMOs are required to cover preventive services.

A POS is similar to a PPA. It functions as a combination of a major medical expense insurance contract, in which the insured/enrollee is unrestricted in the choice of providers, and an HMO contract, in which the choice of providers is restricted to the HMO's in network providers. If the insured/enrollee chooses to use the HMO's network of providers, the insured/enrollee will generally receive a lower deductible and higher coinsurance percentage. However, to get the in-network benefits, the insured must generally coordinate his or her care through a primary care physician.

A POS or provider sponsored network (PSN) is an organization composed of providers of health care which contracts with an entity (e.g., a self-funded employer, Medicare, Medicaid) to provide comprehensive health care services. A PSO is similar to an HMO; however, it is not clear whether it is subject to the same regulatory requirements.

E. Trends

A recent trend in medical expense insurance is the concept of a Medical Savings Account (MSA). A medical savings account develops as part of an arrangement whereby an employer will offer two types of medical expense insurance plans: a low deductible plan and a high deductible plan. If an insured selects the high deductible plan, the employer establishes a medical savings account into which he or she contributes the difference in premiums between the low deductible and the high deductible plan. The amount accumulated in the medical savings account may be used to pay for future medical expenses, premiums and long term care insurance. Several states have allowed the insured a tax deduction for the amounts contributed to the medical savings account. Recent federal legislation allows a tax deduction from federal income taxes for amounts contributed by the employer to medical savings accounts on a test basis.

MSAs have sparked a significant amount of controversy. On one side of the debate are those who believe that MSAs will be used by the healthy and the wealthy since they will be the only ones who can withstand the cost of the high deductible while the MSA is building. On the other side of the debate are those who say that MSAs will go a long way in the effort to contain health care costs by giving the insured a direct incentive to monitor the care they are receiving.

Managed care has already been attributed with significantly decreasing the cost of health care in the United States. Now that health care costs appear to be getting under control, the focus has shifted to quality of care. There are several significant issues with respect to quality of care including access to providers, specialists, hospitals and emergency room treatment; standards for approval or disapproval of care; gag clauses, which limit treatment options that may be discussed with enrollees; requirements for quality assurance programs; and grievance procedures.

II. PUBLIC FINANCING OF HEALTH CARE

A. Medicare

Medicare is a federal health insurance program established by the 1965 amendments to the Social Security Act. It has grown at a phenomenal rate rising to about $166.1 billion of personal health care expenditures funding in 1994 (Williams and Torrens). This program is administered by the Health Care Financing Administration (HCFA, 1993) and is designed to provide health insurance for people age 65 or older, people of any age with permanent kidney failure, and certain disabled people under age 65, who are eligible for Social Security. Medicare has two major components: Hospital Insurance (Part A) and Medical Insurance (Part B).

1. Medicare Part A

Medicare Part A provides coverage for medically necessary inpatient care in a general hospital, skilled nursing facility, psychiatric hospital or hospice care. In addition, Part A pays the full cost of medically necessary home health care and 80% of the approved cost for wheelchairs, hospital beds, and other durable medical equipment (DME) supplied under the home health care benefit. Coverage is also provided for whole blood or units of packed cells, after the first three pints, when furnished by a hospital or skilled nursing facility during a covered stay.

Medicare hospital and skilled nursing facility benefits are paid on the basis of benefit periods. In general, a benefit period begins the first day an individual receives a Medicare-covered service in a qualified hospital and ends when the individual has been out of the qualified hospital for 60 consecutive days. If an individual enters a hospital after the end of a benefit period, a new benefit period begins. With each new benefit period, Medicare Part A hospital and skilled nursing facility benefits are renewed except for any lifetime reserve days or psychiatric hospital benefits which have been used.

a. Inpatient Hospital Care

If an individual is hospitalized, Medicare will pay for all covered hospital services during the first 60 days of a benefit period after the deductible has been satisfied. The Part A deductible for 1996 was $736 per benefit period. For the 61st through the 90th day, Medicare Part A will pay for all covered services except for a coinsurance amount of $184 per day in 1996.

Under Medicare Part A, an individual has a lifetime reserve of 60 days for inpatient hospital care. The lifetime reserve days may be used if an individual is in the hospital for more than 90 days in a benefit period. When a reserve day is used, Medicare Part A will pay for all covered services except for a coinsurance amount of $368 in 1996.

b. Psychiatric Hospital Care

Medicare Part A will pay for no more than 190 days of inpatient care in a Medicare-participating psychiatric hospital in an individual's lifetime. However, psychiatric care provided in a general hospital, rather than in a psychiatric hospital, is not subject to the 190-day limit.

Medicare Part A will pay for part of up to 100 days of skilled nursing care in a skilled nursing facility during a benefit period. All covered services for the first 20 days of care are fully paid by Medicare. All covered services for the next 80 days are paid by Medicare, except for a daily coinsurance amount which must be paid by the Medicare beneficiary. The daily coinsurance amount in 1996 is $92. If more than 100 days of care are required in a benefit period, the individual is responsible for all charges beginning with the 101st day.

A skilled nursing facility is different from a nursing home. It is a special kind of facility that primarily furnishes skilled nursing and rehabilitation services. It may be a separate facility or a distinct part of another facility such as a hospital. Medicare will not pay for the stay if the services received are primarily personal care or custodial services, such as assistance in walking, getting in and out of bed, eating, dressing, bathing, and taking medicine.

c. Home Health Care

Medicare pays the full cost of medically necessary home health visits by a Medicare approved home health agency. A home health agency is a public or private agency that provides skilled nursing care, physical therapy, speech therapy and other therapeutic services in the patient's home. These services are usually provided on a periodic basis by a visiting nurse and/or home health aide.

To qualify for coverage, an individual must have a need for intermittent skilled nursing care, physical therapy, or speech therapy or be confined to his or her home and under a physician's care. There is no deductible or coinsurance amount (except for durable medical equipment), and no prior hospitalization is required for home health care benefits. Medicare will also cover a portion of the cost of wheelchairs, hospital beds and other durable medical equipment (DME) provided under a plan-of-care set up and periodically reviewed by a physician.

d. Hospice Care

Medicare pays for hospice care for terminally ill beneficiaries who choose to receive hospice care rather than regular Medicare benefits for management of their illness. Under Medicare, hospice is primarily a program of care provided in the patient's home. The focus is on care, not cure. Hospice services covered under Medicare Part A include physician's services, nursing care, medical appliances and supplies, drugs (for pain and symptom relief), short-term inpatient care, medical social services, physical therapy, occupational therapy and speech/language pathology services, dietary and other counseling. There is no deductible for these hospice care benefits.

Medicare Part A is financed by part of the Social Security payroll withholding tax paid by workers and their employers and part of the Self Employment Tax paid by self-employed workers. Medicare Part A is available free of charge to individuals entitled to Social Security benefits, Railroad Retirement benefits, or benefits under a federal, state or local system with some conditions. Individuals not entitled to receive Medicare Part A free of charge, may purchase the coverage under certain conditions. In 1996, the monthly premium for Medicare Part A for individuals with at least 30 and fewer than 40 quarters of Medicare covered employment was $188. The 1996 monthly premium was $289 for individuals with fewer than 30 quarters of covered employment.

B. Medicare Part B

Medicare Part B pays for a wide range of medical services and supplies, the most important of which is physician services. Medically necessary physician services are covered no matter where they are received. Medicare Part B also covers outpatient hospital services, x-rays and laboratory tests, certain ambulance services, durable medical equipment, such as wheelchairs and hospital beds used at home, services of certain specially qualified practitioners who are not physicians, physical and occupational therapy, speech/language pathology services, partial hospitalization for mental health care, mammograms and pap smears, and home health care if you do not have Medicare Part A. While Part B generally does not cover outpatient prescription drugs, it does cover some oral anti-cancer drugs, certain drugs for hospice enrollees, and non-self-administrable drugs provided as part of physician's services. Certain drugs furnished during the first year after an organ transplantation and epotein for home dialysis patients are also covered, as part of antigens, and flu, pneumococcal, and hepatitis B vaccines. Coverage is also provided for blood after you meet the 3-pint annual deductible.

1. Part B Deductible and Coinsurance

As of calendar year 1996, individuals receiving Part B benefits, were required to pay the first $100 of charges for each calendar year. This deductible must be based on the Medicare-approved amount for covered services and supplies, not the actual charges billed by the physician or medical supplies.

After the deductible has been met, part B generally pays 80% of the Medicare-approved amount for all covered services received during the rest of the year. The individual must pay the remaining 20%. This 20% is called coinsurance. If home health care services are required under Medicare Part B, the deductible and coinsurance are waived. However, the individual must pay 20% of the Medicare approved amount of any durable medical equipment supplied under the home health benefit.

In addition to the deductible and coinsurance, the insured is responsible for any amounts which the physician or medical supplier charges over Medicare's approved amount. This difference is the excess charge.

2. Medicare-Approved Amount

The Medicare-approved amount for physician services covered by Medicare Part B is based on the lesser of the physician's actual charge or the fee schedule amount. The fee schedule assigns a dollar value to each physician service based on services performed, the cost of funding a practice, and malpractice insurance costs. Medicare generally pays 80% of the approved amount.

3. Accepting Assignment

In general, physicians and medical suppliers can decide whether or not to accept assignment of the Medicare-approved amount. They may accept assignment on a case-by-case basis or sign a participation agreement with Medicare and accept the Medicare-approved amount as full payment on all Medicare claims. Physicians and medical suppliers who sign these agreements are called "participating" physicians and suppliers and are listed in The Medicare Participating Physician/Supplier Directory.

Physicians or suppliers who accept assignment are reimbursed directly by Medicare, except for the deductible and coinsurance amounts which must be paid by the Medicare beneficiary. Those who do not accept assignment collect the full amount from the participant. Medicare then reimburses the participant for its share of the approved amount for the services or supplies received. Regardless of whether the physician or supplier accepts assignment, they must file the Medicare claim for the beneficiary.

In certain situations non-participating physicians and suppliers who do not normally accept assignment are required by law to do so. For instance, all physicians and laboratories must accept assignment for clinical diagnostic laboratory tests covered by Medicare. Physicians must also accept assignment for covered services provided to beneficiaries with incomes low enough to qualify for Medicaid payment of their Medicare cost-sharing requirements.

4. Physician Charge Limits

Physicians who do not accept assignment of a Medicare claim can charge more than physicians who do. However, there is a limit to the amount they can charge for services covered by Medicare. They are permitted to charge only 15% more than the Medicare-approved amount. This is the limiting amount.

Under a new law all Medicare carriers are required to screen physician bills for overcharges and notify the physician and the patient within 30 days of any overcharge. The physician is then required to refund the overcharge within 30 days or credit the beneficiaries account for it. Physicians who knowing, willfully and repeatedly charge more than the legal limit are subject to sanctions.

Some states have also enacted charge limit laws. By 1996, Connecticut, Massachusetts, Minnesota, New York, Ohio, Pennsylvania, Rhode Island and Vermont had enacted such laws.

5. Other Charge Limits

Physicians who do not accept assignment for elective surgery are required to give a written estimate to the beneficiary of the cost of the surgery if the total charge will be $500 (in 1996) or more. If an estimate is not given, the beneficiary is entitled to a refund of any amount paid in excess of the Medicare-approved amount. Additionally, any non-participating physician who provides services that he or she knows or has reason to believe Medicare will determine to be medically unnecessary, and thus will not pay for, is required to inform the beneficiary in writing before performing the service. If written notice is not given, the beneficiary cannot be held liable for payment of that service. However, if the beneficiary did receive written notice and signed an agreement to pay for the service, he or she will be held liable to pay.

Medicare Part B is a voluntary program. Individuals eligible for Medicare Part A are automatically enrolled in Medicare Part B, unless they indicate that they do not want the coverage. Medicare Part B is financed, in part, by the premiums paid by persons enrolled in the program. The 1996 monthly premium was $42.50. The rest of the program is financed by the federal government.

C. Health Insurance-Private

There are several private insurance options available to help Medicare recipients pay all or part of those medical expenses which are not covered by Medicare. The most important of these are Medicare Supplement (Medigap), Medicare SELECT, and Managed Care Plans

1. Medicare Supplement (Medigap)

Medigap insurance, which most beneficiaries buy because it is specifically designed to supplement Medicare's benefits, is regulated by federal and state law and must be clearly identified as Medicare supplement insurance. It provides specific benefits that help fill the gaps in Medicare coverage.

2. Standard Medigap Plans

To make it easier for consumers to comparison shop for Medigap insurance, nearly all states, U.S. territories and the District of Columbia limit the number of different Medigap policies that can be sold in any of those jurisdictions to no more than 10 standard Medigap plans. The plans were developed by the National Association of Insurance Commissioners and incorporated into state and federal law.

The plans have letters designations ranging from A through J, with Plan A being the basic benefit package. Each of the other plans includes the basic package plus a different combination of additional benefits. The plans cover specific expenses either not covered or not fully covered by Medicare, with A being the most basic policy and J being the most comprehensive.

3. What Medigap Plans Cover

Medigap policies pay most, if not all, Medicare coinsurance amounts and may provide coverage for Medicare's deductibles. Some of the 10 standard plans pay for services not covered by Medicare such as outpatient prescription drugs, preventive screening and emergency medical care while traveling outside the United States. Coverage is also provided in some plans for provider charges in excess of Medicare's approved amount and for at-home personal care services. Some of the benefits have dollar limits. For example, the at-home recovery benefit available in some plans pays up to $40 per visit for up to seven visits a week and can be used for up to 8 weeks. The services covered by the Medigap policy must be ordered by the insured's doctor.

Both the basic and the extended outpatient prescription drug benefits also have payout limits. Under basic coverage, the insured is responsible for a $250 deductible each calendar year, after which the policy covers 50% of outpatient prescription drug charges up to a maximum of $1,250 in benefits per calendar year. The extended prescription drug benefit also pays 50% of the insured's drug bills up to a maximum of $3,000 per year after the insured pays the first $250 .

The preventive screening benefit pays a maximum of $120 per year for physician-ordered health care screenings. The foreign travel emergency benefit covers 80% of the costs of emergency medical care begun during the first 2 months of each trip outside the United States after the insured pays the $250 annual deductible. The lifetime maximum benefit is $50,000.

Unlike some types of health coverage that restrict where and from whom the insured can receive care, Medigap policies generally pay the same supplemental benefits regardless of the insured's choice of health care provider. If Medicare pays for a service, wherever provided, the standard Medigap policy must pay its regular share of benefits. The only exception is Medicare SELECT.

4. *Medicare SELECT*

Another Medicare supplement health insurance product, Medicare SELECT, is permitted to be sold by insurance companies and HMOs throughout the country. Medicare SELECT is the same as standard Medigap insurance in nearly all respects. If insureds buy a Medicare SELECT policy, they are buying one of the standard Medigap plans.

The only difference between Medicare SELECT and the standard Medigap insurance is that each insurer has specific providers, and in some cases specific hospitals, that must be used by the insured except in emergency in order to be eligible for full benefits. Medicare SELECT policies generally have lower premiums in comparison to other Medigap policies because of this requirement.

When a policyholder uses the insured's preferred providers, Medicare pays its share of the approved charges and the insurer is responsible for the full supplemental benefits provided for in the policy. In general, Medicare SELECT policies are not required to pay any benefits if the insured does not use a preferred provider for non-emergency services. Medicare, however, will still pay its share of approved charges regardless of the provider selected by the insured.

Congress designated Medicare SELECT as an experimental program and initially approved its availability in 15 states. In 1995, Congress expanded the program to include all 50 states and extended the program for another three years. Even if Congress decides not to continue Medicare SELECT, insurers will be required to honor all existing Medicare SELECT policies. If an insured has a Medicare SELECT policy and the program is terminated in 1998, the insured will be able to either keep the SELECT policy with no changes in benefits or, regardless of the status of health, purchase any other Medigap policy offered by the insurer, if the insurer issues Medigap insurance other the Medicare SELECT. To the extent possible, the replacement policy would have to provide similar benefits.

5. *Managed Care Plans that Contract with Medicare*

Managed care plans are sometimes called "coordinated care," or "prepaid plans," or "HMOs." They might be thought of as a combination insurance company and doctor/hospital. Like an insurance company, they cover health care costs in return for a monthly premium, and like a doctor or hospital, they provide health care services.

Each plan has its own network of hospitals, skilled nursing facilities, home health agencies, doctors and other professionals. Depending on how the plan is organized, services are usually provided at one or more centrally located health care facilities or in the private practice offices of the doctors and other health care professionals that are part of the plan.

Most managed care plans allow the insured to select a primary care doctor from those that are part of the plan. If the insured does not make a selection, one will be assigned. The primary care doctor is responsible for managing the insured's medical care, admitting the insured to the hospital and referring the insured to specialists.

The insured may pay a fixed monthly premium to the plan and small copayments each time he or she goes to the doctor or uses other services. The premiums and copayments vary from plan to plan and can be changed each year. The insured also must continue to pay the Part B premium to Medicare. The insured does not, however, pay Medicare's deductibles and coinsurance.

Usually there are no additional charges no matter how many times the insured visits the doctor, is hospitalized, or uses other covered services. The insured will get all of the Medicare hospital and medical benefits to which he or she is entitled through the plan, and retain all Medciare protections and appeal rights.

There are two types of contracts that a plan may have with Medicare: a risk or a cost contract. Plans with risk contracts have lock-in requirements. This means that the insured is generally locked into receiving all covered care through the plan or through referrals by the plan.

In most cases, if the insured goes outside the plan for services, neither the plan nor Medicare will pay. The insured will be responsible for the entire bill. The only exceptions recognized by all Medicare-contracting plans are for emergency services, which may be received anywhere in the United States, and for urgently needed care, which may be received while temporarily away from the plan's service area.

A third exception is now offered by a few risk plans: the point-of service (POS) option. Under the POS option, the plan permits the insured to receive certain services outside the plan's established provider network and the plan will pay a percentage of the charges. In return for the flexibility, the insured must pay a portion of the cost, typically 20% of the bill.

Unlike risk plans, cost plans do not have lock-in requirements. If an insured enrolls in a cost plan, the insured can either go to health care providers affiliated with the plan or go outside the plan. If the insured goes outside the plan, the plan probably will not pay, but Medicare will. Medicare will pay its share of charges it approves. The insured will be responsible for Medicare's coinsurance, deductibles and other charges just as if the insured was receiving care on the fee-for-service system. Because of this flexibility, a cost plan may be a good choice for the insured, if the insured travels frequently, lives in another state part of the year, or wants to continue to use a physician who is not affiliated with a plan.

While benefits vary from plan to plan, all plans that have either a risk or cost contract must provide all of the Medicare benefits generally available in the plan's service area. Whether or not the insured is entitled to Parts A and B, or Part A only, the insured can get all Medicare benefits through the plan. In addition, many plans promote preventive health care by providing extra benefits such as eye examinations, hearing aids, checkups, scheduled inoculations and prescription drugs for little or no extra fee.

D. Medicaid

Medicaid is the name used to refer to the medical assistance program which was established by the 1965 amendments to Title XIX of the Social Security Act. The

Medicaid program provides assistance to individuals unable to afford the cost of medical care due to insufficient income and assets. The program is administered at the state level. However, the cost of the program is shared between the federal and state governments. The amount which the federal government contributes is based on the state's per capita income and varies between 50% and 83% under the current formula (NAIC, p. 4; Social Insurance, p. 364). In order to qualify for federal funding, state programs must meet certain standards with respect to eligibility and benefits provided.

1. Eligibility

State programs generally cover individuals who are determined to be either categorically needy or medically needy. Categorically needy individuals include those individuals receiving payments under the Aid to Families with Dependent Children (AFDC) program, certain groups of individuals who meet AFDC criteria but do not receive payments under the AFDC program, and most individuals receiving income under the Supplemental Security Income (SSI) program (Social Insurance).

The AFDC program is a federal public assistance program which provides a monthly payment and Medicaid to poor families in which the children are deprived of the care and support of at least one parent. Individuals who meet AFDC criteria but do not receive a monthly payment include, but are not limited to pregnant women and individuals who are denied a monthly payment because the AFDC check would be less than a certain amount (e.g., $10). The Supplemental Security Income (SSI) program is a federal public assistance program which provides a monthly payment to poor individuals who are aged, blind and disabled (South Carolina).

Medically needy individuals include individuals whose incomes exceed those required to qualify for the AFDC or SSI program, but are not sufficient to cover their medical bills. Benefits to medically needy individuals are provided in more than 75% of the states (NAIC).

Since eligibility for Medicaid is need-based, many people who are not poor attempt to qualify for Medicaid by transferring assets and/or diverting income from their estates. OBRA 93 curtailed this practice by increasing the lookback period for asset transfers from 30 to 36 months and set the lookback for trusts at 60 months (Medicaid Planning).

2. Benefits

Medicaid will pay for medically necessary services and medical supplies within certain limits. To qualify for federal funding, the Medicaid program must provide basic medical services and supplies to the categorically needy. These services include, but are not limited to, hospital services (in-patient and out-patient), physicians' services, and x-ray and laboratory services (Social Insurance). However, the program may provide additional medical services and supplies as it deems necessary including early and periodic screening, diagnosis, and treatment (EPSDT) program, vision care, dental services, rural health clinic services, family planning services, durable medical equipment, prescription drugs, ambulance transportation, medical transportation, podiatrists' services, skilled nursing facility services, intermediate care facility services, home health services, certain types of therapy, inpatient hospital services for individuals age 65 or older in institution for tuberculosis or mental disease, inpatient psychiatric services for individuals under the age of 22, mental health clinic services, case management, and certain home and community-based services. It should be remembered, however, that Medicaid will only pay for twelve total visits in a year for these types of services.

3. Choice of Providers

In general, the Medicaid recipient has the freedom to choose his or her own doctor, hospital, drugstore, and other medical providers. However, the provider must typically practice within the state or within a certain distance of the state's borders (e.g., 25 miles). Special approval is generally required for medical services which the Medicaid beneficiary receives outside of the state.

The provider must also agree to accept Medicaid as full payment for services rendered. If the provider agrees to accept Medicaid as payment, he or she may not bill the Medicaid beneficiary for any excess charges. However, the provider may bill the Medicaid recipient for any services which are not covered by Medicaid.

4. Medicaid Managed Care

In an effort to control the costs of Medicaid Programs, many states have experimented with providing medical services to beneficiaries through managed care arrangements. In order to use a managed care arrangement, the states must receive a waiver from the Health Care Financing Agency (HCFA). A Section 1115 waiver allows the state to test extensive reform on a statewide basis. A Section 1915(b) waiver is more restrictive and allows a state to waive a patient's freedom to choose a provider. Both of these waivers are only granted for a limited time period.

Several types of managed care arrangements have emerged. The most common are the full-risk capitation arrangement, the partial capitation arrangement and the primary care case management (PCCM) arrangements.

Under the full-risk capitation arrangement, the state contracts with an organization to provide a broad range of medical services to Medicaid beneficiaries for a fixed prepaid fee. Under the partial capitation arrangement, the state contracts with an organization to provide a limited set of medical services for a fixed prepaid fee. The rest of the services are provided on a fee-for-service basis. Under a primary care case management arrangement, providers are paid a fee for monitoring and approving the use of covered services by Medicaid beneficiaries. In addition, providers are reimbursed on a fee-for-service basis for all medical services rendered.

One of the features which distinguishes the arrangements described above is the amount of financial risk which is transferred from the state to the organization providing the medical services. The full-capitation arrangement allows for the most financial risk to be transferred from the state to the organization providing the medical services. The primary care case management arrangement allows for the least amount of financial risk to be transferred from the state to the organization providing the medical services.

SUMMARY

Since its emergence in 1850 in Massachusetts, the health insurance industry has grown into one of the largest employers and industries in the country. Private insurance has evolved from traditional indemnity plans with payment based on fee-for-services provided and determined by the providers of health care, to various generations of HMO's, or managed care organizations, who seek to provide comprehensive, quality care while maximizing containment of costs through population enrollment and payment per person per period of coverage for all services. Since the introduction of the Medicare and Medicaid programs in 1965, national health care expenditures in the United States have increased exponentially from 5.1% of the gross national product in 1960 to almost 14% in 1994. Pressures from increasing costs for health care continue to plague the system and answers to questions regarding the most effective, efficient, fair and comprehensive methods of reimbursement for health care services that maximize prevention, diagnosis, treatment, rehabilitation and well being continue to evade a simple answer. Most Americans today receive some of the highest quality of care anywhere in the world, yet too many of our citizens remain either uninsured or underinsured. Responding to the everpresent threats of rising costs and growing limits to access as well as developing strategies and methods to address overall health care needs must be approached within the constraints of limited resources combined with expanding technology. The impact of rising health care costs on all payers--private insurance, public funding sources and personal patient payments for financing--will continue to be the subject of much debate and controversy as we move into the next millenium.

END NOTE

1.   The information on Medicare was reprinted with minor modifications from the 1996 Guide to Health Insurance for People with Medicare developed jointly by the National Association of Insurance Commissioners and the Health Care Financing Administration of the US Department of Health and Human Services.

REFERENCES

American Academy of Actuaries. (1996). *Medicaid managed care: Savings, access and quality. American Academy of Actuaries.*. Washington, DC.

Black Jr., K. and Skipper, Jr., H. (1994). *Life Insurance, 12th Edition*. Prentice Hall, Inc., Englewood Cliffs, NJ.

Department of Social Services. (1995). *South Carolina Department of Social Services Medicaid Handbook*. Department of Social Services., Columbia, SC.

Families USA Foundation. (1996, July). HMO Consumers At Risk: States to the Rescue.. FamiliesUSA Foundation.

Health Insurance Association of America. (1994). Group life and health insurance. *The Health Insurance Association of America. (Publication Part A, 5th Edition, 21-55)*. Washington, DC.

Health Insurance Association of America. (1994). Individual health insurance. *The Health Insurance Association of America.* (Part A, 5th Edition,, 47-66). Washington, DC.

Health Insurance Association of America. (1994). *Managed care: Integrating the delivery and financing of health care.* The Health Insurance Association of America, (Publication: Part A, 1st ed., 1-139). Washington, DC.

Health Insurance Association of America. (1995). 1995 *Source book of health insurance data.* The Health Insurance Association of America, 35th Edition, pp. 1-139. Washington, DC.

Hunter, G. and Netzer, G. (1996). Medicaid Planning Directs Clients to Secure Future, *Best's Review, Life Health Insurance Edition, 97,* May, 74+.

National Association of Insurance Commissioners. (1989). Model laws regulations and guidelines. *National Association of Insurance Commissioners Health Insurance Shoppers' Guide 1,* 45-1 to 45-15. Kansas City, MO.

National Association of Insurance Commissioners. (1989). Model laws regulations and guidelines. *National Association of Insurance Commissioners: Health Maintenance Organization Model Act.,1,* Kansas City, MO.

National Association of Insurance Commissioners. (1989). Model regulation to implement the individual accident and sickness insurance minimum standards act. *National Association of Insurance Commissioners.* (Publication: Model laws regulations and guidelines, 1, 171-1 to 171-32). Kansas City, MO.

National Association of Insurance Commissioners. (1989). NAIC Model Health Insurance Shopper's Guide for Senior Citizens. *National Association of Insurance Commissioners Model Laws Regulations and Guidelines, 1,* 45-1 to 45-15. Kansas City, MO.

National Association of Insurance Commissioners. (1995). Medicaid managed care: Perspectives of the national association of insurance commissioners' state and federal health insurance legislative task force. *National Association of Insurance Commissioners.* Kansas City, MO.

National Association of Insurance Commissioners. (1996). *1996 Guide to Health Insurance for People with Medicare,* pp. 1-27. Kansas City, MO and the Health Care Financing Association, Washington, DC.

National Association of Insurance Commissioners. Preferred Provider Arrangements Model Act. *National Association of Insurance Commissioners Model laws regulations and guidelines, 1.* Kansas City, MO.

Prescott, F. M. (1997). PSNs: A new model for medicare risk contracting. *Healthcare Financial Management,* (March).

Rejda, G. E. (1988). *Social Insurance and Economic Security,* (3rd ed, 213-228). Prentice Hall, Inc., Englewood Cliffs, NJ.

Rejda, G. E. (1992). *Principles of Risk Management and Insurance, (4th Ed).* HarperCollins Publishers Inc., New York, NY.

Social Security Bulleting. (1986). *Social Security Programs in the United States,* Social Security Bulleting , 49 (1), 55.

South Carolina Department of Insurance. (1995). *South Carolina Health Insurance Buyer's Guide,* 1-22. South Carolina Department of Insurance, Columbia, SC.

Williams, S. and Torrens, P. (1993). *Introduction to Health Services, (4th ed.).* Delmar Publishers, Albany, NY.

APPENDIX

Benefit	A	B	C	D	E	F	G	H	I	J
Basic Benefit	Basic Benefit	Basic Benefit	Basic Benefit	Basic Benefit	Basic Benefit	Basic Benefit	Basic Benefit	Basic Benefit	Basic Benefit	Basic Benefit
Skilled Nursing Coinsurance			Skilled Nursing Coinsurance	Skilled Nursing Coinsurance	Skilled Nursing Coinsurance	Skilled Nursing Coinsurance	Skilled Nursing Coinsurance	Skilled Nursing Coinsurance	Skilled Nursing Coinsurance	Skilled Nursing Coinsurance
Part A Deductible		Part A Deductible	Part A Deductible	Part A Deductible	Part A Deductible	Part A Deductible	Part A Deductible	Part A Deductible	Part A Deductible	Part A Deductible
Part B Deductible			Part B Deductible			Part B Deductible				
Part B Excess						Part B Excess (100%)	Part B Excess (80%)			
Foreign Travel Emergency			Foreign Travel Emergency	Foreign Travel Emergency	Foreign Travel Emergency	Foreign Travel Emergency	Foreign Travel Emergency	Foreign Travel Emergency	Foreign Travel Emergency	Foreign Travel Emergency
At Home Recovery				At Home Recovery			At Home Recovery			
Preventive Care					Preventive Care					
Basic Drug Benefit								Basic Drug Benefit ($1,250 Benefit)	Basic Drug Benefit ($1,250 Benefit)	Basic Drug Benefit ($3,000 Benefit)

The information in this section was reprinted with minor modifications from the 1996 Guide to Health Insurance for People with Medicare developed jointly by the National Association of Insurance Commissioners and the Health Care Financing Administration of the US Department of Health and Human Services.

7.
CHALLENGES OF HEALTH FINANCE AND MANAGED CARE

Walter J. Jones, *Medical University of South Carolina, Charleston, SC*

Robert L. Barber, *Carolinas Hospital Network, Charlotte, NC*

Since the late 1970s, no area of U. S. health care has been analyzed and agonized over more intensely than its financial "system." The U. S. both raises and expends its health care funds through a relatively uncoordinated set of private and public sector mechanisms and revenue sources. These mechanisms have broken down in key areas during the last thirty years. Consequently, the shortcomings of health finance are central factors which must be considered in addressing the nation's problems in cost containment, access and quality.

In the U. S., the health insurance status of the individual largely depends upon individual or family income, employment status, whether or not employers provide health insurance as part of a benefits package (if employed), or whether or not the individual qualifies for Medicaid (if unemployed) (Torrens, 1993). An individual's age, occupational type, and pre-existing health status are also critical variables. No other country makes insurance coverage of its citizens so contingent on individual circumstances (National Leadership Commission, 1989). Only those over 65 years of age, who generally qualify for Medicare, have a standard and comprehensive health insurance package.

I. THE MANAGED CARE IMPERATIVE

A. Early History

While what we know today as managed care has its roots as far back as the Civil War, the imperative of managed care is largely a phenomenon of the last ten years.

Indeed, a search of the HealthPLAN database, which contained references to articles for the period 1985 through August 1995 at the time of the search, yielded a list of 3,912 articles on the subject. As might be expected, the volume of articles steadily increased with each year of the decade covered.

Prepaid health plans for employees had been tried by railroad and lumber companies during the Civil War, and coal companies tried such plans in the 1880s (Currey, 1992). The first modern prepaid health care plans are thought to have been those developed independently in three American cities in 1929. One of those plans was a prepaid hospitalization plan developed by Baylor University for school teachers in Dallas (Weeks and Berman, 1985). Two others were a plan established by Dr. Michael Shadid of Elk City, Oklahoma and a group practice prepayment plan developed by Drs. Donald Ross and H. Clifford Loos of Los Angeles, California. Dr. Shadid developed a cooperative plan for rural farmers, while Drs. Ross and Loos contracted to provide prepaid health care services to local water company employees (Kongstvedt, 1993).

Although preceded in 1937 by the Group Health Association of Washington, DC, (Kongstvedt, 1993), the most successful of the early plans that were to become widely known as health maintenance organizations (HMOs) was developed in 1938 by Dr. Sidney Garfield for Henry J. Kaiser. Kaiser and his associates were under contract for the construction of the Grand Coulee Dam across the Columbia River in Washington State. As the project's medical contractor, Dr. Garfield hired other physicians and a staff and developed an organization to provide care for some 5,000 workers. Ultimately, he and his staff provided a full range of medical services to the workers and their families on a prepaid, contract basis (Currey, 1992).

Following completion of the Grand Coulee project in 1942, Dr. Garfield followed Kaiser into the ship-building business, developing a plan for Kaiser's Oakland, California, and Portland, Oregon, shipyards. The plan became known as the Kaiser-Permanente Medical Care Program, named after Kaiser and Southern California's Permanente Creek, a favorite of Kaiser's. By 1944, the plan had 200,000 subscribers (Currey, 1992). Other successful plans followed including the Group Health Cooperative of Puget Sound in Seattle in 1947, the Health Insurance Plan of Greater New York also in 1947, and the Group Health Plan of Minneapolis, 1957 (Kongstvedt, 1993).

The organizational structure of the early plans followed one of two models. They were either what is today known as the staff model, in which the physicians are employed by the plan, or the group model, in which the plan contracts with an organized physician group practice for services to its members, usually on an exclusive provider basis. As might be expected, lack of access to the patients of the plan did not sit well with the portion of the medical community not included as providers under the plan. One response to this dissatisfaction was the development of open panel plans. In 1954, an independent practice association (IPA) was developed as an HMO by the county medical society in the San Joaquin Valley of California. Under the IPA model, the association is formed of, or contracts with, independent practitioners, who provide care to the HMO's subscribers in their own offices (Kongstvedt, 1993). This model grew rapidly and most of today's HMOs follow this organizational pattern.

B. Mid-Century HMOs

While many of the early plans were developed with either somewhat altruistic or purely practical motives, the success of the Kaiser plan and others was viewed as a dangerous assault on fee-for-service medicine by the medical establishment. For that reason, growth of HMOs was slowed during the 1950s and 1960s by attacks by the American Medical Association and its state and local counterparts. The result was that as late as 1973, only about 5 million subscribers had enrolled in HMOs (Kongstvedt, 1993). However, at the same time, other changes in the medical establishment were taking place. Spurred by the availability of veterans' educational benefits, thousands of physicians were taking further medical training and residencies in order to practice as specialists within particular areas of medicine. The result was that by 1966, 70 percent of physicians considered themselves specialists (Kongstvedt, 1993).

While this change in the composition of the medical establishment was taking place, an economic change was also taking place. Perhaps driven by the physicians' expectations of greater compensation for their additional training and specialized knowledge, perhaps by the specialists' tendency to practice their specialties to unprecedented levels, perhaps by the widening availability of health insurance as an employee benefit or government entitlement, the national cost of health care began to rise. As costs rose, cost containment became a growing issue, particularly with the Federal government, which in 1965 had assumed responsibility for care of the nation's elderly and poor under the Medicare and Medicaid programs. With the passage of the HMO Act of 1973, HMOs were encouraged with the expectation that they would decrease costs without government intervention by providing free-market competition in medical care.

Beyond the obstacles to HMO growth presented by the medical establishment during the period of the 1950s and 1960s, HMOs also faced certain growth impediments in the market. As the national cost of health care moved past ten percent of gross domestic product in the early 1980s, employers began to show increasing interest in the cost control possibilities of managed care. However, the stringent controls and access limitations of HMOs were often considered too extreme. Many employers, still operating in something of a paternalistic mode, were not willing to impose drastic limitations on an employee population that was accustomed to the freedom of choice inherent in indemnity coverage. One marketplace response to the desire of employers for a form of managed care that offered some of the benefits of HMOs without what were perceived as draconian controls was the formation of a new type of managed care organization known as the preferred provider organization (PPO).

C. Growth of PPOs

The fundamental difference between HMOs and the new PPOs was the element of choice of providers afforded by the new PPOs. While HMO members were strictly limited to the providers participating in the plan, PPO members could elect to utilize other non-network providers, albeit at a cost. The cost members paid for using outside providers was a reduction in coverage levels. For example if services of a network provider were covered at 90 percent, services of a non-network provider were covered at 70 percent or less, providing choice, but with a guiding financial incentive. This

financial incentive is known as patient steerage. PPO members also had no requirement to have all care managed by a primary care physician, meaning that they could
obtain services of specialists at will, rather than only by referral of their primary care
physician.

Among the first PPOs were those developed by providers. Concerned about the
ability of HMOs to shift care settings and even reduce utilization and recognizing the
control of patient populations potentially exercised by third-party payers, providers
organized PPOs to market their services to the third-party payers as an alternative to
HMOs. Indeed, the term *"alternative delivery system"* soon came into use among
providers to describe this new form of managed care organization. The form of these
new PPOs was much like the IPA, that is, a network of providers joined together to provide health care services to the populations represented by the third-party payers.
Participation in the networks was linked to willingness to provide services at a discount.
And the availability of discounted services gave the PPOs their market attractiveness.
Thus, as Douglas L. Elden, J.D., put it, "The basic purpose of these provider PPOs was to
exchange discounts for patient volume and to fill physician offices and hospital beds,
that is to protect and maintain the providers' market share" (Cobbs, 1989).

Regrettably, the early PPOs were often perceived as no more than discount mechanisms, although they often did incorporate utilization review and case management
programs and thus were able to provide some real management of care and thereby
achieve cost reductions. Like the development of the PPO itself, the utilization review
and case management programs were instituted by providers as much in response to
market demands as in response to fear of external utilization management programs.
In any event, the early PPOs were successful enough in the market to attract widespread adoption of the PPO as the dominant form of managed care. By 1992, 39 percent of employers participating in the A. Foster Higgins & Co. Health Care Benefits
Survey were offering PPOs. Another 5 percent planned to offer a PPO by 1994 (Bader,
1993). According to the results of the PULSE Survey conducted by Inforum, Inc., by
1994, approximately 30 percent of U.S. households were covered by a PPO plan
(Inforum, 1994). With approximately 80 million households in the U.S. and an average
household size of approximately 3 persons, Inforum's results suggest over 70 million
persons covered by PPOs.

D. Recent Developments

By the early 1990s, growth in HMO enrollment had reached about 36 million persons (Kongstvedt, 1993). There was clear evidence that the HMOs were reducing
costs. A Johnson and Higgins study of health care costs in mid-sized employers,
reported in the November 1993 issue of *Business & Health*, showed that for 1992 HMOs
were producing about a 16 percent cost savings over traditional indemnity insurance
plans. PPOs were also saving health care costs, but at only about half the rate of the
HMOs.

The rapid growth of PPO membership, from zero in the late 1970s to a number
about double that of the HMOs in the early 1990s, was a testament to the interest in
cost savings available through managed care. It also demonstrated the market's preference for the less restrictive controls and limitations of the PPO over the stringent

controls of the HMOs. However, the market also coveted the greater savings achieved by the HMOs. This led to the development of a hybrid type of managed care plan known as the point-of-service (POS) plan.

These new POS plans combined the cost saving benefits of the HMOs with the expanded choice of providers available under the PPOs. The POS plans used panels of preferred providers and primary care physicians to manage the care of assigned members. But, they also allowed members to opt for care from non-network providers and to bypass the primary care physician gatekeepers in obtaining care. They did, however, use the mechanism of differential benefits to steer members to network providers and to their assigned primary care physicians. The POS plans, then, drew their name from the fact that differential levels of benefits were available depending on the point at which the member accessed the system for service.

Existing HMOs and PPOs both have seized upon the POS plan as a way to enhance their own attractiveness to the market and thus expand the number of members that they cover. The new POS plans are relatively easy to establish since they often use the same provider network as the existing plan. The HMOs, therefore, see them as a way to offer a new plan in their family which allows greater patient choice but still utilizes their infrastructure of cost control procedures. The PPOs, likewise, see the POS plans as a way to protect their market share by creating a new, related plan that offers increased savings but with their traditional choice of providers. According to the Johnson and Higgins study, the young POS plans appear to save slightly more than the established PPO plans. They are expected to increase in cost saving efficiency.

Despite the cost saving success of the managed care plans, by the early 1990s, national spending on health care was approaching 15 percent of gross domestic product. This fact, along with local health care concerns, became the defining issue in a Pennsylvania senatorial special election. The Democratic Party candidate Harris Wofford, promising health care reform, was a substantial winner. The managers of the 1992 Democratic Presidential campaign took notice of the power of the issue and propelled health care reform to the forefront of the national consciousness. Meanwhile, the nation's large corporations, having astutely discovered that health benefits costs were consuming the equivalent of 38 percent of corporate profits (*Business & Health*, 1993), joined the hue and cry for health care reform. As an aside, one wonders how the fact that corporate income taxes in actuality consuming 43% of corporate profits did not lead to an equally vociferous demand for tax reform.

Although the Democrats' expansive drive for national health care reform was abortive, the exercise focused national attention on the high and rising cost of health care. The nearness of the threat of such massive restructuring of health care delivery under the control of the federal government kicked off a massive, internally driven focus on cost control and restructuring by the health care industry. At the same time, the national attention sparked a rapid growth in the size and power of the managed care industry. The attention to cost control paid off, as by 1994, employers realized their first decline in health care costs in over two decades (Appleby, 1995).

The massive restructuring of health care is now driven by the managed care industry. Managed care organizations are not only the forces driving the changes in health care delivery, but they are also fully involved in those changes. Restructuring comes in the form of a great consolidation among both managed care organizations and providers and in the form of a massive trend toward integration in health care delivery.

From 1993-1995, there were massive, billion-dollar mergers and acquisitions among the managed care organizations. For example, in 1994, The Travelers Insurance Group formed a health insurance joint venture with The Metropolitan Life Insurance Company known as MetraHealth. In 1995, United Healthcare bought MetraHealth in a billion dollar plus transaction. Many insurance companies and HMOs are building national networks and plans. The Blue Cross/Blue Shield Association, not to be outdone, has, through the mechanism of interplan billing agreements, also fashioned a national PPO out of its individual local plans. With each merger or acquisition among the managed care organizations, the increased size has produced increased clout in the health care marketplace.

Faced with the increased clout of the third-party payers, providers, too, have become fully involved in a massive move toward consolidation. The financial pressures, which caused a wave of hospital closures in the early 1990s, have produced an unprecedented wave of hospital mergers and acquisitions in the mid-1990s. Prior to 1994, annual hospital mergers and acquisitions generally numbered under 40 (Healthcare Advisory Board, 1995). In 1994 that number exploded to 184 transactions, involving over 300 hospitals. The explosion increased in 1995 to 230 transactions, involving 735 hospitals. In effect, about 20 percent of the nation's community hospitals were involved in changes of ownership in 1994 and 1995 (Lutz, 1995).

The nation's for-profit hospital chains led the way with their own multi-billion dollar merger and acquisition transactions, such as the 1994 $5.6 billion acquisition of Healthtrust by the giant Columbia/HCA Corporation (Lutz, 1995), which now owns 337 hospitals according to the January 1, 1996, issue of *Modern Healthcare*. American Medical International was also purchased in 1995 by National Medical Enterprises in a $3.3 billion transaction creating Tenet Healthcare Corporation. The for-profit chains have also been extremely aggressive in their acquisitions of community hospitals. Buoyed by their impressive success in the financial markets, the for-profit chains, their shares often selling for twenty-five times earnings or more, have moved into virtually every major market in the country and have strong rural penetration, often as the sole community provider.

Threatened by the twin demons of massive third-party payer consolidations and massive for-profit provider consolidations with their aggressive market expansions, the not-for-profit providers have countered with their own wave of mergers, acquisitions, joint ventures, and other combinations aimed at bolstering their strength and market viability. Foremost among these would probably be the $3 billion merger of Catholic Healthcare West and Daughters of Charity National Health System-West, although an even larger proposed merger of Sisters of Charity Health Care Systems, Catholic Health Corporation and Franciscan Health System is still pending (Lutz, 1995).

Although the mega-mergers gain the majority of attention and newsprint, an unprecedented extent, combinations of various forms are occurring among the nation's not-for-profit community hospitals. These have taken the form of straight mergers, straight acquisitions, joint-ventures, partnerships, or alliances, forming various types of local or regional networks. However, regardless of the form, the trend is clear: the days of the free-standing, independent community hospital are limited. Bernstein Research projects that about two-thirds of hospitals will be part of multi-hospital systems before the end of the millennium.

Most of these consolidations are promoted, defended, and often approved on the basis of cost savings and reduction of costly duplication of services. It is interesting to note that the free market appears to be accomplishing that for which two decades of regulation and certificate-of-need laws were spectacular in their failure.

The hospitals were not alone in the move to consolidation. Also in the mid-1990s, the organization of the practice of medicine among physicians began a major wave of consolidation. Some of the consolidation came in the form of growth of staff model HMOs and their increasing employment of physicians. However, other forms of consolidation were much more fundamental and startling.

In the early 1990s, a new form of for-profit health care organization emerged: the physician management company (PMC). These PMCs use investor capital to purchase the assets, including receivables and goodwill, of physician practices and employ or contract with the former physician-owners of the practice for provision of medical services to the patients of the practice. The physicians have the opportunity to "cash out" on the value they have built in the practice and turn over the increasingly troublesome business of managing the practice to the professional managers employed by the PMC. The service contracts either provide for salaried compensation for the physicians or some form of sharing of either gross revenue or net income between the physicians and the PMC. Nashville, Tennessee-based PhyCor is a leading example of the new PMCs, now owning the practices of several hundred physicians and managing the practices of over 1,000 more through ownership of IPAs. These PMCs often form alliances with national hospital systems, managed care organizations, and third-party payer systems, further solidifying the for-profit threat to the not-for-profits and the independent physicians.

This threat has, in turn, propelled physicians to form a variety of organizations intended to protect their independence and autonomy, at least as physicians--if not as entrepreneurs. These physician organizations or POs take a variety of forms, from IPAs to partnerships to management service organizations (MSO). They may include physicians in a single specialty or multiple specialties. They may include physicians in a single community, a regional market, or even statewide. The fundamental purpose of the POs is, however, to create leverage in negotiating with managed care organizations, third-party payers, and hospitals to protect the physicians' autonomy and, not coincidentally, their incomes.

A third form of physician consolidation is the rapid development of physician-hospital organizations (PHO). These new provider organizations usually consist of a new entity, jointly owned and controlled by a number of physicians, individually or in partnership, and a hospital. The hospitals generally claim that the purpose of the organizations is to align the interests of the physicians and the hospital, although the opportunity to cement the loyalty of its medical staff is undoubtedly a consideration. Regardless of the ostensible purpose of these unions, the operative purpose is usually to develop contracting leverage to deal with managed care organizations and third-party payers. Indeed, some observers believe that the real purpose of the 3,000 PHOs that have been formed is to "wrest the control of healthcare from the managed care industry" (Findlay, 1995, p. 55).

A fourth, fundamental change in the organization of the practice of medicine presents an interesting historical juxtaposition. Whereas the early hospitals were often developed and owned by physicians, nowadays hospitals are purchasing physician practices and most often employing the physicians. This, too, has become a wide-spread trend in the health care industry. The most frequently purchased practices are those generally classified as primary care--family practice, internal medicine, pediatrics, obstetrics, and gynecology.

The objectives of the physicians in selling are often the same as discussed above in the case of physician sales to the physician management companies although they often feel some greater comfort in selling to known, local management rather than the out-of-state managers of the PMCs. The hospitals' objectives are often to control the flow of specialty referrals, which, in turn, tends to secure a flow of admissions to the hospital. Regardless of the form or objectives of the participants of the consolidation in medical services, one thing appears to be certain: Like the independent community hospital, the entrepreneurial bastion of free enterprise that the nation's physician's practices formerly represented seems to face a limited future.

Whatever the stated or operative objectives and whatever the form taken by the joining of physicians and hospitals, the larger objective has been the development of health care systems that can, on an integrated basis, respond to both the health care needs of patients and the market's demand for cost-effectiveness in delivery of health care. These consolidated organizations have become known as integrated delivery systems. Their integration also usually goes beyond physicians and hospitals and may include such ancillary services as outpatient diagnostic and surgery facilities, home health agencies, and long-term care facilities. The more mature systems often include an owned managed care plan, such as an HMO. The systems may speak of patient care and service in terms of "seamless delivery systems." These seamless systems are those which can provide a continuum of care under a single organizational structure. The market often prefers the simplified dealing of a single, more accountable entity (DeMuro, 1994). However, the real imperative has been the development of systems which can cope with the demands of the managed care market.

The new integrated systems provide an organizational structure for the alignment of incentives between physicians and hospitals. This alignment of incentives usually comes in the form of shared financial risk. The primary mechanism for sharing of financial risks is the capitated contract for the provision of health care services. Under a capitated contract, the integrated organization is paid a fixed monthly amount per enrolled member, or per capita. This fixed payment is generally expected to be compensation in full, in advance, for any and all covered health care services the member may need. It is expressly in lieu of any fee for services provided. Thus, having been paid in advance, the incentive for all providers is to control utilization of all services in order to ensure that the cost of providing the services does not exceed the amount of the capitation payment. The primary tools for controlling utilization are strong internal utilization review and case management activities and strong data systems that allow close tracking of utilization and referral patterns by provider. A growing focus of data systems is in outcomes measurement and management systems, while the current trend in case management activities has a prospective orientation, focusing on the development of care maps or pathways.

E. Summary

The current health care system is characterized by a tumultuous restructuring. Health care providers of all kinds are joining together as never before in a broad range of integrative combinations. The combinations include horizontal consolidations of like providers as well as vertical consolidations of various elements in the continuum of care. All of the organizations have the common objectives of improving the delivery of care and respond to the market demands for more cost-effective delivery of care.

Regardless of the forms of consolidation, the objectives of the participants or the resulting organizations, or the tactics employed, it is clear that meeting the demands of the market, as manifest in the popularity of modern managed care plans, is the new imperative in the business side of health care delivery.

II. CREATING THE FUTURE OF U. S. HEALTH CARE: POLITICS AND VALUES

At the turn of the century there do not appear to be any effective countervailing forces to the managed care imperative that is rapidly reshaping health services in the U. S. There are, of course, significant concerns about managed care, both on the political left and right. Managed care has been criticized by some liberals as tantamount to corporatized rationing of care to the middle classes and an abandonment of the community service mission of health care (Starr, 1982; Stephens, 1989). On the right, some conservatives have called it organizationally socialistic and anti-individualist (Ponnuru, 1995). However, to date this opposition has not resulted in the establishment of any economically viable systemwide alternative that could win sufficient popular and political support.

A. The Liberal Response

During the twentieth century, American liberals have generally felt that the access and financial weaknesses of the U. S. health care system were signs of deep sociocultural weaknesses and pathologies. The U. S. could only redeem itself and provide reasonable access and cost-containment through the establishment of a unified and comprehensive system of national health insurance (Rothman, 1993). At some points, it did seem to follow logically from the precedents of the Franklin Roosevelt's New Deal, from Social Security to health security.

Liberals have largely abandoned the notion, popular in the '70s, of establishing a U. S. national health service similar to that found in the United Kingdom. However, in recent years, they have found the single payer Canadian health care system to be particularly attractive (Grumbach, 1991). The Canadian system, unlike the British, does not nationalize health services delivery; most care is provided by nonprofit and private entities, as in the U. S. However, government does monopolize most health insurance options, and significant health care charges are paid by the nation's federal and provincial governments. By centralizing health care insurance and financing in government, the single payer system gives the government monopoly market power as a purchaser, which undoubtedly enhances cost containment (Jacobs, 1991; Jones, Reilly and Broyles, 1992). Since it eliminates employer-based insurance, a single payer system also permits the establishment of universal insurance coverage, with common standards of access and care for all citizens --a cherished ideological goal of liberals (Evans, 1992). Since establishing such a system in the '60s, Canada has had a lower health care inflation rate than the U. S., while providing access to high quality care, particularly with respect to primary care services (Jacobs, 1991).

B. The Conservative Response

The conservative response has been to note that the single payer system does not eliminate the need for rationing of care. Waiting times for advanced medical procedures can be lengthy, and Canadians have less access to some types of high technology care than Americans (at least, insured Americans). More generally, conservatives ridicule the potential competence of the U. S. federal and state governments to manage such a system. ("If you like the U. S. Postal Service, you'll love the U. S. Health Care Service.") Liberals retort that U. S. managed care networks are increasingly carrying out the same technology rationing that conservatives criticize in Canada, and that universal access in such a system would reduce the need for high technology acute care by enhancing preventive and primary care services.

Both sides have made reasonable arguments for and against a single payer system. The chief weakness of the liberal position is essentially political. With the single payer system, as well as for other comprehensive reform options, liberals have repeatedly failed to make a persuasive case for their proposals to the American people and a majority of their elected representatives. Liberalism in general has declined as a viable political/ideological force in the U. S. in the last twenty years (Ladd, 1989; Barone and Ujifusa, 1995). Whatever the merits of their case, liberal blueprints for national health insurance were considered at some level in almost every decade since the '30s, and were rejected each time--most recently, in 1994, with the demise of the Clinton Administration's Health Security Act. That rejection, along with the subsequent Democratic Party losses in the 1994 Congressional elections, has probably ensured that the liberal ideal of a national system of health care for all citizens is politically dead, at least for the forseeable future. Even most liberal health policymakers are now reconciled to developing and promoting incremental reforms that are more politically attractive and that might lead to universal coverage at some point in the future (Feder and Levitt, 1995).

Conservatives have their own complaints about the managed care revolution. Many of them are traditionally sympathetic with the physicians (who are themselves disproportionately well-to-do conservatives). They are deeply disturbed by the apparent impact that managed care is having on the autonomy of physicians and patients. Under the prevailing system of health services organizations during most of the twentieth century, the physician was highly respected and paid, with almost complete professional autonomy. Patients have had a great deal of freedom to choose their own physician, at least theoretically. Government was restricted to a supportive role--subsidizing health services technology and physician training, and preserving physician control over the system through regulation (Johnson and Jones, 1993).

That arrangement was never completely stable. One might argue that third-party insurance payers would have inevitably demanded a greater say over physician decisionmaking, given the constantly increasing demand for resources by the health care sector. Nonetheless, traditional physician autonomy was greatly damaged by the establishment of Medicare and Medicaid in the '60s. The provision of wider access without adequate financial controls greatly hastened the onset of the turmoil currently taking place within health care. While conservatives might criticize big government, they could not ignore the impending public bankruptcy of Medicare and Medicaid. It was in fact big government--headed by the most popular conservative President in this century, Ronald Reagan--which used its regulatory and market power to impose prospective payment on hospitals. It was also the business community--traditionally conservative--which found spiraling health care costs to be intolerable, and thus demanded greater controls on medical decisionmaking (Starr, 1982). These sentiments, however, have led to managed care systems that some conservatives consider corporate collectivism, profoundly antagonistic to traditional values in health care.

Comprehending the potentially revolutionary impact of managed care organizations, some conservatives have cast about for alternative system reforms that would preserve both physician and patient autonomy, while introducing effective market controls over costs. At this time, one of the most widely discussed conservative alternatives to current forms of managed care is the Medical Savings Account (MSA) (Goodman and Musgrave, 1994). The variations on MSA proposals are too many and too complex to cover here, but most MSAs would provide for tax-sheltered savings accounts that individuals would use to cover out-of-pocket medical expenses. These accounts could be funded by employer and employee contributions, as with current employer-based insurance, or they could be entirely funded by the individual. In most plans, remaining medical insurance policies would primarily cover catastrophic expenses, and deductibles would be much higher than is customary today--$2000 to $3000, as opposed to current averages of $200 to $500. Since they would be paying most non-catastrophic medical expenses out of pocket from their MSAs, individuals would have to directly make more of their own health care spending decisions. They would therefore presumably have greater incentives to shop carefully (Pauly and Goodman, 1995). In many plans, MSA holders could keep the difference between contributions and expenditures, and use the money for other purposes, or roll it over into the next enrollment year.

For some conservatives, the advantage of MSAs is that they would theoretically provide for consumer cost containment incentives while avoiding the aggregation of individuals into large plans as is the case with most managed care plans today. (However, some forms of MSAs are in fact designed to fit into managed care systems, so the basic concept does not depend on their elimination.) Since individual consumers could purchase services independently, the overwhelming systemwide incentives for large managed care networks would be greatly reduced. Liberals strongly oppose MSAs, arguing that such an insurance option would provide an incentive for healthy and affluent individuals to drop out of conventional insurance plans, leaving them with relatively poorer and sicker clients and those less economically viable (Chollet, 1995; Nichols, 1995). Liberals contend that employer-based and/or governmental insurance is fairer since everyone has access to a wide range of health services. Conservatives respond that such fairness is really a large redistribution of wealth and service access from healthier and wealthier to poorer and less healthy people and consider this to be an unacceptable restriction on individual freedom to choose (Goodman and Musgrave, 1994). Although at this time the case for at least an experimental approach to MSAs is gradually gaining acceptance, it is unlikely that they will be strongly supported by the federal government with either branch of Congress or the Presidency controlled by the Democratic Party.

C. The Future

The apparent inevitability of managed care is thus not based on the ideological enthusiasm of liberals or conservatives. Even most nonideological moderates are aware (often from firsthand experience) that managed care often involves disturbing restrictions on enrollee choice of care and caregivers, possible negative impacts on the quality of care delivered, and significant gatekeeping and other bureaucratic obstacles. However, at the present managed care is in the same position with respect to U. S. health care organization that former British Prime Minister Winston Churchill saw democracy in with respect to government organization--the worst option, except for all of the rest. Despite managed care's very real problems, all other major reform options are politically unacceptable to one or another blocking faction in the national health policymaking arena. And most politically influential groups, particularly those paying for health care, find the old fee-for-service, cost-plus reimbursement system to be simply unsustainable.

In the near future, the most important and interesting policy and management debates will not be over the existence of managed care. Rather, they will be concerned with the best ways in which managed care networks can accommodate their cost containment mandate with national concerns about the quality of and access to care. There is a now a growing and sophisticated understanding within the managed care industry of the need to cultivate more customer friendly services. Successful managed care networks, like other viable service industry organizations, will have to provide quality services that their enrollee customers value (Roper, 1995). If they succeed, they will dominate health services delivery for the foreseeable future. If they do not--if health care is fundamentally incompatible with modern capitalist organization or if large numbers of middle class citizens find that they are excluded from necessary medical services--then unpredictable and radical change may in fact occur in the U. S. health care system, either from the political left or right.

Even assuming that the managed care imperative proves long-lasting, there are still major issues that government policymakers, in collaboration with the American public, must resolve.

1. The Problem of the Uninsured

This most serious problem must be addressed by public policymakers. However efficient and effective a market-oriented managed care system is, it cannot account for the needs of those who do not have the money to participate in it. This is the biggest weakness of the U. S. system of employer-provided insurance. In the long run, the basic legitimacy of a health care system which does not provide tens of millions of citizens with necessary services can be seriously questioned. The lack of some level of universal access will also continue to create excessive public health costs through the neglect of primary/preventive health care by the uninsured, as well as fear among currently insured middle class citizens about the consequences of unemployment in the dynamic turn-of-century U. S. economy.

On the other hand, those who would remedy this with comprehensive, systemwide reform need to remember that the vast majority of Americans are generally satisfied with their own health care arrangements and will not accept their disruption by governmental fiat. A gradual extension of Medicaid or the provision of health insurance purchase vouchers to low income citizens have been promising options under discussion (Pauly, et al., 1992; Holahan, et al., 1995). At this point, however, there is no public consensus on a proper path to follow on this critical issue. Equally importantly, there is no national political willingness to pay the costs for any such reforms. Perhaps the widespread state-level experimentation currently underway with Medicaid will lead to viable innovations that can be nationally reproduced at a price that a majority of middle-class voters can accept.

2. The Ground Rules of Health Services Rationing

Establishing ground rules associated with rationing of health services,particularly of costly life-and-death high technology procedures, will have to be gradually worked out in the public arena. In the last few years, the state of Oregon has provided a useful example of government developed and publicly agreed upon criteria for allocating limited health services dollars on the basis of clinical justification and social need (Thorne, 1992). As critics have noted, however, the Oregon rationing guidelines fall only on Medicaid recipients, not politically influential middle class citizens with private insurance (Rosenbaum, 1992). There are also major moral questions with explicit rationing systems that need to be thoroughly debated and resolved within society before they can be considered truly legitimate (Daniels, 1991; Engelhardt, 1992). Of course, those debating the morality of rationing care need to keep in mind that all health care systems ration in one way or another. It is not obvious why explicit rationing as used in Oregon is somehow less moral than the implicit rationing through insurance status that this nation currently uses.

It is likely that public policymakers will have to extend their considerations of proper rationing to the private sector since managed care networks are applying everbroader controls on high cost services. The mid-'90s controversy in several states over HMO refusal to reimburse automatically for normal childbirth hospital stays of greater than 24 hours is only one of many such issues which lawmakers will have to confront (Nordheimer, 1995). Given the difficulties of conducting serious political debates in an electoral system that emphasizes sound-bite campaign slogans, it is likely that the U. S. will be struggling with public policy toward rationing for some time to come.

3. The Environment of Effective Health Care

Ideally, effective health care is only part of an environment that protects and empowers individuals, families and communities. As public health advocates have noted, most major causes of morbidity and mortality are significantly connected to lifestyle choices with respect to diet, exercise, sexual expression, and consumption of cigarettes and alcohol (U. S. Department of Health and Human Services, 1991; Koop, 1995). Effective health education would contribute more dramatically to human well-being and save more money than the most careful services rationing scheme. The concern for healthy communities must also include efforts to address issues that are not normally thought of as health care matters such as violence and environmental degradation.

SUMMARY

Ultimately, the U. S., like other nations, will best advance and safeguard health by creating and preserving communities and families which care for each other's well-being and growth. Though it will inevitably entail controversy in specific cases, government policymakers, along with all citizens, will have to be willing to develop and clearly articulate standards of right and wrong. Though it should have compassion for those involved, a healthy society cannot consider individually and socially destructive behavior such as teenage pregnancy, drug addiction, unsafe sex and domestic violence to be morally acceptable lifestyle choices. Nor can it consider, whatever their constitutional/legal status, capitalist activities that foster such behavior (be they popular entertainment that glorifies amoral and predatory behavior or the legalized drug-dealing of cigarette manufacturers) as morally acceptable business practices. A society must ceaselessly work to reconcile the values of liberty and community, freedom and responsibility, if it to be truly healthy. Part of this effort concerns positive change within the U. S. health care system. But another more important part will involve individual and collective transformation within American society itself.

REFERENCES

Appleby, C. (1995, May 5). Health care's new heavyweights. *Hospitals and Health Networks, 26.*

Bader, N. (1993, December). Retaining freedom of choice in a managed care plan, *Business & Health*, 62-66.

Barone, M. and Ujifusa, G. (1995). The Almanac of American Politics 1996. *National Journal,* Washington, DC.

Business & Health (1993). *Issues and trends (November)*, 20.

Chollet, D. (1995). Why the Pauly/Goodman proposal won't work. *Health Affairs, 14,(2):* 273-274.

Cobbs, D. L.. ed. (1989). *Preferred Provider Organizations: Strategies for Sponsors and Network Providers.* American Hospital Association Publishing, Inc., Chicago, IL.

Currey, R. (1992). Medicine for sale. *Whittle Direct Books*, 8-11.

Daniels, N. (1991). Is the Oregon rationing plan fair? *Journal of the American Medical Association,* 265: 2232-2235.

DeMuro, P. R. (1994, January). Provider Alliances: Key to health care reform. *Healthcare Financial Management*, 27-32.

Engelhardt, H. T. (1992). *Why a two-tier system of health care delivery is morally unavoidable. In Rationing America's Health Care: The Oregon Plan and Beyond.* (M. A. Strosberg, et al., eds.). Brookings Institution, Washington, DC: 196-207.

Evans, R. G. (1992). Canada: The real issues. *Journal of Health Politics, Policy and Law, 17:* 739-762.

Feder, J. and Levitt, L. (1995). Steps toward universal coverage. *Health Affairs, 14*(1): 140-149.

Findlay, S. (1995, November). A bend in the river. *Business & Health,* 55.

Goodman, J. C. and Musgrave, G. L. (1994). *Patient Power: The Free Enterprise Alternative to the Clinton Health Plan.* Cato Institute, Washington, DC.

Grumbach, K. (1991). Liberal benefits, conservative spending: The Physicians for a National Health Program proposal. *Journal of the American Medical Association, 265:* 2549-2554.

Healthcare Advisory Board. (1995). Hospital Networking: Strategy Briefing for Chief Executives. Health Advisory Board, Washington, DC.

Holahan, J. F., Coughlin, T., Ku, L., Lipson, D. J. and Rajan, S. (1995). Insuring the poor through Medicaid 1115 waivers. *Health Affairs, 14*(1): 200-217.

Inforum, Inc. (1994). *Inforum's PULSE Managed Care Summary.* Inform, Inc., Nashville, TN.

Jacobs, P. (1991). *The Economics of Health and Medical Care.* Aspen Publishers, Inc., Gaithersburg, MD.

Johnson J. A. and Jones, W. J. (1993). *The American Medical Association and Organized Medicine.* Garland Press, New York, NY.

Jones, W. J., Reilly, B. J. and Broyles, R. W. (1992). Cost containment, access and American health care financing: Getting beyond the shell game. *Journal of Health and Human Resources Administration, 14:* 290-306.

Kongstvedt, P. R., ed. (1993). The managed health care handbook , 2nd ed. Aspen Publishers, Inc., Rockville, MD.

Koop, C. E. (1995). A personal role in health care reform. *American Journal of Public Health 85:* 759-760.

Ladd, E. C. (1989). The American Polity, 3rd ed. W. W. Norton & Company, New York, NY.

Lutz, S. (1995). 1995: A record year for hospital deals. *Modern Healthcare (12/18-25):* 43-44.

National Leadership Commission (1989). *For the Health of a Nation.* Health Administration Press, Ann Arbor, MI.

Nichols, N. M. (1995). Medical savings accounts and risk segmentation. *Health Affairs, 14*(2): 275-276.

Nordheimer, J. (1995). New mothers gain second day in hospital: Whitman signs a bill to fight curbs on care. *New York Times, June 29:* B1.

Pauly, M. V., Danzon, P., Feldstein, P. J. and Hoff, J. (1992). *Responsible National Health Insurance.* American Enterprise Institute Press, Washington, DC.

Pauly, M. V. and Goodman, J. C. (1995). Tax credits for health insurance and medical savings accounts. *Health Affairs, 14*(1): 126-139.

Ponnuru, R. (1995). Mediacare. *National Review, 47:* 24-26.

Roper, W. L. (1995). Quality assurance in the competitive marketplace. *Health Affairs, 14*(1): 120-122.

Rosenbaum, S. (1992). Poor women, poor children, poor policy. In *Rationing America's Medical Care: The Oregon Plan and Beyond* (M. A. Strosberg et al., eds.), Brookings Institution, Washington, DC: 91-106.

Rothman, D. J. (1993). A century of failure: Health care reform in America. *Journal of Health Politics, Policy and Law, 18:* 271-287.

Starr, P. (1982). *The Transformation of American Medicine.* Basic Books, Inc., New York, NY.

Stevens, R. (1989). *In Sickness and in Wealth.* Basic Books, Inc., New York, NY.

Thorne, J. I. (1992). The Oregon plan approach to comprehensive and rational health care. In *Rationing America's Medical Care: The Oregon Plan and Beyond* (M. A. Strosberg, et al., eds.), Brookings Institution, Washington, DC:24-36.

Torrens, P. R. (1993). Historical evolution and overview of health services in the United States. In *Introduction to Health Services* (S. J. Williams and P. R. Torrens, eds.), Delmar Publishers, Inc., Albany, NY: 3-28.

U. S. Congressional Budget Office (1995). *Reducing the Deficit: Spending and Revenue Options.* Government Printing Office, Washington, DC.

U. S. Department of Health and Human Services. (1991). *Healthy People 2000.* U. S. Government
   Printing Office, Washington, DC.
Weeks, L. E. and Berman, H. J. (1985). *Shapers of American Health Care Policy: An Oral History.*
   Health Administration Press, Ann Arbor, MI.

8.
MANAGED CARE

Winfield C. Towles, *The Horizon Group, Inc., Mt. Pleasant, SC*
Veronica Elliott, *Birch and Davis Associates, Inc., Silver Spring, MD*

Managed care is defined as "any organized, systematic intervention that can favorably affect the quality or cost of health care by linking purchasers, insurers and providers" (Council on Graduate Medical Education: Sixth Report, 1995). This definition captures the essential characteristics of all managed care: concerns about quality and cost within a construct of formal organizational linkages. Managed care organizations are typically of three types: Health Maintenance Organizations (HMOs), Preferred Provider Organizations (PPOs) and Managed Indemnity Plans (MIPs).

This chapter traces the evolution of managed care, describes the types of organizations that implement the managed care approach, distinguishes the essential components of any managed care model, and predicts the future of this concept. It does so at a time of rapid and dramatic change in the overall health care industry in the United States.

The American health care system is in a period of significant adjustment, with the basic tenets of many of the traditional approaches being challenged and the roles of many of the traditional players being re-cast. The emergence of managed care is both a cause and an effect of much of this turmoil. The coming together of the concepts that encompass managed care has principally occurred only in the past five to ten years; both the concepts themselves and their synergistic relationship within the managed care model continue to evolve.

I. THE EMERGENCE OF MANAGED CARE AS THE DOMINANT MODEL

The seeds of many of the elements of today's health care system are found in earlier times. A little less than 100 hundred years ago, physicians collected payment for their services by billing patients once or twice a year according to a fee-for-service (FFS) schedule established by the local medical society. Care was often given to the poor at no charge, with the rich being expected to pay a little extra—this was the original concept of cross-subsidy. A small number of Americans were covered by insurance through fraternal organizations, trade unions, or commercial insurance carriers. These plans were designed to give income protection with occasion fixed cash benefits for medical expenses. The benefit to cover wage loss was typically about three times that to cover hospital expenses. A few remote lumber and mining companies sponsored "prepaid plans" through the establishment of contracts with physicians, who were paid at a fixed rate per member. This forerunner of capitation was heartily condemned by organized medicine. At least two cities, New York and Philadelphia, paid per diem rates for hospital care of the injured. Generally, however, Americans paid 90 percent of their medical expenses out-of-pocket. It is worth noting that Germany adopted compulsory health insurance in 1883, followed by England in 1911.

About this same time there was some initial support in the U.S. for national health insurance, even among physicians. However, this support abated, in part due to disappointment with the bureaucracy of Workman's Compensation, as well as fear of future wage losses by physicians. With the coming of World War I, organized medicine defeated national health insurance in the United States by suggesting that it was a German notion.

By the early 1920s hospital costs and deficits had increased. During the Depression, both hospital occupancy and receipts plummeted. Out of economic necessity, hospitals developed prepaid arrangements with consumers, with members contributing a certain amount each month in exchange for 21 days of guaranteed coverage. During the mid-1930s, multi-hospital arrangements were established and, in many states, these organizations received exemption from insurance regulation and tax exempt status in exchange for service to the entire community. This was the beginning of Blue Cross, giving them a competitive edge over other organizations offering health insurance. Under these plans, hospitals were paid in full but there was no coverage for out-of-hospital expenses. The premiums were the same to all subscribers, regardless of the potential expense of the group--a rating system known as community rating. Later, Blue Shield was established with similar arrangements in order to pay physicians.

To compete during this same time, commercial insurance carriers established indemnity coverage. Indemnity coverage reimburses the patient, not the hospital, for medical costs incurred by the patient. The amount reimbursed was often a fixed dollar amount per hospital day, a concept that became per diem or per admission, later known as global payment and a forerunner of today's DRG. The person enrolled in the program paid the provider and was responsible for those provider charges that were above and beyond the insurance payment, a concept known as balanced billing. Towards the end of the 1930s, payments by many insurance companies were extended to cover surgery and other physician services (comprehensive coverage) or to cover expenses such as prescription drugs and physician office visits.

Several prepaid plans were initiated in the 1930s. However, growth was slow due to opposition by organized medicine. Providers of prepaid plans were often barred from membership in medical societies, such membership being a prerequisite for hospital privileges. During World War II, wartime price stabilization policies capped wages. These caps encouraged employers and workers to bargain over noncash benefits (i.e., insurance, disability), resulting in the spread of health insurance to many millions of workers. Although Blue Cross and Blue Shield had initially seized the market and had special tax status and an established network of hospitals, indemnity insurers were now able to compete with lower prices. This was due in part to the nature of indemnity insurance with enrollees being reimbursed for a specified percentage of charges, premiums being determined on the basis of the past cost experience of the group (a concept referred to as experience rating), and employers being involved in plan administration and benefit design.

Harry Truman made national health a campaign issue in the 1950s, but the proposed legislation was defeated. It is felt that President Truman's initiative led to the eventual passage of Medicare and Medicaid in 1965 (Starr, P.,1982). Recognizing the rapid rise in health care costs during the Nixon administration, the HMO Act of 1973 was passed to develop competition in health care. The focus of this legislation was to stimulate the interest of consumers and providers in making health care delivery available through HMO plans.

National interest in managed care in the 1970s and 1980s derived from a growing concern for both cost and access. Health care costs were increasing consistently at a rate considerably higher than inflation while simultaneously, large numbers of people were without access to care because they lacked comprehensive health insurance. Generally, employers were under pressure to offer insurance to their workers, but could not tolerate the high rates being charged for indemnity programs. Managed care, with its emphasis on efficiency, preventive care and predictable, competitive premiums, emerged as a powerful response to these pressures.

In 1994, about 55 million Americans were enrolled in an HMO and a further 79 million in a preferred provider organization (PPO), bringing the total percentage of Americans belonging to a managed care program to 51.4 percent. By way of contrast, note that 38.9 million (15 percent) were uninsured, 32 million (12 percent) were covered by Medicare, and 37 million (14 percent) were covered by Medicaid.

Managed care organizations are more likely to flourish in metropolitan markets, especially in the 30 largest metropolitan areas. California currently has greater than 85 percent of its eligible population statewide enrolled in managed care. The managed care industry continues to consolidate, although at a slower pace than in the early 1990s, through merger, acquisitions and closings, resulting in fewer but larger managed care organizations. Currently, there are 556 HMO plans operating in the United States and about 799 PPO plans, with the majority of HMO plans being owned by chains.

Enrollment in managed care continues to grow with the introduction of out-of-network options to the basic HMO plan. These PPO-like options are commonly referred to as point-of-service plans (otherwise known as "leaks" or "opt outs"). These point-of service plans allow enrollees to choose within a network of HMO providers or out-of-network providers of their choice but at a lesser coverage if they do so. This lesser coverage may be in the form of a higher copay, coinsurance or deductible, or between the difference in what the plan pays and the provider charges (a term known as balance billing). More than half the nation's HMOs now have point-of-service products. These point-of-service plans have been credited with an increase in HMO enrollment of 20 percent in 1994, as opposed to PPO growth of only 3 percent. The trend toward blurring the differences between the PPO and the HMO models of managed care will continue (Hoechst Marion Roussel, 1995).

Some observers have identified and categorized differential stages of managed care growth and penetration that are experienced across geographic areas (see Figure 1). These stages provide useful insight into the changes which cities and regions can expect as managed health care delivery and financing systems mature (Council on Graduate Medical Education, 1995).

Figure 1 - Stages of Managed Care Growth

Stage I: Unstructured	Stage II: Loose framework	Stage III: Consolidation	Stage IV: Managed competition
Low (<20%) HMO Penetration	HMO enrollment balloons (20%-40%)	A few large HMOs emerge	Employers from coalitions to purchase health care
Independent Providers Hospitals Physicians Fragmentation of care	Providers experience: Price pressures Network formation Hospitals Physicians Some excess capacity	Providers: capitation of group practice with some IDS formation Hospitals: erosion of margins Economic credential	Providers form Integrated delivery systems
Employer activity: none	Employers activity: Purchasing coalitions	Employers demand data on quality	Formal coalitions
Few Payer demands: fragmented	Payers less fragmented: demand for greater price predictability	Consolidated Payers: Elimination of excess testing with evidence of long-term efficiency	Highly consolidated payers

II. TYPES OF MANAGED CARE ORGANIZATIONS

One of the ways in which managed care is distinguished from other forms of health insurance is its dependence on linkages among purchasers, insurers, and providers. This section discusses the many forms these linkages take, the organizational structures that have evolved to accommodate these linkages, and the differences between the various types.

There are three basic managed care delivery systems: The Health Maintenance Organization (HMO), the Preferred Provider Organization (PPO), and the Managed

Indemnity Plan (MIP). HMOs provide prepaid health care, making a defined package of health services available to its members (or enrollees) in exchange for a fixed monthly premium. Care may be provided directly by the HMO or through contract with a network of physicians and other providers. PPOs are networks through which health insurance companies and employer health benefit plans contract with a panel of independent physicians for discounted health care services. MIPs are indemnity plans that use varying degrees of utilization management.

There are two major types of HMOs: the Staff or Group HMO and the Network or IPA HMO. They are distinguished by the relationship between the HMO and the physicians who provide services to members. Both types are usually at risk for the costs of care and therefore most often control costs by requiring patients to be referred to specialists through primary care doctors (also known as gatekeepers) who accept some risk-sharing agreement. This is referred to as a closed access model. A few HMOs allow members to seek care from existing primary care or specialists without referral which is known as an open access model.

Staff or Group HMOs use physicians in fully integrated multispecialty group practices and doctors are usually salaried and receive a bonus based on productivity. They may work either directly for the plan (Staff Model HMO), or for a physician group practice which has an exclusive contract with the plan (Group Model HMO). These physicians manage their own utilization with the help of their own medical directors and physician committees. Group models have shown significant gains in utilization control in California by using a collaborative approach with hospitals in coordinating care.

IPA and Network HMOs do not have physician providers on salary. Rather, IPA HMOs use community-based solo or small group practices while the Network HMOs use larger group practices to provide services to members. IPAs frequently use fee for service (FFS) or capitation while network models most often use capitation to pay each group, which then pays the individual physician. The IPA/Network model with almost 75 percent of current total membership is said to create the majority of their savings from utilization review and discounts, although more recent reports suggest improvement in cost consciousness due in part to provider profiling and feedback and greater usage of financial risk in more advanced markets (Gold, 1995).

A PPO consists of a network of doctors who agree to provide services to the managed care organization's members for discounted fees and the acceptance of utilization review. The member has the option of pursuing care outside of the network and paying more for this option. On the other hand, an MIP offers free choice of providers and FFS, with no prepayment for care, but the insurer exercises some degree of utilization control to manage costs.

In reality, one fifth of HMOs are combination model types. For example, a group model plan may subcontract with an IPA or network plan to get coverage in a certain area, resulting in a combination plan. Point-of-service (POS) plans are now available in about half of all managed care plans. Thirty-eight percent of all HMOs offer employers triple option plans. Triple option plans include a choice of HMO, PPO, or indemnity plans (Hoechst Marion Roussel, 1995).

A more recent innovation in managed care is the introduction of integrated delivery systems. An integrated delivery system is a system of organizations, practice groups, and professionals that assume responsibility for delivery of a complete array of health care services including primary, specialty, hospital care and other related health services. They in fact take full risk (capitation) for contracted services that may include only the professional services (primary and specialty), institutional services (i.e., hospital, subacute, rehab, emergency room and home health) and other services. Integrated health systems have been more likely to contract with network model HMOs and Group model HMOs due to the ease of single signature and capitation payments.

Other forms of physician organizations (PO) and physician hospital organizations (PHO) are subsets of the integrated delivery system. These entities contract various third party payers, managed care plans, or self insured groups to make the services of the POs and PHOs available to persons covered by those payers.

III. MANAGED CARE PLAN OPERATIONS

All managed care organizations and plans have common administrative functions. Several forces are shaping the relative importance of these functions and the way that they are performed. The most potent force in the mid-1990s is the pressure to reduce both medical and administrative costs (lower the medical loss ratio) in order for the managed care organization to be more competitive. (An additional powerful force is the availability of technology that streamlines operations and connects payers, providers, and consumers.) The availability of technology can have a very significant effect on both cost and quality of care as an additional powerful force.

Administrative functions common to all managed care organizations are
- Benefit design
- Premium development
- Payment methods
- Marketing
- Claims administration
- Customer support
- Contracts
- Risk and underwriting
- Medical management

A. Benefit Design

Managed Care Organizations (MCOs) offer rich benefits to their members at lower costs which is accomplished by plan design. HMOs, in particular, offer access to all effective forms of care including preventive care, routine office visits, pharmacy, physical therapy, and mental health treatments through a series of contracts with providers. This benefit design includes incentives and disincentives, such as deductibles and copayments, utilization requirements, the use of provider panels, no benefit or benefit differentials for out-of-network, and formularies.

Controlling the volume and intensity of services provided by physicians and others has been, and will probably remain, the primary method employed to contain health care costs. To do this, however, without paying close attention to quality of care, does not lead to long-term gains. This section describes some of the methods used in controlling unnecessary expenses while maintaining continuous improvement in quality of care.

Copayment is an amount of money that the member or insured person pays directly to a provider at the time services are rendered. Copayments are important in reducing overall utilization because as out-of-pocket costs to the patient decrease and the cost of care for the actual service is dissociated from the cost of care, demand for more services is stimulated. In economics this phenomenon is referred to as moral hazard. Free care results in a 40% increase in health care expenditures. Evidence suggests that the effect of copayments on expenditures is nearly twice as great as that of capitation. Moral hazard can be thought of in terms of a sale. As the cost of service to the recipient is reduced, the number of services increase up to a point. Copayments can be either of two types: (1) deductible–amount the patient must pay before insurance plans pay anything; (2) coinsurance–a percentage of provider charge paid by the patient after the deductible has been paid. For example, a plan may require payment by the patient of the first $250 of care in any given calendar year with the patient paying 25 percent of any charges thereafter.

A rise in copayment, while reducing the plan liability results in several outcomes:
- It reduces the total services provided by the plan.
- It may reduce the competitiveness of the insurance company with other insurers.
- Raising copayments within a company amounts to a reduction in benefits and may cause some distrust.
- Raising copayments reduces health care access for lower paid workers more than for management.
- Copayments can be offset by other insurances (if available).

B. Premium Development

At the most basic level, an HMO's actual financial results can vary from expected levels since revenues or expenses can also vary from predicted levels. Revenues and expenses will vary from predicted levels because assumptions underlying revenue and expense forecasts may not be realized. A useful way to identify key factors that give rise to variations from expected revenues and expenses is to analyze HMO premium development. Step one of the process requires estimating the cost of providing covered health services for an average enrollee. Figure 2 depicts a typical premium development. The second step involves allocating the average monthly cost per member to the various contract categories used in an HMO rate structure. This is referred to as day rate and is expressed as monthly amounts per person, or per member per month (PMPM). Once these allocated monies are made to the different categories, they are then combined with a contribution for administrative expenses and profit which then gives the tentative gross premium. A gross premium is developed for each contract category which should carry its own financial burden. While there is no legal requirement that an individual premium category contains a close relationship between cost and price, the fundamental objective should be to control each of those categories.

There are two restraints on pricing. They are 1) a need to get the premium approved by the regulatory authorities and 2) a need to be competitive within the marketplace. The final step, therefore, in the pricing process compares the tentative growth premiums to the prevailing premiums of competitors and modifying tentative premiums as appropriate (van Steenwyk, 1989).

Figure 2 - Development of an Estimated Gross Premium

30%	Hospital Inpatient
10%	Outpatient Services
33%	Physician & Professional Services
8%	Outpatient Drugs
4%	SNF, Home health, DME, OP Ancillary
14%	Administration & Profit

C. Payment Methods

There are a variety of methods used by managed care organizations to reimburse for the services received by its members. The most common of these are charge-based, cost-based, and prospective payment methods.

1. Charge-Based Reimbursement

Physician payment for health care has traditionally been based on fee for service (FFS) — a fee is rendered for each service delivered. Under the FFS system, expenditures increase not only if the fees themselves increase but also if more units of service are charged or more expensive services are substituted for less expensive ones. FFS is also referred to as charge-based reimbursement because the payer pays billed charges. In the past, payments to physicians by insurers were based on historical charges from the individual physician as well as those from colleagues in the same speciality and geographic area — a system known as customary, prevailing and reasonable (CPR) or usual, customary and reasonable (UCR). The CPR system encouraged inflationary billing so that the amount charged would gradually increase, allowing the profile to calculate future CPR charges higher and resulting in increased payments. It also encouraged interregional differences in pay schedules and a shift in incentives toward procedural services like cardiovascular surgery.

In 1992, Medicare introduced the resource-based relative-value scale (RBRVS) as its new fee schedule. Developed by HSIAO, this schedule considers such factors as physician time, effort, training, practice experience, malpractice and the payment schedule. RBRVS is fast becoming the industry standard for physician payment, with payers establishing conversion factors that are easily multiplied by the updated HCFA relative value unit. Thus, for example, a payer can agree to pay the RBRVS plus or minus a given percentage for the performance of a particular service.

Other methods which have been developed to alter payment schedules, include
- Balance billing–the amount that physicians are permitted to receive from patients in excess of the amount the plan will pay;
- Expenditure targets–the desired level of total expenditures is determined and budgeted prospectively and spending is limited to that amount;
- Negotiated charges–a percentage of discount from billed/UCR in exchange for higher volume.

Virtually all managed care organizations have a contract clause prohibiting balance billing, as does Medicare. Expenditure targets are used by Medicare and a similar methodology is used by managed care plans when they receive a cap and pay their physicians. For example, if one provider within the group is found to be a high utilizer, his fee-for-service payment could be decreased by a percentage of over-utilization to reach a budget neutral position. The negotiation of charges likewise can be exchanged for a lower conversion factor against the Medicare Relative Value Unit (RVU), thus replacing this as a payment methodology in the future.

Charge-based reimbursement can also apply to institutions such as hospitals. Full FFS charges or percentage from billed charges is frequently used by hospitals in early managed care markets and/or rural areas where managed care organizations have little negotiating room. This methodology is also frequently used by PPOs.

2. Cost-Based Reimbursement

Cost-based reimbursement can be either retrospective or prospective. Under the retrospective cost method, the payer agrees to pay a provider certain costs that are incurred in providing services to the payer's enrollees. Typically, the insurer makes periodic interim payments to the provider, and then a final reconciliation is made after the contract period expires and all costs have worked their way through the provider's accounting system. In general, under this methodology, reasonable costs are defined as (1) operating costs for labor and material, (2) capital costs for depreciation, interest-expense, lease payments, and return on equity for investor-owned hospitals, and (3) costs associated with medical educational programs.

Under the prospective cost method, costs are determined in advance, so insurers know beforehand what the cost will be for services, but they do not know which services, and in what amount, will be consumed. This method includes a provision for retroactive adjustment when cost increases exceed some pre-set limit.

Both retrospective and prospective cost-based reimbursement systems provide little incentive to reduce excessive services and overly long hospital stays. Fortunately, these methods have become less and less common in managed care situations.

3. Prospective Payment Reimbursement

In a prospective payment system, rates paid by insurers are determined in advance and are tied neither directly to reimbursable costs nor to billed charges. Prospective payment includes four common payment units.

a. Per Diagnosis or Per Procedure (Outpatient)

Per diagnosis or per procedure, the provider is paid a rate based on the patient diagnosis (procedure). This method of payment is used by Medicare under the DRG system for inpatient care and Ambulatory Surgical Groupings (ASG) for outpatient surgery and places the risk with a provider for any costs which exceed the payment of each patient's diagnosis or procedure. In theory, higher cost diagnoses and procedures carry higher prospective payments commensurate with level of difficulty. The DRG, however, is infrequently used in HMOs due to its fixed length of stay and utilization problems. ASGs are increasing in popularity with managed care organizations due to their widespread use by Medicare and the ease of using a multiplier to negotiate contracts.

Another example of a prospective payment option is a global price that covers physician, outpatient facility, laboratory, etc., with a negotiated fee being paid for the procedure (for example coronary artery bypass at $16,500). Global prices stimulate efficiency to cost containment by reducing level of service and shortening length of stay and perhaps by providing outpatient service or by avoiding hospitalization altogether for money-losing cases.

b. Per Diem

In this scenario the provider is paid a fixed amount for each day of patient-care, usually categorized by service (e.g., OB, medicine, ICU). Since the nature of service can vary widely, the provider bears the risk that costs associated with the services provided on any day may exceed the per diem rate that has been agreed upon. The incentive for the provider, therefore, is to develop greater efficiency; however, there is no incentive to reduce length of stay.

c. Per Admission

This method is a single payment made for each admission, regardless of the services provided or the length of stay. Under this method, the risk to the provider is higher than under the per diem method, since the diagnoses and consequent level of care are generally unknown at the time at which the rate of payment is established.

d. Capitation

A fixed payment is made for each covered person under this prospective payment system. Payment is made in advance regardless of whether or not the covered person becomes an active patient and regardless of the number and mix of services utilized by the patient. While FFS methods pay providers after the fact on a claim-by-claim basis and usually without questions being asked, capitation pays monthly based on the number of people in their health care panel and their history of expected utilization. Thus, the incentive under FFS is for providers to provide as many services as possible and to emphasize costly services. Under prospective capitation, the incentive for the provider is to control both the cost and utilization of services for any given patient by providing the most efficient care.

Advantages of capitation to the payer include shared risk with the provider more predictable expenses (a predictable medical loss ratio); decreased administrative costs, and the opportunity to develop a partnership with providers. Advantages to the provider include improved cash flow, clinical economy, guaranteed volume, increased market share, and the opportunity to partner with the payer to develop prevention programs.

Capitation rates are essentially determined from previous payment and utilization data and vary from region to region, as utilization has been noted to vary in numerous studies. If previous payment and utilization data are used, the derived rate is then discounted 20-25% to arrive at the capitation rate for a provider. However, several problems can be found with this methodology. Accurate data are sometimes not available in the aggregate and are even less available for the sub-specialty that is being capitated and often derive from hospital and physician charges that were developed under the FFS system, with its incentive to use more services in order to generate charges and therefore income.

To calculate what a contract is actually worth using the capitation method the following formula is used:

annual capitation revenue =
PMPM rate $\times$ 12 (month/year) $\times$ average enrollment $\times$ 75-80%.

Unfortunately, accurate data are not always available to the health plan. In this case, the best way to calculate the rate is through the expected utilization for each service and the target payment rate per unit or payment multiplied by use. Payment is the easier of the two variables to determine. In the case of RBRVS, the payment used is that for each of the CPT codes. That use, however, is dependant on the relevant CPT code for the contract and their frequencies. This necessary information can be obtained in two ways: actual experience of the enrolled population or published regional data.

There is recently, however, a movement toward a second way of setting capitation, that of the establishment of a national benchmark. This method for determining capitation rate relies on statistical data from the marketplace because it is the marketplace that drives price. In this method, a market price is established by using information on the going rate for contracts in a metropolitan area and/or state and then negotiating a rate about 80% of that determined rate. Under capitated arrangements, providers become cost centers and must decide how to cut their costs in order to live within a market driven payment system.

Capitation can be applied in institutional services such as acute care, rehabilitation, skilled nursing facility, home health, outpatient surgery and emergency care. Each of these institutional services can be substitutable; therefore, they should be capitated as one to prevent shifting from one category to another. Under capitation, the institution has an incentive to develop clinical care pathways and disease management programs and, through these and other means, to become more efficient and effective service providers. This efficiency and effectiveness improves when managers of the institution and health care providers meet regularly to set goals and establish performance standards, to exchange data and to collaborate on problems. Through these means, the institution may stay within the institutional cap by, for example, adding a home pain management program to encourage more outpatient surgeries or starting disease management programs for diabetes and congestive heart failure in order to prevent unnecessary admissions to acute care facilities or to allow people to be admitted to a lower level of care, such as a skilled nursing home facility.

Occasionally, a managed care organization will establish risk pools that set aside a percentage of the capitation paid usually to the primary physician because of overutilization or to encourage limits on utilization. The entire amount set aside (called the withhold) or some portion of it may become payable based on performance criteria. Once the performance criteria are met, these withheld monies can be paid in whole, or some percentage retained in a stabilization pool to cover overutilization from period to period or to smooth out unexpected experience fluctuations. Other risk pools may be created, depending on the incentives that are seen as being useful to maintain a balanced prospective capitation system of payment (Bader, 1994).

D. Marketing

Marketing is a social and managerial process by which individual and groups obtain what they need and want through creating, offering, and exchanging products of value with others. Marketing costs can consume as much as a quarter to a third of a managed care organization's administrative costs.

Managed care frequently markets a variety of plans (indemnity, PPOs and HMOs) to meet the needs of the consumer. These options can range from two traditional indemnity plans with varying levels of deductibles and coinsurance to a true dual choice of a traditional indemnity plan with a PPO or HMO option. The triple option is referred to as the indemnity plan, the HMO and the PPO plan. Multi-choice plans create significant problems for the employer (if self insured) or the insurer by introducing the opportunity for adverse selection by offering an HMO because sicker patients will want to stay with their current doctor where they feel safe rather than switch to an unknown panel of providers with perceived restrictions.

Employee's select insurance plans based on benefit design, access to providers and out-of-pocket expense. The relative importance of each varies with the individual employee's need. Individuals with known major medical health problems will emphasize benefit design and access to care over out-of-pocket cost in selecting a health plan. The logic could go this way. Which plan provides a benefit for my condition? Plans with no benefits are eliminated. Which plan has the best or highest benefit for my condition? If multiple plans have comparable benefits, emphasis will shift to access. Do any of these plans offer direct access to my personal physician or facility currently treating my problem? Maintenance of provider relationships can be a strong influence, although not as much as in the past. Which plan offers the easiest access to specialty care? High risk patients consider cost last; low risk consider cost/access.

Recent trends have seen employers begin shifting to defined contribution plans for all benefits. In a defined plan, an employer can offer different health care plans that vary by premium and choice. Many large national companies would prefer to have a single managed care plan; however, due to the local nature of the medical market place they are unable to do so. In order for a health plan to be successful, it must be able to sell both the employer and employee on its product viability.

Employers have a variety of concerns in their relationships with HMOs:

- Employers want to exert control over their outlays for health benefits and pay for what their employees actually cost;
- Employers would prefer retrospective experience rating or options for self-insurance/risk sharing based on actual claims experience;
- Employers want employer-specific utilization and cost data to justify premium rates;
- Many fear that HMOs will shadow price or charge what the market will bear;
- Employers want documentation of efficiency and cost effectiveness;
- Employers want assurance that the plan is not skimming;
- Employers don't want to pay excessive overhead loadings;

- Some employers want more flexible coverage (options for less);
- More flexible cost sharing;
- Satisfaction proof;
- Quality;
- Long term business partners/can negotiate with issues of concern.

Marketing health plans requires specialization not only in selling but also in developing advertising and promotion, developing rates and underwriting, and in managing complaints from the customers and maintaining long lasting clients and preserving their business relationships.

E. Claims Administration

Benefits of Claims Administration is probably the most underestimated functional division in the operation of a managed care health plan. The functions grouped under claims administration include member eligibility verification, benefits interpretation, provider request for services adjudication and payment, provider support and system file maintenance, member reimbursement for services, coordination of benefits, third party liability recognition and collection, capitation accounting and payment, liability accrual estimation, and the preparation of various reports and profiles. These functions are essential for the efficient and effective management of the managed care organization.

Claims can be handled internally by the managed care organization or externally by third party administrators. Typically, third party administrators are information system companies that work under contract with one or more managed care organizations.

Advantages to the managed care organization of contracting with a third party administrator are lower cost from administrative economies of scale, lower capital outlays for equipment, and often less costly personnel and space. Staffing for claims administration requires a director, claims examiner, claims control clerk, data entry clerk, coordination of benefits/third party liability (COB/TPL) clerk, a membership clerk, a coder and financial clerk. These personnel are hired according to certain ratios that follow industry standards.

One of the most important contributions made by claims administration to the managed care organization is benefits interpretation. Ideally, the schedule of benefits will be clear and well documented so that the administration of claims can be routine and payments promptly made. More often, however, the managed care organization has to accommodate charges that are inappropriately billed or claims for services that are not, in fact, covered. The claims administration function includes the interpretation of benefits and development of the managed care organization's response to common problems such as lack of preauthorization, lack of notification of services rendered, questionable use of emergency services, charges for services not routinely covered under benefit plan, incomplete or inaccurate claims data or documentation, potential and third party liability/coordination of benefits.

Standard claims forms used include UB-82 for inpatient care, HCFA-1500 for physicians/other services, and NCPDP for prescription billing. Although hard copy claims are still the predominant form of billing, electronic claims transmission is on the increase especially among managed care organizations. The claims administration function also includes responsibility for a number of management reports: claims payment lag analysis, provider and member utilization statistics, productivity reports, and explanation of benefits reports.

1. Claims Recovery

Managed care organizations want to limit the care that they pay for to that for which the consumer has no other source of payment. Therefore, it is important for the staff of any managed care organization to be trained to recognize other coverage. This is especially true of staff who perform customer/member services, claims processing, utilization review, and QA analysis as well as providers of health care services. Training should include ways to identify the type of claims and how to make contact with the managed care plan so that plan personnel are alerted to query the system for recovery information. A good claim recovery system will bring between 6 and 10 percent of the total premium back into the plan.

a. Coordination of Benefits

As health insurance coverage expands, the likelihood that a person has dual coverage increases, making it in the interests of managed care organizations and others to add the coordination of benefits (COB) to its administrative functions. Dual coverage means that individuals could receive duplicate payment or reimbursement for the same medical service because they have insurance through more than one arrangement. For example, a child might be covered by health insurance purchased by two employers--one employing the mother and the other the father. To insure proper benefit payment and reduce the likelihood of an individual profiting from dual coverage, the National Association of Insurance Commissioners (NAIC) has developed payment guidelines that delineate the types of insurance that can and cannot be coordinated, the procedures for determining which health plan is primary (and therefore should pay), the procedure for determining allowable charges, and the benefits payable by each plan coverage.

b. Third Party Liability

COB is not part of third party liability, as COB indicates a shared liability with another carrier because of dual coverage. Under third party liability (TPL), the liability is transferred in full or recovered. The identification of third party liability allows the managed care organization to transfer liability for expenses related to injuries and illnesses suffered by members to the source or party causing injury. In the case of work-related injuries and illnesses, this is known as worker's compensation, and shifts the responsibility to the worker's compensation insurance carrier. In the case of expenses related to injuries and illnesses that are caused by the negligence or willful acts of a third party, it is known as subrogation.

Proper administration of these provisions requires initial identification of situations that are or could be work-related or involve third party liability. Any accident or injury to a member should be questioned. For example, a member falls at the supermarket and fractures an arm. If the member is an employee of the supermarket , it is a worker's compensation claim; if a customer, subrogation. Certain illnesses should be questioned dependent on occupation because of worker's compensation potential, for example lung disease among mining or textile workers, coronary disease among police and fire workers, cancer among people working with nuclear or other toxic products.

c. Reinsurance

Reinsurance protects against the managed care organization incurring large catastrophic expenses. Often called stop-loss, this form of reinsurance provides protection for medical expenses above a certain limit. Thus reinsurance allows the managed care organization to recover some or all of the expenses incurred after that limit is reached.

2. Claims Abuse

The extent of claims abuse is unknown, but is probably in the range of two to five percent. The most common types of abuse follow:

- Unbundling: The breaking of a procedure into its component parts for the purposes of maximizing payment by claiming each part separately. For example, a physician submitted a bill for a total hysterectomy: $1,600 for a hysterectomy, $1,000 for a oophorectomy, $1,000 for a salpingectomy, and $1,000 for an exploratory. A reviewer would know that the oophorectomy (removal of the ovary), salpingectomy (removal of the fallopian tube), and laparotomy (exploration of the abdomen) should all be included in the surgeon's fee for hysterectomy.
- Bilateral or multiple procedures: When bilateral procedures are performed (for example, a bilateral hernia repair), postoperative care is provided for both parts of the procedure at the same time. It is customary to discount the second and subsequent procedures by 50 percent. Modifiers are used to denote the bilateral procedure.
- Assistant surgeons: Assistant surgeons are only occasionally needed. A list of those procedures requiring an assistant surgeon should be published in the agreement between the managed care organization and providers. Any exception to this list should be approved by the managed care organization's medical director prior to the procedure.
- Patient churning: This term denotes asking the patient to return for follow-up visits much more frequently than is necessary.
- Gaming and code creep: Upcoding to get higher reimbursement.

Techniques that compare claims against standards or customary practices are used by managed care organizations to limit claims abuses. If abuses are consistently detected, providers may well be deselected from the managed care organization's network.

F. Provider Relations

Responsibilities of the provider representatives include training medical providers to follow proper billing procedures; communicating with providers and other departments such as claims, utilization management, and quality assurance regarding payment policy and procedural problems; and communicating with providers concerning outstanding claims or billing problems. Provider representatives often perform contracting functions in smaller managed care organizations.

G. Member Services

The primary function of member services--or customer relations--is to communicate with the members of the managed care organization. Member services should serve as an advocate for the member as they research denied claims, provide information about benefits, and act on the member's behalf in the review of complaints.

H. Contracts

The development, negotiating and oversight of contracts is a major component in the operations of any managed care organization. Contracts determine the relationships between the managed care organization and the groups purchasing care from the organization; they also establish the relationships between the managed care organization and the providers of care to people enrolled through these groups. These contracts are the group master contract (GMC) and provider agreements.

1. Master Contract

The GMC is an agreement between the managed care organization and a subscribing group. It contains rates, performance covenants, relationships among parties, schedule of benefits and other conditions. The group purchasing insurance is able to control some of the cost of health care through this document.

Typically, the GMC contains a statement of coverage services; definition of limitations, exclusions and pre-existing conditions; required cost sharing by covered individuals; restrictions on access to physicians and non-physician medical care, providers, pre-admission screening and authorization procedures for both inpatient and outpatient services; delineation of an agreement on coordination of benefits, subrogation and requirements of claim payer audit and billing audit. The GMC also specifies access and who coordinates the delivery of care. It is prepared in conjunction with state guidelines (and federal in case of federal qualification), and approved by the state insurance commissioner, and will contain all mandated covered services and requirements of the state. All marketing and other brochures should reflect the terms of the GMC. The GMC itself is given to the purchaser (employer); the individual member receives a certificate of coverage.

2. Provider Agreements

Managed care organizations are arranged in managed networks of providers to deliver the health care benefit designated in the GMC in accordance with provisions detailed in the provider agreement. Typically included in provider agreements are terms that reflect cost and quality considerations, such as restrictions on member access to providers, requirements for utilization control, and requirements for reporting, documentation and communication.

In the agreement, the provider agrees to certain payment arrangements, to billing procedures, and may agree to risk/incentive agreements. These agreements are designed to control unnecessary services and provide incentives for quality. Primary care providers (PCP) require information to manage the risk/incentive arrangement. This necessitates tracking referral activity, utilization activity, payment and withholds from payment for individual providers. Payment methods include fee schedules, discounted fees and capitation. Providers agree to accept assignment of benefits and to accept payment in full. They also agree not to bill the balance of submitted charges except for allowed co-payments, co-insurance and deductible amounts.

I. Placement of Risk and Underwriting

Financial consequences of the various risks may rest with the managed care organization, the hospital providers or the physician providers. Conceptually, the risk ought to fall to the party that has the greatest control over the actual results achieved. The reimbursement methodology employed by a managed care organization determines the locale of the risk inherent in the delivery of health care on a prepaid basis. In FFS payment, the financial consequences of variances from what is expected from the allocated amount lies with the HMO. Under a capitated methodology, however, the financial consequences of variances from what is expected are the provider's responsibility.

1. Underwriting

People seek health insurance because they want to avoid taking risks. Health insurance prevents a family from suffering financial ruin as a result of expensive medical care. Unlike other types of coverage (life, homeowners), health insurance also has become a mechanism of financial payment for care, thus determining the patient's access to the health care system. Because of this characteristic, the managed care organization providing health insurance has an incentive to include in its covered population people who are generally representative of the entire population. This is known as community-based coverage.

Selection bias, which occurs when a managed care organization does not obtain a random sample from the population of those persons eligible to make a choice, can be either favorable or adverse. Selection bias is favorable when individuals with lower than average expected risk enroll. For example, if all of the younger, healthy members of a business sign up for a particular HMO, that HMO has a favorable selection bias. Selection bias can also be adverse. Adverse selection occurs when the individuals who are the most likely to have poorer than average health expectations apply for or continue coverage to a greater extent than the persons with average or better than average expectations. For example, people without health insurance are likely to be more motivated to seek out insurance when they know that they are in need of costly surgical procedures. A certain type of adverse selection bias can occur within an insurance group if the individuals in that group are permitted to select from among different insurance options. For example, an employer offers a self-funded group an HMO option. The younger, healthier employees choose the HMO option. The self-funded group now experiences adverse selection because it retains the older, sicker patients who have regularly established doctors and who do not want to leave the security of that relationship.

Insurers often deny small businesses health insurance because of the nature of the work, the rate of claims, or the administrative costs. Those businesses excluded in this way might involve hazardous work situations; low paying or seasonal businesses having higher than average claims to doctors and dentists; and groups such as government, finance, nonprofit organizations and municipalities since they tend to have higher administrative costs. From a practical standpoint, small groups are more costly because of higher turnover with associated administrative costs and the uncertainty of risks. Large groups are more attractive because they include many individuals under a single contract, thus being more representative of the population as a whole.

Redlining is the name given to denying coverage to people in certain interest groups or certain geographic areas perceived as high risk. The insurer attempts to control adverse selection by underwriting provisions (the selection and classification of candidates for insurance). For example, suppose that an insurer intends to insure all individuals for the same premium charge regardless of the individual's (or group's) age, sex, geographic location, line of work, smoking habits, genetic predisposition, and so on. The premium charge would need to be sufficient to cover all expected outlays plus administrative expenses and profit. In this example, cross-subsidy clearly exists, because the premiums of the younger and healthier clearly exceed the cost of their care while older, sicker individuals pay premiums that are less than their expected costs. This single premium model is the basis for community rating.

If perfect information was available, insurers could charge a premium to each subscriber on the basis of the subscriber's projected health care costs. Healthy individuals would have low costs, and therefore low premiums, while sick individuals would have higher costs. Projecting the expected costs of care for a group based on indicators leads the insurer to arrive at a group rate based on experience. Premiums based on group claims experiences are known as experience rating. Blended premiums include both community and experience rated premiums.

Another way of protecting against adverse selection is through the use of preexisting clauses. A preexisting condition clause excludes coverage of that particular physical or mental condition for a period of time. This limits the likelihood that a person will join the health insurance plan just because they know that they have a condition that requires costly care.

There has been a movement in this country towards according health care special status as a fundamental right, like education, and thus guaranteeing access to all without regard to ability to pay. If one accepts this principal, certain barriers to health care, such as experience rating and preexisting conditions, must be changed. Further, health insurance organizations would need to stop a number of current practices such as cherry picking or cream skimming (offering lower rates only to groups of young, healthy, low risk persons); bait and switch (attracting customers by offering discount rates and then raising them substantially upon renewal); redlining (denying coverage to people in certain industries and geographic areas perceived as high risk); no guarantee of renewal (insurers can drop anyone for any reason).

J. Medical Management and Quality Assurance

Managed care organizations review the provision of health care to their enrollees in order to control cost and to monitor the quality of services being provided. Medical management is a complex and interactive process. A few integrated medical groups in advance markets who are paid on a capitated per-member per-month basis for professional services, hospital service, home health and pharmacy services have been shown to handle utilization more effectively that others. This model of medical management is performed by their own medical directors and physician committees, allowing decisions to be based on more detailed clinical information than is available to outside reviewers. A cooperative approach such as this has been shown to reduce the often adversarial nature of utilization management and encourage the use of disease management programs as well as clinical guidelines and clinical care pathways (Robinson, 1995).

However, not many managed care organizations presently employ a cooperative approach such as this. More often, the medical management function is performed by the managed care organization itself, rather than by an integrated medical group. The overall function of medical management and quality assurance can usefully be broken down into several component parts: utilization management, provider profiles, guidelines/pathways/disease management programs, customer surveys, provider selection and credentialing and prevention programs. Figure 3 depicts the function between the plan types for both medical management and quality.

1. Utilization Management

Utilization management review varies markedly between plans. Some plans review only hospital admissions. Others review selected services such as ambulatory surgery and outpatient treatments for psychiatric disorders or substance abuse. In a

Figure 3 - Comparison of Different Functions Between Plan Types

Type of MCO	Richness of Benefits	Premium	Cost Control Methods	Quality Prevent /Outcome	Customer Satisfation Survey	Credentialing
MIP	+	+++	Deductible/ copay Underwritting Utilization Management	0	0	0
PPO	++	+++	Add: Selective Network No Balance Billing	0	0	+
HMO	++	+	Add: "Gatekeeper" Capitation/ Withhold Deselection Multiple Contracts Provider Profiles/ Guidelines	+	+	+

few, only expensive outpatient treatments (radiation therapy and diagnostic tests such as CT and MRI) and home care may be reviewed. Regardless of its scope, the system of utilization management involves data collection, review and/or authorization of these services, and coordination with other plan activities such as contracting, provider and member services, and interpretation of the group master contract for benefits.

a. Utilization Review

Utilization review (UR) is a collection of techniques in which a third party, other than the patient and the patient's physician, determines the appropriateness of medical services suggested to or provided to the patient by the attending physician. The primary objectives of UR are to

- Provide a monitoring and control system to assure the delivery of medical services at the appropriate level of care in a timely, efficient and cost-effective manner;
- Monitor and give feedback to providers regarding their medical practice patterns and utilization of health services;
- Educate patients on prevention;
- Identify opportunities to educate physicians regarding cost containment such as preadmissions, testing or home care instead of inpatient stays;
- Reduce length of stay by preventing avoidable inpatient days and avoid unnecessary admission by use of ambulatory surgery and outpatient treatment.

UR programs seek to lower the rate of medically unnecessary admissions and days by requiring patients and physicians to participate in different levels of review: preadmission review; concurrent, retrospective review; and case management. Preadmission review takes place before a service is provided and includes precertification, procedural review and second surgical opinion programs. Preadmission review procedures are intended to affect the location and timing of inpatient admissions by assessing the appropriateness of a decision to admit a patient before the admission takes place.

UR programs typically include the following procedures:
- Patient- or physician-initiated contact with the review organization as notification of intention to admit;
- Initial screening of the proposed admission, usually by a nurse reviewer, that will result in approval of the case if it conforms with established criteria;
- Physician review of cases that do not conform with the criteria; and
- An appeals process for proposed admission judged to be inappropriate.

Precertification review for outpatient services are similar to preadmission review. Emphasis here is made on adherence to explicit guidelines for both outpatient surgery and high cost outpatient procedures such as MRI. Precertification review also considers location (contracts, site), need and timing of services.

After a patient is admitted, the managed care organization monitors inpatient stay to avoid unnecessary days and to foster appropriate substitution of less intense outpatient surgeries and more efficient inpatient care, thus resulting in shorter lengths of stay. This is referred to as concurrent review. Its objective is to alter the pattern of service to be rendered in the future.

Evidence in the past has shown that the number of hospital admissions and days of inpatient care are reduced as a result of UR, although its effect on overall cost and quality of care are unknown. Recent evidence suggests that significantly few of utilization review targeted outpatient procedures are performed with no compensatory increase in the number of these same procedures in the following year. Second opinions appear to reduce the number of elective procedures performed and are reported by patients to assist them with their own decision-making. Patients, their physicians, or both may choose more efficient options for care when they expect that care to be reviewed, suggesting that requirements for review act as a deterrent either to the physicians (against performing the procedure or possibly looking for more efficient methods of treatment) or to the patient who might sometimes have been seeking cosmetic or other services that are not covered or indicated (Rosenberg, 1995).

Utilization review can be done by the managed care organization using preauthorization criteria or, in the case of a capitated network, by one of those providers affected. For example, a marked reduction in MRI and CT scans occurred when mandatory requests were instituted requiring contact with the radiologist prior to the ordering of such procedures. Prior authorization has also been used outside of the institutional setting in controlling drug costs. For example, prior authorization reduced the cost of nongeneric NSAIDS by more than half (53%) in the Tennessee Medicaid program in 1989 through the substitution of generic agents (Smalley, 1995). In fact, the Omnibus Budget Reconciliation Act of 1990 requires states to provide claims-based drug utilization review to all Medicaid enrollees in managed care organizations prior to dispensing drugs as a means of preventing or minimizing inappropriate prescribing.

b. Case Management

Concurrent review is often combined with case management. Case managers are usually non-physicians who are employed by managed care organizations to promote more cost-effective and appropriate modes of care for patients with illnesses that can be very costly, for example, when a person receives a hand injury or is partially paralyzed. Case management is intended to insure continuity of services, to overcome fragmentation of services, and to minimize the misutilization of facilities and resources. It also attempts to match the appropriate intensive services with patients' needs over time.

When necessary, case management can authorize services not normally covered by insurers in an attempt to reduce the number of patients with extremely high overutilization and cost. The case management process may also authorize supplemental benefits (such as refurbishing a home to enable a person using a wheelchair to recuperate or receive treatment) in order to make it possible to provide treatment in a setting less expensive than the hospital. Such benefits can save money for providers; however, in most studies it is suggested that they are only supplemental and therefore only improve quality of care for patients by providing a more integrated coordinated approach (Rosenberg, 1995).

c. Retrospective Review

Retrospective review is the process of reviewing the necessity and appropriateness of medical services based on review of the medical record, treatment plan, claims or authorization log after medical care is rendered. Retrospective review may include hospital and institutional review, professional practice review, physician referral patterns and ancillary services review including laboratory and x-ray treatment. Retrospective review is labor intensive and should be used judiciously due to the small or nonexistent savings that it generates.

d. Provider Profile

Provider profiles are informational tools that help providers compare their performance against their peers in costs and utilization. By providing ongoing feedback to providers of their own performance and aggregate performance of their peers, the provider gains greater insight into the process of medical care and begins to focus on best practices and methods for improvement.

2. Quality

The potential for lesser quality in a managed care organization, due to an emphasis on utilization control, has long been an argument against managed care. A limited number of studies to date, however, do not substantiate that claim. In fact, existing studies of Group Health of Puget Sound suggest a slightly higher standard of care. Although Total Quality Management (TQM) has recently appeared on the scene, Quality Assurance (QA) is still the standard program in most managed care organizations. HMOs are required to have a QA program in order to be federally qualified if they are located in a state that has regulations for quality. Regardless of such a requirement, some HMOs use quality to differentiate themselves from their competitors through proven service delivery excellence. Quality has two components—quality in fact and quality in perception. Excellence in both is essential and can be defined by three key elements: the ability of the HMO to meet or exceed expectations, the managed care organization ability to maintain its customers, and its ability to attract and retain qualified physicians.

A number of management tools are used by managed care organizations to promote quality. They include guidelines, pathways and disease management programs, member satisfaction surveys, assessments of outcomes, and the promotion of preventive care.

a. Guidelines, Pathways and Disease Management Programs

Investigators have long noted substantial variations in the use of medical and surgical procedures, hospital resources and medications at local, regional and international levels. For example, there may be as much as a two-to threefold difference in the consumption of medical care resources within a busy cardiology group practice with no relationship between the use of invasive cardiac procedures and crude measures of outcome. Another example is regional variation in the use of certain cardiac medications that have been shown to improve the outcome after heart attack (myocardial infarction—MI) (Guadagnoli, 1995).

Patients, managed care systems and physicians are all interested in delivering and receiving the best quality of care. Payers are demanding increasing accountability and quality along with lower prices. Variation in the use of diagnostic and therapeutic procedures can be of three types: difference in the health care system, the practice style of the physician, and characteristics of the patient.

Varying incentives in the health care system encourage different behavior. Fee for service (FFS) does not encourage cost accountability nor does it encourage providers to be efficient and control cost. High copayments for members and capitation for providers encourage lower use rates. For example, the Advisory Board has suggested that as much as a 50% reduction in cardiac services might result from capitation without any change in medical outcomes (Advisory Board, 1994).

Physicians differ in their beliefs about the effectiveness of a health care intervention, especially when good evidence of efficacy is lacking. Even when high quality of information is known, practice styles of physicians can vary in their interpretation of that evidence. Not surprisingly, physicians also differ in individual levels of skills, including technical skills and knowledge.

Patient's individual characteristics also influence the use of medical services. In general, neither severity of illness or case mix among regions is a significant factor. Instead, characteristics such as attitudes toward pain, aggressive surgical approach and timing of intervention play significant roles.

To control the variations that result from these differences, a number of means have been developed. The most common are clinical practice guidelines, clinical care or critical care pathways and disease management programs.

Clinical practice guidelines are systematically developed statements that assist practitioners and patients in the outpatient setting as they make decisions about appropriate health care for specific clinical circumstances. Clinical guidelines are used to accomplish two major goals: (1) improvement of clinical quality by closing the gap between current practice and optimal practice; and (2) control of the associated medical care costs. One guideline developed by Park Nicollet Medical Center, Minneapolis, to improve quality and reduce costs eliminated 70% of traditional patient-physician interaction by giving nurses the primary responsibility for treating 11,000 annual cases of urinary tract infections. These interactions now take place via telephone, a change which has resulted in high patient satisfaction and total savings estimated at $150,000 on their prepaid patient population by reducing the annual treatment charge from $67 to $39 (Physician Manager, 1994).

Clinical practice guidelines are developed by consensus or evidence. One of the better known consensus statements is that of the ACIP Guidelines for Immunization. A number of speciality organizations also turn out statements, such as the American College of Physicians Clinical Efficacy Assessment Project.

Clinical care (critical) pathways has been referred to as a step-by-step sequencing of patient care for a specific diagnosis or DRG, which can be used by the hospital to meet patient, provider and payer needs. A clinical pathway introduces a more rational and systematic process of care, thus reducing variance of the care provided and improving practice patterns and efficiency indexes. Clinical care pathways have been used to assist in the transition to total quality improvement, to increase the focus on system issues, to improve databases, to encourage physician participation by collaboration, to improve patient outcomes by reduction in variation in practice patterns, to build teams and promote collaboration, to provide education to multiple hospital levels, to meet community service requirements and to influence positively the cost of care.

While clinical care pathways were designed initially only to meet specific goals on a specific unit, the trend has been to expand these pathways beginning with the initial physician contact through hospitalization and on to the discharge phase. The basic intent is, therefore, to identify the optimal way to deliver and coordinate every step of the care.

Patient and provider expectation and feedback are critical to pathway success, and their input is used in achieving this success. For example, one hospital invited former patients who had undergone total hip replacement to a breakfast meeting with the intent of sharing with them the clinical pathway development. The patients were pleased with the pathway but recommended that new patients have an opportunity to speak with former patients who had undergone total hip replacements because they said that although the education and support received from the medical and nursing staff was excellent, it was not the same as patients speaking with peers. As a result, a program was developed in that hospital pairing new total hip replacement patients with former ones either by telephone or in person, thus establishing a total hip replacement support group (Healthcare Leadership, 1995).

Disease management programs are a comprehensive, integrated approach to care and reimbursement based on the natural course of a disease with treatment designed to address the illness by maximizing the effectiveness and efficiency of care delivery. Emphasis is on preventing disease and managing it aggressively when intervention will have the greatest impact. While traditional care has focused on treatment intervention at the onset of disease recognition, disease management encompasses the entire course of a disease, whether acute or in remission and whether care is given in the hospital or at home. Disease management, thus, differs from care in traditional FFS because diagnosis and treatment is based on disease process not reimbursement. Further, it provides an education and compliance program for chronic disease aimed at patients, their families, providers and caregivers, cutting across care settings and providing full continuity of care.

A number of diseases are ideal candidates for disease management including asthma, diabetes, AIDS, hypertension, chronic obstructive pulmonary disease (COPD) and congestive heart failure (CHF). These diseases are ideal because they create highly visible costs in both the inpatient and outpatient setting, comprise a large patient population, can be improved by both patient and provider education and lend themselves to outcome measurements and improvement.

Clinical guidelines, clinical care pathways and disease management programs depend on acceptance by physicians, patients, other providers and, to some degree, the payment mechanism. Acceptance is improved when physicians are involved in the development and implementation of the process itself, when feedback on practice patterns compared to peers is used, when tied to small group or personal CME; when opinion leaders are in agreement; when reminders are given; when patients are part of the team; and when certain administrative procedures are applied. Compliance with clinical guidelines, clinical care paths and disease management programs are improved when aligned with financial incentives. For example, if primary care physicians are paid by capitation, they could be encouraged to provide immunization by the ACIP immunization schedule if this service were paid for under FFS. Hospitals and integrated delivery systems are more likely to adopt clinical care paths and disease management programs when financial incentives change making them cost centers rather than revenue centers.

b. Customer Satisfaction Surveys

The term "patient satisfaction" has taken on broader significance in the '90s. The current focus is on quality of care from the patient's point of view (patient perception). This information is useful for three reasons: oversight of access and quality, as a way for consumers and purchasers to make informed choices among competing plans, and to allow managed care organizations to incorporate these findings into both their operations and marketing efforts. A number of surveys have been developed to assess satisfaction; however, there exists no uniform standard to date. It has become common practice among managed care organizations to issue report cards based on consumer satisfaction findings and other data. Usually these compare performance of the particular managed care organization with that of the industry as a whole.

c. Provider Selection and Credentialing

At the heart of managed care is the selection of providers. Providers chosen should be willing participants having good reputations and wanting to be partners. Staff and group model HMOs generally are more selective requiring board certification or eligibility as well as the ability to secure hospital privileges and maintain positive professional relationships. Network or IPA models often investigate professional reputation and patterns of care in addition to examining some of the above criteria. While the staffing ratios of the past have been one primary care physician to three specialists, primary care physicians (general internists, family practitioners, pediatricians, and possibly obstetricians) will comprise about half of a successful network of the future to get more predictable expense and services. Initially, because of excess specialty supply, some networks may have more specialists than needed to serve a covered population, but over time, credentialing needs tightening so that physicians who practice high-quality, efficient medicine will be rewarded with more patients. Today, physician turnover within HMOs has been less than 5 percent in most plans with the highest turnover rates noted in group/staff model HMOs.

Physician credentialing is tantamount to providing quality health care services. Prior to any hire physicians and other providers should be credentialed. Credentialing is done in the managed care environment for a number of reasons including the desire to provide high quality services to the membership or to achieve National Committee for Quality Assurance (NCQA) accreditation, regulatory requirements verifying credentials of practitioners and facilities, payer demand for cost-effective networks, and the desire to minimize tort liability. Credentialing begins with the creation of written policies and procedures for initial affiliation and for the recredentialing process of providers. These policies and procedures are then reviewed and approved by the managed care organization's governing body or its delegate. Because members of an HMO can only go to select network providers chosen by the HMO, the HMO assumes greater risk as a result. From a risk management standpoint, provider selection and credentialing is one of the most important processes in quality.

Every HMO must check the qualifications of its providers. At a minimum their investigation should include the following: a scope which is inclusive of all licensed practitioners included in the managed care organization's literature, a statement from the applicant as to their disciplinary activity, physical and mental status, license history, criminal record, lack of impairment, and the correctness and completeness of the application; inquiries to the National Practitioner Data Bank, the applicable licensing board and Medicare and Medicaidabout sanction activity; a visit to each primary care physician's office to review the site and the medical record-keeping practices. The initial credentialing process should review and verify information regarding licensure, DEA or CDS certification, medical school, residency or other training, work history, professional liability claims history, and malpractice coverage. A recredentialing process which is implemented at least every two years and which includes verification of the base line data and the information provided in the applicant's statement should be part of HMO general policy; the use of an integrated appraisal process including member complaints, quality reviews, utilization management records and member satisfaction surveys should be maintained.

Credentialing and recredentialing is the cornerstone of the HMO's selection and deselection process. These policies set the standard for fair process procedure and quality throughout the program. HMOs will experience greater challenges to fair process in the future due to any willing provider and economic credentialing. Many successful systems of the future will be physician-driven, and physicians should be involved in key leadership, clinical management, and administrative management roles such as credentialing.

d. Prevention

Prevention is an essential key element in reducing medical care costs and improving quality. It is estimated that over 70% of all illness is preventable. For example, childhood immunizations are said to prevent more than 3.3 million cases of measles, 2.1 million cases of mumps and 1.5 million cases of rubella annually. Cost estimates of treatment for these thwarted diseases would have been in excess of $14 billion. Preventative services include childhood and adult immunizations, cholesterol screening, mammography screening, hypertension screening in the workplace and pap smears for cervical cancer. In the past decade there has been an effort to develop and disseminate information on indicators of quality, a report card type of approach. This information on performance is seen as an aid to purchasers seeking value when they make contract decisions and to consumers making their personal health care choices (Preventive Medicine, 1995).

IV. FUTURE TRENDS IN MANAGED CARE

The future of health care promises to be exciting in the managed care arena. The primary care physician has taken on a new role as a leader of the health care team. Multispeciality groups will continue to grow at a rapid pace as physicians abandon their independence. Health plans will grow in value as capital moves out of hospitals and into delivery systems and as they accumulate health data that will help caregivers make better decisions. Hospitals will become cost centers and will lose value. They will experience difficulties in obtaining expansion funds. Physicians, health plans and hospitals will continue to consolidate, merge and form alliances. Provider-supplier relationships will improve as managed care groups consolidate suppliers through long term contracts, reduced prices and reduced utilization.

Health care of the future must focus on community needs rather than the needs of the organization. Hospitals, who have in the past used consensus to satisfy their internal stakeholders—hospital staff, specialists and subspecialists—must remain focused on the needs of the health care buyers. They will rely on the reengineering efforts to improve patient care through patient-focused care, reaggregation of patients with similar conditions into homogenous patient units to reduce availability of care, the use of multi-skilled teams, the expansion of clinical pathways to encompass an entire episode of care and aligning authority and accountability to allow self-directed teams to make decisions at the point of contact.

The health care system of the future must demonstrate that it can prevent illness and cure disease better than other systems within the area. In the past it has been sufficient to have a reputation based on anecdotal information or historical contributions. The future will demand more objective and measurable data. In order to prove superior quality services, integrated systems must develop and enforce standard protocols of care (clinical guidelines, clinical care pathways, and disease management programs) so that multiple patients receive the same care and results provided are better than the industry standard.

Although the concept of managed care has been in existence for some time, managed care as we know it today is in its infancy as it evolves from a piecemeal uncoordinated system to a more efficient model of care. While the HMO is to date the most effective, efficient, reliable system available in the dynamic evolutionary process of health care management, it certainly won't be the endpoint of our system.

REFERENCES

Bader, B. and Matheny, M. (1994). *Health System Leader*, 4-16.

Beckham, D. (1995). *Healthcare Leadership Review*, 14 (7): 1-15.

Council on Graduate Medical Education: Sixth Report. (Sept 1995): 1-36.

Dueck, R. (1994). *Physician Manager*, 5 (8): 1,8.

Gold, M., Hurley, R., Lake, T., Ensor, T., and Berenson, R. (1995). *New England Journal of Medicine*, 333 (25): 1678-1683.

The Governance Committee. (1994).

Guadagnoli, E., Hauptman, P., Ayanian, J., Pashos, C., McNiel, B., and Cleary, P. (1995). *New England Journal of Medicine*, 333 (9): 573-578.

Hoechst Marion Roussel, Inc. (1995). *Managed Care Digest Series: HMO- PPO Digest*: 1-72.

Manning, W., et al. (1987). Health insurance and the demand for medical care: Evidence from a randomized experiment. *American Economic Review.* 77 (3): 251-277.

Preventive Medicine: Strategies for Quality Care and Lower Costs (1995). 1-32.

Robinson, J. and Casalino, L. (1995). *New England Journal of Medecine*, 333(25): 1684-1687.

Rosenburg, S., Allen, D., Handte, J., Jackson, T., Leto, L., Rodstein, B., Stratton, S., Westfall, G., and Yasser, R. (1995). *New England Journal of Medicine*, 333(20): 1326-1330.

Smalley, W., Griffin, M., Fought, R., Sullivan, L., and Ray, W. (1995). *New England Journal of Medicine*, 322(20): 1612-1618.

Starr, P. (1982). *The Social Transformation of American Medicine.* New York: Basic Books.

van Steenwyk, J. (1989). *The Managed Healthcare Handbook*, Aspen Publishers, Gaithersburg, MD: 225-229.

9.
INDIGENT HEALTH CARE

Joy A. Clay, *University of Memphis, Memphis, TN*

Medical indigency has been a public policy issue in the United States since colonial times. The issue is complex and requires policy solutions that go beyond merely extending insurance, since medical indigency is often related to other social problems, including poverty, illiteracy and under education, homelessness, and substance abuse. These social problems compound health access issues. Current programs, although well-intentioned, have created a system marked by fragmentation, gaps, and inequities. Consequently, effective policy solutions require that underlying structural and individual behavioral issues which serve as barriers be addressed.

This chapter identifies issues related to medical indigency, including an overview of health access issues, a description of the characteristics of the medically indigent, and a brief assessment of the public programs which presently serve as the "safety net" for the medically indigent. The chapter ends with an analysis of the challenges facing policy makers.

I. MEDICAL INDIGENCY—A PUBLIC POLICY PROBLEM

A commonly accepted definition of "medical indigency" is the inability to afford needed health care services due to insufficient income and/or lack of health insurance. Defining the public policy issues associated with medical indigency in this way would lead one to assume that overcoming the financial aspects of health access would solve health access problems for the medically indigent. Several studies, however, have shown that having insurance does not guarantee access, especially to specialized services (Cykert, 1995, Haas, 1993).

Health access is generally defined as the degree to which persons are able to obtain needed health care services (Institute of Medicine, 1993). Aday, Fleming and Anderson (1984), for example, categorize the personal characteristics that influence health-seeking behavior into predisposing factors such as age and education; enabling factors such as insurance coverage and income; and need, which addresses health status. Lack of access to health services for the indigent can be due to the unavailability of health professionals, facilities, or specialized services in a reasonably nearby location and/or the inadequacy of affordable transportation to get residents to where the health professionals are located (Clay and Norris-Tirrell, 1995). In addition, some Americans experience poor access due to the nature of their health care problem, e.g., pre-existing conditions excluded by insurance provisions, AIDS, substance abuse or serious mental disorder. These may not be covered, or inadequately covered, by their specific insurance plan or by public assistance programs. Moreover, the medically indigent, who are generally at the lower socioeconomic levels of society, are also more likely to become ill or disabled (Aday, 1993; Mentnech, 1995). In general, poor, uninsured, or non-white children face more barriers to access to preventive or general medical care than do children from affluent or white families and use community clinics, emergency rooms, and hospital outpatient departments as their usual source of care (Wood et al., 1990). Such providers form the health "safety net" in their communities. Public programs which pay for health care for the poor and health care providers who serve those who cannot pay or pay very much for their care are described as providing a "safety net" for these individuals when they become ill. Both public and non-profit hospitals, for example, have traditionally served this population and have been willing either to subsidize or defray unreimbursed care. Cost containment pressures applied by private insurers as well as the increasing need to compete in aggressive managed care marketplaces, however, have made it increasingly difficult for safety net providers to continue to serve indigent patients or make it necessary somehow to avoid those with health conditions, such as AIDS, at-risk pregnancies, or serious mental health disorders, that place the provider at financial risk.

Access to health services is a local, state, and national public health issue since populations already socially vulnerable are made more vulnerable due to the risk of ill-health and disability. For example, success in having this population move from welfare to work requires people to be healthy. Additionally, access to appropriate and timely health services for the medically indigent is important because lack of preventive care or early intervention can prove more costly in the long term. Attention to the economic impact of significant bad debt and charity care is critical to maintaining sufficient network of stable health providers, furthering community development, and protecting the public's health overall.

Part of the challenge to solving the problem of medical indigency in the United States is to reach a national consensus regarding whether health care is a right, a privilege related to work, or a social welfare benefit. Current programs, such as Medicare and Medicaid, which were designed to address health access problems for the medically indigent still have gaps in coverage and have proven to be very costly government programs. Since the 1970s, fiscal pressures have been the driving force for health care policy. Consequently, policy decisions currently are focused on curbing physician autonomy and privilege as well as restricting patient access to the health care system as a means to restrain costs (Wilsford, 1995). Although the "Health Insurance

Portability and Accountability Act" steered by Senators Robert Kennedy (D-Mass.) and Nancy Kassenbaum (R-Kan.) may address one serious gap in insurance coverage, that of losing coverage when changing jobs, the new law which took effect July 1, 1997 does not assure affordability and thus individuals may not be able to realize access. Further, the new law does not address the needs of those remaining uninsured.

To be successful, policy solutions must address not only financial/insurance issues but also the underlying socio-medical and structural issues related to reaching these vulnerable populations. Given budgetary constraints, disillusion with nationally designed public programs, and pending welfare reform, partnerships among business leaders, community officials, and health industry representatives must forge to develop state-wide and local programs that better coordinate services for the medically indigent and attempt to reduce barriers to needed services. If states are allowed sufficient flexibility to design their own systems, however, the result will be an even greater patchwork with the potential for serious inequities across the nation. Those states having greater numbers of citizens in poverty will face significant funding challenges.

A. Magnitude of the Problem

The Center for Health Economics Research reports that in 1990 the public sector spent $367 billion on health services for the elderly and poor, a 40-fold increase since 1966 when Medicare and Medicaid began (1994, p. 14). Moreover, the Center notes that "A new Medicare retiree in 1990 can expect to receive $4 for every $1 paid into the program in taxes and premiums "(1994, p. 21). Although many have been served by these public programs, medical indigency remains a problem due to gaps in service coverage for eligible beneficiaries of both programs as well as the Medicaid eligibility limitations faced especially by the working poor. Low reimbursement levels and charity care result in higher costs for everyone as institutions transfer these expenses as much as possible to the insured.

The financial strain placed on safety-net institutions due to uncompensated care further affects the financial viability of such institutions. The Health Care Advisory Board reports that uncompensated care costs have more than tripled since 1980, costing $9.5 billion in 1990 and that government subsidies used to help cover uninsured costs have fallen from 28% in 1980 to only 20% in 1990 (1992b). Even more staggering is the Advisory Board's finding of the magnitude of uneven distribution among hospitals shouldering the burden: "5% of hospitals carry 37% of national uncompensated care costs" (1992b, p. 5). As states are allowed more flexibility in managing Medicaid, the safety-net institutions already carrying a disproportionate burden in their respective communities may be further burdened, potentially to the degree that their financial position becomes seriously threatened.

Estimates of the number of uninsured, or those unable to pay for needed health services, range from 10 per cent to 19.8 per cent of the U.S. population (Ries, 1993; Freeman et al., 1990; Melnick, Mann and Golan, 1989). The 1987 National Medical Expenditures Survey reported that 34-36 million persons were without health coverage at different periods while the March 1990 Current Population Survey indicated that 33.4 million persons were uninsured in 1989 (Ries, 1993). Other health experts estimate the number of uninsured at 31 million to 36.8 million, with an increase of almost 10 million in this group since 1977 (Barrilleaux and Miller, 1992; Brown, 1991; Hubbell et al., 1989; Health Care Advisory Board, 1992b). In contrast, the 1986 Robert Wood Johnson Foundation Survey estimated that there were 16 million adults of working age who were uninsured at any point in time, with 25 million uninsured at some time during a given year (Freeman et al., 1990).

The research findings summarized above do have some limitations and probably underestimate the extent of the problem. Telephone surveys will under-report the homeless and institutionalized and the reliance upon self-reported information also may be unreliable. These design limitations illustrate the complexity of assuring an accurate estimate of the uninsured (Hayward et al., 1988; Pane, Farner and Salness, 1991; Makuc, Freid and Kleinman, 1989; Melnick, Mann and Golan, 1989; Powers, 1988; Gelberg et al., 1990). Moreover, Aday (1993) found that estimating the number of vulnerable people is difficult due to the questionable quality and completeness of data. Although data constraints affect our ability to know for certain the magnitude of the policy problem, we do know that AIDS cases have increased, homelessness has worsened, over five million people have immigrated to the United States, families have further fragmented, the number of abused children has increased, and substance abuse remains a national problem.

II. CHARACTERISTICS OF THE MEDICALLY INDIGENT

Health researchers commonly use socio-demographic characteristics such as gender, race, education, age, income, access to a regular source of care, health status, employment status, geographic location, and insurance status to analyze the type and extent of utilization of health care services (Barrilleaux and Miller, 1992; Ries, 1993; Clay and Norris-Tirrell, 1995). Each of these predisposing, enabling, and need factors offer not only insights into the problems faced by various subpopulations but demonstrate the complexity of the issue. They remind us that a variety of solutions will be necessary if the community is to address the specific problems posed by the medically indigent.

A. Gender, Race, Age, Income and Education

Researchers generally describe the uninsured as consisting of an equal number of males and females, who tend to be younger (less than 25 years of age) than the insured population, and are predominantly unmarried (Brown, 1991; Freeman et al., 1990; Ries, 1993). Based on the 1989 U.S. Bureau of the Census National Health Interview Survey, families with lower incomes account for a higher proportion of the uninsured. About 27.7 percent of families with an annual income of $5,000-$9,999 are without health insurance while only 3.6 percent of families with an income of $50,000 or more are uninsured (Ries, 1993). Ries further reports that 36.0 percent of the people who are in poverty have no health care coverage. Of children under 18 years of age in poverty, 32.5 percent lack health care coverage (Ries, 1993). The Health Care Advisory Board reports that a "majority of the uninsured are poor or near poor with 60.1% having incomes below 200% of the poverty level" (1992, p. 12). As welfare reform is implemented, health access for poor families is likely to become a greater problem.

Whites and the elderly generally have better access to care than do non-white or poor children (Hayward et al., 1988; Pane, Farner and Salness, 1991; Makuc, Freid and Kleinman 1989; Barrilleaux and Miller 1992; and Hubbell et al. 1989). Blacks and Hispanics face comparably more barriers to health access than whites (Freeman et al., 1990; Akin et al., 1989). In an extensive review of the literature, Davis (1991) concluded that elderly Blacks have more physician visits but shorter hospital lengths of stay. Andersen and his colleagues (1987) found that Blacks, especially those who are indigent, have a higher incidence of chronic medical problems than Whites. Blacks also tend to inappropriately use the emergency room for primary care (White-Means and Thorton, 1989). Mitchell and Kandker (1995) found an uneven use of high technology cardiac procedures for white and black beneficiaries. Eggers report that black ESRD beneficiaries "are the least likely to get on the national wait list, and have longer wait times once they do get wait listed. Consequently, their overall transplant rates lag far behind the other racial groups" (1995, p. 101).

Schur and her colleagues found that financial factors are the most significant barrier to care for Hispanics. Moreover, they reported that the lack of health insurance is an even greater issue for Hispanics than for Blacks. "The proportion of uninsured Hispanic persons has grown from 8 percent in 1977 to 20 percent in 1992" (Schur, Albers, and Beck, 1995, p.75). Of particular interest, these researchers found that "approximately one-third of elderly Hispanics rely on Medicare as their only source of [insurance] coverage compared with about 10 percent of the elderly as a whole" (1995, p. 86). Consequently, restrictions and changes to Medicare could have an especially significant impact upon the Hispanic population.

In a study conducted at two urban public hospitals in Atlanta, Williams (1995) found that a high proportion of patients were unable to comprehend basic written medical instructions. Almost 60% were unable to understand a standard informed consent document. Williams estimates that over 40 million adults in the United States are functionally illiterate and that another 50 million are only marginally literate. The study found that literacy skills were highly correlated with age and education. Inability to understand prescription, appointment, health education, and informed consent information is a significant burden on the elderly and other vulnerable populations.

Predominantly black and Hispanic communities have few physicians regardless of income (Komaromy, 1996). Moy and Bartman (1995) found that racial and ethnic minorities also are more likely to receive care from non-white physicians, as were low-income, Medicaid, and the uninsured. Moreover, the patients treated by non-white physicians tend to be sicker, have chronic conditions, functional limitations, and psychological symptoms, all of which tend to require longer visits. The uneven burden on non-white physicians is of concern because taking care of this population places them at risk financially, especially if exposed through aggressive managed care capitation negotiations, and may also lead to dissatisfaction with medical practice (Moy and Bartman, 1995). Further, the General Accounting Office found that the Health Professional Shortage Areas (HPSAs) and Medically Underserved Areas (MUAs) are not effective in targeting federal resources. GAO found data and methodological problems with both systems and an inability to accurately match which program was best suited to a particular community's needs (1995). Although Medicare does allow a 10% premium to its fee schedule for physicians in MUAs, without further government assistance, urban and rural communities may find it difficult to assure the continued presence of primary care providers in medically underserved areas.

B. Employment

The uninsured are primarily unemployed (Freeman et al., 1990; Brown, 1991). Ries reports, however, that employment does not necessarily equate to being insured and vice versa. Ries found that of persons surveyed who were between 18-64 years of age and unemployed, 39.2 percent were without health care coverage, 47.6 percent had private health coverage, 9.8 percent had public assistance coverage, and 2.0 percent had military-VA coverage (Ries, 1993). In contrast, of those employed, 14.3 percent lacked health care coverage, 83.5 percent had private coverage, 1.0 percent had public assistance coverage, and 2.0 percent had military-VA coverage (Ries, 1993).

Similarly, the Health Care Advisory Board found that the number of uninsured full-time workers has shown a steady trend upward with "1.2 million more full-time workers uninsured in 1990 than in 1988" (1992b, p. 9). In a related finding the Health Care Advisory Board reports that employers are facing per employee health insurance costs that have doubled since 1984: "$1,645 in 1984 to $3,605 in 1991" (1992b, p. 9). Moreover, the majority of employed uninsured work in firms with fewer than 100 employees (1992a, p. 12).

C. Health Utilization

Health services researchers describe the uninsured and the poor of all ages and races as generally having more chronic and more serious medical problems at presentation than the insured, often because of late diagnosis. Late diagnosis when the health problem has become severe can lead to higher medical costs and could be related to access barriers to preventive health care. For example, uninsured women tend to have fewer physical examinations, fewer pap smears and breast exams, and less prenatal care, particularly in the first trimester of pregnancy. Black women are less likely to have prenatal care in the first trimester regardless of age and education. Of special interest, the uninsured visit physicians two-thirds as often as the insured, with the low-income uninsured visiting physicians only one-half as frequently as the insured (Freeman et al., 1990; Pane, Farner and Salness, 1991; Makuc, Freid and Kleinman, 1989; Brown, 1991; Akin et al., 1989).

Such lack of access can serve as a significant barrier to routine preventive care services such as cholesterol, prostrate, and hypertension checks. Aday describes the medically vulnerable as "those for whom the risk of poor physical, psychological, or social health has or is quite likely to become a reality" (1993, pp. 9-10). Aday characterizes the current system of financing health care for these vulnerable populations inadequate, both from a parity and equity standpoint. Lack of adequate resources, uneven quality of service provision, fragmentation, and often overly complex procedures can create organizational barriers to access (Aday, 1993). At the same time, the uneven coverage and quality of care for this population will most likely continue until policymakers recognize the association between the uninsured and increased costs (Tuckman and Chang, 1991, Iglehart, 1984). Although Congress expanded Medicaid eligibility for pregnant women in the late 1980s, Elmwood and Kenney, for example, found that substantial numbers of women continue to enroll late in their pregnancy. Moreover, Elmwood and Kenney convincingly argue that increases in Medicaid coverage do not address "underlying socioeconomic and behavioral factors that affect prenatal care and birth outcomes" (1995, p. 27).

D. Rural Health Access

Rural communities face serious challenges in assuring access to quality health care services. A number of factors contribute to this problem: "declining population, economic stagnation, shortages of physicians and other health care professionals, a disproportionate share of elderly, poor, and underinsured residents, and high rates of chronic illness" (Weisgrau, 1995, p. 1). Even when transportation presents no barrier to the elderly in rural areas, costs of care still present a significant and persistent barrier despite Medicare (Blazer et al., 1995). The shift in patient care from hospital to outpatient care and competition from nearby urban providers has taken its toll on rural hospitals. Although Rosenbach and Dayhoff (1995) found some decline in inpatient and outpatient utilization by Medicare beneficiaries in a rural hospital closure area, they suggest that hospital closures may have a more serious impact on the vulnerable rural population, such as Medicaid beneficiaries or the uninsured. These researchers also argue that more research needs to be done to determine the long term consequences of hospital closure on rural residents, including possible high readmission rates due to lack of medical and social support systems and higher potential for negative outcomes, such as higher mortality rates (Rosenbach and Dayhoff, 1995).

Although urban providers are reaching out to include rural providers in networks (Moscovice et al., 1995) and managed care companies are including some rural residents in their markets, especially if adjacent to populated centers, access remains an issue for rural Americans. For example, Ricketts and his colleagues found that the least populated and remote counties are not likely to be included in health management organization markets, areas estimated to house almost 17.8 million rural residents (1995). Moreover, the lower supply of mental health providers in rural areas has led to a greater reliance on primary care providers to deliver these services. In a recent study of AFDC Medicaid beneficiaries in Maine, Lambert and Agger found that rural beneficiaries had a significantly lower utilization of mental health services than did their urban counterparts (1995).

III. THE SAFETY NET

Medicare was implemented in 1965 to assure economic security to elderly Americans through the provision of health insurance coverage. Congress has added benefits and expanded eligibility. The Kaiser Foundation (1996) reports that more than 97 percent of America's elderly have enrolled in Medicare, which translates into approximately 38 million Medicare beneficiaries, including 4.8 million disabled individuals and persons with ESRD. Additionally, Medicare expenditures are expected to be $199 billion in 1996 (1996). Clearly, Medicare forms a major part of the safety net for many Americans. Although a very popular program with the elderly, recent concerns about the financial health of the program is generating public discussion about modifying and curtailing Medicare benefits and further curtailing payments to providers. Recent congressional efforts are tending to focus on reducing provider fees, further adding to the financial pressures on the already fragile safety net.

In the United States, health coverage offered through public assistance is generally related to Medicaid, which was implemented with the Medicare legislation. Medicaid is a means-tested entitlement program financed by state and federal governments and administered by each state. Federal guidelines specify coverage and mandate benefits. States willing to meet the mandates receive federal matching payments based on the state's per capita income, the federal share ranging from 50 to 80 percent of Medicaid expenditures (Kaiser, 1995). Since each state determines eligibility and reimbursement levels for Medicaid, coverage of health services varies across states resulting in access and utilization differentials (Barrilleaux and Miller, 1992; Howell, Baugh and Pine, 1988). Public assistance health coverage does not resolve, however, the various problems indigent patients face when meeting a fragmented system with transportation barriers and health provider shortages, due either to provider availability or insufficient acceptance of Medicaid reimbursement by providers. In addition, Medicaid has become an important source of long term care funding, a benefit for which it was not originally designed. This factor has added significant costs to the program but has also increased the safety net for the elderly and other vulnerable populations.

There were 27.4 million Medicaid person-year equivalent enrollees in 1992, a 60 percent increase since 1975 (Cromwell, 1995). The Kaiser Commission on the Future of Medicaid reports that Medicaid, in its role as a safety net, "finances care for over 32 million people: 16 million children and 7 million adults in low-income families, 5 million blind and disabled persons, and 4 million elderly" at a cost of $125.2 billion in 1993 (1995, p. v). Consequently, Medicaid is the "major public financing program providing health and long-term care coverage to millions of the nation's poor and vulnerable populations" (Kaiser, 1995, p. v).

The Omnibus Budget Reconciliation Acts (OBRAs) of 1980 and 1981 gave States greater flexibility in setting eligibility criteria and service coverage. The unintended consequence of legislative change was declining enrollments. This led to more Congressional action, including the Deficit Reduction Act of 1984 which extended coverage to pregnant poor women and infants, subsequent OBRAs and the Medicare Catastrophic Coverage Act of 1988, all of which extended coverage mandates (Cromwell, 1995). Although States have always had the option to pay Medicare premiums and deductibles for Medicaid-eligible beneficiaries, Congress enacted the Qualified Medicare Beneficiary program to increase participation by those qualified: "Medicare beneficiaries whose income do not exceed 100 percent of the Federal poverty rate and whose resources do not exceed twice the amount established for Supplemental Security Income (SSI) eligibility" (Neumann et al., 1995, p. 169). Over 2 million eligible beneficiaries are not participating and unfortunately, beneficiaries who do participate tend to be those most in need of assistance, that is those who have the lowest incomes, high utilization rates, less education, and are rural residents (Neumann et al., 1995).

IV. THE POLICYMAKING CHALLENGE

Since their inception in the mid-1960s, Medicare and Medicaid have improved the coverage of health care for the elderly and low income, helped to expand health services throughout the country, and served as a significant safety net for the vulnerable. However, uneven access is still a problem for many Americans, especially for the indigent. Not all persons eligible become enrolled in these two major public programs.

Many do not understand Medicare and Medicaid's complexities or are ill-informed about benefits. Many others face geographic, cultural, and/or administrative barriers. Nor do those enrolled necessarily get into the health care system in a timely way due to various enabling factors, such as transportation, provider availability, etc. In addition, there are gaps in coverage of services for both programs and growing provider frustration with complex requirements and relatively low reimbursement levels.

Unfunded federal mandates further stress state budget capacity. Friction between centralized control and decentralized flexibility further exacerbates the federal-state tension. Here the public policy dilemma stands. On the one hand, the rising costs of health care and the resulting drain on Federal and state budgets lead to increased public demand for health reform, that is, reduced expenditures. On the other hand, Medicare and Medicaid beneficiaries and their families as well as public health advocates are anxious about further barriers to health care, especially increased out-of-pocket expenses. Although managed care organizations offer the potential to improve access to preventive care and effective case management, skepticism about this approach remains. Many public health advocates argue the solution to be increased coverage and benefits, with some supporting a universal health system or systems similar to those in Canada, Germany, or Japan (Glaser, 1993). However, the negative response of middle-class elderly Americans to the Catastrophic Act and the strong negative public response to the Clinton health reform proposal signals that the public may not be ready to lose benefits, pay higher premiums, or significantly restructure the health systems. Clearly, health care reform will require deft hands and ingenious design if it is to resolve the conflicting expectations of the various stakeholders. Increasing constraints on consumer choice, limits on provider autonomy, and gaps in insurance coverage, however, may finally result in the public pressure for major restructuring of the health system.

Tennessee and its Medicaid managed care program, TennCare, offers an interesting case study in the challenges facing designers of health care reform programs and important lessons for health reformers (Clay, forthcoming). A focus on Tennessee is especially relevant because many states have expressed interest in Tennessee's Medicaid managed care program and Tennessee was the first state to shift its Medicaid program to a statewide demonstration project. Although TennCare has resulted in savings to the State budget, the effects of its implementation on communities still remain to be evaluated and problems resolved. Lessons to be learned from the Tennessee experience are that: health reform is messy, is highly political, causes unexpected shifts in structural alliances, and unevenly affects the provider community.

The federal government, however, is caught in a dilemma. On the one hand, during the beginning of his administration in the early 1990s, President Clinton was on record encouraging states to experiment with health care reform. The President and Congress also appeared ready to devolve more responsibility to the states for public programs. However, key public policy challenges related to medical indigency continue, whether addressed nationally or individually by states:

- What is the appropriate role for government in public health care? Just payor? Provider of last resort? The First Report of the National Commission on the State and Local Public Service (1993) lamented the national Medicaid crisis that has resulted from increasing federal cutbacks and recommended: "Begin to deal with the financing crisis in health care, with the federal government leading, following, or getting out the way."

- How should the government relate to the private sector and the non-profit sector? Regulator? Facilitator? What degree of oversight should be implemented?
- Should public assistance for health care be removed from its tie to welfare? Is health care a right or a privilege?
- Can states serve as laboratories if serious inequities result? Can we afford to have states risk disaster? How will we evaluate success? What about urban centers, such as Memphis, that serve more than its state?
- Should states allow local communities to have flexibility? If so, how does the state assure accountability? If not, can statewide programs meet and satisfy local situations?
- How do we fund services such as trauma units and neonatal centers that provide services to a whole region?
- How do we allocate funds for medical education? Can we rely on the market to affect individual medical career decision-making?
- Should something be done to help providers (hospitals, nursing homes, physicians, etc.) that are providing an disproportionate share of health care services to the medically indigent? Should government do more to target areas where there is a shortage of primary care providers?
- Given the current public and political mood, how realistic are proposals for health reform that will assure access to care when and where needed?

Answers to these questions need to be addressed if we are to eventually solve the problem of parity and equity of health services to vulnerable populations in our nation. Resolution of financial/insurance issues is not sufficient since other problems, structural and individual, compound the policy issue of medical indigency. At the same time, financial barriers are key barriers for many in accessing primary and preventive care. The theory of managed care, with its associated case management, lends itself to overcoming barriers to cooperation and communication among providers. Like most issues, however, the "devil" is in the details of implementation. TennCare has shown that Medicaid Reform can extend insurance coverage and constrain cost escalation. TennCare also demonstrates that information systems are essential if the public is to hold payers and providers accountable. Gaps in coverage and service fragmentation may still be occurring; provider availability remains a problem, especially, specialty care; effects on providers vary; and, individual behavioral issues remain. Medico-structural and behavioral issues continue to be thorny policy challenges, not easily resolved and not addressed by programs focused on insurance coverage.

REFERENCES

Aday, L. A. (1993). *At Risk in America.* Jossey-Bass, San Francisco.

Aday, L. A., Fleming, G., and Anderson, R. (1984). *Access to Medical Care in the U. S.: Who Has It, Who Doesn't,* Pluribus Press, Chicago.

Andersen, R., Chen, M., Aday, L. A., and Cornelius, L. (1987). "Health Status and Medical Care Utilization." *Health Affairs, 6:* 136-156.

Akin, B.V., Rucker,L., Hubbell, F. A., Cygan, R., and Waitzkin, H. (1989). Access to medical care in a medically indigent population. *Journal of General Internal Medicine, 4:* 216-220.

Barrilleaux, C. J. and Mark, M. (1992). Decisions without consequences: Cost control and access in state Medicaid programs. *Journal of Health Politics, Policy and Law, 17:* 97-118.

Blazer, D., Landerman, L., Fillenbaum, G., and Horner, R. Health services access and use among older adults in North Carolina: Urban vs rural residents, *American Journal of Public Health, 85:* 1384-1390.

Brown, L. D. (1991). The medically uninsured: Problems, policies, and politics. In *Health Policy and the Disadvantaged* (Lawrence D. Brown,ed.), Duke University Press, Durham, 169-183.

Clay, J. A. and Norris-Tirrell, D. (1995). *Maternal and Infant Needs Assessment: West Tennessee and Crittenden County, Arkansas,* March of Dimes Birth Defects Foundation, Memphis.

Cromwell, J. and Butrica, B. (1995). Hospital department cost and employment increases: 1980-92. *Health Care Financing Review, 17:* 147-165.

Cykert, S., Kissling, G., Layson, R, and Hansen, C. (1995). Heal insurance does not guarantee access to primary care. *Journal of General Internal Medicine, 10:* 345-348.

Davis, K. (1991). Inequality and access to health care. *Milbank Quarterly, 69:* 253-273.

Eggers, P. W. (1995). Racial differences in access to kidney transplantation. *Health Care Financing Review, 17:* 89-103.

Ellwood, M. R. and Kenney, G. Medicaid and pregnant women: Who is being enrolled and when, *Health Care Financing Review, 17:* 7-28.

Freeman, H. E., Aiken, L. H., Blendon, R. J. and Corey, C. R. (1990). Uninsured working-age adults: Characteristics and consequences. *Health Services Research, 24:* 811-823.

Gelberg, L., Linn, L. S., Usatine, R. P., and Smith, M. H. (1990.) Health, homelessness and poverty, *Archives Internal Medicine, 150:* 2325-2330.

Glazer, W. A. (1993). Universal health insurance that really works: Foreign lessons for the United States, *Journal of Health Politics, Policy and Law, 18:* 695-722.

Haas, J., Udvarhelyi, I., Morris, C., and Epstein, A. (1993). The effect of providing health coverage to poor uninsured pregnant women in Massachusetts, *JAMA, 269:* 87-91.

Hayward, R. A., Shapiro, M. F., Freeman, H. E., and Corey, C. R. (1988). Inequities in health services among insured Americans, *New England Journal of Medicine, 318:* 1507-1512.

Health Care Advisory Board. (1992a). *America's Uninsured: Issue Brief-Platinum Medicaid Sign-Up Program,* Author, Washington.

Health Care Advisory Board. (1992b). *America's Uninsured: Special Report for Civic and Business Leaders,* Author, Washington.

Howell, E.M., Baugh, D. K., and Pine, P. L. (1988). Patterns of Medicaid expenditures in selected states: 1980-84, *Health Care Financing Review, 10:* 1-16.

Hubbell, F. A., Waitzkin, H., Mishra, S. I., and Dombrink, J. (1989). Evaluating health-care needs of the poor: a community oriented approach. *American Journal of Medicine, 87:* 127-131.

Iglehart, J. (1984). Cutting costs of health care for the poor in California, *NEJM, 311:* 745-748.

Institue of Medicine. (1993). *Access to Health Care in America* (M. Millman, ed.), National Academy Press, Washington.

Institute of Medicine. (1988). *The future of public health,* National Academy Press, Washington.

Kaiser Foundation. (1996). *The Medicare and Managed Care,* Author, Washington.

Kaiser Foundation. (1995). *The Medicaid Program at a Glance,* Author, Washington.

Komaromy, M., Grumbach, K., Drake, M., Vranizan, K., Lurie, N., Keane, D., and Bindman, A. (1996). The role of Black and Hispanic physicians in providing health care for underserved populations, *NEJM, 334*: 1305-1310.

Lambert, D. and Agger, M. S. (1995). Access of Rural AFDC Medicaid Beneficiaries to Mental Health Services. *Health Care Financing Review, 17*: 133-145.

Makuc, D. M., Freid, V. M., and Kleinman, J. C.(1989). National trends in the use of preventive health care by women, *American Journal of Public Health, 79:* 21-26.

Melnick, G. A., Mann, J., and Golan, I. (1989). Uncompensated emergency care in hospital markets in Los Angeles county, *American Journal of Public Health, 79*: 514-516.

Mentnech, R. (1995). Overview: Access to Health Services for Vulnerable Populations. *Health Care Financing Review, 17*: 1.

Mitchell, J. B. and Kandker, R. K. (1995). Black-White Treatment Differences in Acute Myocardial Infarction. *Health Care Financing Review, 17*: 61-70.

Moscovice, I., Christianson, Johnson, J., Kralewski, J., and Manning, W. (1995). Rural Hospital Networks: Implications for Rural Health Reform. *Health Care Financing Review, 17*: 53-67.

Moy, E. and Bartman, B. A. (1995). Physician Race and Care of Minority Indigent Patients, *JAMA, 273*: 1515-1520.

National Commission on the State and Local Public Service. (1993). *Hard Truths/Tough Choices: An agenda for state and local reform,* Sponsored by the Nelson A. Rockefeller Institute of Government, State University of New York, Albany.

Neumann, P. J., Bernardin, M. D., Evans, W. N., and Bayer, E. J. (1995). Participation in the Qualified Medicare Beneficiary Program, *Health Care Financing Review, 17*: 169-178.

Pane, G. A., Farner, M. C., and Salness, K. A. (1991). Health care access problems of medically indigent emergency   department walk-in patients. *Annals of Emergency Medicine, 20*: 730-733.

Powers, R. D. (1988). Emergency department patient literacy and the readability of patient - directed materials. *Annuals of Emergency Medicine, 17*: 124-126.

Ries, P. (1993). Characteristics of Persons With and Without Health Care Coverage: United States, 1989. In *Contemporary Issues in Health Services*, (S. J. Williams, ed.), Delmar, Albany, 160-169.

Schur, C. L., Albers, L. A., and Berk, M. L. (1995). Health care use by Hispanic adults: Financial vs. Non-financial determinants, *Health Care Financing Review, 17*: 71-88.

Tuckman, H. and Chang, C. (1991). A proposal to redistribute the cost of hospital charity care, *Milbank Quarterly, 69*: 113-142.

U. S. Government Accounting Office. (1995). *Health Care Shortage Areas: Designations Not a Useful Tool for Directing Resources to the Underserved,* U. S. Government Accounting Office, Washington, DC.

Weisgrau, Sheldon. (1995). Issues in Rural Health: Access, Hospitals, and Reform, *Health Care Financing Review, 17*: 1-13.

White-Means, S. and Thornton, M. C. (1989). Nonemergency visits to hospital emergency rooms: A comparison of blacks and whites. *Milbank Quarterly, 67*: 35-57.

Williams, M. V. (1995). Inadequate functional health literacy among patients at two public hospitals, *JAMA, 274*: 1677.

Wilsford, (1995). States facing interests: Struggles over health care policy in advanced, industrial democracies, *Journal of Health Politics, Policy and Law, 20*: 571-613.

Wood, D. L., Hayward, R. A., Corey, C. R., Freeman, H. E., and Shapiro, M. F. (1990). Access to medical care for children and adolescents in the United States, *Pediatrics, 86*: 666-673.

10.
INTEGRATED HEALTH CARE SYSTEMS

Yvonne J. Kochanowski, *SteelEdge Business Consulting, Placerville, CA*

Today's health care delivery systems are changing; increasing numbers are form-ing some sort of integrated model. But what is integration? It does not look exactly the same in each system. Oftentimes each application of integration is unique. The next generation of system design and organizational challenge in health care is diffi-cult to define and even harder to foster with consistent, predictable results. And as health care futurist Jeff Goldsmith states:

> "In business, the correct organizational structure is the one that most
> elegantly and simply encourages the creation of value. In health
> care, we are only now learning that structure must follow from strat-
> egy, not precede it or somehow mystically embody it" (Goldsmith,
> 1994, p. 31).

Intuition, the sixth sense, should be present in an integrated health care system — not mandated in structure but consistent in the substance of achievements in organiza-tion. For example, components of care may be provided through programs owned and operated by the system. They may also be provided by contractors independent of the system. Factors of participation, models of integration, and motivations behind these new age health care partnerships differ from case to case. Quality care, provided in a cost-effective manner with measurable and qualitative outcomes — these are the results systems hope to achieve. The reality is too often very different from these goals. In an atmosphere of rapid change, Merry (1994) offers a ray of hope: "The most obvious benefit of unsettled times is the unique opportunity they afford to create rapid change," (p. 32). Out of the historical roots and strong traditions of the past, American health care reforms itself into new structures which will model the concepts and values of practice in the future.

The key today is combine, collaborate and coordinate as part of a system. Health care has transitioned from high levels of independence and autonomy in the early years of the United States to a focus on integrated systems of care which incorporate community needs, government participation, facility and provider services, physician group cooperation, and payor system partners. How did health care delivery become an integrated model? What features and criteria of integration are appropriate to expect in a successful partnership? Is this collaboration the way of the future or another passing fad in the provision of services?

This chapter will attempt to answer such questions. While much is written today on the status of integrated systems, few absolutes in terms of structure and content emerge. Innovation and collaboration are the watchwords; with financial resources becoming scarcer by the day, health care providers and payors at all levels are challenged to provide quality care in a cost-effective manner with outcomes that are successful from the patient's perspective.

I. HOW HAS THIS TREND EVOLVED?

To understand the evolution of today's integrated systems, it is important to study the development of the uniquely American health care system. This historical analysis of trends provides a frameworkto interpret the features which drive and motivate stakeholders in integrated systems and encourage or discourage their participation in the integration process.

A. Historical Basis

The American system of health care, comprised of physicians, providers and payors, was born out of the same spirit which gave birth to the country — individualism, autonomy, and survivalist instincts. As new frontiers opened in the early 1800's, few physicians were available for care. A member of each extended family, typically one of the women, became the resident expert on all things healing related. When someone fell sick, these experienced lay healers were called upon to provide health services with herbs, folk medicines, and experience originating from self-reliance.

If one was lucky enough to live near a town, a doctor may have been called to attend the sick. However, the practice of medicine by physicians was also very different during these early times. A fledgling physician would apprentice with an experienced doctor and would then practice alone, often in an area with few colleagues available for consultation. There were no medical groups, and learning was shared through professional journals which charted progress with early medicines, pharmacology, and healing practices. While the standard of individual practice remained, several events contributed to the reorganization of medicine:

- The advent of medical schools after the War of 1812,
- Credentialing and standards of practice with a medical license in the mid-1800s, and
- Consultations between physicians in the mid to late 1800s.

Meanwhile, facilities were making other strides towards organization. Early hospitals were dying wards for those who could not recover. Later, facilities became charitable projects of the wealthy. Large physician capital investments in facilities after the Civil War and a trend from social welfare to medical science transitioned hospitals from charities to formal places of healing. Nursing, antiseptic surgery and increased reliance on physician referrals similarly supported phases of development which changed hospitals from voluntary structures to religious and ethical organizations, and eventually evolving into for-profit businesses run by physicians and corporations by the turn of the century. This trend continues today as health systems have become segmented in markets representing non-profit organizations, for-profit chains, teaching institutions, and independent hospitals.

From a payor perspective, insurance has its roots in social programs as well. Originally intended to cover individual losses of income, medical fees, and indirect costs of illness to society, insurance became a right to benefits in the early 1930s. The focus shifted from stabilizing income and guaranteed wage replacement to financing and expanding access to medical care. By the 1950s, health insurance became a standard employment benefit extended to the family as well as the wage earner. The development of a sophisticated risk insurance market provided the third component of today's integrated systems.

B. Trends and Directions

According to Starr (1982), five trends shifted the individualized pieces of the health system towards the integrated structures existing today:

- Changes in type of ownership and control from non-profit and government organizations to for-profit companies.
- Horizontal integration of like providers into multi-institution systems.
- Diversification and corporate restructuring to corporations which strongly influence a geographic market.
- Vertical integration across the continuum of care at all levels of services.
- Industry concentration covering multiple regional and national geographies.

Three recent significant trends can be added to this list:
- Shifts from facility-based to outpatient, ambulatory and home care services, reducing the hospital power base;
- Changes in staffing patterns of care providers, reducing the impact of specialist physicians and increasing emphasis on physician extenders and alternative staffing models; and
- Increased pressures to reduce insurance premium costs, placing greater burdens on insurance companies to manage limited financial resources without being accused of withholding quality patient care.

Within this new framework the need for collaboration and alliances between physicians, providers, and payors to serve the patient have arisen. This framework begs integration between all levels of patient care and all stakeholders interested in the efficiency and effectiveness of the American health care system.

II. WHAT IS AN INTEGRATED DELIVERY SYSTEM?

Integrated health care delivery models are patterned on horizontal and vertical combinations of different levels of the continuum of care, types of providers, categories of payors, and needs of patients. This organizational realignment, traditionally performed to dominate the market, provides services to a greater portion of the patient population in a given geographic area. Theoretically, this realignment reduces the costs of services and improves service delivery for patients as well as the satisfaction of clients of the system. It occurs in response to the economics of managed care pressures within the health care marketplace.

A. Definitions

A fully integrated delivery system is most typically defined as a system which ties the financing for services to the provision of all services; all parties share risk. Care is provided at the most appropriate level of clinical and financial care. Accountability for the community health status — wellness as well as treatment of illness — is also a cornerstone. Conrad and Dowling (1990) expanded this definition:

> A vertically integrated health care system is an arrangement whereby a health care organization (or closely related group of organizations) offers, either directly or through others, a broad range of patient care and support services operated in a functionally unified manner....Full functional integration requires both administrative and clinical integration.

While this definition identifies the clinical continuum and support services of an integrated structure, little is mentioned about cost-effective provision of care. In responding to economic realities, the financial component must be built into the integration paradigm.

> Coddington, et al. (1995) define an integrated system as a system that combines physicians, hospitals, and other medical services, along with a health plan (or the ability of the system to enter into risk contracts), in order to provide the complete spectrum of medical care for its customers. In a fully integrated system, the three key elements — physicians, hospital(s), and health plan(s) — are kept in balance by common management and financial incentives so they can match medical resources with the needs of payers and patients.

Key characteristics of this definition include providers and payors, shared risk for the success of the venture, and cost effectiveness and information management systems which can maintain the efficacy of the system overall. Shortell, et al. (1994) add the following key characteristics to the definition:

We define an organized delivery system as a network of organizations that provides or arranges to provide a coordinated continuum of services to a defined population and is willing to be held clinically and fiscally accountable for the outcomes and the health status of the population served (p. 47).

These researchers further indicate that common ownership is not mandatory; in fact a variety of strategic alliances and contractual arrangements is appropriate. Expanding the organization further, this structure takes the perspective from the individual to the organization, and from the organization to the industry overall. This world view comes closer to reality. Since health systems are growing from regional to national alliances, the broadest handshakes possible must be considered.

B. Structure and Degrees of Integration

What does an integrated system look like? In asking graduate health care management students to draw a picture of the system's design, a variety of different structures develop. A traditional model is often the baseline (Figure 1).

Some will draw a pyramid (Figure 2), with the corners being the physician, the hospital, and the payor. The patient is centered inside the structure. Others will draw

Figure 1 - Traditional Health System Model

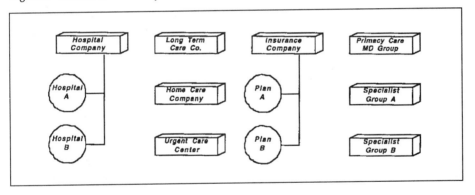

Figure 2 - Informal Health System Model

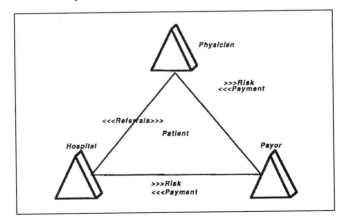

a modified human form, with the payor serving as the blood supply, the physician at the head, and the appendages and other body parts representing the provider parts of the continuum. The patient is at the heart of the form. Still others will draw a complex system of pulleys, fulcrums and levers.

None of these pictures is right per se, and all factually represent different versions of integrated systems. A more global interpretation of any graphic integrated system representation identifies major stakeholders and relationships, open to modification as the system and its internal and external factors evolve.

Rather than attempt to determine finite models, integrated health care systems need to incorporate a variety of features and elements which indicate that the action of combining organizational structures has begun to take place. Devers, et al. (1994) have identified three models of achieving integration. The first, functional integration, refers to the combination of support systems and business operations, including accounting and finance, human resources, planning, marketing, contracting and information systems. A second model looks at physician-system integration to foster a collaborative structure through economic links, risk sharing, governance, and administrative commitments. Clinical integration, the third model, focuses on coordinated patient care, multi-disciplinary treatment modalities, a full continuum of available services, and infrastructures such as medical records.

Research has further catalogued the degree of integration that has developed within each of these classifications. Functional systems are most likely to be integrated, with financial systems, strategic planning and support services exhibiting the greatest organizational standardization. Information systems, the skeletal structure of any coordinated system, are the least integrated (Devers, et al., 1994). In the physician-system relationship, physicians are most likely to be involved in management and governance, but Devers' research finds that little of this extends beyond more than one or two operating units (1994). Physician participation is high at the unit operating level in management and governance, but administrative involvement is low across the levels of the continuum. And while most health care organizations have formed networks and systems to provide an array of services across the continuum of care, clinical integration is the least integrated dimension of the three. Low to moderate levels of clinical integration exist across the continuum, exhibited by the difficulties in negotiating critical paths for care and other coordination tools. Ironically that the primary purpose of these systems — the provision of health care services — is the area where change is slowest to occur.

What are the important features of any definition of an integrated health care system? System wide success in financial and clinical purpose, greater effectiveness, clinical resource controls and maximization of resources all appear to be critical. However, the impact of integration on the physician, the provider system, and the payor must be considered in light of its effect on the key customer the patient.

III. WHAT FACTORS DETERMINE AN INTEGRATED STRUCTURE?

In a 1994 study, 71% of hospital and health network leaders said that their organizations trended towards integrated delivery systems that 81% felt would not exist as standalone institutions within five years (Bartlling, 1995). How, then, does an organization identify the appropriate time to integrate, and what format should this coordination take?

Four indicators can be used to gauge an organization's readiness for integration and the market's ability to cope with the restructuring. Strategic direction, economic processes, organizational culture, and unique clinical knowledge and capabilities provide evidence that the organization is ready to integrate and become part of a larger system.

A. Strategic Direction

Vision and values guide the strategic direction of an organization. The structure and design of the organization, its mission and objectives, and its intentions for the future are derivatives of the strategic direction. Some describe the strategic direction as the map which leaders and their constituents follow in walking (or running) the road into the future. Others describe it as a decision tree or flowchart of key activities and steps which will be required.

Direction is set through a consensus within a group of organizational leaders or through the vision of an individual awarded the intellectual and/or authoritative leadership of the group. This direction translates into a structure typically representing a cross-functional team responsible for managing a business, a geographical area, a function, or a core competence. Unfortunately, today's decision to join an integrated structure is most often made based on fear and uncertainty. When leadership identifies a level of risk which it deems to be high enough to warrant a move, change will take place. The decision is not necessarily too late or improper; it's simply that it takes a strong jolt to move out of the comfort zone.

B. Economic Processes

A number of economic forces lead to integration. The advent of more extensive managed care in a market creates a need to be more cost competitive. Cost containment, a concept which breeds concern about quality patient care, can be achieved through economics of scale in business office functions of the organization, better purchasing power, improved market share, and analysis of clinical treatment and patient outcomes. Enhancement of the bottom line is a strong lure towards opportunities realized in being part of a larger, integrated structure.

Coupled with cost concerns are patient flow control issues. An integrated network can offer the provider increased access to patients through a formal referral network, contractual relationships for preferred provider and exclusive relationships, and technological links through telemedicine, epidemiological studies, and critical paths which encompass a variety of patient care models. This patient control paranoia produces a fight for market share to improve the competitive edge of the individual provider organization. Preparation of an integrated model allows greater market flexibility in referral coordination which works through and around the problems typically limited by regulatory constraints.

C. Organizational Culture

The shared vision of an organization must be prepared to accept partnership and sustainability as part of its culture. Typically, health care providers have been encouraged to cultivate an atmosphere of individualism, competition, and incentive compensation based on the volume of care provided. Under an integrated culture, equal representation of partners, flexible structures of patient care across the continuum, craft work which moves beyond the assembly line patient care approach, and advanced information technology are necessary.

To be prepared for integration, the organization must reflect readiness to adopt a new set of norms and rituals consistent with this positive cultural change. Recognition of the roles and responsibilities of all parties in the new organization, acceptance of interactions with others, readiness to give up sole direction and leadership, and willingness to create positive human structures are signs that the organizational culture is ready to expand its knowledge and sphere of influence with other partners.

D. Unique Clinical Contribution

Synergism between levels of care are the primary reasons why organizations integrate. However, simply being ready to share patients is not enough preparation for the unique clinical care changes that an integrated structure provides. In addition to cost savings and coordination of service benefits, clinical coordination means operational stability within the chaos that is health care, a strong primary care physician base which encourages partnership, efficient delivery of medical services, and geographic access to physicians and other providers through the integrated network.

Readiness for clinical integration is fostered through coordinated patient care plans and true case management, formation of intraorganizational teams to develop and continuously improve patient care, support through technology providing a single medical record, and discharge planning which recognizes all patient care levels of the continuum. Information sharing between all levels improves the acceptance of care at different levels. Each party must also have knowledge and understanding about the continuum to assure that the patient is receiving the best available care.

Figure 3 - Four Phases of Integration

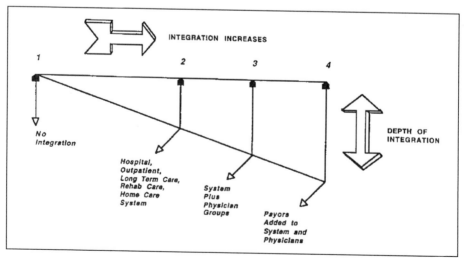

IV. HOW DOES INTEGRATION HAPPEN?

The creation of an integrated delivery system does not occur overnight. It is a multi-phased process with steps or levels occurring simultaneously in a market. Phases of integration development are captured in Figure 3.

A. A Four-Phased Approach

The first phase of integration is actually no integration. Providers and physicians are reimbursed for services on a discounted fee-for-service basis. Reimbursement for services is typically fee for service and discounted care. While some integration occurs in this phase through contracts for services not available from the caregiver, by and large the model is one of economic competition.

The second phase most often occurs at the hospital and associated program level. In this phase, a continuum of care is formed, including acute inpatient, ambulatory and outpatient, rehabilitation care, skilled nursing facility, and home care service components. Because of cost controls and the influence of managed care and associated changes in the delivery of care, providers begin to contract with each other to fulfill requirements within the provider continuum. Hospitals begin to contract with physicians, and the network becomes more sophisticated. Integration at this point in system development is primarily horizontal.

The third phase exhibits closer organizational alliances between the continuum provider network and physicians in the community. Shared risks and incentives require a system of financial alignment, and because the network represents a full spectrum of services, patients' cases can be managed to provide care in the most quality and cost-effective level within the continuum. Integration at this phase becomes vertical as well as horizontal in structure.

The fourth phase combines the providers and physicians with payors. Preventive care, outcomes measurement, quality incentives and service incentives characterize this phase. Equilibrium is maintained through management and financial balance between the provider system, the physicians, and the payors in order to exercise appropriate care in servicing the preventive and curative needs of the health plan member.

B. Where Processes Begin

Organizational integration and formation of a system network can begin in a number of ways: patient coordination, legal structure, office and administrative support functions and market driven moves. While no one indicator is more efficient than another, certain guidelines can strengthen the effectiveness of the actions taking place.

One most obvious process which leads to integration is the coordination of referral patterns across geographic coverage. For example, a physician admits a patient to the hospital where he or she has privileges. A hospital discharge planner sends the patient to a rehabilitation facility which meets the patient's specific care needs and is geographically appropriate or convenient for the patient. A home care agency receives the referrals for patients within its service area.

Another process which leads to integration is the formation of a new or reorganized legal structure. These legal relationships might include the purchase of another organization, interest shares in an organization, or common patient organizations. Single ownership organizations give way to shared ownership, management contracts, external party contracts, affiliation agreements, informal memorandums of understanding, and formal acquisitions and mergers.

Clinical integration occurs as a process for overall organizational integration. Development of critical paths, care tracks, and collaborative case management plans result in an interactive patient care process by addressing needs such as improved quality, more efficient delivery of care, and greater standardization. Oftentimes a provider cannot meet all patient needs. With appropriate system size and a mix of primary care physicians, specialists, and caregivers at all levels, joining together at a clinical level can develop into system integration.

Financial incentive alignments produce management structures which encourage integration. For example, payment systems such as capitation reimburse the primary provider for all services within the range of patient care for each enrolled member. These services may not be available within the organization, in which case contracting for the service is critical. Shifting from a contractual arrangement to a more formal close relationship can enhance financial performance and allow greater control for the managing organization.

Integration of information systems also brings about structural combinations. The current health care move towards greater focus on community health information systems (CHINs) encourages discussion of opportunities to compare and coordinate both data and services at other levels. Such recent advances in technology as speeding the transfer of data, allowing telemedicine connections in remote areas, and protecting confidentiality encourages providers to work together.

Operational guidance with common management and coordination of system elements has created integration processes. Coordinated marketing activities, shared high tech equipment, joint strategic planning, and shared administrative and management leadership positions create an organizational framework for integration. Issues such as team management, cross functional positions, and work group style can encourage the combination of organizations at the highest levels of the joint structure.

C. Critical Integration Tools

A number of human resources and organizational tools are critical to the integration process. These include staff empowerment, strong support systems, shared partnerships, and a focus which looks outward into the community as well as inward in the organization.

Staff empowerment, while often an overused term is critical to the concepts and effective implementation of integration as an organization becomes part of a larger integrated system. The role of a single manager expands to include more positions, greater responsibilities, and broader decision-making needs. With these broader responsibilities come more programs to overview, more people to review, and more information to process. An individual's ability to manage is finite, and the manager must rely on staff to assist in the expanded workload. Without staff empowerment and their acceptance of the new responsibilities and accountabilities, a manager is doomed to burnout and failure.

Planning also assists in effective integration implementation. Having a strategic plan which directs the organization and a tactical plan which guides daily operations, the organization can focus on implementation rather than constantly determining direction. This organizational planning process must incorporate the vision and judgments of stakeholders from all levels of the organization to assure a factual, formal and participative process. Actual operations and external environment must be continually assessed against the plan to assure that midcourse corrections are made appropriately and in a timely fashion. To accomplish this, a good information system to support decision making is required. This system includes clinical, cost, and competitive data, both internal to the integrated organization and external in the market.

Creating a flexible organizational structure, one in which physicians, hospital, continuum providers, and payors all play a flexible role which adapts to the changing needs of the marketplace, is another tool. This approach can begin from a hospital or health system, a physicians' group, a payor, or an existing integrated structure. For example, in some situations, physicians may take a leading role in developing a particular clinical specialty which assures a referral pattern for the system as a whole. In other cases, the health system may develop a contractual relationship which encourages use of multiple levels of the continuum of care. Each participant has a role to play in both developing and supporting the integrated structure.

Focusing on community as well as organizational needs is critical to integration effectiveness. The community needing a large network of primary care providers and the organization attracting specialist providers will not be competitive within the community in the provision of care. Similarly, re-engineering the cost of health care delivery at the expense of community programs will disconnect the organization from its greater purpose. As community report cards become more prominent, providing and maintaining measurable, superior health care quality will become a measure of strength. Improved communications and requisite data collection will similarly meet community needs.

Overall, integrated providers must think from a health care system focus, not limiting themselves to a perspective which only reflects a hospital or physician. Building consensus between internal and external partners, evaluating an integration strategy, selecting partners wisely, and performing due diligence will allow partners in the integrated approach to implement a business plan which concentrates on effective patient care while providing cost-efficient services.

V. IS INTEGRATION BENEFICIAL?

Integration maintains and grows market share within the service area, improves services available to patients, and reduces the costs of providing those services, allowing the system to realize a more healthy contribution to cost coverage. However, researchers disagree on the effectiveness of integrated systems in achieving these goals.

Goldsmith believes that systems actually add costs through additional layers of management and worsened access by fostering greater distances between care givers and patients. Market share has driven integration and provides little economic benefit to clients. Additionally, integrated systems cost millions of dollars to develop. Better results were achieved through models of "virtual integration" as coined by Steven Burrill from Ernst and Young, describing systems which are flexible and product or service driven (1994).

Shortell, et al. (1994) found evidence that early integrated systems did not demonstrate lower costs, higher care quality, or better access when compared to independent hospitals. These researchers maintained that four conditions needed to occur to achieve a greater degree of integration:

- members identify with the mission and values of the organization;
- strategic planning processes are in place that promote relevant input from across the system;
- information systems attempt to provide clinical data across the system; and
- budgeting policies and practices promote coordination across service lines (p. 15).

The result would be better clinical coordination and better financial performance in comparison to competitors.

Other researchers have discovered additional results. Coddington, et al. (1995) have found evidence that integrated systems are more cost effective and provide value added to payors and patients. This occurs through closer alignment of financial incentives, less duplication of expensive technologies and services, less inappropriate and unnecessary care, lower malpractice premiums, a more cost-effective mix of physicians, less use of inpatient days, more efficient use of assets, and lower premiums to members. Less data is available on the impact of integrated systems on quality of care, but organizations are committing significant resources to the improvement of information technology to measure patient outcomes. Integrated systems have been shown to make health care more accessible by improving convenience, increasing the number of primary care sites, providing smoother patient transition between levels of care, and offering other services such as urgent care and longer office hours. The financial investment is substantial to create an integrated system, but overall, it appears that the institution of these systems improves the provisions of health care in the U. S.

On a more practical note, integrated systems must judge the market correctly and meet the needs of the various stakeholders they serve. Having an appropriately sized network of providers, either through contracts or ownership, and being able to offer adequate access to patients throughout its geographic coverage area are also important features. Without this base coverage, the integrated system will not attract the referrals to its network of patient services. Tracking quality outcomes from patient care and acknowledging both excellence and areas for improvement in services will assist in setting future goals and appropriate tactics for addressing the organization's growth.

From a business perspective, the integrated system must be able to provide cost-effective care. This encompasses both understanding the current standard costs of providing care and being able to adjust costs and operations to respond to new payor restrictions. The legal structure can vary, including physician-hospital structures such as management services organizations, physician-hospital organizations, practice acquisition models, and equity models. Benefits include coordination of patient care, integrated clinical and financial resources, consolidated fixed costs and better buying power, outcomes management and patient satisfaction, support systems, and shared values.

VI. HOW CAN THE SYSTEM OVERCOME BARRIERS TO SUCCESS?

Success is now defined as becoming and remaining a financially viable, ongoing business concern. This means creating acceptable bottom line returns for the services and products provided. The key to this success is thinking flexibly, providing vision beyond what past models offered, and creating a structure which surpasses the best efforts of individual partners in the integrated delivery system. It creates synergy; the sum of the parts adds up to more that the individual pieces.

Integration models must respond to the needs of the community and the purchasers of the health plan. Critical links between provider systems, physicians and payors must be established. High quality delivery of care is necessary. However, barriers to effective collaboration in an integrated model include mixed financial incentives, undeveloped clinical information systems, lack of geographic coverage, ambiguous roles and responsibilities, an acute care paradigm, lack of strategic alignment, inability to execute the system's strategy, and an inability to mandate managed care (Shortell et al., 1994).

A. Mixed Financial Incentives

Different providers within the health care continuum receive compensation for services based on alternative methods. For example, most hospital reimbursement for Medicare services is based on a Diagnosis Related Group (DRG) which limits reimbursement to a set figure for all care required for a specific diagnosis. This model encourages cost controls and standardized care. Physicians paid under a fee-for-service model, have incentives to provide services but within a more limited cost structure. Home health agencies, paid under a cost reimbursed model, are encouraged to incur appropriate costs for care up to the limits of their caps, but are given fewer authorizations for visits and therefore may look more closely at the care plan. Many argue that insurance companies want to control both costs and quantity, but are willing to concede quality as a result.

When each component of the system realizes different financial incentives for its services, the alignment of both intentions and resources is difficult to achieve. Moves towards incentive structures such as capitation may modify and realign these incentives. However, capitation is not a financial incentive alignment mechanism which appeals to all parties. For example, Health Maintenance Organizations (HMOs) are interested in moving risk to the provider level. Responsibility for authorizing care would similarly move to the provider, and HMOs would lose control over both the services provided and the costs of care. For aggressive cost containment providers, capitation can assure a regular revenue stream while covering an array of patient services. Again, alignment may not be achieved even under these evolving structures.

B. Undeveloped Clinical Information Systems

Effective management runs on information — for health care, clinical information, cost accounting data, and quality outcomes tracking. However, the ability of information technology to provide what management needs have been lacking. In the best of all worlds, an insurer can tell contracted providers about their plan members, including what types of illnesses, injuries and kinds of preventive care to expect, frequency of services required, and other coverage factors. The provider, in turn, would plan staffing and products to meet these assumed needs. The provider could assess needs on an activity based costing model, and would adjust future requirements by changing volume environments. As care is provided, clinical records would be shared by physicians and other clinical staff, even in situations of remote geographic care coverage.

In reality, most payors have incomplete information on the health status of their plan members. Information that exists is usually not available to the provider in an automated format. Providers have staffing and product information, but cost accounting is not tied to the services provided. In essence, providers cannot determine the projected cost of care based on expectations about future critical, diagnostic and preventive care needs. Variance analysis is weak, since the information system is not structured to analyze data in a three-dimensional or matrix fashion. Similarly, the patient's clinical information cannot be shared in a real-time basis, and longer term information sharing often relies on paper reports rather than online services. Until information technology allows for ease of access while controlling confidentiality, and until costs for hardware, software and custom programming become financially feasible for all health care provider levels, organizations will continue to require staffing to manage and share data in an inconsistent and incomplete fashion throughout the network of payors and providers.

C. Lack of Geographic Coverage

Often, an integrated system stops at the borders of its service area. For care outside the area, out-of-network providers take over the patient's care. In some cases, the patient may elect continuing coverage outside the network. While this problem begs a solution, broader coverage can be offered through ownership and contractual relationship with equally good results.

Because of regulatory constraints, contracting challenges, and lack of common goals, health systems experience holes in their provider networks. Physician groups, allied hospitals, and other components of the continuum of care cannot offer broad coverage for all insured plan members, and consequently, multiple contracts and overlapping management and administrative systems are required. Until organizations align both vertically across the continuum and horizontally offering coverage in broader geographies, efficient systems integration will be difficult to achieve.

D. Ambiguous Roles and Responsibilities

In some care structures, the physician is the gatekeeper, gauging the appropriate care required by a patient, the specialists and tests needed, and the length of service required. Other structures maintain this control in the hands of the payor authorizers for care. Hospitals accept the rigors of care for those without insurance coverage, and other providers separately control the access of patients to the system.

Similarly, contracting for services is often confusing. Hospital systems agree to provide care and are held financially responsible for services over which they have no control, such as physicians' services. Similarly, physicians are asked to cover outpatient services and products for which they must contract separately. Roles and responsibilities of all parties must be clearly defined and structured to encourage cooperative arrangements which make sense for appropriate patient care.

E. Acute Paradigm

In many health systems, the transition to outpatient and ambulatory services has been slow. Some integrated systems maintain that the appropriate site for care occurs in the acute or hospital-based setting. It is difficult to change this paradigm when organizations have made significant financial investments in bricks and mortar. Fear of major shifts in patient care further blocks the ability of integrated systems to change their focus.

The health care provider community's ability to meet patient needs is exhibited by the increasing use of ambulatory surgeries, outpatient rehabilitation and home based care. Most of these changes have occurred without significant deterioration of patient outcomes, and in many cases, the patient appears to have benefited from the change. However, these sites of care require fewer staff, less administration, and smaller investments in the traditional physical plant. Moving towards alternative sites for care requires providers to change traditional thinking in the integrated system of the future.

F. Lack of Strategic Alignment

Many organizations face differing views from within their organizations and face additional challenges in the scope of vision and values they often do not share with their organizational partners. Since goals vary, strategic alignment for purposes of creating integrated patient care models is difficult to achieve.

Health care leaders are asked to inspire and challenge their stakeholders and partners, staff and employees, and external constituents to buy in to the organization's mission and objectives. When internal parties do not agree on the mission of an organization, external groups are less likely to find common ground. Common vision and values to motivate the organization's future depend on strategies for collaboration.

G. Inability to Execute the System's Strategy

Many of the shortcomings listed above lead to difficulties in successfully operationalizing the integrated system's strategy. When a system cannot put its plan into action, whether this is due to regulatory and legal hurdles, unresponsive organizational partners, or fiscal limitations, the move towards integration is slowed. Future ability to integrate must necessarily be based on appropriate consideration of options and alternative tactics for those situations in which structural problems occur.

H. Inability to Mandate Managed Care

Despite the industry's best efforts to control escalating costs of services, managing patient care is not an option in many areas. For example, patients without adequate insurance coverage will always enter at the emergency room door, and the hospital must provide the basic care requirements of that patient. Similarly, certain geographic areas, particular disease processes, and entitlements to care will continue to foster fee-for-service arrangements with few limitations. When an existing health care system attempts to integrate in order to address these specific challenges, it also must realize that some portion of the system will continue to operate in the traditional model.

VII. PROGNOSES, BOUNDARIES, AND RISKS FOR THE FUTURE

The health care arena is shifting rapidly, and like a patient who rises from the hospital bed too quickly, stakeholders are dizzy with the rapid changes and paradigm shifts which we are experiencing today and will continue to face into the future. Clinical pathways, health care as a business, financial realignment, quality as a cost saving measure, and institutional entrepreneurship have become the new buzzwords.

Future industry risks will evolve around a seeming inability to understand the changes occurring, unwillingness to accept those changes, and confusion over the myriad structural and process changes. Roles and responsibilities, strategies, and alignments must shift to reflect new partnership goals. Only then can the structural changes made to create an integrated delivery system take the most profound effect. Shared leadership framed within a new collaborative approach for the future and recognition and incorporation of future trends will be critical to the system's present recovery and ongoing health.

A. Shared Leadership Model

Shared leadership through a collaborative structure will be critical to future success. Evolving new practices of leadership will incorporate both the traditional clinical leader — the physician — and the health system administrative — the scientific manager. The characteristics of individuals within this shared leadership approach will include the following:

- Ability to manage complex managerial tasks, including financial management, people management and systems development throughout the integrated network.
- Strong values for leadership capabilities of others, expressed as both verbal belief in others, and practice of the organization in its daily operations.
- Knowledge and skills for the field, exhibited by an understanding of the clinical, management, and payor perspectives in the provision of health services.
- Wisdom about people and a sense of inspiration, to bring all stakeholders to the table looking towards the future of the process.
- Ability to get along with people of many different viewpoints, since the field attracts and will continue to attract individuals from all walks of life and all belief systems to its ranks.

A more collaborative leadership structure, one which relies less on the vision of the individual and more on the vision of the group as the values-creating process, will allow enhanced organizational performance for the future.

B. Future Trends

The future will bring continued change to the integrated system environment. Patient centered outcomes, preventive care, ties to clinical critical paths, investment in technology, and staff at the system entry level as well as the curative level remain buzzwords of this future period. Seamless integration of administration and management, education, clinical and public health service will similarly change the dynamics between public and private providers. Success factors will include making the system the right size, interfacing with the community needs, sharing risk, developing new management and governance models, and developing regulatory models of licensure and certification which accommodate integrated systems.

The trends throughout this text will offer the critical reader options for selecting a path along which future goals and objectives can be realized. From an integrated perspective, the road will be bumpy. However, the patient should make a full recovery, and perhaps even gain greater functionality than before.

REFERENCES

Anthony, M.F. and Sheridan J.F. (1994). Essentials for PHO Success. *Health care Executive, 9*(3): 16-19.

Bartling, A.C. (1995). Integrated Delivery Systems: Fact or Fiction. *Healthcare Executive, 10*(3): 6-11.

Beckman, J. D. (1995a). Altered States. *Healthcare Forum Journal, 38*(5): 70-79.

Beckman, J. D. (1995b). Redefining Work in the Integrated Delivery System. *Healthcare Forum Journal, 38*(3): 76-82.

Bureau of National Affairs, Inc., The. (1994) Voluntary Purchasing Alliances Gaining Momentum in California. BNA California - *Health Care Report, June 10*: 242-243.

Burns, L.R. and Darrell P.T. (1993). Trends and Models in Physician-Hospital Organization. *Health Care Management Review, 18*(4): 7-20.

Cave, D.G. (1995). Vertical Integration Models to Prepare Health Systems for Capitation. *Health Care Management Review, 20*(1): 26-39.

Coddington, D.C., Moore K.D. and Fischer, E.A. (1994a). Costs and Benefits of Integrated Healthcare Systems. *Healthcare Financial Management, 48*(3): 21-29.

Coddington, D.C., Moore K.D., and Fischer E.A. (1994b). In Pursuit of Integration. *Healthcare Forum Journal, 37*(2): 53-59.

Coddington, D.C., Moore, K.D. and Fischer E.A. (1995). Integrating? Hang in There — The Odds Are In Your Favor. *Healthcare Forum Journal, 38*(1): 72-76.

Coile, R.C., Jr. (1994). Guiding the Integrated Delivery Network. *Healthcare Forum Journal, 37*(6): 16-23.

Conrad, D.A. and Dowling W.L. (1990). Vertical Integration in Health Services: Theory and Managerial Implications. *Health Care Management Review, 15*(4): 9-22.

Cummings, K.C. and Abell R.M. (1993). Losing Sight of the Shore: How a Future Integrated American Health Care Organization Might Look. *Health Care Management Review, 18*(2): 39-50.

Devers, K.J., Shortell S.M., Gillies R.R., Anderson D.A., Mitchell J.B. and Morgan K.L. Erickson. (1994). Implementing Organized Delivery Systems: An Integration Scorecard. *Health Care Management Review, 19*(3): 7-20.

Flower, J. (1995). Built to Last: A Conversation with James C. Collins. *Healthcare Forum Journal, 38*(5): 62-68.

Friend, P. M. and Spence M. (1994). Driving Forces Behind Integration: Weigh Your Options. *Healthcare Executive, 9*(3): 12-15.

Griffith, J.R. (1995). The Infrastructure of Integrated Delivery Systems. *Healthcare Executive, 10*(3): 12-17.

Goldsmith, J.C. (1994). The Illusive Logic of Integration. *Healthcare Forum Journal, 38*(50): 26-31.

Goldstein, D. (1995). Moving Beyond Generic Integration Models. *Healthcare Financial Management, 49*(4): 56-62.

Kaufman, N. (1995). Competing in an Integrated Healthcare Market: Four Strategies for Success. *Healthcare Executive, 10*(3): 18-22.

Menard, B. and Kathleen D. (1994). Eleven Key Strategies for Joining or Forming a Network Venture. *The Remington Report, April/May*, 25-31.

Merry, M.D. (1994). Shared Leadership in Health Care Organizations. *Topics in Health Care Financing, 20*(4): 26-38.

Rynne, T.J. (1995). Bringing an Integrated System to Market: The Fundamental Things Apply. *Healthcare Forum Journal, 38*(6): 52-59.

Scanlan, L. Jr. (1995). Building Consensus for Integration. *Healthcare Financial Management, 49*(1): 33-43.

Schultz, D.V. (1995). The Importance of Primary Care Providers in Integrated Systems. *Healthcare Financial Management, 49*(1): 58-63.

Sheehy, J.P. (1994). Health Care Leaders Work on 'the Vision Thing'. *Hospitals & Health Networks, 68*(1): 47-59.

Shortell, S.M., Gillies, R.R. and Anderson, D.A. (1994). The New World of Managed Care: Creating Organized Delivery Systems. *Health Affairs, 13*(5): 46-64.

Starr, P. (1982). *The Social Transformation of American Medicine*, Basic Books.

Tweed, S.C. and Weber, A.J. (1994). Integration, Autonomy, and a Seamless Health Care system: Models and Strategies for Redefining Your Organization. *Outreach, July-August*: 5-6.

Wachel, W. (1994). The Leadership Challenge of Integrated Delivery Systems. *Healthcare Executive, 9*(5): 12-15.

Wilford, D.S. and Annison, M.H. (1995). The Collaborative Competitors. *Healthcare Forum Journal, 38*(6): 28-31.

11.
COMMUNITY-BASED PLANNING

Bruce W. Kieler, *University of Southern Mississippi, Hattiesburg, MS*

Ishak Saporta, *Tel Aviv University, Tel Aviv, Israel*

Zakiyyah El'Amin, *Alameda County Department of Public Health, Oakland, CA*

The rapidly changing health care industry in the U.S.A. suggests a dynamic and turbulent organizational environment. Into this complex and unpredictable environment an unusual type of planning organization is being embedded, namely, the community-based participatory planning entity. This type of entity is also called the participatory community planning entity or organization. Establishment of these new organizations is being mandated by both federal and state legislation. The premier examples of these new entities are the HIV Health Services Planning Council mandated by Title I of the Ryan White Comprehensive AIDS Resources Emergency Act of 1990 (the CARE Act) (Public Law 101-381), as amended in 1996, and the HIV Health Care Consortium mandated by Title II of the CARE Act. Another such planning entity is the HIV Prevention Community Planning Council that is mandated by the Centers for Disease Control and Prevention. The HIV Prevention Planning Council has responsibility for addressing the needs for education about and prevention of HIV infection in almost all public health jurisdictions in the U.S.A.

Community-based participatory planning entities have many of the characteristics that define a coalition (e.g., Brown, 1984; Feighery and Rogers, 1989). Definitions of each of these entities, as well as enumeration of their respective roles, responsibilities, and mandates, are usually provided in the specific legislation or program announcements authorizing their use. Specific instructions to local health jurisdictions about establishing these entities are often contained in the program guidance issued by the federal or state agency responsible for implementing the program. (For example, see Academy for Educational Development, 1994, and McKay, 1994, for extensive discussions on the HIV prevention community planning process.)

In reporting on a multi-year observational study of the Oakland HIV health services planning council, Kieler et al. (1996) note that at the time the CARE Act was enacted by the U.S. Congress, the use of community-based participatory planning entities was popular with HIV/AIDS advocates, HIV/AIDS service organizations, and federal officials alike. This model of health care and support services planning provided a way for community-based organizations and public sector agencies, as well as individuals infected and affected by HIV disease, to play key roles in these newly initiated and federally mandated planning councils. Additionally, this model appealed to local agencies because it offered local control over the allocation of funds to meet local needs for health care and support services. The model appealed to federal officials because it placed AIDS constituency groups in the position of having to work collaboratively at the local level to achieve expanded availability of services rather than constantly appealing to Congress and the federal executive branch in an ad hoc fashion for more funds.

The experiences of a number of planning councils in different parts of the country, most notably the Oakland HIV Health Services Planning Council, suggest that this model of planning does work, but not in the collaborative, rational fashion envisioned in the CARE Act. As Kieler et al. (1996) report, local control of the program in the Oakland area was accompanied by interorganization conflict, accusations of personal and organizational misconduct, frequent challenges to the legitimacy of the process, and a general sense that local political factors played too great a role in priority setting, in resource allocation decisions, and in contracting for services. However, despite these difficulties, the Oakland planning council was able to distribute funds approximately on schedule to local service providers, and the availability of needed services was increased. The findings of the Oakland study suggest a number of ways that a planning council could be structured in order to increase its effectiveness while reducing the interpersonal and interorganizational stress among service providers that the process induced in the past. (For a detailed analysis of the outcomes associated with a previous federally sponsored program implemented in the Oakland metropolitan area, see the classic report entitled *Implementation: How Great Expectations In Washington Are Dashed In Oakland; Or, Why It's Amazing That Federal Programs Work At All,* by Pressman and Wildavsky, 1973.)

Several papers on Title I planning councils look at the various issues and challenges that confront planning councils (Bowen et al., 1992; Kieler et al., 1996), the initial stages of development of a typical planning council (Kachur et al., 1993; Kieler, 1994), institutionalization and legitimation of a planning council process (Kieler, 1994), decision making by a planning council (Kieler, 1994), and the organizational environment and organizational form of a planning council (Kieler, Rundall, and Saporta, 1996). Other papers on the Title I process focus on the types and availability of HIV/AIDS services before and after the allocation of Title I funds (Marconi et al., 1994; Gentry and Rundall, 1995; Rundall et al., in press) as well as on the impacts of the various CARE Act titles (Fleishman et al., 1992; Penner, 1992a, 1992b; McKinney, 1993; McKinney et al., 1993; Mor et al., 1993; Mor et al., 1994). Several major unpublished manuscripts focus on the implementation of the various CARE Act titles, including a report submitted to the AIDS Action Foundation (Doughty, 1993) and a report submitted to the Kaiser Family Foundation (Ryan White Study Group, 1994).

Much additional work needs to be done to develop a theory-based literature that will document, explain, and analyze all aspects of the establishment, operation, development, and effectiveness of these newly mandated community-based participatory planning entities, and guide the establishment and development of future participatory planning entities. Such a literature might also serve as the basis for building organizational theory specific to participatory planning entities.

The study of community-based participatory planning entities can be based on a wide variety of theoretical perspectives, including the literature on small group formation, authority in groups, procedural justice, group decision making, conflict resolution, organizational environment and form, institutionalization of new organizational forms, population ecology of organizations, organizational innovation and change, organizational alignment with the environment, management of strategic alliances, and coordination of services. The goal of this chapter is to examine several of the leading theoretical perspectives that are relevant to the study of the expanding organizational population of community-based participatory planning entities.

I. AN INTEGRATED THEORETICAL MODEL

Federal and state programs mandating the use of community-based participatory planning entities in local-level health care and support services environments are only a part of the major changes that are resulting in the restructuring of health care and health-related services. Scott (1993) observes that the medical care field is a multifaceted and dynamic scene, that it is complex and rapidly changing, that health care organizations in the U.S.A. have undergone a revolution during the past half century, and that particularly dramatic changes have occurred during the past two decades. In order "to throw some light on the current situation," Scott describes the nature of the changes that have occurred in health care organizations, particularly those in the medical care delivery system. He is convinced that "we will not make much headway in our understanding of complex societal systems until we begin to examine the ways in which institutional and technical environments, organizational fields, [organizational] populations, organizational sets, and individual organizations act and interact to constrain and change each other" (p. 296).

In describing the nature of the changes that have occurred in health care organizations and the medical care delivery system, Scott (1993) formulates a general theoretical framework within which to view, interpret, and explain such changes. This framework may provide us with a basis for studying the formation, operations, and organizational development of the numerous new organizations, including participatory planning entities, that are emerging in the health care and support services environment.

Scott (1993) begins by noting that the various organization theories (population ecology, strategic management, resource dependency, transactions costs, and institutional theory), which are used by analysts to account for one or another feature of the changing health care scene, "have only recently been developed [most appeared after 1975] and are typically treated by organizational analysts as offering contradictory or competing explanations" (p. 272). Scott feels, however, that each of these perspectives is limited and provides only a partial account of the complex phenomena being observed. While development of unified theory is beyond the scope of his paper, he does propose that "the search for an improved, detailed understanding and for verifiable accounts will be advanced by the development of more integrative frameworks that seek to define where and when — to what types of phenomena and under what conditions — the various theory fragments apply" (p. 272). He proposes that the "effort to understand the medical care system should begin at the most comprehensive level — the institutional environment — and then proceed to examine more and more delimited systems and units" (p. 273).

The key features of the organizational analysis model that Scott proposes include three levels, namely, the organizational environments level, the organizational fields/populations level, and the organizational sets/organizations level. For each level, he identifies the appropriate theoretical perspective to use in discussing activities at that level.

Scott then goes on to identify the major trends in the development of the U.S. health care sector. These include such features as the increased scale of the medical care system, the increased concentration of the medical resources devoted to the delivery of health services, and the increased specialization of both individual providers and medical care organizations. These trends also include greater diversification, such as in the range of services and types of clients served. Scott points out that other trends in the health care sector include increased linkages among provider organizations, increased governmental involvement in the health care system, increased privatization, increased managerial and reduced professional influence, and increased market orientation of the health care system.

Within this rapidly changing health care sector are embedded the newly established community-based participatory planning entities to which so many must now turn for health care, support services, and prevention/education.

II. ORGANIZATIONAL ENVIRONMENT AND FORM

Bidwell and Kasarda (1985) note that organizational form is composed not only of the interpersonal relations of the members of the organization, but also contains properties which pertain to the organization conceived of as a collectivity with a unitary character. Some of these properties can be regarded as aggregates of interpersonal relations, such as the division of labor and hierarchy. Others may not be so regarded, such as the size and composition of an organization's membership, its stock of technological and material resources, its own institutional characteristics (structure, bylaws, rules, policies, and processes), and the technological, physical, demographic, and institutional properties of its environment. The authors caution against using a behavioral approach to a theory of organizational form because of the likelihood that such an approach would yield a theory of "unmanageable complexity and intellectual difficulty." Instead, they espouse a macro-social approach which allows the treatment of the aggregative properties of the organizational collectivity without appeal to the mediation of interpersonal ties or exchanges. They note that in "taking this step other properties of the collective unit (such as technology, rules, and laws) are introduced into the web of systemic relationships at the level of the collectivity" (p. 25).

Bidwell and Kasarda next define organizational environment to include all external phenomena that affect or could affect an organization. They identify four aspects of the environment, namely, the supplies of resources, the actors who supply them or who in other ways may affect their supply, the flows of resources to and among the various populations of organizations within the environment, and the relationships among the environmental actors that influence the flow and utilization of resources. The first two are compositional aspects of the environment and the third and fourth are relational aspects (p. 38).

Bidwell and Kasarda (1985) divide the organizational environment into an "internal" and an "external" environment. The internal environment is synonymous with the structure of the organization itself. They posit that organizational structure is the locus of opportunities for and constraints upon the organization's further morphological evolution. The existence of the external environment in its relational aspects — that is, the surrounding social and normative order — is another principal source of these opportunities and constraints (p. 39).

If participatory planning entities, such as the CARE Act/Title I planning councils, are viewed as organizations, then this population of organizations is continually expanding as additional metropolitan areas turn to this type of organization to address local needs for health care, support services, and disease prevention/education. The specific organizational form that characterizes all participatory planning entities is not a unique form. Although at first glance an argument might be made that these entities have the characteristics of "synthetic" organizations as defined in Thompson (1967), their apparently increasing permanence and institutionalization in the local health care environment suggest something more. All such entities appear to have many of the characteristics of what is known in the organizational behavior literature as a "minimalist" organization.

The minimalist organizational form is clearly identified by Halliday, Powell, and Granfors (1987, 1993) in a study of the vital events observed in the organizational population of state bar associations. Furthermore, Aldrich et al. (1990) use a similar approach in their study of U.S. trade associations. Both of these studies focus on minimalist organizations in the private sector and use the population ecology of organizations perspective. (For discussions on population ecology of organizations, see Hannan and Freeman, 1977, 1984, and 1989; Hannan and Carroll, 1992; Singh, 1990; and Tucker, Singh, and Meinhard, 1990.)

The studies of minimalist organizations note that such organizations are structurally flexible, frequently exist in relatively noncompetitive environments, and have long life spans. These organizations may not demonstrate the patterns of foundings and failures characteristic of most business organizations and especially not the liability of newness. They are called "minimalist" because they require minimal resources for founding and sustenance.

In the case of Title I planning councils, the boundaries of each respective eligible metropolitan area define the area in which a particular planning council has the responsibility and authority to plan, prioritize, and allocate resources for health care and support services for persons with HIV disease. Except for the required annual submission for a supplemental grant application, through which the metropolitan areas participating in the Title I program receive additional grant funds based on the merits of their application, there is supposedly no competition among the organizational population of Title I planning councils or the eligible metropolitan areas in which they operate.

Kieler, Rundall, and Saporta (1996) posit that the HIV health services planning council, as mandated by Title I of the CARE Act, have all four of the core dimensions manifested by minimalist organizations as well as the dimensions of the subclass of minimalist organizations enjoying a monopoly in a particular environmental niche. They conclude that the Title I planning councils represent a new organizational population of mandated minimalist organizations in the public sector. Use of the population ecology of organizations perspective in the study of these planning councils could contribute to a greater understanding of this particular organizational population, as well as other organizational populations of participatory planning entities.

III. COORDINATION OF SERVICES

The responsibility for developing a regional comprehensive plan for the delivery of health care and support services for persons with HIV disease makes the HIV Health Services Planning Council mandated by Title I of the CARE Act a key element in the coordination of such services at the local level. It can, therefore, be expected that the planning council could face many of the same problems and barriers that Aiken et al. (1975) found to be impeding efforts in the planning and implementation of integrated and coordinated mental health service delivery systems. These barriers include fragmentation of services, inaccessibility of services, lack of accountability of service delivery agencies, discontinuities in services, dispersal of services, wastefulness of resources, ineffectiveness of services, short-term commitments, and multiple local governments. Barriers to coordination are linked to aspects of the service delivery system, including organizational autonomy, professional ideologies, conflicts among various client interest groups, and conflicts over who is to control the resources (p. 4). Many of these same barriers to coordination and issues of ideology that Aiken et al. observed in the 1970s were also observed during the Oakland Planning Council case study in 1992-95, or 20 years after they were first identified in a study of mental health service delivery systems. Kieler et al. (1996) discuss the challenges and issues faced by the Oakland Planning Council.

Aiken et al. (1975) note that professional ideologies often prevent professionals in one field from wanting to cooperate with professionals in another field. They observe that competing client interest groups may be working at cross-purposes, cancel out each other's efforts, and present a less than united front in the community. They also note that service organizations frequently put their own survival and prestige ahead of the needs of the clients. They point out various studies that show that acceptance of clients by service organizations depends on social, cultural, and historical factors, and not just on the needs of the clients; that agencies refer clients to places that profit the agency, rather than to places good for clients; and that agencies like to have the right clients rather than those with the most pressing problems.

Aiken et al. suggest that one way to conceive of a coordinated delivery system was to view it as a change process having several stages. These stages of development are identical to those noted by Hernandez and Kaluzny (1994) and include awareness, initiation of effort, implementation, and routinization or institutionalization. In each stage, specific critical problems emerge:

- Awareness stage. The coordination effort usually has an initial period of increasing agitation by community groups and awareness by professional groups that treatment requires specialized services and new programs (p. 22).
- Initiation of effort stage. Problems of gaining power, legitimacy, and funding usually occur in the initiation stage of the coordination effort (p. 22).
- Implementation stage. The problems that arise during implementation usually stem from the choice of the organizational structure for the service delivery system, internal conflicts among the key participants, and lack of effective control over other organizations, that is, resistance to implementation by some of the participants. Another problem that might arise is the transformation of the goals of the change agent. As failures in achieving objectives occur, goals of the program may become displaced; that is, the change agent might scale down its objectives and begin to concentrate on particular goals that reflect its inherent interests and values (p. 23).
- Routinization stage. The primary problem that might emerge lies with the resource controllers. Without their continued support, even the best of programs or service delivery systems would be jeopardized (p. 23).

Not only could the Title I planning council process in a particular metropolitan area face the various problems associated with the first three stages noted by Aiken et al. (1975), it could also face the uncertainty of continued funding. In spring 1995, efforts were begun in the U.S. Congress to secure reauthorization of the Ryan White CARE Act for an additional five-year period. As of January 1996, the fate of the CARE Act had not yet been decided, nor had any funds been appropriated for the Act's various titles for the fiscal year to begin in fall 1996. Non-reauthorization of the CARE Act would have resulted in major changes in the organizational environment of all Title I planning councils, and possibly in their demise as a regional planning and coordinating process for health care and support services for persons with HIV disease. Fortunately, however, final reauthorization was approved by the Congress in March 1996.

IV. IMPLICATIONS OF THE OAKLAND CASE FOR PRACTITIONERS

Analysis of the data pertaining to the Oakland metropolitan area's HIV Health Services Planning Council includes a systematic examination, discussion, and critique of several key aspects of the Ryan White CARE Act, the organizational form of the planning council, and the organizational environment in which a planning council must function. It also includes a description of the organization of the Title I process in the Oakland eligible metropolitan area and a discussion on the major issues that the planning council successfully dealt with during the period 1992 through 1994. It applies a process model of organizational development and change to the planning council's efforts to reform its organizational structure, bylaws, processes, and procedures, and it examines the planning council's efforts to assure adherence to the planning council's own bylaws and Robert's Rules of Order, and to assure the compliance by all planning council members with the conflict-of-interest requirements.

The Oakland study also presents the implications for practitioners of the issues that arose to challenge the planning council during the period of observation. The primary issues and challenges that the Oakland HIV Health Services Planning Council faced are probably typical of all such participatory planning entities established in multicultural urban areas. These include multiple, complex interorganizational relationships, conflict of interest, pre-existing societal tensions, factionalism and competition for influence by the major social groups in the area, changing trends in the epidemic, consumers' conflicting demands for services, competition among service providers for funding, membership burnout, accountability, compliance with bylaws and rules of order, dealing with financially troubled service providers who were understandably reluctant to relinquish grant funding, and competition with other metropolitan areas for a fair-share of the Title I funds. Kieler (1994), Kieler, Rundall, and Saporta (1996), and Kieler et al. (1996) present discussions on each of these issues.

In mandating the establishment of the HIV Health Services Planning Council as the mechanism for assessing needs, setting priorities, and allocating Title I funds to health care and support service providers in an eligible metropolitan area, the CARE Act mandated the creation of a population of new minimalist organizations in the public sector. The CARE Act embedded this new organizational population in local HIV/AIDS-related health care and support services environments that are characterized by the uncertainties and limitations of multiple complex interorganizational relationships, the rivalries between service providers competing for limited funds, and the conflicting demands of the various populations that the planning council is mandated by Title I to serve. In other words, the CARE Act set the planning council into a multifaceted, diverse, and dynamic environment — that is, a turbulent environment. Such an environment can have unpredictable impacts on the membership, functioning, credibility, and viability of the planning council process.

Any new organization, including community-based participatory planning entities, may face a liability of newness. A new planning entity could conceivably face an enormous burden in establishing its organizational legitimacy, in settling upon an appropriate organizational structure to facilitate the accomplishment of its legislative mandates, and in adopting a standard operating procedure that would accommodate and satisfy its various stakeholders. The effort to achieve organizational legitimacy could consume an inordinate amount of time and effort during the first years of such an organization's existence.

The Oakland data suggest that a Title I planning council, even though it is a government-mandated organization, can have serious organizational legitimacy problems. These problems with legitimacy were reflected both in the various letters of complaint and in the opinions of providers and consumers about the planning council's prioritizations, its allocations of funds, its request-for-proposals process, its appeals process, and its contracting process. Additionally, the periodic efforts to change the planning council's organizational structure, prompted by internal opinion as well as by concerns expressed by federal program monitors, indicated a minimalist organization that was attempting to structure itself in response to environmental challenges to its legitimacy. The challenges to the legitimacy of the Oakland Planning Council stemmed primarily from the planning council's involvement in the direct allocation of Title I funds to local-level service providers, a role that more appropriately should have belonged to the grantee. However, removal of the planning council from involvement in provider-specific allocations served to increase the perceived legitimacy of the planning council process in the Oakland metropolitan area.

If the organizational ecology concept of failure to survive could be defined to include abrupt and significant changes (that is, massive changes) in a planning council's membership, organizational structure, bylaws, policies, processes, and/or interorganizational relationships (that is, its core features), then strong evidence of failure to survive by certain members of this new organizational population could be expected and probably at a much higher rate than is found in the event histories of other populations of minimalist organizations. However, it should be noted that an initial high rate of organizational death typifies many organizational populations, but that this initial high rate declines over time as the population of organizations is legitimated and as the population's members successfully compete with each other for limited resources.

Since it is almost inconceivable that the chief elected official of an eligible metropolitan area and the various stakeholders in the Title I planning council process would condone a non-functional or dysfunctional planning council for very long, massive changes in a planning council's core features might suggest that the planning council is in the process of rapidly adapting itself — it is being adapted —to fit the specific social and organizational environment in which it must function. That is to say, the planning council is evolving to fit the local environment, and its evolutionary track is characterized by punctuated patterns of morphological change. In other words, it is experiencing periods in which changes are unusually significant when compared to its prior state.

However, given the event history of the Title I planning council in the Oakland metropolitan area, the case for evolution seems weak. The Oakland data suggest an alternative hypothesis concerning massive changes in a particular planning council's core features, namely, that a replacement of an existing planning council by a successor planning council occurred. Furthermore, it appears that replacement of a planning council by a successor planning council is highly feasible, basically without cost, and might even serve to enhance the acceptability, credibility, and viability of the Title I process in an eligible metropolitan area. Swift replacement of an existing planning council, a dysfunctional planning council, or a collapsed planning council does not appear to jeopardize either the area's Title I status and eligibility, or its Title I-funded health and social services delivery system. The ramifications of the replacement procedure on perceptions of empowerment of the HIV/AIDS community are, however, yet to be articulated.

An examination of the event histories of other Title I planning councils — or other similar participatory planning entities — might provide additional evidence of the occurrence of replacement of an established planning entity by a successor planning entity. Quite possibly, it might be found that, in certain metropolitan areas and jurisdictions, there have been repeated replacements of the local participatory planning entity. Additionally, elaboration and analysis of the phenomenon of replacement of a planning council by a successor council may provide additional support for the hypothesis that environmental selection is occurring in this new population of public sector minimalist organizations.

ACKNOWLEDGMENTS

Preparation of this manuscript was begun during the Oakland HIV Health Services Planning Council study and was supported, in part, by a grant from the

Henry J. Kaiser Family Foundation, Menlo Park, California. Additional support came from the U.S. Public Health Service and the University of California's AIDS Research Program. Technical support was provided by the Institute of Industrial Relations at the University of California at Berkeley.

REFERENCES

Academy for Educational Development. (1994). *Handbook for HIV Prevention Community Planning*, Centers for Disease Control and Prevention, Atlanta, GA.

Aiken, M., Dewar, R., DiTomaso, N., Hage, J., and Zeitz, G. (1975). *Coordinating Human Services*, Jossey-Bass, Inc., Publishers, San Francisco, CA.

Aldrich, H., Staber, U., Zimmer, C., and Beggs, J. J. (1990). Minimalism and Organizational Mortality: Patterns of Disbanding Among U.S. Trade Associations, 1900-1983, in *Organizational Evolution: New Directions* (J.V. Singh, ed.), Sage Publications, Inc., Newbury Park, CA, pp. 21-51.

Bidwell, C. E., and Kasarda, J. D. (1985). *The Organization and its Ecosystem: A Theory of Structuring in Organizations*, JAI Press Inc., Greenwich, CT.

Bowen, G. S., Marconi, K., Kohn, S., Bailey, D. M., Goosby, E. P., Shorter, S., and Niemcryk, S. (1992). First Year of AIDS Services Delivery Under Title I of the Ryan White CARE Act, *Public Health Reports*, 107(5): 491-499.

Brown, C. (1984). *The Art of Coalition Building: A Guide for Community Leaders*, The American Jewish Committee, New York, NY.

Centers for Disease Control and Prevention (1994). *Supplemental Guidance on HIV Prevention Community Planning for Noncompeting Continuation of Cooperative Agreements for HIV Prevention Projects*, U.S. Department of Health and Human Services, Atlanta, GA.

Doughty, R. (1993). *Lessons From the First Two Years: Issues Arising in the Implementation of Ryan White CARE Act Titles I and II*, AIDS Action Foundation, Washington, DC.

Feighery, E., and Rogers, T. (1989). *Building and Maintaining Effective Coalitions (published as Guide No. 12 in the series How-To Guides on Community Health Promotion)*, Stanford Health Promotion Resource Center, Palo Alto, CA.

Fleishman, J. A., Mor, V., Piette, J. D., and Allen, S.M. (1992). Organizing AIDS Service Consortia: Lead Agency Identity and Consortium Cohesion, *Social Science Review*, 66(4): 547-570.

Gentry, D., and Rundall, T. G. (1995). Staffing in AIDS Service Organizations: The Volunteer Contribution, *Journal of Health and Human Services Administration*, 18(2): 190-204.

Glaser, B. G., and Strauss, A. L. (1967). *The Discovery of Grounded Theory: Strategies for Qualitative Research*, Aldine Publishing Company, Chicago, IL.

Greenwood, R., and Hinings, C. R. (1996). Understanding Radical Organizational Change: Bringing Together the Old and the New Institutionalism, *Academy of Management Review*, 21(4): 1022-1054.

Halliday, T. C., Powell, M. J., and Granfors, M. W. (1987). Minimalist Organizations: Vital Events in State Bar Associations, 1870-1930, *American Sociological Review*, 52(4): 456-471.

Halliday, T. C., Powell, M. J., and Granfors, M. W. (1993). After Minimalism: Transformations of State Bar Associations From Market Dependence to State Reliance, 1918 to 1950, *American Sociological Review*, 58(4): 515-535.

Hannan, M. T., and Carroll, G. R. (1992). *Dynamics of Organizational Populations: Density, Legitimation, and Competition*, Oxford University Press, New York, NY.

Hannan, M. T., and Freeman, J. (1977). The Population Ecology of Organizations, *American Journal of Sociology*, 83: 929-964.

Hannan, M. T., and Freeman, J. (1984). Structural Inertia and Organizational Change, *American Sociological Review, 49(2):* 149-164.

Hannan, M. T., and Freeman, J. (1989). *Organizational Ecology,* Harvard University Press, Cambridge, MA.

Hernandez, S. R., and Kaluzny, A. D. (1994). Organizational Innovation and Change, in *Health Care Management: Organization Design and Behavior* (S.M. Shortell, A.D. Kaluzny, and Associates), Delmar Publishers Inc., Albany, NY, pp. 294-315.

Kachur, S. P., Sonnega, A. J., Cintron, R., Farup, C., Silbersiepe, K., Celentano, D. D., and Kwait, J. (1992). An Analysis of the Greater Baltimore HIV Services Planning Council, *AIDS & Public Policy Journal, 7(4):* 238-246.

Kieler, B. W. (1994). The Oakland CARE Act Title I HIV/AIDS Planning Council: A Minimalist Organization Functioning in a Turbulent Environment, University Microfilms Inc., Ann Arbor, MI.

Kieler, B. W., Rundall, T. G., and Saporta, I. (1996). The Oakland HIV/AIDS Planning Council: Its Organizational Form and Environment, *International Journal of Public Administration, 19(7):* 1203-1219.

Kieler, B. W., Rundall, T. G., Saporta, I., Sussman, P. C., Keilch, R., Warren, N., Black, S., Brinkley, B., and Barney, L. (1996). Challenges Faced by the HIV Health Services Planning Council in Oakland, California, 1991-1994, *American Journal of Preventive Medicine, 12(4):* 26-32.

Marconi, K., Rundall, T., Gentry, D., Kwait, J., Celentano, D., and Stolley, P. (1994). The Organization and Availability of HIV-related Services in Baltimore, Maryland, and Oakland, California, *AIDS & Public Policy Journal, 9(4):* 173-181.

McKay, E. G. (1994). *Do's and Don'ts for an Inclusive HIV Prevention Community Planning Process: A Self-Help Guide,* National Council of La Raza, Center for Health Promotion, Washington, DC.

McKinney, M. M. (1993). Consortium Approaches to the Delivery of HIV Services under the Ryan White CARE Act, *AIDS & Public Policy Journal, 8(3):* 115-125.

McKinney, M. M., Morrissey, J. P., and Kaluzny, A. D. (1993). Interorganizational Exchanges as Performance Markers in a Community Cancer Network, *Health Services Research, 28(4):* 495-478.

McKinney, M. M., Wieland, M. K., Bowen, G. S., Goosby, E. P., and Marconi, K. M. (1993). States' Responses to Title II of the Ryan White CARE Act, *Public Health Reports, 108(1):* 4-11.

Mor, V., Fleishman, J. A., Allen, S. M., and Piette, J. D. (1994). Consortium Structure and Operation, in *Networking AIDS Services,* Health Administration Press, Ann Arbor, MI, pp. 55-74.

Mor, V., Fleishman, J. A., Piette, J. D., and Allen, S. M. (1993). Developing AIDS Community Service Consortia, *Health Affairs, 12(1):* 186-199.

Penner, S. J. (1992a). A Study of Coalitions Among Voluntary AIDS/HIV Service Organizations in California, University Microfilms Inc., Ann Arbor, MI.

Penner, S. J. (1992b). Problems with Planning for the HIV Epidemic, *AIDS & Public Policy Journal, 7(2):* 120-127.

Rundall, T. G., Kwait, J., Marconi, K., Bender-Kitz, S., and Celentano, D. (no date). Changes in the Availability of HIV/AIDS Services in Baltimore, Maryland, and Oakland, California After Receipt of Ryan White CARE Act Title I Funds (under review).

Ryan White Study Group (T.G. Rundall, Principal Investigator) (1994). *Implementation of Title I of the Ryan White CARE Act of 1990: A Report to the Kaiser Family Foundation,* The Kaiser Family Foundation, Menlo Park, California.

Scott, W. R. (1992). *Organizations: Rational, Natural and Open Systems (3rd edition),* Prentice-Hall, Inc., Englewood Cliffs, NJ.

Scott, W. R. (1993). The Organization of Medical Care Services: Toward an Integrated Theoretical Model, *Medical Care Review, 50(3):* 271-303.

Singh, J. V. (ed.) (1990). *Organizational Evolution: New Directions,* Sage Publications, Inc., Newbury Park, CA.

Thompson, J. D. (1967). The Synthetic Organization, in *Organizations in Action: Social Science Bases of Administrative Theory*, McGraw-Hill Book Company, New York, NY, pp. 52-54.

Tucker, D. J., Singh, J. V., and Meinhard, A. G. (1990). Organizational Form, Population Dynamics, and Institutional Change: The Founding Patterns of Voluntary Organizations, *Academy of Management Journal, 33*(1): 151-178.

12.
COMMUNITY HOSPITALS AND NETWORKS

William E. Aaronson, *Temple University, Philadelphia, PA*

Edward R. Balotsky, *Winthrop University, Rock Hill, SC*

The health care delivery system has changed considerably in recent years as a result of health services market, governmental regulatory and payment reforms (Mechanic, 1993). The role of the community hospital in the continuum of services has also changed. Purchasers of health services are demanding more value for their investments. Clinical services coordination and integration appears to be one option for providing a cost effective delivery system (Conrad, 1993). The hospital is in a good strategic position to become the fulcrum of such organizational forms as integrated service delivery systems or community care networks (CCNs). When justification for hospital leadership among CCNs and the potential for hospitals to exercise such leadership are explored from the perspective of organization theory, the hospital clearly emerges as the pivot point of a community care system. It must, though, overcome an increasingly burdensome history in order to do so.

I. CONTEXT OF HOSPITAL LEADERSHIP IN COMMUNITY CARE

Recent health care market reform, state health reform and governmental regulatory changes have resulted in rapid, unprecedented transformation of the health care system. The potential for federal health reform, while diminished, serves to exacerbate market reforms. According to Hurley (1993), major structural reconfigurations of service delivery are already being engineered as a result of aggressive purchasers of care. Regional health care systems change almost daily (Gaul, 1994). Indicators of the breadth and depth of this change are everywhere. For example, Hospitals, the journal of the American Hospital Association, officially changed its name to Hospitals and

Health Networks on June 5, 1993; content differences were immediately apparent. Hospitals should be viewed as the key link in a community-based, integrated service delivery system. Consequently, the challenge to hospitals, physicians and insurers is to radically rethink organizational structure and interorganizational relations (Wolford et al., 1993).

Traditional functions performed by acute care hospitals have diminished in importance. Health needs have shifted from short-term, acute to long-term, chronic. Payment methods have emphasized shorter hospital stays and alternative care sites. Shortell et al. (1993) believe that acute care is no longer the core business of health care, having been displaced by the growing emphasis on primary care and wellness, to which we add prevention and long-term chronic care. They identify the organized delivery system as one that will provide a comprehensive and coordinated system of care. However, the source of community health system leadership is not clear. Major participants in the system include hospitals, physicians and payers, and the communities they serve; other participants include a host of health and social service providers. Transformational leadership for health system development must come from among these participants.

Historically, health services organizations were designed primarily to provide discrete services to consumers, not to provide community-focused coordinated care networks with easy and appropriate access into a continuum of care. The hospital, as the dominant provider of services in existing community care systems (Griffith, 1992), is a logical choice to serve as the fulcrum, or pivot point, of a seamless system. Kenkel (1993) suggests that hospital systems are positioning themselves to provide medical services to large groups of consumers on a fixed budget, based on capitated payment. While community care networks do not necessarily depend on hospital-based leadership, hospitals are the only participants sufficiently capitalized to provide the support for community care network development while simultaneously warding off "takeover" by external forces. If hospital executives fail to recognize the potential for system leadership, hospitals will become more subject to micromanagement by increasingly powerful managed care organizations (Wolford, 1993; Robinson, 1994).

II. FOCUS ON THE HOSPITAL'S ROLE

Our objective is to focus on the community hospital's role in developing and managing a continuum of services within its constituent community. We contend that 1) hospitals are in the best position to negotiate and manage integrated, community-based service delivery systems, and 2) community-based, provider-sponsored managed care systems are more consumer-focused, hence, qualitatively better than purchaser-sponsored systems. Hospital participation in integrated community care organizations is distinguished from previous efforts at service diversification and vertical integration (Clement, 1988); hospitals are envisioned as leading partners in newer structural forms that are community health, not hospital, centered. Further, hospitals will be incapable of controlling the system or remaining the hub. Rather, hospitals must become "servant organizations," giving and receiving empowerment from others (Shortell, Gillies and Dever, 1995). We prefer the "fulcrum" metaphor in that it describes the hospital as performing a delicate balancing act among a number of healthcare organizations that participate in integrated health systems. The fulcrum influences relative relationships, but is not necessarily in the center. We explore the likelihood of hospital structural transformation necessary to become an integral part of the continuum of care from a population ecology and a transactions cost perspective.

III. A POPULATION ECOLOGY PERSPECTIVE

The population ecology perspective is based in the biological sciences. It assumes that the behavior of organizations is largely determined by their environments (Hannan and Freeman, 1977; 1989). Because individual organizations are subject to strong inertial forces, evolution occurs primarily at the organizational population level as new organizational forms replace older forms. The model suggests that only organizations with environmentally consistent structures will survive (Hannan and Freeman, 1989). As environmental conditions change, so do the optimal structures needed to meet the demands of the new environment. Structural inertia renders suboptimal organizations unable to change organizational design and structure rapidly and radically enough to adopt environmentally determined optimal structures (Hannan and Freeman, 1984).

The growing aggressiveness of health services purchasers (Hurley, 1993), changes in Medicare and Medicaid payment, and the potential for health reform legislation indicate that resources will decline and service mandates will increase; thus, change already being experienced in the health services delivery environment will accelerate. However, structural inertia is expected to inhibit the transformation of hospitals into comprehensive community care providers, a view consistent with population ecology theory (Hannan and Freeman, 1977). That is, it is unlikely that hospitals can alter organizational culture and modify structure sufficiently to provide the range of services needed to manage community health. In applying a population ecology perspective, Alexander et al. (1986) hypothesized that as the environment becomes more unstable and turbulent, organizational interconnections increase and a multiplicity of authority and accountability relationships are formed. Since crucial patient care decisions cannot be made without the participation of a variety of organizational types, more diversified organizations will form. Their focus will be the integration of clinical services. These newer forms are likely to be dynamic, resembling the "virtual corporation" (Davidow and Malone, 1992), rather than the traditional static, bureaucracy most familiar to health services executives. Unfortunately, the source of vision and leadership necessary to foster this formation is far from clear.

IV. REDEFINING THE ENVIRONMENT

The population ecology perspective is useful in assessing hospital structural response for another reason. Hannan and Freeman (1989) suggest that an application of this model requires an identification of "boundaries" that produce uniformity within populations. Health services organizations are classified by structural characteristics such as inpatient or ambulatory, length of stay, services provided. Organizations within a specified class are uniform and are bounded from other health services organizational types. Hospitals, nursing homes, and physician practices belong to different populations of health services organizations, but have sufficient commonalties within the organization type to produce uniformity within the population boundaries.

Within the bounded environment organizations occupy niches. Competition occurs when niches overlap. For example, community hospitals occupy geographic spaces which will support a given level of acute inpatient care use. Hospitals in a unique niche (e.g., rural and small community hospitals) will be noncompetitive since they do not need to share environmental resources (patients, physicians, capital, labor). However, when niches overlap, hospitals must compete for resources. Hospital-to-hospital and hospital-to-alternative-provider (e.g., surgicenters or emergicenters) competition occurs.

Historically, hospitals occupied a unique space, protected from other health services organization types by a fee-for-service payment system. Fee-for-service rewarded health services organizations for providing a patient with a discrete service unrelated to other health and social services. For example, hospital payment was not related to physician payment or to home health agency payments for provision of services within a single episode of illness. Thus, overlap between hospital niches and other organizational niches was minimized. Hospitals did not need to compete with other providers. Since resources were not shared, the hospital environment was resource rich. The introduction of a case-based prospective payment system (DRG) encouraged hospital cooperation with other service providers in order to reduce financial risk, but left the boundaries between organizational types intact.

Managed care promised to redefine system boundaries by creating integrated care systems. In reality, most managed care organizations (MCOs) utilize selective contracting with providers and micromanagement of services delivered by the individual contractors (Wolford, 1993). Thus, boundaries are not affected. However, the confluence of environmental forces, including government intervention and the growing aggressiveness of health purchasers, has profoundly affected relationships among health services organizations.

State and local regulatory and tax reforms have also had an effect on health service providers. Several states have begun to examine health reform proposals that emphasize managed care. Pennsylvania has proposed legislation that calls for contracting with community-based, health care networks (HCNs) for services to Medicaid recipients, to the uninsured, and to the underinsured (Casey, 1993). Florida has recently enacted legislation which created community health purchasing alliances, based on the premise that health service providers, insurers and purchasers must take the initiative to reorganize the health care system at the community level (Brown, 1993). A host of other states have recently enacted or are contemplating legislation for health reform based on purchase of competitive service packages (managed competition). Taxing authorities at all levels of government have attempted to alter the conditions for tax exemption. For example, Texas requires hospitals to periodically assess the health of their communities as a condition for tax exemption (Sigmond and Seay, 1994). Community health assessment leads logically to accountability. Accountability creates incentives to build more effective systems.

Federal regulatory changes such as implementation of the Americans with Disabilities Act of 1990 and the Clinical Laboratory Improvement Act have made operation of small HSOs less viable. Application of the Occupational Health and Safety

Act to health services organizations not previously regulated has produced the same effect. Most physician practices cannot financially afford compliance with these regulatory requirements. These pressures combined with existing market pressures are redefining the optimal health services organizational structure. Medical practice organizations are therefore under equal or greater pressure for structural transformation as are hospitals.

V. THE OPTIMAL ORGANIZATIONAL STRUCTURE

Tying economic and social incentives to the management of care for a discrete population redefines internal and external system boundaries. Given the nature of governmental regulatory and payment reform, and the structural transformations already under way (Hurley, 1993), organizations which can offer integrated service packages, not just facilities and personnel, will be most likely to improve community health status; thus, they will be more likely to perform well in the evolving health care marketplace.

Astley (1985) suggests an inherent weakness in population ecology theory: an environment is internally stable only when coexisting with a larger, diverse range of environments. Astley's criticism is particularly important when assessing community hospital environments since the service is not portable across geographic boundaries[1] like other products or services. Instead, the hospital is part of a natural, geographically bound ecosystem known as a community. Hospitals and other health service organizations are part of an infrastructure which supports and maintains the productive capacity of the larger social and economic system; they enhance quality of life within the community. Thus, the appropriateness of hospital structure and the effectiveness of hospital organizations can only be assessed on a higher environmental plane. That is, hospitals are effective to the extent that they contribute to the larger organizational ecosystem, the community. Community and population health are likely to become the relevant environments within which hospital performance is evaluated (Seay and Sigmond, 1989; Shortell and McNerney, 1990; Longo, 1994).

Integration of clinical services across both health and non-health organizational boundaries is critical to the cost-effective delivery of services to a geographically defined region or community (Conrad, 1993). The optimal health services organizational structure provides a clinically integrated continuum of care; however, no one organization can offer a full range of services given the needed mix of medical, public health, social and psychological services. Thus, hospitals must participate in the vertical integration of clinical services to best meet the health needs of the community. Conrad believes that administrative structures which support managerial integration across organizational lines are necessary to support a clinically integrated system of care. However, the larger health services environment has been rendered unstable due to the demise of historically recognized system boundaries. Population ecology theory predicts that a generalist organization is more easily adaptable than a specialist structure (Hannan and Freeman, 1989). Since diversification and integration in the 1980s caused hospitals to be more generalized than other health services organizations, they may be better able to lead community health system reform.

VI. CLINICAL INTEGRATION AND SERVICE MANAGEMENT

Integrated delivery systems must be based on the vertical integration of patient care (Conrad, 1993). This integration of clinical services creates a continuum of care, not the integration of administrative structures. Gillies et al. define integration as

> "the extent to which functions and activities are appropriately coordinated across operating units—that is, any organization within the system that is involved in the provision of health care services such as acute care and specialty hospitals, home health agencies, nursing facilities and medical group practices—to maximize value of services delivered to the patient" (1993, p. 492).

Thus, integrated delivery systems are those which have "the capacity to plan, deliver, monitor, and adjust the care of an individual over time" (Conrad, 1993, p. 492).

According to Hurley (1993), a continuum of care can be implemented by provider-sponsored integrated care systems or by purchaser-driven provider networks such as MCOs. That is, integrated delivery structures can be fostered by community-based providers entering into service networks, or they can be fostered by service purchasers who enroll providers into integrated networks.

VII. PROVIDER-SPONSORED INTEGRATED SYSTEMS

The provider-sponsored, fully integrated system is less developed, but may be a more appropriate vehicle for developing a fully responsive community-based care continuum. As an example of a provider-sponsored system, Shortell et al. describe what they call organized delivery systems (ODS). An ODS is

> "a network of organizations that provides or arranges to provide a coordinated continuum of services to a defined population and is willing to be held clinically and fiscally accountable for the outcomes and the health status of the population served," (1993, p. 447).

The American Hospital Association defines community care networks (CCNs) as:

> "A system of health care delivery that has made great progress toward community care network vision, especially by planning and operating itself through the pursuit of improving community health. It delivers or enables the delivery of a comprehensive array of health and health-related services from preventive to acute to chronic services, in a well-coordinated, high quality, cost effective manner. It operates within the constraints of a budget fixed by capitated payments or a global budget,"(1993).

While community hospitals may belong to horizontally integrated hospital systems or alliances, the extent of hospital affiliation with community care providers will

Figure 1 - Community Care Networks, Managing the Health of the Community

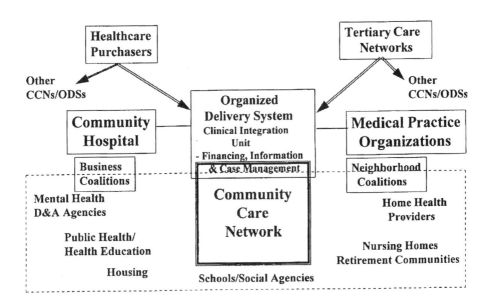

determine the breadth of delivery offered within a geographically concentrated sphere of health care interest. The hallmark of provider-sponsored, community-focused care systems is that the population of a culturally and geographically bound community is the denominator in the health status measures used for purposes of accountability (Sigmond and Seay, 1994).

Figure 1 provides a vision of a community care system in which purchasers negotiate a comprehensive service package with the CCN. The CCN, itself a network of service organizations, has access to tertiary care systems. Shortell (1991) used physician-hospital organizations (PHOs) as an example of an alternative structural form supporting hospital-physician integration. He believed that PHOs would evolve into higher level, more integrated organizations, which would become responsible for the delivery of comprehensive service packages. Given the changes in the environment, the evolution of PHOs and CCNs is congruent with population ecology theory in that this new organizational entity compensates for organizational inertia inherent in hospitals and medical practice organizations.

VIII. PURCHASER-DRIVEN INTEGRATED SYSTEMS

Purchaser-driven systems are those systems in which the purchaser organizes the delivery system for an enrolled population, most likely spread over several communities (Sigmond and Seay, 1994). Service delivery occurs through purchaser owned subsidiaries and/or service contracts with local health services providers. The purchaser (hereafter called the managed care organization—MCO) coordinates and integrates services into a logical continuum. Provider contracts are likely to be consummated on an at-risk basis; the purchaser and provider share the financial risk of service use by the enrolled population.

Purchaser-driven systems of care tend to focus on efficiency and cost, primarily due to the ease with which costs can be modeled. While quality is an important consideration, quality management focuses on the development of critical paths and clinical outcomes. (In 1992, Coffey et al. defined critical path as an optimal sequencing and timing of interventions by physicians, nurses and other staff for a particular diagnosis.) Clinically defined pathways or medical practice guidelines can be easily monitored with modern information technology, thus simplifying the MCO's task of managing services. Sigmond prefers to call this process "managing benefits," rather than care (Kovner, 1994).

Current managed care systems directed by MCOs make primary care physicians formally responsible for case management. Physicians receive incentives for managing efficiently in accordance with practice guidelines. The physician serves as the first gatekeeper. MCOs have an incentive to reduce financial risk through oversight of the gatekeeper function. At the very least, this incentive creates an ethical dilemma for both the MCO and the primary care physician since it places the physician in a position to balance the demands of MCO and personal economic health against the legitimate professional and consumer expectations of quality and accountability (Rakich, Longest and Darr, 1992; Golenski and Cloutier, 1994). While most physicians are not directly motivated by financial incentives to prescribe the lower cost treatment, MCOs indirectly increase leverage on physicians by refusing to pay for a higher cost alternative. Considerable concern has been generated recently about direct incentives that MCOs provide for undertreating patients and for covering up economic incentives inherent in the physician-provider agreement.

The emerging focus on subacute care provides an illustration. Patients requiring intravenous antibiotic therapy and close medical supervision may be treated either in an acute care hospital or in a lower cost skilled nursing facility (SNF). The role of the MCO as backup gatekeeper enters, protecting the MCO from the uncertainties of opportunistic physician behavior. Primary care physicians may be given no choice in treatment site if the MCO refuses to pay for hospital admission. Thus, MCOs have the incentive and ability to restructure use of services by the way in which payment for services is determined and by carefully monitoring or micromanaging the use of services.

IX. SERVICE MANAGEMENT, FINANCIAL RISK AND UNCERTAINTY REDUCTION—THE ROLE OF TRANSACTIONS COSTS

Purchasing services for consumers is a primary financial transaction for any health services organization that provides or pays for services. All transactions entail costs in addition to the monetary value of the exchange. Non-monetary costs are incurred as a result of uncertainty created by the potential for opportunistic behavior by one or more parties to the transaction. For example, physicians may provide more services than the consumer needs. The consumer who is unconcerned about the financial risk of purchasing unneeded services will be a neutral party to the exchange. The insurer, however, will bear the full monetary cost of the service purchase and will incur an additional cost in future transactions. Williamson (1981) suggests that as the costs of interorganizational (market) transactions increase, so will a tendency to incorporate these transactions within a unified organizational hierarchy. Thus, care purchase decisions become bureaucratized as a means to control the uncertainty of the transaction. In other words, the service purchaser incorporates some of the activities into the purchaser's organization. The MCO can "control patient flows through selective contracting, gatekeeper and referral mechanisms" (Robinson, 1994, p. 273), so that transaction decisions which allow physicians to act opportunistically are bureaucratized.

In purchaser-driven integrated systems, the purchaser takes a lead in managing services. The purchaser is seldom resident in the community; services are managed from a central office though professional, usually nonphysician staff who monitor medical decisions and use of services. The process has been referred to as micromanagement of services (Wolford et al., 1993). Micromanagement by case managers external to the community may incur unforeseen costs. By nature, medical decisions are fraught with uncertainty (Eddy, 1986). The identification of medical need becomes less clear as the condition moves from emergent to long-term or chronic, the predominant medical needs in post-industrial societies (Harper and Lambert, 1994). Service is affected by measurable medical conditions (pathophysiology) and intangible social support needs. Coordination of services for older and chronically ill clients becomes integral in assuring that service needs are identified and met equitably (Koff, 1989).

Care managers working for MCOs make service decisions based on critical path analysis, clinical protocols, medical practice guidelines or least-cost options. As medical conditions become more complex, critical pathways become more obtuse, clinical decisions less clear, and outcomes more uncertain (Falconer et al., 1993). Case managers external to the care system have less ability to manage care; therefore, outcome uncertainty and financial risk to the MCO increase. Since knowledge of community services comes at great cost to organizations external to the community, MCO decisions also frequently fail to take advantage of the full network.

A community-oriented primary care (COPC) delivery system in which medical, public health and other community care services are integrated is becoming more important as the health needs of the population have shifted from acute, intermittent care to long-term, chronic care (Rundall, 1994). Incorporating uncertain market transactions into an organization or hierarchy is likely to reduce costs because individual physicians have less ability to act opportunistically in this constrained hierarchy. An additional reduction in systems costs results from greater access to information available through upgraded and easily accessible information systems. That is, a community-organized delivery system has greater likelihood of obtaining sufficient information about all potential configurations of medical, hospital-based, long-term care and social service programs than does the MCO external to the community.

X. PROVIDER AND PURCHASER SPONSORED SYSTEMS

While critical path analysis is useful for configuring services and for controlling opportunistic provider behavior, community-based case management systems are more likely to identify personal, cultural or community factors which affect care outcomes. Managing care outcomes may be more efficient since the target population

Figure 2 - Community Health Accountability: Who Is Responsible?

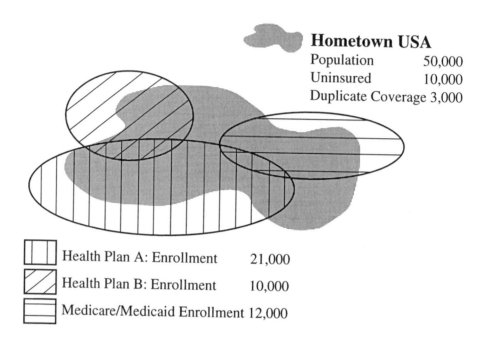

Hometown USA
Population   50,000
Uninsured   10,000
Duplicate Coverage 3,000

Health Plan A: Enrollment   21,000
Health Plan B: Enrollment   10,000
Medicare/Medicaid Enrollment 12,000

belongs to one geographically defined community rather than a number of distinct communities. Figure 2 shows the differences in community health accountability engendered by purchaser-driven and community-sponsored care systems. Without governmentally guaranteed universal insurance coverage, community members are more likely to be left out of purchaser-driven systems. Defining the community as the relevant unit of organization results in universal inclusion (Kovner, 1994; Sigmond and Seay, 1994). Excluded persons become a drain on their respective communities if exclusion results in greater risk of social and health morbidities. Since most of the major medical morbidities (cancer, HIV, etc.) have behavioral components, the social system supporting adverse health behaviors must be influenced (Becker, 1993). Clearly, integrating public health and medical services at the community level influences the health status of the whole community (Rundall, 1993).

Community-based systems are more likely to allow access to a broader range of community-based voluntary and proprietary agencies since participants can attain information at lower cost than can MCOs. As a result, locally sponsored care management efforts have a greater likelihood of applying clinical practice guidelines flexibly and effectively. Locally organized care management strategies which focus on use of nurse specialists or interdisciplinary clinical teams to coordinate care are more likely to be perceived as augmenting, rather than controlling, the primary medical care practice (Conrad, 1993). Guidelines will emerge through consensus, not by edict, and will incorporate a broader range of options for practitioners than would be possible given the information limitations of externally controlled care systems. Thus, local control of service access is likely to be more cost effective than external control due to the greater ability to compensate for uncertainty in medical decisions, the greater likelihood of attaining physician participation in the continuum and clinical service integration across a broader community care constituency. These factors, critical to the successful development of CCNs, bring all parties into a voluntary, partially bureaucratized structure that reduces cost.

While provider-sponsored CCNs may be appealing due to the likely impact on community health, hospital leadership of such coalitions has been questioned. The high cost of capital-intensive hospitals filters down to the cost structure of lower cost services (skilled nursing services, case management, etc.) operated by hospitals (Robinson, 1994). Hospital diversification into related industries and subsequent vertical integration of services has produced diseconomies of scope[2] for two reasons (Robinson, 1994). First, input costs (capital and personnel) for hospital-based outpatient, home health and nursing home services are higher than for nonhospital-based. Second, more capital intense hospitals are likely to use opportunistic cost and revenue accounting to spread costs into outpatient, subacute and long-term care units. Consequently, Robinson (1994) rules out unified ownership in favor of a less bureaucratized structure based on contracting. He concludes that "[T]he importance of continuity and coordination rules out spot contracting for particular services, but leaves open the possibility that complex relational contracting mechanisms will outperform vertical integration" (Robinson, 1994, p. 273).

XI. NEW IMPERATIVE: HOSPITALS AND COORDINATION OF CARE

Read and O'Brien (1989) challenged hospitals to become the focus of integrated, comprehensive and coordinated care systems. The driving forces propelling integration of health services are well documented. However, the concept of a continuum of care, despite its widespread use, has lacked clarity of definition. Evashwick defined a continuum of care as "an integrated, client-oriented system of care composed of both services and integrating mechanisms that guides and tracks clients over time through a comprehensive array of health, mental health, and social services spanning all levels of intensity of care," (1987, p. 23). Complete clinical integration, then, implies the coordination of services across the continuum of care (Conrad, 1993). The system of care at present is compartmentalized, not by client need, but by the predominant mode of service required and/or the payment source or method that is available to those providing services.

The hospital's link to the range of community-based health and social services has historically been through the post-hospital care planning process and physicians on the hospital's medical staff. The critical nature of these links, which became more apparent as a result of the Medicare Prospective Payment System (PPS), has caused many hospitals to explore diversification[3] options (Giardina et al., 1990; Capitman et al., 1988). Forward integration and diversification (e.g., acquisition of nursing homes or home health agencies) helped control hospital length of stay by providing easier access to post-discharge placement options. Backward integration (e.g., acquisition of medical practice organizations or managed care plans) has become important as a result of the growing power and system control exercised by MCOs (Wolford, 1993; Kenkel,

1993). Despite the obvious need for diversification and integration, hospital response has been mixed as has been the resulting performance (Shortell et al., 1990).

XII. EVALUATION OF HOSPITAL-BASED COORDINATED CARE

Payment and market incentives challenge hospitals to become more heavily involved in coordinating care within the community. However, the effectiveness of this hospital involvement has not been well researched. Early results from the Health Systems Integration Study (HSIS) were reported recently (Shortell et al., 1993; Gillies et al., 1993). Relatively little is known about organized health care delivery systems that embrace all levels of care: primary, secondary, tertiary, social and rehabilitative care services (Shortell et al., 1993). But evidence suggests that some hospitals have developed sophisticated methods of care coordination and case management (Christianson et al., 1989; Evans and Hendricks, 1993). Social models of case management have become more sophisticated as a result of federal long-term care demonstration projects such as the Community Long-Term Care Project and the Medicaid 2176 waiver program (Capitman et al., 1988). However, applications of lessons learned from these projects to hospital-based coordinated care have not worked well, partly because program planners have not adequately factored important organizational contingencies, such as hospital-physician relations, into the program designs.

Two projects—the Robert Wood Johnson Foundation Hospital Initiative Program in Long-Term Care and the Flinn Foundation Hospital-Based Coordinated Care Program—focused on the hospital's role in coordinating care for persons with long-term needs (Coombs et al., 1989; McAdam et al., 1989). While encountering short run successes, the projects were not sustained beyond the grant periods. The failure of grant-funded demonstration projects may be a function of the approaches taken. First, the projects did little to encourage or facilitate hospital structural change or managerial paradigm shifts. For example, they encouraged expansion of hospital efforts in care management but did not require integration with other services such as medical practice organizations or community long-term care programs. Second, the projects failed to incorporate physicians into program planning and implementation. Without physician support, efforts to coordinate care were doomed.

The critical role of physicians in affecting system integration is further supported in the HSIS study (Gillies et al., 1993) which found that the level of physician integration influences both clinical and functional integration. Thus, the success of care coordination is linked to physician participation and integration into the delivery system. Newly emerging structures must be based on partnerships between physicians and hospitals. New delivery models could result in financial ruin for hospitals if the major source of revenue and cost generation (the physician) is not co-opted into the process of structural redesign (Kenkel, 1993).

Hospitals best positioned to take advantage of newer constituent preferences will be those who have developed parallel structures for supporting community care orientation, thus avoiding the limitations of organizational inertia. As envisioned in Figure 1, the community care organization is a structure parallel to both hospital and medical practice organizations. It incorporates community-based public health, social services and healthcare organizations. This organization's purpose is to focus on the care needs of the community (Sigmond and Seay, 1994). In this respect, the purpose is a logical extension of the Community Benefits Standards Program (Seay and Sigmond, 1989; HRET, 1994). That is, community care networks bring to fulfillment the efforts initiated under the CBSP, which is the underpinning of the Kellogg grant to HRET. Since the community care network takes on a life of its own, organizational legitimacy must be established. Sigmond and Seay (1994) have identified the issues of organizational legitimacy and tax exemption as important for health care reform at the community level. Organizational legitimacy issues aside, hospital leadership in the formation and management of community care networks is the manifestation of the organizational birth process that can be best understood from the population ecology perspective.

XIII. CAN HOSPITALS PRODUCE LEADERSHIP?

Population ecology theory suggests that organizations are relatively powerless to undergo radical structural change. An inherent weakness in this theory is that it fails to recognize that organizations are contrived entities, more fluid than biological systems (Young, 1988; Katz and Kahn, 1978; Hannan and Freeman, 1977). Thus, while population ecology theory is necessary to understand issues of organizational birth and death, it is not sufficient to explain organizational growth, survival and death. New structural forms evolve not only from environmental selection but as a result of managerial vision, innovation and investment. Leibenstein (1987) states that if enough external pressure is applied, organizations will be "shocked" into nonroutine behavior aimed at adjusting to the change. If the external threat is severe enough, organizations may be able to overcome inertia. Amburgey et al. (1993) demonstrated that older organizations may have a greater resource base protecting them against change-induced organizational failure. Thus, given the extreme environmental turbulence, many hospitals, as long-standing entities, have the opportunity to break structural inertia and develop new, more appropriate organizational designs. The new structures will incorporate hospitals into a network of organizations with more fluid boundaries resulting from negotiated alliances.

Hirschhorn and Gilmore (1992) describe how boundaries may be redefined in new "boundaryless" organizations. In remapping organizational boundaries, four important boundaries must be considered: authority, task, political and identity. While the need to erase task boundaries among health services organizations (i.e., clinical integration) is understood, authority, political and identity boundaries remain problematic. Political rancor among health services organizations may intensify as resource commitments to those organizations change or are withdrawn. An organizational and professional identity crisis is also likely to heat up as demands increase on organizations and professionals to become full participants in a seamless system of care. The demise of system boundaries, outside the control of individual health services organizations, has created an authority vacuum, perhaps the most serious concern of all. New authority and leadership boundaries must emerge to assure that the system's purpose is fulfilled. This perceived loss of autonomy will not be easy.

The newly emerging authority figures may appear more like what Miles and Snow (1986) call "brokers" within a "dynamic" network of health services organizations. The broker plays a lead role in creating linkages among partners in such a way as to allow individual components to pursue their distinct competencies while fulfilling the purpose of the organized delivery system. Each network component must perceive that it complements the other components rather than competing with them. The broker must convince potential health service organization partners that the emerging network will enhance the power of each participant relative to other market or organizational arrangements, such as purchaser-driven managed care networks. At the same time, the broker must demonstrate that the new partnerships will reduce uncertainty for each participant (Zajac and D'Aunno, 1994). Historic associations and animosities among health service providers make these strategic alliances fragile at best. However, the emerging authority of purchasers will provide the leverage for brokers to negotiate provider-sponsored integrated delivery systems rather than succumb to purchaser-driven systems.

All health care providers present in the ecosystem are constrained by the same inertial forces. Leadership for newer organizational forms must spring from one of the existing providers. Hospitals, a natural pivot point or fulcrum in the system, were tainted in the 1980s as predator organizations that acquired, merged and dominated less powerful health services organizations. Despite a critical assessment of hospital performance in this century, Stevens (1989) suggests that hospitals are the best hope for health care reform. The W.K. Kellogg-sponsored Community Benefits Standards Program has shown that hospitals are capable of providing community health system leadership (Sigmond and Seay, 1994). Hospitals respond to public policy incentives when their survival is threatened; they can be expected to respond in ways that reflect their idealism and their communities' moral values.

Hospitals are a rich time, capital, technology, and talent resource to the community. They are the dominant provider of services in the existing system. Well-managed hospitals continue to have credibility with community constituents (Griffith, 1987). As the most visible community care provider, hospitals are held accountable for community health (Seay and Sigmond, 1989), necessitating the assumption of a leadership role. As a natural fulcrum in the system, they can lead by assessing community health needs as well as negotiating partnerships and alliances with medical practice organizations, medical societies, public health agencies, nursing homes, ancillary service organizations, home health providers, community-based long-term care providers, area agencies on aging, mental health providers, schools and political leaders. Discussing emerging organizational forms in a dynamic network, Miles and Snow (1986) argue that "Prospector" organizations play the designer role within an industry. Thus, hospitals that have had a history of diversification and service integration may be more likely to assume the role of system re-designer and become the broker of CCNs.

Recent literature has engaged in hospital-bashing. A number of critics have suggested that hospitals are incapable of assuming a leadership role; however, hospitals are the only community-based care system that has a critical mass of information and clinical technology necessary to support community care decisions. The question is not whether hospitals are in the best position to lead, but whether they have the will and political skills necessary to overcome a jaded history and again present themselves as moral leaders of community health reform.

XIV. LEADERSHIP CHARACTERISTICS

New community health system leadership roles will require the development of community organization skills and a broader vision. Continued focus on hospital beds as the primary profit center of the system, referred to as the "hospital paradigm" by Shortell et al. (1993), will inhibit meaningful change (Goldsmith, 1989), a view consistent with population ecology theory. Opportunistic accounting and cost allocation methods, in conjunction with predatory behavior, will increase the transactions cost to nonhospital organizations entering spot contracts with hospitals (Robinson, 1994). Early results from the HSIS are not very encouraging in terms of the degree to which hospital systems have formed ODSs fostering a clinically integrated continuum of care.

Cummings and Abell (1993) envision a future hospital-led integrated health care organization providing a continuum of clinical services. CCNs will require a set of core capabilities including systems thinking, interorganizational management skills, population-based community health assessments, patient care management, technology and information linkage management, and continuous quality improvement process (Shortell et al., 1993). While recognizing that administrative and managerial integration will be far more daunting than clinical integration, Cummings and Abell (1993) conclude by citing Andre Gide. This French novelist said that in order to discover new lands, we must be willing to lose sight of the shore. Leadership must come from the source that envisions an integrated care organization. Despite their shortcomings, hospitals are the social institutions which have the greatest likelihood of taking on the mantle of community health and meeting health care policy objectives. Hospitals will be successful in leading the development of integrated delivery systems only if they are willing to "lose sight of the shore."

XV. CATHEDRALS IN THE NEW ORGANIZATIONAL ORDER

The development of integrated community systems of care from the ashes of the monolithic hospital, referred to as the leveling of cathedrals by Hurley (1993), requires a paradigm shift. This current situation resembles Renaissance religious reform movements. Just as the Cathedrals, the central churches of the Roman Catholic dioceses and seats of the bishops of the Church, were in the best position to affect religious reforms, hospitals are in the best position to reform the modern health care system. However, their power is only as strong as their willingness to empower partners in an integrated system. The hospital's role will work best when it becomes "relatively invisible"—hidden within the context of more integrated health systems (Shortell, Gillies and Dever, 1995).

A population ecology perspective suggests that hospitals may be incapable of the types of structural changes that would facilitate a community-based continuum of care. Just as structural inertia, lack of vision and the feared loss of control allowed the birth and spread of Protestant reformation movements throughout Europe, similar organizational characteristics might stifle hospital leadership. Transformational leaders must envision leadership and broker roles for the hospital in integrated delivery networks. While that may mean relinquishing some control and prestige, the evolving organization forms, such as CCNs, will be better able to meet constituent needs and experience enhanced positions within local communities.

XVI. ORGANIZATIONAL EVALUATION: THE NEXT AGENDA

Given the radical changes in the health care environment and the likely changes in environmental boundaries, a population ecology perspective suggests that newer organizational forms will evolve to meet changed environmental demands (Alexander et al., 1986). The types of organizational forms and the conditions for health care structural change at the community level will be influenced by the need to reduce transaction costs (Robinson, 1994). The course of structural change raises several research issues. First, under what conditions will hospitals join in partnership with medical practice organizations, long-term care providers, public health agencies, home care providers, social service agencies, pharmacies, and others to form integrated delivery networks? For example, are community-based integrated delivery networks more likely to form where managed care organization penetration is greater or lesser? Where the financial risk of selective contracting is high? Where physicians are organized in large single and multispecialty group practices, or where solo practice is the predominant mode? Where long-term care services are in ample supply or in short supply? Where hospital capacity is in excess or in short supply? In states where health reform focuses on integrated delivery?

Second, organizational effectiveness analysis historically has focused on the quality and outcomes of hospitals, physicians, nursing homes and HMOs as discrete organizational entities. While there is some evidence that integrated service delivery systems do produce more cost-effective services, this question needs to be explored more fully in light of the growing emphasis on managed competition in health reform proposals. The assumption of responsibility for community health will require new approaches to definition and measurement of effectiveness. In particular, it will be important to study the degree to which communication and integration within CCNs improve the health outcomes of constituent communities while controlling costs.

Finally, how will hospital organizational culture either facilitate or constrain CCN development? Are geographically concentrated ODSs (CCNs) more likely to develop where the community hospital has a history of "prospector" behavior? These questions provide fertile ground for organizational research. However, the questions also present a challenge and opportunity to health services executives and to health services management researchers. Undoubtedly, partnerships between academics and executives/managers will be necessary in assessing the need for and impact of newer organizational forms. This is new territory for both groups; only through solid program development and evaluation can the best possible outcomes be achieved. Health reform at the community level depends on it.

ENDNOTES

1. This rationale applies to community hospitals only, tertiary care hospitals have broader constituencies that cross geographic boundaries.

2. Diseconomies of Scope occur when two services produced simultaneously cost more than producing the services independently.
3. For a more comprehensive discussion of hospital diversification and vertical integration, see Clement (1988).

ACKNOWLEDGMENT

Partial support for the development of this paper was received through a Gerontological Society of America Technical Assistance Program Research Award funded by a private foundation and Mercy Health Corporation of Southeastern Pennsylvania. The views expressed here are those of the authors and not necessarily those of the supporting organizations. GSA, a private anonymous foundation and Mercy Health Corporation are gratefully acknowledged for their generous support.

REFERENCES

Alexander, J. A., Kaluzny A. D., and Middleton S. C. (1986). Organizational growth, survival and death in the U.S. hospital industry: A population ecology perspective. *Social Science and Medicine, 22*(3): 303-308.

Amburgey, T. L., Kelly, D., and Barnett, W. P. (1993). Resetting the clock: The dynamics of organizational change and failure. *Administrative Science Quarterly, 38*(1): 51-73.

American Hospital Association. (1993). *Transforming Health Care: Toward Community Care Networks.* Chicago: AHA.

Astley, W. G. (1985). The two ecologies: Population and community perspectives on organizational evolution. *Administrative Science Quarterly, 30*(2): 224-241.

Becker, M. H. (1993). A medical sociologist looks at health promotion. *Journal of Health and Social Behavior, 34*(March): 1-6.

Brown, L. (1993). Commissions, clubs, and consensus: Florida reorganizes for health reform. *Health Affairs, 12*(2): 7-26.

Capitman, J. A., Prottas J., MacAdam M., Leutz W., Westwater D., and Yee D. L. (1988). A descriptive framework for new hospital roles in geriatric care. *Health Care Financing Review,* (Annual Supplement): 17-25.

Casey, R. (1993). *Health Security Act for Pennsylvania.* Office of the Governor, Harrisburg.

Christianson, J. B., Warrick, L. H., Netting, F. E., Williams, F. G., Read, W., and Murphy, J. (1991). Hospital case management: Bridging acute and long-term care. *Health Affairs, Summer*: 173-184.

Clement, J. P. (1988). Vertical integration and diversification of acute care hospitals: Conceptual definitions. *Hospital and Health Services Administration, 33*(Spring): 99-110.

Coffey, R., Richards, J., Remmert, C., LeRoy, S., Schoville, R. and Baldwin, P. (1992). An introduction to critical paths. *Quality Management in Health Care, 1*(1): 45-54.

Coombs, C. A., Eisdorfer C., Feiden K. L., and Kessler D. A. (1989). Lessons from the Program for Hospital Initiatives for Long-Term Care. In Eisdorfer, C., Kessler D. A., and Spector A.N. (Eds.) *Caring for the Elderly: Reshaping Health Policy.* Baltimore: The Johns Hopkins University Press.

Cummings, K. C. and Abell, R. M. (1993). Losing sight of the shore: How a future integrated American health care organization may look. *Health Care Management Review, 18*(2): 39-50.

Davidow, W. and Malone, M. *The Virtual Corporation.* New York: Harper Collins Publishers.

Devers, K., Shortell, S., Gillies, R., Anderson, D., Mitchell, J. and Morgan Erickson, K. (1994). Implementing organized delivery systems: An integration scorecard. *Health Care Management Review, 19*(3): 7-20.

Eddy, D. M. (1986). "Variations in Physician Practice." *Health Affairs, 3*(2): 74-89.

Evans, R. and Hendricks, R. (1993). Evaluating hospital discharge planning: A randomized clinical trial. *Medical Care, 31*(4): 358-370.

Evashwick, C. J. (1987). Definition of the continuum of care. In Evashwick, C. J. and L. J. Weiss (Eds.). *Managing the Continuum of Care.* Rockville, MD: Aspen Publishers, Inc.

Falconer, J., Roth, E., Sutin, J., Strassner, D., and Chang, R. (1993). The critical path method in stroke rehabilitation: Lessons from an experiment in cost containment and outcome improvement. *Quality Review Bulletin,* (January): 8-16.

Gaul, G. (1994). Regional health-care system changing, even before reform. *Philadelphia Inquirer, February 1, 1994*: C1,8.

Giardina, C., Fottler, M., Shewchuk, R. and Hill, R. (1990). The case for hospital diversification into long-term care. *Health Care Management Review, 15*(1): 71-82.

Gillies, R., Shortell, S., Anderson, D., Mitchell, J. and Morgan, K. (1993). Conceptualizing and measuring integration: Findings from the Health Systems Integration Study. *Hospital and Health Services Administration, 38*(4): 467-490.

Goldsmith, J. (1989). A radical prescription for hospitals. *Harvard Business Review,* May-June, 104-111.

Golenski, J. D., and Cloutier, M. (1994). The ethics of managed care. *Medical Group Management Journal,* September-October: 24-28.

Griffith, J. (1992). *The Well-Managed Community Hospital.* Ann Arbor, MI: Health Administration Press.

Hannan, M. and Freeman J. (1977). The population ecology of organizations. *American Journal of Sociology, 82*(5): 929-964.

Hannan, M. and Freeman J. (1984). Structural inertia and organizational change. *American Sociological Review, 49*(2): 149-164.

Hannan, M. and Freeman J. (1989). *Organizational Ecology.* Cambridge, MA: Harvard University Press.

Harper, A. C., and Lambert, L.J. (1994). *The Health of Populations: An Introduction, Second Edition.* New York: Springer Publishing.

Hirschhorn, L. and Gilmore, T. (1992). The new boundaries of the "boundaryless" company. *Harvard Business Review, May-June*: 104-115.

Hurley, R. (1993). The purchaser-driven reformation in health care: Alternative approaches to leveling our cathedrals. *Frontiers in Health Services Management 9*(4): 5-35.

Katz, D. and Kahn, R. (1978). *The Social Psychology of Organizations, 2nd Edition.* New York: John Wiley.

Kenkel, P. (1993). Filling up beds no longer the name of the system game. *Modern Healthcare* (September 13): 39-48.

Koff, T. H. (1988). *New Approaches to Health Care for an Aging Population.* San Francisco: Jossey-Bass.

Kovner, A. (1994). Community care networks and health care reform: An interview with Robert Sigmond. *Journal of Health Administration Education, 12*(3): 353-371.

Longo, D. (1994). The measurement of community benefit: Issues, options and questions for further research. *Journal of Health Administration Education, 12*(3): 291-317.

Mechanic, D. (1993). America's health care system and its future: The view of a despairing optimist. *Medical Care Review, 50*(1): 7-48.

Miles, R. and Snow, C. (1986). Organizations: New concepts for new forms. *California Management Review, 3*(1): 62-73.

Peters, G. (1994). Organizational and business issues affecting integrated delivery systems. *Topics in Health Care Financing, Spring*: 3-12.

Rakich, J., Longest, B., and Darr, K. (1992). *Managing Health Services Organizations.* Baltimore: Health Professions Press.

Read, W. A. and O'Brien J. L. (1989). The involved hospital. In Eisdorfer, C., Kessler, D.A. and Spector, A.N (Eds.) *Caring for the Elderly: Reshaping Health Policy.* Baltimore: The Johns Hopkins University Press.

Robinson, J. C. (1994). The changing boundaries of the American Hospital. *The Milbank Quarterly,* 72(2): 259-275.

Seay, J. D. and Sigmond, R. (1989). Community benefit standards for hospitals: Perceptions and performance. *Frontiers in Health Services Management,* 4(3): 3-39.

Shortell, S. M. (1991). Revisiting the garden: Medicine and management in the 1990s. *Frontiers in Health Services Management,* 7(1): 3-32.

Shortell, S. et al.. (1990). *Strategic Choices for America's Hospitals.* San Francisco: Jossey-Bass.

Shortell, S., Gillies, R., and Anderson, D. (1994). The new world of managed care: creating organized delivery systems. *Health Affairs,* Winter: 45-64.

Shortell, S., Gillies, R., Anderson, D., Mitchell, J. and Morgan, K. (1993). Creating organized delivery systems: The barriers and facilitators. *Hospital and Health Services Administration,* 38(4): 447-466.

Shortell, S., Gillies, R., and Dever, K. (1995). Reinventing the American hospital. *The Milbank Quarterly,* 73(2): 131-160.

Shortell, S., and McNerney, W. (1990) Criteria and guidelines for reforming the U.S. healthcare system. *New England Journal of Medicine,* 322: 463-467.

Sigmond, R. and Seay, J. (1994). In health care reform, who cares for the community? *Journal of Health Administration Education,* 12(3): 259-268.

Stevens, R. (1989). *In Sickness and in Wealth: American Hospitals in the Twentieth Century.* New York: Basic Books.

Williamson, O. (1981). The economics of organization: The transaction cost approach. *American Journal of Sociology,* 87: 548-577.

Wolford, G. R., Brown M., and McCool, B. P. (1993). Getting to go in managed care. *Health Care Management Review,* 18(1): 7-19.

Young, R. C. (1988). Is population ecology a useful paradigm for the study of organizations? *American Journal of Sociology,* 94(1): 1-24.

Zajac, E. and D'Aunno, T. (1994). Managing strategic alliances. In Shortell, S. and Kaluzny, A. (Eds.) *Health Care Management: Organization Design and Behavior.* Albany, NY: Delmar Publishers.

13.
URBAN PUBLIC HOSPITALS

Anne Osborne Kilpatrick, *Medical University of South Carolina, Charleston, SC*

Lynn W. Beasley, *Newberry County Memorial Hospital, Newberry, SC*

Elliot C. Roberts, Sr., *Louisiana State University Medical School, Baton Rouge, LA*

The nation's urban public hospitals have significantly changed during the past two decades. Initiated as places for the dying poor, they have served as the place of last resort, the primary care physician for the uninsured, and a major supplier of teaching resources for academic medical centers. Since the introduction of a competitive health care system, the emergence of investor-owned corporate hospitals, and the decline of local and state controls over construction and new facility development, many urban hospitals are moving into yet another period of major uncertainty. This chapter reviews the evolution of public hospitals, explains innovations or stabilizing efforts to influence public hospitals, describes the history and status of health reform, and identifies new challenges and opportunities for public hospitals entering the 21st century.

I. HISTORY OF PUBLIC HOSPITALS

Hospitals began as part of the provision of general care for the poor and medical care for the acutely ill. Local communities built infirmaries in the "poorhouses" that housed the poor. For example, Virginia opened one in 1612; Philadelphia's opening was in 1732, and New York City's followed in 1736. "The first public institution designed solely for the care of the sick was the 'pesthouse' built on the same grounds as the New York City workhouse. . . . [In] 1848 the administration of the two institutions was formally separated and an independent hospital created" (Enright and Jonas, 1981). Private voluntary hospitals began in the eighteenth century and were mostly occupied by the poor. Among the first were the Pennsylvania Hospital in Philadelphia, established in 1751, followed by the New York Hospital in 1769 and Boston's Massachusetts General in 1811. By 1873 only 178 hospitals existed (Enright and Jonas, 1981).

Until the turn of the century, hospital patients had less than a 50/50 chance of survival. People entered hospitals to die when they had nowhere else to go. However, with the development of improved institutional hygiene, asepsis, and surgical anesthesia, patients had an increasing chance of survival in a hospital (Enright and Jonas, 1981).

In 1909, more than 4,359 hospitals encompassed more than 421,000 beds. Growing urbanization, increased medical knowledge resulting in further complexity of care, and the need to consult with specialists were major reasons for this growth. By 1943, about 655 hospitals had been established sponsored by local governments with subsidies from states (Altman et al., 1989). The federal government's direct involvement in funding and supporting local hospitals was precluded by law from 1935 to 1965. Under the Social Security Act regulations, all health care money had to be paid directly to recipients. In-kind services from hospitals were not allowed.

II. FEDERAL GOVERNMENT INVOLVEMENT

The turn of the century marks the beginning of a relationship between the federal government and public hospitals--a relationship that has grown throughout the century and resulted in an expanding financial relationship and dependence. The major types of involvement are described below.

A. Research

In 1902, the Hygienic Laboratory, which later became the National Institutes for Health, was established to create a biomedical research system and provide research support to teaching institutions. Results of the funding included a dependence on federal subsidies by medical schools, encouragement of specialization, a belief that good medicine is the key to good health, and a growing emphasis on technology (Johnson, 1978). This technology has become a burgeoning business, particularly as competition became the modus operandi during the late '70s and throughout the '80s. Advances in medical science have changed the focus of treatment in hospitals: e.g., insulin with diabetes (1923), liver extract for pernicious anemia (1929), sulfonamide for pneumonia and other infectious diseases (1935), and antibiotics (1943) (Enright and Jonas, 1981).

B. Health Services Funding

The Social Security Act was passed in 1935, broadening participation in public programs by granting money to states and territories for public health programs. The Act resulted in as many as 1,000 programs in the federal government, including such "categorical programs" for targeted groups as maternal and child health and crippled children (Johnson, 1978).

C. Health Manpower Training

In 1943, training subsidies were established to educate and train nurses for the armed forces, government services, and the private sector. Veterans were included through the GI Bill of 1944. Finally in 1963, the Health Professions Educational Assistance Act was passed. This Bill was designed to address the perceived physician shortage and to assist in financing medical schools.

D. Construction Support

In 1946 the Hill-Burton Act (Hospital Survey and Construction Act, PL 79-725) provided funds to survey and construct hospitals in areas with inadequate facilities. Between 1947 and 1971, the Hill-Burton program provided $3.7 billion for the construction of facilities under the auspices of public agencies and not-for-profit organizations. Its mission was to replace aging and deteriorating facilities where they existed and establish new ones where the need was unmet (Johnson, 1978). State health plans were required to identify bed shortages and noncomplying beds.

The Hill-Burton program served as a tremendous impetus in improving access particularly in rural underserved areas. In return, the program required recipient providers to serve and document uncompensated patient care and community service provisions under the law (Rohrer, 1987). The Hill-Burton program existed until 1974 when it was folded into the Comprehensive Health Planning Law, P.L. 93-641. During its life, the Hill-Burton program changed its focus from rural, newly constructed hospitals to nursing homes, urban hospitals, academic medical centers, and finally to primary care. By the early 1970s, concerns of oversupply, system duplication, inefficiencies, rising costs, and competition for Medicare and Medicaid funds signaled its demise.

E. Private Insurance

During the 1940s, third party insurance coverage emerged for two reasons: 1) the insecurity of hospitals in the post-Depression era, resulting in the establishment of Blue Cross and 2) the view by business and industry that health insurance could be a fringe benefit in lieu of paying increased wages. Business became a major purchaser of health insurance. This involvement expanded after 1959 when the government provided insurance coverage to all federal employees through the Federal Health Benefits Program (Johnson, 1976).

Health care insurance, particularly of the type based on community rating practices (as in the case of Blue Cross/Blue Shield initially) had a favorable impact on all U. S. hospitals by increasing financial access to the population and thus net receivables to providers. In multiple hospital communities, however, insurance tended to stratify the population. Higher income groups who could better afford insurance gravitated toward private hospitals and left the uninsured to be served predominantly by public hospitals. This situation was confounded when commercial insurers entered the market and began selling policies based on demographic divisions and other health risk factor rating practices. Over time, there have been numerous attempts to regulate insurers through a complex set of public policy restrictions governing the industry.

F. The Government as Insurer

The passage of Medicare and Medicaid in 1965 created the most substantial impact to U. S. hospitals in the last 50 years. It firmly established both the federal government and the states as insurers and payers of health care for major segments of the U. S. population. These sectors included the elderly, the catastrophically poor as well as blind and disabled individuals. Many administrators of public hospitals thought that the enactment of Medicare and Medicaid would represent a panacea to their institutions and bring additional revenue to cover expenses generated by their heretofore medically indigent patients. However, the reverse occurred at first as these newly insured patients left their public caregivers to obtain care from private providers (Johnson, 1993). Over time many of these patients returned to public facilities for their care--not always out of choice, but rather based on refusal of service from private providers. Private providers became increasingly disenchanted with the following:
- federal rules and regulations associated with this revenue source,
- inadequacy of payment,
- patient noncompliance with treatment schedules, and
- economic and racial class discrimination.

Even so, Medicare and Medicaid provided a massive economic injection to the U.S. hospital and health care industry of a size never before experienced. Initial cost-based reimbursement under these programs also set off an inflationary reaction of the magnitude only few ever imagined. Providers quickly learned that the more they spent in the delivery of care, technology acquisition, and plant capitalization, the more revenue they would be reimbursed under these programs. Within a very short time, large increases in patient demand for services, technology and plant; system inefficiency; and overcapacity resulted.

G. Regulation

The government responded by countering growth with increased rules and regulations. Regulation and payment controls revised how physicians and hospitals would be paid for Medicare and Medicaid patients. Cost containment in health care became a main agenda of government policymakers and bureaucrats alike. Many states began to restrict eligibility under Medicaid and passed Certificate of Need laws to help stem the tide. The federal government enacted a nationally directed health planning and Section 1122 review in an attempt to slow down the geometric growth of the health care budget. Professional Standards Review Organizations (PSROs), created during this period, were charged with reviewing hospital admissions for medical necessity, quality, length of stay, readmissions, and efficiency. Also, increases in Medicare and Medicaid payments were constricted to cover annual increases in provider costs. National price freezes were enacted and several states adopted rate review processes as efforts to tighten the screws on health care inflation. However, federal health expenditures have continued to increase at exponential rates each year since 1965.

One of the results of these cost-control efforts was the closing of some community hospitals--156 between 1980 and 1984. Most were not members of multi-hospital systems and had fewer than 199 beds. These facilities were, for the most part, investor-owned or not-for-profit. They were nonteaching hospitals that had been open for 35 years. Further, they were not the only community hospitals located in their county (Whiteis and Salmon, 1987).

H. The Era of Competition

Much interest in competition and privatization was raised as governmental expenditures and costs of health care rose faster than increases in the Gross Domestic Product (GDP) from the late 1970s on. The national perception was that competition from other providers would control the costs of care; thus, no local regulation on community health planning was needed. The investor-owned hospital emerged and began to compete with public hospitals for paying patients.

Since the early 1980s, privatization has caused a growth in patient bumping or dumping. When patient coverage expires, the patient is moved or "bumped" to a public hospital to open a bed and remove the cost from the rolls. In Cook County Hospital in Chicago, patient bumping rose from 100 a month to 450. Additionally, as funding changed and competition for the paying patient increased, visits to emergency rooms from indigent, minority, unemployed, and sicker patients increased (Whiteis and Salmon, 1987). The working poor, unemployed, racial minorities, elderly women, children, and the homeless are most negatively affected by competition.

To assist in overcoming these inequities, Congress finally passed "anti-dumping amendments" as a part of the OBRA Amendments of 1989 which established severe monetary penalties should hospitals not follow specifically set requirements in patient transfer. In addition, South Carolina and other states had previously passed statutes requiring hospitals to give emergency care "regardless of ability to pay" (South Carolina Code of Laws, 1988).

The decline of public hospitals began in the 1950s and continues into the '90s. Enright and Jonas (1981) credit this decline to five factors:
- growth in the proportion of indigent and dependent patients in hospital populations;
- departure of the middle class population base to the suburbs resulting in the erosion of the tax base;
- the movement of private community hospitals to the suburbs in response to population shifts;
- loss of medical research and faculty to private and university teaching facilities; and
- change in demand for services.

Other reasons included the complex and cumbersome nature of local government administrations and the reduced competitive advantage of public hospitals with private ones for loans and government subsidies. As previously discussed, the decline of local community health planning in the 1980s and the lack of regulation at the state and local levels for new construction were also major contributing factors. According to Allison (1993), the largest number of public hospitals existed in 1976 when 1905 institutions were listed in the U.S.

Altman et al. (1989) cite two contributing factors that emerged in the '80s: 1) growing numbers of the uninsured including the recently unemployed, legal and illegal aliens, the urban poor, and changing regulations which disenfranchised some insured groups and 2) the DRG system which revised Medicare policy, affecting length of stay, maximum payouts for specific diagnoses, and payment differentials between urban and rural hospitals. Patient dumping was only one result. Another was a need to absorb more costs of care while receiving less money. Altman et al. (1989) write, "An analysis of the effect of DRG payment methodology on 27 public hospitals indicated that in the first year of the system, average Medicare revenues decreased almost $2.5 million, while average Medicare costs increased $1.1 million" (p. 8).

Enright and Jonas (1981) also attribute the problems of public hospitals to

- poor management resulting from the political structure and a cumbersome civil service;
- the "pauper stigma," i.e., serving the poor may dissuade middle class patients from selecting the public hospital for care;
- staffing by specialists, hampering comprehensive care; and
- location--in urban inner cities and underserved rural areas which affects amenities, surroundings, overall staffing, buildings, equipment, and budgeting.

Altman et al. (1989) report on a 1980 survey noting that nonfederal public hospitals which make up about one-third of the nation's community hospitals, accounted for 43 percent of all bad debt and charity care. The nation's network of public hospitals serves as a less costly surrogate to national health insurance. . . an implicit acknowledgment that, due to economic circumstances or special health needs, a significant proportion of the populations falls between the cracks of the current health insurance system (p. 8). They continue:

> [T]here are approximately 1700 nonfederal public hospitals in the U.S. Of these, 90 hospitals in 1978, and only 60 hospitals in 1985 were located in large cities. Thirty of these had either closed or transferred ownership during those seven years. These urban public hospitals average over 500 beds, and are major teaching institutions. (Altman, 1989, p. 2).

According to the editors, these urban public hospitals also serve the poor and near-poor. While they receive approximately 25 percent of their revenues from Medicaid and 30 percent from state and local government appropriations for indigent care, they also provide 65 percent of the charity or unreimbursed care (Altman, 1989).

The treatment of persons with AIDS has grown exponentially in public hospitals. From 1985 to 1987, AIDS admissions increased 114 percent with a corresponding increase in patient days of 82 percent. National estimates in 1989 projected 450,000 cases of AIDS by 1993 (Andrulis, 1989). Additionally, urban public hospitals provide 45 percent of all hospital-based ambulatory care visits and a significant portion of all specialty care, including burn, alcoholism, neonatal intensive care units, psychiatric emergency and inpatient care, trauma and emergency care (Altman et al., 1989).

These urban public hospitals provide teaching and training laboratories which result in their involvement in "one-fifth of all medical and dental residents and one-tenth of other health professionals" (Altman et al., 1989, p. 3). The dependence this relationship creates was described by Allison (1993) in the case of Philadelphia General

Hospital. Five medical schools used PGH for teaching and research, but each withdrew during the period of decline as a result of "interinstitutional rivalries and tensions [which] led to problems in division of responsibility and later to virtual warfare" (Allison, 1993, p. 600). The hospital ultimately closed.

III. DISPROPORTIONATE SHARE

Over time, financial pressures took their toll, and providers complained bitterly that they were losing large sums of money under these federal and state initiatives. Public hospitals complained that reimbursement did not adequately cover the costs associated with care to sicker populations and that Medicaid did not cover many medically indigent patients. More hospitals began to close (many of these public); some discontinued services which were most inadequately funded. Cost shifting to privately insured patients became commonplace for hospitals, particularly not-for-profit and investor-owned facilities. These hospitals also began severely restricting admissions to Medicare and Medicaid patients. Since the pool of privately funded patients was small or nonexistent for urban public facilities, cost shifting was a limited option. As early as 1981, Congress formally addressed the concern that certain hospitals were being inadequately reimbursed for the "disproportionate" service to disadvantaged population groups with special health needs through passage of an Amendment to Section 1902(a)(13)(A) of the Social Security Act of 1981 (OBRA, 1989; Coleman and Riley, 1993). It was not until 1988, however, that Congress passed further Amendments, including adequate definition, directions to the Secretary, and funding to address "disproportionate share hospitals."

Coleman and Riley (1993) outline the process by which South Carolina facilities qualified for the program which provided substantial fiscal support for those hospitals. State plans and methods were required by Medicaid agencies and varied considerably among states. For the most part, however, many urban and rural hospitals, teaching facilities, and a few for-profit and investor-owned hospitals benefitted. For many of the public facilities, only the disproportionate share program stood between them and closure during these very tight fiscal times.

By 1992, the pendulum had clearly swung too far in many places. Several disproportionate share providers had taken the Congressional intent beyond its original purpose; major federal cutbacks and corrections were instituted. Further, some facilities were being propped up even though their economic viability, efficiency, and need within their communities had been outlived. Even so, the disproportionate share program served as an excellent example of the best-intentioned public health policy being utilized to the maximum or "gamed" by providers when proper incentives for efficiency in the delivery of quality care are not thoroughly preplanned.

At the same time, private employers were increasingly vocal about cost increases and unfair cost shifts. To help solve the ever-growing health care crisis, business coalitions were organized to encourage or require employee enrollment in managed care alternatives (HMOs/PPOs). Private employers needing help also began to lobby Congress and State Legislators. They restricted further coverage for alcohol/drug abuse and psychiatric services as well as increasing employee deductibles. This crisis among large

employers affected middle America and small employers more and more by further limiting health insurance as an employee benefit or by discontinuing it all together. Thus
employers began to demand more aggressive public health policy reform.

IV. STAGE SET FOR HEALTH REFORM

By the early 1990s, societal ills converged to create a fertile environment for major
national attention and calls for action from a number of quarters. Although these societal
issues were not traditionally considered to be within the health care arena, most directly
contributed to the increasing crisis within the health system. Many of these problems
were not only inadequately addressed but also appeared to be worsening. Problems such
as urban decay and rising unemployment, worsening crime and violence, teenage pregnancy and infant mortality, HIV/AIDS, and homelessness portrayed graphically that our
health and welfare systems were not making a substantial difference.

These conditions set the stage for health care reform to become a major
Presidential platform plank during the 1992 campaign. The primary tenets of National
health care reform centered around the following:
- issues of the lack of universal access;
- continued spiraling health care costs and the need for improved efficiency;
- the need for documented improvements in quality, particularly as relates to
  outcomes; and
- efforts to create "seamless" delivery mechanisms across the many
  sub-components of our local and regional delivery systems.

However, Congress adjourned without completing the process of implementation. As
a result, the number of mergers and acquisitions both by the not-for-profit as well as
the for-profit sectors of the health field have rapidly accelerated.

V. PLAN FOR SURVIVAL

A. Description of a National Study

In 1993-1994 eight urban public hospital systems representing 26 urban public
hospitals were surveyed to assess their plans for survival. This first attempt to deter-
mine what was being done to anticipate the changes being proposed through health
reform legislation included the following hospitals:
- Parkland Memorial Hospital--Dallas (1)
- Louisiana Health Care Authority--LA (11)
- Harris County Hospital District--Houston (3)
- The Regional Medical Center--Memphis (1)
- Cook County Hospital--Chicago (1)
- NYC Health and Hospitals Corporation--New York (2 of 11)
- LA County Department of Health Services--LA (6)
- Truman Medical Center--Kansas City (1)

A number of strategies characterized this study:
- Establishing/expanding primary care services,
- Effecting transition from disproportionate share,
- Renovating and expanding outpatient areas,
- Broadening outreach to community, and
- Improving Management Information Systems

In 1995, hospital systems were contacted to evaluate the progress made in the intervening period as well as to learn of managements' perspective on the future of their individual organizations and their prediction for the future of public sector hospitals. Table 1 describes the findings:

Table 1 - Planned Activities by Hospital Systems

Establish and expand primary care services	100%
Effect transition from disproportionate share	87.5% (7 of 8)
Renovate/expand outpatient areas	75% (6 of 8)
Broaden outreach to community	87.5% (7 of 8)
Improve Management Information Systems	62.5% (5 of 8)

Three variables were identified as critical to organizational survival:
- Governance: Management flexibility free of political restrictions (interference) so as to allow an entity to make timely operational decisions;
- Tax Support: Financial strength--limited dependence upon tax support for operating capital; and
- Community Support: Positive relationship with and support of three entities: legislative body to which it is accountable; hospitals and the health care community; patients.

B. Results of the Study

The results of the study revealed important information. First, while legislative approval of the budget was required for all, in some cases, the process amounted only to a review of the budget. The purpose of the review was to establish a basis for determining the level of additional financial support needed from the taxing authority. To this end, the cost of unsponsored care became dependent on the receipt of tax support.

Legislative approval for entering into contracts and agreements was also required-specifically, 62.5% (5/8) of the cases. In addition, approval to buy and/or sell real estate was required in 87.5% (7/8) of the cases. Interestingly, all states had applied for 1115 waivers, but only one had approval and a program implemented. Eighty-seven and a half percent of the hospitals were already providing managed care to a population.

Finally, all hospitals felt that it was important to be a part of an integrated system or a network. The expectation that they would actually be invited varied with the location and the level of activity in the state. The key ingredient was the role the public hospital could play and how this would be supported by the taxing authority. Each felt that the failure of public hospitals would be followed by the failure of private hospitals because of the indigent patient load left for the private sector to absorb.

VI. OUTLOOK FOR THE FUTURE

A driving force for change in the delivery of health care services is the cost and the source of payment. In the public sector, politics continue to influence decisions.

How will managed care affect those so often disenfranchised--the poor, the elderly, minorities, persons with AIDS, trauma patients? Will public hospitals once again be a place to die rather than to live? Will technology and skills training be provided at places other than public hospitals? Will state and community planning re-emerge to develop an alternative scenario which might address all the needs of a community and eliminate excess supply/unnecessary duplication, negative competition, and galloping costs? Will we be able to involve VA Medical Centers in the planning and implementation of a comprehensive community health and "caring" system which addresses the health care needs of the uninsured, the homeless, the drug abuser, the veteran, the pregnant teen, and the trauma patient? What will a new Administration and Congress do to plan for the future?

In a recent health policy seminar, the director of a community hospital observed that administrators are responsible for being community leaders and that we must plan together to improve the health of our community. The time is now not only to begin that planning, but to ensure its healthy implementation. Public hospitals can survive. However, they will need public support and resources as well as broadened community services. They will also have to provide quality care. Dowling's (1982) question, then, still remains for us to answer: "Does anybody care?"

ENDNOTE

1.   Portions of this chapter were originally published in the Journal of Health and Human Services Administration. Used with permission of publishers.

APPENDIX

Questions for CEOs

1. Does your organization require legislative approval of your budget? Do you depend upon tax revenue to support your budget?

2. Do you require legislative approval for contracts and agreements?

3. Can you buy and/or sell real estate without the approval of your legislative body?

4. Does your state have a 1115 waiver for Medicaid? Is your hospital providing managed care service to the Medicaid population? To any population?

5. Is your hospital currently or do you intend in the future to be a part of an integrated health network and/or alliance? If not, why not? How might this type of activity affect our success in the future?

REFERENCES

Allison, F. Jr., (1993). Public hospitals - past, present and future. *Perspectives in Biology and Medicine 36*(4): 596-610.

Altman, S., Brecher, C., Henderson,M. and Thorpe, K. (Eds.). (1989). *Competition and Compassion: Conficting Roles for Public Hospitals.* Health Administration Press: Ann Arbor, MI.

Andrulis, D. (1989) . *Crisis at the Front Line: The Effects of AIDS on Public Hospitals.* New York: Priority Press Publications.

Applebaum, A.L. (1978). Commission Report Addresses Future of Public General Hospitals. *Hospitals* (May 16):95.

Baker, D., Stevens, C., and Brook, R. (1991). Patients Who Leave a Public Hospital Emergency Department Without Being Seen by a Physician. Causes and Consequences. *Journal of the American Medical Association. 266*(8): 1123-1125.

Battistella, R. and Rundall, T. (Eds.). (1978). *Health Care Policy in a Changing Environment.* Berkeley, CA: McCutchan.

Coile, R. (1990). The New Medicine: *Reshaping Medical Practice and Health Care Management.* Rockville, MD: Aspen.

Coleman, C. Jr. and Riley, N. (1993). Disproportionate Share Funding: The Case of South Carolina from 1986-1992. *Carolina Health Services Review 1*(1) (Summer): 52-62.

Dowling, H. (1982). *City Hospitals: The Undercare of the Underprivileged.* Cambridge, Mass.: Harvard University Press.

Enright, M. and Jonas, S. (1981). Hospitals. In Steven Jonas (ed.). *Health Care Delivery in the United States.* (2nd ed.). New York, NY: Spinger.

Farber, S. (1978). The future role of the VA hospital system: A National health dilemma. *New England Journal of Medicine, 298*(1):625-628.

Felix, M. J.R. and Burdine, J. (1993). Creating Partnership for Community Health: *The Strategy for Strategy for Survival in the New Health Paradigm.* Chicago: American College of Healthcare Executives, Health Administration Press.

Friedman, E. (1987). Public hospitals often face unmet capital needs, underfunding, uncompensated patient-care costs. *Journal of the American Medical Association, 257*(13):1698-1701.

Green, J. (1994). ProMedica agrees to acquire toledo public hospital for $60 million. *AHA News, 30*(4) (Jan. 24):4.

Greenspan, B., and Dubey, D. (1993). Parents and communities. *Health Management Quarterly.* (3rd Quarter):24-28.

Gronvall, J. (1989). The VA-medical school partnership: The VA perspective. *Journal of Medical Education, 62* (March): 158-162.

Gronvall, J. (1989). The VA's affiliation with academic medicine: An emergency post war strategy becomes a permanent partnership. *Academic Medicine.* (February):61-66

Hollingsworth, J., William, J. and Bondy, P. (1990). The role of Veterans Affairs hospitals in the health care system. *New England Journal of Medicine, 322*(4):1851-1857.

Johnson, R. B. (1993). Health care reform: What it might mean to urban public hospitals. *Journal of Health Care for the Poor and Underserved, 4*(3):172-176.

Johnson, S. C. (1978). Introduction: Perspectives on the health policy process. In R. M. Battistella and T. G. Rundall (Eds.). *Health Care Policy in a Changing Environment.* Berkeley, CA: McCutchan.

Kerr, H. and Byrd, J. (1989). Community hospital transfers to a VA medical center. *Journal of the American Medical Association, 262*(1):70-73.

Kilpatrick, A. O. (1993). The Future of the Department of Veterans Affairs Health Care System and Public Hospitals: Quo Vadis? Paper presented at the Annual Meeting of the American Public Health Association, San Francisco, October 24-28.

Kilpatrick, A., Mirvis, D. and Magnetti, S. (1992). Anticipating change: effects of uncertainty on VA leadership. *Journal of health and Juman Resource Administration,*14(3) (Winter):327-339.

Mahairas, E. P. (1986). Case Study of a VA Medical Center Changing from Chronic to Acute Care: Professional Reactions to Discharge Planning. Doctoral Dissertation, Bryn Mawr College.

Mather, J. and Abel, R. (1986). Medical care of Veterans: A brief history. *Journal of the American Geriatrics Society, 34*(10): 757-760.

OBRA: 1989 Amendments. Title 42, Section 1395(ee)(dd).418-431.

Reddy, A. and Campbell, D. (1993). Positioning hospitals: A model for regional hospitals. *Journal of Health Care Marketing,* (Winter): 40-44.

Rohrer, J. E. (1987). The political development of the Hill-Burton program: A case study in distributive policy. *Journal of Health Politics, Policy, and Law, 12*(1) (Spring): 137-175.

Salit, S and Marcos, L. (1991). Have general hospitals become chronic care institutions for the mentally ill? *American Journal of Psychiatry, 148*(7):892-897.

Saltman, R. B. (1992). Recent health policy initiatives in nordic countries. *Health Care Financing Review, 13*(4) (Summer):157-163. *South Carolina Code of Laws* as amended (1988). Section 44-7-260 (E). 56-57.

Starr, P. (1984). *The Social Transformation of American Medicine.* New York: Basic Books.

White House Domestic Policy Council (1993). *The President's Health Security Plan.* New York: Times Books.

Whiteis, D. and Salmon J. (1987). The proprietarization of health care and the underdevelopment of the public sector. *International Journal of Health Services, 17*(1):47-64.

Wright, R.A. (1993). Community-oriented primary care: the cornerstone of health care reform. *Journal of the American Medical Association, 269*(19) (May): 2544-2547.

14.
ACUTE CARE HOSPITALS

Leonard H. Friedman, *Oregon State University, Corvallis, OR*

Larry A. Mullins, *Good Samaritan Hospital, Corvallis, OR*

Hospitals in the United States are at the center of the debate on strategies designed to reduce overall health spending. America has witnessed the transition of hospitals from revenue centers to cost centers. The number of community hospitals has shrunk from a high of 5,881 in 1977 to 5,261 in 1993 (Hospital Statistics, 1995). Despite the steady increase in total expenditures since 1960 (Figure 1), the percentage of hospital spending as a fraction of all health care expenditures and rate of hospital spending from the previous year have both declined since 1980 (Figure 2). Hospitals are no longer primarily being reimbursed on a fee for service basis. Now, payment in the form of capitation, per diems, discounted fee-for-service, and diagnosis-related groups are the predominant methods of funding.

Coupled with the changes in the financial side of hospital operations has been the continued move towards consolidation in the form of mergers, acquisitions, and growth of integrated delivery systems. An example of rapid expansion in the 1990s was Columbia/HCA, a for-profit chain with 327 hospitals in 36 states (Columbia/HCA, 1995). A survey of hospital and health network executives conducted by Deloitte and Touche in 1994 indicated that 71% of the respondent hospitals either belonged to or were in the process of constructing an integrated delivery system. Eighty-one percent of the respondents believed that their hospital would not be a stand-alone institution within the next five years (Bartling, 1995).

Figure 1 - Total National Health Expenditures

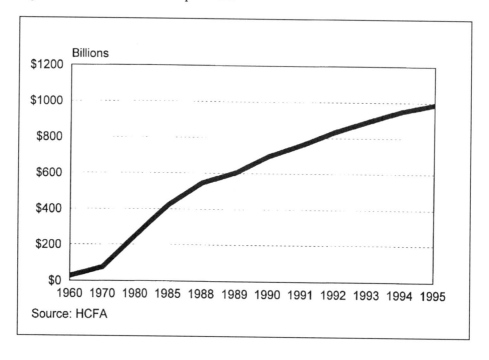

Figure 2 - Hospital Expenditures

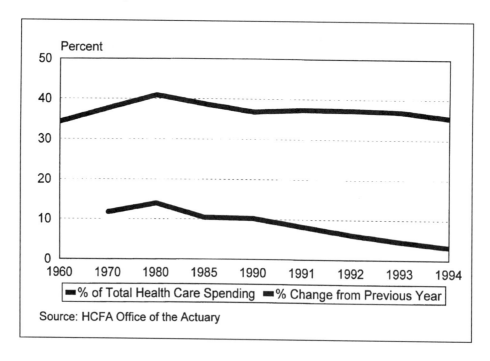

I. ROLE OF THE CONTEMPORARY HOSPITAL

Hospitals have traditionally focused on their role in treating illness and disease. The advent of scientific medicine early in the twentieth century moved hospitals to the forefront in this arena where the latest technological advances and most highly trained personnel provide care. While the primary emphasis for the hospital had been on admitting patients for treatment, recent shifts in reimbursement have forced hospitals to move a greater percentage of their activity into outpatient arenas including same day surgery and rehabilitation.

A newer role is that of health promotion and disease prevention. Research in this field continues to substantiate the critical role of exercise, nutrition, stress reduction, and avoidance of high risk behaviors in prolonging good health, preventing illness, and reducing the severity of disease (McKeown, 1994). Hospitals are realizing that it makes good sense to engage in these activities as part of a more holistic approach to health. While childbirth education classes are commonly provided , a wider range of education programs are now in place. In 1993, over 82% of all hospitals reported offering community health promotion programs, 90% had some form of patient education, and 61% engaged in worksite health promotion (AHA, 1994).

Hospitals have also traditionally embraced the role of educating new health practitioners. Physician education occurs at academic health centers and large teaching hospitals. However, a wide range of practitioners receives clinical training in hospitals including nurses, pharmacists, physical and occupational therapists along with other health professionals. A number of health care administration students also choose to do their internships or residencies in hospital settings.

The fourth role for hospitals involves providing a site for important clinical research. Prior to approval by the Food and Drug Administration (FDA), new medical technology, procedures, and pharmaceuticals must go through lengthy clinical trials on human subjects. Academic health centers, teaching hospitals, and specialized research hospitals are the focus for this type of activity.

Finally, hospitals are increasingly responsible for upholding the health of their community. The transition of health care from in-patient to out-patient treatment requires that hospitals relate to their communities in new and different ways than before. In the "old days," patients had little or no choice about when or where they were to be hospitalized and certainly no say whatsoever regarding the way in which they were treated. Today, a much more educated and cost-conscious consumer is demanding that hospitals (and all health providers for that matter) deliver care at the lowest cost and in the highest quality manner possible. Hospitals have to treat their patients as valued customers.

II. ORGANIZATION

Hospitals have traditionally been classified in one of three ways: length of stay (short stay or long term); service (general or special); or ownership (public or private). Short stay (acute care) hospitals are defined by the American Hospital Association as those facilities where the average length of stay is 30 days or less. In 1993, acute care

Table 1 Distribution of Acute Hospitals

Number of Beds	Numbers of Hospitals - 1983	Numbers of Hospitals - 1993	Percent Change
< 25	224	227	1.3
25-49	986	894	-9.3
50-99	1,414	1,147	-18.9
100-199	1,726	1,575	-8.7
200-299	726	730	0.5
300-399	438	402	-8.2
400-499	274	205	-25.2
>500	339	285	-15.9
Total	5,783	5,261	-9.0

Source: American Hospital Association Statistics 1994/95
Excludes federal hospitals, non-federal long term hospitals, and hospital units of institutions

hospitals made up 86% of all non-federal hospitals (AHA, 1994). Table 1 shows the distribution of acute care hospitals differentiated by bed size and the changes that took place between 1983 and 1993. Immediately evident from these data is the fact that the number of hospitals has decreased by 9% over the 10 years measured with a significant decline occurring in hospitals with less than 100 beds. The majority of these smaller hospitals are in rural communities and contribute to the overall crisis in rural health care currently being experienced (Haugland and Dowling, 1993). Long term hospitals generally include psychiatric and rehabilitation facilities and constituted 862 facilities in 1993 (AHA, 1994).

The second means of characterizing hospitals is by service orientation. General hospitals are usually thought of as providing a full range of medical and surgical services. Among the most common services offered are obstetrics and gynecology, ambulatory surgery, community health promotion, geriatric services, and rehabilitation.

Another way of categorizing general hospitals is by the mix of services or complexity of treatment provided. Most small, community-based hospitals are considered to be primary facilities. They offer a basic set of services including most common medical/surgical procedures, obstetrics, and a range of outpatient and rehabilitation programs. The next level of general hospitals are secondary or regional facilities. These hospitals are generally larger than primary or community hospitals. In addition to the full range of services found in community hospitals, regional hospitals may include radiation therapy, open heart surgery, neonatal intensive care, oncology services, magnetic resonance imaging, or psychiatric care. The final level of general hospital is the tertiary facility. In addition to all the services provided by regional hospitals, tertiary hospitals typically conduct organ transplants, staff trauma centers, and have access to the most sophisticated medical technology available. In many cases, tertiary hospitals are the sites of medical education and are consequently part of academic health centers.

Finally, hospitals are classified by ownership. Thy are either government or non-government owned. Government ownership occurs at the federal, state, or local levels. In 1993, there were 286 federally owned general hospitals and included military hospitals, the Veterans Administration hospitals, hospitals run by the Indian Health Service, and hospitals attached to the federal prison system. State governments operated 84 general hospitals in 1993 and local governments operated 1,305 general hospitals in that year. Typically, state hospitals are affiliated with medical schools as part of academic health centers. Local government hospitals are also used as training grounds for medical professionals, but far and away, the majority make up the county hospitals that provide service to the poor and medically indigent. In 1993, the 1,305 local government hospitals reported in excess of 4.2 million admissions, for an average of 3,218 admissions per hospital (AHA, 1994).

Government ownership represented only 31% of all hospitals operated in 1993. Without question, the largest number of hospitals are owned by non-government (private) entities. Private hospitals continue to be either for-profit or not-for-profit. For-profit hospitals are operated for the financial benefit of those persons who own shares of stock in the parent company. In this instance, the operation of a hospital may represent only one portion of the business interests of the parent. In 1993, 641 investor owned hospitals with 93,184 beds were operating in the United States. The vast majority of for-profit hospitals are in the 100-199 bed range and make up 42% of the total number of all such hospitals currently open. In 1997, the largest for-profit hospital chain was Columbia/HCA with over 300 hospitals and in excess of $14.5 billion in revenue in 1994 (Annual Report, 1995).

Not-for-profit (or voluntary) hospitals represent the largest percentage of all hospitals in the United States. In 1993, 3,026 or 57% of all acute care, general hospitals were classified as not-for-profit. The 637,579 beds served almost 22.5 million admissions. It is useful to subdivide not-for-profit hospitals into two groups: religious and non-sectarian. Religious hospitals are governed by a particular religious group or order. The historical significance of religious hospitals in America has been tremendous as the fundamental mission of most religious hospitals is one of service to the poor and needy. It is within this context that many religious hospitals are located in urban, inner-city environments and strive to meet both the medical and religious needs of their patients.

Non-sectarian or community hospitals are typically governed by groups of volunteer community leaders or by a corporate board of directors in the instance when the not-for-profit is part of a not-for-profit multi-hospital system. In either case, the rules are the same. Any revenue in excess of expenses (typically in the form of returned overhead) must be rolled back into the organization and not distributed to shareholders in the form of dividends as is the case in for-profits. In exchange for potentially decreased access to capital as a result of not being able to sell shares of stock, the Internal Revenue Service (IRS) provides community and religious hospitals with a special 501(c)(3) tax-exempt status. This status exempts the hospital from paying federal or state taxes on any of the revenue made during the course of operations. In addition, not-for-profits are permitted to engage in philanthropic activity whereby they can approach individuals and corporations for cash, real property, stock, or other items of value. The IRS requires that any not-for-profit hospital demonstrate that they are serving the "community good" in order to continue its tax exempt status. The General

Accounting Office estimates that the benefit of 501(c)(3) tax exempt status to not-for-profit hospitals is worth billions of dollars in tax savings, access to tax exempt bond financing, and charitable donations. This concept of community good is the subject of considerable debate. While community good has ordinarily meant charity care, many hospitals apply a somewhat looser interpretation and include services such as community health education, health fairs, and sponsorship of community activities, as well as other marketing-oriented activities. Given the move of not-for-profits into joint ventures, strategic alliances, and integrated delivery networks, the IRS is beginning to question where not-for-profit community benefits end and outright cash flow begins (Hudson, 1992). As a means of summarizing the descriptive information provided, Table 2 lists the various types of hospitals along with selected utilization data.

Table 2 Hospitals, Beds, Admissions, and Outpatient Visits by Ownership Type, 1993

	HOSPITALS		BEDS		ADMISSIONS		OUTPT. VISITS	
	Number	Percent	Number	Percent	Number	Percent	Number	Percent
All Hospitals	6,040	100	1,033,827	100	32,859,632	100	430,239,768	100
Federal	290	4.8	71,868	7.0	1,544,780	4.7	57,876,524	13.5
Non-Federal								
Psychiatric	460	7.6	41,337	4.0	543,837	1.7	3,995,474	0.9
Tuberculosis	1	0.2	115	<0.1	681	<0.1	10,249	<0.1
Specialty	233	3.9	23,367	2.3	451,340	1.4	7,226,801	2.0
Other General								
Not-For-Profit	3,026	50.1	637,579	61.7	22,438,862	68.3	265,629,417	61.7
For-Profit	641	10.6	93,184	9.0	2,861,191	8.7	23,369,147	5.4
State & Local Government	1,389	23.0	166,377	16.1	5,018,941	15.3	72,132,156	16.8

Source: American Hospital Association Statistics, 1994-95

Beyond differentiation of the roles assumed by hospitals and the distinction between public vs. private and for-profit vs. not-for-profit is the importance of the organizational structure of contemporary hospitals. Regardless of the type of hospital under study, three basic elements are always present: governing board, administrative staff, and medical staff. Prior to examining each of these parts, it is worthwhile to digress for a moment to review some of the fundamental ideas of organization theory and organization design and explore how they apply to the structure of modern hospitals.

III. ORGANIZATION THEORY AND DESIGN

A. Organization Theory

Organization theory provides an important contribution to our understanding of how hospitals are managed and managers would be well advised to draw from the wealth of information available in order to administer their organizations in the manner most appropriate for their setting. Questions about how to design organizations in a manner to provide the highest possible level of economy and efficiency have been formally asked since the turn of the 20th century. The study of organizational forms arising from the Industrial Revolution inspired thinkers such as Max Weber and others to develop the notion of ideal bureaucratic forms. The word bureaucracy has come to be a derisive phrase in the English language, yet it originated from a technical term referring to a specific form of social organization for administrative purposes (Nigro and Nigro, 1984). The ideal form of organizational structure contained a number of necessary elements including clear division of labor, hierarchical organization of positions, formal rules and regulations, impersonal relationships, and competence as the "hallmark" of managers within this type of system. These principles became part of the "classic" requirements for organization design made up of division of work, authority and responsibility relationships, departmentalization, span of control, and coordination.

Traditionally coupled with ideal organizational structure was the concept of scientific management developed originally by Frederick Taylor, an engineer who concentrated on empirical studies of work at the level of the industrial shop and individual worker during the early 20th century (Taylor, 1967). Taylor believed that a rigorous investigation of work performance would eventually lead to "one best way" of doing work. While his ideas and methods have been repudiated as being inhumane and depersonalizing, his work in scientific management served to move efficiency to the forefront as a guiding principle for contemporary organizations. Perhaps as a harbinger for management practice to come, Taylor urged a "mental revolution" in the attitudes of managers and workers wherein the two groups stop pulling against one another and instead, cooperate in order to gain greater wages for the workers and higher profits for the owners.

A third school of thought was represented by the ideas found in the principles of administration. While the emphasis of scientific management was on the individual, a group of scholars began to look at the organization as the primary unit of analysis. To this group, represented by Henri Fayol, Luther Gulick, and Lyndall Urwick, formal organizational structure was when the organization and efficiency depended on the proper initial arrangement and later readjustment of various subdivisions. Seven principles arose from their collective work including:

1. Organizational structure is the key to rational and efficient management;
2. Organizations should be structured according to the purposes they serve, processes they use, persons and things worked with, and place where the work is done;
3. Unity of command or direction by only one supervisor is essential;
4. Responsibility for completing a task must be accompanied by authority;
5. A narrow "span of control" is desirable;
6. Systematic planning is a necessary administrative function; and
7. Human psychological variables must be taken into consideration

It was from this model that Gulick developed his famous POSDCORB acronym containing the first letters of the seven administrative functions that included planning, organizing, staffing, directing, coordinating, reporting, and budgeting (Gulick and Wrwick, 1937). As was the case for bureaucracy and scientific management, the ideas embodied in the principles of administration school were attacked and discredited by a number of scholars including Herbert Simon who claimed that this latest idea lacked any scientific validity whatsoever (George, 1968).

A fourth significant influence on organizational theory and design began to appear in the late 1920s at the Harvard Business School and was based on research of Elton Mayo at the Hawthorne plant of the Western Electric Company. Work conducted by Mayo and those who followed made up the human relations movement. An underlying premise of this movement was to focus on the organization as a social system and help explain the importance of informal groups as a significant influence on the behavior of persons in organizations. One of the chief advocates of the human relations movement, Chester Barnard, maintained that organizations were systems of consciously coordinated personnel activities of two or more persons held together by its capacity to generate a common purpose and effective communications (Barnard, 1938). While the human relations movement was criticized for lack of empirical rigor and somewhat naive assumptions of human behavior, it, along with the three models that preceded it, helped provide a historic framework for the design of contemporary organizations including hospitals. While a number of other theories have surfaced over the past 30 years including contingency theory, resource dependence, strategic management, population ecology, and institutional theory (Shortell and Kaluzny, 1994), the way that hospitals have been structured and are operated appear to employ many of the principles first explained almost 100 years ago.

Bernard's organizational design coupled with the study of organization theory is the field of organization design. How should hospitals be structured so as to take greatest advantage of the internal strengths and weaknesses and external opportunities and threats? Although there is no "one best way" to configure the organizational structure, there is a measure of consistency seen in virtually every hospital. Functional designs differentiate between various departments (Duncan, 1979). Department managers oversee the activities in their particular area of the hospital and report to either an assistant administrator or the administrator. The number of department managers and number and title of assistant administrators is most often a function of the size of the hospital.

In larger facilities such as teaching hospitals, the facility may be organized into a divisional design (Shortell and Kaluzny, 1994). Divisions are typically arranged around various product lines or clinical services such as medicine, pediatrics, oncology, and others. In this structure, each particular service has the capability of drawing on the resources from various support structures in the hospital to help efficiently coordinate their operations.

A third traditional design configuration is the matrix organization (Griener and Schien, 1981). Matrix organizations have most frequently been used to manage special and complex projects drawing on multiple services in the hospital which require a high degree of innovation. Most structures of this type have dual authority systems with both a functional and project manager. Possible confusion and ambiguity resulting from multiple managers and high project costs make this design difficult to maintain except under extraordinary circumstances.

Beyond the classical organizational structures common to most business students, a new way of thinking about organizations has evolved over the past 25 years. Rather

Figure 3 - Good Samaritan Hospital, Corvallis - Organizational Chart

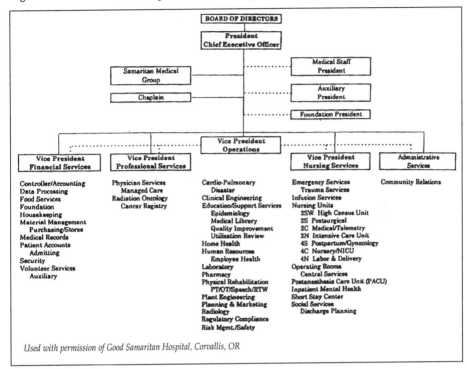

Used with permission of Good Samaritan Hospital, Corvallis, OR

than thinking of organizations as fairly unidimensional entities that fall neatly into one or another neat box, it makes sense to examine interactions between and among smaller operating units and groups. According to Henry Mintzberg, perhaps the most influential thinker in this area over this period of time, there are seven fundamental organizational configurations which are made up of combinations of six different pieces (Mintzberg, 1989). These six basic parts to every organization include:

1. Strategic Apex - provides oversight to the organization
2. Operating Core - persons who perform the basic work of the organization
3. Middle Line - represents a hierarchy of authority between the strategic apex and operating core
4. Technostructure - analysts or staff who provide technical support to the organization
5. Support Staff - provide internal support including clerical, physical plant, and others
6. Ideology - traditions and beliefs of the organization (also referred to as culture)

These six parts, found in virtually every hospital in the country, can be combined into seven different configurations that include entrepreneurial organizations, machine organizations, diversified organizations, professional organizations, innovative organizations, missionary organizations, and political organizations (Mintzberg, 1989). Hospitals tend to configure themselves as professional organizations where power is decentralized to the operating core (physicians) requiring a large support staff to sustain the work of the operating core. Multi-hospital systems can be configured as diversified organizations wherein a small strategic apex in the corporate office oversees the work of the member hospitals.

In addition to the seminal work of Mintzberg, two new organizational designs have recently emerged in response to the demand for both high quality and low cost. While originally developed to help promote quality of work life, parallel design is currently being used in hospitals that have adopted quality improvement (QI) as a significant part of the organization's culture (Stein and Kanter, 1980). Here, cross disciplinary teams are continuously being formed, dissolved, and reformed in an effort to effectively deal with improving work processes. Functional organization remains intact while, concurrently, front line workers and managers from different departments work together to improve the quality of services provided to customers.

Product line management (MacStravic, 1986) wherein a single person is responsible for a particular product or group of products is another recent organizational development. Here, the individual is in charge of all aspects of the product including revenue, expenses, planning, human resources, marketing, and any other services required. Upper management's goal is to discover the points where various product lines intersect and then take advantage of the resulting synergies. This type of organization structure is seen most distinctly when hospitals clearly define single product (or service) lines such as open heart surgery, women's health, rehabilitation, pediatrics, and oncology among others. Lamont and colleagues (1993) reported the enhanced performance of hospitals which had clearly defined product lines in response to the needs of their customers.

B. Hospital Governance

In the case of governance, there are a number of roles that are common to all hospitals regardless of ownership. Differences in board composition and relationship with the chief executive officer are most clearly seen in for-profit hospitals as opposed to not-for-profits.

All hospital governing boards operate under rules established by the American Hospital Association (1990). The governing board's responsibilities can be summarized as follows:

- Organize itself, adopt policies and procedures in order to function, and adopt whatever bylaws are necessary;
- Select a qualified chief executive officer and delegate to that person the authority to effectively manage the hospital;
- Be responsible for clinical care through an organized medical staff;
- Establish and maintain external relationships with outside stakeholders to monitor and influence public policy;
- Establish and revise the hospital's mission, goals, and objectives;
- Properly develop, utilize, and control resources within the hospital;
- Organize, protect, and enhance human resources; and
- Provide health care education and research programs that further the mission.

In all cases, the governing board is composed of a number of different committees which may include finance, quality improvement, executive, and professional staff. Perhaps the single most important committee is the executive committee which provides leadership to the other committees. Generally, membership on the executive committee includes the chair of the governing board, chairs of the various board committees, chief of the medical staff, and the hospital CEO who serves in an ex-officio capacity. The role of the CEO and medical staff is critical to the effectiveness of the governing board in that they provide an informational advantage to the board members (Molinari, et al, 1993). The structure of the governing board in terms of number and types of committees has also been shown to be strongly linked with hospital strategy (Young, et al, 1992).

Differences between governing boards occur primarily as a function of whether the hospital is operated as for-profit or not-for-profit. The most common difference is in terms of board composition. For-profit hospital boards are generally made up of officers from the parent corporation, physician members of the professional staff, and (on occasion) influential community members. Not-for-profit hospital governing boards typically select important members from the community who bring special expertise to the hospital in areas such as law, philanthropy, and finance. The by-laws of religious hospitals generally require that leaders of the particular religious group sponsoring the hospital also be part of the governing board. Not-for-profit governing boards typically operate in a mixed corporate-philanthropic model where aspects of both types are combined into a hybrid that meet the needs of these hospitals (Weiner and Alexander, 1993). Variation in size of the governing board represents an additional difference. The average number of board members in public hospitals is eight, for-profits is ten, and not-for-profits is eighteen, with the average among all hospitals being fifteen (Alexander, 1990).

C. Administrative Staff

The administrative staff is critical to the ability of the governing board to realize its vision for the hospital. Central to this activity is the person occupying the position of chief executive officer, administrator, president, or whatever title might be assigned. This person serves at the pleasure of the governing board and is responsible for managing virtually every activity in the hospital with the exception of the professional staff organization (PSO) or medical staff. The CEO has the ability to hire a team of persons to assist him or her in managing the hospital. Figure 3 displays an organization chart from a community hospital that uses corporate titles for the various executives.

All members of the administrative staff ultimately answer to the CEO, however a number of noteworthy exceptions are evident with the most glaring example being the relationship between the administration and medical staff. The dotted line suggests a consultative relationship between the CEO and medical director. This relationship must be carefully managed to encourage free and open communication between both parties. A consulting relationship also exists between the CEO and the foundation (in this case the hospital is not-for-profit). It is the opinion of the authors that a hospital CEO has the most challenging administrative job currently available. The difficulties inherent in managing a complex organization coupled with a turbulent and uncertain environment serve to make hospital administration more challenging now than at any other time in the history of the industry (Friedman and Mullins, 1995).

D. Professional Staff Organization

The final piece to the contemporary hospital triad is the professional staff organization (PSO) or medical staff. As is the case in the governing board, the PSO is organized into committees, has a set of by-laws, and elects its own officers. Members of the PSO are persons (typically physicians) who are authorized to act independently. Traditionally, members of the PSO were encouraged to admit patients to the hospital particularly when the patient had good, third-party insurance and costs were reimbursed on a fee-for-service basis. The transition to a capitated, per-diem, or discounted fee-for-service model, however, has moved hospitals away from seeing themselves as revenue centers to a point where today, they are considered cost centers. Admissions are carefully managed and there is tremendous pressure on physicians to treat patients in the most cost-efficient manner possible.

Responsibilities of the PSO include granting membership to physicians wishing to admit their patients at the hospital as well as credentialing all members of the medical staff. The PSO is authorized to determine what types of privileges will be granted to all PSO members. PSOs are also responsible for disciplining its members with the ultimate sanction being the withdrawal of all hospital privileges. This issue of membership, credentialing, and privileges has become more important as persons other than MDs and DOs have begun to join PSOs. One of the largest group of non-physician caregivers seeking accreditation by hospital PSOs are those advanced practice nurses (including nurse practitioners, certified nurse midwives, clinical nurse specialists, and certified nurse anesthetists), physician assistants, dentists, podiatrists, and chiropractors. As Medicare and Medicaid relax payment restrictions to these groups, pressure will continue to be brought to bear on PSOs to allow these practitioners to function autonomously within the hospital.

Two final observations complete this section on the PSO and its relationship to the organization as a whole. First is the increasingly important role of the hospital physician in the planning, implementation, and evaluation of system-wide continuous quality improvement initiatives. Abundant evidence exists to show that QI is being integrated into the culture of a large number of hospitals across the country (Counte et al., 1995; Haddock et al., 1995; Shortell et al., 1995). However, despite the diffusion of CQI methodologies into hospitals, physician involvement has been sporadic at best (Shortell et al., 1995). Coile is clear that successful health care providers, including hospitals, will be differentiated on the basis of quality, not price (Coile, 1990). PSOs have to recognize that physician members must learn to work as part of cross-disciplinary teams and encourage their members to understand the importance of systemic quality improvement.

The final consideration for hospitals is the growing importance of PHOs or physician-hospital organizations. One of the difficulties which hospitals have traditionally faced has occurred when a physician belongs to the medical staff of several different hospitals (Conomikes, 1988). Despite the recent transition to prospective payment, physicians remain the hospital's primary consumer of services. Physician loyalty and patient referrals are potentially spread among various hospitals where the physician has admitting privileges. In the late 1980s and early 1990s, the concept of "physician bonding" began to be a concern for hospital executives (Coile, 1990). The result of a Delphi study conducted in 1987 predicted that hospitals would attempt to identify their "first team" of preferred physicians and begin locking them into long-term relationships (Coile, 1987).

Hospitals recognize the importance of maintaining close linkages with physicians a connection which often comes in the form of a physician hospital organization (PHO). A study done in 1994 indicated that 54% of all U. S. hospitals had already formed PHOs (Coile, 1994). PHOs generally function to bind physicians to hospitals via financial arrangements and strategic alliances. Baker (1990) identified five types of PHO arrangements including affiliations, contracts, limited partnerships, development of a new corporation, and vertical integration with affiliations as the loosest arrangement and vertical integration the tightest. Defining features of any PHO include the following:

- A jointly owned entity formed to undertake cooperative business initiatives
- Sharing of risk and rewards;
- Physicians may participate either individually or through a medical group or IPA;
- PHOs often do not involve all members of the medical staff (Dowling, 1995).

While there are a number of legal issues to be resolved in any PHO, particularly potential anti-trust violations (Gorrell, et al, 1995), the majority of hospitals are moving towards developing PHOs (Unland, 1995). McManis and Stewart (1992) point out that successful PHOs will include those who have done the best job in developing economic integration between the hospital and physician members. Involving physician staff in both service quality and the financial success of the hospital are key to the future of hospitals in the next century.

IV. FUTURE OF THE U.S. HOSPITAL INDUSTRY

In his cover letter to the 1996 annual meeting of the American Hospital Association, President Dick Davidson stated, "We are here when you need us," (Davidson, 1995). While the statement refers to the role of the AHA as a support mechanism for its member hospitals, the quote has a much more significant implication. That is, can hospitals and health care systems keep their promise to America that they will be able to continue their current mission to serve the communities in which they are located? It is a profound question, as there is little doubt that America's hospital industry and health care delivery systems are undergoing dynamic change and that the system, as it is currently configured and financed, will in the future be vastly different from what people have experienced the latter part of the twentieth century.

The objective of this section is to provide an opportunity to reflect on changes currently affecting the hospital industry and ask how those changes will affect health care delivery in the future. We assume that the hospital industry is indivisible from the health care delivery system and the forces that affect one, affect the other. There is no pretense that we can accurately predict the future. Rather, our intent is to provide the reader an opportunity to examine the forces impacting the industry today and project how those forces will create new organizational forms and strategies.

A. Forces of Change

Health care delivery systems are buffeted by a sea of change made up of multiple currents including governance, costs, standards of care, equity versus non-equity models, and sovereignty over care of the patient. While there is no doubt that change is occurring, there is ongoing debate as to the form of this change and the impact it will have on providers, payers, and patients. Furthermore, it is unclear as to who should make the decisions which will design the infrastructures for health care delivery in the future. Issues surrounding the delivery and financing of health care have existed since the beginning of the industry, and while great difficulties continue to confront contemporary health care administrators, a measure of comfort should come from the experiences of prior generations of health care leaders. As with generations before, it must be to insure that health care services will continue to be a valued and viable service to the public. What is of less certainty is the form or shape the healthcare delivery systems of the future might take as a result of both the current delivery models in use and the nature of change itself.

There is little doubt that health care costs will continue to be a driving force in the reformation of the nation's health care delivery system. Providers are confronted with increasing pressures to lower the overall and per capita costs of their service while providing care to an increasing population base with high expectations as to outcomes. Notwithstanding legitimate reservations about the effect of cost reductions on standards of care and recent questions regarding the impact of managed care programs potential negative impact on patient care, the costs of health care and the questions associated with funding will continue to dominate for the foreseeable future. Payers and patients question whether the value they receive for their health care dollar is worth the expense they are being asked to pay. Another reason health care costs will remain a focal issue is the problem of intergenerational subsidization of health services where younger workers are compelled to pay for health care costs incurred by the elderly who no longer actively fund the system. Reallocation of existing resources and alignment of economic incentives through managed care approaches, while not popular with some, are believed to be a model that will be with us for the foreseeable future.

Economic alignment, physician loyalty issues, and patient responsibility will also continue to act as forces in the future evolution of health care systems. Complicating the economic alignment question is the issue of whose economic interest will be aligned with whom and what entity will maintain ultimate responsibility for the patient. Conflicting and competitive "camps" appear to be developing claiming responsibility for the patients or "covered lives" and the economic stream that flows with those covered lives. The newest groups attempting to accomplish this goal of ownership are the providers themselves in the form of independent physician associations (IPAs) and physician hospital organizations (PHOs). These physician arrangements assume that if providers lose control of the administration of the health care plan itself, they run the risk of losing not only their current responsibility for the care of the patient, but their economic position as well.

Payers are also cognizant of economic forces. The expansion of health maintenance organizations (HMOs) throughout the country and alignment of some HMOs with hospitals and physicians show they are also attempting to position themselves so that doctors and hospitals will be dependent upon them for access to patients and administration of plans.

To add further intrigue is the question of whether non-profit hospitals will be able to continue their unique mission and advantageous tax status while attempting to compete with the for-profits. The latter have the backing of the investment market, and equity models have been successful in aligning economic risks and rewards, resulting in increased standards at lower costs.

While the for-profit versus not-for-profit model represents an interesting dynamic, the role of health insurance companies will continue to change as more providers develop the capability to produce their own "insurance" product or contract directly with major payor groups as evidenced by the growth of exclusive provider organizations (EPOs). Traditional insurance companies which are at greater and greater risk for their own survival will no doubt develop new and innovative health program designs.

B. Potential Scenarios

Given the forces acting upon the system and provision of health services, there are four possible scenarios that might serve as road maps for the future direction of the hospital and health care industry. These scenarios include: enhanced government control; control by the free market; expansion of non-profit networks; and community benefit delivery systems.

1. Enhanced Government Control

The role that federal and state governments will play in the future is one which will certainly affect the design, structure, and implementation of any plan that is formulated by payers or providers, and, depending on the direction of public policy, can be either very empowering or very restrictive. As one of the largest payers of health services, as well as the ultimate regulator, the question arises whether the government will be content to let the desires of the private sector define the future shape of health care delivery, or will government step in to regulate or legislate to a greater degree than at the present time? One thing is reasonably certain. If the private sector cannot control costs and maintain quality, and if the public does not perceive that they are doing so, state and federal government will not hesitate to assume they can and will take over these processes. For those who disagree with this assessment, one can recall how the government intervened in the Medicare and Medicaid programs to mandate and provide services for those whom the private sector did not appear to be providing an adequate level of care. While some might argue whether government involvement is a better or worse approach to our health care delivery dilemma, it is clear that government will not sit quietly on the sidelines if progress is not made, and providers may be facing increased nationalization of health care that will reduce the private sector's role to that of contractors with little or no control over patients, policies, or payments.

2. Control by the Free Market

An alternative view to that of greater government involvement is a delivery system driven by the investment market bringing the full power of the free enterprise system to bear to accomplish alignment of economic interests coupled with increased value for the service. This view includes the emergence of huge conglomerates of health care providers utilizing corporate practices and large size to achieve economies of scale in the provision of hospital care, physician, and other services. In this model, hospitals and doctors are driven by equity participation in the organizations they belong to and the value of their equity is the motivating force in accomplishing significant cost reductions as well as increasing productivity and establishing benchmarks for higher patient care standards. For this model to be successful, it would require the tacit approval of the government in changing many of the regulatory and statutory constraints that currently inhibit the formation of such conglomerates. In addition, a demonstrated effort will be required to provide many of the community based activities that non-profits engage in, coupled with a willingness to (on occasion) forgo profits in the interest of patients. In this scenario, we see the active participation of third party payers with their substantial access to capital and familiarity with corporate models, as well as their demonstrated ability to market or promote a concept or program to the public.

3. Expansion of Non-Profit Networks

The third scenario centers around the formation of large non-profit corporations that seek to achieve the same benefits as for-profits in terms of network coverage and economies of scale. The key difference is their reliance upon traditional reinvestment value to the community to offset the attraction of for-profits with their establishment of non-profit benefit foundations. There is also the possibility of involvement of non-profit insurance payers such as Blue Cross in the formation of these networks who would bring to the table not only their substantial capital but also expertise in marketing and management of health plans.

4. Community Benefit Delivery Systems

The final, and perhaps ideal, model of health care delivery would incorporate the best features of all three systems previously described and provide significant community benefit under a non-profit governance structure. At the same time, economic benefit would accrue to providers for standards of care and quality related issues and secondarily for economic gain. The underlying premise of this model includes the principles embodied in the discipline of public health. That is, the system continually asks what it is doing to enhance to health of the community. Answers might lie in the areas of childhood immunization programs, wellness activities, tobacco cessation, community clinics, or other activities designed to help improve the health status of the community and consequently reduce the expense of delivering costly diagnostic and treatment services. This model would not only require significant changes in the laws and tax codes, but would also necessitate a significant paradigm shift for many organizations and their corporate cultures. Rather than dealing with patients as individual entities, hospitals and health care organizations would be responsible for protecting the health of an entire community. Health education and disease prevention, environmental protection, and early diagnosis and treatment of disease would all be part of the organization's mission.

SUMMARY

What is certain is that with contraction of the health care dollar and increased expectations as to outcomes, a greater emphasis will be placed on healthier communities and disease prevention than on costly interventions or heroic measures without clear justification. To that end, changes can be expected in not only the delivery and payment of health care but also in how the public perceives the job in maintaining health. Does health care administration place greater value on the health status of our communities or on our own economic status? A decision to concentrate our efforts at maintaining our economic value at the expense of the health of our communities is not only wrong, but would probably prove to be the only change that neither providers or the public could sustain. A healthy future must envision an environment where hospitals achieve a healthy balance between margin and mission. Operating the organization with the primary goal to make the highest possible return for investors is short sighted and ill advised. On the other hand, hospitals can not afford to operate in anything but the most cost-efficient manner possible. The challenge for hospital executives and health care administrators, regardless of the organizational setting, will be to achieve the simultaneous needs of serving their communities and maintaining their own economic health. The means by which those goals are attained will be the key to survival in this highly competitive and dynamic industry.

REFERENCES

Alexander, J. (1990). *The Changing Character of Hospital Governance.* The Hospital Research and Educational Trust, Chicago, IL.

American Hospital Association (1994). *Hospital Statistics.* Chicago, IL.

American Hospital Assocaition (1990). *Role and Functions of the Governing Board.* Chicago, IL.

Baker, G. (1990). "Hospital Physician Organizations." *Group Practice Journal*, 4.

Barnard, C. (1938). *The Functions of the Executive.* Harvard University Press; Cambridge, MA: 172.

Bartling, A. (1995). "Integrated Delivery Systems: Fact or Fiction?" *Healthcare Executive, 3*: 7-11.

Coile, R. (1987). "The New Medicine." *Healthcare Forum Journal, 5*: 14-17.

Coile, R. (1990). *The New Medicine: Reshaping Medical Practice and Health Care Management.* Aspen Publishers, Rockville, MD: 341.

Coile, R. (1994). "Transformation of American Healthcare in the Post-Reform Era." *Healthcare Executive, 4*: 9-12.

Columbia/HCA Health Systems (1995). Annual Report Nashville, TN.

Conomikes, G. (1987). "Hospitals Should Adopt Marketing Plans That Target Both Physicians and Patients." *Modern Healthcare, 2*: 36.

Counte, M., Glandon, G., Oleske, D., and Hill, J. (1995). "Improving Hospital Performance: Issues in Assessing the Impact of TQM Activities." *Hospitals and Health Services Administration, 1*: 80-94.

Davidson, D. (1995). "Keeping The Promise" American Hosptial Association, Chicago, IL.

Dowling, W. (1995). "Strategic Alliances as a Structure for Integrated Delivery Systems", in *Partners for the Dance* (Kaluzny, A., Zuckerman, H., and Ricketts, T., eds.) Health Administration Press, Ann Arbor, MI: 152-155.

Duncan, R. (1979). "What is the Right Organizational Structure? Decision Tree Analysis Provides the Answer." *Organizational Dynamics, 4*: 35-48.

Friedman, L., and Mullins, L. (1995). "Development of A Local Integrated Health Network." *Hospital Topics.*, 2: 22-27.

Gorrell, J., Herschman, G., and Goldstein, W. (1995). "The Purposes, Formation, and Legal Implications of PHOs." *New Jersey Medicine*, 5: 322-325.

Griener, L. and Schien, V. (1981). "The Paradox of Managing a Project-Oriented Matrix: Establishing Coherence Within Chaos." *Sloan Management Review*, 2: 17-22.

Gulick, L. and Wyrick, L. (1937). Papers on the Science of Administration Institute of Public Administration, New York, NY.

Haddock, C., Nosky, C., Fargason, C., and Kurz, R. (1995). "The Impact of CQI on Human Resources Management." *Hospital and Health Services Administration*, 1: 138-153.

Haglund, C. and Dowling, W. (1993). "The Hospital" in *Introduction to Health Services (4th ed.)* Delmar Publishers; Albany, NY: 165-167.

Hudson, T. (1992). "Hospitals Strive to Provide Communities with Benefits." *Hospitals*, 13: 102-106.

Lamont, B., Marlin, D., and Hoffman, J. (1993). "Porter's Generic Strategies, Discontinuous Environments, and Performance: A Longitudinal Study of Changing Strategies in the Hospital Industry." *Health Services Research*, 5: 623-640.

MacStravic, R. (1986). "Product-Line Administration in Hospitals." *Health Care Management Review*, 1: 23-32.

McKeown, T. (1994). "Determinants of Health." in *The Nation's Health* (P. Lee and C. Estes, eds.) Jones and Bartlett Publishers; Boston, MA: 6-13.

McMannis G. and Stewart, T. (1992). "Hospital-Physician Alliances." *Healthcare Executive*, 2: 15-21.

Mintzberg, H. (1989). *Mintzberg on Management.* The Free Press; New York, NY.

Molinari, C., Morlock, L., Alexander, J., and Lyles, C. (1993). "Hospital Board Effectiveness: Relationships Between Governing Baord Composition and Hospital Financial Viability." *Health Services Research*, 3: 358-377.

Nigro, F. and Nigro, L. (1984). *Modern Public Administration.* Harper and Row Publishers, Cambridge, MA: 142.

Shortell, S. and Kaluzny, A. (eds) (1994). *Health Care Management: Organization Design and Behavior (3rd ed.).* Delmar Publishers, Inc, Albany, NY.

Shortell, S., Levin, D., O'Brien, J., and Hughes, E. (1995). "Assessing the Evidence on CQI: Is the Glass Half Empty or Half Full?" *Hospital and Health Services Administration*, 1: 4-24.

Simon, H. (1957). *Administrative Behavior: A Study of Decision Making Processes in Administrative Organizations (2nd ed.).* Free Press, New York, NY: 20-24.

Stein, B. and Kanter, R. (1980). "Building the Parallel Organization: Creating Mechanisms for Permanent Quality of Work Life." *Journal of Applied Behavioral Science*, 16: 371-386.

Taylor, F. (1967). *Principles of Scientific Management* Norton Press, New York, NY.

Unland, J. (1995). "Hospitals Versus Physicians, POs versus PHOs: The Provider's Struggle for Control of Managed Care Contracting." *Journal of Health Care Financing*, 3: 17-36.

Weiner, B. and Alexander, J. (1993). "Corporate and Philanthropic Models of Hospital Governance: A Taxonomic Evaluation." *Health Services Research*, 3, 325-355.

Young, G., Beekun, R., and Ginn, G. (1992). "Governing Board Structure, Business Strategy, and Performance of Acute Care Hospitals: A Contingency Perspective." *Health Services Research*, 4: 543-564.

15.
ACADEMIC HEALTH CENTERS

Roger J. Bulger, *Association of Academic Health Centers, Washington, DC*

Elaine Rubin, *Association of Academic Health Centers, Washington, DC*

In recent years, both the rhetoric and reality of health care reform have been catalysts for reshaping and reconfiguring the delivery of health care services in the United
States. "Access, quality, and cost" became a virtual slogan of change as policymakers
and the public demanded access for uninsured populations, greater quality of care,
and lower health care costs. Swift, dramatic changes in the health care environment
have occurred with the dual drives toward cost containment and competition stimulating the spread of managed care and organized delivery systems. Consumer involvement has also been reflected in the priorities of the nation's health care agenda.

These forces of change, having confronted academic health centers for years, are
now sweeping forward at a dramatic rate. Change has occurred so rapidly that it is
threatening the survival into the 21st century of many academic health centers.
Leaders of academic health centers—the nation's major institutions for health professions education, biomedical and health services research, and patient care services—
have been seeking aggressively to evaluate, define, and preserve the special missions,
roles, and values of these unique institutions while responding to the challenges of the
new environment.

I. ACADEMIC HEALTH CENTERS: DEFINITION AND ROLES

While the concept of an integrated research, education and service institution first
emerged in the post World War II era, the health care reform debate of 1994 focused
public attention on the mission and the institution. "Academic health center" became

a commonly used term in the health care arena after the Health Security Act of 1994 provided specific financing to these institutions. However, more than 25 years ago the Association of Academic Health Centers defined the term as divisions of higher education that are the health complexes within universities. An academic health center comprises at least an allopathic or osteopathic school of medicine, one or more other health profession schools or programs, and one or more owned or affiliated teaching hospitals (Association of Academic Health Centers, 1969). These institutions have for decades been dedicated to multiprofessional tripartite research, education, and service mission. By this definition, there are more than 120 such institutions in this country (Association of Academic Health Centers, 1994).

Academic health centers educate a major portion of the nation's highest level health professionals, including allied health and public health professionals, dentists, nurses, pharmacists, and physicians. In addition, most biomedical research scientists are graduates of schools within the academic health center. In terms of patient care services, academic health centers have shouldered a disproportionately heavy burden of care for the sickest and poorest members of their communities. Although the 282 major teaching hospitals most closely affiliated with academic health centers represent only 18 percent of all set-up and staffed hospital beds in the nation, they nevertheless provide 45 percent of the nation's charity care (Association of American Medical Colleges, 1996). In the research arena, academic health centers have been recognized as national resources for the advancement of the biomedical sciences, the development of health care technology, and the provision of the most advanced and complex health care services. Academic health centers, in fact, have been viewed as the institutions that are consistently on the leading edge of technology development, a condition that has ensured America's worldwide domination of advanced health care.

More than one half of the entire extramural research budget of the National Institutes of Health is funneled through the nation's medical schools. Additional resources go to the other health professional schools as well as scientific laboratories of the parent universities of academic health centers. In a 1994 survey of its members, the Association of Academic Health Centers reported that the NIH was the largest single source of funding, providing 44 percent of the total reported expenditures for reporting institutions. Given the breadth of their mission and scope of services, these institutions are a unique and integral part of America's health care system (Association of Academic Health Centers, 1994).

A. Models of Organization and Structure

No two academic health centers are exactly alike. They are public or private universities; they may be university-based with a parent university or they may be free-standing universities of the health sciences. These institutions consist of from two to five schools of the health professions and have one or more owned or affiliated teaching hospitals. They have a variety of governance and organizational structures.

To analyze the response of academic health centers to the changing health care market and to explore the benefits and risks associated with the many organizational models, we might classify the member institutions of the Association of Academic Health Centers according to six broad categories of organizational models. Each model can be further subdivided and differentially characterized in other important ways.

- Models I and II are both a wholly-owned teaching hospital and a medical school (allopathic or osteopathic) as well as at least one other health professions school. These can be public or private institutions which is the distinction between Model I and II. Approximately 50 percent of the members fit this model.
- Models III and IV have the same criteria as Model I except that the academic health center does not own its hospital. Again, these can be public or private. Approximately 30 percent fit this model.
- Model V is a freestanding academic health center or university of the health sciences whose CEO is the president of the enterprise. In this model, the hospital is owned by the university. About 10 percent of the academic health centers fit this model.
- Model VI is similar to Model V except that the hospital is not owned by the university; between 5 and 10 percent of academic health centers are examples of this model.

Within this broad framework, various governance structures exist that add another dimension to the models. Some have a vice president of health affairs who reports to the university president who ultimately reports to a board of regents. The freestanding academic health centers have chief executive officers (CEOs) who are the presidents of the institution and therefore report to the board of trustees. Some of the CEOs have control over all education, research, and service components of the institution; others do not.

These models reflect the myriad organizational and governance structures, administrative positions, and hospital and university relationships that currently exist. Other important characteristics which differentiate these institutions one from another include the internal organization of clinical services, the structure of governing boards, the relationships with the parent university, state financing, and the structure of the research enterprise.

B. Future Options

The changing nature of health care poses questions about future appropriateness and viability of these models. Academic health centers must confront profound changes in the culture, structure, and behavior of faculty and staff within the various components of the institution as they struggle to survive and develop. The future is uncertain. Are some, many, or all academic health centers bound for extinction? Or will they emerge transformed in the next century? These are the issues at hand.

To better understand the options for the future and to shed light on the uniqueness and complexity of the issues facing academic health centers, we will review the history of academic health centers including many of the forces for development and change.

II. EMERGENCE OF ACADEMIC HEALTH CENTERS (1945-1970)

Society signaled its agreement and commitment to biomedical research and growth in the health sciences following World War II. The three prongs of the academic health center mission—education, research, service—developed and matured at different rates and by differing pathways, but eventually became inextricably tied to one another to form the foundation of the modern institution. Changes in health professions education, including the expansion of university-based nursing programs, the emergence of new allied health disciplines, and the increased need for medical schools to expand teaching resources were forces that helped to hasten the evolution of academic health centers to their present form (Ebert and Brown, 1983). The policies and programs of the federal government also had a profound influence on their development.

A. The Research Mission

Post-World War II policies directed at the development of science and technology abandoned the idea of establishing a European model of private or state-owned research institutions in favor of developing America's established universities and medical schools as primary research sites (Bush, 1945). The success of university-run, federally-supported studies related to the war effort bolstered this decision. These policies ultimately strengthened the research emphasis in medical education, an emphasis that had evolved since the turn of the century and was reflected in the employment growth of full-time clinical faculty. The publication of the Flexner Report in 1910 had given credence to this model, ensuring its expansion in institutions throughout the nation (Barondess, 1991; Flexner, 1910).

The benefits of combining research with teaching and patient care became ever more apparent in the decades following the war. As medical education relied more on the clinical experience, the relationship between medical school and teaching hospital grew; the charity mission of the teaching hospital was also strengthened (Knowles, 1966). The marriage of scientific technology and innovation at the bedside took place in the university hospital as it often rapidly became a sort of clinical court of last resort for difficult or complex cases.

Numerous forces encouraged growth in the health sciences and the explosion of biomedical research within the university setting. This era, which began with a belief in the power of reductionist science to uncover nature's secrets at the molecular level, fed on the American can-do spirit and love of technology. Scientists in universities and other research institutions created useful interventions; medical and surgical specialists tailored interventions and new technologies to the needs of patients. Money appeared to be no object in the American quest to defeat individual disability and to restore the seriously ill to good health.

Based on a peer-review system comprising faculty from the nation's medical schools, the National Institutes of Health (NIH) not only increased in stature but also became the engine that drove biomedical research in this country. The NIH budget went from about $42 million in 1950 to $7 billion in 1989; it currently exceeds $12 billion annually (National Institutes of Health). In addition, the federal government financed the capital investments in the research facilities of universities and medical schools, often encouraging through its policies that laboratories be contiguous with the clinical sciences and the university teaching hospitals (P.L. 835, 84th Congress, 1960). These forces stimulated transfer of knowledge from the bedside to the bench, enhancement of quality clinical care, and transformation of advances from the basic sciences into clinically practical interventions. An eager public hungered after such advancements then just as they do today.

As the investments in basic biological sciences yielded new disciplines within the medical and scientific arenas and as new frontiers opened for science, clinical competence in the academic health center became associated with competence in both the basic and applied sciences. Together, the basic sciences, the clinical applied sciences, and the appropriate clinical specialty practices achieved new heights and status. State policies favored these developments in the 1950s and 1960s, often creating university research enterprises which became powerful local and regional engines of economic growth, contributing jobs and other economic benefits to a wide geographic area.

Growth in federal support through the 1960s was attributed to a general belief in the capacity of the research enterprise to solve a number of important medical problem (Shannon, 1973). The 1960s also saw a concurrent expansion of federal health efforts with the 1965 passage of Medicare and Medicaid amendments to the Social Security Act. Ironically, until the passage of Medicare and Medicaid legislation, the increasing support for biomedical research had been accompanied by a continued rejection of efforts to obtain a substantial engagement of the federal apparatus with significant programs related to medical education (Shannon, 1973). Thus the mechanisms for vigorous federal expression in health were limited to the categorical research and training programs of the NIH. Shannon (1973) noted that the NIH programs of the 1950s and early 1960s may have served in part as a surrogate for the inherently controversial but rapidly growing desire of the country to undertake a substantial national effort to improve the health of its citizens.

B. Patient Care Services

Societal expectations about health services helped design and strengthen the academic health center's patient care mission. The post-World War II society demanded increasing numbers of hospital beds, modern technology, and access to the latest services and technologic advances. In the first half of the century, government and industry were minimally involved in health care financing. Health insurance was traditional indemnity medical insurance; fee-for-service medicine was the mode of health care delivery. Insurers paid for care on the basis of reasonable local practices, and the result was a capacity to support technical innovations.

The third-party payment system is credited with unleashing an unprecedented demand for hospital services because it removed considerations of cost constraints from hospital billings (Stevens, 1989). Payments by the third-party commercial and mutual insurance companies has been described as the "pot-of-gold" that encouraged hospitals to respond to the demand by providing more expensive, improved care in areas that were most likely to be reimbursed (Stevens, 1989). Cost-based reimbursement incentives meant that no one entity would really feel the pinch of spending—a situation that would change considerably in the 1980s.

One result of this intense demand is that today the nation has perhaps double the number of hospital beds needed. More important, academic health centers became the medical courts of last resort, responding to the demand and thriving on the need for high technology and the specialists who controlled its use. Academic health centers became the flagships of quality as they increased their staffs, equipment, and facilities.

The teaching hospital was viewed as the model by medical professionals. Thus, these standards were in turn duplicated in other types of hospitals (Stevens, 1989). Increasingly over the past fifteen years, specialty practice and high technology medicine has extended beyond university teaching hospitals to community hospitals and other non-academic settings, thus breaking the academic health center monopoly on advanced practice.

C. Health Professions Education

As early as 1951, legislation was introduced to support educational programs for the health professions. However, it was not until 1963 that Congress enacted the Health Professions Educational Assistance Act that authorized federal funds for the construction and rehabilitation of medical and dental schools as well as loans for students in dentistry and allopathic and osteopathic medicine (P.L. 88-129 Health Professions Educational Assistance Act of 1963).

Responding to the national perception of a physician shortage, Congress passed the Health Manpower Training Act of 1968. This law provided financial support for institutions to increase the enrollment of students in medicine, nursing, and other health professions (P.L. 90-1490, 1968). The subsequent Comprehensive Health Manpower Training Act of 1971 continued this trend with federal assistance given in the form of capitation grants (P.L. 92-157), a per capita payment for each enrolled student.

By the late 1960s and early 1970s, the reorganization of Public Health Service placed the budgets for manpower and research in competition with one another. Education won. Reports and commissions pointed to insufficient health manpower for the nation. The assistant secretary of the U. S. Department of Health, Education, and Welfare stated that the U. S. needed 50,000 more physicians, "a couple of hundred thousand more nurses and almost 150,000 more technicians" (U.S. News and World Report, 1970; Carnegie Commission on Higher Education, 1976).

In nursing, for example, over an 18-year period beginning in 1965, more than $1.6 billion was appropriated under the Nurse Training Act, the primary intent of which was to expand the supply of nurses as well as to improve the quality and distribution of the supply. These goals would be accomplished by increasing the capacity of educational institutions, providing student financial assistance, and increasing the opportunities of nurses to obtain advanced training as nurse practitioners or clinical nurse specialists (Institute of Medicine, 1983). By the early 1970s, the need for more health professionals appeared to dominate the policymaking scene, thus enlarging the educational dimension of the academic health center (Shannon, 1973).

The perceived need for more physicians, particularly in underserved regions, coupled with voter demand in many states for places in medical schools for their children resulted in increased class sizes in all health professions schools. Forty new medical schools opened between 1965 and 1982 (Stevens, 1989). The Veterans Administration Medical School Assistance and Health Manpower Training Act of 1972, which provided financial support for the creation of new state schools affiliated with Veterans Administration hospitals, prompted the establishment of five of those 40 schools. The federal government's contribution to the finances of medical schools reached its peak in 1965-1966 when it represented approximately 54 percent of total revenues (Association of American Medical Colleges, 1981). By the end of the 1970s, the proportion of support would drop to 29 percent. The number of first-year medical students rose from approximately 5,000 in the mid-1960s to more than 15,000 in 1980 (Association of American Medical Colleges, 1981).

III. GROWTH AND EARLY WARNING SIGNS OF FISCAL TROUBLE: 1970s AND 1980s

Through the 1970s the societal credo for research, education, and health care services seemed to be "more or bigger is better." The growth that occurred within the nation's major universities often played out as follows: a state funded the buildings for the medical school and other health professions schools. They provided basic operating support for faculty and support staff. Federal funds were available to at least partially support construction for research facilities, medical schools, and associated teaching hospitals. Federal reimbursement for indirect costs provided further subsidies for maintenance and capital investment in the institution. The university pointed to these facilities to attract leading scientists and academic clinicians to the institution, who in turn formed the core faculty that generated grant support, usually from the National Institutes of Health or other federal agencies.

Administrators in both new and old medical schools targeted faculty recruitment as a way to gain national prestige in the research arena. The faculty recruitment game included benefit or incentive packages designed to attract academic superstars—packages that represented a coordination between the administration of the hospital and the medical school or academic health center. The capacity to parlay state, private, research, and academic funds to enhance the image and status of the institution was key in recruitment efforts for medicine. Such prestige frequently generated more patients for the hospital and for a variety of specialists on the faculty. Success often generated surplus funds that allowed for further investments and a recurring round of growth. Similar, if less dramatic, strategies were successfully applied to dentistry and nursing. Thus the societal pressure to grow and to concentrate on high technology and superspecialization tended to call the tune into the 1980s.

In some states, economic impact studies clearly indicated that every dollar the state invested in the academic health center generated between $8-$15. Economic well-being for the community and for the state resulted from the fact that personnel received seventy percent of the dollars spent in these institutions (Academic Health Centers, 1990).

During this growth era of the 1970s, the teaching hospital became an increasingly dominant force within the academic health center. Bringing education, research, and service together, the teaching hospital, often the recipient of much federal and state funding, became the cash cow for the rest of the academic health center and, to some extent, the university. As technology became the watchword for education and clinical care, medical education became even more imbedded inside the hospital. The Medicare program, as part of the payment for Medicare beneficiaries, paid teaching hospitals for direct and indirect costs of the graduate medical education that occurred in these institutions. Then a delicate balance of cross-subsidization of public and private funds covered excess costs incurred by the teaching hospital. The balance has been threatened since the 1980s when monies for education and research started to constrict.

By 1978-79, the proportion of federal support of medical school finances dropped to 29 percent; at the same time, clinical revenues, tuition, and university fees increased to account for approximately 30 percent of the total. Clinical revenues alone continued to increase during the 1980s and 1990s such that they more than compensated for cuts in federal and state funding. Today, in fact, they provide the single largest source of support for medical schools and their academic health centers. Clinical revenues average about 31 percent of medical school budgets (Association of American Medical Colleges, 1993).

Experts have long noted that academic health centers have surprisingly fragile economic foundations caused by the cross-subsidization required over the years to pay for much of the costs of research and education (Lombardi, 1991; Iglehart, 1995). Academic health centers increasingly rely on clinical revenues, thus building what might be considered a financial house of cards.

IV. CHANGING MARKETS AND MISSIONS: 1990s AND BEYOND

Over the past few years, political debates regarding cost, quality, and access call into question basic tenets of the mission of academic health centers and the organization and structure of these institutions. In addition, market economics are changing a fee-for-service delivery system to a managed care environment.

While definitions of managed care vary, they generally assume a model of care that uses contracts with selected physicians and hospitals to furnish comprehensive health care services to an enrolled population for a fixed, predetermined premium. The price, site of care, and rate of use are determined by the purchaser of health care (Fox, 1993). The managed care trend often begins with prior authorization for hospitalization, second opinions case managers, and utilization review procedures.

The growing demand of the business community, particularly large corporations, to control the cost of health care for their current and retired employees helped stimulate this dramatic change. In addition to the economic savings that many believed could be realized from prepaid capitated and managed health care, many people became convinced that primary care plus disease prevention and health promotion strategies were more valuable in the effort to sustain and improve the population's health than were the myriad technological interventions for the treatment of the sick individual. Clearly, the altered economic incentives of managed care tend to support such activities. Thus, in health care delivery, the reductionist biomedical approach is now tempered by the epidemiological, population-based perspective on care.

President Clinton and the Health Security Act of 1994 have encouraged this new phase in health care delivery where market forces are preeminent. By championing health care as the major domestic policy issue and highlighting managed competition as the solution to problems of access and escalating health care costs, Clinton galvanized the business community to rebuff big government and to reassert market forces into the health care scene.

The managed care model is transforming the market with a force and momentum that appear to be unstoppable. Demographic shifts in the pattern of insurance coverage of the U.S. population, as well as payment policies of both public and private payers, now threaten the viability of the academic health center. Federal and state policies are designed to produce more generalist physicians and primary care providers. In the private sector, managed care plans emphasize the role of primary care and non-physician providers above that of physician specialists. This renewed emphasis of public policy on what has been labeled primary care practice is intended to improve health through better access to needed services, to moderate escalating costs, and to improve both the quality of care and patient satisfaction (Donaldson, 1994). Health care experts and policymakers have been calling for academic health centers to expand their horizons into community-based public health, which may seem to run counter to the basic sciences focus of many institutions (Bulger, 1995; Schroeder et al., 1989).

Pressures to reduce cost and excess provider capacity drive forces within the market. High costs challenge health maintenance organizations, insurers, employers, and purchasers to reduce provider payments, utilization, and choice (University Hospital Consortium, 1995). Excess capacity gives insurers and purchasers the needed leverage to reinforce behaviors that reduce costs (University Hospital Consortium, 1995). With such change under way, these market forces are not only transforming the health care industry but also the economies of many regions. Hospitals are finding their margins squeezed. Downsizing is occurring. The consolidation of providers is taking place in many regions, often with the formation of hospital chains or the establishment of integrated delivery systems that involve horizontal and vertical integration of health care providers, insurers, and practitioners.

Some experts believe that insurers, using modern computing methodology and management know-how, can convert a fee-for-service market to a managed care, prepaid capitated environment in a matter of months rather than decades. Such a transition to managed care could redistribute and perhaps dramatically reduce the cost of health care, perhaps by as much as 30 cents on every health care dollar. Such a number wields tremendous power on Wall Street, which exacerbates the economic pressure to change (Sokolov, 1996). Teaching hospitals and their academic health centers are particularly threatened by a market that potentially reduces the share of health care dollar by 30 percent. Thus, they are seeking strategies to change, compete, and survive.

A. Academic Health Centers and Managed Care

Managed care challenges the costs, productivity, efficiency, patient base, services and ultimately the mission of academic health centers, which are being forced to restructure and reorganize to survive in a price competitive market. Change is made more difficult by decreased federal and state support, the pressures to orient education and training of health professionals to primary care, the movement of services and training sites outside the teaching hospital, and the decreased demand for specialists (Weiner, 1994).

The impact on the academic health center is profound. Some are positioned outside of newly-consolidated markets and are looking in! The university hospital, forced into economic competition, has moved from being a "cash cow" to a cost center. Many research and educational activities and programs that once relied on excess hospital revenues are now without financial support.

At risk is the focus of medical innovation to benefit society. A drying up of research monies combined with this shortfall in clinical revenues has meant that academic health centers must require researchers to pay their own way—that is, to bring in money by seeing patients. Pressure to see patients may cause researchers to leave institutions or the profession. A National Research Council study reported that in 1993 grant applications were at an all time low; only 21.7 percent of applications to the NIH for R01 grants from young scientists 36 years old or younger were funded (The National Research Council, 1994). This situation is another threat to the future of biomedical research and the academic health centers. Finally, these budget constraints have made it extremely difficult for many hospitals to fund clinical trials, which tend to be expensive and involve long commitments of money and time. Who will pay for the untried but promising therapeutic innovation, a cost previously absorbed through the various cross-subsidies from academic clinical income?

In the future, these conditions which are causing reconfiguration should also raise the ante for academic health centers and their faculties to become more involved in clinical evaluative studies, outcome measures, and studies of the effectiveness and efficiency of new technologies and innovations. Universities are the institutions the public depends upon for data and critical analyses. For-profit or investor-owned enterprises tend to maintain their "trade secrets" of data, technology, and patient outcomes.

In this context, the large medical faculties of the academic health center suddenly seem overpopulated with researchers and specialists and undersupplied with primary care practitioners, epidemiologists, and public health experts. Thus, a time of retrenchment and reconfiguration is at hand for the faculties of the nation's medical schools, swollen from approximately 12,000 full-time equivalents in the 1960s to more than 87,000 full-time equivalents in the early 1990s. Economic forces have added weight to the need for educational change. Medical education particularly must move out of the hospital and become more community-oriented. Health professions education must focus on interdisciplinary, team-oriented, patient-centered training and care. These concepts are not new, but they are now receiving higher priority on the educational agenda. Clinical educators are turning their attention to the community.

Faculty recruitment strategies that produced growth and research orientation have dramatically changed. Institutions now must consider research, education, and health care delivery in terms of separable funding streams, each of which must be adequate to support the efforts assigned to it. Surpluses are rapidly becoming obsolete. Though the future can be very successful and bright, it may never again include the phenomenal growth and synergy among research, service, and educational functions that characterized the last 50 years in academic health centers.

B. Academic Health Centers Respond to Change

Academic health centers are responding in myriad ways. Whether or not managed care has penetrated every market in the country, leaders of academic health centers believe that it will gain a certain degree of supremacy are therefore laying the groundwork for change within their institutions. These chief executive officers are recognizing that the era of cross-subsidization is essentially over. To compete, leaders are focusing on the clinical enterprise, seeking ways to ensure organization and governance structures that allow the academic health center greater flexibility and independence from the university in terms of operations and functions.

Invariably, a trickle-down effect will be felt throughout the organization as resources constrict and are more accountably targeted to specific areas of activity. Transformations in the delivery system also present new pedagogical challenges at a time when the financial resources are not available to pay for such activities. Certainly, no one can foretell the result and certainly much good can come from the stimulant of such momentous change. On the other hand, some unintended consequences may transpire and some otherwise healthy babies will get tossed out with the bath water.

We are rationing high-tech medicine through market incentives now; paradoxically we are rationing the time necessary to carry out successful low-tech treatments which are more labor intensive. Furthermore, the current systems of managed care tend to reward economic benefits and efficiency as measured in months rather than in years. Providers do not generally invest in many preventive strategies because too often lower costs and charges lure patients to change health plans each year, long before the patient can realize the benefits of improved health status from preventive interventions. Nevertheless, the thrust of the change persists: fewer hospital beds, fewer specialists, increased number of primary care providers, increased difficulty in gaining access to highly specialized procedures or technology.

C. Impact of Managed Care on the Teaching Hospital and Clinical Services

The significance of the teaching hospital component of the academic health center cannot be minimized, for they have integral value to the mission. The political and economic policies currently laying siege to the viability of these institutions is not fully known, but many scenarios are possible.

The primary teaching hospitals of academic health centers are particularly vulnerable to changes in public policy and market place economics because of their educational, research, and service needs. Teaching hospitals have traditionally been higher cost institutions (Iezzoni, et al., 1990; Epstein, 1995). Higher charges reflect the higher costs related to the patient mix, which in teaching hospitals means patients who are sicker and require more complex care. Medical students and residents add to the costs; additional space is required along with higher use of facilities and equipment. Finally, paid staff spend more time with students, thus adding to the expense. The market trends are toward lower utilization of secondary and tertiary services, fewer hospital admissions, and short lengths of stay; therefore, university hospitals are being confronted with a decrease in revenues by as much as 50 percent in an aggressive managed care market (University Hospital Consortium, 1995). As specialist contributions to patient care revenues decline, funding for education and research is threatened. Teaching hospitals are faced with lowering their costs substantially in order to remain financially viable.

Until recently, the chiefs of clinical departments and the heads of sub-specialty divisions have exercised tremendous governing control in their responsibility for both academic and service functions. They are, in fact, the source for a substantial amount of funding from both research grants and faculty practice plans for the departments (Ebert, 1983). This model worked well for several decades, but it may not be the most appropriate or workable approach for the future.

The following scenario illustrates the critical problem areas for academic health centers and their teaching hospitals in today's market. Let us imagine a wholly-owned university teaching hospital with 700 beds, a major trauma center and emergency facility, and the regional neonatal intensive care unit. The hospital has an esteemed reputation in high-technology care, with a prestigious cardiology department known for diagnosis, surgery that includes coronary bypass procedures, and a vast array of other treatment methodologies.

The hospital's operating budget is $500 million a year and, until recently, had an end-of-the-year surplus of between $30 and $50 million. Five years ago, the hospital surplus built a new clinical research wing, which now houses more than 100 research laboratories and associated educational activities for graduate students in the biomedical sciences, senior fellows, and residents in training. The medical school and its faculty—who hold the staff positions in the hospital—have focused their research energies and funds on neonates, heart disease, and trauma care. The total research budget is approximately $50 million per year; clinical earnings of the faculty have been increasing annually and totaled $100 million a year. Of the $100 million in clinical revenues, $30 million are devoted to research and educational support. The dean of the school of medicine receives $7 million of the $30 million which is then used to fund basic science departments or ambulatory teaching sites.

Thirty percent of the hospital's patients are Medicare beneficiaries, and managed care is making significant inroads with this population. Fifty percent of the city's indigent population receive care in the hospital. The care of the poor has been relatively well supported by the state's Medicaid program. However, Medicaid enrollees, a traditional patient base for the hospital, have been given broader provider options and are now choosing to receive care at other hospitals and through managed care networks which exclude this teaching hospital.

Managed care has penetrated the hospital's market area. Fifty-five percent of the population including Medicaid enrollees, is enrolled in managed care with more than half in capitated arrangements. The hospital had failed to make arrangements with any of the large employers in the region and had not joined or been invited to join any of the three major organized delivery systems that give evidence of dominating the local market.

Since clinical revenues, which in the past helped to support the university's health professions schools, have significantly decreased, educational support of the medical, dental and nursing schools and students is no longer possible. Teaching is being curtailed due to the shortage of clinical teaching staff. Integrated private health care systems are also contributing to squeeze the hospital's sources of revenues by negotiating discounts that eliminate subsidies for the extra costs of teaching and research. Managed care organizations are referring patients to lower-cost community hospitals.

As a result, a major reorganization has led to a separation of the hospital from the university with the establishment of a separate management and board to run the service enterprise and to contract with payers for services. The new management is dedicated to maintaining the academic presence of the institution, but has just joined a system of local private, not-for-profit hospitals. The university hospital does not control this system, but is a part of it.

Already, several things are apparent: the hospital workforce is being downsized from 3000 to 800 as the bed complement is reduced to 385. Academic personnel within the hospital are also at risk of losing their jobs because the three-year strategic plan calls for a 5 percent reduction of clinical staff each year. The neonatal center is being closed, and the cardiac surgery program is being cut by 50 percent. New contracts with payers will reduce clinical income for physicians by an estimated 30 percent, and the hospital is projecting no surplus at year's end.

We may assume, then, that the total clinical professional income earned by the physician faculty will be markedly reduced. The reduction of specialty referrals and procedures will mean a concomitant reduction in trainees. These reductions will undoubtedly cause a major reduction in the number of full-time faculty in the clinical departments. If the dean of the school of medicine is allowed to sustain the traditional 7 percent dean's tax, the clinicians will exert more pressure to spend those dollars on the clinical departments, not on the basic sciences. One can envision a 40 percent drop in income to a total of $60 million. The dean will be fortunate to salvage $2 million for general educational and research purposes, leaving perhaps $15-$18 million to supplement departmental efforts, most of which will be moved into direct salary for the clinicians.

The other challenge will be to find a way to conduct the requisite clinical education programs in the ambulatory setting such that teaching is patient-friendly and cost-effective. If the universities lose heart and retreat from the educational world, a bleak picture emerges—industry-run education invariably perpetuates the present way of doing things.

If this hospital were part of the only academic health center in the state, it might survive because of support from the state government or local philanthropists. Its students, however, would receive much of their clinical education outside the hospital. If this hospital were only one of several teaching hospitals affiliated with more than one academic health center, one or two other university hospitals might also need to close, having lost out in the redistribution of patients and financial resources caused by managed care. The economic fall-out is great as it spreads across the health professions and eventually creates a large number of unemployed in a small geographic area. The large, complex research infrastructure arrangements would crash or disintegrate more slowly. Because this scenario is a possibility, we are seeing consolidations within institutions and new alignments and relationships. Many hospitals which are part of academic health centers are merging or consolidating with one another rather than simply playing winner-takes-all.

The hospital in the new era will have no surpluses for building new research buildings or capitalizing investments in promising new technologies. Funds to cross-subsidize clinical education and research will have rapidly dried up. Thus the educational and research enterprises associated with the academic health center and its teaching hospital will have lost upwards of $60 million dollars a year!

Such change, necessary for the survival of many academic health centers, would mean major reductions in faculty, research output, and technological interventions. In another scenario, with a different local environment, the university might contrive to sell the hospital to a for-profit hospital chain or other organized delivery system, hopefully recouping enough money from the sale to offset the loss of service dollars previously used to cross-subsidize research and education. In still another scenario, already played out more than once over the past few years, the university may close the hospital and merge the educational and research programs with another institution.

Alternatively, some academic health centers are positioned to be "winners" in the health care reform sweepstakes, having been fortuitously placed in a favorable market environment or having implemented a strategically sound approach through which the institution either owns or is securely partnered in an organized delivery system with a patient population sufficient to support its education and clinical research efforts.

One can only hope that the reductions that emerge by the turn of the century have a critical mass of academic health centers to ensure a steady, if reduced, flow of new technologies and the clinical evaluation expertise and apparatus necessary to assess the innovations at hand.

There seems to be little doubt that the academic health center will shrink over the next decade in large measure because of the reshaping of the health care delivery system. To adjust to the future, many organizational transformations are occurring that may change the nature of academic health centers.

D. Strategies for Change

Experts have noted that ownership, governance, organization and leadership of academic health centers must meet and beat market demands, including the need for speed and decisiveness, ability to take and manage risk, primary care capacity, unified response, collaboration with other providers and insurers, and demonstrated value in terms of cost, quality, and service (University Hospital Consortium, 1995). We are already seeing a strong movement to free the service component from state or university bureaucratic controls.

In the service arena, academic health centers will need access to income from health premiums. Those institutions that do not hold the contracts of the employers in their market or own a system of clinical sites and hospitals may be forced to become part of service networks. In some instances, academic health centers are selling their clinical facilities to a system, provided the system reimburses them for educational and research costs. However, conflict arises since the academic orientation can often be at odds with a corporate, for-profit business outlook.

Some academic health centers are moving toward integration within their institutions, forming highly organized, multispecialty group practices capable of interfacing with other organized delivery systems or primary care networks. These institutions also have patient-friendly ambulatory services that may be part of or independent from the teaching hospital. Some centers have already organized strong physician-hospital organizations with their primary teaching hospital or its affiliated system. Most try to connect their physicians and their hospital in a single or coordinated entity, but some (especially those that have sold or do not own their hospital and service system) see fit to operate the physicians' organization independently.

A 1994 survey of members of the Association of Academic Health Centers revealed diverse responses to current transformations. Eighty percent of the responding institutions reported an expansion of linkages to the community and managed care entities as well as the downsizing of the primary teaching hospital (Ball and Rubin, 1995).

These changes within the service system continue to raise issues of cost and accountability within the educational and research domains. Market forces will continue to pressure these components of the academic health center perhaps causing major transformation in the health professions schools and the research enterprise in the not-too-distant future.

V. A RECONFIGURED ACADEMIC HEALTH CENTER

Changing times will require that leaders of academic health centers have a broad perspective on the future workforce. An interdisciplinary rather than a discipline specific outlook will be more valued. The infrastructure attached to the departmental system of organization may no longer be affordable. Leaders will be needed to move toward a centralized structure in terms of finances and administration. The academic health center may reorganize so that its academic component is centralized, interdisciplinary, dedicated solely to education. The same will be true for the research component. Both will be forced to function very efficiently and in a cost-effective manner, thus drawing their operations closer to the standards of the market.

For the future, CEOs of academic health centers will play key but different roles. They may serve as coordinators, integrating the education, service, and research functions with the chiefs of the service, academic, and research divisions reporting to them. What has been described as risk-oriented leadership in the service sector will also be true in the educational and research arena (University Hospital Consortium, 1995).

For some institutions, the position of CEO may be transformed into an academic provost or provost for the health sciences position, with the CEO heading all academic divisions as well as the board of the academic coordinating committee that relates to the director of the clinical enterprise or the health care system. In addition, a vice provost for research, who might also be the dean of graduate studies, would report to the academic provost.

Current trends suggest that research and educational funds will be carefully sequestered to be used only for those designated activities. Deans of the health professions schools, medicine in particular, will be forced to identify and carefully manage educational dollars. Educational funds may be husbanded and dispensed from a central source, most likely the CEO, to accomplish educational goals in the most efficient manner. The need for accountability of educational monies may lead some academic health centers to consolidate their faculties into a single health sciences faculty, with divisions for the basic sciences and each of the various health professions on the campus. A common academic calendar would be instituted to ensure that broad interdisciplinary education and training could take place.

The teaching faculty may be smaller with some faculty members devoting their time solely to teaching. The requirement for every faculty member, particularly in medicine, to be a teacher, researcher, and clinician may no longer remain a viable concept. Such an approach suggests that deans and department chairpersons of medicine in particular will have more restricted roles than is now the case in most institutions.

The vice provosts for research would have responsibilities for all research and development, grants and contracts, space management, technology transfer, and start-up companies and industry relations. Again, collaboration and sharing of common resources among departments and institutions will be required for survival.

In summary, the dramatically rapid pace of health care reform is forcing equally dramatic changes upon all components of academic health centers. The changes in the funding for and organization of clinical services require setting the clinical services apart from education and research and ending the tradition of cross-subsidy among education, research and practice dollars. Since both education and research dollars are in short supply, a dramatic reduction in clinical income will greatly impact the other two functions

Academic health centers continue to demonstrate strong commitments to the tripartite education, research and service mission even as they restructure to meet the challenges of a highly competitive market for patient services (Ball and Rubin, 1995). This commitment, however, is problematic for the future. Reduced enrollments in medical and other health professions schools may be in order. Residency programs will probably be reduced or amalgamated. Less expensive models of education with a redesigned curriculum may be demanded. All-payer funding for physician education, in particular, may be required. Information technology will probably change the face of education, accelerating collaboration and cooperation among and within institutions. Some schools will close; research and innovation will be reduced in quantity; traditional specialties and the clinical "courts of last resort" will be reduced or disappear. In this setting, many academic health centers will have the opportunity to seize the day, anticipate the future, and organize to be of maximum utility to the city or region.

Academic health centers can become the central focus for new health care alliances or educational networks within given geographic areas. As coordinators of educational networks, academic health centers can also enrich the professional lives of health care practitioners in surrounding communities by building the infrastructure for educational, clinical, and professional linkages. Such support will remain particularly important in rural or isolated areas. There will continue to be pressures for health professions schools to develop courses or programs emphasizing new bodies of knowledge or needs.

In the history of health care delivery, this market-dominated phase will no doubt be one of the great turning points. With the environment still in flux, health care leaders must remain flexible and imaginative to keep pace and to ensure that quality, value, ethical practices and patient concerns remain part of whatever health care system evolves. And academic health centers should be part of whatever that system is. Society is responsible for advancing education, research, and service. Academic health centers can and should be the institutions to develop and implement plans to meet these societal needs.

How all this will play out in the next five years remains to be seen. The times are both exhilarating and risky not only for individual academic health centers, but also for the overall well-being of society.

REFERENCES

Association of Academic Health Centers (1969). Bylaws.
Association of Academic Health Centers. Economic and Social Impact of Academic Health Centers (1990). Association of Academic Health Centers, Washington, D.C.
Association of American Medical Colleges (1981). *Medical Education: Characteristics and Programs: A Background Paper*. Washington, D. C.: Figure 23.
Association of American Medical Colleges (1993). *Data Book: Statistical Information Related to Medical Education*. Association of American Medical Colleges, Washington, D.C.

Ball, J., and Rubin E. (1995). Academic Health Centers: Structures and Strategies for Coping with the Managed Care Environment. Association of Academic Health Centers, Washington, D. C.

Barondess, J. (1991). *Annals of Internal Medicine, 115:* 962.

Bulger, R. (1995). *Academic Health Centers In: Encyclopedia of Bioethics, Vol. I.* (W. T. Reich, ed.), Simon & Schuster MacMillan, New York, N. Y., p. 53.

Bush, V. (1945). *Science - The Endless Frontier.* National Science Foundation, Washington, D.C.

Carnegie Commission on Higher Education (1970). *Higher Education and the Nation's Health.* McGraw-Hill Company, New York., N.Y.,

The Comprehensive Health Manpower Training Act of 1971. *Public Law,* 92-157.

Country's No. 1 Health Problem: Interview with Top Presidential Adviser. *U. S. News and World Report, February 23, 1970,* pp. 68-73.

Donaldson, M., Yordy, K. And Vanselow, N. eds. (1994). Defining Primary Care: An Interim Report, National Academy Press, Washington, D.C.

Ebert, R. H., Brown, S. S. (1983). *NEJM, 308:*1021.

Ebert, R. H., Brown, S. S. (1983). *NEJM, 308:*1206.

Epstein, A. (1995). "U. S. Teaching Hospitals in the Evolving Health Care System." *JAMA: 1995; 273:*1204.

Flexner, A. (1910). Medical Education in the United States and Canada. *Carnegie Foundation for the Advancement of Teaching.* Bulletin 4.

Fox, P. D, Wasserman, J. (1993). Academic Medical Centers and Managed Care: Uneasy Partners. *Health Affairs,* Millwood. 1993.

Health Manpower Training Act of 1968. *Public Law,* 90-1490.

Health Professions Education Assistance Act. *Public Law* 88-129, 88th Congress, 1963.

Health Research Facilities Construction Act. *Public Law* 835, 84th Congress, 1960.

Iezzoni, L. I., Shwartz, M., Moskowitz, M., Ash, A., Sawitz, E., and Burnside, S. (1990). "Illness Severity and Costs of Admissions at Teaching and Nonteaching Hospitals." *JAMA. 264:* 1426.

Iglehart, J. (1995). Rapid Changes for Academic Medical Centers. Part II, *NEJM, February.*

Institute of Medicine (1983). *Nursing and Nursing Education: Public Policies and Private Actions.* National Academy Press, Washington, D.C.

Knowles, J., ed. (1966). *The Teaching Hospital. Evolution and Contemporary Issues.* Harvard University Press, Cambridge, MA.

Lombardi, J. V. (1991). Science, Doctors, and the University: New Alliances for a Competitive Age. In *Preparing for Science in the 21st Century.* Association of Academic Health Centers, Washington, D. C., p. 54.

National Institutes of Health. Office of Program Planning and Evaluation Basic Data Realting to the National Institutes of Health.

The National Research Council (1994). *The Funding of Young Investigators in the Biological and Biomedical Sciences.* National Academy Press, Washington, D. C.

Schroeder, S. A., Zones, J. S., and Showstack, J. A. (1989). "Academic Medicine as a Public Trust." *JAMA, 161(6):*803-812.

Shannon, J. A. (1973). *Science and the Evolution of Public Policy.* Rockefeller University Press, N.Y.

Sokolov, J. (1996). Merging Financial and Clinical Objectives.: A Strategic Market Based Overview. Presentation at the Society of Medical Administrators, Naples, FL, 1996.

Stevens, R. (1989). *In Sickness and in Wealth: American Hospitals in the Twentieth Century.* Basic Books, New York, NY.

University Hospital Consortium (1995). *Hospital Consolidation: Implementation Strategies.* University Hospital Consortium. Oak Brook, IL.

University Hospital Consortium, 1995 Research Conference. St. Petersburg, FL. February 2-3, 1995.

The Veterans Administration Medical School Assistant and Health Manpower Training Act of 1972.

Weiner, J.P. (1994) Forecasting the Effects of Health Reform on U.S. Physician Workforce Requirement: Evidence from HMO Staffing Patterns. *American Medical Association.* 272:222-230.

16.
VETERANS HEALTH CARE

Evelyn P. Mahairas, *VA Medical Center, Coatesville, PA*

In these days of intense public debate on the need for health care reform, both private and public sectors are generating forums to consider ways to reduce health care costs, without jeopardizing quality of care in the process. In the midst of these challenges, the issue of entitlements is often raised as a means of eliminating unnecessary expenditures. One entitlement that is often included in this debate is that of veterans' health care.

However, such challenges to the need for veterans entitlements as a unnecessary cost to the national economy could represent an uninformed viewpoint that does not take into account the significant role played by the veterans health care system in the United States of America. Moreover, those health care benefits, already established for veterans, represent a long-standing tradition that has evolved over time; assuring a continuum of care for veterans not always available through other public health care delivery systems.

It is important to note that without a system such as the Veterans Health Administration (VHA), under the Department of Veterans Affairs which was formerly known as the VA (Veterans Administration), ongoing needs of veterans and their families might not be met. In addition, if this system of veterans health care benefits was threatened with dissolution, it could be considered a breach of promise from a nation's agreement: "[T]o care for him who shall have borne the burden and for his widow and his child,..." (Lincoln's second Inaugural Address, March 4, 1865, in Richardson, 1899, Vol. VI, pp. 276-277).

Essentially, precedent has been set by the U.S. government, in establishing a covenant to provide care for veterans. This implicit covenant originated in order to acknowledge a nation's gratitude to veterans who have served their country and provided military protection, while sacrificing personal needs in response to national needs. Unfortunately, traditional public representation in favor of veterans' interests has eroded in support of a veterans' constituency. In part, the waning of public support for veterans benefits is an offshoot of political debates stemming from the Vietnam War era.

In large part, however, this decrease in public support is also reflective of changing demographics; defined by an aging veteran population and a diminishing need for large numbers of military personnel in recent decades. That is to say, there is less need for military actions requiring large troop maneuvers while, at the same time, there continues to be significant increase in scientific technologies that create technological substitutes as replacements for direct use of military personnel.

Still, even as the number of veteran cohorts dwindle, there may be a greater need to advocate on behalf of retaining veterans benefits as established by tradition. Clearly, it is important to address these issues and provide clarification of veterans benefits so as to ensure an informed public. In this way, greater understanding about the significance of these evolving benefits and their significant contributions to U.S may occur. Moreover, it is important to provide the context in which these benefits were generated. By presenting the actual circumstances of immediate times when benefits transpire, it will be evident that a cumulative emergence of a broadening spread in veterans benefits ultimately led to the formation of a major health care system, the VHA. The existence of such an organization signifies a nation's expression of appreciation for those who have served it well; helping to preserve this country's national security for its citizenry.

I. HISTORICAL PERSPECTIVES

As is already noted, throughout the course of U.S. history, from colonial times on, each achievement in veterans benefits was established through public acceptance of documented need. Ultimately, a collection of veterans legislative enactments passed into the twentieth century; emerging as a unified organization, known as the VA (Veterans Administration). Although this paper will not present all legislative enactments over the course of U.S. history, it will identify pertinent highlights and major shifts of policy leading to benchmark legislations referred to above; giving shape to today's VA.

A major part of this analysis will discuss those public laws that inform us of the development of a three-pronged system of benefits consisting of: compensation, shelter, and health care. As indicated, these major legislative enactments signify increments of veterans benefits that form the foundation for entitlements that evolved over the course of over three and one half centuries.

It will also be valuable to present briefly some of the outstanding hallmarks of the emergent VHA during the final years of the 20th century. It will be useful, as well, to include VA contributions to the health care delivery system, along with accomplishments of note in research, education, and clinical care of veterans.

A full and detailed picture of veterans benefits, as they are currently in place, cannot be addressed in this paper. Yet it will be valuable to gain an understanding of how veterans needs received broad attention through development of public dialogue and creation of a public forum. Thus, as each benchmark is identified in the progressive development of veterans' benefits, a contextual or historic perspective is provided to enhance insights on this evolving expansion of veterans benefits. This analysis suggests that as each change occurs in the public domain and new legislation is enacted, there are likely to be specific events or changes taking place in the environment that lead to policy shifts. This gradual increase in benefits also evolves with growing public acceptance as needs continue to be demonstrated.

A. Theoretical Perspectives

Frequently, underlying assumptions are made about bureaucracies; they are presumed to be fixed and rigid, based on organization behavioral concepts (Katz and Kahn, 1966). Such myths can be seen as stereotypical in light of the following discussion. It will be seen throughout this contextual analysis that, as external changes take place in the organizational environment, the organization itself must respond, internally, with changes in its own behaviors.

Moreover, it is often assumed that a military organization is a reliable constant that consists of only one type of military membership. Yet, it is clear that in early centuries, western civilization relied on mercenary armies for protection or conquest against foreign domains or states. Such a structure relied on troop retention by means of granting rewards that were acquired through accepted pillage and plunder. Early forms of organized armed forces were expressions of military might that were used during the rise of city states; culminating in the dominant military power manifested during the era of the Roman empire.

In contrast, associated with the rise of national governments, a shift occurred with the transformation from a mercenary style army to a professional career military force designed to defend territorial interests and, eventually, national boundaries. Still later, as more democratic style governments arose, interest in a professional or career style military began to diminish. Instead, it became necessary to seek volunteers for a citizen style army. Hence, the citizen army was conceptualized as a new military formation; rallying short term, non-professional military support during brief periods of defense when a nation's boundaries was being threatened.

As a consequence, with the decline of the large career military support, and as more democratic governments prevailed, it became necessary to solicit military reinforcements from ordinary citizens as volunteers or conscripts for military service. As this newer type of citizen recruitment emerged, a system of incentives was needed in establishing compensations to ordinary citizens for time spent away from family and community as well as offering rewards for losses, not only in terms of income, but for potential sacrifices in loss of life or limb. Hence, it is clear that the mode of military strength shifted significantly over the centuries in western civilization. This system of incentives and rewards continued to unfold in parallel development to that of the U.S. as a nation.

II. TODAY'S CHALLENGES

The above documentation is indicative of significant contributions made by the VA in advancing program development to meet veterans' health care needs through the first half of the 20th century. At this juncture, it is important to identify some of its major achievements and accomplishments that followed in the latter part of the 20th century.

A. Updated Status: Achievements

Despite some inevitable controversies that usually accompany the issues of veterans' benefits, the VA's place in health care has been a highly significant one.

1. Legacy in Health Care

Although an extensive description of today's VA is not possible in this chapter, it is important to note its role and contributions to the public good and the U.S. health care delivery system; particularly since the establishment of the D.M.S. at the end of World War II. The following discussion reveals the development of a major health care delivery system designed to provide comprehensive care to veterans.

For example, the extent of this hospital system continued to flourish with a total of 172 medical centers and in-patient facilities being made available to veterans nationwide within the next four decades. Out-patient services were also extended to veterans through the development of 365 out-patient, community, and outreach clinics, 128 nursing homes, and 37 domiciliaries. However, within another decade, federal budget cutbacks began focusing on veterans benefits as well. Currently, issues related to health care reform are bringing new challenges to the VA and its traditional ways of providing services to veterans.

2. Promoting Health Care Advances

It is clear from the above discussion that generating therapeutic approaches to improve veterans' care is correlated with those medical and technological advances associated with each war era.

a. Rehabilitative Therapies

The onset of rehabilitation and the growth of allied health disciplines are principally associated with the post W.W. I era. This period of time, in the aftermath of wartime recovery, ushered in many innovative therapies that would help veterans re-enter U.S. society. Thus, the emergence of allied health professions, introduced in the early part of this century, were strengthened through newer techniques and services designed to assist veterans to become more independent and self reliant, even if physically disabled.

b. Medical and Surgical Advances

World War II's achievements are more notable in the development of surgical procedures and medication treatments being advanced, along with further developments in scientific technologies. Also, more extensive programs were available to care for veterans suffering from chronic medical or psychiatric illnesses and disabilities. These were highly instrumental in helping to absorb the immense W.W. II cohort; surviving combat and re-entering civilian life in unheard-of numbers. This growing health care system was to become the largest in the western world, outside the system established under communism. Through the establishment of the D.M.S., quality of care would be assured.

c. Shifts in Program Developments

Each decade since W.W. II represents a fresh emphasis in veterans' services. They reflect changing demographics and new veteran cohort needs. Benefits are also seen to change, with fewer benefits available to those cohorts following the special thrust of the "GI Bill," with its emphasis on universally agreed-to post war recovery efforts.

The VA's unique position of being a public agency has both advantages and disadvantages. Being in the public domain signifies that events occurring anywhere within the system generate great public interest. Clearly, since all of its services are governed by congressional laws, its services and the care offered to veterans or their families are subject, typically, to broad public scrutiny. On the other hand, it has enjoyed a remarkable position within the public domain and serves as a major resource in the health care delivery system. The next segment of this paper will amplify this public position; highlighting major program achievements as relevant.

B. Leadership Roles in Health Care

The following section will provide a brief overview of the VA's outstanding contributions to the U.S. health care delivery system. As noted above, much of this information is found in government documents; substantiated with pertinent data. Yet, some mention of VA achievements will be of interest in this context.

1. Geriatrics

While new veteran cohorts were emerging from the Korean and Viet Nam eras, it was also evident that the W.W. II cohort was advancing in age. Due to new legislation regarding eligibilities based on age, this cohort was anticipated to reach its watershed year in health care eligibility by 1985. This demographic projection was documented with the support of an extensive study conducted by the National Academy of Science in 1977 (Sen.Com., 1977; Vets H.Act, 1973).

Implicit within this congressional report by the National Academy of Science is a likely budgetary crisis, related to anticipated increased demands on the system. Recent legislation had determined that chronological age alone would suffice for older veteran entry into the VA system, rather than reliance on a means test (Vets Pens. Adj. Act, 1976). This shift in eligibility was in contrast to former requirements that permitted entry into VA facilities to non-service connected veterans based on availability of beds and inability to pay for services due to lack of income.

Unless such generous conditions were altered, a tidal wave of aging W.W. II veterans would place inordinate demands on limited government resources as they reached age 65 and became eligible for unrestricted health care benefits (H.R., 1969). Hence, this breach of past eligibility stipulations, allowing chronological age to be the sole proviso for eligibility, was soon to be rectified. A return to a means test for elderly veterans would be re-introduced in order to avert a fiscal overload to this system which could lead to inordinate demands on government resources.

2. Expansion of Clinical Services

To augment existing in-patient programs, additional out-patient services were developed to assure continuity of care and prevent unnecessary, costly in-patient care.

a. Out-Patient Care

Emerging programs to serve older veterans while remaining in the community included: Adult Day Care, Respite Care, Hospice, Hospital-Based Home Care, and Home Health Aid Services. Thus, the evolving concept of a continuum of care became a reality, based on the creation of new programming to address the needs of an aging veteran population.

b. Viet Nam Era Needs: PTSD and SATU

Other program developments centered around the special needs of the Viet Nam era veteran cohort. Because of controversy surrounding this cohort, different in-patient programs were essential for addressing the unique experiences of this besieged cohort. Out-patient residency programs, such as domiciliaries, remained an important aspect of enabling greater opportunity for veterans to gradually return to more independent living arrangements.

Due to the unpopularity and controversy surrounding the Viet Nam conflict, negative attitudes regarding this cohort were shaped based on perceptions related to the fermenting anti-war movement. These negative associations, in turn, lead to the scapegoating of this particular veteran cohort by its own peer group. At the same time, these same veterans were being excluded from participation with earlier veteran cohort groups. Ultimately, its own symptomatology was addressed by in-patient psychiatric care to veterans for PTSD (Post Traumatic Stress Syndrome) and SATU (Substance Abuse Treatment Unit).

Moreover, specific legislation was needed to enable this cohort to become more fully integrated into the community and to promote its ability to become as self supporting as possible. Therefore, a new enactment was passed to provide educational and vocational rehabilitation assistance and financial supports for disabled Viet Nam veterans and their families. (Veterans Rehabilitation and Education Amendment, 1980).

As has been demonstrated from the above discussion, each veteran cohort may face different challenges that call for special government attention. For example, this discussion can only allude to controversies surrounding reports such as: exposure to environmental toxins such as Agent Orange; questions raised pertaining to symptoms associated with what is referred to as the Persian Gulf syndrome; problems related to homelessness; or, more recently, relating to the possibility of sexual traumas experienced by female veterans (U.S. Department of Veterans Affairs, 1995).

Many of these most recent challenges reflect the push and pull of ongoing veterans' needs. These in turn represent dynamic changes in the ebb and flow of veterans' programming which shift in emphasis; dependent on public reactions, congressional and other governmental responses, as well as available resources at any given point in time in the evolution of veterans' programming.

C. Leadership Roles in Education and Research

Before concluding this analysis in the evolution of veterans programming, it will be valuable to identify some cutting edge innovations achieved through VA contributions.

1. *Education: A National Resource*

Critics of the VA are often unaware of the invaluable contributions to public educational needs made by this organization while serving its veterans. It is a little known fact that the VA also serves as a major educational facility that promotes academic and clinical programs intended to prepare health care disciplines for clinical practice.

a. Affiliations

Through academic affiliations, with a variety of accredited clinical programs, at least fifty percent (50%) of all health care disciplines receive some clinical training through VA facilities. In the field of medicine, this ratio is higher. In medical education, seventy-five percent (75%) of all physicians and over ninety percent (90%) of specialities have spent some portion of their educational and clinical training in VA medical centers.

b. Geriatrics

With the onset of the wave of aging veteran cohorts being anticipated, other innovative programs emerged in the 1980s:

1) GEMs (Geriatric Evaluation and Management Units): intended to assess the multiple needs of older veterans and develop interdisciplinary team care plans for dealing with the complexities of aging and to assure comprehensive care of the older veteran patient.
2) GRECCs (Geriatric Research, Education, and Clinical Care) Centers of Excellence: designed to address research focusing on a special focus area of study within the field of geriatrics/gerontology (Vet. Adm., 1979).
3) ITTGs (Interdisciplinary Team Training in Geriatrics) programs: intended to promote an interdisciplinary team approach to deal with the complex needs of an aging population (Feazell and Mather, 1986).

2. *Research*

Outstanding contributions made through VA associated researchers must also be included. Many research accomplishments are routinely conducted in laboratory and clinical trial studies that are notable in creating bench-mark research efforts as in the following areas:

a. **Advanced scientific technologies developing the following:**
   1) Cardiac pacemaker;
   2) CT scan;
   3) Magnetic source imaging and brain surgery;
   4) Prosthetics;
   5) Electric stimulation for muscular activation.

b. **Surgical advances as seen in research and development for:**
   1) Liver transplant;
   2) Vagus nerve stimulation;.

c. **Clinical research in:**
   1) Autoimmune system: gene therapy;
   2) Spinal cord injury: protein therapy;
   3) Ulcers: ranitidine drug therapy;
   4) Cancer: chemical compounds;
   5) Alcoholism: chromosome and genetic makeup studies;
   6) Schozophrenia and Bi-polar disorders: Psychotropic medications;
   7) Hypertension, heart attack, laryngial cancer, and chochlear
      implants: Cooperative studies;
   8) Post-Traumatic Stress Disorder (PTSD), AIDS, Alzheimer's
      Disease: Ongoing studies (Dept. of Vets. Affrs., 1994; AMVETS,
      DAV, PVA, VFW, 1995)

D. Department of Veterans Affairs Cabinet Post Status

The next benchmark in the VA's development is the establishment of the Department of Veterans Affairs through a series of enactments beginning in 1988 (The Dept. of Vet. Affrs. Act, 1988, with ensuing amendments 1989, 1990, and 1991).

These major enactments represent administrative changes that redefine the VA as an executive department; leading to its establishment as a cabinet post, rather than, as before, an independent agency reporting separately to the President. Thus the VA Administrator role is now designated as Secretary of the Department of Veterans Affairs, held by Secretary Jesse Brown, until recently. The position originally entitled Chief Medical Director is now referred to as Under Secretary of Health, a position currently held by Kenneth Kizer, M.D., M.P.H., who oversees the former D.M.S., now referred to as the Veterans Health Services and Research Administration [V.H.A.].

Other organizational changes relating to administration of veterans benefits and budgetary concerns can be found in both governmental references cited above and under Dr. Kizer's *Vision for Change* (Kizer, 1995).

III. CHALLENGES TO THE VA: DESIGNING STRATEGIES FOR THE FUTURE

By now, it is clear that the myth of fixed, rigid bureaucracy is a misnomer and hardly addresses the ebb and flow of a dynamic organization that must respond to changes in its environment. New shifts in the delivery of care lead to innovations in approaches for addressing health care needs of veterans and their families. They also represent progressive responses to growing demands for health care reform.

A. Innovations in Program Development

Several changes in the way health care is provided have surfaced in recent years. These changes have contributed to creative programming that actually expand on veterans' options for services through a variety of modalities, rather than being limited to a few traditional venues relied upon in the past. The following approaches have all developed during the 1980s or early 1990s. Many of them have been adapted within the VA system in an effort to remain consistent with trends seen in other organizations and in compliance with JCAHO (Joint Commission on Accreditation of Health Organizations) standards for accreditation purposes, or as a means of reducing costs by utilizing less costly provision of services or lower salaried health care disciplines (JCAHO, 1992).

1. ITTP (Interdisciplinary Team Training Program)

One of the earlier innovative programs established by the VA is ITTP. This was originally referred to as ITTG (Interdisciplinary Team Training in Geriatrics). It is designed to promote a generation of team-oriented clinicians who would lead the way toward a more cooperative approach and provide a more holistic, comprehensive system of care for patients with complex or multiple problems (Mahairas, 1989; 1994).

An interdisciplinary health care team approach gives recognition to the importance of bringing together expertise from a variety of disciplines in order to promote collaboration across disciplinary lines. It emphasizes shared leadership in the decision making process. This is especially relevant for those veterans with multiple problems that require input from various disciplinary perspectives (Ducanis and Golin, 1979).

The team approach to problem solving is being adapted in a variety of applications throughout the system. Where, before it was limited to a geriatric focus, its use has expanded significantly to capture its broad applicability throughout the system (Mahairas, et al., 1996).

2. Primary Care

Another shift in health care delivery is under greater emphasis on primary care. This approach usually assigns patients to a specific physician and associated team of health care disciplines. This represents the current trend in medical education aimed on reducing the number of specializations within the field of medicine. Its purpose is to assure continuity of care for veterans so that the same health care provider remains a constant, regardless of where the patient is assigned for treatment (Department of Veterans Affairs, 1995). This shift holds broad implications for health care in general.

3. Out-Patient Services

The third shift in the delivery of health care services is seen in a growing emphasis on the provision of care through out-patient services. The goal is to encourage veterans to remain in the community and avoid lengthy in-patient stays as much as possible. Such innovations may permit the VA to substantially reduce its expenditures for costlier in-patient services as well as utilization of interventions by more cost-effective, health care disciplines (Kizer, 1997; 1996, b).

All of these organizational changes require further study to determine their impact on the care of veteran patients and their families. Whatever the eventual impact of service delivery will be, other organizational changes are important to mention, though their outcomes may be difficult to predict at this point in time (U. S. Department. of Veterans Affairs, 1995).

B. A Paradigm Shift: Patient-Centered Care

Recent trends, guided, in part, by JCAHO standards, are giving a new emphasis to a patient-centered care delivery system. Essentially, this shift to a patient-focused care system has led to organizational changes based on principles adopted from industry (Ingraham and Romzek 1994; Lathrop, 1993).

1. TQM (Total Quality Management)

Trends from industry are being applied within the VA. Strategic planning methods have been applied to support administrative decision making processes. Principles from Total Quality Management (TQM) are being adapted. While discussion precludes TQM theories and methodologies espoused by Deming and others, customer satisfaction as the over-riding goal in the decision making process for industry is being carried over into health care as well (Deming, 1986; Cohen and Brand, 1993).

2. Health Care Applications

CQI (Continuous Quality Improvement). These principles of customer satisfaction, established in industry, are being adapted for health care delivery systems. The acronym, CQI (Continuous Quality Improvement), essentially represents a new paradigm in the delivery of health care. Indeed, goals of emphasizing customer satisfaction in health care can lead to a patient-centered delivery system; aiming for effective provision of services, presumably at lower cost (Gaucher and Coffey, 1993; Martin, 1993). At the same time, questions regarding quality of health care under a managed care system are surfacing (Arndt and Bigelow, 1995; Bigelow and Arndt, 1995).

C. Restructuring

In order to accomplish the goal of reducing the rise of health care costs in today's delivery systems, both private and public sectors have been downsizing significantly. These trends are seen in the VA itself; leading to major shifts within this organization. At this time, considerable reorganizing is taking place. Several administrative and fiscal strategies have begun to take hold (Department of Veterans Affairs, 1994):

1. *Decentralization*

Reduction in the work force in Washington's Central Offices is leading to a shift in controls from Washington, D.C., with four regional offices managing local medical centers to 22 VISNs (Veterans Integrated Service Networks) that have more direct control over field operations.

2. *Consolidations*

Many medical centers are combining or consolidating in an effort to reduce administrative costs while developing strategies for shared resources.

3. *Functional Product Lines*

This reorganization strategy represents a cost-cutting effort to flatten hierarchical organization layers in order to reduce unnecessary levels of middle management and eliminate discipline-specific service lines or departments. Along with emphasizing function rather than departmental lines, this organizational change is expected to give greater emphasis to team effort.

4. *Third-party Reimbursements*

This represents efforts to design financial reimbursement strategies for reclaiming third-party reimbursement funds from insured veterans for provision of services, which are now collectable but being returned to the U.S. Treasury at the present time.

D. Health Care Reform: A New Mandate

1. *Current Issues*

A dominant theme in health care during these uncertain times must take into account ongoing budgetary considerations. Since all decisions regarding veterans health care must be approved by legislative action, VA responses to new demands on its anticipated expenditures and allocation of resources are permitted only through congressional enactments. Paradoxically, the VA remains responsible to federal laws pertaining to veteran benefits and already established entitlements; yet, without full control over how its resources are developed or allocated. At the same time, it must remain vigilant to the needs of veterans and their families, as stipulated within the bounds of the most recent legislative dictates (AMVETS, et al., 1995).

2. *Competing in Today's Health Care Market*

Many of the above shifts within the VA represent administrative changes taking place throughout health care. As health care reforms and HMO or case management concepts continue to guide the industry's efforts to reduce escalating costs in service delivery, the VA is now expected to compete under new mandates applied to its own health care delivery system.

Dr. Kizer's recent publication, *Prescription for Change*, challenges the VA to compete in today's health care delivery system (Kizer, 1996, a). Indeed, the VA must respond to external pressures in its environment in a timely manner in order to retain its status as a major health care provider. Hence, it is being called upon to respond to pressures from public health care reform debates by becoming more effective in its delivery of services. It is clear that many of the principles that govern TQM/CQI, relating to customer satisfaction, are shaping the emerging VA as it prepares for the new millennium. This over-arching influence is apparent in Dr. Kizer's recent message to VHA employees, stating:

> The future of our health care system depends on whether our
> patients feel we are meeting their needs as well as, or hopefully bet-
> ter than, another health care provider might. Much of their percep-
> tion in this regard will be dictated by the quality of their caregiver's
> communication... (I)mproving our patients' satisfaction with their
> care is one of the most important things we can do to help ensure
> VA's future (Kizer, 1996c).

The above analysis raises many questions when considering current tensions and queries regarding the future of veterans health care programming. In the face of a shrinking veteran population, how will a system of entitlements survive in the wake of governmental cutbacks and downsizing? Is it likely that a veterans health care system can remain viable under the current public climate which is opposed to allocation of resources, if dependent on increased taxes. Nor is public opinion in agreement on supporting federally funded programs for special interest groups. These questions hold implications for maintaining the traditions of a covenant intended to support a citizen military force that expands and contracts in size based on elastic demands for national security and military protection.

Clearly, uncertainties remain regarding the viability of the VA as an organization. Challenges to maintain quality of care must be met while, at the same time, the VA is being faced with an emerging competitive health care market. Unfortunately, the VA is restrained by a legislative decision making process that limits its ability to respond to change or make adjustments in a timely manner. Hence, it is important to consider whether this organization can maintain its convenant in the face of these external forces interacting in its environment.

An additional dilemma that veterans health care programming must deal with is the loss of a strong veteran constituency in the face of reductions in veteran demographics over the latter part of the 20th century. In order to face the new millennium, can the VA, as it stands today, survive in isolation from other health care facilities? Moreover, can it continue serving as a major force in public health care without broadening its mission? Furthermore, are veteran groups and the American public willing to share this national resource with other needy groups? If so, then the existing system might survive.

Perhaps it would be well to consider this organization as a prototype for a national health organization. Such a suggestion might produce some adverse reactions, particularly from veterans groups. However, in order to survive, as Dr. Kizer suggests, major changes will continue to be necessary if the VA is to respond satisfactorily to public demands for reductions in budgetary appropriations and shifting resource allocations.

REFERENCES

AMVETS, DAV, PVA, VFW (1995). Independent budget for Department of Veterans Affairs: Fiscal Year 1995. *Washington, D.C.: AMVETS, DAV* (Disabled American Veterans), PVA (Paralyzed Veterans of America), and VFW (Veterans of Foreign Wars).

An Act To incorporate a national military and naval Asylum for the Relief of the totally disabled Officers and Men of the Volunteer Forces of the United States, ch. XCI, 13 Stat. 509: (1865).

An Act making appropriations for the support of the Army for the year ending the thirtieth of June, eighteen hundred and sixty, ch. LXXXIII, 11 Stat. 431 (1859).

An Act To authorize the establishment of a Bureau of Risk Insurance in the Treasury Department, ch. 293, Pub.L. No.193, 38 Stat. 711 (1914).

An Act To authorize the Secretary of the Treasury to provide hospital and sanitarium facilities for discharged sick and disabled soldiers, sailors, and marines, ch. 98, Pub.L. No.326, 40 Stat. 1302 (1919).

An Act providing additional hospital facilities for patients of the Bureau of War Risk Insurance and of the Federal Board for Vocational Education, Division of Rehabilitation and for other purposes, ch. 156, Pub.L. No.394, 41 Stat. 1364 (1921, a.).

An Act To provide for the vocational rehabilitation and return to civil employment of disabled persons discharged form the military or naval forces of the United States, and for other purposes, ch. 1, Pub.L. No.109, 42 Stat. 327 (1921, b.).

An Act To establish a Veterans' Bureau and to improve the facilities and service of such bureau, and further to amend and modify the War Risk Insurance Act, ch. 57, Pub.L. No.47, Stat. 147 (1921, c.).

An Act To amend Veterans Regulation numbered 10, as amended, to grant hospitalization, domiciliary care, and burial benefits in certain World War II cases, ch. 16, Pub.L. No.10, 57 Stat. 21 (1943, a.).

An Act To amend Title I of Public Law Numbered 2, Seventy-third Congress, March 20, 1943 and the Veterans Regulations to provide for rehabilitation of disabled veterans, and for other purposes, ch. 22, Pub.L. No.16, 57 Stat. 43 (1943, b.).

An Act To establish a Department of Medicine and Surgery in the Veterans Administration, ch. 658, Pub.L. No.293, 59 Stat. 675 (1946).

An Act To authorize the establishment of internship in the Department of Medicine and Surgery of the Veterans Administration, ch. 553, Pub.L. No.722, 62 Stat. 536 (1948, a.).

An Act To authorize assistance to certain veterans in acquiring specially adapted housing which they require by reason of the nature of their service-connected disabilities, ch. 533, Pub.L. No.702, 62 Stat. 500 (1948, b.)

An Act To provide certain additional rehabilitation assistance for certain seriously disabled veterans in order to remove an existing inequality, ch. 536, Pub.L. No.286, 63 Stat. 688 (1949).

Arndt, M. and Bigelow, B. (1995). The implementation of total quality management in hospitals: How good is the fit? *Health Care Management Review, 20(4):* 7-14.

Bigelow, B., and Arndt, M. (1995). Total quality management: Field of dreams? *Health Care Management Review, 20(4):* 15-25.

Cohen, S. and Brand, R. (1993). *Total quality management in government: A practical guide for the real world.* San Francisco: Jossey-Bass.

Daniels, R. (1971). *The bonus march: An episode of the great depression, Contributions in American History, No. 14.* Westport, Connecticut: Greenwood.

Department of Veterans Affairs Act, ch. 3, Pub.L. No.102-83, Sec. 2(a), August 6, 1991, 105 Stat. 378 (1991). (Codified as amended at 38 USCA, sec. 310, Title 38, Part I, ch. 3 and renumbered from section 1101, sec.5(a), Pub.L. 102-83 (1991), with references to: Pub.L. 100-527, Oct.25, 1988, 102 Stat. 2635, as amended Pub.L. 101-94, Title IV, sec.401, Aug. 16, 1989, 103 Stat. 628; Pub.L. 101-576, Title II, sec. 205(c)(2), Nov. 15, 1990, 104. Stat. 2845; Pub.L. 102-83, sec.3, Aug. 6, 1991, 105 Stat. 402).

Department of Veterans Affairs and Foundation for Health Services Research (1995). *Primary care in VA: Primer.* Management Decision and Research Center, Health Services Research and Development Service, Washington, D.C.

Department of Veterans Affairs (1994). *Annual report of the Secretary of Veterans Affairs: Fiscal Year 1994.* Department of Veterans Affairs, Washington, D.C.

Ducanis, A. J. and Golin, A. K. (1979). *The interdisciplinary health care team: A handbook.* Germantown, Maryland: Aspen.

Feazell, J. H. and Mather, J. H. (1986, May). Interdisciplinary Teams for geriatric and long-term care. *VA Practitioner,* 15.

Gaucher, E. J. and Coffey, R. J. (1993). *Total quality in health care: From theory to practice.* San Francisco: Jossey-Bass, Health Series.

House Committee On Veterans Affairs, Medical Benefits For Older Veterans. H.R. Rep. No. 693, 91st Cong., (1969).

H.R.J. Res. 390, *Making additional appropriations for the fiscal year 1947,* and for other purposes, ch. 870, Pub.L. No.663, 60 Stat. 910 (1946).

Ingraham, P. W. , Romzek, B. S. and Assoc. (1994). *New paradigms for government: Issues for the changing public service.* San Francisco: Jossey-Bass.

Joint Commission on Accreditation of Healthcare Organizations [JCAHO] (1992). *Quality improvement in long term care: How quality improvement care help fulfill OBRA '87 requirements.* Joint Commission on Accreditation of Healthcare Organizations, Oakbrook Terrace, IL.

Katz, D. and Kahn, R. L. (1966). *The social psychology of organizations (1978 ed.).* New York: John Wiley.

Kizer, K. W. (1995). *Vision for change: A plan to restructure the Veterans Health Administration.* Department of Veterans Affairs, Washington, D.C.

Kizer, K. W. (1996, a). *Prescription for change: The guiding principles and strategic objectives underlying the transformation of the Veterans Healthcare System.* Veterans Health Administration, Washington, D.C.

Kizer, K. W. (1996, b, April 10). Transforming the Veterans Health Care System; The 'new VA'. *Journal of the American Medical Association, 275*(14): 1069.

Kizer, K. W. (1996, c, April 30). *Message from Kenneth Kizer, MD, MPH, Under Secretary for Veterans Health Administration.* Department of Veterans Affairs, Washington, D.C.

Kizer, K. W. (1997, January) VA becomes true 'system' of care. *U.S. Medicine, 33*(1 & 2): 10-11.

Lathrop, J. P. (1993). Restructuring health care. *The patient-focused paradigm.* Jossey-Bass, San Francisco.

Lawton, E. A. (1914). *History of the Soldier's Home.* Knickerbocker Press, New York.

Lincoln, A. (1865, March 4). *A compilation of the messages and papers of the Presidents: 1789-1897, Vol. VI,* in Richardson, J.D. (Ed.),(pp. 276-277) (1899 ed.). U.S. Congress, Washington, D.C.

Mahairas, E. P. (1986/1987). Case study of a Veterans Administration Medical Center changing from chronic to acute care: Professional reactions to discharge planning. *Dissertation Abstracts International, 42,*(11): University Microfilms No. OA8704532.

Mahairas, E. P. (1989). Applying interdisciplinary perspectives to professional reactions in discharge planning: Chronic/Acute dilemmas in a medical setting undergoing change. In C.R. Willis, M.P. Rastatter, L.L. Crawford, C.M. O'Hara, and H.A. Hoffman (Eds.), Proceedings, *The Tenth Annual Interdisciplinary Health Care Team Conference,* September 15-17, 1988, (pp. 163-185). Toledo, Ohio: College of Health and Human Services, Bowling Green State University, Bowling Green, Ohio.

Mahairas, E. P. (1994). Resolving differences for teams in decision making: An interdisciplinary health model, in Mahairas, E.P., Symposium Organizer. Health care teams: Dynamic models in a changing environment. In S.G. Amin, P.B. Barr, and D.L. Moore (Eds.). *World Business Trends, Proceedings of the 1994 International Conference* (pp. 942-957), Academy of Business Administration, Wembley, England, June 3-8, 1994. Maryland: Academy of Business Administration.

Mahairas, E. P., Gurule, M., Skoloda, T., Morgan, L., Zavorski, R., Laky, L., Nagaraj, S., Leszczynski, S., Joyce, F., Olearsek, M., and Haftl, C. (1996). The dynamics of change under health care reform: Impact of TQM and primary care on the interdisciplinary health care team. *Paper presented at the 18th Annual Interdisciplinary Health Care Team Conference*, Minneapolis, Minnesota, September 26-28, 1996. (Submitted for publication to the Journal for Interprofessional Care.)

Martin, L. L. (1993). Total quality management in human service organizations. *Human Services Guide*, 67. Sage, Newbury Park, CA.

McAdoo, W. G. (1931). *Crowded years: The reminiscences of William G. McAdoo*. Houghton Miflin, (The Riverside Press), Boston.

Morrison, S. E. and Commager, H. S. (1942). *The growth of the American Republic, Vol. 2* (pp. 527-528). Oxford University Press, New York.

National Service Life Insurance Act of 1940, *Title VI of the Second Revenue Act of 1940*, ch. 757, Pub.L. No.801, 54 Stat. 974-1018, 1008 (1940).

Selective Training and Service Act of 1940, ch. 720, Pub.L. No.783, 54 Stat. 885 (1940).

Servicemen's Readjustment Act of 1944, ch. 268, Pub.L. No.346, 58 Stat. 284 (1944). Senate Committee On Veterans Affairs, Study Of Health Care For American Veterans. S.REP. No.4, prepared by the National Academy of Sciences, National Research Council, 95th Cong., 2d Sess. (Committee Print 1976).

Hearing before a Subcommittee of the Committee on Government Operations, 100th Cong., 1st Sess., on H.R. 3471, To Establish the Veterans' Administration as an Executive Department, October 27, 1987.

U.S. Department of Veterans Affairs (1995, January). Vanguard. Office of Public Affairs, Department of Veterans Affairs, Washington, D.C.

Veterans Administration (1979). Geriatrics: VA challenge of the 80's, Proceedings, September 11-12, 1979, Washington, D.C. Northeast Regional Medical Education Center, Veterans Administration, Washington, D.C.

Veterans and Survivors Pension Adjustment Act of 1976, Pub.L.No.94-432, 90 Stat. 1369, (1976).

Veterans Health Care Expansion Act of 1973, Pub.L.No.93-82, 87 Stat. 179, (1973).

Veterans Rehabilitation and Education Amendments of 1980. Pub.L.No.96-466, 94 Stat. 2171, (1980).

World War Veterans' Act of 1924, ch. 320, Pub.L. No.242, 43 Stat. 607, (1924).

Wilson, W. (1983). Presidential Address to a Joint Session of Congress, April 2, 1917. In A. S. Link (Ed.), *The papers of Woodrow Wilson, Vol. 41*, January 24 to April 6, 1917 (pp. 519-527). Princeton, New Jersey: Princeton University Press.

17.
RURAL HEALTH CARE

Esther M. Forti, *Medical University of South Carolina, Charleston, SC*

Erin Silva, *Medical University of South Carolina, Charleston, SC*

The American health care system is undergoing tremendous changes. This transformation will directly affect rural health care delivery and services as well as external and intracommunity forces. External forces are changes in the overall health care system and in the changing demographic, social, and economic structure of America's small towns and rural communities. Intracommunity factors such as poor leadership and ineffectual performance on the part of providers are also assumed to be responsible for our failing rural health care system (Amundson, 1993).

Health care needs of rural residents are generally less well met than those in more urban areas except for inner-city neighborhoods. No rural community can be totally self-sufficient in meeting the health care needs of its population. How each rural community acts on the future should be based on an understanding of past and present events and the desire of rural people to act. The goal of this chapter is to provide an overview of the challenges confronting rural health and the proposed options for creating a successful rural health care system.

I. TRENDS IN SMALL RURAL COMMUNITIES

Rural and community are defined within a multidimensional conceptual framework. Rural comprises three components: a spatial element characterized by low population size and density in wide-open spaces; an employment element consisting of agriculture, manufacturing, and extractive industries; and a sociocultural element consisting of social interactions viewed within a context of varying traditional values, beliefs, and close-knit relationships (Willets and Bealer, 1967). Similarly, community can be defined as comprising three components: a localized territory, organizational structures to meet daily needs (although not all daily needs must be met to fulfill this criteria), and a local group of people collectively working together to solve problems and maintain or enhance social well-being (Kaufman, 1959).

Factors associated with the rural environment that affect rural health are: diversity among rural communities (Moscovice, 1989a), fragile economies (Cordes, 1989), high poverty rates with high unemployment and underemployment (Deavers & Hoppe, 1991), a lack of adequate transportation (Wimberly, 1991), an increase in the number of elderly people, and shifts in population with out-migration (Falk & Lyson, 1991). Ninety-five percent of Americans lived in rural areas when the first Census was taken in 1790. Since then there has been a notable decline or shifts in population. According to the 1991 U.S. Census, 25% of America's population reside in rural areas. Nevertheless, the phenomenon of population shifts of in- and out-migration in rural areas are more important than numbers. These shifts result in a low unstable population base that contributes to an inability of rural communities to sustain adequate health services and infrastructures.

Aging of the rural population has been occurring. The percentage of the population over 60 years of age is higher in rural areas (19 percent) than in urban areas (16 percent) according to the 1990 U.S. Census. The dependency ration is higher in rural areas because of the increasing number of elders. And yet, federal funding programs are known to disperse less monies for needy persons residing in rural communities than in urban ones (Cordes, 1989). These events have strained the ability of rural communities to provide basic health services.

II. TRENDS AND ISSUES IN RURAL HEALTH CARE

It is a well-documented fact that rural areas suffer from a lack of basic health services. Factors that might trigger a health care system crisis or failure in rural communities include the following: shortage of health professionals, lack of resources and technology, instability of rural hospitals, inequity in federal reimbursement favoring urban areas, unsuitable or lack of transportation infrastructures, inability of small rural community leadership to act in providing basic services to its residents, and structural changes in the health care delivery system.

Changes in the overall health care environment have impacted on rural health; these changes include an increased use of technology, inequitable reimbursement mechanisms, and health reform efforts associated with managed care (Hicks, 1990). Diversity among rural areas is the key to understanding much of the continued problems that exist between rural and health care (Cordes, 1989). An appropriate axiom expresses this diversity—"If you've seen one rural community, you've seen one rural community." We can no longer think about rural in a "one size fits all" context. No single strategy or solution meets the health needs of all rural communities. Rather, each works with a unique set of resources and faces unique challenges.

III. BARRIERS TO RURAL HEALTH CARE

In addition to inadequate transportation systems, other barriers affect rural health care and delivery: shortage of primary care physicians, traditional and cultural norms and values, fragile status of the rural hospital, poor health status of rural populations, poor quality of care, and an inability of rural communities to act.

A. Primary Care Physicians

Rural communities have had and still have great difficulty in attracting and retaining primary care physicians (Forti et al., 1995; Pathman et al., 1994). Availability of primary care physicians is essential because they are the first to treat most rural health problems and also act as gatekeepers. Several factors have been associated with physicians leaving rural practice: professional isolation (Crandall et al., 1990), lack of technological support, demanding practices and excessive on-call hours (Cooper and Johnson, 1986), lower incomes and federal reimbursements for similar services as those in more urban sites (Cordes, 1989), and spousal dissatisfaction (Ogle et al., 1986). See Table 1 for comparisons in numbers of primary care physicians according to place of residence.

Table 1 - Trends in Distribution of Nonfederal Physicians in Metropolitan and Nonmetropolitan Areas, 1994

Activity Specialty	Metropolitan Percent	Nonmetropolitan Percent
Total Physicians	88.5	11.5
Total Patient Care	88.7	11.3
Office-based practice	86.8	13.2
General/Family practice	72.5	27.5
Medical Specialty	90.0	10.0
Surgical Specialties	87.3	12.7
Other Specialty	90.2	9.8
Hospital-based practice	94.4	5.6
Other professional activity	94.7	5.3
Not classified	82.9	17.1
Inactive	82.9	17.1

Source: Physician Characteristics and Distribution in the U.S., American Medical Association, 1995/96

B. Cultural Norms and Values

The rural health orientation differs from urban in that rural persons are either less knowledgeable about health conditions or they complain less about symptoms and disabilities. This spirit of independence is characteristic of many rural people who are less likely to seek help or take part in health programs (Weinart and Long, 1987). Socioeconomic factors (income, educational level), values and beliefs, slow diffusion of new information, and diversity within rural communities also negatively influence access to and utilization of health care.

C. Rural Hospitals

The rural hospital has always been regarded as the foundation on which rural health care delivery systems operate. More than 200 rural community hospitals have closed since 1980 (Moscovice, 1989a). These hospitals closed for a variety of reasons: inequitable reimbursements in Medicare and Medicaid resulting in higher proportions of uncompensated care and higher outlays of monies relative to patient revenues; failure of many rural hospitals to link with other rural institutions and health care providers; a declining population base; and an outmigration of residents to larger medical centers for care and treatment.

D. Health Status of Rural Populations

Rural areas are disadvantaged in terms of health status and increased health risks. Rural people have a higher prevalence of chronic illness and higher injury rates than their urban counterparts. Poor health status of those living in rural areas may result from inadequate access and availability of health services in addition to their health belief orientation. A medically uninsured status suggests a further decrease in utilization of services. Rural residents who are also poor and uninsured are at triple jeopardy (Rowland and Lyons, 1989). Health status characteristics among persons residing across four residence categories are displayed in Table 2.

E. Quality of Care

Quality of care is a controversial issue for rural hospital performance, the crux of which is the ability to balance the trade-off between maintaining an acceptable level of quality and offering a full range of inpatient services (Moscovice, 1989b). The challenge of assuring adequate quality of care is directly linked to determining the appropriate scope of services. The substance of quality assurance (QA) and peer review in rural hospitals differs from urban because of inadequate resources: limited resources to monitor, collect, and analyze QA data, inadequate knowledge about the QA process, and insufficient funds to purchase equipment to perform the tasks involved with QA monitoring (RWJ Foundation, 1993).

F. Community Empowerment

According to Amundson (1993), intracommunity factors such as the following are the prime reasons for a failing rural health system: ineffectual performance by

Table 2 - Selected Health Status Indicators for Adults Ages 18-64 by Place of Residence, U.S.

Health Status Indicator	Core Metropolitan	Other Metropolitan	Urbanized Non Metro	Rural Population
Perceived Health Status				
Excellent/Good	84.1	86.4	82.1	78.6
Fair/Poor	15.9	13.6	17.3	21.4
Physician-Diagnosed Chronic Condition				
Any chronic condition (1)	31.1	33.4	34.9	36.7
Hypertension	18.1	18.9	20.3	21.1
Arthritis/Rheumatism	13.0	15.0	16.4	19.1
Diabetes	3.6	3.4	4.2	4.6
Cardiovascular Disease	5.1	5.1	6.0	6.0
Cancer	3.0	3.2	2.9	4.5

Source: *Agency for Health Care Policy and Research. National Medical Expenditure Survey, 1987.*
(1) Includes emphysema and gallbladder disease in addition to those specified.

providers, poor community leadership, turf issues (chronic conflict among local providers), and problems with quality of care. A lack of expertise of many leaders and managers of health and human service agencies magnifies the problem. Inadequate human infrastructures for providing services, little or no margin for providing new services, and an inability to compete with larger metropolitan areas for state and federal monies tend to leave rural communities at a disadvantage in the kind and quality of health services they are able to offer. Professional domain turf issues (with competition and duplication) also lead to the inability of rural communities to provide comprehensive health services. Amundson (1993) contends that other factors and problems are secondary to the rural health demise created by these issues.

IV. OPTIONS FOR A VIABLE RURAL HEALTH CARE SYSTEM

According to the advisory committee of the National Rural Health Association, creativity, innovation, and flexibility in their responses to the dilemmas in rural communities are hallmarks of successful rural health systems. These systems should be consumer focused, attentive to the professional and personal needs of their health care professionals, and require a variety of health care professionals working in an environment of mutual respect and support, an interdisciplinary framework (NRHA, 1992).

Options proposed to address several of the health care problems plaguing rural communities are rural community-based training programs for health professionals, diversification of rural hospitals through alternate delivery systems, technological advances, community empowerment strategies, and integrative rural health networks.

A. Health Professions Training and Education

Professional training and practice should focus on developing generalists trained to practice in ambulatory and community-based settings. Several groups have recommended specific actions regarding the role and responsibility of American colleges and schools of medicine: implementing curricular activities exposing medical students to rural health needs and practice; admitting a higher ratio of rural students; offering rural community-based training; providing continuing medical education programs; developing service linkages with other rural health care providers; and developing a practice support system (AAMC, 1993; NRHA, 1990).

Utilization of nonphysician providers (physician assistants, nurse practitioner, nurse midwives) is a viable means of addressing the shortage of primary care physicians. Research findings reveal that these practitioners improve access to care and quality of care, are cost-effective, and yield high responses of patient satisfaction (Conway-Welch, 1991; Ricketts, 1990). However, State Practice Acts need to be examined and revised to allow reimbursement to nonphysician providers for providing primary care health services in rural communities.

B. Alternate Delivery Systems

Rural hospitals can avoid closure and remain viable if they provide essential services to their communities by remaining diverse and flexible in their offerings (Kernaghan, 1992). Outpatient services, Medicare swing-bed programs, long-term care facilities, home health care services, hospice care, urgent care centers, satellite clinics, multi-hospital arrangements, and managed care systems are alternate delivery options available to small community hospitals (Gibbons, 1990). Crucial concerns in defining alternate models include determining the scope of services and Medicare regulations and State licensure and certification (AHCPR, 1991).

A number of alternates sustain access to primary care services in small rural communities. Emergency medical services can be coordinated with local ambulance services. They can provide basic life support services and transport patients to medical facilities that render services for higher levels of trauma and acute care (AHCPR, 1991).

Managed care has grown in popularity as costs of health services have skyrocketed. Rural communities are attempting to adapt managed care to meet the needs of their residents. In some communities, clinics, health professionals, and hospitals are forming networks to jointly negotiate contracts with managed care organizations.

C. Technological Advances

Telemedicine is one of the most innovative advances of technology for medical education and patient services. Telemedicine has great potential in minimizing perceptions of professional isolation by linking physicians and other practitioners in remote and small communities to specialists in urban medical centers for consultation. Telemedicine also has the possibility for longterm cost savings by eliminating or decreasing hospital stays and by reducing transportation costs to major medical centers (Colby, 1994). However, without continued economic subsidies, this form of technology in small rural communities may not be able to support itself. Many rural practitioners report that such technology is of little interest to their practices (Forti et al., 1996). One possible reason for this lack of interest may be an unfamiliarity with these methods. If so, peer marketing, trial demonstrations, and technical assistance should be available to address these concerns.

D. Community Empowerment Strategies

Unstable economies, limited range of services, and an inability to collectively organize for effective action strongly identify a need for community organization. It is vital to recognize the role that rural community variables such as social organization—supportive leadership, community cohesion, and volunteer groups—can play in providing services to residents. Solutions to rural health care delivery must carry a community's unique imprint or they will probably not take root in the community (AHA, 1993). Sociological theories of community should be utilized in developing community-based health services. Principles and tactics employed in community organization include: use of community analysis to understand community weaknesses and strengths, provision of concrete assistance to accomplish community change, and use of and reinforcement of local structures that will remain to carry on programs (Bracht, 1990; Kinne et al., 1989).

E. Integrative Rural Health Networks

Since no rural community can be self-sufficient in meeting the health care needs of its populace, cooperative arrangements are a meaningful option. New forms of health alliances have been emerging under the rubrics of networks, coalitions, consortia and other names. An integrative rural health network implies an arrangement based on a range of organizational structures that may become formalized over time depending on the success of the network.

Rural areas have more difficulty forming networks than urban areas for at least two reasons: they have a smaller pool of organizations to draw from and they have more difficulty acquiring the right mix of partners (Moscovice, et al., 1996). One effective, longstanding rural network that is not well known or is underutilized by health professionals is the Cooperative Extension Service (CES). This community-based network has a history of program delivery capacity and rural legitimacy. Each state's CES receives funding from federal, state, and county sources to support practice-oriented research-based educational programs. One of eight initiatives involve programs to improve nutrition, diet, and health of rural people.

V. FEDERAL AND STATE INITIATIVES

Increased concern for the status of rural health care has prompted federal, state, and local policymakers and public and private organizations to act. Major rural health service policies and initiatives have been established to address the problems confronting rural health. The USDHHS established the Office of Rural Health Policy in 1987. At the same time, Congress mandated the National Center for Health Services

Research and the Health Care and Technology Assessment to develop a research agenda to address rural health issues.

Initiatives developed to address health manpower shortages in rural underserved areas include the National Health Service Corps (NHSC), and federally designated health manpower shortage areas. The NHSC was established in 1970 in response to the shortage of health manpower and inadequate access to health services in rural and urban poverty areas. Legislation was passed to enable students to obtain scholarships for training costs in return for field service with the NHSC. Two basic types of shortage and underserved areas federally designated are: health professional shortage areas (HPSAs) and medically underserved areas (MUAs). These designated shortage areas receive federally subsidized programs and monies in an attempt to correct such shortages (Lee, 1991).

Area Health Education Center (AHEC) programs, established in the 1970s, are funded by the DHHS, Bureau of Health Professions. They provide a variety of innovative community-based training and educational programs to support health professionals in underserved rural and urban communities (Patton, 1988).

Many states have established offices of rural health. These offices offer technical assistance and act as advocates as well as planners, coordinators and evaluators of rural health programs. Several states in concert with offices of rural health and health departments support the development of primary care initiatives. Activities can include: loan forgiveness programs for health professionals who practice in rural areas; financial support for telecommunications access between major medical centers and small rural communities for medical consultation, referral, and continuing education; seed funds for medical facilities and community capacity building and leadership programs; data collection coordination efforts to document health status; financial and regulatory incentives for health providers to form networks; and assistance in developing rural health advocacy groups.

Table 3 - Rural, Urban, Metropolitan Population of the United States, 1990

	Metropolitan	Nonmetropolitan	Total
Rural	26,525,155 13.8% of Metro	35,133,175 62.7% of Nonmetropolitan	61,658,330 24.8% of total
Urban	166,201,175 86.2% of Metro	20,850,368 37.3% of Nonmetropolitan	187,051,543 6.2% of total
Total	192,926,330 77.5%	55,983,543 22.5%	248,709,873 100%

Source: What is "Rural" and How to Measure "Rurality": A Focus on Health Care Delivery and Health Policy. North Carolina Rural Health Research and Policy Analysis Center, 1997.

VI. DEFINING RURALITY

One of the research issues of major interest to health researchers and policymakers is the continued lack of a uniform definition for rural. The need for precision has escalated because today's rural America is much more diverse than yesterday's (Cordes, 1989). The typologies most commonly used are rural-urban or metropolitan-nonmetropolitan dichotomous groupings. However, rural and nonmetropolitan are not synonymous. For example, nonmetropolitan areas include urban populations (small cities) and Metropolitan Statistical Areas (MSAs) contain portions of rural populations (Fuguitt, Brown, and Beale, 1989). See Table 3.

Such crude dichotomous codings of residence make identification of differences in health outcomes across the range of diverse rural communities impossible (DeFriese and Ricketts, 1989). Adding further to the confusion, values defining areas as rural are diverse and varied from one government agency to another (Bushy, 1991; Hewitt, 1989).

DISCUSSION

The goal of this chapter was to provide an overview of the relevant issues related to rural health care and to present options assumed to minimize these problems. Several important aspects of rurality must be weighed, i.e., the social and economic context of the rural community and the diversity among rural communities, when programs and research projects are developed to meet the health care needs of rural communities.

The future of rural health relies on a system of networks staffed by health professionals who have been trained in an interdisciplinary manner to meet the unique needs of a diverse rural America. Survival mandates that rural communities develop community empowerment strategies, innovative alternate delivery systems, and integrated rural health networks to solve their health care system problems and to provide comprehensive health services to its populations. Ultimately, each community as a unique entity will decide what it will accept and support as a quality health care delivery system. Solving the problems in our rural health care system is a challenge of balancing broad public policy with focused local needs. As Tilly (1973) contended, the situation improves when threatened communities do act because rural people have a longstanding tradition of coming together to solve their problems.

REFERENCES

Agency for Health Care Policy and Research (AHCPR). (1991). *Delivering essential health care services in rural areas: An analysis of alternative models.* USDHHS, PHS. MD: Rockville.

American Academy of Family Physicians. (1989). *Rural family practice: You can make a difference.* Kansas City, MO: American Academy of Family Physicians.

American Association of Medical Colleges Generalist Physician Task Force. (1993). AAMC policy on the generalist physician, as adopted October 8, 1992. *Academic Medicine. 68*, 1-6.

American Hospital Association (1993). *Working from Within: Integrating rural health care. Hospital Research and Educational Trust.* Ill: Chicago, pp 83.

Amundson, B. (1993). Myth and reality in the rural health service crisis: Facing up to community responsibilities. *Journal of Rural Health.* 5, 176-187.

Bracht, N. (Ed.) (1990). *Health Promotion at the Community Level.* Newbury Park, CA: Sage.

Bushy, A. (1991) *Rural Nursing,.* Newbury Park: Sage Publications.

Colby, M. (1994). Telemedicine is poised to revolutionize the practice of medicine. *Health Data Management. 2(6),* 40-41, 43-47.

Conway-Welch, C. (1991). Issues surrounding the distribution and utilization of nurse non-physician providers in rural America. *Journal of Rural Health. 7,* 388-401.

Cooper, J., and Johnson, T. (1986). Evaluation of medical center support for rural physicians. *Journal of Rural Health. 2(2),* 47-54.

Cordes, S. (1989). The changing rural environment and the relationship between health services and rural development. *Health Services Research. 23(6),* 757-784.

Crandall, L., Dwyer, J., and Duncan, R. (1990). Recruitment and retention of rural physicians: Issues for the 1990s. *Journal of Rural Health, 6 (1),* 19-38.1980s: A context for rural health research. *Journal of Rural Health. 6,* 357-63.

Deavers, K. and Hoppe, R. (1991). The rural poor: The past as prologue. In C.B. Flora and Christenson, J. (Eds.), *Rural Policies for the 1990s.* Boulder: Westview.

DeFriese, G.H., and Ricketts, T.C. (1989). Primary health care in rural areas: An agenda for research. *Health Services Research. 23(6),* 931-974.

Dwyer, J., Lee, G., and Coward, R. (1990). The health status, health service utilization, and social support networks of the rural elderly: A decade review. *Journal of Rural Health. 7,* 379-398.

Forti, E., Martin, K., Jones, R., and Herman, J. (1996). An assessment of practice support and continuing education needs of rural Pennsylvania family physicians. *Journal of Rural Health. 12,* 43-437.

Forti, E., Martin, K., Jones, R., and Herman, J. (1995). Factors influencing retention of rural Pennsylvania family physicians. *Journal of the American Board of Family Practice. 8,* 469-474.

Frenzen, P.D. (1992). Rural areas gained doctors during the 1980s. *Rural Development Perspectives. 8 (1):* 16-21.

Fuguitt, G. Brown, D., and Beale, C. (1989). *Rural and Small Town America.* New York: Russell Sage.

Graduate Medical Education Reform to Increase Providers in Rural Areas. (1993, February). Working paper of the National Rural Health Association, Task Force on Health Professions Education Reform.

Gibbons, B. (1990). Change and adaptation: Contexts for rural health. Center for Rural Health, University of North Dakota.

Hewitt, M. (19~9). *Defining "rural" areas: Impact on health care policy and research.* Washington, D.C.: U. S. Government Printing Office.

Hicks, L. (1990). Availability and accessibility of rural health care. *Journal of Rural Health 6,* 485-505.

Kaufman, H. (1959). Toward an interactional conception of community. *Social Forces. 38,* 8-17.

Kernaghan, S. (1992). *Healthy People 2000 in rural America.* American Hospital Association. IL: Chicago.

Kinne, S. Thompson, B., Chrisman, N., and Hanley, J. (1989). Community organization to enhance the delivery of preventive health services. *American Journal of Preventive Medicine. 5,* 225-229.

Moscovice, I., Wellever, A., and Christianson, J. (1996). Rural Health Networks: Concepts, Cases, and Public Policy. Rural Health Research Center, University of Minnesota.

Moscovice, I. (1989a). Strategies for promoting a viable rural health care system. *Journal of Rural Health. 5,* 216-30.

Moscovice, I. (1989b). Rural Hospitals: A literature synthesis and health services research agenda. *Health Service Research, 23,* 891-930.

National Rural Health Association (1992). Executive Summary: A Rural Health Agenda for the Future. MO: Kansas City.

Nichols, A. and Geller, S. (1990). Area health education centers: Research issues in the 1980s: An agenda for 1990s. *Journal of Rural Health. 6*, 543-552.

Ogle, K.S., Henry, R.C., Durda, K., and Zivick, J.D. (1986). Gender specific differences in family practice graduates. *Journal of Family Practice, 23*, 357-360.

Pathman, D.E., Konrad, T.R., and Ricketts, T.C. (1994). Medical education and the retention of rural physicians. *Health Services Research. 29 (1)*, 39-58.

Patton, L. (1989). Setting the rural health services research agenda: The Congressional perspective. *Health Service Research, 23*, 1005-1051.

Patton, L. (1988). The Rural Health Challenge (report no. 100145). Senate Special Committee on Aging. Washington, D.C.: U.S. Government Printing Office.

Robert Wood Johnson Foundation. (1993). *Rural health challenges in the 1990's: Strategies from the Hospital-Based Rural Health Care Program*, V. Weisfeld (Ed.). NJ: Princeton.

Ricketts, T.C. (1990). Education of physicain assistants, nurse midwives and nurse practitioners for rural practice. *Journal of Rural Health, 6*, 537-542.

Rhoades, J., and Day, F. (1989). Locational decisions of physicians in rural North Carolina. *Journal of Rural Health, 5*, 137-153.

Rowland, D. and Lyons, B. (1989). Triple jeopardy: Rural, poor, and uninsured. *Health Service Research, 23*, 975-1004.

Tilly, C. (1973). Do communities act? *Sociological Inquiry, 43*, 209-240.

The role and responsibility of America's colleges of medicine in addressing rural health. (1990, August). Position paper, National Rural Health Association Research and Education Constituency Group.

Weinert, C. and Long, K. (1987) Understanding the health care needs of rural Families. *Family Relations, 36*, 445-455.

Willets, F. and Bealer, R. (1967). An evaluations of a composite definition of "rurality". *Rural Sociology, 32*, 165-77.

18.
COMMUNITY HEALTH CENTERS

Leon Burton, *Franklin C. Fetter Community Health Center, Charleston, SC*

The community-based health center model is now being used as the health care model to develop community-oriented primary health care practices to develop health care networks in preparation for managed care in the United States. Community oriented primary health care provides comprehensive health care services that are accessible to communities. Administrative and clinical resources are maximized to reduce operational cost and improve efficiency of community-based practices.

During the eighteenth and nineteenth centuries, upper and middle class Americans received care in the home. Hospitals that evolved during the eighteenth and nineteenth centuries were primarily established to serve the poor or strangers. Significant medical treatment using antiseptic operating rooms and laboratories in hospitals did not take place until just before the end of the nineteenth century. Treatment was primarily provided in dispensaries or free standing clinics that offered limited treatment such as minor surgery, tooth extractions, and prescription of drugs for common ailments (Rosenberg, 1974).

Beginning in or about 1890 there was a campaign against dispensaries alleging that they were being abused by patients who could afford care elsewhere. The campaign was from physicians who had gone to medical school and completed their internship or residency. In many instances these internships were done in dispensaries, hospitals, or free standing physician practices. Physicians whose economic livelihood was dependent upon paying patients, claimed that dispensaries that were primarily established to serve the poor were also treating patients who could afford care in the private sector. Therefore, dispensaries were considered as a threat to their personal interest. Dispensary activities were primarily attributed to the large scale influx of immigrants, the migration of people from the south and a number of economic depressions. In 1899, laws were enacted that regulated hospital clinics and dispensaries to limit the provision of services to those who could prove that they were unable to purchase private medical care. By 1920, free standing dispensaries no longer existed (Fegain, 1975).

I. SOCIAL MEDICINE

The first neighborhood health centers were established in 1910 by the New York City Health Department. These centers were established in communities where the residents were poor, offering patients maternal and child care, treatment for venereal diseases, and tuberculosis testing. As this type of center gained rapid acceptance, maternal and child care became accepted as other basic functions of the public health service. By 1926, there were more than a thousand of these centers across the country. They did not compete with the private sector since they provided basic preventive services. Being set up in central locations by public and private agencies, services were more accessible to community residents. The health care focus was on the prevention of disease through education, maternal and child health care, food inspection, and immunization. The number of health departments increased as society became more industrialized and urbanized.

This ever increasing number of health departments precipitated a need to define the level of services that were to be offered by this organizational system of care. A special committee of the American Public Health Association chaired by Haven Emerson, who at that time was a public health officer, issued a set of standards identifying the minimal acceptable services to be offered by health departments. The committee's report known as the Emerson report, defined five basic functions that local health departments should exemplify:

(1) the recording, tabulation, interpretation, and publication of essential facts of births, deaths, and reportable diseases known as vital statistics.
(2) provide screening and testing for communicable diseases, such as tuberculosis, venereal diseases, malaria, and hookworm,
(3) monitor the sanitation of milk, water, and restaurants or eating places,
(4) provide basic laboratory services,
(5) provide maternal and child hygiene services, including the supervision of the health of school-aged children, and provide basic health education.

The use of emergency rooms increased as well. In addition to treating true emergencies, they began to care for patients who could not afford care by private physicians, or access the hospital speciality clinics because of overcrowding or closure. Emergency room doctors also functioned as backup for private physicians who were not available for call or were not equipped to treat patients under certain circumstances.

II. THE NEIGHBORHOOD HEALTH CENTER PROGRAM

In 1964, the Economic Opportunity Act was passed by Congress resulting in the creation of the Office of Economic Opportunity (OEO) within the federal government. The Economic Opportunity Act was legislation sponsored by the Johnson Administration's "WAR on Poverty." Its objective was to provide basic education, job training, and other services to low-income individuals by funding community agencies serving the poor. Health care was not one of the initial areas planned for funding, but because an overwhelming number of local agencies submitted proposals that included significant purchases of health care services from the private sector, OEO decided that it would be more economical to directly fund health care projects (Donovan, 1967).

The first health care project was funded by a grant awarded to Tufts University Medical School (Klaw, 1976). The University proposed to establish a health center model of care that would provide comprehensive health care services, train and employ residents, and include community participation. Subsequent to the Tufts University grant, six additional health care grants were awarded the following year. In that same year, the 1964 Economic Opportunity Act legislation was amended as a result of an amendment sponsored by Senator Edward Kennedy. The amendment provided monies for the planning and operation of comprehensive health programs in urban and rural low-income areas that lacked adequate health services. It discussed the importance of consumer participation and the need to provide employment opportunities and other social services in addition to health services. It also provided 50 million dollars for neighborhood health center programs.

By 1968, more than 50 health centers had been funded. That number was up to 100 funded health centers by 1971 (Anderson, et al., 1976). Neighborhood health centers were to be a new model of providing health care services that were dignified, accessible, comprehensive and community based. They were to have three community-based elements:

(1) community health services,
(2) community economic development, and
(3) community participation (Klaw, 1976).

In 1968, OEO established guidelines adding preventive services, transportation, environment health, patient and community education, to complement medical and social services offered by neighborhood health centers.

Even though health centers provided an array of services at one facility and were centrally located in communities, they were viewed as a decentralized system of care compared to the traditional public and private health care system. This was one of the principles used by the health center movement, however, it was not a new idea. Like those health centers created by the establishment of health departments in 1910, the 1964 neighborhood health centers served a defined population or catchment area (Anderson, et al., 1976). In contrast with earlier health centers, the 1964 health centers provided treatment as well as preventive care and they involved community residents in the center's operation. Neighborhood health centers employed residents of the community that visited patients in their homes, and acted as liaisons between the patients and the centers' professional staff. These workers were called family health workers, and functioned as part of a health care team along with a physician and public health nurse. They provided bedside care, health education, and social advocacy services such as assistance with housing, welfare, and other aspects of the patient's social environment. The most important and innovative approach in the establishment of community health centers was the mandate of community participation in their operation. This involvement allowed for community input in the resolution of their health care needs.

The neighborhood health center concept challenged the health care system that existed by its approach to providing health care. First, preventive, primary, environmental and outreach services were being offered in one facility, versus being traditionally performed at several facilities and providers. Secondly, by providing care to all residents, the boundaries established between public and private medicines were disregarded. A means test was not required to determine if a patient was poverty stricken, or fell into a certain disease category. Thirdly, neighborhood health centers were a form of group practice that employed physicians and was inconsistent with the traditional fee-for-service solo practice concept. In addition to all of the above (composed of teams of physicians, nurse practitioners, and family health workers), this approach challenged the traditional medical hierarchy where the physician is normally at the top. Finally, the dominance health professionals were being challenged by having consumer participation in decisions on operating health centers.

III. PROGRAM SURVIVAL AND INSTITUTIONALIZATION

The political challenges that faced health centers on a local and state level began to be an even greater challenge on the national level beginning with the President. During his 1968 presidential campaign, Nixon promised to reduce the federal government's role in social policy. His proposal in 1969 was intended to dismantle the categorical grant structures that had been established by previous Democratic administrations (Iglehart, 1973). As part of the health policy, Nixon's goal was to radically reduce the federal subsidies in health activities, while stimulating the private sector to restructure health care to reduce costs. He proposed two major health programs, one was the national health insurance plan and the other was health maintenance organizations or prepaid group plans.

In 1973, Congress passed a bill extending the major health programs that Nixon had discontinued for one year. Included was the Hill Burton program for hospital construction, the regional medical program, community mental health center program, migrant health center program, and the neighborhood health center program. The very next year, instead of re-authorizing the general legislation under which the health centers had been funded, the Senate and House Subcommittees wrote new legislation that specifically described community health centers and authorized separate funding for them. It was in 1975 that Public Law 94-63 was enacted. Health centers had withstood the assaults under the Nixon and Ford administrations and then expanded under the Carter administration. During 1975 and 1976 however, no new health centers were funded (Iglehart, 1973).

In 1977, the Rural Health Clinic Act (Public Law 95-210) was passed by Congress and implemented in 1978 (Iglehart, 1973). It encouraged the utilization of midlevel practitioners such as nurse practitioners, nurse midwifes, and physician assistants by providing reimbursement for their services. It created a cost-based reimbursement mechanism to generate additional primary care practices located in rural areas with an underserved area designation. There are two types of Rural Health Clinics (RHC): one independent and the other provider-based. The independent RHC is a freestanding practice; not part of a hospital, skilled nursing facility, or home health agency operated under common licensure, governance, and professional supervision. Provider-based clinics are reimbursed as a cost center of a hospital or other provider (Iglehart, 1973).

During the Reagan era, the number of health center grantees was reduced from 800 in 1981 to 600 by 1990 (Plaska and Veith, 1995). This reduction was caused by the administration's policy to reverse the growth of the federal government and turn the administration of social programs over to the states. The number of centers was downsized by eliminating small, inefficiently managed centers either through mergers with other centers or by the defunding of centers. There were 186 centers defunded by 1986 (Plaska and Vieth, 1995).

After almost ten years of stagnation and constant budgetary threats, the Federally Qualified Health Centers program was enacted under the 1989 Omnibus Budget Reconciliation Act (OBRA) and expanded under OBRA 1990. OBRA provided reimbursement of reimbursable cost (up to a cap) for legislatively specified services covered by Medicare and Medicaid. OBRA 1990 clarified that FQHCs could be entities or facilities, and provide a safe harbor for an FQHC that discounts the Medicare co-insurance for sliding fee scale patients. It also clarified the FQHC right to reasonable cost reimbursement in Medicaid-managed care arrangements and clarified that reasonable cost reimbursement cannot be waived through a state application for freedom of choice waivers (Travers and Ellis, 1992). Although OBRA legislation occurred in 1989, many states did not implement cost-based reimbursement for health centers until 1992 and 1993.

IV. COMMUNITY HEALTH CENTER ORGANIZATIONAL STRUCTURE

As one of the three elements of the comprehensive health care model, all federally funded health centers are mandated to have a governing board. Boards are required to carry out certain responsibilities which include strategic planning, policy making, and monitoring and evaluating health center operations. After 1975, neighborhood health centers were referred to as community and migrant health centers (Medicus, 1982). They must be governed by representatives of the community of which at least 51% whom are users of the center's services. As a nonprofit corporation under corporate law, a health center governing board can make financial commitments for the center's debts and obligations and can enter into legally binding agreements. It may sue or be sued. The individual board member is largely protected under corporate law from most lawsuits that may occur as a result of a board decision or action; however, the board member may still be liable for failure to fulfill duties.

V. COMMUNITY HEALTH CENTER PRIMARY SERVICE POPULATION

Since their inception in the 1960s, community health centers have served as a primary care safety net for the nation's poor and underserved populations in the inner cities and in rural America. They are called various names including neighborhood health centers, community health centers, migrant health centers, family health cen-

ters, and rural health clinics. There were approximately 550 C/MHCs serving an estimated seven million people in 1993, including 30% of the nation's indigent population.
Their patients were primarily drawn from minority groups: 29% African American,
28% Hispanic, and 5% other minority. Anyone may receive care at a C/MHC. All
C/MHCs employ a sliding fee schedule based on a patient's income and seek direct
and third party reimbursement for services. Nationally about 40% of the Center's
income is derived directly from the federal government through funds authorized
under section 330, 329, and 340 of Title III of the Public Health Service Act. Remaining
funds come from Medicare, Medicaid, private insurance, direct patient fees, and state
and local support (Travers and Ellis, 1992).

Today, poor and medically underserved Americans face great unmet health care
needs just as they did a quarter century ago when the health center program was first
authorized. At least 33 million significant groups of populations served by health cen-
ters include low-income children, migrant farm workers, homeless persons, persons
with HIV disease, those with drug and alcohol problems, and the frail and elderly.
Services provided by Community Health Centers include the following:
- Primary health care services
- Primary care for all life cycles
- Basic Laboratory
- Emergency Care
- X-ray
- Pharmacy
- Preventive Health
- Preventive Dental
- Transportation
- Case Management
- Inpatient/Speciality Care

VI. COMMUNITY ORIENTED PRIMARY CARE (COPC)

By examining the evolutionary trends and patterns in health care that has been
provided by this country, one can begin to understand the Community Oriented
Primary Care Model which is the cornerstone of health care reform (Wright, 1993).
COPC is population based and requires the following:
1. a community based, primary care practice
2. an identifiable population or community for which the practice
   assumes responsibility for affecting change in health status
3. a planning, monitoring, and evaluation process for identifying and resolving
   health problems.
COPC centers apply epidemiology to assess community health problems, collaborate with community residents and leaders to identify needs, plan intervention strategies, prioritize resources, and rely on program evaluation and outcomes research to
progressively and systematically modify the health care services and to redirect health
care resources. This model promotes collaboration and coordination which are in
direct opposition of the competition promoted by current forces. Preventive and pri-

mary care are emphasized by COPC. While our current system empowers providers, organizations and payers, COPC empowers individuals and communities to engage in a decision making process that affects health care. This model was utilized to implement current integrated delivery systems for Community and Migrant Health Centers within the United States. The COPC model has no equal in the competitive marketplace. The primary focus is on the community's health rather than the entrepreneurial interest of physicians, hospitals, or managed care plans. This being the case, the model has an internal planning process that targets resources to high priority needs.

Policy makers, politicians and Americans are focusing on primary and preventive care services rather than acute hospital care which has been the emphasis for more than 50 years. Socially responsive community medicine is now at a pivotal point in its evolution and it is possible that this may likely become a paradigm for reforming the delivery of health care services in America (Wright, 1993).

VII. COMMUNITY HEALTH CENTERS FUTURE IN MANAGED CARE

A. Surviving in a Managed Care Delivery System

Many physicians today are realizing the dynamics of managed care will require them to restructure their practices if they are to prosper in today's market (Braender, 1997). The federally funded and non-federally-funded health center of the future will be faced with new challenges. New areas of exploration are opening up as a result of the nationwide push toward managed care. New forms of practice management and contractual arrangements with providers will be vertical and horizontal.

Administrators, medical directors, clinicians, and most importantly, board members will move into new roles including:
1. Clinicians and board members will be required to understand complex financial issues involving risk management.
2. Administrators, on the other hand, may have to take a back seat to the emphasis on clinical process and outcomes.
3. Everyone will have to keep up with technology explosions that may define all parts of the health care arena (Braender, 1997).

B. Medicaid Managed Care

In the absence of comprehensive national health care reform, many states have begun to move toward statewide, integrated managed care systems by enrolling their Medicaid populations in managed care plans. States are looking toward managed care as a way of controlling their Medicaid program costs while integrating approaches to improve quality and access to care. The enrollment of Medicaid programs have more than doubled since 1993 (Schauffler, et al., 1996). Forty-two states including the District of Columbia have some type of Medicaid managed care plan, enrolling a total of 4.8 million persons, or 15% of the Medicaid population, in full risk capitation programs, with an additional 2% enrolled in partially capitated arrangements.

By 1995, all but eight states had implemented Medicaid managed care; Tennessee and Arizona however, were the only two that had 100% enrollment of Medicaid enrollees in capitated plans (Schauffer et al., 1996). Along with Oregon these two states were the only ones with more than 20% of Medicaid dollars paid through capitation arrangements. It may be unrealistic for C/MHCs to continue to their argument for complete independence and autonomy from private managed care plans.

To survive C/MCHs will have to continue to work collaboratively at the national, state, and local levels, through existing networks, by sharing resources and staying abreast of policy development in health care reform.

As the country moves rapidly from fee-for-service to a managed care system, C/MHC's survival will require specific safeguards at the federal and state levels that ensure their ability to develop their own networks or that require health plans to incorporate them into existing networks. Federal provisions to maintain funding to continue care for the uninsured is also needed.

C. Strategic Plan for C/MHCs on the National Level

To accomplish its mission in today's environment, BPHC stated that it must assume a national leadership role, promoting models of care that work to increase access and improve health in communities served by its resources as well as those with remaining gaps in services. They are looking outward to partnerships with other providers, policy makers and researchers. They are also looking to build integrated systems and are currently judging health center programs by industry standards.

D. Strategic Plan for C/MHC on a Local and State Level

To succeed in managed care on a local and state level C/MHCs must understand how to serve a changing community. This can be accomplished by doing a market analysis or needs assessment and by reprogramming existing resources and securing new resources and staff.

Ongoing reviews of board composition as it relates to users and the community served should be conducted. C/MHCs will need to develop expertise, seek additional funding sources for special population groups and explore and develop partnerships with other health care providers such as hospitals, HMOs, private practices, mental health centers, and substance abuse providers. Education is also critical in their struggle for success.

Capacity building among C/MHCs is another important factor in building success in a managed care environment. Health centers should establish a strategic plan to identify opportunities for expansion, identifying and securing resources (including establishing reserves) to fund expansion projects. Plans should be developed for recruitment and retention of staff to support expansion projects. One alternative for expansion is through establishing appropriate relationships and partnerships. Facilities and access to capital are issues that should be considered when considering alternatives for expansion.

Health centers have played an important role since the early nineteenth century in providing care for individuals and families who are economically disadvantaged as a result of poverty, lack of access, or the lack of adequate health insurance. The roles of health centers were expanded to include preventive care, primary care, environmental health, screening, testing, and outreach; they are now recognized by many as the safety net for millions of Americans needing basic health care services. I believe one of the most significant factors in the continued success of health center is community participation which was mandated by law.

Individuals within their communities have assisted in identifying their communities health needs, and provide direction to address them. The community based health center model is now being used as the model to develop community oriented primary care practices in developing health care networks and delivery systems across the country in preparation of managed care. This basic model provides comprehensive health care services and increased access to care for community resources and allows better utilization of both clinical and administrative resources. As this country seeks to reduce its health care cost, it is ironic that the same system that was established for the economically disadvantaged as a separate health care system is now being mainstreamed as the model of care for all Americans.

REFERENCES

Anderson, E. J., Judd, L. R., May, J. T., and New, P. K. (1976). *The Neighborhood Center Program, It Growth and Problems: An Introduction.* NANHC, Washington, D.C.

Braender, L. J. (March, 1997). Surviving in the Managed Care Environment: the push for physicians to combine. *Group Practice Journal*, 25-31.

Bureau of Health Care Delivery and Assistance, 1983.

Burrow, J. G. (1977). *Organized Medicine In the Progressive Era: The Move Toward Monopoly.* John Hopkins University Press, Baltimore, MD.

Donovan, J. C. (1967). *The Politics of Poverty.* Pegasus Books, New York.

Feagin, J. R. (1975). *Subordinating the Poor, Welfare and American Beliefs.* Prentice-Hall, Englewood Cliffs, NJ.

Iglehart, J. K. (1973). Health Report/Executive Legislative Conflict Looms Over Continuation of Health Care Subsidies. *National Journal, 5*: 645-652.

Marcus, I. (1981). *Dollars for Reform: The OEO Neighborhood Health Centers.* Lexington Books, Lexington, MA.

Jonas, S. (1986). *Health Care Delivery in the United States.* (3rd ed). Springer, New York.

Klaw, S. (1976). *The Great American Medicine Show.* Penguin Books, Harmondsworth.

Larkin, H. (1997). Community Care Gets Competitive. *American Medical News v40, 7*(3).

Merrill, J. (1995). Helping Community Health Center Adapt to Changing Environments: one foundation's response. *Journal of Ambulatory Care Management, 18*(2): 1-2.

National Association of Community Health Centers, (March 1997). *The 22nd Annual Policy Issues Forum: America's Health Centers: Preserving the Mission in the Marketplace.* Author, Washington, DC.

National Association of Public Hospitals, National Association of Community Health Centers, National Association of Children's Hospitals and Related Institutions, National Association of Rural Health Clinics and The George Washington University, Center for Health Policy Research, (1995). *America's Essential Providers: The Foundation of Our Nation's Health System:* Author, Washington, DC.

Plaska, M., Vieth, E. A. ,and Roundtree, M. J., (1995). Overview of the Program to Strengthen Primary Care Health Centers: A profile of the grant-making process, the recipients, and their activities. *Journal of Ambulatory Care Management, 18*(2): 9-14.

Rosenberg, C. E. (1974). Social Class and Medical Care in Nineteenth Century America: The Rise and Fall of the Dispensary. *Journal of the History of Medicine and Allied Sciences, 29*: 32-54.

Schauffler, H. H., and Wolin, J. (1996). Community Health Clinics Under Managed Care: navigating uncharted waters *21,3:* 461-488

Stevens, R. (1971). *American Medicine and the Public Interest.* Yale University Press, New Haven, CT.

Travers, K., and Ellis, R. (1992). *Comparison of the Rural Health Clinic and Federally Qualified Health Center Programs.* NACHC, Augusta, ME.

Williams, S. J., Torrens, P. R., (1993). *Introduction to Health Services, 4th ed.* Delmar Publishers Inc., Albany, NY.

Wright, R. A. (1993). Community Oriented Primary Care: the cornerstone of health care reform. *The Journal of the American Medical Association, 269*(19): 2544 (4).

What Barriers Are C/MHCs Facing Within Managed Care?
Http://158.72.85.159/MC/MC_2.htm 4/13/1997

19.
COMMUNITY HEALTH NURSING

Rebekah Damazo, *California State University, Chico, CA*

Over the past century, community health nursing practice has evolved to meet the changing needs and demands of society. Contemporary public health issues--epidemics such as AIDS, and teenage pregnancy, and an aging population--are complicated by an increasingly diverse society and a rapidly changing health care system. Changes in the financing of health care require shorter hospital stays, and it has been predicted that there will be a marked decline in hospital employment of nurses (Maraldo and Solomon, 1987). Community health nurses face significant demands for change as health care expands into the community.

The current period of health care reform has involved changes in both public health and personal health care services. These changes are creating tremendous opportunities and challenges for nurses as they strive to be leaders in health care policy development (Primomo, 1995). As more nurses seek employment in community based agencies, the question becomes whether to provide acute care nursing at home or to educate nurses to provide communities and clients care from a wellness perspective. Nurses continue to be the largest group of health care workers, numbering 2.2 million (American Nurses Association), and thus have the ability to impact and influence politics to promote wellness as public policy (Irurita, 1994). Community health nurses are in a position to assist the U.S. Health Care system in the necessary transition from a disease oriented model to one that is health oriented (Clark, 1995).

I. ECONOMIC IMPLICATIONS FOR COMMUNITY HEALTH NURSES

Quite clearly, the cost of providing health care to the U.S. public has skyrocketed in the last 50 years. The federal government has placed the burden of escalating cost back on the health care industry by restructuring reimbursement for both Medicare and Medicaid. In the past, nursing ignored teaching or providing input into the development of health care policy and most nurses had only a minimal understanding of the overall health care system (Smith and Maurer, 1995, p. 111). Nurses focused on the "care" component of their profession rather the "cost" component. The financial element of health care was considered irrelevant to the "planning and distribution of good nursing care." Nurses believed that all persons should be provided with "the best and most appropriate nursing care" without concern for one's ability to pay for those services (Smith and Maurer, 1995, p. 111). Health planners, however, were already addressing the reality of cost when figuring the health care bill. Professional nursing care for inpatient services was seen as a line item that could be reduced. Eventually, as the nursing profession felt the direct impact of financial cuts, they developed an interest in the economics and politics of health care delivery.

Physicians and hospitals responded to governments' reduction in reimbursement through prospective payment systems, by decreasing the patients' length of stay or by denying services all together. Hospitals unable to recoup costs from third party payers elected to close emergency rooms and/or maternity services in an effort to remain financially viable in the changing health care environment. Those hospitals that continued to provide high cost, less profitable services began to discharge patients early in an effort to contain costs. The correlation between length of hospital stays is directly proportional to the patient's hospital costs; therefore, the longer a patient stays, the greater the cost. Since 1982, with the advent of Diagnostic Related Groups (DRGs), all providers have become aware of the need to decrease the length of hospital stay in consideration of the economic advantages (Lutjens, 1993). Increasingly, the focus and demand of society has become to contain the nation's health care costs and one strategy advanced has been to discharge patients from hospitals as soon as possible. As a result of concerns over the cost of inpatient hospital care, the number of in-patient hospital days per 1000 population is less than two thirds the level of 30 years ago (Fuchs, 1994). Hospitals have responded by opening hospital-based home care agencies in an effort to capture dollars potentially lost to non-affiliated home care agencies. Hospital administrators and boards of directors progressively became involved in home care. What had traditionally been "community"-focused care for clients evolved into an extension of hospital care. This evolution has major implications for expectations in care delivery.

Economic changes have significantly impacted all areas under the umbrella of community health nursing practice leading to expanded opportunities for nurses practicing in the community setting (Gill, 1995; Meister, et al., 1995). Nurses who work in the community fill a variety of care roles including Home Health, Public Health, School Nursing, Hospice Nursing, Occupational Health Nursing, Nurse Practitioners and the newly emerging specialty of Parish Nursing.

A. Home Health

Because nursing constitutes the largest segment of the health care profession, it is important to examine how this significant work force will function as the setting for health care is moved from hospital to home. As hospitals discharge patients earlier and sicker, the burden of illness care and recovery is transferred to the home health agency. While homecare still accounts for a small portion of the nation's health care expenditures, it is the fastest growing sector in the medical market (Gill, 1995; Meister, et al., 1995; Weinstein, 1993). In 1995 alone, more than 7.1 million Americans received medical care at home (Schnack, 1995). Our nation's growing elderly population and the need for cost containment have helped fuel home health's 31 billion dollar industry.

Today, the demand for skilled home health nurses has once again exceeded the supply. Home health hiring trends reflect a need for nurses able to manage acute medical problems at home and therefore, solicit nurses with acute care and high-tech experience (Stulginsky, 1993). Qualifications specifically related to community nursing and/or a baccalaureate nursing degree are frequently preferred but not required by home health employers (Kalnins, 1989). To suggest that the same set of skills and knowledge base is required in both acute care and community health practice is naïve, yet many nurses are coming to home health assuming they possess all the requirements for independent practice (Stulginsky, 1993). Recent market demand for nurses willing to work in the home care setting has brought large numbers of nurses out of acute care and into community health nursing with little or no preparation for the role.

Simultaneously, seasoned home health nurses have been thrust into home situations requiring knowledge of advanced medical equipment and procedures with little transitional thought, educational training or planning. Many nurses have been overwhelmed and staff turnover rates have been high. As care has shifted to the home, home health nurses have become tangled in government regulation, documentation and competition. Government's involvement in care regulation has brought burdensome paperwork and care delivery requirements that impede practice and result in fewer home visits per day, low job satisfaction, increased nursing staff turnover, decreased quality of care, and a change in the spirit of community nursing from an emphasis on caring and community service to a focus on reimbursement (Baldwin and Price, 1994; Congdon, and Maglivy, 1995). Overwhelming requirements for documentation leave less time for the patient, depersonalize care and exhaust providers. Nurses report that paperwork is the single most frustrating aspect of home health care nursing. Some nurses believe the changes in service priorities are so profound that the value system of nursing is being jeopardized (Morrissey-Ross, 1988; Baldwin and Price, 1994).

Historically, public health nurses, educated in family-oriented services with a preventive and holistic community focus, made home visits. Today, the home health nurse is from an acute care setting where the emphasis is individualized and focused on curative, short-term outcomes (Kenyon, et al., 1990). Responsibility for a patient's care in a home environment is challenging at best. Even locating a client's place of residence can be a formidable task (Zerwekh, 1992b).

Once in the home, nurses are faced with situations that are not always conducive to prescribed treatment protocols. A home may have no running water, and conditions may be less than optimally sanitary. Children, who may be the patient's only care givers, may resist cooperating with smoking protocols around situations requiring oxygen. Infants discharged from neonatal intensive care units may go home to a family without a telephone to contact emergency services. Doctors may not be willing to renew treatment plans for elderly patients who no longer meet Medicare requirements that must be provided "under the care of a physician." In addition, patients themselves may resist compliance with prescribed treatment after returning home. While the acute care home health nurse may be skilled in operating equipment and dispensing care, she may be hindered by an inability to navigate the client's environment. The community health nurse is a guest in the clients' home and must relinquish control to the client, while endeavoring to provide quality nursing care.

Working in the community can be both rewarding and lonely. The home health nurse typically interacts with other nurses and health professionals for only a few minutes at the start of the day. The role requires independence and self sufficiency. As a case manager, responsibility for quality care rests directly with the nurse and her ability to coordinate necessary services. After services are provided, she must effectively document care to assure reimbursement for the agency.

Nurses working in the home health care setting require continued support and continuing education to keep abreast of rapid changes in all areas of home health nursing practice. Supervisors for home health field nurses are rarely effective leaders without direct experiences with the types and acuity of clients in this setting. An understanding of the range of encounters that front line nurses manage on a daily basis is critical to effective home care management.

B. Public Health

Public health nurses are professionals who work to develop healthful communities. Public health nurses, because of their preventive, holistic community focus have been historically the profession called on to visit the sick in their homes (Stulginsky, 1993). Los Angeles (in 1898) and New York City (in 1908) were the first cities to employ public health nurses whose work specifically focused on the control of communicable disease and meeting the needs of the poor (Pickett and Hanlon, 1990). Community health nurses make up the largest percentage of health care workers in more than 2200 local health departments (Stanhope and Lancaster, 1995). Public health nurses continue to address communicable diseases and new epidemics such as AIDS and teenage pregnancy. Although the terms *community health nurse* and *public health nurse* are used interchangeably, nurses that work for government-sponsored agencies typically prefer the original title public health nurse (Stanhope and Lancaster, 1995).

Assuring basic health services to citizens is seen as a part of public health. As health care dollars diminished in the 1980s, persons who rely on government assistance through the Medicaid program have increasingly been denied health care services due to low government reimbursement structures. In addition, the increased cost of services has resulted in unprecedented growth in the number of uninsured and underinsured citizens. Because of decreased access to care, additional demands have been placed on local health departments as they struggle to meet the basic health care service needs of communities (Stanhope and Lancaster, 1996).

Since public health nursing is functional, its responsiveness to society has led public agencies and public health nurses to assume a more clinical, illness-oriented role rather than the traditional community prevention or public health role (Salmon, 1993). As a consequence of practitioners' refusal to treat individuals without health insurance, the nation has struggled with ways to provide care to its poor. Public agencies have gradually moved into the medical model of health care provision in an effort to provide necessary primary care. The move to provide direct clinical care to individuals had the positive effect of generating reimbursement dollars for public health care services. However, there was a corresponding negative effect for communities as public agencies diverted attention to secondary prevention efforts, rather than focusing on health promotion (Stanhope and Lancaster, 1995; Zerwekh, 1993). As health departments began to look like any other type of delivery system, public health nurses have been distracted from the primary role of prevention (Salmon, 1993).

While nursing faces changes and seeks a position on the future health care agenda of the country, it is important, as a profession, to define what role public health nurses intend to play in the overall picture of community based health care services. Difficulty in describing the mission or even the public served has plagued efforts to determine the destiny of the public health nurse (Zerwekh, 1992a; Reverby, 1993).

Public health nurses are the largest group of public health professionals practicing in local communities, outnumbering physicians, administrators, social workers and therapists. In spite of their numbers, Zerwekh (1993) describes public health nursing as an "invisible profession," for although public health nursing has demonstrated clear benefits to communities, the role of public health nursing and its accomplishments are difficult to explain. It is imperative that community nurses grapple with controversies that affect the way they practice.

C. School

School nursing began at the end of the 19th century and became one of the earliest specialties to emerge from public health nursing practice. Private physicians felt threatened by school nurses diagnosing and treating problems in children and strongly discouraged treatment of illness in the school setting. Early school nurses faced pressure from the private medical sector to limit their scope of practice. The lack of support from the medical community impacted on the school nurse's ability to provide more than a minimal role in treating health problems and maintaining a healthy school environment (Clark, 1996). Government budgetary cuts in education and related services since the 1970s have seriously affected the number of school nurses practicing throughout the country. Increasing optimism has developed recently, however, as the federal government has expanded their role in health promotion in school settings (Smith and Maurer, 1995). The role of the school nurse has emerged stronger, and school nurses are now leading community care for children by advocating for school based health clinics, access to immunizations and early intervention for health problems that may interfere with a child's ability to learn. The school-based clinic is seen as an important tool to reach the nation's children and youth (Walter, et al., 1995).

School nursing continues to be a changing field. Case management has evolved as a natural way of assuring that a child receives necessary services. After implementation of the Education for All Handicapped Children Act (EHA) became law in 1975, children with handicaps have access to a free and appropriate education. Children with chronic illnesses were integrated (mainstreamed) into regular classrooms and illness care progressively has become an emerging focus, even in the school setting. School nurses, along with other community health nurses, now question their priorities for practice. In spite of the new epidemics of illicit drugs, alcohol and teen pregnancy, school nurses continue to have the responsibility of keeping children well and in school.

There is tremendous potential to impact the health of the entire community as school nurses promote the health of children. However, if school nursing is to survive, efforts must be made to secure funding outside of the traditional education budget. Direct reimbursement from third party payers is one avenue that school nurses are exploring to provide for comprehensive school health programs.

D. Hospice

Hospice nursing is a philosophy that promotes caring for clients and their families to ease the pain of dying. The first hospice program in the United States began in 1974. Today, more than 2,800 hospice programs provide multiple services. The National Hospice Organization estimates that hospice programs serve over 340,000 terminally ill persons and their families each year. In the past five years, hospice growth has averaged nearly 17 per cent. Hospice offers help and support to dying individuals and their families on a 24-hours-a-day, seven-days-a-week basis. Patients routinely receive periodic in-home services of a nurse as well as a multidisciplinary team. While the hospice movement began as a volunteer effort, today hospice care is a covered benefit under most private insurance plans, including HMOs, managed care organizations and Medicare. In 1994 Medicare spent $1.2 million on hospice services. Hospice services are offered by eighty-two percent of managed care plans. More than ninety percent of hospice care hours are provided in home based care. This care enables patients to remain in familiar surroundings while in the final phase of a terminal illness. A study commissioned by the National Hospice Organization in 1995 showed that for every dollar Medicare spent on hospice, it saved $1.52 in Medicare Part A and Part B expenditures (National Hospice Organization, 1996).

The hospice movement evolved in the United States as a volunteer organization designed to provide those individuals with terminal illness the opportunity to die with dignity. Small community organizations were founded with private funding and donations. Hospice nurses functioned freely to provide necessary services to terminally ill clients and their families. Those who worked to develop this important community nursing role have watched their work erode as government reimbursement and subsequent regulation has filtered into hospice practice. Because of required government regulations and controls, hospice nurses are frustrated as the important work of caring for the dying has been shadowed with increased documentation requirements and limits on covered services. It is difficult to measure or regulate the humane and compassionate care implemented by the hospice nurse. Hospice uses sophisticated methods of pain control that enable the patient to live as comfortably and fully as possible. How a family is able to cope with illness and death affects both the individual's health and the health of the entire family (Burns and Gianutsos, 1987; Whyte, 1992).

Today, hospice employs more than 25,000 paid professionals nationwide. Additionally, 96,000 volunteers, logging in more than 5.25 million hours of service annually, continue to be a driving force behind the remarkable growth of the hospice movement (National Hospice Organization, 1996).

E. Occupational Health

Occupational health nurses have become important care providers for industry. Nurses caring for workers was officially entitled Industrial Nursing in 1888. Industrial nurses initially were responsible for both worker and their family. Nurses hired by coal and manufacturing companies would visit sick employees, provide emergency care and educate mothers about childcare and healthy living. Companies realized that a healthy workforce was a productive one, and industrial nursing grew rapidly during the first half of the twentieth century. By World War II there were approximately 4000 industrial nurses. In the 1960s and 1970s the federal government enacted several laws to protect the health and well being of its workers. In particular, the passage of the Occupational Health and Safety Act in 1970 stimulated an increased need for occupational health nurses (Stanhope and Lancaster, 1996).

The role of occupational health nurse continues to evolve with American industry. The occupational health nurse is influential and instrumental in creating a safe workplace. Ethical conflict may develop as nurses attempt to care for the employees' needs while maintaining company loyalty. The occupational health nurse's role in the community may vary from providing emergency treatment and follow-up of work site injury to developing employee health promotion programs that prevent health problems. In addition, the task of maintaining a safe work environment free from potential hazards is a continuing challenge. The most recent national survey of registered nurses indicates that there are more than 19,000 occupational health nurses (U.S. Department of Health and Human Services, 1992). In this survey 70% of occupational health nurses report that they are employed as staff nurses; most of these manage one-nurse units in a variety of businesses. The American Association of Occupational Health Nurses describes five job titles for occupational health nurses: solo practitioner, administrator, educator, researcher and consultant (AAOHN, 1988). The role of occupational health nursing is changing in the emerging managed care environment. In the future, more time will be spent keeping workers and their families well rather than treating their problems.

F. Nurse Practitioner

Nurse practitioners have expanded their scope of practice beyond that of the registered nurse and are in demand as cost-effective primary health care providers (Brush and Capezuti, 1995). A nurse practitioner (NP) is a registered nurse who has advanced education and clinical training in a health care specialty area. NPs are primary health care providers who provide nursing and medical services to individuals, families and groups, emphasizing health promotion and disease prevention, as well as the diagnosis and management of acute and chronic diseases.

The nurse practitioner movement began in 1965 at the University of Colorado and opened a new era for nursing's involvement in primary care. The first nurses to work as nurse practitioners were community health nurses with additional skills in the diagnosis and treatment of common illnesses (Stanhope and Lancaster, 1996). Studies have shown that nurse practitioners rate high in consumer satisfaction (Kulal and Cleaver, 1974). In a review of 15 studies, Record (1979) concluded that between 75% and 80% of adult primary care services and up to 90% of pediatric primary care services could be performed by nurse practitioners. Patients respond favorably to treatment by a nurse practitioner because NPs reportedly spend more time with them and create a relaxed atmosphere where they (the patients) are more comfortable asking questions which might be regarded as too trivial for a physician (Robin and Hadley, 1980).

Nurse practitioners are registered nurses with advanced education and certification. The length of training required for this advanced practice role varies according to the practice specialty. NPs function under the rules and regulations of the Nurse Practice Act of the state in which they work. Many NPs are also nationally certified in their specialty area and have masters or doctorate degrees. Nurse practitioners make up approximately 30% of the 77,000 physician extenders practicing in the United States (Smith and Maurer, 1995). Nurse practitioners provide cost-effective primary care to consumers. Many nurse practitioners work with physicians, some are employed by clinics or hospitals and some practice independently. The use of nurse practitioners in decentralized outpatient medical clinics resulted in 50% fewer hospitalized days for their patients compared to the control group (Runyan, 1975). Effective utilization of NPs has the potential to provide efficient, accessible health care to consumers at a substantial cost-savings (Writson, 1981). Medically underserved communities that do not attract physicians may employ nurse practitioners to meet their primary care needs.

A direct outgrowth of the nurse practitioner movement is the nursing center. Nursing centers were first conceived in 1971 as a way for nurse practitioners to gain control of their practice arena. The trend towards nursing centers as a location for independent nursing practice continues to gain momentum as Americans have difficulty accessing cost-effective primary care. These centers are staffed by nurses, have a client centered focus and have been shown to be effective in providing important health maintenance, promotion and education services.

NPs may be found in all 50 states. A large number of research studies over the past 20 years have documented that NPs providehigh quality, cost-effective care. As primary care providers become the gatekeepers for the managed care industry, nurse practitioners have received increased responsibility and attention within the health care arena.

G. Parish Nurse

Parish nurses have arrived on the community health care scene as increasing parallels are drawn between social support, spirituality and healing (Miskelly, 1995; Macrae, 1995). The parish nurse is typically supported by a religious congregation or group of congregations and is employed to care for the health of church members. Types of services members receive depends on the health care goals set by the congregation in association with the parish nurse. Health education as well as health advocacy are frequently part of a parish nurse's job description. The parish nurse movement is spreading as government is increasingly unable to meet the growing needs of society. Church congregations are contracting with trained professional nurses in a trusting care relationship. Parish nurses are an important resource for communities as they can help fill in the gaps in services for clients where reimbursement is an issue.

Community nurses in all fields of practice continue to change and develop as health care delivery systems evolve. The case management practice model can improve quality, cost-effective care delivery in any practice environment.

II. COMMUNITY HEALTH CARE DISEASE VS. WELLNESS MODEL

Community health nursing is concerned with the complex relationships that exist between individuals and their communities. As the nation plans for health reform, it is important to recognize that health is more than the absence of disease and health care is more than medical care (Smith 1994). If we continue to ignore health promotion and prevention as a part of service delivery, we can expect to see an even greater resurgence in age-old problems such as tuberculosis and rabies, compounded by new epidemics caused by super organisms such AIDS, Ebola and Hanta virus. By putting the health care dollar in curative medicine rather than prevention, we, as a nation, stand vulnerable to epidemics with far reaching consequences--problems that can be triggered by something as simple as a weather change (Cowley, 1995). As more and more organisms become resistant to pharmacological treatment, it would be unrealistic to expect that these deadly diseases will be eradicated by medical advances alone. By focusing on curing disease, rather than preventing disease, we stand to lose the battle on both disease and economic fronts. We need to remind ourselves, government and consumers, of the functions of a viable public health system (Smith, 1994).

The rationale for the above changes in the way health care does business seems obvious, yet as a nation we continue to support an annual per capita expenditure for medical care that is 34 times what is spent for public health (Congressional Budget Office, 1993). In spite of the glut of spending for disease treatment, public health efforts are responsible for 80-90 per cent of the nation's improvement in morbidity and mortality in the last century (Office of Disease Prevention and Health Promotion, 1993). With all the focus on distribution of services and models of care delivery, we as consumers must remember that public health is not a branch of medicine. Rather, medicine and medical care services are better seen as a branch of public health in its broadest sense (Navarro, 1994).

Population-focused, community-based health care is the core of community health nursing. However, because of the rapid expansion of community care agencies and the increased demand for nurses willing to practice in the community, the focus on "community as client" has been lost or at least temporarily misplaced. When the client is the center of care, concentration moves from treatment of illness to maintaining health and wellness. By changing the measurement of outcomes, that is, from disease eradication to wellness, the nurse is able to determine the overall benefits of nursing interventions implemented. It is much easier for health care practitioners to treat disease than to focus on individual, family and community wellness. For example, if a child is treated in a clinic for a urinary tract infection, the disease can usually be eliminated with the simple use of an antibiotic. However, a community nurse, to practice to the full extent of her charge, must examine the source of the infection, perhaps sexual abuse, and the cause of the infection, possibly an organism typically transmitted sexually. A simple treatment now becomes a complex issue that requires skill and training. How much better for the overall well-being of the client to promote healing from a person perspective, rather than from a problem perspective. This is where client centered care from a public health nursing viewpoint becomes important.

The clinic-based practitioner can treat repeated episodes of staphylococcal skin infections—a result of insect bites--where the nurse with an understanding of prevention will assess the environment, convince the landlord to place screens on windows, teach the family the importance of hand-washing and how to prevent further spread of infection. In addition, she may also work with the county mosquito abatement program in the client's community to help control the problem for everyone in the neighborhood. By planning for the client's wellness rather than simply treating disease, the community nurse has prevented further disease episodes and empowered the family and community. This "teach a person to fish" model of care also proves invaluable in terms of cost-effective services. From one professional nursing visit a community problem has been addressed and, not only did the client benefit by preventing the recurrence of infection, but the entire neighborhood benefited.

This type of client centered, wellness model is appropriate for any setting where nurses choose to practice and is indispensable for "population-based" services. Modern medicine treats illness outside of the context of home and community (Zerwekh, 1993). Yet how can health care practitioners expect to make a lasting difference without considering the communities and families where their clients live and work? Community health nurses in diverse settings have the ability to change a disease oriented model into one that emphasizes wellness. The benefits of such a model cannot be measured. For example, the school nurse who focuses on a child with attendance problems that she thinks are related to illness may discover that the child is actually home caring for a sick family member. She then has the opportunity to plan interventions for the family that will ultimately benefit the child.

An occupational health nurse may discover a similar problem when a company employee has hypertension. The employee may be manifesting symptoms of disease secondary to difficulty or stress in caring for an elderly parent or new baby. The impact of intervention should then be at the family level, rather than an individual level with the emphasis on preventing problems, not treating them. Working with the company and others, the occupational health nurse can positively impact the entire community by obtaining funds to begin a day care center with the additional benefit of decreasing employee stress.

In the acute care setting, a 67-year-old mother of six will be treated for cardiac disease the appropriate number of days then released. Next, the home health nurse will assess the limited financial resources available and establish protocol for a successful diet and medication plan. She may also discover that this woman is caring for grandchildren and a medically frail spouse in addition to managing her own health, tasks which contribute to her own disease process. The well-prepared community nurse, functioning in the home health setting, would be able to educate family, plan care and move the client toward a healthier lifestyle in addition to providing treatment for the disease condition. Additional benefits occur when the whole family is able to profit from nutrition education and stress reduction methods advocated by the community health nurse. The circle of influence this type of consumer-oriented care will have on future costs can be measured in terms of healthier individuals, families and communities.

One of the unique differences between public health nursing and acute care nursing is the ability to look beyond disease to the person, family or community.

Population focused health promotion and primary prevention designed to be provided throughout the community, are essential to public well being. Worksites, schools, churches and community centers are increasingly becoming the place nurses and other health professionals reach consumers. The healing of communities is a primary goal of community health nursing, in general, and public health nursing, in particular. Nurses promote the development of a healing environment. A healing environment can only exist when communities cease to be victims and become empowered to identify and solve problems at their source (Quinn, 1992; May, Mendelson and Ferketich, 1995).

Society continues to ignore the proven return on investments in public health's efforts at disease prevention (Pender, 1987). Yet, in spite of the nation's financial focus on disease treatment there has been little reward in terms of health outcomes. National efforts to educate the public about the dangers of cigarette smoking, excessive drinking and the need to control dietary fats and cholesterol have done more to prolong life and assure positive health outcomes than any treatment effort.

A nation struggling to develop a new health care system must include a vision for where it is going. Consumers must become partners with health care providers in our efforts to control cost and prevent disease. Damaging lifestyle choices currently account for 50 - 75% of the mortality in the U.S. population (Gallagher and Kriedler, 1987). It is time to encourage consumers to be responsible for their own health. Our medically based patriarchal system, where the physician assumes responsibility for health and illness decision making, has not been effective in dealing with ancient or modern plagues such as violence and substance abuse (Smith, 1994). A new system needs to evolve out of the current health care system. For that to happen community health nursing leaders, with their own vision for the future of health care, and preserving the best of what we've learned from the past, need to surface to guide the reconstruction.

III. COMMUNITY HEALTH NURSES AS HEALTH CARE LEADERS

In a health care system that is rapidly changing, nursing should not ignore its leadership responsibility. While nurses have never lacked opportunities for leadership, they have been reluctant to take the reins. Nurses spend a greater amount of time in direct contact with clients than any other health professionals (Smith and Maurer, 1994). Because of their knowledge base and the exposure to both clients and communities, nurses hold valuable information for health planning. By assuming a participative role in the transformation of the health care delivery system, nurses have the opportunity to advance the principles of health promotion and prevention in the policy arena.

Community health nurses possess both the education and vision required for leadership in the area of health care. With competition for the health care dollar steadily increasing, consumers need to be educated regarding how much can be accomplished with relatively low cost prevention. Nurses should be in the forefront to inform our citizens about health promotion and prevention activities as important aspects of cost-effective health care.

The changes in health care provide an opportunity for nurses to put aside internal arguments which pit technological nurses against professional nurses and instead unite to promote healthy individuals, families and communities (Martin, 1989).

Nurses cannot afford to be infighting over areas of practice rather than designing collaborative roles between acute and community nurses as well as other health care professionals. It is clear, as health care evolves putting energy into labor disputes rather than working with the business community to produce appropriate, high quality, cost-effective care would only be counterproductive. Our profession must be willing to step into the political arena and rally the nurse voter to become involved in political change or we will be merely victims. It is also clear that we need leaders to guide us in the process. As professional nurses continue to learn leadership principles and study management practices, we must also be willing to step forward with vision and the determination to make changes happen in health care delivery systems.

A. Leadership Effectiveness

As community health nurses measure their leadership effectiveness (Table 1), they need to examine existing and potential leadership opportunities. In addition to leadership in health care policy and politics, community health nurses need leadership at the local level. Leaders with a clear understanding of community care can facilitate the effective movement of nursing care from the confines of an acute care setting to the community. Community nurses have been keen on questioning the status quo, but little is documented in terms of solutions. Technology, often faulted for soaring medical costs (Fuchs, 1994), may ultimately be our salvation. The ability to connect agencies and providers through advanced electronic technology is a benefit few currently use to full advantage. As care moves to the community, nurses can eliminate the isolation experienced for decades. The ability to connect with a similar agency or cohort and conference on plans or evaluate outcomes could bring about creative solutions in health care.

Table 1 - Practices of Effective Leaders

- Challenging the process: being on the cutting edge of technology, taking risks, being innovative, experimenting, finding new and better ways of doing things, and questioning the status quo.
- Inspiring a shared vision: identifying a mission and goals that others can share, building excitement, describing the future in colorful ways, and involving everyone in the vision.
- Enabling others to act: building teamwork, involving others in the tasks and empowering staff to feel strong and capable;
- Modeling the way: making values and standards very clear and providing an excellent example, always being consistent with stated values and practicing what is advocated; and
- Encouraging the heart: supporting and encouraging follower, providing praise, and celebrating accomplishments.

McNeese-Smith, 1993; Kouzes and Posner, 1988

B. Leadership with Vision

To make progress toward our national goals of healthier people and communities requires leadership with vision. Community health nursing needs leaders capable of showing the way to the future. The spiraling influence of such leadership cannot be overemphasized. By becoming partners with other health professions and community members we can move forward to create a plan for the future. Collaboration and collegiality between health care professionals should be sought on all levels. Every health care provider has a sphere of expertise that is valuable (Fagin, 1992). Nursing has the opportunity to develop a panoramic view of the health needs of a community by teaming with other disciplines such as business, communications, rural and urban planners to broaden its perspective (Schoultz, Hatcher and Hurrel, 1992). Communities and individuals need to be educated regarding what community nurses have to contribute to the construction of a better health care industry. The future of an improved health care system demands that all health professionals increase multidimensional, health promoting, collaborative coalitions and partnerships with the communities they serve.

IV. COMMUNITY HEALTH NURSING CHALLENGES

The dichotomy between "healthy living" (Hygeia) and "cure" (Panacea) that originated in Greek times continues to challenge health care delivery today (Swanson and Albrecht, 1993; Smith, 1993). Lack of funding, limited leadership and medicine's political maneuvering are concerns of those practicing in the health promotion/prevention arena. Florence Nightingale commented that it was more spiritual and certainly more effective to clean the gutter to prevent cholera from spreading, in keeping with God's laws, than to pray for the disease to disappear (Macrae, 1995).

The focus on disease rather than health has permeated all levels of health care. In spite of a remarkable foundation established by nursing pioneers such as Wald and Nightingale, modern nursing has been swept up in the expansive and expensive technical delivery of illness care to single individuals. This trend has cost both society and the profession.

The current period of health care reform has created opportunities for those willing to seize them as the economy driven move to managed care has brought forward the idea that managed competition will contain health care costs (Fuchs, 1994). In a "name that tune" format, managed care companies compete to provide that procedure through progressively fewer inpatient days. It should not be surprising that quality of care issues are beginning to surface where market forces and cost control are the primary incentives for health care change. The nursing community has limited resources and should focus energy on removing economic and political barriers to community nursing practice and make critical decisions about what skills are needed to compete in today's health care market (Maraldo and Solomon, 1987).

The spectrum of illness and health care is so broad that responsibilities for care must be shared by nurses, clients and caregivers (Rice, 1996). Our greatest challenge will be synthesizing the pieces to provide integrated community nursing care. Community health nurses with varying educational preparation can work together to develop necessary partnerships that set the stage for a continuum of care that maximizes the client's and community's potential for health.

REFERENCES

American Association of Occupational Health Nurses. (1988). *A comprehensive guide for establishing an occupational health service.* Atlanta: AAOHN.

Auriolio, L. (1985). Power through participation. *Nursing Success Today, 2(10):* 20.

Baldwin, D. and Price, S. (1994). Work excitement: The energizer for home healthcare nursing. *Journal of Nursing Administration, 24 (9):* 37-42.

Brush, B. and Capezuti, E. (1996). Revisiting "A Nurse For All Settings": The nurse practitioner movement, 1965-1995. *Journal of the American Academy of Nurse Practitioners, 8(1):* 5-11.

Buchanan, L. (1996). The Acute Care Nurse Practitioner in Collaborative Practice. *Journal of the American Academy of Nurse Practitioners, 8(1):* 13-20.

Burns, P. and Gianutsos, R. (1987). Reentry of the head-injured survivor into the educational system: First steps. *Journal of Community Health Nursing, 4(3):* 145-152.

Cejka and Company. (1995). 1995 Physician Recruitment Practices Survey. Sponsored by Cejka and Company, St. Louis, MO, and Modern Healthcare, 1995.

Clark, M. (1996). *Nursing in the Community* (2nd ed.). Stamford, CT: Appleton and Lange.

Cogden, J. and Maglivy, J. (1995). The changing spirit of rural community nursing: Documentation burden. *Public Health Nursing, 12(1):* 18-24.

Committee for the Study of the Future of Public Health, Institute of Medicine. (1988) *The Future of Public Health.* National Academy Press, Washington, DC.

Consensus Conference on the Essentials of Public Health Nursing Practice and Education. (1985). US Department of Health and Human Services. Bureau of Health Professions, Division of Nursing: Rockville, MD.

Cowley, J. (1995). Outbreak of fear. *Newsweek ,* (May 22): 48-55.

Council on Community Health Nursing, American Nurses Association. (1991). CHN Communiqué. American Nurses Association, Washington, DC.

Erikson, G. (1987). Public health nursing initiatives: Guideposts for future practice. *Public Health Nursing, (4):* 202-11.

Fagin, C. M. (1992). The Myth of superdoc blocks health care reform. *Nursing and Health Care, 13(10):* 542-3.

Feingold, E. (1994). Health Care Reform—More than cost containment and universal access. *American Journal of Public Health, 84(5):* 727-728

Fuchs, V. R. (1994). Health system reform: A different approach. *Journal of the American Medical Association, 272(7):* 560-563.

Gallagher, L., and Kriedler, M. (1987). *Nursing and health: Maximizing human potential throughout the life span.* Norwalk, CT: Appleton and Lange.

Gill, H. S. (1995). Home care's place within an integrated delivery system. *The Journal of Care Management, 1(3):* 17-22.

Goeppinger, J., Lassiter, P., and Wilcox, B. (1980). Community health is community competence. *Nursing Outlook, (30):* 464-467.

Hickman, P. (Ed.). (1990). *Essentials Of Baccalaureate Nursing Education For Entry Level Community Health Nursing Practice..* Association of Community Health Nursing Educators, Louisville, KY.

Irurita, V. F. (1994). Optimism, values and commitment as forces in nursing leadership. *Journal of Nursing Administration, 24(9):* 61-71.

Kalnins, I. (1989). Home health agency preferences for staff nurse qualifications and practices in hiring and orientation. *Public Health Nursing, 6*(2): 33-39.

Kouzes, J., Posner, B. (1988). *The Leadership Challenge.* Jossey-Bass Publishers, San Francisco.

Kulal, S., Clever, L., (1974). Acceptance of the Nurse Practitioner. *American Journal of Nursing,* (March): 251-256.

Lutjens, L. (1995). Determinants of hospital length of stay. *Journal of Nursing Administration, 25*(4): 14.

Macrae, J. (1995). Nightingale's spiritual philosophy and its significance for modern nursing. *Image, 27*(1): 8-10.

Maglacas A. (1988). Health for all, nursing's role. *Nursing Outlook, 36.*

Maraldo, P., and Solomon, S. (1987). Nursing's window of opportunity. *Image, 19*(2): 83-86.

Martin, B. (1989). Power, politics and nursing's future. *Imprint, 36*(4).

May, K., Mendelson, C., and Ferketich, S. (1995). Community empowerment in rural health care. *Public Health Nursing, 12*(1): 25-30.

McNeese-Smith, D. (1993). How effective are your leadership skills? *Journal of Nursing Administration, 23*(2): 9-10.

Meister, S., Rodts, B., Gothard, J., and Maturen, V. (1995). Home care steps protocols: Home care's answer to changes in reimbursement. *Journal of Nursing Administration, 25*(6): 33-42.

Miskelly, S. (1995). A parish nursing model: Applying the community health nursing process in a church community. *Journal of Community Health Nursing, 12*(1): 1-14.

Morrissey-Ross, M. (1988). Documentation: If you haven't written it, you haven't done it. *Nursing Clinics of North America, 23*(2): 363-371.

Murphy, M. (1995). Get the head for leadership. Unique Opportunities: *The Physicians Resource. May/June:* 18-28.

Navarro, V. (1994). The future of public health in health care reform. *American Journal of Public Health, 84*(5): 729-730.

O'Rourke, M. W. (1996). Who holds the keys to the future of health care? *NurseWeek, 9*(1): 1,26-27.

Pender, N. (1987). *Health promotion in nursing practice (2nd edition).* Norwalk, CT: Appleton and Lange.

Pickett, G., and Hanlon, J. (1990). *Public health administration and practice* (9th ed.). St. Louis: Times-Mirror/Mosby College Publishing.

Primomo, J. (1995). Ensuring Public Health Nursing In Managed Care: Partnerships for healthy communities. *Public Health Nursing, 12*(2): 69-71.

Public Health Service. (1990). *Healthy People 2000: National health promotion and disease prevention objectives.* USDHHS, Washington, D.C.

Quinn, J. (1992). Holding sacred space: The nurse as healing environment. *Holistic Nursing Practice, 4*(6): 26-36.

Record, J. C. (Ed.). (1992). Provided Requirements, Cost Savings and The New Health Practitioner in Primary Care. National Estimate for 1990. Contract 231-77-0077. Washington, D.C.: DEHEW.

Reverby, S. (1993). From Lillian Wald to Hillary Rodham Clinton: What will happen to public health nursing? *American Journal of Public Health,* (83): 1662-1663.

Rice, R. (1996). *Home Health Nursing Practice, Concepts and Applications.* (2nd ed.). St. Louis, Missouri: Mosby-Year Book, Inc.

Rich, M., Beckham, V., Wittenberg, C., Leven, C., Freedland, K., and Carney, R. (1995). A multi-disciplinary intervention to prevent the readmission of elderly patients with congestive heart failure. *New England Journal of Medicine,* 333: 1190-1195.

Robyn, D., Hadley, J. (1980). National Health Insurance and the New Health Occupations: Nurse Practitioners and Physician Assistants. *Journal of Health Politics, Policy and Law, 5*(3): 450.

Runyan, J. W. (1975). The Memphis Chronic Disease Program: Comparisons in Outcome and the Nurse's Extended Role. *Journal of the American Medical Association, 231*(3): 264-267.

Salmon, M. E. (1993). Editorial: Public Health Nursing—The opportunity of a century. *American Journal of Public Health, 83*(12): 1674-1675.

Sawyer, L. M. (1995). Community participation: Lip service? *Nursing Outlook, 43*(1): 17-22.

Shoultz, J., Hatcher, P. and Hurrell, M. (1992). Growing edges of a new paradigm: The future of nursing in the health of the nation. *Nursing Outlook, 40*(2): 57-61.

Sills, G. and Goeppinger, J. (1985). The community as a field of inquiry in nursing. *Annual Review of Nursing Research, 3*: 1-23. Springer, New York.

Smith, C. and Maurer, F. (1995). *Community Health Nursing, Theory and Practice*. Philadelphia, PA: W.B. Saunders Co.

Smith, D. R. (1994). Porches, politics and public health. *American Journal of Public Health, 84*(5): 725-726.

Spradley, B. (1991). *Readings in Community Health Nursing*, (4th ed.). Philadelphia, PA: J.B. Lippincott, Co.

Stanhope, M. and Lancaster, J. (1996). *Community Health Nursing: Promoting Health Of Aggregates, Families And Individuals*, (4th ed.). St. Louis, MO: Mosby Year Book, Inc.

Stuck, A., Arownow, H., Steiner, A., Alessi, C., Bula, C., Gold, M., Yuhas, K., Nisenbaum, R., Rubenstein, L., and Beck, J. (1995). A trial of annual in-home comprehensive geriatric assessments for elderly people living in the community. *New England Journal of Medicine, 333*: 1184-1189.

Stulginsky, M. M. (1993). Nurses' home health experience: Part I: The practice setting. *Nursing and Health Care, 14*(8): 402-407.

Swanson, J. and Albrecht, M. (1993). *Community Health Nursing: Promoting the Health of Aggregates*. (1st ed.). W.B. Saunders Co.

Taylor, M. W. (1996). Physician compensation and managed care: Win, lose, or draw? *Hospital Physician, 32*(1): 45-49.

U.S. Department of Health and Human Services (USDHHS). (1991). *Healthy people 2000: National Health Promotion and Disease Prevention Objectives*. U.S. Government Printing Office, Washington. D.C.

Walter, H. Vaughan, R., Armstrong, B., Krakoff, R., Tieszzi, L., and McCarthy, J. (1995). School-based health care for urban minority junior high school students. *Archives of Pediatrics and Adolescent Medicine, 149*: 1221-1225.

Weinstein, S. (1993). A coordinated approach to home infusion care. *Home Healthcare Nurse, 11*(1): 15-20.

Whyte, D. (1992). A family nursing approach to the care of a child with a chronic illness. *Journal of Advanced Nursing, 17*: 317-327.

Williams, C. (1977). Community health nursing — What is it? *Nursing Outlook, 5*(April): 250-254.

Writson, S. (1981). Nurse Practitioner Reimbursement. *Journal of Health Politics, Policy and Law, 6*(3): 444.

Zerwekh, J. V. (1991). Tales from public health nursing true detectives. *American Journal of Nursing, 91*: 30-36.

Zerwekh, J. V. (1992a). Community health nurses—A population at risk. *Public Health Nursing, 9*(1): 1.

Zerwekh, J. V. (1992b). Public health nursing: historical practical wisdom. *Nursing and Health Care, 13*: 84-92.

Zerwekh, J.V. (1993). Commentary: Going to the people—public health nursing today and tomorrow. *American Journal of Public Health, 83*(12): 1676-1678.

20.

PRIMARY CARE NETWORK DEVELOPMENT AND MANAGEMENT SERVICE ORGANIZATIONS

Wes McKenna, *Care Alliance Medical Services Organization, Charleston, SC*

Roseann Carothers, *Care Alliance Medical Services Organization, Charleston, SC*

Dramatic changes in the health care environment over the past decade have created the need for effective management to ensure not just survival but financial viability of future delivery systems, traditional hospitals, and individual physician practices. Increased competition among medical providers and rising health care costs are creating innovative approaches to making health care more affordable to purchasers, namely patients and employers.

Health care providers are combining resources and management expertise into single entities such as integrated delivery systems (IDSs) because of uncertain times of health care reform and impending managed care. To further complicate the environment, rapid technological changes, increased intricacies of third party payment plans, widening discrepancies between health care costs and reimbursement, and increased quality expectancies of patients have challenged administrators to adapt to change while responding to opportunities. Therefore, management of the IDS must facilitate responses to change in the external environment while preserving quality, containing costs, and operating within changing legal requirements.

In addition to health administrators, primary care physicians (PCPs) struggle with changes in payer relationships, managed care arrangements, and increasing complexity of business issues in their practices. PCPs are enjoying their important status as the essential gatekeeper in these new managed care arrangements, but they fear loss of professional autonomy and financial security as the terms of the plans are delineated. They are therefore looking for ways to combine resources with other physicians and health systems in order to protect their revenues and avoid being left behind as the health care market changes.

I. THE MANAGEMENT SERVICES ORGANIZATION

Health care providers and facilities may align within several structures to reach the common goals of both physicians and health care organizations. One of the most prevalent models in today's environment is the management services organization (MSO). Although the level of integration under an MSO model may vary, the common goals are to provide management and administrative services to physicians, hospitals, and other providers within an integrated delivery system.

The most integrated MSO is called the comprehensive or turn-key MSO. In this model, the MSO purchases all tangible assets of physician practices, hires all the acquired practice's employees, and manages all the operations. In effect, the practitioner turns the key, walks in the door, practices medicine, and leaves the administrative services to the MSO. These services include practice management, facilities management, provision of information systems, benefits administration, utilization review and quality assurance, marketing and advertising, third party contract negotiation, compliance with regulatory guidelines, financial analysis of practice operations, centralized billing and collection, and physician recruitment. For purposes of this chapter, the MSO described will be specific to the operations of the comprehensive or turn key MSO.

Under the MSO, a previously decentralized system of providers can now act structurally as a common entity linked together by centralized management (Niederman et al., 1994). Economies of scale can be enjoyed by all parties through collective purchasing of services and supplies and the sharing of management expertise not usually available to the traditional independent PCP. Consolidation of managed care contracts will enable higher reimbursement and capitated payments to the providers within the MSO through the stronger negotiating power of the singular group. However, forming an MSO and strategically aligning a group of providers is a challenging and demanding process which requires carefully formed strategy, commitment to common goals, and thorough understanding of both the internal and external environment.

A. Development of an MSO

Successful integration of physicians and health care organizations into a prosperous MSO requires attention to a number of issues: the type of governance and leadership, changes necessary in the delivery of patient care, capital for start up and continuing operations, ownership definition. McManis et al. (1995) conducted a forum of medical group leaders in which key components to successful integration of providers with traditional organizations were defined. Involvement of physicians in development and management issues was cited as an one very important factor. Therefore, the initiation and development of the MSO should begin by bringing together key physicians with leaders of health care organizations under the common goal of combining resources in order to positively impact patient care in the face of health care reform. Participants in the new system should be committed to its goals at each step in the process.

According to Cimasi (1995), the MSO must be established and operate in a manner that emphasizes collaboration and cooperation among providers and organizations. A clear vision of what the MSO and network should achieve must be defined, and expectations and performance objectives should be clearly delineated. The MSO should work to eliminate duplication of administrative services and reduce overhead costs, but adequate staff and resources must be committed to facilitate this goal. The MSO should also be financially structured in such a way as to allow both hospitals and physicians to share in the risk of capitated contracts of third party payers. Finally, organizational structure should allow for adaptation to changes in the marketplace while accommodating the needs of the community and its culture.

B. Legal Issues

Once the decision has been made to form and operate an MSO, competent legal counsel must be employed to address the complex legal issues. Although specific legal analysis should be left to the attorneys, it is essential that health administrators involved with the start up of an MSO thoroughly understand the legal implications of integration.

Primary legal risks include the purchase transaction, the leaseback of space and equipment, and the management services provided by the MSO (Johnson, 1995). Administrators should always ensure that the fair market value for the physician practice acquisition and facilities and equipment lease be determined and paid in every transaction. The determination of the fair market value should be well documented with a professional, independent consulting group involved in the process. Payments are strictly delineated in contracts with physician sellers to ensure that the monies exchanged do not represent or imply the inducement of referrals of any type, including ancillary and inpatient services (1995). A management services agreement between the MSO and providers must be established to clearly outline responsibilities, and a fair market value of fees must be determined and methods for payment defined.

II. NETWORK DEVELOPMENT

A. Environmental Analysis

One of the first steps in the development of an integrated network of primary care physicians is careful analysis of the community, its physicians, and its patients. Especially vital is examining the delivery system area and determining population growth or decline trends, employment opportunities or reductions, key demographic data, and even traffic patterns. This information can sometimes be found at the public library or Chamber of Commerce since most cities track such trends for the purposes of attracting employment prospects to the area. Questions about future land use must be considered. For example, are new subdivisions being planned or built? Are new business parks and shopping complexes being arranged? Are new road improvements being designed. In short, a profile or description of local characteristics that affect patterns of community development should be acquired and examined.

The existing network of primary care physicians also must be reviewed. One excellent source of this information is the admitting physicians on active staff at the hospitals to be part of the IDS. Those physicians who are loyal to the facilities through inpatient admissions, referrals to specialists, or voluntary service on hospital committees, board activities and community education programs are more likely sources for the inaugural group of physicians. An advisory committee of these physicians may be a beneficial way to gain the trust of the primary care physicians who will be forming the integrated group.

B. Physician Supply and Demand Analysis

After the initial group has been included in the advisory process, every physician in the area should be identified and considered for affiliation. Physician supply and demand models should be determined. Several data sources might provide this information.

1. Visit Rate Model

Information may be collaborated from the National Health Interview Survey (NHIS) and the National Ambulatory Medical Care Survey (NAMCS). Visit rates are regionally adjusted to four census regions in the US. The model should reflect age, sex, income, and race composition of patients.

2. Productivity Rate Model

The average number of office visits per physician per week by primary care specialty should be estimated based on average productivity data from local physicians. The AMA Socioeconomic Survey and the Medical Group Management Association are also good sources to consult when estimating productivity. For example, in the South, family practice physicians averaged 5300 ambulatory visits per year, pediatricians averaged 4200 visits, and internal medicine physicians averaged 3100 visits. This model assumes that physicians are operating a full-time medical practice with average acuity levels of patients. All inpatient visits, nursing home visits, and services provided by mid-level practitioners should be excluded.

3. Physician Supply

A complete listing of physicians, usually found through any state or county agency which tracks licensed physicians practicing in the immediate service area as well as surrounding counties, should be obtained. The database should be reviewed carefully for accuracy and enhanced with the addition of primary and secondary office addresses as well as FTE complements. Physicians involved primarily in teaching and research should be eliminated from the database as should those primary care physicians for whom retirement is imminent.

Once the above data sources have been identified, the following calculations may be made to determine physician supply and predict patient demand:
- Estimated Visit Volume = Market Area Population × Visit Rate Model
- Physician Visit Potential = Physician Supply × Productivity Rate Model
- Unmet Visit Demand = Estimated Visit Volume − Physician Visit Potential
- Number of Physicians Needed = Unmet Visit Demand/Productivity Rate Model (The Sachs Group, 1995)

C. Physician Recruitment Plan

Upon completion of physician supply and demand analysis, a detailed physician recruitment plan should be compiled. This plan assesses the current status of physician coverage in defined market areas, determines the need for relationships with existing practitioners, and highlights the market areas with significant unmet patient demand requiring recruitment of new physicians. This instrument, a reference point for planning and management decisions, aids in the initial network formation as well as subsequent addition of new physicians. It should be specific enough to define a strategy for the recruitment necessary to meet the pre-determined goals of the affiliated organizations, yet flexible enough to adjust to significant changes in the market. One person annually revises the plan as the patient population changes, as managed care becomes more prevalent, or as competitors' strategies are realized.

Next, the existing physician productivity rate is compared with the goals of the IDS. This comparison will help define the estimated number of existing physician practices to be acquired in order to meet system goals. For example, if the goal of the system is to capture fifty percent of the patients in a defined population or geographic area, then approximately half of the physicians within that area or specialty should in some way affiliate with the network. This simplified goal assumes that the physicians in the defined area are operating at capacity or near the productivity rate model defined in the initial stages of the analysis. Any deficiencies or unmet patient demand will indicate growth potential; therefore, recruiting new physicians to the area will be necessary in meeting the goals of the system. The number of affiliations and new physicians necessary to meet the system goals should be calculated and designated into key areas. Recommendations for each planning zone will then be prioritized and time frame goals attached to each recommendation. Delineating the capital and human resource requirements for each recommendation allows the MSO or designated entity to develop the network budget accordingly.

D. Recruitment of Physicians

After defining the number of physicians necessary to meet network goals, the organization must identify which existing physicians should be potential acquisitions. Simply considering loyal physicians or heavy admitters may unjustly eliminate candidates who would enhance the network. A physician criteria worksheet should be developed to help with decision making. This worksheet should include data regarding the reputation and quality of the practitioners, utilization review and specific quality assurance indicators as well as geographic location data including strategic need for coverage, accessibility for patients, and office surroundings. The criteria should also include details regarding the operation of the practice, such as appointment hours, call responsibility, managed care orientation, and physician willingness for change. Profitability factors should be analyzed: revenue and expenses, assets, liabilities, equity, depreciation, outstanding loans, staff compensation, patient statistics including age, sex, and insurance, accounts receivable aging report, type of computer system available, and projection of capital requirements. The goals of the physician and his practice must be consistent with the goals of the organization. Also, the competitors' strategy and physician's relationship to the competitor must be a factor. Potential alternative strategies to purchasing the practice should be analyzed. The data on this physician criteria worksheet should be carefully obtained and analyzed by the organization before additional steps are taken to acquire the practice.

Once the organization has concluded the criteria analysis on existing practices in the community, administration may find an insufficient resource of physicians in a particular specialty or area of the network. Often the outlying areas or secondary markets will be underserved with physicians, causing patients seeking care to drive distances. These outlying physician practices, although not heavy admitters to the hospital, may be loyal referral sources to the IDS, either through the use of specialists, ancillary services or outpatient procedures. Therefore, recruitment of new physicians to this market may be necessary. In order to meet the long-term needs of the community, specific criteria must be considered.

The first step in the process of recruiting a new physician is to identify the needs and credentials that will adequately serve the population. Many third year residents look for employment in primary care and are eager for practice opportunities. Usually, turn key practices are most attractive for residents since little capital and no up-front buy-in costs are required. Also, most residents have minimal business skills or experience with operating a practice, so practice management services provided by the MSO will be the best option for these new physicians. In addition, foreign medical graduates are a good resource for placement in the underserved areas since quality foreign-trained physicians in US residency programs must practice in an underserved community in order to maintain work status in the United States. However, specific criteria must be met in order to qualify for these programs, so an attorney must interpret the most recent requirements from the Immigration and Naturalization Service.

Once a particular type has been identified, the organization must try to compile a qualified pool of candidates through advertisements in medical journals, physician magazines, opportunity listing services (either hard copies or Internet), and medical school newspapers. Less expensive means of advertising an opportunity within the system include contacting residency programs, participating in recruitment fairs, and word of mouth. Physicians already in the group practice may contact their residency chairman and ask for potential candidates, or newly hired residents may advise their peers of the opportunity.

If these efforts are unsuccessful or advertisements go unanswered, physician recruitment firms might assist with the search for a candidate. These firms are eager to work with organizations since most recruiters work on commission. Although the search may cost a substantial amount (approximately $20,000 per placement), such firms become necessary when an organization is unable to identify qualified candidates. Both retained or contingency firms will initiate the relationship with a contract, so again an attorney is necessary to ensure that the organization's best interests are protected. Early termination provisions, guarantee clauses, or reduction in fees for length of contract may be negotiated at the beginning. Both the recruitment firm and the organization must be committed to recruiting a qualified candidate to the system in order for the effort to be successful. The use of a firm does not eliminate work for the organization; it simply provides broader access to resources not readily available.

The interview process is an essential part of identifying the perfect candidate for the organization. It can also be time consuming and expensive if not done carefully. Once the curriculum vitae and letter of interest have been reviewed by the organization, an interview must be conducted. For local candidates, a personal interview is optimal in determining if the candidate is a good fit for the practice opportunity. The candidate will then be able to ask questions and equally determine if the opportunity will meet personal and professional needs. Issues such as call schedules, inpatient requirements and practice styles must be discussed at this meeting. Organization details such as history of the group, patient acuity level, and provider expectations should be reviewed. If the candidate preliminarily meets the needs of the MSO, a benefits sheet and sample employment agreement may be shared. This will provide an occasion for the candidate to carefully review these documents before proceeding with the process.

The next step is to invite the candidate for a site visit. These meetings work best in small groups and should include opportunities for the candidate to experience community restaurants, real estate options, and entertainment. Any special touches provided are often appreciated, such as bed and breakfast overnight stays, welcome baskets, and personal meetings with other group physicians. These site visits do provide an opportunity to wine and dine potential candidates, but more importantly, they test the appropriateness of a particular candidate.

Once a candidate has been identified as a potential match for the organization, credentials must be verified. Of course, references from the medical school and residency are necessary as are verification of licenses. A query of the National Practitioner Data Bank will ensure that no fraudulent or negligent activities have been reported. A release of information statement from the candidate, essential before a query may be performed, provides legal protection to both parties. Most medical attorneys will have access to this statement, which can be easily tailored to meet the organization's individual needs.

Assuming the process continues with the potential candidate, an offer should then be created. Offers may be made informally in person or by letter to accompany an employment agreement. As in any business negotiation, written offers preclude misunderstandings. The offer should include base salary, benefits paid by the organization as well as the out-of-pocket costs to the physician, term of agreement, bonus structure, minimum productivity requirements, office site location, moving allowance, and signing bonus, if any.

Base salary determination is often the most difficult figure to determine although several sources might assist inexperienced organizations in this task. For example, surveys by such groups as the Medical Group Management Association (MGMA), American Medical Association, the Hay Group, and Medical Economics help gauge physician compensation expectations. MGMA and the Hay Group specifically target salary expectations of physicians in the first through third years of practice, so they are good resources when recruiting medical residents. Often a combination of survey information and local salaries will determine the compensation necessary to recruit the best candidates. A compensation structure which incorporates increasing salary as the physician becomes more established with patients benefits both the organization and the individual. Finally, compensation beyond the predetermined salary in the form of a bonus will also create a win-win situation. With advanced planning, careful negotiations, and care in selecting the best match for the health system, the organization should be able to develop long term relationships with new physicians who will be able to meet the needs of the patients and community through the constant changes created by a managed care environment.

III. THE TRANSITION FROM PRIVATE PRACTICE TO THE MSO

The transition process should begin once the physician has signed the employment agreement and asset purchase agreement. This dynamic process is where network development blends with the operations of the practice sites being absorbed into the MSO. The MSO team must be very focused on the objective of moving the independent practice to a group practice. Nearly every aspect of the practice is structurally changed when it is transitioned to the MSO's methods of doing business: billing, accounts payable, accounts receivable, purchasing, information systems, banking services, human resources policies and procedures, benefits administration, payroll, facilities management, and practice management.

If the transition team is to incorporate many individual practices into the MSO, planning should concentrate on the following three criteria: medical specialty (family practice, internal medicine, pediatrics), the existing computer system in the practice, and the size and complexity of the practice.

In the early stages of the development of an MSO, the staff might incorporate many practices into the MSO within a short period of time. Since the MSO will have a monthly maximum absorption rate, the above criteria will create a reasonable time frame for accomplishing this task. First, all three medical specialties should be represented during the transition process. Blending the specialties helps to prevent physician groups perceiving they are being left till last and helps the transition team uncover any unique characteristics about each specialty. Experience teaches that blending large, medium and small practices together each month is also wise.

Additionally, each MSO needs to decide on a practice management information system to be used by all of the practices. Deciding which system to use and obtaining the necessary capital funding must precede the transition of any practices to the MSO. In today's environment, a primary care network made up of some 30 practice sites could easily cost between $750,000 and $1,000,000 for the practice management information system. Those practices that already have the system chosen by the MSO should be first in line for transition. The remaining practices will require more effort in purchasing the system, training the staff, converting existing data, and providing follow-up training. Surprisingly, many practices, some very large, have no computer system, thus no existing computer orientation on the part of the staff. Typically, these practices are transitioned last.

SUMMARY

In today's economy, health care providers, especially primary care physicians, seek new alternatives to partner with other providers in an effort to continue to provide quality, cost-effective care in an extremely complex environment. The Management Services Organization affords a means for the primary care physician to maintain a degree of professional autonomy while gaining access to resources and information provided within the shared system of the MSO. With vigilant planning, analysis, and strategic collaboration of health administrators and physicians, the MSO may be the mechanism with which the entire health care system will benefit.

REFERENCES

Johnson, B.A. (1995). The legal issues of integrated delivery systems. *Medical Group Management Journal, 42(1):* 16-18, 20, 22.

McManis, G. L., Pavia, L., Ackerman, F. K., and Connelly, I. L. (1995). Integration, opportunities and issues for medical group practices. *Medical Group Management Journal, 42(6):* 42, 44, 46.

Neiderman, G. A., and Johnson, B. A. (1994). Integrated provider networks - a primer. *Medical Group Management Journal, 41(6):* 62-64, 66, 68.

21.
NURSING HOME ORGANIZATION AND OPERATIONS

David R. Graber, *Medical University of South Carolina, Charleston, SC*

David M. Ward, *Medical University of South Carolina, Charleston, SC*

This chapter will provide an overview of the U.S. nursing home industry. The historical development of the modern nursing home will be reviewed along with current demographic information concerning both facilities and patients. Financing and regulatory requirements will be explained to help guide students, administrators and policy makers through the complexities of the system. The goal of this chapter is to provide a basic introduction to the nursing home industry.

I. BACKGROUND

Nursing homes have traditionally been the principal provider of extended long-term care for the elderly. Long-term care has been defined as "the provision of diagnostic, preventive, therapeutic, and supportive services to patients of all ages with a severe chronic disease or disability involving substantial functional impairment" (Somers, 1987). Fundamentally, long-term care is oriented toward assisting people who have substantial functional impairment. According to the 1989 National Long-Term Care survey 22.6% of the population 65 and over needed assistance for 90 days or more with one or more activities of daily living (ADLs), self-care activities vital for maintaining independence (Malone-Rising, 1994). In addition, since infirmity increases with age (Birenbaum, 1993) and the oldest-old (those over the age of 85) are the fastest growing portion of the elderly population (Malone-Rising, 1994; Aiken, et al., 1985) the need for nursing home care and alternative long-term care will grow in the coming years.

This assistance can take many forms and can be provided in many different settings. Data from the 1987 National Medical Expenditure Survey reveals that the majority (70%) of the elderly in need of assistance receive help from family and friends and another 10% get help through formal homecare agencies (Birenbaum, 1993). Nursing facilities are another form of long-term care. Approximately five percent of the elderly in the United States live in nursing facilities (Birenbaum, 1993). Table 1 presents the number and proportion of elderly residing in nursing homes by age, category, and gender.

Table 1- Number and Proportion of Elderly Residing in Nursing Homes by Age Bracket and Gender

	Number of Elderly in Nursing Facilities			Percent of Elderly in Nursing Facilities		
	1963	1973	1985	1963	1973	1985
All Ages	445,600	961,500	1,318,300	2.5	4.5	4.6
65 - 74 Years Old	89,600	163,100	212,100	0.8	1.2	1.3
75 - 84 Years Old	207,200	384,900	509,000	4.0	5.8	5.8
85 and over	148,700	413,600	597,300	14.8	25.7	22.0
Gender						
Male	141,000	265,700	334,400	1.8	3.0	2.9
Female	304,500	695,800	983,900	3.1	5.5	5.8

Source: National Center for Health Statistics. Health, United States, 1994. Hyattsville, Maryland: Public Health Service. 1994.

As can be seen in Table 1, both the number and the proportion of all elderly residing in nursing homes have increased since 1963. The most significant growth has taken place in the 85 and over age group which increased from just under 150,000 residents in 1963 to just under 600,000 residents in 1985. Significantly, the proportion of all elderly 85 and over also increased from 14.8% in 1963 to 22.0% in 1985. Table 1 illustrates the importance of distinguishing amongst the different age brackets within the elderly population. Nursing homes have served and continue to serve primarily the very old.

While the overall percentage presented in Table 1 may appear somewhat low, these figures represent the proportion of the elderly in a nursing facility at any given time. Arnold Birenbaum estimates that over half of all people who survive to age 65 will at some point in their lifetime enter a nursing home (1993). In addition, a study by Kemper and Murtaugh estimated that one out of every eleven Americans who turned 65 in 1990 will spend five years in a nursing facility (1991). So while only 5% of the elderly population may be in a nursing facility at any one point, many, if not most, will spend some time as nursing home residents.

A. Overview of the U.S. Nursing Home Industry

The nursing home industry can be traced back to the late Nineteenth and early Twentieth centuries. At that time, five types of facilities existed: county poorhouses,

Table 2- Distribution of Nursing Home Residents by Selected Facility and Resident
Characteristics: 1964, 1973-74, 1977, and 1985

Facility Characteristics	Percent of Residents			
	1964	1973-74	1977	1985
Ownership:				
Proprietary	60.2	69.8	68.2	68.7
Nonprofit and Government	39.8	30.2	31.8	31.3
Bed Size:				
Less than 50 beds	—	15.2	12.9	8.9
50-99 beds	—	34.1	30.5	27.6
100-199 beds	—	35.6	38.8	43.2
200 beds or more	—	15.1	17.9	20.2
Resident Characteristics				
Age:				
Under 65 years	12.0	10.6	13.6	11.6
65-74 years	18.9	15.0	16.2	14.2
75-84 years	41.7	35.5	35.7	34.1
85 years and over	27.5	38.8	34.5	40.0
Sex:				
Male	35.0	29.1	28.8	28.4
Female	65.0	70.9	71.2	71.6

Adapted from Health Care Financing Administration, "Recent Trends in Medicaid Expenditures." Health Care Financing Review.
(Annual Supplement 1992):Table 138.

state mental hospitals, voluntary homes for the aged, early proprietary boarding houses, and hospital affiliated nursing homes (Waldman, 1985). The first steady source of
income for this industry came in 1935 with the passage of the Old Age and Survivors
Insurance and the Old Age Assistance programs (Harrington and Swan, 1985). The
enactment of Medicaid and Medicare in 1965 brought with it a dramatic growth in the
supply of nursing home beds (Harrington and Swan, 1985; Aiken, et al., 1985).
Between 1963 and 1980, the number of nursing home beds grew by 197% (Harrington
and Swan, 1985).

The type of nursing facilities operating in the United States has been fairly constant over time. Table 2 shows the percent of nursing home residents by selected resident and facility characteristics. In 1985, 68.7% of nursing home beds were in proprietary facilities while 31.3% of the beds were in nonprofit or governmental facilities
(HCFA, 1992). It is important to note, though, that the proprietary facilities represent
77% of the total number of facilities (Lloyd and Greenspan, 1985). The discrepancy
between the mix of beds and number of facilities exists because nonprofit and governmental facilities tend to be larger (Lloyd and Greenspan, 1985).

Table 2 shows that the largest proportion of residents were in facilities that ranged
from 100 to 199 beds. There has, however, been a slight trend toward larger facilities.
The gender mix of nursing home residents has been constant over time; roughly 70%
of all residents are female. Table 2 also reveals the aging of the nursing home popula-

tion in recent years. In 1964, the oldest-old (85 and over) represented only 27% of all nursing home residents. By 1985, this group made up 40%.

From 1976 to 1991 the number of nursing facilities fell by 1,347 (an 8% reduction) while the total number of available beds increased by 260,426 (a 20% increase). The only areas of the country that had an increase in the number of facilities between 1976 and 1991 were the three Southern regions (South Atlantic, East South Central and West South Central). Although given the dramatic growth (as high as 50%) in the number of beds within the three Southern regions, the increase in facilities within these regions was relatively small.

The growth in the number of nursing home beds has not kept pace with the overall growth in the population over the age of 85. The beds per 1,000 people over age 85 has fallen from 685 in 1976 to 495 in 1991. Given nursing home occupancy rates as high as 96% in a number of states, some researchers and policy makers have begun to look more closely at the supply of nursing home beds. The reduction in the supply of nursing home beds per 1,000 people and high occupancy rates does not, in and of itself, imply a shortage of beds. One must consider both the growth of non-institutionalized care and the fact that improved health status may account for an actual reduction in demand.

When looking at the demand for nursing home beds, one must assess the prevalence of functional disability in the entire elderly population. In a 1993 study by Manton, Corder and Stallard, data from the National Long-Term Care Survey (NLTCS) was used to determine the prevalence of disability in persons age 65 and over living in the community and in nursing facilities. The authors defined disability as "the inability to perform an Activities of Daily Living (ADL) or an Instrumental Activities of Daily Living (IADL) without assistance for 90 or more days." The study found that "the total prevalence of U.S. chronically disabled, community-dwelling, and institutionalized elderly populations declined from 1984 to 1989, overall, for each of three age strata

The trend toward larger facilities can be seen in Table 3 which shows the number of nursing facilities, the number of beds, and the number of beds per 1,000 resident population 85 years of age and over (by geographic region).

Table 3- Nursing Homes, Beds, and Beds per 1,000 by Geographic Region

	Nursing Homes		Beds		Beds per 1,000	
	1976	1991	1976	1991	1976	1991
United States	16,091	14,744	1,298,968	1,559,394	685	495
New England	1,435	1,157	93,418	108,194	732	550
Middle Atlantic	1,607	1,497	178,323	220,241	527	424
East North Central	3,184	3.029	288,352	331,278	807	602
West North Central	2,185	2,108	163,231	187,639	803	610
South Atlantic	1,749	1,883	140,161	210,534	531	393
East South Central	867	890	65,037	93,932	562	491
West South Central	1,758	1,935	157,492	199,056	914	666
Mountain	630	611	47,662	59,113	681	423
Pacific	2,676	1,634	165,292	149,407	669	361

Source: National Center for Health Statistics. Health, United States, 1994. Hyattsville, Maryland: Public Health Service. 1994.

and after mortality adjustment" (Manton, Corder and Stallard, 1993). However, the decline was not consistent across levels of disability. The percentage of elders with three or four ADL deficits actually increased over the five year period. In addition, the decrease in disability does not compensate for the overall growth in the elderly population over the same five year period (Malone-Rising, 1994).

A 1992 study by Zedlewski and McBride used dynamic microsimulation techniques to project the elderly population's characteristics, incomes, and long-term care needs through the year 2030. The simulations accounted for projected changes in demographic risk factors (fertility history, living arrangements, and age distribution) as well as changes in health status (number of elderly living in the community with ADL limitations). According to researchers, the number of elderly requiring nursing home care will increase from 1.8 million in 1990 to approximately 3-3.4 million in 2010 and 4.3-5.3 million in 2030. As the authors point out, "the need for nursing home care could nearly triple from 1990 to 2030, despite the fact that the elderly population will only increase by 125 percent over the same period" (Zedlewski and McBride, 1992). The study predicts that the proportion of elderly requiring nursing home care will expand most dramatically between 1990 and 2010 because the proportion of the elderly who are very old, unmarried, and with health limitations will increase faster during this period (Zedlewski and McBride, 1992).

Dramatic growth in non-institutional care combined with functional improvements in the elderly population allows states to constrict the growth of nursing home beds. If state resources for the non-institutional health care needs of the elderly become increasingly scarce and the number of elderly in need of nursing home care grows, the issue of an adequate supply of nursing home beds will become critical.

Regardless of the relative supply beds, today's nursing homes provide a level of care significantly higher than that provided ten or fifteen years ago. Table 4 shows the 1977 and 1985 percentages of nursing home residents who need some level of assistance with the various activities of daily living.

Table 4- Percent of Nursing Home Residents Requiring Assistance with ADLs, 1977 and 1985

	Percent of Residents	
	1977	1985
Required assistance with:		
Dressing	69.4	75.4
Toileting	52.5	60.9
Mobility	66.1	70.7
Continence	45.3	51.9
Eating	32.6	39.3

Source: National Center for Health Statistics. Health, United States, 1994. Hyattsville, Maryland: Public Health Service. 1994.

Nursing homes are clearly caring for a population that is both older and less independent. There is also evidence on the state level that nursing homes have continued the trend of caring for an increasingly dependent population (Schultz, Ward, and Knickman, 1994).

II. NURSING HOME ORGANIZATION AND MANAGEMENT

Although there is great variety in the nursing home industry, most nursing homes are remarkably similar in organizational structure. The formal head of a facility is the administrator. Under the administrator the organizational chart includes the department heads of nursing, dietary, housekeeping and maintenance, social services, activities, the business office, medical records, and in many facilities, rehabilitation. The composition and size of these departments can vary substantially depending on such factors as the size of the facility and the level of care provided. In a small facility, some of the departments may have only one employed member (e.g., social services, activities, medical records). An independent facility may have a rather large business office to carry out payroll functions, accounting duties, and billing while a chain-owned facility will usually carry out most business functions at a central location.

A. Nursing and Rehabilitation

The *raison d'être* of the nursing home—to provide nursing care—is performed by the nursing department, the largest department in almost every facility. Directed by a Director of Nursing (D.O.N.), it is staffed by charge nurses (or shift supervisors), registered nurses (RNs), licensed vocational nurses (LVNs), and certified nursing assistants (CNAs). In some states, these titles or acronyms vary (e.g., licensed practical nurse-LPN).

The responsibilities of the D.O.N. are considerable; often the individual in this position possesses informal authority comparable to or greater than the administrator. Because nursing homes are continually staffed, the D.O.N. interacts with and directs three shifts. The D.O.N. must assure that the facility is always staffed with nursing personnel at regulated levels. Attracting and retaining qualified nursing personnel can be difficult, as nursing home staff are not typically paid at comparable levels to nursing staff in hospitals or ambulatory care clinics.

Nursing staff must assess, develop, and implement a comprehensive plan of care for each resident. In addition, they must administer multiple medications several times a day to each resident. Virtually every task must be documented to satisfy regulatory agencies and to substantiate that adequate care is being provided.

The job of the nursing assistant demands physical vitality for moving and repositioning, transferring, bathing, and dressing residents. Assisting residents who are unable to feed themselves also requires considerable time. Because of the nursing staff's close interactions with residents and their families, social skills and sensitivity are useful, important qualities. Poor human relations skills of a few nursing home staff will often lead to complaints by upset residents and families, unannounced inspections, and even lawsuits.

The two current licensure categories of nursing homes are skilled nursing facilities (SNF) that typically serve both custodial care and highly disabled residents and nursing facilities (NF) that primarily provide custodial care. The SNF that serves many medically unstable residents and has a high Medicare census may have a large rehabilitation department. Rehabilitation services may also be contracted out, or the department will primarily consist of individuals not employed by the facility. On the other hand, resident care needs might not warrant a rehabilitation department in a Nursing Facility (NF).

B. Management Challenges

Nursing home management is a unique experience with its own challenges and rewards. A nursing home administrator is paid considerably less than a hospital administrator; however, salaries for good administrators are not inconsiderable. Within the facility, a nursing home administrator usually holds more power and freedom to effect change than does a hospital CEO, whose authority is counterbalanced by the medical staff and other high-level administrators. Because of negative publicity about nursing homes, the position is not highly regarded outside of the work setting. The nursing home administrator (and other staff) may often feel their work is unappreciated.

Unlike the hospital setting, no cadre of management personnel in nursing homes represents financial and operational imperatives of the organization. Typically, one individual—the administrator—does this. He or she must be a leader to staff members whose orientations, concerns, and professional cultures are focused on patient care issues. The more successful nursing home administrators are good communicators and listeners; they secure support from key department heads, particularly nursing managers. The Director of Nursing who attends Board meetings, is privy to financial statements, and has input into how financial goals are achieved will be far more likely to support the administrator than one who primarily receives directives.

In chain operations, nursing home staff have historically been expected to implement directives and new programs emanating from the "home office." To an even greater degree, staff members and managers have become focused on regulatory compliance due to pervasive nursing home regulation. Rapid change in regulation and government programs is said to have "tired" front-line health workers (Filipczak, 1994). These external demands may leave little remaining energy and enthusiasm for internal programs to improve the quality of residents' lives. Administrators who expect staff to implement new programs must watch the timing and pace of management changes; they must also successfully communicate their values and vision.

When asked to name the most important element of running a good facility, a highly successful Idaho nursing home administrator stated simply, "Keep the families happy." Family members often visit daily and may intimately know the staff and the facility. The nursing home resident may not return to the community, but the family member does—every day. Inadequate care, staff insensitivity, and other facility weaknesses will inevitably be shared in the community. Even in the best-run nursing homes, the administrator and D.O.N. must often attend, with surprising effort, to issues raised by family members. Generally, a family member has already unsuccessfully sought to resolve these problems with line staff before contacting the administrator. However, if family members' requests are neglected or regularly denied, the facility will soon receive unannounced inspections by the state health department or ombudsman's office. An attorney may even pursue a family's concerns a fortiori.

Due to the relatively small size of most nursing homes, administrators know in some depth their department's operations and staff. Limited managerial and business staff means that the administrator must personally carry out, rather than delegate, a number of tasks. In times of staff shortages, the administrator must do the unexpected, including (in the experience of one of the authors) washing dirty linen, admitting patients, and assisting with activities. If the evening and night shift staff are to feel that management is interested in their concerns and performance, the administrator must also be prepared to come in at unusual hours.

III. QUALITY OF CARE

Quality is an elusive entity, generally defined in terms of the interaction of structural and process components to produce outcomes (Donabedian, 1966). Structure refers to established or relatively stable features of a facility such as the physical plant, organizational form, staffing ratios, policies and procedures, and patient mix. Process refers to the procedures and actions carried out by the providers of care: delivering treatments, passing medications, using restraints, documenting services. Outcomes refer to the changes in health status or mortality which are influenced by antecedent care.

Studies carried out in the 1970s and '80s sought to determine what types of facilities provided the best care. Typically, violations or deficiencies received on the annual survey were employed as the dependent variables and quality measures. Complaints and composite measures were also employed in several studies as quality measures. Defending any of these measures as pristine, objective indicators of quality is difficult. Survey deficiency measures have been employed, obviously due to their easy accessibility. Nursing home quality assurance and inspections have traditionally focused on structure and process measures (Lesage and Barhyte, 1989; Peters, 1989); however, there is a movement toward measuring outcomes (Lohr, 1988; Kane, 1990). The OBRA regulations were designed to improve quality of care and focus on resident outcomes in nursing homes, but their actual impact remains to be evaluated.

Although not conclusive, using the above-mentioned quality indicators, the results of most studies indicate that non-profit facilities provide higher quality care than for-profit facilities (Graber and Mutran, 1995; Hawes and Phillips, 1986). Chain affiliation (as compared to independent facilities) has not been identified as being associated with poor quality; however, considerable variance in quality among chains has been noted (Consumer Reports, 1995; Hawes and Phillips, 1986). Larger facilities have also received more deficiencies (Graber and Mutran, 1995; Nyman, 1988; Riportella-Muller and Schlesinger, 1982), possibly due to survey procedures: more patients assessed in larger facilities, more records studied, and more resident interviews carried out. Thus, the probability of finding problems increases.

Nursing homes are characterized by a total absence of physicians in day-to-day operations: patient care is largely carried out by nursing assistants and licensed vocational nurses (LVNs). The presence of RNs, who have more comprehensive training in caring for highly unstable patients, varies widely. The nursing home may seek to attenuate the impact of increased admissions and patient severity through hiring additional staff or increasing RN coverage. In 1977, Linn and colleagues found more RN hours associated with an increase in the likelihood of resident survival, discharge, and improved function. Spector and Takada (1991) found a stable RN staff associated with improvements in resident functioning. Graber and Mutran (1995) found an interaction of RN staffing and admission rate to be negatively related to violations. Thus, there is some evidence that nursing home quality may be improved through higher levels of RN staff.

Patient information taken from the Minimum Data Set (MDS) assessment form is being used as the foundation for the development of quality indicators. Current research conducted at the University of Wisconsin is directed towards developing patient and facility-level quality indicators to be used for nursing home surveys and monitoring (Zimmerman et al., 1994). For example, health departments may soon have online, up-to-date data on a variety of facility-level indicators such as the number of patients in the facility with decubitus ulcers (pressure sores) or who are receiving psychotropic drugs, the number of resident falls, and the proportion of residents with recent declines in functioning. Similar patient-level indicators will enable facility and regulate oversight of individual patients.

Computerized programs that automatically identify facility problems should be operational in the early 2000s; they will significantly reduce the element of chance in facility surveys. Review of resident outcomes, such as acute illnesses and mortality, in relation to facility structural indicators and processes of care will be improved substantially. Indicator analysis may also be used by facility administrators for quality improvement and by consumer groups in monitoring and rating facilities.

IV. FINANCING OF THE U.S. NURSING HOME INDUSTRY

Nursing facilities are clearly a significant component of long-term care in the United States. Not only do many elderly depend on them, but the financial resources devoted to them also prove their significance to the overall system. In 1993, total national expenditures on nursing facilities was $69.6 billion (HCFA, 1994).

As described in the chapter by Barbara Holt, the financing of nursing home care in the United States is dominated by two sources: out-of-pocket payments by individual consumers and state-run Medicaid programs. Of the $69.6 billion in national expenditures on nursing home care, 33% is paid for with private finances and 52% is financed through state-run Medicaid programs (HCFA, 1994). The $35.9 billion in Medicaid payments for nursing homes represent 33% of all Medicaid expenditures. This percentage varies from state to state from a low of 22% in Kentucky and Michigan to a high of 56% in Connecticut. In most states, Medicaid expenditures for nursing homes exceed Medicaid expenditures for inpatient hospital care (HCFA, 1994).

While many have called for increasing the role of private health insurance in the financing of nursing facilities (Zedlewski and McBride, 1992; Knickman, 1987; Mechanic, 1987; Brecher and Knickman, 1985), as of 1993, private health insurance paid for only 2.5% of national expenditures on nursing home care (HCFA, 1994). This percentage has remained relatively unchanged since 1984. Prior to 1984, private health insurance funded less than 1% of nursing home expenditures.

Much like private health insurance, the role of Medicare has remained small over the last two decades. Current Medicare regulations limit the reimbursement of nursing homes to patient stays that immediately follow discharge from a hospital and that focus on rehabilitation. The strict limitations on funding has kept the Medicare share of total expenditures on nursing home care below 8.8% (HCFA, 1992).

The current financing system for nursing home care has resulted in a system in which an individual's stay is either paid for by the consumer, by state-run Medicaid programs, or by a combination of the two (referred to as "spend-down"). Consumer spend-down occurs when the individual enters the nursing facility as a private pay patient and essentially uses all the financial resources before becoming eligible for

Medicaid. Since the eligibility criteria for Medicaid is based on an individual's financial resources, consumers appear impoverished by their stays in nursing facilities. Various studies have estimated that half or more of all nursing home patients on Medicaid were private pay until they spent down to poverty (Branch et al., 1988; DHHS, 1987). However, several studies indicate a smaller rate of impoverishment among nursing home residents (Spence and Wiener, 1990; Burwell, Adams and Meiners, 1990; Liu and Manton, 1989). A 1985 study by Thomas Rice estimated that 18.2% of initial private pay patients spent down to Medicaid eligibility. Rice correctly emphasizes that 36% of all patients began as Medicaid eligible. He points out that "this indicates that many elderly either spend-down when they are still in the community, or have done so during previous nursing-home stays" (Rice, 1989). Regardless of which analysis on consumer spend-down is accurate, the fact remains that over 84% of all expenditures on nursing home care are either paid for directly by the consumer or by state-run Medicaid programs on behalf of consumers who do not have the financial resources to pay.

A. Medicaid Reimbursement Systems

Every state has its own unique Medicaid reimbursement system with wide variation in both their methods and the resulting rates (Swan, 1993). The reimbursement systems can be grouped into two broad categories: retrospective systems and prospective systems. Retrospective payment systems ultimately reimburse the nursing facility all allowable costs of care. The manner in which this happens may vary from state to state, but the end is the same—full reimbursement of allowable costs. Prospective payment systems, on the other hand, set reimbursement rates in advance. Payments are based on the rates rather than the costs incurred by the nursing facility. In a prospective payment system, rates are often based on historical costs (a base year) and trended forward for inflation. Cohen and Dubay (1990) correctly point out that "prospective reimbursement systems can resemble retrospective systems if the base from which rates are determined is updated yearly." Prospective reimbursement is the most common form of Medicaid payment system, and most include payment ceilings to provide cost containment incentives (Buchanan, 1992).

Since the mid 1980s, states (as well as HCFA) have begun studying payment systems linked to the level of care provided. These systems, typically called case-mix systems, function in a similar manner to the DRG systems used by Medicare to reimburse hospitals. Residents are grouped into different reimbursement categories based on assessments of their functional status. Facilities that care for residents who require a higher level of care are reimbursed at a higher rate than facilities with residents who require lower levels of care. The rationale behind case-mix systems is straightforward. Under systems that do not tie payment levels to the functional status of residents, facility administrators have an incentive to admit residents who require the least amount of care. Under case-mix systems the incentive is reversed so that facility administrators are financially encouraged to admit residents in need of a higher level of care. The incentive to admit heavy care residents was identified in a study of the New York State case-mix system in which researchers found that in the five-year period after the introduction of a case-mix system, the statewide case-mix index (a measure of resident functional status and resource consumption) increased by 9% (Schultz, Ward and Knickman, 1994).

Since out-of-pocket payments from residents are usually greater than Medicaid reimbursement rates (Harrington, Swan and Grant, 1988) one might assume that nursing home administrators give preference to residents paying with private funds. Some theorize that nursing homes will maximize the number of private pay residents and fill the remaining beds with Medicaid beneficiaries (Scanlon, 1980). Given the inherent incentive to favor private pay residents over Medicaid residents, it is encouraging to note that in a 1990 survey of state Medicaid programs, Buchanan found that "the use of case mix systems typically increased the access that Medicaid recipients with heavy care needs had to nursing facilities" (1992).

V. NURSING HOME REGULATION AND MONITORING

A. Inspections

The nursing home industry has been highly regulated for many years. State inspection efforts have generally followed a deterrence model (Hawkins and Thomas, 1984) characterized by punishment of wrongdoing, adversarial relationships, and frequent recourse to legal proceedings. Counseling or assistive educational strategies by the inspecting agency are discouraged. In this climate, conformity to rules is more important to nursing home survival than technical proficiency (Scott, 1983) or internal quality improvement approaches. In fact, internal improvement efforts and innovation may be subtly or overtly discouraged by the regulations (Kane and Wilson, 1993). Similarly, a widespread negative public perception of nursing homes provides a strong disincentive to state health departments to moderate or modify punitive inspection processes.

In most states, annual inspections to assure compliance with Medicare and Medicaid certification standards are carried out by a certification branch of the state health department. The annual survey in a given facility generally identifies a number of deficiencies or unmet standards.

Facilities which fare poorly on annual surveys receive follow-up surveys. On the follow-up survey, the inspecting agency may issue fines for violations and may revoke a facility's license, although this is rare.

B. Complaints

In most states, nursing facilities are required to post a placard listing a telephone number for reporting complaints. Depending on severity, complaints may prompt an unannounced inspection. After the inspection, deficiencies and fines may be issued to the facility found culpable in regard to the reported complaint.

Another monitoring mechanism is the long-term care ombudsman program. In many states an ombudsman will periodically visit nursing homes, talk to staff and patients, and elicit concerns and complaints. Due to law requirements, the phone numbers of the ombudsman's offices are often posted in the facilities. A reported complaint may prompt an investigation from the ombudsman's office or be turned over to the state health department for investigation.

C. Implementation of the OBRA Survey

In 1986, HCFA directed nursing facility surveyors to de-emphasize compliance with structural measures of quality of care and to focus on evaluating patient care outcomes. This directive was an initial step towards more comprehensive reform of the annual survey process, which assesses facility compliance with the requirements for participation in the Medicare and Medicaid programs. The new survey process is a result of regulatory changes in requirements for participation, first proposed by HCFA in October 1987, and to Congressional mandates for nursing home reform in the Omnibus Budget Reconciliation Act of 1987 (OBRA).

A number of key areas of the OBRA survey represent significant modifications of the previous survey process:

- A greater emphasis on resident rights and on the promotion of resident autonomy.
- Use of a Uniform Minimum Data Set (UMDS) as a nationwide resident assessment instrument. The UMDS allows surveyors to examine how facilities assess patient needs and the extent to which facilities achieve appropriate outcomes based on those needs.
- An emphasis on the substantial reduction of restraint and psychotropic medications use.
- A review of the physical environment focusing on the "fit" between the environment and the residents' needs and residents maintaining independence and competence.
- More rigorous national standards for nurse assistant training programs.

Transition to the OBRA survey requirements has had a number of positive effects.

The proportion of restrained nursing home residents dropped from about 40% in 1988 to 20% in 1994 (Schoeneman and Graber, 1995). In Minnesota, antipsychotic drug use declined by one-third after the OBRA survey took effect (Garrard et al., 1995). The Minimum Data Set (MDS) assessment form, introduced through the OBRA legislation, is now used in nursing homes (and by inspectors) to track the care and condition of residents.

The OBRA survey has encouraged an increasing emphasis on outcomes, but the nature of health department/nursing home interactions and survey enforcement remains largely unchanged. Computerized monitoring of facility nursing care will provide regulators with a powerful tool for nursing home oversight. On the other hand, the facility monitoring function may in time evolve to be a more cooperative process, with exemplary operators rewarded for achieving patient care and outcome objectives.

In the late 1900s, Congressional budget discussions considered the conversion of Medicaid into block grants to the states. Devolution of programmatic and regulatory authority to the states could have extensive impact on nursing home regulation. Of particular concern is whether the 1987 Nursing Home Reform Act provisions would be continued by the states. Increased training for nursing home aides, restraint and psychotropic drug use controls, patient assessment by nursing staff, patient autonomy policies, and bed transfer policies are just a few areas that may be weakened or abandoned by the states under a block grant program.

D. Consumer Groups and Regulatory Reform

Health care consumerism was spawned during the tumultuous decade of the 1960s. A central criticism of health care providers during that time was that they were not responsive to community needs (Arnold, 1994). This criticism could be directed at the nursing home industry for failing to assess consumer wants and needs. Nevertheless, the increased expression of consumer assertiveness in American culture positions the patient and family member in a key decision-making role (Paul and Wong, 1994). In the last decade, consumer groups have significantly influenced new regulations and nursing home reform. The National Citizens' Coalition for Nursing Home Reform and similar state-level organizations have emerged as formidable counterweights to nursing home lobbies. The strong emphasis in the OBRA survey on the reduction of physical restraints and psychotropic drugs is due in part to their activities. Consumerism and the growth of citizen "watchdog" groups will continue to exert pressure on nursing home managers to provide quality care and be attentive to the needs of patients and family members.

VI. NURSING HOMES AND THE FUTURE

The distribution and mix of elderly health services in the next century will certainly vary from that of today. Through the first decade of the twenty-first century, nursing home bed demand should increase. From 2010 to 2020, the small Depression-era cohort will be reaching 80 years of age. During this period, the moderate population growth of ages 80 and older, if accompanied by increases in community care and assisted living programs, should attenuate the need for major increases in nursing home beds. However, by 2030, an elderly population of more than double the current population will demand marked growth in health services including nursing home care. The ultimate size of these elderly cohorts is not certain, and will be dependent on such factors as lifestyle changes, medical care advances, and immigration patterns.

Since nursing homes may be increasingly pushed to provide two distinct levels of care, two classes of facilities may emerge. Subacute facilities will proliferate due to their clear savings over hospital-based care. More nursing homes will care for head injury, post-surgical, stroke rehabilitation, cancer, and AIDS patients. Adequate case-mix reimbursement systems developed for Medicare or Medicaid would also spur the growth of high acuity nursing homes.

The ubiquitous custodial care nursing home will come under increasing competition from home and assisted-living alternative models of care, as elaborated in the chapter by Holt on community-based long term care.

Nursing home regulations and consumer oversight should both increase. Satisfying the regulators and caring for sicker, less stable patients should make nursing home management even more challenging. A growth toward higher levels of care requires that managers be capable of providing such care to health providers, insurers, and the public—not a simple task, considering the negative image of nursing homes. If states are given the freedom to monitor nursing homes (with minimal federal oversight), highly uneven quality of care could result. Cuts in Medicaid funding could also make it difficult for the nursing home industry to fulfill society's expectations.

For the higher-level facilities, nursing home managers will be expected to possess a greater knowledge of medicine and more sophisticated modalities of care. Recruitment and retention of well-trained staff will be even more critical. Managers of facilities with fewer disabled residents will need to improve facility atmosphere and care to compete with increasingly attractive alternative models. A broader spectrum of residential options and programs in the coming years should make the long-term care market more interesting and also provide more appropriate individual care options for our elderly.

REFERENCES

Aiken, L. H., Mezey, M. D., Lynaugh, J. E., and Buck, C. R. (1985). Teaching nursing homes: prospects for improving long-term care. *Journal of the American Geriatrics Society, 33*(suppl 2): 196-201.

Arnold, A. (1994). The "big bang" theory of competition in health care. In Cooper P, ed. *Health Care Marketing: A Foundation for Managed Quality*. Aspen Publishers, Gaithersburg, MD.

Birenbaum, A. (1993). *Putting Health Care on the National Agenda*. Praeger, Westport, CT .

Branch, L. G, Friedman, D., Cohen, M., et al. (1988). Impoverishing the elderly. *Gerontologist, 28*(suppl 4): 648-652.

Brecher, C., Knickman, J. (1985). A reconsideration of long-term-care policy. *Journal of Health Politics, Policy & Law, 10*(suppl 2): 245-273.

Buchanan, R. J. (1992). Medicaid payment policies for nursing home care: case mix, access, and heavy care. *The Journal of Health Administration Education, 10*(suppl 4): 623-648.

Burwell, B. O., Adams, E. K., and Meiners, M. R. (1990). Spend-Down of assets before medicaid eligibility among elderly nursing-home recipients in Michigan. *Medical Care, 28*(suppl 4): 349-362.

Cohen, J. W., Dubay, L. C. (1990). The effects of medicaid reimbursement method and ownership on nursing home costs, case mix, and staffing. *Inquiry, 27*(suppl 2): 183-200.

Consumer Reports. (1995). In search of the right home. *August*: 519-527.

Department of Health and Human Services (DHHS). (1987). *Report of the Task Force on Long-Term Health Care Policies*. U.S. Government Printing Office, Washington, DC.

Donabedian, A. (1966). Evaluating the quality of medical care. *Milbank Memorial Fund Quarterly, 44*: 166-206.

Filipczak, B. (1994). Weathering change - enough already. *Training, September*: 23-29.

Garrard, J., Chen, V., and Dowd, B. (1995). The impact of the 1987 federal regulations on the use of psychotropic drugs in Minnesota nursing homes. *Am J Public Health, 85*:6.

Graber, D., and Mutran, B. (1995). The influence of nursing home characteristics on health survey violations. *Carolina Health Services Review, 3*.

Harrington, C., and Swan, J. J. (1985). Institutional long-term care services. In: Harrington et al .

Harrington, C., Swan, J. H., and Grant, L. (1989). State medicaid reimbursement for ICF-MR facilities in the 1978-1986 period. *Mental Retardation, 27*(6): 353-67.

Hawes, C., and Phillips, C. (1986). The changing structure of the nursing home industry and the impact of ownership on quality, cost, and access. In: Gray, B., ed. *For-Profit Enterprise in Health Care*. National Academy Press, 492-541.

Hawkins, K., and Thomas, J. M. (1984). *Enforcing Regulation*. Clarendon Press, Oxford.

Health Care Financing Administration (HCFA). (1992). Recent trends in medicaid expenditures. *Health Care Financing Review, Annual Supplement*.

Kane, R. L. (1990). Rethinking long-term care. *J Am Geriatr Soc, 38*: 704.

Kane, R. A., and Wilson K. B. (1993). *Assisted Living in the United States: a New Paradigm for Residential Care for Frail Older Persons*. American Association of Retired Persons, Washington, DC.

Kemper, P., and Murtaugh, C. M. (1991). Lifetime use of nursing home care. *New England Journal of Medicine, 324*(suppl 9).

Knickman, J. (1987). Insurance against impoverishment: a new policy for long-term care. *New York Affairs, Winter*: 96-107.

Lesage, J., and Barhyte, D. Y. (1989). *Nursing Quality Assurance in Long-term Care*. Aspen Publishers, Rockville, MD.

Linn, M. W., Gurel, L., and Linn, B. S. (1977). Patient outcome as a measure of quality of nursing home care. *Am J Public Health, 67*: 337-344.

Liu, K., Manton, K. (1989). The effect of nursing home use on medicaid eligibility. *Gerontologist, 29*(suppl 1): 59-66.

Lloyd, S., Greenspan, N. T. (1985). Nursing homes, home health services, and adult day care. In: Vogel, R. J., Palmer, H. C., eds. *Long-Term Care: Perspectives from Research and Demonstrations*. Aspen, Rockville, MD.

Lohr, K. N. (1988). Outcome measurement: concepts and questions. *Inquiry, 25*: 37.

Manton, K. G., Corder, L. S., and Stallard, E. (1993). Estimates of change in chronic disability and institutional incidence and prevalence rates in the U.S. elderly population from the 1982, 1984, and 1989 National Long Term Care Survey. *J Gerontol, 48*(4): S153-66.

Mechanic, D. (1987). Challenges in long-term care policy. *Health Affairs, 6*(suppl 2): 22-34.

Nyman, J. A. (1988). Excess demand, the percentage of medicaid patients and the quality of nursing home care settings. *Journal of Human Resources, 23*: 555-574.

Paul, T., and Wong, J. (1994). The retailing of health care. In: Cooper P, ed. *Health Care Marketing: A Foundation for Managed Quality*. Aspen Publishers, Gaithersburg, MD.

Peters, D. A. (1989). An overview of current research relating to long-term care outcomes. *Nurs Health Care, 10*: 132.

Rice, T. (1989). The use, and economic burden of nursing-home care in 1985. *Medical Care, 27*(suppl 12): 1133-1147.

Riportella-Muller, R., and Schlesinger, D. P. (1982). The relationship of ownership and size to quality of care in Wisconsin nursing homes. *Gerontologist, 22*: 50-53.

Scanlon, W. (1980). A theory of the nursing home market. *Inquiry, 17*(suppl 1): 25-41.

Schoeneman, K., and Graber, D. R. Restraint prevalence in U.S. nursing homes. Submitted to: *Am J Public Health*, October, 1995.

Schultz, B., Ward, D., and Knickman, J. (1994). RUG-II impacts on long-term care facilities in New York State. *Health Care Financing Review, 16*(suppl 2): 85-99.

Scott, W. R. (1983). Health care organizations in the 1980s: the convergence of public and professional systems. In: Meyer J. W., Scott W. R., eds. *Organizational Environments: Ritual and Rationality*. Sage, Beverly Hills.

Scott, W. R. (1983). Reform movements and organizations: the case of aging. In: Meyer, J. W., Scott, W. R., eds. *Organizational Environments: Ritual and Rationality*. Sage, Beverly Hills.

Spector, W. D., and Takada, H. (1991). Characteristics of nursing homes that affect resident outcomes. *Journal of Aging and Health, 3*: 427-454.

Spence, D. A., and Wiener, J. M. (1990). Estimating the extent of medicaid spend-down in nursing homes. *Journal of Health Politics, Policy & Law, 15*(suppl 3): 607-26.

Somers, A. R. (1987). Insurance for long-term care: some definitions, problems, and guidelines for action. *New England Journal of Medicine, 327*(suppl 1): 23-29.

Swan, J. H., et al. (1993). Trends in medicaid nursing home reimbursement: 1978-89. *Health Care Financing Review, 14*(suppl 4): 111-132.

Vogel, R. J., and Palmer, H. C. (1985). *Long-Term Care: Perspectives from Research and Demonstrations*. Aspen, Rockville, MD.

Waldman, S. (1985). A legislative history of nursing home care. In: Vogel, R. J., and Palmer, H. C., eds. *Long-Term Care: Perspectives from Research and Demonstrations*. Aspen, Rockville, MD.

Zedlewski, S. R., and McBride, T. D. (1992). The changing profile of the elderly. *The Milbank Quarterly, 70*(suppl 2): 247-273.

Zimmerman, D. G., Arling, T., Collins, S., et al. (1994). Development, analysis, and use of residents' assessment-based quality indicators. Proceedings: *Fifth International Conference on Systems Science and Health - Social Services for the Elderly and Disabled*. Geneva, Switzerland.

22.
COMMUNITY-BASED LONG TERM CARE

Barbara J. Holt, *West Virginia University, Morgantown, WV*

An area of health care that is experiencing dramatic growth and change is the range of services called long-term care. In 1992, 3.3 million Americans were over the age of 85. By 2050, this number will increase by 500 percent, including 1.2 million over the age of 100. The growth of the elderly population is directly reflected in the use of long-term care. In 1990, seven million elderly in the United States required assistance. With the increased demand for services, the focus is shifting to the provision of services outside of a nursing home environment. By 2040, it is estimated that there will be 13 million elderly and disabled requiring services; of these, 10 million are likely to need home and community-based services (Federal Council on the Aging, 1994).

As a result of its growing pains, these activities are either misunderstood or not considered at all by many in and out of the health care field. The name itself can be misleading; many services that fall under this label are required for short periods, do not necessarily mean nursing home care and are often non-medical in nature. Therefore, the growing demand for such care has necessitated a hurried education by administrators, legislators and most of all, family members. As of yet, the field of long-term care has yet to be organized, structured or, in many cases, even identified. There is no national long-term care policy, only assorted and sometimes conflicting federal, state and local policies, offering future health care policy makers and administrators a "new frontier."

Long-term care is an accumulation of social, health, housing and personal services utilized by persons without the capacity for total self care. The level of need by the client for each type and the level of skill required to perform each service varies case by case. It is this individualized care that creates the popularity of long-term care services; it also results in a lack of standardization which has implications for service delivery, quality control and outcome measurement.

I. INSTITUTIONAL BIAS

The history of long-term care in the United States has always operated under an institutional bias, particularly in regard to the care of the elderly. Beginning with the "poor houses" of the 1800s and continuing with the state asylums of the 1940s and 1950s, the solution for care of the elderly without sufficient family support was to remove them from society and "warehouse" them in institutions. Even today, while the results may not be so drastic, one can see many biases in the long-term care system which emphasize institutional placement rather than community services.

A. The Medical Model

The development of sophisticated medical treatment has focused health care on the hospital setting rather than the community setting, making "cure" rather than "care" the major intent (Chichin, 1989). Physicians have tended to recommend placement because they operate from a medical model rather than a social one, and because many physicians are simply not aware of community-based resources.

B. Financial Incentives

A principal reason for this approach is a system of financial incentives that favor medical services over social services and institutional over non-institutional care. The services reimbursed by Medicaid and Medicare are primarily care in acute facilities or nursing homes; over half of nursing home placements are financed by Medicaid. In 1992, there were 1.6 million beds in 16,000 nursing homes - 94 percent of these were certified Medicaid reimbursable (Fralich, 1995). Until recently, Medicaid programs would only pay for nursing home costs, not community based ones and there are still caps on the numbers which can be served in the community while none are placed on the numbers which can be institutionalized. Additionally, the eligibility requirements for community care are often more stringent than those required for nursing home admission (Spector, Reschovsky and Cohen, 1996). Therefore, unless sufficient family resources exist, the decision of whether to care for an elder in the home with no external assistance or have them institutionalized with no internal cost amounts to no real decision at all.

C. Lack of Options

Finally, there has been a simple lack of choices. Those elderly without family or requiring more skilled care than could be managed by informal caregivers became at risk of institutionalization. Though it might be a distasteful decision, there were few alternatives. Professionals faced a lack of options also; while screening of potential nursing home admissions to determine the appropriateness of institutionalization may be present in theory, the absence of alternative care makes the process futile.

D. Increasing Attention to Home- and Community-Based Services

Political, financial, social and ethical factors have combined to draw attention and support to the creation and maintenance of home-based long term care. Following the move to deinstitutionalize the mentally ill came the idea to keep the elderly and physically disabled in the community as well. Termed "aging in place," this movement may have been prompted by social service professionals but it was quickly adopted by the elderly and disabled themselves. As the older population became larger, as politicians realized that the elderly are the most reliable voters and as organizations representing the elderly and disabled came into operation, this group was in a stronger position to demand an alternative to institutional care.

E. Client-Based Decisionmaking

There has also been a change from seeing the clients as persons with physiological and medical abnormalities and more focus on the manner in which the social environment impacts on the individual. This has led to a move away from a medical model, which dictated institutionalization, to the premise that the least restrictive environment is in the client's best interest, or a social-legal model. The attitude shift has been spurred by the interests in the rights of an individual to determine his own care. It is no longer the authority of a social or health care worker to make final judgments on what is best for a client; it has now become accepted for the client to have the final say in what services he or she will receive and where they will be provided. In many cases, the elderly and disabled prefer to remain in the home and community rather than enter a nursing home.

F. Role of the Primary Caregiver

Societal changes have also increased the need for home and community based assistance. In the first part of the century, the elderly family member was cared for by the female who also functioned as the "housewife," usually a daughter or daughter-in-law who was at home with children while her husband supported the family. The elderly parent was able to move in and receive necessary care. Although the additional responsibility might be burdensome, the wife was expected to accept it as her duty. Economic changes in the last two decades have removed the housewife from the domestic circumstances and placed her in the work force.

Today, the primary caregiver may be employed when the need for care by a parent or spouse becomes evident, requiring them to decide to leave employment and remain at home without income or leave the disabled family member to care for themselves during work hours. The need for a second income often outweighs the need for family-provided child care and elder care, creating a demand for alternative services.

In some cases, the caregiver is simply unable to handle the responsibilities of caring for a frail family member. As many caregivers are siblings or spouses of the patient, they may themselves suffer from disabilities which inhibit their ability to provide assistance or to pay for in-home care. Or a lack of knowledge of the skills and processes may inhibit caregiving. Those caregivers who attempt to care for the elderly at home have seldom had exposure to the frail population and therefore have little prior experience and few role models.

In the past, adult children tended to remain in the vicinity of their elderly parents. Often living in the same town, same neighborhood or even next door, the need to provide supplemental care to the older family members could be accommodated. The evolution of the family unit from the extended, stable group of the early part of the 20th century to the nuclear and highly mobile systems we now see has left the elderly living alone, distant from family support. The pursuit of employment opportunities has moved the younger generation to large cities, often across the country; many retirees have migrated to the Sunbelt while they are physically and economically healthy, only to develop chronic illnesses in later years. Both events have left the elderly without close family contact.

G. Financial Considerations

From a historical perspective, the emphasis on home care is not a new idea, it is a return to a time when people had all their health care needs met at home. This system changed with the advent of technological advances which were thought to be deliverable only in an institutional setting. Fee-for-service insurance covered services in hospitals so that patients were encouraged to remain in that setting until they were stable enough to manage without continuing care.

Before Medicaid and Medicare, the nursing home bills were paid by family members or local charities. The county home was the last resort for the indigent. After the two federal programs came into existence in 1965, tax monies were used to finance institutional care for a large percent of placements. The rising cost of care became a significant budget item in the Medicaid budget, both on the state and federal levels. Insurance companies began to feel the pressure of long hospital stays. The need for a cost effective alternative became evident.

Finally, in 1983 Medicare stopped reimbursing hospitals based on the actual charges they reported and started paying a fixed fee for a patient's hospitalization based on her diagnosis. Under this Prospective Payment System, hospitals now make or lose money depending on whether the patient's treatment cost is higher or lower than the Medicare rate. So the advent of the diagnosis related groups (DRGs) restricted the willingness of hospitals to retain patients past the first possible discharge opportunity since the payment was fixed, regardless of the hospital days needed. Many critics of the system have used the phrase "quicker and sicker" to describe the process which encouraged earlier discharges. These changes have made home care more important because people are released before they are completely healed or are not admitted to begin with.

Another financial change is the adoption of case-mix reimbursement for nursing homes: higher pay for higher levels of care. This has prompted nursing homes to prefer the more disabled client and avoid those needing fewer services and thereby generating less income.

There have been many studies to determine the financial costs or savings of community based programs as compared to institutional care. Several factors make such evaluations difficult. First there is the argument that more persons are served in alternative programs than would have actually been placed in a nursing home (called the "woodwork effect" to indicate these persons crawl out of the woodwork to take advantage of the program), thereby increasing rather than decreasing the government cost.

Studies have also tended to compare the cost of formal services alone, not including the costs of informal care to the client and to the family. A recent analysis which estimated informal costs based on equivalent services delivered by an outside provider as well as living expenses concluded that "for the majority of elders [75%], community care is less costly than nursing home care; for some severely disabled elders, however, nursing home care might be a cost-effective alternative to community care, if no informal support is available" (Harrow, Tennstedt and McKinlay, 1995). It could be argued that informal costs should include not only the cost of supplies, medication, transportation, food and lodging, but also the forfeited income of outside employment. In addition, there is no way to set a price on the emotional and social costs to the caregiver.

II. WHO SEEKS LONG-TERM CARE?

The underlying cause of most chronic disability is either disease or the debilitating consequences of old age itself. However, the impact of such disease or infirmity on an individual's ability to function independently varies enormously, depending upon his or her access to various social and economic supports. It is estimated that 42.6 million residents of the United States qualify as disabled. Of these, 12.6 million report difficulty in completing the Activities of Daily Living and the Instrumental Activities of Daily Living due to chronic conditions which limit their physical and mental abilities and require some degree of long-term care (United States General Accounting Office, November, 1994). Although long-term care is generally considered a service for the elderly, it is actually required by those with AIDS, technologically-dependent children, the mentally retarded, persons experiencing serous mental illnesses or substance abuse as well as a variety of other serious disabilities. In fact, 42.1 percent of this number represents working age adults or children. However, the elderly account for 75 percent of the expenditures (Vladeck, Miller and Clauser, 1993).

Long-term care is called for when an individual can no longer perform the usual tasks necessary for independence. Commonly used as a standard measure, it is assumed that limitations in the ability to perform daily tasks are more indicative and reflective of the severity of disability than medical diagnoses. For example, a cancer patient with a terminal prognosis may be able to perform all tasks while a bone fracture, which is not life-threatening, may totally disable an individual.

These life responsibilities are divided into two categories: ADLs and IADLs. Activities of Daily Living (ADLs) refer to seven tasks relating to personal care: eating, toileting, dressing, bathing, walking, transferring (getting in and out of a bed or chair) and going outside. Instrumental Activities of Daily Living (IADLs) include tasks related to controlling one's environment: preparing meals, shopping, managing money, using the telephone, cleaning the home and doing laundry. It should be noted that a number of persons may possess the physical capacity to perform ADLs and IADLs but lack the mental acuity to do so. Table 1 reports the age progressive of difficulty in these measures.

Table 1 - Distribution of Elderly Persons Exhibiting Difficulty and Receiving Assistance

Age	One or More ADLs		One or More IADLs	
	% having difficulty	% receiving help	% having difficulty	% receiving help
All 65+	23%	10%	28%	23%
65-74	17%	6%	21%	17%
75-84	29%	14%	35%	30%
85+	45%	29%	58%	53%

Source: adapted from United States General Accounting Office, November, 1994.

Most persons requiring long-term care services are those with chronic conditions; those disabilities which require continuing treatment or attention but which are not necessarily life threatening. By definition, a chronic illness is never cured. Ironically, the improvements in medical care over the last decades have eliminated many of the causes of early deaths, allowing people to exhibit chronic conditions in an old age they would not have previously reached. The path to physical or mental incapacity is not necessarily straight nor steady. An individual will have periods of total independence, interrupted by episodes which compel increased assistance.

Many items in current literature form a consensus that the factors which tend to place a frail individual at risk of nursing home placement are cognitive impairment, lack of mobility and the lack of a caregiver (Branch, and Jette, 1982; Braun, Rose and Finch, 1991; Greece and Ondrich, 1990; Kane, Matthias and Sampson, 1983; Wolinsky, Callahan, Fitzgerald, and Johnson, 1992). Cognitive impairment affects the ability to self-medicate, to handle business affairs, to schedule services and sometimes even to identify family members. The inability to ambulate restricts performance of most ADLs such as toileting or self-feeding as well as all of the IADLs.

When coupled with an absence of a family member to assist in the performance of these activities, the individual is unable to maintain a healthy and safe existence in the community. Experiencing longer life spans, women usually outlive their spouses and often their children, leaving them without informal caregivers. These differences are displayed in Table 2.

Table 2 - Living Arrangements of Persons 65+: 1993

Living Arrangement	Men	Women
Living with spouse	75%	41%
Living with other relatives	7%	17%
Living with nonrelatives	3%	2%
Living alone	16%	41%

Source: United States General Accounting Office, November, 1994

Research has shown an additional factor which places individuals at risk of institutional placement is low financial resources. Most persons with severe disabilities have low incomes: nearly one-third live below poverty, and fewer than one in four have incomes at or above 300 percent of poverty, about $22,000 a year for a single person in 1994 (United States General Accounting Office, November, 1994). Women and persons of advanced age often have lower incomes, resulting in sub-standard housing, poor nutrition and less access to medical and pharmaceutical care (Ford, Roy, Haug, Folmar and Jones, 1991).

Understanding which clients are most at risk will provide more accurate targeting and more appropriate care plans to offset deficiencies in the client's support environment. Networks that included a paid provider modestly offset the impact that multiple Independent Activities of Daily Living impairments had on being admitted to a nursing home (Pearlman and Crown, 1992), a feature which is attractive to states which often bear the burden of nursing home payments.

III. COMMUNITY-BASED LONG TERM CARE SERVICES

A. Informal Supports

When policy makers speak of long-term care services, they are usually referring to those provided by nursing homes, home health agencies, social welfare agencies - professionals who arrange, provide and sometimes fund the care and are reimbursed by the client or a third party. It is important to note, however, that the majority of long-term care is provided by family members, estimated from 70 percent (Richardson, 1990) to 80 percent (Bartlett and Greenberg, 1985).

Over one half of adults with a surviving parent can expect to provide care to that parent at some point in the future. Parental caregiving is rare at any point; however, among older women with a surviving parent, parental caregiving is common (Himes, 1994). Adult children are more likely to provide care to a parent of the same gender and infirm elders are more likely to receive care from a child of the same gender. Daughters are a traditional source of assistance in the care of their elderly parents. They were 3.22 times more likely than sons to provide ADL assistance and 2.56 times more likely to provide IADL assistance (Dwyer and Coward, 1991). Because the substantial majority of elderly parents requiring care from children are mothers, this tendency toward gender consistency in the caregiving relationship partially accounts for the fact that daughters are more likely than sons to be involved in parent care (Lee, Dwyer and Coward 1993).

B. Caregiver Stress

Some can handle the task alone; others can manage with limited assistance from formal providers. Both the physical and emotional stress of caregiving take serious tolls on the provider.

A strong source of stress in caregiving is the financial need for caregivers to work outside of the home. Gorey, Rice and Brice (1992) report that approximately one-fifth to one-quarter of persons in the work force provide care for an elderly dependent. Whether they would be able to work without supportive services, or whether those who are not employed would be if not for caregiving responsibilities is a popular topic in policy discussions. This number also lends credence to the growing attention to providing support to adult children in the workplace It is proposed that interrole conflict is predicted by physical and psychological involvement in elder care and predicts both partial absenteeism from work and psychological strain (Barling, MacEwen, Kelloway and Higginbottom, 1994).

To facilitate the continued availability of family members, several states have initiated programs which provide incentives for care. Some states allow state income tax deductions for the cost of elderly care, similar to the deductions allowed for child care. Other individual programs have provided compensation for care by a family member; the premise is that the individual must generate income to survive and it is financially beneficial for the state to pay for their duties in the home rather than have them seek employment in the marketplace and force the elder to the institutionalized.

C. Formal Types of Services

As in the institutional setting, services delivered in the community exhibit several levels of skill as shown in Table 3. It should be stressed that a single individual may need different levels at the same time as well as over time. In addition, the progression of care to a higher level may be for a short term only; individuals are likely to go through crisis periods as well as times of self-sufficiency.

D. Case Management

Case management has become so popular so fast because it addresses the two issues dearest to the hearts of Americans: it promotes freedom and it saves money. Almost all proposals for health care reform contain some case management component (Vladeck, Miller and Clauser, 1993).

Case management is a service, usually performed by a social worker or a registered nurse, which begins by assessing the physical, environmental, financial, cognitive and functional level of the client. The next step is the determination of the services needed to enhance the current support system and maintain the client in his or her environment. Care is then arranged with appropriate providers by locating, developing, arranging and coordinating services, monitoring the provision of those services on a regular basis, as well as changes in the recipient's condition, and, adjusting the service plan as needed.

The growth of case management as a distinct concept can be linked to the increase in human service programs in the 1960's which focused on the individual's right to services and resources. Programs were designed to treat one distinct problem, to address a small target population, creating a jumble of programs with varying eligibility requirements. Persons with multiple problems, a characteristic of the elderly, were served by several programs, sometimes working at cross purposes and duplicating efforts while other needs remained unmet. This was particularly true in the gap between health and social service agencies. It was unrealistic that a client, already suffering from a disability, would be able to locate, apply for and receive assistance from all programs for which she was eligible. These events resulted in two discoveries: having a service in the community did not mean it would be utilized by those needing it and granting independence did not assure the health and safety of the client.

The goal of case management is the enabling of a chronically impaired person to remain in the least restrictive environment, while maintaining the greatest amount of independence and human dignity, in a cost-effective and service-efficient manner. These goals are accomplished with sensitivity to the client's own personal preference and choice and based upon the strengths present in the client himself or herself along with those of the caregivers.

The duties of a case manager extend far beyond a scheduler of services and the maintenance of organized case records. The competent case manager schedules services to address identified needs in the client's physical and social environment to ease the tension caused by the deterioration of some aspect of the client's condition. The unstable nature of the clients cared for in a case management system require an insight into the source of difficulties and constant attention to fluctuations in the degrees of seriousness that they take. This is accomplished by the establishment of a trusting relationship and an accurate assessment of the functioning levels of clients and resources, and an on-going adjustment of services as needed. The case manager must be aware of events such as death or illness of a relative (or even a pet), eviction, loss of benefits which can negatively impact the client's physical and emotional condition.

The cost of case management varies according to the provider. When the management is provided under Medicaid or as a part of private insurance, there is usually no direct cost to the consumer. Case management provided through Area Agencies on Aging or other governmental agencies may be free or offered on a sliding-scale based on the individual's income. The cost of private geriatric care managers ranges from $50 to $150 per hour (United States General Accounting Office, November, 1994).

E. Continuing Care Retirement Communities

The growing population of elderly in this country has attracted the attention of developers who are interested in building retirement communities, many of which offer a "continuum of care." This phrase refers to all of the services that people need as they age being available through one service provider or on one campus. A continuing care retirement community (CCRC) offers various levels of social activities and health services to the residents in their own homes or in communal areas. Potential residents are solicited by assuring them that as their physical and mental capacities deteriorate, they will be cared for without having to be transferred out of the development. In addition to housing for the healthy, younger population, the communities contain assisted living facilities and skilled nursing facilities for the older and more frail residents.

The continuing care retirement community offers a lifestyle that appeals to a wide variety of older persons. This type of community offers a long-term contract providing for housing, services and health care, usually all on one site. Services are tailored to individual needs, but typically include nursing and other health services, meals, housekeeping, transportation and personal assistance activities. Most also offer a wide variety of social, educational and recreational events which appeal to the retiree. The CCRCs are licensed and authorized by the states to contract for the provision of care. Within the CCRC category are the life care facilities which meet higher standards regarding fees and covered services.

The agreement between the CCRC and its residents is a combination of a homeowner's association and an insurance policy, offering variations in the amount of health care and the method of payment. The rates vary significantly depending upon the type of accommodations and services and the extent to which health care is provided. Health care coverage can be extensive (providing all services including meals and skilled nursing care), modified (offering fewer meals and lower levels of health services), and fee for service (additional payments for services as they are received). Financial arrangements may include an entry fee and a monthly fee with residents either renting or buying the living space. In 1991, 43 percent of CCRCs offered extensive service plans, 26 percent featured modified plans and 28 percent were still using fee-for service (Health Care Financing Review, 1993). A survey of CCRCs by the American Association of Homes and Services for the Aging found that the extensive service contract facilities have more affluent elderly while fee-for-service communities attract the less wealthy. There was also a 15 percent reduction in the use of nursing home level of care by the extensive contract residents over the usage of the fee-for-service category (Sloan, Shayne and Conover, 1995).

While the earliest models of continuing care communities involved moving a resident to different parts of the development as higher levels of care were indicated, a more recent design views the congregate housing available to the independent elderly as an appropriate location for delivering the additional services commonly attributed to assisted living facilities. Under the concept of "aging in place," this model eliminates constant moves to different facilities triggered by deterioration or improvements in the residents' capacities to meet their own needs. Keeping the more frail clients in the active population not only encourages their involvement in community activities, it allows healthier residents to provide socialization and supportive care to their neighbors. Until a resident deteriorates to the point of being disruptive to his neighbors or becomes a risk to himself without constant skilled care, the provider can supply almost all social and health care services in the home (Holt, 1995).

There are now about 900 CCRCs in the United States (U.S. Department of Commerce, 1996), ranging from high rises to expansive campuses, from 100 residences to over 700, from a couple of acres to over 100. The residences can be apartments, cottages, townhomes, clusters or single family homes in urban, suburban, and rural areas. Communities will offer different services and programs, but common ones are a dining room, sundry shops, activity and exercise areas, outdoor recreation and swimming pools.

F. Assisted Living

Assisted living facilities provide housing arrangements for individuals who need varying levels and intensities of care or supervision. Bridging the gap between housing and nursing home care, assisted living facilities serve those who need daily assistance but do not need continuous nursing care. Also known as personal care homes, board and care, foster care, domiciliaries or congregate care, these facilities offer fewer skilled services than nursing homes but strive to create a more homelike environment (Spector, Reschovsky and Cohen, 1996). It is this lack of standardization that limits accurate information on the numbers, types and services of assisted living facilities.

Assisted living facilities are usually considered a middle level of care, offering assistance with activities of daily living such as bathing, dressing, eating, toileting, continence, medications management, escort service, wake up and tuck in supervision. Residents can also receive housekeeping, shopping, laundry, and meal preparation services. Most facilities require that the resident be able to perform at least some self-supporting activities, be ambulatory to a moderate degree and not require constant supervision. Residents needing the higher levels of skilled services are usually placed in skilled nursing facilities.

The lastest models of assisted living provide features that enhance tenants' autonomy, such as lockable doors, full bathrooms, temperature control, and single occupancy. Other features include cooking facilities in individual units, flexible visiting hours; a requirement that staff knock before entering tenants' units; and provisions for pets, smoking in the units or in designated areas, and the use of alcoholic beverages. Perhaps the most independence-enhancing feature of this type of housing is that the wide variety on the market offers the potential resident wide choice in selecting the social setting, the size of accommodations, the types of social and recreational activities and level of health services

Assisted living facilities are most often licensed by the states, but are called a variety of different names in different areas. Charges in assisted living facilities generally reflect the level of service required, the size of one's living quarters and whether the facility is modest or more luxurious. In some states, the Supplemental Security Income (SSI) grant is supplemented for those individuals residing in an assisted living facility. In a few states, Medicaid funds this mid-level of care. However, most residents of these facilities are middle-income elderly who can self-pay the fees (Heumann and Boldy, 1993).

The state of Oregon is a leader in the development of assisted living. Oregon's assisted living settings provide private apartments and serve tenants with higher levels of disability than tenants of assisted living settings in other states. Some of these facilities provide up to 16 hours of nursing care a day (Spector, Reschovsky and Cohen, 1966).

G. Adult Day Care

Adult day care services are provided to the elderly during the day at a center facility. Often utilized by families in which the caregiver is employed, day care centers offer an assortment of social, recreational, health and nutritional services. Participants range from mildly impaired to severely disabled. While most centers accept a variety of populations, certain facilities specialize in serving those of a certain diagnosis (such as Alzheimers) or of a certain culture (such as Asian or Hispanic). Most adult day care centers are non-profit, supported in some degree by public funds such as Medicaid or Social Security block grants, and are often dependent on participant contributions and outside grants.

Centers vary in size, from six to over 40 participants, with the average just under 20 persons. An individual attends an average of three and one-half days per week for about six hours, with more dependent individuals attending at a higher rate. The cost per day exhibits a wide range, with $29.50 as the mean (Weissert, Elston, Bolda, Zelman, Mutran, and Mangum, 1990).

Adult day care centers may be classified under three models: health-based, social-based and special needs. A comparison of the first two (and most utilized) models in Table 3 shows major differences all elements, although it should be stressed that each has components of the other.

Table 3 - Models of Adult Day Care Centers

Type	Health Care Model	Social Model
Affiliation	Nursing home or rehabilitation hospital	General hospital, social services or housing agency
Client Population	Physically dependent, older, white, few with mental disorders	Unmarried, female, high proportion of minority, under 85, minimally disabled, over 40% mentally disabled
Funding source	Philanthropic, self-pay	Governmental, particularly Medicaid
Services	Nursing, therapies, therapeutic diets, transportation	Case management, nutrition education, professional counseling, transportation, health assessment

Source: adapted from Weissert, Elston, Bolda, Zelman, Mutran, and Mangum, 1990

Special purpose centers target one type of diagnosis or client. Examples include mentally retarded, mentally ill, blind, veterans or non-English speaking centers. The services are designed specifically to meet the special needs of the clients and funding sources vary. As the chronically disabled population grows, resulting in larger numbers of specific clients, special purpose centers are expected to increase.

The evaluations of these programs vary. While many elderly enjoy the daily interaction with peers, others would prefer to remain in their homes and attend solely to please family members or to delay an institutional decision. The staff/client ratio also appears to have a direct influence on client satisfaction; however, it also impacts the costs of attendance (Weissert, Elston, Bolda, Zelman, Mutran, and Mangum, 1990). It should be understood that the physical environments, recreational activities, cultural programs, meal quality and rehabilitation activities are not consistent between centers which obviously impacts the diverse assessments.

H. Nutritional Services

The most well-known nutritional support is the home-delivered meals program, often called meals-on-wheels. Operated by area agencies on aging through Title III-C (1) of the Older Americans Act as well as by religious and civic organizations, these services seek to assure the provision of one nutritionally complete meal per day to elderly and disabled persons who are unable to prepare meals themselves or travel to a central site. In Fiscal Year 1993, 102.5 million home-delivered meals were served to some 794,500 persons of whom 77 percent were frail and disabled; 58 percent were low-income; 45 percent were rural residents; 19 percent were minority; and 15 percent were low-income minority (Greenberg, 1995). Most programs utilize volunteers for the daily delivery process although there are several localities which have provided microwave ovens and weekly deliveries of frozen meals. This change is seen as cost effective and allows the client to chose his or her own meal each day but is criticized for increasing isolation by reducing the incidence of contact with another person.

Seniors may also receive congregate meals in group settings at community centers, churches and senior centers under Title III-C(2). Usually these meals are provided on a Monday through Friday basis and the participants are offered additional activities such as recreational and educational programs. There is substantial private sector, state, and local financial and volunteer support for the congregate meals program. While participants are not charged a fee, the Administration on Aging (AoA) requests donations to help defray the cost of services. Other participants volunteer as nutrition site managers or deliver meals to further support the program. AoA reported that in Fiscal Year 1993, 126.3 million congregate meals were served to 2.36 million older persons of whom 28 percent were frail and disabled; 47 percent were low-income; 42 percent were rural residents; 18 percent were minority; and 13 percent were low-income minority (Greenberg, 1995). Transportation is a major cost factor in these programs, particularly in rural areas, and the difficulty of disabled persons in attending can affect utilization and the ability of the agencies to target those most in need.

I. Respite Care

One manner of describing respite care is that the caregiver is the actual beneficiary; these are a variety of activities designed to provide relief to caregivers of the elderly and disabled. Provided in a community setting such as a day care center, nursing home or in the client's home, the respite worker assumes the responsibility for care to allow the primary caregiver to attend business, medical or personal activities or to simply provide a break to relieve the stress of continual demands. Care can be provided for a few hours or a few weeks, on a scheduled basis or in response to an emergency (Kane and Penrod, 1993). Such a service may be thought of as a preventive measure to decrease incidences of elder abuse as well as lengthening the period of family care before institutional solutions are sought.

Funding for respite services can come from Medicaid, Social Security block grants, state funds or private payment. Often regulations are attached which restrict the amount of hours, the cost of care or the purpose of the respite; for example, respite may not be available to allow the caregiver to work. While respite care receives popular approval, there has been little evaluation as to its effectiveness in reducing nursing home placement or reducing elder abuse. The few studies which have assessed respite outcomes have not determined a positive impact on these two factors (Richardson, 1990).

J. Caregiver Support

An associated but important element in this mixture is the availability of support for caregivers of the homebound. The most well-known resource is the availability of group meetings designed to provide emotional support, educational material, advice and often services in a setting of peers. While some groups target a certain type of individual, such as the caregiver of an Alzheimer's patient, others are more generic. Education on managing the patient and the patient's environment is a common feature of these programs. The stress generated by a caregiving situation can often be relieved by a mixture of these services which are usually delivered by volunteers or agents of other programs.

Evaluations of these programs have been mixed. While earlier studies reported no significant effect on patient care, recent evaluations of respite programs as well as reconsideration of previous research have determined more positive results; nursing home admission was delayed or avoided, caregiver self-esteem was increased and caregiver stress was decreased (Kosloski and Montgomery, 1995).

Another variety of such groups are national networks designed to refer long distance caregivers to services in the locality of the client. With the mobility of society and the need for young adults to relocate in order to secure employment, the concern for an elderly parent is heightened by the distance and a frustration is created, sometimes compounded by guilt. These referral services are designed to relieve this concern to a degree by assisting the caregiver in selecting and securing assistance. Often a local case manager can be obtained to handle matters, usually at an hourly fee.

A major example of this service is the Eldercare Locator (1-800-677-1116) which is a service of the Administration on Aging, operated by the National Association of Area Agencies on Aging and the National Association of State Units on Aging. Established in 1991, the Eldercare Locator is a nationwide, directory assistance service designed to help older persons and caregivers locate local support resources for aging Americans. This service offers initial screening to determine the type of service needed and provides callers with the names and phone numbers of organizations within a desired location, anywhere in the country. Many states also sponsor central referral sites of the services available within their boundaries.

There are also several financial supports for caregivers. While some are indirect such as tax credits or vouchers for future services for oneself, some programs provide direct payment for caregiving (Kane and Penrod, 1993). Cash payments to family members draw a large measure of criticism as it is seen as a family responsibility to care for the young, disabled and elderly. For a spouse or a parent living in the same household, it becomes problematic to determine what tasks are reimbursable and which are a normal family function. Monitoring and accurately assessing these services is very difficult, making supervision and accountability a dilemma.

K. Funding Sources

Monk and Cox (1993) report a minimum of 80 federal programs related to long-term care. The major programs - Medicare, Medicaid, Social Security Block Grants, and the Older Americans Act - provide a variety of services which, unfortunately, are rarely coordinated with each other. In addition, many states and localities have other in-home programs targeting specific ages, diagnoses, locations and other points of eligibility. A recent entry into the field is the private long term care insurance policy.

1. Medicare

It is an unfortunate fact (and a very frustrating one for those in the field) that the common American assumes that when and if the time for nursing home care comes, it will be paid for by Medicare. So too are the assumptions that Medicare will supply whatever in-home services are needed in one's later years. In fact, Medicare is authorized to reimburse for "intermittent skilled care," primarily following hospitalization. Further, the patient must be classified as homebound, a term which carries a very strict definition. Finally, there are limits on eligibility for certain types of services; a patient may be in need of home health services, not nursing services provides by a registered nurse, excluding chronically dependent persons or Alzheimer's victims (Monk and Cox, 1993).

2. Medicaid

Medicaid is a federal program which is funded to a great extent by state matching funds. In FY 1994, Medicaid programs paid for 41 percent of all long-term care services delivered in the United States; 85 percent of that amount went to institutional care, representing the single largest expenditure in the Medicaid program (Fralich, 1995).

Since states pay a significant portion of the Medicaid bill, their budgets are undergoing pressure similar to that experienced at the federal level. The eight million persons who receive long-term care under Medicaid are primarily those over 65 years of age, although a number of persons with physical disabilities and developmental disabilities are included in this number. In 1993, one-third of Medicaid dollars ($42.5 billion) were spent on long-term care services, including both institutional and home care (United States General Accounting Office, November, 1994). Lengthening life expectancies are likely to increase both the prevalence of caregiving and the ages at which it occurs (Himes, 1994). The explosion of the AIDS/HIV caseload among the younger population has further strained resources. These needs will by necessity increase the demand for state administered programs to either support existing caregiver or substitute in their absence.

Due to the ability of states to determine the mix of services they will offer under the Medicaid program, there is a wide variety of the types and amounts of assistance offered. In-home care under Medicaid is required to include part-time nursing, home health aide services, medical equipment and supplies (Monk and Cox, 1993). Some states offer only those services that are federally mandated, while others cover as many as 31 additional optional services. For example, disabled Medicaid beneficiaries in Wisconsin are eligible to receive personal care services (as well as 30 other optional services) but Medicaid beneficiaries in Wyoming are not. The populations served also differ; persons in similar circumstances in different states confront different eligibility criteria. For example, in Texas, a family of three with an annual income above 17 percent of the federal poverty level (i.e., $184 per month) would not be eligible for Medicaid. However, this same family might be covered in Connecticut where eligibility is set at 58 percent of the poverty level or $581 per month (United States General Accounting Office, November, 1994). Dissolving federal directives to states and replacing mandates with block grants allowing local determination of programs will create an even wider assortment of assistance to different populations.

For many persons, the ability of Medicaid to cover long-term care services, both institutional and non-institutional, is the last level of assistance. Under the "spend down" idea, an individual with resources in excess of the allowable limit, must utilize these assets before applying for Medicaid. Unfortunately, with the high cost of care, this process can go quite quickly and has become the safety net for middle income as well as low income persons. In an attempt to curb the growth in Medicaid long-term care expenditures, states have enacted a variety of rules prohibiting the transfer of assets in order to become financially eligible.

The increasingly tight state budgets have enticed many states to begin focusing on community based services as economic alternatives; other states have not included non-institutional care as part of their regular Medicaid program and deliver these services only under Medicaid waivers.

3. Medicaid Waivers

Most states did not provide significant Medicaid home and community-based long-term care services until after 1981, when Congress specifically provided the option of states securing waivers to the normal programs so that non-medical assistance (such a housekeeping and personal care) could be provided in locations other than institutional settings. These services are not considered a part of the regular Medicaid program and therefore can be limited in eligibility, expense and number of recipients. As of May 1994, 195 waiver programs were being administered, with applications for 34 more under consideration by the Health Care Financing Administration (United States General Accounting Office, August, 1994).

The model most often cited is the Medicaid Waiver of Section 2176 of the Omnibus Budget Reconciliation Act of 1981. This is a waiver of Medicaid program regulations so that states may administer in-home services of both a medical and a social nature to persons who would otherwise be placed in a nursing facility. An element of this program is the requirement that it is "budget neutral," that is, community services must not exceed what would have otherwise been spent on nursing home care. This necessitates targeting those persons who may avoid or delay institutionalization by receiving services outside of a nursing home.

Part of the concern expressed by policy makers was that the offering of such a program would not strictly serve those persons who would have otherwise gone into a nursing home at Medicaid expense; this would result in the serving of a different population and therefore not represent a cost savings to the federal and state budgets. Termed the "woodwork" effect, it was feared that applicants would "come out of the woodwork" to use services for which they were not originally targeted. Subsequent research has shown that this may indeed be the case (United States General Accounting Office, August, 1994; Monk and Cox, 1993) but it is argued that cost savings alone should not be the only criteria for judging the effectiveness of the program.

4. Social Services Block Grant

Funded under Title XX of the Social Security Act, this is a state-administered program which reflects the wide variance of other programs with local priority setting. Approximately ten percent of each state's allocation is budgeted for in-home care even though most states reported an extensive waiting list for services (Monk and Cox, 1993).

5. Older Americans Act

Passed in 1965, the purpose of this program was the creation and coordination of services for the elderly. In addition to the nutrition program discussed earlier, Title III of the Older Americans Act supported the network of 600 area agencies on providing home and community based care as well as leveraged resources from other federal, state and local entities. Most supportive services fall under three broad categories: access services, such as transportation, outreach, information and assistance, and case management; in-home services, including homemaker and home health aides, chore maintenance, and supportive services for families of older individuals who are victims of Alzheimer's disease; and community services such as adult day care, legal assistance and recreation. Once again, decisions on the state and local level hold the final say in the distribution of funds and services.

Supportive services are designed to maximize the informal support provided by caregivers and to enhance the capacity of older persons to remain self-sufficient. During FY 1993 information and assistance services were provided to over three million older persons and their caregivers. Over three million outreach contacts were also made to identify those older persons who needed to gain access to services. Transportation continued to be one of the most heavily used services. Over 800,000 older persons received more than 40 million units of transportation services to their doctor, clinic or senior center.

In FY 1994 over $7 million was provided via Title III for in-home services to frail older individuals, including victims of Alzheimer's disease. The main objective of in-home services to the frail elderly is to direct resources to those older Americans most at risk of losing their self-sufficiency. Services include homemaker and home health aides, visiting and telephone reassurance, chore and maintenance services, in-home respite care and adult day care respite, minor modification of homes to facilitate continued occupancy by older individuals, personal care and other in-home services as defined by the state and area agencies on aging (Greenberg, 1995).

6. Private Long-Term Care Insurance

Long-term care insurance is private insurance sold by insurance companies designed specifically to pay for long term care services. There are approximately 135 companies nationwide that currently sell this type of insurance, with an estimated customer base of three million. Policies typically cover some part of nursing home care and home health care; occasionally they will also cover other benefits such as some adult day care benefits and temporary respite care. Long-term care polices are typically indemnity policies, which means the insurer pays for a certain dollar amount of covered services per day.

A long-term care insurance policy can cost between $400 and $4,000 dollars per year depending upon age, health and selected benefits. A policy that covers a good portion of the daily cost of a nursing home or a policy with inflation protection will increase the cost. There are no federal standards governing the sale of long-term care insurance policies, but some standards do exist in most states. Currently, less than two percent of national long-term care expenditures are covered by private insurance.

There have been many criticisms of private long-term care insurance. It is argued that it is not available or affordable for those who need it most, such as those persons who already have disabilities or those of advanced age. Critics continue that the value of many policies erode over time. If the popularity of these policies continue to grow, it is possible that an increased pool of insured will reduce the cost to an individual.

IV. SYSTEM FRAGMENTATION

As topical as the long-term care system has become, it still exhibits many difficulties in its operation. First, the long-term care continuum only works when there are a wide range of social and medical services available to meet the individual needs of the patients. As has been discussed, there is no continuity of services from one locality to another, no standardization of eligibility. Programs coexist with varying qualifications and no incentive for coordination. Most initiatives are the result of state and local organizations trying to assist those who have fallen through the cracks. The system can err in two directions. A person with disabilities can be maintained in setting offering a much higher level of care than is appropriate, while another may exist without sufficient care to maintain health and safety.

The lack of coordination is reflected in the lack of standards for quality. Without uniform guidelines for service delivery or training, there is a concern that low cost will mean low quality. Care delivered outside the constant supervision of physicians or nurses is difficult to regulate. While professional supervision may be scheduled biweekly, it is often accomplished during a short visit and may not include observation of care being provided. It should also be noted that most in-home workers are homemakers or home health aides; even if they are provided by a Medicare-certified agency, these activities are not regulated. One study showed that complaints of inadequate staff screening, theft, high rates of worker turnover, poor coordination of services, and unprofessional conduct were as common in licensed agencies as in unlicensed ones (Monk and Cox, 1993).

Furthermore, it is hard to develop standards and outcome evaluation tools when the process is based on the philosophy that care is individualized and customized to each patient's resources and needs. Particularly hard to quantify are the sometimes stated goals such as "personal dignity" or "maximized independence." Added to the mix is the focus on self-determination which dictates that the client and family have the right to decide which, if any, services should be delivered. With these system characteristics, formulating standards, uniform plans of care, optimal practices and standardized outcomes become a futile exercise.

SUMMARY

Despite these issues, the most attractive feature of home care to many of the community stakeholders is that it costs much less than institutional care. Whether state officials are seeking a reduction in Medicaid costs or family members are trying to avoid personal expenditures, the rising costs associated with nursing home care have made community-based services an appealing alternative.

To the clients themselves, the opportunity to remain in the home or in the community is an important option. In a society which values independence and self-determination, it is likely that this trend will continue to grow as more persons face long-term care decisions.

REFERENCES

Barling, J., MacEwen, K. E., Kelloway, E. K., and Higginbottom, S. F. (1994). Predictors and outcomes of elder-care-based interrole conflict. *Psychology and Aging, 9:* 391-397.

Bartlett, L., and Greenberg, J. (1985). The elderly and long term care: Present and future state directions. In *New Federalism and Long-Term Health Care of the Elderly,* Burton D. Dunlop, ed. Project Hope, Millwood, VA.

Branch, L. G. and Jette, A. M. (1982). A prospective study of long-term care institutionalization among the aged. *American Journal of Public Health, 72:* 1373-1379.

Braun, K. L., Rose C., and Finch, M. (1991). Patient characteristics and outcome in institutional and community long-term care. *The Gerontologist, 1:* 648-656.

Chichin, E. (1989). Community care for the frail elderly: The case of non-professional home care workers. *Women and Health, 14(3/4):* 93-104.

Dwyer, J. W., and Coward, R. T. (1991). A multivariate comparison of the involvement of adult sons versus daughters in the care of impaired parents. *Journal of Gerontology: Social Sciences 46:* S259-269.

Executive Office of Consumer Affairs and Business Regulation. (1996). Questions and Answers about Long Term Care Insurance, Commonwealth of Massachusetts (web).

Federal Council on the Aging. (1994). The Need for Home and Community-based Long Term Care: A Rural Perspective. Issue Brief, 1(1), Washington, DC.

Ford, A. B., Roy, A. W., Haug, M. R., Folmar, S. J. and Jones, P. K. (1991). Impaired and disabled elderly in the community. *American Journal of Public Health, 81(9):* 1207-1209.

Fralich, J. (1995) *Reducing the Cost of Institutional Care: Downsizing, Diversion, Closing and Conversion of Nursing Homes.* National Long Term Care Resource Center, Portland, ME.

Gorey, K. M., Rice, R. W. and Brice, G. C. (1992). The prevalence of elder care responsibilities among the work force population. *Research on Aging, 14:* 399-418.

Greece, V. and Ondrich, J. (1990). Risk factors for nursing home admissions and exits: a dicrete-time hazard function approach. *Journal of Gerontology 45:* S250-S258.

Greenberg, S. (1995) Title III- State and Community Programs. Administration on Aging (Web).

Harrow, B. S., Tennstedt, S. L. and McKinlay, J. B. (1995). How costly is it to care for disabled elders in a community setting? *The Gerontologist, 35(6):* 803-813.

Health Care Financing Review (1993). Study shows retirement communities expanding, offering more choices. *14(4):* 275.

Heumann, L. F. And Boldy, D. P. (1993) *Aging in Place with Dignity.* Praeger, Westport.

Himes, C. (1994). Parental caregiving by adult women. *Research on Aging 16:* 191-211.

Holt, B. J. (1995). An integrated service model for continuing care communities. *The Agenda, 2(1):* 2-3.

Hughes, S. (1986). Long-Term Care: Options in an Expanding Market. Dow Jones Irwin, Homewood, IL.

Kane, R., and Penrod, J. D. (1993) Family caregiving policies: Insights from an intensive longitudinal study. In *Caregiving Systems: Informal and Formal Helpers,* Zarit, S. H., Pearlin, L. I., and Schaie, K. W., eds. Lawrence Erlbaum Associates: Hillsdale, NJ.

Kane, R., Matthias, R. and Sampson, S. (1983). The risk of placement in a nursing home after acute hospitalization. *Medical Care, 21:* 1005-1061.

23.

HOSPICE AS PALLIATIVE CARE FOR THE TERMINALLY ILL

Kathleen M. Reding, *Western Michigan University, Kalamazoo, MI*

In the United States, the one-page death certificate and the death notice in the daily newspaper usually identify the person's date of birth and death, the cause of death, and when, where and how the body will be disposed. "What is missing from these pages—what is always missing—is the description of how they died. Was the teacher in pain or at peace? Did the executive have a living will and a doctor who listened? Did the civic leader linger attached to a machine?..." (Goodman, E. 1995, p. 8.)

Hospice programs address concerns about how people die. Hospice attempts to improve on both monitored medicide and intransitive dying, terms introduced by Ivan Illich in 1992. Monitored medicide uses so-called *heroic measures* to keep an individual alive primarily through technological interventions. Advanced medical and surgical technologies available in hospital settings, can prolong life and even maintain an individual in a vegetative state for several years (Brock, 1993).

Two highly publicized and prolonged court cases, the Karen Anne Quinlan case (1976) and the Nancy Cruzan case (1990) brought these end-of-life issues to the attention of the general public. The *real hero of these heroic measures* has never been identified. Is the hero the patient who is subjected to these technological intrusions when "there is such little hope?" Or is the hero the physician who makes every effort to keep the patient alive? "For many patients and families, prolonging life unnecessarily without offering an opportunity to prolong a meaningful life, is not a tolerable option" (Veatch, 1976, p. 112).

At the other end of the spectrum, intransitive dying is dying one's "natural" death, i.e., without any intervention, whether heroic or not, in nature's course. While monitored medicide fails to address the patient's dignity and autonomy, intransitive dying fails to address the patient's pain and discomfort. Even when intransitive dying is chosen, the dying patient tends to be deserted.

Sponsored by the Robert Wood Johnson Foundation, the Study to Understand Prognoses and Preference for Outcomes and Risks Treatments (SUPPORT), a controlled trial to improve care for terminally ill hospitalized patients, identified serious problems with the care of the terminally ill. Foremost among these problems was the failure of physicians to respect the patient's autonomy, i.e., to carry out the hospitalized patient's wishes, even when the patient's advanced directives were available. The researchers were left with a troubling situation. They preferred to "envision that, when confronted with life-threatening illness, the patient and family would be included in discussions, realistic estimates of outcome would be valued, pain would be treated, and dying would not be prolonged" (Editorial, JAMA, 1995, p. 1635). However, this form of consultation seldom occurred. Even when a systematic protocol was developed to alert the physicians to patient and family end-of-life preferences, the physicians tended to ignore these preferences (JAMA, 1995).

Studies which compared the benefits of terminal care in a hospital and in a hospice program found that hospice provided the terminally ill patient and family with greater comfort, improved quality of life, with little, if any, negative experience for the patient (Traille, 1991).

I. HOSPICE CARE DEFINED

The concept of patient-centered medicine, versus provider-centered medicine, has received more attention since the passage of the Patient Self-Determination Act in 1991 (Omnibus Budget Reconciliation Act, 1990). Patient-centered medicine refers to medicine which emphasizes the patient's wishes, needs and preferences. In the patient-centered age, the emphasis shifts from patient compliance to patient participation in the medical decision-making process (Angell, 1997). The assumptions are that the patient will be fully informed by the physician about the choices available so that an informed decision will be reached (Laine and Davidoff, 1996) and that the physician will comply with the patient's treatment preferences.

A prime example of patient-centered medicine, hospice care integrates dying with living, as it used to be when home was the place where most persons died, physicians made home visits, and family members and friends stayed with the dying patient to provide care and comfort. In some cultures, the body of the deceased is then cleansed and dressed by family members and is laid out in the patient's home before burial.

Hospice might best be defined as a program designed to meet the medical, psychosocial, and spiritual needs of the terminally ill patient and of the patient's family. Throughout the terminal stages of the illness, the patient and the family are cared for by an inter-disciplinary team of medical and non-medical professionals and volunteers. Following the patient's death, a hospice volunteer or staff member continues to provide support to the family during the period of bereavement.

Hospice provides care to all terminally ill individuals and to their families "regardless of age, gender, nationality, race, creed, sexual orientation, disability, diagnosis, availability of a primary caregiver or ability to pay" (National Hospice Organization, 1994, p. 39). Thus, hospice provides an alternative to monitored medicide and to intransitive dying. This option is available to terminally ill persons who choose palliative care either after curative interventions have been tried and failed, or after the patient decides to forego further therapeutic attempts and their unavoidable side-effects.

Palliative care is defined as "treatment that enhances comfort and improves the quality of the patient's life. No specific therapy is excluded from consideration. The test of palliative treatment lies in the agreement by the patient, the physician, the primary caregiver, and the hospice team that the goal is to relieve distressing symptoms, alleviate pain, and enhance the quality of life. The decision to intervene with an active palliative treatment is based on the treatment's ability to meet the stated goals rather than its effect on the underlying disease" (National Hospice Organization, 1995). Once symptoms are under control, the patient and the family can devote their time and energy to caring and to taking leave (Rhymes, 1993, p. 16).

The individual who chooses hospice knows that the disease is terminal and is requesting hospice care as the end-of-life care. Hospice provides a plan-of-care to and with the patient and the family through a team comprised of physicians, nurses, home health aides, social workers, counsellors, chaplains, and volunteers. As needed, physical therapists, occupational therapists, dietitians, and other trained professionals participate in the patient's care.

The values and beliefs of the patient and of the family take precedence over those of the health professionals in the selection of the palliative care pursued. For example, some patients who are no longer capable of taking food orally, might consider tube-feeding to be extraordinary and unduly invasive, whereas others might receive it as a welcome alternative (Maillet and King, 1993, pp. 38-39). Unlike the more traditional medical model, with its focus on the physician and the nurse as the intervenors, hospice is implemented by a multidisciplinary team.

II. IMPLEMENTATION OF THE HOSPICE PHILOSOPHY

Hospice emphasizes that care is delivered by a team of hospice professionals and volunteers whose task is "to meet the physiological, psychological, social, spiritual, and economic needs of hospice patient/families facing terminal illness and bereavement" (National Hospice Organization, 1994, p. 42). Hospice services are delivered with a sensitivity to the fact that hospice professionals enter people's lives and homes during a period of heightened need and potential vulnerability.

A. Hospice Education

Welk (1991) developed a model to educate health care professionals and the general public about hospice (p. 14). The model identified four issues that the terminally ill patient and the patient's family face. These issues address the physical, emotional, social and spiritual support needs. Physical care includes the control of pain and the management of symptoms that cause physical discomfort, so that suffering decreases. "Unless pain is controlled, other issues cannot be addressed" (p. 15). Emotional support allows the patient to express fears about dying, especially fears about dying alone, and assures the patient that hospice will not abandon him/her during the dying process. Social support offers the person opportunities to complete unfinished business, including the resolution of interpersonal conflicts, and divisions. Finally, spiritual support is provided, although the author recognizes that "not everyone agrees that this is a part of human functioning" (p. 17). Spiritual support, which is not necessarily associated with religion, maximizes the quality of time that the patient has remaining. These approaches allow the patient to "live peacefully until the moment of death" (p. 14).

Sontag, in her 1993 study of Oregon hospice found that the hospice programs did not uniformly provide the total care which hospice philosophy purports to offer. Nurses were the primary providers of care. Other members of the interdisciplinary team felt that their roles and functions had not been fully developed or understood within the hospice program. In some instances the nurses were perceived to be assuming the role of social worker, and counselor.

B. Hospice Settings

Where possible, "the focus of hospice care is to enable an individual to remain in the familiar surrounding of his/her own home as long as it is possible and appropriate," (Kohut and Kohut, 1984, p. 58). The goal is to maximize the patient's level of independence, while making physical and other accommodations within the home to assist the patient in coping with the constraints imposed by his/her illness.

Hospice services in the United States are provided in five settings: the home-based care or hospice-without-walls; the extended care facility or nursing home hospice; the free-standing independent hospice; the hospital-affiliated free-standing hospice; and the hospital-based hospice which might include a separate hospice unit, or counseling services provided to hospice patients dispersed throughout the hospital, or a home care program provided by a staff trained in hospice care (Kohut and Kohut, 1984). The inpatient setting "allows terminal patients without a strong family support system to be served in a hospice" (Mor, 1988, p. 27.)

As of June 1995, the Health Care Financing Administration (HCFA) reported that 55 percent of the hospices are freestanding, 25 percent are part of a home health agency, 17 percent are hospital based, and only one percent are located in skilled nursing facilities. The average number of days a beneficiary remains in hospice care, weighted by the number of beneficiaries in each hospice service, showed that in free-standing hospices the average was 63.7 days, as compared to 55.4 days in hospital-based programs, 45.4 days in a skilled nursing facility program, 45.5 days and 53.3 days in a home care program (Table 1, Vladeck, 1995, p. 449).

Table 1 - Average Number of Patient Days in Hospice by Program Site

Free-standing programs	63.7
Hospital-based programs	55.4
Skilled nursing programs	45.5
Home care programs	53.3

Source: Health Care Financing Administration (1995).

C. Hospice Patients

In 1994, in the United States, hospice programs cared for an estimated 300,000 patients (Vladeck, 1995). Seventy-eight percent of the patients receiving hospice care in the United States were diagnosed with cancer; 10% with heart-related diagnoses, 4% with AIDS, 1% with kidney diseases, 1% with Alzheimer's and 6% with various other illnesses. Hospices cared for close to one out of every three cancer and AIDS patients who died in 1994 (Hospice, 1996).

Although only one % of patients with end-stage dementia are presently served by hospice, such patients represent ideal candidates for hospice: "their prognosis is poor, aggressive medical treatment is not indicated and they have significant medical problems associated with their underlying condition" (Hanrahan and Luchins, 1995, p. 48.). However, the survival time of dementia patients is perceived to be more uncertain than that of individuals with cancer or AIDS. "A criteria for enrollment in many hospices is that a physician certify that the patient is expected to die within six or seven months" (Hanrahan and Luchins, 1995, p. 48).

In 1995, 68% of patients served by hospice were men 65 years and older, and 72% were women 65 and older (National Hospice Organization, 1995). According to the 1990 census, there are 31 million persons 65 years of age and over, as compared to 25 million persons in 1980, and this age group continues to increase. Over 7 million of those persons are 80 or more years of age (U.S. Census, 1990). With the rapid increase in the elderly population, it seems apparent that the need for hospice care will continue to increase.

D. Case Studies of Two Hospice Patients

Case #1: Claire, age 81, had worked as an administrator. Susan, her only child, said: "When my Mother retired at the age of 65, she came home, sat in her chair and wanted to be waited on by her husband, until he died five years ago; then Mother came to live with me." Claire was a home hospice patient for eight months; she suffered from severe arthritis and a deteriorating cardiac condition. She had several mini-strokes, each one leaving her weaker. The medication kept her comfortable, although she said that the arthritic pain was always with her. Five days a week, a home health aide came to give her a bath and to make her bed. A nurse and a social worker also visited. Although Claire knew that pastoral services were available, she was not interested.

Claire used to say "I want to live while I am waiting to die." Eventually, Claire's failing eyesight did not permit her to read. She loved to chat and to be waited on, always saying that she did not like to get up from her lounge chair more than was necessary. She was never at a loss for words when she had a good day and enjoyed the visits from the hospice team members including the volunteer's weekly visit. Claire always insisted that on her weekly visits, the hospice volunteer prepare and eat lunch with her saying; "the rest of the time, I eat alone in the middle of the day, and that is no fun."

On one of the volunteer's visits, Claire asked if she could visit the volunteer's farm. Years ago, her grandparents lived on a farm, and Claire had fond memories of her visits there. The following week, the volunteer picked her up and drove her around the farm to watch the cattle. When it was time for lunch on the volunteer's patio, Claire had verified with her hospice nurse beforehand, that it was all right for her to have a "real drink"-her favorite, vodka and tonic. Several times in the succeeding months, Claire mentioned how much she had enjoyed "going to a real farm."

Claire's daughter used the hospice staff and the volunteer as a sounding board, admitting that it was difficult to see her Mother giving up and wanting to die. With the encouragement of the staff, she took a part-time job that kept her away from the house, three times a week for four hours. On weekends, Claire's grandsons came over to spend time with their grandmother, so that Susan and her husband would have some time to themselves. After her Mother's death, Susan told the social worker: "My Mother died as she lived. My Dad and I spoiled her. She always came first. I was an only child and I felt that I had to take care of my Mother until she died. I am glad that I was able to keep her at home where she was happy. The hospice team's home visits made it possible for me and my family to take care of my Mother at home."

Case #2: Jim, age 84, a religious man who looked forward to the monthly visits of his young pastor, had worked as a manual laborer all of his life. After he retired, he enjoyed reading biographies, puttering around on his pontoon boat, on his garden tractor, and in the woodworking shop which adjoined his home. In the months following his diagnosis with bone cancer, the home health aide came daily to help bathe and dress him; a physical therapist came twice a week; and the nurse and the social worker visited him regularly.

Jim walked with difficulty. Most of the time, he used a walker. His wife, age 80 and in good health, and his daughter who lived nearby, were afraid that he would fall. They would forbid him to go around doing what he felt like doing. However, during the weekly visits of the hospice volunteer, Jim did as he pleased, including going down a flight of wooden stairs to find a tool that he needed to repair something, and enlisting the volunteer's help to complete the repair work; walking to the edge of the lake to inspect his boat, which he had painted the summer before; eating two desserts with his lunch, and planning what he and the volunteer would do on her next visit.

One week, Jim told the volunteer that when they thought he was asleep, he overheard his wife and daughter talking about his funeral. The volunteer asked him how he felt about that incident; with tears in his eyes, he told her that he wished they would talk about it in front of him. Asked whether he had ever discussed his funeral with his family, he replied that he had tried to, but his wife's response had been "I do not want to talk about that." Jim told the volunteer that there was a particular dress that he wanted his wife to wear at his funeral, and it was not a black dress either. The volunteer suggested that he might want to tell his wife that that was what he wanted. A week later, Jim had a big smile on his face when the volunteer arrived. "I spoke to my wife, and she agreed that she would wear the dress that I want her to wear. Now, I feel better," he said.

One of Jim's last gestures before he slipped into a coma, was to make a trip down the wooden stairs (it took him 15 minutes to negotiate that staircase) to bring up a spark plug. He insisted that the volunteer take it home with her, as she would need it in the spring time for her garden tractor. Jim knew that he would not be around in the spring.

E. The Role of Volunteers

Volunteers are an integral part of the hospice movement in the United States, and are required in Medicare-certified hospices. Hospice volunteers come from the local communities where the hospice programs are located, and from the family, relatives and friends of the patients, including those who had experienced bereavement (Hanna, 1981).

Individuals become hospice volunteers for a variety of reasons. Some are motivated by a general desire to help others (Knight, 1990), others are looking for personal growth and self-actualization (Seibold, 1987), and still others list less positive reasons, such as a personal dread of becoming afflicted with cancer (Jimenez and Jimenez, 1990).

Hospice volunteers go through close to 25 hours of training prior to being assigned a hospice patient. They represent the outside world for the patient whose contact with that world is increasingly limited as the patient's clinical condition deteriorates. The relationship between the volunteer and the hospice patient and family is often similar to that of a friend, who visits regularly and willingly without financial reward. Thus, the volunteer who works in an in-home hospice plays a significant role, not only in the life of the patient, but also in the life of family members. Hospice patients tend to use hospice volunteers and staff as their confidants, persons with whom they share those thoughts, feelings, and experiences, which they do not feel free to discuss with family members (Sander, 1991). In addition, the volunteer offers respite care for the family and is a link with an environment that differs from that of the daily caregivers.

Like the other members of the hospice staff, the volunteer submits a brief weekly written report to the coordinator of volunteers and maintains telephone contact, to apprise the coordinator of any changes in the patient's condition, or to alert the coordinator to impending problems. The coordinator also keeps the volunteer aware of any changes in the patient's condition.

III. EXTENT OF THE HOSPICE MOVEMENT IN THE UNITED STATES

According to the National Hospice Organization, as of June 1996, there were 2573 hospices in the United States, in urban and rural areas (Table 2). Eighty-two percent were Medicare certified and 18% were not Medicare certified. Approximately one-fourth of these hospices admit terminally ill children and 22 hospices throughout the United States specialize in the care of terminally ill children (Miller-Thiel, J. , Glover, J.J., and Beliveau, E., 1993). More than three-fourths (77.7%) of the hospice organizations are non-profit entities (Table 3).

Table 2 - Hospices in the United States

Medicare Certified	2099	82%
Non-Medicare Certified	474	18%
Totals	2573	100%

Source: National Hospice Organization, Statistical Report, June 1996.

Table 3 - Hospice by Ownership Type

Non-profit	77.7%
For-profit	13.0%
Government	3.0%
Other unreported	6.3%

Source: National Hospice Organization, Statistical Report (1996).

IV. FUTURE ISSUES

As the hospice programs adapt to local needs and to societal changes, several emerging issues confront providers of hospice care. These issues fall into five categories. Who should be eligible to receive hospice services? When should patients be referred? What end-of-life services should be provided? Who should provide hospice services? Should hospice programs become specialized?

A. Who Should Be Eligible for Hospice Services?

The primary recipients of hospice care are individuals who fit into the existing Medicare requirements. "Thus if one does not have a home, or if family members need to work, or if one's physician has trouble certifying the six-month life expectancy, one can be declared ineligible for taking advantage of the Medicare hospice benefit" (Sachs, 1994, p. 21). In some instances, the in-patient hospice is an alternative for those who do not have a primary care giver, whether a family member, a colleague, or a friend. The provision of hospice services to patients in institutional settings, primarily hospitals and nursing homes, also accommodates individuals who no longer have a home outside of the institutional setting. However, the primary group served by hospice programs continues to be those who have a primary caregiver, thus excluding individuals in a less traditional family.

It has been found that Hispanics (including Mexican Americans, Puerto Ricans, Cubans, Central and South Americans) and African-Americans fail to access hospice services as often as Caucasians. Researchers suggest several reasons for this finding: lack of trust, fear, hopelessness, insufficient knowledge, an inability to identify providers who share the same heritage and religious beliefs about death and dying (Burrs, 1995, Talamantes, M.A., Lawler, W.R. and Espino, D.V. 1995). Greater attention needs to be given to insure that these populations have continued access to hospice. Efforts to reach these populations with providers and volunteers who are members of these ethnic communities, may broaden the utilization of hospice services.

B. When Should Patients Be Referred to Hospice?

Of continued concern is the perceived reluctance of physicians to refer patients to hospice until the course of dying is well advanced, thus minimizing the time allotted to hospice team members to provide services to dying patients and to their families (Speer, Robinson and Reed, 1995). It is not clear whether postponing entrance into hospice is the result of physician reluctance to refer, or of the patient's refusal to follow the physician's recommendation to seek hospice care.

C. What End-of-Life Services Should Be Provided?

Effective pain management is a primary goal of hospice care programs. Nevertheless, studies indicate that inadequate and unrecorded pain assessment is a persistent problem (Petrosino, 1985; Berry and Ward, 1995; McMillan and Tittle, 1995).

Euthanasia and physician-assisted suicide in their various forms are discussed in hospice programs; some ethicists, and some physicians, who were formerly associated with hospice, favor these end-of-life choices (Quill, 1993). However, many hospice clinicians do not believe that these choices have any place in the continuum of end-of-life care available to hospice patients. Byock (1994) suggests that "the issue extends far beyond mere legalization of physician-assisted suicide. It incorporates the comprehensive consideration of how a society cares for its dying," (p. 3). Some view euthanasia and physician-assisted suicide as a threat to the hospice philosophy, others believe that hospice should be open to participate in the ongoing public debate about these end-of-life issues, and still others look upon these choices as options available, only to individuals who do not choose hospice care.

At least one hospice program in Oregon has announced that, while it will provide counseling services, it will not provide nursing care to patients who ask for physician-assisted suicide. Nevertheless, the author recognizes that nurses are being called upon "to re-examine our commitment to assuring people choice and control over their dying process" (Holden, 1995, p. 14).

Both within and without the hospice movement, there continues to be much conflict of opinion concerning the rights of the patient to choose when and how he/she will die. This conflict arises whether or not pain management has been successful. Patients who wish to choose the time, place and means of their death may do so because they experience loss of functioning as eliminating all meaning from their lives. When the question of euthanasia or physician-assisted suicide arises among providers, disagreement still prevails as to who should decide when enough is enough (Wanzer, Federman, Adelstein, Cassel, Cranford, Hook, Lo, Moertel, Safar, Stone, and Van Eys, 1989; Laine and Davidoff, 1996; Foley, 1997).

D. Who Should Provide Hospice Services?

From the perspectives of the terminally ill patient and of the patient's family, the presence of individuals who provide physical care and physical comfort to the patient, i.e., the home-health aide and the nurse, lowers the family's level of stress. Concern has been voiced by those who fear that the traditional provider-centered model (as opposed to the patient-centered health care delivery model) may dominate the development of hospice to the effect that physical care, which includes pain control, may blind the hospice providers to the psychological, emotional and spiritual issues faced by the dying patient and by the family. The medical model does emphasize the patient's physical comfort and the alleviation and control of physical pain primarily through appropriate medications. Although this model does not preclude the use of interdisciplinary personnel, their roles and functions may be viewed as ancillary rather than as essential (Sontag, 1993).

From the perspectives of the professional hospice caregivers, the roles and functions of each team member may require ongoing clarification. Where do the roles and functions of each member of the interdisciplinary team overlap? Where do they complement each other? To reach a clear definition of the connections between the roles of the professionals, these issues need to be discussed openly among staff members, before the nature of the services provided by each staff member is explained to the patient and to the family.

E. Should Hospice Programs Specialize?

Torrens (1985) suggests that, in the future, as hospice matures, "what will most probably emerge will be a full spectrum of hospice programs that range from the most general, community-based, non-specialized programs that provide a broad base of care to all dying patients, through several more specialized variations, and finally reaching a small number of highly specialized referral units where vigorous research and teaching are actively carried on," (p. 65). The question will then be: "Which dying patients should be served by which hospices?" rather than "Which dying patients should hospices serve?" (p. 65).

The need for research and teaching should not require the adoption of a "medical model of hospice care," which Torrens appears to suggest. Caution needs to be exerted so that meeting the terminally ill patient's non-medical as well as medical needs continue to be the goal of all hospice programs.

SUMMARY

For Sachs (1994), "real progress will come only when death is reintegrated into American society and into medical care" (p. 19). He believes that "all older people deserve good care when dying, not just those with the good fortune to have a home, with family members available to serve as caregivers." The existing Medicare coverage favors those who require aggressive and even inappropriate in-patient care and those who are diagnosed with a terminal illness and are certified by a physician as likely to die within six months.

The care of the aged who are chronically ill, and not benefitting from a six month medical verdict of death, but need palliative care, is not covered under existing Medicare benefits. Palliative care for the chronically ill falls between the cracks, with their Medicare coverage restricted almost exclusively to acute care in a hospital, whereas in Great Britain, St. Christopher's hospice provides non-terminally ill elderly patients with such palliative care. A necessary and progressive step will take place in the United States health care system when government extends its funding of home-based support programs to provide palliative care to persons afflicted with chronic and debilitating medical problems, especially, but not exclusively, the aged. Such programs would offer home care services and respite care, to enhance or maintain the quality of life of both the chronically ill patient and of his/her caregiver. Hospice programs for the chronically ill, delivered primarily in the patient's home will require greater flexibility because the services, though intermittent, may extend over several years.

Already, hospice constitutes a direct affront to the medicalization of dying. In Great Britain and in the United States, it began as a social movement. Hospice was not integrated in the United States health care system until 1983, when hospice services became a covered health care benefit under Medicare, and also under Medicaid in the majority of the states. The hospice movement presently faces some greater challenges, as end-of-life issues are given increasing attention by all strata of society, including ethicists, medical providers, legislators, lawyers, the courts, the terminally ill patients themselves and their relatives.

REFERENCES

Angell, M. (1997). The Supreme Court and physician-assisted suicide—the ultimate right. *The New England Journal of Medicine, 336*(1): 50-53.

Back, A., Wallace, J., Starks, H., and Pearlman, R. (1996). Physician-assisted suicide and euthanasia in Washington state: Patient requesnts and physician responses. *Journal of the American Medical Assoication, 275*(12): 919-925.

Beach, D. (1995). Caregiver discourse: Perceptions of illness-related dialogue. *The Hospice Journal, 10*(3): 13-25.

Berry, P. E. and Ward, S. E. (1995). Barriers to pain management in hospice: A study of family caregivers. *Hospice, 10*(4): 19-34.

Brock, D. (1993). *Life and Death.* Cambridge University Press, Great Britain.

Burrs, F. A. (1995). The African American Experience: Breaking the barriers to hospice. *The Hospice Journal, 10*(2): 15-18.

Byock, I. R. (1991). Physician involvement in assisted suicide decisions. *American Journal of Hospice & Palliative Care, Jan.-Feb.:* 6-7.

Cruzan v. Director. (1990). Missouri Department of Health 110 S. Ct. 2841.

Donovan, M. Dillon P. and McGuire, L. (1987). Incidence and characteristics of pain in a sample of medical-surgical inpatients. *Pain, 30:* 69-78.

Editorial. (1995). Improving care near the end of life: Why is it so hard? *Journal of the American Medical Association, 274*(20): 1634-1636.

Foley, K. (1997). Competent care for the dying instead of physician-assisted suicide. *The New England Journal of Medicine, 336*(1): 54-58.

Goodman, E. (1995). Seeking a humane way to die. The Kalamazoo Gazette. Kalamazoo, MI p.A14

Hanna, S. (1981). The volunteer as part of a hospice team. In *The role of the volunteer in the care of the terminal patient and the family.* Arno Press, NY. 106-110.

Hanrahan, P., and Luchins, D. J. (1995). Feasible criteria for enrolling end-stage dementia patients in home hospice care. *The Hospice Journal, 10*(3): 47-54.

Holden, C. (1995). Must Physician-assisted suicide affect our willingness 'to comfort always'?" *Fanfare ix (1):* 14.

Hospice. (1996). *Newsbriefs, Winter:* 3-4.

Illich, I. (1992). *In the mirror of the past.* Marions Boyars, Publ., NY.

Jimenez, M. A., and Jimenez, D. R. (1990). Training volunteer caregivers of persons with AIDS. *Social Work Health Care, 14*(3): 73-85.

Knight, C. F. (1990). Networking with the gay community to meet the needs of AIDS patients: Special considerations for volunteer training. *American Journal of Hospice Care, 7*(1): 31-35.

Kohut, J. M. and, Kohut, S., Jr. (1984). *Hospice: caring for the terminally ill.* Charles C. Thomas, Publisher, Illinois.

Laine, C., and Davidoff, F. (1996). Patient-centered medicine: A professional evolution. *Journal of the American Medical Association, 275*(2): 152-156.

Maillet, J., and King, D. (1993). Nutritional care of the terminally ill adult. *Hospice, 9*(2/3): 37-54.

McMillan, S. C., and Tittle, M. (1995). A descriptive study of the management of pain and pain-related side effects in a cancer center and a hospice. *The Hospice Journal, 10*(1): 89-107.

Miller-Thiel, J. Glover, J. J., and Beliveau, E. (1993). Caring for the dying child. *The Hospice Journal, 9*(2-3): 55-72.

Mor, V. (1988). Participating hospices and the patients they serve. In *The hospice experiment.* (ed. Mor, V., Greer, D.S., and Kastenbaum. R.). John Hopkins University Press, Baltimore, p. 16-27.

National Hospice Organization. (1994). Standards of a hospice program of care. *The Hospice Journal ,9*(4): 39-74.

National Hospice Organization (1995). *Hospice Code of Ethics.* National Hospice Organization, Arlington, VA.

National Hospice Organization. (1995). *Organizational Vision, Mission Statement and Goals.* October.

National Hospice Organization. (1996). *Facts about Hospice.*

Omnibus Budget Reconciliation Act of 1990. Title 4, Section 4206. *Congressional Record, October* 26: 12638.

Petrosino, B. M. (1985). Characteristics of hospice patients, primary caregivers, and nursing problems: Foundations for future research. *The Hospice Journal, 1*(1): 3-19.

Quill, T. E. (1993). *Death and Dignity.* W.W. Norton, New York.

Quinlan, Karen v. State of New Jersey. (1976). 355 A 2d 647.

Rhymes, J. (1990). Hospice care in America. *Journal of the American Medical Association, 264*(3): 369-372.

Rhymes, J. A. (1993). Hospice care in the nursing home. *Nursing Home Medicine, 1*(6): 14-24.

Robert Wood Johnson Foundation, Support Project. (1995). A controlled trial to improve care for seriously ill hospitalized patients: The study to understand prognoses and preferences for out-comes and risks of treatment. *Journal of the American Medical Association, 274*(20): 1591-1598.

Sachs, G. A. (1994). Improving care of the dying. *Generations, Winter:* 19-22.

Sander, C. P. (1991). Hospice life: Terminally ill and the quality of life (Doctoral Dissertation, New York University, 1991). *Dissertation Abstracts International, 52*(06B): 3279.

Seale, C. and Cartwright, A. (1994). *The year before death.* Ashgate Publishing Co., Brookfield, VT.

Seibold, D. R., Rossi, S. M., Berteotti, C. R., Soprych, S. L., and McQuillan, L. P. (1987). Volunteer involvement in a hospice care program: An examination of motives, activities. *American Journal of Hospice Care, 4*(2):43-55.

Sontag, M. E. (1993). Oregon hospices: Medicare certification, program characteristics, and staff perceptions (Doctoral Dissertation, University of California Berkeley, 1993). *Dissertation Abstracts International, 55*(07A): 2145.

Speer, D.C. Robinson, B.E. & Reed, M.P. (1995). The relationship between hospice length of stay and caregiver adjustment. *Hospice Journal 10*(1): 45-58.

Talamantes, M. A., Lawler, W .R. and Espino, D. V. (1995). Hispanic American Elders: Caregiving norms surrounding dying and the use of hospice services. *The Hospice Journal, 10*(2): 35-49.

Torrens, P. R. (1985). "Which dying patients should hospices serve? In *Hospice Patients and Public Policy.* (ed. Torrens, P.R.). American Hospital Association, IL, 63-72.

Traille, J. M. (1991). Palliative care for the terminally ill. (Doctoral Dissertation, The Union Institute, 1991). *Dissertation Abstracts International, 52*(01B): 188.

U.S. Government Census. (1990).

Veatch, R.M. (1976). *Death, dying and the biological revolution: Our last quest for responsibility.* Yale University Press, New Haven.

Vladeck, B. C. (1995). End of life care. *Journal of the American Medical Association, 274*(6): 449.

Wanzer, S., Federman, D., Adelstein, S., Cassel, C., Cranford, R., Hook, E., Lo, B., Moertel, C., Safar, P., Stone, A., and Van Eys, J. (1989). The physician's responsibility toward hopelessly ill patients: A second look. *The New England Journal of Medicine* 320(13): 844-849.

Welk, T. A. (1991). An educational model for explaining hospice services. *The Journal of Hospice & Palliative Care, Sept./Oct:* 14-17.

24.

SOCIAL AND ETHICAL CHOICES IN HEALTH CARE

Ruth Ellen Bulger, *Uniformed Services University of the Health Sciences, Bethesda, MD*

Complex processes affect how social and ethical decisions related to health care treatment are made in the United States. Various kinds of decisions that patients and families must make can lead to perplexing social and ethical dilemmas for the nation. These issues need careful consideration by various people, including the involved individuals, their care givers, and the administrators of health care institutions. In some cases, state and national venues also contribute.

I. SOURCES OF SOCIAL AND ETHICAL DILEMMAS

A recent Institute of Medicine Report, Society's Choices: Social and Ethical Decision Making in Biomedicine (1995), finds that such dilemmas involved with social and ethical issues emanate from a variety of situations. First, new or novel scientific developments raise unique ethical concerns. For example, in the United States, the development and use of renal dialysis or transplantation of a kidney are always paid for by the government. However, this payment for treatment of one particular disease has given rise to an interesting question: Why does the federal government not pay for the transplantation of other body organs or for the care of other diseases?

Second, social and ethical dilemmas can also arise when there is early diffusion of newly developed innovations before the related ethical issues are resolved. For example, the use by an infertile couple of an unrelated female as a surrogate mother raises questions about parental identity for the subsequent child.

Ethical dilemmas can also result from the aggregate effect of many small developments. For example, the routine use of immunization, antibiotics and good hygiene have reduced the risk of early death due to infectious diseases; thus, people live longer. Longevity, in turn, raises questions about quality of life for the very old and end-of-life care issues.

Finally, organizational changes can be accompanied by ethical problems. An example of this in the United States would be the restructuring of the health care system to reduce health care costs in such a way that allocation of health care resources for the poor and rationing of resources have become major ethical dilemmas (IOM, 1995).

Abundant unsolved social and ethical issues confront the hospitals and other medical care institutions in our country. What is appropriate care at the beginning and end of life, how much or how little care is required, who makes decisions, who should get available organs for transplantation, and the complications that arise from recent genetic study are just a few of the issues that demand daily decisions within health care organizations. Health care administrators need to ensure that mechanisms within their institutions establish and carry out appropriate, functional policies and procedures. Ethical dilemmas experienced by patients, staff, and community must be dealt with in an appropriate and sensitive manner. The exact mechanisms will depend on the institution's relationship to other institutions—health science centers, companies, other hospitals—or other more complex associations.

A. Managed Care Raises Ethical Dilemmas

Particularly pressing is the problem of handling the increasing costs of health care and the rapidly changing environment of managed care while also providing appropriate care for Americans not covered by medical insurance. In the U.S. we spend about 15% of our gross domestic product on health care or, more accurately, on the care of those who are sick. By world standards, our care is enviable. At the same time, the country does not provide universal access to health care for all its citizens, allowing gross inequities to exist. The rejection of the Health Security Act proposed by the Clinton Administration has accelerated market penetration by various kinds of managed health care organizations, with hopes of slowing the rate of increase in health care costs. These unfettered market forces in health care have created an environment where entrepreneurs and investors can also reap profits, sometimes at the expense of quality. Brook et al. (1996) point out that over 50 million people are currently enrolled in managed care organizations (20% of all Americans). They also stress the importance of maintaining quality of care in the new managed care environment. The enormous growth of managed care organizations has brought with it fundamental changes to medical care and a variety of new social and ethical decisions. Johnson (1995) suggests that hospital-based acute care bioethics has encountered problems in translation to a managed care system since such systems need to address not only the issues of individual treatment decisions, but the ethical issues of allocation of scarce resources, financial health, growth of the whole institution providing the care, insurance risk, and limitations on care.

A diverse set of present managed care organizational forms (MCO) have been described by Christensen (1995). These forms include the preferred provider organization (PPOs), in which physicians contract with the MCO and are paid on a fee-for-service basis. Incentives tend to increase health care costs with fees often deeply discounted by the health plan. Income security is low, but professional involvement in decision making is high. Another form consists of the independent practice associations (IPSs), in which physicians contract with one or more MCOs, but the practice association gives them negotiation power. Pay is often reimbursed on a capitated basis, yet physician autonomy is high. Group model health maintenance organizations (HMOs) are another form; here the physician is part of a group that contracts with the HMO and is paid a salary plus bonuses on a capitated basis in advance of providing services, but retaining professional involvement as physicians. Finally, in the staff model HMO physicians are employed by the MCO (again with incentives), but with job security as employees. They tend to have little professional involvement as physicians.

Christensen (1995) concludes that structured features neutralizing incentives to undertreat patients and maximizing incentives to provide quality medical care include the following:

- non-profit status
- salaried physicians
- sharing the risk of capitation across a large group of physicians
- clinical practice managed by physicians with utilization review not serving as a barrier to providing health care services
- patients or members of the MCO having a role in operations of the organization at a number of levels, including receiving full disclosure about incentives to limit treatment and restrictions on coverage as well as being included in discussions of benefit coverage and conflict resolution procedures.

Patients or members should also be involved with related ethics committees as well as having health education on improving health and financial tradeoffs in treatment and benefit decisions.

Mariner (1995) discusses the problems involved with developing ethics standards for MCOs. These standards combine business ethics such as those related to insurance and management with ethics of health care delivery expected as part of the doctor/patient relationship. She points out that existing codes do not answer whose needs take precedence for the manager when the financial needs of the organization conflict with the needs of the patients. She suggests that basic features to be considered include recognizing that MCOs have non-delegable medical responsibilities as an organization. They must provide good health care to individual enrollees although officers and staff still remain bound by personal ethical obligations. Ethical standards should give priority to its medical mission. Organizational standards should reflect ethical principles that apply to all human endeavors. Mariner lists fairness, honesty, truthfulness, respect, and justice as such standards. Justice would ensure that all enrollees receive appropriate care from an ethical viewpoint, not from financial self-interest. Honesty and fairness might require complete disclosure of terms and conditions of the contracts that the organization offers, such as detailed information on specific treatments that are and are not covered as well as criteria for making decisions about coverage for new therapies.

Morreim (1995) argues that the relationship between distributive justice in health care—justice that emphasizes the needs of vulnerable individuals who may be denied specific interventions—must be balanced with contributive justice that observes the legitimate expectations of the many whose contributions create the common resource pool. He believes that health care must now be conceived in terms of trade-offs.

B. Mechanisms for Considering Ethical Issues Beginning with the Patient

The most pressing ethical issues change; what they are depends on the eye of the viewer. Hence, workable mechanisms must be used on all levels to help resolve social and ethical dilemmas related to health care. The mechanisms will also be most useful if they are associated with the institutions that can bring about resolution of the problem, whether that be at the level of the patient and family, the hospital, the health care organization, the courts, the state, or the nation. The health care administrator needs to know how such mechanisms have been used in the past, the results previously generated, and how they might function to solve new dilemmas that arise.

In the U.S. these dilemmas are accompanied by a situation in which the patient is intimately involved in the process of health care decision making. Since patients bear the pain of illness and side effects, they frequently become the main factor in the decision-making process. In order to understand the view of the relationships between the patient and the health care provider, certain societal and cultural elements that occurred in key moments in the history of American thought need to be considered. Examples include the emphasis that is placed on respect for patient autonomy, the fundamental role accorded the patient in giving informed consent prior to medical care on research being done to him or her, and finally, the growth of various groups in America that demand rights. In a recent book entitled Habits of the Heart, Robert Bellah and co-authors (1986) reflect on three central strands of thought in America: biblical, republican, and modern individualist. They assert that Americans feel conflict between individualism and the need to be part of a community committed to the common good.

II. RESOURCES FOR ETHICAL PROBLEM SOLVING

Differences of values about problematic ethical issues that occur in the health care arena do exist among parts of our society; however, public resources can be used at various levels in society to consider what responses are appropriate. A variety of reports and articles have described and evaluated past national bioethics bodies to identify which ones have been successful. Two of the most recent analyses include the Office of Technology Assessment report entitled Biomedical Ethics in U.S. Public Policy (1993) as well as the recent Institute of Medicine (IOM) report entitled Society's Choices: Social and Ethical Decision Making in Biomedicine (1995).

A. Functions of Ethics Deliberative Bodies

The 1995 IOM study discusses a variety of mechanisms categorized by source of sponsorship or authority as (1) political and legal such as federal commissions, (2) professional and institutional such as Institutional Review Boards, or (3) grassroots such as individual and community initiatives. The report provides a variety of functions that such ethics or public deliberative bodies, have been created to fill including but not limited to the following:
- to bring to the larger public opportunity and responsibility previously belonging to elite groups;
- to identify ethical issues at stake in areas of societal controversy;

- to undertake a careful analysis of an issue;
- to develop and/or document areas of consensus;
- to expose and document areas of disagreement;
- to unify the expertise of authorities from a wide variety of relevant fields;
- to represent competing interests;
- to generate public awareness and debate;
- to be a lightning rod for public concern;
- to educate;
- to correct misunderstandings and errors in reasoning;
- to develop factual bases for public policy;
- to offer guidance for decision making;
- to develop recommendations for action;
- to recommend new legislation or improvements in existing public policy;
- to sanction delays or recommend unpopular policies;
- to dignify and legitimize official action;
- to overcome bureaucratic obstacles; and/or
- to justify the expenditure of money.

B. Performance Criteria

While the evaluation of a particular public ethics body depends upon its context (nature of the controversy, specific tasks of the body, social setting, legal environment), the IOM report (1995) developed criteria that could be used in establishing, participating in, or judging the performance of public ethics bodies.

The IOM criteria covers a number of areas. First, the intellectual integrity of the report is of utmost importance. Logic is a prerequisite including soundness of reasoning and coherence of the report. Logical analysis can help clarify the terms and nature of the debates. The dimension of scholarship, including coherence, competence, knowledge of the interdisciplinary field of bioethics and solid, empirical, state-of-the-art information is crucial. Ethical consideration is often complicated by uncertainty, lack of information, and conflicting values; sound judgment manifests the ability to discern the unique particularities of the problem, to reframe, to reason by analogy, to acknowledge the interest of affected parties, and to balance competing considerations. Another criteria is sensitivity to democratic values, representation of diverse views, and openness whenever possible. The reports communicate if they are written clearly, trenchantly argued, and comprehensible to as wide an audience as possible.

Effectiveness is based on an understanding of the group's purpose, the public need, the social context, and ability to communicate. They must also be well disseminated to a broad audience. Authority can come from the appointing source such as the President, the individual reputation of members and staff or from a successful history of accomplishment (IOM, 1995).

C. Levels of Ethics Deliberative Bodies

In health care decision making, attempts are generally made to keep the decision-making process as close to the autonomous patient as possible. The patient, the family, the patient's religious advisor, and immediate health care providers are most often involved in the decisions. Hospital Ethics Committees make decisions that consider broader local issues as well as issues affecting individuals other than the patient. Professional societies provide guidelines for decision making. In some cases, legal and ultimately political mechanisms become necessary. Nagel (1995) and Brock (1995) both look at the way public ethics bodies in present day pluralistic America can face ethical challenges from the points of view of moral epistemology and philosophy as a way to justify the value of the group.

In America the patient is central to the decision-making process. Understanding the United States' view of the relationships that have developed between patient and health care provider necessitates consideration of the following:

- societal and cultural elements in key moments in the history of American thought;
- the fundamental role of informed consent;
- the emphasis on the respect for patient autonomy; and
- the growth of various rights groups that have worked together to place the patient in the center of decision making.

However, many complex ethical decisions affect more than the individual. Should one use organs of a brain-dead individual or a primate to keep another individual alive? Should society pay a large hospital bill to keep a brain-dead person alive by the use of modern machines for long periods of time at the request of a family member? What, if any, limits to shared funding of health care should be paid by group insurance or public funding? In these cases decisions involve more than just the particular patient or local groups.

The first requirement for decision makers is to recognize which components are based on scientific considerations and which ones on social or ethical issues. Take, for example, the practice of using adult white males as the only subjects in clinical trials of a medication that in clinical practice would be used in males and females (both pregnant and nonpregnant) of various ages and racial or ethnic groups. For an adequate decision to be made about the acceptability of the data obtained, one would need to have scientific data on whether the results are also valid for additional groups. Other scientific issues that could relate to the decision include whether administering a certain drug to a pregnant women is known by scientific experiments to cause fetal damage.

At the same time these same health decisions have a number of social and ethical issues that must also be confronted; concerns about justice, autonomy, beneficence, non-maleficence, caring, and responsibility must be balanced. Who is best able to balance these ethical principles during the decision-making process? Who decides if a pregnant woman should be included in a clinical trial of a drug, thereby exposing the fetus—the woman, the physician, an Institutional Review Board, some other part of society, or a combination of sources? These are decisions we face daily.

D. Use of Courts, Legislatures, and Executive Branch Agencies

Obviously, we need appropriate mechanisms to address these ethically charged issues as they arise in health care. Health care administrators must also be familiar with ethical analysis and the results produced when these mechanisms have been used. Currently, health care solutions to social, legal, and ethical issues are made by (1) the courts, (2) state or national legislatures, (3) the executive branch, and occasionally by (4) ethics deliberative bodies appointed to consider these complex decisions. Each has strengths and weaknesses. Gostin (1995) points out the expansive range of policy making bodies and groups that seek to influence health policy, thereby making it impossible to offer a systematic and comprehensive analysis of health policy formulation. He finds that a robust society valuing freedom of expression should not exclude those who wish to participate in the formulation of health policy. He believes that sound health policy is based on objectivity, understanding of the data and arguments, a fair balance between competing values, well-considered criteria for decision making, and public accountability for decisions.

Gostin (1995) discusses the strengths and weaknesses each of the three branches of government has in making ethical decisions. He believes that the particular branch used is determined more by chance and how a question is raised than by the effectiveness of the mechanism for the particular question being posed. Policy that fundamentally affects human rights may require judicial rather than majoritarian determinations since courts are suited to protect the rights of individuals and groups. When little established policy exists, courts can answer questions case-by-case. They can interpret, construe, and apply the law, remaining aloof from controversy and relying on neutral legal doctrine. Courts focus on the concerns of individuals or groups involved in specific cases, not the broader implications and overall objectives of the health care system.

In analyzing the role of the legislature, Gostin (1995) believes that after years of case law, the legislature can clarify and codify policy choices. The legislature is publicly accountable, has the capacity to collect full information, has a mandate to protect and promote the health of the public, and can engage deliberative processes in enacting legislation. However, as we have repeatedly witnessed, legislators belong to partisan political parties, may be indebted to individuals or groups such as special interest groups, and tend to operate on a short horizon related to their term of office (Gostin, 1995).

The executive branch, Gostin (1995) finds, can also be objective and accountable. It can marshal evidence and reasoning with power to develop, shape, and expand health policy via executive orders, rule making, and interpretive guidance. Yet here again, the process is conducted on the platform of the executive. Advisory ethics bodies are appointed by various executive branch agencies.

E. Other Resources for Decision Making

In America, we have devised many decision making approaches in addition to those provided by the judicial, legislative, and executive branches of the government. Several different levels may be needed since decisions depend on the number of people involved. Specifically, The IOM report (1995) favors a multilevel approach to bioethics deliberations; the levels include local, institutional, professional, community, state, and national levels.

The first level includes the patient making the decision concerning a personal moral dilemma. If only that person is involved, much latitude is given for determining the decision. The family, health care provider, and religious advisor can provide increased input for the individual patient. Yet the decision remains as close to the individual as possible (IOM, 1995). However, Levinsky (1996) points out that the growth of managed care magnifies potential forces outside the doctor-patient relationship that can influence or infringe upon this right including insurance companies and managed care organizations.

If disagreements arise concerning an ethical dilemma while a patient is in a hospital, ethics committees help evaluate the patient's situation, prognosis, and the community norms in order to provide advice to the patient and caregivers. As individual health care institutions form groups that provide not only acute care, but chronic or nursing care, such ethics committees need to address issues across the various institutions, but still remain advisory by nature, situated at the proper level to have an optimal effect (IOM, 1995).

Of particular importance to hospital administrators are the roles that the multidisciplinary institutional ethics committees, frequently called Hospital Ethics Committees, have evolved over the past twenty years both in the U. S. and Canada. Institutions should share in the responsibility of morally charged treatment, and caregivers who know a great deal about the condition of the patient are valuable members of these committees. The Joint Commission on Accreditation of Health Care Organizations, for example, requires that hospitals have some mechanism like the hospital ethics committee.

Although the function of Hospital Ethics Committees varies, they are helpful in confirming clinical diagnoses and prognoses as well as reviewing treatment decisions and mediating conflicts over patient care. They frequently serve as a forum to discuss ethical issues, and they formulate institutional procedural guidelines on decision making. Further, the committee can educate staff, families, and the community about ethical problems.

Community preferences can be involved in decision making when communities have certain moral or social views. For example, hospitals supported by certain churches may not provide family planning education or abortion services. On a more general level, professional societies, such as nursing or medical associations, become involved by promulgating professional standards and practice guidelines for their members. These practice guidelines help ensure an adequate standard for care. State laws also can be involved in certain decisions since such laws control many aspects of provider behavior, medical licensing, and institutional standards. Certain states have appointed ethics commissions such as the New York State Task Force on Life and the Law or the New Jersey Commission on Legal and Ethical Problems in the Delivery of Health Care.

National guidelines are involved in some cases since Congress has frequently provided laws related to medical care. National Commissions debate ethical issues and provide guidance to health care professionals and legislators who make these laws. Certain commissions are agency-specific, making recommendations on issues related only to one agency as was the case of the National Commission for the Protection of Human Subjects of Biomedical and Behavioral Research. Others examine issues that have cross-agency concerns such as the President's Commission for the Study of Ethical Problems in Medicine and Biomedical and Behavioral Research.

Historically, commissions, task forces, and ad hoc advisory bodies on national health policy decisions have not only been supported by various parts of the government but also by private foundations. Using interviews, media reports, government documents, and scholarly literature, Feldman et al. (1992) studied five major foundation-funded commissions that were established in the post-World War II period with the primary purpose of influencing government policy related to health care. In addition to policy analysis, these authors give implicit purposes for such commissions. The purposes include long-range education or agenda setting; legitimizing and mobilizing support for an initiative to which some policymakers were committed; investigating the cause of a crisis and giving reassurance; managing an issue by providing time for cooling-off while objective analysis occurs; and creating the appearance that something is being done. The authors concluded that all five of the commissions produced usable knowledge: two had a diffuse impact on policy, and three had a discernible impact on legislation, especially those that took advantage of a policy window in which the public perceived a problem, the government believed action was appropriate, and political activists and policy people agreed on the broad lines of a solution.

When values related to problematic ethical issues in health care clash, these ethics deliberative bodies consider decisions. Resources provide different types of guidance. They can identify the ethical issues in societal controversies, undertake a careful analysis of the issues, stimulate discussion, ensure the representation of competing interests, generate public awareness and debate, and educate the public. Through discussion, they can develop and document areas of public consensus, draw on the expertise of authorities from a wide variety of fields, and develop factual bases and recommendations for public policy (IOM, 1995).

However, public debate of contentious issues may have negative results. For example, a report could be unduly influenced by a particular special interest group; hence it would not be representative of the public at large. A report might also attempt to deliver a moral certainly that it is not really equipped to produce (IOM, 1995).

F. Clinical Trials Regulation by Institutional Review Boards

Frequently the best treatment options are available only if the patient takes part in a clinical trial as part of a clinical research protocol. To safeguard these human subjects, Institutional Review Boards (IRBs) have been mandated by the National Research Act of 1979 (P.L.93-348) in all research institutions receiving federal funds. Each IRB must include individuals as members who are not involved in research. The IRB also includes members with professional competence in pertinent aspects of human subjects research as well as those of various ethnic and racial backgrounds. Edgar and Rothman (1995) suggest a variety of reforms for the IRB process, including more effective oversight mechanisms such as examining a sample protocol from research settings or interviews of the research subjects about the consent process and their understanding of the research. Such protection was not always mandated, and history has demonstrated that certain safeguards are necessary to protect patient rights that have too often been ignored. A variety of responsibilities now fall to Institutional Review Boards:

- assessing risks and benefits of the proposed research;
- looking at the process of asking the subject for informed consent including the written material that each subject must sign;
- assuring the privacy and confidentiality of participants;
- monitoring and observing the research; and
- ensuring that the incentives offered to subjects do not unduly coerce them into becoming subjects.

Special consideration protects such vulnerable subjects as children, prisoners, pregnant women, mentally disabled persons, economically and educationally disadvantaged persons. To be approved, research must carry minimal risk or benefit subjects directly.

Informed consent took center stage after terrible lapses in the protection of patients' rights seen in such heinous human experiments as those undertaken by the Nazis during World War II. The abuse suffered by prisoners of war and civilians constantly reminds us of what can and does occur. During the Nuremberg military criminal trials, the Nuremberg Code of 1948 was developed as a standard to judge the action of the perpetrators of these experiments (1949).

Despite the code, further infractions of human rights occurred in the United States. In 1932 the infamous Tuskeegee study began, a study in which rural black males with syphilis were allowed to go untreated long after penicillin had been discovered and treatment had been shown to work for this condition (1973).

In 1966, debilitated elderly patients at the Jewish Chronic Disease Hospital in Brooklyn were injected with live cancer cells to determine if the cells would be rejected. No proper informed consent was obtained from the subjects (Faden and Beauchamp, 1986).

Clearly, vigilance is required to ensure that advances be made in human subjects research, but only with careful protection of their rights and welfare. To this end, the U.S. government is launching a three-year $6 million grant program for research on how to help potential subjects understand the purpose, methods, procedures, risks, and benefits of research using human subjects.

G. Ethics Commissions Established by Congress

The first U.S. Government federal guidelines for research on human subjects was written in 1953 for research at the Clinical Center at NIH. This document, entitled "Group Consideration for Clinical Research Procedures Deviating from Accepted Medical Practice or Involving Universal Hazards," was the first that required committee review of human subjects research. The requirement extended to all medical institutions funded by the government in 1966. Rights for research subjects were bolstered after a series of hearings was held at the United States Senate in 1973. The discussion encompassed a variety of topics including sterilization of the mentally retarded, research on human fetuses, and the use of prisoners in research.

Partially in response to these hearings, Congress passed the National Research Act of 1974 (P.L.93-348), establishing Institutional Review Boards as a requirement. The U.S. Congress authorized a National Commission for the Protection of Human Subjects of Biomedical and Behavioral Research. The Commission had several functions: identifying ethical principles underlying the conduct of biomedical and behavioral research involving human subjects, developing guidelines so that the research is done in accordance with the underlying principles, and making recommendations to the Secretary of DHEW on regulations that should be developed. The scope of concern of the National Commission was focused within one agency and was limited to research funded by Department of Health Education and Welfare and topics mandated by Congress. The National Commission, chaired by Kenneth J. Ryan, M.D., wrote a series of valuable reports summed up in what is known as the Belmont Report (1978). This report had three organizing principles for clinical research:

- Autonomy: Individuals should be treated as autonomous agents capable of self determination; persons with diminished autonomy are entitled to protection;
- Beneficence: Beneficence is the making of efforts to secure the well being of persons and protect them from harm; and
- Justice: Justice requires that burdens and benefits be equally distributed among subjects.

The President's Commission for the Study of Ethical Problems in Medicine and Biomedical and Behavioral Research followed the National Commission. The President's Commission functioned from 1980-1983 under the U.S. Congress's Biomedical Research and Training Amendments of 1978 (P.L.95-622). Its function was to advise both the President and Congress on bioethical issues, some of which were mandated by Congress, some undertaken on the Commission's own initiative. Its scope crossed several federal agencies and included patient care issues. This commission was chaired by Morris B. Abram, J.D., L.L.D. Many of the reports of both the National Commission and President's Commission remain extremely valuable resources for those interested in issues of human subjects research and biomedical ethics.

In January 1994, a 15-member Advisory Committee on Human Radiation Experiments (ACHRE) was appointed by President Clinton and chaired by Ruth Faden, Ph.D., to ascertain if unethical radiation experiments were sponsored by the federal government between 1946-1974. The Committee, having submitted its final report on ethical and scientific standards in radiation-related experiments in October 1995, made recommendations for improving current policies and procedures that provide protection for human research subjects. They also recommended many improvements including the following (JAMA, 1996; ACHRE report, 1996):

- IRBs should allocate time so that careful attention can be directed to studies with more than minimal risk for subjects.
- Clinical treatment must be clearly distinguished from clinical research in the minds of potential human subjects.
- Agencies supporting the research and the purpose of the research should be clearly presented to the subjects.
- IRBs should be responsible that the quality of the science to be conducted is high enough to warrant exposure of the subject to risk or inconvenience.
- Subjects would be provided with as much benefit as they would have if they did not participate in the research.

The opinions voiced in the ACHRE report served as one stimulus for President Clinton to appoint a new National Biomedical Advisory Commission (NBAC) to be chaired by Princeton's President Harold Shapiro. The new advisory group is charged with the protection of the welfare of human research subjects, but will also consider other topics such as those related to genetic information.

H. Ethics Groups Appointed Within the Executive Branch

Executive agencies have appointed ad hoc ethics advisory groups which provide advice in handling biomedical ethics issues. The Director of NIH established a Recombinant DNA Advisory Committee (RAC) that advises on recombinant DNA research, just as the present NIH Director has appointed a new panel to advise on whether this committee should continue to function in the present capacity. In 1988, the Ethical, Legal, and Social Implications (ELSI) Working Group was established at the National Center for Human Genome Research at NIH. Presently, another ad hoc advisory group is evaluating the role being played by the ELSI group. The NIH Human Fetal Tissue Transplantation Research Panel was appointed in 1988 to consider federally supported research that involved transplantation of human fetal tissue. Although most members of the Panel supported this research when the decision to abort a fetus was separated from the research, the Panel's recommendations were not made into policy; in fact, a moratorium on such research with federal funds continues.

III. RESOURCES PROVIDED BY PROFESSIONAL GROUPS

Additional resources help hospital administrators with social and ethical decision making. On the first level, a rich environment of biomedical ethicists have been trained over the last decade. Many are presently involved with research and analysis of ethical dilemmas related to biomedical ethics and clinical research. Training has occurred both in the University environment but also in important ethics centers. The Hasting Center in New York, established in 1969 as an independent, nonprofit institution, is an important example. Hastings Center sponsors conferences, internships, visiting investigator programs, and two publications: Hastings Center Report and IRB: A Review of Human Subjects.

Another valuable resource is the Joseph and Rose Kennedy Institute of Ethics, which began in 1971 at Georgetown University in Washington, D.C. The Kennedy Institute maintains an exclusive National Reference Center for Bioethics Literature; publishes the Kennedy Institute of Ethics Journal, Bibliography of Bioethics, and the Encyclopedia of Bioethics and conducts courses in beginning and advanced bioethics with faculty members from a broad area of biomedical ethics. Georgetown University also houses the Center for Clinical Bioethics.

Professional specialty associations, voluntary organizations, and a variety of foundations have taken the handling of bioethics issues related to the disciplines seriously. Both clinical practice guidelines and ethics policies or statements are published to help their members handle difficult situations. For problems related to specific issues, these groups form important resources. Numerous courses, publications, and newsletters address social and ethical issues in health care.

Professional groups that have been active in considering social and ethical issues in biomedicine include the American College of Obstetricians and Gynecologists (ACOG); they have produced a variety of reports and guidelines for practitioners (ACOG, 1992). An offshoot of ACOG is the National Advisory Board on Ethics and Reproduction (NABER) that provides a forum for debate and counsel on ethical issues in reproductive sciences and technology. The American Medical Association (AMA) supports a Council on Ethical and Judicial Affairs that addresses a variety of ethical and legal concerns of interest to clinicians. Guidelines and recommendations are published in their Journal of the American Medical Association. The American College of Physicians (ACP) has published several editions of the American College of Physicians Ethics Manual as well as policies in the Annals of Internal Medicine.

SUMMARY

Public bodies that deliberate on health issues play an important continuing role in addressing health care dilemmas at a variety of levels. Health care administrators have many resources available to aid in decision-making for ethical and social dilemmas.

ADDITIONAL RESOURCES AND REPORTS

Reports of the National Commission for the Protection of Human Subjects of Biomedical and Behavioral Research (National Commission).

Report and Recommendations: Research on the Fetus, 1975.

Appendix to Report and Recommendations: Research on the Fetus, 1975.

Proceedings of the March 14-15, 1975 Meeting

The Belmont Report: Ethical Principles and Guidelines for the Protection of Human Subjects of Research, 1978.

Appendix (Volumes I and II) to the Belmont Report: Ethical Principles and Guidelines for the Protection of Human Subjects of Research, 1978.

Report and Recommendations: Research Involving Prisoners, 1976.

Appendix to Report and Recommendations: Research Involving Prisoners, 1976.

Report and Recommendations: Research Involving Children, 1977.

Appendix to Report and Recommendations: Research Involving Children, 1977

Report and Recommendations: Psychosurgery, 1977.

Appendix to Report and Recommendations. Psychosurgery, 1977.

Disclosure of Research Information Under the Freedom of Information Act, 1977.

Report and Recommendations: Special Study. Implications of Advances in Biomedical and Behavioral Research, 1978.

Report and Recommendations. Research Involving Those Institutionalized as Mentally Infirm, 1978.

Appendix to Report and Recommendations: Research Involving Those Institutionalized as Mentally Infirm, 1978.

Report and Recommendations. Institutional Review Boards, 1978.

Appendix to Report and Recommendations: Institutional Review Boards, 1978.

Report and Recommendations: Ethical Guidelines for Delivery of Health Services in DHEW, 1978.

Appendix to Report and Recommendations: Ethical Guidelines for Delivery of Health Services by DHEW, 1978.

Reports of the President's Commission for the Study of Ethics, Problems in Medicine and Biomedical and Behavioral Research (President's Commission).

Defining Death: A Report on the Medical, Legal, and Ethical Issues in the Determination of Death, 1981.

Protecting Human Subjects: The Adequacy and Uniformity of Federal Rules and their Implementation, 1981.

Whistleblowing in Biomedical Research: Policies and Procedures for Responding to Reports of Misconduct, 1981.

Making Health Care Decisions: A Report on the Ethical and Legal Implications of Informed Consent in the Patient-Practitioner Relationship. Volume 1: Report, 1982.

Making Health Care Decisions: A Report on the Ethical and Legal Implications of Informed Consent in the Patient-Practitioner Relationship. Volume 2: Appendices, 1982.

Making Health Care Decisions. A Report on the Ethical and Legal Implications of Informed Consent in the Patient-Practitioner Relationship. Volume 3: Appendices, Studies of the Foundations of Informed Consent, 1982.

Splicing Life: A Report on the Social and Ethical Issues of Genetic Engineering with Human Beings, 1982.

Compensating for Research Injuries. The Ethical and Legal Implications for Programs to Redress Injured Subjects, 1982.

Deciding to Forego Life-Sustaining Treatment: A Report on the Ethical, Medical, and Legal Issues in Treatment Decisions, 1983.

Implementing Human Research Regulations: Second Biennial Report of the Adequacy and Uniformity of Federal Rules and Policies, and of their Implementation, for the Protection of Human Subjects, 1983.

Screening and Counseling for Genetic Conditions: The Ethical, Social, and Legal Implications of Genetic Screening, Counseling, and Education Programs, 1983.

Securing Access to Health Care: The Ethical Implications of Differences in the Availability of Health Services. Volume 1: Report, 1983.

Securing Access to Health Care: The Ethical Implications of Differences in the Availability of Health Services. Volume 2: Appendices, Sociocultural and Philosophical Studies, 1983.

Securing Access to Health Care: The Ethical Implications of Differences in the Availability of Health Services. Volume 3: Appendices, Empirical, Legal, and Conceptual Studies, 1983.

Summing Up: Final Report on Studies of the Ethical and Legal Problems in Medicine and Biomedical and Behavioral Research, 1983.

REFERENCES

Abram, M. B. and Wolf, S. M. (1984). Public involvement in medical ethics: A model for government action. *New England Journal of Medicine*, 310: 627-632.

Advisory Committee on Human Radiation Experiments. (1996). The Human Radiation Experiments: Final Report of the President's Advisory Committee. Oxford University Press, New York, NY.

A.G.O.G. (1992). *List of Committee Opinions (December).* ACOG Resource Center, Washington, D.C.

Altman, L. K. (1993). Fatal drug trial raises questions about informed consent. *New York Times* (Oct. 5): C3.

Bellah, R. N., Madsen, R., Sullivan, W. M., Swidler, A., and Tipton, S. M. (1986). *Habits of the Heart: An Individualism and Commitment in American Life,* Harper and Row Publishers, New York.

Beecher, H. K. (1966). Ethics and clinical research. *New England Journal of Medicine,* 274: 1354-1360.

Brock, D. W. (1995). Public Moral Discourse. In: *Society's Choices: Social and Ethical Decision Making in Biomedicine.* National Academy Press, Washington, DC.

Brody, B. A. (1995). Limiting life-prolonging medical treatment: A comparative analysis of the reports of the President's Commission and the New York State Task Force on Life and Law. In: *Society's Choices: Social and Ethical Decision Making in Biomedicine*, Institute of Medicine. National Academy Press, Washington, D.C.

Brook, R. H., Kanberg, C. J., and McGlynn, E. A. (1996). Health system reform and quality. *JAMA, 276*: 215-240.

Bureau of National Affairs. (1993). Number of uninsured persons increases to 36.6 million in 1991. *Daily Labor Report*, January 12.

Charo, A. (1995) La Penible False Hesitation: Fetal Tissue Research Review and the Use of Bioethics Commissions in France and the United States. In: *Society's Choices: Social and Ethical Decision Making in Biomedicine*, Institute of Medicine. National Academy Press, Washington, D.C.

Christensen, K. T. (1995) Ethically Important Distinctions Among Managed Care Organizations. *Journal of Law, Medicine and Ethics, 23*: 223-229.

Courts and Health Policy. (1992). *Health Affairs*, 96-110.

Edgar, H., and Rothman, D. (1995). The Institutional Review Board and Beyond: Future Challenges to the Ethics of Human Experimentation. *The Milbank Quarterly, 73*: 489-506.

Faden, R. R., and Beauchamp, T. L. (1986). A History and Theory of Informed Consent. Oxford University Press, New York.

Feldman, P. H., Putman, S., and Gerteis, M. (1992). Grantwatch. I. The Impact of Foundation-Funded commissions on Health Policy, *Health Affairs, Winter*: 207-225.

Gostin, L. (1995). The formulation of health policy by the three branches of government. In: *Society's Choices: Social and Ethical Decision Making in Biomedicine*, Institute of Medicine. National Academy Press, Washington, D.C.

Gray, B. H. (1995). Bioethics commissions: What can we learn from past successes and failures? In: *Society's Choices: Social and Ethical Decision Making in Biomedicine*, Institute of Medicine. National Academy Press, Washington, D.C.

Hanna, K. E., Cook-Deegan, R. M., and Nishimi, R. Y. (1993). Finding a Forum for Bioethics in U.S. Public Policy, *Politics and the Life Sciences, 12*: 205-219.

Hanna, K. E. (1995). The Ethical, Legal, and Social Implications Program of the National Center for Human Genome Research: A missed opportunity. In: *Society's Choices: Social and Ethical Decision Making in Biomedicine*, Institute of Medicine. National Academy Press, Washington, D.C.

Institute of Medicine. (1995). *Society's Choices: Social and Ethical Decision Making in Biomedicine*. Edited by Bulger, R. E., Bobby, E. M., and Fineberg, H. V., National Academy Press, Washington, D.C.

Johnson, S. H. (1995). Managed Care as Regulation: Functional Ethics for a Regulated Environment, *Journal of Law, Medicine and Ethics, 23*: 266-272.

Levinsky, N. G. (1996). Social, Institutional, and Economic Barriers to the Exercise of Patients' Rights. *New England Journal of Medicine, 334*: 532-534.

Mariner, W. L. (1995). Business vs. Medical Ethics Conflicting Standards for Managed Care, *Journal of Law, Medicine and Ethics, 23*: 236-246.

Morreim, W. H. (1995). Moral Justice and Legal Justice in Managed Care: The Ascent of Contributive Justice, *Journal of Law, Medicine and Ethics 23*: 247-265.

Nagel, T. (1995). Moral Epistemology. In: *Society's Choices: Social and Ethical Decision Making in Biomedicine*. National Academy Press, Washington, DC.

National Commission for the Protection of Human Subjects of Biomedical and Behavioral Research. (1978). *The Belmont Report: Ethical Principles and Guidelines for the Protection of Human Subjects of Research*. National Commission, Washington, D.C.

Nuremberg Code. (1949). *Trials of War Criminals Before the Nuremberg Military Tribunals Under Control Council Law No. 10. Vol. 2*, U.S. Government Printing Office, Washington, D.C., 181-182.

Office of Technology Assessment. (1993). *Biomedical Ethics in U.S. Public Policy.* U.S. Government Printing Office, Washington, D.C.

Research Ethics—Advisory Committee on Human Radiation Experiments. (1996). *JAMA, 276:* 403-409.

Senate Committee on Labor and Public Welfare. (1973). *Quality of Health Care-Human Experimentation; Hearings Before the Subcommittee on Health, 93rd Congress. 1st Session (February 21-23, March 6-8, April 30, June 28-29, July 10).* U.S. Government Printing Office, Washington, D.C.

U.S. Department of Health, Education, and Welfare. (1973). Final Report of the Tuskeegee Syphilis Study Ad Hoc Advisory Panel. Washington, D.C.

25.
AMERICAN HEALTH CARE GOVERNANCE

Margaret F. Mastal, *Kaiser Permanente, Springfield, VA*

The term *governance* is a recent addition to the lexicon of health care management, its use common only within the last two decades. Its conceptual and operational definitions remain vague. However, notions from fields of study extant to health care offer fertile grounds for building strong conceptual, operational frameworks for the governance of health care organizations. For example, governance has long been an integral part of political science studies in mankind's search for better ways to govern nations and states. As a part of these studies, politics and political theory are adaptable to health care organizations, offering a viable perspective for understanding and articulating the multiple interactions which occur.

The purpose of this chapter is to present a conceptual framework defining health care governance in terms of two basic concepts, elements and patterns. Seven elements of health care governance define its essence, its basic ingredients: power and authority, leadership, organizational values, communication, decision making, ethics, and conflict.

The second concept, patterns of health care governance, includes three distinct patterns: feudal, bureaucratic, and ethocorporate. These patterns form a gestalt of values, interests and attitudes which direct governing processes. Feudal patterns are associated with paternalism, philanthropy, traditional authority and community commitment. Bureaucratic patterns emphasize organizational hierarchy, management expertise, and rational rules for directing operational concerns. Ethocorporate patterns integrate modern business principles with the rational order of bureaucracy while also attempting to salvage the moral dimension of feudal community commitment as the industry grapples with the allocation of limited resources in the delivery of quality health care services.

The basis for the paradigm explicated here is a research study which analyzed samples of the content of articles in three journals commonly read by health care board members and managers: *Hospital and Healthcare Networks, Trustee, Hospital and Health Services Administration.* Articles were drawn randomly from each journal at five year intervals between 1948 and 1993 for a robust sample of 1,044 articles. The findings of the study identified statistically significant associations between the patterns and specific time frames. Feudal patterns, were most common prior to 1965 when the amendments to the Social Security Act mandated governmental reimbursement of providers for reasonable costs incurred in the care of the aged and the poor (i.e., Medicare and Medicaid). The bureaucratic motif dominated all sample years except 1948 and 1993; however, they were most frequent between 1965 and 1983 when additional amendments to the Social Security Act mandated the Prospective Payment System (PPS). The ethocorporate gestalt emerged in 1978, rose steadily over the intervening years and became the dominant pattern in 1993 (Mastal, 1996). In short, paradigmatic shifts in how the industry approached governing their institutions most likely occurred from dynamic interaction with the environment. Such shifts are reminiscent of political shifts seen in the course of governing nations and states. Politics and political action are core concepts to the notion of health care governance.

I. POLITICS OF HEALTH CARE ORGANIZATIONAL GOVERNANCE

Political science theories offer health care a solid base for launching its own governing strategies. According to political science, governance implies an "ordered polity," that is, a political community. In general, polity refers to both the institutions of government and the socio-cultural milieu in which they occur (Hult and Walcott, 1990). These notions are certainly relevant to organizations as today's environment calls for integrating plural and diverse external forces with the modern organization's mission and operations.

Organizational governance implies political activity, not politics limited to gaining advantage in turf struggles (although these activities abound), but politics as a positive force in achieving institutional mission and goals (Hult and Walcott, 1990; Cleveland, 1980). The term *governance*, rooted in Platonic thought, implies that rigorous reason and action rather than faith and improvisation determine the best structures and systems for achieving goals (Ebenstein, 1969).

Politics, organized by a logic of appropriateness, can be viewed as a system for aggregating individual preferences through voluntary and involuntary exchanges, channeling diverse interests so that individuals and the organization realize their goals (Morgan, 1986). Political institutions are collections of logically interrelated rules and routines which define the appropriateness of actions in terms of relations between roles and situations. Rules are both formal and informal. Formal rules are specific and clear, such as a nation's laws or an organization's by-laws and policies; informal rules, less explicit, are those understandings which exist among participants (Hult and Walcott, 1990). Political action calls for determining the nature of the situation and what role is being fulfilled, subsequently defining the nature of that role in the situation. Through rules and a logic of appropriateness, political institutions strive to realize order and stability while achieving flexibility (March and Olsen, 1989).

Politics and political action abound in health care organizations although the forthright discussion of politics in health care management is a recent phenomenon (Hadelman, 1992; Heymann, 1987). Previously, health care discussed these phenomena in terms of interpersonal theory or styles of management and leadership, and little attention was paid to comparing changes over time.

II. INSTITUTIONALIZATION OF HEALTH CARE GOVERNANCE

The internal political systems within health care organizations evolved as a function of interaction between them and their environment (Mastal, 1996). This evolution supports the view of health care organizations as living forms that have adapted over time to changing circumstances; they have a "natural history" (Scott, 1987).

Health care governance has been shaped both by the characteristics and commitments of participants as well as by external influences and constraints. Central to the adaptive process is the infusion of values resulting in institutionalization (Selznik, 1975).

Institutionalization is a process of organic growth wherein adaptations are made between the strivings of internal groups and the values of external society. However, this adaptation creates tension between inward focused forces and outward-looking forces laden with community values. These forces include the myriad subterranean processes of informal groups, conflict between groups, recruitment policies, dependencies on external constituencies, the striving for prestige, community values, the local community power structure and legal institutions (Perrow, 1986). Health care governance calls for statesmen who guide their organizational boards through existing tensions into a distinct, committed polity—a prized institution (Hult and Walcott, 1989; Hadelman, 1992).

External forces influence many of the rules by which governing bodies shape their institution's politics. As external forces shift, so do internal politics, gradually forming different patterns.

III. AN EMERGING PARADIGM OF HEALTH CARE GOVERNANCE

The paradigm's two major concepts—patterns of governing behavior and elements—address the substance of health care governance and those behaviors, values and attitudes assumed when governing health care organizations. Three governance patterns are woven throughout seven elements of health care governance. The patterns, both their labels and definitions, are rooted in political paradigms seen across history; the elements were synthesized from general and health care-specific management and leadership literature.

A. Health Care Governance Patterns

The patterns define the activities, values, beliefs and attitudes which distinguish three different approaches for governing health care institutions. These patterns, *feudal, bureaucratic and ethocorporate*, were synthesized from political science and organizational governance literature (Perrow, 1986, Morgan, 1986, Selznick, 1957; March and Olsen, 1972; Hult and Walcott, 1990; Kanter, 1989). Each health care governance pattern is associated with events that altered the nature of governing behaviors, values, attitudes. Each pattern is a confluence of beliefs, values, attitudes and behaviors which animate the elements, giving them substance and unique definition. Each evolved in response to social, political, technologic and economic changes in the hospitals and health care environment. The patterns reveal governing bodies' proficiency in adapting to environmental events, initially reacting but gradually moving toward adaptation, even anticipation and proactivity (Hult and Walcott, 1990; Mastal, 1996).

1. Feudal Patterns: Doing Right

Patterns of feudal governance, prevalent in hospital life prior to 1965, persisted until the late 1980s. They are likened to the practices of feudal knights. Medieval feudal values were threefold:
- Military prowess was a social good.
- The bonds of personal loyalty between the lord and the vassal were the sinews of social order, sanctioning political and legal obligations.
- These bonds of loyalty were arranged in ascending-descending order (Cantor, 1993).

Early twentieth century board members were community elites, authoritarian and paternalistic. Their philanthropic gifts and humanitarian leanings earned them the hospital as their "fief" and its superintendent as their "vassal." Close social ties served their business and philanthropic purposes well, but at times gave way to cronyism. Tradition and precedent guided feudal governing performance; honorable behavior demanded that wealth be used to care for the indigent. Their organizational oversight and fiduciary activities fulfilled a moral obligation to the community's poor. Feudal board patterns touted beneficence and justice; the physician-patient relationship was revered. Health care issues were left to the physician; board members were the overlords of administrative and business concerns.

In short, the feudal-type board of directors rarely questioned the rightness of what they were doing and how they were doing it. However, the architecture of "right" as tradition and precedent, social position and philanthropy no longer sufficed as environmental shifts of the 1960s emerged, creating a need for order and precision. The more mechanistic structure of bureaucracy seemed appropriate.

2. Bureaucratic Patterns: Improving on "Right"

External changes during the 1960s and 1970s brought internal changes to hospitals. These external changes included a shifting economic base, the beginning of legislative regulation of health care operations, the development of sophisticated technology, the professional growth of health care managers and paramedical workers, and social pressures to grant equality to women and other minorities. Health care organizations focused on the application of management principles, improving their physical plants and operations, investing in advanced health care technology and defining the roles of personnel, thus supplanting feudal notions of tradition, social position and philanthropy.

Rather, bureaucratic-like boards of directors focused on clear rules and organizational charts. Feudal authoritarianism gave way to delegation of authority, cooperation and interchange, staff development, antidiscriminatory behavior, operational efficiency. Bureaucracy extolled individual rights, quality of care, physician credentialing; it de-emphasized the sacredness of physician-controlled patient relationships by enforcing mandated quality assurance audits. Bureaucratic governance behaviors brought order to hospital and health care organizational life; they specified the methods for better ways to do "right." However, bureaucratic methods came into question abruptly with the sociopolitical and economic changes of the 1980s.

In 1983, efforts to contain escalating health care costs were taken out of the hands of the industry. The Prospective Payment System (PPS), legislated by the 1983 Social Security Act Amendments, banished reasonable cost reimbursement, replacing it with a predetermined amount based on Medicare/Medicaid patients' diagnoses. Private insurance carriers quickly followed the federal government's lead and applied the capitated system to all hospitalized patients, forcing hospitals into a more competitive posture with emphasis on business concerns (Fuchs, 1988).

Turmoil ensued, competitive approaches emerged, innovation became the prized organizational characteristic and business methods surfaced as prized activities. A new pattern began to dominate governance thought, seeking to balance the moral provision of care with business imperatives.

3. Ethocorporate Patterns: What Is Right?

The third pattern, ethocorporate, indicates the tensions experienced and the balance sought between business methods and the ethical delivery of quality health care. This pattern has changed since the 1980s when it emerged as a dominant motif. Its hallmark is a search for redefining "right."

The new business era of the early 1980s called for a balancing act between seemingly antithetical notions—delivering high quality care with scarce funds. Hospital governing boards initially sought ideas and models from the private, for-profit sector. They established corporate boards, streamlined hospital board size, incorporated financial and health industry leaders into their membership as well as nurse executives and physicians and modified meeting agendas to focus on strategic planning, business and financial plans and government and public relations (Alexander, 1986; American Hospital Association, 1989; Wyatt Company, 1986).

Some hospitals survived, a few thrived and many closed—over seven hundred across the nation by 1990. To remain financially solvent, hospitals initially took on a more competitive and market-oriented mantra, engaging in ascribed business-like practices—advertising their services, enhancing the look of facilities, emphasizing service-oriented attitudes with staff—as well as some heretofore unheard of activities such as refusing emergency care to the uninsured or transferring the underinsured to public institutions (Fuchs, 1988).

Since the late 1980s, ethocorporate patterns have modified the hardline aspects of this business or enterprise model, adapting them to the unique institutions of caring for American health. Resulting behaviors are more egalitarian and ethical; community and organizational leaders unite to integrate community health needs with the organizational mission and financial integrity. The 1990s have brought significant change:

defining new goals and integrating them with relevant existing goals, discarding the traditional authority of organizational hierarchy for the authority of proven professional expertise, redefining board member roles, integrating health care operations with local, even global circumstances, defining the ethics of allocating scarce health care resources and looking outward as well as inward (Kanter, 1989; Etzioni, 1993).

B. The Elements of Health Care Governance

The elements of governance were synthesized from general and health care management literature. They include sources of power and authority, leadership, organizational values, communication, decision making, ethics and conflict management (Cleveland, 1980; Houle, 1989; Carver, 1990). They spell out the essence of health care governance, providing labels for understanding governing bodies' concerns. The patterns of governance behaviors are identifiable within each element with the exception of conflict management, a new concern for health care (Perrow, 1986).

1. Sources of Power and Authority

Sources of power and authority are a primary concern of governance; they are the origin of governing bodies' right to act. Sources of health care power and authority have seen dramatic shifts in the latter half of this century.

a. **Feudal Power.** Prior to the mid 1960s, external power sources included corporation law, philanthropic largesse, private insurance funds and the community elites overseeing hospital business concerns. Each organization was autonomous; each translated external power sources to internal power sources: by-laws, centralized authority, fiduciary activities, fund raising and reverence of the physician-patient relationship. Power, originating from time-honored mechanisms, was applied internally by conscientious, wealthy community leaders.

b. **Bureaucratic Power.** Social, political, economic and technologic changes of the 1960s caused power and authority concerns to became bureaucratic in nature. External power sources lay in public and private insurance agency reimbursement policies, government subsidies for education, tort and tax law, regulatory agency surveillance measures, science and technological advances, and the needs of the greater community. Internally, health care governing bodies saw power in containing costs, specifying organizational structures and semantically correct policies and procedures, designing efficient, effective physical plants, defining professional competence, allocating just salaries, applying prudent management principles, and delivering patient-centered care. Institutional autonomy experienced erosion as multihospital partnerships were launched while each organization protected its independent status. The hallmark of bureaucratic power and authority lay in the ability to identify relevant external events and implement appropriate internal processes to meet requirements.

c. **Ethocorporate Power.** In contrast, ethocorporate authority lies in the ability to proactively affect external events. External power sources exist largely in economic principles with capitated reimbursement, marketing, consumerism and payer demands, controls and sanction as central forces. Power lies in developing internal and external coalitions and constituencies of providers, consumers and purchasers. Where the goals are mission-centered, shared power reduces costs, and professional expertise meets population needs.

In essence, sources of power and authority evolved from a limited number of external forces which directed the simple oversight of hospital business through events which called for bringing order to internal mechanisms and culminating in a complex system of diverse external elements that compel the interaction of governing bodies with local or even global conditions.

2. Leadership

Health care leadership characteristics, the second element of governance, have evolved sharply over the past fifty years. The leadership journey, originating in feudal notions of paternalism and noblesse oblige, has progressed through the coordination and formal interchange of bureaucracy to realize ethocorporatism's energetic, creative involvement in organizational and community life.

a. **Feudal Power.** Feudal leadership patterns reflect traditional notions of patriarchal authoritarian benevolence. These board members were dignified community elites revered for their philanthropy and business acumen. They were conscientious and sensible about the stewardship of the hospital's fiscal affairs. They conducted board affairs as they did their businesses with close careful oversight. Their close social connections admitted fellowship and cronyism as accepted manners in the conduct of business and philanthropic life. They supported and valued the continuing education of physicians as key to a strong hospital staff.

b. **Bureaucratic Leadership.** Banishing authoritarian benevolence, bureaucratic leadership characteristics emphasized cooperation, coordination and methodical consistency. Bureaucratic leaders value the education of the hospital staff as well as physicians; thus staff evolved into qualified specialists accountable for the competent execution of duties. In contrast to their specialized staffs, hospital leaders adopted systems thinking approaches, holistically perceiving, coordinating and improving internal operations. Sensitivity to the political realm grew as legislation with attendant administrative policies increasingly governed the reimbursement of health care costs and the expansion of facilities. Cooperation, facilitation, coordination and consistency also enjoyed status as hallmarks of bureaucratic leadership.

c. **Ethocorporate Leadership.** In contrast, ethocorporate leadership features creativity and innovation, valuing capabilities to strategize proactively in the political arena as well as in organizational and community life. Bureaucratic coordination gave way to notions of energetic involvement and collegial teamsmanship where leaders act as coaches, catalysts and statesmen in the creation of stakeholder constituencies. Further, board member education joined physician and staff development as critical to organizational growth.

3. Organizational Values

Governing health care organizations requires articulating institutional values—values that have adapted to changing circumstances.

a. **Feudal Organizational Values.** Feudal organizational values incorporated a sense of civic pride and moral duty with organizational fealty translated as volunteerism and generosity. These values, common in America's early years, are enjoying renewal in a new search to reclaim community roots and rediscover moral social interactions (Etzioni, 1993). Further, hospitals and other health care organizations have long prized their volunteer force whose value increases their healthy links to the community. However, these values experienced repression in the governance forums of the 1960s, 1970s and early 1980s as other environmental forces garnered their attention.

b. **Bureaucratic Organizational Values.** Bureaucratic values eschewed moral obligation for a sense of legal responsibility, embracing efficiency and effectiveness as central bywords for creating internal order. Bureaucratic organizations prized safety, utility, productivity, uniformity and objectivity in the pursuit of incremental progress. These values, basically the heritage of the scientific management school of thought, fostered the development of methods to improve facility design and technology which in turn assured a safe, cost-effective milieu for the delivery of care.

c. **Ethocorporate Organizational Values.** Ethocorporate organizational values are an evolution and a composite of feudal and bureaucratic patterns. While legal duty remains inherent organizational responsibility, the modern arcane financial climate has gathered remnants of feudal fiduciary activities and fashioned a pointed sense of fiscal responsibility. Ethocorporate fiscal responsibility goes beyond the stewardship of funds from insurance payers and philanthropy; it requires a sophisticated ability to weave a financial infrastructure from multiple sources. Today's health care organizations also have retrieved a value for their community roots, seeking guidance and support as they consolidate resources but diversify services (Etzioni, 1993). Calculated risk-taking has replaced incremental approaches as organizations seek proficiency, not just efficiency and effectiveness, in an ongoing search for development. An organization's values form the foundation for internal and external action and communication.

4. Communication

Communication is the fourth element of health care governance, one that has received limited recognition until recent years. Yet it is through communication techniques that we project our values and our message.

    a. **Feudal Communication.** Feudal patterns emphasized social occasions and frequent meetings. Camaraderie and verbal interactions formulated the basis for disseminating rules, news and expectations. Dinners and weekend excursions with board members were frequently used as physician recruitment tools. Interactions among social elites, centered around entertainment, were considered appropriate opportunities for judging each other's mettle in gracious settings.

    b. **Bureaucratic Communication.** Bureaucratic patterns jettisoned informality for precise clarification and codification using written vehicles: reports, memos, bulletins, meeting agenda and minutes, legal contracts and formal agreements. The objective was clarity of the message through mutual understanding and formal interchange. Because organizational business was confidential, written communication was primarily internal.

    c. **Ethocorporate Communication.** Ethocorporate communication patterns blend some of the feudal and bureaucratic characteristics while adding today's technology. Candor creates interdependent networks as health care turns to the media for advertising services and reengineering public image. Sharing information is a key bartering tool. Creating accurate databases and adeptly applying computer technology is a prime concern as health care organizations link with others. In essence, communication as a governance element has adapted traditional human methods to technology.

5. Decision Making

Decision making has not received the attention in health care governance literature that it has in general management literature. In health care, making decisions was both a process and an outcome of governance; however, it did not serve as a paradigm to explain plural governing activities. Neither decision models nor decision processes were foci of discussion. While decision making in health care governance literature seemed largely an assumed activity, patterns around issues requiring decision making were discernible.

    a. **Feudal Decision Making.** Feudal patterns focused mainly on the evaluation of personnel. Considering the authoritarian, paternalistic styles of the leaders in health care during the feudal years and the personal nature of communication patterns, making decisions about staff evaluations would naturally surface as a principal interest. Additionally, tacit recognition of organizational decision making in terms of consensus and maintaining harmony existed.

b. **Bureaucratic Decision Making.** Bureaucratic patterns are far more concrete—quantitative analysis of retrospective internal audits with extensive presentation of data in tables and graphs. Logic and reason, not consensus, is a hallmark, the rigors of scientific methodology critical.

c. **Ethocorporate Decision Making.** Ethocorporate decision making expands on bureaucratic processes, focusing on comprehensive marketing analyses (internal and external audits and evaluation). Sophisticated prediction and forecasting techniques supplant retrospective analysis of data as the basis for logical, reasonable decision making. Further, prioritizing decisions is endorsed as a reality of organizational life since limited resources force difficult choices (Ramage, 1983).

6. Ethics

Ethics, traditionally perceived as the purview of clinical providers, has not received formal recognition as a health care governance issue until recently. Medical ethics is rooted in Hippocrates with ethical codes well articulated for physicians, other professional providers and associated health care organizations (Pellegrino, 1993). Health care organizational ethics is still amorphous.

a. **Feudal Ethics.** Feudal ethical patterns centered around the epochal principles of beneficence and nonmaleficence where the personal virtue of providers protected the individual worth and dignity of patients and maintained the confidentiality of their health information. Codes of ethics for physicians and other health care workers assured ethical health care practices while boardroom members' humanitarian pursuits fulfilled their ethical responsibilities.

b. **Bureaucratic Ethics.** In the late 1960s and 1970s, governing board ethical concerns began to diverge from the bioethical model, and organizational issues surfaced. Rather than principles allied to physician-patient interactions, boards focused on providing quality care, the legal rights of individual physicians, staff and patients, physician credentialing, informed consent practices, board member and physician conflict of interest issues, and antidiscriminatory employment practices.

c. **Ethocorporate Ethics.** Ethocorporate concerns have a distinctly societal flavor. Ethocorporate ethical values seek to define the social mission of the institution, improve clinical outcomes, enhance the role of caring as an element of social justice, revive honesty and personal integrity, acclaim cultural diversity, and enjoin communal society to participate in health care rationing decisions (Reiser, 1994; Woodstock Theological Seminary, 1995; Thomas, 1991). Ethics separates health care from other industries as the thorny issue of allocating limited resources creates personal and organizational conflict.

7. Conflict and Conflict Management

Until very recent times conflict and its management in health care, as in most other fields, have been either ignored as organizational social realities or perceived as failures of leadership (Perrow, 1986). Perrow (pp. 135-136) cites the "garbage can" model of organizations as articulated by March and his colleagues Cyert and Olson as a breakthrough for organizations in perceiving conflict objectively. This model sheds light on the micro-organizational processes of group dynamics, intergroup relations and the dilemmas of leadership. It adds the human dimension to the static skeleton of more rational and structural frameworks, offering some sense to the bewildering shifts, turns and unexpected outcomes of daily organizational experiences.

Since the late 1970s, conflict has been mentioned in the health care governance literature, but only in very objective terms. Threats from government legislative and regulatory intervention were acknowledged as were controversies among physician groups and between physicians and health care management. However, resolution of intraorganizational conflict was prominent by its absence.

Rather, conflict management was cited in terms of formal compromise, arbitration, lawsuits and collective bargaining. No substantive recordings addressed managing daily conflict or resolving intergroup dispute. Dealing with conflict, a concern of organizational governance, is embryonic in constructive approaches.

IV. SUMMARY

Politics and political actions are valid, if novel, metaphors for health care governance. They offer a different perspective for looking at the organization as a whole, how the different parts function separately and together, how people influence each other, and how the organization and the environment maintain dynamic equilibrium. Through political perspectives, we can more clearly visualize how internal tensions and external pressures exert synergistic energy to achieve organizational change.

A. Conceptual Value

Together, the elements and the patterns form the conceptual substance of health care governance, a notion rooted in the political thoughts of ancient Greece whereby governing bodies guided their ships of state (Hult and Walcott, 1990). That notion serves as a framework for the governance of health care organizations. (See Figure 1.)

The diagram depicts the environmental forces as interactive with governing bodies, shaping patterns of governance behaviors as boards dealt with the substance of governance concerns. At the heart of governance is the organization's mission, realized by political interactions between and among board members.

Additionally, a political governance metaphor allows specific definition—health care governance is defined as a confluence of political values, structures, actions and interactions which lead and guide the work and performance of the health care organization. This confluence operates within the governance elements, through and among internal and external groups of stakeholders as they balance the tensions between competing values, beliefs and attitudes (Selznick, 1975; Perrow, 1986; Fennel and

Figure 1 - Model for the Governance of Health Care Organizations

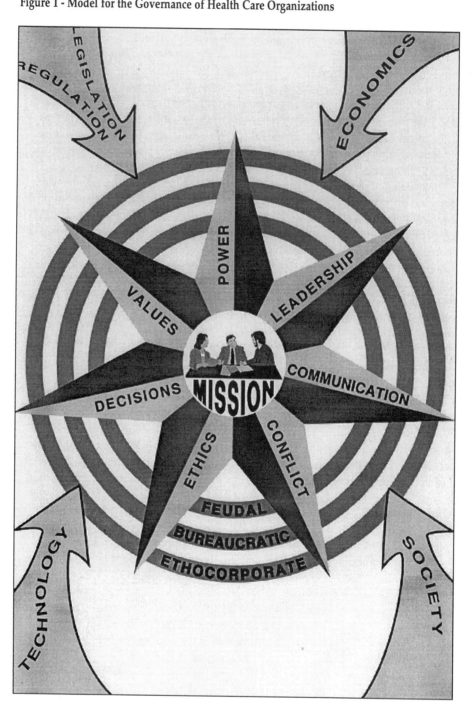

Alexander, 1989; March and Olsen, 1989; Carver, 1990; Hult and Walcott, 1990; Weiner and Alexander, 1993; Arrington, Gautam and McCabe, 1995). In short, defining health care governance and articulating a framework fills an existing conceptual void, offering a new focus for the study and research of the industry's governing beliefs, values, structures and activities and the education of those who govern America's health care organizations. Conceptual clarity offers operational value as well.

B. Operational Value

Governing bodies can use such a framework to fashion the values, structures and processes that enhance organizational performance, the achievements of personnel, and the organization's position in the community. Considering both global and local circumstances, governing bodies need to explore questions that effect richer, more robust governance strategies:

- What environmental forces are most relevant—the consumer society, the financial infrastructure, or legal and regulatory mandates? Are we just adapting to environmental circumstances or affecting them proactively?
- What are our sources of power and authority? What gives us and our organizational operations legitimacy—management principles, corporate structures and business proficiencies, well-conceived and well thought-through innovations?
- What are our leadership approaches? What are the optimal structures and processes for governing our institution? Will we govern using only selected experts or include providers, staff and consumers? Will we relate informally, formally or as stakeholders who bring unique perspectives?
- What does our organization value and in what priority—loyalty, efficiency, economic growth, human resources? What do we find of worth for our organization's climate and culture? How can we adopt those values now missing?
- How will we best communicate our values and worth to internal and external constituencies? What technology best meets our communication needs? How will we develop proficiency with the selected technologies?
- What is our moral position regarding types and costs of health care services? What outcomes do we and our constituents and consumers expect? Are care and organizational ethical issues compatible? What is our basis for making ethical choices—individual concerns, organizational concerns or society's concerns?
- How are decisions made? By whom? What are our major sources of information for making choices? What structures and processes best serve effective decision making in our organization?
- What are the sources of conflict within our organization and in our environment? What are our beliefs and attitudes about conflict? How can we best confront, manage, even avoid conflict?

These are only a few questions that governing bodies might ask in refashioning the governance systems that will ensure healthy organizational performance in today's slippery environment. Answers will be a function of resolving tension between internal and external stakeholders—partnerships of providers, managers, staff and citizens who work together in fashioning the health systems of their community (Bader, 1993).

Health care's governing bodies must carve out the practices that will guide their institutions; they must specify economic purposes, outline standards of competent proficiency, and define human values for conduct of moral business. The modern era calls for a balancing act which retains those practices that preserve internal order while developing practices which generate innovative zeal.

Health care faces multiple tasks: searching for new goals and integrating them with relevant standing goals, discarding the authority of organizational position and fashioning a constituency of relevant shareholders, integrating organizational operations with local and global community circumstances, looking outward as well as inward, developing those statesman-like behaviors which will guide the institutional delivery of quality, cost-effective care in an ethical environment. Politics is a tool for governing bodies to use as organizations exercise the means to achieve these ends.

REFERENCES

Alexander, J. A. (1986). Current issues in governance. (Cat. #597191). *Hospital Research and Educational Trust*, American Hospital Association, Chicago, IL.

American Hospital Association. (1989). *Hospital governance.* Author, Chicago, IL.

Andrews, K. R. (1989). Ethics in practice. *Harvard Business Review, 89*: 99-104.

Arrington, B., Gautam, K. and McCabe, W. (1995). Continually improving governance. *Hospital and Health Services Administration, 40*: 95-110.

Bader, B. S. (1993). CQI progress reports. *Healthcare Executive, 8*: 8-11.

Beauchamp, T. and Childress, J. (1989). *Principles of biomedical ethics (3rd ed.).* Oxford University Press, New York.

Cantor, N. F. (1993). *Civilization of the middle ages.* Harper Perennial, New York.

Carver, J. (1990). *Boards that make a difference.* Jossey-Bass Publishers, San Francisco.

Chait, R. P. and Taylor, B. E. (1989). Charting the territory of nonprofit boards. *Harvard Business Review, 89*: 44-54.

Chandler, R. L. (1980). Filling empty board seats. *Hospital and Health Services Administration, 25*: 69-85.

Cleveland, H. (1980). *Learning the art of leadership.* Twin Cities Magazine.

Dayton, K. N. (1984). Corporate governance: The other side of the coin. *Harvard Business Review, 84*: 34-37.

Downs, A. (1967). *Inside bureaucracy.* Little, Brown & Co.: Boston, MA.

Drucker, P. F. (1974). *Management: Tasks, responsibilities, practices.* Harper & Row Publishers, New York.

Drucker, P. F. (1980). *Managing in turbulent times.* Harper & Row, Publishers, New York.

Drucker, P. F. (1985). *Innovation and entrepreneurship.* Harper and Row, Publishers, New York.

Drucker, P. F. (1989). *The new realities.* Harper and Row, Publishers, New York.

Drucker, P. F. (1992). The new society of organizations. *Harvard Business Review, 70*: 95-104.

Ebenstein, W. (1969). *Great political thinkers.* Holt, Rinehart & Winston, New York.

Eggers, P. W. (1987). Prospective payment system and quality: early results and research strategy. *Health Care Financing Review, Annual supplement.*

Enthoven, A. C. (1988). Managed competition: an agenda for action. *Health Affairs, 7*: 25-47.

Ermann, D. and Gabel, J. (1984). Multihospital systems: issues and empirical findings. *Health Affairs, 3*:: 54.

Etzioni, A. (1993). *The spirit of community.* Simon and Schuster, New York.

Fennel, M. L. and Alexander, J.A. (1989). Governing boards and profound organizational change in hospitals. *Medical Care Review, 46*: 157-187.

Fuchs, V. R. (1988). The competition revolution in health care. *Health Affairs, 7*: 5-24.

Gilligan, C. (1982). *In a different voice.* Harvard University Press, Cambridge, MA.

Ginzberg, E. (1985). The restructuring of U.S. health care. *Inquiry, XXII*: 272-281.

Hadelman, J. (1992). Boards in transition. *Healthcare Executive, 7*: 32-34.

Hafertepe, Sr. E. C. (1987). Systemwide board assessment. *Health Progress, 68*: 82-86.

Heymann, P. B. (1987). *The politics of public management.* Yale University Press, New Haven.

Hoffman, P. B. (1995). Performing an ethics audit. *Healthcare Executive, 10*: 47.

Homes and Gustafson. (1990). Philosophical critique of bioethics. *Journal of Medical Philosphy, 15*: 236.

Houle, C. (1989). *Governing Boards.* Jossey-Bass, San Francisco.

Hult, K. M. (1988). Governing in bureaucracies the case of parental notification. *Administration and Society, 20*: 313-334.

Hult, K. M. and Walcott, C. (1990). *Governing public organizations.* Brooks/Cole, Palisades, CA.

Kanter, R. M. (1989). *When giants learn to dance.* Simon & Schuster, New York, NY.

Kinzer, D. M. (1986). Where is hospital leadership coming from? *Frontiers of Health Services Management, 3*: 3-25.

Kovner, A. R. (1981). Hospital governance and market share. *Inquiry, 18*: 255-265.

Kovner, A. R. (1985). Improving the effectiveness of hospital governing boards. *Frontiers of Health Services Management, 2*: 4-33.

Lemieux, C. L., Meslin, E., Aird, C., Baker, R. and Leatt, P. (1993). Ethical issues faced by clinician/managers in resource-allocation decisions. *Hospital and Health Services Administration, 38*: 267-285.

March, J. G. and Olsen, J. P. (1989). *Rediscovering institutions.* The Free Press, New York.

Mastal, M. F. (1996). *Governance in American healthcare organizations 1948-1993 elements and patterns.* Dissertation Abstracts 9712181. UMI Microforms, Ann Arbor, MI.

Miller, I. (1988). Lessons from Benjamin Franklin's civic leadership: the Pennsylvania hospital story. *Hospital & Health Services Administration, 33*:: 498-503.

Morgan, G. (1986). *Images of organizations.* Sage Publications, Inc., Beverly Hills, CA.

Morlock, L., Alexander, J., and Hunter, H. (1985). Formal relationships among governing boards, CEOs, and medical staffs in independent and system hospitals. *Medical Care, 23*: 1193-1213.

Nederman, C. J. (1992). Freedom, community and function: communitarian lessons of medieval political theory. *American Political Science Review, 86*: 977-986.

Nelson, C. A. (1978). Wanted: strong trustees for strong boards. *Trustee, 31*: 21-25.

Nigosian, G. J. (1980a). New data on hospital governing boards. *Trustee, 33*: 18-25.

Nigosian, G. J. (1980b). How boards conduct their business. *Trustee, 33*: 35-38.

Nutt, P. C. (1984). Types of organizational decision processes. *Administrative Science Quarterly, 29*: 414-450.

Nutt, P. C. (1989). *Making tough decisions.* Jossey-Bass Publishers, San Francisco.

Parcesepe, C. L. (1976). American hospitals: A 200-year odyssey. *Trustee, 29*: 14-18.

Pellegrino, E. D. (1993). The metamorphosis of medical ethics. *Journal of the American Medical Association, 269*: 1158-1162.

Perrow, C. (1965). Hospitals: technology, structure and goals. In James G. March (Ed.), *Handbook of Organizations.* Rand McNally & Company, Chicago, IL.

Perrow, C. (1986). *Complex Organizations: a Critical Essay (3rd ed.).* Random House, New York.

Ramage, R. C. (1983). United we stand; divided, the outcome is less clear. *Trustee, 36*: 19-23.

Rehm, J. and Alexander, J. (1986). New trends in governing board-medical staff relations. *Trustee, 39*: 15-18.

Reiser, S. J. (1994). The ethical life of health care organizations. *Hastings Center Report, 24*: 28-35.

Ritvo, R. A. (1980). Adaptation to environmental change: the board's role. *Hospital and Health Services Administration, 25*: 23-37.

Robinette, T. K. (1985). Adapting to the age of competition: a paradigm shift for voluntary hospitals. *Hospital and Health Services Administration*, 71-19.

Russell, J. A. and Ebner, G. H. (1985). Adapting to a 1980's style of governance. *Trustee, 38*: 29-31.

Schlesinger, M., Marmor, T. R. and Smithey, R. (1987). Nonprofit and for-profit medical care: shifting roles and implications for health policy. *Journal of Health Politics, Policy and Law, 12*: 427-457.

Scott, W. R. (1975). The adolescence of institutional theory. *Administrative Science Quarterly, 32*: 493-511.

Scott, W. G., Mitchell, T. R. and Birnbaum, P. H. (1981). *Organization theory a structural and behavioral analysis (4th ed.).* Richard D. Irwin, Inc., Homewood, IL.

Selznick, P. (1975). *Leadership in administration.* Harper and Row, New York.

Slade, G. R. (1973). Governance. *Hospitals, 47*: 51-55.

Shortell, S. M. (1989). New directions in hospital governance. *Hospital & Health Services Administration, 34*: 8-23.

Weil, P. and Douglass, S. (1994). The governance team: a firsthand look at leadership practices. *Healthcare Executive, 9*: 6-19.

Wesbury, S. A. (1988). Meeting the challenge: the health care executive's role. *Hospital and Health Services Administration, 33*: 276-281.

Wildavsky, A. (1987). Choosing preferences by constructing institutions: a cultural theory of preference formation. *American Political Science Review, 81*: 3-21.

Woodstock Theological Center (1995). *Ethical considerations in the business aspects of health care.* Georgetown University Press, Washington, DC.

Wyatt Company. (1986). Practices of boards of directors/trustees in the health industry. (Survey conducted by Executive Compensation Service, Inc. a subsidiary of the Wyatt Co.). Author, Fort Lee, NJ.

Zuckerman, H. S. (1989). Redefining the role of the CEO: challenges and conflicts. *Hospital and Health Services Administration, 34*: 26-38.

26.
RISK MANAGEMENT IN HEALTH CARE

Alysia Olshinski, *Medical University of South Carolina, Charleston, SC*

Individuals face risk at every turn. Decisions are constantly being made to avoid risk exposure. The health care industry is no different. However, due to the nature of the services provided in the health care industry, a special set of risks has evolved for those who work in this arena. Daily risks that can be involved in health care include medication errors, falls, surgical procedures, confidentiality issues, diagnoses, and general medical treatment. As the health care industry continues to branch into new ventures, the possibility of risk can be heightened. This has led to an increasing need for prevention and management of those risks. An overview of the definition and history of risk management is helpful in discussing exactly what risk management comprises and how it evolved.

I. DEFINITION AND HISTORY

Risk management might be easily defined as simply the management of risk. However, risk can have many definitions. In general, risk is the possibility or the probability of a loss occurring. Risk can also be described as the uncertainty arising from the possible occurrence of a given event. Webster has described risk as the possibility of suffering harm or loss. The Centers for Disease Control and Prevention (1994) have more specifically defined five levels of risk for health care organizations, based upon the numbers of tuberculosis patients in the facility. With these various interpretations for risk, it is clear that the definition of risk management is quite complex and variable. The American Society for Healthcare Risk Managers defines risk management as "the process of making and carrying out decisions that will assist in the prevention of adverse consequences and minimize the adverse effects of accidental losses upon an organization." The process of health care risk management also has the goal of improving the quality of care while protecting the institution and its employees.

The health industry has always been careful to exercise some form of risk management, although it did not experience organized risk management until the mid-1970s. This was in response to the escalating medical malpractice claims. As medical malpractice suits increased in number, the insurance industry that protected physicians and hospitals experienced depletion of its cash reserves. To try to control the exposure of the their clients to risk, most companies began to mandate that risk management programs be initiated and organized. Thus began the difference between risk management and risk financing. Risk financing involves the purchase of policies to protect the organization when there has been a risk exposure. However, risk management tries to prevent the exposure from occurring in the first place, or if it is impossible to prevent the exposure, risk management tries to minimize such exposure. When institutions eventually realized the true value of the risk management approach, it became a driving force in quality improvement and cost reduction for the health care industry.

Currently, risk management approaches are used in all health care settings, from physician offices to insurance agencies. Different settings use various techniques to minimize risks. For example, a physician office might encourage better patient relations in the form of more patient education to prevent lawsuits based mostly on bedside manner. A hospital has a wide variety of risk management strategies that can be employed, from training and education of staff to the hiring of safety officers who ensure that regulatory standards are being met. Long-term care facilities may concentrate on the reduction and prevention of patient falls, as well as study and implement any new legislation concerning living wills and do-not-resuscitate (DNR) orders. Managed care organizations are concerned with many risk issues, such as legal issues regarding written contractual agreements, and the extent of liability that the organization holds for risk exposures of member practices and hospitals. Clearly, risk management today encompasses many more areas than it did even ten years ago. An in-depth discussion of some of the specifics associated with risk management and methods for risk management techniques to different areas of health care follows.

II. FUNCTION OF THE RISK MANAGER AND RISK MANAGEMENT PROGRAM

An effective risk management program will always have several purposes. According to Benton and Bunting (1996), the three most important purposes of any risk management department are:

- Identify risks in a systematic multi-disciplinary manner
- Determine the most effective way to manage identified risks
- Monitor the effectiveness of the program

To serve the purposes of a risk management program, the manager must identify loss exposures, examine potential risk management techniques, select viable techniques and implement them, and monitor the results of those techniques. In order to meet these goals, the risk manager must engage in several activities. A 1992 American

Society for Healthcare Risk Management (ASHRM) survey detailed many areas in which risk management involvement was deemed to be important, including insurance purchasing, claims management, acquisitions/mergers, affiliation agreements, workers' compensation, joint ventures, legal issues, and contract reviews. This chapter will cover some of these activities.

In order to be effective, a risk manager must first be able to correctly identify exposures and other forms of risk. Employee education is imperative in the reduction of losses. Staying knowledgeable about changing legislation regarding the healthcare industry is also necessary in protecting the organization and its employees. Providing a functional system for reporting incidents or exposures will help all the employees to participate in risk management for the organization. Effectively handling patient complaints includes: proper investigation of incidents and complaints. When a claim cannot be settled, the risk manager must be able to work effectively with the legal office throughout the entire process of litigation. Finally, the risk manager must stay abreast of new trends in the industry to minimize losses to the institution and its employees.

A. Risk Identification

In order to properly identify risks, risk managers must understand exposures. An exposure is the state of being subject to loss because of some hazard or contingency. There are several types of exposures that an organization might face. They include property, net income, liability, and personnel exposures. Specific problem areas can include destruction of property, dishonesty of employees, injuries to visitors, liability of directors and officers, vehicle liability, machinery malfunction, and disability or death of employees. There are several methods of identifying exposures. Formal methods of identification include incident reports and occurrence reports, while informal methods of identification can include looking at history of prior claims. Patient complaints can also show a pattern of exposures. Standardized surveys and questionnaires are also helpful in identification (Benton and Bunting, 1996). Flowcharts can provide the risk manager with a clear pattern for exposure identification, and personal inspection of the facilities can provide a concise view of problem areas. Finally, experts such as risk management or insurance brokerage specialists can help to identify exposures in health care organizations.

This risk identification process is the "process through which the risk manager becomes aware of risks in the health care environment that constitute potential loss exposures for the institution" (Harpster and Leach, 1990). These processes have dual purposes for the risk manager. First, risk identification can flag adverse occurrences that will alert the risk manager to begin an investigation. Secondly, risk identification can help the risk manager to develop a database of trends and patterns of risk within the institution. This information can be invaluable in the development of risk reduction and prevention programs.

III. LEGISLATION

The major liability of health care institutions lies with the legal doctrine of respondeat superior. This doctrine states that the "master" (the health care organization) is liable for the actions of its "servant" (the employees). Under this doctrine, an organization can be sued for the action of its employees in the course of their employment. Even if the facility was careful to select a competent and qualified individual, it can still be held responsible for the actions of that individual (Medical Device, 1996). This doctrine does not give the employee complete immunity from his or her actions or from being sued (Dodero, 1994), which can be a particularly sticky legal issue when agency personnel are working for another institution. The "captain of the ship" doctrine can also apply, and has generally been used to hold surgeons responsible for the actions of their subordinates in the operating room. However, it has more recently been the trend to hold the individuals responsible for their actions in these instances.

Another important function of the risk manager is to ensure that all federal, state, and local laws are being followed by their institution. Federal level legislation includes Occupational Safety and Health Administration (OSHA) standards that govern if a facility is safe and is performing at a minimum level of care. The Joint Commission for Accreditation of Health Care Organizations (JCAHO) also has standards for the health care industry. While these standards are not legal in nature, many certificates of need state that an organization must have a minimum level of accreditation from this organization. Finally, local and state laws differ for types and locations of organizations.

OSHA standards encompass several facets of an organization - from facilities maintenance to patient care. OSHA deems that employees have a right to a safe environment in the workplace. All health care organizations must meet minimum OSHA requirements, and have a listing of those requirements available for their employees. Some OSHA requirements that are particular to health care include, but are not limited to: sterilization of equipment, use of protective gear, disposal of hazardous material, proper labeling of chemicals, etc. The bloodborne pathogen standard also includes information regarding control plans, post-exposure evaluations, Hepatitis B vaccine, hazard communication warning labels, continuous education, and record keeping of events (Peterson and Cohen, 1996). Most risk management programs familiarize their employees with OSHA standards in the initial orientation process. This is commonly in the form of a film or demonstration of various OSHA techniques and/or equipment. Participants learn how to follow OSHA standards and how to report incidents when they find their workplace lacking of standards and/or equipment. The risk manager, along with an environmental safety officer or other appropriate staff member, must conduct inspections to be sure that OSHA standards are being met. Although most larger organizations have a separate individual assigned to insuring that OSHA standards are followed, it is also the responsibility of the risk manager. The risk manager knows the organization best and is partially responsible for these guidelines being met, so the risk manager should tailor a checklist fitted to the needs of the specific organization. OSHA imposes large fines on organizations that fail to meet the guidelines, so enforcing standards and guidelines can save the organization a great deal of money This is particularly an issue for smaller organizations that might not have a separate OSHA safety officer to ensure compliance on a daily basis.

Another important piece of Federal legislation that affects health care organizations is the Safe Medical Devices Act of 1990 (SMDA). This act affects hospitals, nursing homes, ambulatory surgical facilities, outpatient diagnostic facilities, outpatient treatment facilities, home health agencies, ambulance companies, skilled nursing facilities, rehabilitation, and hospice programs (New FDA Reporting, 1996). Currently, the SMDA does not cover private physicians' offices. This act states that if there is failure or malfunction of a medical device, it must be reported to the FDA within ten days of the incident. This is an important factor for the risk manager, because it makes prompt reporting of incidents imperative. The SMDA was revised in July of 1996 to include human-error-related malfunctions of equipment (Federal Register, 1995). This is not to penalize the employees who operated the equipment; rather, it is to warn the manufacturers of the equipment that instructions for use may not be detailed enough. There has also been an amendment that relates to tracking implantable medical devices. This amendment applies to permanently implantable devices, life-supporting or life-sustaining devices, and FDA designed devices. This amendment is designed to protect patients should an implantable device be recalled. The risk manager should consult with the Chief Information Officer to create a database of patients with such devices. The database should include names, address, emergency names, the device, the manufacturer, date of implant, and any other relevant information. The risk manager can use several forms to report an incident, such as FDA Form 3500A, FDA Form 3500, and FDA Form 3419 (Richter, P. 1996). An electronic equivalent of these forms is also available for reporting purposes.

The Patient Self-Determination Act was legislated in 1991. This act mandates that patients must be informed of their legal rights to participate in and direct health care decisions affecting them, such as the right to have an advanced directive. An advanced directive includes information about the patient's wishes for care in the event that the patient can not speak for themselves. A do-not-resuscitate (DNR) would be an example of an advanced directive. These directives also include information about life support and donation of the organs. To help ensure that the wishes of patients are carried out, a system for marking the outside of records which contain advanced directives could be implemented.

The Americans with Disabilities Act (ADA) ensures that individuals with disabilities be reasonably accommodated. For health care institutions, this act is very critical, because an individual can file a complaint with the Department of Justice at any time if they find a facility lacking in accessibility. For a health care facility, access signs are particularly important. These can include parking spaces, loading areas, and entrances for the disabled that are clearly marked with the international symbol for disabled accessibility (Richter, 1996). Restrooms that are accessible by disabled individuals should be clearly marked and identified with raised Braille letters, except in the case that every restroom in the facility is accessible. Finally, elevator control panels must have raised Braille letters to indicate emergency controls, alarms, and floors. The sides of the elevators must also have floor indicators in Braille letters.

The Joint Commission for Accreditation of Health care Organizations also has a set of standards that most health care organizations follow. There are several reasons for this: the organization that receives JCAHO accreditation tends to receive a deemed status in the community, many bond holders require a certain level of accreditation *for continuation of bond issuance, employees may be more easily recruited to a JCAHO accredited organization, and liability of the organization may be reduced due to the strict licensure requirements of JCAHO* (Fritz, 1996). The Joint Commission inspects all aspects of the organization - from human resources to clinical abilities. Risk managers can prepare for Joint Commission inspections by conducting their own inspections of the facilities.

In addition to the inspection of the facilities, clinical procedures are subject to inspection. This inspection area would be concerned with documentation of proper procedures in the medical records. A new issue that is of particular concern to risk managers is the use of restraints. In facilities such as psychiatric hospitals and geriatric units, the use of restraints can be warranted to protect the patients and staff. However, there must be extensive documentation of physician's orders for the use of restraints. Improper use of restraints can increase the liability of the organization. Because policies regarding the use of restraints are constantly being revised, the risk manager needs to stay informed of current policy and procedure.

The Consolidated Omnibus Budget Reconciliation Act was a statute that was enacted in 1985 by the federal government. This statute attempts to govern how and when physicians can transfer patients. More specifically, COBRA laws affect health care organizations, and were enacted to ensure that patients who were in medical crisis and needed treatment could receive it, regardless of ability to pay. These laws, known as the anti-dumping laws, state that a patient presenting with an emergency medical condition has a right to a screening exam and stabilization before he is transferred (Pfaehler, K., 1996). Of course, a patient still has the right to refuse the proposed treatment or transfer, but should do so in writing to reduce the liability of the organization. The most productive way for the risk manager to insure compliance with COBRA standards is to initiate a checklist that is part of all transfer and discharge paperwork. This checklist should adequately cover the important aspects of the COBRA statutes, such as: results of triage examination, stabilization procedures, and transfer information with physician notes and/or orders.

Because there are so many federal laws and statutes, the wise risk manager must devise a way to stay abreast of any new legislation. The Federal Register provides information regarding new legislation, and is updated periodically. Subscriptions are also available for electronic services that can provide this type of information. The Internet provides other information such as current Supreme Court decisions that can affect health care organizations. The risk manager should consult with the Chief Information Officer to ensure adequate access to needed information.

Local and state laws vary for type and size of the health care institution. Licensure requirements also vary, depending on the type of clinician. The risk manager should have a close relationship with the legal office to ensure that all local and state ordinances are being followed. Local and state licensing will become an increasingly controversial issue as health care continues to advance technologically. Telemedicine is a good example of medical care that will not be confined by state boundaries, and issues concerning licensure and credentialing will be affected. Also, increasing national affiliations between health care organizations are making it difficult to create uniform policies for those organizations. Other state regulations cover topics such as advance directives, medical/surgical consent procedures, informed consent procedures, HIV policies, and sterilization policies.

IV. EDUCATION OF EMPLOYEES

Education of employees is vital in the reduction of liability of the organization. Employees must be taught what risk management is and how it will affect them. The risk manager should have an active role in any orientations for new staff or residents. First, the risk manager should work with the personnel coordinators and the human resources department to ensure that applicants for employment are properly educated as per the position description. Also, credentials must be documented and updated in the personnel files. The risk manager should ensure that all training specified by the Occupational Safety and Health Administration (OSHA) and the Joint Commission for the Accreditation of Healthcare Organizations (JCAHO) is provided and documented in the personnel files of the employees. Finally, the risk management department should provide education about the key issues of risk management.

Risk managers could provide an introduction to risk management at the initial orientation for employees. The function of the risk management office should be described, as well as the physical location of the office. The manager should provide a basic definition of risk management, and describe some specific issues that risk managers handle (this could be tailored to the types of employees present--physicians might be particularly interested in medical malpractice). Incident reports should be introduced at this orientation. The employees should be given an extensive explanation of the process of incident reporting. It should be emphasized that the incident report is not to be mentioned in the medical record. Patient confidentiality issues should also be discussed. Employees need to be aware that they are not allowed to discuss any patient information with anyone other than the relevant caregivers without the written consent of the patient. Willey and Youngberg (1994) also suggest describing the " Golden Rules" of risk management during this orientation which include:

1. Know the procedures and policies that govern your practice.
2. Listen to your patients. If you ignore their concerns or they perceive you as callous, your chances of being sued increase dramatically.
3. Do not offer patients unrealistic expectations. Choose your words carefully, and do not make false promises.
4. Comply with incident reporting to guarantee early intervention and resolution of problems.
5. Learn to recognize patient and family behavior that suggests a litigious propensity. Involve patient relations, social services, and the risk management department with these persons early on in the continuum of care.
6. When in doubt, err on the side of caution and always draw upon the expertise of others.
7. Treat each of your patients in the same way as you would like yourself or your family to be treated.

Practitioners should be more specifically taught to establish and keep a good rapport with patients, involve patients in decision-making, and to recognize their own limitations - physically, mentally, and emotionally (Risk Management Pearls, 1991). Practitioners should also be given intensive information regarding informed consent. Clinical workers should be taught to never overestimate the patient's ability to understand what they have been told. The patient must be informed of the nature of the procedure or treatment, the benefits of the procedure, why that particular procedure is being recommended, the risks that can reasonably be expected to exist, and any alternative modalities available (Risk Management Pearls, 1991). At this orientation, a good overview of policies and procedures should be given as well. Proper documentation should also be discussed at length.

Risk managers should also conduct inservice educational programs. These can be regularly scheduled, such as a monthly update on legal rulings in the state that affect the health care industry, or they could be tailored to fit a particular department's needs, such as a program on the reduction and prevention of falls. Other areas that could be covered include: medical malpractice, living wills and DNR orders and their impact on the liability of the individual and the organization, communication issues, emergency department issues, patient confidentiality, and HIV testing and disclosure. The wise risk manager has a good line of communication with every department, and will know what types of seminars will benefit the employees in each area. A suggestion box can also be used to determine topics for upcoming seminars.

V. INCIDENT AND OCCURRENCE REPORTING

Incident and occurrence reports are essential for risk managers who wish to identify and track trends in their institution. It should be remembered that incidents are any events which occur that are not consistent with the normal operating procedures of the facility or routine patient care (Identifying, 1996), while occurrences also include patient medical interventions, intensities of care, or health care impairments (Benton and Bunting, 1996). However, these terms are used interchangeably. Many institutions are now combining incident and occurrence reporting on the same form for the reason that any deviation from normal procedure could be considered a potential occurrence. There are several reasons that incident reports are important. First, incidents are symptoms of an underlying problem. If incidents are reported, it becomes much easier to track information to determine the underlying cause. No incident is too small to report because each incident can help to identify and track trends. Every incident can be a potential threat to an employee, the patient, or the institution. Incident reporting can also help to determine the areas in which problems exist. For example, many medication errors that are reported may be due to an error by the pharmacy, the physician, or the giver of the medication. A properly completed incident report would show where the problem lies so that corrective action can be taken. Also, an incident report can be a valuable tool if a lawsuit is filed. Often, medical lawsuits are not filed until many years after the occurrence. The incident report might be the only record of the events surrounding the incident. Finally incident reports provide a mechanism for risk managers to identify and track problem areas of the institution in an effort to improve the quality of patient care.

Employees should be educated extensively about incident reporting. The orientation program for new employees should include a presentation by the risk manager about the risk management department, with information on what incident reports are and how to use them. It should be emphasized that incident reports are not punitive measures and exist to protect the employee and to improve overall quality of patient care. Employees should also be aware that incident reports are generally not discoverable in a court of law, if they are not noted in the medical record. However, there have been exceptions to this rule in cases that report medication errors (Pfaehler, 1996). Incident reports are not part of the medical record, and no reference should be made to them in that record. The person filing the report should simply state what occurred and include any relevant factual information about the incident. It is also important that no copies be made of the incident report for any reason, as additional copies of the report can invite discovery of the document or leakage of the information. Finally, the timeliness of the report should be emphasized. The report needs to be filed as soon as possible after the incident occurs. This serves two purposes: the incident is recorded while the information is still fresh in the memories of the witnesses, and the risk manager can take more prompt action to resolve the problem.

After incidents have been reported and investigations have been made to resolve the problems, the incident report is still of great use to the risk manager. By using computerized data, the risk manager can perform a trend analysis to discover underlying information about incidents within the institution. The data can be manipulated to produce reports for individual departments to assist them in improving patient care. The risk manager can create useful information by employing tables, graphs, or charts for departmental occurrences. However, the information distributed should not include any identifying patient information. Information concerning a particular unit should be distributed to that unit only, unless the risk manager has permission to give the information to others.

Through the use of information contained in incident reports, risk managers can be of assistance to any department in the institution. If the risk manager educates employees about the proper use of an incident report, and educates departmental managers about the information available from those reports, a proactive risk management stance can be taken to avoid future problems.

VI. DOCUMENTATION

Proper documentation in the medical record is very important to the risk manager. There are several purposes for documentation. Most importantly, documentation provides accurate and complete information about the care and treatment of patients. This can provide a basis for treatment planning of each patient. By following the patient through his stay at the institution, documentation can also provide an ongoing means of communication among all caregivers involved in the treatment of an individual patient. Finally, a documented medical record is of extreme importance to risk managers as a legal document that can be subpoenaed for use in a court of law.

Because the medical record is a legal document, many caregivers engage in defensive documentation. This means that the caregiver documents everything with the knowledge that the information contained in the record may be the only defense if a lawsuit is filed at a later date. The caregiver will see hundreds of patients between the time that care is rendered and the time that the patient files a lawsuit. The information in the record may be the only specifics that the provider can recall in order to defend himself. In fact, the medical record has been referred to as "the one witness that never dies and never lies." The patient may have family or friends as witnesses to back up their testimony. Often, the medical record may be the only tool that will substantiate a caregiver's testimony. The provider must also remember that the medical record may be used against him or his peers, subordinates, or superiors. For this reason, opinions about other caregivers should not be included, and no reference should be made in the medical record if an incident report is filed concerning the patient. Also, the medical record should not contain any inaccuracies, inconsistencies, or contradictions that could be misconstrued as improper care. Finally, the physician should review daily entries made by other caregivers (Physician's Guide, 1995). This is of particular importance in a hospital setting, where various caregivers may be documenting in the same record. If there are errors or problems, they should be corrected as quickly as possible.

Caregivers need to be aware of what specifically should be included in the medical record. The record should contain the initial history and physical examination of the patient. This should include significant surgical and medical conditions, allergies, drug reactions, current medications, recently used medications, and any over-the-counter drugs being used by the patient (Physician's guide, 1995). The medical record should also include reports of diagnostic procedures (lab results, x-rays, tests, etc.), progress reports, consultations, and referrals. Telephone consultations and advice should be documented including time of the conversation, personnel involved, nature of the problem, and service provided. All consent forms, and notes documenting informed consent processes should be included. For each patient visit, the chief complaint, purpose of the visit, date, time, vital signs, and a physician signature, or department/service identifier should be included.

The caregiver should then document diagnosis or impression of the patient's symptoms and the studies or tests ordered for the patient (Physician's guide, 1995). Ultimately, therapies administered, patient instructions, and the signature of the practitioner (title included), should be present at the end of each entry.

Caregivers also need to be aware of what should not be included in the medical record. No erasures should be present and entries should not be "whited out". The proper procedure for making a correction is to draw a single line through the error (while keeping the error legible), with the correction to the side or above it. The date and reason for the correction should be noted. Do not blame or belittle others in the patient record (Risk management, 1991). No mention of the insurance or billing status of a patient should be part of the medical record, except for the information appearing on the face sheet (Willey and Youngberg, 1994). A description of a patient in an inflammatory or prejudiced manner should never be present in a medical record. If the patient is rude or threatening, or otherwise acts inappropriately, make note of it through quotes or specific descriptions of the actions of the patient. Finally, never make reference to the fact that an incident or management report has been filed. If the report is referenced in the medical record it can be legally discovered as part of the medical record itself. No matter what the circumstance, the physician should never attempt to delete or alter existing information after a legal action has been initiated. This can arouse undue suspicion (Physician's guide, 1995).

VII. COMPLAINT HANDLING

One of the most important skills of the risk manager is that individual's ability to effectively handle complaints from the customers of the organization. Because a satisfied patient tells four other people about the organization and a dissatisfied patient tells twenty other people about their care, effective handling of patient complaints is vital (Benton and Bunting, 1996). There are several things that a complaining customer seeks: a serious response to his complaint, immediate action, compensation for his inconvenience, a solution for the problem so that no one has to go through the same thing, someone to be reprimanded, and most importantly, a complaining patient wants to be heard (Leebov, 1990). Therefore, patient complaints should be responded to immediately.

Before a risk manager handles a complaint, he or she should remember what health care customers want. First, health care customers want control over their lives. Giving informed consent, which includes education concerning the medical condition, helps the patient regain some control over health care situations through knowledge. Patients also wish to be treated fairly, just as a customer in any other industry wants. Patients also want a friendly reception, to be appreciated, and to have a sense of belonging (Leebov, 1990). It is important for the risk manager to make all employees aware of this important patient need. Through basic demeanor and attitude, every employee that comes into contact with a patient can help fulfill this need. Finally, customers want to know what is happening to them. In a health care organization, procedures are done to a patient, and this creates the lack of control. When a patient is sufficiently aware of what is occurring, part of that control is regained, producing a sense of security.

Customers who have any of the above needs violated or ignored will probably complain. Risk managers should see this as an opportunity to encourage return business. The fact that the customer is taking time to complain indicates that he is willing to return to the organization for care. When a customer's complaint is satisfactorily resolved, the instance of repeat business can zoom to 95% (Leebov, 1990). To ensure that this opportunity is used to its fullest advantage, the risk manager needs to avoid some common pitfalls of complaint handling. Whoever receives the complaint should not become defensive. This makes the customer equally defensive, if not more so. The recipient of the complaint should remain cordial and neutral, and not overreact or side against the organization. Such behavior can undermine the customer's faith that problem will be resolved, and can also lead to a lawsuit if the customer believes that the employees think the organization is lacking in some respect. The manager should not cite organizational policy as a response to a customer's complaint (Benton and Bunting, 1996). This can make the customer feel like a number or unit of service instead of a human being with a viable concern. The risk manager should address the complaint clearly and concisely. However, if it is necessary to contact other individuals or conduct an investigation, the risk manager should articulate that, and indicate how long it might take to resolve the problem to the satisfaction of the customer (Benton and Bunting, 1996). If it is not possible to estimate this information, the risk manager should at least negotiate a date to contact the customer with an update on how the complaint is being handled. Finally, when dealing with customers, employees must be conscious of their non-verbal behaviors. Body language is very revealing, and crossing of arms, avoiding eye contact, and fidgeting can all indicate that the complaint is not important to the person receiving it (Leebov, 1990).

Once the risk manager understands successful complaint protocol, he or she is ready to handle complaints. The first step is to listen carefully to the customer without interruption. After the complaint has been stated, the risk manager should always use a "sad but glad" statement, such as "I'm sorry that you are not satisfied with your care, but I'm glad that you're bringing it to our attention" (Leebov, 1990). Risk managers should also express some type of empathy, or demonstrate an ability to see the situation from the customer's point of view. This makes the customer feel that the complaint is appreciated and understood. Questions that clarify the problem should then be asked. These could include more specifics such as time and place of the occurrence, or staff members involved in the incident. What the customer wants should also be determined. After all of this information has been gathered, the risk manager should explain what he can and cannot do, and fully discuss alternatives with the customer (Benton and Bunting, 1996). After the customer has left, the risk manager should take action and then follow up to ensure satisfaction. If the resolution of the complaint is taking longer than previously expected, the manager should contact the customer and alert them to this fact. This information is always appreciated, and the customer does not feel "left out in the dark."

VIII. CLAIMS HANDLING / CRISIS MANAGEMENT

After a complaint has been lodged, or an incident report has been filed, the risk manager begins the process of claims handling, also called crisis management, depending upon the severity of the incident. The medical record should be sequestered immediately and become the property of the legal department to prevent discovery of the document. This is done for two other reasons as well: to allow the risk manager to see what has occurred, and to protect the integrity of the document. The billing department should also be contacted to hold billing for that patient (Benton and Bunting, 1996). This is done as a courtesy to the patient, and can improve patient relations, even if the organization is not found at fault. Next, the staff involved in the incident should be interviewed to get facts that may not have been included in the medical record. A Polaroid camera is always a good tool for the risk manager. If an incident is reported in a timely enough manner, the camera can produce concrete evidence of the surrounding scene, the injury, or other pertinent information. All staff should then be counseled regarding confidentiality. The risk manager should coordinate all communication with the patient and/or the family. If the risk manager is unable to be the go-between, he should assign one individual to the duty to ensure consistent communication with the patient/family. If the incident has become public, the risk manager should also consult with the public relations department of the institution.

After an investigation has been conducted, the risk manager should consult with the legal office concerning the findings. If the institution is at fault, then the risk manager should commence negotiations with the family or patient. The bill for the care can be written off or adjusted to assist in compensation. This is usually the first line of defense against legal action. Many times, this satisfies the displeased parties, without undue additional costs to the institution. There should never be an admittance of fault due to the ramifications if legal actions are later pursued. If the institution is not deemed to be at fault, they may refuse to compensate for the claim. However, sometimes nuisance claims are filed that would be expensive to battle in court. On such occasions, the legal office will help to determine which will be more cost-efficient – settling with the family, or defending the institution in court. Depending on the policies and reporting relationships of the institution, the risk manager should consult with the necessary administrative personnel to advise them of the state of the claim.

In general, if a claim goes to litigation, the legal and risk management departments work closely together to protect the institution and its employees.

IX. NEW TRENDS / ISSUES IN RISK MANAGEMENT: PROACTIVE RISK MANAGEMENT

As risk management emerged on the health care scene in the 1970s, it was generally a reactive measure to reduce losses already incurred by the institution. Typically, nothing was done to prevent a problem from occurring. Most risk managers practiced damage control. Because most employees had contact with the risk manager only when something was wrong, the relationship between the risk manager and the employees of the institution was strained. Consequently, risk managers were seen in a negative light. However, risk management departments are seeing the advantage of a team-like relationship with their employees. Instead of reactively contacting employees about incidents that have already occurred, most risk managers are now working to create a proactive risk management department. This advantageous approach should begin with the risk manager getting to know the employees and the units of their organization before an incident occurs. As a positive relationship with the employees emerges, the risk manager should encourage employees to come to them with any concerns or problems they have with their performance, their unit, overall safety, or any other risk issue. By teaming up, employees and risk managers can create risk reduction plans specific to each unit, and help prevent some exposures from occurring at all. As detailed by Sharon Barnes and Kathleen Finch (1995), the success of this approach is exemplified in the design of the emergency department risk management plan at the Duke University Medical Center.

The approach taken by the emergency department at Duke University Medical center was a success. The partnership was cited as a significant innovation by the external auditors, who noted that the project provided risk reduction through strengthening of loss control measures and effective incident report and claims management. The project was also slated for expansion into other high risk areas such as pediatrics, the operating room, and OB/GYN. The emergency department/risk management program also fostered mutual respect between emergency department leaders, the staff, and the risk manager which raised the level of trust in participating in the process. Finally, this program enhanced the continuity of care from the emergency department to the inpatient setting.

A. The Electronic Medical Record

The electronic medical record is one of the newest and most controversial technology advances today. Because of the shifting nature of health care due to spiraling costs, rapid and inexpensive access to information is necessary. Advances in information technology are making a completely electronic medical record possible. Currently, there are several types of electronic medical information available. Picture archiving and communication systems (PACS) are currently used for storage, retrieval, and transmission of images (Austin, 1992). This technology can use images such as computed tomography scans, MRI scans, and nuclear medicine studies. These images can be transmitted to other locations outside of the storage facility, such as homes or offices of physicians or workstations on patient floors. Technology also exists to create "smart cards" that contain a patient's pertinent medical information. Telemedicine is another type of evolving technology that will permit the transmission of data and images in a two-way digital format. This two way interactive screen based technology is intended to bring medical expertise to geographically remote areas. Rural health care will be one area to benefit from such technology Finally, security issues are being addressed with information technology. Some systems now have a fingerprint recorder for access to databases. The provider simply places their finger on a mouse-like device, and instead of a password, the computer reads the print (Turnbull, 1996). This technology is currently available at an inexpensive, cost-effective price. All of these technologies can be combined to create an entirely electronic medical record.

Electronic health information will be used in many different ways in the future of health care. It will facilitate hospital admission and discharge planning, especially from the physician's office. It will be able to document health care services provided, as well as coordinate billing and collection of medical services. Electronic information will assist in clinical decision-making, identify the most likely diagnosis for a given set of symptoms, and advise physicians of treatment alternatives (Garlock and Stockton, 1996). With this type of information, organizations will be able to compile clinical practice profiles and assess physician compliance with practice guidelines and utilization standards. All of this information will enable comparison of health plan performance by health care purchasers.

As health care organizations increase their utilization of information technology in the ways listed above, the entire operation of health care will change by decreasing office visits and inpatient days, and changing the way in which patients are monitored. As more electronic data is available to health care institutions, organizations will be required by payors to produce data regarding cost, quality, and access of care for their patients (Austin, 1992). Researching this type of data can also facilitate decision making related to cost-efficiency and projections for capital and other investments. As the health care industry shifts to capitation, electronic information will become increasingly important. The type of information now available helps to track true costs for procedures or types of patients. This information is invaluable when trying to negotiate contracts with new organizations, or renegotiate old contracts to fit the capabilities of the organization and the market. Finally, electronic claims processing reduces time and costs for both providers and payors.

Although health care information technology obviously has many benefits, there are many drawbacks as well. The emergence of the electronic medical record can be a security and confidentiality nightmare. Currently, there is a lack of standards governing the use of electronic information. Decisions related to information access are also a problem. Once a decision has been made about access, it is difficult to police access to electronic information. The fingerprint password increases security and tracking processes, but it does not solve all of the problems associated with electronic health information. While the technology is still relatively new, confidentiality issues will increase costs and slow progress of electronic health information. As technology progresses, however, the costs should decrease because security measures will be pre-installed.

Electronic medical records pose their own set of unique risks. Although access to information may be gained more quickly, the health care provider continues to have the same duties and liabilities related to confidentiality issues. Most proponents of electronic information state that it is harder to access this type of data because of passwords, and if the data is accessed, it is easier to track who accessed it through audit trails built into the system (Garlock and Stockton, 1996). However, opponents still contend that electronics will provide greater access to all of a patient's information, increasing the liability of the organization. When a patient's medical information is involved, the provider must be concerned with two areas of confidentiality. The first is the physician-patient privilege, which states that all information shared with a physician is privileged, unless a patient gives authorization to release that information. Also, access to a patient's medical record is restricted to the patient, the patient's authorized representative, and the attending physician and others with a legitimate need to know, including participants in health care delivery. Financial information about the patient is also considered confidential, and is subject to the above restrictions (Garlock and Stockton, 1996). Of particular concern to the national health networks is the lack of consistent confidentiality laws between the states.

With all of the concerns listed above, the risk manager begins to see the various areas of liability which an organization that uses electronic health information faces. General handling of information, whether electronic or on paper, can lead to risks such as accidental or intentional unauthorized disclosure of information, entering inaccurate information, unauthorized modification or destruction of information, and negligent failure to disclose information (Garlock and Stockton, 1996). However, with the advent of technology, new risks are faced by health care organizations. First, computerization makes it possible to store large amounts of data in a small space, so much greater amounts of information are potentially at risk during one unauthorized episode than with paper records. Additionally, misdirecting one paper file has more limited consequences than erroneously and instantaneously sending huge amounts of data to the wrong recipient (Garlock and Stockton, 1996). Improper linkage of data can also pose problems. For example, employers could gain access to unauthorized information through improper linkage of health care information. Finally, system failure can lead to a large loss of information.

Through unauthorized access, the risk manager can be looking at a variety of liability issues. Breach of confidentiality is the most obvious form of liability, because the health care provider has a responsibility to take reasonable measures to ensure confidentiality. Unauthorized disclosure can constitute medical malpractice in itself, and also violate the standard of care for that area. Breach of contract can be a liability issue because of the implied contract of medical records confidentiality between the physician and the patient. The organization or provider could also be liable for invasion of privacy. Several statutes exist that impose criminal or civil liability for unauthorized disclosure of medical information, leading to possible statutory penalties for providers (Garlock and Stockton, 1996).

B. The Impact of Managed Care on Risk Management

Managed care continues to increase its market share in health care. Health care institutions are now competing against each other to win managed care contracts. Managed care organizations base contractual negotiations on the cost-efficient delivery of quality care by the institution. Quality of care is also important. However, as health care organizations compete to decrease their spiraling costs, quality of care sometimes suffers. This is illustrated by the downsizing of health care organizations. Numbers of both clinical and support personnel are being decreased, and the health care workers that remain have more responsibilities than their predecessors. All of these factors create difficult risk management issues.

The risk manager should be involved as organizations downsize for cost cutting purposes. An adequate number of personnel to care for patient loads should be determined and adhered to. The use of physician extenders such as nurse practitioners and physician assistants must be closely monitored. Credentials should be kept on file, and competencies should be listed. If these caregivers practice outside the realm of their education, the institution can be held liable under respondeat superior. Also, the use of agency and pool employees must be monitored closely. New Joint Commission regulations for 1996 state that caregivers must be trained in age-specific competencies. If a pool nurse typically works in the adult unit, but is needed in the pediatrics ward due to a staffing shortage, organizational liability increases. The risk manager should also be present during layoffs. Disgruntled employees can and have become violent as a result of termination. Security issues should be noted in cases where this may be a problem.

When a health care facility has a contract with a managed care organization (MCO), the practices of the MCO can increase the risks at the facility. For example, the gatekeeping policies of many MCOs can adversely affect the liability of the emergency department, by increasing exposures to personal injury lawsuits, or fines stemming from COBRA violations. To help prevent this, risk management should ensure that the emergency department staff is sufficiently trained in screening, documentation practices, stabilization, and decision-making procedures for admitting, transferring, or releasing patients (Pfaehler, 1996). Also, when negotiating a contract, the risk manager should require that the MCO provide a clear definition of what constitutes an emergency. The health care facility could also face increased liability and exposure from utilization and quality review requirements of the MCO. Karl Pfaehler (1996) suggests that risk managers diligently monitor these three risk exposures: unauthorized access to confidential patient information by "others" who profess to have the right to see such data, disputes about what is considered over-utilization or an outlier, and use of utilization and quality data generated by MCOs in medical staff credentialing.

To prevent many of the above problems from occurring, the risk manager should be involved in any contractual negotiations with managed care organizations. As part of an administrative team, the risk manger can assess any clauses for referrals, treatment patterns, length of stay mandates, and number of patients being provided. The risk manager can then advise the rest of the administrative staff regarding risk issues related to these clauses. The risk manager should also ascertain the liability of the institution if the managed care organization demands that agency personnel are used. Contractually-imposed clinical practice guidelines and credentialing requirements should also be noted by the risk manager (Pfaehler, 1996). With the assistance of the legal department, the risk manager must also determine if there are any illegal clauses in the proposed contract, such as a gag order. Gag orders prevent a physician from discussing alternative forms of care that might be in the best interests of the patient, if those forms of care are not covered under the patient's policy. If a health care institution is prudent in regard to their contract signing processes, and careful during the negotiation process, the liability of the organization can be minimized.

SUMMARY

Risk managers of today are faced with a variety of tasks. Overall, risks to the patients, staff, and an organization must be minimized. To accomplish this, risks must be identified and defined. Legislation and regulatory issues must be addressed and processes must be standardized to meet these statutes. New legislation and its effect on an organization must be closely monitored. Employees must be educated about risk issues including documentation, complaint handling, patient relations, OSHA standards, and occurrence reporting. All training and education must be documented. Finally, risk managers should be proficient in complaint and claims handling and crisis management.

Risk managers must also be considering the future issues and trends that can affect an organization. Managed care will continue to be a risk issue for many years to come, as will other contracting arrangements being made by health care organizations. Electronic medical records and other similar technology are also a security concern. However, as the future arrives, risk managers will also find many tools at their disposal. Although it poses a security risk, information technology can help the risk manager track and forecast trends within an organization or network. Benchmarking between and within networked organizations will also be an important quality improvement tool. By using these tools and continually seeking new solutions for risk issues, the risk manager can create a truly proactive department.

Risk management can be a challenge for any health professional. Because risk management encompasses a variety of activities, all employees of an organization must participate in the prevention and management of risk. By involving everyone, harm to patients, staff, and the institution can be minimized.

REFERENCES

American Society for Healthcare Risk Management. (1992). *An analysis of ASHRM's insurance survey: criteria for accepting a health care entity as an insurable risk.* American Hospital Association: Chicago.

American Society for Healthcare Risk Management. (1990). Harpster L. M. , and Veach, M., eds. *Risk management handbook for health care facilities.* American Hospital Publishing Inc., Chicago.

Austin, C. J. (1992). *Information systems for health services administration. (4th ed.).* Ann Arbor, MI: AUPHA Press.

Barnes, S. L., and Finch, K. G. (1995). ED risk management: A practical, comprehensive program for a high-risk area. *Journal of Healthcare Risk Management. Fall:* 9-15.

Benton, J. and Bunting, R. (1996). Fundamentals of risk management. Presented at the Southeastern Regional Risk Management Conference, May 1996.

Dodero, F. (1994). Preparing for the risks of tomorrow's technology. In Barbara J. Youngberg (Ed.), *The Risk Manager's Desk Reference,* Aspen Publishers, Inc., Gaithersburg, MD, 315-323.

Federal Register. (1995) Dec. 11; 60[237]: 63577-606.

Fritz, A. (1996). Human resources standards: Effective JCAHO survey preparation. Presented at Management of Human Resources - Meeting the JCAHO Standards. Columbia, SC: PHTS.

Garlock, B. B. and Stockton, P. (1996). *Electronic health care information: Minimizing security and confidentiality risks.* Unpublished manuscript presented at the North Carolina ASHRM Fall Conference, November 1996.

Identifying and managing risks. (1996). *Healthcare Risk Control, vol 2*, 1-11.

Leebov, W. (1990). *Effective complaint handling in health care*. American Hospital Publishing, Inc.: Chicago.

Managing risks and the liability in the delivery of managed care. (January, 1996). *Risk Management Newsletter, (Reeves, K., ed.)*, 6:1, 1-2.

Medical Affairs Committee of the American Society for Healthcare Risk Management. (1991). Risk management pearls for physicians [Brochure]. Author, Chicago..

Medical device liability. (1996, January). Healthcare Risk Control: Laws, Regulations, and Standards.

New FDA reporting rule, new risk management concerns. (1996, February). *The Risk Management Reporter, 15*(1): 1-5.

Patient Self-Determination act of 1990 (P.L. 101-508; U.S.C. Sec. 4206).

Peterson, R. D., and Cohen, J. M. (1996). The complete guide to OSHA compliance. CRC Press, Boca Raton.

Pfaehler, K. (1996, October). Medication incident report is subject to discovery. *Risk Management Newsletter, 6*(4): 1-2.

Pfaehler, K. (1996, April). Managed care in the emergency department. *Risk Management Newsletter, 6*(2): 1-2.

Pfaehler, K. (1996, April). Risk exposures from utilization and quality review requirements. *Risk Management Newsletter, 6*(2): 4-5.

Pfaehler, K. (1996, April). Clinical risk management. Presented at the Basic Risk Management Workshop at the South Carolina Hospital Association, April 1996.

PHICO. (1995). Physician's guide to risk management. Author, Mechanicsburg, PA.

Richter, P. V. (1996, April). Does your signage meet ADA requirements? *Risk Management Newsletter, 6*(2): 5-6. South Carolina Hospital Association.

Richter, P. V. (1996). Basic risk management for support services. Presented at South Carolina Hospital Association Basic Risk Management Workshop, April 1996.

Turnbull, J. (1996). [Information systems technology for health care facilities]. Unpublished presentation.

Willey, E. L., and Youngberg, B. J. (1994). Education as a valuable risk management resource. In Barbara J. Youngberg (Ed.), *The risk manager's desk reference*. Aspen Publishers, Inc., Gaithersburg, MD: 67-95.

27.
THE BEHAVIOR OF PHYSICIANS

David M. Mirvis, *University of Tennessee, Memphis, TN*

Understanding the dynamic and complex factors determining physician behavior is critical to the effective management of health care organizations, especially with the expansion of programs that alter the traditional relationships between physicians, patients and organizations. For example, the introduction of prospective payment systems, expansion of contractual arrangements between patients and provider organizations, and the expanding direct employment of physicians by for-profit as well as not-for-profit health care organizations have all introduced new complexities in the interactions between physicians,patients, and health care organizations (Sheldon, 1986).

Knowledge of the elements motivating physicians can be used to understand observed behavior and to predict the consequences of organizational changes as well as to guide that behavior to better meet new needs. In this review, we shall 1) describe the classical elements of physician behavior; 2) analyze the implications of these forces on the role of physicians within the health care system in general and, in particular, within structured health care organizations; 3) consider the forces that are changing the traditional determinants of physician behavior; and 4) examine some of the new organizational models and forces that are developing based on the changes in physician roles.

I. CLASSICAL MODELS OF PHYSICIAN BEHAVIOR

Classical approaches consider five major factors that drive physician behavior: the doctor-patient relationship, professional autonomy, professional dominance, self-interest, societal issues. Each interacts with the others to result in the complex behavior that uniquely distinguishes physicians.

A. The Physician-Patient Relationship

The driving force behind physician behavior has long been the physician-patient relationship. Its singular features are largely responsible for the physician behavior pattern that is different from virtually all other professionals. It is perhaps unique among all interpersonal relations. As described by Kirsner, "[I]t is not a routine encounter, not a legal arrangement or business transaction, and since medicine is not a mathematical discipline, the relationship is not a computer exercise. The physician-patient relationship rather is an evolving person-to-person interaction, transcending ethnic, economic and sociocultural differences, an interchange generating confidence, mutual trust, and respect" (1992).

The basic structure and the importance of the physician-patient relationship have been recognized for centuries. This relationship is an essential component of virtually every religious and professional code of ethics. The Hippocratic Oath, for example, demands that physicians "will prescribe regimens for the good of ... patients according to [their] ability and judgment ... In any house where [they] come, [they] will enter only for the good of [their] patients."

Six elements define the "ideal" physician-patient relationship (Emanuel and Dubler, 1995). First, patients may expect to have choices in their care, including choice of physician, choice of practice setting and, most importantly, choice between treatment alternatives. These alternatives are based on personal autonomy, guided by but not forced by the advice of physicians. Second, patients may expect their physicians to be competent. This competence includes not only technical capability but the ability to make decisions for the patient based on the best available information. Third, patients may expect physicians to exhibit good communication, including listening to and understanding their concerns and values as well as symptoms. Fourth, physicians are expected to exhibit compassion in addition to technical proficiency. Fifth, the relation with a physician should be durable, permitting an effective and understanding relationship to develop. Finally, and most critically, the relation should be single-mindedly for the good of the patient, without conflicts of interest with monetary or other personal interests of the physician or interests of other third-parties (Gabbard and Nadelson, 1995).

Because the patient is in need and cannot fully assess the quality of the service that is delivered, the relationship is intrinsically asymmetric with the physician assuming a fiduciary responsibility. That is, the physician acts as the patient's agent, obtaining for the patient what the patient would want if he or she had the physician's knowledge and skill. Thus, the relation is enormously complex, assuming not only therapeutic and humanitarian values, but also legal and ethical dimensions. The relationship is characterized most simply as one of trust that the physician will act solely on behalf of and advocate for the physical, psychosocial and spiritual good of the individual patient.

This relationship may be modeled after any of four general prototypes (Emanuel and Emanuel, 1992). In the paternalistic model, the physician acts as the patient's guardian, determining what is best and presenting that conclusion to the patient. In the informative construct, the physician is a teacher who presents information to the patient about the options for care, and the patient is left to choose without further intervention or guidance by the physician. In the interpretive model, the physician acts as a counselor, seeking to understand the patient's wishes and helping the patient to choose the care that best matches these needs. Finally, in the deliberative model, the physician persuades but does not coerce the patient to follow what the physician determines to be the best option. Each may be appropriate for certain patients and under certain conditions.

A key component of each of these models is advocacy for the needs of the patient. Physicians classically view themselves as "single mindedly serving the patients' needs" (Preister, 1992) and as "required to do everything that they believe may benefit each patient without regard to costs or other societal considerations …The physician's master must be the patient" (Levinsky, 1984). Thus, advocacy may be viewed as having no limits. Any intervention that may benefit the patient should be used, regardless of likely success or the cost to be incurred. As summarized by Fried, "the physician who withholds care that it is in his power to give … breaks faith with his patient" (1975). This advocacy, in its purist form, cannot tolerate external intervention and is blind to outside constraints. Indeed, patient advocacy may commonly be used as a justification for deceiving third party payers when patient needs are considered to be at stake (Novack et al., 1989).

This advocate role is a closely guarded one-to-one relationship. A physician will have many patients, each with a different physician-patient relationship. At any one moment, the needs of one particular patient are paramount and are considered independent of the needs of any other patient, whether of the same physician or of another; the physician's behavior is focused on individual patients, one at a time. Thus, in the pure form of advocacy, needs of the patient currently being treated take precedence over possible conflicting needs of others.

These characteristics of the physician-patient relation would result in physician behavior that is directed solely toward the health and well-being of the patient. This is, however, subject to constraints. Patients may want something that would not otherwise be recommended or provided by the physician. This may include performing unnecessary tests to reassure patients that they have no illness, prescribing unnecessary treatments because of patients' expectations based on outside influences, or requesting unneeded referrals to specialists to assuage patients' anxieties. Alternatively, it may include the refusal of the patient to accept the recommendations of the physician, choices which may be to the physical detriment of the patient (Brock and Wortman, 1992). In some situations the physician may decline to do what the patient asks or demands. For example, there may be conflicts between the patient's requests and the physician's ethical standards or because the requested treatment would be futile or inhumane (Paris et al., 1992).

The second constraint is the limited information available to the physician. Repeatedly, experts acknowledge that much of what physicians do is not based on rigorous scientific knowledge and that, for precious few conditions, is the single best definitive approach known (Eddy, 1982; Wennberg, 1984). Rather, decisions on behalf of patients involve considerable judgment based on personal experience, habits, and attitudes even when the practitioner is exceptionally well versed in the medical literature. Other limitations will be considered later in this paper.

B. Professional Autonomy

This beneficent motivation is accompanied and tempered by other forces related to the physician as a professional. The first and most important concept is that physicians, like other professionals (Raelin, 1994), strive for autonomy. The definition and scope of autonomy vary from author to author. At a minimum, it consists of "the ability to deliver medical care to a patient without the uninvited imposition of outside influences" (Grumbach and Bodenheimer, 1990). This freedom may include, in addition to the right to diagnose and prescribe for a patient without interference, the ability to control the organization of the work, the freedom from control by other organizational or external influences, and the ability to self-regulate and self-govern. Autonomy may also be expressed in terms of freedom to set fees (Grumbach and Bodenheimer, 1990) and to generate income (Reed and Evans, 1987).

Thus, the realm of autonomy is very broad, including virtually all components of the health care delivery system. Through it, the medical profession determines what shall be done (by establishing the knowledge base of physicians and standards of practice), who shall join (by establishing admission and education criteria and licensing practices), why the work shall be done (by codes of ethics and the service orientation of the profession) and how the work shall be done (O'Connor and Lanning, 1992).

These patterns of autonomy have been maintained by five interrelated factors: a monopoly over information; public respect; legal protections; internal cohesiveness and representation of the profession; and organizational control. First, the medical profession has maintained a relative monopoly over specialized knowledge and skills that are not readily mastered or even comprehended by the lay public (Freidson, 1970; Starr, 1982). This cognitive basis for autonomy is enhanced by the intellectual connection of medicine to modern science and the general reliance of modern society on scientific advancements to improve standards of living (Starr, 1982).

Second, the public grants deference and respect to physicians for their work because of the value society places on health care and the public's confidence that the profession will act in the public's best interest. The latter is strengthened by activities such as complex educational requirements, codes of ethics, professional societies, and peer review processes that strive to assure appropriate professional behavior. The standardization of the medical education system after the Flexner report also significantly enhanced the public's confidence in the training of the individual practitioner who could now be assumed to follow professionally mandated and accepted guidelines (Freidson, 1970; Starr, 1982).

Third, a legal basis for autonomy is provided by the state through functions such as licensing regulations. The state grants these privileges to the profession in response to general acceptance of the value and public-mindedness of the profession, as well as the recognition that only members of the profession have the knowledge and skill to practice. Thus, the professional autonomy initially rooted in specialized knowledge takes on the force of law because of the public's need for, acceptance of and trust in the medical profession. This legal protection is granted to the profession as a whole but, in effect, confers autonomy to the individual practitioner (Light and Levine, 1988). The withdrawal of the state from involvement of health affairs after granting autonomy is a major factor in the maintenance of physician autonomy (Duran-Arenas and Kennedy, 1991). The state uses its power to support the profession's own standards and to maintain an environment relatively free of serious competition (Freidson, 1970).

This withdrawal is greater in the United States than in other countries (Yishai, 1992) because the importance placed on the freedom of the individual to function without coercion is greater than in other countries.

Fourth, the profession has maintained tight internal cohesiveness with powerful local and national representation. Thus, the profession is able to secure legislative privileges and protection, and to influence economic and social conditions beyond the normal scope of medical expertise (Starr, 1982; McKinlay and Arches, 1985). The American Medical Association has been the preeminent leader in presenting the cohesive interests of the medical profession in the United States. Such organizations have greatest impact when other professions and health care functions are not so tightly organized (Duran-Arenas and Kennedy, 1991).

Finally, medicine has been able to sustain its autonomy by gaining control over organizations that might otherwise have threatened its position. For example, the medical profession has until recently been able to structure the potentially conflicting roles of hospitals and health insurance in ways that serve their interests and protect their autonomy. The result is a broad and well-protected sphere of autonomy.

C. Professional Dominance

A third motivator is professional dominance (Freidson, 1970), the notion that physicians have been traditionally placed in a dominant, controlling position in health care. The medical profession "is portrayed as dominant in a division of labor in which other occupations [are] obliged to work under the supervision of physicians and take orders from them" (Freidson, 1985). Social codes as well as law enforce this dominance; for example, only physicians can order tests and procedures that are performed by other health care practitioners. Thus, a physician defines the work content and may intercede in the work of others, but nonphysician groups may not reciprocate.

This tradition of dominance may also be expanded to include an "intellectual hegemony" in which the medical profession induces health care needs that only they can then provide, that is, an intellectual as well as an organizational dominance (Freidson, 1985). Thus, physicians dominate their clients as well as other workers. Physicians exert what Starr (1982) calls "cultural authority," the ability to influence the "definitions of reality" by shaping the patient's understanding of his or her own condition. Cultural authority contrasts social authority, which is controlling actions by giving commands. The ability of physicians to exert both cultural and social authority over patients is based not only on their presumed superior competence, but also on the emotionally dependent condition of the patient when ill and the physician's function as a gatekeeper to nonmedical resources such as insurance reimbursement, employment certification, etc. This analysis also extends the concept of physician-induced demand (Eisenberg, 1986), discussed below, from only an economic to a sociological phenomenon.

Dominance also commonly includes social patterns that extend both to nonprofessional and professional activities. Physician managers, for example, are typified as needing influence and dominance; they seek to be the focal point of discussions and to impose their positions on others. More importantly, physicians commonly attempt to extend dominance to all aspects of health care such as finance and policy decisions. Such issues are, however, outside the specialized scope of professional medical knowledge; the physician therefore does not have a monopoly on this knowledge so that the fundamental basis for autonomy and dominance is missing (Mirvis, 1993).

This view of dominance is based on organizational authority. Dominance may also exist because of the economic leverage physicians have within health care organizations (Greer, 1984). In hospitals, for example, physicians control the inputs [i.e., the admission of patients], the outputs [i.e., the number of tests and procedures performed], and main parts of internal processes, all of which determine the fiscal health of the organization (Pauly and Redisch, 1973).

Autonomy and dominance, once granted, confer responsibility as well as privilege. Privileges include the relative isolation from external interference by legislative regulation and from other professions. Even individual physicians resist examination from nonprofessionals as well as from other physicians.

Responsibilities include, most notably, the obligation of self-governance. Self-governance is mandated as no other necessarily subordinate profession can regulate it. Since the monopoly over information ensures that only members of the profession know the work to be done, nonmembers cannot evaluate the functions of the profession and hence cannot interfere with its activities (Freidson, 1970). This self-regulation includes maintaining professional competence as well as maintaining the public interest in its activities.

D. Self-Interests

Fourth, physicians, like all people, behave in ways that reflect and maximize their own self-interests. For physicians, each of the above characteristics is part of the system of self-interest. Thus, maximizing patient well-being is in the self-interest of the physician as well as in the best interest of the patient. Other self-interests are, however, more typical of all persons and not particular to professionals or to physicians. These include the desire for income, the desire for a certain practice style and setting, the desire to fulfill certain personal characteristics, the desire to emulate practices of clinical leaders, and the desire to avoid litigation (Eisenberg, 1986).

The most talked about self-interest is income generation. Physicians can actually induce demand for their services rather than simply meet needs generated by external factors. Physicians initiate most, perhaps as much as 90%, of orders for medical care and are directly paid for many of these orders. While most of these orders are initiated because of patients' health (Rossiter and Wilensky, 1983), physicians are capable of altering practice for personal financial gain.

This ability to generate demand can be studied by analyzing physician responses to changes in reimbursement systems. For example, when reimbursement rates are lowered, the intensity, both in terms of quantity and complexity, of services performed by practitioners rises, partially replacing previously lost income (Rossiter and Wilensky, 1983). The Congressional Budget Office estimated that only 44% of the expected cost savings caused by a drop in reimbursement rates will actually be realized because utilization rates will rise (Christensen, 1989). Conversely, an increase in reimbursement rates leads to falls in utilization, suggesting that physicians act to maintain a certain level of income rather than to maximize income (Eisenberg, 1986).

Most of this behavior is consistent with the role of the physician as a patient advocate. While medical practice is largely based on sound scientific principles, relatively little is known about what tests are minimally necessary or maximally appropriate and what treatments are truly best. Thus, when treating a patient, the physician generally determines what tests to perform and what procedures to order. Physicians may thus alter behavior within the fairly broad bounds of acceptable practice in accordance with the personal incentives included within the health care delivery system, yet not conflict with professional norms (1980). The increase in demand may include economically beneficial substitutions in services ranging from office visits to laboratory procedures or from drug therapy to invasive procedures, as well as the addition of new services. Conversely, demands of managed care organizations may influence physicians to reduce services to maximize corporate profits as well as personal perquisites (Hillman et al., 1989).

In other cases, however, physician practice may fall outside of acceptable norms. Examples include unnecessary referral of patients to laboratories owned by the referring physician, a practice shown to increase utilization and cost (Relman, 1992). Prepaid or capitation systems may also result in unacceptable restriction of services (Council on Ethical and Judicial Affairs, 1995). Patient interests and ideology are often used to justify actions, but these arguments only mask the underlying primary economic and other self interests of physicians (Globerman, 1990)

Physicians also act to meet personal preferences as to style and setting of their practices. Variables include personal aggressiveness, interest in certain types of patients, convenience, and habits. For example, physicians with offices in hospitals hospitalize patients more often than do those with offices elsewhere. Practices in university hospitals differ from those in community hospitals; those in fee-for-service practices differ from those in capitation-based delivery systems. Older physicians order fewer laboratory tests than to younger ones while specialists tend to order more procedures than do generalists (Greenfield et al., 1992). Practitioners in different specialties or trained in different countries may treat similar patients differently. For example, physicians in Canada are less aggressive in ordering cardiac catheterization than are those in the United States (Pilote et al., 1995). Peer pressure, especially from clinical leaders, socialization within the practice group (Eisenberg, 1979) to perform in certain ways, and access to different technologies may account for these differences.

A final behavior based on self-interest is the avoidance of malpractice suites, that is, defensive medicine. Some practices that are not medically necessary are performed either to reduce the likelihood of being sued or to provide a better defense if sued. The quantitative impact of defensive medicine on overall physician behavior is unknown. Estimates range from assertions that as many as 27% of physicians practice some defensive medicine (Special Task Force on Professional Liability and Insurance, 1984) to claims that only 1% of laboratory tests are ordered to avoid or to defend malpractice cases (Wertman et al., 1980). Regardless of the actual cost or volume of defensive medicine, fear of litigation significantly affects physician behavior. Some estimate that a physician will be under indictment for 40% of his or her professional life, a value exceeding that of most habitual criminals (Sheldon, 1986).

E. Social Responsibility

A final determinant of physician behavior is a limited attempt to meet social and societal interests. Traditionally, physicians have advocated for improvements in public health, for achievements in biomedical research, and for advances in health delivery systems.

These activities are consonant with patient advocacy. However, attending to societal interests in areas that impede autonomy or patient-centered practice is resisted. For example, restricting care, even that of marginal benefit, because of the impact on health care finances is typically resisted. Levinsky (1984) says physicians are "required to do everything that they believe may benefit each patient without regard to cost or other societal considerations."

II. PHYSICIAN BEHAVIOR IN ORGANIZATIONS

When physicians enter into health care systems as employees or as clients, these behavioral characteristics come into direct contact with those of the organization. For example, professionals strive to maintain their goals of patient advocacy, autonomy and dominance when they function within organizations as they do in individual relationships with patients and other professionals. These behavioral motives are significantly different from those that characterize most of the organizations in which physicians function, so conflicts are common.

The importance of these strains is emphasized by the interdependence of physicians and health care systems. Physicians practice in hospitals, and hospitals remain largely dependent on physicians for patient referrals. Physicians also have a considerable stake in the success of the organization; the success of the system determines, to a significant extent, the ability of the physician to do his or her work and thereby to further career goals and professional reputation. Changes in health care systems are more intrinsically integrating physicians into various organizational systems, either as employees or as significant stakeholders in the fiscal and operational well-being of the organization.

A. Differences Between Professionals, Professional Organizations and Nonprofessional Organizations

Many differences in behavior between physicians, nonprofessionals [and at times other professionals], and the organization in which they work exist. These differences have been conceptualized by Mintzberg (1983) and others as forming two distinct organizational models. Organizations dominated by professionals operate under a system of expertise. Accomplishing the work of the organization depends upon the specific, unique skills of individual professionals, not upon formalized procedures or the detailed direction of supervisors. Power rests with the individual workers and flows "upward"; power is highly decentralized and is greater at the bottom than at the top of the organizational chart. Each practitioner has a considerable degree of authority to act independently. For example, over 50% of medical school faculty, i.e., physicians employed in a structured bureaucratic environment, could not identify a supervisor in the area of patient care (Weisbord, 1976). Power is also fluid, shifting from patient to patient and issue to issue.

Administrative functions, in contrast, operate under a system of authority. In the classic, although somewhat outdated model, power is maximized at the top of the organizational chart. The chief executive establishes concrete goals and the "whole organization is then consciously designed as a logically integrated chain of means and ends to accomplish them" (Mintzberg, 1983). All subordinates are expected to conform to the established goals, policies and procedures of the organization; line workers have little authority to control their work.

While these descriptions may represent the extremes of organizational forms, they do illustrate the problem at hand. Stereotypically, physicians may be viewed as individualistic professionals who apply a specific body of highly specialized knowledge to unique conditions for the maximal benefit of individual clients. Organizations, in contrast, strive for predictability and efficiency; they seek the routine and the typical so that behavior of individual as well as groups of workers can be patterned and monitored in a system of hierarchical control that maximizes the good of the overall organization.

Conflict may result. First, attempts to apply routine procedures to care delivery, even those intended to optimize basic systems and ultimately improve care, may be resisted as encroaching on the physician-patient relationship and upon professional autonomy. As summarized by Raelin (1991), physicians "are hired to apply specialized knowledge to a host of unstructured problems. Solutions to such problems are ordinarily developed through individual problem-solving processes. No amount of administrative procedure or regulation will necessarily cause the problems to be solved more quickly or more efficiently." Not uncommonly, this conflict leads physicians to defy authority and overtly or passively disregard organizational policies and procedures.

Physicians resent close supervision of practice as encroachment on autonomy. While physicians may accept management's right to specify the broad goals of the organization, they resist specification of the means to achieve those goals (Raelin, 1991). The role of the supervisor is to promote professional growth and to remove bureaucratic obstacles to individual practice, not to monitor or direct clinical activities. Professionals also seek an egalitarian organizational structure in which differences are based on competence rather than on position within an organizational hierarchy. Although hierarchical authority is thus minimized, power based on reputation among colleagues is important (Bucher and Stelling, 1969). Physicians will respect and follow the leadership of peers with professional qualifications, but commonly not respond to nonprofessionals at managerial or executive levels.

Most importantly, physicians work to meet professional rather than organizational standards. For example, physicians work toward unbridled advocacy for individual patients at whatever the cost—a key element of classical physician-patient relationship—rather than the organization's attempts to manage resources needed by populations of patients. As summarized by Levinsky (1984), "in caring for the individual patient, the physician must act solely as the patient's advocate, against the apparent interests of society as a whole, if necessary." The goal is to meet or exceed established professional standards of practice, ignoring if necessary the constraints imposed by bureaucratic systems.

Similarly, professionals gain most of their nonmonetary rewards from outside the organization, while nonprofessionals receive rewards from the organization itself. While organizations expect the allegiance of their workers, physicians show allegiance and loyalty first to the profession and only secondarily to any organization. When they allocate loyalty between more than one organization, they pay greater allegiance to the more professionally oriented organization; for example, loyalty will be greater to a university than to a hospital. Wilson (1989) has indeed defined a "professional" as one who seeks rewards from outside the organization in contrast to a "bureaucrat" who obtains rewards from the organization itself. Raelin (1991) similarly considers professionals as "cosmopolitans" who seek reward outside as opposed to "locals" who seek rewards inside the organization.

Because of these numerous and pervasive differences, professionals and large organizations may be intrinsically incompatible (Begun, 1985; Scott, 1982). As summarized by Harries-Jenkins (1970), "[T]he individual [professional] in these bureaucracies retains a distinctive frame of reference, so that as a professional, he participates in two distinct, irreconcilable systems. He is a member of two institutions: the profession and the organization. Each of these attempts to control his occupational activities, and the manner in which the former establishes standards and norms for the conduct of professional activities, contrasts with the way the latter specifies work objectives."

B. The Dual Firm Model

Several organizational paradigms have been developed to address these issues. One mechanism is for the hospital to function as two separate, parallel organizations rather than as a single institution i.e., a dual firm model. Two distinct lines of authority exist side by side: an administrative one controlled by management and a professional one dominated by the medical staff. Administrators run one firm that provides input into a second one run by physicians; the physician-run firm combines this input with professional forces to produce health care (Harris, 1977).

Thus, physicians are able to maintain their autonomy. The hospital delegates to the medical staff considerable responsibility for working independently as well as for goal setting, as reflections of the special nature of the work to be done (Scott, 1982). Administrators act as facilitators of the professionals rather than as classical managers, seeking to provide an operationally and financially stable place for physicians to work (Weiner et al., 1987). Physicians then work within the bureaucratic organization by remaining functionally outside of its administrative structure (Goss et al., 1977). Thus, hospitals have been described as the "physicians' workshop" (Pauly, 1980) functioning primarily to maximize the profit of physicians. As a secondary result, the hospital itself succeeds.

The major advantage of this dual system is that most responsibility for decisions is placed in the hands of those professional workers who make the decisions. Because these professionals are largely service-oriented, the needs of individual patients are emphasized (Scott, 1982). The separation of powers also minimizes conflict between professionals and administrators.

Negative consequences are, however, serious. Although physician-oriented management will pay great attention to needs of individual clients, the macro-level needs of the organization such as planning may be inappropriately de-emphasized especially when they conflict with needs of individual patients (Scott, 1982).

In addition, decisions in these organizations are made by complex negotiations and compromises between the parties rather than by a single management hierarchy. Response to both external or internal threats and opportunities is sluggish, loosely coordinated. These organizations, then, tend to be characterized by inertia, inefficiency and reactive posturing. They have been termed satisficing organizations; the conflicting goals of key groups limit the hospital's ability to make appropriate and important decisions.

Another characteristic of decision making in dual firm models is the high prevalence of political activity. In the absence of an organized system of authority, political "games" frequently emerge, games promoted, as described by Mintzberg (1983), because power allocated based on expertise is fluid as needs and competencies change. Political activity is also supported by the allegiance of physicians to specific professional groups based on specialty with political conflicts developing between specialties.

C. The Conflictive Power Equilibrium

The two systems in the dual firm model are not and cannot be fully separate. Physicians commonly have involvement in administrative functions; administrators commonly take actions that affect or are interpreted as interfering with the prerogatives of the professional. Thus, organizational models based on conflict evolve.

One such model is the conflictive power equilibrium construct developed by Young and Saltman (1985). This paradigm is based on the exchange model of the hospital proposed by Jacobs (1974). In it, the hospital is viewed as a neutral forum in which various professional groups compete for power. The result is a conflictive environment in which groups compete to gain control over resources and to make the decisions that directly affect them.

Greatest power is gained by those who introduce the most uncertainty into the organization, i.e., those groups whose appropriate performance is most critical and, conversely, those whose absence or inadequate performance would most jeopardize the organization. In hospitals, the medical staff introduces the most uncertainty and thus have the most power; only they have the skills most central and immediate to the delivery of health care because of their specialized knowledge and legal protection.

However, intergroup conflicts are moderated to ensure survival of the overall organization. One method for achieving moderation is to routinize day-to-day organization of authority and responsibility. Thus, groups subordinate their power maximizing behavior at some point, so that a "conflictive power equilibrium" exists, with "permanent internecine conflict within the framework of a stable systematic equilibrium" (Saltman and Young, 1985).

To maintain their position of power, physicians act to defend their position from incursions by other groups. In this model, the results of an action by management or such groups as nurses are largely determined by the effect the action has on groups dominating the hospital power equilibrium. For example, cost containment efforts by management that introduce financial control on physicians will provoke new efforts by physicians to evade the controls.

The conflictive approach suggests a Marxian type of interclass struggle (Lammert, 1978). In this model, conflicts develop between divergent "social" strata. Some positions are empowered to exercise control over others. This power distribution then "invariably stimulates social conflicts analogous to class conflicts in the traditional Marxian sense" (Lamment, 1978).

D. Hybrid Organizations and Shaky Alliances

The necessary or forced interaction of different power groups or classes within a single organization may also be modeled as a hybrid organization (Mintzberg, 1983). The result is a shaky alliance between the components to address each other's goals for the overall good of the organization. This construct is intrinsically unstable; as summarized by Mintzberg (1983), "outright conflict is never far from the surface. Should one side falter, the other will quickly move in to usurp its prerogatives." Thus, moderate levels of conflict pervade the organization. If this conflict is moderated, the organization can continue to function; if it becomes more intense, political forces commonly lead to the death of the organization.

E. Professional Segmentation

The models described above relate to conflicts between professional and non-professional components of an organization. Important conflicts also exist within the professional structure (Bucher and Stelling, 1969; Freidson, 1985). Lumping all issues into a professional versus nonprofessional construct masks the underlying diversity of physician subgroups. Significant differences in physician behavior exist, for example, between generalists and specialists, between hospital based and community based practitioners, between physicians in private practice and those employed by health care systems.

These differences lead to segmentation of the profession and result in intraorganizational conflicts. These conflicts are particularly prominent when the workspaces of different physician cohorts overlap or when determining significant organizational policy is at stake. Differences are also significant when members of various specialties serve on teams; working together may cause painful redefinition of roles and threaten autonomy of subgroups (Bucher and Stelling, 1969).

F. Physician Inclusion Models

In contrast to these conflictive models of physician-organization interaction, other models in which physicians and administrative organizations work well together have been developed. The goal is to manage with professionals rather than manage professionals and to emphasize the ways in which clinicians and organizations are interdependent rather than the ways in which they are different. This model has several advantages (Begun, 1985). First, conflict that results in organizational inefficiency and that impedes the ability of the organization to meet challenges is reduced. Second, including professionals in the management structure increases creativity and innovation needed to meet, for example, the clinical challenges of cost reduction and market share. Physicians are responsible for over 80% of medical care costs (Young and Saltman, 1983) by the application of their specialized knowledge and skill; this knowledge should best be included in the decision making process so that decisions will be informed ones and so that results will be appropriate. Third, including physicians in organizational processes enhances buy-in and may mediate resistance against actions perceived to impact autonomy.

One particularly appealing nonconflictive organizational model developed by Scott (1982) is the conjoint organization. In it, professionals and nonprofessionals serve as equals, coexisting in "a state of interdependence and mutual influence." Each group has primary responsibility for certain hospital functions, but with considerable overlap. Thus, "no administrator should be completely governed by administrative [macro] values; and no practitioner should subscribe exclusively to professional [micro] values" (Scott, 1982).

Physicians are thereby granted considerable professional autonomy while recognizing the growing interdependence of professional and administrative functions needed to coordinate macro-level goals of the organization. Such coordination is optimized by keeping the primary advocates of patient care and macro-level objectives in close contact at equal levels of organizational power; the impact of one upon the other can be readily discerned and negotiated without one side imposing solutions on the other. As summarized by Scott (1982), this type of organization "provides overlapping roles and structures that allow administrators to co-opt professionals in the decision bodies stressing macro-level goals, and professionals to co-opt administrators in decision areas stressing micro-level goals." Thus, these organizations are pluralistic with multiple, loosely coupled centers of power. Certain centers represent the needs of administrators, others reflect the goals of physicians, and still others permit both groups to work together.

In addition, matrix structures exist in which both clinical and administrative staff members report simultaneously to clinical and administrative supervisors. Members thus simultaneously consider both types of organizational needs and objectives to provide a broad base of decision making for both operational sectors (Young and Saltman, 1983). The matrix structures likewise combine hierarchical control needed for some nonprofessional tasks with the participative management approach best suited for professional activities (Neuhauser, 1972).

III. CHANGES IN THE DETERMINANTS OF PHYSICIAN BEHAVIOR

Dramatic changes in health care finance and delivery systems have occurred during the past decade. Inevitably, these changes have affected and will continue to affect all factors that motivate physician practices.

A. The Physician-Patient Relationship

The tightness of the physician-patient relation has been eroded by changes in patient characteristics, in the practice of medicine, and in delivery systems. Several factors have led to a more active patient role in health care and to greater questioning of physician authority (Freidson, 1989): greater public sophistication in science and matters of health, increased consumerism and consumer advocacy in health, and the lessening of social status gap between physicians and patients. The result is less tolerance for the paternalism of classical physician-patient relations. Evidence includes widespread publication of self-help material, mandates for patient-rights information, and compelling arguments to the public for involvement in clinical decision making (Cousins, 1979; Reiser, 1992).

Changes in the practice of medicine have likewise affected the relationship. Greater reliance on technology has reduced the personal role of the patient's physician. Dependence on technology may also reduce the physician, in the eyes of the patient, to the level of a technician who relies on machines rather than personal skill and knowledge. This attitude has been described by Siegler (1993) as "airplane medicine" —just as any competent pilot can get an airplane from one city to another, any competent physician can manage a patient. Physicians, like pilots, become interchangeable. Technology has also introduced an unattainable expectation of physician perfection, a condition termed plupractice by Sheldon (1986). Thus, any error, including common, unavoidable bad outcomes, is viewed as failure by the physician and of medicine. The ability to quantify practice patterns and outcomes and the public reporting of results of specific physicians likewise makes the physician-patient relationship less personal and more statistical (Relman, 1988).

Changes in health systems have also markedly affected physician-patient relationships. Employer supplied insurance may limit patient choice. Managed care structures, in particular, act to determine patient flow and guide clinical practice so that the traditional bilateral physician-patient relation has become a trilateral physician-patient-health care organization relationship (Sheldon, 1986). Previously, third-parties were operative, their role limited to financing health care; now, the third-parties rather than the physician often attract patients to a practice and guide practice patterns. As a result, the patient-health care organization axis may be stronger than the patient-physician axis.

General dissatisfaction with the health care system also detracts from the physician-patient relation. Physicians may be viewed as businessmen acting primarily for their own financial self interest and treated with the same skepticism as are "used car salesmen" (Blendon, 1991). Isolated episodes of physician abuse and fraud reported in the media are commonly generalized to represent all physicians.

Finally, the judicial system has affected the relationship through the threat of malpractice suits. Another more direct intervention is the legal restriction of counseling patients in certain settings concerning specific family planning methods (Annas, 1991). The effect of these factors is a dramatic change in the most basic determinate of physician behavior, the physician-patient relationship.

B. Physician Autonomy and Dominance

The dual management structure has been tolerated, even fostered, in most settings. The costs of dealing with autonomy and dominance were less than the resulting organizational inefficiency. However, several recent changes in the societal role of physicians and in the health care environment make continuation of this dual model more problematic.

1. Changes in Society

The enhanced consumer role has led to a deprofessionalization of physicians. As patients acquire more information, they not only begin to act for themselves, but they also become skeptical about others' claims to specific knowledge. Haug (1976, 1988) and others have emphasized the effects of increased public literacy and access to medical information; the profession's monopoly over knowledge has been fractured. These changes reduce public deference and trust in the profession as well as authority. Indeed, consumerism and professional dominance are intrinsically inconsistent with each other; the former stresses the rights of patients whereas the latter optimizes the prerogatives of the provider.

Second, the public has begun to constrain the autonomy of physicians when their specialized areas of expertise do not automatically lead to authority. While medical science provides a unique basis of physician dominance in scientific areas of pathophysiology and therapy, it does not necessarily do so in moral or evaluative concerns of social policy (Freidson, 1970; Mirvis, 1993), such as systems of health care delivery. In these subjects, society has an important role in determining policy. Thus, the expansion of public interest into health care financing and prioritization of delivery services represents attempts by society to constrain physician autonomy.

2. Changes in Medical Practice

Specialization of medical practice may also significantly reduce autonomy while attempting to increase the skills of physicians and the quality of care delivered to patients (Light and Levine, 1988; McKinlay and Stoeckle, 1988). Specialization makes individual physicians more dependent on other physicians, limiting the power of the individual physician. Thus, a patient has several physicians rather than one, reducing the intensity of the physician-patient relationship. Similarly, specialization requires sophisticated supporting technical and management systems, diffusing the power of the medical profession as a whole. Specialization breaks the knowledge base of the physician into smaller manageable segments, some of which may be mastered by non-physicians, for example, initial patient assessments and follow-up by nurses, physician assistants, etc. Clinical decisions are no longer the exclusive province of the physician. Specialization also fragments the cohesiveness of the profession; specialists show greater allegiance to their particular field than to the profession as a whole (McKinlay and Stoeckle, 1988). This leads to increases in intraprofessional conflict as well as a decrease in the ability of the profession to present a unified position to the public on important matters. Common axes of diversity include generalists vs. specialists, hospital-based vs. community-based practitioners, and private practice vs. employed physicians.

3. Public Attitudes Toward the Profession

Public concern over the performance and the attitudes of the profession has also increased. Issues over quality of health care, including the prevalence of unnecessary deaths (Dubois and Brook, 1988), have shaken the public's confidence in the scientific bases of medicine. Similarly, public concerns over the altruistic nature of the profession with such issues as self-referral (Iglehart, 1990), involvement with commercial for-profit enterprises (Relman, 1991), the high prevalence of unnecessary procedures (Winslow et al., 1988) with a possible pecuniary basis, and rapidly rising health care costs have lead to doubts. Blendon (1991), for example, reported that whereas in 1960, 73% of Americans had a high level of confidence in medical leaders, in 1989 only 30% did so. More recently, in the debate over national health care reform, physicians were viewed as battling to preserve their self interests. Iglehart (1994) noted, "[S]ome in ranks of organized medicine...are more inclined to rely on the [AMAs] formidable lobby to press the pocketbook issues than to enter the struggle over universal coverage."

The ability and practice of the profession to self-regulate and self-discipline itself are also being questioned by the public. Many of the concerns about quality and ethics have not, in the view of the public, been adequately dealt with by the profession itself. For example, the profession tends to address truly deviant errors and to accept routine errors (Sheldon, 1986). This discrepency apparently violates the implied commitment of the profession as a whole to self-regulate in return for being granted autonomy.

The result is that "if the physician is not trusted to know what is best, nor to always choose ethically even when he or she does know, then the social and economic system will step in with alternatives that constrain the physician's ability to define quality of care" (O'Connor and Lanning, 1992); thus, the autonomy granted by the public is reduced or withdrawn (Wolinsky, 1988). Examples include legislated regulations on housestaff work hours and supervision (Asch and Perker, 1988) and mandated systems for tracking professionally impaired physicians (Oshel et al., 1994).

4. Changes in the Health Care Environment

Additional factors affecting autonomy and dominance include changes in the general health care environment. First, changes in payment systems affect hospitals and physicians differently. Under prior retroactive, cost-based payment schemes, the hospital was shielded from or benefitted from the financial impact of the costs of clinical decisions. However, prospective payment systems have placed the hospital at financial risk from physicians' decisions. Because physicians are cost centers, hospital management must pay more attention to medical staff activities.

Second, the rise of corporate health care providers has changed the nature of the physician-patient relationship. These corporate structures directly contract with patients (or their employers) to provide care; hence, the fundamental relation is shifted from the physician-patient axis to the organization-patient axis (Sheldon, 1986).

Third, the increase in the number of physicians allows hospitals to be more selective in granting staff privileges and more involved in medical affairs. Individual practitioners have lost their irreplaceable status as the number of physicians and specialists has risen.

Fourth, expanded corporate involvement in health care has introduced more direct hierarchical management systems to maximize efficiency and profits. This leads to the bureaucratization of medicine.

Last, methods to quantify key aspects of medical care and of physician performance have evolved. These include such productivity measures as number of patients seen and the resulting costs (Relman, 1988), as well as the emphasis on outcomes of therapy (Elwood, 1988), development of patient treatment protocols, etc. While these tools are intended to improve patient care, they may also place physicians under the same scrutiny as nonprofessional workers.

All of these factors have reduced physician autonomy and dominance both in society as well as within the organizations. As professional autonomy falls, health care organizations increase their ability to control the work of the profession.

IV. RESULTING MODELS OF PHYSICIAN BEHAVIOR IN ORGANIZATIONS

These changes in the determinants of physician behavior have changed the way physicians function in society within organizations. Selected models will be considered in this section.

A. Bureaucratization

The corporatization or bureaucratization model considers the effects of corporate and bureaucratic structures on physician behavior (McKinlay and Arches, 1985). The move to bureaucratization is manifest by the increasing number of physicians who are employees rather than individual practitioners, the growing essentiality of complex medical centers to provide care, and the entrance and growing dominance of corporate entities into the health care market. The hospital, rather than being the physician's "workshop," becomes the physician's "workmaster."

Such changes may be needed to provide health care to large numbers of people efficiently or to gain a needed measure of social control over employees so that corporate goals can be met (McKinlay and Arches, 1985). The measures of control vary. At a minimum, the organization sets for itself overall goals and creates the organizational structure for accomplishing its work. A second level involves control over the work of employees by establishing an organizational hierarchy and operational procedures. Finally, the activities of clients themselves become regulated.

Bureaucratization has several consequences. First, bureaucratic medical settings have multiple interests, including budget balancing, profit making, and delivery of patient care. Physicians in such situations may be pressured to sacrifice interests of individual patients for those of the organization. They may withhold necessary treatments because of financial constraints imposed by organizations or for personal gain (Kassirer, 1995). Thus, macro-level issues may take precedence over micro-level needs of individual patients (Scott, 1982). This not only interferes with the traditionally straightforward physician-patient relationship, but also dilutes the personal responsibility of the physician who may blame the organization for failures in care delivery (Mechanic, 1977).

B. Proletarianization

Proletarianization reduces the status of physicians to that of worker rather than leader. This model is based on the Marxist concept that in a capitalist system all workers eventually become either the agents of capital (the bourgeoisie) or those who perform the productive labor and who are exploited for the purposes of profit and expanding capital (the proletariat). Medicine is viewed as no different than any other production industry, responding primarily to the same profit motives as any capitalist industry. McKinlay and Arches (1985) define proletarianization as "the process by which an occupational category is divested of control over certain prerogatives relating to the location, content and essentiality of its task activities and is thereby subordinated to the broader requirements of production under advanced capitalism." Physicians are no longer the primary force in health care; they are a secondary source of power subordinate to the primary force of capitalism. Thus, proletarianization corresponds to corporatization with a political overlay (Mechanic, 1991).

In contrast to the deprofessionalization model, this construct focuses on the relation of physicians to supervisors and employers. Physicians are just one component of the medical industry that operates under capitalistic controls, not the dominant group in the traditional view (McKinlay, 1977). For example, the importance of physicians to hospitals as referrers of patients is diminished as hospitals directly negotiate with payers for group hospitalization contracts. Physicians are free to act in such environments only as long as their actions benefit the organization.

McKinlay and Arches (1985) suggest that proletarianization is the result of bureaucratization. Bureaucratic activities force physicians to yield control over their own work. They become subject to the same procedural dependency and work measurement and control techniques as are other "nonprofessional" employees.

C. Combined Models

Physician behavior probably does not correspond to any one of these conceptual models but rather to a blend of all (Freidson, 1985). Indeed, aspects of all coexist in a state of internal tension and conflict. This tension is captured in the model of countervailing forces discussed by Light (1991). This concept represents a dynamic interaction between forces and "points to a historic dynamic that begins with one party accumulating such power that it prompts other parties to muster forces and attempt to control the first." Thus, such forces as deprofessionalization are responses to the amassing of autonomy by the medical profession.

Clearly the self-governing ability of physicians has decreased in recent years. Physician behavior has come under increasingly intense scrutiny and regulation by agencies ranging from Congress to the courts to individual hospital boards of directors and consumer groups. As the public questions the abilities and motives of the medical profession, autonomy and dominance will be reduced.

However, despite growing concerns about health care and the practices of physicians, little has been done to formally reduce legal dominance of the physician (Freidson, 1985). More clinical privileges have been granted to nonphysician fields, such as clinical pharmacy, psychology and optometry, but the fields of practice of these groups have remained highly constrained. Thus, even if the medical profession cannot fully block emergence of other dominant fields, it has been able to restrain their purview. Efforts to enforce greater control over physician practices have focused on greater self-regulation, greater control of physicians by other physicians. Examples include peer review of hospital admissions and of personal impairment.

The public also has developed considerably greater involvement in health care. Thus, consumerism is a major motivation for increased regulatory oversight of the medical profession. However, the public's knowledge remains limited as the scope of medical information and technology grows at a rapid rate. Nonprofessionals remain heavily dependent on the specialized knowledge of the physician professional. Further, despite increased knowledge, legal statutes still require physician approval for access to even basic health care resources.

Elements of proletarianization also exist. Physicians in highly structured organizations do have reduced control over their work; production guidelines and work quotas are similar to those of other nonprofessional workers. However, it is unlikely that true proletarianization will occur. As described by Navarro (1988), true proletariats have no control over their work, do not supervise others, do not make decisions and have no skills that require credentialling. Physicians, however, are needed by hospitals and health care organizations. The Joint Commission on Accreditation of Healthcare Organizations explicitly requires involvement of the medical staff in hospital governance.

The effect is internal tension between all models. Physicians strive to maintain their autonomy while the public seeks greater involvement in health care and the corporate sector attempts to control physician behavior.

D. Effects on Physicians

Changes in the forces acting on physician practices have induced changes in the profession. On one hand, physicians have become disillusioned with the practice of medicine. One survey reports that only 23% of physicians in the United States thought the health system worked well (Blendon, 1993). In a survey of New England internists, 76% reported that "physicians' prerogatives are being so restricted that it will become increasingly difficult to practice good medicine," 36% indicated an interest in early retirement, 41% reported a negative sense of the public's respect for physicians, and 24% were negative about the general, global future of medicine (Hershey et al., 1989). These feelings are significant contributors to, until recently, a fall in interest in medicine as a career (Stimmel, 1990) particularly in primary patient care fields (Colwill, 1992).

On the other hand, many professional groups are calling upon physicians to meet the challenges of health system change. Cluff (1991), for example, called for physicians to recognize "the social context and societal consequences of the care they provide," noting that "too many physicians, it seems, are fiddling their familiar tune while the edifices of medicine are set ablaze by outsiders." Actions have included increased stringency in peer review and greater accountability for costs as well as development of specific agendas for participation in system reform (Berwick, 1994).

SUMMARY

This review has considered the major factors affecting physician behavior and the conflicts that these patterns produce within organizations. None of these motivations can be considered right or wrong; all are deeply ingrained in the physician persona. Some are laudatory; others are not. All represent challenges and must be managed to result in productive, nondestructive interaction for the good of all parties.

REFERENCES

Annas, G. J. (1991). Restricting doctor-patient conversations in federally funded clinics. *New England Journal of Medicine, 325*: 362-364.

Asch, D. A., and Perker, R. M. (1988). The Libby Zion case. One step forward and two steps backward? *New England Journal of Medicine, 318*: 771-775.

Begun, J. W. (1985). Managing with professionals in a changing health care environment. *Medical Care Review, 42*: 3-10.

Berwick, D. M. (1994). Eleven worthy aims for clinical leadership of health system reform. *JAMA, 272*: 797-802.

Blendon, R. J. (1991). The public view of medicine. *Clinical Neurosurgery 37*: 225-231.

Blendon, R. J. (1993). Physicians' perspectives on caring for patients in the United States, Canada, and West Germany. *New England Journal of Medicine, 328*: 1011-1016.

Brock, D. W., and Wartman, S. A. (1990). When competent patients, make irrational choices. *New England Journal of Medicine, 322*: 1595-1599.

Bucher, R., and Stelling, J. (1969). Characteristics of professional organizations. *Journal of Health Soc. Behavior, 28*: 3-15.

Christensen, S. (1989). *Volume Responses to Exogenous Changes in Medicare's Payment Policies.* US Congressional Budget Office, Washington, DC.

Cluff, L. E. (1991). Physicians, patients, and society. *Annals of Internal Medicine, 114*: 805-806.

Colwill, J. M. (1992). Where have all the primary care applicants gone? *New England Journal of Medicine, 326*: 387-393.

Council on Ethical and Judicial Affairs, American Medical Association (1995). Ethical issues in managed care. *JAMA, 273*: 330-335.

Cousins, N. (1979). *Anatomy of an Illness as Perceived by the Patient*. Norton, New York.

Dubois, R. W., and Brook, R.H. (1988). Preventable deaths: who, how often and why? *Annals of Internal Medicine, 109*: 582-589.

Duran-Arenas, L., and Kennedy, M. (1991). The constitution of physician's power: A theoretical framework for comparative analysis. *Social Science Medicine, 32*: 643-648.

Eddy, D. M. (1982). Clinical policies and the quality of a clinical practice. *New England Journal of Medicine, 307*: 343-347.

Elwood, P. M. (1988). Outcomes management. A technology of patient experience. *New England Journal of Medicine, 318*: 1549-1556.

Eisenberg, J. M. (1979). Sociological influences on decision making by clinicians. *Annals of Internal Medicine, 90*: 957-964.

Eisenberg, J. M. (1986). *Doctor's Decisions and the Cost of Medical Care*. Health Administration Press, Ann Arbor, MI.

Emanuel, E. J., and Dubler, N. N. (1995) Preserving the physician-patient relationship in the era of managed care. *JAMA, 273*: 323-329.

Emanuel, E. J., and Emanuel, L. L. (1992) Four models of the physician-patient relationship. *JAMA, 267*: 2221-2226.

Freidson, E. (1970). *Profession of Medicine: A Study in the Sociology of Applied Knowledge*. Dodd, Mead, New York.

Freidson, E. (1985) The reorganization of the medical profession. *Medical Care Review, 42*: 11-35.

Freidson, E. (1989). *Medical Work in America*. Yale University Press, New Haven.

Fried, C. (1975). Rights and health care - beyond equity and efficiency. *New England Journal of Medicine, 291*: 241-245.

Gabbard, G. O., and Nadelson, C. (1995). Professional boundaries in the physician-patient relationship. *JAMA, 273*: 1445-1449.

Globerman, J. (1990). Free enterprise, professional ideology, and self-interest: An analysis of resistance by Canadian physicians to universal health insurance. *Journal of Health Social Behavior, 31*: 11-27.

Goss, M. E. W., Battistella, R. M., Colombotos, J., Freidson, E., and Riedel, D. C. (1977). Social organization and control in medical work: a call for research. *Medical Care, 15*: 1-10.

Greenfield, S., Nelson, E.C., Zubcoff, M., Manning, W., Rogers, W., Kravitz, R. L., Keller, A., Tarlov, A. R., and Ware, J. E. (1992). Variations in resource utilization among medical specialists and system of care. *JAMA, 267*: 1624-1630.

Greer, A. L. (1984). Medical technology and professional dominance theory. *Social Science Medicine, 18*: 809-817.

Grumbach, K., and Bodenheimer, T. (1990). Reins or fences: A physician's view of cost containment. *Health Affairs, 9*: 120-126.

Harries-Jenkins, G. (1970). Professionals in Organizations. In *Professions and Professionalization*. (J.A. Jackson, ed.), Cambridge University Press, Cambridge.

Harris, J. (1977) The internal organization of hospitals: Some economic implications. *Bell Journal of Economics, 8*: 467-482.

Haug, M. R. (1976). The erosion of professional authority: A cross-cultural inquiry in the case of the physician. *Milbank Memorial Fund Quarterly, 54*: 83-106.

Haug, M. R. (1988). A re-examination of the hypothesis of physician deprofessionalization. *Milbank Memorial Fund Quarterly, 66 (Supplement 2)*: 48-56.

Hershey, C. O., McAloon, M. H., and Bertram, D. A. (1989). The new medical practice environment. Internists' view of the future. *Archives of Internal Medicine, 149*: 1745-1749.

Hillman, A. L., Pauly, M. V., and Kerstein, J. J. (1989). How do financial incentives affect physicians' clinical decisions and the financial performance of health maintenance organizations. *New England Journal of Medicine, 321*: 86-92.

Iglehart, J. K. (1990). Congress moves to regulate self-referral and physicians' ownership of clinical laboratories. *New England Journal of Medicine, 322:* 1682-1687.

Iglehart, J. K. (1994). Health care reform. The role of physicians. *New England Journal of Medicine, 320:* 728-731.

Jacobs, P. (1974). A survey of economic models of hospitals. *Inquiry, 11:* 83-97.

Kassirer, J. P. (1995). Managed care and the morality of the marketplace. *New England Journal of Medicine, 333:* 50-52.

Lammert, M. H. (1978). Power, authority and status in health systems: a Marxian-based conflict analysis. *Journal of Applied Behavioral Science, 14:* 321-333.

Levinsky, N. G.(1984) The doctor's master. *New England Journal of Medicine, 311:* 1573-1575.

Light, D. (1991). Professionalism as a countervailing power. *Journal of Health Polit. Policy Law, 16:* 499- 518.

Light, D., and Levine, S. (1988). The changing character of the medical profession: A theoretical overview. *Milbank Memorial Fund Quarterly, 66 (Supplement 2):* 10-38.

McKinlay, J. B. (1977). The business of good doctoring or doctoring as good business: Reflections on Freidson's view of the medical game. *International Journal of Health Services, 7:* 459-483.

McKinlay, J.B., Arches. J. (1985). Towards the proletarianization of physicians. *International Journal of Health Services, 15(2):* 161-195.

McKinlay, J. B., and Stoeckle, J. D. (1988). Corporatization and the social transformation of doctoring. *International Journal of Health Services, 18:* 191-205.

Mechanic, D. (1977). The growth of medical technology and bureaucracy: Implications for medical care. *Milbank Memorial Fund Quarterly, 55:* 61-78.

Mechanic, D. (1991). Sources of countervailing power in medicine. *Journal of Health Polit. Pol. Law, 16:* 485-498.

Mintzberg, H. (1983). *Power In and Around Organizations.* Prentice-Hall, Englewood Cliffs.

Mirvis, D. M. (1993). Professional autonomy - the relation between public and professional expectations. *New Engl. J. Med., 328:* 1346-1349.

Navarro, V. (1988). Professional dominance or proletarianism? Neither. *Milbank Mem. Fund Quarterly, 66 (Supplement 2):* 57-75.

Neuhauser, D. (1972). The hospital as a matrix organization. *Hospital Administration, 17:* 8-25.

Novack, D. H., Detering, B. J., Arnold, R., Forrow, L., Ladinsky, M., and Pezzullo, J. C. (1985). Physicians' attitudes toward using deception to resolve difficult ethical problems. *JAMA, 261:* 2980-2985.

O'Connor, S. J., and Lanning, J. A. (1992). The end of autonomy? Reflections of the postprofessional physician. *Health Care Management Review, 17(1):* 63-72.

Oshel, R. E., Croft, T., and Rodak, J.: The National Practitioner Data Bank: the first 4 years. *Public Health Review, 110:* 383-394.

Paris, J. J., Crone, R. K., and Reardon, F. (1990). Physicians' refusal of requested treatment. *New England Journal of Medicine, 322:* 1012-1015.

Pauly, M. V. (1980). *Doctors and Their Workshops: Economic Models of Physician Behavior.* University of Chicago Press.

Pauly, M. V., and Redisch, M. (1973). The not-for-profit hospital as a physician cooperative. *American Economic Review 63:* 87-99.

Pilote, L., Granger, C., Armstrong, P. W., Mark, D. B., and Hlatky, M. A. (1995). Differences in the treatment of myocardial infarction between the United States and Canada. *Medical Care, 33:* 598-610.

Raelin, J. A. (1991). *The Clash of Cultures. Managers Managing Professionals.* Harvard Business School Press, Boston.

Reed, R. R., and Evans, D. (1987). The deprofessionalization of medicine. Causes, effects and responses. *JAMA, 258:* 3279-3282.

Reiser, S. J. (1992). Consumer competence and the reform of American health care. *JAMA, 267*: 1511-1515.

Relman, A. S. (1988) Assessment and accountability. The third revolution in medical care. *New England Journal of Medicine, 319*: 1220-1222.

Relman, A. S. (1991). The health care industry: where is it taking us? *New England Journal of Medicine, 325*: 854-859.

Relman, A. S. (1992). "Self referral": What's at stake? *New England Journal of Medicine, 327*: 1522-1524.

Rossiter, L. F., and Wilensky, G. R. (1983). A reexamination of the use of physician services: the role of physician-initiated demand. *Inquiry, 20*: 162-172.

Scott, W. R. (1965). Reactions to supervision in a heteronomous professional organization. *Administrative Science Quarterly, 10*: 65-81.

Scott, W. R. (1982). Managing professional work: three models for control of health organizations. *Health Services Res., 17*: 213-240.

Sheldon, A. (1986). *Managing Doctors.* Dow Jones-Irwin, Homewood, IL.

Siegler, M. (1993). Falling of the pedestal: What is happening to the traditional doctor-patient relationship? *Mayo Clinic Proc., 68*: 461-467.

Special Task Force on Professional Liability and Insurance (1984). *Professional Liability in the '80s.* American Medical Association, Chicago.

Starr, P. (1982) *The Social Transformation of American Medicine.* New York: Basic Books.

Stimmel, B. (1990). The study and practice of medicine in the twenty-first century: ask not for whom the bell tolls. *Mount Sinai Journal of Medicine, 57*:11-24.

Weiner, S. L., Maxwell, J. H., Sapolsky, H. M., Dunn, D. L., and Hsiao, W. C. (1987). Economic incentives and organizational realities: Managing hospitals under DRGs. *Milbank Memorial Fund Quarterly, 54*: 463-487.

Weisbord, M. (1976). Why organization development hasn't worked (so far) in medical centers. *Health Care Management Review, 1*: 17-28.

Wennberg, J. E. (1984). Dealing with medical practice variations: a proposal for action. *Health Affairs, 3*: 6-31.

Wertman, B. G., Sostrin, S. V., Pavlova, Z., and Lundberg, G. D. (1980). Why do physicians order laboratory tests? A study of laboratory test request and use patterns. *JAMA, 243*: 2020-2082.

Wilson, J. Q. (1989). *Bureaucracy.* Basic Books, New York.

Winslow, C. M., Kosecoff, J. B., Chassin, M., Kanovse, D. E., and Brook, R. H. (1988). The appropriateness of performing coronary artery bypass surgery. *JAMA, 260*: 505-509.

Wolinsky, F. D. (1988). The professional dominance perspective revisited. *Milbank Memorial Fund Quarterly, 66 (Supplement 2)*: 33-47.

Yishai, Y. (1992). Physicians and the state in the USA and Israel. *Social Science Med., 34*: 129-139.

Young, D. W., and Saltman, R. B. (1983). Prospective reimbursement and hospital power equilibrium: A matrix-based management control structure. *Inquiry, 20*: 20-33.

Young, D. W., Saltman, R. B. (1985). *The Hospital Power Equilibrium.* Johns Hopkins University Press, Baltimore.

28.
GENDER ISSUES IN HEALTH CARE

Meredith A. Newman, *Washington State University, Vancouver, WA*

Mary E. Guy, *Florida State University, Talahassee, FL*

Gender is the silent partner in health care, affecting treatment, service delivery, and utilization. While women always outnumber men — there are 95.4 men for every 100 women in the United States — women disproportionately deliver and use health services (Friedman, 1994; Heim, 1995; Roberts and Group, 1995; U.S. Department of Commerce, 1993, 1995; West, Holoviak, and Figler, 1995.)

Women comprise
- 60% of all office visits to physicians
- 60% of Medicare enrollees
- 75% of Medicaid recipients (including children under the age of 6)
- 77% of all hospital employees
- 79% of health workers employed outside of hospitals
- 97% of RNs

On the other hand, men disproportionately direct, govern, and make the most money from health services.

Men comprise
- 81% of all physicians
- 96% of hospital administrators

Directed by men and done by women, health service delivery is filled with gendered assumptions. This chapter shines a light on these assumptions, showing how they sculpt and influence America's health care system. The issues revolve around the following questions:

> Who administers health care services?
> Who delivers services?
> Who uses services?
> Who benefits?

The examination concludes with a discussion of how health care roles are proscribed by gender. Health administrators are advised to be cognizant of the role that gender plays in utilization, job classification and compensation schemes, promotion opportunities, decision making, service delivery, and consumer spending.

Physicians and health services administrators, most of whom are men, have controlled policy debates while nurses and "ancillary" health professionals, most of whom are women, have been encouraged to sit on the sidelines as spectators. Women are expected to be helpmates rather than drivers; they are to play the supportive role while the limelight shines on others. This confluence of gender, power, and leadership is considered normal in the U.S. health care system.

Gender power among health professionals is an exaggeration of power relations embedded in the culture at large. Women are to be heard through the voices of physicians and health administrators, rather than through their own voices as consumers, nurses and "ancillary" care givers. The chains of influence that drive health policy converge in a tightly woven knot — a knot that harbors a number of threads and loops all entangled: gender, medical tradition, health delivery systems, and economic power.

I. WHO ADMINISTERS HEALTH CARE SERVICES?

The chief executive in a health care organization will have one of several titles: administrator, director, Chief Executive Officer (CEO), president, or superintendent. Whatever the title, it is likely to be held by a man (Heim, 1995). Boards of trustees, most of whom are men, select and delegate authority to the CEO. The CEO may also be a voting member of the board and the chair. This crossover between CEOs and hospital boards serves as a powerful barrier to outsiders and newcomers.

Moreover, the size of salaries being paid to senior executives of HMOs predicts that the positions are held by men. Cash and stock awards to the CEOs of the seven biggest for-profit HMOs averaged $7 million in 1994 (Freudenheim, 1995). The more fundamental perception that men are rightful leaders, not women, perpetuates the status quo.

The future for women in the executive suite is not optimistic. Consolidation brought about by managed care may propel more chief medical officers into the role of CEO. Thus women may find it even harder to advance from a position which already finds them two steps back and to the left when it comes to leadership positions.

II. WHO DELIVERS SERVICES?

The interrelation between gender and health service delivery is well established. Gender differences exist both between and within occupations, such that there are women's jobs and roles and men's jobs and roles. Health occupations are characterized by gender stratification and sex discrimination. Take nursing, for example. Men rise to the top more than women, even when they are the minority in the profession (Walby and Greenwell, 1994). Within nursing, men on average earn more money than their female counterparts; they are concentrated in the most prestigious specialties; and they are overrepresented in administrative positions (Williams, 1995).

Nurses (mostly women) struggle to achieve equality and to be acknowledged and heard, but they work in settings where physicians (mostly men) dominate. In fact, more than three-quarters of all health care workers are female, including 97 percent of nurses and the majority of home health aides, nurse's aides, medical librarians, and laboratory technicians (Friedman, 1994).

The perpetuation of gendered roles is aided by both women and men. Despite the fact that in 1992-93, women earned more than four out of five degrees awarded (83% of the associate through doctoral degrees in nursing, physical therapy, pre-medicine studies, and health administration), almost all writings of nurses refer to physicians as male; pictures in nursing journals invariably depict male physicians; and until recently, even research does not usually distinguish between male and female physicians (Roberts and Group, 1995). The glorification of physicians characterizes the masculine.

A. Women in Medicine

Opportunities for women in medicine have improved since 1848, when Elizabeth Blackwell became the first American woman to receive a medical degree. Women now represent a significant part of the medical work force, making up 18 percent of all physicians and nearly 42 percent of all enrolling medical students (Friedman, 1994). Nevertheless, only 3 percent of medical school deans and 5 percent of department heads are women. At Harvard Medical School, the 1994 class was 52 percent female; yet only 7 percent of the tenured professors were women (Angier, 1995).

Table 1 - Physicians by Gender, United States, 1970-1994

	1970	1980	1990	1994
Men	92%	88%	83%	81%
Women	8%	12%	17%	19%

Data Source: Physician Characteristics and Distribution in the U.S., 1995/96 ed.

As can be seen from Table 1, the number of women physicians in the United States has more than quadrupled in the past 25 years. In 1970, there were slightly more than 25,000 female physicians in the U.S. By 1980, that number had more than doubled to 54,284. Between 1980 and 1990, the number of physicians grew by 31.6 percent, while the number of women physicians increased nearly 92 percent.

This increase resulted from the growing number of women who had been admitted to medical schools following passage of the Civil Rights Act of 1964 and subsequent implementation of equal employment opportunity policies. In the 1969-70 class, 9.2 percent of those enrolled were female. By 1979-80, that number had risen to 28.3 percent and by 1989-90, to 39.2 percent.

Table 2 - Specialties with Highest Numbers of Women M.D.s, 1994

	Women	Men	Median Income-1992
Pediatrics	43%	57%	$112,000
Obstetrics/Gynecology	27%	73%	$190,000
Pathology	26%	74%	$170,000
Psychiatry	26%	74%	$120,000
Internal medicine	23%	77%	$130,000
General or Family Practice	19%	81%	$100,000
Anesthesiology	19%	81%	$220,000

Data Source: Physician Characteristics and Distribution in the U.S., 1995/6 ed.; Dorgan, 1995.

If there is a trend afoot, however, it has a distinct limp. Despite the increase in overall representation of women in medicine, these women are concentrated within a limited number of specialties. As shown in Table 2, almost 60 percent of all women physicians in 1992 were in one of seven specialties: pediatrics, obstetrics/gynecology, pathology, psychiatry, internal medicine, general or family practice, and anesthesiology. Moreover, while the number of women physicians has increased in each of these specialties, the rank order has remained the same since 1980. Prior to 1980, pediatrics was the specialty choice of women, followed by internal medicine; otherwise, the ranking was the same (Friedman, 1994).

Women are about three times as likely as men to be pediatricians, making up 43 percent of the total specialty (almost 20 percent of all women physicians versus 5 percent of all men physicians); they are less than half as likely to be in general surgery or a surgical subspecialty. Emily Friedman (1994) suggests that the medical profession should work to increase gender diversity and eliminate specialty selection barriers that deter women from surgery and other subspecialties.

B. Women in Nursing

Just as it is impossible to examine women and health care without discussing nursing, so it is impossible to discuss nursing without considering its femaleness. The nursing profession's struggle to grow in stature and gain autonomy is linked to the relationship between gender and professional roles as these have changed over time. The terms "woman" and "profession" seem mutually exclusive to many — nurses are not professionals because they are women. According to Roberts and Group (1995), physicians have argued that nursing could never be a profession and should remain a form of supportive labor. "To sustain this myth, the distinct contributions of nurses have been attributed to medical skill," (p. 239).

Table 3 - Percentage of Women Among Full-Time Workers in Allied Health Professions

Health Occupations	% Women
Dental Assistants	99
Dietitians	90
Medical Records Librarians	93
Laboratory Techs	75
Radiological Technicians	75
Physical Therapists	73
Inhalation Therapists	58
Physician Assistants	32

Data Source: Friedman, 1994

Throughout its history, nursing has been "women's work." The stereotypical nurse is a self-sacrificing caretaker, nurturer, a "beloved imbecile" intellectually inferior to physicians and unable to make informed clinical judgments. Muff (as cited in Roberts and Group, 1995) categorizes nurse stereotypes into six areas including angels of mercy, filled with selfless devotion and affirming compassion but negating nurses' own interests; handmaidens to physicians, involving traditional "feminine" deference and submission to masculine authority to the exclusion of autonomy; and women in white, emphasizing purity and cleanliness in a simplistic, limiting, and impractical way. (The remaining three categories are battle-axes, sex symbols, and torturers.) Obviously these roles impede attainment of personal and organizational outcomes in health care organizations, especially when they block the effective use of power and women's leadership potential (Cummings, 1995). Such stereotypes are symbols that circumscribe the role of nurses and perpetuate powerlessness.

In addition to the continuing struggle to counteract these symbols, nursing leaders are pushing for professional autonomy and greater accountability and control, increased sophistication of nursing education and research efforts, and legislation for entry-into-practice and third-party reimbursement. Their challenge is to uncover the fallacious dichotomy between nursing care and medical treatment, and to debunk the myth of women's subordination to men as played out in physician-nurse relationships. Otherwise, the value of nursing will continue to be negated, and nurses' voices will be but a whisper in shaping health policy. Indeed, nurses are often invisible in policy debates. For example, in much of the literature on integrated delivery systems, references to nurses are conspicuous by their absence. The marginality of the nursing profession was further evidenced in a 1984 television series of twenty, ten-minute health sequences on health assessment, disease prevention, detection, and nutrition. Physicians, psychologists, dietitians, pharmacists, and safety council representatives were represented, but "nurses were neither involved as presenters nor pictured in the series. The word "nurse" was used only once" (Turnbull, as cited in Roberts and Group, 1995, p. 282). Thus the role of 1,600,000 nurses was ignored.

C. Women in Allied Health Professions

Women are overrepresented not only in nursing but also in non-nursing health care professions such as technicians and technologists, therapists, dietitians, physician assistants, and home health care workers. Allied health occupations comprise those fields in which staff assist, facilitate, or complement the work of physicians. This definition almost assures that it is "women's work." Not surprisingly, women make up a large proportion of the labor force in these fields.

Table 3 shows the number of full-time workers by gender in major allied health occupations in 1990. In three of the listed occupations (dietitians, medical record librarians, and dental assistants), 90 percent or more of full-time workers are female. Among the other allied health fields in Table 3, three-quarters of the physical therapists and radiological technicians and three-fifths of the inhalation therapists are female (Friedman, 1994).

Further evidence that gender issues have not been put to rest comes from dental service occupations. Dentistry has remained predominantly male, and dental hygienists and dental assistants are almost exclusively female. Ninety-nine percent of dental assistants and dental hygienists are female. These two dental-supportive occupations are the most classically sex-typed fields in allied health (Friedman, 1994).

Taken together, the current delivery of health services relies upon the maintenance of a strict dichotomy between physicians and non-physician professionals — between medical treatment and "ancillary" care. The system is founded (foundered) on gendered norms: physicians call the shots, nurses comply. Does the gendered nature of health care delivery spill over into utilization? It is to this that we now turn.

III. WHO USES SERVICES?

The Women's Research and Education Institute (1994) assessed women's utilization of health care services and found that women of childbearing age are more likely to use health care services than their male counterparts. Out-of-pocket expenditures are higher for women of childbearing age than for their male contemporaries and women spend a larger proportion of their income on out-of-pocket health expenditures than men. Reproductive services account for a large portion of women's health spending. Since many health insurance plans fail to adequately cover preventive and reproductive services, women of reproductive age spend a larger proportion of their income on health care than men.

Table 4 shows that women utilize health services more frequently than men. While almost 84% of all women see a physician within the span of a year, only 73% of all men see a physician within a year's time. Women are greater consumers of health services than are men.

Table 4 - Interval Since Last Physician Contact: 1991

	less than 1 yr	1 to 2 yrs	2 to 5 yrs	over 5 yrs
Women	83.7%	8.5%	5.7%	2.1%
Men	73.0%	11.4%	10.7%	4.9%

Data Source: Dorgan, 1995, p. 134.

Despite its advances and the fact that women consume health services more than men, American health care does not do a very good job with women's health. Extraordinarily little is understood about menstrual cycles and menopause. Cancers unique to women have yet to come close to being conquered. The prevalence of cancer in men is 1,930 per 100,000 adults while it is 4,412 cases in women per 100,000 adults (Byrne, Kessler, and Devesa, 1992). Breast cancer accounts for 32% of all cancers in women, and 18% of all cancer deaths in women.

Even though women make more visits to the physician and spend more money for medical services than men, medical research has focused more on men's health than on women's. One of the most egregious examples is that of a widely publicized study of heart disease that omitted women subjects. Done by Harvard Medical School and Brigham and Women's Hospital in the 1980s, the study concluded that moderate doses of aspirin may prevent cardiovascular disease. The whole story is that the sample included 22,071 men and not a single woman. The researchers justified their exclusion of women by saying that women's menstrual cycles alter the effect of medications in the body and, thus, the true effect of a drug is confounded by the inclusion of women.

Only if women's health is irrelevant can one justify the exclusion of women from medical studies such as the heart study. In 1990, the number of deaths from heart disease was 360,788 for men and 359,270 for women, a difference of 1,518 or two-tenths of one percent! (Dorgan, 1995, p. 59). Nevertheless, the results were immediately generalized to both women and men in spite of the fact that the chemistry of women's bodies differs from that of men's and the study had failed to test the therapeutic effect on women (Walker, 1996).

IV. WHO BENEFITS?

The gender power imbalance between physicians and other health professions has dollars and cents consequences. Prior to the emergence of integrated delivery systems and networks (which are complex, multi-faceted organizations that encompass medical group practices along with a hospital component and a managed care component), physicians had always been able to bill fee-for-service (Blair, Fottler, Paolino, and Rotarius, 1995). As Roberts and Group (1995) emphasize, the issue has been control of dollars. The AMA has insisted on physician supervision because while nurses stress humane, caring values, this leaves physicians free to reap the rewards by getting the first dollar (p. 329).

With the establishment of health maintenance organizations around the nation, revenue streams will be capitation-based and the health care environment will be payor-driven (Blair, et al., 1995). Capitation is the chief method that managed care plans use to control fees paid to physicians. The system pays the physician or physician group a flat rate per patient per month regardless of service utilization.

Nurses, on the other hand, are paid salaries by physicians and hospitals, regardless of the number of enrollees that are seen or the number of procedures performed. Nurses have been prohibited by state law from billing for services provided. Only in the case of Advanced Practice Nurses are there exceptions made. It is expected that the move towards integrated care networks will challenge this practice since most health care will be delivered through managed care. But managed care may not be such a bitter pill for physicians to swallow. According to Coile (1994), salary levels for primary care physicians will jump as networks compete to hire them out of residencies and private practice.

At the same time, the potential exists that integrated care networks will not only depress nurses' salaries but will result in nurse lay-offs if, for example, a network is closing a year over budget. And as hospitals respond to ever-tighter restrictions, skilled registered nurses are being replaced with cheaper less-skilled workers (Papazian, 1995). Of significance, too, is the fact that DRG payment schedules bring a reduction in the total number of registered nurses (RNs) on hospital staffs. To lower costs, nursing budgets are cut first, even though hospitals with a higher proportion of registered nurses have been shown to provide better quality care, measured by lower mortality rates. The consequences of excluding nurses while over relying on physicians extends beyond health economics to professional control of a business enterprise.

Moreover, under many managed care plans, physicians receive bonuses by limiting the number of patient referrals to specialists and the number of diagnostic tests or hospital stays. According to Caputo (as cited in Sullivan, 1995, p. 6), these bonuses are nothing more than "an outrageous system of camouflaged kickbacks in which physicians are paid not to provide health care." Because they are included in policy decisions, physicians gain more than they lose in health reform because they are guaranteed a seat at the table to protect their economic interest. In a zero-sum market, nurses are seen as economic threats to physicians and excluded from policy making.

An analogy between the work that women do in their homes and nurses' work is revealing. Smoyak (as cited in Roberts and Group, 1995) asks why such "house" work is not recognized as contributing to the Gross National Product. "The parallel to why nurses' work has not been billed separately in hospitals (i.e., why nurses' work is a part of the bed fee) is so striking that it needs no further explication" (p. 265). Economists see households as non-economic units, presumably because they are regulated by altruism and affection. This parallels the arguments for paying nurses low salaries. Nurses' costs must be separated from general hospital accounts in order to assess the value of women's work in nursing. [Salary expenses for nurses as a percentage of hospital expenses have declined since 1968 (Roberts and Group, 1995).]

The gender power imbalance is not confined to physicians and nurses, of course. Within medicine, women physicians are twice as likely as men physicians to be employees and less likely to be self-employed (Friedman, 1994). Female physicians continue to earn less than male physicians. Their lower income levels can be attributed largely to their overrepresentation in the lower paid primary care specialties, generally younger age and lower level of experience, and lower number of patient visits and work hours. When these factors are controlled for, the income gap shrinks; nevertheless, disparities remain, indicating some level of gender bias in professional pay (Friedman, 1994).

According to the AMA Council on Ethical and Judicial Affairs' 1993 report Gender Discrimination in the Medical Profession, "women in medicine are generally not advancing to the highest levels of the profession and are continuing to encounter subtle and overt forms of discrimination in their training and careers" (Friedman, 1994, pp. 130). Gender-based economic and professional discrimination, sexual harassment, and a wide range of more subtle acts of discouragement continue to impede the professional progress of many women physicians.

Beyond the fact that women's earnings are lower than men's, the root of the problem lies earlier. Throughout the century, women have had to excel in tasks that men had only to perform as average in order to be seen as a viable medical school student. As health became medicalized in the twentieth century, women were actively relegated to the role of helpmate and their admission into medical schools was resisted (Glazer and Slater, 1987). As medicine converted from a healing art to a "science" women were judged to be unsuited for "a dispassionate inquiry" and lacking in the innate capacity for objectivity that is called for as physicians ply their trade (Glazer and Slater, 1987).

Women's nineteenth century roles as midwives, healers, and doctors tied women to the natural world, argued those who were enthralled with the "science" of medicine. In the name of science, male practitioners proclaimed that women lacked the higher order intellect required for scientific investigation (Glazer and Slater, 1987). The "fragile female constitution" with its delicate sensibilities could not be exposed to the horrors of death and disease.

A. Sexual Harassment

With gender power pervading the health care workplace, sexual harassment is frequent. Women are the primary victims of sexual harassment. Since the health care workforce is predominantly women and since men are the power players, healthcare settings are prime sites for violations. Surveys indicate that two-thirds of nurses have experienced unwanted sexual attention to the extent that it led to discomfort or humiliation or interfered with their job (West, Holoviak, and Figler, 1995). These results indicate that the incidence and severity of sexual harassment may be more widespread in health care environments than has previously been thought.

Administrators are advised to stop harassment and discrimination from occurring, deal effectively with complaints when they occur, and to stay abreast of this area of the law as it evolves to ensure that institutional policies and procedures are timely. Most nurses report that they have experienced sexual harassment. Victims of sexual harassment are filing claims in increasing numbers and receiving judgements in their favor. In 1992, 1340 cases filed with the EEOC were settled with $12.7 million in awards. In 1993, 1500 settlements yielded $25.2 million in awards (West, Holoviak, and Figler, 1995).

Both categories of sexual harassment, quid pro quo and hostile environment, result in morale problems that produce lower productivity, higher error rates, and increased operating costs. It is incumbent on administrators to have a clear, unambiguous policy prohibiting sexual harassment, an effective training program, and an effective means for addressing complaints. Additionally, employers have been held responsible for the harassing behaviors of vendors, contractors, and/or customers when the employer failed to take possible corrective actions (West, Holoviak, and Figler, 1995).

B. Which Professions Rule?

Professional hegemony and gender hegemony converge in health care, for it is an industry governed by men but delivered by women. The traditional male power structures in the health-care industry are well entrenched. As dominant groups, physicians and hospital administrators control resources and access to them — money, media attention, and public opinion. Witness the differences between press coverage of medical and nursing news and of the unequal allocation of federal funds for medical and nursing research. Dominant groups not only define themselves, but situations and other groups as well.

Subjugated groups (such as nurses) may accept or reject such definitions. However, as Greenleaf (cited in Roberts and Group, 1995) states, "when medicine is defined as encompassing all health care, any challenge to nursing to define its own uniqueness is a futile effort" (p. 296). Medicine, then, determines where the boundary is between medicine and nursing, and sets limits to the skill and influence of nursing so as to ensure its own dominance (Walby and Greenwell, 1994).

This model of domination/subjugation is the most persistent loop in the tangle of health care; it supports and even legitimizes the gendered norms of the health care establishment. While females comprise the vast majority of health care workers, they are employed in relatively low paying occupations. For example, 97% of nurses are women, and despite investing one-third to one-half the time in education as does a physician, nurses receive only one-fifth of physicians' average earnings. It is significant that the gap between nurse and physician salaries is widening: in 1945 nurses' salaries were one-third of physician incomes (Roberts and Group, 1995).

The old model of conforming to the establishment and the new order of confrontation and negotiation clash on the hospital floor. In the past nurses were trained to accept a subordinate role at work and do as the physician ordered. Now nurses are trained to perform as professionals, making informed decisions. As newly trained nurses join the workforce, the complexion of cooperation between the professions will change, challenging the administrator's skill at teambuilding.

Moreover, health care pricing mechanisms are built around physicians, even though a patient will have more contact time with a nurse than with a physician (Hafner-Eaton, 1993), and will be more dependent on a nurse than on a physician for the provision of services. Most reimbursement schedules are predicated on whether the physician orders the services of the "ancillary" professional. If a physician does not prescribe the service, reimbursement is usually not allowed. It is doubtful that there is any other industry as lucrative as health care where one discipline has had such occupational and financial control over the income of all other professionals.

Nurses (along with other women) have had to deal continually with their exclusion from medical, political, economic, and social power structures. For example, the vast majority of directors of nursing do not control their departmental budgets — they have the title without the authority (Cleland, as cited in Roberts and Group, 1995). And while high-level titles, such as Vice President for Patient Services, may suggest broader power than Director of Nursing, this is more a euphemism than a reality since the majority of women still have little power to influence or evaluate those who are actually in charge. The three major power centers of any hospital are the governing board, top administration, and medical staff. Power is increasingly becoming centralized within the board of trustees and hospital administration. The emergence of independent practice associations (IPAs) is part of the realignment of power among the three power centers (Wolper, 1995). At this writing, there is little indication that women will gain a stronger toehold on decision making than they have had in the past.

C. Gender and Governance

Hospital boards, like the rest of the country's corporate power structure, live and reproduce by the mirror image concept. That is, the concept of homomorphy, the "cloning effect," prevails. Before the 1970s, hospital boards of directors, in general, did not make a notable difference in shaping health policy. Any influence associated with hospital boards was more perceived than real. Now, the picture is changing. According to Bader (as cited in Friedman, 1994, p. 252), "Powerful changes in the economic, social, and political environment have turned boardsmanship from a prestigious pastime into a serious endeavor of heavy responsibility." After all, the board bears the ultimate legal and fiduciary responsibility for the performance and accountability of the hospital.

Women remain largely tokens on hospital boards, while physician participation on hospital boards has been required by the Joint Commission for Accreditation of Healthcare Organizations (JCAHO) since 1986. Whether the number of women directors increases depends on the extent to which women become more visible, more vocal, more political, and more influential. Women represent a vital dimension in the health care equation (Friedman, 1994). Their partnership in the governance of health care is long overdue.

D. Hospital Administrators

The hospital executive suite is still very much a male bastion. Women's successful integration into top-level administrative positions is handicapped by, among other things, a perceived lack of power, trained helplessness, lack of role models, and lack of support. The old-boy network in hospitals is traditionally dominated by physicians and career administrators. This network is being breached, however. For example, in 1988 the first female Commissioner of Health and Hospitals and CEO of Boston City Hospital was appointed (Gabor, 1995).

E. Medical Staff

In an age of managed care, physicians are positioning themselves to protect their income and authority. Proposals exist to allow physicians to engage in business enterprises that have been forbidden in the past. Backed by the AMA, proposed legislation would allow doctors to start physician-run health groups without the financial and regulatory requirements that states impose on similar organizations (Gottlieb, 1995). This would make it easier for physicians to set prices in ways that would otherwise violate antitrust rules. It would permit local medical groups to define standards in ways that curb competition and raise prices to patients. That is, the proposal gives physicians the opportunity to start their own physician service networks without having to put up the capital reserves or meet the detailed mandates often required of managed care companies. These networks would be exempt from state regulations and, hence, are opposed by insurers and managed care companies (Gottlieb, 1995). In the meantime, Physician-Hospital Organizations (PHOs), economic alliances between physicians and hospitals, have sprung up to ease any perceived or real financial burden. Taken together, the autonomy and power of physicians will likely be maintained or increased, while nurses will remain largely invisible in this struggle for economic power.

F. Licensure

Professional hegemony is upheld by a phalanx of governmental regulation. Health care is currently one of the most heavily regulated enterprises in the country. Licensure, registration, certification, and other professional standards have mushroomed in the last 60 years (Wolper, 1995). But the licensure playing field is far from even. Restrictive licensing of nurses and permissive licensing of physicians reinforces the limitations on the nursing profession and its comparative narrowness of clinical judgment and functional activity (Porter-O'Grady, 1995).

The American College of Surgeons, created in 1913, is the major certification board of the surgical profession. The requirements of the American College of Surgeons have been translated into minimum requirements for state licensure. The American Medical Association, through its Council on Medical Education and Hospitals during the 1920s and 1930s, developed standards for hospital-based internship and residency programs. The Joint Commission on Accreditation of Healthcare Organizations, formed in 1952, is the single most influential accrediting organization in the hospital industry.

The effect of the regulatory activity of these three organizations has been to emphasize medical staff autonomy, a natural result of the fact that much of the energy driving regulatory reform originated within the medical profession itself. The combined effects of these regulations has cemented the division of the U.S. hospital into an administrative sphere controlled by the hospital's lay administration, and a clinical sphere under the control of the medical staff (Wolper, 1995). The expression of gender power is clear — physicians' dominance over nurses became formalized.

The state regulatory landscape mirrors that at the national level. State Boards of Medical Examiners license physicians and are empowered to discipline individual doctors. Conflicts of interest abound, since state licensing boards are governed by physicians. In the early 1990s, state medical boards came under criticism for failing to be sufficiently aggressive in disciplining physicians with problems related to their professional activities (Rakich, Longest, and Darr, 1994). The license granted by a state is unlimited in terms of activities a physician may undertake. It is only in the health services organization that the scope of this otherwise unlimited right to practice medicine is modified.

The licensure of non-physician health services workers may be divided into two groups: those licensed to treat patients independently (called LIPs) and those who may or may not be licensed, but who are dependent on the orders of a physician or non-physician LIP to allow them to deliver health services. Dependent caregivers include medical technologists, pharmacists, radiographers, licensed practical nurses, and nursing assistants. In many states, nurse-midwives and some types of nurse-practitioners are LIPs (Rakich, Longest, and Darr, 1994).

In very recent years, nurses and consumers are gaining more of a toehold. The creation of the Community Health Accreditation Program (CHAP), discussed below, represents one chink in the regulatory armor of physicians.

G. Nurses as Policy Advisors

In the past, health care has been an industry where women stay in the background while policy decisions are made, despite the fact that women are the primary consumers of health care. President Clinton's Task Force on Health Care Reform reached into the states and brought state nursing directors and key nursing initiatives to the table. The inclusiveness of the Task Force was a major political victory for nurses' activism, and changed the face of the health care debates. The fee-for-service providers (physicians and hospitals) had less of an influence than that to which they had grown accustomed. The AMA was aggravated when representatives from nursing associations and Deans of Nursing Schools were invited to a meeting of the Health Reform Task Force (Birmingham Post-Herald, 1993). At that time, the Task Force was considering how to increase the utilization of Advanced Practice Nurses (APNs), such as nurse practitioners, nurse midwives and nurse anesthetists, who are underutilized in the current system. The American Nurses Association (ANA) wanted the services of Advanced Practice Nurses as a covered benefit for consumers; use of Graduate Medical Education funds for nursing education; stronger language on preempting state regulatory barriers to nursing practice; clarification of the term "health professional"; and broader criteria for provider participation on the National Health Board (Roberts and Group, 1995). The Health Security Act bill included nurses as "essential community providers" of health care, allowing APNs to be reimbursed directly for their services as primary care professionals. The Act essentially overrode state regulatory barriers to reimbursement of several primary health-care professionals. The slogan that appeared in the Spring of 1993, "In the future your family doctor may be a nurse," threatened both the professional power and personal finances of physicians. In December 1993 the AMA House of Delegates released a report that opposed autonomy for APNs, as well as for psychologists, social workers, chiropractors, and podiatrists. AMA opposition to greater use of APNs also included clinical nurse specialists, certified nurse midwives, and certified registered nurse anesthetists.

The issues of autonomy and control are at the crux of this physician/nurse conflict, of course. The intrusion by nurses into the health policy arena threatened to upset the traditional (im)balance of power enjoyed by physicians. According to ANA President Betts, "The issue is control, especially control of dollars. The AMA wants physician supervision because then the physician gets the first dollar" (Mechan, 1994, p. 3 as cited in Roberts and Group, 1995, p. 329). The American Nurses Association estimated that APNs could deliver primary care as competently as physicians and at 40 percent savings if they were not limited by barriers to reimbursement and limits on prescriptive authority. Social workers, psychologists, chiropractors, and physician assistants also asked for more latitude in their practice and prescriptive authority. Threatening the economic status quo too directly, health reform self-destructed.

If the Community Health Accreditation Program (CHAP) is evidence, however, there are moves afoot to change physicians' lock on standard-setting. CHAP is an alliance of consumers and purchasers of home health-care services. It successfully challenged the tradition that accreditation of health-care organizations should be established and controlled by the medical profession, rather than by consumers or nurses. Nurses' role in defining standards of care in community home-care agencies, however, represents only a marginal victory. The physician-dominated Joint Commission on Accreditation of Health Care Organizations remains intact.

Indeed, the policy route for nurses is arduous because many potential inroads remain uncharted. For example, Faye G. Abdullah, former deputy surgeon general, U.S. Public Health Service, deplored nursing's powerlessness to influence DRG parameters, pointing to the exclusion of nursing service as a component of all 467 Diagnostic Related Groups. Not one of these included a nursing service component with related predetermined costs (Kippinbrock, as cited in Roberts and Group, 1995).

SUMMARY

Health administration is a gendered enterprise. Any analysis of the health care system that ignores the power and presence of gender is incomplete. To break through the walls that limit our understanding of health, we must be aware of gendered norms — norms that drive medical research, the provision of services, notions about pricing, billing, and treatment protocols. Sexist assumptions, the trivialization of nurses and "allied" health professionals, stereotypes of the intellectual male and emotional female, and inequities in income, define the health arena and shape if not predict the character of health administration.

Table 5 - Summary of Points

Point 1	Women disproportionately deliver and use health services:
	60% of office visits are made by women
	97% of registered nurses are women
Point 2	Men disproportionately direct, govern, and benefit financially from health services:
	96% of healthcare administrators are men
	81% of physicians are men
Point 3	Given the complicated spectrum of health policy questions, the health arena should tap the leadership strengths of all its members, not just administrators and physicians.

Gender often is wrapped in the garb of some other topic. Medicine remains a powerful cultural paradigm in the United States. It dominates the public's conception of health and disease. It condones the present system of enforced and subordinated silence in which physicians overcharge for what nurses can do instead, take credit for what nurses actually do, and deny patients access to nurses' expertise; a system in which hospital administrators demand more and more competence from nurses and increase their responsibilities but expect nurses to do their work without full authority or the economic rewards to make it worthwhile (Roberts and Group, 1995).

We currently have a system of care heavily weighted to high-technology curative care in contrast to the promotion of function and quality of life (Mechanic 1989, as cited in Mechanic, 1994). A level playing field for the health care workforce, as well as for consumers, would lead to better health for everyone. Awareness of this fact helps to define more effective, more humane and more inclusive approaches to service delivery.

Gender cross-cuts the U.S. health care system. This chapter has demonstrated that, although women consume more health services than men, and although women deliver health services more than men, men are the more fortunate beneficiaries of the system. There are a number of loops in the tangle of gender and health administration: gender, medical establishment, institutionalized sexism, and trained helplessness. In an attempt to untangle these strands, we have discussed the nexus between gender and health administration by examining who delivers services, who uses services, and who benefits.

Those who stand to gain most by the maintenance of the status quo have been effective at resisting the efforts of those who are poised to upset that balance. As more women graduate from professional schools, as they gain an economic toehold in the workplace, as they contribute their wages to household income, gender power shifts and women expect to be accorded the same respect and influence as that which men possess.

Women and men in health administration must work to ensure that women participate in agenda setting and policy making as well as caregiving and teaching. We encourage those in health administration to promote qualified women, to include nurses and other women's professions in decision-making, and to encourage women in the health arena to understand the gender politics of health care. Given the complicated spectrum of health policy questions, the health arena needs to tap the leadership strengths of all its members. Women would be well advised to heed an early warning by Florence Nightingale: "Let us take care not to be left behind, crying 'Forward, Forward,' every two minutes...," and never stirring a step (Roberts and Group, 1995, pp. 335).

The health care system is a mirror to the values, tensions, and conflicts that characterize our daily lives. Gender power relations in medicine are an exaggeration of power relations embedded in the political culture. The relations between the structures we develop and the arrangements of power, influence, and control in our society are all reflected in this mirror.

REFERENCES

American Medical Association. (1996). *Physician Characteristics and Distribution in the U.S.* AMA, Chicago, IL.

Angier, N. (1995). Why Science Loses Women in the Ranks. *The New York Times, May 14, 1995*, Section 4: 5.

Blair, J. D., Fottler M. D., Paolino A. R. , and Rotarius T. M. (1995). *Medical Group Practices Face the Uncertain Future: Challenges, Opportunities and Strategies.* Center for Research in Ambulatory Health Care Administration, Englewood, CO.

Byrne, J., Kessler, L. G., and Devesa, S. S. (1992). The Prevalence of Cancer Among Adults in the United States:1987. *Cancer, 69*: 2154-2159.

Coile, R. C., Jr. (1994). The New Governance. *Strategies for an Era of Health Reform.* Health Administration Press: Ann Arbor, MI.

Cummings, S. H. (1995). Attila the Hun Versus Attila the Hen: Gender Socialization of the American Nurse. *Nursing Administration Quarterly, 19(2)*: 19-29.

Dorgan, C. A. (Ed.) (1995). *Statistical Record of Health & Medicine.* Gale Research Inc.: New York.

Freudenheim, M. (1995). A Bitter Pill for the HMO's; Swallow Hard and Cut Your Costs, Customers Say. *The New York Times, April 28, 1995, Section D*: 1.

Friedman, E. (ed.). (1994). *An Unfinished Revolution. Women and Health Care in America*. United Hospital Fund of New York: New York.

Gabor, A. (1995). Crashing the 'Old Boy' Party. *The New York Times, January 8, 1995, Section 3*: 1.

Glazer, P. M., and Slater, M. (1987). *Unequal Colleagues: The Entrance of Women into the Professions, 1890-1940*. Rutgers University Press: New Brunswick, NJ.

Gottlieb, M. (1995). Republican Bills on Health Bow to Wishes of Doctors. *The New York Times, October 31,1995, Section A*: 1.

Guy, M. E. (1995). Hillary, Health Care, and Gender Power in Duerst-Lahti, In Georgia and R.M. Kelly (Eds.) *Gender Power, Leadership, and Governance,* The University of Michigan Press, Ann Arbor, MI: 239-256.

Hafner-Eaton, C. (1993). Will the Phoenix Rise, and Where Should She Go? *American Behavioral Scientist, 36(6)*: 841-856.

Heim, P. (1995). Getting Beyond 'She Said, He Said'. *Nursing Administration Quarterly, 19(2)*: 6-18.

Mechanic, D. (1994). Inescapable Decisions. *The Imperatives of Health Reform*. Transaction Publishers, New Brunswick, NJ.

Papazian, E. (1995). Are Nurses Being Phased Out? *Ms., September/October, 1995*: 35.

Porter-O'Grady, T. (1995). Reverse Discrimination in Nursing Leadership: Hitting the Concrete Ceiling. *Nursing Administration Quarterly, 19(2)*: 56-62.

Rakich, J. S., Longest, Jr., B. B., and Darr, K. (1994). *Managing Health Services Organizations. 3rd Ed.,* Health Professions Press, Baltimore, MD.

Roberts, J. I. and Group, T. M. (1995). *Feminism and Nursing. An Historical Perspective on Power, Status, and Political Activism in the Nursing Profession,* Praeger, Westport, CT.

Sullivan, J. F. (1995). Officials Scrutinizing Doctor Bonuses in Managed Care Plans. *The New York Times, September 21, 1995, Section B*: 6.

U.S. Department of Commerce. (1995, September). *Statistical Abstract of the United States.* Government Printing Office: Washington, D.C.

U.S. Department of Commerce, Bureau of the Census. (1993). *Statistical Abstract of the United States, 110th ed.,* Government Printing Office, Washington, D.C.: 409.

Walby, S. and Greenwell, J. (1994). *Medicine and Nursing. Professions in a Changing Health Service.* Sage Publications Inc.: Thousand Oaks, CA.

Walker, P. V. (1996, March 15). NIH Reports Greater Diversity of Participants in Clinical Studies. *Chronicle of Higher Education*: A32.

West, C. T., Holoviak, S. J., and Figler, R. A. (1995). Sexual Harassment Among Nursing Professionals: Evidence and Prescriptions for Administrators. *Journal of Health and Human Services Administration, 18(2)*: 163-177.

Williams, C. L. (1995). Hidden Advantages for Men in Nursing. *Nursing Administration Quarterly, 19(2)*: 63-70.

Women's Research and Education Institute. (1994). Women's Health Care Costs and Experiences. Report available from *The Women's Research and Education Institute,* 1700 18th Street, N.W., Suite 400, Washington, D.C. 20009.

Wolper, L. F. (1995). Principles, Practices, Structure, and Delivery. In *Health Care Administration, Second Ed.,* Aspen Publishers, Inc.: Gaithersburg, MD.

29.
HEALTH SERVICES RESEARCH AND APPLICATIONS

Leiyu Shi, *University of South Carolina, Columbia, SC*

Health services research is an applied multidisciplinary field that produces knowledge about various components of health services at the population level including health services resources, provisions, organizing, financing, and policies (White, 1992; Frenk, 1993; Institute of Medicine, 1979). Health services research may be conducted at the organization level or policy level. Research at the organization level focuses on the micro- and intra-organizational elements of health services, which include health resources, provisions, organizing, and financing. Research at the policy level focuses on the macro- and inter-organizational elements of health services. Its purpose is to investigate the social, political, and economic determinants of health and health services. Policy level research also involves the formulation, implementation, and evaluation of the consequences of health policies related to health resources, provisions, organizing, and financing. In this chapter, the four major characteristics of health services research – scientific, multidisciplinary, population based, and applied – will be described first (Shi, 1997). Then, the major components of health services will be delineated and applications of health services research presented.

I. CHARACTERISTICS OF HEALTH SERVICES RESEARCH[1]

A. Scientific

Health services research is scientific inquiry. The conceptual and logical foundations of science provide guidance to health services researchers. The scientific principles of positivism, theory, empiricism, and objectivity, apply to health services research

477

as well. As with any scientific inquiry, health services research is founded on the premise that there are regularities in the delivery of health services. Scientific theories, many of which are from the social sciences, provide guidance for health services research which in turn contributes to the development of theories as related to the health phenomena. The series of stages typically associated with empirical research, including problem conceptualization and formulation, measurement and data collection, and analysis and interpretation, are also essential components of the process of health services research. Maintaining objectivity is crucial for health services researchers in light of the human nature of health services and the diverse interest groups involved.

As in social science disciplines, the application of scientific principles in health services research is not without constraints. The complexity of problems addressed in health services, and their variations in time and place, complicate analytic research efforts in health services research. Because health services research takes place in particular places and periods, particular studies cannot satisfy the needs and interests of all potential audiences. Often, due to circumstances peculiar to the site the study was conducted, findings from a study done in a particular health care institution, community, or state cannot be generalized to other settings. For the same reasons, data from national studies often do not apply to local levels.

Health services research is also constrained by the state-of-the-art of the theories and methods of disciplines that contribute to health services research. Since much of health services research is based on the theories and methods of social sciences, its ability to explain events is limited by the level of development of these sciences. The uncertainty is compounded because research in health services often addresses issues that are elusive and judgmental, such as the general health status of populations, quality of care, and access to care, the human element in health services delivery, and the economic value of life.

Limitations in the availability of data also contribute to the difficulty. Data for health services research are drawn principally from population surveys, records, documents, and direct observation. Each of these methods admits biases and unreliability. Answers to seemingly straightforward questions may not be found from existing data sources. Special studies may be necessary, which are often expensive and time-consuming. Moreover, results derived from such data may have questionable validity due to missing values or incomplete disclosure of certain types of information because of legal requirements to protect the respondents' privacy or organizational interests to protect the economic and political well being.

Although the classic experimental design remains the ideal foundation on which to conduct scientific research. studies in health services are primarily based on nonexperimental or quasi-experimental designs due to the difficulty of establishing truly experimental situations. Often, practical and ethical problems prevent investigators from controlling events and circumstances that are extraneous to the principal research questions. Thus, it is difficult to draw strong conclusions regarding cause and effect. These inherent difficulties to a large extent account for the seemingly inconclusive results in most studies. A multidisciplinary approach helps overcome some of these difficulties.

B. Multidisciplinary

Health services research is multidisciplinary since both biological and social factors converge in the delivery of health care. Often, no conceptual framework from a single discipline takes into account all aspects of a health services problem or is inherently superior to others. A cohesive combination of diverse disciplines that encompass a variety of perspectives is often required to carry out health services research successfully. Health services research may be considered as the application of the biomedical, social, and other scientific disciplines to the study of how to deliver health services to groups of people.

The first of these disciplines are those of biomedical sciences. Input from biomedical sciences is important for several reasons. First, humans have a biological dimension, which is expressed, among other phenomena, in the distribution of genetic characteristics, herd immunity, and the interaction of humans with other populations, such as microorganisms (Frenk, 1993). To achieve a proper understanding of any health condition in a population (a particular disease, for example), we must understand the biological processes that underlie the condition. Biological sciences contribute to the understanding of human populations through the study of biological determinants, risk factors, and consequences of health processes in populations, as well as the use of methods and techniques derived from the biological sciences to characterize such phenomena. Examples of such applications include health surveys that require laboratory tests to measure the prevalence or incidence of a given condition, and toxicological analysis of environmental risks. Second, medical sciences also contribute to health services research in important ways. For example, the normative clinical standards of care as accepted by the medical professions have to be taken into account before any assessment of health services can be made. Practice patterns of individual doctors must be known before data can be aggregated coherently.

Social science disciplines contribute significantly to health services research (Choi and Greenberg, 1982; Bice, 1980). First, since human populations are organized in societies, social sciences are indispensable for fully understanding health services in populations. Second, similar to health services research, social science disciplines are more likely to focus on groups rather than individuals. Third, many health services researchers were trained in social science disciplines including sociology (e.g., medical sociology), economics (e.g., health economics), law (e.g., health law), psychology (e.g., clinical psychology), political science (e.g., health policy), and management (e.g., health finance, health administration). Their research is influenced by the conceptual frameworks, theories, and methods espoused by those disciplines.

Demography, the study of population, can also be of benefit to health services researchers (Choi and Greenberg, 1982). First, the facts about population size, composition, rates, etc., that demographers produce are needed for good health planning. Planners need data about current and projected population to estimate needs for health services and potential use of these services. National health legislation has had a direct impact on demographers' work. Because of increasing emphasis on local and regional health planning, demographers are producing more data with local-level detail and are developing estimation techniques for small populations. Second, health researchers and planners with some training in demography can, for instance, compute rates or map population distribution. For example, with data on hospital patients and estimates of population size, local health professionals can compute hospital discharge rates for their areas. Thus, demographers provide important descriptive information for health services researchers and planners, and they have developed methods that health workers can use to describe their populations.

In addition to biomedical and social sciences, significant contributions to health services research have also come from the quantitative sciences including mathematics, statistics, operations research, and computer sciences. Advances in computerized multivariate analyses, for example, have opened possibilities for investigating certain types of questions that previously could not be addressed.

Behavior sciences are crucial to the understanding of health services. Behavioral research draws upon knowledge from epidemiological studies that identify behavioral determinants of illness, such as diet and smoking habits, and examines their social and psychological components. The interests of behavioral and health services research come together in studies of effects of lifestyles on the use of health services and in research on the effects of health services on individuals' health-related habits.

The influence of the physical sciences should also be considered, particularly in the study of problems with an environmental component. Knowledge from studies of environmental causes of health problems is important in health services research, because it gives insight into the kinds of health problems for which people seek care and the types of services that must be provided by the personal health services industry.

Administrative sciences, which themselves are an amalgam of the social and quantitative sciences, have made significant contribution to the study of health services, through the refinement of a body of knowledge related to organization theory, decision theory, information theory, and financial analysis. The impact of educational sciences cannot be ignored. Effective educational programs should be directed toward groups of people, health services institutions, and health professionals.

The fact that many biomedical and social sciences disciplines can be involved in health services research does not mean that every health services research encompasses all (or even a majority) of the disciplines mentioned. Health services research addresses a broad spectrum of problems. Therefore, it is natural that a given research problem would be dominated by theories from the disciplines most relevant to the problems. However, the challenge remains that there is a great need for integration, which in practice, can best be achieved through collaboration of researchers trained in different disciplines. Thus, the challenge for health services research is to enhance interaction among different scientific disciplines and approaches. Significant advances in knowledge and theory can only be achieved more rapidly through the application and integration of theoretical perspectives and methods across scientific disciplines and approaches around comprehensive health problems.

C. Population Based

Health services research focuses on population rather than individuals. The focus on population differentiates health services research from other health related researches. For example, clinical research focuses primarily on studying the efficacy of the preventive, diagnostic, and therapeutic services applied to the individual patients (Institute of Medicine, 1979). Biomedical research is primarily concerned with the conditions, processes, and mechanisms of health and illness at the subindividual level.

Environmental health research concentrates on services that attempt to promote the health of populations by treating their environments rather than by treating specific individuals.

D. Applied

Health services research is an applied field. Its priorities are established by societal questions and problems about health services for population groups. Studies in health services research are frequently occasioned by existing problems related to specific populations identified by societal groups and decision makers. Research is aimed at solving the problems. The application of knowledge generated through health services research can be found in specific populations, such as children, pregnant women, the poor, elderly, and migrants; particular problems, such as AIDS, mental, or dental health; or specific programs, such as community, environmental, occupational, and international health. The products of health services research are often assessed primarily in terms of their usefulness to people with decision making responsibilities, whether they be clinicians, administrators of health care institutions or government programs, or officials charged with formulating national health care policy. Indeed, the institutionalization of health services research within the nation's major universities and institutions and the sharp increase in health services research activities over the past two decades are primarily due to the increased funding from the federal government as a result of its expanded roles in health care delivery, financing, planning, and regulation, and its desire for relevant research to guide future decision making.

II. APPLICATIONS OF HEALTH SERVICES RESEARCH

Health services differ from other commodities in a number of ways. First, the demand for health care stems from a demand for a more fundamental commodity— health itself. The demand for health care is, therefore, a derived demand. Health care is not the ultimate goal; rather it is a surrogate for health. Its link to health should be proven rather than taken for granted.

The second complication refers to an agency relationship (Sorkin, 1992). Because the patient lacks the technical knowledge to make the necessary decisions, he must delegate this authority to the physician. It is likely that the physician's decision will reflect not only the preference of the patient, but also his self-interest, the pressure from professional colleagues and institution, a sense of medical ethics, and a desire to make good use of available resources.

The third complication concerns financing. For most health services, the money paid out-of-pocket at the point of usage is often significantly lower than the total eventual payment, largely due to insurance coverage. It is generally believed that the combination of comprehensive insurance for patients and fee-for-service payment for providers has driven the health care system to its current state—a voracious black hole for economic resources. Thus, the use of health care services is related to how the services are financed.

Finally, health services are influenced by the environment in which they are provided—the social, economic, demographic, technological, political, and cultural con-

Table 1 - Classification of Health Service Concepts, Topics, and Policy Concerns

	KNOWLEDGE COMPONENT	POLICY COMPONENT
1. Health Services Resources	• Physicians (generalists, specialists, DOS) • Dentists, nurses, pharmacists, therapists • Nonphysician primary care providers: nurse practitioners, physician assistants, certified nurse midwives • Medical technology (drugs, equipment, procedures) • Physician requirement forecast: need versus demand	• Market justice versus social justice • Physician surplus and shortage by specialty and geographic distribution • Access to providers and other resources • Productivity • Recruitment and retention • Coordination of services • Coordination of technology • Government health professional regulation
2. Health Services Provisions	• Preventive services: health promotion, disease prevention, health protection • Primary care and community oriented primary care • Long-term care (home, community, institution) • Mental health • Home care, dental care, vision care, foot care, drug dispensing, hospice • Special segments: rural health, urban health, school health, prison health, Indian health, migrant health, HIV/AIDS patients • Medical practice guidelines and standards • Total Quality Management, Continuous Quality Improvement, reengineering • Models of health services utilization: Aday and Anderson behavior model, the health belief model, and social learning theory • Health administration, cost containment, acquisition of medical technology	• Market justice versus social justice • Access to services (availability, accessibility, acceptability, affordability, contact, effectiveness) • Rationing • Equity of access and rationing • Ethics in health care • Quality of care (structure, process, outcome, patient satisfaction) • Community needs assessment • The impact of health promotion and disease prevention on risk and disease reduction
3. Health Services Organizing	• System: system for the employed, insured; system for the unemployed, uninsured, and poor; system for active duty military personnel; system for retired, disabled veterans • Types of hospitals: community (proprietary, nonprofit, multihospital system), government • Hospital integration: vertical versus horizontal • Diversification: related versus unrelated • Integrated delivery system • Nursing homes • Mental health facilities • Managed care approaches: HMO, PPO, IPA, EPA • Ambulatory care facilities (clinics, outpatients, surgical centers, physician group practices, community and migrant health centers) • Community based programs: local and state health departments, home health agency, hospice programs • Supportive organizations: government, business, regulatory organizations, insurance companies, educational institutions, professional associations, pharmaceutical and medical equipment suppliers • Regulatory approaches: subsidies, entry controls, rate setting, quality controls, social regulation, market preserving controls, Certificate of Need • Public health department	• Market justice versus social justice • Competition versus regulation • Effectiveness and efficiency • Fiscal and clinical accountability • Health care reform • Impact of managed care on cost and quality • Organizational networking

Table 1 - continued

KNOWLEDGE COMPONENT	POLICY COMPONENT
4. Health Services Financing	

4. Health Services Financing

KNOWLEDGE COMPONENT
- How much are we spending?
- Financing sources: private health insurance, out-of-pocket payment, Medicare, Medicaid
- Financing objects: hospital care, physician services, nursing home care
- Sources of personal health care expenditures
- Sources of hospital care expenditures
- Sources of physician care expenditures
- Methods of physician reimbursement: fee-for-service, capitation, salary, RBRVS
- Retrospective (cost based) versus prospective payment (DRGs)
- Public health financing: block grant versus categorical grant
- Health insurance terms: risk, moral hazard, adverse selection, deductible, copayment, experience-rated, community-rated
- Health insurance types: voluntary (Blue Cross and Blue Shield, private, HMOs), Social (Medicare, Workers Compensation, CHAMPUS), Welfare (Medicaid)
- Cost containment approaches: cost sharing, utilization review, case management, selective contracting

POLICY COMPONENT
- Market justice versus social justice
- Financial incentives for organizations
- Financial incentives for professionals
- Financial incentives for patients
- Effectiveness and efficiency
- The feasibility and impact of financing reform
- Long term care financing
- Impact of provider reimbursement methods on volume and quality of services
- Health care as a right versus the insurance principle
- Financing reform: one-payer system, "laissez-faire" free market approach, employer based approach ("play or pay")

texts surrounding the provision of health services. For example, among the major forces shaping the health care industry, the social reality of the growing number of uninsured is one of the major factors spearheading the recurrent debate about health care reform. The economic picture of the country and the large federal deficit necessitate greater cost containment and fiscal accountability in addition to clinical accountability. Globalization of the economy results in the increasing prominence of big business which is more involved with both the financing and delivery of medical services. The growing proportion of the elderly projects additional need for the professional labor force. Technological growth contributes to improving quality and increasing expenditures at the same time. The distinctive American political culture tends to distrust power, particularly government power, and prefers market mechanisms, voluntarism, and self-rule. This implicit American assumption that self-rule in small groups maximizes freedom is one reason we have so many sub-systems in the U.S. rather than a national health care system. However, many Americans do believe that health is a basic human right and that access to health care should be guaranteed. This belief in the social nature of health may explain the large role of the government in health care. Indeed the conflicts between market and social justice account for many of the problems and contradictions surrounding the provision, organizing, and financing of health services.

The major components of health services include health services resources, provisions, organizing, and financing. Important concepts related to each of the components are summarized in Table 1.

A. Health Services Resources

Health services resources can be classified into two major categories: human and non-human. Both are required for the provision of health services. Human resources consist of both physician and nonphysician providers. Physicians include allopathic and osteopathic; each is characterized by a diversity of specialties. Osteopathic medicine differs from allopathic medicine in that osteopaths traditionally emphasize treatments that involve corrections of the joints or tissues. Theyn stress diet or environment as factors that might destroy natural resistance. Allopathic medicine views the physician as an active interventionist attempting to neutralize effects of a disease by using treatments that produce a counteracting effect. It is organized in a variety of ways and practiced in a number of settings: private practice, group practice, health maintenance organizations, emergency rooms, outpatient clinics, hospitals, nursing homes, health departments, and home health agencies.

Nonphysician primary care providers include nurse practitioners, physician assistants, and certified nurse midwives. Among the issues that need to be resolved before nonphysician primary care providers can be used fully are legal restrictions to practice, reimbursement policies, and relationships with physicians (Shi et al., 1993). Other nonphysician providers include dentists, nurses, pharmacists, podiatrists, chiropodists, chiropractors, public health and social workers, optometrists, and physical therapists.

Medical technology is a major nonhuman resource. Such technology as techniques, drugs, equipment, and procedures used by health care professionals in delivering medical care to individuals are an expensive component of the health care system. The systems within which care is delivered may also be considered medical technology.

The basic health professional manpower problem in the U.S. is that the supply of providers such as physicians is largely determined by a need-based model (social justice principle), but medical services are actually delivered under the supply-demand model (market justice principle). The need-based model assumes even distribution of providers, but the market model is based on supply and demand. The inconsistency between the two models largely contributes to provider surplus in certain areas (metro, suburban) and shortages in other areas (rural, inner-city). Distributional shortages of physicians and other health professionals are likely to persist throughout the 1990s in many rural and selected inner-city areas.

Health services research studies strategies for creating balance to promote adequate access to available resources. Health services resources, both human and nonhuman, are expensive. The number and composition of providers are directly associated with medical care spending. The assessment, diffusion, and use of medical technology also significantly influence the cost of medical care. The surplus of resources will drive spending unnecessarily. Their shortage, however, will adversely affect the delivery of health care.

Health services research has contributed significantly to solving the professional shortage problem. In the late 1960s, research identified several problems in the health manpower needs of the nation, and action was subsequently taken in an effort to resolve them. To alleviate the shortage of physicians, for example, new medical schools were instituted in the underserved areas (inner city and rural). Financial support for family medicine programs was increased after research established its efficacy relative to more highly specialized areas of medical practice. Nurses in expanded roles (e.g., nurse practitioners) emerged as a viable option to remedy the many facets of the health manpower problem after research showed that the clinical skills of nurse practitioners were comparable to those of physicians when employed for conditions cared for by both. Furthermore, patients seemed to be more satisfied with the care received from nurse practitioners than from physicians (Office of Technology Assessment, 1986, 1991).

Research indicates that the surplus and shortage problem may be reduced through a combination of various policy options including health care professions regulations, reimbursement policies, targeted programs for underserved areas, and health professional schools (Conway-Welch, 1991; Wennberg et al., 1993; Kindig and Yan, 1993; Blumenthal and Meyer, 1993; Weiner, 1993). Regulations specify the tasks different health professionals are permitted to perform and the form of supervision required for each task. Of particular significance in reaching underserved areas is expanding the scope of practice for advanced nurses, including the right to prescribe drugs. Regulations affect the attractiveness of the profession to potential students as well as the locations in which they choose to serve.

Reimbursement policies affect practice-related choices of current and future physicians. Reimbursement methods that pay a premium for physicians serving in urban areas, for specialized rather than primary care, and for inpatient rather than ambulatory care provide incentives for physicians to be specialists associated with an urban hospital. Reimbursement is also crucial to nonphysician health professionals. The possibility of being reimbursed at a rate not substantially lower than that received by physicians for the same procedure attracts and retains advanced nurses.

Targeted programs for underserved areas include setting up task forces or commissions, offices of rural health, and incentive programs. Financial support for medical and nursing schools can promote rural-focused training programs, target dollars to family practice physician training, and incorporate in medical curriculum the unique concerns of practicing in underserved areas.

Policy makers and decision makers at all levels will have to use the above strategies with increased ingenuity and creativity. A broad conceptual framework must recognize the interests and perspectives of many diverse groups—patients, physicians, nurses, other health professionals, employers, insurers, labor, and government.

B. Health Services Provisions

Health services may be classified as primary, secondary, or tertiary. They may be targeted at different segments of the population, for example, maternal and child, elderly (long-term care), mentally ill (mental health), and terminally ill patients (hospice). Health services may be institution based (hospital, nursing home), ambulatory based (either institution based including outpatient and ambulatory clinics, ambulatory surgery centers, emergency medical services, and community and migrant health centers or non-institution based ambulatory services including physician offices, prison health services, vision care, dental care, foot care, and drug dispensing from pharmacists), community based (school health services, adult day care), or home based.

Ethical decision making is often involved in health services provisions, for example, when dealing with death and dying, organ transplantation, mental health services, trauma care, drug abuse, prescription drug pricing, professional-patient relationship, health care, reproductive rights (contraception and abortion), resource allocation (access and rationing), acquired immune deficiency syndrome (AIDS), mental health, and confidentiality.

Health services research related to service provisions include access to and quality of medical services. Access to appropriate and affordable health services has long been a topic of national attention and research (U.S. GAO, 1991). Access to care refers to the ability of persons needing health services to obtain appropriate care in a timely way. Care is considered appropriate care when it contributes to the well-being of those receiving it. These services may include primary care including health promotion, preventive and screening services; specialized secondary and tertiary services including inpatient and outpatient care of acute, chronic, mental, and emotional illness or disorders; long-term institutional care; various types of sociomedical services that aim at maintaining patients in their homes and communities rather than in institutions. Such services include home health care, adult day care, hospice and respite care. Access to care can be described as a continuum of coverage by availability (people for whom the service is available), accessibility (people who can use the service), acceptability (people who are willing to use the service), contact (people who actually use the service), and effectiveness (people who are cured of the disease) (Hongvivatana, 1984).

Much of health services research is concerned with utilization. Who uses health services? With what frequency? Of what sort? With what cost and quality outcome? Health policy makers face these focal questions; answers represent a central area of health services research. There are a number of distinct approaches to studying utilization behavior: the demographic approach, emphasizing variables such as age, sex, and family size; the social-structural approach, emphasizing variables such as education, occupation, social class, and ethnicity; the economic approach, focusing on variables such as price and income related to demand and supply; and the organizational approach, emphasizing the organization of provider practices, referral patterns, and interorganizational linkages.

Quality of care refers to the degree of excellence or conformity to established standards and criteria. The two policy concerns regarding health care quality are quality assessment and assurance. Quality assessment includes the processes of defining how quality is to be determined or measured, identification of specific measurement variables, collection of data, and analysis and interpretation of the results of the assessment.

Quality measurement in health care mainly consists of such structural measures as inputs used in production of health or various organizational and professional factors, process measures (what is done to and for patients with respect to diagnosis, treatment, rehabilitation, and palliation), and outcome measures (health status, health-related quality of life, patient well-being) (Donabedian, 1985; Caper, 1988; Berwick, 1989; McNeil et al., 1992). Structural and process measures are merely intervening variables; their validity and reliability should be established before adoption. The validity of a measure is the extent to which it actually assesses what it purports to measure. If a measure is supposed to reflect the quality of care, one would expect improvements in quality to affect the measure positively. Reliability reflects the extent to which the same result occurs from repeated application of a measure to the same subject.

Patients, the consumers of health care, are the final judge of quality. The clinical judgment of experts may be used to inform patients in their evaluation. Patient and provider satisfaction can in turn relate to a broad set of questions concerning accessibility, availability, and costs of care in addition to ratings of the technical and interpersonal performance of clinicians and institutions.

Quality assurance is the ongoing process of institutionalizing or conducting quality measurement activities followed by feedback mechanisms. It aims at assuring continuity and coordination of care and is concerned about the flow from illness to wellness. It also studies the services sought and rendered through an entire episode of care across time and settings of care. Examples of quality assurance include risk management and total quality management (TQM) or continuous quality improvement (CQI) (Whetsell, 1991; Kaluzny et al., 1992).

Another important research interest related to quality of care is the promotion of community oriented primary care (COPC). COPC incorporates the elements of good primary care delivery and adds to this a population-based approach to identifying and addressing community health problems. In addition to medical or treatment intervention, it includes educational and preventative intervention, political intervention (lobbying, interest group politics, and coalition building), community organizing and involvement, organizational intervention (fit health care organization to community needs), and financial intervention (location of funding sources for community programs).

An important area of health services provision research has to do with medical practice guidelines and standards of practice. Earlier research has demonstrated a high degree of variation in patterns of medical practice. These variations have been the stimulus for a relatively new field called outcomes research or effectiveness research (Guadagnoli and McNeil, 1994). Outcomes research involves linking the type of care (for example, medical, surgical, diagnostic, preventive, or rehabilitative care) received by patients to positive and negative outcomes (for example, mortality, morbidity, physical functioning, mental well-being) in order to determine the most effective care for patients with particular characteristics.

Through analysis of the actual effectiveness of alternative treatments for specific conditions, as measured in both physiological and functional health status dimensions, outcomes research promises to provide clinicians with practice guidelines and standards which represent the crucial link between outcomes research and clinical practice. Outcomes research can provide patients with important information that can help them choose health plans, individual providers, and treatments. Outcomes research can also aid managers and policy makers in the design of systems and incentives that promote the use of the most effective and appropriate health services and identify ineffective care so that it can be eliminated and medical expenditures reduced. Managers can use outcomes data as part of continuous quality improvement activities to improve or change services. Payers may link health care outcomes with reimbursement for care and reward or penalize hospitals on the basis of their performance. Effectiveness results can be used to rank different types of care and to ration care by paying only for those that meet certain cost benefit criteria.

C. Health Services Organizing

The system under which medical care services are provided in the United States may be described as a patchwork of subsystems serving many: regularly employed, middle-income families with continuous health insurance coverage; poor, unemployed (or underemployed) families without continuous health insurance coverage; active-duty military personnel and their dependents; and veterans of U.S. military service (Williams and Torrens, 1993).

In the past three decades, this patchwork of subsystems have operated under a semi-competitive and semi-regulatory environment. Examples of competition include insurance plan copayments that make consumers more cost conscious; Health Maintenance Organizations (HMOs); competition and the proliferation of alternative managed care approaches to cost containment including Independent Practice Associations (IPAs), Preferred Provider Organizations (PPO), and Exclusive Provider Arrangement (EPA) (Weiner and Lissovoy, 1993; Iglehart, 1992). Examples of regulation include subsidies (e.g., medical education), rate setting (e.g., prospective payment based on DRG), quality controls (e.g., professional standard review), social regulation (e.g., hospital fire and safely codes), market preserving controls (e.g., anti-trust laws), and entry controls (e.g., licensure, Certificate of Need or CON program). CON is a process by which hospitals or other health care providers seeking a substantial expansion of their scope of services or physical facilities will require prior approval from a government-endorsed entity.

Health services research related to organizing has focused on health care reform. The ineffectiveness of the semi-competitive and semi-regulatory approach either in containing cost or in expanding access prompts policy makers to seriously consider fundamental health care reform. Health services researchers and analysts have reviewed various options of organizing medical care systems: a laissez-faire free-market approach, the single payer approach, health planning, financing mechanisms, the public utility approach, incrementalism, the employer based approach or "play or pay," and managed competition. They have compared alternative national health care systems (in particular, Germany and Canada) to find the best "cure" for the U.S. (see Table 2). The final shape of health care delivery depends on a number of factors including the role of Presidential and Congressional leadership, the medical community, business, and the American public. The historical tendency toward incremental reform in health care suggests that any federal initiative will preserve and build on important features of the current health care system including employment-based insurance, the private health insurance industry, a pluralistic delivery system including fee-for-service practice of medicine, and a strong role for state government.

Assessing the effectiveness of managed care is another important health services research topic. Managed care is being touted as an effective approach to both cost control and quality improvement. Existing research demonstrates that most forms of managed care are effective in reducing health care utilization, especially inpatient care (Altman and Reinhardt, 1996). Health Maintenance Organizations (HMOs) tend to reduce utilization of tests, procedures, or expensive treatments without lowering quality of care. However, little evidence shows that lower managed care costs lead to lower systemwide health care costs. Future health services research can study the cost-effectiveness of different managed care approaches on different kinds of patient populations, delivery settings, and health conditions.

D. Health Services Financing

Health care financing includes a number of areas: the magnitude, trend, and sources of medical care spending, as well as both public and private sector funding sources. The magnitude of spending answers questions about how much we are spending on health care and compares our performance with that of other developed

Table 2 - Major Health Care Reform Approaches

Approach	Pros	Cons
A laissez-faire free-market approach ("piecemeal")	• Builds on, rather than replacing, current system • Promotes managed care concept (HMOs, PPOs) which sets fees and budgets to control costs • Gives people incentive to price-shop for insurance and medical care, improving individual choice and reducing personal costs • Maintains private market-based approach • Significantly restricts government involvement and regulation compared with other approaches	• Doesn't mandate coverage for everyone • Requires consumers to have a sophisticated knowledge of insurance plans • Relies primarily on questionable cost-control strategies already in place • Doesn't address administrative waste • Continues two-tier medical system in which those who can afford it have greater coverage, but low-income people receive minimum coverage • Lacks long-term care coverage
Governmentally controlled health care system ("single payer")	• Guarantees access to care for all individuals • Eliminates exclusions for pre-existing conditions • Reduces or eliminates many out-of-pocket costs • Controls costs by setting payment rates or limits on health-care spending • Removes employers' responsibility to provide health insurance, though they continue to pay for coverage through taxes • Greatly reduces insurance companies' role, thus lowering administrative costs • Spreads risk and cost across entire population • Ensures coverage if people lose or change jobs	• Increases taxes substantially • Puts government in charge of whole system, which could lead to budgetary constraints affecting choice, quality, use of new technologies, waiting lists, and shortages • Significantly curbs need for private insurance coverage, resulting in thousands of lost jobs throughout insurance industry • Could allow political and ideological biases to influence scientific decisions
Employer based approach ("play or pay")	• Provides coverage for everyone • Builds on, rather than replacing, current system • Eliminates exclusions for pre-existing conditions • Reduces out-of-pocket costs substantially for many groups of people • Maintains competition among private-market insurance companies • Spreads risk and cost across entire population	• May offer no real incentive for some employers to "play" because tax route may be cheaper which could shift millions of employed people into government pool • Requires small business to pay, through either health insurance ("play") or more taxes ("pay") • Enables many insurance companies to continue to operate, which means some of the administrative costs (e.g., advertising) also continue • Increases taxes, although less than in government based approach

nations. Trends look at the patterns of medical care spending over time. The major sources of spending include hospital care, physician services, and nursing home care. The major funding sources are private health insurance, out-of-pocket payment, government programs such as Medicare and Medicaid, and other private funding. These financing sources may be classified as either public sector which includes both social health insurance and public welfare program or private sector which includes voluntary health insurance and fee-for-service.

Social health insurance reflects participation in a government entitlement program linked to previous employment. Examples include Medicare and Workers' Compensation. Public welfare health care programs connote lack of employment or the inability to gain employment stemming from a disabling condition. Examples include Medicaid for the poor.

Voluntary health insurance or private health insurance in the United States usually denotes current employment; it can be subdivided into three categories: Blue Cross and Blue Shield, private or commercial health insurance, and HMOs or prepaid managed care plans that provide fairly comprehensive coverage in return for a prepaid fee.

The upward escalation in health care expenditure and cost of care is a critical concern confronting health services researchers and policy makers. U.S. health care expenditures significantly exceed those of other industrialized countries. For example, in 1990, per capita health expenditure in the U.S. was $2,567. The similar expenditure in Canada was 45 percent less, Germany was 77 percent less, United Kingdom 164 percent, and Turkey 1,845 percent (Schieber et al., 1992).

Unfortunately, these disparities in spending have not translated into better health outcomes as reflected in standard measures. Among twenty-four industrialized counties, the U.S. ranked twentieth in infant mortality rate, sixteenth in perinatal mortality rate, sixteenth in female life expectancy, and seventeenth in male life expectancy. Satisfaction with health care system is also lower in the U.S. than in other industrialized countries. The sharp increase in spending has generated criticism that the health care system is inefficient. Rationing for services, particularly among the poor is debated and experimented.

Health services research seeks to explain causes for the upward spiral of health expenditures. Explanations include the following:

- Changing demographics of the population and the growing proportion of the elderly in particular
- Consequence of third-party insurance coverage in insulating individuals from the true cost of care
- Advancement in and duplication of sophisticated medical technology
- Ability of health care providers to generate demand for their services
- Lack of knowledge about the efficacy and appropriateness of health care interventions
- Rising expectations about what health care can do to extend and enhance the quality of life.

The challenge for researchers is to sort out the impact those factors have on cost and to isolate those most amenable to change.

Health services researchers have looked at the many attempts to control rising health care expenditures, including the shift from cost-based reimbursement for Medicare hospital care to DRG-based prospective payment system, fee schedules for physician services, cost-sharing imposed by third-party payers, and various approaches of utilization review and managed care. The challenge is to ascertain the relative impact of these and other attempts at cost containment and to provide more definitive answers to the question of effectiveness.

Significant progress has been made in health services financing research, especially by health economists. Research indicates the demand for medical care is price-inelastic; in other words, the degree of responsiveness of use to price is less than proportional. With physicians' services, for example, a ten percent price increase might lead to a one or two percent decline in the quantity demanded. The quantity of hospital services demanded appears to be somewhat more responsive, but still inelastic—about a three to five percent quantity response for a ten percent price change.

Most demand studies have found that income elasticity—degree of responsiveness of quantity demanded to income—for medical care expenditures in general is near 1.0. In other words, a given percentage increase in income should lead to a proportional increase in the amount expended on medical care. In the case of hospital services, income elasticity is generally lower. Moreover, the effect of income on medical care expenditures appears to have declined over time, undoubtedly because insurance coverage has increased significantly.

Another example of health services financing research is cost-effective analysis of screening programs and early diagnosis. Some claim that early diagnosis can reduce costs for many conditions by intervening in the disease at a less expensive point, thus avoiding the development of more expensive health problems later on. Over the years, many studies have been conducted on the efficacy of specific diagnostic tests as well as on more general health-screening programs (Canadian Task Force on the Periodic Health Examination, 1988; Preventive Services Task Force, 1989; Eddy, 1991; Sox, 1994). Most have found them to be cost-effective (Dietrich et al., 1992; Mandel, Bond and Church, 1993; Nichol et al., 1994).

Financing long-term care is another critical research and policy concern (Porter and Witek, 1991; Wiener and Hanley, 1991; McCall et al., 1991). Two major sources of nursing home payments are Medicaid (about 47%) and out-of-pocket (about 43%). Public and private programs currently do not provide sufficient benefits or financial coverage to meet the long-term care needs of the elderly and chronically ill, including those covered by Medicaid. As a result, family burdens, both financial and human, are substantial. To compound this problem, the costs of long-term care are also increasing rapidly, making available services less accessible to more people. Both public- and private-sector decision makers need to know how long-term care costs for the elderly and the chronically ill can be financed most effectively and efficiently. Through analysis of policy options, health services researchers help identify and evaluate the implications of alternative roles for both public and private sectors in financing long-term care programs, the integration between public and private approaches, and the coordination between current funding sources and long term care services.

Health services researchers, synthesizing the growing knowledge about provider reimbursement systems, might inform us about other public and private insurance and indemnity systems. In an increasing number of states, however, Medicaid reimbursements have been changed (both increased and decreased), thus providing a natural experiment for health services research by which to gauge the positive and negative effects of altering Medicaid physician reimbursement levels. A synthesis of the research already conducted on these experiment would be very useful to state policy makers. For instance, policy makers would like to know how changing Medicaid reimbursement levels will impact the rate of provider participation in the Medicaid program and the provision of medical services to Medicaid beneficiaries.

SUMMARY

Perhaps the ultimate gratification for health services researchers is to see their findings implemented in policy decisions. One of the major goals of health services research is the application of multidisciplinary knowledge to the task of solving current and emerging health related problems. Resources can then be better utilized to improve the health status of the population. The synthesis and dissemination of health services research have played and continue to play an important role in health policy formulation and implementation (Ginzberg, 1991). To further enhance policy implementation of findings, researchers need to establish a close rapport with decision makers, communicating policy priorities and research scope, and setting timetables and reporting style. Researchers and decision makers need each other. Decision makers rely on researchers to assist them in making sound, legitimate decisions based on scientific evidence and existing knowledge. Researchers need decision makers to identify, conduct, and implement research, including selecting research problems, obtaining funding, gaining access to research sites and subjects. The sooner both sides recognize this inter-dependency and work towards collaboration, the greater will be the value of health services research to policy formulation and implementation.

ENDNOTE

1. This section is adapted from my book Health Services Research Methods. (Chapter 1, pp. 15-22), reprinted with permission from Delmar.

REFERENCES

Altman, S. H., and Reinhardt, U. E. (1996). *Strategic Choices for a Changing Health Care System.* Health Administration Press, Chicago, IL.

Berwick, S. M. (1989). Health services research and quality of care. *Medical Care,* 27: 763-771.

Bice, T. (1980). Social Science and Health Services Research: Contribution to Public Policy. *Milbank Memorial Fund Quarterly, 56(Spring):* 173-200.

Blumenthal, D., and Meyer, G. S. (1993). Transforming the size and composition of the physician work force to meet the demands of health care reform. *New England Journal of Medicine, 329:* 1810-1814.

Canadian Task Force on the Periodic Health Examination. (1988). The periodic health examination: 2. 1987 update. *Can Med Assoc J, 138:* 618-26.

Caper, P. (1988). Defining quality in medical care. *Health Affairs, 8*: 49-61.

Choi, T., and Greenberg, J. N. (1982). Social Science Approaches to Health Services Research. Health Administration Press, Ann Arbor, MI.

Conway-Welch, C. (1991). Issues surrounding the distribution and utilization of nurse non-physician providers in rural America, *Journal of Rural Health, 7*: 388-401.

Dietrich, A. J., O'Connor, G. T., Kelly, A., Carney, P.A., Levy, D., and Whaley, F. S. (1992). Cancer: Improving early detection and prevention: a community practice randomized trial. *BMJ, 304*: 687-91.

Donabedian, A. (1985). Twenty years of research on the quality of medical care. *Evaluation & the Health Professions, 8*: 243-265.

Eddy, D. M. (1991). Common Screening Tests. Philadelphia: American College of Physicians.

Frenk, J. (1993). The new public health. *Annual Review of Public Health, 14*: 469-90.

Ginzberg, E. (1991). Health Services Research: Key to Health Policy. Cambridge, MA: Harvard University Press.

Guadagnoli, E. and McNeil, B. J. (1994). Outcomes research: Hope for the future or the latest rage? *Inquiry, 31*, 14-24.

Hongvivatana, T. (1984). Data analysis: Social science perspective. in Evaluating Primary Health Care in Southeast Asia, Proceedings of a Regional Seminar. New Deli: Regional Office WHO.

Iglehart, J.K. (1992). The American health care system: Managed care. *New England Journal of Medicine, 327*: 742-747.

Institute of Medicine. (1979). Health Services Research. Washington, DC: National Academy of Sciences.

Kaluzny, A. D., McLaughlin, C. P., and Simpson, K. (1992). Applying total quality management concepts to public health organizations. *Public Health Reports, 107*: 257-264.

Kindig, D., and Yan, G. (1993). Physician supply in rural areas with large minority populations. *Health Affairs, Summer*: 177-184.

Mandel, J. S., Bond, J. H., and Church, T. R. (1993). Reducing mortality from colorectal cancer by screening for fecal occult blood. *New England Journal of Medicine, 329*: 672.

McCall, N., Knickman, J., and Bauer, E. J. (1991). Public/private partnerships: A new approach to long-term care. *Health Affairs, 10*: 164-176.

McNeil, B. J., Pedersen, S. H., and Gatsonis, C. (1992). Current issues in profiling quality of care. *Inquiry, 29*: 298-307.

Nichol, K. L., Margolis, K. L., Wuorenma, J., and Von Sternberg, T. (1994). The efficacy and cost effectiveness of vaccination against influenza among elderly persons living in the community. *New England Journal of Medicine, 331*: 778-84.

Office of Technology Assessment (OTA). (1986). *Nurse Practitioners, Physician Assistants, and Certified Nurse Midwives: A Policy Analysis.* (Health technology case study 37) U.S. Government Printing Office, Washington, DC.

Office of Technology Assessment (OTA). (1991). Health Care in Rural America. OTA-H-434, U.S. Government Printing Office, Washington, DC.

Porter, M., and Witek, J. E. (1991). The nursing home industry: Past, present, and future. *Topics in Health Care Financing, 17*: 42-48.

Preventive Services Task Force. (1989). Guide to Clinical Preventive Services: Report of the U.S. Preventive Services Task Force. Williams & Wilkins, Baltimore.

Shi, L., Samuels, M. E., Konrad, T. R., Ricketts, T. C., Stoskopf, C. H., and Richter, D. L. (1993). The determinants of utilization of nonphysician providers in rural community and migrant health centers. *Journal of Rural Health, 9*: 27-39.

Shi, L. (1997). *Health Services Research Methods.* Delmar Publishers, Albany, NY.

Schieber, G. J., Pollier, J. P., and Greenward L. M. (1992). Health expenditure performance: An international comparison and data update. *Health Care Financing Review, 13*(4): 1-87.

Sorkin, A. L. (1992). An Introduction to Health Oconomics. New York, NY: Lexington Books.

U.S. General Accounting Office (GAO). (1991). *Access to Health Care: States Respond to Growing Crisis.* (GAO/HRD-92-70) U.S. Government Printing Office, Washington, DC.

Weiner, J. P., and Lissovoy, G. (1993). A taxonomy for managed care and health insurance plans. *Journal of Health Politics, Policy and Law, 18:* 75-103.

Weiner, J. P. (1993). The demand for physician services in a changing health care system: A synthesis. *Medical Care Review, 50:* 411-449.

Wennberg, J. E., Goodman, D. C., Nease, R. F., and Keller, R. B. (1993). Finding equilibrium in U.S. physician supply. *Health Affairs, Summer:* 89-103.

Whetsell, G. W. (1991). Total quality management. *Topics in Health Care Financing, 18:* 12-20.

White, K. L. (1992). Health Services Research: An Anthology. Pan American Health Organization, Washington, DC.

Wiener, J. M., and Hanley, R. J. (1991). Long-term care financing: Problems and progress. *Annual Review of Public Health, 12:* 67-84.

Williams, S. J., and Torrens, P. R. (eds). (1993). *Introduction to Health Services.* 4th edition. Delmar Publishers Inc., Albany, NY.

30.
HEALTH CARE TECHNOLOGY ASSESSMENT

Mary Ellen Uphoff, *University of Nebraska Medical Center, Omaha, NE*

Dale Krane, *University of Nebraska at Omaha, Omaha, NE*

The rapid development of complex and expensive medical procedures and technologies poses significant challenges to health care managers and policy makers. Selection of appropriate modes of treatment is intertwined with issues of access, cost, safety, and overall quality of care delivery. Without adequate means of assessment and monitoring, managers and policy makers may make faulty decisions. Health Care Technology Assessment (HCTA) consists of a diverse array of research tools and investigative procedures which permit systematic, data-based judgments to be made about the feasibility and utility of medical practices, technologies, treatments, and delivery systems.

This chapter examines the demand for HCTA, its importance and significance for health policy and administration, and its utilization by health decision makers at various levels of medical practice and delivery. Second, the principal assessment methodologies are described with an emphasis on the types of evaluation procedures commonly used to determine the safety, effectiveness, and costs of different medical devices and practices. Third, the types of medical organizations that perform HCTA are reviewed. The chapter concludes with a discussion of how HCTA fits in with the movement to adopt strategic management and process redesign in health organizations.

I. THE NATURE AND SIGNIFICANCE OF HEALTH CARE TECHNOLOGY ASSESSMENT

The United States Office of Technology Assessment (OTA) defines medical technology as "the set of techniques, drugs, equipment and procedures used by health care professionals in delivering medical care to individuals, and the systems within which such care is delivered" (OTA, 1976). Inclusion of delivery systems acknowledges the importance of the context in which a health intervention takes place, and that a number of individual technologies grouped together (e.g., intensive care unit, or outpatient surgical center) could be considered a complex technology (Power, Tunis, and Wagner, 1994).

Technology assessment is a systematic process to develop evidence by which to form a conclusion as to the merits of a particular technology. This includes the evaluation of new and innovative technologies, as well as existing practices. The merit and role of the evaluated practice or technology are considered in relation to the clinical value, return on investment, and reimbursement implications. The product of an assessment effort is information regarding various characteristics of the technology in question (Matuszewski and Vermeulen, 1996). Banta's (1987) conceptualization of technology assessment highlights this broader impact perspective:

> "...technology assessment is analysis primarily of social rather than technical issues, and it is particularly concerned with unintended, indirect, or delayed social impacts.
> Its goal is to provide policy makers with information on policy alternatives regarding matters such as allocation of research and development funds, formulation of regulations, and development of legislation."

Basic evaluation of any device, drug, or procedure rests on several criteria including present and future need for the product, safety, efficacy, effectiveness, accuracy (for diagnostic products), and cost conditions (Perry, Pillar, and Radany, 1990). Safety is measured in terms of risk-to-benefit ratios. A low risk technology may be unacceptable if the potential benefit is also low, whereas a high risk technology may be acceptable if the potential benefit is also high. In relation to the medical condition for which a technology is being considered, a high risk technology may be considered acceptable if applied towards the treatment of a disease that if untreated will prove fatal (Perry, Pillar, and Radany, 1990). Efficacy measures the probability of benefit to individuals in a defined population under ideal or laboratory conditions. This may include employment of the technology under a research protocol, or use at a center of excellence by a highly trained physician. Effectiveness is the ability of the technology to render the desired benefit in a less controlled day-to-day clinical setting. (Perry, Pillar, and Radany, 1990). A technology may prove to be efficacious but not effective. Levels of performance and success may vary significantly when applied to a more diverse patient population and by practitioners with differing levels of skill in a variety of settings (Franklin, 1993; Goodman, 1993; Hillman, 1995).

Cost analyses of technology estimate both the direct costs of health care such as physician fees and medical supplies, as well as indirect costs such as the value of work time lost by the patient. HCTA may also be used to generate information about opportunity costs, production costs, research and development costs, overhead, and marginal valuation. Of course, the quality of cost analysis depends on the quality of the data used and the assumptions made (Perry, Pillar, and Radany, 1990).

The purpose of cost-effectiveness analysis in health care is to compare various investments in order to find the most efficient and effective. By combining information about both the costs and the health effects of various forms of treatment one acknowledges a "trade-off" (Garber, 1996).

Researchers have tried to standardize tradeoffs between a year of life spent in one state of health versus another. The quality adjusted life year (QALY) saved has become the most accepted unit of comparison. This approach attempts to quantify the aspects and states of health that are of value to the patient. Those years of life gained that are less acceptable to the patient due to pain and suffering, functional limitations, and other burdens related to ill health are weighted in such a way as to indicate that they are less valuable than those spent in good health (Garber, 1996). Once this general measure of output is determined, the results of widely different therapies and programs can be compared (Fryback, 1990).

Cost-effectiveness analysis requires identification of the costs that go into a procedure: direct costs, transaction costs, indirect costs such as morbidity and mortality (Hillman, 1995), and the intangible but significant costs of pain and suffering. In recent years, HCTA has been broadened in scope to incorporate clinical effectiveness (as compared to efficacy), considerations of quality of life, patient preferences, cost/benefit analysis, implications for services paid for by insurers, protection of the individual, principles of distributive justice, and the concepts of benevolence and mercy (Perry, Pillar, and Radany, 1990).

Currently, benefit/cost analysis is driven by the pressure to cut costs while maintaining quality and enhancing the provider's productivity and clinical outcomes (Veluchamy and Saver, 1990). But the impacts of new health care technologies ripple out beyond the care of an individual patient. New medical treatments also possess the capacity to shape the larger cultural and social realms of behavior. The consequences of technology application on the surrounding community or society at large may encompass issues as controversial and diverse as access to health care, the norms of interpersonal relations (e.g., "safe sex"), or environmental impacts (e.g., disposal of nuclear materials). Likewise, new health practices such as organ transplantation or treatment for infertility can lead to changes in medico-legal standards of care and bioethical issues (Franklin, 1993; Fuchs, 1990; Jennings and Weinstein, 1991; Reiser and Ross, 1992).

A. The Demand for Health Care Technology Assessment

Available evidence supports the view that the rate of technological change has been particularly rapid since the end of World War II (Gelijns, 1994; Terry, 1994). Challenges to conventional wisdom and the application of scientific methodology and research have led to significant innovations in medical technology. Once occurring decades apart, technological breakthroughs now occur on a weekly or even daily basis (Misener, 1990).

In recent years, the health care reform debate in the United States has focused its attention on technological advances. Considered both a blessing and a curse, advances in medical knowledge and technological innovation over the last several decades have significantly improved health, but have contributed to skyrocketing health care costs (Gelijns, 1994; Misener, 1990; Perry, Pillar, and Radany, 1990). During this period, real U.S. health spending per capita has advanced at an average 4.5% annually, more than twice the rate of growth in the gross domestic product (Terry, 1994). The cost of a day in the hospital has almost quintupled during the past 30 years, suggesting that patients are receiving more care. This price rise also extends beyond hospitals. According to the U.S. national government's Prospective Payment Commission, from 1985 to 1990 increased intensity of services raised actual inpatient costs by 41%, outpatient expenditures by 31%, nursing home costs by 33%, and physician charges by 38% (Terry, 1994). It is estimated that health care will comprise 15% United States GNP by the year 2000, and quickly continue its rise to reach 20% soon after (Misener, 1990; Schwartz, 1994).

A growing skepticism about the value derived from US health care expenditures, coupled with observations of substantial geographic variation in the frequency with which various medical procedures are performed, highlight a pronounced need for clinical management and policy strategies capable of containing costs while preserving or enhancing health care quality (Steinberg and Graziano, 1990). However, according to health economists, even with a health care system operating at maximum efficiency, medical advances would continue to drive expenditures upward (Terry, 1994). Many fear that the inevitable results of an environment characterized by inexorably rising costs will include either planned or de facto rationing of care (Misener, 1990).

Technology's contributions to cost increases in health care services are due to several factors. The cost of the technology and the equipment itself do not stand alone, but increase when personnel expenses and facilities costs are added. Additional costs are incurred when technology is made available throughout the population (McGregor, 1989).

New technologies may provide the option of treatment to a sizable population formerly unserved (Gelijns, 1994). The introduction of laprascopic cholecystectomy illustrates this point, as it increased the overall level of gallbladder removals by an estimated 60 percent in a large HMO. Suggesting that this procedure became partly prophylactic, the application of this technology moved from sicker to mildly symptomatic patients, as well as to higher risk patients (such as the elderly) once considered ineligible for the procedure. Therefore, although laparoscopic cholecystectomies have shortened hospital stays and reduced unit costs by 25%, their introduction resulted in an increase, not a decrease in aggregate expenditures (Legorreta, et al. 1993).

Non-technological factors also increase health care expenditures. These include the growth and aging of our population (Hendee, 1990; Terry, 1994), widespread availability of heath insurance including access to high tech care (Terry, 1994), price increases of health care goods, services, and labor above the general rate of inflation, higher costs for professional liability insurance (Hendee, 1990) and the public's fascination with technologies of all kinds (Coile, 1990). These factors make the careful evaluation of technology an absolute necessity, if decisions regarding its appropriate application are to be made and rational public policies for the allocation of health care resources are to be written (Coile, 1990; Perry, Pillar, and Radany, 1990). Technological change has been identified as the most important controllable component of health care, and as such, no plan to limit the health care budget will be successful unless it influences the application of medical technology.

There are ways to confront the dilemma of controlling technology costs while delivering quality care (Coile, 1990; Perry, Pillar, and Radany, 1990). In order to reap the maximum benefits of health expenditures, more information is required about what works, in what settings, and at what cost. The number of well designed clinical trials has increased in recent years; however, many technologies are not subjected to rigorous evaluation and random trials leave substantial uncertainty about generalizability of findings (Misener, 1990). Premature adoption of some technologies leads to inappropriate use, the potential for harm to patients, and a waste of resources (Perry, Pillar, and Radany, 1990). One can hypothesize that the limitation of ineffective technologies and the replacement of older effective technologies when newer ones demonstrate the ability to improve quality of care and to yield cost savings will enhance not only the quality of health care delivered to patients, but do so in a more cost effective manner.

B. Health Care Technology Life-Cycle

Health care technologies often follow a common life cycle — they are developed, promoted, diffused into medical practice, become obsolete, and dropped from use as superior alternatives emerge (Banta and Thacker, 1990; Matuszewski, 1995). In the investigational stage, the new technology is created, tested, and packaged. This includes laboratory work and clinical studies. The promotional stage begins when the technology is introduced and marketed to the consumer/practice community. Acceptance and utilization follow when the technology becomes incorporated into general medical practice. In the decline phase, the technology is eventually replaced by superior new technology and falls out of general use. The final stage is obsolescence, and the technology is no longer considered appropriate because newer technologies offer greater benefits and/or less harm. Health care technologies can be assessed at different phases in their development and assimilation into practice. The most useful assessment occurs in the late investigational phase and the early promotional phase.

This may imply that all innovation in medicine flows in a linear fashion; however, a high percentage of new medical devices have emerged through the transfer of technologies that were developed elsewhere. Computer technologies, lasers, and ultrasound were all developed outside the medical venue, and then modified to suit the particular needs of the medical sector (Gelijns, 1994). The linear model may also imply a neat distinction between research and development on one hand, and adoption on the other, when in fact much uncertainty associated with a new technology can be resolved only after extensive use in practice (Gelijns, 1994). The endoscope provides one example of this technological evolution. First introduced in the 1950s, major incremental improvements have occurred over the last three decades and have resulted in today's highly sophisticated diagnostic and therapeutic tool. The incremental and continuous process of numerous small advances over time will affect the manner of use, the clinical results achieved, and the resource costs associated with technological intervention. This argues for an evaluative approach that emphasizes periodic reassessment of an intervention during its life-cycle (Gelijns, 1994). This allows for potential adjustments, improvements, and replacements to be made in a timely manner.

C. Technology Assessment and Quality Assessment

Technology assessment and quality assessment are interrelated because medical technologies need to be evaluated if standards for their improved use are to be developed. Perry, Pillar, and Radany (1990) explain that "By scrutinizing technologies and fostering their appropriate use, technology assessment enhances the quality of care for the patient." Comprehensive assessment of any health care technology must include both primary issues (safety, efficacy, efficiency, cost/benefit) and second order consequences (social impact, ethical choices, and legal implications) in order to provide for optimal quality of patient care. Indeed, HCTA supports quality assessment of health care by establishing standards for the use of technology. Perry, Pillar, and Radany (1990) argue

> "In the case of high risk technologies, which carry the potential for harm when mis-used, attention to information gathering and the refinement of standards for their use is particularly critical to the quality of patient care. When these high-risk technologies are also high in cost, the need for technology assessment is even greater because of the implications for national resource allocation availability of scarce resources, and access by the underprivileged."

According to Schwartz (1994) determining what technologies are useless is a relatively simple task, with the challenge being elimination of high-cost, low-benefit care.

Announced with great fanfare and promise, some medical breakthroughs quickly become failures or are soon replaced by other, newer technologies. The list of such disappointments is lengthy, but a few examples are worth noting. Extracorporeal shock wave lithotripsy (ESWL) to remove gallstones was rapidly accepted; but ESWL soon proved disappointing because it was less effective and more painful than originally promised, and was quickly replaced by laparascopic surgery techniques. Optic nerve decompression surgery (ONDS) to treat nonarteritic anterior ischemic optic neuropathy in elderly patients was diffused into practice without the benefit of adequate clinical trials, which when later performed proved the surgical technique to be less effective than watchful waiting, and sometimes even detrimental to the patient. Some technologies, although they initially appear to be promising, are often displaced by other technological or pharmacological innovations. The iron lung provides a classic example of a technology that, while life saving to polio victims during the historical period of polio epidemics, became virtually obsolete with the development of a polio vaccine. In the not so distant future, the same may prove true for kidney dialysis, as there is now the expectation that gene therapy may eradicate diabetes, a primary cause of renal disease and failure.

The previous examples contain a common thread. All are illustrative of medical technologies that no longer are, or in the foreseeable future will be, part of the repertoire of care. In evaluating the merits of medical technologies, assessments of costs and quality of care are essential. As in the cases of ONDS and ESWL, some technologies enter into practice before safety, efficacy, and effectiveness have been established. At best, the implementation of these technologies is costly. At the very worst, the health of the patient may be put at risk, either by the application of an unsafe treatment, or because employment of one technology precludes the offering of another, more effective alternative. In a more positive vein, some technologies such as the emerging possibility of gene therapy may provide the ability to diagnose and treat medical problems in less invasive ways, improve or enhance quality of life, increase human life expectancy, and alleviate much pain and suffering.

The developments in treatment practices during the past decade, if prudently assessed and adopted, can be of great value to efforts aimed at reducing health care costs (Veluchamy and Saver, 1990). This can be demonstrated in the recent shift of patient care to the most cost-effective setting, perhaps ambulatory care centers, primary care clinics or home care (Cerne, 1995). From assessments it should be possible for health care providers to identify whether certain new delivery arrangements will be cost increasing or cost decreasing (Veluchamy and Saver, 1990). As an example, the introduction of new and effective biotechnology drugs has doubled hospital pharmacy budgets in recent years (Lumsdon, 1992). HCTA can also assist decision makers in establishing clinical and social policy because it can address the broader effects of a technology on the health care system and society. The Agency for Health Care Policy and Research (AHCPR) was established in 1989 with the goal of selecting technologies for assessment and providing federal leadership (Banta and Thacker, 1990). These "broader effects may be considered the second concern of quality assessment" (Perry, Pillar, and Radany, 1990).

However, excellence in clinical process requires that highly effective technologies be applied appropriately, correctly, and with skill. Furthermore, potentially effective technology cannot improve health outcomes unless patients have access to it in a timely manner (Misener, 1990). Furthermore, not only must the application of a particular technology achieve a desired outcome for the patient, but the care giver should also be able to identify the steps in the clinical process that contributed to that outcome, and retain them, while eliminating those steps that either add nothing or impede progress. Through careful planning, diligent monitoring, and rapid resolution of identified problems, quality care can be maintained, while providing patients with innovative medical treatment. Major hospitals and health care systems, that utilize proactive assessment and adoption of new technologies will find opportunities to respond to the fast-growing managed care environment. They can become more competitive through team/multi-disciplinary treatment programs and cooperative arrangements with other providers for selected new technologies, helping to deliver efficient care and lowering operating costs (Veluchamy and Saver, 1990).

II. TECHNIQUES OF HEALTH CARE TECHNOLOGY ASSESSMENT

In one fundamental sense HCTA has been an integral part of medical practice since its prehistoric origins. Medical knowledge advanced as humans discovered which herb or root cured or killed the injured or sick person, and how much of the "magical" substance was helpful or harmful. As scientific practice and technology progressed, so did the diversity, power, and utility of methods which could be applied to the study of medicine. Today, the established theoretical approaches and methodologies available for HCTA are extensive and increasingly sophisticated (Weinstein, 1988).

However, in another sense, HCTA is a relatively new subdiscipline closely related to the more general field of technology assessment. The notion of technology assessment came into accepted use in the mid-1960s, and represented a new conceptual and epistemological framework that was soon transferred to health care, bringing with it many advantages. Notably, it emphasized the message that health technologies could be thoroughly evaluated, not only for their immediate health benefits and costs but also for their short- and long-term social consequences (Panerai and Pena Mohr, 1989).

The techniques commonly used by HCTA run the gamut from those which rely on subjective judgment such as various ways of systematically using expert opinion to complex statistical studies relying on multivariate modeling to fiscally-based analyses of benefits and costs. Of course, this growing tool kit is in addition to the long-standing methods of clinical trials and laboratory experimentation.

Earlier it was pointed out that many different criteria can be used to guide HCTA. The choice of criterion — e.g., affordability, effectiveness, quality, safety, social impact — usually shapes the choice of technique. That is, different techniques answer different questions. Consequently, as concerns about medical devices and practices have expanded from the earliest efforts to discover what cures to contemporary questions about cost, risk management, or quality of life, the number of different methodologies adopted for HCTA has increased concomitantly. To a large extent there is task specialization and division of labor in the methods used depending on the question asked and the professional background of the evaluator. Rigorous experimental methodology such as "double-blind" experimentation is the "gold standard" followed by physician-researchers in the determination of the efficacy and safety of a new medical procedure. Benefit/Cost analysis is more likely to be the method of choice by hospital managers when affordability is at issue. Work flow analysis is often used to examine and improve patient management procedures. "Health values" are a key part of the analytic thinking used by health policy planners interested in fostering personal wellness and public health.

Similarly, the choice of HCTA technique is also influenced by the type of decision-making process for which it is intended to provide information, or what is referred to as the level of analysis. Most immediate, HCTA can guide the choice of therapy a physician selects for an individual patient. It is now widely accepted that clinical practice will be guided by the results of HCTA (OTA, 1994). The hospital provides another venue for analysis, especially for decisions about the acquisition of new equipment or the case management of patients. HCTA can also inform health decisions at the community or occupational level, where questions of access or risk management may be under consideration. In its broadest application, HCTA can generate valuable information for use in health policy decisions that have nationwide impact. Developing nations with their very limited financial resources rely increasingly on HCTA to make budget allocations about what type of medical equipment to import or how many new practitioners in a given specialty (e.g., neurology) should be trained during the next five year plan (Panerai and Pena Mohr, 1989).

There are, then, a multitude of assessment approaches and, as might be expected, certain advantages and disadvantages associated with each approach (Hendee, 1991). Any one investigator or any one assessment project may employ a single method or a combination of several techniques, depending on the scope of the issues to be examined (UHC Technology Monitor, 1996). The breadth and scope of these assessment processes and techniques cannot be covered in detail in this chapter. Instead the following subsections briefly describe the more commonly used approaches and illustrate the range of HCTA methodology.

A. Safety Research

Because no health technology is completely safe, the determination of acceptable levels of risk is a vital area of HCTA. How much "undue harm" is acceptable and what is the probability of its occurrence is the focus of safety research. On the surface, what constitutes safety may appear to be quite straightforward, but the degree of safety rests on judgments that balance the nature of the medical problem (e.g., life-threatening) with the likelihood that the medical procedure will be successful, while inflicting only an acceptable level of discomfort (temporary pain instead of death). Of course, these judgments are also influenced by the population affected (children versus the elderly) by the problem (OTA, 1978).

Safety research relies heavily on the use of random controlled clinical trials (RCCTs) and the application of statistical estimates of event probabilities. RCCTs are a complex form of classic experimental designs. Laboratory experiments offer the highest level of internal validity because they physically eliminate the effects of any factor other than the treatment itself. Many different designs for setting up experiments exist, but all rely on the random assignment of subjects (n.b.: random assignment is different from random selection) to the "experimental group" that receives the treatment or to the "control group" that does not receive the treatment. Randomization of subjects to experimental and control groups insures that the variation in personal attributes (e.g., age, race, sex, intelligence, socioeconomic background) are equally distributed among both groups, and therefore their effects are canceled out (Langbein, 1980).

The control group is usually given a placebo, or non-active substance, to insure that positive results are not due to the well-known psychological lift created when attention is given to an individual (the so-called "Hawthorne effect"). Another technique for minimizing bias in experiments is "blinding", or insuring that either the patient ("single-blind"), or both the patient and the physician/researcher ("double-blind), are not aware of which treatment is received.

Safety research, as well as effectiveness research, raises ethical questions of patient comfort, consent, and selection. Because safety research attempts to estimate the risk of a new device or procedure, patients may experience more than just discomfort, they may suffer harm, even if it is by accident. The issue of what constitutes informed consent, especially where the outcomes are still uncertain, has provoked a vociferous debate among health researchers (Bunker, Barnes and Mosteller, 1977). Since the World Medical Association's 1975 Helsinki Declaration on guidelines for doctors engaged in biomedical research on human subjects, the level of protection and information accorded to patient/subjects has been raised to a very high level. Hospitals and other research facilities typically follow a set of institutional guidelines for the protection of human subjects. [see the *Handbook's* chapter on Social and Ethical Choices in Health Care]. An important recent development in the study of the safety of medical practices is the examination of the psychological impact of the procedure or therapy on the patient/subject.

B. Effectiveness Research

In 1989 when the U.S. Congress created the Agency for Health Care Policy and Research (AHCPR), it charged (Public Law 101-239) the agency with the evaluation of clinical practice for the specific purpose of identifying effective care and disseminating knowledge about effective care patterns (OTA, 1994: 2). The tools for studying the effectiveness of health technologies fall into four broad categories, each of which has application to particular issues and makes use of distinctive analytic techniques.

The first and most basic approach to assessing effectiveness "requires an evaluation of whether the health-related outcomes resulting from the use of that intervention are better than would have been expected without it" (OTA, 1994). Now the simplest outcome measure is death, but since a prime goal of medical practice is to avoid high fatality rates, health status measurement emerged early on as an important indicator of effectiveness. Beginning in the 1940s and 1950s with indices such as the Karnofsky Index and the Activities of Daily Living, these physician-based assessments have been supplemented by patient self-reporting of health. With the development of modern public opinion polling and survey research, patient self-assessment has been transformed into multi-faceted questionnaires such as the Quality of Well Being Scale and the Sickness Impact Profile. These types of questionnaires seek information about a person's level of functional ability, perceived health, psychological well-being, and role functioning. Currently, these self-assessment tools are deemed to be reliable and valid for monitoring health status and for comparing the outcomes of different therapies in clinical trials. There is some debate over the use of quality of life surveys as the basis for community or national health policy decisions.

A second major category of effectiveness research relies on the epidemiological studies of patient outcomes. Observational and experimental studies are well developed methodologies and familiar to all in the health professions. Random Controlled Clinical Trials (RCCTs) are used primarily to establish the general efficacy of a device or drug. However, because experimental results do not always hold in general practice, effectiveness research also relies on observational techniques such as case-control and cohort analyses.

The crucial distinction between efficacy and effectiveness comes into play with the study of safety once the drug or procedure enters general use. A drug or practice which was very efficacious in the laboratory may result in terrible tragedies when used in general practice, as exemplified by the classic case of the drug Thalidomide. In other words, a medical procedure which relieves a given condition based on laboratory tests may well exhibit a much lower level of benefit once the procedure enters clinical use. Consequently, much of the focus of HCTA is on the workings of normal medical practice outside the totally controlled world of laboratory experiments.

Statistical analyses of public health records provide another powerful tool for monitoring the effectiveness and safety of health care technologies, once they enter into widespread use. In the last decade health researchers have attempted to exploit the extensive administrative databases compiled by government health agencies and by private insurance companies as a means of statistically testing the effectiveness of given treatments. The case for substituting database analysis for random clinical trials rests on the advantages of information drawn from large numbers of persons, about the ordinary world of general practice, the unobtrusive availability and low cost of the data, and the ability to track the health of individuals over time (OTA, 1994). Although classic laboratory experiments no longer are the sole method in effectiveness studies, newer and simpler forms of large-scale random trials have been developed to permit the widespread testing of a given treatment. Also growing in popularity are so-called "firm trials" in which patients are randomized among entire clinics or other institutional settings such as jails (Neuhauser, 1991; OTA, 1994).

A third major category of effectiveness research relies on synthesizing the results of previous research. A review of the existing literature on original research or on previously conducted evaluations helps immeasurably in the preparation of the design, methods, data analysis, and interpretation of results.

> "The basic idea behind these synthesis methods is that through the use of systematic and comprehensive retrieval practices (accumulation of prior studies), quantification of results using a common metric such as effect size, and statistical aggregation of the collection of results, it is possible to derive a more accurate and useful portrayal of what is known and not known about a given topic" (Cordray and Fischer, 1994).

Meta-analysis is a quantitative method used to answer specific questions about a particular technology. The evaluator's interest may be on such topics as treatment effectiveness, group differences, and test validity. This method "assumes that certain questions can be addressed by combining several reports that individually yield only equivocal answers to the questions" (Hendee, 1991). Through a systematic review of previous research on a given topic, evaluation synthesis provides a summary or synthesis of the types of studies conducted, methodologies used, population samples, location and demographic traits, and results obtained. Evaluation synthesis (ES) differs from Meta-Analysis in that ES takes a more programmatic level approach to summarizing previous studies. Instead of a focus on treatment effectiveness at the patient level, ES explores cost-effectiveness, identifies exemplary treatments, and analyzes components deemed to be critical to success or failure (Cordray and Fischer, 1994).

A fourth methodological strategy to assessing effectiveness relies on quantitative decision analysis, which consists of a class of models that can illuminate the problems of choice under conditions of uncertainty. Panerai and Pena Mohr (1989) observe:

> "The method was initially applied to problems involving the clinical management of individual patients, where uncertainties of diagnosis and treatment make its use extremely appealing. More recently, it has been recognized that decision analysis can also be useful in dealing with public health problems and, undoubtedly, in the evaluation of health technologies."

Proposed by Lusted (1971) as a method for HCTA, decision analysis has become widely adopted because it helps lay out options and outcomes so that the utility or value of different courses of action can be weighed one against the other. It should be noted that determination of the various options and the value of their outcomes is a function of the preferences the analyst incorporates into the analysis. A continuing criticism of decision analysis is that different analysts may well use different estimates of preferences when modeling the same problem.

C. Cost-effectiveness Research

Consumers and providers of health care are equally concerned about its costs. While in the past it may have been possible to provide care regardless of cost, contemporary decisions about all aspects of health care increasingly include a fiscal calculus. Combining cost figures with effectiveness research produces an important class of HCTA techniques. Cost-effectiveness (CE) analyses are more than mere accounting exercises. They seek to answer questions of efficiency and productivity. Even without patient and taxpayer pressure to hold down the price of medical care, physicians and hospital managers need to estimate the benefits and costs of alternative technologies in order to maximize their available resources as well as to maximize the positive effects provided by the physician and the hospital (Garber, 1996).

There are several variants of CE analysis, each with its own strengths and weakness. The oldest form of CE analysis is benefit/cost analysis which "is an applied branch of economics that attempts to assess service programs by determining whether total societal welfare has increased (in the aggregate more people have been made better off) because of the project or program" (Kee, 1994). Benefit/Cost (B/C) analysis follows three deceptively simple steps (1) determine the benefits of the intervention or treatment and their dollar value, (2) compute the total costs of the treatment, and (3) compare benefits to costs, usually by computing a B/C ratio (Kee, 1994).

The challenge in B/C analysis as applied to HCTA is to estimate the dollar value of many intangible benefits and costs associated with health technologies. Evaluators often use an accounting technique known as shadow pricing, by which a substitute value is computed when an actual market price can be directly determined (Chambers, Wedel, and Rodwell, 1992). Four analytic techniques are commonly used to estimate the value of life and limb for purposes of B/C analysis (Eastaugh, 1992). One of the most common pricing strategies is the 'willingness to pay' (WTP) approach developed by Schelling (1968) which uses opinion polling to estimate how much people would be willing to pay to receive a service if the person was faced by a known risk of some danger or probability of avoiding some specified injury. One of the oldest forms of pricing intangibles is the discounted future earnings (DFE) technique which is used extensively for computing the cost to an individual of a health event such as a stroke. A third method of price estimation is labor market imputed willingness to pay (LWTP) which attempts to calculate what someone else might be willing to pay for one's life or limb, as exemplified by higher wages.

More recently, a fourth approach to health care prices tries to measure the quality of life. The typical procedure for Quality-Adjusted Life Years (QALY) analysis relies on statistical analysis to compute survival rates and sum the quality-weighted years of life per capita for a given treatment group. The key to QALY analysis is the development of an index of life quality which takes into account such factors as life-style, degree of pain, and support required. Cost-utility analysis, a variant of cost-effectiveness analysis, relies on QALY indicators in order to compare procedures or practices which yield outcomes that are not particularly similar (the apple and oranges problem). Cost-utility analysis (CUA) attempts to take cost analysis beyond simple accounting costs by converting qualitatively different outcomes into a standard unit of health. CUA's appeal derives from its ability to permit the comparison of health technologies while avoiding the problem of having to assign a dollar value to a given life.

HCTA at the communitywide level uses cost of illness (COI) computations "to convey in some quantifiable way the impact of illness on the U.S. economy" (Kenkel, 1994). COI analysis measures medical expenditures and foregone earnings due to illness, and then goes on to project the benefits of any health practice or program against these costs. Kenkel (1994) explains "The reasoning is clear: if illness imposes the costs of medical expenditures and foregone earnings, a reduction in illness yields benefits equal to the costs saved." Although COI analyses are very useful in estimating communitywide costs due to inattention to a health problem, COI analysis is less helpful in making the case for individual financial contributions to the acquisition of new health technology because COI estimates usually do not take into account willingness to pay.

None of these approaches to cost analysis are simple and all involve trade-offs of values that are differentially important to different persons. Beyond the well-known methodological issues related to benefit/cost analysis that economists have wrestled with for years, the growing reliance of HCTA on cost analysis poses other important issues which must be resolved. Two obvious problems are comparability and quality. The almost daily announcements about biomedical research which claims to have found the cure for a dreaded disease or the means to extend life has made the general public wary of competing studies and their often contradictory results. Similarly, cost analyses conducted by different researchers need to incorporate similar approaches and standard measures, otherwise their generalizability will be minimal. Likewise, analyses which do not follow accepted, basic principles of sound research and cost accounting will not yield results with credible validity. Finally, the growing popularity of cost-utility analysis "introduces two dangers: decision-makers may not fully understand the implications of the values that CUA incorporates; and they may not fully realize that although some values are quantified and incorporated into CUA results, other equally important values are not" [bold in the original] (OTA, 1994). Eastaugh (1992) summarizes the general value of cost-effectiveness analysis to HCTA by noting "At the present time technology assessment does not provide the individual doctor with a court-sanctioned set of guidelines to make cost or quality trade-offs at the patient's bedside...Technology assessment mainly assists reimbursement decisions for what services should be covered by government or the company insurance plan."

To briefly summarize about assessment methods, it is important to point out that authors of technology assessment reports attempt to minimize errors by following the steps expected of any scientific study. Data and criteria used in the evaluation are made public. Investigators are expected to include clear descriptions of the assumptions, definitions, measures, techniques, and results. Use of a sensitivity analysis to demonstrate the consequences of altering uncertain assumptions is highly recommended when possible to perform. Because the decisions of health policy makers, hospital administrators, and individual care givers all depend on the availability of systematic evidence about the effectiveness, affordability, and safety of new as well as established health technologies, HCTA professionals must adhere to the norms of sound evaluation methods in order to produce the very best possible analysis that is permitted by the time, money, and skill allocated to the assessment. "Impartiality, critical judgment, expertise in the form of technology discussed and its alternatives, and command of the relevant methods distinguish the best assessors; the best evaluations are complete, explicit, and balanced" (Fuchs, 1990).

SUMMARY

Decisions about the use of expensive technologies continue to be made without the analysis of their safety, effectiveness, or affordability. As recently as 1994, it was reported in the Annals of Internal Medicine that not a single study examining the effect on patient outcomes of the use of magnetic resonance imaging (MRI) could be found. Astonishingly, more than 2,000 MRI scanners, at an average cost of $1.5 million each, were being operated around the United States, and patients were being charged approximately $900 to $1,200 per scan. Yet, "not one controlled study of diagnostic accuracy or changes in therapeutic choices documented patients benefits" had been conducted as of 1994 (Sultz and Young, 1997)!

Technology assessment functions at the intersection of several issues that dominate decisions about the delivery of health care (Institute of Medicine, 1996). Whether the concern is the well-being of the individual patient, the quality of care available to a community, or the ability to provide sufficient resources to make adequate care available to all citizens, legitimate decisions about these issues are not possible without the use of HCTA. As society attempts to balance price, consumer value, and health status improvement, HCTA must become an integral component of health policy-making and medical practice. Until this happens at all levels of the health community, decisions will continue to be made with less than sufficient information.

REFERENCES

Agency for Health Care Policy Research. (1990). AHCPR Program Note. NSDMMS, PHS., Rockville, MD.

Banta, D. (1987, March). Clinical Trials and Technology Assessment. *Quality Review Bulletin*, 94-98.

Banta, H. D., and Thacker, S. B. (1990, July 11). The Case for Reassessment of Health Care Technology: Once is Not Enough. *Journal of the American Medical Association*, 264(2): 235-239.

Bunker, J. P., Barnes, B. A., and Mosteller, F. (Eds.). (1977). *Costs, Risks, and Benefits of Surgery*. Oxford University Press, New York, NY.

Cerne, F. (1995, July 20). Transforming Vision Into Achievement. *Hospital and Health Networks*, 25-30.

Chambers, D. E., Wedel, K. R., and Rodwell, M. K. (1992). *Evaluating Social Programs*. Allyn and Bacon, Boston, MA: 242.

Coile, R. C. (1990, Jan./Feb.). The 'Racers Edge' in Hospital Competition: Strategic Technology Plan. *Healthcare Executive*, 21-24.

Cordray, D. S., and Fischer, R. L. (1994). Synthesizing Evaluation Findings. In J. S. Wholey, H. P. Hatry, and K. E. Newcomer (Eds.). *Handbook of Practical Program Evaluation*. (198- 231). Jossey-Bass, San Francisco, CA.

Eastaugh, S. R. (1992). Health Economics: Efficiency, Quality, and Equity. Auburn House, Westport, CT: 377-387.

Franklin, C. (1993). Basic Concepts and Fundamental Issues in Technology Assessment. *Intensive Care Medicine*, 19: 117-121.

Fryback, D. G. (1990). Technology Evaluation-Applying Cost-effectiveness Analysis for Health Technology Assessment. *Decisions in Imaging Economics*, 1: 4-9.

Fuchs, V. R. (1990). The New Technology Assessment. *The New England Journal of Medicine, 323* (10): 673-677.

Garber, A. M. (1996, Jan.). Cost-Effectiveness Analysis as a Measure of Value. *Technologia*, 1-6. Blue Cross and Blue Shield Association, Chicago, IL.

Gelijns, A. (1994, Summer). The Dynamics of Technological Change in Medicine. *Health Affairs*, 29-46.

Goodman, C. S. (1993). Technology Assessment in Healthcare: A Means for Pursuing the Goals of Biomedical Engineering. *Medical and Biological Engineering and Computing*, 31, HTA3-HTA10.

Hendee, W. R. (1990, June). Technology Transfer and Cost Constraints in Medicine. *Investigative Radiology*, 25: 745-747.

Hendee, W. R. (1991). Technology Assessment in Medicine: Methods, Status and Trends. *Medical Progress Through Technology*, 17: 69-75.

Hillman, A. L. (1995, Mar./April). Economic Analysis in Technology Assessment. *Imaging Economics*.

Hospital Association of New York State (1991, May). Medical Technology Assessment—A Model for Informed Decision Making.

Kee, J. E. (1994). Benefit-Cost Analysis in Program Evaluation. In J.S. Wholey, H.P. Hatry, and K. E. Newcomer (Eds.). *Handbook of Practical Program Evaluation*. (456-488). Jossey-Bass, San Francisco, CA.

Kenkel, D. (1994). Cost of Illness Approach. In G. Tolley, D. Kenkel, and R. Fabian (Eds.). *Valuing Health for Policy: An Economics Approach*. (42-71). University of Chicago Press, Chicago, IL.

Jennings, J. R., and Weinstein, A. (1991). Technology Assessment. Why Hospitals Must Get Serious. *Decisions in Imaging Economics*, 31-35.

Langbein, L. I. (1980). *Discovering Whether Programs Work: A Guide to Statistical Methods for Program Evaluation*. Goodyear Publishing Co, Santa Monica, CA.

Legorreta, A. P., Silber, J. H., Costantino, G. N., Kobylinski, R. W., and Zatz, S. L. (1993, Sept. 22/29). Increased Cholecystectomy Rate After the Introduction of Laparoscopic cholecystectomy. *The Journal of the American Medical Association*, 270(12): 1429-1432.

Lumsdon, K. (1992, Aug. 5). Beyond Tech Assessment: Balancing Needs, Strategy. *Hospitals*, 66: 20-26.

Lusted, L. B. (1971, Feb.). Decision Making Studies in Patient Management. *New England Journal of Medicine*, 284,(8): 416-424.

McGregor, M. (1989, Jan. 12). Sounding Board-Technology and the Allocation of Resources. The *New England Journal of Medicine*, 320(2): 118-120.

Misener, J. H. (1990, June). The Impact of Technology on the Quality of Health Care. *Quarterly Review Bulletin*, 209-213.

Neuhauser, D. (1991). Parallel Providers, Ongoing Randomization, and Continuous Improvement. *Medical Care*, 29(7): JS5-8.

Office of Technology Assessment. (1976). *Development of Medical Technology: Opportunities For Assessment*. U.S. Government Printing Office, Washington, DC.

Office of Technology Assessment. (1978). *Assessing The Efficacy and Safety of Medical Technologies*. (OTA-H-75). U.S. Government Printing Office, Washington, DC.

Office of Technology Assessment. (1980). The Implications of Cost-Effectiveness Analysis of Medical Technology. Background Paper #4: *The Management Of Health Care Technology In Ten Countries*. (OTA-BP-H-7). U.S. Government Printing Office, Washington, DC.

Office of Technology Assessment. (1993). *Researching Health Risks*. (OTA-BBS-571). U.S. Government Printing Office, Washington, DC.

Office of Technology Assessment. (1994). *Identifying Health Technologies That Work: Searching for Evidence*. (OTA-H-608). U.S. Government Printing Office, Washington, DC.

Office of Technology Assessment. (1995). *Tools for Evaluating Health Technologies: Five Background Papers.* (OTA-BP-H-142). U.S. Government Printing Office, Washington, DC.

Panerai, R. B., and Pena Mohr, J. (1989). *Health Technology Assessment Methodologies for Developing Countries.* Pan American Health Organization, Washington, DC.

Perry, S., Pillar, B., and Radany, M. H. (1990, June 16). The Appropriate Use of High-Cost, High-Risk Technologies: The Case of Total Parenteral Nutrition, *Quarterly Review Bulletin,* 6: 214-217.

Power, E. J., Tunis, S. R., and Wagner, J. L. (1994). Technology Assessment and Public Health. *Annual Review of Public Health, 15:* 561-79.

Reiser, S. J., and Ross, G.T. (1992, Aug. 5). *Out of Chaos: A Rational Approach to Assessing Technology. Hospitals, 66:* 22-23.

Schelling, T. (1968). The Life You Save May Be Your Own. In S. Chase (Ed.), *Problems in Public Expenditure Analysis* (127-162). Brookings Institution, Washington, DC.

Schwartz, W. (1994). *Interviewed as quoted in Terry* (1994), 124.

Steinberg, E. P., and Graziano, S. (1990, June). Integrating Technology Assessment and Medical Practice Evaluation Into Hospital Operations. *Quarterly Review Bulletin,* 218-222.

Terry, K. (1994, March 21). Technology: The Biggest Health-Care Cost-Driver of All: Can We Curb Its Rise? *Medical Economics,* 124-137.

University Hospital Consortium. (1996). UHC Technology Assessment Monitor-A Guide to Published Technology Assessments, 1995. Author, Oak Brook, IL.

Veluchamy, S., and Saver, C. I. (1990, June). Clinical Technology Assessment, Cost-Effective Adoption, and Quality Management by Hospitals in the 1990's. *Quality Review Bulletin-228.*

Weinstein, M. C. (1988). Economic Techniques for Technology Assessment. In F.F.H. Rutten and S. J. Reiser (Eds.), *The Economics of Medical Technology* (p. 44). Springer-Verlag, Berlin.

31.
OUTCOMES ASSESSMENT AND QUALITY OF LIFE MEASUREMENT

Judith T. Barr, *Northeastern University, Boston, MA*

Outcomes assessment and health-related quality of life are two of the most timely issues in American health care today. These two topics are interconnected, one a subset of the other. Broadly stated, outcomes assessment is a comprehensive and integrated system of assessments to measure the efficiency and effectiveness of health care services and interventions. Health-related quality of life is a more focused, patient-centered, multidimensional concept that should be measured and included in an outcomes assessment system.

Outcomes assessment asks the question: are the services and therapies we provide patients improving their status or at least preventing or slowing further deterioration of their conditions and are they provided as efficiently as possible? In other words, are our treatments effective? Are patients better because they receive these services? Have we made a difference in patient's end results or "outcomes?" Because the answers to these questions will be used to shape health policies and reimbursement decisions, the outcomes assessment process requires that the results can be generalizable to a broad population. Therefore, unlike clinical trials or efficacy research that is conducted in ideal and controlled conditions, outcomes assessment or effectiveness research is conducted in the "real world" by average practitioners under ordinary circumstances with typical patients.

Notice that the "outcomes" in outcomes assessment is plural. This indicates that the outcomes assessment process generally uses more than one measure to determine the effectiveness of a service or intervention; it is an outcome assessment system. A comprehensive battery of outcome measures, appropriate for the clinical condition and intervention being assessed, is included in the assessment. Outcomes assessment requires that more than a biologic or pathophysiologic variable be measured to judge the effectiveness of treatments or interventions; it means more than pulmonary function tests, range of motion, grip strength or activities of daily living. Epstein describes outcomes assessment, effectiveness research, and the outcomes movement in this way:

> Perhaps the most important effect of the outcomes movement has been a broadening of our focus to include a wider range of outcomes...We have seen a dramatic expansion in the range of outcomes that physicians and policy makers are willing to consider valid indicators of health. These go beyond traditional clinical indexes and include a series of variables assessed through interviews: functional status, emotional health, social interaction, cognitive function, degree of disability, and so forth. There is a growing appreciation in the medical community that instruments based on subjective data from patients can provide important information that may not be evident from physiologic measurements and may be as reliable as — or more reliable than — many of the clinical, biochemical, or physiologic indexes (Epstein, 1990).

This chapter will first describe why there is an "outcomes movement" and review some earlier strategies for including measures of outcomes in quality of care assessments. Then we will define the concept of "health" which serves as the foundation for the development of health-related quality of life measures. We will compare the health model to models of disability/handicap and discuss the implications of the different approaches to the design of outcomes assessment measures. We will describe the construct of health-related quality of life (HRQL), summarize the content of several HRQL measures, and review some operational characteristics that should be considered when selecting measures to assess patient status and to evaluate the effectiveness of clinical interventions. Lastly we will link outcomes assessment to quality assurance and total quality management programs.

I. WHY IS THERE AN OUTCOMES ASSESSMENT MOVEMENT?

The outcomes assessment movement is a powerful force in health care today. It is fueled by two principal objectives — one economic and one humanistic. While these two objectives originate from different constituencies, they converge in a demand to evaluate our health care practices and provide only cost-efficient and effective, patient-centered health care.

A. The Economic Objective

American health care is expensive. In 1996, the United States spent more than $1 trillion on health care services. That averages to more than $3,600 for every man, woman, and child in this country and more per person than any other country on earth. Perhaps if we as a country had the best health in the world, the expenditure could be justified. But, we don't. Compared to twenty other industrialized countries, the United States is near the top in infant mortality and low birth-weights as a percent of births and only in the middle of the pack as measured by years of life expectancy (Schieber, Poulier and Greenwald, 1994).

We are investing more in health care than any other country, but it appears that we are not getting the most value for our money. Nearly 25 years ago, Wennberg and colleagues found early indications of a disconnect between the quantity of health care inputs and the quality of patient outcomes. In studying surgery rates in different counties in New England, they detected huge variations in the rates of elective surgeries such as hysterectomies and tonsillectomies after adjusting for differences in population density, income and age (Wennberg and Gittelsohn, 1973). Here's an example so you understand what this means. Imagine you could exactly duplicate 100 children and then place one group of 100 children in County A and the other group in County B. Over time, 80% of the children in County A had tonsillectomies, but only 40% of the same children in County B had the surgery, with no difference in outcome. It is likely that this implies that half of the surgeries performed in County A were not necessary and that the money associated with that care was wasted.

Since then, the use of Wennberg's analytic technique, called variation analysis, has detected wide differences in how clinicians use other health care services. Insurance companies, seeing these large variations in inputs (health care services) with no apparent differences in outputs (patient outcomes), question why they should pay for services that do not improve patient outcome. In addition to variations in practice, they see health care dollars being wasted on treatments and interventions which have never rigorously been proven to be of clinical benefit. For example, few rehabilitation practices have been evaluated for their efficacy in carefully controlled circumstances or for their effectiveness in typical clinical situations (Fuhrer, 1995). Therefore, third party payers argue that all services should be evaluated and if a therapeutic intervention is found to be ineffective or diagnostic procedures do not provide useful information, payments for those services should be discontinued and the money either saved or transferred to support other interventions or procedures which have been proven to be effective.

Thus cost reduction is the economic objective behind outcomes assessment — a need to create a more cost-efficient, and clinically effective, national health care delivery system. Our nation is spending more on health care services than any other country, but it appears that we are not getting our money's worth. Variation analysis tells us that there is waste in the system; clinical effectiveness research will tell us what health care services are of little or no value. Based on this information, third party payers such as insurance groups, self-insured businesses and federal and state governments will demand that clinically ineffective services and areas of waste be identified and eliminated. Then, health care expenses can be reduced by not paying for those services.

These economic issues affect clinical practice. Either directly or indirectly, economic evaluation of health care practices will affect what services are provided, the frequency with which they are provided, and the payment that will be received. As more health care is delivered through managed care systems and as more health clinicians are paid by capitation systems, there will be even further scrutiny of the value received for the health care dollar. Therapists, including rehabilitation and other therapists, will have to demonstrate that the services they provide are clinically effective and that the recommended duration of treatment is necessary. If the effectiveness of a treatment is not established, payment will no longer be made for that service. Over time, the economic pressure to reduce costs and the outcomes assessment pressure to demonstrate clinical effectiveness will modify professional practices of all health professionals.

II. THE HUMANISTIC COMPONENT

The inclusion of the individual patient's perspective is the humanistic objective behind the outcomes movement. This humanistic component considers the patient's, rather than only the provider's or insurer's perspective in the assessment of the clinical effectiveness of procedures and interventions. Providers traditionally have used mortality, morbidity, physiologic, other biomedical, or limited physical functional measures to judge the effectiveness of their services. Rarely are patients queried as to what values they place on different health states and what changes in their clinical condition they perceive to be most beneficial. If they are consulted, patient-identified and provider-identified priorities are frequently in conflict. Further problems arise when effective team communication is inhibited by each health profession's use of its own discipline-specific measurement tools; providers do not speak a common assessment language. Patient-centered outcomes measures would not only introduce a patient perspective into clinical effectiveness studies, but would also provide a common assessment vocabulary for cross-disciplinary discussion of patients needs, planning of treatment strategies, and assessment of clinical effectiveness.

Patient-centered outcomes assessment builds upon the World Health Organization's definition of health as "a complete state of physical, mental, and social well-being and not merely the absence of disease" (WHO, 1948). From this perspective, health is a multidimensional concept. Patient-centered outcomes assessment requires that clinical effectiveness studies evaluate these components of health and that more than a biologic or pathophysiologic measurement be performed before and after treatments or interventions. No longer are pulmonary function tests, range of motion, grip strength, or exercise endurance sufficient outcome measures to evaluate clinical effectiveness.

Traditionally, as shown in Figure 1, the practice community evaluates an intervention using such outcome measures as efficacy (evaluation under ideal conditions, frequently relying upon physiologic measures), safety, and costs. However, a patient-centered outcomes assessment recognizes that patients have their own values, beliefs and judgments which can filter the impact of an intervention in different ways. To patients, the effectiveness of an intervention is judged by its effect on their physical status, mental status and psychological well-being, social interactions, and economic stability. Because assessment measures and values of importance to the practice community and patient populations may vary, different conclusions may be reached by the two groups concerning the same intervention. Clinicians may judge a cardiac rehabilitation program to be successful if a patient loses weight, improves his diet, and increases exercise endurance. However, the heart attack has been a severe jolt to the patient who now has come face-to-face with his own mortality. He may be believe that a return to his high stress position may cause a reoccurrence. If the patient's values and beliefs are not incorporated into the assessment system, these concerns, if undetected, could lead to depression and functional limitations in his professional role. The patient's physical function may improve as a result of the program, but a more complete, patient-centered assessment of health will detect that he still has psychological and role functioning problems.

While physical functional assessment is not new to such allied health professionals as physical therapists and occupational therapists, studies incorporating broader

Figure 1 - Impact of health intervention as typically judged by the health care system, then filtered by patient's values, beliefs, and judgements (WHO, 1948, modified).

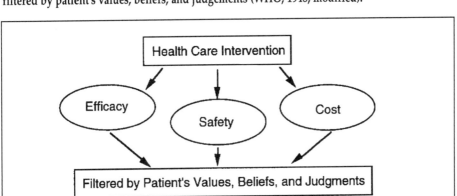

assessments of health are rarely found in the allied health literature (Barr, 1993). Ellwood described these broader measures as "a technology of patient experience designed to help patients, payers, and providers make rational medical care-related choices based on better insight into the effect of these choices on the patient's life. It would routinely and systematically measure the functioning and well-being of patients, along with disease-specific clinical outcomes." Ellwood proposes that these types of measurements be central to the development of a longitudinal type of outcomes assessment based on patient-centered assessment: "The centerpiece and unifying ingredient of outcomes management is the tracking and measurement of function and well-being or quality of life" across healthcare locations (Ellwood, 1988).

In summary, there has been a convergence of two communities of interest: the economist's interest to reduce health care costs and the humanist's interest to include patient's values and beliefs in the evaluation of health care services. The result is the patient-centered, outcomes assessment movement. When the two interests work in harmony, they produce a more cost-efficient and effective delivery system that directs attention specifically to individual patients and their well-being.

III. EARLIER APPROACHES TO MEASURING OUTCOMES

The measurement of patient outcomes was an important element in the evaluation strategies of two early pioneers of quality of care assessment. Neither was motivated by cost-reduction concerns; rather, they both were interested in using measurement strategies to improve the quality, and to standardize the delivery of care. And both have important messages that we should consider as we develop cost-efficient, patient-centered, outcomes assessment programs.

A. The "End Result" Proposal: the Codman Approach

In 1913 Dr. E. A. Codman proposed the "End Result" approach (Codman, 1914). Codman, an early pioneer in quality of care measurement, was concerned with the lack of information concerning the effectiveness of medical practices, the skill of practitioners, and the quality of American hospitals. He suggested that hospitals adopt a business approach and issue an annual report detailing the products or "end results" of their care. He argued that the information contained in annual reports of the times (the number of patients treated, the annual budget, the number of residents trained, and the number of papers published by the staff) was of no value. What was needed was a new approach to determine if the procedures were effective and to measure if patients improved, the ultimate "end result."

Codman's "End Result" proposal was based on patient outcomes. If the mission of medical care was to cure patients, Codman reasoned that the evaluation of the care should not be based on what procedures the patient received, but rather what was the patient's outcome. Therefore, the effectiveness of care was not based on whether the patient was admitted to the hospital or whether surgery was performed. To Codman, the ultimate evaluation of the medical care provided, the "end result," was a "satisfied and relieved" patient, one who could resume function in the community after receiving medical treatment. To operationalize the "end result" proposal, Codman trained a group of social workers who followed the patient into the community after hospital discharge to measure the "end result" of care. If "satisfied and relieved" patients returned to their former function, then the treatment they received could be considered to be effective and the practitioners who provided that care were judged to be skillful.

Codman had all the stature and credentials to force serious consideration of this proposal by the organized medical community. He was a faculty member at Harvard Medical School, a surgeon at Massachusetts General Hospital, chairman of the local medical society, and a delegate to the American Medical Association. However, all of that was not enough. Codman's End Stage Idea was judged too radical, or perhaps too much of a threat to physician autonomy. He was asked to resign from his positions at both Harvard Medical School and Massachusetts General Hospital. Nearly 10 years later, he wrote "Although the End Result Idea may not achieve its entire fulfillment for several generations...I am able to enjoy the hypothesis that I may receive some honors from a more receptive generation," (Codman, 1914).

There are important lessons from the "End Result" proposal. First is the need to evaluate the effectiveness of our practices by measuring the therapeutic impact on patients in their everyday functioning. That involves a broad assessment of functioning — not only physical functioning, but also psychological and social functioning. Now that valid and reliable, patient-centered outcome measures are available, we can perform this type of assessment; we just have to use them. However, if and when we do use them, the assessment frequently is performed within the health care setting after the health intervention has been completed. Codman's End Result Idea tells us that this is too soon and in the wrong location. In addition to the discharge evaluations, assessments also should be conducted in the home and work environments, in the "community," 3 to 6 months after the end of the treatment. That would provide enough time to determine the true effectiveness of the intervention. This measurement strategy is more challenging and perhaps more costly, but it will yield a more accurate reflection of the value of health care services to patients. Self-administered, multidimensional assessments may be economical methods to accomplish this goal.

And of course, another lesson from Codman is never to give up on a good idea. Its time will come.

B. Outcomes as a Component of Quality of Care: the Donabedian Approach

Alexis Donabedian is the father of the traditional quality of care measurement model, a model based on the evaluation of three components of care: structure, process, and outcome (Donabedian, 1966). A solid structure must be provided to provide care, the proper processes must be followed to deliver that care, and then the outcomes must be measured to evaluate the effectiveness of the care. In this model, the quality of the structure component includes factors related to the structure of a health care delivery system including its buildings, equipment, and staff. This can consist of an assessment of physical features such as the adequacy and quality of facilities and equipment and conformance to building codes and other standards, as well as the qualifications and experience of staff, personnel staffing patterns, organizational reporting and financing arrangements, and other administrative elements. In allied health practices, examples of structure components include adequacy of rehabilitation equipment, characteristics and location of treatment sites, and qualification and organization of the clinical staff.

The *process* component consists of activities involved in the process of delivering health care services, including the technical and interpersonal actions of health providers and patients, as well as organizational processes within the health care system. If clinical pathways have been developed, the quality of the process of care can be assessed by determining how closely the health provider has followed the designated course of care. Other process examples include the number of hours of therapy, the type of treatment modalities used in providing care, individual versus group therapy sessions, and the temporal placement of treatments within the disease course.

The *outcome* component of the Donabedian model examines the effect of a health care intervention on the outcome of the patient and, from a delivery system or societal perspective, the impact on the economic performance of the health care system. While the health status of the individual is the ultimate criterion to assess the outcome of an intervention or service, the economic impact is an important societal outcome.

Donabedian's structure-process-outcome model of quality of care assessment does not include a clear definition of health status which could be used to guide the outcome measurement component. Generally, the traditional measurement of rehabilitation outcomes has taken a provider-oriented approach and has focused on physiologic variables, range of motion, gait, grip strength, activities of daily living, and independent activities of daily living. In the structure-process-outcome model, evaluators tend to independently measure narrow individual elements rather than recognizing and assessing the interplay among the three components.

The important lesson from Donabedian is that the outcomes of an intervention are influenced by a host of structural and process factors. In many cases we do not know what is the best way to provide a service, but we can use outcomes information to help us. For example in cardiac rehabilitation, how soon after the heart attack should a person begin a program? How many hours are necessary? Should it include psychological counseling in addition to exercise strengthening and diet modification? Do individual versus group sessions make a difference? What patient co-morbidities and other characteristics affect outcomes? Does it make a difference if physical therapists, exercise physiologists, occupational therapists, or physicians are in charge of the program? To answer these questions, researchers are studying variations in the outcomes of care to identify the most efficient and effective structures and processes that produce the best outcomes of care. The use of outcomes information to improve the structure and process of care will be developed in a later section of this chapter.

IV. COMPARING MODELS OF HANDICAP / DISABILITY TO A COMPREHENSIVE OUTCOMES ASSESSMENT SYSTEM

In most parts of the world, rehabilitation studies rely upon the World Health Organization's International Classification of Impairment, Disabilities, and Handicaps (ICIDH) to provide a framework to organize and classify information about the consequences of disease (WHO, 1980). However, in the United States, the Nagi model of disability is used for descriptive classification purposes in rehabilitation assessment. This has led to confusion in the rehabilitation literature because the two models have different classifications and names for essentially the same functional state. Both models use practitioner-assessed, descriptive systems and generally do not incorporate patient-centered, self-assessments of functional abilities. However, they are presented to enable the reader to make the connections between the two rehabilitation models and then compare both to a more comprehensive, operational model of patient outcomes that links clinical variables with patient-centered, health-related quality of life outcomes.

V. THE WORLD HEALTH ORGANIZATION'S HANDICAP MODEL

The World Health Organization's International Classification of Impairments, Disabilities and Handicap (ICIDH) provides a model for considering the consequences of chronic disease. It is based on four levels of limitation: disease, impairment, disability, and handicap (WHO, 1980). Disease is a result of an abnormal happening within the individual which changes the structure and functioning of the body. An impairment is any loss or abnormality of psychological, physiological, or anatomical structure or function at the organ level. A disease becomes an impairment when it is "exteriorized" and someone becomes aware of it; however, an impairment may exist without any underlying disease. For example, in some patients hypertension is a "silent" disease, unrecognized by the patient. When detected by a practitioner as a result of a blood pressure reading, it becomes an impairment because it has been exteriorized or recognized.

If the impairment is not corrected, disability may occur. In the WHO/ICIDH model, disability refers to a restriction in the ability of a person to carry out a function or activity in a manner considered normal for a human being. If a person with untreated hypertension suffers a stroke, disability results if the stroke renders that individual unable to communicate via normal speech or maintain a normal walking gait. If the disability limits the individual's ability to function within a normal social and work role, then a handicap is present. Handicap refers to a disadvantage resulting from an impairment or disability that limits or prevents the fulfillment of a role that is normal (depending on age, gender, and sociocultural factors) for the individual. For example, if an altered speech pattern prevents an individual from resuming work or other role responsibilities or if the work environment can not accommodate a the disability, such as being wheelchair accessible, then the individual can not resume his occupational or social responsibilities. The disability, in relation to other people, has become a handicap.

VI. THE NAGI DISABILITY MODEL

The Nagi disability model, more commonly used in the United States, consists of a framework of four distinct but interrelated concepts to describe and classify disease and limitation: active pathology, impairment, functional limitation, and disability (Nagi, 1964; 1991). The state of active pathology develops when an interruption or interference occurs in normal physiologic processes. An impairment indicates a loss of normality of an anatomical, physiological, mental, or emotional nature. Impairments occur as a result of an active pathology, as a residual of a previous active pathology, or as abnormalities not associated with pathologies. Therefore, every pathology involves an impairment, but not every impairment involves a disability.

Functional limitation refers to limitations manifested at the level of the organism, the person, as a whole, not at the level of the tissues, organs, or systems. The same level of functional limitation may result from different impairments. For example, an abnormally low 6-minute walking test could be a result of angina as well as chronic obstructive pulmonary disease. Disability refers to social rather than organismic functioning. It denotes an inability or limitation of an individual to perform socially defined roles within a sociocultural and physical environment such as roles with the family, the employment setting, education, and recreation. Not all functional limitations lead to disability; that depends on the individual's reaction to the functional limitation, the environmental modification to accommodate the functional limitation, and the social support and acceptance of the functional limitation.

VII. THE WILSON-CLEARY OUTCOMES MODEL

While the WHO and Nagi models provide methods to describe and classify disease, Doctors Ira Wilson and Paul Cleary (Wilson and Cleary, 1995) have developed a five part causal pathway to explain and quantitate the relationships between clinical variables and measures of health-related quality of life and the relationships of intervening variables that mediate these effects. Incorporating elements of the WHO/Nagi approaches while expanding the model into areas of patient health perceptions and quality of life, Wilson and Cleary present an integrated outcomes measurement approach that initially can be used to measure patient status, then monitor patient

Figure 2 - The Wilson/Cleary model of patient outcome measures linking clinical variables to health-related quality of life. Reproduced with permission.

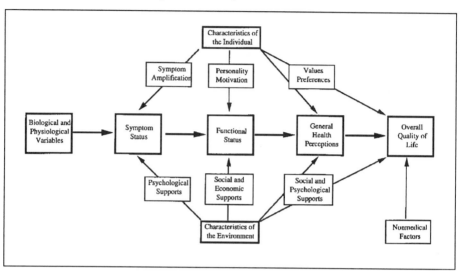

progress during a treatment regimen to determine the effectiveness of care, and finally to manage future patients based on the comparative effectiveness of various treatment strategies. The model is displayed in Figure 2.

The Wilson/Cleary model provides a taxonomy of outcome measures that links the biomedical world of disease causation to the social science world of complex behavior, feelings, and quality of life. As they state:

> We present a taxonomy of patient outcomes that categorizes measures of patient outcome according to the underlying health concepts they represent and proposes specific causal relationships between different health concepts, thereby integrating the two models of health described (biomedical and social science). Because our model focuses on relationships among aspects of health, the taxonomy we develop is not necessarily related to other classifications of health status measures. There is a conceptual difference between identifying the dimensions of health that are necessary to comprehensively and validly describe health and specifying a series of critical concepts on a causal pathway. The latter is our goal. It is not possible to create a one-to-one relationship between our levels and existing health-related quality of life measures because our causal model and the numerous existing measures have fundamentally different, though complementary goals (Wilson and Cleary, 1995).

In the causal pathway (Figure 2), measures of health are presented as existing on a continuum of increasing biological, social, and psychological complexity. Starting on the left, biological and physiological variables can be measured by such traditional methods as laboratory tests that can be used to assess the functioning of cells, organs, and organ systems. Although there is not a direct relationship between the presence of abnormal biologic change and the presence and intensity of symptoms, some of these biological changes may progress to produce symptoms at the organism level. Symptoms, the second level, are the patient's perceptions of an abnormal physical, emotional, or cognitive state and often bring the patient to the practitioner. The intensity of the subjective symptoms can be measured by pain scales, dyspnea indexes, and other measures which are specific for the disease symptom.

The third level of the model is functional status measured by the ability of individuals to perform defined physical, social, psychological, and role tasks. The presence and intensity of symptoms can affect functional ability. For example, severe shortness of breath in a person with chronic obstructive pulmonary disease (COPD) may reduce that person's ability to walk up stairs, play with their grandchildren, enjoy a good laugh, or continue in their job. The degree of functional decline can be influenced by a person's personality, tolerance for the symptoms, and motivation to perform the task. Also family and social support as well as economic and environmental factors can affect the individual's ability to perform selected functions. In COPD, the impact of shortness of breath on a person's functional status can be lessened if the individual is motivated to maintain function, if economic resources are available to modify the living and working space to prevent overexertion, and if family and coworkers are supportive in maintaining the individual's functional ability and sense of self-worth. Physical function is assessed by such objective measures as activities of daily living (ADL), instrumental ADLs, and 6-minute walking tests. Additional objective measures are available to determine social, psychological, and role functioning.

The fourth component assesses the impact of the disease on patient's perceptions of their health. Health perceptions are patient-generated, subjective ratings and are influenced by the cumulative effect of the severity of the condition, the intensity of the symptoms, and the degree of functional limitation. However, all of these factors can be moderated by the values and preferences of the patient as well as the amount of social and psychological support. For example, given two individuals with the same clinical symptoms and functional status, the person who also is a hypochondriac will have a lower subjective health perception than the other individual who is not a hypochondriac.

The fifth and final component is overall quality of life. This encompasses not only health issues but life as a whole including economic viability, family matters, and spirituality. Following the causal model chain, patients' assessments of their overall quality of life depend on the severity of the physiologic problem, the amount of symptoms, whether the symptoms affect functional status, and patient's perception of their health. However the overall quality of life also is influenced by three other groups of factors: the patient's values and beliefs, the social and psychological supports needed to help them to continue to function in all aspects of their lives, and nonmedical factors such as economic stability, family relationships, and spirituality. While instruments are available to assess overall quality of life, when evaluating the effectiveness of health care interventions, investigators do not query these nonmedical influences but rather use more focused, health-related quality of life (HRQL) measures to assess what physical, psychological, and social impact the disease has on patients as well to assess the effectiveness of health care services. Characteristics of these HRQL measures are described in the next section.

As an example, we can use the Wilson/Cleary model to guide the selection of measures to include in an outcomes assessment system to evaluate the effectiveness of an clinical intervention such as cardiac rehabilitation program? As one moves from left to right in this model, from physiological and functional status measures (objective assessments) to health perception and quality of life (subjective assessments) one moves outward from the cellular level to the individual, and then to the global interaction of the individual in society. Therefore, a complete evaluation of a clinical intervention should include measures from each level of the model. For example a comprehensive outcomes assessment system could include lipid profile, blood pressure, and body mass index as biological and physiological variables; exertional dyspnea as a symptom measure; capacity on a treadmill as a physical functional measure and Profile of Mood States (McNair et al., 1971) as a psychological function measure; and the Short Form-36 Health Survey (Ware and Sherbourne, 1992) as a measure of health perception and health-related quality of life.

VIII. INTEGRATING THE WHO/ICIDH, NAGI AND WILSON-CLEARY MODELS

There are many similarities among these three models. All move from micro to macro characteristics of the individual; from cellular abnormalities to functionality to performance within society. All recognize the importance of the physical and social environments and their influences on enhancing or limiting the capabilities of our patients and clients. All have well developed measures to assess the early stages — physiologic variables, symptom indicators, and measures of functionality. Fewer measures have been developed to assess the more conceptually complex levels of handicap, disability, and quality of life.

However, it is at these higher levels of handicap/disability and health-related quality of life where differences in conceptualization do occur. The WHO/ICIDH and Nagi models are rooted in a more social perspective — the ability of the individual to function within society. On the other hand, the Wilson/Cleary model, while recognizing the role of society and the environment, places more emphasis on the individual and how individuals views their health-related quality of life. Of course that involves how they function within society, but now the emphasis is more on the patient-centered interpretation of that function combined with their evaluation of their physical, social, and psychological functioning.

A comparison of two assessment measures will illustrate this point. The London Handicap Scale (Harwood et al., 1994) was developed to measure the effectiveness of reducing handicap in chronically ill populations. The authors include the six dimensions of handicap in their scale: mobility, orientation, physical independence, occupation, social integration, and economic self sufficiency. Compare these variables with those included in the SF-36, a health-related quality of life scale (Ware and Sherbourne, 1992): physical functioning, role limitations due to physical functioning, pain, vitality, general health perceptions, social interactions, role limitations due to emotional functioning, and mental health. The latter balances assessments of how individuals are functioning within society with assessments of their general health perceptions, vitality, and mental health. The handicap/disability measures have more of an objective, occupational focus, while the health-related quality of life measures combine occupational aspects with patient-centered, holistic and subjective assessments.

IX. HEALTH-RELATED QUALITY OF LIFE

No clear and concise, generally accepted, and universally used definition exists for the concept, "quality of life." However, most authors agree that five major domains compose quality of life:

- physical status and functional abilities,
- psychological status and well-being,
- social interactions,
- economic factors, and
- religious and/or family status (Spilker, 1996).

However, when investigators develop quality of life measures to be used to assess patients and evaluate health care practices, they generally do not include the last two domains. Health interventions primarily are targeted at creating change in the first three domains, and the content of the measures reflect that intent. These more focused quality of life measures are called health-related quality of life (HRQL) or health status measures. Valid and reliable HRQL measures include three important characteristics: 1) they assess multiple dimensions of health; e.g., physical, mental/psychological, and social; 2) they are a patient-centered form of assessment and are intended to measure the effect of the clinical condition on the patient as perceived by the patient, not a health care provider or a relative of the patient, and 3) they provide a standardized method of patient assessment that can be used by different health professionals in different patient populations at different times. These multidimensional, patient-centered, standardized HRQL measures offer new opportunities for more comprehensive clinical assessments.

Multidimensional HRQL measures provide an opportunity to move beyond the traditional professionally grounded assessments of physical function and other objective measures and now include a broader assessment of patient status, as objectively and subjectively perceived by the patient. As described in the Wilson/Cleary model, patients with the same physical function, because of their different values, beliefs, and expectations, may have very different perceptions of their health and their health-related quality of life. It is important that health professionals obtain this information to develop patient-specific treatment plans and to evaluate the effectiveness of interventions.

Health-related quality of life measures can be designed to assess health in general or to focus on disease-specific consequences of individual clinical conditions. Because general health-related quality of life measures can be used across all conditions, they enable clinicians and policy makers to determine the relative impact of different disease states and treatment options on patient populations and resource allocation. On the other hand, disease-specific health-related quality of life measures can focus on those aspects of health that are most affected by a specific clinical condition. Both types are useful in a comprehensive assessment of the effectiveness of clinical interventions.

The MOS short-form, 36-item health survey (SF-36) is an example of a general HRQL measure (Ware and Sherbourne, 1992). It is a self-administered, 36-item questionnaire that takes approximately 10 minutes to complete. The SF-36 yields a profile of eight components of health: physical functioning, role limitations due to physical functioning, pain, health perceptions, vitality, social functioning, role limitations due to emotional status, and mental health. Two summary scores can be created from the 36 items: the first four domains are combined to yield a physical component summary score and the last four domains produce a mental component summary score. At present, a method to obtain a single, composite, summary score for health status as measured by the SF-36 has not been developed.

Spilker (1996) and McDowell (1996) are good sources for information concerning other general HRQL measures. Spilker also describes disease-specific outcome measures that have been developed to assess symptomatic, functional, and HRQL outcomes measures for more than 20 clinical conditions.

X. CONSIDERATIONS FOR SELECTING OUTCOME MEASURES

With the increased awareness that health-related quality of life is an important characteristic of patient health status, researchers and clinicians are beginning to include instruments to measure this multidimensional factor in patient assessment batteries. However, the quality of the measures and the feasibility of their administration are quite variable, and care must be taken when selecting a HRQL measure. While excellent HRQL measures are available, instruments may appear in the literature or be developed by local institutions that are less than comprehensive in their assessment of health-related quality of life concepts or have incompletely evaluated the performance of the instrument. Consider these eight questions, based on criteria developed by the Medical Outcomes Trust, as you evaluate instruments for possible incorporation into an outcomes assessment program.

1. What is the population for which the instrument was developed? Some HRQL measures have been developed for a general population, while others have been targeted for subpopulations. For example, a general population HRQL instrument could be used with geriatric patients, but a HRQL measure developed for a geriatric population should not be used in a general population study. The geriatric measure, while adequate for its intended population, may be limited in the extent of activities assessed by the instrument. You will want to match your population to the population for which the instrument was developed.

2. Are the HRQL concepts or domains that you wish to measure, included in the instrument? Before you begin searching for outcome measures, determine what concepts or domains you want to assess in your patient population. Do you want to evaluate only physical functioning or do you want a more general and/or disease-specific health-related quality of life measure? Besides the three HRQL domains of physical, social, and psychological functioning, do you want the measure to include an assessment of pain, well-being, or other concepts?

3. Do each of the sections within the instrument measure a unique concept or domain? The developer of an instrument should provide evidence that each section of the instrument measures a unique concept or domain and does not overlap with other sections. Also the questions within a domain should have a higher correlation with that domain's score than it has with the scores of other domains.

4. Is the instrument reliable? Three types of reliability should be examined when selecting an instrument: intra-rater, inter-rater, and internal reliability. Is the

score of the measure consistent when given to the same patient under the same conditions when the clinical status has not changed (intra-rater or test-retest reliability)? Is the score of the measure reproducible when administered by different staff members to the same patient, under the same conditions and without change in patient status (inter-rater reliability)? Are the items within the instrument consistent with one another; do they measure the same concept across patients and across time (internal reliability)?

5. Is the instrument valid? Does the measure accurately assess what it is intended to measure? If it is a HRQL measure, does it sample important elements from the physical, psychological, and social dimensions? If it is a disease-specific health status instrument, does it question the patient about the multidimensional aspects of that specific disease? Is the measure a comprehensive assessment of all important elements associated with general health or aspects of health adversely affected by a specific disease? Does the instrument discriminate among various levels of health or severity of illness?

6. Can the instrument detect change in patient status when it occurs? Is the instrument sensitive enough to detect clinically significant changes across the range of illness severity?

7. Is it administratively and economically feasible to use the selected instrument? Different assessment measures require different administrative protocols. Some instruments are quite lengthy and require that they be administered to patients by trained staff. At the other extreme, others can be completed independently by the patient in a short period of time. Therefore, the site should determine if there is an adequate budget and staff to properly administer the selected health status instrument and whether or not the measure is of reasonable length for the target patient population.

8. Is the instrument acceptable to the patient population? Will the instrument be easy to understand by the intended patient population? Is it written for an appropriate reading level? Will patients be comfortable answering the questions contained in the instrument?

XI. IMPLICATIONS FOR HEALTH ADMINISTRATION AND POLICY

Health administrators should encourage the use of outcomes assessment systems in routine clinical practice. Such systems should not be viewed as research tools; rather they should be considered essential components of contemporary methods to improve the effectiveness and efficiency of health care practices. Clinicians should use a comprehensive "outcomes" assessment system to evaluate patients prior to treatment. Based on these baseline results, they should develop individual treatment plans, monitor the effectiveness of the interventions, and make midcourse adjustments as necessary. Administrators should combine the results of similar interventions, and, in consultation with clinicians, determine the effectiveness of clinical interventions. Using total quality management techniques, they should feed this information back to clinicians and encourage, if not require, the discontinuation of ineffective treatments. This cycle of measuring patient status, monitoring the course of the intervention, and then managing future patients based on earlier results leads to an increase in effective and efficient care.

But a comprehensive outcomes assessment system does require measuring physiologic, symptomatic, functional, health perceptions, and general and disease-specific HRQL measures. Focusing only on the traditional physiologic or functional variables without assessing the impact on more patient-centered outcome measures could produce a distorted picture of the effectiveness of an intervention. For example, some medication may produce improvement in physiologic variables, but the patient may report adverse drug reactions with no perceived benefit. Or, due to physical therapy sessions, patients who experienced a stroke may improve their grip strength or range of motion, but their HRQL remains low. On the other hand, in chronic obstructive pulmonary disease, patients who complete a pulmonary rehabilitation program rarely see changes in their pulmonary function tests, but their symptoms, physical function, and HRQL all improve.

Outcomes assessment involves a system of measurement. If it is to produce the twin benefits of increased effectiveness and efficiency, administrators must encourage and clinicians must use all components—from clinician-preferred physiologic variables to patient-centered HRQL measures— in the outcomes measurement system.

REFERENCES

Barr, J. T. (1993). *Critical Review of Health Services Literature Related to the Allied Health Professions.* Agency for Health Care Policy and Research: Washington, DC.

Codman, E. A. (1914). The product of a hospital. *Surgery, Gynecology, and Obstetrics, 18,* 491-496.

Donabedian, A. (1966). Evaluating the quality of medical care. *Milbank Quarterly, 44,* 166-203.

Ellwood, P. M. (1988). Outcomes management: a technology of patient experiences. 1988. *New England Journal of Medicine, 318,* 1549-1556.

Epstein, A. M. (1990). The outcomes movement: will it get us where we want to go? *New England Journal of Medicine, 323:* 266-270.

Fuhrer, M. J. (1995). Conference report: an agenda for medical rehabilitation outcomes research. *Journal of Allied Health, 24,* 79-87.

Harwood, R.H., Jitapunkul, S., Dickinson, E., and Ebrahim, S. (1994). Measuring handicap: motives, methods, and a model. *Quality in Health Care, 3,* 53-57.

McDowell, I. and Newell, C. (1996). *Measuring Health: A Guide to Rating Scales and Questionnaires, 2nd Ed.* Oxford Press: New York.

McNair, D., Lord, M., and Droppleman, L. F. (1971). EITS manual for the Profile of Mood States. San Diego, CA: Educational Testing Service.

Nagi, S. Z. (1964). Some conceptual issues indisability and rehabilitation potential: Concepts, methods, and procedures. *American Journal of Public Health, 54,* 1568-1579.

Nagi, S. Z. (1991). "Disability Concepts Revisited: Implications for Prevention" in Pope, A.M. and Tarlov, A. R. (eds). *Disability in America: Toward a National Agenda for Prevention.* National Academy Press: Washington DC.

Schieber, G. J., Poulier, J. P., and Greenwald, L. M. (1994). Health system performance in OECD countries, 1980-1992. *Health Affairs, 13,* 100-112.

Spilker B. (1996) *Quality of Life and Pharmacoeconomics in Clinical Trials, 2nd Ed.* Lippincott-Raven: Philadelphia.

Ware, J.E and Sherbourne C.D. (1992). The MOS 36-item short-form health status survey. *Medical Care, 30:* 473-483.

Wennberg, J. and Gittelsohn, A. (1973). Small area variations in health care delivery. *Science, 182,* 1102-1108.

Wilson, I. and Cleary, P. (1995). Linking clinical variables with health-related quality of life: a conceptual model of patient outcomes. *Journal of the American Medical Association, 273*, 59-65.

World Health Organization. (1948). Constitution of the World Health Organization. World Health Organization, Geneva, Switzerland.

World Health Organization. (1980). International Classification of Impairments, Disabilities and Handicaps: A Manual of Classification Relating to the Consequences of Diseases. *World Health Organization: Geneva*, pp. 25-29.

32.
QUANTITATIVE DECISION ANALYSIS IN ADMINISTRATION

Charles J. Austin, *Medical University of South Carolina, Charleston, SC*

Stuart B. Boxerman, *Washington University School of Medicine, St. Louis, MO*

Health care managers face complex, demanding tasks in planning and supervising services provided by their organizations. Challenged by pressures to expand access, control costs, and improve quality, administrators must have the knowledge and skills required to utilize modern principles of management. Quantitative decision analysis (QDA) comprises a set of techniques that should be a standard part of the arsenal of tools used by health care managers in today's constantly changing environment.

Quantitative analysis for managerial problem solving developed during World War II when mathematical models and statistical methods were applied to military planning, tactical operations, and weapons' utilization (Feldstein, 1963). The term "operations research" was used to describe this emerging discipline, and departments of "management science" were formed at university business and engineering schools across the country. Techniques of operations research were first applied to health care in the 1960s and 1970s (Flagle, 1962; Fries, 1976; Shuman et al., 1975). The need for continuous quality improvement and process re-engineering has lent quantitative decision analysis in health care organizations increased importance during the 1990s.

Few health administrators will have the mathematical background to employ quantitative decision analysis on their own. However, they can become intelligent consumers of the technology and advocates for its use in their organizations by encouraging partnerships between managers and technical specialists for problem identification and problem solving.

I. AREAS OF APPLICATION

There is no shortage of management problems to which QDA can be applied in health care. The list which follows is illustrative but by no means constitutes an exhaustive set of potential areas of application.

A. Market Analysis

Health care organizations must understand current and potential future markets for their services. QDA can be used to describe the demographic and cultural characteristics of populations in the geographic service area. Understanding of markets is essential as integrated delivery systems are established and strategic alliances are formed by multiple providers of care in the community.

B. Strategic Planning

Several quantitative techniques can be used to support strategic planning. These include forecasting demand for services, analyzing an organization's case mix, and simulating the effects of potential managed care contracts on costs and revenue.

C. Resource Allocation

Given careful market analysis and service planning, QDA can assist in allocating resources to achieve optimum efficiency in the delivery of services. Examples include financial simulation, linear programming models for assigning personnel and allocating financial resources, and budget variation analysis.

D. Productivity Enhancement

Cost reduction requires that health care organizations improve their productivity in delivery of services. Operations improvement has been a major focus of quantitative analysis since World War II. Techniques include simulation, queuing theory, transportation and assignment models, and inventory control. Increasingly, programs of patient-focused care and process re-engineering have been initiated to reduce costs and ensure that the primary focus of all activities continues to be on the patient.

E. Quality Improvement

Continuous quality improvement has become the clarion call of United States industry as it competes increasingly in world markets. Health care organizations have answered this call. QDA is being applied to studies of quality including measurement of patient satisfaction and monitoring of clinical and service quality throughout the organization.

F. Program Evaluation and Outcomes Measurement

Quantitative measures are being used to assess the effectiveness of health care programs at the local, regional, and national level. Health care organizations and integrated delivery systems have initiated programs of outcomes analysis by which the clinical effectiveness and costs of alternative treatment modalities are compared in order to provide high quality care in the most efficient manner.

II. QUANTITATIVE DECISION ANALYSIS: A GENERALIZED PROCESS[1]

The procedures followed in quantitative analysis for managerial decision making parallel the scientific method used by investigators in basic and applied research. There are also close parallels to the process of systems analysis employed by management engineers in the study of organizational processes.

The general framework for analysis includes the following steps:
1. Preliminary observation.
2. Problem definition.
3. Model formulation.
4. Determination of data requirements and availability.
5. Preliminary examination of data.
6. Selection of appropriate analytical techniques for solving the problem.
7. Selection of computer software to be used in the analysis.
8. Running the analysis.
9. Analyzing and interpreting results (sensitivity analysis).
10. Application of results to management decision(s).
11. Post-implementation evaluation of decision.

A. Step 1: Preliminary Observation

Organizational problems or decisions that may lend themselves to quantitative analysis must first be identified by managers involved in the decision process. If managers believe that analysis and modeling may be useful to the decision, they will consult with appropriate technical staff (management engineers and analysts) who will conduct preliminary observation and discussion with individuals in the organization to be studied. The purpose of this step is twofold: (1) to determine (in a preliminary way) the feasibility of the study; and (2) to help establish the basic parameters for defining the problem to be solved.

B. Step 2: Problem Definition

This step involves establishment of objectives for the analysis stated in functional (managerial) terms. For example, objectives for a study of managed care contracting might be stated as follows:

> "The purpose of this study is to estimate the financial impact of contracting with the Tri-County Health Maintenance Organization for the provision of inpatient services to members of the HMO for two years. Objectives of the analysis include: (1) estimating incremental demand for inpatient services and additional revenue generated as a result; (2) estimating incremental costs associated with provision of these services; and (3) determination of the level of service required for net revenue from the contract to be positive."

During this step in the process, analysts should assist managers in stating clear functional objectives and should avoid the tendency to begin casting the problem in mathematical terms.

C. Step 3: Model Formulation

Working from a clearly-stated set of functional objectives, the analysts assigned to the study should develop a model of the process to be studied. A model is a representation of some real world process expressed in physical, graphical, or mathematical terms. For the managed care contracting example described in Step 2, the model might take the form of a set of mathematical equations expressing the relationship between incremental costs and incremental revenue resulting from the proposed new contract.

D. Step 4: Determination of Data Requirements and Data Availability

Quantitative analysis requires data as basic input to the process. A critical step in the process (and one frequently ignored or minimized in many operations research textbooks) is the determination of: (1) what data are required for the model or analytical process; and (2) where these data can be obtained. In the previously cited example, data will be required on the direct and indirect costs of providing inpatient services from the internal information systems of the hospital considering the managed care contract. In addition, the hospital must have access to external data from the HMO on the number of members, basic demographic characteristics of the membership, and previous utilization history, if available. Ideally, much of the internal data required for analyses can be obtained from the organization's information systems, but unfortunately this is not always the case. Collection of data required for an analysis is possible but is often an expensive and time-consuming process. If extensive data collection is required, then management must determine if the costs involved will be worth the benefits to be obtained from conducting the study.

E. Step 5: Preliminary Examination of Data

Frequently in the conduct of a management study, much can be learned by preliminary examination of raw data before any models are constructed and solved. Simple grouping of information using descriptive statistics (e.g., means and frequency distributions) along with "eyeballing" of data may provide important insights into the problem to be solved and may result in reformulation of study objectives or model development. In the managed care contracting problem described above, if information on inpatient utilization of the HMO membership is inadequate or not available, then it may be necessary to obtain additional data from external sources on utilization of services by other populations with similar demographic characters (age, sex, income, etc.) to the HMO membership in order to develop estimates of probable utilization.

F. Step 6: Selection of Analytical Techniques

Given a problem definition, study objectives, model formulation, and preliminary examination of data, then those conducting the study will determine the appropriate techniques to be used for the analysis. For the managed care contracting example, the analysts might choose to use the mathematical technique of breakeven analysis. "WHAT-IF analysis" might also be employed if the hospital wanted to forecast alternate cost/revenue break even points using different assumptions about future utilization patterns by the HMO membership.

G. Step 7: Selection of Computer Software

Operations research relies heavily on the computational power of computer technology for modeling and problem solving. Most studies will involve computer processing of data. Although some analysis may require the development of special computer programs, most studies can be carried out using standard computer software available from commercial or nonprofit sources. Thus, one step in the process is determining and obtaining appropriate computer software for problem analysis and solution.

H. Step 8: Running the Analysis

After obtaining data, completing the final model formulation, and selecting computer software, the next step in the process is running the model and obtaining a solution. This often involves multiple repetitions (iterations) of the process as preliminary results are obtained and modifications are made to the model.

I. Step 9: Analyzing and Interpreting Results

This step, often referred to as sensitivity analysis, should be carried out as a joint effort of the analysts and managers involved in the study. It involves careful examination of the results of the analysis in terms of its sensitivity to study design, quality of data, assumptions built into the model, and any compromises necessary in data collection and quantification (Warner, Holloway, and Grazier, 1984).

J. Step 10: Application of Results to Management Decisions

After managers and analysts are satisfied with the sensitivity of the results and alternative runs have been made if necessary, managers can use the information obtained from the analysis to support management decisions. For the managed care contracting example, information on cost/revenue breakeven points under alternate assumptions about utilization should assist the hospital CEO and other executives in reaching a decision about whether or not to contract with the HMO. Data obtained in the analysis may also help the management team formulate its negotiating strategy with regard to prices and discounts to be included in the contract.

K. Step 11: Post-implementation Evaluation

The use of analytical studies should be evaluated at an appropriate point after the results have been applied to organizational decisions. For the example used in this section, management should evaluate their decisions regarding the managed care contract after the contract goes into effect to determine how well the breakeven analysis has forecast actual financial experience in the provision of inpatient services under the contract.

III. QUANTITATIVE TECHNIQUES EMPLOYED

This section describes a limited number of quantitative models and techniques often used to support managerial decision-making in health care organizations. The first set is particularly useful in supporting strategic planning activities. The second set is often used in programs of operations improvement. The models described do not constitute an exhaustive set of possible quantitative decision tools but do represent those available to health care managers.

A. Strategic Planning Applications

As the health care system becomes increasingly complex, the strategic planning function of the health care executive grows in importance. Not only must decisions be made about current situations, but the executive must also be able to anticipate and respond to a variety of future situations. This section contains a discussion of four quantitative techniques which assist executives in their planning role.

1. Breakeven Analysis

In many planning situations, the executive is considering two alternatives, each of whose cost (or revenue) varies with a volume measure. The question is which alternative should be chosen. The criterion for making this choice is typically to minimize cost or maximize revenue. In the simplest case, the cost (or revenue) associated with each alternative will vary with the volume measure in a linear fashion. Thus, a graph of cost versus volume measure for the two alternatives will contain two straight lines as illustrated in Figure 1.

Figure 1 - Graph of Cost vs Volume for Two Alternatives

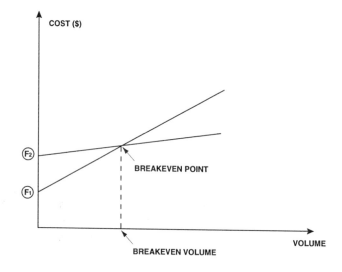

The linear relationship between cost and volume, shown in Figure 1, occurs when the total cost is the aggregate of two categories of cost components—fixed costs and variable costs. Fixed costs are those that occur, regardless of the level of the volume measure. They are associated with capital costs of facilities or equipment, overhead costs such as electricity and repairs, and salaries of the minimum personnel required even if the volume measure equals zero. Variable costs are associated with the resources expended for each additional unit of volume. The costs of labor, materials, or energy required for each additional unit of volume would be classified as variable costs. In the simplest case, this incremental cost per unit remains the same no matter what level of volume is chosen.

When the linear cost curves for the two alternatives under consideration are drawn on a single graph (see Figure 1), one observes that the two lines will typically intersect. (Only if the two alternatives have exactly the same variable costs and two different fixed costs will the lines be parallel.) At the point of intersection, the two alternatives have exactly the same cost. This point is known as the breakeven point, and the corresponding volume level is known as the breakeven volume. The goal of breakeven analysis is to locate this breakeven point and its associated breakeven volume. For volumes smaller than the breakeven volume, one of the alternatives will always be optimal, while for volumes larger than the breakeven volume, the other alternative will be best. Thus, once the breakeven volume has been found, the health care executive can attempt to specify the probable range of volume levels, thus identifying the best alternative.

For example, consider a hospital which, in response to the pressures of managed care in the region, is seeking the lowest cost way of providing a new radiology procedure. Under alternative A they can lease a piece of equipment at an annual fixed cost of $75,000. The variable cost per test using this equipment is $80. With alternative B, the variable cost per test will be only $65, but the annual fixed cost of leasing this equipment is $90,000. We want to obtain the breakeven point.

The solution is found by equating the cost expressions for the two alternatives:

$$\$75,000 + \$80(X) = \$90,000 + \$65(X)$$

where X denotes the breakeven volume. Solving for X, one obtains the value of 1,000. Thus, the two alternatives will have identical costs when the annual volume is 1,000. For volumes less than 1,000, alternative A has the lower cost (the alternative with the lower fixed cost is always best for low volumes), while for volumes above 1,000, one would choose alternative B. Finally, the breakeven cost is $155,000.

This basic breakeven model can be modified in several ways. First, consider a situation in which one must choose between using an outside contractor to provide a new service or providing the service in house. Often, the contractor will negotiate at a specific rate independent of volume of service. In some cases, no additional capital would be required to provide the service in house. Thus, for this particular case, the two alternatives are characterized by one having only a fixed-cost component while the other has only a variable cost component. This problem, often known as a make-buy problem, occurs quite frequently when decision makers are looking at adding a new service.

Another variation to the basic breakeven model occurs when one or both of the cost-volume curves are non-linear. Then it is possible for the two curves to have more than one point of intersection, hence more than one breakeven point. Thus, there will be ranges of volume level for which one alternative is best and other ranges of volume level where the second alternative would be preferred.

Finally, another model of breakeven analysis is one in which a plot of revenue versus volume level and cost versus volume level are drawn on the same graph. The point at which revenue equals cost (the two curves will cross) corresponds to the breakeven point. The corresponding volume level is the breakeven volume. This type of analysis allows the decision maker to examine the level of volume necessary for a proposed venture to just break even.

Breakeven analysis has been touted in the literature as a valuable management tool. Gapenski (1989) indicates that breakeven analysis gives health care financial managers a tool for weighing the potential profitability of adding a new service. Alternate courses of action can be evaluated and compared to determine the best route under various expansion proposals. Carpenter (1990) describes the role of breakeven analysis as part of a cost analysis for the smaller laboratory for which computerized methods may be unavailable or unappealing. Other discussions of breakeven analysis have appeared in the dental literature (Caplan, 1988) and the nursing literature (Lukacs, 1986) and (Jones, 1994).

2. Decision Analysis and Decision Trees

The preceding discussion of breakeven analysis dealt with models for choosing between two alternatives. Frequently, the health care executive has a number of alternatives from which to choose and confronts varying degrees of uncertainty regarding volume levels associated with the decision. Quantitative decision models can help guide the executive in making an appropriate choice. The models can employ either an algebraic or a graphical orientation.

An algebraic approach is used to model "single-stage" problems in which the decision-maker must choose from a finite number of available alternatives. Once an alternative is selected, a powerful force often dubbed "Nature" will cause one of a finite number of "events" to occur. The specific event that Nature will choose is not known in advance by the decision maker. It is also assumed that the decision maker is fully aware of the consequence which results from a particular combination of "decision maker's alternative/Nature's chosen event."

The problem is typically modeled with a payoff matrix. Rows correspond to the alternatives under consideration, and columns represent the events available, events frequently referred to as alternative states of Nature. The cells denote the cost or profit resulting from the choice of a given alternative by the decision maker and a particular state of Nature. As in breakeven analysis, the decision maker seeks to choose the alternative which will yield the lowest cost or highest profit. The discussion will be based on cost minimization, but profit maximization proceeds in an analogous way.

Suppose that a planner has three alternative ways of funding the development of a given service. The cost associated with each alternative depends upon the economic conditions prevalent at the time the service is developed. A payoff matrix such as that in Table 1 might be developed to model the decision making problem:

Table 1 - Cost (in Millions of Dollars) for Each Plan by Economic Condition

Plan	Economic Conditions			
	Poor	Fair	Good	Excellent
Plan A	7	9	14	17
Plan B	12	14	11	16
Plan C	10	15	13	14

If the decision maker knew for sure which economic condition would occur, the solution would involve merely choosing the lowest cost plan for that condition. Thus, if Fair economic conditions were to occur, the optimum choice would be Plan A. Problems where the state of Nature is known for sure are called decision making under certainty.

In many cases the state of Nature is not known; in fact, no knowledge of probabilities associated with these states is available or can be assumed. In this case the decision making problem is known as decision making under uncertainty. The optimum choice of plan depends upon the criterion of goodness chosen by the decision maker. The choice of criterion depends on the relative degree of optimism possessed by the decision maker.

An optimistic decision maker would choose the mini-min criterion which presumes that Nature's choice will be maximally beneficial. Using this criterion, the decision maker determines the minimum cost associated with each alternative. For the sample problem, these minimum costs are $7, 11, and 10 million, respectively. The smallest, $7 million, corresponds to Plan A, which is thus the optimal choice using the mini-min criterion. When profit figures comprise the payoff matrix, corresponding criterion is the maxi-max criterion.

A pessimistic decision maker assumes that Nature's choice will be maximally detrimental to the decision maker. The decision maker seeks the alternative which does the "best job it can" under these adverse conditions. To that end, the decision maker obtains the maximum cost associated with each alternative. For the sample problem, these maximum costs are $17, 16, and 15, respectively. The smallest, $15 million, corresponds to Plan C, which is therefore the optimal choice using the mini-max criterion. The mini-max criterion typically justifies the purchase of insurance or extended warranties since the cost of the policy is lower than the highest possible expense without the policy. When the payoff matrix contains profit values, the corresponding criterion is known as the maxi-min criterion.

If the decision maker has access to reasonable estimates of the probabilities of the states of Nature, then the decision making problem is known as decision making under risk. The optimum alternative is defined as the one having the minimum expected cost. (For a problem involving profits, the maximum expected profit would be obtained.) For the sample problem, assume that the four economic conditions are likely to occur with probabilities 0.2, 0.1, 0.6, and 0.1, respectively. Then the expected costs of the three plans are $12.4, $12.0, and $12.7 million, respectively. Thus, the optimum plan would be Plan B.

The dollar figures in the payoff matrix can be replaced with a dimensionless quantity indicative of the decision maker's preference for money. This quantity is known as utility. The preferred plan chosen on the basis of dollars expended frequently differs

Figure 2 - Sample Decision Tree

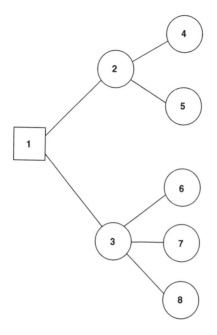

from the plan preferred on the basis of utility values. A detailed discussion of utility theory can be found in a number of decision analysis texts, for example Clemen (1991).

When the problem to be solved is a multi-stage decision problem, a graphical approach is more appropriate. The complexities of the decisions which health care executives must make often require this model. The graphical orientation of these multi-stage models allows for the display of every possible choice that the decision maker can make as well as every possible event that Nature can select. These choices and events can occur in any logical sequence as dictated by the circumstances of the problem. The graphical model is known as a decision tree.

A sample decision tree is shown in Figure 2. It consists of nodes (the squares or circles) and arcs (the lines between the nodes). Square nodes correspond to decision nodes and represent choices made by the decision maker. Circular nodes correspond to chance nodes and denote events selected by Nature. The sequence of these decisions by the decision maker and selections by Nature are depicted by the logic of the tree diagram itself.

The nodes at which the various paths through the tree diagram end are known as terminal nodes. Each terminal node will typically be associated with a profit or cost figure which corresponds to the economic consequence of the decision maker choosing a sequence which concludes at that node. The choices made by Nature have a probability distribution associated with them, and these probabilities are typically affixed to the branches leaving the chance nodes. Once the decision maker has constructed a tree appropriate to this problem, the values of these probabilities and profit or cost figures must still be obtained.

The goal of decision tree analysis is to determine the appropriate set of choices for the decision maker so that the minimum expected cost (or maximum expected profit)

Figure 3 - Example of "Solved" Decision Tree

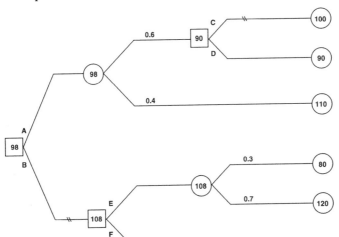

is obtained. The procedure for identifying these appropriate choices involves working backwards through the network averaging out the chance nodes and folding back the decision nodes. The computations can best be understood by referring to Figure 3.

The tree in Figure 3 corresponds to a hypothetical decision-making problem in which the dollar values assigned to the terminal nodes correspond to costs. The goal is to minimize cost. The folded back value for node 3 would be $90, the smaller of $90 and $100. The averaged out value for node 2 is found from [$90(0.6) + $110(0.4)] or $98. In a similar fashion values are affixed to nodes 8, 7, and finally node 1. Notice that when a folded back value is affixed to a decision node, small cross marks are drawn across the non optimal branch(es) leaving that node.

The solution has now been found. The minimum cost decision has a cost of $98 and consists of choosing alternative A, and if the chance presents itself, choosing alternative D. In practice, these computations are performed on a computer using one of several available decision tree software packages. Examples are DATA (Tree-Age Software, 1994) and DPL (ADA Decision Systems, 1995). While these programs simplify the computational phase of decision tree analysis, the health care executive is still responsible for ensuring that the logic of the tree accurately reflects the decision flow present in the problem under consideration.

Health care literature abounds with articles which utilize decision analysis and decision trees. Many of these articles report cost-benefit or cost-effectiveness studies of alternative treatment modalities or programs. For example, Barrett et al. (1994) used a decision tree model to estimate the incremental cost per quality-adjusted life (QALY) of low—as opposed to high—osmolality contrast media for cardiac angiography. Nutting et al. (1994) employed a decision tree in their study of the implications of annual screening mammography for cost and mortality in American Indian populations with differing baseline breast cancer rates. Other applications include a cost-benefit analysis of smoking cessation programs during pregnancy for the prevention of low birthweight (Hueston et al., 1994), a comparison of the cost-effectiveness of alternative drug regimens in the treatment of duodenal ulcers (Sintonen and Alander, 1990) and the use of decision analysis in quality assessment (Coleman, 1989).

3. Simulation

The quantitative models employed to address planning and operational problems are designed to provide a realistic representation of the real-world issues under consideration. The models are chosen so as to represent these issues as accurately as possible while still having sufficient simplicity so that a solution can be obtained using analytical quantitative methods. Modeling is employed because it is cheaper, faster, and less disruptive than manipulating the real-world system itself.

Unfortunately, problems confronting the health care executive are often too complex to be handled by available analytical modeling techniques. Nevertheless, these problems must be addressed. The decision maker might, in these cases, resort to an experimental approach using the real-world system itself. This could be relatively costly, consume a great deal of time, and be disruptive to, if not destructive of, the system being studied. It would be nice if the real-world system could somehow be represented in a laboratory setting to whatever level of detail the decision maker might choose. Once this laboratory representation of the system was constructed, the decision maker could perform experiments which would indicate the outputs that result when the system is modified in a specific way or when the inputs assume a particular form. In this way, the actual real-world system need not be disturbed.

A computer environment provides just such a laboratory; the process of developing and running the appropriate program to guide the computer-based experimentation is known as simulation modeling. (Simulations can be performed with pencil-and-paper techniques, but reasonable performance estimates generally require computer implementation.) Ideally, if the components of a real-world system along with their interactions can be described, the real-world system can be studied using simulation methods.

The development of a simulation model begins with the construction of a flowchart depicting the elements of the real-world system and the interconnection of these elements. The detail with which this flowchart is constructed will be one determinant of the match between the results obtained from the simulation and those that would be obtained by experimenting on the real-world system itself. The flowchart displays the logic of the system under study and thus serves as a blueprint for the logic which must be incorporated into the simulation model. In addition, the flowchart highlights the inputs to the system, the parameters which must be quantified, and the outputs which are generated by the system. Each of these system components must also be incorporated into the model.

For most real-world systems, one or more of the inputs will involve randomness. Simulation models, which incorporate such randomness, are usually referred to as monte carlo simulation models. They have three major components: the capability to generate values from given probability distributions which emulate the randomness in the real-world system; a logical flow built into the computer program which emulates the logic within the real-world system; and a bookkeeping and report-generator function which accumulates output and other characteristics of interest to the decision maker, displays these results, thus serves as the answer to the study.

Figure 4 - Process Chart for Clinical Model

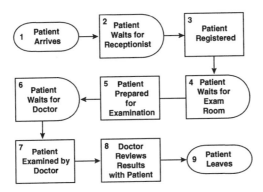

Figure 5 - Medical Model Output Segment - Clinical Model

```
                                          D:\SIMULATE\CLINIC.RES
MedModel 1.11 Results for D:\SIMULATE\CLINIC.MOD [Clinic

Date: Sep/05/1994    Time: 02:13:09 PM

Replication     :     60 of 60
Warmup Time     :      0 Hours    0.00 Minutes
Simulation Time:       8 Hours   47.94 Minutes


SINGLE CAPACITY LOCATIONS

              Sche-            Final  Avg                        Avg
              duled   Total    con-   Minutes                    Minu
Name          Hours   Entries  tents  Per Entry   Std Dev        Per
--------      -----   -------  -----  ---------   -------        ----
Recep           8       10       0      8.07       1.24
Office          8       10       0     17.47       4.56
Exam_rm         8       10       0     35.64      14.40


MULTICAPACITY LOCATIONS

              Sche-                           Avg
              duled   Capa-    Total    Minutes      Avg
Name          Hours   city     Entries  Per Entry    Contents
--------      -----   -----    -------  ---------    --------
Recept_Q        8       4        10       1.29        0.02
Waiting         8       6        10      73.08        1.38


RESOURCES

                       Sche-    Total    Avg       Avg
                       duled    Times    Minutes   Travel    %
Name        Units      Hours    Used     Per Use   To Use    In Use
------      -----      -------  ------   -------   -------   ------
Doctor        1          8       10       34.81     0.85      69.91
Nurse         1          8       20        6.60     0.09      25.00
```

The actual simulation run consists of a relatively large number of executions of the program's logical flow, each iteration corresponding to one trial of the system. At the end of each iteration, the counters and bookkeeping entries are updated to reflect the impact of that trial. If the number of iterations is sufficiently large, the random components of the model will have generated values reflective of all possibilities for those components. In this way, the bookkeeping entries will represent the range of values which would be observed over the long range for the real-world system.

With an easily read report generator built into the computer program, the decision maker will be able to readily interpret the output and obtain the desired answers. Some of the professional simulation programs offer not only sophisticated output reports but also displays of animated figures flowing through the simulated systems. This graphical display allows the decision maker to see the flow through the system and verify the logic of the program.

A simple illustration of simulation modeling, developed by Tee H. Hiett, Ph.D., can be found in Chapter 11 of Austin and Boxerman (1995). The system being simulated is a clinic located in a hospital and staffed with one nurse and one doctor. Patients arrive from several locations between 8:00 am and 2:00 pm so the clinic can close by 4:30 pm. A variety of complaints about the clinic's operation has prompted a study.

A process chart (Austin and Boxerman, 1995) is shown in Figure 4. It serves as the basis for building the logic into the simulation model so that the system is accurately represented.

Hiett built this simulation model using the professional simulation software package MedModel. This program incorporates animation which adds a dramatic quality to the analysis. Icons representing patients, nurses, and doctors move on the screen. In addition, the software provides statistical tabulations. An example of part of such a report is shown in Figure 5. For this run, patients waited in the waiting room an average of 73 minutes, they waited to see the receptionist an average of about 1.3 minutes, and they spent an average of 34.81 minutes with the doctor.

A number of interesting health care applications of simulation modeling have been reported. Song and Rathwell (1994) describe a simulation model designed to estimate the demand for hospital beds and doctors in China between 1990 and 2010. The model compares deterministic sensitivity analysis and stochastic simulation for assessing inherent uncertainty in health projections. Jeang (1990) used a simulation model to describe the behavior of the inpatient admission system in a hospital. A simulation model was developed by Goldberg et al. (1990) to evaluate a set of emergency response vehicle base locations. The authors have performed an analysis evaluating two alternative sets of locations for a system in Tucson. Finally, Saunders, Makens, and Leblanc (1989) have analyzed emergency department operations using simulation software. Their model incorporated patient priority, individual assignment to a nurse and physician, standard tests, procedures, and consultations. A variety of output measures were generated, and the value of simulation modeling in analyzing emergency department systems was clearly established.

4. Forecasting

The planning function of the health care executive involves looking toward the future. Health care planners must anticipate the demand for services, technological changes, future economic conditions, demographics, and medical advances. While guesswork is certainly one approach by which the planner can look to the future, more systematic approaches to forecasting would certainly be beneficial. Five approaches might assist the health care planner and decision maker in the forecasting effort. These approaches are

- use of historical analogies
- delphi methods
- extrapolation of historical data
- simulation modeling
- operations research models

The first two approaches are intuitive, not based on formal modeling, while the remaining three are model-based.

The two intuitive approaches do have a systematic basis. The rationale for using historical analogies to develop a forecast is that the specific situation faced by the decision maker is probably similar to one faced previously by another decision maker. For example, as one looks ahead to the growth of managed care in a specific market, it is quite likely that another market was at the same level of managed care in a previous year. By consulting with health care executives in that other market, the executive can gain an understanding of the evolution that took place and that is likely to occur in his or her own market. There is no guarantee, of course, that the pattern experienced in the more mature market will repeat itself in the newer market. But certainly the decision maker trying to forecast developments in his or her own market profits from the input received from the mature market.

The second intuitive approach utilizes a group of experts whose collective input generates a forecast. These experts may be assembled in a single location or they might communicate by mail, voice mail, or e-mail. The key to this approach, known as the delphi approach, is that participants are provided with some specific issues to discuss. Their input is aggregated; the summary is redistributed to the group along with some additional points to consider. After several iterations, the process concludes in a forecast which reflects the group's perspective.

The first model-based forecasting approach extrapolates historical data. These data, tabulated as a function of time, constitute a time series. This time series can be represented as a sum (or product) of four components: trend, a seasonal component, a cyclical component, and a random or noise component. For long-term forecasting (more than a year, but less than the period of cyclical behavior), it is often sufficient to identify the trend component. Frequently this component will be linear, so that a simple linear regression computation can be used to obtain a forecast equation of the form: $Y = b0 + b1t$.

For short term forecasting (less than a year) of monthly values, for example, several models can be considered. If there is no trend present, next month's value might be forecast using this month's forecast and this month's actual value with a method known as exponential smoothing. The forecast is based on a weighted average of this month's actual value and this month's forecasted value. The relative weight given to each is determined by a quantity, known as the smoothing constant, whose value is assigned by the decision maker. If a trend is present, one employs double smoothing, and if a seasonal component is present, a third smoothing constant is added to the model.

The regression model is an approach used to forecast monthly values where a trend and seasonal component are present. This model contains a time term along with 11 dummy variables which account for the monthly variation. The number of dummy variables is always one less than the number of periods in the season cycle. Thus, quarterly data (values per year) would include three dummy variables.

In some cases time alone is not sufficient to explain the past behavior of the process under study. Other variables must be added to the regression model to forecast future values of the process. Economic factors, demographics, and medical science advances are three variables which can influence future demands for particular health services. They might be significant components of a model to forecast demand for these services. Using such models is sometimes referred to as prediction by association, and the formulation of these models involves multiple regression. Of course, when these models are used as a forecasting tool, the decision maker must be able to forecast future values of the variables in the model. Forecasting the values of these model variables might be as difficult as forecasting the level of demand for the services directly.

A fourth approach to forecasting also uses simulation modeling. With this approach, a model is developed which represents current conditions. Key system and environmental components are identified, and probability distributions are assumed which describe likely patterns of change during the forecast time period for these components. By running the model for a reasonably large number of trials, the decision maker can obtain a forecast for the variables of interest described as a probability distribution.

Finally, other operations research models can be used as the basis for forecasting. One example is the Markov model. This model describes a process which is assumed to be a series of stages; at each stage the process is in one of a number of possible states. An example of such a process is a patient's stay in a critical care unit, when each day might be equated to a stage, and the level of severity of the patient on a given day might be defined as the state. The goal would be to forecast, for example, the patient's length of stay.

Wilson and Schuiling (1992) use multiple regression models to obtain monthly forecasts of laboratory procedures. They claim that their forecasts provided the basis for better resource planning and enhanced operating efficiency. Schmitz, Masters, and Dilts (1989) describe accurate forecasting methods that integrate clinical and financial data to ensure profitability and high-quality patient care. Born (1981) looks at the applicability of several techniques to forecasting within the dental field. Elwell (1979) considers forecasting applicability as a tool for the laboratory manager.

B. Operations Improvement Applications

1. Queuing Problems

Waiting for service seems to be an intrinsic component of the health care delivery system. Patients wait in physicians' offices, physicians wait for laboratory results, laboratory technicians wait for machines to process tests, and administrative personnel wait to obtain authorization for patients to receive care. In some instances, these waits are merely a source of inconvenience. In others, however, waiting might be life-threatening. Health care executives, therefore, are increasingly interested in configuring their systems so as to reduce waiting time to the lowest possible value.

Figure 6 - The General Queuing System

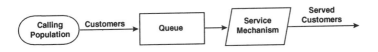

Obviously, waiting time can be reduced by simply adding additional serving capacity to the system. The problem, of course, is that this additional capacity has cost associated with it. The goal is to add only that additional capacity necessary to achieve performance characteristics deemed acceptable by management. Queuing models provide the analytical framework for determining the required capacity.

A general queuing system is shown in Figure 6. Such a system consists of a source of customers, a line or queue where customers wait to be served, and a mechanism for rendering service to the customers. The population can be either finite or infinite. Simpler mathematics occur when the population is infinite. The members of the population can be either homogeneous or heterogeneous relative to their needs for service, and the customers can arrive either singly or in groups (batched). Finally, the arrival sequence can either be deterministic (follow a predictable pattern) or be random. For random arrivals, the decision maker must identify an appropriate probability model.

The queue can also be either finite or infinite. An arriving customer can not enter a finite queue if it is full. This customer is blocked. Even when a customer is not blocked, if the line is quite long, the customer might decide not to enter the queue. This decision is known as balking. Customers who grow tired of waiting and leave the queue are said to be reneging. Also of importance is the rule by which customers are drawn from the queue to be served. This rule might be first-in, first-out (FIFO); last-in, first out (LIFO); or follow some priority rule. Patients calling the physician referral service would typically be served on a FIFO basis, while arrivals to the emergency room would usually be treated according to priority based upon severity of illness or injury.

In the study of queuing system behavior, several characteristics are important. First is the number of servers in the service mechanism. The simplest case has a single server while more complicated systems have multiple servers or channels. The time required to render service to a single customer can be either deterministic or stochastic. Again, for stochastic case must identify the appropriate probability distribution which describes the serving process. Finally, the service mechanism may possess some additional characteristics including the possibility of a breakdown, the tendency to modify the rate of rendering service when the waiting line grows, or the capability of rendering service to multiple customers (batch processing).

The basic single-server queuing system provides a good example with which to illustrate the properties and output characteristics typically of interest to the decision maker. Assume that a medical clinic is located within a large manufacturing facility and serves the injured or ill workers. The clinic operates 24 hours per day. Assume further that the clinic is characterized by the following:

1. The number of workers is large so it is appropriate to consider the population who arrive at the clinic to be infinite.

Figure 7 - Basic Single-Server Queue Steady-State Algebraic Formulas

1. Percent utilization of the medical clinic -

$$\rho = (\frac{\lambda}{\mu})(100) = (\frac{4}{5})(100) = 80\%$$

2. Average number of workers in the medical clinic -

$$L = \frac{\lambda}{\mu - \lambda} = \frac{4}{5 - 4} = 4$$

3. Average number of workers in the waiting room -

$$Lq = \frac{\lambda^2}{\mu(\mu - \lambda)} = \frac{4^2}{5(5 - 4)} = 3.2$$

4. Expected time in the medical clinic -

$$W = \frac{1}{\mu - \lambda} = \frac{1}{5 - 4} = 1 \; hour$$

5. Expected time in the waiting room -

$$Wq = \frac{\lambda}{\mu(\mu - \lambda)} = \frac{4}{5(5 - 4)} = 0.8 \; hour$$

2. The severity of illnesses and injuries treated varies so little that the population can be considered homogenous; since arrivals occur individually, there are no batched arrivals.

3. Workers arrive at the clinic according to a statistical model known as the Poisson probability distribution. (Details on the Poisson distribution can be found, for example, in Berenson and Levine, 1992, p. 245-48). The arrivals occur at a rate of 4 per hour. In general, the arrival rate is often designated with the Greek letter lambda.

4. The waiting room is so large that it is valid to assume an infinite queue capacity.

5. Workers enter the clinic no matter how many other workers are waiting (no balking). They are always seen by the physician (no reneging).

6. Workers are treated in a first-come, first-served order (FIFO).

7. The clinic is staffed by a single physician.

8. The time required for the physician to treat a worker follows a stochastic model known as the exponential probability distribution. (A discussion of the exponential distribution is available in Keller, Warrack, and Bartel, 1994, pp. 203-6). The rate with which the physician treats workers is 5 per hour, denoted in general by the Greek letter mu (μ).

9. The physician suffers no breakdowns, and does not vary the rate of rendering service if the waiting room becomes crowded. No more than one worker is treated at a time.

Because the clinic has these nine properties and is thus a basic single-server queuing system, a number of interesting output properties can be obtained with simple algebra: the percent utilization of the medical clinic, equals 80%; the average number of workers in the medical clinic, L, is 4; the average number of workers in the waiting room, Lq, is equal to 3.2; the expected time in the medical clinic, W, is equal to 1 hour; and the expected time in the waiting room, Wq, is equal to 0.8 hour. The formulas from which these quantities were obtained are tabulated in Figure 7. These formulas hold if $< \mu$, and describe the steady-state behavior of the system.

An important application of these results is to examine the economic consequences. Observe that an average of 4 workers is in the medical office. If these workers earn $10 per hour, the cost to the plant is $40 per hour. Suppose that it were possible to increase the rate of treating patients from the current rate of 5 per hour to 6 per hour. How much should we pay? To answer this question, look at the average number in the medical clinic when the service rate (μ) = 6. This will equal 4 divided by (6-4) or 2 persons. Thus, the cost of waiting per hour is now $20, a savings of $20. Therefore, any investment which increases the service rate to 6 can be justified so long as its hourly cost is no more than $20.

A number of queuing systems of interest to the health care executive represent slight variations from this basic model. For example, when there is more than one server, the multiple-server basic queuing system can be analytically described, or the queue capacity can be assumed finite. A practical example is a telephone system with a limited number of hold positions. Similarly, the calling population can be assumed finite. This is the case when the servicing of laboratory test equipment is considered. The finite number of laboratory units constitute the calling population. This situation can also be solved analytically. Descriptions of analytical models for these systems, as well as others, are given in a number of references, such as Winston (1991). In many cases, however, the queuing system which the health care executive is working with cannot be modeled analytically. In these cases, simulation modeling must be used in order to study the system.

Relevant applications of queuing systems are reported in the literature. Culmer (1975) has suggested that many organizations within the Department of Defense exhibit properties of multi-channel, time dependent queuing systems as in the Army's Acute Minor Illness Clinic (AMIC). Models of this system would allow one to determine optimum staffing levels and to upgrade the quality of service. The usefulness of queuing analysis in radiology has been discussed by Rosenquist (1987). In this study, the characteristics of examination time and interarrival time were determined for an emergency room radiology service. Weiss and McClain (1987) used a queuing-analytic approach to describe the process by which patients leaving an acute care facility await extended care services.

2. Inventory Control

Health care organizations use large quantities of supplies and equipment in the delivery of services. They must maintain an inventory of pharmaceuticals, medical supplies, blood plasma, office supplies, food and dietary supplements, and spare parts for equipment maintenance and repair. Therefore, cost-effective inventory control is an important component of the materials management program.

Quantitative decision analysis provides tools for decisions about the level of supply to be maintained for various items in the organization's inventory. The basic inventory model has two primary objectives:

- to provide information that will help minimize the costs of ordering and storing items of inventory;
- to provide information necessary for determining reorder points.

Figure 8 describes the basic economic order quantity (EOQ) model. This model provides the materials manager with information on the quantity of a supply item that

Figure 8 - Economic Order Quality (EOQ) Model

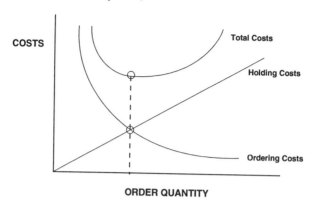

Figure 9 - Determining Reorder Point

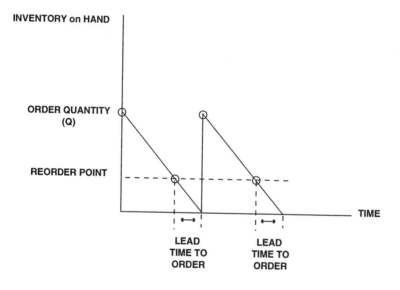

should be purchased in order to minimize the total costs of ordering and holding that item in inventory. Ordering costs include the costs of preparing requisitions and purchase orders, transmitting the order to the supplier (mail or electronic order), receiving and checking the material when received, and maintaining necessary records. Holding costs include the costs of handling and storing the supply, maintaining inventory records, and the cost of invested capital. The latter is a measure of the opportunity cost of having cash tied up in inventory that otherwise could be used for other purposes by the organization, including short-term investment.

Note from Figure 8 that ordering costs decline as the order quantity is increased, but holding costs increase as order quantity is increased since larger inventory levels must be maintained. The EOQ is the point at which these two cost functions intersect, the point at which the total of both costs is the lowest.

The second objective of the inventory model is to determine when to reorder. The reorder point (see Figure 9) is the minimum level of inventory that can be maintained while insuring that the supply will not be depleted. The demand pattern for drawing items from inventory is plotted against time. The lead time to order is determined by the maximum time required to place an order and receive the material from a supplier. The reorder point is that level of inventory which is on hand when the lead time for an order is reached.

In Figure 9, the demand pattern for drawing items from inventory is continuous and uniform, an unlikely situation in the real world. The lead time to order will be affected by the pattern of demand which may be completely random or may follow mathematical patterns. Recent advances in the use of computer technology and electronic data interchange between purchasers and suppliers have significantly reduced lead time. Just-in-time ordering systems have been adopted by many hospitals and other health services organizations working in collaboration with their major suppliers.

Many variations to the basic inventory model described in this section exist. The reader interested in the mathematical formulas or in more detail on model variations is directed to such sources as Austin & Boxerman, 1995. Inventory control computer software is readily available from commercial vendors.

Inventory models have been used by a number of health care organizations and by medical suppliers as well. For example, Kwak, Durbin, and Stanley (1991) describe the use of EOQ models in a 220-bed teaching pediatric hospital for the purchase of intravenous fluids. Storage space and capital requirements for inventory were reduced without affecting the quality of service provided.

3. Linear Programming

Efficient allocation of resources is an essential component of cost containment for health services organizations. Linear programming models assist managers in allocating resources in the most efficient manner within the limits of resources available to them. Organizational objectives often include the following:
- Providing service at the lowest possible cost
- Providing the largest quantity of service possible with available resources
- Assigning staff to service units in the most efficient manner
- Maximizing net revenue in the provision of services.

The basic linear programming model is made up of two components—an objective function and a set of resource constraints. The objective function describes the variable to be optimized (maximized or minimized) in the form of a linear equation. The constraints are a set of linear inequalities and/or equations that determine the range of feasible solutions in which the optimum solution will be found. These functions are expressed in terms of decision variables whose values are determined when the model is solved.

An illustration will show how a linear programming model is formulated. An outpatient clinic provides physical examinations as part of its service program. Both adult employment physicals and preschool physicals for children are offered. Certain resources are required for each type of exam:
- Each adult physical requires 20 minutes of physician time and 40 minutes of support staff time.
- Each preschool exam requires 40 minutes of physician time and 20 minutes of support staff time.

These exams are scheduled once a week on Monday. For the upcoming Monday, time available includes 8 hours of physician time and 10 hours of support staff time. The clinic administrator wants to schedule the maximum number of examinations within these limitations.

This problem is expressed mathematically as follows:
The objective function is SVC = X1 + X2 where
    X1 = the number of adult exams to be scheduled,
    X2 = the number of child exams to be scheduled, and
    SVC = the totals number of exams to be provided.
The objective is to maximize SVC.

There are two resource constraints for this problem, one for each of the two types of resources required: physician time and support staff time. These are expressed mathematically as:
    20X1 + 40X2 < 480 (Physician Time Constraint)
    40X1 + 20X2 < 600 (Support Staff Time Constraint)
The physician time constraint states that physician time required for adult exams (20 minutes times X1) plus physician time required for child exams (40 minutes times X2) must be less than or equal to the total physician time available, 480 minutes (8 hours). The support staff time constraint indicates that support staff time required for adult exams (40 minutes times X1) plus staff time required for child exams (20 minutes times X2) cannot exceed 600 minutes (10 hours), the total support staff time available.

The solution to this problem is obtained mathematically using the Simplex Method. The Simplex solution is an iterative process in which an initial feasible solution is found and successive improvements are made until an optimum solution is obtained. Good computer software is available for solving these problems.

The solution to the example problem using the QuickQuant computer software (Lapin, 1994) is shown in Figure 10. The solution which maximizes total service provided is:
    X1 = 12 adult physicals and
    X2 = 6 child exams.
A total of 18 exams can be scheduled for next Monday.

Note that this problem was solved using integer programming, a special case of linear programming in which one or more of the decision variables must take on whole number or integer values. Since scheduling a fraction of a patient for a physical exam is impossible, integer programming was used to solve the model.

The reader interested in more detail on linear programming and the solution techniques involved is referred to Austin and Boxerman, Quantitative Analysis for Health Services Administration.

Linear programming requires that the objective function and constraint inequalities/equations be linear, that is graphed as straight lines. Not all problems in the real world meet this condition. Mathematical programming models can be used in solving nonlinear optimization problems (Lee, Moore, and Taylor, 1990).

Transportation and assignment models are special cases of linear programming (Austin & Boxerman, 1995). The transportation model is used in solving problems which involve multiple supply and demand locations. For example, a multi-hospital system might contract with a supplier of pharmaceuticals with multiple warehouse locations. In preparing a shipment plan to supply the hospitals, a matrix of supply

Figure 10 - QuickQuant Report-Solution to Integer Program

Problem: Clinic Schedule   Date: 01-16-1996

FORMULATED INTEGER PROGRAM

Maximize P =

$+ 1\ X_1$ $+ 1\ X_2$

Subject to:

C1: $+ 20\ X_1$ $+ 40\ X_2$ < 480

C2: $+ 40\ X_1$ $+ 20\ X_2$ < 600

DETAILED RECORD OF LINEAR PROGRAMS EVALUATED IN SOLVING INTEGER PROGRAM

Problem Number	Profit Upper Bound	Parent Problem	Branching Variable	Problem Status
1	18.000		Integer	

SOLUTION TO INTEGER PROGRAM

Original Variable	Value	Status
X_1	12.00000	integer
X_2	6.00000	integer

Objective Value: P =   18.00000

Figure 11 - Statistical Control Chart

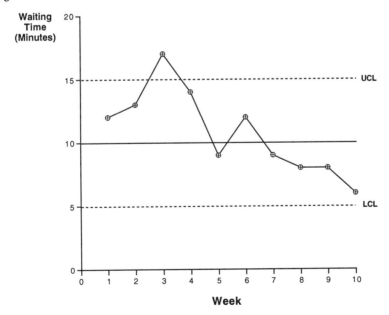

and demand requirements is developed with the transportation costs shown for each possible shipment combination. The solution to the transportation model will minimize transportation costs by minimizing the miles that material will travel in filling the order. The assignment model is a second special case of linear programming used to assign employees to work stations, one employee per station, with the objective of minimizing labor costs.

Linear programming has been applied to a number of problems in health care management. Hospitals use linear programming to analyze the impact of patient case mix on revenue and resource usage (Brandeau and Hopkins, 1984; Hughes and Soliman, 1985). Other applications include blood allocation systems from regional blood banks (Sapountzis, 1989) and nurse staffing models (Leiken, Sexton, and Silkman, 1986).

4. Statistical Process Control

Programs of continuous quality improvement (CQI) have become very important in the delivery of health services. One important quantitative technique which is an essential component of a quality management program is statistical process control.

Statistical process control is a tool to assist managers in monitoring the performance of organizational systems and processes in reference to predetermined standards of quality. Health services organizations have used statistical process control to monitor measures of patient satisfaction, clinical quality, and financial performance. Once a quality standard is established, actual performance is measured periodically and compared to the standard. Variations are reviewed to determine whether they occurred by chance (random events) or were the result of some other assignable cause (system failure) that can be corrected.

Statistical control charts are a commonly used graphic tool for plotting performance measures against standards with values falling outside an acceptable range of random variation. Repeated samples of the variable to be monitored are taken at periodic time intervals with the sample means plotted in reference to the average of all observations.

Figure 11 is an example of a statistical control chart for monitoring patient waiting time for service at an outpatient clinic pharmacy. A random sample of 20 patients is selected each week, and the waiting times for these patients are recorded. Mean waiting times are plotted each week on the control chart, which includes three reference lines:

- The center line is the average of all observations taken over the course of the study.
- The upper control limit (UCL) and lower control limit (LCL) are plotted at a distance of three standard deviations from the center line (overall mean).

Assuming that waiting times are normally distributed, the probability that any weekly value would fall outside of the area between the control limits is less than 1%. (See Austin and Boxerman, 1995.)

Figure 11 indicates that the mean waiting time for week three of the study exceeded the upper control limit indicating that there might have been a problem to be investigated during that period (staffing shortage, inadequate supervision, etc.) The control chart can be used to monitor trends as well. In the example, mean waiting time declined from weeks 6 through 10 indicating continuous improvement in service during this period.

A second type of control chart used in quality monitoring programs is the attribute chart. The attribute chart monitors services or activities that either conform or do not conform to specifications; that is, they take on binary values (conforming or non-conforming). The control chart plots the proportion of non-conforming events for periodic time intervals for management review and corrective action as necessary. For example, a hospital might use an attribute chart to monitor the proportion of patients who required re-admission to the hospital after an initial hospitalization.

Statistical process control charts have been used by health care organizations for a variety of purposes including infection control, employee performance monitoring, monitoring of medication errors, patient satisfaction monitoring, and financial performance review. For example, Latter Day Saints Hospital in Salt Lake City, Utah, used control charts as part of a study to determine how the timing of antibiotic administration affects the risk of surgical wound infections of patients in the Hospital (Classen et al., 1992).

SUMMARY

Quantitative analysis provides an important set of tools for managers in strategic planning and operations improvement; however, limitations do exist. Not all decisions and areas of potential improvement lend themselves to quantitative modeling. In some cases, the costs of modeling may exceed the benefits. Models require data not readily available from the organization's information systems.

Quantitative decision analysis may suggest solutions which call for significant organizational change. Managers must consider human factors and the organization's culture in implementing solutions suggested by the analysis.

The health care industry has become extremely complex and competitive. Recognizing the limitations of quantitative analysis in some situations, managers need to work with technical specialists in their organizations to use these tools for making better strategic decisions and continuously improving organizational performance.

ENDNOTE

1. This section is reprinted with permission from Austin & Boxerman, Quantitative Analysis for Health Services Administration, Ann Arbor, Michigan: Health Administration Press, 1995, pp. 8-12.

REFERENCES

ADA Decision Systems (1995). DPL. ADA Decision Systems, 2710 Sand Hill Road, Menlo Park, CA.
Arthur Andersen & Co. and American College of Healthcare Executives. (1987). *The Future of Healthcare: Changes and Choices.*

Austin, C. J. and Boxerman, S. B. (1995). *Quantitative Analysis for Health Services Administration*, AUPHA Press/Health Administration Press, Ann Arbor, MI.

Barrett, B. J., Parfrey, P. S., Foley, R. N., and Detsky, A. S. (1994). An Economic Analysis of Strategies for the Use of Contrast Media for Diagnostic Cardiac Catheterization. *Medical Decision Making, 14*(4): 325-35.

Berenson, M. L. and Levine, D. M. (1992). *Basic Business Statistics: Concepts and Applications*, Prentice Hall, Englewood Cliffs, N. J.

Born, D. O. (1981). Issues in Forcasting Graduate Dental Education Manpower Supply and Requirements. *Journal of Dental Education, 45*(6): 362-73.

Brandeau, M. L. and Hopkins, D. S. P. (1984). A Patient Mix Model for Hospital Financial Planning. *Inquiry, 21(Spring)*: 32-44.

Caplan, C. M. (1988). Practice Expansion. The Decision-Making Process and Related Strategies. *Dental Clinics of North America, 32*(1): 85-97.

Carpenter, R. B. (1990). Laboratory Cost Analysis: A Practical Approach. *Clinical Laboratory Management Review, 4*(3):168-77.

Classen, D. C. et. al. (1992). The Timing of Prophylactic Administration of Antibiotics and the Risk of Surgical-Wound Infection. *The New England Journal of Medicine, 326*: 281-86.

Clemen, R. T. (1991). *Making Hard Decisions: An Introduction to Decision Analysis*. PWS-Kent Publishing Co., Boston.

Coleman, R.L. (1989). The Use of Decision Analysis in Quality Assessment. *Quality Review Bulletin, 15*(12):383-91.

Culmer, B. B. (1975). A Simulation Model for Multi-Channel, Time-Dependent Queueing Systems and an Application to Test and Evaluate an Analytical Model of the U.S. Army Acute Minor Illness Clinics. *NTIS AD-A018 310/3*, (September).

Dasbach, M. S. and Gustafson, D. H. (1989). Impacting Quality in Health Care: the Role of the Health Systems Engineer. *Journal of the Society for Health Systems, 1*(1): 75-84.

Duncan, A. J. (1986). *Quality Control and Industrial Statistics* (5th ed.), Richard D. Irwin, Inc., Homewood.

Elwell, G. R. (1979). Forecasting: Which Type is For You?, *American Journal of Medical Technology, 45*(2): 131-5.

Feldstein, M. S. (1963). Operational Research and Efficiency in the Health Service. *The Lancet, (2 March)*: 491-93.

Flagle, C. D. (1962). Operations Research in the Health Services. *Circulation Research, 11*: 621-28.

Fries, B. E. (1976). Bibliography of Operations Research in Health-Care Systems. *Operations Research, 24*: 801-14.

Gapenski, L. C. (1989). Analysis Provides Test for Profitability of New Services. *Healthcare Financial Management, 43*(11): 48, 52-4, 58.

Goldberg, J., Dietrich, R., Chen, J. M., Mitwasi, M., Valenzuela, T., and Criss, E. (1990). A Simulation Model for Evaluating a set of Emergency Vehicle Base Locations: Development, Validation, and Usage. *Socio-Economic Planning Sciences, 24*(2): 125-41.

Grant, E. L. and Leavenworth, R. S. (1980). *Statistical Quality Control* (5th ed.), McGraw-Hill, New York.

Hammer, M. and Champy, J. (1993). *Reengineering the Corporation: A Manifesto for Business Revolution*, Harper-Collins, New York.

Healthcare Information and Management Systems Society (1995). *Guide to Effective Health Care Management Engineering*, The Society, Chicago.

Hueston, W. J., Mainous III, A. G., and Farrell, J. B. (1994). A Cost-Benefit Analysis of Smoking Cessation Programs During the First Trimester of Pregnancy for the Prevention of Low Birthweight. *Journal of Family Practice, 39*(4): 353-7.

Hughes, W. L. and Soliman, S. Y. (1985). Short-term Case Mix Management with Linear Programming. *Hospital and Health Services Administration, 30* (January-February): 52-60.

Jeang, A. (1990). Inpatient Admission System Model Using SIMAN Software. *Journal of Medical Systems, 14(6):* 365-74.

Jones, K. R. (1994). Breakeven Analysis. *Seminars for Nurse Managers, 2(2):* 53-4.

Jones M. and Simmons, P. (1994). Preparing a Successful Satisfaction Survey. *Healthcare Information Management, 8(4):* 61-68.

Keller, G., Warrack, B., and Bartel, H. (1994). *Statistics for Management and Economics,* Duxbury Press, Belmont, CA.

Kwak, N. K., Durbin, E. and Stanley, D. (1991). An Inventory Model for Optimizing Purchasing of Intravenous Fluids for Hospitals: A Case Study. *Journal of Medical Systems, 15(2):* 171-81.

Lapin, L. L. (1994). *QuickQuant Version 4.1,* Alamo Publishing Co., Pleasonton, CA.

Lee, S. M., Moore, L. J. and Taylor, B. W. (1990). *Management Science,* Allyn and Bacon, Boston.

Leiken, A., Sexton, T. R. and Silkman, R. H. (1986). A Model to Assess the Quality-Cost Trade-off in Nursing Homes. *Health Services Research, 21(2):* 145-60.

Lukacs, J. (1986). Breakeven Analysis. *Nurse Practitioner, 11(2):* 48, 53.

Nutting, P. A., Calonge, B. N., Iverson, D. C., and Green, L. A. (1994). The Danger of Applying Uniform Clinical Policies Across Populations: The Case of Breast Cancer in American Indians. *American Journal of Public Health, 84(10):* 1631-6.

Pratt, M. L. and Grindon, A. J. (1982). Computer Simulation Analysis of Blood Donor Queueing Problems. *Transfusion, 22(3):* 234-7.

Rosenquist C. J. (1987). Queueing Analysis: A Useful Planning and Management Technique for Radiology. *Journal of Medical Systems, 11(6):* 413-9.

Sahney, V. K. (1993). Evolution of Hospital Industrial Engineering. *Journal of the Society for Health Systems, 4(1):* 10.

Sapountzis, C. (1989). Allocating Blood to Hospitals. *Journal of the Operational Research Society, 40(5):* 443-9.

Saunders, C. E., Makens, P. K., and Leblanc, L. J. (1989). Modeling Emergency Department Operations Using Advanced Computer Simulation Systems. *Annals of Emergency Medicine, 18(2):* 134-40.

Schmitz, V., Masters, G. M., and Dilts, W. (1989). Better Forecasting Ensures Profitability, Quality of Care. *Healthcare Financial Management, 43(1):* 60, 62, 64-6.

Scott, D. W., Factor, L. E., and Gorry, G. A. (1978). Predicting the Response Time of an Urban Ambulance System. *Health Service Research, 13(4):* 404-17.

Shuman, L. J., Speas, R. D. and Young, J. P. (1975). *Operations Research in Health Care: A Critical Analysis,* The Johns Hopkins University Press, Baltimore.

Sintonen, H., and Alander, V. (1990). Comparing the Cost-Effectiveness of Drug Regimens in the Treatment of Duodenal Ulcers. *Journal of Health Economics, 9(1):* 85-101.

Song, F., and Rathwel, T. (1994). Stochastic Simulation and Sensitivity Analysis: Estimating Future Demand for Health Resources in China. *World Health Statistics Quarterly - Rapport Trimestriel de Statistiques Sanitaires Mondiales, 47(3-4):* 149-56.

Thomas, W. H. (1968). A Model for Predicting Progress of Coronary Patients. *Health Services Research, 3(3):* 185-213.

Tree Age Software (1994). *Data For Windows.* Tree Age Software, Inc., PO Box 329, Boston, MA.

Vogel, L. C., Sjoerdsma, A. C., Swinkels, W. J., and W'Oigo, H. O. (1979). Operational Experiments in the Outpatient Department. *Tropical & Geographical Medicine, 31(3):* 23-31.

Warner, D. M., Holloway, D. C. and Grazier, K. L. (1984). *Decision Making and Control for Health Administration: The Management of Quantitative Analysis* (2nd ed.), Health Administration Press, Ann Arbor, MI.

Weiss, E. N., and McClain, J. O. (1987). Administrative Days in Acute Care Facilities: A Queueing-Analytic Approach. *Operations Research, 35(1):* 35-44.

Wilson, J. H., and Schuiling, S. J. (1992). Forecasting Hospital Laboratory Procedures. *Journal of Medical Systems, 16(6):* 269-79.

Winston, W. L. (1991). *Operations Research: Applications & Algorithms* (2nd Ed). PWS-Kent Publishing Co., Boston, MA.

33.
ANALYSIS OF CLINICAL JUDGMENT

Krishna S. Dhir, *Pennsylvania State University at Harrisburg, Middletown, PA*

Subjectivity plays an important role in practically every aspect of medical practice, including the physician's tasks of diagnosing, assessing, and treating. This is not to say that objective measurement tools are absent in the medical profession. On the contrary, clinical as well as laboratory techniques continue to achieve increased sophistication and precision in this area. Nevertheless, integration of information obtained by decision makers in the medical and health care fields remains a subjective process. For such integration, physicians must rely on their own judgment. Recent studies on the process of human judgment have demonstrated its limitations. These studies have major implications for the decision making process in the medical profession.

However, new tools based on theories in applied psychology, policy sciences, computer oriented data handling and graphic displays, and multiple regression analyses make possible the investigation of the judgment process. This enables the assessment of the role of subjectivity in decision making and facilitates development of effective support systems for clinical judgment.

I. THE PROCESS OF HUMAN JUDGMENT

Human judgment is a process through which an individual uses social information to make decisions. The social information is obtained from an individual's environment and is interpreted through the individual's cognitive image of the environment. The cognitive image provides a representation of the environment based on past experiences and training and essentially predisposes the person to respond to social information in predictable ways. These patterns are represented by an individual's policies or beliefs about the environment.

Human judgments are based, then, upon one's interpretation of available information. In this light, judgments are probability statements about one's environment and how one reacts to it. Clearly, the human judgment process is inherently limited. It is fundamentally a covert process; individuals seldom describe their judgment process accurately. Ordinarily, the only means of actually explaining judgments are introspection and guessing at reasons. These explanations are generally incomplete and misleading. Subjective reporting is fallible. Judgments are thus inaccurately reported and generally observed to be inconsistent. Identical circumstances do not always lead to identical judgments. Observations of inconsistent judgment might send an observer in search of hidden motives or incompetence on the part of the decision maker.

Psychological theory of human behavior, however, finds such assumption unnecessary. Judgment is inconsistent because its process is not fully analytical and controlled. Inconsistency is, therefore, an inherent characteristic. While covertness, inaccuracy of reporting, and inconsistency may not completely describe the human judgment process, these characteristics make clear that decision aids would prove enormously useful in overcoming the limitations of human judgment.

A. Parameters of Human Judgment

If the parameters of one's judgmental policy orientations could be identified, then we might model the process of that person's judgment and develop support systems to aid clinical judgment. This process may be explored by posing the following questions:

- What factors influence the individual's judgments? Answers will identify variables that influence the individual's assessment of the severity of diseases. These factors should have mutually exclusive characteristics or properties (Hammond et al., 1975).
- What relative emphasis or weight does the individual put on each of these factors? This question refers to the relative weights assigned to the factors in question. One source of disagreement between decision makers arises from the fact that different weights are likely to be attached by different decision makers to the factors (Nisbett and Wilson, 1977; Slovic and Lichtenstein, 1973).
- How does the individual integrate the information regarding each factor to arrive at an overall judgment? Identification of the mathematical relationship which describes the dependence of the overall judgment on the factors considered is important. The relationship between each factor and the overall judgment may be linear or nonlinear, and the contribution of each factor to the overall judgment may be positive or negative. The nature of dependence of the overall judgment on each factor is referred to as that factor's function-form.
- How consistent is the individual in making judgments? An individual may make different judgments about the same situation on different occasions. At least two characteristics of the judgment task are known to affect consistency: task complexity and task uncertainty. Studies show that consistency is lower when the judgment task is complex and when the task requires use of nonlinear rather than linear function forms (Hammond et al., 1975; Hogarth, 1980). Even

when a decision maker intends to use a specific judgment rule as defined by a specific set of factors, relative weights and function forms, his or her judgments or assessments may deviate from those suggested by that rule. In absence of explicit and immediate feedback on judgment, the decision maker may be unaware of the degree to which the actual judgment or assessment deviates from that intended (Nisbett and Wilson, 1977).

Consistency is different from accuracy. A decision maker can be accurate but inconsistent, consistent but inaccurate, both consistent and accurate, or neither. Consistency has to do with the reliability of the decision maker in executing the intended judgmental policy as defined by specific set of factors, relative weights and function forms. When deviation between the actual judgment and that intended is low, consistency is greater. On the other hand, accuracy has to do with the validity of the policy itself—whether the judgmental policy executed (the specific set of factors, relative weights and function forms) is indeed the one that was to be executed.

II. ALTERNATIVE THEORIES

Alternative theories available for the analysis of judgment and decision making include decision theory and multiattribute utility theory (Keeney and Raiffa, 1976), behavioral decision theory (Edwards and Tversky, 1967), psychological decision theory (Kahneman and Tversky, 1979), information integration theory (Anderson, 1974), attribution theory (Jones and McGillis, 1976), and social judgment theory (Hammond et al., 1975; Brehmer and Joyce, 1988). While a brief description of these theories is presented below, a detailed discussion can be found in Human Judgment and Decision Making (Hammond, McClelland and Mumpower, 1980). Readers may also wish to explore literature about the analytic hierarchy process (Saaty, 1980), fuzzy decision theory (Zadeh, 1973), and others not described in this chapter (Cooksey, 1996).

Decision theory literature evaluates unidimensional utility functions over single attributes. True to decision theory's prescriptive nature, multiattribute utility theory, too, seeks to maximize the overall utility derived from a set of attributes. Behavioral decision theory is based on the subjective expected utility concept, and like decision theory and multiattribute utility theory, attempts to prescribe rational decisions. Zeleny (1982) describes it as the "poor person's" multiattribute utility theory. Psychological decision theory moves beyond description of decision making process to explanation and prediction of decision behavior. Seeking the cognitive sources of departure from the criteria of rationality, it attempts to make decision makers aware of their own errors and biases.

The goal of information integration theory is to discover the metric form of cognitive algebra employed in cognitive activities. For example, it asks whether information is integrated in one situation by one algebraic principle and in another situation by another algebraic principle. Attribution theory draws from gestalt psychology. It views people as observing events in their environment and seeking causes of events by evaluating available information. It does not seek models of individual judgment or decision and offers no relative weights or component functions.

Like policy capturing (Stewart, 1975; Zeleny 1982), social judgment theory evolved from Brunswik's lens model. The emerging body of literature explores interpersonal conflict arising from different judgments and lends itself to applications in policy analysis. The social element in social judgment theory is derived from the interaction it affords among two or more individuals through improved communication. While policy capturing uses the lens model to make an individual's judgmental orientations explicit through multiple regression analysis, social judgment theory extends policy capturing to communication of the judgmental orientations and facilitates social interaction. While policy capturing applies to single-person systems, social judgment theory applies to systems consisting of two or more decision makers. The social judgment theory communicates overt judgment differences among decision makers as, for instance, in the DELPHI technique (see Linstone and Turoff, 1975). It also communicates the covert policy differences in terms of its parameters, such as relative weights and function-forms (unlike the DELPHI technique).

Social judgment theory application requires the separation of relative weights from function-forms, a separation unnecessary in policy capturing (Stewart, 1975; Zeleny, 1982). Through this separation, however, social judgment theory allows identification of the sources of differences among decision makers—whether their policy differences arise due to differences in weights assigned to specific factors (relative weights) or differences in the manner in which the information on specific factors is utilized (function-forms). Availability of such information facilitates the development of alternative approaches to social interaction. Exchange of the information may or may not require face-to-face interaction among decision makers (Hammond, 1976).

This chapter describes an application of the social judgment theory that is preferable for a number of reasons. Decision theory and multiattribute utility theory are prescriptive; they indicate how rational decisions should be made. Behavioral decision theory and psychological decision theory explore why decision makers depart from rational prescriptions. The objective here is not to develop a prescriptive approach to clinical judgment or decision making. It is not to compare observed decision behavior against a rational prescription. Rather, the primary objective is to describe the observed process involved in clinical judgment. Social judgment theory works well for such description since it neither prescribes, nor does it seek to explain deviations from rational behavior.

Some controversy surrounds the approach taken by multiattribute utility theory which elicits the relative weights used in making judgments through direct interrogation of the decision maker. The highly influential work of Nisbett and Wilson (1977) sheds suspicion on verbal elicitation. They argue that decision makers' accounts do not explain or clarify their own judgments and decisions. Certain social psychologists do not accept this claim. Ericsson and Simon (1980) argue that useful verbal data can be obtained from decision makers' verbal accounts of their subjective thoughts if investigative techniques are correct. In contrast to the approach of the multiattribute utility theory, the social judgment theory seeks these relative weights indirectly, separate from function-forms, through analysis of the decision maker's judgments on a set of alternative scenarios. For a comparative analysis of multiattribute utility theory and social judgment theory, see Zeleny (1982).

For the purposes of this chapter, social judgment theory is also preferred over attribution theory and information integration theory. Social judgment theory offers means of obtaining a model of individual judgment process—a model useful in developing judgment and decision aids. Attribution theory, on the other hand, generally assumes that cognitive processes underlying causal judgments are not influenced by the person making the judgment. The information integration theory has generally stayed away from applications. For additional discussion, see Hammond, McClelland and Mumpower (1980).

Social judgment theory is also easy to use. The methodology involved in its application yields relatively straightforward, easily understood, mathematically clean results. Further, literature reports that the simple additive models of decision making based on regression analysis seem to be at least as accurate as the more complex models and are preferred by many users with respect to most criteria of desirability (Zeleny, 1982).

Applications based on social judgment theory have had considerable success in the development of decision and judgment aids. For instance, such analyses have proven quite efficient in reducing conflict and increasing agreement among decision makers. These analyses have been found superior even to the DELPHI technique (Rohrbaugh, 1979). Cook and Stewart (1975) compared seven different approaches to obtaining descriptions of judgmental policy and found that the statistical descriptions, such as obtained through the application of social judgment theory, were preferable. For examples, see Kaplan and Schwartz (1977), Arkes and Hammond (1986), Brehmer and Joyce (1988), Cooksey (1996).

III. ANALYSIS OF THE PHYSICIAN'S COGNITION

Consider a situation in which a physician is faced with a patient who has a previously diagnosed case of bacterial pneumonia. The physician must rely on his or her own judgment to assess the severity of the patient's affliction. The analysis of a physician's cognitive system involves the following steps: identification of the clinical problem, exercise of judgment, analysis of judgment, and display of results.

A. Identification of the Clinical Problem

The physician is asked to identify those factors which seem pertinent to the assessment of severity of bacterial pneumonia in afflicted patients. The physician may wish to discuss the attributes of bacterial pneumonia with colleagues or refer to the literature prior to specifying an exhaustive list of factors to be considered in judging the severity. Let us assume that this list is as follows: x-ray of the patient's chest, analysis of sputum, body temperature, respiratory rate, white cell count, red cell count, and age of the patient.

A set of patient profiles, say twenty five in all, is randomly generated; each represents a patient suffering from bacterial pneumonia. A sample profile is shown in Figure 1. In these profiles, x-ray and sputum are rated on a three-point scale, where a rating of 1 represents a mild condition of affliction, 2 a moderate level, and 3 a severe level. Since all patients are afflicted, none represent normal. The patient's body temperature is represented on a scale from a minimum of 38°C to a maximum of 43°C. Rate of respiration is represented on a scale from 30 per minute to 40 per minute. The scale used for white cell count is 10,000 per cubic millimeter to 40,000 per cubic millimeter. Red cell count is 3 million per cubic millimeter to 6 million per cubic millimeter. The patient's age is represented on a scale from 10 to 90 years.

Figure 1 - A Sample Profile of a Bacterial Pneumonia Patient

Case 16

Factors	Values	Scales
X-RAY	2	1 = mild; 2 = moderate; 3 = severe
SPUTUM	1	1 = mild; 2 = moderate; 3 = severe
TEMPERATURE	40°	38 to 43°C
RESPIRATORY RATE	34/min.	30 to 40/min.
WHITE CELL COUNT	35,000/cu.mm.	10,000 to 40,000/cu.mm.
RED CELL COUNT	4 million/cu.mm.	3 to 6 million/cu.mm.
AGE	15 years	10 to 90 years

Please indicate your assessment of the severity of bacterial pneumonia on a scale from 1 to 4, where a rating of 1 represents a *nearly normal* patient, 2 represents a *mild* affliction, 3 represents a *moderate* affliction, and 4 represents a *severe* affliction:_____

To minimize the effect of intercorrelation among the factors, profiles are tested for orthogonality. The objective is to establish the absence of significance among all correlations. The Pearson product-moment correlation coefficient may be used to estimate the population correlation coefficient (Hays and Winkler, 1970). Correlation coefficients are computed for all possible pairs of factors. If the highest correlation coefficient is established not to be significantly different from zero, then we may conclude that none of the correlation coefficients are significantly different from zero. Therefore, a significance test is performed on the highest correlation coefficient observed by computing the t-statistic as follows:

$$t = r_{ij} \bullet [\{ (n - 2) / (1 - r_{ij}2) \} 0.5]$$

where r_{ij} is the sample correlation coefficient (Pearson product-moment coefficient) for variables i and j and n is the number of observations.

B. Exercise of Judgments

The physician is now asked to indicate the a priori subjective estimate of weights when making judgments about the severity of bacterial pneumonia to be described through the twenty-five patient profiles. By distributing 100 points among the seven factors described above, the points assigned to each indicate its importance relative to others. The physician is also asked to indicate the a priori estimates of the function-forms for each factor. From a menu of graph displays the physician may select the one which, in his or her own judgment, best represents the relationship between each factor and the severity rating. (See Figure 2.) Thus, through the relative weights for each factor and the respective relationship with the severity assessment criterion, we obtain the a priori description of the physician's policy regarding assessment of the severity of bacterial pneumonia.

The physician is now asked to rate each patient profile for severity of bacterial pneumonia. This rating may be indicated on a scale from 1 to 4, where 1 represents a nearly normal patient, 2 a patient with a mild affliction, 3 moderate affliction, and 4

Figure 2 - A Menu of Graph Displays

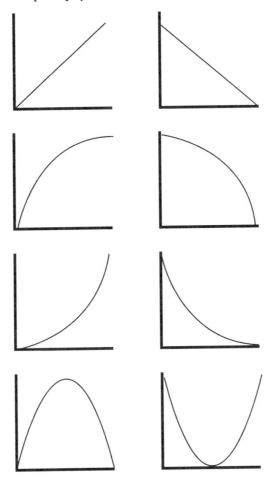

severe affliction. Fractional values for severity ratings may be allowed. After all patient profiles have been rated for severity, the physician may review the 25 patient profiles and make revisions in the severity ratings.

C. Analysis of Judgment

After the physician expresses satisfaction with the severity ratings assigned to patient profiles, the next task is to extract from these judgments a policy orientation description. This task is accomplished through nonlinear multiple regression analyses. In regression analyses, the severity ratings assigned to the different profiles are dependent variables, and the seven factors are the independent variables. These analyses yield the parameters of the decision maker's executed judgmental policy. The regression model consists of first- and second-order terms for each factor. The weights as measures of the emphasis given to the different factors and the function-forms for the different factors are derived from algebraic transformation of the regression model.

For detailed description of the mathematical basis and development of these measures see Hammond et al. (1975).

An issue emerges at this point. Why should a nonlinear model be preferred over a linear model for multiple regression analysis? After all, linear models are used in a large variety of analytical approaches to decision analysis (Zeleny, 1982). Many studies have demonstrated that a linear model accounts for nearly all of the explainable variance in descriptive models of decision making (Stahl and Zimmerer, 1983) and compete well with alternative models using higher order terms (Goldberg, 1971; Goldberg, 1986). At a descriptive level, the linear model is accurate in predicting individual judgments (Laughlin 1978; Dawes, 1979; Einhorn, Kleinmuntz and Kleinmuntz, 1979). It has also been suggested that "linear models are insensitive to deviations from underlying assumptions and thus can reproduce judgments generated by other processes to a remarkable degree of accuracy" (Hogarth, 1980).

Linear models, however, require a process of explicit computation and trading off of factors which, even in moderately complex judgment tasks, is not feasible for unaided judgment (Einhorn, Kleinmuntz and Kleinmuntz, 1979; Hogarth, 1980). Studies show that preferences based on subjective judgment differ from those constructed by a linear model. Zeleny (1982) questions the claim of superiority of linear models because of their robustness as, for instance, made by Dawes (1979) and Laughlin (1978). He suggests that this robustness may be situation-dependent and describes cases where linear models are not capable of reaching correct predictions of human judgment and preference. For discussions on nonlinear representations of judgment and their use within the regression framework, see Hammond et al. (1975).

In the analysis of judgmental policies, consistency in exercise of judgments should be measured and reported whenever possible. Stahl and Harrell (1983) present a discussion on the use of squared multiple correlation coefficient as a measure of a decision maker's cognitive consistency. However, Hammond and Summers (1972) distinguish between cognitive consistency and cognitive control. While cognitive consistency refers to the similarity between repeated judgments of identical profiles, cognitive control is the similarity between an individual's judgments and predictions based on a specific model. The variance about the mean is always less than the variance around any other point; therefore, consistency is the upper bound for control with respect to any model. When the predictions from a model coincide with the mean of the distributions of repeated judgments of identical profiles, the measure of control becomes a measure of consistency.

Cognitive control exercised by a participant with respect to the particular model obtained through nonlinear multiple regression analysis is measured in terms of the multiple correlation coefficient, R (Hammond and Summers, 1971). Hammond et al. (1975) propose that to determine whether the multiple correlation coefficient will provide a measure of cognitive consistency, a test for lack of fit of the specific model obtained through multiple regression analysis should be performed (Draper and Smith, 1981). If there is no evidence of lack of fit, the multiple correlation coefficient provides a measure of both consistency and control.

D. Display of Results

The physician can now be provided with feedback on the components of his or her judgment process regarding the assessment of severity of bacterial pneumonia as follows:

- The relative weights associated with each factor obtained from the ratings of the patient profiles are now available, so the physician may compare his or her own set of weights with a priori weights. The physician is also able to compare these weights with the weights obtained from other physicians. See Figure 3 for a sample of the format used for this feedback.
- Function-forms for each factor obtained from the physician's judgments are available. Again, the physician may compare his or her own set of function-forms with the a priori function-forms as well as with those of others.
- The physician can receive feedback regarding his or her own cognitive control as measured by the multiple correlation coefficient. A high value for multiple correlation coefficient, near 1.0, would indicate that the person was relatively consistent in making judgments, and that the regression model provided a good "fit" or description of those judgments. However, even slight inconsistencies can lead to perceived conflicts and disagreements where little conflict really exists, clearly a source of confusion in clinical assessment.

IV. APPLICATION OF ANALYSIS

The analyses described above offer interesting possibilities for the study of clinical judgment and decision making. For example, the relationship between the cognitive models of two individuals may be analyzed through lens model equation (Hammond et al., 1975; Brehmer and Joyce, 1988):

$$r_{12} = G \bullet R1 \bullet R2 + C \bullet [\,(1 - R1)2 \bullet (1 - R2)2\,]0.5$$

where r_{12} is the correlation between two variables, say Y1 and Y2 (the variables may be two individuals' judgments or an individual's judgment and an environmental criterion); G is the correlation between the components of Y1 and Y2 that are predicted from a linear regression on the factors; R1 and R2 are the linear multiple correlations between the factors and Y1 and Y2 respectively; and C is the correlation between the residuals from the linear regressions of Y1 and Y2 .

R1 may be interpreted as a measure of the fit of the specific model. G is the correlation between predictions based on two models. C measures the relation between the components of Y1 and Y2 that is not accounted for by the regression analysis. If the regression analysis is based on a linear model, a high value of C would suggest presence of nonlinear variation shared by the two systems. In such cases, inclusion of nonlinear terms in the model may be considered. If two individuals have identical policies represented by linear models, then G becomes 1. If no shared nonlinearity exists, then r12 would become (R1 • R2), i.e., a measure of agreement between two individuals.

We have already distinguished the concept of cognitive control a physician exercises over his judgment policy from the concept of consistency with which the physician applies it. If R1 measures cognitive control, R2 measures consistency, and we ignore the second term in the equation above. Then the correlation between ratings suggested by the policy and the ratings assigned by the physician judgment, ra, may be described as:

$$ra = G \bullet R1 \bullet R2$$

G may be considered a measure of the physician's knowledge of the policy.

Correlation between the judgments made by two physicians over the same set of

Figure 3 - A Sample of Format Used to Provide Feedback on Relative Weights Obtained From Judgments of Severity of Bacterial Pneumonia

RELATIVE WEIGHT PROFILE

A: PHYSICIAN 12'S WEIGHTS FROM INITIAL JUDGMENT POLICY
B: PHYSICIAN 12'S WEIGHTS FROM A PRIORI POLICY

0.0_____0.5_____1.0	WEIGHT	FUNCTION FORM
X-RAY		
AAAA	0.11	POSITIVE LINEAR
BBBBBBB	0.18	POSITIVE LINEAR
SPUTUM		
AAAA	0.11	NONLINEAR
BBBBBBB	0.18	NONLINEAR
TEMPERATURE		
AAAA	0.11	NONLINEAR
BBB	0.10	NONLINEAR
RESPIRATORY RATE		
AAA	0.08	NONLINEAR
BBBBBBB	0.20	POSITIVE LINEAR
WHITE CELL COUNT		
AA	0.06	NONLINEAR
BBBBB	0.15	NONLINEAR
RED CELL COUNT		
AAAAAA	0.15	NONLINEAR
B	0.05	NONLINEAR
AGE		
AAAAAAAAAAAAAAAA	0.38	NONLINEAR
BBBBB	0.14	NONLINEAR

0.0_____0.5_____1.0

patient profiles can be used as a measure of the degree of consensus among the two physicians or the similarity between their respective policies. A number of studies demonstrate that aids to judgment enhance consensus among decision makers through application of social judgment theory.

A number of studies have also shown that decision makers are unable to describe accurately their own judgment process. However, their judgmental policies become explicit through relative weights and function-forms. Once made explicit, the decision makers can modify their policies in a controlled manner by specifying changes in weights and/or function-forms. To appreciate the uniqueness of the approach presented in this chapter, we might compare it to the DELPHI technique (Linstone and Turoff, 1975; Rohrbaugh, 1976) would be useful. The DELPHI technique was an outgrowth of a series of studies at the RAND Corporation. By 1970 it was widely acclaimed as a means to generate a consensus of judgment in a group. The DELPHI technique is characterized by three distinct features: a guarantee of anonymity to the participants in the group; a primarily statistical compilation of the group's response, and controlled, iterative feedback of the group's response to each member prior to another set of judgments.

The approach described here meets the same criteria. It can guarantee anonymity to a group of physicians attempting to build consensus. It can also be used to compile statistics on the participating physicians' judgmental responses. In fact, the data compiled would include information not only on overall judgments (as in the DELPHI technique), but also on the components or parameters of the judgments (unlike the DELPHI technique). Finally, the approach can include controlled feedback of the participating physicians' judgmental policies to each member of the participating group prior to another set of judgments. In this way, not only are the overt judgment differences made explicit (as in the DELPHI technique), but the covert policy differences, too, may be explicit (unlike the DELPHI technique). This would identify those specific parameters (i.e., factors, relative weights, and function-forms) of the individual judgmental policies which contribute to disagreements among the physicians. Explicit parameters allow physicians to control policy to be implemented by revision of their judgmental policies. The DELPHI technique, limited to revising overt responses, does not offer such opportunities. As in the DELPHI method, our approach, or a modification, may be repeated until the desired level of consensus is reached or alternative policies explored.

SUMMARY

This chapter presents an alternative approach to clinical judgment for the assessment of disease severity. Describing policies in terms of the parameters of the human judgment process provides an operational definition of decision makers' cognitive sets. Investigation of the judgment's parameters enables the development of judgmental aids to assist in the exercise of human judgment in two ways:

- The judgment process of the individual, though covert, internal and subjective, is clarified, externalized, and explained so that it can be examined and under stood.
- Desired changes in the judgment policy motivated by change of insights,

self-understanding, group discussions, and feedback about judgment policy can be specified and executed consistently as desired.

A decision maker may therefore define severity as well as assess it as defined by another. To the extent that a chosen set of trade-offs or weights are executed consistently, the policies would be implemented with improved effectiveness, thus yielding better decisions. To the extent that a group of decision makers agree on policy, relevancy of decisions can be taken with a greater degree of confidence.

REFERENCES

Anderson, N. H. (1974). Cognitive algebra. In L. Berkowitz (Ed.) *Advances in Experimental Social Psychology, 7.* Academic Press, New York.

Arkes, H. R., and Hammond, K. R., (Eds) (1986). *Judgment and Decision Making: An Interdisciplinary Reader.* Cambridge University Press, New York.

Brehmer, B., and Joyce, C. R. B. (Eds) (1988). *Human Judgment: The SJT View.* Elsevier Science Publishers B.V. (North-Holland), New York.

Cook, R. L., and Stewart, T. R. (1975). A comparison of seven methods for obtaining subjective descriptions of judgmental policy. *Organizational Behavior and Human Performance, 13*: 31-45.

Cooksey, R. W. (1996). *Judgment Analysis: Theory, Methods, and Applications.* Academic Press, San Diego, CA.

Dawes, R. M. (1979). The robust beauty of improper linear models in decision making. *American Psychologist, 34*(7): 571-582.

Draper, N. and Smith, H. (1981). *Applied Regression Analysis,* Second Edition. Wiley, New York.

Edwards, W., and Tversky, A. (1967). *Decision Making: Selected Readings.* Penguin Books, Middlesex, England.

Einhorn, H. J., Kleinmuntz, D. N., and Kleinmuntz, B. (1979). Linear regression and process tracing models of judgment. *Psychological Review, 86*: 465-485.

Ericsson, K. A., and Simon, H. A. (1980). Verbal reports as data. *Psychological Review, 87*: 215-251.

Goldberg, L. R. (1971). Five models of clinical judgment: An empirical comparison between linear and nonlinear representations of the human inference process. *Organizational Behavior and Human Performance, 6*: 458-479.

Goldberg, L. R. (1986). Simple models or simple processes? Some research on clinical judgments. In H. R. Arkes and K. R. Hammond (Eds). *Judgment and Decision Making: An Interdisciplinary Reader,* 335-353. Cambridge University Press, New York.

Hammond, K. R. and Summers, D. A. (1972). Cognitive control. *Psychological Review, 79*: 58-67.

Hammond, K. R., Stewart, T. R., Brehmer, B., and Steinmann, D. O. (1975). Social judgment theory. In M. Kaplan and S. Schwartz (Eds.) *Human Judgment and Decision Processes,* 271-312. Academic Press, New York.

Hammond, K. R. (1976). Externalizing the parameters of quasi-rational thought. In M. Zeleny (Ed.), *Multiple Criteria Decision Making: Kyoto 1975,* 75-96. Springer-Verlag, New York.

Hammond, K. R., McClelland, G. H., and Mumpower, J. (1980). *Human Judgment and Decision Making.* Praeger, New York.

Hays, W. L., and Winkler, R. L. (1970). *Statistics: Probability, Inference, and Decision, Volume II.* Holt, Rinehart and Winston, New York.

Hogarth, R. M. (1980). *Judgement and Choice: The Psychology of Decision.* Wiley, New York.

Jones, E. E., and McGillis, D. (1976). New directions in attribution theory research. In J. H. Harvey, W. J. Ickes and R. F. Kidd (Eds.). *New Directions in Attribution Research.* Erlbaum, Hillsdale, NJ.

Kahneman, D., and Tversky, A. (1979). Prospect theory. *Econometrica, 47*: 263-291.

Kaplan, M. F., and Schwartz, S. (Eds.) (1977). *Human Judgment and Decision Processes in Applied Settings.* Academic Press, New York.

Keeney, R. L., and Raiffa, H. (1976). *Decisions with Multiple Objectives: Preferences and Value Tradeoffs.* Wiley, New York.

Laughlin, J. E. (1978). Comment on estimating coefficients in linear models: It don't make no nevermind. *Psychological Bulletin, 85*(2): 247-253.

Linstone, H. A., and Turoff, M. (1975). *The DELPHI Method: Techniques and Applications.* Addison-Wesley, Reading, MA.

Nisbett, R. E., and Wilson, T. D. (1977). Telling more than we can know: Verbal reports on mental processes. *Psychological Review, 84*: 231-259.

Rohrbaugh, J. W. (1976). Conflict management in decision-making groups: A comparison of social judgment analysis and the DELPHI technique. Unpublished doctoral dissertation, University of Colorado.

Rohrbaugh, J. W. (1979). Improving the quality of group judgment: Social judgment theory and the DELPHI technique. *Organizational Behavior and Human Performance, 24*: 73-92.

Saaty, T .L. (1980). *The Analytic Hierarchy Process.* McGraw-Hill, New York.

Slovic, P., and Lichtenstein, S. (1973). Comparison of Bayesian and regression approaches to the study of information processing in judgment. In L. Rappaport and D.A. Summers (Eds.) *Human Judgment and Social Interaction,* 16-108. Holt, Rinehart, and Winston, New York.

Stahl, M. J., and Harrell, A. M. (1981). Modeling effort decisions with behavioral decision theory: Toward an individual differences model of expectancy theory. *Organizational Performance and Human Performance, 27*: 303-381.

Stahl, M. J., and Zimmerer, T. W. (1983). Modeling product development decision policies of managers and management students: Differences between subjective and relative weights. *IEEE Transactions on Engineering Management, EM-30*(1):18-24.

Stewart, T. R. (1975). Policy capture. In C. McMillan, *Mathematical Programming,* Second Edition, 635-646. Wiley, New York.

Zadeh, L. A. (1973). Outline of a new approach to the analysis of complex systems and decision processes. *IEEE Transactions on Systems, Man, and Cybernetics, 3,* 28-44.

Zeleny, M. (1982). *Multiple Criteria Decision Making.* McGraw-Hill, New York.

34.
MANAGING POPULATION HEALTH

Suzan D. Boyd, *University of South Carolina, Columbia, SC*

Carleen Stoskopf, *University of South Carolina, Columbia, SC*

The changing health care paradigm requires a change in the accountability of health service organizations (HSOs) from managing illness to managing health, from organizations that are responsible for treating individuals to ones that are not only responsible to the individual but also for the health of populations. In this new paradigm, the basic mission of the hospital changes from providing excellence in acute care to assuming responsibility for collaboration with others in the ongoing effort to improve community health. The hospital must facilitate the development of a continuum of health care services and create an organization that can manage the health of populations.

This transition has occurred for several reasons. National health care reform has failed. Health care costs are escalating. And financing mechanisms have changed from fee-for-service to forms of managed care and capitation. The latter places health services organizations and associated providers at risk for the cost of the health care services they provide. As a result, hospitals and/or integrated systems must develop mechanisms for managing the health of groups and individuals in defined communities. This management is currently being accomplished through the development of community health initiatives and alliances or integrated networks of providers that will assume responsibility for providing care to "defined groups of individuals" throughout a continuum of services (Shortell et al., 1996).

Defining community is a critical first step. Hospitals historically have defined their community simply as the town or neighborhood in which they are located. Their primary market has been defined as either the geographic area from which a significant percentage of their patients come or the area physically surrounding the hospital. The Hospital Community Benefit Program at New York University defined community as "all persons and organizations within a reasonably circumscribed geographic area, in which there is a sense of interdependence and belonging" (Kovner, 1995).

Responsibility for the health of populations (population health) requires re-thinking the definition of community. Initial thought indicates that membership in an integrated network or an alliance may simply change the definition of community to encompass a broader geographic area or a defined service population. Gamm points out that the changing structure of health care and the development of partnerships of providers, insurers, and sometimes consumers changes the definition of community health populations from a defined geographic population or a disadvantaged and vulnerable group to groups of health plan enrollees and care-seeking populations (Gamm, 1996). This may be correct, but a complicating factor is that while networks may be contractually responsible for a defined population, the individuals in that group can change insurance; may or may not be insured; and can utilize hospital and provider services without regard to contractual services. Hospitals, through their emergency rooms or by being a sole community provider, will be called upon to provide care for all individuals who seek or need such care, not just the population enrolled in their network or those that represent an insured population. Thus, the attempt to manage health only for an enrolled population will not, over the long run, have a major effect on reducing the costs of health care in a community. Networks or hospitals must in a true sense assume responsibility for improving the health of three groups: the broader community, actual service users, and populations enrolled in their network or affiliated insurance products. The community to be served, then, will cover a range from the broad geographic area of network members to the neighborhood/vicinity in which its participating hospitals and providers are located.

Managing this changing health care paradigm and playing a role in community health requires addressing health care issues at both the macro/community and micro/individual level. It requires an understanding of macro level community health issues affecting the entire population such as clean air, water, schools, housing, and access to health care, as well as to micro level health risks and behaviors of individuals. This shift places an emphasis on health promotion and prevention for the community and the individual at the primary, secondary, and tertiary level. Such a broad scope will require collaboration of all public and private HSOs and other service organizations in a community. Community resources, primary care, and health promotion and prevention are tools that will enable the hospital to facilitate change in community health.

This chapter will discuss how an HSO can manage the health of a defined population, assuming that the HSO is responsible for the health of the community in which it is located in addition to the population served by a network, alliance, or particular business or contractual relationship. The discussion will cover five areas basic to managing the health of populations:

- Community assessment as a component of strategic planning;
- Managerial epidemiology to provide a new managerial framework based on the use of epidemiological analysis of the population and provider characteristics, as well as assessment of prevention activities, and monitoring of outcomes;
- The role of clinicians in providing population-based prevention both in planning for population health and in managing the individual patient;

- The role of data in planning and epidemiology, and the need for data as a link between the community, networks, hospitals and clinicians;
- Managing care toward achieving pre-defined population goals and objectives as related to the levels of prevention.

I. COMMUNITY ASSESSMENT

Community assessment should be completed as part of the external environmental assessment in a strategic planning process. Traditionally the external environmental assessment has analyzed the economic, political, technological, stakeholder, and competitive issues and indicators of the community and market (Duncan, et al., 1995). The changing health care paradigm requires that in addition to the traditional areas of market analysis the hospital must develop a detailed understanding of critical health risks and community needs. Only with community health data can the hospital begin to plan for management of population health in a way that will meet both short and long term goals of improving health and reducing cost to the community.

Community assessment includes two steps: assessment and action. It provides a framework for gathering primary and secondary data, both quantitative and qualitative, that yields a detailed description and picture of the current health problems and needs of the community. Data should include measures of morbidity, mortality, incidence and prevalence of disease, relevant measures of socioeconomic status, health and social service capacity, and community perceptions about the health needs of that community. Published models of community assessment include the Social Accountability Budget of the Catholic Hospital Association; the American Hospital Association framework; PATCH (Planned Approach to Community Health) from the CDC; and APEXph: Assessment Protocol for Excellence in Public Health (Catholic Hospital Association., 1991; Rice, 1993; U.S. Dept. Of Health and Human Services, 1993; National Association of County Officials, 1991). Community assessment involves a collaborative data-driven measurement process. This process contains elements of assessing the community organizational structure, involving the community for problem-solving and action, assessing health needs using science-based data, setting priorities in light of local resources, developing intervention strategies, and using a system of monitoring and evaluation (CDC, 1991).

Community assessment by definition includes community involvement both in the process and in the prioritization and implementation of services (Rice, 1993; CHA, 1989). To have an impact on macro and micro health levels affecting the population and ultimately to change community and individual behavior, the network or hospital must collaborate with other social and health services providers, business, government, and individuals in the community. No one hospital, network, or health department can assume responsibility for the complex social, community and individual issues that affect health. Thus, collaboration must build bridges over traditional organizational boundaries, and traditional roles of leadership and accountability must shift as a response to the community's priority health needs.

The theoretical framework outlined by CDC is reflected in approaches to community assessment relative to both process and the acquisition of "science-based data." A community assessment process optimally contains the elements outlined in Table 1.

This model was developed based on an extensive review of the literature and interviews with hospital CEOs (Boyd, 1997).

Table 1 - Community Assessment Processes and Information

---

1. Community:
   A. Select/identify community partner(s)
   B. Form a community assessment committee
   C. Define the community assessment process
   D. Define the community
2. Obtaining, Organizing, and Analyzing Data
   A. Complete an:
      1. Analysis of community health services
      2. Analysis of community social services
   B. Gather and review secondary data:
      1. Demographic data
      2. Socioeconomic data
      3. Morbidity and mortality data
   C. Obtain primary data:
      1. Conduct focus groups
      2. Conduct interviews with community residents and leaders
      3. Complete citizen surveys (mail or telephone)
      4. Town meetings/community forums
3. Identify Problems and Priorities
   A. Identify major health problems in the community
   B. Determine the priority problems to be addressed
      1. Nominal groups
   C. Identify benchmarks such as in Healthy People 2000
4. Program Planning
   A. Plan programs addressing priority problems
   B. Initiate programs addressing priority problems
5. Evaluation
   A. Plan for short term evaluation
   B. Plan for long term evaluation

(Boyd, 1991)

Information from the community assessment should be included in the external environmental analysis used to develop the hospital strategic plan. Identified areas of risk and need should then guide the HSO, with input from the community, in developing specific goals and objectives for improving health. This community input should come from a community advocacy group (community assessment committee) that has participated not only in planning the community assessment but also in determining the community health priorities identified by that assessment. The plan must have explicit goals and objectives that allow for intervention at both the community and individual level. The priority objectives and strategies should emphasize population-wide interventions that can protect entire communities (McGinnis and Lee, 1995). At one level, the development of objectives and strategies serves to educate stakeholders and managers to the needs of the community. In addition, budgeting needs are identified as an HSOs strategic plan sends a clear signal to allocate resources for accomplishing these objectives.

Objectives should be realistic, measurable, and economically feasible. Data should be collected for each objective. The data should reflect the current status for a particular disease or morbidity statistic, what that statistic would be without intervention given the current trend, the projected trend and the target goal by a time five years hence. Benchmarks such as Healthy People 2000 can aid in establishing health criteria and goals (CDC, 1991). "CDC's Consensus Set of Health Status Indicators" provides another source when comparing local to state and national indicators (Carson and Zucconi, 1993). (See Table 2.)

Table 2 - CDC's Consensus Set of Health Status Indicators for Assessing Community Health Status and Monitoring Progress Toward Objectives

---

Indicators of health status outcome:
   1. Race/ethnicity-specific infant mortality, as measured by the rate (per 1,000 live births) of deaths among infants < 1 year of age.

Death rates (per 100,000 population) from:
   2. Motor vehicle crashes
   3. Work-related injury
   4. Suicide
   5. Lung Cancer
   6. Breast Cancer
   7. Cardiovascular disease
   8. Homicide
   9. All causes

Reported incidence (per 100,000 population) of:
   10. Acquired Immune Deficiency Syndrome
   11. Measles
   12. Tuberculosis
   13. Primary and secondary syphilis

Indicators of risk factors:
   14. Incidence of low birthrate, as measured by percentage of total number of live-born infants weighing < 2,500 grams at birth.
   15. Births to adolescents (females aged 10-17) as a percentage of total live births.
   16. Prenatal care, as measured by percentage of mothers delivering live infants who do not receive prenatal care during first trimester.
   17. Childhood poverty, as measured by the proportion of children <15 years of age living in families at or below the poverty level.
   18. Proportion of persons living in counties exceeding U.S. Environmental Protection Agency standards for air quality during previous year.

(Carson and Zucconi, 1993)

These types of objectives are measurable; they require strategies that address the social context giving shape to personal attitudes and choices. HSO approaches will differ. Because the health of the community requires collaboration, the plan should determine who in the hospital and/or community is responsible for each objective, who must be collaborated with, and what the hospital will assume primary rather than secondary responsibility for.

One model of goals and objectives is reflected in the North Carolina *Healthy Carolinians 2000: The Report of the Governor's Task Force on Health Objectives for the Year 2000.* For many years North Carolina had one of the highest infant mortality rates in the nation. In November 1992, the Governor's Task Force prepared the Objectives and Baseline Data from which an excerpt is outlined in Table 3 (Healthy Carolinians, 1992). The task force also developed general strategies and activities for attaining these objectives.

Table 3 - Maternal and Infant Health: Primary Goals and Special Targets

Primary goals: Reduce total infant mortality rate by 30%
                Reduce non-white infant mortality rate by 40%
Special Targets: Reverse trend of low birth weight.
                Reverse trend of pregnancies among girls less than age 18

Baseline Data			
Indicator	1990	2000 Current Projection given current trend	2000 Objectives
Deaths per 1,000 live births (Number of deaths)			
Total	10.6 (1,110)	8.6 (954)	7.4 (666)
Nonwhite	16.6 (530)	14.5 (483)	8.7 (290)
Percent low birthweight (Events)			
Total	8.0% (8,358)	8.2% (7,650)	7.0% (7,200)
Nonwhite	12.4% (4147)	13.7% 4568)	10.4% (3468)
Pregnancies per 1,000 girls age 15-17 (Pregnancies)			
Total	72.0 (9,453)	85.0 (11,958)	63.0 (8,862)
Nonwhite	107.8 (4,433)	123.8 (5,092)	86.7 (3,566)

A plan for monitoring, evaluation and regular reporting of progress should be developed. Inter-agency and inter-organization collaboration requires defined leadership and structure. Sustained long-term change in environmental and individual health behavior is a complex, slow process. Thus, evaluation must reflect the time needed to achieve change in health status indicators.

One approach is to evaluate the processes, impacts and outcomes associated with a specific strategy or intervention. This approach is outlined in PATCH (Planned Approach to Community Health: Guide for the Local Coordinator) (DHHS, 1993). Process evaluation looks at the development and structure of programming for targeted objectives "aimed at understanding the internal dynamics of program operations and identifying areas for improvement (DHHS, 1993). It provides an ongoing examination of what is delivered and how it is delivered, including program conception, staff, methods and activities, effectiveness and efficiency in reaching the target group. Impact evaluation looks at the short term effect on the population or "program effects on intermediate objectives such as changes in knowledge, skills, attitudes, behaviors or policies" (DHHS, 1993). It assess the overall effectiveness of a program in producing favorable cognitive, belief, and behavioral effects in the target population. Outcome is aimed at assessing program effects on the ultimate goals or results, including changes in health status, health status indicators, and quality of life" (DHHS, 1993). It is an assessment of change in health status indicators, such as morbidity and mortality, for a specified population and indicators such as those included in the CDC set of indicators. For example, process would look at whether appropriate program structures are in place; impact would look at whether the target population is attending health education classes and whether those who do attend evaluate the classes positively; outcome would look at a change in the actual health status indicator relative to the health problem being addressed. Since achieving measurable change in health status indicators usually takes several years from the actual time of program implementation, PATCH and other assessment models emphasize the use of process and impact approaches to evaluation.

As will be discussed later, the development of an integrated community health information system will allow for the collection, quantification, analysis and evaluation of the health status of the community. Development of integrated data systems not only allows for the monitoring of health status indicators and program impact as reflected through changes of these indicators, but an integrated system also allows for analysis of data relative to cost.

II. MANAGERIAL EPIDEMIOLOGY

Since managed care is well established, providers continue to consolidate through mergers and alliances. The level of charity care providers offer is declining; a new role for epidemiology is rapidly being defined in the health care delivery system. Through market forces not even envisioned ten years ago, fragmentation between the public health sector and the private sector is being bridged at an astounding rate. The resulting challenges fall squarely on the shoulders of health care managers who need to develop a population-based epidemiologic viewpoint as they explore the emerging role of public health.

Traditionally, epidemiology has established connections between environmental factors and personal characteristics and the etiology of disease (MacDowell and Lutz, 1993). It is a discipline well entrenched in public health. As Voelker (1994) points out, "In a burgeoning era of accountability through outcomes, the provision of preventive and primary care services is taking on an epidemiologic twist." To manage effectively in the future, resources of the organization must be based on an understanding of epidemiology. In fact, some epidemiology data is already used by insurers as part of their actuarial efforts.

This section will explore the emerging role of epidemiology in the private sector as managers grapple with this new tool and its implications for the well-being of their health care organizations. The concept of managerial epidemiology is based on a blending of two disciplines: epidemiology and the management of health services of organizations. Clearly, we must link the science of epidemiology to the planning, delivery, and evaluation of health services with particular emphases on outcomes measures.

First, a good working definition of epidemiology is necessary. In the 1980s, the definition expanded to include the study of the etiology of disease and its relationship to health services and social environment as well as the traditional relationships to personal characteristics and the physical and biological environment (Ibrahim, 1985). Today, Oleske (1993) includes control of adverse outcomes caused by personal characteristics, the environment (social, physical, and biological), and health services. Her definition focuses managers on control, a function central to all managers in today's environment of continuous quality assessment and improvement. Oleske (1993) proposes that we control adverse outcomes through use and management of information; education of health consumers and providers; and delivery of health care services based on assessment of need, planning, and evaluation of appropriate primary, secondary, and tertiary preventive and acute health services. Knowing the etiology of diseases and the factors contributing to them is no longer enough. Managers must design health care systems that actively manage and, when possible, interrupt chains of disease.

III. THE EPIDEMIOLOGIST ON THE HEALTH CARE MANAGEMENT TEAM

Oleske states that the epidemiologist sits on the window ledge of the organization gazing outside to the population served by the health service organization. Simultaneously, they look inside to measure and monitor patient outcomes and to evaluate the effectiveness of prevention activities (Oleske, 1993). Epidemiologists track the incidence and prevalence of disease in a given population. Mausner and Kramer define prevalence as the number of existing cases per 1000 population and incidence as the number of new cases per 1000 population in a given time period (1985). The prevalence and incidence of disease rates provide the health care manager with two very important and readily accessible measures for planning health services and for a standard by which to measure performance. This concept is reflected in Table 4 (Oleske, 1993).

Table 4 - On the Window Ledge of the Organization

Looking Outside	Looking Inside
1. Disease burden in the community: a.) Population specific disease rates b.) Benchmarks	1. Monitoring patient population outcomes
	2. Evaluation of HSO prevention programs
2. Assessment of prevention activities in the community	3. Selection of clinical pathways that are most effective and efficient
3. Assessment of the effectiveness of different types of prevention activities/programs	4. Data collection and monitoring
	5. Selection of measures for control and evaluation
	6. Feedback to clinicians through meaningful presentation of data members

The second focus for the epidemiologist is the description and understanding of the "chain of disease." The chain of disease includes the etiological agent, modes of transmission, intermediate hosts, and the infectivity rates for each disease process. This model for transmission of disease was initially developed for communicable diseases such as staphylococcal infection, influenza, and malaria.

The emergence of antibiotics, methods of vector control, and new levels of sanitation that followed World War II caused a reduction in communicable diseases, so the attention of public health refocused on chronic disease. But the chain of disease model is still appropriate for viewing genetic predisposing factors and lifestyle as etiological agents for heart disease, food and advertising in our culture as modes of transmission. In the late 1980's public health professionals expanded their view of disease to include unwanted pregnancy, malnutrition, injury, and violence. This view was changed to look for the causes and facilitating factors in the incidence and prevalence of these social diseases (Mausner and Kramer, 1985). Of course, with the advent of HIV/AIDS and drug resistance of many old and familiar etiological agents, we are experiencing a renewed interest in infectious diseases.

Once a disease process is understood, a plan of attack can be developed to prevent transmission, looking for the weakest link in the chain. For the health care manager this approach forms the basis for planning preventive and acute services at the primary, secondary, and tertiary levels (Mausner and Kramer, 1985)

A third function of the epidemiologist is to monitor scientific literature for evaluation of prevention programs and activities. According to Oleske (1995), they must ask important questions of the literature:

- What prevention programs work and in what populations?
- What outcome measures are used?
- How have programs been implemented and what resources were consumed?
- Is a specific prevention program appropriate to the populations we serve?
- How might prevention programs cited in the literature be modified to fit our special population needs?

Fourth, the epidemiologist selects measures to monitor the incidence and prevalence of disease and the outcomes of specific prevention programs. The key to this function is finding measures that are population specific, easy to collect, and readily understood by health care providers.

The epidemiologist on a management team also collects community and health care delivery system data. That information must then be presented, in a meaningful way, to other members of the health care team. Success of prevention programs is linked to the provision of timely, clear feedback to clinicians who need to know how their prevention efforts effect change in both community and patient populations (Thompson et al., 1995). Benchmarks selected by the epidemiologist represent the best efforts in the larger health care community as a comparison for performance of primary, secondary, and tertiary prevention programs and a comparison of the communities' health with other comparable communities (Gift and Mosel, 1994).

Finally, epidemiology as a health care management tool helps evaluate the merits of different prevention efforts in terms of outcomes and inputs (resources). This consideration focuses precious resources on the most effective, most efficient prevention initiatives. Table 5 outlines the relationship between traditional managerial function and epidemiology. The relationship between the two demonstrates the applicability of both in managing the health of populations (Rakich, et al., 1992; Mausner and Kramer, 1985; McLaughlin and Kaluzny, 1994; Oleske, 1995)

IV. PRIMARY, SECONDARY, AND TERTIARY MANAGEMENT AND PREVENTION

The results of a community health assessment based on data and an epidemiologic approach will be used to develop primary, secondary, and tertiary approaches to health education and prevention. In addition, at the secondary and tertiary level of illness, care will be provided in hospitals and managed according to traditional managed care approaches outlined and utilized by health insurers and managed care organizations. As the managed care market has matured, so has the ability to manage acute inpatient care. Two key areas of growth are the prevention and management of chronic disease and illness.

Primary prevention is identification of mitigating circumstances that lead to the development of disease before the disease or injury occurs. Primary prevention activities consist of two major categories: health promotion and specific protective measures (Mausner and Kramer, 1985). Primary prevention is generally targeted towards the community as a whole. Examples of such programs include bicycle helmet and safety programs designed to reduce head injuries, immunization efforts, teen health clinics that provide counseling, birth control, and education about HIV infection. Other large community level primary prevention activities include smoking cessation, nutritional

Table 5 - The Managerial and Epidemiological Functions

Managerial Functions	Epidemiological Functions
1. External environmental assessment inclusive of community assessment	1. Collection of all pertinent data on the health of the community, stratified to reflect special populations
2. Planning of prevention activities and health services	2. Assessment of literature for effectiveness (of strategies and programs) as measured by changes in health indices
3. Evaluation and control	3. a. Selection of "measures" or data to be collected based on meaningful population statistics b. Recognizing the best efforts in other communities and adopting benchmarks c. Collection of data on programs and patient outcomes and presentation of this data in a meaningful manner to clinicians and other stakeholders
4. Resource allocation	4. Assessment of resources needed to implement prevention programs and cost/benefit analysis, emphasizing the measurement of "benefit"
5. TQM/CQI	a. Team member development of measures and data systems b. Evaluation of "effectiveness"

information, promotion of exercise, and campaigns for seat belt utilization. But primary prevention isn't limited to the community. The role of the primary care physician in preventive activities is rapidly expanding. Periodic visits for health care, whether precipitated by illness or a general physical examination, provide an opportunity for the primary care physician to assess behavioral and lifestyle factors that contribute to disease and to provide needed education and counseling (Thompson, 1995). Further, health care organizations can sponsor wellness programs to selected populations or the community at large.

Secondary prevention is the early detection of disease coupled with timely, efficient, and effective care. It prevents further deterioration along the disease process, protects against the transmission of infectious disease, and improves outcomes (Mausner and Kramer, 1985). Traditionally focused on the individual, secondary prevention includes interventions that preclude relapse or another episode of disease. Secondary prevention remains primarily in the purview of the health care delivery system. Screening programs for breast cancer, rectal cancer, and cholesterol/triglyceride levels are examples of such programs. Also included in secondary prevention is educating patients about their disease processes as well as follow-up and evaluation of interventions.

Tertiary prevention targets reduction in recidivism and repeat incidence of disease incidents. It consists of "limitation of disability and rehabilitation where disease has already occurred and left residual damage. . . Its major theme is maximal utilization of the individual's residual capacities" (Mausner and Kramer, 1985). One aspect of tertiary prevention is correctly providing the appropriate acute care during a disease episode.

Focusing on prevention of a recurrence or prevention of further deterioration may include consultation on lifestyle and behavioral changes, adherence to medication schedules, and appropriate monitoring and follow-up of patients. Examples of tertiary prevention include cardiac rehabilitation (following a heart attack or cardiac surgery) that includes diet modification, exercise, and medication in an effort to both rehabilitate and to prevent a second attack. The success or failure of tertiary prevention programs are directly related to positive or negative organization performance outcomes.

Not surprisingly, tertiary prevention brings us full circle. When we view the health care delivery system it its entirety, the complexities of wellness, health, and diseases and the interrelationships within the health care system as well as the relationship between the system and the social and physical environments make it an ever-evolving, dynamic system that mirrors almost every aspect of human existence and community.

V. IMPLEMENTATION OF CLINICAL PREVENTIVE SERVICES

Community assessment and an epidemiologic perspective allow the management team to gather data helpful in planning for changing health behaviors at both the macro and micro level. Macro level issues such as education and housing need to be addressed in collaboration with community service agencies, government and other appropriate community organizations and individuals. In addition, "experts are urging physicians to consider the population as their patient and begin documenting its incidence and prevalence of disease. . . Physicians increasingly will have to focus on the provision of clinical preventive services in practice to maintain their communities' health and on community-wide data collections to monitor health status" (Voelker, 1994). In the past few years, HMOs have placed increasing emphasis on the development of primary care prevention approaches and protocols. Group Health of Puget Sound, for instance, has developed a sophisticated system of "population-based management of care at the level of individual practice" (Voelker, 1994). Activities at Group Health in Puget Sound (GHC) described by Voelker (1994) include "Dividing [the] population into clinically important subgroups. . . tailoring preventive services proven effective for each one and devising a careful planning scheme for the provision of those services. . .The system is a team approach in which physicians, registered nurses, and licensed practical nurses all have distinct roles in planning and providing services. This is the population-based management of care at the level of individual practice."

Hospitals involved in networks may or may not employ physicians; therefore, the ability to engage physicians in an organized approach to population-based medicine will be more complicated than working with physician employees or those in closed-panel HMOs. Employee relationships, Medical Service Organizations (MSOs), Physician Hospital Organizations (PHOs), and shared contracts with managed care and capitated products mechanisms will need to be developed to foster and provide incentives for increased attention to prevention in primary care practice. Data gathered through community assessment and epidemiological assessment, which demonstrated the incidence and prevalence of disease, coupled with hospital and physician practice information can identify high risk and clinically important subgroups in the practice population. Collaboration between clinicians, hospitals, health departments and other community based health services organizations can link community/population based health promotion efforts to individual primary care prevention efforts. Table 6 outlines GHCs "Critical Elements for an ideal Preventive Care Provision System" (Thompson, et al., 1995).

Table 6 - Critical Elements for an Ideal Preventive Care Provision System

1. Population-based planning.
2. Directed toward major causes of morbidity and mortality, epidemiologically determined. This includes the epidemiology of "needs" (the diseases and the risks) and the epidemiology of the "wants" (the desires of the enrollees).
3. Evidence for intervention effectiveness.
4. Functioning at multiple levels, including one-to-one level of primary care, infrastructure level, organization level, and external community.
5. Prospective and automated to the maximum extent feasible.
6. Health is a by-product of a shared endeavor between practitioners and patients. Informed discussion and consent are maximized.

(Thompson, et al., 1995)

Clinician education of the practice community and high risk populations targeted for intervention must be persistent and ongoing. Whereas some prevention activities should be community based, some clinical preventive services priorities represent those counseling, screening, immunization, and chemoprophylaxis interventions that are best provided through clinical settings (McGinnis and Lee, 1995).

Frequently cited barriers to providing prevention service in private practice include cost, time and inability to measure outcome. As hospitals develop integrated networks, they must work with physicians, nurses, and health educators to plan for clinical primary prevention. Appropriate educational programs, data systems, feedback and reward must be planned and initiated. In hospitals and integrated networks where physicians are not employees and where the system and practitioner financial incentives are not always aligned, the hospital or network will probably have to hire personnel to be responsible for coordinating health promotion, prevention education and activities for physicians and other primary care providers.

VI. THE ROLE OF DATA IN MANAGING THE CARE OF POPULATIONS

Data, both inside and outside the health care delivery system, is vital to all aspects of managing prevention activities, including community assessment, assessment of populations, planning of programs and services, and ongoing evaluation of prevention efforts (Tan, 1995).

Public health data may come from a myriad of sources at the local, county, state, and national levels. Data appropriate to public health and prevention issues may be found in health departments, law enforcement agencies, state and federal bureaus of statistics, insurance agencies, state Medicaid agencies, Social Security and Medicare, the Census and a plethora of other groups such as departments of labor, occupational health and safety as well as such private organizations as consumer groups, advocate groups, labor unions, and local industries. Managerial epidemiologists must make sense out of the seemingly endless data—no small task to be sure (Carson and Zucconi, 1993; Healthy People 2000, 1991).

Unfortunately, some of the data available from the above sources is not in an immediately usable form and requires considerable manipulation. Often, data is not specific enough to an individual community, nor is it stratified to account for subtle differences such as disease incidence and prevalence variations between population subgroups based on race, age, and social economic status. This phase of assessment requires the use of an epidemiologist/biostatistician. Good numbers are an essential basis for all prevention activities.

Internal data management plays an important role in prevention program evaluation, education of providers, continuous quality improvement, and resource allocation. Managerial activities are often characterized by brevity, discontinuity, and reliance on soft data (Mintzberg, 1975). In today's environment, the assessment of community health, selection of prevention efforts, and evaluation of programs, requires more than soft data. Careful planning of the collection and dissemination of good measures is vital to success.

The success of internal planning of an evaluation rests on bridging technical and managerial skills through the efficient and effective use of management information systems (MIS). HSOs lie along a continuum in their development of MIS. Most HSOs fall no lower than Stage III or IV on the continuum below:

- Stage I—initiation, introduction of computer technology into the organization with basic transactional processing;
- Stage II—contagion, applications become more sophisticated than mere transaction processing; more resources are needed;
- Stage III—control, the beginning of planning, restricted use of computing capability and the development of efficiency standards for computer technology;
- Stage IV—integration, the proliferation of computing technology with structured planning for its use;
- Stage V—data administration, the establishment of data administration functions assigned to an individual(s);
- Stage VI—maturity, technology and management are fully integrated to function as one (Tan, 1995).

Three layers of application exist: stand-alone financial-oriented systems; networked patient-oriented systems, and integrated future-oriented systems. Regardless of where an institution is in terms of MIS development, the epidemiological approach to management requires an extensive understanding of data sources within the organization and the ability to consolidate information across functional areas of the institution, its affiliated organization, and constituencies. Several types of MIS applications are most useful in the community health/epidemiological approach to health services management. Case management systems integrate data both vertically across providers and horizontally across departments of the same types of institutions. Case mix systems integrate clinical and financial data for groups of patients. Health data base management systems are depositories of logically organized facts and figures with querying capacity (Tan, 1995). A major task for an epidemiologist and/or biostatistician in an HSO is to play an active role in the continuous development and management of MIS data systems.

SUMMARY

Sigmond notes that health care necessarily "involves not only patient care and care of enrolled populations, but also care of communities. If only patients and enrolled populations were involved it seems clear that mainstream management methodology would be sufficient. Caring for patients, populations and communities involve quite different mind sets and data sets and methodologies that are not readily compatible through purely business management techniques" (Sigmond, 1996).

Continued escalation of the costs of health care in this country has renewed the need to manage public health. This management can be accomplished through the development of integrated health networks dedicated to improving the health of the communities they serve. The definition of community, while including necessary subsections, basically includes the geographic area in which the hospital is located and those in which their patients live. The management of the health of this population must be based on integrating community assessment and community involvement in establishing priority community health needs, the use of managerial epidemiology, and a plan to address primary, secondary, and tertiary care and prevention.

HSO administrators will need to develop collaborative approaches with community organizations to address priority macro level issues that affect large populations subgroups with problems such as hypertension, poor housing, and teen pregnancy. Collaboration is a complicated and difficult process. These problems will have to be addressed by multiple community organizations willing to transcend traditional organizational barriers. No single organization has the resources and skills, stakeholders, or knowledge of community to solve the problems. One organization attempting such management would probably not engender the necessary community involvement and ownership to initiate sustainable longer term change. Thus, public health agencies, community service organizations, schools and agencies of government must work with both public and private HSOs. In addition, HSOs will have to develop management processes and information systems to aid clinicians in working with high risk groups and individuals. Strategic planning and epidemiology can provide a strong foundation for planning these needed approaches. Evaluation must be based on science-based data, community and regional data which establishes targets for change in health status linked to national benchmarks. Looking at management with this new perspective will facilitate effective management of the health of populations.

REFERENCES

American Public Health Association, Association of State and Territorial Health Officials, U.S. Department of Health and Human Services, U.S. Public Health Service, Center for Disease Control, U.S. Conference of Local Health Officers. (1991). *Assessment Protocol for Excellence in Public Health.* National Association of County Health Officials, Washington, D.C.

Boyd, S. (1997). Hospital Community Assessment and Community Health Initiatives. Unpublished Manuscript.

Catholic Hospital Association and Levin ICF. (1989). *Social Accountability Budget for Not-for-Profit Healthcare Organizations.* Catholic Hospital Publishing, St. Louis, MO.

Carson, C. A., and Zucconi, S. (1993). Epidemiologic Indicators of Health Status to Guide Health Care management Decision Making. *Journal of Health Administration Education. 11*(4), 551-574.

Duncan, J., Ginter, P. and L. Swayne. (1995). *Strategic Management of Health Care Organizations.* Blackwell Publishers, Cambridge, MA.

Gamm, L. (1996). The Pursuit of Community in Leadership of Partnerships for Community Health. Presentation at the Association of University Programs in Health Administration Annual Meeting. Atlanta, Georgia, June 9.

Gift, R. and D. Mosel. (1994). *Benchmarking in Health Care: A Collaborative Approach.* American Hospital Publishing, Chicago, IL.

Healthy Carolinians 2000: The Report of the governor's Task Force on Health Objectives for the Year 2000. (1992). North Carolina Department of Environment, Health and Natural Resources. Raleigh, N.C.

Healthy People 2000; National Health Promotion and Disease Prevention Objectives. (1991). DHHS (PHS) Publication No. 91-50212. U.S. Government Printing Office, Washington, D.C.

Ibrahim, M. A. (1985). *Epidemiology and Health Policy.* Aspen Publishers, Rockville, MS.

Kovner, A. (1994). Community Benefit and Health Care Reform. *The Journal of Health Administration Education. 12*(3): 253-258.

MacDowell, N. M., and Lutz, J. (1993). Applications of Epidemiology in the Operation and Marketing of Managed Care Plans. *Journal of Health Administration Education. 11*: 4.

Mausner, J. S., and Kramer, S. (1985). *Epidemiology: An Introductory Text.* Second Ed., W. B. Saunders Co., Philadelphia, PA.

McGinnis, J. M., and Lee, P. (1995). Healthy People 2000 at Mid Decade. *Journal of the American Medical Association. 273*(14): 1123-1129.

McLaughlin, C. P., and Kaluzny, A. D. (1994). *Continuous Quality Improvement in Health Care.* Aspen Publishers, Inc., Gaithersburg, MD.

Mintzberg, H. (1975). The manager's job: folklore and fact. *Harvard Business Review. July-August:* 49-61.

Oleske, D. M., (1995). *Epidemiology and the Delivery of Health Care: Methods and Applications.* Plenum Press, New York.

Oleske, D. M., (1993). Linking the Delivery of Health Care to Service Population Needs: The Role of the Epidemiologist on the Health Care Management Team. *The Journal of Health Administration Education. 11*(4): 531-539.

Public Health Service, U.S. Department of Health and Human Services. (1991). *Healthy People 2000: National Health Promotion and Disease Prevention Objectives.* U.S. Government Printing Office, Washington, D.C.

Rakich, T. S., Longest, Jr., B. B., and Darr, K. (1992). *Managing Health Services Organizations.* Third Ed., Health Professions Press, Baltimore, MD.

Rice, J. (1993). *Community Health Assessment: The First Steps in Community Health Planning.* American Hospital Association Publishing, Chicago, IL.

Shortell, S., Gillies, R., Anderson, D., Erickson, K., and Mitchell, J. (1996). *Remaking Health Care in America: Building Organized Delivery Systems.* Jossey-Bass Publishers, San Francisco, CA.

Sigmond, R. (1996). The Andrew Patullo Lecture. Presentation at the Association of University Programs in Health Administration, Atlanta, GA. June 8.

Tan, J. K. H. (1995). *Health Management Information Systems: Theories, Methods, and Applications.* Aspen Publications, Gaithersburg, MD.

Thompson, R., Taplin, S., McAfee, T., Mandelson, M., and Smith, A. (1995). Primary and Secondary Prevention Services in Clinical Practice, *Journal of the American Medical Association.* 273(14): 1130-1135.

U.S. Dept. of Health and Human Services. (1993). *Planned Approach to Community Health (PATCH): Guide for the Local Coordinator.* U.S. Department of Health and Human Services, Department of Health and Human Services, Centers for Disease Control and Prevention, National Center for Chronic Disease and Prevention, Atlanta, GA.

Voelker, R. (1994). Population-Based Medicine Merges Clinical Care, Epidemiologic Techniques. *Journal of the American Medical Association.* 271(17): 1301-1302.

35.
MANAGING CHANGE

Evelyn T. Dravecky, *University of California Los Angeles School of Medicine, Los Angeles, CA*

Joanne C. Preston, *Pepperdine University, Culver City, CA*

Although futurist thinkers tell us that describing what will happen in society and health care cannot be predicted, patterns of change can be anticipated. They point out that we can anticipate scientific breakthroughs such as mapping the human genome and understanding healthy aging. But we can't predict the exact timing of these breakthroughs or when they will be integrated into medical practices. Changes in societal values, public policy and individual behaviors are even more uncertain and often more important to health and health care provision than medical breakthroughs. Health care policy and financing may evolve in ways that directly impact people's health in the future (Begeld, 1996).

If the only certainty we have is that change and uncertainty will always be with us, how can we plan for change? How can we manage it? As Charles Handy points out (1996), we can wait around for great people to come up with great visions and ideas and while we're waiting allow ourselves to be pulled in different directions by external circumstances and events. If we look at the history of health care organizations since the 1970s, they have reacted to external forces and conflicting views of how health care provision should be transformed. The major thesis of this paper is that instead of reactive change, change can be anticipated, planned for and managed effectively if the principles described in Table 1 are considered.

Table 1 - Principles for Managing Change

A. **Systems Perspective**

Any change process must be considered from a systemic perspective. Every organization consists of a dynamic interaction among technical, social, psychosocial systems, internal and external environments. The critical task of a change effort is to understand how all the different parts fit together and the impact they have on each other. Systemic thinking provides a framework for restructuring the internal environment of the organization.

B. **Stakeholders**

Anticipating, planning and implementing change can be successful if it is based upon the goals and values of all the key stakeholders in the organization and outside of the organization who can impact the success of the change process.

C. **External Environment**

Anticipating and preparing for change requires ongoing monitoring of the organization's external environment. This means gathering information not only related to health care, but regional demographic shifts, opening and closing of industries, political/social policies. It requires futurist behaviors such as seeking information across boundaries for a sense of what will transform the environment.

D. **Social System Issues**

Feelings and emotions are an integral part of change. When people in organizations are asked to do something different than they have before, their reactions include shock, disbelief, anger, depression, cynicism – and for some – the excitement of change. Whatever the reactions are, addressing people issues is an important part of managing the change process.

E. **Planning**

Planning for change considers reviewing peoples' roles, tasks and competencies from new perspectives to determine how best to accomplish the organization's values and goals. The challenge for health care organizations is how to move from fragmentation and overspecialization to developing core competencies and capabilities that go beyond individual jobs, careers, professions, groups, departments, and organizational boundaries (Shortell et al., 1996).

Whether the organization is a small community clinic or a large complex health network, HMO, or public health system, each individual needs to think, feel and do something different if change is to occur. The challenge is to enable people with their individual differences and organization beliefs to create a new kind of organization.

Managing change is unlike any other task that managers face. Operational and financial models are not good fits for managing change because change does not easily fit the linear approaches of these models. Managing change is like looking at a dozen computer screens, transferring information from one to the other, correcting errors and inputting new information – simultaneously. This picture of change is compounded when it is applied to health care because of the present chaotic nature of this system. Managing change effectively requires shifts in organizational paradigms and learning how to be a discontinuous thinker in order to adapt to the continuous change of turbulent environments. Being a discontinuous thinker means revising the ways each of us views, experiences and learns in an environment that is less predictable and manageable. New rules, new behaviors and new ideas are required to work successfully in this kind of an environment. Since the changes occurring are themselves discontinuous, that is, not part of a familiar pattern, they call for fresh and innovative approaches (Handy, 1995).

I. THE NATURE OF CHANGE IN HEALTH CARE ENVIRONMENTS

All organizations change. They grow, people come and go, environments, cultures and services change. But the kinds of changes occurring in health care are more dramatic than evolutionary models imply. They require that embedded behavior patterns be dramatically altered. Change of this kind is seen as "frame breaking." In general, when a dramatic change in or reversal of an organization's external behavior takes place, the greater the need for changing its internal behavior (Herman-Taylor, 1985).

Health care services literature in the 1980s and 1990s documents fundamental changes in organization forms, shifts in authority and control patterns and an increased emphasis on cost containment and sound business practices. This documentation emphasizes the transformation of a cottage industry to that of a larger, more organizaed system (Alexander and D'Aunno, 1990). Because of these rapid and unpredictable changes in their environments, health care organizations are finding that the traditional response modes, such as downsizing and piecemeal structural and process rearrangements are not sufficient for meaningful adaptability. Other time honored management models from an industrial era such as authoritarian-style leadership and hierarchical structure are also inadequate for meeting today's health care issues. The environment is so dynamic that a flatter structure with boundary spanners is required to channel information back quickly to decision makers.

A number of potentially transformative management philosophies, including Total Quality Management (TQM) and Socio-Technical Work Redesign, frequently lose effectiveness and do not produce expected results by becoming the change technique of the month. These management models are often not successful because, while the environments for health care organizations have changed dramatically, mental models used by people trying to implement change are self perpetuating and therefore resistant to change (Dravecky and Fadem, 1980; Senge, 1990; Nevis et al., 1996).

For change to be optimally managed, health care managers must think, see, plan and understand the world from a new paradigm. They can no longer make changes as a series of independent pieces or programs that are decided at the top and then implemented as fast as possible without concern for the consequences to the rest of the organization. Surviving in a world of continuous change requires a new organizational reality and a resocialization of organization members and stakeholders to participate in change. It requires health care managers to adopt a change paradigm that emphasizes a systems view of organizations, communication and participation by everyone, role modeling, structural redesign and continuous assessment of internal and external environments.

II. STRATEGIES FOR MANAGING CHANGE IN HEALTH CARE ORGANIZATIONS

Current thinking tends to view change activities as rationally controlled, orderly processes. However, it is more accurate to say that change activities have a more chaotic quality and often involve shifting goals, discontinuous and even surprising events, and unexpected combinations of changes (Nevis, et al., 1996b). For example, a community clinic in the middle of an organizational redesign may experience the loss of a major funding source, requiring reassessment of budgets, staffing, services and a rethinking of the redesign.

Although many models for improving the effectiveness of health care organizations have been proposed in the last several years, these efforts show that the complexities of health care systems make change efforts difficult. These are described in Table 2 below.

Table 2 - Key Difficulties Encountered by Previous Change Efforts

1. Science based professional work is different from product-related work which makes work technology more ambiguous.
2. Levels of information skills and even goal priorities in patient care differ.
3. In the 1990s, the arrival of Health Maintenance Organizations and emphasis on containing health care costs have shifted the direction of patient care from professional leadership to an industrial-based model of administration and management (Cummings and Worley, 1993; Dravecky and LaBorde, 1992).

These kinds of emergent situations make managing change a complex and dynamic process that requires a willingness to modify and refine management plans as new circumstances arise, and to embrace innovative ways of thinking and planning for change implementation.

Taking a systems view of organizations and management of change, studies related to health care organizations are frequently based on the assumption that organizations have coping mechanisms to integrate new structures and processes to reach organization goals and even fulfill individual members' needs and expectations (Chisholm and Ziegenfuss, 1986). However, experiences in implementing change efforts within health care organizations show that failure often stems from an incomplete understanding of the multiple causes of organization problems and responses to change efforts. The following example will help clarify the importance of understanding the complexity of organizational systems and the long range planning needed to sustain change.

The change project was a long-term effort to improve treatment services of a free standing Alcohol and Drug Dependency program in a major HMO in the western states. Program staff wanted to understand the growing pains of the program so as to continue to provide high quality services. Program administrators identified several areas that needed improvement:

1. Lack of clarity regarding organizational expectations about the program.
2. Different treatment philosophies among the staff.
3. Ambiguity about the relationship between the program and the psychiatric department.
4. Heavy counselor work load and related staff "burn-out" (Dravecky and LaBorde, 1992).

The initial change effort was successful with the implementation of self-directed service teams and new procedures. However, an independent evaluation identified a major flaw in the process. Managers and staff had not considered that the changes in the program required ongoing monitoring in order to meet new organizational and environmental realities. Although the initial redesign appeared to be effective for more than six years, questions arose about the effectiveness and costs of the program in today's environment.

Any organization, in this case, a health care organization, is a dynamic entity that is continually interacting with its environment, changing and adapting to establish congruence between people, process, structures and internal and external environments. Acknowledging and understanding that organizations are dynamic entities helps explain why bureaucratic organizations, the traditionally dominant form in health care, are under stress and new organizational forms are evolving. Traditional bureaucratic methods can no longer survive in the present health care environment!

Healthy organizations sense changes in both their environments and make adaptations in how they function in order to meet new organization demands. Based on their capacity to respond, they may also choose to interact with only parts of a larger environment based on their capability to respond (Cummings and Worley, 1993).

A. Managing Political Aspects of the Environment

From a political perspective, health care organizations, as all organizations, are composed of loosely structured coalitions of individuals and groups that have different preferences and interests. Nursing staff desire secure, high paying jobs; physicians are concerned with maintaining professional autonomy; and top executives seek effective and efficient practices to cut costs and diversify services. Each of these different groups or coalitions competes with the other for scarce resources and influence in the organization. Each tries to preserve or enhance its own self-interests while managing to achieve a balance of power sufficient to sustain commitment to the organization and maintain overall effectiveness (Cummings and Worley, 1993).

From this perspective, attempts to change an organization can threaten the balance of power among and between the groups and result in political conflicts. Individuals and groups look at change efforts from the standpoint of how these changes affect their own power and influence. Those who perceive threat to their power may attempt to minimize change as unnecessary or seek only minor adjustments in the organization. Others who believe that they might gain power from change try to legitimize the need for change. As a result, significant organization changes are frequently accompanied by conflicting interests, distorted information and political turmoil. These issues will not go away; however, they can be addressed in the following ways:

1. Determining the change agent sources of power;
2. Identifying internal and external stakeholders;
3. Obtaining stakeholder support – appreciative inquiry process;
4. Using appreciative inquiry to initiate change;
5. Implementing action plans;
6. Managing change.

B. Determining the Change Agent Sources of Power

Who is going to lead the change activity – the designated leader, informed leaders of the organizations or of a department, or professional consultants outside of the organization? What is the change agent's power base that can be used to influence others to support changes?

The individual or individuals leading the change effort, has various sources of power which can be beneficially used. First of all, his/her charisma, reputation and professional credibility provides a personal source of power. Having expertise that is valued by other people and controlling information is a knowledge base of power. Connections with informal networks that can provide people, informational and material resources contributes to the personal source of power and can be important to encourage people to support and participate in change efforts.

Because health care systems have a complex power culture, the change agent must become involved in the use of power and political tactics to address the change issues as they arise. The important question for the change agent is how he or she will choose to use these personal power bases. Will they be used to enable organizational members and stakeholders to develop skills to lead and manage change? Or will they be used to manipulate and create dependency on a particular change agent and change techniques?

These are questions that are not often publicly expressed. However, for change to have positive results for the organization, ways to use power and politics and change techniques ethically must be a part of initial planning (Preston and DuToit, 1994).

C. Identifying and Including Key Stakeholders Within and Outside of the Organization in the Change Process

No change effort can occur or be managed effectively without including those individuals and groups who stand to gain or lose the most from it. At the initial stage of designing the change activity, particular attention must be paid to identifying stakeholders who can block or support change. This assessment and obtaining broad-based support is a critical component of planned change. Within the organization, key stakeholders are top management, department managers, staff groups and unions. External to the organization are recipients of services, suppliers, community groups who relate to it, benefactors who support the organization, government agencies that regulate health care, and organizations which purchase health care services. If the health care system is part of a large network, the network itself is a stakeholder. Nadler (1987) has suggested that developing a stakeholder relationship map can clarify who influences whom both inside and outside of an organization.

Gaining initial buy-in of key stakeholders and attending to their continued support is one of the most important components in effectively managing change. The time spent identifying and including them in determining direction and focus contributes to the ultimate success or lack of success in implementing change. Change does not occur simply because top management decrees it.

D. Developing Stakeholder Support: The Appreciative Inquiry Process

Once key internal and external stakeholders are identified, these diverse interests must be brought to agreement regarding the direction of change. A most productive approach – the appreciative inquiry process – can be used to do this. The major purpose of this process is to focus on creative outcomes and divergent thinking, rather than convergent thinking. As a systematic process, appreciative inquiry results in clarifying and articulating organizational values that support committed action toward change. It focuses on designing the future through what has been most effective and valued in the past. Appreciative inquiry creates a dialogue among organization members and stakeholders about what the organization is and can become. It emphasizes organizational strengths, successes, capabilities and the creation of a more dynamic entity (Cooperrider and Srivastva, 1987). Traditional change approaches concentrate on defining problems, setting targets, planning strategies and overcoming barriers. Focusing only on what is not working well, on organization failings and stakeholders' major differences can result in a demoralized environment and the feeling that there is no hope for improvement. This often leaves an organization with a sense of an inferiority complex and little hope for a bright future. Consequently, when little is done to improve the situation, stakeholders in the organization become less enthusiastic about sharing their problems and they avoid risks for fear of failure.

From another perspective, because each stakeholder helps determine which are the important historical values and successes that will go into the future state, the appreciative inquiry process contributes to preparing the organization for a large-scale change effort. This creates an exciting climate since all the stakeholders paint the picture of success rather than problems. Appreciative inquiry also puts the use of external consultants into a clearer perspective. Rather than allowing outside experts to determine change goals and activities, those with the greatest commitment and enthusiasm for the organization determine the direction of change. External expertise then becomes the means rather than the driver of change.

E. Using Appreciative Inquiry to Initiate a Change Process

Appreciative inquiry uses three major steps to initiate a change process. These are described in Table 3 below.

Table 3 - Steps for the Appreciative Inquiry Process

1. *Identifying a team to organize and carry out the activity.* This team should be composed of key people from within the organization plus internal and external consultants. It is the team's task to identify the key stakeholders who will participate in the appreciative inquiry process and organize the meeting for these groups.

2. *Preparation.* This step consists of identifying and collecting success stories about the purpose of the health care organization, the economic and service impact that it has on the community or communities around it. Sources that can contribute to this information base include Chambers of Commerce in the community, universities and independent groups that carry out projects related to business trends and demographic changes in the area. Key themes from these success stories are then summarized and sent to the planning committee for review. The external consultants provide guidelines for reviewing the themes, enabling the group to envision the future state with all the successes and minimal problems.

   Depending upon the number of stakeholders interviewed, the scale of the change process, ease of access and volume of the stories to be summarized and distributed, the time period for this preparation phase can be from one to three months.

3. *Inquiry Conference and Development of an Action Plan.* Stakeholders attending the actual inquiry conference must represent the internal and external individuals and groups who can influence and are impacted by any change effort. If, for example, the change process is to occur in a large public health system, the number of stakeholder participants could be five hundred people, since the organization internally consists of many programs and people and has wide impact into the community. An example of one design model would suggest that the group work for three days over a three week period so that participants can review information generated at each meeting and prepare for the next session.

   On the first day the Inquiry Conference team explains the purpose of the conference, summarizes major success themes from the interviews and states the major questions to be addressed by the attending stakeholders. Using the example of a large public health system, questions such as the following can be asked:

   - What role should the public health system play in providing health care in our community?

   - What strengths and accomplishments can provide direction for a redesign of the system?

   - How can the purpose of public health be reframed and retooled to reflect the new reality of a health care industry?

   - What organization structure will best serve meeting the purpose, community needs and expectations?

It's important to point out that the process established at the beginning of the inquiry conference described in Table 3 must be fluid and open-ended. The major purpose is to allow creative productivity or divergent thinking to emerge not focus on the past or convergent thinking. Participants work in large and small groups during the conference sessions. The ideas they produce are then synthesized into a new vision and future state for the organization: something unique and special that they can agree upon. The entire group does not have to agree, but among the guidelines emphasized in conference activities is that each participant must think broadly of the whole system, and go beyond thinking of each individual's advocate group. Appreciative inquiry sets up the potential for greater buy-in by those who are being asked to support it.

The final day of the inquiry conference concentrates on developing an overall plan to implement a new vision and its strategic components. This plan outlines implementation steps, clarifies accountability, lists resources available and needed, and establishes a time-line. The outcome of this activity should give the organization's managers and staff a "blueprint" for creating a revitalized and relevant health services organization with internal and community support for its new direction as well as a clearer picture of accountabilities.

Skilled conference facilitators for each working group are a necessary component in the success of the appreciative inquiry process. This is an area where synergy between internal and external resources can happen.

F. Implementing Action Plans

Implementing change in an organization means requires that a number of concurrent projects be initiated as part of the change effort. But success in managing change demands that each project or change activity connect and balance with all of the effort. This requires an understanding of how the parts relate to one another, and of how each part can affect the direction, sequence and pace of the whole structure. A Transition Management Team (TMT), which can maintain the big picture of change and coordinate all the different activities, facilitates this effort. Duck (1993) describes such a team as a group of company leaders, who report to the organization's top leader and commit all their time and energy to managing the change process. The TMT works together until the change process has been integrated into the organization. The team is responsible for ensuring that there are clear communication channels between those who are leading the change process and those who are given the job of implementing the new strategies. They manage the organizational context in which the change occurs and the emotional connections necessary for any transformation. This requires a major commitment of the organization's time, talent and money.

The major contribution of a Transition Management Team is that it provides a committed leadership group which has a clear vision of the future and understands the steps needed to make the vision a reality. The TMT's activities send a powerful message to others in the organization that leadership commitment to change is real. It is imperative, when a transition team/task force is established, that attention be paid to establishing communication lines to the implementation groups and to keeping them informed about the planning process. If two-way communication isn't established, rumors may abound about, how and when change activities will occur. Others in the organization who are not part of the change planning must be regularly informed about the goals, design elements and tradeoffs made in planning the change process. Although the change management plan may be very good and plausible, it is quite likely to fail because the people who are expected to implement it haven't bought into it. This was the situation in a large hospital system whose executive group was interested in improving productivity in the organization and cutting costs. A well-respected consulting group designed a very solid and practical transformation plan. The consultant group had gathered information carefully from people in the organization and studied the situation extensively. They guaranteed success. However, the plan was never implemented. No one felt ownership in the plan, not even top management.

G. Moving from Concepts to Action

Using the Transition Management Team model described above, the group oversees the change effort and ensures that all of the change initiatives fit together. The TMT is not another layer of bureaucracy or a job for executives on their way out (Duck, 1993). It is composed of eight to twelve talented organizational leaders who commit their time and skills to making the change process a reality. The group has trust and support from top management. This support is publically and formally given by the top executive or CEO when the context and rationale for a new organizational direction is announced. The TMT's task consists of working out the guidelines and ensuring that they are understood by managers in the organization who are expected to carry them out.

Leadership of the TMT is critical. The leader must be someone who has proven talent and credibility among peers. The leadership role requires an understanding of long term vision and values of the organization, thorough knowledge of the business (in this case the health care industry), and the complete trust of the top manager or administrator.

The TMT reports directly to the head of the organization on a regular basis. The CEO or top executive is an ex officio member of the group and an external consultant participates as facilitator. The TMT has funding authority, and the power to alter or stop change projects that don't fit the goals of the change process. It also contributes to the evaluations of projects and the individuals and people who are implementing them.

In addition to effective leadership, the TMT must pay particular attention to emotional and behavioral issues that emerge during change. One or more skilled facilitators usually fill this role. Facilitators also need to understand the business, be sensitive to people issues, be well respected and connected in the organization. They ensure that people issues are not ignored or compromised. Facilitators work with the various leaders of different change projects in the organization, i.e., information technology, process redesign, human resources, and communication. Organization members who participate in these change projects are drawn from all levels of the organization and represent diverse skill and information levels.

The TMT ensures that coordination of change activities is widespread. It needs to anticipate and be prepared to manage the reactions, questions and concerns that change generates. The point of having a TMT member responsible for attending to socio-emotional issues is acknowledgment of the importance of these issues and recognition that unless someone owns an issue, no one is responsible for it (Duck, 1993c).

Another approach to managing change is to utilize a network of managers throughout the organization as the key implementers of change in their throughout the organization as the key implementers of change in their areas of responsibility. This throughout the organization as the key implementers of change in their areas of responsibility. This approach, however, still requires a core planning group who works with the managers in structuring the change process. Subsequent training of managers and their key staff on leadership, organizational systems and requisite skills for effectively implementing change processes must be a part of this approach.

Whatever model for change is used, a change planning group is the major component in guiding and integrating activities in the organization. To ensure that all the organizational parts involved in the change process keep in mind the overall goal they are working toward, there are several major responsibilities that this group has and shares with top management. These responsibilities are summarized in Table 4.

Table 4 - Top Management and Change Planning Team Shared Responsibilities

Certain responsibilities must be shared by the team members and management. These responsibilities include the following:

1. A clear and established organizational vision must be shared with everyone often utilizing every available communication channel so that each person and group can align their own activities with the new direction.

2. Communicate across levels and functions to generate support for new ideas, insights and creative thinking.

3. Ensure that adequate resources are provided to support change. Resources often times are not monies needed. Managers and groups involved in the change process generally need information, support, and help to get unstuck.

4. The planning group's job is to keep everyone's eye on the "overall prize." They must coordinate and align change activities so that they fit together and inform the entire organization about the "big picture," how the different activities are integrated, so that everyone can understand that this is a carefully thought out plan. This is a key responsibility because change programs rapidly escalate into a melange of task forces, teams and projects.

5. Everyone in the organization must contribute to the creation of a new approach to work together if change is to be successful. The core planning group is a resource for information, education, cross-linkages for managers and staff to assess, redesign and implement changes in their areas.

6. Help managers and staff to anticipate, identify and address people issues that are endemic to change processes. The core planning group must use all means at their disposal, particularly people in Human Resources and communication. When issues of redesigning work roles, consolidating services, outsourcing, changing compensation emerge, time is needed to discuss and consider alternatives for addressing the consequences of these changes on all parts of the organization.

In summary, implementing change programs requires commitment to change, a clear vision from those in executive roles, and a core planning group representative of all parts of the organization. It requires ongoing communication to keep people focused on the goal of the change process. It means tending to the emotional issues of change, continuing education and most importantly to providing leadership.

H. Leading Change

"Everyone" says that leadership is important, but there are as many definitions for leadership as there are management theorists. In health care, the dual leadership of medicine and administration contributes to even more ambiguity about leadership responsibility. With the industrialization of health care, corporate stakeholders have different aspirations, different goals than health care administrators or physicians. But the challenge of reconciling conflicting values is common to all leaders and this is particularly true during times of change. There will be conflicting views on identifying the purpose of the organization, e.g. whether it should provide preventive or high-risk care, teach future health care providers, and/or provide care to the poor. There will be resistance to changing anything in the organization because people there have a self-interest in maintaining status quo; they are comfortable, secure in what they do, have an identity and resist change. Change means confusion, chaos and uncertainty. So what is a leader to do since a leader must lead?

James O'Toole (1996) points out that great leaders recognize that the perpetual lot of organizations in today's world is continuous uncertainty and disagreement among those with conflicting values about the proper direction. Consequently, the process of leadership involves an ongoing struggle to balance the constant demands of those with different objectives. Leaders live in a state of perpetual tension because they cannot completely satisfy conflicting demands of all interested parties in the system. But, if leadership is to be accepted and seen as legitimate, every member in the organization must believe the leader will treat him or her fairly and with respect at all times. Poor leaders cannot tolerate this uncomfortable position. They tend to resolve the tension and conflict by either giving in to demands of those who are most powerful or by issuing an edict that represents their own will. "Change will be what I say it is."

O'Toole suggests that effectively leading change means providing leadership that is values-based. Values-based leadership creates a symmetry among those with conflicting values. Values-based leadership means listening to all sides, but being dictated to by no one side. It means creating transcendent values that provide a tent large enough to hold different aspirations. Values-based leadership in health care requires creating systems that maintain higher order values that reflect the origins of caring for people with current concerns for illness prevention and resource management.

The role of leadership in managing change is to keep the focus on the anticipatedresults, explaining the purpose of change, listening and walking the talk. A major responsibility of the Transitional Management Team, who represent top leadership in the organization, is to model values-based leadership to other key leaders and staff within the organization. As the TMT plans the change process, it must define value-based leadership for itself and how team members can acquire behaviors that reflect this kind of leadership. External consultants can play a key role in this education process. They can provide information and experiences to assist TMT members to develop new leadership behaviors and approaches to effect organizational change.

III. THE STRATEGIC MIDDLE MANAGER

Implementing organizational strategy or change has been perceived as a process that is more mechanical than bureaucratic (Floyd and Wooldridge, 1996). In reality, details of top management's goal or intent must be developed so that middle managers and staff can effect a plan of action. Middle managers in particular are given the responsibility of ensuring agreement among organization members and managing conflict and resistance to change constructively. Top managers often assume that by simply stating new directions and priorities that middle managers can then provide the leadership necessary for effective implementation requires. However, if middle managers lack understanding about the meaning of new directions and the kind of impact change will have on the organization, it can create problems for effecting change. System wide changes in work mechanisms, performance standards and leadership techniques require a "paradigm shift" in those given the responsibility of implementing change. A "paradigm shift" necessitates revising their beliefs about organizational identity values and goals (Floyd and Woolridge, 1996b).

A. The Middle Manager

Middle managers are critical to effective organization change. As noted in Table 5, they play pivotal roles in their interactions with top management, key stakeholders and employees.

Table 5 - Key Role of the Middle Manager

1. Middle managers represent the organization's identity to other members.

2. Middle managers are the major links between top management, policy makers, and those who carry out the organization's work.

3. Middle managers are representatives of the organization's current belief system. They model the dominant social norms.

4. Leading change for middle managers requires changing themselves.

5. Middle managers have a "synthesizing role" because they interact across management levels and with outside groups. They are continually receiving information about the ways others see the organization.

Because of these pivotal roles, middle managers frequently are the first to recognize or appreciate the subtleties related to organization change and are in an excellent position to see the need for change, but also unanticipated consequences. They can identify the gap between an ideal organization and the existing organization. Middle managers are in a unique position to suggest and reorient attention to underlying concerns and priorities of employees and outside stakeholders. Including middle managers in the planning of the change process, and developing their leadership skills, will have a dramatic effect on the success of implementing change.

B. Addressing Resistance to Change

Resistance is an anticipated component of any change process. Frequently individual and organizational resistance is treated as monolithic and unidimensional; in reality, resistance is a highly complex, multidimensional phenomenon. Three reasons people might resist change include:

1. They see the change from a different perspective than those promoting change;
2. They are expressing a normal, common fear of the unknown; and
3. They disagree substantively with the specifics of the proposed change.

Identifying any of these reactions as negative or wrong fails to respect the reality and validity of these responses. If the change effort is to be successful, it is important to know and understand the thoughts and feelings of organizational members who are reluctant to accept what others consider as highly desirable change. Appreciative inquiry model described above provides one of the most powerful forms of addressing resistance issues.

The three types of resistance noted above are often treated as if they stemmed from one single cause. Everyone who questions the change process is categorized as a deviant. Thus, the usual response is to mount a counterattack on any one who has reservations about the change process. Those who support the change process say, "If you're not with us, get out of the way. The train is leaving the station." They categorize resisters as people the organization can do without. This, unfortunately, only leads to more entrenched resistance and, at times, loss of effective talent.

A more effective approach to addressing resistance to change is to begin with the premise that middle managers and other organization members may know their work areas very well but generally do not have general understanding of the organization and its goals. Involving middle managers in an ongoing participative communication process creates opportunities to assist them in broadening their ideas about the organization and their individual work worlds and develop a new, shared perspective for supporting the change process. They are then better prepared to explain organizational changes to their staffs and the external stakeholders who interact with them. Middle managers will also see themselves as informed participants with multiple ways to influence the change process.

Ongoing communication also enables the Transition Management Team to identify exactly where disagreements exist and how they can be addressed. Disagreements which cannot be easily resolved can provide insights into the reasons or causes for them. If discussion cannot resolve differences, exploring the issues minimizes the negative impact on the change process.

Communication and participation also reduce the sense of loss, anxiety and fear at the middle manager and staff levels (Nevis, et al., 1996b). People find that they are not alone in their feelings and concerns; knowing that others share their concerns reduces the intensity of these feelings.

Middle managers assume new leadership roles through their involvement in the design and implementation of the change process. Numerous war stories about change recount how middle managers simply dig in and won't cooperate with the change efforts because they know change can have a negative impact on them. They are well aware that re-engineering projects have eliminated layers of middle management in other organizations. Total Quality Management and Socio-Technical systems methods shift large parts of the traditional supervisory role to employee groups. Creating accountable work teams means that the traditional management role is no longer required. Consequently, resistance behaviors become tactics to save face and save jobs. However, the middle manager's attitude toward change can be a positive one if given an opportunity to contribute to the change process and be accountable for his/her personal future in the organization. Two different examples explain how this can occur.

In the first example, Organization Alpha anticipated middle management resistance to change and involved them as implementation leaders. While participation did not guarantee any middle manager a job in the re-engineered organization, it did give each one an important role to play in the transition. Training and coaching was provided for the new role and an implementation leaders' network (ILN) was developed and sanctioned. The tasks included identifying changes necessary in company policy to support the re-engineering efforts, design any new procedures and reporting relationships needed and create any tasks forces necessary to address transition issues. The network also was responsible for determining new skills needed to manage the change process i.e. facilitation, problem solving, conflict resolution, and team building skills. The middle manager network communicated through small group telephone conferences and periodic face-to-face meetings.

The network also publicized implementation successes throughout the organization, supported joint problem-solving when issues arose, and monitored the progress of implementation. Through involvement as important players in the re-engineering project, middle managers could knowledgeably support change efforts in their work areas and provide expertise to prototyping re-engineering processes. This example does not indicate any specific downsizing in the middle management ranks.

The second example took place in a large, public-sector health organization that experienced several major staff reductions in recent years. Those who remained, including middle managers, were dispirited and confused regarding the future of the organization. There was a general feeling that everyone had hit rock bottom and work lives were beyond their control. In this case, a group of middle managers from several clinical areas in the largest health care facility sought guidance from outside resources and a strategic plan emerged from these discussions. The managers acknowledged that change needed to occur if the organization was to survive; but they were afraid their individual roles and their employees' jobs might now be eliminated.

The first step of their plan was to accept the givens of the situation – that further downsizing will occur, people will move to other parts of the organization, and some will seek employment elsewhere. The second was to allow emotional reactions to the change process to be shared, by their employees and themselves. The third was to identify specific steps that these managers individually and as a group could take to plan their futures. They would also conduct these sessions with their employees. The objective was to be accountable and to have alternatives. Even though the organization did not involve them in any change planning, the managers took charge of their responses to any organizational decisions.

These two examples show that resistance to change can be addressed through multiple perspectives. The common theme through any successful organization change process is middle management involvement. Effective involvement, on the other hand, requires specific skills on the part of participants (Nevis, et al., 1996).

C. The Importance of Building Skills to Implement Change

As previously discussed, initiating, implementing and managing change requires a paradigm shift in the way everyone in the organization considers change. Thus top managers need to be vision oriented and values based leaders and transfer this leadership model to middle managers who will carry out and interpreting the change process throughout the organization. Consequently, an education program is included in the planning phase of the change process which is directed at the learning needs of top management, middle managers and all participants in change implementation. In addition to an initial needs assessment, a program to implement and manage change consists of four major topical areas. These concepts are described in Table 6.

Table 6 - Implementing and Managing Change: Educational Program

- **Large-scale change in organizations.** Understanding the dynamics of organizations, paradigm shifts, the importance of identifying and including internal and external stakeholders in planning for change, addressing resistance to change, and consequences of change for the organization. These concepts provide a framework for planning, implementation and evaluation.

- **Team Building: group facilitation.** Included are group dynamics, the leadership role, participating as a follower, accepting and using diversity on a team; developing group norms decision making.

- **Dealing with conflict, resistance to change.** Basic competencies in conflict management techniques and addressing resistance to change behaviors.

- **Technical skills related to specific methodologies used in change processes.** Information regarding specific change methodologies used in implementing change (i.e. TQM, job redesign, etc.). Concepts and techniques related to planning and implementing change.

The expected outcome of the educational program is to facilitate the change process and build an organizational infrastructure which can systematically and appropriately adapt to environmental challenges. Education for managing change cannot be an afterthought; successful change projects are built on a foundation of knowledge and capabilities to implement them.

The time required to develop these abilities depends upon the previous experiences and skills people in the organization have had in the educational topics described in Table 6. Eliminating or short-circuiting skills development can have dramatic impact on the success of the change process because participants will not be able to effectively address new expectations or changing roles. They will continue to respond as they did in the past to a new situation. These behaviors are often categorized as resistance to change.

D. Empowering People to Do Their Jobs

Anyone who has participated in a management workshop, meeting, or class in the last several years has heard about empowerment. Some organizations say that they have implemented empowerment but are unable to provide a clear description of how empowerment has changed the organization. It's a word that can mean everything and nothing. Jay Conger (1989), who has done extensive research on concept of empowerment, suggests that empowerment is having decision making power and/or access to resources necessary to carry out those decisions in the work areas of the organization. He notes that empowerment is a relational and a motivational concept. It is a function of the dependence or independence of a person or a group as they try to address the issues faced in the workplace and the levels of the organization they must refer to before a decision can be made. Empowerment also refers to the resources (financial, expertise, information, symbolic) which are available to an individual or a group which enables them to carry out their work.

Health care organizations have traditionally been considered hierarchical organizations with physicians and administrators having the most empowerment because of their organizational roles, access to information and financial resources. Everyone else in the organization, nurses, technologists, and support staff, have different levels of empowerment. A number of these levels are dictated by state licensing laws, others by the formal structure of the organization.

Major decision makers in organizations often perceive employee empowerment as usurping their traditional management powers of control and direction. In the turbulent environment of health care organizations, the traditional roles that were empowered to provide all the decisions related to patient care are seeing their empowerment shifting to other groups. For example, the physician's role as major decision maker for patient care is supported by state laws of licensure but is now governed by insurer cost guidelines and administrative regulations. Nursing staff, also regulated by state licensure laws, consist of different levels of nursing expertise with different limitations on decision making, use of health care resources.

The issue of empowerment within a health organization structure is thus complicated by the involvement of two powerful external stakeholders – state government and health maintenance organizations and insurers. Consequently, staff/employee empowerment must be defined by the work context and legal constraints. Empowerment in the Personnel Department will have a different definition than in the Emergency Room.

SUMMARY

This chapter began with the thesis that change is inevitable and learning to accommodate and adapt to uncertainty and ambiguity is a new reality. Health care organizations, as all other organizations, face the dilemma of creating and recreating themselves as they meet new challenges from changing and diminishing resources, scientific breakthroughs, patient expectations, and the "business-izing" of operations. But planning and managing change still begins with fundamental concepts:

- What is the purpose of the organization?
- Whom do we serve?
- How do we maintain our standards and values throughout the change process?
- How do we prepare ourselves for continuous change?

Clear-cut methodologies will lead health care organizations through the maze of change outlined in this chapter. The required ingredient for effective change is the commitment of each individual in the organization to a change process to build organizational capability to adapt to a fluid, fast-paced external environment.

REFERENCES

Alexander, J. A. and D'Aunno, T. A. (1990). Transformation of Institutional Environments. In Mick, S. A. and Associates: *Innovations in Health Care Delivery*, Jossey-Bass, San Francisco: 53-85.

Begeld, C. (1996). Your Health Scenarios. *The Futurist, 30:* 35-39.

Chisholm, R. F. and Ziegenfuss, J. T. (1990). A Review of Applications of Sociotechnical Systems Approach to Health Care Organizations. *The Journal of Applied Behavioral Science, 22(3):* 315-327.

Conger, J. (1989). Leadership: The Art of Empowering Others. The Academy of Management *EXECUTIVE, III(1):* 17-24.

Cooperider, D. L. and Srivastva, S. (1987). Appreciative Inquiry in Organizational Life. In Woodman, R. W. and Pasmore, W. A., *Research in Organizational Change and Development, Vol. 1,* JAI Press, Inc., Greenwich, CT: 129-169.

Cummings, T. G. and Worley, C. (1993). *Organization Development and Change, 5th Ed.* West Publishing Co., St. Paul, MN.

Dravecky, E. T. (1985). Socio-Technical Systems Analysis: Health Care Applications. In Buback, K. and Grant, M. K, Eds., *Quality of Work Life: Health Care Applications.* The Catholic Health Association of the United States, St. Louis, MO.

Dravecky, E. T. and Fadem, J. The Quality of Working Life in Hospitals. Presented to the Conference on Health Care and Industrial Relations, UCLA Institute of Industrial Relations and School of Public Health, June 20, 1980.

Dravecky, E. T. and LaBorde, A. (1992). Improving the Quality of Work and Productivity Through the Self-Designing Team Concept. *The Journal of Health and Human Resource Administration, Part II, Fall:* 327-360.

Duck, J. D. (1993). Managing Change: The Art of Balancing. *Harvard Business Review, November-December:* 109-118.

Floyd, S. and Woolridge, B. (1996). *The Strategic Middle Manager: How to Create and Sustain Competitive Advantage.* Jossey-Bass Publishers, San Francisco, CA.

Herman-Taylor, R. J. (1985). Finding New Ways of Overcoming Resistance to Change. In Pennings, Johannes M. and Associates, *Organizational Strategy and Change.* Jossey-Bass Publishers, San Francisco, CA: 383-411.

Handy, C. (1995). *The Age of Paradox.* Harvard Business School Press, Boston, MA.

Nadler, D. (1987). The Effective Management of Change. In Lorsch, Edward J.: *Handbook of Organization Behavior.* Prentice-Hall, Inc., Englewood Cliffs, NJ: 358-369.

Nevis, E. C., Lancourt, J., and Vassallo, H. G. (1996). *Intentional Revolutions.* Jossey-Bass Publishers, San Francisco, CA.

Preston, J. C. and DuToit, T.L. (1994). Power and Politics in Large Systems Change: The Old and New Perspective. In Cole, D., Preston, J.C. and Finlay, J., Eds., *What Is New In OD*, ODI, Cleveland, OH: 151-175.

Senge, P. M. (1990). *The Fifth Discipline.* Doubleday Publishing Group, Inc., New York.

Shortell, S. M. et al. (1996). *Remaking Health Care in America: Building Organized Building Systems.* Jossey-Bass Publishers, San Francisco, CA.

36.
THE *VALUE* MODEL IN STRATEGIC MANAGEMENT

Ken Czisny, *California Lutheran University, Thousand Oaks, CA*

Health care leaders need to manage strategically in order to meet the demands of rapidly changing environments. Strategic management is a way of focusing resources to improve quality and reduce costs. It has three purposes that go beyond the intent of traditional management. The first is to align organizational resources so that costs are reduced and goals more easily achieved. The second is to respond to a dynamic, competitive environment. The third is to develop a long-term customer competitive response that is favorable to the organization. Health care leaders recognize quality improvement and cost reduction as long-term challenges to their leadership abilities. This chapter describes a strategic management model that enables health care leaders to better provide high-quality health care services at a reasonable cost.

I. THE VALUE MODEL

Strategic management is most easily understood using a process model. Models identify factors, establish relationships, and enhance understanding of the dynamic nature of a phenomenon. A model for the strategic management process is presented as Figure 1. The purpose of this model is to describe the factors that must be addressed if one is to manage strategically. Therefore, the model does not address the circumstances under which strategy is formulated. Health care leaders are encouraged to read *Strategic Choices For America's Hospitals* to better understand the dynamics of strategic adaptation (Shortell, Morrison and Friedman, 1992).

The VALUE model presented in Figure 1 identifies 11 processes that conceptually describe strategic management. Each of the processes is defined, discussed, and categorized in accordance with the way they assist an organization in its efforts to identify a vision, conduct assessments, leverage resources, achieve understanding, or evaluate performance. The acronym VALUE is a composite of the first letters of the words vision, assessment, leverage, understanding, and evaluation.

Health care leaders have always established a raison d'être, identified customers, developed goals and objectives, allocated resources, and monitored organizational performance. The difference between traditional management and strategic management is that the latter also evaluates external and internal factors, identifies primary and secondary businesses, develops specific strategies and a long-range plan, establishes the relationships between the long-range plan and the organization's culture and work processes, and evaluates the effectiveness of the strategy. The following sections describe the strategic management process using the combined model presented as Figure 1.

A. Vision Statement

Vision is essential to every enterprise. The concept of vision is as old as Moses: "A nation without vision will perish" (Proverbs 29:18). Contemporary writers emphasize the need for leaders to provide visions for their organizations (Mintzberg, 1994; Duncan, Ginter and Swayne 1995). Unfortunately, organizational visions are not

Figure 1 - Strategic Management: The VALUE Model

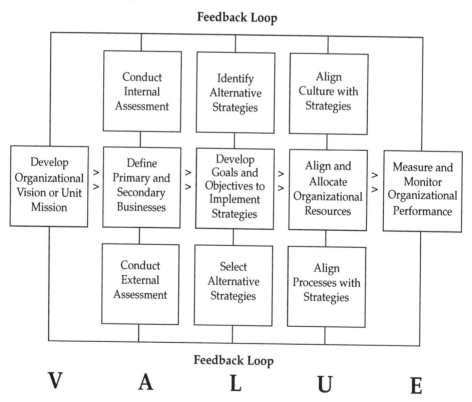

always clear, and leaders are seldom able to provide lucid pictures of the future for their followers. However, when leaders create visions of a positive and achievable future, they serve to motivate followers and provide direction for their performance (Kouzes and Posner, 1995).

Vision statements establish what an organization strives to achieve. A recent study defined a vision statement as "a cognitive image of the future which is positive enough to members so as to be motivating and elaborate enough to provide direction for future planning and goal setting" (Thomas and Greenberger, 1995).

Vision statements are used to establish the nature of the relationship between an organization and its stakeholders. The concept of organizational stakeholders was developed by Freeman in a study of Fortune 500 companies (Freeman, 1984). Several researchers have identified organizational stakeholders for health care organizations, and stakeholder maps have been developed to show the dynamic relationships between the organization and its stakeholders (Fottler, Blair, Whitehead, Laus, and Savage, 1989; Donaldson, 1995).

Organizational stakeholders are usually categorized into four groups: customers, co-workers, contributors, and community. Each group represents a separate constituency for the organization, and therefore the relationship between the organization and the group must be carefully defined to achieve a coherent organizational vision. An organizational vision statement usually has one paragraph that describes the relationship between each stakeholder group and the organization. The Arroyo Vista Family Health Center is a federally-funded community health center located in Los Angeles, California. Their vision statement exemplifies a vision statement that addresses all stakeholder groups. It is presented as Figure 2.

The nature of the stakeholder relationship depends on the values of the organizational leaders. The values held by an organization's leaders establish the basis for the relationships between the organization and its stakeholders. If the organization's leaders value fairness, this value is reflected in vision statement clauses such as " (the organization) recognizes patients rights" or "provides effective managers who value diversity, fairness ..." The organizational vision statement combines the values of the leadership (Board of Directors or management) with the needs of the stakeholder group. The first stakeholder group are the organization's customers. Relationships with customers need to be defined so that other stakeholder groups recognize the importance of this group. All organizations exist to meet human needs; the needs of the customer. When an organization fails to meet customers' needs, it disappears as soon as its resources are depleted. Health care organizations must provide high-quality, cost effective services to their customers in order to survive. The consolidation of the health care industry demonstrates the need to constantly understand the changing needs of health care customers.

Co-workers constitute the second stakeholder group addressed by an organization's vision statement. The term co-workers encompasses a number of different groups. First, there are the employees of the organization who most directly assist management in achieving organizational goals. Second, there are the legal and regulatory agencies who act in the best interests of the organization by interfacing with competitors, interest groups, and the general public. Third, there are suppliers, vendors, and contractors who provide the organization with high-quality, cost-effective, dependable, and accessible products and services. Each of these co-worker stakehold-

Figure 2 - Arroyo Vista Family Health Center Vision Statement

ARROYO VISTA FAMILY HEALTH CENTER strives to serve patients by providing prompt access to high quality preventive and primary health care services regardless of ability to pay. We deliver health care services in a courteous and friendly manner that respects patient's rights and encourages them to assume responsibility for their health.

ARROYO VISTA FAMILY HEALTH CENTER recognizes its responsibility to its employees by maintaining policies that ensure equal opportunities for professional development and advancement, fair and equitable compensation, avenues for open communication, and a clean, orderly, and safe working environment. We continuously provide effective managers and leaders who value and respect diversity, fairness, individual dignity, team effort, and outstanding performance.

ARROYO VISTA FAMILY HEALTH CENTER contributes to the community by sharing clinical, technical, administrative and legislative information with other community health professionals and organizations and by developing and maintaining a mutual referral and resource base. We promote academic excellence by providing clinical experiences for students and health professionals.

ARROYO VISTA FAMILY HEALTH CENTER promotes opportunities for fair competition to those who provide us with products and services. We establish relationships with vendors and suppliers that result in trust and the delivery of high quality, cost-effective, dependable, and accessible products and services. We compensate vendors and suppliers on a timely basis, inform them about the mission of the Center, encourage their support, and recognize their contributions.

ARROYO VISTA FAMILY HEALTH CENTER encourages the support of private foundations and government agencies by making them aware of community health needs, available resources, and our ability to respond. We develop strategies that encourage growth, enhance service accessibility and availability, and respond to individual health care needs. We comply with all grant award requirements and provide accurate and timely data to those funding sources to reflect our commitment to service and our appreciation of the investment they make in our community.

Figure 3 - Arroyo Vista Family Health Center Mission Statement

ARROYO VISTA FAMILY HEALTH CENTER provides high-quality, cost-effective health care services to residents of Northeast Los Angeles.

ers has a vested interest in the success of the organization and provides guidance and assistance for the firm.

The third group of organizational stakeholders are the contributors. This group is comprised of venture capitalists, shareholders, and bondholders in for-profit health care organizations and foundations, funding agencies, and donors in not-for-profit health care organizations. Regardless of the legal status of the organization, contributors are an important constituency and have a powerful influence on the goals of the organization.

Community is the fourth stakeholder group that affects health care organizations. This stakeholder group is comprised of special interest groups, individuals, and community leaders who influence the goals of a health care organization. Public and peer pressure are important social forces that need to be recognized by health care leaders. It is essential that organizations respond to this stakeholder group in a way that demonstrates competence, creativity, and concern.

Health care leaders that manage strategically define and understand their relationship with each of the stakeholder groups. The vision statement is the vehicle that defines stakeholder relationships. If stakeholder relationships are not keenly defined and delineated, they cannot be managed. Health care leaders need to manage their stakeholder relationships in order to achieve organizational goals.

In summary, the vision statement is a vehicle for communicating what the organization strives to achieve and how it interacts with different stakeholder groups as it accomplishes its goals. The vision statement establishes the values of the leaders and provides guidance for operationalizing organizational values through organization-stakeholder interactions. The four major stakeholders groups for health care organizations are: customers, co-workers, contributors, and the community. Strategic relationships with each stakeholder group need to be defined and managed.

B. Mission Statement

Mission statements establish the purpose and scope of an organization or unit. Mission statements do not duplicate vision statements because they do not define organizational statkeholder relationships. The Arroyo Vista Family Health Center mission statement is presented as Figure 3.

A unit's mission statement needs to be consistent with the vision statement of the organization. A unit mission statement may be developed for any organizational entity that wishes to manage strategically. A mission statement allows a unit to align its mission with that of the organization and establish goals that are consistent with its mission.

In summary, mission statements are developed for either an organization or an organizational unit. Whereas the vision statement communicates what the organization is striving to achieve (what the organization intends to do), the mission statement establishes purpose and scope (what the organization is doing).

Health care organizations complete the vision phase of the strategic management process by establishing a vision or mission statement for their organization or unit. The next steps depicted by the VALUE model are to assess internal and external environments and define the core businesses of the organization.

C. Internal Assessment

The internal assessment focuses on the strengths and weaknesses of the organization. A particular factor (e.g., use of technology) may be both a strength and weakness for the organization. Health care leaders conduct internal assessments in order to identify the specific strengths and weaknesses that can create the future success of the organization. Some of the factors considered in the internal assessment are:

• **Human Resources** - Health care is a labor intensive industry. Therefore, the foremost asset of the health care organization is its ability to attract, employ, and retain talented people. Successful organizations attend to environmental work factors and compensation issues, and motivate employees who are dedicated, reliable, and interested in their work. Strategically, the experience, flexibility, and growth of health care workers is especially important. Initial education and training combined with continuing professional education are important to the ability of the organization to adapt to new requirements. Health care organizations that are able to build a workforce that is flexible are in a better position to take advantage of new opportunities.

• **Technology** - Technology assessment is important for the preservation of assets. Health care leaders conduct technology audits to determine the extent to which organizational processes use technology to add customer value. Technology audits are important supplements to committees that evaluate and recommend new technologies (Bolton, 1995).

• **Processes** - Process assessment is an important step toward the improvement of health care services. Health care leaders who wish to save time and money while improving quality need to identify organizational processes. Because process improvement is a complicated subject, it is discussed in a separate section headed *Evaluate Organizational Processes*. Health care leaders need to be able to name their organization's processes and provide a qualitative evaluation of effectiveness.

• **Finances** - Finances usually attract the most attention when an internal assessment is conducted. There are at least three reasons for this. First, the organization's financial information is usually closely guarded (although information on new initiatives is more valuable strategically). Second, financial information is quantitative whereas information on processes is qualitative, or worse yet ambiguous. Third, financial information is guarded by a CFO who usually reports to a CEO, and therefore, the information must be important. In reality, financial information is important, but its true value becomes evident when it is combined with other information from an internal assessment in order to determine organizational strengths and weaknesses.

A health care leader performing an internal assessment may conduct a functional analysis to help assess the organization's strengths and weaknesses. Functional areas include management, finance, human resources, marketing, research, development and operations. The functional analysis is a proactive audit that determines how well different components of the organization are working together. Critical success indicators are developed and applied to each functional area. Management is evaluated by its contribution to process effectiveness and systemic alignment. Finance is assessed using industry and market financial ratios. Human resources is evaluated using benefit burden and employee turnover ratios. Marketing is evaluated using market share and stakeholder relations information. Operations is assessed by an evaluation of improvements in process efficacy and customer satisfaction. Organizational alignment is assessed by the time it takes for an organization to assimilate a management initiative (e.g., Continuous Quality Improvement).

Functional analysis is useful for determining the relative position of an organization vis-à-vis its market competitors. Benchmarking is used to determine the organization's relative industry position and how well the organization is working as a whole. Positive interaction between functional areas is an important determinant of organizational capabilities, competitiveness, and competitive advantage. Each of these concepts is explored below.

• **Capabilities** - The capabilities of an organization are not predetermined by available resources. Health care organizations extend resources by collaborating with other organizations (including competitors), leveraging organizational resources, and engaging in organizational learning. Collaboration allows an organization to successfully overcome a deficit or larger competitor. Whether collaboration is undertaken to combine the resources of smaller organizations or explore an expensive technology, the results will be positive if both organizations are clear about why they are working together. Leveraging organizational resources occurs in many ways: concentrating, focusing, blending, balancing, recycling and shielding resources, and expediting success (Hamel and Prahalad, 1993). For example, organizations concentrate and focus resources by creating multi-disciplinary task groups that address specific issues.

Organizational learning is perhaps the most important way to leverage an organization's capabilities and expedite success. Organizational learning occurs when adaptive or generative activities are implemented (Senge, 1990). Examples of adaptive activities include critical path analyses and market focus groups. Generative activities include human resource development and community health risk assessment. Senge encourages health care leaders to manage organizational resources so a "creative tension" exists between current resources and those needed to meet the vision. The tension results from an artificially induced shortfall of organizational resources. If managed correctly, the organizational resources will be "stretched" to achieve the vision.

• **Competencies** - Competencies are derived from the organization's human resources. People, not technologies, drive the competencies of health care organizations. Some competencies (e.g., patient relations) are at the core of health care organizations. Core competencies provide a health care organization with an identity that is different from other organizations. Although short-run advantages are derived from the price versus performance tradeoffs of current services (e.g., HMO services) long-run competitiveness drives from the ability to build core competencies. The same core competencies also contribute to the long-term prosperity of an organization, make a major contribution to customer perceived value, are competitively unique, and are extendible to current and future markets (Prahalad and Hamel, 1990). An organization's core competencies are identifiable because they relate to a core organizational process. For example, risk management (a core competence) is related to patient information flow (an organizational process).

• **Competitive Advantage** - Competitive advantage results from the combination of organizational resources, human resources, and leadership. Quality improvement programs provide competitive advantage by identifying market segments, emphasizing customer preferences, and accentuating reliability. Cost reduction programs provide competitive advantage by comparing competitor performance, stressing the efficiency of internal operations, and advancing the role of technology. However, sustain-

Figure 4 - Organizational Evolution

Organizational Phase	What accounts for growth	What accounts for crisis	Problem Resolution
Emerging	Creativity	Leadership	Outside leader
Growth	Direction	Control	Decentralization
Maturity	Management	Bureaucracy	Empowerment
Decline	Collaboration	Less creativity	Rethinking

able competitive advantage is also derived from changes in service, distribution, reputation, innovation, functionality, durability, and flexibility. Each of these factors provides competitive advantage for health care organizations. Two issues need to be underscored. First, competitive advantage is unique (within a particular market). Second, competitive advantage is sustainable; discounting the price of services is not sustainable.

Other factors also affect the competitive strength of an organization. For example, organizations evolve at different rates and in different ways. The rate of organizational evolution is affected by factors such as organizational age, size, growth rate of industry, etc. The manner in which an organization evolves is determined by whether it is in an evolutionary or revolutionary period (Greiner, 1989). According to Greiner, organizations move through four identifiable phases, are driven by a specific force, encounter a particular problem, and resolve the problem in specific way. These phenomena are depicted in Figure 4.

Figure 4 was constructed to portray Greiner's ideas by depicting the different phases of organizational development and identifying the factors that usually account for growth in a specific phase. Figure 4 also identifies the major challenge faced by the organization in each growth phase and its resolution. Understanding organizational development is essential to developing specific leadership skills, anticipating future crises, and recommending well-considered solutions to problems as they evolve.

In summary, the internal assessment process identifies organizational factors that affect the organization's ability to successfully compete. The most important factors for health care organizations are people, technology, processes and finances, and their interrelationship. Functional audits are used to determine the relative performance of each functional area and the synergistic result of coordination. Coordination enhances organizational capability, competitiveness and competitive advantage by focusing organizational resources. Health care leaders consider organizational development when assessing organizational strengths and weaknesses.

D. External Assessment

External assessment focuses on the opportunities and threats that face the organization. It should be noted that a particular factor (e.g., a specific demographic trend) may represent both an opportunity and a threat to the organization. Organizational leaders conduct an external assessment in order to identify opportunities and threats that affect the future success of the organization. Some of the factors considered in the external assessment are:

- **Geography**--The physical location of health care facility impacts the success of the health care organization by enhancing or limiting the customer base. This factor is very important for health care organizations since most depend on the local market for customers. The decline in the number of rural hospitals in the US demonstrates one impact of geography (Pasley et al., 1995).

- **Economics**--The impact of the local economy on the use of health care services is well documented (Luke et al., 1995). An individual's copayment level often determines use of health care services (Briggs et al., 1995; Institute of Medicine, 1993).

- **Politics**--Health care is profoundly affected by political and regulatory activity. The use of health care services is partially determined by the coverage available through private or government insurance. Health care organizations monitor and influence private and government payors to ensure recognition of important trends.

- **Social Trends**--Population demographics and the beliefs and values of individuals dramatically affect the use of health care services. Health care leaders track a variety of demographic trends (e.g., birth rate) to learn more about the populations for which they are responsible. Health care leaders also monitor and understand the cultures of the communities they serve. This information is assimilated and analyzed so the organization's health care programs are responsive to the unique needs of the community. Recently, legislation in some states requires hospitals to monitor a number of specific social trends (e.g., crime rates) in an effort to integrate community health programs.

- **Technology**--Health care and technology are intertwined. Because health care is a labor intensive industry, the use of technology to leverage the time of the health care professional is inevitable. Health care leaders need to understand the technologies that enable them to leverage the time of the processes they control. Health care leaders also need to understand information technologies to conserve resources.

- **Competition**--Organizational competitors usually receive the most attention when an external assessment is conducted. Focusing solely on competitors skews the assessment process and fails to emphasize the importance of other factors.

Nevertheless, because competitors are easy to identify and understand (being similar to the organization), they are the focal point. Health care leaders need to understand three things about their competitors. First, they need to know the competitor's capabilities; this implies an understanding of the competitor's physical, financial, and technological resources. Second, they need to know the competitor's competencies; this implies an understanding of the competitor's human resources. Third, they need to know the source of the competitor's competitive advantage; this implies an understanding of how the competitor's leadership will combine all available resources with a sense of entrepreneurship to create a unique quality for the organization that is sustainable over time.

Health care leaders who conduct external assessments use several standard information sources to evaluate important trends. Generally, professional journals (e.g., *Healthcare Executive*) provide secondary data on economic, political and social trends in articles written by practitioners and consultants. Other information sources provide primary data based on survey research. The list provided in Figure 5 identifies some available data sources.

Figure 5 - External Assessment Information Sources

Annual Publications
- Statistical Abstract of the U.S.
- Statistical Abstract of the World
- United States Industrial Outlook (1974-1994)
- SEC 10K Reports

- Moody's Publications

- Dun & Bradstreet Publications
- European Marketing Data & Statistics
- International Marketing Data & Statistics

- Hoover's Handbook of American Business
- Hoover's Handbook of World Business

Social, demographic, political and economic information
Industry forecasts, profiles, data, trends and projections by SIC code
Descriptive and financial information on specific organizations
Information on capital structures, histories and financial conditions
Reference indexes

Country demographic, economic and financial information
Company balance sheet information and competitor listing

Published Monthly/Weekly/Daily
- Value Line Investment Survey

- Funk & Scott Index of Corporations and Industries
- Public Affairs Information Service Bulletin

- Facts on File
- Federal Register (published daily)

- Federal Reserve Bulletin

Investor information on companies and industries; forecast data included
Information on organizations and industries by SIC codes
Indexes books, periodicals, pamphlets and government publications
Summaries of world business news
Federal agency regulations and legal notices
Congressional reports, staff studies, announcements

Electronic Databases
- ABI/ Proquest
- Dow Jones
- Lexis/Nexis
- InfoTrac General BusinesFile

- National Trade Data Bank

Indexes scholarly research articles
Company and industry information
Legal, business, and news information
Journal articles, company and SIC profiles, investext reports
Global trade information, country commercial guides, and market research

Internet Addresses:
- http://www.sec.gov/edgarhp.htm
- http://www.doc.gov/Commerce HomePage.html
- http://stats.bls.gov/blshome.htm
- http://www.bea.doc.gov/

- http://www.access.gpo.gov/congress/ cong002.html

SEC EDGAR Database

U.S. Department of Commerce
U.S. Bureau of Labor Statistics
U.S. Bureau of Economic Analysis (BEA) Home Page

Economic Indicators

Figure 6 - Competitor Matrix

Key Success Factors	Weight	Hospital 1		Hospital 2		Hospital 3		Hospital 4	
Market Share	.20	1	.20	3	.60	3	.60	1	.20
Price Competitiveness	.15	2	.30	3	.45	4	.60	2	.30
Quality	.15	1	.15	3	.45	3	.45	1	.15
Quality Improvement	.10	4	.40	3	.30	1	.10	3	.30
Service Level	.10	4	.40	2	.30	1	.10	3	.30
Responsiveness	.10	1	.10	2	.20	4	.40	1	.10
Financial Position	.10	2	.20	4	.40	1	.10	2	.20
Medical Staff	.05	1	.05	1	.05	3	.15	2	.10
Technology	.05	3	.15	4	.20	2	.10	2	.10
Total	1.00	1	.95	3	.05	2	.60	1	.75

Rating: 4 = firm's position is superior; 3 = above average; 2 = average; 1 = poor
Scoring: Multiply weight* rating to obtain score; add scores to obtain total.

None of the information resources listed in Figure 5 provides specific information on local competitors. Since health care is a localized business, competitive intelligence needs to be gathered discretely. Information is routinely gathered by: networking with other health professionals; interviewing competitor employees (or recent hires); using consultants to conduct surveys, etc. In California, the state Office of Statewide Health Planning and Development (OSHPD) collects competitive information from hospitals and, to a lesser extent, medical clinics. However, most of the data are spurious until the state agency audits the data. By that time, the data are 2 years old and their competitive use is limited. Consequently, consultants are often used to gather competitive information. Competitive information is often displayed in a matrix similar to Figure 6.

In summary, the external assessment process identifies environmental factors that affect an organization's ability to compete successfully. The most important factors for health care organizations are geography; the state of the local economy; local, state and national politics; social trends; new technologies and local market competitors. Health care organizations need to focus on these factors in order to understand their environment. Understanding the capabilities, competencies, and competitive advantage of competitors is key to completing an external assessment that assists organizational growth.

E. Define Primary and Secondary Businesses

Once a health care organization sets a vision, conducts an external assessment to delineate environmental opportunities, and threats and conducts an internal assessment to determine organizational strengths and weaknesses, the leadership needs to decide if the organizational resources are being used in the best possible way. For new organizations, the strategic question is "What are the right primary businesses for our organization?" For all other organizations, the strategic questions are "Are we in the right primary businesses?" "Why do we think that we are in the right primary businesses?" "What other primary businesses should we be in?" Primary businesses are those endeavors that define the essence of the organization. Secondary businesses are those in which an organization has a lesser financial interest.

Most health care organizations manage multiple primary businesses Too often, managers believe that the primary business is "health care" which is separated into "service areas" or "product lines". Health care services are provided by health care professionals; they are not produced like products (France and Grover, 1992). Thinking about health care as a product strengthens a paradigm that is not congruent with the characteristics of health care services. These characteristics include nonstandard output, a high level of customer contact, decentralized facilities located near customers, subjective measures of effectiveness, and a high level of personal judgment. Using the "service area" concept does not recognize that a unique set of critical success factors controls each primary business.

A health care organization answers three basic questions when it defines its primary businesses: What are we selling? To whom? How? Without clear answers to these questions, health care leaders are not able to address the strategic questions: What do our customers particularly value? Why are they willing to pay for our services? Will we still have these advantages in the future? Which advantages will we be able to defend? Which advantages will we not be able to defend? How can we transform our competitive advantages? Each of these questions needs to be answered to determine if an organization should remain in a specific primary business (Hamel and Prahalad, 1994).

The answer to questions about the primary businesses evolves through analyses of organizational strengths and weaknesses and environmental opportunities and threats. For example, decreasing profit margins may signal the organization to redesign the service, increase revenues, decrease expenses or, if the organization has 100% of the market and a hyper-efficient operating unit, to find other primary businesses. Another example, increasing regulatory activity, may signal the organization to explore other primary businesses lest over-regulation cause profit margins to fall to unacceptable levels. Too often, leaders choose to continue in primary businesses they know about (or are certified or licensed to operate) because they do not want to erode or share organizational power.

In summary, analyses are performed to help define the primary businesses of an organization. Health care leaders need to ask the hard questions: "Are we in the right primary businesses?" "Why do we believe that we are in the right primary businesses?" "What other primary businesses should we be in?" The vision statement, internal assessment, and external assessment provide information that make these questions easier to answer. It is imperative that health care leaders move their organizations into those primary businesses that align organizational resources with the needs of the environment.

Health care organizations complete the assessment phase of the strategic management process by conducting internal and external evaluations and defining their primary businesses. The next step in the VALUE model is to identify the alternative strategies that may help the organization adapt to its environment.

F. Identify Alternative Strategies

Strategists differentiate between two types of strategies: generic and specific. Generic strategies are broad and general. For example, an organization may pursue strategies that are aggressive (cost leadership) or conservative (staying in a niche). Specific strategies are narrow and focused. For example, an organization may pursue a strategy of horizontal integration. Specific strategies emerge from analyses that identify, weigh and quantify factors that influence an organization's ability to succeed in its environment.

Specific strategies have a standard nomenclature in all industries although implementation differs. For this reason, health care leaders look to non-health care industries (e.g. financial services) to identify the strategies of organizations that won in a period of industry change (e.g. consolidation). Health care leaders also use a concept examined earlier, organizational evolution, to understand organizational responses to growth.

An organization usually pursues only one or two specific strategies. A listing of 12 specific strategies identified by David appears as Figure 7 (David, 1995). Figure 7 identifies the strategies, provides a definition for each one, specifies when the strategy should be used, and provides an example of strategy use by a health care organization. Health care leaders in organizations that have not engaged in strategic management may find their organizations pursuing as many as seven or eight specific strategies at the same time. Pursuit of multiple strategies usually results in suboptimal organizational performance. The pursuit of multiple strategies also recognizes the fact that some organizations react to events in their environment rather than take actions to control their future.

In summary, health care leaders identify generic strategies and specific strategies for their organizations. Specific strategies emerge from quantitative analyses of factors that influence an organization's ability to succeed in its environment and have standard nomenclatures but industry-specific goals. Health care organizations that pursue more than two specific strategies risk suboptimal performance.

G. Select Alternative Strategies

Two analytic tools that are useful for selecting generic strategies are the SWOT Matrix and Industry Analysis. The SWOT Matrix uses information from the internal and external assessments to evaluate possible strategic responses to environmental and organizational factors. A variant of SWOT Matrix is the TOWS Matrix (Weihrich, 1982). In practice, it is more useful to refer to the instrument as a SWOT Matrix because managers are familiar with the acronym. Also, it is easier for an organization to study its own strengths and weaknesses (the SWs) before addressing the more complex opportunities and threats that exist in the environment (the OTs). A diagram of the 2X2 table used for SWOT Matrix is presented as Figure 8.

Figure 7 - Strategic Options

Strategy	Defined	When to use	Example
Forward Integration	Increasing control over providers	• Expensive, unreliable or incapable providers • Limited quality providers • Resources are available • Demand is predictable • High profit margins exist	HMO develops/buys primary care clinics
Backward Integration	Increasing control over suppliers	• Expensive, unreliable or incapable suppliers • Limited # of suppliers • Resources are available • Prices are stable • High profit margins exist • Org. needs supplier now	Hospital group purchasing coops
Horizontal Integration	Increasing control over competitors	• Economics of scale • Resources are available • Competitors are faltering	Columbia/HCA hospital purchases
Market Penetration	Increasing market share through marketing efforts	• Markets not saturated • Usage may be increased • Competitor share down • Economics of scale	Increase community presence through community education
Market Development	Introducing services into new geographic areas	• Reliable and inexpensive distribution channels exist • Org. knows value chain • Market not saturated • Resources are available • Org. has excess capacity	Hospital expands services in new service area
Concentric Diversification	Adding related services	• Industry is slow-growth • New enhances current • Current is cyclical • Strong mgmt team	Hospital adds long-term care services
Conglomerate Diversification	Adding unrelated services	• Industry is slow-growth • Resources are available • Investment resources are available • Existing market saturated	Development of Integrated Delivery Networks
Horizontal Diversification	Adding unrelated services for present customers	• Significant $ are possible • Low industry profits • OK distribution channel • New are countercyclical	HMO offers life insurance to enrollees

Figure 7 - Continued

Strategy	Defined	When to use	Example
Joint Venture	Two + companies form separate organization	• Legal or $ advantages • Merge core competencies • Benefits > resources • Need for new technology	Physician-Hospital Organizations
Retrenchment	Regrouping through cost and asset reduction to reverse declining profits	• Failure to meet $ goals • Clear core competencies • Org. is weak competitor • Org. has grown quickly	HMO Mergers
Divestiture	Selling assets of the organization	• Retrenchment fails • Unit does not match org. • $ needed quickly • Govt. threatens antitust	Tenent Corporation sells hospitals
Liquidation	Selling all assets of the organization	• Retrenchment and divestiture fail • Alternative is bankruptcy • Losses are minimized through asset sale	Columbia/HCA closes hospital

Figure 8 - SWOT Analysis

	Strengths	Weaknesses
Threats	Confront	Avoid
Opportunities	Exploit	Search For Solutions

Threats

External Environment

Opportunities

Strengths   Weaknesses

Internal Environment

SWOT analysis allows an organization to establish a general course of action. Two alternatives are available when an individual or organization meets a threat: fight (confront) or flight (avoid). As the threats and opportunities in the organization's environment are placed on the 2X2 table, SWOT analysis helps the organization develop a general course of action. Organizational strengths and weaknesses and environmental opportunities and threats may be rank ordered or combined (e.g. S+T). SWOT analysis

Figure 9 - Industry Analysis Matrix

Broad Target Population		
Narrow Target Population		

Cost   Differentiation

assists health care leaders generate generic strategies and organizational goals by providing a greater understanding of how the organization needs to respond to its environment.

In practice, most organizations do not fully utilize the information gained from a SWOT analysis. Some organizations simply list the SWOT factors and move on to goal setting never fully analyzing the SWOT information. Other organizations stop their strategic management efforts after completing a SWOT analysis because they begin to understand the amount of effort needed to fully understand the organization and its environment. Health care leaders need to acknowledge that understanding the relationship between an organization and its environment and taking action to align the organization with its environment is management's value-added to the business enterprise.

A second analytic tool used to identify generic strategies is Industry Analysis. Industry Analysis was developed to understand the dynamics of an organization's industry (Porter, 1979). Industry analysis evaluates the relative impact that suppliers, buyers, new entrants, and substitutes have on an organization. An organization estimates the strength of each of the four factors and takes actions to position the organization in its environment, anticipate shifts in the factor strength, and influence the power of suppliers, buyers, new entrants, and producers of substitutes.

Porter identifies cost and differentiation as two generic strategies used to position an organization in its environment (Porter, 1985) Cost and differentiation strategies may be pursued with broadly or narrowly defined populations. Figure 8 summarizes Porter's generic strategy matrix.

A health care organization that uses Porter's generic strategies might pursue actions that target a broad population with services that are low cost compared with other providers (e.g. a public health department). Alternatively, a health care organization might differentiate itself as a high quality provider and target a narrow population based on ability to pay (e.g. Cleveland Clinic). An organization may segment its market by population, cost, or a differentiating characteristic (e.g. service design). When a health care organization selects a generic strategy it is important to avoid the "crosshairs" at the center of Figure 6 because organizations that position themselves in that area become all things to all people; a sure way to lose credibility and money. Two analytic tools that are useful for selecting specific organizational strategies are the Strategic Position and Action Evaluation (SPACE) Matrix and the Grand Strategy Matrix. The SPACE Matrix was developed by Dickel to identify industry factors and assign each a score from -6 to +6 (Dickel, 1984). The average scores for Financial Strength (FS) and Environmental Stability (ES) are totaled and placed on the Y-axis. Similarly, Competitive Advantage (CA) and Industry Strength (IS) scores are totaled and placed on the X-axis. A line is drawn to the point where the two scores intersect. This point is in one of four quadrants labeled aggressive, conservative, defensive and

Figure 10 - Space Analysis Matrix

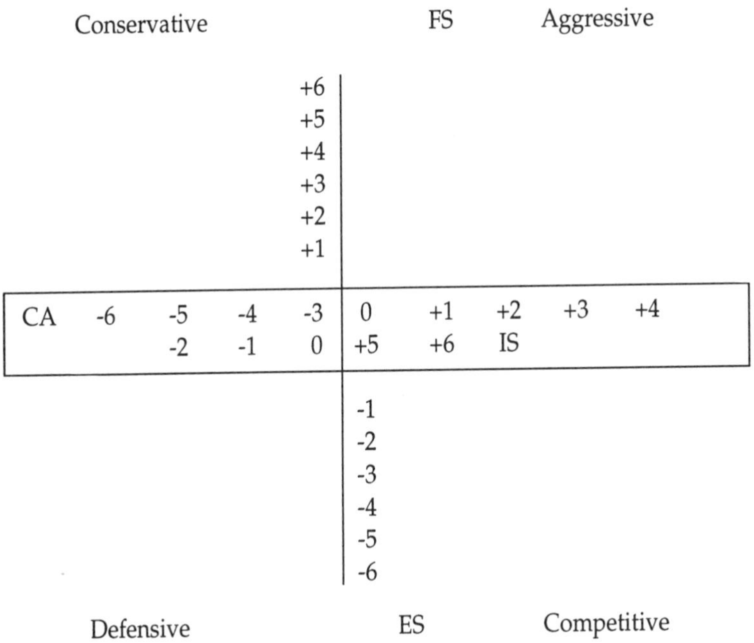

Conservative FS Aggressive

```
                              +6
                              +5
                              +4
                              +3
                              +2
                              +1
  CA   -6    -5   -4   -3 | 0    +1   +2   +3   +4
             -2   -1   0  |+5    +6   IS
                              -1
                              -2
                              -3
                              -4
                              -5
                              -6
```

Defensive ES Competitive

FS = Financial Strength
ES = Environmental Stability
CA = Competitive Advantage
IS = Industry Strength

Internal Strategic Position	Rating	External Strategic Position	Rating
Financial Strength (FS)	(+)	Environmental Stability (ES)	(-)
• Return on investment		• Technological change	
• Asset leverage		• Inflation rate	
• Asset liquidity		• Demand variability	
• Working capital		• Price variability	
• Cash flow		• Competitive pressure	
• Risk		• Barriers to entry	
Competitive Advantage (CA)	(-)	Industry Strength (IS)	(+)
• Market share		• Growth potential	
• Service quality		• Profit potential	
• Customer loyalty		• Financial stability	
• Technological know-how		• Resource utilization	
• Control over suppliers		• Capital intensity	
• Control over service time		• Capacity utilization	

Scoring X axis = average CA + IS scores Y axis = average FS + ES scores
Plot point where scores meet; insert directional arrow

competitive. Organizations select strategies from the listing in Figure 7 that are consistent with the quadrant label. Figure 10 identifies some factors and a SPACE Matrix that might be used to select a specific strategy for a health care organization.

The Grand Strategy Matrix uses two factors to determine strategy: rate of market growth and competitive position. An organization selects the quadrant that matches its relative rate of growth and strength in the marketplace. Each quadrant contains strategies rank ordered by their attractiveness to the organization. Since the quadrants of the Grand Strategy are similar to those of the SPACE Matrix, the two tools are often used together. Figure 11 adapts the Grand Strategy Matrix, developed by Christensen, to a health care environment.

In summary, health care leaders select strategies for their organizations using qualitative and quantitative methods. The decision whether to select a generic or specific strategy is based on management insight and the amount of information available for analysis. If there is little information, the strategies are usually generic, broad and general. If data are available, collected, and analyzed, the strategies are usually specific, narrow and focused. Generic strategies allow organizations to compete in emerging and growth industries.

Specific strategies conserve organizational resources and enhance survival rates for organizations in mature and declining industries.

H. Develop Goals and Objectives to Implement Strategies

Health care leaders develop organizational strategies by identifying ways that specific strategies might be implemented and conducting analyses to verify that a course of action is logical. Since strategies are selected in part on the basis of what makes the leaders of an organization feel most comfortable, strategic analyses are necessary to ensure that organizational assets are not used improperly. Strategic analyses also assist health care leaders in the development of goals, objectives, and activities to implement strategy.

Strategy development is more than developing goals and objectives or establishing a rational and supporting analysis. Strategic development also takes into account the factors and activities that explain organizational growth and market position. Mintzberg asserts that combining the activities that accounted for past success with new activities that are responsive to organizational strengths and environmental opportunities encourages agreement between constancy and change (Mintzberg, 1979). Health care leaders evaluate the "goodness" of their organizational strategies by identifying the extent to which the strategies: maintain long-term consonance with the environment, gain sustainable competitive advantage for the organization, achieve organizational alignment, and seem feasible for the organization (Rumelt, 1980). Health care leaders also use ethics audits to evaluate strategies.

Organizational goals and objectives are essential for implementation of strategy. Goals are statements of what the organization hopes to accomplish during the next 3-5 years. When detailing goals, health care leaders begin with the end point and work backwards. For example, if the goal is to build a medical practice of 2000 patients within three years, one estimates the number of patients that must be seen by the end of the second and first years. It is also useful to establish monthly or quarterly markers to determine if goals are being met.

Figure 11 - Grand Strategy Matrix

Rapid Market Growth

1. Market development	1. Market development
2. Market penetration	2. Market penetration
3. Service development	3. Service development
4. Horizontal integration	4. Forward integration
5. Divestiture	5. Backward integration
6. Liquidation	6. Horizontal integration
	7. Concentric integration

Weak Competitive Position ———————————————————— **Strong Competitive Position**

1. Retrenchment	1. Concentric integration
2. Concentric diversification	2. Horizontal integration
3. Horizontal diversification	3. Conglomerate diversification
4. Conglomerate diversification	4. Joint ventures
5. Divestiture	
6. Liquidation	

Slow Market Growth

Goals increase the effectiveness of organizations by providing challenges and standards, guiding and directing behavior, serving as a source of legitimacy, defining a rationale for organizational structure, reflecting what goals setters think is important, and anticipating, identifying and linking resource allocation with stakeholder needs. Goals need to be shared with all members of the organization in order to increase organizational performance.

In some organizations goals are set by management with minimal input from other organizational stakeholders. Management needs to consider the advantages of having customers, co-workers, contributors, and the community participate in the goal-setting process. Each of these stakeholder groups adds value to a health care organization and therefore the health care leader needs to formally recognize their contribution. Usually, a stakeholder group wants to influence only those goals that pertain to a specific area of concern. Therefore, health care leaders are usually not overcome when they seek input from stakeholders. Conversely, health care leaders may find their resources strained when they choose to not respond or seek the counsel of a stakeholder group.

Most customers are not interested in influencing an organization's goals. Most are interested in ensuring that a particular situation is addressed. If a similar situation presents itself, it may represent an opportunity to redefine the process that is creating the concern.

Co-workers are recognized formally or informally depending on the strength of their ideas and the management style of the organization. For example, a health care leader with a hierarchical management style may choose to post organizational goals in a unit and propose that ideas be submitted via the suggestion box. Another health care leader may choose to meet with co-workers in a series of "Brown Bag Lunches" in order to better understand and provide feedback on co-worker contributions. Successive iterations help insure co-worker "buy-in."

Contributors usually influence the goals of the health care organization by providing funds for specific areas of interest. Health care leaders need to shape the influencing behaviors of contributors by educating them about the needs of the organization. This process, like all educational processes, is time-consuming and requires patience and tenacity. The payoff for the health care leader occurs when contributors understand the organization better and modify regulations, guidelines, or restrictions on their gifts.

Communities influence the goals of health care organizations by demanding services that meet their needs. Both general and special community populations ask community health care organizations to respond to their needs. If the organizations fail to respond, community groups unite and force a response that invariably requires organizational attention and resources. Therefore, health care leaders hold meetings to derive input from subgroups within the community and demonstrate that the organization is responding (at the goal level) to the communities' concerns. It is more important to "close the communications loop" with the community than any other stakeholder group because they have the capacity to close a business that does not meet their needs.

Goals may be evaluated by asking the following questions:
- Are they measurable?
- Are they simple, clear, and easily understandable?
- Are they consistent with the organization's vision?
- Are they consistent with the organization's strategy?
- Do they focus organizational resources?
- Do they have a performance feedback mechanism?
- Do they express a sense of action?
- Do they reflect high standards of excellence?
- Do they challenge organizational members?
- Do they build a gateway to the future?

These questions provide useful information to those who set organizational goals and may be used as a "screen" for current goals. However, the best set of wordsmithed goals will not serve a health care leader who does not communicate well. Personal experience suggests that when communicating new organizational goals, one needs to create a learning environment, anticipate problems, accept criticism gracefully, strive to reduce ambiguity, use organizational networks, be ceremonial, use symbols, accentuate and reinforce the positive, and focus on the future.

When health care leaders articulate what is needed to succeed in a changing environment, it provides a sense of direction, discovery, and destiny for the organization. Hamel and Prahalad use the term "Strategic Intent" to describe the leadership actions that focus an organization's resources on critical success factors. By creating a sense of urgency, encouraging innovation, focusing on competitors, providing resources, monitoring progress, and providing an opportunity for celebration of success, health care leaders demonstrate strategic intent (to win) (Hamel and Prahalad, 1989).

Objectives are statements of what the organization hopes to accomplish during a one year period. Objectives contribute to the attainment of goals. Similarly, activities are actions that take less than one year to accomplish and contribute to the attainment

Figure 12 - Strategic Planning Form

Strategy:
Goal:

Objectives	Activities	Resources	Responsible	Evaluation
1.	1. 2. 3. 4.	1. 2. 3. 4.	1. 2. 3. 4.	1. 2. 3. 4.

Figure 13 - Gantt Chart

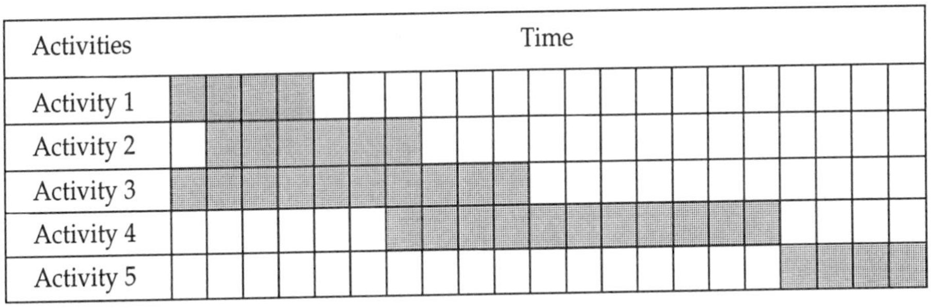

Activities	Time
Activity 1	
Activity 2	
Activity 3	
Activity 4	
Activity 5	

of objectives. Goals, objectives and activities are usually presented in a way similar to the format presented in Figure 12. The format shown in Figure 12 allows management to quickly review the attainment of goals and identify why a specific goal was not achieved (i.e. specific activities did not occur on time which means that an objective was not met which means a goal was not attained). The format also ensures that an end point (product or process) is identified. The Gantt chart (Figure 13) is another useful device for tracking goal implementation, especially if the goal has numerous objectives and activities.

In summary, health care leaders develop strategic analyses, goals, objectives and activities for specific strategies. Strategic analyses identify the purpose of the strategy, resources needed for implementation, and how the strategy will be evaluated. Strategic analyses also consider past activities that contributed to organizational growth and market position. Goals, objectives, and activities are necessary for implementation of a strategy. Selecting the right goals is important to full implementation of the strategy. All stakeholder groups (customers, co-workers, contributors, and community) need to be involved in the goal-setting process or the organization will expend additional time and resources as the stakeholder group either inserts itself into the goal-setting process or rejects the programs of the organization. Goals and objectives need to be understandable, measurable, and action-oriented to maintain the interest of the stakeholder groups. Communication is an important key to goal attainment; goals increase the effectiveness of the organization when they are developed and shared openly. Clarity, humility, and a positive attitude help health care leaders communicate goals well. The right goals, objectives, and activities help the organization leverage its resources and position itself in the environment.

Effective organizations have goals relating to: customer creation, innovation, human resources, capital resources, physical resources, productivity, social responsibility, and profit/surplus.

Once strategies are developed, the development process and final product are evaluated using consonance, alignment, feasibility, competitive advantage, and ethics as screens. The development of strategies allows the organization to leverage its resources and position, thereby achieving sustainable competitive advantage. Health care leaders use the VALUE Model to develop an organizational vision or unit mission statement, conduct internal and external assessments, define primary businesses, identify alternative strategies, select primary and secondary strategies, develop analyses and documents to support strategies, and establish goals, objectives, and activities. The goals, objectives, and activities provide an initial estimate of the resources necessary to implement the strategies. The goals need to be modified after the organization's current culture and processes are aligned with the new strategies. Some health care leaders, especially those in organizations where culture and processes are grossly inconsistent with new strategies, evaluate culture and processes before establishing organizational goals, objectives, and activities.

I. Align Culture With Strategy

Culture represents the shared philosophies, values, norms, and behaviors of an organization. Organizational philosophies are expressed in statements that express the essence of stakeholder relationships. Values are expressed in the written and unwritten rules that govern the organization (e.g. honesty). Norms are based on values and represent expectations of the organization (e.g. long work days). Organizational behaviors often take the form of symbols, rituals, and language (e.g. CQI). Each of these "threads of culture" is woven into the fabric of the organization. Each thread strengthens the organization at some time in its history. Therefore, it is essential for the health care leader to recognize past accomplishments and consider previous alignments of culture and strategy.

Health care leaders need to consider how organizational culture is affected by factors external to the organization. All of the factors considered in the external assessment affect the culture of the organization. Predominant among the factors are social trends. Social trends affect organizational culture the most because individuals determine the philosophies, values, norms, and behaviors of an organization. When an individual or group changes, the culture of the organization changes. Therefore, it is essential that the health care leader attends to organizational language, power relationships, group membership, and individual needs.

A health care organization that needs to change its culture because it is inconsistent with new strategic initiatives may find the task difficult. Consideration must be given to the old culture. Health care leaders need to understand the managerial frames (paradigms), rules, and expectations of the old culture in order to establish a baseline for change. Once the baseline is established, leaders can define new culture goals, activities that achieve the goals, and methods that measure goal attainment. For example, an organization could initiate a continuous quality improvement program to better align the current culture with a concentric diversification strategy.

Health care leaders manage and change the culture of their organization by following several steps. First, they understand the current culture by learning about its paradigms, rules, assumptions, and expectations. Second, they provide support for new ideas that are consistent with organizational vision, strategy and goals. Third, they use effective subcultures as examples of what the new organizational culture might be like. Fourth, they recognize that the process of cultural change is long-term (10 years for major changes) and the futility of frontal advances and force to bring about change. Fifth, they live the new culture by providing support for role models, teachers, and coaches and ensuring that organizational rewards and punishments are consistent with organizational vision. Basically, health care leaders know that the right changes have occurred when their culture can be described as high performance - high commitment. Attributes of this type of culture include: participation and delegation; cross-functional teamwork; empowerment and responsibility; integration of people and technology; and a shared sense of purpose consistent with organizational vision.

In 1990 Peter Senge described the dynamics of a learning organization in which leaders assume the roles of visionary, designers of strategies and creators of learning environments (Senge, 1990). Senge believes that organizational learning may be the only sustainable source of competitive advantage. Therefore, it is important for health care leaders to provide both an accurate picture of the current reality and a compelling picture of a desired future. Within their learning environment, health care leaders help restructure organizational reality by changing the structure of systems, patterns of behavior, and individual events. These actions encourage organizational commitment, defuse routines, and allow leaders to focus on areas of high leverage.

In summary, culture is determined by the shared philosophies, values, norms, and behaviors of an organization. Each of these factors have value for the organization and need to be recognized and celebrated. Changing social trends affect organizational cultures more than other factors. Organizational language, group membership, and power relationships are important indicators of social change. New cultural goals emerge from careful analyses that identify previous managerial frames, rules, and expectations.

Health care leaders align organizational culture with vision, strategy, and goals. Individuals in the organization will resist change because it is natural to do so: fear of uncertainty and fear of loss often overcome good intentions. Health care leaders understand the current culture, provide support for new ideas, use subcultures as examples, recognize the complexity of cultural change, and live the new culture when they attempt cultural change. Strategic cultural change is achieved when organizational vision, strategy, goals, and culture are aligned. Leaders that build learning organizations use educational processes to achieve organizational alignment.

J. Evaluate Organizational Processes

Service organizations are processes bound together for a common purpose (e.g. improvement of health). Health care leaders need to understand an organization's processes and the effect of the processes on customers. The focus on processes is relatively new. Since the 1950s, management gurus have advised business leaders to focus

Figure 14 - Refocusing Organizations

<u>Organizational Focus</u>
- Employees are the problem
- Employees
- Doing the job
- Knowing the job
- Measuring the employee
- Changing the employee
- Finding better employees
- Motivating employees
- Controlling employees
- Don't trust anyone
- Who made the error?
- Correct errors
- Bottom-line driven

<u>Process Focus</u>
- The process is the problem
- People
- Help to get things done
- Knowing the job and entire process
- Measuring the process
- Changing the process
- Improving the process
- Removing barriers
- Developing people
- We are all in this together
- What allowed the error to occur?
- Reduce variation
- Customer driven

Figure 15 - Health Care Processes

<u>Functional Area</u>	<u>Process</u>	<u>Output</u>
Board	Policy Development	Policies
Administration	Risk Management	Insurance Data
Operations	Physical Examination	Medical Record
Finance	Accounts Receivable	Patient Bill
Marketing	Market Research	Demographic Data
Personnel	Employee Orientation	Personnel File

on a variety of topics: management skills (1950s); resource allocation (1960s); resource/cost balance (1970s); costs (1980); quality (1985); customers (1990) and process (1995). The dates represent the high points of each of the trends, not the point at which they were first introduced. Together, focus on quality, customers and processes represent a movement toward strategic management and cause organizations to look beyond internal needs to the environment. The changing paradigms are presented in Figure 14.

Today, health care leaders manage processes more closely than in the past. Process improvement teams, value chain analysis, and re-engineering are now part of our daily life. The core of these activities is the process. Processes are what we identify, model, chart, and improve. One definition of a process is: any activity that takes an input, adds value to it, and provides an output to an internal or external customer. Several health care services processes are presented in Figure 15.

Although organizational definitions for processes vary, each type of health care organization, e.g. hospital, has essentially the same processes. Therefore, health care organizations learn how to identify and improve their own processes by assessing the efforts of collaborators and competitors. Health care leaders also improve their processes by evaluating improvements made in other service industries (e.g., financial services).

Figure 16 - Cross-Functional Processes

Cross-Functional Process	Functional Areas			
	Board	Adm	Ops	Finance
Strategic Planning Process	X	X	X	X
Clinical Forms Completion Process		X	X	X
Insurance Forms Completion Process			X	X

Processes have several important characteristics including: recognized owners; defined boundaries; defined interfaces and responsibilities; documented procedures, tasks and training requirements; defined measurement and feedback controls; customer-related measurements and targets; known cycle times; formalized change procedures; and benchmarked performance levels. In addition, processes are a source of sustainable competitive advantage.

Although most processes have boundaries, some processes cut across functional areas. Understandably, these processes are called cross-functional processes. Several examples of cross-functional processes are presented in Figure 16.

Health care leaders manage and improve the processes of their organization by following several steps. First, they organize by: establishing an executive process improvement team; appointing a process improvement champion; providing executive training; developing an improvement model; communicating goals to employees; reviewing strategy and customer requirements; selecting critical processes; appointing process owners; and selecting process improvement team members. Second, they attempt to understand the process by: defining process scope and purpose; defining process boundaries; providing process improvement team training; developing a process overview; defining and providing measurements for customer expectations; creating a flow diagram of the process; collecting cost, time and value data; performing process walk-throughs; resolving differences; and updating process documentation. Third, they streamline the process by: providing process improvement team training; identifying improvement opportunities (i.e. errors, high costs, poor quality, time delays); eliminating duplication; eliminating activities that do not add value for the customer; simplifying the process; reducing process time; error-proofing the process; upgrading equipment; standardizing; automating; documenting the process; and selecting and training process employees. Lastly, they develop process measurements and controls by: developing measurements and targets; establishing feedback systems; developing audit cycles; and identifying poor-quality costs.

To continuously improve the process they: define and verify the process; perform periodic qualification reviews; define and eliminate process problems; evaluate impacts on customers and business; and benchmark the process. The goals of process improvement management are to improve: effectiveness by producing desired results for customers; efficiency by minimizing resources used (0 errors); and adaptability by meeting changing customer needs (Harrington, 1990; Shaw, 1991).

The efficiency of processes is evaluated by measuring timeliness (# of rings before telephone is answered), accuracy (# of errors), performance (# of complaints), reliability (no-error consistency), costs (below standard), responsiveness (time to appointment), adaptability (adjusting to customer expectations) and dependability (consistency over time).

The effectiveness of processes is evaluated by measuring processing time, resources/unit of output, value-added/unit of output, percentage of value-added time, and poor-quality cost. Understanding the cost of poor quality is useful for establishing organizational value-added and for quantifying cost center savings.

The adaptability of processes is evaluated by measuring exceeded standards or protocol expectations and rate of continuous improvement. Continuous adaptation to customer expectations improves flexibility and sustainable competitive advantage.

Evaluating process improvement using measurements of efficiency, effectiveness, and adaptability is one way to determine the organizational effectiveness. Organizational effectiveness is enhanced when vision, strategy, goals, culture, and processes are aligned. Total alignment is achieved when organizational structure and systems (e.g. compensation), become "vision-centered" and use organizational processes as the basis for change.

In summary, health care leaders need to align organizational processes with vision, strategy, goals, and culture. This is accomplished by organizing a process team, understanding the process, streamlining the process, developing process measurements for efficiency, effectiveness and adaptability, and motivating and rewarding employees. Health care organizations are repositories of the processes that improve health. Successful health care leaders know how to manage and improve the efficiency and effectiveness of the processes. Some processes occur within a functional area whereas others cut across functional areas. Both functional and cross-functional processes are sources of sustainable competitive advantage.

Health care leaders using the VALUE model align organizational goals, objectives, and activities with culture, processes, and strategy before allocating organizational resources.

K. Align and Allocate Organizational Resources

Health care leaders align and allocate resources on the basis of organizational goals and objectives. Ensuring that adequate human, financial, and technological resources are available to employees trying to accomplish the work of the organization is essential to effective management. Process and culture alignment identifies the need for resources and ensures effective allocation. Alignment of goals, objectives, activities, culture, and processes with strategy ensures effective designation of human, capital, and physical resources.

Intra-group and inter-group rivalries along with power plays disrupt effective allocation of organizational resources. Health care leaders need to be vigilant lest resources be drawn to old processes that are not aligned with organizational goals and objectives.

In summary, goals and objectives provide the rationale for the allocation of organizational resources. Process and culture alignment identifies the resources needed to execute the strategies on which the goals and objectives are based. Health care leaders need to constantly monitor performance to ensure that organizational goals are met.

L. Measure and Monitor Organizational Performance

Health care leaders regularly evaluate the effectiveness of their organizations. Most evaluations focus on financial strength (e.g. financial ratios), market position (e.g. percent of market share), and human resource information (e.g. turnover data). Although these data are important for determining the efficiency of specific functions (Are we doing things right?), they do not address the issue of organizational effectiveness (Are we doing the right things?) (Drucker, 1974).

Process evaluations address organizational effectiveness because they are customer-centered and real-time oriented. Process evaluations are based on predetermined targets (goals and objectives), feedback systems (quarterly reporting) and regular analyses of costs and cycle-time. Process cost analyses use activity-based costing techniques developed to determine how resources are employed to support organizational processes (Burns, 1992; Burns, 1991). By using activity-based accounting, health care leaders ensure that all direct and indirect costs are identified and allocated to specific processes. This allows the identification of expensive resources, resource variances, and resource demand patterns. By using cycle-time analysis, health care leaders identify the process-time and wait-time components of a process. Each component contributes to customer dissatisfaction and service cost (Cooper and Kaplan, 1988).

Kaplan and Norton offer a perspective on measuring the strategic contribution of management to organizational success (Kaplan and Norton, 1996). They feel that management is responsible for translating the vision, linking strategy to unit objectives, integrating financial objectives and unit business plans, and assisting organizational learning. Organizations using the Kaplan and Norton approach would also measure and monitor success indicators for these areas.

In summary, traditional measurement and control systems tend to measure elements that are useful for determining functional area efficiency but are not terribly useful for assessing organizational effectiveness. Measurement and control systems need to be aligned with organizational vision, strategy, goals, culture and processes to correctly identify levels of effectiveness. Activity-based cost analysis and cycle-time analysis provide health care leaders with tools for evaluating organizational effectiveness. Used in concert with an awareness of organizational culture and change techniques, they provide health care leaders with methods to improve the strategic management of their organizations.

II. WHERE CAN WE GO FROM HERE?

Health care leaders recognize the fundamental strength of strategic management. Alignment of organizational vision, strategy, goals, culture, and processes produces increases in revenues, employee commitment, and customer satisfaction. But, when a health care organization is the "only game in town," strategic management seems like just another management fad. However, when a local health care organization is besieged by national competitors with deep pockets, strategic management is essential for organizational survival. Therefore, the decision to shift to a strategic management paradigm is tempered by the volatility of the organization's environment.

Leadership vision also affects the implementation of strategic management initiatives. Seen from one perspective, strategic management is a way to help the organization blend with its environment. From another perspective, strategic management is a management philosophy based on the principles of awareness, coordination, and focus. The perspectives are different because the education and experience of individual health care leaders are different. Strategic perspective depends on where one is sitting (literally). Strategos, which is the linguistic base of strategy, means "generalship" in the Greek language. Greek generals tried to place themselves at the highest point so they could understand how the battle was progressing. Today the management team occupies the high ground of the organization chart and has the responsibility for organizational success. The education, experience, and personality of the management team determines their perspective and ability to align the activities of the organization in a way that promotes growth and effectiveness. This calls for a change in perspective and the abandonment of traditional critical success factors for new measures that promote organizational change and effectiveness.

Drucker comments on the need for leaders to change their perspective and embrace new assumptions that fit current realities. The assumptions describe markets, customers, competitors, values, technology, and organizational strengths and weaknesses. These assumptions are referred to as the organization's theory of business. Drucker feels that the assumptions about environment, mission, and core competencies must fit reality and one another, be understood throughout the organization, and be tested constantly by management (Drucker, 1994). The VALUE strategic management process model assists health care organizations test their theory of business.

REFERENCES

Bolton, L. (1995). An IT Aid to Accountability. *Accountancy.* 113: 545.

Briggs, L., Rohrer, J., Ludke, R., Hilserath, P. and Phillips, K. (1995). Geographic Variation in Primary Care Visits. *Health Services Research.* 30(5): 657-671.

Burns, W. Jr., (1991). A Brief Introduction to Cost Accounting. Note 9-192-068. Harvard Business School.

Burns, W. Jr., (1992). Activity Accounting - Another Way to Measure Costs. Note 9-193-044. Harvard Business School.

Christensen, R., Berg, N. and Salter, M., (1976). *Policy Formulation and Administration.* Richard D. Irwin. Homewood, IL.

Cooper R. and Kaplan, R. (1988). Measure Costs Right : Make the Right Decisions. *Harvard Business Review.* Harvard Business School. 88503.

Dickel, K., Rowe, A., and Mason, R. (1984). *Strategic Management and Business Policy: A Methodological Approach.* Addison-Wesley, Reading, MA.

Donaldson, T. and Preston, L. (1995). The Stakeholder Theory of the Corporation : Concepts, Evidence and Implications. *Academy of Management Review.* 20(1): 65-91.

Duncan, W., Ginter, P., and Swayne, L. (1995). *Strategic Management Of Health Care Organizations.* Blackwell, Cambridge.

Drucker, P. (1994). Theory of Business. *Harvard Business Review.* Harvard Business School. 94506.

Drucker, P. (1974). *Management.* Harvard Business School Press, Cambridge.

Fottler, M., Blair, J., Whitehead, C., Laus, M. and Savage, G. (1989). Assessing Key Stakeholders: Who Matters To Hospitals And Why? *Hospital & Health Services Administration.* 34(4): 530.

France, K. and Grover, R. (1992). What Is The Health Care Product? *Journal Of Health Care Marketing*. 12(2): 32.

Freeman, R. (1984). *Strategic Management : A Stakeholder Approach.* Pitman, Boston.

Hamel, G. and Prahalad, C. (1994). *Competing For The Future*, Harvard Business Press, Cambridge.

Hamel, G. and Prahalad, C. (1993). Strategy As Stretch & Leverage. *Harvard Business Review*. Harvard Business School. 93204.

Hamel, G. and Prahalad, C. (1989). Strategic Intent. *Harvard Business Review*. Harvard Business School. 89308.

Harrington, H. (1991). *Business Process Improvement.* McGraw Hill, New York.

Institute of Medicine. (1993). *Access To Health Care In America.* National Academy Press, Washington, D.C.

Kaplan, R. and Norton, D. (1996). Using The Balanced Scorecard As A Strategic Management System. *Harvard Business Review*. Harvard Business School. 96107.

Kouzes, J. and Posner, B. (1995). *The Leadership Challenge.* Jossey Bass, San Francisco.

Luke, R., Ozcan, Y. and Olden, P. Local Markets and Systems: Hospital Consolidation in Metropolitan Areas. *Health Services Research*. 30(4): 555-576.

Mintzberg, H. (1994). *The Rise And Fall Of Strategic Planning.* Free Press, New York.

Mintzberg, H. (1987). Crafting Strategy. *Harvard Business Review*. Harvard Business School. 87407.

Pasley, B. Lagoe, R. and Marshall, N. Excess Acute Care Bed Capacity and Its Causes : The Experience of New York State. *Health Services Research*. 30(1): 115-132.

Prahalad, C. and Hamel, G. (1990). Core Competence Of The Corporation. *Harvard Business Review*. Harvard Business School. 90311.

Porter, M. (1985). Generic Competitive Strategies" Competitive Advantage. Free Press. New York.

Porter, M. (1979). How Competitive Forces Shape Strategy. *Harvard Business Review*. Harvard Business School. 79208.

Quinn, J. (1980). *Strategies for Change: Logical Incrementalism.* Richard D. Irwin. New York.

Rumelt, R., (1980). The Evaluation of Business Strategy. (In W.F. Glueck, ed.) *Business Policy and Strategic Management*. Mc-Graw-Hill, New York: 359-67.

Senge, P. (1990). The Leader's New Work: Building Learning Organizations. *Sloan Management Review*. MIT Press. 90211.

Shaw, J. (1991). *The Service Focus.* Dow-Jones Irwin. Homewood.

Shortell, S., Morrison, E. and Friedman, B. (1992). *Strategic Choices For America's Hospitals.* Jossey-Bass. San Francisco.

Thomas P. and Greenberger, D. (1995). Training Business Leaders To Create Positive Organizational Visions Of The Future: Is It Successful? *1995 Proceedings Of The Academy Of Management.*

Weihrich, H. (1982). The TOWS Matrix: A Tool For Situational Analysis. *Long Range Planning*. 15(2): 61.

37.
STRATEGY: PLANNING, MANAGEMENT, AND CRITICAL SUCCESS FACTORS

Thomas F. McIlwain, *Medical University of South Carolina, Charleston, SC*

James A. Johnson, *Medical University of South Carolina, Charleston, SC*

The concept of strategy is found in early military writings dating back to the Greeks and early Chinese. These first discussions of strategy appear as military concepts dealing with the tactics of winning territory and defeating enemies. This militaristic view of the concept as one of enemy and enemy action and the resultant reaction with an ultimate outcome of winning a battle, operation, or war is not too far removed from today hearing a sportscaster talk of a ball team's strategy in defeating a rival.

In the health care industry, organizations are now concerned with strategic choices such as market development, market penetration, or service development. It has been well established that there are strategic choices for America's hospitals (Shortell, Morrison, and Friedman, 1990). Hardly a meeting in a health care organization goes by without the discussion of some aspect of a strategic decision. Bob Dylan wrote of social change and upheaval in the late '60s and early '70s when he said, "You'd better start swimming or you'll sink like a stone, for the times, they are a changing." Now, like never before health care organizations have to make strategic choices and act (swim) or they will not meet the challenges (sink like a stone) of these new and changing times.

The purpose of this chapter is to introduce the reader to the meaning of strategy, strategic planning, and strategic management. In addition to discussing the benefits of strategic management, the chapter focuses on the elements of the strategic management process. The chapter concludes by providing a specific model for implementing strategies in the health service organization that uses critical success factors.

I. THE MEANING OF STRATEGY, STRATEGIC PLANNING AND MANAGEMENT

The concept of strategy is not simply defined. Merriam-Webster Dictionary (1994) offers no less than six definitions, but also defines other concepts such as strategem, strategic, strategist, and strategize. Specifically, Merriam-Webster contains the following definitions:

1. The science and art of employing the political, economic, psychological, and military forces of a nation or group of nations to afford the maximum support to adopted policies in peace or war.
2. The science and art of military command exercised to meet the enemy in combat under advantageous conditions.
3. A variety of or instance of the use of strategy.
4. A careful plan or method: a clever strategem.
5. The art of devising or employing plans or strategems toward a goal.
6. An adaptation or complex of adaptations (as of behavior, metabolism, or structure) that serves or appears to serve an important function in achieving evolutionary success (foraging strategies of insects).

Additionally, a strategem is defined as "an artifice or trick in war for deceiving and outwitting the enemy; a cleverly contrived trick or scheme for gaining an end; skill in ruses or trickery," (Merriam-Webster's, 1994). The breadth of meaning attributed to this concept is most certainly related to the vast amounts of usage of the term.

In management, strategy implies a decision making process which takes into account current and emerging issues both inside and outside the organization which will have an impact on its success. The organization is a system which must undergo an adaptation or complex of adaptations to achieve evolutionary success including survival, growth, and change. Therefore, strategy is a systematic management process of making decisions and carrying out those decisions to ensure the continued growth and survival of the organization.

Strategic management is generally considered a broad concept encompassing strategic planning. This broad concept of strategic management is a philosophy of management which is externally focused so that the organization can make changes to help shape its future. Thus, a strategy is organizational behavior of interacting with the environment in a way that not only ensures current survival but ensures the future survival of the organization as well.

II. THE IMPORTANCE OF STRATEGIC PLANNING AND MANAGEMENT

Strategic planning and management are not a panacea for saving troubled health care organizations. It is, however, a systematic approach to analyze an organization's situation and develop appropriate responses to improve its situation. The ultimate goal of strategic planning and management is the survival and growth of the organization, but in some cases the organization may not have a viable mission, have appropriate resources, or have the capabilities to continue to exist. Therefore, its strategic behavior may be to dissolve. The importance of the strategy process is to help an organization develop a philosophy, process, and procedures for being more efficient and effective in its environment while carrying out its purpose with a sense of vision and values. All organizations, whether formally or informally, deliberately or not, knowingly or unknowingly, develop and implement strategies. Every organization has a strategy, but those that do not develop them from a more formal process in a deliberate and knowing manner, generally react poorly to rapid change in their environments.

Although the benefits from strategically managing an organization are not always quantifiable, the process helps bring the organization together in a common purpose and mission. This common purpose provides a consistent platform for decision-making which increases the propensity for success. When an organization plans and manages strategically, it requires a heightened degree of communication both vertically and horizontally thus improving coordination of effort. Most importantly, strategic management develops in people a reduced resistance to change, and thus encourages innovative thinking and solutions to problems. Strategic organizations understand that change means opportunity.

III. APPROACHES TO STRATEGIC MANAGEMENT

There are numerous perspectives about the concept of strategy and strategy making. Ten schools of thought were identified by Mintzberg (1990), and these perspectives are categorized as either prescriptive or descriptive. The prescriptive category emphasizes how strategies should be formulated and the descriptive category characterizes how strategies actually get made. As this chapter is concerned with how strategies should be formulated, only the prescriptive schools of thought will be outlined.

The three prescriptive schools of thought are the design school, planning school and positioning school. The design school approaches strategy formation as a product of the conceptual and analytical efforts which is the result of the implementation of SWOT analysis (strength, weakness, opportunities, and threats). Organizations use this process to help guide the organizational structure and the allocation of resources. The planning school embodies a more technical process in a formal and complex manner. The results of the process is a rational planning process using extensive data analysis which generates a blueprint for action by the organization. The positioning school was described by Michael Porter (1980) and is based on a framework that organizational performance is the result of firm conduct which is influenced by the market structure.

The merits of all three prescriptive schools is important in strategically managing an organization. Each suggests that strategies can be identified, planned, and analyzed before being implemented. However, Mintzberg and Waters (1985) suggested that in reality, strategies emerge as an outcome of learning. The authors describe a process where strategies are intended, deliberate, and emergent. Emergent strategies are those that are produced from a learning process and reality testing rather than of the conceptual analytical process. Managers should understand that the strategic management process which works for one organization may not work for another. In addition, managers may pick and choose certain techniques and procedures which work best for their personality types, organization resources, and organizational environments.

IV. THE STRATEGIC MANAGEMENT PROCESS

The strategic management process generally has four stages. Each of these stages is a separate but interrelated process. They deal with how the organization analyzes its environment, determines appropriate strategies, implements the chosen strategies, and then evaluates the success or failure of the chosen action. The fours stages are: situational analysis, strategy formulation, strategic implementation, and strategic control.

By definition, when an organization undertakes a strategic endeavor, it has to take into consideration its organizational setting. This setting is usually referred to as the environment. Health care organizations do not exist in a vacuum, and their environments can be analyzed either as general environmental or specific health care environmental issues. Health care organizations face environments from both a general and industry specific nature. In the general environment, health care organizations are affected by trends and issues that are common to other industries. The organization also faces issues and is affected by information that is specific only to the health care industry. This specific environment has been referred to as the health care environment. The general and health care environments of the health services organization provides information for the situational analysis.

A. Situational Analysis

Analysis of the health care organization's current situation requires a thorough audit of its mission, vision, and values, in addition to four other fundamental groups of variables within the context of its environment. The four groups of variables are sometimes referred to as SWOT or TOWS analysis and represents analysis of the organization's strengths, weaknesses, opportunities, and threats.

As a first step in a health services organization's situation analysis is the articulation of its mission, vision, and values. The mission defines the organizations fundamental purpose for existence. Usually a mission statement will contain reference to what business the organization is in, who the customers are, where (geographically) and how the organization provides value to its customers. As a supplement to the mission, an organization should identify its vision of the future as an indication of what the organization wants to do. And finally, a discussion of the organization's values, or guiding principles, should be identified.

The second step in the organization's situation analysis is the external environmental analysis. This process of looking outside the organization should identify changes which reflect both opportunities and threats to the organization. Environments will always be changing, and those changes can be perceived by the organization as creating opportunities or presenting threats for the existing way of doing things. Threats as well as opportunities are issues which drive what the organization should do to be successful.

A third step in situational analysis is looking internally at the organization's strengths and weakness in relation to its external opportunities and threats. By looking at this "internal environment" the organization identifies what it can realistically accomplish both from an existing inventory of resources but also based on what it might realistically acquire as a means of taking advantage of external opportunities or of avoiding impending threats. In meeting some challenges, the health services organization (HSO) may already possess certain strengths and have few weaknesses. Yet in other cases the organization may be very vulnerable because it cannot take advantage of an opportunity due to lack of human, financial, or other resources. The organization's competition may be well positioned to take advantage of the situation. In this case, a weakness must be eliminated. Strengths should be exploited to the benefit of the organization in either taking advantage of an opportunity or overcoming a threats.

B. Strategy Formulation

Given a thorough situational analysis, the health services organization is prepared to decide on the best course of action or strategy. The organization first revisits its mission, vision, and values. These decisions provide the direction for the organization. All other decisions regarding strategy should be in congruence to these statements of beliefs about the organization. It would be ill-advised for an organization to choose a strategy that did not conform to its basic philosophies and values. Once these decisions are made, the organization must choose, given its situation, whether to pursue growth strategies, consolidation strategies, or status quo strategies. These strategies have been labeled adaptive strategies because they represent how the organization will adapt to its environment given its situation. If an organization chooses a growth strategy, it can do so by penetrating existing markets with existing services, developing new markets with existing services, developing new products in existing markets, or diversifying into other types of businesses by providing new services to new markets. Diversifying usually suggests an organization is not familiar with the new product or service and may be better off by entering in a strategic alliance or joint venture with other organizations.

Consolidation strategies are methods of adapting to an environment by shrinking the organization. The HSO may choose to divest or sell off a service line, retrench by withdrawing from certain markets, or harvest whereby the organization generates cash from the existing service while not investing new resources until the service no longer meets a need in the marketplace. Each of these consolidation strategies requires the organization to reduce the number of resources it spends on providing the good or service.

There are a wide variety of alternative methods used in analyzing the organization's current situation and then choosing or developing appropriate strategies. Several widely accepted methods are the Boston Consulting Group Portfolio Analysis Matrix (McStravic, Mahn, and Reedal, 1983) and the General Electric Business Screen (Desai, and Margenthaler, 1987). Each of these methods involves choosing among alternative strategies based on an analysis of an organization's market share and market growth rate. The GE Business screen is more complex and uses a multidimensional approach labeling its matrix dimensions as market attractiveness and business strength. These two models are only an example, and the reader is encouraged to study other methods of evaluating strategic alternatives.

C. Strategy Implementation and Control

After strategic alternatives have been decided, management must implement functional level strategies (sometimes called tactics) which support or nourish the business level strategies. These functional level strategies must be carried out in the financial, marketing, information systems, and human resources areas related to the overall strategy (McIlwain and McCracken, 1997). If a HSO chooses to develop a new service in a new marketplace (usually a very costly undertaking), then plans must be made to have appropriate funding, personnel, marketing, and information to carry out those plans. In addition, managers have to be aware of how strategies affect individuals in the organization and how individuals affect the implementation of strategies. The culture of an organization can affect the success or failure of a given strategy the same as a given strategy can affect the culture.

Finally, the organization must have control mechanisms in place to evaluate the effectiveness of its strategic actions. During the strategic planning stage, objectives are established which serve as standards to be achieved by the organization. The process of evaluating the success of any strategy is to measure actual performance to the given standard. If there is a significant gap in performance and standards, then corrective action must be taken.

The use of critical success factors is comprehensive strategic planning and management model which touches on all of the previously discussed stages. The next section of this paper defines and discusses the use of critical success factors in the strategic management of successful organizations.

V. CRITICAL SUCCESS FACTORS

In their book *The Success Paradigm: Creating Organizational Effectiveness Through Quality and Strategy*, Friesen and Johnson (1995) point out that to be truly successful any strategic planning process should have four cornerstones: vision, focus, quality improvement, and organizational learning. Vision is essential in creating a mental model that can be articulated and shared with others to engage their support and participation. Focus is critical to concentrate the thought, energy and resources needed for accomplishment of the mission and goals. Quality improvement assures that the plan will address operations and customer satisfaction as well as facilitate the use of data in decision making. Lastly, organizational learning is important in strategic planning. As Mintzberg (1994), in his Harvard Business Review article "The Fall and Rise of Strategic Planning" points out, "We think in order to act, to be sure, but we also act in order to think. We try things and those experiments that work converge gradually into viable patterns that become strategies"(p. 111).

With these four cornerstones in mind it is important to consider how one might go about incorporating them into the planning process. The typical strategic plan does not include quality improvement and organizational learning models. Friesen and Johnson (1995) provide a methodology that does address these key elements of successful planning efforts. As with most strategy models, theirs begins with the establishment of a mission statement for the organization. It follows the five step process described below.

Step 1: Establishing the Mission
The mission statement describes the nature and concept of the organization and its future activities. It also delineates what the organization plans to do and for whom.

Step 2: Identify Critical Success Factors
> *This entails the identification of the core or essential factors that are*
> *absolutely critical to the accomplishment of the organization's mission.*
> *Critical success factors (CSFs) are usually limited in number and serve to*
> *focus resources and effort.*

Step 3: Strengths and Weaknesses Profile
> *Each CSF undergoes an analysis to assess its strengths and weaknesses.*

Step 4: Goals and Action Plans
> *Goals are established and action plans for each are implemented.*

Step 5: Quality Improvement Efforts
> *Continuous quality improvement efforts are designed to address weakness*
> *and to improve strengths for each of the CSF areas.*

This model has been utilized in a number of hospitals and health care networks with great success. One example is a hospital that identified its CSFs as:

1) patient satisfaction;
2) managing financial resources;
3) community relations;
4) quality medical and professional staff;
5) employee attitudes and abilities;
6) managerial leadership and planning; and
7) physical environment.

They then assessed the strengths and weaknesses in each of these areas and set out to develop goals as well as design CQI interventions. After considerable success with their efforts the hospital then inspired their network to adopt the same planning model.

The CSF approach to focusing attention and effort can be used at the macro level as well. Shortell, et al (1996) identifies critical success factors for organized delivery systems. They are the need to streamline the governance process, redefine management roles, develop strong physician leaders, and implement broader performance accountability criteria. Given these CSFs as the "skeleton" an integrated delivery system could follow the Friesen and Johnson Model in designing a strategic plan which would identify the relative strengths and weaknesses of the system and develop CQI interventions and action plans to address them.

In summary, there are approaches that can be taken to develop a strategic plan. However, when doing so the efforts remain focused on what is critical or key to the accomplishment of the organization's mission and where there are weaknesses and improvement opportunities in these areas they should be addressed in a way that facilitates organizational learning.

VI. SUMMARY

This chapter introduces the associations among strategy, strategic planning, and strategic management. Additionally, the chapter focuses on the elements of the strategic management process, concluding with a discussion of a specific model for implementing strategies. Knowing and applying the managing elements of the strategic management process are key to successfully managing an HSO. A wealth of information from process models to complex quantitative evaluation techniques may be used in the formulation of successful strategies. The HSO manager must be able to identify and use those methods which are appropriate to the organization based on its external and internal environments. In this way, the organization can take deliberate actions for continued survival and growth.

REFERENCES

Desai, H. and Margenthaler, C. (1987). A framework for developing hospital strategies. *Hospital and Health Services Administration, 32(2)*, 235-48.

Friesen, M. E. and Johnson, J. A. (1995). The Success Paradigm: Creating Organizational Effectiveness through Quality and Strategy. Westport, CT and London: Quorum Books

McIlwain, T.F. and McCracken, M.J. (1997). Essential dimensions of a marketing strategy in the hospital industry. *Journal of Hospital Marketing, 11(2)*, 39-59.

McStravic, R., Mahn, E. and Reedal, D. (1983). Portfolio analysis for hospitals. *Health Care Management Review, 8(4)*, 69-75.

Merriam-Webster's Collegiate Dictionary, 10th Edition. (1994). Springfield, Massachusetts: Merriam-Webster, Incorporated.

Mintzberg, H.I. and Waters, J.A. (1985). Of strategies, deliberate and emergent. *Strategic Management Journal, 6*, 257-272.

Mintzberg, H. I. (1990). Strategy formation schools of thought. In: Fredrickson, J.W., ed. *Perspectives on Strategic Management*. New York, NY: Harper Business, 105-236.

Mintzberg, H. (1994). The Fall and Rise of Strategic Planning. *Harvard Business Review*. 107-114 (Jan-Feb).

Porter, M. (1980). *Competitive Strategy: Techniques for Analyzing Industries and Competitors*. New York, NY: Free Press.

Schendel, D. and Hofer, C. (1979). *Strategic Management: A New View of Business and Policy and Planning*. Boston: Little, Brown, and Co.

Shortell, S.M., Gillies, R.R., Anderson, D.A., Erickson, K.M., and Mitchell, J. B. (1996). *Remaking Health Care in America*. San Francisco: Jossey-Bass.

Shortell, S.M., Morrison, E.M., and Friedman, B. (1990). *Strategic Choices For America's Hospitals*. San Francisco: Jossey-Bass.

38.

TOTAL QUALITY MANAGEMENT AS A HEALTH CARE CORPORATE STRATEGY[1]

James A. Johnson, *Medical University of South Carolina, Charleston, SC*

Vincent K. Omachonu, *University of Miami, Coral Gables, FL*

I. TQM MUST BECOME A PART OF CORPORATE STRATEGY IF IT IS TO BECOME A WAY OF LIFE IN HEALTH CARE

While health care organizations grapple with the success or failures of total quality management (TQM), it is becoming increasingly clear that TQM must become a part of corporate strategy if it is to become a way of life in health care. Total quality management is a leadership philosophy. It is driven by the following nine key principles (Omachonu, 1991):

1. The need for top management to mobilize its workforce towards the achievement of the mission vision, long-term and short-term goals of an organization.
2. Pursuant to (1) is the need for every individual, function, department and division, to become inextricably linked to the organization's mission, vision, long-term goals, short-term goals and guiding principles.
3. The recognition that the organization's most important reason for existence is its customers, and that its employees are its most valuable asset.
4. Once adopted, TQM should become a way of life. It is a process, not a program. It is not something an organization does to pass inspection by the Joint Commission for the Accreditation of Health Care Organizations (JCAHO). It is a never-ending process.
5. TQM is driven by an understanding of the needs, wants and expectations of the customers (internal and external). It aims to create services that meet or exceed the expectations of the customers. It also aims to bridge the gap between the expectations of customers and what the organization is capable of delivering.

6. It relies on the use of teams to solve problems. It is driven by the notion that no one knows the problems in a process better than those who work and live with the process on a daily basis. Every problem is treated as a defect in the system, and must be eliminated. It aims for long-term solutions to problems by seeking to eliminate the root cause of the problems rather than quick fixes. It is the empowerment of workers. Everyone is involved in and affected by the transformation; receptionists, housekeeping, technicians, physicians, nurses, etc.

7. Everything is a process. Every process requires inputs which then become transformed to produce some output. Processes are interrelated and depend on a series of cross-functional interventions. Pursuant to (6), it is the notion of work interrelatedness which drives the need for cross-functional teams. It calls for the breaking down of departmental barriers.

8. It is the use of statistical thinking to manage processes. It is management by facts, not opinion, guesswork or gut feel.

9. It is the elimination of waste and rework. It is when "good enough" is never good enough. It is the relentless pursuit of excellence in everything an organization does.

The type of transformation which TQM brings about cannot occur in isolation and certainly cannot be sustained unless it is part of a business strategy. Pearson (1990) notes that "business strategy is concerned with how to make an individual business survive and grow and to be profitable in the long term. " The main considerations are as follows (Pearson, 1990):

- the creation of customers;
- the identification of appropriate market niches where no competition exists;
- the identification of customer needs and how best they can be satisfied;
- the application of technology and its future development or substitution;
- the understanding of competitors and how direct competition may be avoided; and
- the motivation of people to put their efforts and enthusiasm behind the strategic aims of the business.

According to Lawrence and Early (1992), "Quality efforts will fail if they are not firmly anchored in the health care organization's strategic direction and executive leadership." Health care organizations principally strive to achieve some or all of the following strategic goals:

- the improvement and management of clinical outcome;
- to attract and retain qualified clinicians;
- cost containment;
- profitability; and
- to achieve customer satisfaction.

The process of continuous quality improvement must be linked to the achievement of these strategic goals. According to Andrews (1980):

> Corporate strategy is the pattern of decisions in a company that
> determines and reveals its objectives, purposes, or goals, produces
> the principal policies and plans for achieving those goals, and
> defines the range of businesses the company is to pursue, the kind of
> economic or human organization it is or intends to be, and the
> nature of the economic and non-economic contribution it intends to
> make to its shareholders, employees, customers, and communi-
> ties...[It] defines the businesses in which a company will compete,
> preferably in a way that focuses resources to convey distinctive com-
> petencies with competitive advantages.

TQM must, first and foremost be seen and implemented as a vehicle for achieving corporate objectives and goals if it is to have any chance of succeeding. Peters and Waterman (1982) define strategy as "a coherent set of actions aimed at gaining a sustainable advantage over competition, improving position vis-a-vis customers, and allocating resources." One of the objectives of TQM is to gain competitive advantage over the competition. The concept of TQM is driven by the notion that if you are not improving, you are falling behind the competition. The improvement of the quality of the services offered to customers and the need to gain competitive advantage are central to the objectives of TQM. Failure to make the TQM process an integral part of business and corporate strategy would confound constancy of purpose. Hax and Majluf (1984) state that: "Strategic management has, as an ultimate objective, the development of corporate values, managerial capabilities, organizational responsibilities, and administrative systems which link strategic and operational decision-making, at all hierarchical levels, and across all businesses and functional lines of authority in a firm."

Pearson (1990) makes a distinction between corporate and business strategy as follows: "Corporate strategy relates to the company's interface with the providers of its capital, while business strategy. . .is concerned with what makes the business prosper in relation to its customers, competitors and technologies."

II. TQM AS PART OF CORPORATE CULTURE

If TQM is to become a way of life for a health care organization, it should be understood in the context of a cultural transformation Schein (1981) explains culture as follows:

> Culture is the set of basic assumptions which members of a group
> invent to solve the basic problems of physical survival in the exter-
> nal environment (adaptation) and social survival in the internal envi-
> ronment (internal integration). Once invented, these basic assump-
> tions serve the function of helping members of the group to avoid or
> reduce anxiety by reducing anxiety and cognitive overload. Once
> invented, those solutions which work are passed on to successive
> generations as ways for them to avoid the anxiety which may have
> motivated the invention in the first place.

Culture is therefore a way in which individuals in an organization respond to external pressures from the environment, by creating rules and a way of thinking which then become the norms of behavior for the group. As new employees become absorbed into the workforce, they too acquire the new culture through the process of adaptation. Some degree of molding of values and ethics take place, formally or informally, and are accepted by everyone. Schwartz and Davis (1981) provide a definition of culture which is fairly consistent with Schein's: "A pattern of beliefs and expectations shared by members of an organization. These beliefs and expectations produce rules for behavior--norms--that powerfully shape the behavior of individuals and groups in the organization." Organizations which choose to ignore the power and influence which culture can produce do so at their own peril. The critical challenge for top management is the creation of a work culture that unites every employee around the needs, wants and expectations of customers. When an organization has adapted successfully to this singleness of purpose in meeting or exceeding the expectations of its customers, the visible evidence can be felt by all customers from admissions to post-discharge, and from the receptionist to the chief executive officer of the organization.

Schwartz and Davis make a distinction between culture and organizational climate. Organizational climate measures the fit between the prevailing culture and the individual values of the employees. If the employees have adopted the values of the prevailing culture, the climate is "good." If they have not, the climate is "poor," and motivation and presumably performance suffer.

TQM calls for a cultural transformation which will lead to new values and a different ethic. In a mature TQM culture, every employee treats every customer as if he or she is the only customer. All employees are engaged in a relentless pursuit of perfection. There is a built-in intolerance for "defects," or customer dissatisfiers. Meeting or exceeding the needs of all internal customers is seen to be critical for the long-term survival of the organization. If the concept of TQM is to have any chance of success, most or all of the individuals in the organization must be culturally socialized on the importance of the customers - internal or external. According to Conrad (1990), some cultures value action, while others sanction activity. In an action-oriented organization the emphasis is on creative work designed to have some positive effects, while in an activity-oriented organization, the emphasis is on merely appearing to be making contributions. The primary goal in an activity oriented organization is to "fill time," regardless of what actually is accomplished. Conrad notes that "construction workers who learn to always keep moving, to always carry a tool in their hands, are part of activity-oriented cultures." So are organizations which reward employees based on some numerical goal or quota rather than the quality of the service provided. The emphasis is on results rather than how well the customers are actually served. Conrad notes that only when the outcomes of activity are also valued does a culture become action oriented. TQM effort can only be sustained by an action oriented culture. If TQM is not viewed as a business strategy as well as a vital process in the cultural socialization of the organization, the results could be disappointing.

Some health care organizations promote a culture which fosters a team approach to providing care, while others value and encourage exceptional individual effort. The concept of TQM is founded-on team accomplishment. According to Lawrence and Early (1992):

The outcome of a surgical procedure will of course, depend on the surgeon's skill, but it will also depend on many other factors, including the speed and accuracy of laboratory tests, the availability of the right information at the right time in the patient's chart, the timely availability of the right material and equipment in the operating room, the appropriateness of prescribed postoperative care, the clarity and precision of the physician's orders, and clinical information from which the surgeon can identify more effective methods of care. Effectively using scientific knowledge to improve clinical outcomes requires a strategic commitment and active, cooperative leadership between physicians and other professional managers.

Some cultures encourage employees to make decisions which minimize risks by making changes in accepted ways of doing things only after carefully, laboriously making the decisions and thoroughly questioning every piece of evidence and every argument supporting the change. These risk-aversive organizations also tend to evaluate decisions only after long periods of time. Others foster high-risk actions by encouraging employees to use temporary "quick fixes" and provide immediate evaluation of employees' actions and decisions (Conrad, 1990). The concept of TQM seeks long-term solutions, not quick fixes. The primary focus is on the prevention of recurrence of problems.

It is not enough to have one person who shows a predisposition to the concept; nor is it sufficient to have one department embracing the philosophy. TQM is not a departmental activity, nor is it one person's job. Effective quality management begins at the top. There is always the temptation of delegating the TQM initiative to others. Godfrey et al. (1992) note:

> It would be a rare, courageous, and perhaps short-lived director of quality management who would make an appointment with the CEO to say, "I've been thinking, boss. The job you are expecting me to carry out is, in fact, your job. You're holding me accountable for changes in culture, behavior, strategic priority, and organizational methods that only you, the physician leaders, and the board can really deliver. In the end, you might think that I let you down; but it's the other way around."

The transformation brought about by TQM requires a shift in paradigm. It calls for a change in management philosophy as it affects human resources, management information system, process design and redesign, customer knowledge systems, and bench marking methods. Strategic planning must then seek to set the organization's priorities and help align the work of teams and departments with those priorities. If the activities of quality teams are not guided by the mission, vision, guiding principles, short-term and long-term goals of an organization, they will have a tendency to be self-serving. Traditionally, decisions in these areas have been made on narrow, tactical grounds, with little attention to business and corporate strategy.

Few health care organizations regard service quality as a source of competitive advantage. As we approach the end of the first decade of TQM implementation in health care, health care organizations which are not able to adapt their strategic vision to the ever-changing health-care industrial landscape will fall by the wayside. An organization's competitive strategy is the path which it intends to follow in achieving its objectives. For health care organizations, competitive strategy usually means a reassessment of the type and quality of services they intend to provide to their internal and external customers. In this sense, TQM can be viewed as a competitive strategy. One of the key factors in gaining a competitive advantage lies in the ability to anticipate the needs of customers many years into the future, and have it ready for them. While there are instances of failure to anticipate the needs of customers in health care, they are not publicized as one would find in manufacturing. In a non-strategy-driven TQM environment, operating decisions are often prompted by an immediate need. A desperate need to contain costs, declining enrollment, and a dramatic increase in medical malpractice suits, are among the factors which help to shape the crises mode. The need is then addressed in a reactive and ad hoc fashion. Choices are based typically on narrow and ill defined financial criteria. In a strategy-driven TQM environment, the choices made by a health care organization are educated by its mission, vision, long and short-term goals, and guiding principles.

III. MANAGEMENT ON THE BASIS OF MISSION AND VISION

The greatest challenge for top management is to create an organization in which every employee, department and function is linked inextricably to the organization's mission and vision. But first, we must understand what is meant by mission and vision. Shores (1988) explains a mission and vision statement as follows:

> The mission statement is an entrepreneurial statement of specific intent, purpose, and reason for an entity, business function, or process. It explains why it exists and usually makes a statement about the market or customer, the product or technology, the competitive goal, and the investors.

Shore notes that: "It is the vision that focuses the goals and strategies for the future." Vision reflects where an organization is going, or what it wants to be in the future. The vision of a health care organization has to be expressed to provide a unifying theme to all organizational units, and serve as a compass and guiding force congruent with the corporate ethic and values. It should become a source of strength and inspiration for all clinicians and non-clinicians to draw on as they confront the challenges of their daily activities. Every health care provider and staff, housekeeping, dietary, receptionist, physician, nurse, pharmacist, etc. has to become an active collaborator in the pursuit of corporate objectives. Each worker must share the vision of the organization, and feel comfortable with the way in which the vision is translated or expressed. The behavior and actions of health care workers will be conditioned by this framework of involvement and partnership through vision. Workers must feel an intimate bonding with this prescription for change and growth as articulated in the corporate vision, and must sense that by following the course charted by the organization's vision, their most personal needs for achievement will be met. It is within the purview of good

Figure 1 - A Framework for Integrating TQM and Corporate Strategy

- It is not possible to have happy customers if you do not have happy employees. Employee relations mirror customer relations.
- The need to focus on process rather than people as the source of problems in the organization.
- The recognition of an internal customer as any person or department that depends on your output in order to do his or her job. It is the realization that everyone is either serving a customer, or serving someone who is. Customer satisfaction is also important for internal customers.
- It is the recognition by every employee that failure to meet or exceed the expectations of customers would ultimately result in the loss of market share and may even lead to the death of the organization. The organization's long-term survival would ultimately be determined by the extent to which the organization's customers are satisfied or dissatisfied. This notion would be ingrained in the mind of every existing and new employee.
- The organization would have a formal training process in place, as well as the necessary support system, to ensure constancy of purpose and consistency in the behaviors and attitudes of all employees regarding the importance of the customers.
- All the required behaviors and attitudes necessary to preserve the supremacy of the customers will not only become part of the organizations training repertoire, but would also become part of the employees job descriptions.
- Establish a formal process for providing adequate, frequent, and timely feedback to employees, regarding all aspects of their work. The establishment of a formal process for routing customer feedback to appropriate employees.
- A built-in mechanism for gathering information on the "voice of the customer." A real commitment to probing the customers constantly for their views on all aspects of the service, and a process for taking corrective action (based on the information gathered) towards meeting or exceeding the expectations of the customers.
- Putting in place performance monitors and indicators to track the extent to which the needs of the customers are being met.
- Employees must be empowered. Employee empowerment should not be misinterpreted as an excuse to abdicate leadership.
- Continuously aiming to find and eliminate the root cause of problems, and prevent their recurrence.
- A focus on outcome management and process improvement.

leadership to articulate the organization's vision so that it has a personal message and meaning for the individuals in the organization.

One of the goals of TQM is to create a customer-driven organization as depicted in Figure 1. In a customer-driven organization, every employee must resolve that his or her most important duty is to the customer; the primary reason for the organization's existence.

Also, top management must resolve that the employees are the organization's most important asset. Any form of weakness in either of these two resolutions would confound constancy of purpose. If TQM is to become part of corporate strategy, top management must create an environment that would foster these ideals. A customer driven environment is based on the criteria listed in Figure 1.

IV. TEAM BUILDING AS PART OF TQM BUSINESS STRATEGY

The use of teams to work on and accomplish organizational objectives has been applauded loudly as one the key benefits of TQM. If TQM is to become part of a corporate strategy, the company strategists and policy makers must integrate the goals of the organization with the problem selection process of the teams. Problem selection can take the following forms:

- Team selects unimportant (low priority) projects.
- Team selects projects with small potential.
- Team selects area in which hospital is already far ahead of competition.

Without strategic direction, a team has a high chance of achieving a disappointing outcome. Team problem selection must be guided by corporate strategy, if it is to avoid disappointing results. TQM activities must directly support strategic business plans. Organizations that do not adopt strategic planning would not have a clear, shared vision or well-defined key objective. Consequently, the quality improvement team projects selected may be the trivial many rather than the vital few. The following prioritization process (proposed by Health Care Advisory Board (1992)) is suggested as a way to integrate problem selection and corporate strategy at a hospital:

- Does the project address the needs of the hospital's top priority customer groups?
- Does the project address important needs of the customer (i.e. which have a meaningful impact on customer's provider selection decision)?
- Is the hospital far ahead of competition in this area already (i.e. will improvement buy the hospital anything)?
- Does this project truly offer the hospital a good chance of making an improvement large enough to change customer behavior?
- Will the project require investment of a size which would wipe out the potential gain?
- How does project rank (on the above criteria) in relation to other possible projects?
- Once the project is selected: is the team continuously assessing whether or not the project is the best one to move the department and hospital towards their goals?

Problem selection, analysis and solution must be pursued as they relate to the mission, vision, long- and short-term goals of the organization. If the strategic interests of a hospital are ignored, problem selection, analysis and implementation would achieve objectives which may or may not be congruent with the overall corporate objectives.

V. REWARD AND RECOGNITION--IMPLICATIONS FOR TQM AND STRATEGY

There is demonstrable evidence of the value of TQM to the organization. The challenge faced by top management is to demonstrate to the individuals within an organization, the benefits of TQM with respect to their personal goals and needs. Gitlow and Melby (1991) state that continuous quality improvement involves a chain of events: improvement in quality leads to decreased costs because of less rework, fewer mistakes, fewer delays and better use of people and materials; productivity improves; better quality and lower price facilitate capturing the market, staying in business and providing more jobs. There should be more emphasis on what is within the individual or environment that stimulates or sustains behavior, i.e. what are the specific things that motivate people?

If a health care manager is to be successful in getting the workers to attain organizational objectives, he or she must understand at least the fundamentals of motivation. However, this is not an easy task. Motivation is an internal psychological process which occurs inside an individual. A manager cannot see motivation; he/she can only assume its presence (or absence) based on observance of worker behavior. But there is a better approach to motivation: it is called need satisfaction. Everyone has needs that require satisfaction. In turn, these needs will cause the person to undertake some form of goal-oriented behavior, which, hopefully, will satisfy the need.

VI. SUMMARY

Change does not occur in a vacuum, and certainly the kind of change needed to sustain a TQM transformation would not take place in the absence of a strategy. TQM is not just teams, nor is it just the commitment of top management. Such a transformation requires a unifying point of focus (mission) to hold it together, a compass (vision) to point the organization to its destination, a customer-driven culture to make it a part of life, and a strategy to sustain it. If TQM is not a part of corporate and business strategy, it is likely to produce disappointing results.

ENDNOTE

1. Originally published in the International Journal of Health Care Quality Assurance. Reprinted with permission of the publisher. For additional information see the International Journal of Health Care Quality Assurance:
http://www.mcb.co.uk/ijhcqa.htm

REFERENCES

Andrews, K.R. (1980). *The Concept of Corporate Strategy*. Homewood, IL: Richard D. Irwin.

Conrad, C. (1990). *Strategic Organizational Communication*. Holt, Rinehart and Winston, Fort Worth, TX: The Dryden Press.

Gitlow, H., and Melby, M. (1991). Framework for continuous quality improvement in the provision of pharmaceutical care. *American Journal for Hospital Pharmacists 48*: 1917.

Godfrey, A., Berwick, D., and Roessner, J. (1992). Can quality management really work in health care? *Quality Progress, XXV* (4): 23.

Hax, A. and Majluf, N. (1984). *Strategic Management: An Integrative Perspective*. Englewood Cliffs, NJ: Prentice-Hall.

Health Care Advisory Board. (1992). *Total Quality Management Volume 11*, The Advisory Board Company.

Lawrence, D. and Early, J. (1992). Strategic leadership for quality in healthcare. *Quality Progress, XXV* (4): 45.

Omachonu, V.K. (1991). *Total Quality and Productivity Management in Health Care Organizations*, Quality Press. Milwaukee, WI: American Society for Quality Control (ASQC), and Industrial Engineering and Management Press, Institute of Industrial Engineers, Norcross, GA.

Pearson, G. J. (1990). *Strategic Thinking*, UK: Prentice-Hall International.

Peters, T. and Waterman, H. Jr. (1982). In Search of Excellence. New York, NY: Harper & Row.

Schein, E. S. (1981). Does Japanese management style have a message for American managers? *Sloan Management Review, 23* (1): 55-67.

Schwartz, H. and Davis, S. M. (1981). Matching corporate culture and business strategy. *Organizational Dynamics, 10*(Summer): 30-48.

Shores, A. R. (1988). *Survival of the Fittest*. Milwaukee, WI: ASQC Quality Press.

39.
STRATEGIC PLANNING IN A VA MEDICAL CENTER

Thomas J. Barth, *University of Memphis, Memphis, TN*

David M. Mirvis, *University of Tennessee Medical School, Memphis, TN*

Kent P. Hill, *VA Medical Center, Memphis, TN*

Kenneth H. Mulholland, Jr., *VA Medical Center, Memphis, TN*

Organizational survival in today's dynamic health care environment calls for a thorough understanding of strategic planning theory and applications. Increased competition, cost constraints, managed care, state and national health care reform, technological advances, and a changing labor market require a continuous strategic posture by health care administrators. For example, McKerrow (1995) discusses the corporate vision and strategic processes necessary to achieve patient centered care and quality improvement; Zuckerman (1994) refers to the need for integrated health delivery systems only achievable by involving physicians constructively in strategic planning; and Veliyath (1992) emphasizes strategic planning orientations that should enable managers to exercise better strategic control and optimize the firm's short-run performance as well as long-term prospects.

What precisely is strategic planning? Bryson (1988) defines strategic planning as "a disciplined effort to produce fundamental decisions and actions that shape and guide what an organization (or other entity) is, what it does, and why it does it" (p. 5). Numerous models appear in the literature; in fact, a database search for the past 15 years revealed over 330 journal articles covering strategic planning in health settings. Most models include common elements: identifying a vision and mission for the organization, assessing the external and internal environment, developing strategies to align the organization with the environment, implementing the strategies, and continuous evaluation of those strategies (Berg, 1989; Bryant, et al. 1990; Fottler, et al. 1990; Henderson and Thomas, 1992; Hillebrand, 1994; Hutchinson, et al., 1989; Jones, 1988; Johnson, 1990; Jones and Crane, 1990; Peoples and Sanders, 1994; Shortell, Morrison and Friedman, 1990; Wood and Robertson, 1992).

Although techniques and models are important, this literature implies that effective strategic planning also requires a certain attitude or approach to doing business—an attitude or approach that includes longer term thinking, proaction, awareness of changing external and internal situations, and mission driven decision making. In short, an organization culture and attention to process is implied.

This chapter moves beyond theory by providing a practical guide to strategic planning. We will examine an ongoing strategic planning process initiated at the Memphis Veterans Affairs Medical Center (VAMC) in the early 1990s. (See Appendix 1 for background informatin on the facility.) Although formal planning sessions and processes had been conducted for years, we will focus primarily on a specific effort to identify the key strategic issues that would facilitate success in the changing health care environment. This story shows a strategic planning process transforming the culture of a large, complex governmental institution. VAMC moved from reacting and focusing on what could not be done to anticipating the environment, setting a focused new direction, and ultimately taking control of its destiny.

The case illustrates the specific steps in the strategic planning process as well as the impact of the initiative in terms of both content (changes in services and programs) and process (how the institution does business). In this chapter we hope to provide both a specific model of the strategic planning process and a discussion of fundamental conceptual issues and challenges inherent in a strategic planning effort.

I. THE STRATEGIC PLANNING PROCESS

Formal strategic planning processes can be the product of an organization's long-term effort to address fundamental challenges. At the VAMC, a comprehensive strategic planning effort occurred only after four years of a series of smaller planning efforts. In 1989, the executive management team (Medical Center Director, Associate Director, and Chief of Medical Staff) determined that a comprehensive, collaborative approach to planning was necessary for guiding the course of the medical center. Service chiefs were brought into the planning process as full participants and annual planning retreats were initiated.

In 1989-1990, the focus of planning was service excellence. At this time an analysis of the corporate culture of the VAMC was completed with preliminary findings shared at the April management retreat. This retreat facilitated the establishment of six task forces to address fourteen key operational issues.

In 1991, the planning process yielded several task forces designed to review a number of key processes and activities within the medical center. The task force topics included primary care, communications, resource allocation, ward design, ward clerks, performance standards, linen availability, uniform room, recruitment and retention, and recycling.

In 1992, the official focus was "The Basics of Service Delivery." Service chiefs and assistant chiefs were charged with identifying how, as managers, they could involve everyone at the medical center in ongoing quality improvement by identifying major process issues which, if resolved, would enable the medical center to consistently deliver better service. An envisioning workshop resulted in the development of the medical center's mission and vision statements.

Still, there was a strong sense among top management that a more structured strategic planning process would both identify and meet VAMC's challenges and opportunities. Fragmented, inefficient patient care processes which resulted from an acute, sub-specialty based, impatient care orientation in the medical center led many medical and administrative staff to conclude that a managed care delivery system based on a primary care model would best facilitate the medical center's planning objectives as well as best satisfy new and changing customer expectations. This planning outcome was reinforced by national and state health care reform discussions which highlighted the need for VAMC to compete in the local health care marketplace.

Given this background, the thrust for the 1993 planning cycle was to engage in a more comprehensive, formalized strategic planning process. As a government institution, VAMC chose a model based on research with government and nonprofit organizations (Bryson, 1988). The VAMC followed the five basic steps seen in some form in most formal strategic planning efforts:

Step 1: Identify External Opportunities and Threats
Step 2: Validate Mission and Vision
Step 3: Identify Internal Strengths and Weaknesses
Step 4: Identify Key Strategic Issues
Step 5: Implement and Follow-Up

Unlike many strategic planning processes, the VAMC chose to discuss the mission and vision of the institution as a step between the identification of external opportunities and threats and internal strengths and weaknesses. This approach served two purposes. First, the examining external opportunities and threats first made participants fully aware of the dynamics in the environment before they revisited mission and vision. Second, validation of the mission and vision was done prior to an examination of internal strengths and weaknesses so as not to constrain participants' creativity. In other words, there was concern that focusing first on weaknesses would dampen the boldness of the visioning process. Finally, VAMC leaders disagreed with Bryson's suggestion that a "vision of success is more important as a guide to implementing strategy than it is to formulating it," (p. 184). They decided that a discussion early in the process on what the medical center should ideally look like in the future was essential for determining the key strategic issues. The general concept was understanding where the medical center currently stood, where it wanted to be, and then identifying those issues that would help them accomplish their goals.

Step 1: Identify External Opportunities and Threats

Effective strategic planning requires a keen awareness of the external environment in which the organization is operating. Shapek (1996) suggests the following trends and events should be examined: technological, economic, social, and political. Bryson (1988) identifies three major categories to monitor: forces and trends; clients, customers, or payers; actual or potential collaborators or competitors.

A practical technique for identifying external opportunities and threats as well as internal strengths and weaknesses is the "snow card" technique developed by Greenblat and Duke (in Bryson, 1988). At the VAMC, the large group of about 36 service chiefs was split into three smaller groups. Group members were asked to individually identify as many ideas as possible which correlated with the topics opportunities, threats, strengths, and weaknesses. Then individuals were asked to transcribe their three most important items onto three separate post-it notes. The small group facilitator (a trained member of the medical center's total quality management staff) then led the group in arranging all the notes on a wall according to categories or themes. The purpose of this process was not so much consensus over the most significant ideas as it was to generate a comprehensive list categorized by themes. Small groups reported their categories to the large group, after which the facilitator generated a second iteration of categories with the help of the large group. Step 1 produced an extensive list of external opportunities and threats that exemplify the type of information derived from this exercise.

Step 2: Validate Vision and Mission

Whether created anew or simply validated, the strategic planning effort requires an examination of the organization's vision and mission. A vision states what the organization aspires to be. Shapek (1996) outlines the following elements of a vision statement:

- Focuses on a better future.
- Reflects the values and beliefs of the organization.
- Encourages the hopes, aspirations, and dreams of its members.
- Represents the views of members and constituents.
- Is inspirational and stated in terms of desired outcomes.
- Generates a sense of ownership, commitment and resolve.

A technique that proved useful at the VAMC for stimulating the visioning process is to have participants individually respond to the following instructions adapted from Bryson (1988):

> Imagine that it is three to five years from now and the VA Medical Center in Memphis has been put together in a very exciting way. It is a recognized premier health institution. Imagine that you are a newspaper reporter assigned to do a story on the medical center. You have thoroughly reviewed the institution's mandates, mission, services, personnel, financing, organization, management, etc. Describe in no more than a page what you see.

The members of each small group shared their statements with each other, and the facilitator recorded the key elements on a flipchart, combining similar elements as much as possible. The purpose of this exercise was not to craft a new mission or vision statement, for prior experience with such efforts in a large group resulted in much wasted time over wordsmithing. Rather, the idea was to expose the entire group to other's ideas for the ideal medical center. A small group of senior staff was then asked to review the results and propose any changes to the existing mission and vision statements.

Although this exercise did not result in any changes to existing mission and vision statements, it did reveal that participants desired new directions for the medical center. This consensus was critical in the ensuing identification of key strategic issues. The vision developed follows: "The VAMC Memphis will be recognized locally, regionally,

and nationally as a premier medical center for comprehensive patient care, medical/
allied health education, health related research and employment opportunities."

The mission of an organization is a more specific description of how the vision
will be achieved. Shapek (1996) describes mission as the purpose of the organization,
and suggests that the following questions be addressed in a mission statement:

- Why do we exist?
- What makes us unique?
- What is our purpose?
- What are our values, beliefs, philosophy?
- What are our goals?
- Whom do we serve?
- Who are we?

The VAMC developed the following mission: "The mission of the VAMC
Memphis is to serve the veteran patient by delivering quality compassionate health
care, training health-care professionals, and conducting health related research." This
statement is supported by a description of core values that underlie everything the
institution does:

VAMC Values
- We put the health care needs of our patients first and foremost.
- We value and respect all VAMC employees.
- We promote teamwork and recognize each employee as an important member
  of our team.
- We wisely manage our available resources.
- We value our teaching affiliations.
- We promote innovation through research.
- We continuously strive to improve all that we do.

Prefacing this step in the process with an identification of the formal and informal
mandates governing the hospital is quite useful. Shapek (1996) notes that formal mandates include ordinances, laws, charters, statutes, rules and regulations. Informal mandates, which Shapek refers to as tradition or organizational culture, include historical
practices, precedent, habits, rules and policies (written or unwritten), and say-so. We
must consider two points here. First, although prefacing visioning with a discussion
of what the organization is required to do by law or regulation might seem logical,
such an approach may limit creativity, especially in an environment of health care
reform where external requirements are rapidly changing. Second, discussing both
formal and informal mandates can be insightful for organizations such as the VAMC
where deeply imbedded traditions are mistakenly accepted as formal mandates that
cannot be changed.

Step 3: Identify Internal Strengths and Weaknesses

The final piece of the assessment process is an audit of the organization's internal
status. Jones (1988) suggests that the areas of focus in a hospital setting should be

organizational design, product-line identification and development, case mix management, financial stability, operational characteristics, and human resources development. Bryson and Roering (1988) suggest the following factors merit examination: resources (people, economic, information, competencies); present strategy (overall, functional, departmental); and performance (results, history). In short, the vision of the hospital provides the context for exploring existing strengths that might be built on and the weaknesses that must be addressed.

Step 4: Identify Key Strategic Issues

The previous steps generate data needed to address the heart of the strategic planning process: the identification of the key strategic issues that will move an institution from where it has been to where it wants to be. Bryson defines a strategic issue as a "fundamental policy choice affecting an organization's mandates, mission, values, product or service level and mix, clients or users, cost, financing, organization, or management" (p. 139). Shapek (1996) uses the term "issues management," but his definition reflects a similar concept—a priority listing derived from an assessment of an organization's mission and mandates, analysis of significant and likely trends and events, and survey of strengths, weaknesses, opportunities and challenges leads to statements reflecting action items that must be addressed to increase mission effectiveness or efficiency. Clearly, issues are the basis of goal setting.

At the VAMC, armed with the information generated by the prior exercises, participants reconvened in small groups and were asked to identify the five most important strategic issues facing the hospital. To initiate this process using the snowcard technique once more, participants first created their individual lists by answering the following questions for each issue:

- What is the issue?
- What factors (mandates, mission, external and internal) make it a strategic issue?
- What are the consequences of failure to address the issue? (Bryson, 1988)

The small groups next attempted to reach consensus on the top five strategic issues facing the VAMC. Following this step, the large group was led by the facilitator through a consensus building process. The key to this process was simply allowing all small groups to explain their list of five strategic issues. Since a number of common themes emerged quickly, the group decided to limit issues presented to three. Too many strategic issues might be difficult to manage and would dilute the focus and energy of the organization in its planning.

Three strategic issues were identified for the VAMC along with a number of corresponding needs to address these issues: to design and implement a managed care system based on the primary care model; to deliver patient centered care; to institute public relations and marketing campaigns.

Step 5: Implementation and Follow-Up

Following the above model with the aid of an effective facilitator, an industrious and cohesive management team may identify core strategic issues facing the institution. The key question then becomes "Where do we go from here to take concrete action to address these issues?" In discussing implementation, Jones (1988) notes that it is necessary to "identify programs, policies, services to be implemented, timing of implementation, responsible parties, and target or expected results" (p. 2). At VAMC participants identified over 300 individual ideas to implement or address the issues. These ideas were grouped into twelve categories that form the basis of the implementation plan (see Appendix 2).

The VAMC leadership then established and chartered 25 interdisciplinary task forces to develop implementation strategies in support of the medical center's mission, vision and strategic initiatives. The 25 groups of more than 100 employees represented a cross-section of the staff.

The energy and momentum created by a strategic planning process must be nurtured by revalidating and reinforcing the vision, mission, and strategic issues at every opportunity. In other words, strategic planning must become part of the institution's culture, the framework for all major decisions. The VAMC has continued to build on the strategic planning outcomes realized in 1993 by conducting formal strategic planning exercises each fall. These planning sessions contain two primary components:

- The mission, vision, and key strategic initiatives are reviewed and reaffirmed. This process involves reviewing the work of various task forces established during the year as well as updating pertinent changes in the external environment which may affect the strategic direction of the facility.
- New challenges being presented to the facility are addressed.

II. ASSESSING THE IMPACT OF STRATEGIC PLANNING

How does one go about assessing whether a strategic planning process is successful? The impact of such planning should be reviewed in terms of both content and process. That is, one has to determine what precisely has changed in the institution as a result of strategic planning (content), and also what has changed regarding how the institution does business (process).

A. Changes in Content

Fottler, et al. (1990) reflect the bottom line or content approach to evaluating strategic planning success by asking whether the process has increased the institution's competitive advantage. For a public or nonprofit institution to measure competitive advantage solely in terms of profit may not be appropriate; however, determining whether the strategic planning process has produced concrete, positive change is possible. Through the identification of the three strategic issues discussed previously and the work of the 25 task forces at the VAMC, the following are examples of changes in content and process that can be attributed to the strategic planning process thus far.

B. Changes in Service Delivery Systems

Perhaps the most important initiative to moving toward a managed care system based on the primary care model (strategic issue #1) has been the establishment of the "firm" concept. Firms are the designated service delivery units of the VAMC's managed care delivery system. Each firm is responsible for managing the health status of each enrolled patient. Mirvis (1994) describes these firms as group practices responsible for the total care of assigned patients. Thus far three firms are operational—two in general medicine and one in geriatric care.

Firms are staffed by a mix of staff physicians and house staff, nurse practitioners and physician assistants, allied health and administrative support personnel. Each firm is jointly headed by a physician and nurse. These two group leaders are accountable for their firm's functions to a management group consisting of the associate chief of staff for ambulatory care, the chief of medical service and the chief nurse. This triad in turn reports to the chief-of-staff. Inpatient and outpatient care is coordinated by nurse case managers and social work staff.

The VAMC expects to expand the number of firms, especially into psychiatry and spinal cord injury. Additionally, the managed care model will be used for VA patients in off-site locations, either in remote VA-operated clinics or in primary care clinics in which VA patients are managed by contract non-VA practitioners under capitated payment arrangements.

Other accomplishments that support moving towards the managed/primary care model include initiatives for the design of electronic medical records and the development of a proposal to establish an off-site primary care clinic through a contractual arrangement.

C. Changes Affecting Direct Patient Care

Accomplishments under this strategic issue include reductions in patient waiting times, establishment of an employee dress code, implementation of an outpatient/escort greeting service, establishment of a women's clinic, and revisions to the medical center's staff performance evaluation system (in process).

D. Changes in Public Perception of the Institution

To address this strategic issue, a contract was awarded to an outside entity to analyze the VAMC market and to develop a marketing plan. As a result, a Consumer Affairs Advisory Board and Patient Education Center has been established, potential satellite clinics and primary care providers identified, performance standards for nurses developed, and a telephone satisfaction survey of recently discharged patients conducted.

E. Changes in Processes

In terms of assessing process or changes in the way an institution does business, a number of factors should be considered. Bryson and Roering (1988) suggest that a strategic planning process is successful to the degree that it focuses the attention of strategic planning teams and key decision makers on what is important for their organizations, helps set priorities for action, and generates those actions. Thomas (1993) identifies the following outcomes of an effective effort:

- understanding of the department's goals and operations,
- easier program planning of units,
- sense of direction,
- professional satisfaction, and
- proaction

Kazemek (1990) suggests the following characteristics reflect a successful process:

- Participation and teamwork among stakeholders (board, management, physicians, nurses and the community) are sought and ample time devoted to them;
- Numerous opportunities for feedback keep the plan on course;
- Internal expertise of organization staff is maximized; consultants fill in the gaps, acting as facilitators of the process and saving significant sums of money;
- The focus for the entire organization is made clear;
- Implementation is likely because resistance to the plan is reduced.

At VAMC, illustrations of each of these outcomes fall into four categories: proaction, sense of common direction or focus, multi-level participation in decisionmaking, and team culture.

F. Proaction

A common barrier to planning in a large institution is the prevailing sense that one has limited control over the future because of the formal and informal mandates imposed on the organization. Formal mandates include the laws, regulations and policies under which the public organization operates; informal mandates are the equally compelling political constraints dictated by powerful stakeholders. According to Bryson (1988) such mandates merit testing, for in his experience few organizational members ever read, let alone understand, the relevant legislation, regulations or contracts that outline the organization's mandates. He concludes:

> It may not be surprising, then, that many organizations make one or both of two fundamental mistakes. Either they believe that they are more tightly constrained in their actions than they are; or they assume that if they are not explicitly told to do something, they are not allowed to do it (p. 49).

The VAMC leadership was very aware of this attitude and stressed to participants in the strategic planning process that the uncertainties in the environment due to health care reform provided opportunities to put aside current mandates and "push the envelope." Leadership also stressed that if the Memphis VAMC came up with innovative ideas, they might, in fact, be able to proactively shape its future environment. Thus the leadership believed it important to discuss the vision and mission of the medical center before, rather than after, the discussion of internal strengths and weaknesses. Leadership expected that participants would narrowly focus on all mandates constraining the medical center and limit the visioning process. The specific structuring of VAMC's strategic planning process fostered a change in attitude from reaction/inaction to proaction.

G. Sense of Common Direction or Focus

Perhaps the most pertinent test of strategic planning evident in the literature is the degree to which the process helps an organization focus on important issues and set priorities. The identification of the three strategic issues for the VAMC during the 1993 session has clearly provided such a focus or "rudder." Not only were the original 25 task forces organized around these issues, but every programmatic and resource decision since has been examined according to its support of the three key issues. Despite the difficulty of quantifying the significance of the change, VAMC leaders are unanimous in asserting that this process has provided a central focus and foundation for all organizational planning and decision making.

H. Multi-Level Participation in Decisionmaking

As the literature suggests, multi-level staff involvement not only provides more comprehensive perspectives, but also enhances commitment to outcomes while reducing resistance to change. In concert with the Total Quality Improvement (TQI) activities initiated in the early 1990s, strategic planning has contributed to a much broader participation in decisionmaking at the VAMC outside of top management (vertically, horizontally, and diagonally). Also interesting is the fact that the entire group sees how much commonality exists among the diverse members. It was not particularly difficult to reach consensus over where the VAMC needs to go or the strategic issues that must be addressed to get there.

I. Team Culture

In large organizations members from different organizational units rarely come together for meaningful discussions about their problems and appropriate institutional responses. A final, albeit somewhat intangible, outcome of strategic planning at the VAMC has been increased camaraderie among the leadership group. Prior to the strategic planning sessions some were concerned that discussions would get hostile, particularly on the topics of resource reductions and redeployment. However, sessions have been overwhelmingly positive—both productive and constructive. This camaraderie has been reinforced by the cross-functional task forces and the firms. A sense of common direction and focus has contributed to a team culture at the VAMC.

SUMMARY

A student or practitioner of health administration must have a thorough understanding of the methods, uses and limitations of strategic planning. In a competitive, rapidly changing health care environment, operating in a reactive manner with unchanging operating assumptions will no longer be sufficient. Thinking strategically means regularly examining operating assumptions by scanning the external and internal environment and revalidating the vision and mission of the institution. Thinking strategically means anticipating the future and identifying the key issues that must be addressed to move the institution from its current position to where it needs to be. Finally, strategic thinking means paying careful attention to the expectations of employees and how the institution's strategic vision is communicated and reinforced throughout all organizational levels.

The VAMC model can be utilized by others; the achievements attributable to the strategic planning effort are significant in terms of both process and content. Chief among these are the establishment of more integrated service delivery systems, the sharper sense of common direction or focus, and the stronger team culture resulting from more multi-level participation in decisionmaking.

Perhaps the most useful component of a detailed case study is unresolved problems; therefore, we conclude with a list of questions for those interested in pursuing strategic planning in a health care setting:

- How does one maintain the momentum of a strategic planning process when changes in the external environment undermine or stall key initiatives?
- What is the appropriate structure and scope of the process used to address the strategic issues identified? (The large number of follow-up task forces at VAMC were difficult to manage, specifically maintaining effective communication, responding to recommendations, and coordinating interrelated projects.)
- How does the leadership of an institution communicate with and enlist professional groups with a strong sense of autonomy and a vested interest in the status quo? The same question applies to lower level but equally important support staff (clerical, janitorial). And how does one deal with those who ultimately do not "buy in" to the program, particularly when some of these individuals are indispensable?
- What is an effective process for linking strategic planning to resource decisions? This question is particularly difficult in a constrained resource environment where little funding is available. This question again ties back to setting realistic expectations and building on small successes.

REFERENCES

Berg, D. (1989). A Search for Soul. Strategic Planning Will Chart the Way. *Health Programs, 70*: 38-41.

Bryant, L., Dobal, M., and Johnson, E. (1990). Strategic Planning: Collaboration and Empowerment. *Nursing connections, 3*: 31-6.

Bryson, J. M. (1988). *Strategic Planning for Public and Nonprofit Organizations.* Jossey-Bass, San Francisco.

Bryson, J. M. and Roering, W. D. (1988). Initiation of Strategic Planning by Governments. *Public Administration Review, 48*: 995-1004.

Fottler, M. D., Phillips, R.L. , Blair, J.D., and Duran, C.A. (1990). Achieving Competitive Advantage Through Strategic Human Resource Management. *Hospital & Health Service Administration, 35*: 341-363.

Henderson, J. C. and Thomas, J. B. (1992). Aligning Business and Information Technology Domains: Strategic Planning in Hospitals. *Hospital and Health Services Administration, 37*: 71-87.

Hillebrand, P. L. (1994). Strategic Planning: A Road Map to the Future. *Nursing Management, 25*: 30-32.

Hutchinson, R. A., Witte, K. W. and Vogel, D. P. (1989). Development and Implementation of a Strategic Planning Process at a University Hospital. *American Journal of Hospital Pharmacy, 46*: 952-57.

Johnson, L. J. (1990). Strategic Management: A New Dimension of the Nurse Executive's Role. *JONA, 20*: 7-10.

Jones, K. R. (1988). Strategic planning in hospitals: Applications to Nursing Administration. *Nursing Administration Quarterly, 13*: 1-10.

Jones, P. G. and Crane, V. S. (1990). Development of an Organizational Strategic Planning Process for a Hospital Department. *Health Care Supervision, 9*: 1-20.

Kazemek, E. A. (1990). There's a Right Way to Do Strategic Planning. *Modern Healthcare, November 12*: 36.

McKerrow, W. (1995). Towards Quality Organizations. *Health Law Can., 15*: 80-3.

Mirvis, D. M. (1994). Organizational Redesign at the Memphis VA Medical Center. *Forum. December*: 4-7.

Peoples, L. T. and Sanders, N. F. (1994). Health Care System Redesign: A Strategic Management Framework. *Hospital Material Management Quarterly, 16*: 1-3.

Shapek, R. A. (1996). The Issues Approach to Strategic Planning for Public Agencies. Paper presented at the Annual Southeastern Conference on Public Administration, Miami, Florida, October 3-5.

Shortell, S. M., Morrison, E. M., and Friedman, B. (1990). *Strategic Choices for America's Hospitals.* Jossey-Bass: San Francisco.

Thomas, A. M. (1993). Strategic Planning: A Practical Approach. *Nursing Management, 24*: 34-38.

Veliyath, R. (1992). Strategic Planning: Balancing Short-Run Performance and Longer Term Prospects. *Long Range Planning, 25*: 86-97.

Wood, V. R. and Robertson, K. R. (1992). Strategic Planning and Marketing Research for Older, Inner-City Health Care Facilities: A Case Study. *Journal of Ambulatory Care Marketing, 5*: 141-59.

Zuckerman, A. M. (1994). Hospital and Medical Staff Strategic Planning: Developing an Integrated Approach. *Physician Executive, 20*: 15-7.

APPENDIX 1: BACKGROUND ON VA MEDICAL CENTER IN MEMPHIS

The VAMC currently has 539 operating beds of which 346 are acute medical and surgical beds, 103 are psychiatric, and 90 are spinal chord injury. The medical center also operates a 120 bed skilled nursing unit providing comprehensive extended care services. The Memphis center, a highly affiliated tertiary care referral center for the veterans of the mid-South, provides primary, secondary, and tertiary care to medical, surgical, neurological, psychiatric, rehabilitation, and spinal cord injury patients, as well as comprehensive primary and consultative medical, surgical, psychiatric, and specialized outpatient services through general, specialty, and subspecialty outpatient clinics. The primary service area is the 55 county area of eastern Tennessee, northeastern

Arkansas, northern Mississippi, and southwestern Kentucky. Over 200,000 veterans reside within this service area. Approximately 28,000 unique patients are treated annually by means of 11,000 inpatient admissions and 234,000 outpatient visits. Approximately 96% of the veteran patients cared for are at the lower end of the socioeconomic scale and medically indigent.

A major training affiliate of the University of Tennessee, Memphis, VAMC contains Colleges of Medicine, Dentistry, Nursing and Allied Health. Over 300 medical students serve clerkships in medicine, surgery and psychiatry. Furthermore, 116 residents, fellows, and allied health trainees are in training at any given time.

Approximately 2,200 full and part-time employees hold positions ranging from the highest skilled medical professionals to unskilled laborers: 400 physicians, 700 nursing personnel, 1,050 other direct care providers, and 650 administrative support personnel. The American Federation of Government Employees (AFGE) and the National Association of Government Employees (NAGE) are the two active unions.

Finally, most of the VAMC physicians are University of Tennessee faculty and researchers. Seventy-five investigators work on 195 individual research projects and are supported by over 35 full-time research technicians, grant supported personnel, and students. The annual research budget is $7.0 million.

The stated mission of the VAMC is to "serve the veteran patient by delivering quality, compassionate health care, training health-care professionals, and conducting health related research." The formal vision follows: "The VAMC Memphis will be recognized locally, regionally, and nationally as a premier medical center for comprehensive patient care, medical/allied health education, health related research and employment opportunities."

APPENDIX 2: IMPLEMENTATION PLAN CATEGORIES

1) Patient Centered Care: A plan to provide patient centered care will be developed. Patient privacy issues will be identified and corrected. Patient education needs will be identified and training provided to support them. Customer expectations will be identified and a plan to address them will be implemented.

2) Define Model of Care: Consensus will be reached on which primary care model(s) will be the foundation of the managed care system. It was apparent from the planning session that there was no shared or common understanding of what is meant by managed care and primary care.

Managed care is a system of care in which patient care expectations are translated into standard. Practitioners, clinics, and hospitals are expected to perform within these minimum standards. Managed care has efficiency as a primary objective which results in increased quality of care as well as reduced resource needs. Preventive care (vaccinations, smoking cessation, cancer screening, etc.) is a significant portion of both primary care and managed care.

Primary care represents a long-term commitment between a practitioner and the patient, in which the practitioner undertakes and/or supervises the comprehensive and complete medical care of that patient, i.e., manages the patient's care. As defined by the Institute of Medicine, primary care is accessible (the patient has access to providers when needed), coordinated (the patient's care needs are met through appropriate referrals and ongoing review of all diagnoses, test results, medications, etc.), continual (medical records are maintained and reviewed regularly in planning care), accountable (the patient's care is monitored and evaluated with the goal of continuous improvement), and acceptable (the patient and/or caregiver participates in the development of the treatment plan).

3) Marketing: A plan to better market the Memphis VAMC both now and in the future will be prepared. We will identify and pursue an external marketing plan and do everything possible to enhance our public image.

4) Referral Base: Community based clinics and/or Preferred Provider Organization (PPO) system will be established. Patient access to the medical center will be enhanced. The feasibility of developing or joining local managed care organizations will be explored.

5) Education/Research: Continuing education and research support for the medical center will be provided. Allied health services research will be utilized to support our strategic planning efforts. After a comprehensive utilization review plan is developed, all involved employees will be trained in its use and their roles. An Ambulatory Care Fellowship will be applied for.

6) Define Service Base: Information about our current and potential patients will be abstracted and provided to all who need to use it for planning purposes.

7) Operational Standards: Specific standards for case management which can be used for utilization review will be developed. These standards will be used to guide case management, and to form the basis of the Utilization review Training Plan.

8) Data Base Management: A comprehensive data base which is essential for planning and decision making will be provided. Input from task groups will be solicited, and common data bases will be assembled and distributed. Input from task groups will be solicited to determine what computer systems support is needed. A plan will then be devised to make the support available.

9) Training: A plan to train all staff to support patient centered/managed care will be initiated. Core supervisory skills will be identified and a training plan developed to provide these skills to new supervisors and enhance the skills of incumbent supervisors. Managed care and patient centered concepts will be developed and all employees trained. Values will be incorporated into operational terms to provide all employees clear performance expectations.

10) Awards: An awards system which supports high level performance and attention to the customer will be implemented. Reward and recognition systems will be revamped to provide meaningful reward and recognition in support of the mission, goals, and values. A functional suggestion awards program in support of the strategic initiatives will be developed and implemented.

11) Plant: A Facilities Improvement Group (FIG) to monitor plant improvements, space assignments/changes, parking, etc. will be created. The Space Committee will be reconstituted. Signage and way-finding throughout the VAMC will be enhanced. Parking will be studied to assure it supports our strategic initiatives. Patient telephone needs will be identified and addressed. Space needs for operating a managed care system based on primary care will be identified and addressed. Interim space renovations in ambulatory care will be identified and addressed.

12) Resources: A cost accounting system to better manage resources (both dollars and FTE) will be pursued.

40.
FUNDAMENTALS OF ACTION RESEARCH

Robert T. Golembiewski, *University of Georgia, Athens, GA*

This chapter transitions through four emphases. It begins with a simple model of a "complete learning cycle," illustrates barriers that commonly lead to incomplete or truncated learning cycles, describes the enhanced role of learning in today's life and economy, and details how "action-research" can serve this growing realization that truncated learning cycles poorly serve both individuals and organizations. The approach is essentially generic, but direct health-care applications get emphasis.

Complete Learning Cycle

Figure 1, patterned on the work of Robert Bruce Shaw and Dennis N.T. Perkins, sketches a simple model of what is here labeled a "complete learning cycle."

Figure 1 - A Complete Learning Cycle

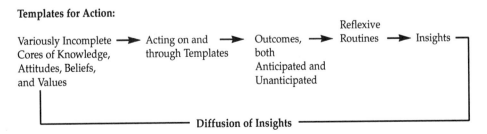

Templates for Action:

Variously Incomplete Cores of Knowledge, Attitudes, Beliefs, and Values → Acting on and through Templates → Outcomes, both Anticipated and Unanticipated → Reflexive Routines → Insights

Diffusion of Insights

In brief, all individuals and collections of them can be said to have "templates for action," which guide choice-making. These templates are variously comprehensive and consistent, but individuals and organizations have to rely on what they have in storage, as it were, when things need doing. Hence, some templates will inform action-taking, for good or ill. However, both anticipated and unanticipated outcomes typically will result, and a reflexive posture toward them can lead to insights that fine-tune or even replace the original templates. Only the major hypothetical causal loop is illustrated. In practice, complex feedback loops also will exist.

I. COMMONPLACE TRUNCATIONS

For a variety of reasons, this complete learning cycle often gets variously impeded or even truncated. Table 1 illustrates common barriers at each of the three points of transition — at action-taking, at reflection on outcomes, and at the diffusion of possible innovations that can enrich or enlarge the available store of templates.

Table 1 - Selected Contributors to Truncated Learning Cycles

I.   Barriers to Acting on and Through Templates

- denial of need to act
- inadequate skills, especially related to communication and feedback
- tendencies toward risk-avoidance
- fixation on failure and its consequences can restrain or even immobilize

- concerns about validity or reliability of data, about their poor quality
- low levels of energy
- feelings of powerlessness
- preferences of autocratic authority figures to restrict local initiative

II.   Barriers to Reflexive Routines

- short time-frames
- "failure of success" syndrome that leads to stereotypic thought/action even

- segmented information flows
- incentives that reinforce narrow behaviors and short time frames as conditions change

III. Barriers to Diffusion of Insights

- emphasis on protecting jurisdictions/roles rather than problem-solving
- organizational fragmentation
- NIH (not invented here) attitudes

- feelings of powerlessness
- low trust
- inadequate opportunities to share information
- competitive vs. collaborative cultures and styles

The examples in Table 1 are largely self-explanatory, but working through one may be useful. Consider the "failure of success" as one barrier to reflection about outcomes. A reflexive posture toward personal, professional, or organizational outcomes is much recommended nowadays (Senge, 1990) but, paradoxically, failure may be the more effective goal. That is, a history of success may discourage reflection, and this can impede or truncate learning cycles. The rationale for this cul-de-sac is obvious: My track record is good, so why should I consider fixing what isn't broken? These fateful words can impede reflection. Indeed, "success" may lead people, as well as collections of them, to take umbrage at suggestions to "be reflexive."

II. A GROWING OPINION

Increasingly, the unacceptable costs of confounding or truncating learning cycles have become a vital part of current commentary. We are all encouraged to "do more with less." For present purposes, this implies the growing costs of the lack of learning cycles that spiral onward and upward.

This new gospel has two targets. Thus, we are all enjoined to exploit all of our own experience, the better to learn from both our failures and successes. At least as important, we are encouraged to reject or at least question central features of our organizational posterity. Thus, traditional notions about organizing emphasize qualities such as stability and regularity — e.g., doing the same things in the same ways. At least in the mythology of organizations, this ideal is clear. Thus, one of the largest U.S. firm's communication system was allegedly built on such public principles:

- Central design: "Do it right, once, starting from the top."
- Stable implementation at lower levels of prescribed designs: "Read, understand, then do."

The times, they are a-changin'. The new watchwords emphasize innovation and flexibility--doing both old and new things in novel and progressively better ways (Golembiewski, 1995). This is the dominant motif of the movement toward "total quality management,"(TQM). Witness also the attention now directed at "learning organizations," which are seen as broadly useful in both public as well as business sectors, and which constitute a polar opposite to the "well-oiled machine" characteristic of Taylorian and bureaucratic approaches to organizing work (Watkins and Golembiewski, 1995). Appropriate norms for their sense and structure take such form (Watkins and Marsick, 1993):

- Learning becomes a growing part of more and more jobs and is increasingly made a part of even lower-level tasks.
- "Job knowledge" gets substantially enlarged. Employees are required to learn the skills/attitudes appropriate for their usual jobs; but employees are also encouraged or required to be "cross-trained"—i.e., to learn the skills/attitudes for several or all jobs in their flow-of-work; and employees are increasingly required to know how their job "fits" with other jobs — not only in their own unit but also in other organizational units—as well as how their jobs fit with broad organizational missions-and-roles.
- Employees are increasingly expected to serve as teachers/ trainers of fellow employees, as well as to learn from their own behavior and that of their co-workers.

III. ACTION RESEARCH AS A VEHICLE FOR ORGANIZATIONAL LEARNING

Action research (AR) seems well-designed to serve as one vehicle to activate this trend toward organizational learning. AR has evolved as a useful complement to conventional science in those many cases in which individuals or systems of people are involved (Evered and Susman, 1978). AR focuses on being rigorously self-reflective about experience in order to permit action planning that leads to desired and desirable changes in the functioning of individuals or human systems.

Three emphases provide useful perspective on the generalization that AR is an apparently simple notion whose profound potential extends to the heart of our individual and collective existences. The first of these emphases describes selected AR features; the second compares AR to conventional science; and the third focuses on several concerns about AR.

A. AR Fundamentals

Any list of basic AR elements risks both overkill and underspecification, depending upon the reader. Some readers come to AR with really open minds. They are either not or somewhat acquainted with the topic and its various complications. Other readers are quite sophisticated about AR. This tension can never be resolved. By way of introduction, however, six features seem minimally necessary to circumscribe AR. In outline, building on an earlier description (Golembiewski, 1996), AR

- Involves a self-reflective inquiry by participants in some collective situation — e.g. members of a medical-surgical ward, inhabitants of a village, etc., who seek to learn about themselves and their collective situation.
- Seeks to improve conditions within the experienced situation by developing better practices in an organization, a profession, or a work unit.
- Strives to improve participant skills relevant to what gets done, how it gets done, and when it gets done in dealing with a shared situation.
- Aspires to generate knowledge about practice as well as improvements in it, to solve local problems, and to build generalizations that contribute to evolving theoretical frameworks or models that inform practice.
- Relies on participants as both subjects and objects of research. In short, AR involves "participant observers" as well as "observant participants" in learning about themselves, from themselves.
- Intends a delicate balance. Participation and involvement are highly valued, but these can be judiciously informed by available experience and theory.
- AR tests the comprehensiveness of available experience and theory and, in the ideal case, can even extend that theory and practice.

Powerful motivators encourage undertaking the difficulties in managing AR. In summary, AR can deal with a broad range of issues, concerning both local preferences and conditions and generalizations from expanding networks of empirical theory. Thus, AR appears under various labels in public agencies and businesses:

Organization Development or (OD), Quality of Working Life or (QWL), and High Involvement Organizations. For example, an action-research application in a medical-surgical ward produced powerfully positive results (Golembiewski and Rountree, 1996). In third-world countries or in less-developed nations, AR often is called participatory or emancipatory research (Brown, 1995). This list could easily be extended.

Four factors illustrate the powerful motivators that induce this impressive diffusion of AR approaches. First, AR at once predates and serves the burgeoning idea that broad ranges of people are usefully involved in understanding their shared conditions, in coping with those conditions and improving those conditions. Even though institutions, like government and employing organizations, can play useful roles, many desired and desirable outcomes are beyond their reach. Hence the growing realization, virtually world wide, is the central need to empower broad ranges of people — from family members and citizens of nation-states, to marginal farmers and professional employees of business and government. AR constitutes a major vehicle for this empowerment as people learn how to learn from themselves about their condition. Typically, this requires developing skills and attitudes appropriate for analysis, and developing competencies and attitudes appropriate for exploiting opportunities for action-taking at low and middle levels of social, political, and economic structures.

Second, AR can serve at two points of critical activity: dealing with issues of practical concern that have theoretical significance; and attacking theoretical issues that have major practical salience. For example, consider the early evaluative work with flexible workhours (Golembiewski, Hilles, and Kagno, 1974; Golembiewski, Billingsley, and Yeager, 1976). That research opened the door to greater responsible freedom at the worksite. It provided a convenient vehicle for decreasing felt-powerlessness, and it met various urgencies, such as traffic congestion or the multiple challenges of affirmative action goals, which often entailed the employment of single heads of families. in addition. Flexible workhours helped with all these sets of problems. In addition, that workaday focus also motivated progress on central theoretical issues, like those related to differentiating kinds of change (Golembiewski, Billingsley, and Yeager, 1976; Golembiewski, 1990).

Third, in an elemental sense, AR gains credibility from the steps it encompasses, which are both generalizable and reasonable to a broad range of situations. Typically, AR involves some client system that is often aided by a skilled facilitator or change-agent. These are some of their action roles relevant to problem solving:

- sensing a learning opportunity;
- contracting between client and facilitator (if relevant) as to what is to be done, who will do it, when it will be completed, and what it will cost;
- preparing diagnoses;
- gathering data;
- giving feedback to all stakeholders;
- exploring data;
- planning action;
- taking action; and
- evaluating.

Note that AR facilitators do not basically act as subject-matter experts, who play the dominant role at each step. Rather, the client is the expert about most aspects of the local condition, both as to what information exists and what is desired or desirable. In sharp contrast, the facilitator provides skills and perspectives that help members of the client system in mobilizing their own skills and energies.

An abstract of an AR application dealing with "river blindness" among inhabitants of a village on the Indian subcontinent is an example of the mix. Villagers associated the disease with rivers. This association was accurate but also imprecise. A water-borne organism was the culprit.

This AR application had two goals: raising villager consciousness about the incidence and character of a particular kind of sight impairment, and developing villager skills to act on that heightened consciousness. In brief outline, approaching the two goals involved certain steps:

- gaining the support of village elders, who were all illiterate, in order to investigate the incidence of river blindness
- contracting with the elders in order to permit participation of newly-literate young villagers. Initially they would help in a survey on the incidence of river blindness in the village in order to mobilize opinion that "something should be done." Later they would help in implementing a program of remediation and prevention, as well as in evaluating the results of that program
- assessing the knowledge base among villagers
- external experts' recommendations or suggestions on additions or changes in the local knowledge base.
- building appropriate attitudes and skills, especially among the young villagers and the elders in order to generate and act relevant information as well as action-taking by all villagers
- surveying by the young villagers to estimate the local incidence of various stages of river blindness
- helping define local programs of remediation and prevention which, after sanctioning by elders, are implemented by young villagers
- assessing program effects by young villagers, who reported their evaluative data to elders for fine-tuning of the follow-on program

Obviously, power, opinional, and knowledge arenas are involved.

Fourth, success rates for AR applications are substantial, if not formidable. Measures of success and AR interventions differ widely, but the estimates of success usually fall in the 50-80% range (Golembiewski, 1990). Most AR applications come from the developed countries, but a large sub-batch has been isolated in even nation states with low Gross National Product per capita (Golembiewski and Luo, 1994).

B. AR and Conventional Science

Even the brief sketch above portrays AR as a useful complement to "conventional," "straight," or "logical-positivist" science, and a few contrasts in Table 2 helps sharpen the point. Although more sophisticated contrasts are available, (Susman and Evered, 1978; Robinson, 1993), Table 2 serves the general purpose.

Table 2 focuses on numerous features differentiating the two kinds of research. In summary, straight science sharply separates the observer from the observed, emphasizes norms of objectivity and impartiality for the observer, and implies low (or zero) capacity for the "objects" observed to reflect on their own behavior. AR basically can be illustrated by one substantial contrast. Straight science pays primary attention to

Table 2 - Contrasting Characterizations of Two Kinds of Research.

		Empirical Research		Action Research
Primary Task	1.	Describe major dimensions of reality; identify causal and moderating relationships.	1.	Define and induce targeted conditions that are desired or desirable in specific hosts.
Range of Applicable Values	2.	The values of science dominate: disinterestedness as to out-comes; honesty in reporting, and so on.	2.	Targeted realities are a composite of generic values such as regenerative interaction of values and definitions of reality characteristic of each host.
Primary Approach	3.	Reduce threats to validity and reliability by distancing observer from the realities observed and by randomly assigning subjects to experimental and control conditions.	3.	Increase applications of relevance to specific hosts, which typically feature close contact between researchers and hosts, and may even require an identity of the two roles. Hence, oberserver/subject differences are moderated or obliterated, and random assignment may be difficult or impossible.
Dominant Emphasis	4.	To replicate proposed patterns of relationships, to test or to reject/extend networks of covariants.	4.	To heighten local involvement and ownership, while producing knowledge of possibly broader applicability.
Overarching Goal	5.	To develop broader networks of covariants.	5.	To produce knowledge that is applicable in specific settings with exportability a desired but not a necessary condition.
Core Abilities/Skills Group	6.	Conceptual and analytic.	6.	Skills in developing individual and group relationships, and for intervening in systems at multiple levels.

Based on Golembiewski, 1986, p. 294, but extending beyond that source.

whether its generalizations and theories are correct or not—that is, whether they mirror some aspects of reality and can be extended by replicated validations into theories of escalating comprehensiveness.

AR basically builds on a concern with heightening the degrees of participation, involvement, and consensus underlying specific change efforts. In order to risk a simplification at a specific site, these heightenings seek to improve the chances that targeted things will be done—in describing an existing state, in prescribing a more desired or desirable state, and in moving toward that state in self-controlling and self-monitoring ways. The "objectivity" and "impartiality" featured in straight science have no direct analog, since the "objects" observed are also active "subjects" in learning by reflecting on those observations.

However the comparisons of straight science and AR are not all clear and sharp distinctions. Consensual processes also play a large role in straight science as when, on notable occasions, powerful forces have supported positions which later came to be seen as mobilized nonsense. Examples include Galilean celestial mechanics vs. religious doctrines or Lysenko biology and communist ideology. Before the new light dawned, severe punishments typically kept non-conformists in line.

Moreover, AR neglects only at great peril real-world barriers that can frustrate even massive mobilizations of human will. For example, on balance AR must overcome temptations to "reinvent the wheel," even if powerful enthusiasms can be generated to support that effort. The issue clearly requires subtle balance, because even ostensible "iron laws" about collective behavior can be merely conventional expressions of a consensus that can be supplanted later by expanding knowledge or by social constructions. For example, much in our ordinary lives is true only by definition. Central concepts, like freedom, equality or justice, can be changed by sufficient human evil and will. Obviously these truths-by-convention can be supported by a determined and well-positioned minority even in the face, the wit and will of the bulk of humanity notwithstanding.

C. Major Concerns About AR

This primer on AR fundamentals suggests a sense of vitality and progress, but major concerns also exist (Robinson, 1993). Good ideas provide the foundation from which extensions can be attempted and must be attempted, even though some extensions can be inconsistent with that core or may negate it. Consider three interrogatives concerning central concerns about AR.

IV. WHAT VALUES PROVIDE GUIDANCE?

Paramountly, as for all human activities, the question is: AR for what? Only values — definitions of the desired and desirable — can provide working answers.

AR researchers do not neglect this key question; neither do they agree about the working answers. Some see AR values in limited and pragmatic terms: the goal is to solve some local presenting problem without creating other problems, especially more formidable ones, with the goals of the solution being defined by local preferences.

Other AR proponents are far more ambitious. They propose to do nothing less than to achieve social justice as variously defined. To oversimplify the present distinction, pragmatists would be content to work on river blindness in the fashion illustrated above—that is, with reduced incidence and virulence of river blindness as the working definition of the desired and desirable. Other AR proponents focus on changing the economic and political systems that induced the huge relative disadvantage of the villagers.

As a first approximation AR at the extremes can be distinguished as either emancipatory or pragmatic. Patently, the difference is consequential. Normatively where one starts matters profoundly. Thus, those committed to emancipatory AR can reasonably see their pragmatic cousins as fiddling with trivia while neglecting the burning issues (Brown, 1985). Similarly, pragmatic AR can view emancipatory AR as promising too much, too soon, and hence as sowing the seeds of disaster, even if with the best of intentions.

My own AR practice inclines toward the pragmatic, but as informed by the detailed normative prescriptions reflected in the useful guidelines for intervenors dealing with individuals as well as human systems (Gellermann, Frankel, and Ladenson, 1990). So a local client's judgment about the desired or desirable is not sufficient to motivate a judgment by this author about signing-on to an AR project.

V. ARE THERE DIFFERENT KINDS OF AR?

We all know where one looks determines what one sees, and may cause a highly-selective perception. We all know the story of the unfortunate looking for a wallet under a street light, not because that is where the wallet was lost but because the light was better there.

And so it is with AR. Pragmatic AR can incline toward a kind of deliberate near-sightedness about seeing problem situations in terms of local trouble-shooting, improving specific relationships, and building local norms. However, one may miss the forest by fixating on a few trees.

In contrast, emancipatory AR favors the macro view. To paraphrase Robinson (1993), those taking that stance will locate barriers to learning or change in the structural features of life—organizational, social, political and, economic barriers. Changes in them constitute the major targets in emancipatory AR.

The ideal is clear enough, but practice is uneven. Both the immediate and broader perspectives are relevant, but they are seldom taken into simultaneous account. For pragmatists, this simultaneity can be viewed as threatening a kind of "paralysis by analysis"—so much to take into account that many useful things get delayed or do not get dealt with. For emancipatory AR, the goals may be so lofty that they induce such great resistance that change is improbable, if not impossible, even if our knowledge base is adequate.

VI. WHAT LEVEL OF INTERVENTION?

A related question involves the level of intervention. At least five such levels can be distinguished:

- improving the relationships between specific individuals and small groups, as in regenerative vs. degenerative interaction which takes into account the levels of risk, trust, openness or truth-telling, and public owning of ideas or feelings (Golembiewski, 1993)
- enhancing the basic problem-solving capacities of individuals or small groups of them, via the development of comprehensive experience and theory about "learning how to learn" (Argyris, et al., 1995)
- institutionalizing a pervasive bias toward self-reflective activity in large collective systems, as in "the learning organization" (Watkins and Marsick, 1993)
- reforming total social and economic systems

This list moves from pragmatic to emancipatory AR.

Again, the ideal choice of levels — that is, all of the above — is both profoundly correct and rare in practice. AR applications usually emphasize either one or a few of these levels, and those differences can serve to stimulate progress as well as controversy.

In summary, AR features and potentialities have motivated growing applications in many realms of human endeavor. The attractions are robust enough to encourage numerous extensions beyond the AR core, but progress remains incomplete in significant senses. The success rates of AR applications remain substantial and permit real optimism that a real beginning has been made in successfully addressing the challenges sketched above.

REFERENCES

Argyris, C., Putman, R., and Smith, D. M. (1985). *Action Science*. San Francisco: Jossey-Bass.

Brown, L. D. (1985). People-centered development and participatory research. *Harvard Educational Review, 55*: 69-75.

Gellermann, W., Frankel, M., and Ladenson, R. (1990). *Values and Ethics in Organization and Human Systems Development*. San Francisco: Jossey-Bass.

Golembiewski, R. T. (1996). Action research. In J. M. Shafritz, (Ed.), *The International Encyclopedia of Public Policy and Administration*. New York: Holt and Company. In press.

Golembiewski, R. T. (1995). *Diversity in Organizations*. University, AL.: University of Alabama Press.

Golembiewski, R. T. (Ed.). (1990). *Ironies in Organizational Development*. New Brunswick, N.J.: Transaction Publishers.

Golembiewski, R. T. (1986). Organizational analysis and praxis: Prominences of progress and stuckness. In C. L. Cooper and I. T. Robertson, (Eds.), *International Review of Industrial and Organizational Psychology*, pp. 279-304. New York: John Wiley & Sons.

Golembiewski, R., Billingsley, K., and Yeager, S. (1976). Measuring change and persistence in human affairs. *Journal of Applied Behavioral Science, 12*: 133-157.

Golembiewski, R., Hilles, R., and Kagno, M. (1974). A longitudinal study of flexi-time effects. *Journal of Applied Behavioral Science, 10*: 503-532.

Golembiewski, R. and Luo, H. (1994). OD applications in developmental settings: An addendum about success rates. *International Journal of Organizational Analysis, 2*: 295-308.

Golembiewski, R. T., and Rountree, B. H. (1996). System redesign. In "Nursing, I: Action planning in a medical-surgical ward," and "System redesign in nursing, II: Impact of action-planning intervention on worksite, shareholders, and costs," *International Journal of Public Administration* (in press).

Robinson, V. (1993). Current Controversies in Action Research. *Public Administration Quarterly, 17*: 263-290.

Susman, G., and Evered, R. (1978). An Assessment of the Scientific Merits of Action Research. *Administrative Science Quarterly, 23:* 582-603.

Watkins, K., and Golembiewski, R. (1995). Rethinking OD for the `learning organization'. *International Journal of Organizational Analysis, 3:* 86-101.

Watkins, K., and Marsick, V. (1993). *Sculpting the Learning Organization.* San Francisco: Jossey-Bass.

41.
HEALTH CARE MARKETING AND PLANNING

Rhonda Walker Mack, *College of Charleston, Charleston, SC*

Marketing in health care has evolved from its early stages of often negatively perceived communications to a broad, aggressive, integral component of all types of health care organizations. This evolution has seen health care marketing professionals move from largely promotional roles and image building campaigns to active, targeted service development activities and present day intensive involvement in quality improvement through relationship marketing and patient satisfaction.

Health care marketing is increasingly becoming the responsibility of the entire organization, from the discharge nurse to the cleaning staff to the physician. Organizations committed to continuous quality improvement with a central customer focus will be somewhere along the continuum from planning quality initiatives to full implementation with marketing functions integration. This type of organization will utilize cross-functional teams in process analysis, improvement and feedback. Customer satisfaction will serve as the ultimate measure in the evaluation process.

I. BASIC MARKETING STRUCTURE

The American Marketing Association defines marketing as follows: Marketing is the process of planning and executing the conception, pricing, promotion, and distribution of ideas, goods, and services to create exchanges that satisfy individual and organizational goals (Bennett, 1988).

While the planning and performance of the marketing tasks will vary depending on the philosophy of the organization, basic activities are similar once the organiza-

tional mission is determined:
- Identify the customer market and relevant needs
- Profile the target customer market
- Determine and develop the full product/service offering
- Develop and carry out the strategy to price, communicate and deliver the offering.

Evaluation and planning are the first and final marketing tasks with both consumer and organizational satisfaction as goals.

Market oriented health care organizations will, like any organization, conduct research to assess market needs. The resulting information may lead to a redefinition of the customer market, curtailment of some services, the repositioning or redefining of services, and cooperative efforts with competing providers to provide services more efficiently. For some organizations with a set mission of a full service community provider, this research step will be less extensive than for other health care organizations with greater flexibility. Even for those with relatively specific full service objectives, research may lead to information enabling the organization to target customer groups with special services, or bundled services, which may improve community health care as well as lead to improvements in future delivery via more desirable demand patterns.

Once the customer is identified, target market profiling is the next step. The information needed depends on the particular customer/market in question. Information can be used to address issues related to products/services to be targeted and related objectives, distribution decisions, pricing/fee decisions, and communications plans.

II. CUSTOMER IDENTIFICATION AND PROFILING

The standard question, "Who is the customer?" is never more relevant than it is today in the various areas of health care marketing. Increased competition necessitates detailed examination of the target customers. Technological advances allow today's managers to reach exactly who they want to communicate and at the precise time desired. This ability requires careful market designation and planning. The customer may be a current patient to the community at large, internal organizational employees, various managed care organizations, physicians, or other medical and government agencies.

Once these customers are identified as targets for the organization, data must be gathered to determine not just their needs, but numerous other aspects related to decision making. Consumer decision making is influenced by factors both internal and external to the individual. These factors must be understood to better meet individual needs as well as to predict and influence buyer behavior (Bearden et al., 1995). This is the case for the individual consumer as well as the professional or organizational buyer. Certain questions should be asked. If the customer is a patient, what is her image of your offering versus her image of the competition? What is important to her in determining satisfaction with the offering? What other people are relevant in decision making, as is often the case with younger and older patients, with respect to communications regarding service offerings, educational materials and other related information? If the customer is a large area employer, what type of people do they employ and what are their most important health care needs? Are they well educated, more likely to be health oriented, and in need of preventive care and fitness programs? Are they likely to have children at home and/or to be caregivers for aging parents? Do they have different needs which should be considered in determining services to be developed and highlighted in efforts to attract the organization for which they work? If the customer is the community, what are the general needs which the organization can provide to improve its image as a vital and valued community member? If the customer is a physician, information such as practice size, location, productivity, physician alliances with payers or managed health organizations, and practice objectives will be useful in developing marketing strategy.

Customer-related data can be gained by the organization itself through conducting primary research, using market research firms to conduct studies, or identifying useful secondary data available from various professional associations and state and local governments. In addition, numerous companies now offer data-based software providing consumer market, physician, payer, and provider information. Such detailed customer information capabilities has led to "relationship marketing" which stresses the close ongoing, individual relationship between the organization and its customers.

The internal customer requires an inquiring focus just as do external customers. The successful delivery of any health care service is dependent upon those involved in its delivery. Not only is their education and product/service-specific training important, but also their commitment to organizational goals and customer satisfaction. Realization of full commitment will only come if the organization is fully committed to its employees via information, support, education, feedback, and compensation. The inability of customers to evaluate the actual service received in many instances of health care offerings increases their reliance on human factors of the delivery in product/service evaluation. Hence, the major emphasis is on the internal customer or employees role in service delivery.

III. PRODUCT/SERVICE STRATEGY

While much of health care marketing concerns the delivery of physical products, much effort is devoted to the marketing of services as in any other industry. The marketing of services is quite similar to that of products, yet a great deal of attention has been given to the differences in product and service marketing and the challenges especially characteristic of services marketing (Lovelock, 1991). Special characteristics of services are important to successful health care service delivery.

A. Recognizing and Planning for the Service Aspects

The intangible nature of services necessitates heavy reliance on subjective delivery factors in service evaluation. Many customers are unable to evaluate the actual health service being received, thus the increased importance of the human factors (internal customer) and environmental factors involved in the delivery.

The inability to inventory services is especially important in marketing. Use of services, such as emergency rooms and obstetric delivery facilities, cannot always be controlled. This problem requires special attention to efforts to influence patterns.

While part-time workers might assist in servicing especially high demand periods, incentives, or promotional programs to increase the use of facilities in low demand periods should be considered. Also, alternative modes of location, such as mobile service delivery, may aid in matching demand and supply. Many lessons can be learned from other service industries such as resorts, entertainment, fitness, and food.

Three additional characteristics of services--inseparability, inconsistency, and customer interaction--also relate to the importance of the internal customer's role in service delivery. Service inconsistency, or the fact that quality control checks along an assembly line are lacking in most health care service delivery, poses a special challenge for the service provider. Continuous quality improvement by health care is focused especially on this issue. Process analysis using various quality tools such as Pareto charts can be especially useful in insuring that the customer is receiving the desired standard of care. The involvement of cross-functional teams is imperative for addressing inconsistency. Until the organization moves in this direction, quality standards are not guaranteed; instead the service received will depend on individuals delivering the service. The definition of quality delivered depends on the personal and professional quality perception of the nurse, doctor, discharge clerk, therapist, receptionist, or volunteer. All too often, this delivery will also be influenced by the personal mood of the employee or how busy the office is on any particular day. Inseparability, the idea that the service delivered is inseparable from those delivering it, and customer interaction, the fact that the customer is also part of and can affect the service delivery, are also relevant. Inseparability, like inconsistency, stresses the need for internal customer involvement. Customer interaction, somewhat different, calls for efforts to influence the external customer via methods such as patient education, positive communications programs, customer involvement, and preventive care programs.

B. Developing Product/Service Offering

Dependent upon the needs of the target market and the mission of the organization, products and services to be offered must be clearly specified along with their accompanying marketing plan(s). Despite some overlapping services and bundling of services to specific markets segments, target customers, product definitions, communications programs, pricing and delivery systems for each should be developed. In some organizations, product/service offerings are planned by product line groupings. A typical Women's Center may include services ranging from gynecology and obstetrics to neonatal and well-baby education, to fitness, and increasingly to grief and life planning counseling in senior years. While each is quite different, they may often be planned and operated from a central focus on one target market, females, with evolving needs. Another example might look at preventive care as a product/service line which would include wellness programs, life planning, fitness and nutrition programs. While these services are related, they could be targeted to multiple markets. A large organization with each of these product lines specified would expect to experience some programs from competition within leading to cannibalization and would need to take precautions in the development of communications programs as well as overall product planning to carefully control costs and product offering proliferation. This emphasizes the importance of the role of the marketing director and organizational chart within the organization in order to maintain an overall perspective of market planning.

C. Product/Service Positioning

Since very few organizations exist in a noncompetitive market, and since few customers are fully aware and informed of all product and service offerings, marketing efforts must position services in the specified target segment (Lautman, 1993). Product position refers to how the product or service is perceived by the consumer relative to its competition. Typically a product's position is based on a limited number of attributes perceived by the target market to be important in defining the product's utility, customer decision making process, and competitive position. Benefit segmentation can be useful in identifying market segments based on the benefits sought by consumers (Miaoulis and Joby, 1992). Tools such as perceptual mapping involving multidimensional scaling can also be used to position the product in its market to identify currently perceived position (by the target market), competitive positions, and repositioning opportunities where "ideal product" market segments exist. The first step in this process is research with the objectives of gathering broad information on the product, the competitions' products, and the customers' needs and perceptions. This useful process should be an ongoing part of every organization's marketing program as market needs and competitive offerings are evolutionary. Quite often, repositioning is necessary to reflect and act on market changes. Traditional nutritional programs are increasingly being "repositioned" as preventive care, fitness, or weight management programs reflective of the changes in customer needs and increased competition from sports fitness facilities as well as other aggressive competitors offering a variety of products/services. Many of the programs had previously been in existence yet had not been positioned properly to the appropriate market segments, nor had they promoted the benefits desired by market.

Marketing professionals in health care must see beyond the required product attributes of health care offerings such as curing abilities, childbirth facilities, hospital beds, and required immunization to those attributes which can be perceived by the customer as relevant and determinant in differentiating "Brand A" from "Brand B" in order to fully utilize the potential of product positioning. Once the determinant attributes and desired position are determined, product management must work with promotions management in developing the appropriate strategies to convey the existence of the product/service and any relevant differential advantages. Some hospitals and physician practices which are repositioning their nutritional programs as described earlier are realizing a differential advantage since their offerings are provided by a reputable medical organization as opposed to their competitions' offerings.

D. Product Awareness and Information Needs

In order to develop marketing plans, one must first know the current awareness level of the consumer segments to determine the effort needed in planning distribution, pricing, and communications programs. For example, in planning for a truly new service, the marketing plan would need to include an extensive education program on what the service is, how it compares to anything else currently available, what it will do for the consumer, where and how to receive the service, etc. While most products and services are typically not new, differences in awareness and information levels exist in the market which should be acknowledged and planned for in developing marketing strategy. These differences will often vary across segments for the same product offering, and marketing research should be used to identify such differences. The information derived from the research will be especially useful in developing promotional programs as well as in planning for service demand. Newer services are less likely to experience a high level of initial demand according to the diffusion of innovation concept (Rogers, 1982). As the consumer market becomes more familiar with the service, the adoption rate, or demand, will rise. The objective, then, for the manager of a new product or service is to increase awareness of the product in order to build demand to the desirable point. This may be for a new type of medical test, piece of equipment, wellness program, a new satellite emergency center, a mobile nursing service, or a newly recommended children's immunization. The target customer must be identified, the product/service offering structured, the information which is lacking identified, and communications designed to distribute the appropriate information. As the market becomes more familiar with the offering through promotions, public relations, word-of-mouth, or trial, the marketing strategy will need to reflect the new level at which consumers arrive along the continuum from building awareness, information, and interest for new service trial to more competitively oriented communications to maintain the desired demand.

E. Mature Product Strategies

As product and services mature, demand may at times become stagnant and even decline. The product life cycle has implications for product planning relative to how long it has been in existence, its competitive situation and demand, and revenue (Bennett, 1988). This concept refers to several stages which represent product sales and revenue over its life: the introductory stage, growth, maturity and the decline stage. Some product life cycle models will represent the introductory stage as two stages, development and introduction, and some will divide the maturity into maturity and saturation stages. Regardless of the number of stages, the product or service goes through various stages of life, each with different marketing implications. The stages may vary in length although the standard model is a typical bell-shaped curve representing sales (and revenue). Similar to the idea of the diffusion of innovation, the introductory stage is characterized by often slow and low demand. As demand increases, the product enters the growth stage. As sales begin to slow, the maturity stage is beginning followed by the decline stage, of course with declining sales.

The introductory stage typically calls for awareness building communications objectives. Pricing strategies may depend on a number of factors at this stage, including anticipated competitive entry into the market and expected acceptance rate for the product or service. If competition is near or the market is ready to accept the new service, then a low introductory price (price penetration policy) may be warranted in order to achieve an early, high market share to carry through the following life cycle. If, however, competitive entry is anticipated to be slow and a slow acceptance rate is expected, a higher, skimming pricing policy will enable the organization to recoup as much of the earlier investment as possible (since a low price would not encourage a much greater demand with the price-inelastic market). As demand increases, as the market is becoming more familiar with the service, and as competition is entering, then highly competitive communications, strong competitive positioning strategies and margins will change accordingly. As the product or service continues to develop and demand peaks and slows, the question is often whether or not to continue allocating organizational time and financial resources to a declining service. Sometimes students of marketing identify a product/service decline stage and immediately assume the product's demise, often prematurely. It is wise to assess the current demand, as well as to examine potential for revitalizing an existing product or service in lieu of extinction. Sales decline may be due as much to lack of attention to a mature product as it is to a real lack of market desire for the product. Often, competition is exiting these markets leaving an even greater opportunity for those who will properly manage mature products and services. In assessing new product development strategies, one of the first lessons to be learned is that it is much less expensive to reposition and remarket a preexisting service than to introduce a totally new one. If the opportunity to revitalize the product to its current target segment is not adequate, attention should be given to opportunities which may exist within new segments or even to product/service alternatives or spin offs to the current market segment. Most marketing texts refer to four company growth strategies:

- market penetration (sell more of current product to current markets),
- market development (sell current products to new markets),
- product growth (introduce new products to current market), or
- diversification (introduce new products to new markets).

Each calls for varying types and levels of investment and planning.

Product and service offerings are central to all other marketing strategy decisions. Their proper fit with the target customers and careful alignment with all other marketing functions determines the organization's success. Special care should be taken in decisions of new offerings, as well as the continuation or severing of mature product lines. The truly market-oriented organization maintains the awareness that the product and the market fit is a dynamic effort which must be continuously examined and improved.

IV. PRICING STRATEGY

Essential to pricing decisions is the full appreciation of the price, quantity, and revenue relationship. Revenue is determined by price and quantity sold. While this concept is straightforward, the determination of price is a complex decision increasingly moving outside the realm of the traditional marketing functions. As health care marketing has less influence over price, its ability to project and influence demand and, thus, revenue necessary for strategic marketing planning, becomes difficult. As control over price may seem to be moving out of the realm of health care marketing, its emphasis on cost control is increasing and becoming a major component of product/service evaluation and planning.

Price is often seen as the exchange value of a good or service or the monetary value received. In very early stages of marketing, exchange existed in a barter society. This is not uncommon in contemporary times with the existence of database barter societies. The health care price decision today is a complicated one, heavily influenced by legislation, ethics, competitive pressure, and market demand. As with other industries, intermediaries are involved in pricing at all levels; discounting and bundling abound. Drug store chains require adequate markups. Upper and lower eyelid bletheroplasty can be had individually for $1500 each, but upper and lower can be had for a discount at the same appointment for only $2500. Insurance costs per employee to employers offering a large number of employees (prospective patients) to an HMO vary substantially when compared to costs available to small employers.

A. Product and Service Cost

Various cost factors must be considered for pricing decisions. Fixed costs are those which remain constant and are not dependent on volume of product or service produced and delivered. Certain equipment and overhead costs fall into this category. Variable costs change with volume. Many supplies and certain personnel costs directly associated with volume fall into this category. Total costs represent the combined total costs derived from fixed and variable costs. Awareness of fixed and total costs is imperative when deciding how to price products and services. Typically, an organization's long run existence depends upon pricing set to at least a breakeven point. Some organizations may in the short run price low to obtain a desired sales level or market share for competitive purposes; they may receive subsidies or grants to enable lower pricing. However, long-term pricing below break even for competitive purposes is risky, but competitive pricing to increase demand beyond the breakeven point is attractive in adding to profit margin.

B. Price Elasticity

Standard marketing textbooks present the concept of price elasticity, the percentage change in demand given a percentage change in price of the good (Simon, 1992; Tellis, 1988). If price is very elastic, a change will result in a demand change either directly or inversely. Also related are the concepts of substitute and complementary products and services. One might see a membership at a local gym as a substitute for entering a nutritional weight-loss oriented counseling program. The benefit derived from the customer purchasing either of these might be increased fitness, slimming down, and a healthier body. Thus, either might be perceived as a way to achieve the desired benefit. A price increase in gym memberships might cause a decrease in their sales and a possible increase in sales for the substitute good, nutritional weight loss counseling programs. In this example, a price change in a service affects the demand of its substitute, positively or negatively. With respect to complementary goods, the purchase of one is likely to be associated with the purchase of the other. The increased use of home health care nursing agencies might be expected to increase the rental or purchase of health care equipment for the home. Thus, an increase in nursing services might result in lower demand for home equipment.

Not all demand is price elastic. With many products and services, a change in price would not result in demand change. For a diabetic, insulin is a necessary product. If the price of insulin were to decrease, insulin sales would not increase dramatically nor would a price increase be likely to result in a substantial decrease in demand. While there may be some demand shift in the short term, the overall demand would vary little. The very inelasticity of many health care products and services is the root of much debate over the ethics in health care pricing today.

C. Pricing Objectives

Various possible objectives exist in developing price strategies. A typical objective is profit or a specific return on investment. Factors such as the anticipated diffusion of innovation and stage in the product life cycle often influence pricing decisions as previously discussed with price skimming. Ethical issues abound, and the decision must be made weighing the profit objective of the organization against possible need of the product or service. The interest of the business and those of society must be balanced.

Another common objective determining price setting is the desired sales level to be obtained. Pharmaceutical companies desiring to expand the use of a particular over-the-counter drug might drop price to complement a new promotional campaign targeted at expanded sales. Similarly, market share objectives are common in health care pricing. Prices set to achieve market share goals are typical in communities with several competing hospitals offering similar services. In fact, such hospitals will often promote themselves as the leader in a particular area as high market share is achieved and certain expertise established and perceived within the medical community. Image pricing, while somewhat less prevalent in health care, does exist. For many products and services, a price-quality relationship--"you get what you pay for"--often exists. While many of us don't mind trading off convenience or price for a less-than-perfect hamburger, we typically don't desire poor quality health care at any price. Many examples, however, are relevant here: generic drugs, health clinics which provide "cheap" sports physicals, and conversely the prestige plastic surgeon who is known to charge more than anyone else in town (and have the longest list of patients). Some pricing decisions in the health care community are set like those in many other industries such as corner gasoline sales, hair cuts, and plumbing services. A status quo pricing system encourages stability within the industry while protecting the margins of the organization and its competitors. Increasingly, health care pricing is moving in the direction of negotiation with large acquisitions, mergers, and health care reform. Quite often, in today's health care industry, the decision to set an initial traditional price or determine when to change price is not in the hands of health care marketing professionals.

D. Strategic Pricing

Several alternative pricing strategies are available to organizations dependent upon their objectives and flexibility in price setting. A flexible versus one-price policy may be used with special care by the organization for adherence to the Robinson-Patman Act prohibiting price discrimination that would hinder competition. With one-price policies, organizations require all customers to pay the same price. A flexible pricing policy allows differential pricing dependent upon negotiation or buying power. This practice may be typical of HMO and employer negotiations. Bundled pricing is typical of health care marketing especially as organizations become larger and offer more varied services through mergers and acquisitions and "bundle," or present, these services together as a package to attract customers. Various forms of discounts may be offered by organizations to its customers as long as they are available to all customers who meet discount qualifications. Discounts for volume purchases, seasonality (or even time-of-day/day-of-week), or performing certain functions (such as helping promote a drug or piece of equipment) are common in health care. Other strategies

Figure 1 - Communications Model

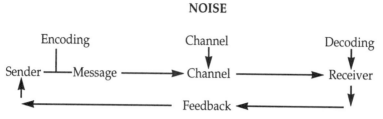

such as price lining, odd-versus-even pricing, and leader pricing are available but are less typical in health care environments.

V. COMMUNICATIONS STRATEGY

Early health care marketing professionals were largely concerned with communications or promotional functions. Communications, implying a two-way flow of information, includes tools such as advertising, publicity, sales promotions, and personal selling. The use of each of these is extensive in health care marketing.

A. The Communications Model

In order to communicate effectively, careful planning must be given to the major communications components. The communications process is often represented by a communications model (Schramm, 1955).

The sender is the person or organization desiring to send a message. While the sender is the organization itself, celebrities or spokespersons are increasingly being used in health care promotions to aid in getting the attention of the target customer. Such representatives, chosen not only for their ability to get attention but for their "fit" with the product/service and their credibility and believability, become "sender" to consumers who associate the spokesperson with the organization. This association can have both negative and positive results dependent upon the spokesperson's continuing image.

The message decision is vital. All too often, communications are planned quickly without considering the appropriateness of the message to be sent. Communications planning must begin with consideration of the objective to be achieved. Is the objective to launch a new product or to increase sales of a mature product? Does the organization want to meet and challenge a competitive offer or simply remind the community of the organization's image? Is the objective to get people in the door immediately to purchase a product or service or to build goodwill? Several "hierarchy of effects" models exist to illustrate the continuum of possible objectives. These models portray the consumer as moving along a continuum from unawareness of a product or service to building awareness and interest, evaluation of a product or service and finally adoption or purchase action to procure the product (Bovee and Arens, 1989). Following the purchase action would be the post-purchase evaluation possibly leading to satisfaction or even dissonance. With such models in mind, the communications director can examine the offering and current level of awareness or action of the market in order to determine the ideal objective of the communications to be planned. "Taking advantage" of discount media time or space requiring quick placement without proper planning can be wasteful of valuable funds. Communications planning should consider what message should be sent to achieve the desired objective and also carefully examine the target customer profile to determine message components.

Many options exist in message planning and encoding. The message ideas need to be developed or translated in the appropriate form. A message can be humorous, "scare tactics" can be used, or fantasy "slice-of-life" strategies played upon. Again, the objective, the product, and the target customer must be considered in making these decisions. Many aspects of health care are not humorous, yet creative advertisers may effectively use humor in advertising. Some products may lend themselves to scare tactics or fright. Special care should be taken in using this appeal, however, to prevent too negative of an association. The use of professional creative people is important in message design and execution. They can be helpful in developing messages with either one-or-two sided presentation which are constructive. One-sided messages present only the positive side of the offering and are useful if there are no major disadvantages of the offering. If the target audience is higher educated, or if there are major disadvantages, counter-arguments to a one-sided message may outweigh the message itself. A well-designed, two-sided message may be more effective in achieving the desired objective.

The encoded message is then sent through one of the many channels available at which point it is decoded by the receiver. The communications channel(s) choice determines a great deal of the decisions to follow. Personal selling can be used, publicity and public relations can be emphasized, or mass media and word of mouth can be utilized. Typically the organization uses a combination of these channels referred to as the promotional mix, to be addressed later in this section. With respect to decoding of the message, one simple rule should always be followed. Care should be taken in keeping the message simple and straight forward. Creativity is wonderful but should never get in the way of the message itself. The target customer should always be kept in mind in designing the message. Vocabulary used should not be above the level of comprehension and care should be taken not to insult the customer with stereotypes or demeaning vocabulary. The product itself should be carefully represented and the chosen source should not overshadow the product and message as it is to be perceived by the receiver.

Two additional communications aspects are noise and feedback. Noise refers to the potential external factors which may influence the likelihood of the message being received properly or even affect its interpretation. Noise is especially prevalent in advertising with competing messages bombarding consumers every minute. It is also prevalent in the most personal channel of communications, personal selling. Pharmaceutical representatives compete with patients, nurses, other reps, and full waiting rooms in attempting to communicate a message to physicians.

Feedback refers to the idea that the receiver provides feedback in some form ranging from increased awareness, to purchase, or even complaint. Aggressive encouragement of customer feedback insures that the organization stays in touch with customer needs and issues of satisfaction or dissatisfaction with products or services. This can be done through the availability of 800 number customer comment lines, customer feedback research, or the promotions of customer service departments. The purpose of the communications model is to stress the importance of the careful planning of each step of the process so that effective communications is encouraged.

B. The Promotions Mix

The promotions mix usually combines one or more channel tools including advertising, publicity, personal selling, or sales promotions. These tools are to be planned to work synergistically with specified objectives and time frame included. The communications budget must be understood in determining the promotions mix to be used with objectives in mind.

Advertising is any paid form of nonpersonal communications representing the organization's goods and services. This is contrasted with publicity which is not directly paid for by the organization being represented, and personal selling which is a paid, but personal, representation of the organization's product or services. Sales promotions has traditionally been a "catch-all" category of promotional efforts not directly falling into one of the previous categories, which are short-term oriented. However, sales promotions are receiving increased attention and budget allocations are moving beyond the typical short-term inducement and becoming integral to the overall mix. Promotions options themselves are becoming broader. Extensive use can be effectively made of sponsorship marketing, the use of events (sponsored by the organization) appropriately targeted to the desired market, to communicate specific products or services or to promote goodwill. The information highway is increasingly familiar with alternatives, like net pages becoming viable tools which, while paid for, presents a way to often present a more personal communication. Direct marketing communications-relationship oriented, is becoming a vital part of many organizations' communications plans (Direct, 1991; Johnson, 1992; and Levin, 1992).

1. Advertising

Advertising is often negatively equated with marketing due to the proliferation of ads and the image of some advertising perceived as encouraging negative stereotypes and the purchase of unnecessary and socially undesirable products and services. Advertising, however, is a powerful tool when properly planned. Advertising can take several different forms. For example, product advertising promotes a particular product or service while institutional advertising is used to build goodwill and enhance the organization's image. Advertising can be competitive (competing to sell versus a competitor's product or service), or it can be used to build primary demand for a product or service category with competing organizations working together in promotions. One familiar form of advertising is comparative where one brand is compared to another. While this may be appealing to the advertiser, there is a risk of negative perception by the consumer.

The use of advertising requires proper target identification to match the choice of media (television, radio, magazine, outdoor, etc.) and scheduling. Advertising research is necessary to prevent wasteful purchases which will not effectively reach the target audience. Planners should request data from media representatives showing audience profiles. Such information is typically made readily available on a local and national basis in the form of media packages. Selection of the most cost-effective media plan will require assessment of information including reach (unduplicated audience reached), frequency (number of times a message reaches the same person during a specified time period), cost-per thousand/CPM (measure the cost of reaching a 1,000 size audience), and gross rating points (allows for comparisons of different sized markets in addition to the profile data (Bearden, et al., 1995). Different media forms can be used effectively to work together to reinforce each other. For example, the billboard can serve to strongly remind the target customer of the more detailed newspaper advertisement or the strong images conveyed in the television commercial. Each media form has its strengths and weaknesses including factors regarding its appeal to various market segments, impact, lead time, costs, appropriateness for message type, etc. and should be selected accordingly. Many organizations are guilty of poor choice of outdoor location and especially guilty of trying to crowd too much information on a billboard with multiple traffic lanes passing at rapid speeds. Similarly, television is a powerful medium with the capability to provide sight and sound, yet typically in a short time on a set budget. Too much information will result in low comprehension. Print media such as newspaper, magazine, direct mail, or even computer screens can be used to present more extensive information when necessary. Here, problems with clutter are major, and advertising professionals can be helpful in developing effective messages and placement strategies.

Other media factors to be considered are issues such as shelf life (length of the exposure or effectiveness of the message), quality of production (sometimes a problem in newspaper but able to be overcome with new printing capabilities or use of inserts), lead time required for ad placement (requiring proper time planning), and lagged effects of advertising (the resulting action desired by the placement may not take place until a good amount of time elapses). This makes it especially difficult to measure the effectiveness of advertising. An advertisement seen today may effect a purchase two days, two weeks, or even two-or-more months later. Advertising research can be used to gauge effectiveness to some extent through measures such as changes in awareness, attitude, and intention to purchase. Pretesting ads as well as posttesting ads using such methods as day-after-recall can be used to gauge effectiveness. Service and product sales (for example, the number of new patients, medical equipment orders, new program membership, or increased immunization rates) can also be tracked if direct sales growth or market share is an objective. However, measuring advertising effectiveness still remains a big problem and often an objection which must be overcome in justifying the advertising budget to upper management.

Many health care organizations use the services of advertising agencies to handle part, or all, of their advertising efforts. Full service agencies will supply all advertising functions to the client working closely with the client at every step. Other limited service agencies, often referred to as boutique agencies, will provide various specialized functions such as creatives, photography and layout, commercial production, or media buying services. Agencies are typically compensated by either a specific fee for service or a typical 15 percent commission of media billings (in effect retained from the total amount paid for the media space and time).

Similar to advertising in many other industries, ethical concerns are a major issue in health care advertising. While there are numerous legal guidelines, across-industry guidelines and various media guidelines, the Alliance of Health Care Strategy and Marketing has established its own set of voluntary guidelines for health care advertising. (Berkowitz 1996). These guidelines regard the documentation of advertising claims, the importance of the patients interests, and the full disclosure of sponsoring advertisers.

2. *Publicity*

Publicity is extensively used by many health care organizations where it is often managed by the public relations department. The importance of positive relationships with local and regional media representatives is recognized by those in charge of the organization's publicity efforts. Even though publicity is not a directly paid for type of communications, it should be aggressively planned and managed. The continual development of news releases and dissemination of all types of organizational news to the various media outlets is vital. Publicity placement should be timed with other components of the promotions mix in order to take full advantage of the mix. The lack of control over its use makes planning difficult, but all attempts should be made to gain good coverage. Quite often the organization may be able to elicit the involvement of the local media in community events which are health-care oriented helping build strong relationships with those in charge. Publicity's greatest advantage is that it is perceived as more credible and objective than other types of promotions. In instances of negative publicity, this credibility holds true as well. Organizations should have publicity managers who are schooled in methods of handling publicity and public relations during crisis management. Health care is receiving increasing scrutiny in recent years and the ability to effectively respond to negative information is vital. The organization should maintain control over information which is disseminated from within and should encourage training of its publicity staff in crisis management. There should, of course, be built in flows of information within the organization to assure that management is aware beforehand of any information which may be perceived negatively by the press as well as the public. This will enable the organization to be prepared to respond and possibly even to prevent negative coverage.

3. *Personal Selling*

While it is the most expensive promotional tool, personal selling allows for direct interaction between the organization and the customer. Explanations can be given, questions can be answered, and objections can be countered. Personal selling can be on a on-on-one basis, or there can be an individual or team presentation to individuals or groups. The presentation can be formal, or it can be informal depending on the product, the needs of the customer, and amount of time available. Different sales approaches include various methods ranging from canned presentations (which provide the same presentation to each customer) to consultative selling (which focuses on the specific needs or problems of the individual customer). Quite often, in selling to health care professionals, time is minimal, so the greater the need to have information presented in a brief yet complete fashion with accompanying materials which can remain with the customer for reference. Follow-up is critical regardless of the sales approach used.

Many industries rely heavily on personal selling and allocate significant resources to sales force management. Decisions must be made beginning with the type and size of the sales force, training needs, and appropriate method of sales force allocation (by geographic territory, by product type, or by customer organization). Sales goals, sales force compensation and benefits, and the type of evaluation to be used must also be examined. While professional sales people are commonly found in pharmaceutical and medical equipment sales, they are also active in many types of health care providers. Hospitals often employ professional sales people to work in areas such as physician relations, as well as final customer and employer relations.

Professional sales people are an important link for the health care organization. They interact with customers at all levels and are a source for gathering vital market and competitive information (Hawes, et al., 1989). It is important that sales management understands the role of sales personal in the organization for full utilization. The sales staff should be properly trained not only in sales methods and the importance of information gathering and follow-up, but they should also understand the industry in which they are working to properly interact with the customer and represent the organization professionally.

Professional sales can be used for all areas of the organization but is especially helpful in areas where products and services are particularly complex, where technology is more complex requiring greater explanation, where the customer market is smaller (physicians and employers versus community households), and where the "purchase/decision" requires a great change or high risk (personal risk but especially financial investment risk).

4. Sales Promotions

Sales promotions has traditionally been labeled a short-term inducement to buy. Expenditures of US companies are almost three times more for sales promotions than for advertising (Mandese and Donaton, 1992). Typical sales promotions tools include coupons, two-for-one offerings, rebates, samples, premiums of all kinds, and contests. These can be targeted to the final customer, or they can be aimed at industrial customers or intermediaries. Sales promotions can be used to increase awareness and involvement of a product, service, or organization, and they can be used as reminders. Sales promotions companies will assist the health care organization in selecting the appropriate items or programs to achieve their objectives. The objective may be as simple as a reminder item, like a refrigerator magnet displaying the organization's name and number for reminder purposes, or it may be as extensive as a nationwide internal customer (employee) recognition program rewarding excellent customer service.

Providing allowances, or discounts, is a common promotional tool to intermediaries in turn for their performing various functions. For example, a manufacturer of a special treatment bed might provide a price discount to a regional hospital which agrees to offer an informational training demonstration of the bed to sister association hospitals. In addition, cooperative advertising is extensively used to encourage intermediary support. A hospital, for instance, may pay a portion of a full page ad in the city newspaper to announce the arrival of a new physician on the medical staff of a local group practice. This would aid the group practice as well as bond the relationship of the practice physicians with the hospital. Similarly, a medical equipment supplier might assist a local HMO in advertising the addition of a new piece of screening equipment to encourage the lease or sale from the perspective of the equipment supplier and in order to increase awareness among potential customers from the perspective of the HMO.

Many sales promotions directors are moving beyond the short-term sales promotions definition as professional planning evolves. Long-term benefits from sales promotions are increasingly being realized as many of the programs become annual events which are accepted and looked forward to by the customer. While events such as health screenings and health fairs are one-time-events in a planning period, they often are perceived as an ongoing community service providing vital positive image impressions in the community. While the use of standard sales promotions items, coupons, sweepstakes, and premiums, does appear to be of short-term character in health care as in other industries, the use of other sales promotions tactics is more evolved in health care as professionals have taken the opportunity to use sales promotions to build community bridges.

Events sponsorship is related to this type of sales promotion. The public responds positively to health-related sponsorships. This information can be used by the organization to attract large corporate, as well as local sponsors, in building bridges to provide community events. Such cooperative sponsorship activities will serve not only to aid the community but to provide positive links to potential corporate employers who represent potential customers as well as links to media representatives who are a channel for publicity and can assist in advertising efforts. In addition, suppliers can often be involved in events providing great potential value. These events can be targeted to specific market segments and used to distribute information about a large number of products and services offered by the organization. To realize the full benefits of sponsorship opportunities, the organization must target and plan them professionally. Some channel sponsorships, such as those used by pharmaceutical companies to reach physicians, have raised ethical questions and should always be carefully examined (Barton, 1993).

5. Word of Mouth

An additional communications method sometimes not listed specifically as a promotions method is word of mouth. Personal information is the most credible type of communications. Most of us have gone to a movie or not gone to a particular restaurant because we were given positive or negative advice based on a friend's experience. Identifying methods of encouraging positive word of mouth should be part of every organization's communications plan. Some medical offices have signs inside inviting patients to tell a friend if they were pleased with the service. Some organizations give discounts, rewards of other type, or thank you cards for referrals. Negative word-of-mouth, on the other hand, is one of the worst things that can happen to an organization. Training programs should be conducted within the organization to impress upon the employees how devastating negative word of mouth can be, and how easily it can be initiated.

C. Push and Pull Strategies

In planning promotional efforts, two basic strategies exist, push or pull. Push strategies refer to efforts which require promotions directed to intermediaries in the distribution channel. Much of health care promotions is of this type. Until recently, pharmaceutical manufacturers relied solely on push strategies for prescription drugs with all efforts aimed at the physician or pharmacist. Manufacturers of medical services, products, and equipment have largely sold to hospitals, pharmacies, skilled care facilities, etc. in the past using push strategies as well. Push promotions would entail the use of tools such as advertising in trade journals and booths at conventions, sales promotions targeted to intermediaries, and heavy personal selling. More recently, pull strategies have begun to increase. Pull strategies involve appeals targeted directly to the final consumer. The idea is that demand will be built at this level relying on the final consumer to pull the product through the distribution system by demand. These efforts may take many forms including mass advertising, sales promotions, publicity, and sales promotions. The final consumer market has long been a target for pull strategies for over-the-counter drugs. For example, Seldane and Rogaine were pioneer brands breaking this mold for prescription drugs using advertising, toll-free numbers and direct mail including videos. Other medical services are also benefiting from pull strategies. Mass television advertisements targeting the final consumer encouraging breast screenings and childhood immunizations, and the use of condoms and smoking cessation are examples. Push and pull strategies are commonly used in combination in order to achieve a more effective promotional program.

D. Promotional Budgeting

As in other types of organizations, promotional budgeting in health care is often a weak point. Just as promotional programs should not be planned without specific objectives in mind, they should not be planned or launched without careful budget considerations. Several methods exist to provide budgetary guidelines. Some firms use a percentage of past sales to determine promotions budgets. The disadvantage of this method is that it assumes that the past determines the future overlooking the desire to launch new products or services or the objective of growth. To overcome this problem, many organizations use an annual sales forecast to determine budget. This is difficult for some health care organizations without a track record of sales, or with a lack of experience in marketing and sales forecasting. This method does, however, acknowledge a relationship between promotional efforts and sales. Some firms use a competitive parity, or status-quo, method of determining promotions budgets which allows the organization to spend similarly to its market competitors with the objective being one of competitive equilibrium. Some organizations use no budgeting method at all, simply spending or not spending when funds are available. With this method, promotions are often the first area to cut in times of financial crunch when this is the opposite of what should happen. Many of these firms will often experience a lack of funds available during the last quarter of the year for needed program promotions, and some will find a great surplus available which is often spent without planning or promotional objectives in mind.

One budget method referred to as "objectives and tasks" is a more ideal method of planning promotional expenditures. Management identifies the objectives to be achieved and then determines the promotional tasks necessary to meet the objectives. Costs of the tasks are then estimated to arrive at the desired budget which is then examined and either accepted or altered. Sometimes this requires alteration of the objectives, and sometimes management simply requests that marketing deliver "more for the money" than planned. Regardless, this method includes a deliberate consideration of promotion components needed throughout the planning period often forcing more structure than would have otherwise been involved in the planning process.

Effective communications strategies are vital for organizations to successfully compete in the growing health care industry. Careful identification of objectives and budget, consideration of the entire promotional mix, and adequate research are necessary. Organizations which successfully communicate with their target markets will be well on their way to realizing their market objectives.

VI. DISTRIBUTION / CHANNEL STRATEGIES

Distribution enables the movement of the product and service from the producer to the consumer. The distribution decision for the health care organization is very broad and typically long-term oriented. This decision includes the distribution method(s) to be used (the "place" decision) including transportation, wholesaling, and retailing as well as the decision of who will perform the specific distribution functions and location specifics (Cokelez and Peacock, 1993). Also to be determined is the decision of how extensive the market coverage will be. This latter decision has many implications, some of which are beyond this discussion regarding logistical issues. Standard marketing textbooks remind the reader that all distribution functions must be performed, that none can be skipped. The use of intermediaries, or middlemen, is common in distribution requiring decisions about who will perform the various functions involved.

A. Channel Length and Intermediary Use

The distribution decisions must reflect the target market, product and service, competition, and organization characteristics. Distribution channels may be direct to the consumer, as is characteristic of various services, or they may be indirect often depending upon the use of intermediaries to move the product through the channel. Channel length refers to the number of intermediaries between the producer and consumer. Many direct channels (using no intermediaries) are used in health care delivery. Typical examples are primary care physician practices and home health care services. These types of examples stress the importance of service versus product characteristics in delivery planning to assure quality. Service production is simultaneous with consumption, thus, quality delivery is dependent upon those delivering the service and the interaction with the customer as previously discussed. Many health care industry distribution systems are indirect such as pharmaceutical, medical equipment or supply manufacturers using middlemen such as wholesalers or retailers to distribute their product. As many hospitals merge into complex corporate structures, delivery systems sometimes become longer with the provision of more diversified and distanced services.

The use of intermediaries requires the organization to determine the decision of "ownership," or who takes title to the product or service through its delivery system. Many intermediaries, like advertising agencies, are full service and provide all aspects of the distribution function including transporting, warehousing and inventory services, and retailing. They will also provide services including everything from packaging to promotions. Often these middlemen will take ownership of the product providing revenue to the manufacturing organization to reinvest in resources required for production. Many manufacturers use intermediaries just for this reason. They realize that their expertise is in the research, design, and production phases and have no desire to diversify into the distribution functions. A major disadvantage of intermediary use is the loss of control to varying degrees over the product or service. The tradeoff is, of course, the lack of responsibility over various functions ranging from shipping, to accounting, to retailing, or purchasing, etc. Whether full or limited service intermediaries are used, information should be gathered in determining their selection. Interviews should take place with current clients represented, and the firm's image should be examined as well as the quality and comparability of the current lines they represent. Their track record and financial condition should be assessed and the philosophical suitability should be considered. The selection of intermediaries should be viewed as a long-term relationship where they serve basically as an extension of the organization and are involved as much as possible to insure a successful relationship.

B. Distribution Intensity

One major decision, reflective of the customer market and competition, is the intensity, or extensiveness, of the distribution system. Three broad categories of distribution intensity are typically suggested: intensive distribution, selective distribution, and exclusive distribution. With intensive distribution, the product or service is available in many outlets to insure that the customer must exert very little effort to acquire the offering. Headache remedies would be a product example in this category. Many hospital associations are moving in this direction with satellite locations providing around-the-clock service and often more extensive services than the early acute care satellite service facilities. Heavy market penetration of ambulatory care services in many regions is rapidly changing the distribution character of health care. Selective distribution products and services are on a somewhat less available basis requiring some shopping around, and often resulting price comparison by consumers. This would be typical of many medical supply offerings to customers. Exclusive distribution provides the product or service on a limited basis in selective outlets and is typical of luxury products. Health care examples might include certain elite, specialized treatment facilities and offerings of higher-priced, specialized medical equipment often under the protection of patents.

Quite often, a service or product offering will be limited to a small geographical area, especially in its early introduction. As demand increases or as resources allow, the organization may want to expand the market coverage to city, county, state, national, or global distribution. Many products and services are introduced at a broad level. Broader, more intensive coverage requires a more intensive distribution network. This network can be provided by the organization, or as previously discussed, intermediaries can be used to facilitate the broad network. This decision requires consideration of the number and type of transporters (such as truck, air, rail, shipping, and inter modal), consideration of warehousing decisions (centralized or decentralized, private or public) and inventory implications, and specifications regarding retailing. Each of these components has time, cost, and location implications. Typically, the more intensive the system, the higher the likelihood that more intermediaries will be used. The length in time of the channel will typically be longer as well. As the channel lengthens and broadens, the organization must set up appropriate information systems to maintain data on the product/service tracking, competitive information, and customer feedback. Information systems management may be provided by the intermediary as well. Continuous feedback on product location, pricing, customer demand, and competitive movement is vital if the organization is to provide quality customer satisfaction and respond with necessary changes as market factors evolve.

C. Channel Control

As in other industries, the location of channel control must be determined in effective health care distribution management. The very nature of distribution systems sometimes encourages conflict. A set of independent organizations joined together, each with their own personality, financial needs, board of directors, and objectives often leads to problems. Members of the distribution channel must maintain the ultimate objective of the channel, customer satisfaction. Without this, the long run existence of the channel will be in danger. The establishment of channel leaders and specific channel member agreements, or contracts, is necessary to lessen the chance for conflict within the distribution channel. Several categories of channel systems have evolved over the years which should be considered in developing a new system or revising an old one. A corporate vertical marketing system places management of the system under one single corporate sponsorship. In this case, the corporation would largely manufacture and fully distribute the product maintaining all control. In health care, vertically integrated delivery systems are moving in this direction combining hospitals, physicians, insurers, and various other health care services under one umbrella. This system is similar to an administered vertical marketing system in which channel management is achieved by coordination through typically one member who is perceived as more powerful or carrying more weight in the system. Many HMO examples evolved around the United States in the 1980s via this method combining forward and backward integration. A third system, the contractual vertical marketing system, achieves channel agreement via contract. None of the members are necessarily larger or more powerful than others, yet the organizations desire to bind together at the same level to realize various benefits.

An additional type of system which is rapidly growing in health care is the franchise. Following in the steps of fast food, hair care, lodging, auto repair, and legal services, many areas of health care are discovering the benefits of a franchise. The franchiser receives a fee for providing the franchise opportunity to the franchisee. While franchise agreements vary, typical aspects included regard product/service specification, advertising agreements, facility design and maintenance, training, and pricing. Tight control over the franchise agreement by the franchiser is important in maintaining the value of the franchise. From the perspective of the franchisee, however, there is a need to have increasing control to tailor the franchise to the characteristics of the local or regional market.

The planning, implementation, and ongoing evaluation of the distribution channel is crucial to the health of the organization. This area of health care marketing is rapidly changing with increasing opportunities and threats as it evolves. Many health care organizations are experiencing mergers and acquisitions, and alliances, and many franchises are flourishing. Such organizations must be alert and responsive as health care industry structuring and regulation continues.

VII. HEALTH CARE PLANNING AND MONITORING

The ongoing analysis and planning of marketing strategies is vital for the long-term success of the health care organization. Constant monitoring of marketing activities and use of various measures will aid in the development and needed changes in the marketing planning process. Measures such as the overall industry market share, as well as market share indicators relative to major competitors, should be monitored on a planned basis. In addition, measures relating to the established goals, such as sales analysis, should be used. Profitability measures including contribution analysis of specific product/service lines will be useful in examining their ongoing performance and importance to the organization's portfolio over time. Analysis of the various marketing functions using measures, such as sales ratios, advertising recall and attitude change, analysis of efficiency of distribution costs, and inventory expenses, will be valuable.

Two major aspects of marketing operations analysis, the marketing audit and customer satisfaction measures are discussed below. Each of these is crucial to organizations in any industry but especially so in health care.

A. Customer Satisfaction

Customer satisfaction is central to health care operations. Previous discussions related to the varying types of customers and the importance of identifying their needs. Attention to both the internal, as well as the external customer in planning and measuring customer satisfaction is important. Market research can be utilized in this effort. Many organizations initially use focus groups to explore customer needs in general. Focus group feedback can provide the organization with rich information to aid in understanding the determinant attributes used by the customer in evaluating the products and services he or she receives. Focus groups usually consist of eight to fourteen participants and consist of a one to one and one-half hour discussion facilitated by a professional. It is wise to use more than one focus group in this phase of research and to make sure that the groups are reflective of the target market demographics. One major caution of focus groups is that they provide only qualitative information from a small sample of the population, and thus the information derived should not be extrapolated to the population at large. Information derived from focus groups is useful in developing a broader survey of the target population to provide needed quantitative data from a larger, reliable sample. The use of professionals in the development, implementation, and analysis of market research is suggested. It is often difficult for employees of the organization to be objective in developing research studies and instruments, and the reliability of the data derived is dependent on a well planned and executed study.

Market research topics to be used in gauging customer satisfaction differ dependent upon the target market and product or service. If a pharmaceutical organization is conducting research, it may be interested in data from physicians, pharmacists, insurance providers, and final customers (and even family members if the user is a child or a senior parent). Careful consideration of the aspects to be included in a survey could be gathered from focus groups. Are questions needed about the packaging, taste, form, color, instructions, side effects, costs, or safety? Since a hospital is concerned about patient satisfaction, research should target all aspects of the patient experience beginning with information obtained before admission, through the admissions process, interaction with all services and employees, food, environment, medical treatment, and the discharge process.

In health care research, continuous quality improvement encourages a process analysis orientation. Each service or product component will be examined as a process with the supplier and customer (internal or external) identified as well as the process needs and satisfiers of the customer. Focus groups and questionnaires, as well as objective measures, can be used to assess the effectiveness of each process. A number of quality tools exist for this purpose. The data derived from continuous quality improvement research is used by each department and cross-functional teams as a quality gauge in order to set standards and to measure continuous improvement. Benchmarks from other industries, as well as competitors, are also valuable in quality research. Increasingly, organizations are sharing information in efforts to improve their own quality and better understand customer satisfaction. More organizations are also benefiting from internal marketing efforts to improve service quality (Shank and Gilbert, 1993).

Central to customer satisfaction and quality improvement is the requirement that data be gathered and examined on a continuous basis. Goals should be set, for instance, based on data derived from one month or quarter for the next time period. At that point, performance is measured against the goals. If goals were not met, what can be derived from the data as related to problems? Possible focus groups or additional surveys might be developed to further probe special problem areas. Internal organizational feedback of quality progress data should be an integral component of the customer satisfaction plan. Employees should be aware of their progress and problem areas. Reward systems are often used to enhance quality performance.

B. The Marketing Audit

A marketing audit is a systematic review of the organization's entire marketing operations. It enables the organization to evaluate operations, objectives, policies and underlying philosophy and assumptions. The marketing audit is useful in identifying opportunities and weaknesses for the organization and pointing to areas in need of change. It addresses various aspects regarding the market and specific targets, the internal organization, products and services offered, direct and indirect competitors, the environment in which the organization operates (including legal, social, industrial, etc. ramifications), and the marketing functions: product planning, pricing, communications and distribution systems. A number of publications are available to assist in the planning and performance of the marketing audit (Berkowitz, 1996; Cooper, 1994; Kotler and Clarke, 1987). The marketing audit is a prerequisite step in the development of the marketing plan which includes the organization's mission and objectives, the marketing audit, the full development of the marketing functions, and the evaluation plan (Perreault and McCarthy, 1996).

SUMMARY

The health care marketing professional is facing new challenges today in an environment unlike that of the past. The professional now needs broad business skills and increasingly some health care background. Schools of business are beginning to offer health care marketing courses and marketing is an integral component of health care administration programs. The evolution of the health care industry has resulted in increased involvement of the health care marketing professional in continuous quality improvement and service development. This evolution, along with the increased cost and complexity of health care products and services, has placed greater responsibility on the professional. In addition, the need for timely and accurate information is greater today than ever before in health care. The role of market research is an important one for aiding decision making under uncertainty. The role of the health care marketer is more vital today than than ever before.

REFERENCES

Barton, L. (1993). Ethics, profit and patients: When pharmaceutical companies sponsor medical meetings. *Journal of Hospital Marketing, 9* (1): 71-82.

Bearden, W., Ingram, T., and Laforge, R. (1995). *Marketing: Principles and Perspectives,* Irwin, Chicago, IL: 104-151, 452-454.

Bennett, P. D. (1988). *Dictionary of Marketing Terms,* American Marketing Association, Chicago, IL: 54.

Berkowitz, E. N. (1996). *Essentials of Health Care Marketing,* Aspen Publishers, Inc., Gaithersburg, MD: 328-329, 383-378.

Bovee, C. and Arens, W. (1989). *Contemporary Advertising,* (3rd. ed.). Richard D. Irwin, Inc., Homewood, IL: 228-233.

Cokelez, S. and Peacock, E. (1993). A Modeling Approach to Hospital Location for Effective Marketing, *Journal of Hospital Marketing, 8*(1): 29-40.

Cooper, P. D. (1994). Health Care Marketing a Foundation for Managed Quality, (3rd. ed.), Aspen Publishers, Inc., Gathersburg, Md., 464-480. The Direct '92 Forecast, (1991), *Direct,* December, 23-29.

Hawes, J., Mast, K., and Swain, J. (1989). Trust earning perceptions of sellers and buyers. *Journal of Personal Selling and Sales Management, Spring:* 1-8.

Johnson, G. (1992). Knowledged-Based Marketing Adds Value to Mailing Lists, *Marketing News, January 20* (15): 18.

Kotler, P. and Clarke, R. (1987). *Marketing For Health Care Organizations,* Prentice Hall, Inc., Englewood Cliffs, NJ: 202-209.

Lautman, M. R. (1993). The ABCs of positioning. *Marketing Research: A Magazine of Management and Applications, Winter:* 12.

Levin, G. (1992). Database Draws Fevered Interest. *Advertising Age, June 8:* 31.

Lovelock, C. H. (1991). *Services Marketing,* (2nd ed.). Prentice Hall, Engelwood Cliffs, NJ: 7-8.

Mandese, J. and Donaton, S. (1992). Media, promotion gap to narrow. *Advertising Age, June 29:* 6.

Miaoulis, G. and Joby, J. (1992). A model for understanding benefit segmentation. *Preventive Health Care, Health Care Management Review, 7* (2): 21-32.

Perreault, W., Jr. and McCarthy, E. (1996). *Basic Marketing: A Global-Managerial Approach,* (12th ed.). Richard D. Irwin, Chicago, IL: 608-612.

Rogers, E. M. (1962). *Diffusion of Innovations,* (3rd ed.). Free Press of Glencoe, New York: 81-86.

Schramm, W. (Ed.). (1955). How communication works. *The Process and Effects of Mass Communication,* The University of Illinois Press, Urbana, IL: 3-26.

Shank, M. and Gilbert, F. (1993). An internal marketing approach to total service quality: A guide for practitioners. *Journal of Health Care Marketing, 8* (1): 113-130.

Simon, H. (1992). Pricing opportunities and how to exploit them. *Sloan Management Review, Winter:* 56.

Tellis, G. J. (1988). The price elasticity of selective demand: A meta-analysis of econometric models of sales. *Journal of Marketing Research, November:* 331-341.

42.

THE APPLICATION OF ORGANIZATIONAL THEORY AND BEHAVIOR

Bruce J. Fried, *The University of North Carolina at Chapel Hill, Chapel Hill, NC*

This chapter explores how organizational theory and behavior can be applied to enhance our understanding of healthcare organizations and management. The fields of organizational theory and behavior deal with issues from an individual employee's motivation and work behavior, to the behavior of large health care networks and health care systems. The goal of this chapter is to describe and to encourage further understanding of the field.

I. COMING TO TERMS WITH THEORY

Theories often connote abstract notions with little basis in reality. Used and applied appropriately, however, theories can be helpful in:
- diagnosing and understanding organizational problems
- designing and implementing interventions aimed at improving organizational, interorganizational, team, and individual effectiveness
- helping managers to learn from mistakes

Theories help us to appreciate the fact that not all behavior and phenomena are random; much behavior is in fact predictable where we are to understand and build upon the experiences of others. Theories suggest patterns, and if we understand those patterns, we may be able to engage in better decision-making and more effective managerial practices. This chapter explains how an understanding of organizational theory and behavior can be useful to managers in health care organizations. A sampling of major perspectives and schools of thought from organizational theory and behavior follow. Various organizational levels addressed by organizational theory and behavior are described with perspectives relevant to specific managerial and organizational challenges. A vignette provides an overview of how theory may be useful to managers. Theory provides a natural complement to the experiences of managers, and with those experiences, can help put the world of organizations and our experiences in those organizations in context.

A. A Brief History of Organizational Theory and Behavior

The objective of this section of the chapter is to provide an historical perspective on organizational theory and behavior. While this field has grown in many different directions over the past century, each stage of growth emerged out of a particular historical context. In most cases, social, economic, and political conditions had a major influence on the development of the field. Each stage of growth also made a new and lasting contribution to theory and to the practice of management. Many current approaches to management are rooted in concepts and theories developed decades ago.

Scott (1978) suggests that a useful way to describe the evolution of organizational theory and behavior is to consider two broad underlying conceptual dimensions. The first dimension reflects the idea that organizations are open systems that interact constantly with their environment. Prior to the 1960s, dominant views of organizations did not consider the external environment as a significant focus of attention; the organization was considered as essentially autonomous and independent of its environment. Later perspectives emphasized the importance of the external environment in influencing organizational goals, strategy, and design. This perspective provides the foundation for strategic planning. The second dimension concerns the issue of rationality. Earlier perspectives viewed organizations as mechanistic goal-directed entities that behaved entirely rationally in pursuit of a well-defined and measurable goal. Later perspectives viewed the organization in political and social terms. Because organizations are populated by and influenced by people (who are clearly not always rational), it is unlikely that organizations will always behave in a rational manner. This perspective accommodates a number of "nonrational" elements, including:

- Organizational goals and other key decisions are determined in a political environment in which conflicting forces, internal and external to the organization, compete for power and control.
- Social relationships, and not just hierarchical managerial controls, influence productivity and organizational effectiveness.
- Leadership skills may be differentiated from management skills; a well-managed organization may lack innovation and creativity because of the lack of effective leadership. An interesting study by Amabile links creativity at the individual level with innovation at the organizational level (Amabile, 1988).
- The formal organizational chart is an inaccurate and incomplete depiction of the manner in which work is really accomplished in an organization, the way in which communication occurs, and the manner in which power is distributed; much work gets accomplished and information communicated through informal channels.

Using these two dimensions, it is useful to divide the field of organizational theory and behavior into four chronological classifications:

1. The Closed System/Rational Model, emphasizing mechanical efficiency
2. The Closed System/Social Model, emphasizing people and human relations
3. The Open System/Rational Model, emphasizing contingency views of organizations
4. The Open System/Social Model, emphasizing power and political considerations

There is naturally some overlap between these models. This framework helps in identifying the unique contributions (and shortcomings) of each model. The central features of each of these models follow.

B. The Closed System/Rational Model (1900-1930)

This earliest attempt at formulating a theory of organizations emerged during the early days of the industrial revolution. North America and Europe were moving from agricultural and craft-based economies to urbanization and mass production. Factories were being established, and there was a dire need at the time to determine how best to organize for the new industrial society. Scientific management, exemplified by the publication in 1911 of Frederick Winslow Taylor's Principles of Scientific Management (Taylor, 1911), developed the belief that productivity could be greatly improved through the use of the scientific method. Emphasizing careful measurement and analysis of tasks and individual potential, Taylor proposed four principles of scientific management:

1. The replacement of rule-of-thumb methods for determining each element of a worker's job with scientific determination.
2. The scientific selection and training of workers.
3. The cooperation of management and labor to accomplish work objectives, in accordance with the scientific method.
4. A more equal division of responsibility between managers and workers, with the former doing the planning and supervising, and the latter doing the actual work.

While certain aspects of scientific management have been discredited because of their inattention to the human element, there are certainly vestiges of Taylorism to this day. Current operations research methods, including mathematical forecasting, inventory modeling, linear programming, queuing theory, and network models are the descendants of scientific management. Modern quality improvement and quality control methods, with their emphasis on measurement and process analysis and improvement, certainly have their roots in Taylor's approach to understanding production processes and the role of people in those processes. Industrial engineering and production management clearly have roots in scientific management. Scientific management also formed the basis for many current personnel practices, such as job design, job analysis, employee selection and placement procedures, and training programs. Although it may have been relevant to the relatively simple workplace of the early 1900s, his call for a strict distinction between managerial and worker roles is in many respects outdated today. As work has become increasingly complex and technologically sophisticated, and as professionals play a more pronounced role in organizations, there has emerged a strong need for lower level workers to become involved in problem-solving and decision-making—areas that previously were in the sole domain of managers and supervisors. Notwithstanding these shortcomings, there are some clear practical lessons for today's workplace that may be extracted from scientific management (Schermerhorn, 1993):

1. Use results-based compensation as a performance incentive.
2. Design jobs and work methods to maximize a person's performance potential.
3. Carefully select people—based on abilities—to do required jobs.
4. Train people to perform jobs according to task requirements and to the best of their abilities.
5. Provide workers with supervisory support, so they can best utilize their abilities to achieve high performance.

In the same vein as Taylor were the fourteen administrative principles developed by the Frenchman Henri Fayol (1916). It was proposed that these principles were universally applicable to all work situations. While many may seem intuitive today, in the early years of the century, they provided a framework for effective organization and management. These fourteen principles were:

1. Division of work: the need for specialization to increase employee efficiency and effectiveness.
2. Authority: the right of managers to give orders and the need to couple responsibility with requisite levels of authority.
3. The need for discipline.
4. Unity of command: employees should receive orders from only one superior.
5. Unity of direction: each group of activities should be directed by a single manager.
6. Subordination of individual interests to the organization's interests.
7. Fair remuneration for employees.
8. Centralization: the need to determine the appropriate balance between centralization and decentralization.
9. Scalar chain: lines of authority and communication flow clearly from top to bottom (lateral communication may be allowed under certain circumstances).
10. Order: people and materials should be in the right place at the right time.
11. Equity and fairness in the workplace.
12. Stability of personnel and avoiding turnover.
13. Initiative: encouraging employees to develop and implement plans.
14. The importance of esprit de corps.

Another major contributor to the development of administrative principles was Mary Parker Follett, who developed a deep commitment to human cooperation in her writings about business and organization (Follett, 1949). She viewed organizations as communities in which managers and workers could work together in harmony.

The German sociologist Max Weber defined the essential features of an effective organization. In his attempts to ameliorate many of the deficiencies in German government organizations, Weber argued that many people were placed in positions of authority not because of their job-related competencies, but because of their social status or "connections" in German society. He developed a new form of organization, the bureaucracy, based on the following principles (Weber, 1947):

1. Clear division of labor.
2. Well-defined hierarchy of authority.
3. Formal rules and procedures.
4. Impersonality: the application of rules in an impartial manner.
5. Hiring and promotion based on merit.

Numerous lessons may be drawn from the work of Fayol, Weber, and other early writers on organizations and management. While the term "bureaucracy" does not carry negative connotations, it should be understood that Weber's description of the ideal bureaucracy was in fact "pre-bureaucratic." In many countries, including the US., corruption and prejudice in hiring and other personnel practices were rampant. The bureaucracy seen by Weber was seen as an innovative cure for these excesses. In fact, while the Civil Service in the US. is today seen by many as a stifling and rigid bureaucracy, in its early days, the Civil Service represented substantial reform. Other insights from these early writers have great relevance today.

> Follett believed that making every employee an owner in the business would create feelings of collective responsibility. Today, we address the same issues under such labels as employee ownership, profit sharing, and gain-sharing plans. Second, she believed that business problems involve a wide variety of factors that must be considered in relationship to one another. Today, we talk about "systems" when describing the same phenomenon. And third, Follett believed that businesses were services, and that private profits should always be considered vis-à-vis the public good. Today, we pursue the same issues under the labels of managerial ethics and corporate social responsibility (Schermerhorn, 1993).

C. The Closed System/Social Model (1930-1960)

While the model described above views organizations largely as machines and humans as essential parts of the machine, the closed system/social model emphasized the human and social aspects of organizations. Often referred to as the human relations school, this model had its philosophical and empirical origins in the Hawthorne studies conducted at Western Electric Company's Hawthorne Works in Cicero, Illinois, between 1924 and 1927. This plant manufactured telephone relay equipment, which was tedious work requiring great concentration. These studies began as scientific management studies focusing on improving worker productivity by identifying the optimal intensity of illumination. Using experimental and control groups, illumination was varied. To the surprise of the researchers, very little association was found between illumination and productivity:

> The conditions of scientific experiment had apparently been fulfilled—experimental room, control room; changes introduced one at a time; all other conditions held steady. And the results were perplexing. . . . Lighting improved in the experimental room, production went up; but it rose also in the control room. The opposite of this: lighting diminished from 10 to 3 foot-candles in the experimental room, and the production again went up; simultaneously in the control room, with illumination constant, production also rose (Mayo, 1945).

The explanation for these findings was difficult to ascertain. Through later studies, it was concluded that a variety of other factors accounted for these strange results, among them being work group norms and expectations, and social relationships.

Perhaps of greatest importance, however, was the fact that these workers were made to feel important—they were given more information than usual and were asked for their opinions. In sum, they felt that they were being cared for by the organization. While there may have been some interest at the time in the humane treatment of workers, there is little evidence that worker productivity could be enhanced by having "happier" workers.

Later studies of this type came out with other interesting findings. In one study, it was found that under certain circumstances some employees would actually restrict their output to avoid group disapproval, even if it meant that their own pay might be in jeopardy. This confirmed the findings of the earlier Hawthorne studies: work group norms and relationships can have a profound impact on worker productivity, attitudes, and motivation. These early studies, while their research designs were not as technically strong as research carried out today, signaled a turning point in organizational theory and management practices. They initiated the perspective that using good human relations could improve productivity.

This line of research prompted many other writers and researchers to define those social and human factors that contribute to productivity. Much of this work was carried out after World War II, in which the allies had defeated fascist, dictatorial regimes. Democracy was popular, both in the international sphere and in the workplace, and the environment was conducive to writers who promoted and could prove that humanistic and participative management was effective in promoting organizational effectiveness.

Abraham Maslow played an important role in reinforcing the importance of the human relations approach. The basic thesis of his and other "need theorists" is that managers who attend to and satisfy human needs will see increased productivity (Maslow, 1970). In other words, productivity could be enhanced to the extent that basic human needs could be met in the workplace.

Douglas McGregor made an important contribution to organizational theory through his distinction between "Theory X" and "Theory Y" managers (McGregor, 1960). Using this framework, he concluded that these two types of managers hold very different assumptions about employees and the factors that affect their motivation. Theory X managers believe that employees by nature:

1. Dislike work.
2. Lack ambition.
3. Are irresponsible.
4. Are resistant to change.
5. Prefer to be led rather than to lead.

Theory Y managers, on the other hand, believe that most employees are:

1. Willing to work.
2. Willing to accept responsibility.
3. Capable of self-direction.
4. Capable of self-control.
5. Capable of imagination and creativity, and that the ability to make good decisions is not necessarily in the sole province of managers.

McGregor encouraged managers to adopt Theory Y principles. He contributed to the eagerness in the 1960s (and continuing to this day) for participative decision-making, the creation of challenging jobs, and the use of more delegation and job autonomy.

The Theory X/Theory Y dichotomy is still used as a simple way of distinguishing between management styles.

In sum, the Closed System/Social Model emphasized factors other than extrinsic rewards, such as pay, in determining job satisfaction, motivation, and performance. Emerging from this model is the idea that human needs and social relationships can have a profound impact on these issues, and that managers and supervisors need to be cognizant of the impact of their management style on their employees. Attention, however, still had not yet focused on the external environment of the organization, and the potential effects of this environment on all aspects of organizational life. It was in the early 1960s that the environment was first considered as a central essential element to consider in management.

D. The Open System/Rational Model (1960-1975)

Earlier approaches to the study of organizations—the mechanistic approach of the scientific management era and the social approach of the human relations school—each carried a certain dogma about the one "best way" to organize and manage. The principles offered by writers and researchers were generally universalistic prescriptions. As the field matured, evidence began to emerge that in fact it was necessary to study the conditions under which sometimes contradictory principles were applicable. For example, is there really one optimal span of control, or might this depend upon specific characteristics of the situation? Beginning the 1960s, the belief that "one-size-fits-all" was replaced by the idea of contingency. As stated simply by Galbraith (1973) and Scott (1981), contingency theory operates under the following three assumptions:

1. There is no one best way to organize.
2. Any way of organizing is not equally effective.
3. The best way to organize depends on the nature of the environment to which the organization must relate.

A central premise of contingency theory is that organizations whose internal features match the demands of the external environment will be able to adapt effectively to environmental changes and maximize their potential. This view of organizations has as its foundation the idea that organizations are open systems (Katz and Kahn, 1978). As open systems, organizations are in a continual state of exchange with their environments and subject to various levels of control by the environment (Pfeffer and Salancik, 1978). Being highly dependent upon their environments, a key task facing all organizations is survival; like life forms (a metaphor frequently used in systems theory), organizations must maintain a steady flow of needed resources into the organization (e.g., money, personnel, customers). Some writers have even defined organizational effectiveness as the ability of the organization to procure scarce resources from the environment (Yuchtman and Seashore, 1967).

In addition to the environment, the idea of contingency applies to other factors. The work of Woodward (1965), Perrow (1967), and the Aston group (Pugh, et al., 1969) in Great Britain suggests there is also a need for a match between organizational design and both the type of technology used by the organization and the size of the organization.

The contingency approach was in many respects the first analytic approach to organizational life. While it assumes a clear set of organizational goals and purposes, (i.e., it operates under assumptions of organizational rationality) its major premise is that there are alternative routes to achieving those goals. The optimal route is one that takes into consideration a host of factors internal and external to the organization. The contingency perspective was originally developed as a means of understanding organizational design. However, this idea has been extended into other areas of management, such as leadership style and motivation. For example, the Hersey-Blanchard situational leadership theory (Hersey and Blanchard, 1988) suggests that successful leaders modify their styles depending on the readiness of followers to perform in a given situation. Similarly, Vroom and Jago (1988) developed a highly structured model to help managers to decide when unilateral decision-making is preferable and when groups or other individuals need to be consulted and involved in decision-making. In this model, the contingency factors include such factors as the relative need for a high quality decision, the importance of subordinate commitment to a decision, the extent to which the leader has sufficient information with which to make a good decision, and the extent to which there is consensus among subordinates on organizational goals. While their model may be viewed as fairly rigid and mechanical, it is the philosophical underpinnings of their approach and other contingency perspectives that is most important. The fundamental challenges facing contingency theorists is to identify those factors that influence choice of strategy and to confirm, through research, the veracity of these factors.

Contingency theorists basically have an inherent belief in the ability of managers and organizations to define their own destiny. According to this view, with sufficient information about the environment and a good understanding of the organization's strengths and weaknesses, organizations are able to adapt their goals and strategies to changing circumstances. In sum, managers can make a difference in assuring the survival of their organization. This strategic choice approach (Chandler, 1962; Lawrence and Lorsch, 1967) is in marked contrast to the population ecology perspective that organizations are severely constrained in the ability to change (Aldrich, 1979; Hannan and Freeman, 1984):

> Certain inertial forces tend to preserve the status quo: investments in current goals, policies, people, technology, structures, and reward systems. These are costly to change, not only financially but psychically as well. People's careers and identities are often linked to preserving the status quo, particularly when the organization has enjoyed past success and has been rewarded for it. Sometimes just two or three key leaders with significant ego investment in preserving current directions are sufficient to create inertia (Shortell, Morrison, and Friedman, 1990).

A central principle in the population ecology perspective is that natural selection processes operate around organizations, and that the environment selects certain populations of organizations for survival and "deselects" others for extinction. Unless an organization can find an appropriate protective niche, it is ultimately vulnerable to environmental forces beyond the control of its leaders. While few managers subscribe to all of the tenets of the population ecology perspective, namely that managers ultimately do not and cannot decide on their own destiny, there are important lessons for managers. First, environmental assessment should not be a periodic process but one that is ongoing and continuous. The population ecology view certainly reinforces this basic requirement. Second, where rapid and dramatic environmental changes are forecasted, the organization must have a process to anticipate these changes and respond in an timely and appropriate manner. Organizations, of course, vary in whether they tend to be proactive or reactive in dealing with their environment. The Miles and Snow typology of organizational strategies (1978) suggests that organizations can be classified as prospectors, defenders, analyzers, or reactors, depending upon how they respond to changes in their environment. Third, it is sometimes possible for organizations to in fact influence and change their environments. This may be done on a micro-level through such strategies as co-optation of important stakeholders, or on a macro-level, using such strategies as vertical integration and mergers.

A final approach that may be classified under the open system/rational model is a view of organizations based on transaction-cost economics (Hesterly, et al., 1990; Williamson, 1975). This rational view of organizations assumes that organizations attempt to minimize transaction costs, which, put simply, refer to the cost of obtaining resources from the environment. These transaction costs become prohibitively high as the environment grows increasingly complex. At some point, organizations engage in "make vs. buy" decisions; that is, it may be more cost-effective for the organization to produce a particular good or service internally, rather than deal with acquiring those resources in an uncertainties marketplace. Thus, if a hospital or other health care organization is having difficulty procuring the services of primary care physicians, it may embark on a strategy of buying primary care practices and subsuming these physicians under a corporate umbrella. This strategy is becoming increasingly common for many health care organizations and may be explained at least in part by the desire of the organization to minimize the costs and uncertainties of transactions and assure that the organization has control over this critical resource. Vertical and horizontal integration strategies may also be explained through a transaction-cost approach. These approaches potentially lower transaction costs, in part by achieving economies of scope and scale.

E. The Open System/Social Model (1975 - Present)

The most recent stage of organizational theory and behavior continues with the open system perspective, but challenges the idea that organizations are necessarily rational entities. As noted earlier in the discussion of the home health agency, managers are not always able to identify optimal decisions. In the words of March and Simon (1958), organizations often "satisfice," implementing strategies or solutions to problems that satisfy organizational constraints. Because of time constraints and the costs of acquiring additional information, organizations are often in the situation of having to settle for the best, rather than the optimal strategy or solution. In a similar vein, the "garbage can" model of decision-making challenged the conventional wisdom that organizational decision-making is logical and sequential (Cohen, et al., 1972). According to this view, problem identification and problem solution may not be connected to each other. An idea may be proposed as a solution when no problem is specified. A problem may exist and never generate a solution. An ongoing problem may persist in an organization and never generate a solution. Organizations instead consist of independent streams consisting of (1) problems, (2) potential solutions (ideas that somebody proposes for adoption), (3) participants, and (4) choice opportunities (occasions when an organization makes a decision). The manner in which these four streams is largely random, leading to the following potential consequences:

1. Solutions may be proposed even when problems do not exist.
2. Choices are made without solving problems.
3. Problems may persist without being solved.
4. A few problems are solved.

Another approach that derives from the open system/social model is the institutional perspective. According to this view, when organizations are faced with high uncertainty, they often imitate other organizations in the same institutional environment. A hospital, for example, facing unprecedented changes in its market, may very well examine and mimic the behavior of its competitors or other hospitals operating in similar markets. The organization may, for example, decide to embark on a joint venture with physician groups, develop strategic alliances with other organizations, develop insurance products, or it may pursue any one of many other strategies that the organization believes to be associated with high performance. In sum, the organization may copy the structure, management techniques, and other organizations that appear to be successful. This view has achieved empirical and theoretical support in recent years (DiMaggio and Powell, 1983; Alexander and D'Aunno, 1990), and is certainly evidenced anecdotally by the frequent fads that cross the business and health care communities.

II. THE HOME HEALTH AGENCY: A BRIEF VIGNETTE

This vignette is presented in an effort to illustrate the variety of applications of organizational theory and behavior to real life problems in organizations and management. The purpose is not to present an exhaustive compendium of theories—that is the work of entire textbooks on organizational theory and behavior. Nor is it the intent to present theory as the answer to all managerial and organizational problems. Organizations are sufficiently complex that a single remedy for an organizational problem is rarely possible. Financial solutions, for example, always include an organizational component, whether this means a new method of compensating employees (this will likely affect employee motivation and job satisfaction) or implementing a new financial management computer program (among other things, this will require the need for organizations and people to adapt to change). This vignette seeks to sample the range of theories that may be used to shed light on organizational issues and to present these theories as diagnostic and strategic tools.

Consider the case of a growing home health organization that finds it increasingly difficult to communicate with employees who are growing more and more detached and alienated from the organization and finds that decision-making is becoming overly cumbersome and slow. What can organizational theory contribute to a diagnosis of this situation? Among the fundamental tenets of organizational theory is that organizations develop the need to decentralize when they reach sufficient size and complexity (Hage and Aiken, 1967). In this instance, organizational theory helps us to diagnose an organizational problem and plan effective interventions or organizational changes.

What may have appeared to be a simple problem may, in fact, have complex origins and complex solutions.

How might organizational theory help to implement interventions aimed at dealing with the situation described above? The issues described above indicates that the problems experienced by this organization may have been caused by an organization that had grown quite large in a relatively short period of time. It is likely as well that the organization had become more complex, possibly having to contend with new types of patients, a broader spectrum of reimbursement procedures, and new types of professional staff. Such a situation may lead to over-dependence upon top managers who became overloaded with decisions. Further, many of these decisions may have been beyond the knowledge and expertise of top managers. Thus, the quality of decisions may have become compromised because of the diversity of tasks in the organization. The rational organization, in these circumstances, might consider decentralizing, forming divisions based on geography, patient characteristics, or some alternative way of organizing. Given the need to decentralize, how should the home health agency go about the process of deciding upon an appropriate organizational design? Another body of organizational theory dealing with organizational change suggests that employee involvement in these deliberations may indeed prove helpful in developing a suitable organizational design and would maximize the probability that what changes are agreed upon would be accepted and implemented in a manner consistent with the intent of those planning the changes (Coch and French, 1948; Nutt, 1986). If managers select an implementation approach according to the demands of the situation, implementation success can be improved (Nutt, 1996).

Again considering the case of the home health agency, it is quite plausible that the organization may decentralize and divisionalize, developing smaller working groups. What should be the appropriate span of control, that is, the number of subordinates that an individual manager should supervise in these work groups? How much and what type of supervision would be required? Several bodies of literature suggest guidelines for addressing these questions. The literature on span of control suggests that the more complex and nonroutine the task, the greater the need for individuals to interact with supervisors, thus suggesting a smaller span of control (Woodward, 1965; Blau and Schoenherr, 1971; Collins and Hull, 1986). Similarly, more routine tasks typically require less supervision, particularly for highly-trained professional staff. The literature on professionals and professional organizations suggests that highly-trained individuals are capable of self-monitoring and require less oversight than other types of employees (Mintzberg, 1993; Greenwood, et al., 1993). A study on the relationships among leadership behaviors and employee productivity, job satisfaction, and organizational commitment has implications for managers in identifying critical skills needed by leaders (McNeese-Smith, 1996).

Once the decision has been made to decentralize the organization, key decisions have to be made about how staff in the organization should be grouped, how these various groupings (divisions or departments) should relate and communicate with each other, and how they should relate to senior management. A specific issue related to the latter concern is how to allocate decision-making responsibility between senior management and divisional staff. A very significant body of organizational theory— organizational design—speaks to these issues. The organizational design literature suggests that the external environment (Terreberry, 1968; Lawrence and Lorsch, 1967), the type of technology employed by the organization (Woodward, 1965; Bowen , et al., 1989; Leatt and Schneck, 1984), and the information processing needs of the organization (Nadler and Tushman, 1988; Galbraith, 1973; 1977) play key roles in determining an appropriate organizational design.

A major challenge facing organizations is how to differentiate its major functions, that is, on what basis should work groups or departments be formed? As noted earlier, a home health agency might organize itself by function (i.e., by professional group), geography, or patient category. The other challenge facing organizations is, once it has differentiated its various roles or functions, to integrate these functions so that the organization exists as a coherent whole rather than a fragmented group of people and departments (Lawrence and Lorsch, 1967). The organizational design literature suggests several prototype designs, including functional, divisional, matrix, and hybrid designs. Attention must be given to avoiding suboptimization of departments or groups at the expense of the organization's overall effectiveness.

Of primary importance in designing an organization is to consider how the organization should respond to its external environment. The external environment facing the home health agency would likely include the patient population, referral sources (physicians, hospitals, individuals), reimbursement organizations (insurance companies, managed care organizations), suppliers of equipment, potential staff, labor and professional organizations, and other home health agencies. This environment as well may be characterized along several dimensions, such as its degree of stability (that is, the extent to which it is likely to change) and level of complexity (or the dissimilarity of external elements) (Duncan, 1972).

For the home health agency under discussion, the external environment would likely be characterized as highly complex and unstable. Under these circumstances, the organization will need to attend to many different types of elements in the external environment, requiring a variety of skill requirements within the organization. If the particular organization is located in a typical urban or suburban market in the U.S., it is likely that aspects of the environment are highly unstable and prone to change. There may be new and different types of organizations paying for services, reimbursement schedules may be changing, and new competitors may be on the horizon. Typically, organizations make decisions about organizational design and consider organizing by professional discipline (e.g., nursing, speech therapy, physical therapy), geography, patient groupings, or some combination of these categories (e.g., matrix structures). Deciding upon the best organizational design for a particular decision is one that takes into consideration a variety of factors related to the environment, technology, size, and goals of the organization (Duncan, 1979).

The technologies employed by the organization, including technical equipment and communications technologies, are also changing. Technological advancements may permit new ways of treating and monitoring patients, which likely would affect the design of individual jobs. Communications technologies may affect the manner in which multidisciplinary teams are organized and the manner in which team members communicate and coordinate with each other and with personnel and organizations outside of the home health agency. For example, face-to-face meetings among team members may no longer be required to meet the information processing needs of the organization. With the use of cellular phones and other communication technologies, team members may in fact become members of several different "virtual teams."

These teams may be fluid in nature and could include individuals outside the formal boundaries of the home health agency. In sum, the technologies used by (and potentially available to) the organization may have a profound impact on the design of individual jobs, work teams, and the organization as a whole.

In considering the environment facing this home health agency, the organization may find that its environment and market have so markedly changed, that a change in mission and goals may be in order. The organization may engage in a strategic planning process, which clearly is a process that is informed by various aspects of organizational theory and behavior. In particular, strategic planning emphasizes environmental assessment and analyzing the organization's internal strengths and weaknesses. Out of this process comes a redefinition of organizational goals, an identification of strategic issues facing the organization, and a set of strategies to be pursued by the organization.

Organizational theory has devoted considerable attention to the problems inherent in identifying and gaining consensus on organizational mission and goals. For example, some of the leading theorists in the field have distinguished between official and operative goals (Perrow, 1961), identified the problems involved in achieving multiple and sometimes conflicting goals, and articulated the different purposes of goals (Thompson, 1967). March and Simon (1958) presented the notion of "satisficing." This perspective suggests that organizations do not always have the time and resources to discover optimal solutions to organizational problems or to achieve goals to their fullest extent; according to this view, goals simply act as constraints for the organization. An organization may be considered effective to the extent that it can satisfy, at least at some minimal level, these multiple goals or constraints. Still other theorists have considered goals as emerging from the interplay and influence of various internal and external constituencies, and that an organization's effectiveness may best be evaluated through the perceptions of and assessments by these key constituencies (Connolly, et al., 1980; Friedlander and Pickle, 1968; Tsui, 1990; Fried and Worthington, 1995).

For the home health agency considering a review and possible reformulation of organizational goals, these perspectives on goals would prove quite helpful. Effective managers, for example, realize that goals serve many purposes above and beyond the assessment of organizational effectiveness. Goals help gain legitimacy for the organization, establish guidelines for decisionmaking, provide guidance for employees and supervisors, and help to establish individual performance expectations. An understanding of organizational theory would also reinforce the idea that consensus on goals is highly desirable but not always easily attainable. In conducting a strategic planning process, we might find the home health agency identifying its major stakeholders and customers and involving them in the process of formulating goals and priorities. Where multiple and conflicting goals emerge, the organization may have to consider alternative ways of satisfying these goals, such as satisficing and perhaps sequential attention to goals. Also impacting considerations in this area is the fit between the organization and its employees and their goals (Cable and Judge, 1996).

Managing a strategic planning process also requires careful attention to issues of group process, consensus-building, and managing multiple and sometimes competing agendas. Important contributions to team management have come from organizational theory and behavior (Fried and Rundall, 1994). An understanding of group and team processes, and the dynamics of conducting meetings, are essential managerial skills. Health care organizations may also need to develop diversity management programs (Wallace, 1996).

A key part of the home health agency's strategy may be the development or reinforcement of interorganizational relationships. For example, the agency may have contractual relationships with referral sources and informal relationships with other organizations. The agency may, in fact, already be part of a vertically integrated health care system or strategic alliance, or may be considering such an interorganizational arrangement. An important subset of organizational theory, particularly relevant to policy and management in today's health care sector, is devoted to understanding interorganizational relationships (Sofaer and Myrtle, 1991). This body of theory addresses such questions as:

- Under what circumstances are interorganizational relationships among organizations successful?
- What are the predictable stages of development in interorganizational relationships?
- What are the facilitating and inhibiting factors in the development of interorganizational relationship?
- What are the costs and benefits of interaction among organizations?
- Are voluntary interorganizational relationships more effective than mandated interorganizational relationships?
- How mechanisms can be used to evaluate the effectiveness of interorganizational relationships?

The study of interorganizational relationships goes back to at least 1961 with early studies of voluntary cooperation among community service agencies (Levine and White, 1961). The field has become increasingly complex in recent years with the emergence of a broad range of interorganizational relationships ranging from tightly coupled arrangements to looser voluntary relationships. Health services researchers have examined a variety of these organizational forms, including voluntary consortia (Provan, 1984); hospital-physician organizations and other types of relationships (Shortell, 1991); strategic alliances (Zuckerman and Kaluzny, 1991); hospital alliances (Zuckerman and D'Aunno, 1990); hospital mergers (Starkweather, 1981); multihospital systems (Longest, 1990); various types of health provider networks, a number of different contractual relationships, and community support networks for individuals with chronic diseases (Morrissey, 1992; Fried, et al., in press).

In sum, a number of lessons from organizational theory and behavior would prove quite useful to this home health agency in its struggle to adapt to a changing environment.

III. CONCLUSION: LEVELS OF ANALYSIS IN ORGANIZATIONAL THEORY AND BEHAVIOR

This chapter has explored through an historical review, a case example, and the breadth of work encompassed in the field of organizational theory and behavior. What are the domains covered by this field? While the distinction between organizational theory and organizational behavior is sometimes blurred, it is useful to differentiate between the two so that the diverse disciplinary roots in this field can be appreciated. Organizational theory tends to focus on the behavior of health care organizations, while organizational behavior attempts to describe behavior in health care organizations. Organizational theory has its roots in the disciplines of sociology, economics, and political science. Analysis in organizational theory usually focuses on one or more of the following levels and the interactions among these levels:

- The external environment, including issues of environmental change.
- Populations of organizations, including the study of whole groups of like organizations.
- Organizational systems, including the health system as a whole and health care systems.
- Interorganizational relationships and networks, including a broad range of interorganizational structures, processes, behaviors, and interorganizational conflict.
- Organizational strategy, including its relationships with the environment and organizational structure.
- Organizational design, including various types of organizational designs, coordinating mechanisms, the manner in which design is influenced by the environment, and the organization's strategy.
- Power and control in and around organizations.
- Organizational culture.
- Organizational subunit relationships, including interdepartmental relationships.

Organizational behavior has its intellectual roots in psychology, social psychology, group process, and industrial psychology. The levels of analysis common in organizational behavior include:

- The individual, including issues of motivation, job satisfaction, stress, and burnout.
- The work group and team, including issues related to team effectiveness and stages of group development.
- Conflict, including various sources and types of conflict, conflict resolution, and negotiations.
- Leadership and leader behavior.
- Role relationships, role conflict, and the behavior of professionals in organizations.
- Communication.

Work being done at the meso level between macro and micro levels is concerned with the integration of the two approaches. "The distinguishing feature of organizational phenomenon is that processes at several levels of analysis are in some way linked" (House, Rousseau, and Thomas-Hunt, 1995, p. 73). The resulting linkages and relationships have great potential for providing better understanding of organizations by explaining behavior within structural properties of the organization and in so doing enriching analysis of individual factors (Pfeffer, 1991, p. 793).

As indicated by the breadth of theories and perspectives summarized in this chapter, organizational theory and behavior contributes to our understanding of organizations on multiple levels. Much of what we know about organizations is in a highly theoretical stage, although in the last 15 years, researchers have become increasingly sophisticated in their research methods. Much theory in earlier years was unverifiable and often simplistic; with the attention given to well designed studies, measurement, and analysis, there is now a substantial amount of empirical literature in this field. Perhaps the most important overall finding is that organizations are not nearly as simple as they were earlier believed to be. The often superficial "proverbs" of management no longer have the appeal that they once had; organizations are, after all, created, populated, and managed by people, and as such, will always be as complex and unpredictable as humans tend to be.

REFERENCES

Aldrich, H. (1979). *Organization and Environments*. Prentice-Hall, Englewood Cliffs, NJ.

Alexander, J. A. and D'Aunno, T. A. (1990). Transformation of institutional environments: perspectives on the corporatization of U.S. health care. In S.M. Mick and Associates, *Innovations in Health Care Delivery: Insights for Organization Theory*. Jossey-Bass, San Francisco.

Amabile, T. M. A model of creativity and innovation in organizations. *Research in Organizational Behavior, 10*: 123-67.

Blau, P. M. and Schoenherr, R. A. (1971). *The Structure of Organizations*. Basic Books, New York.

Bowen, D. E., Siehl, C., and Schneider, B. (1989). A framework for analyzing customer service organizations in manufacturing. *Academy of Management Review 14*: 79-95.

Cable, D. M. and Judge, T. A. (1996). Person-organization fit, job choice decisions and organization entry. *Organizational Behavior and Human Decision Processes 67(3)*: 294-311.

Chandler, A. D. (1962). *Strategy and Structure: Chapters in the History of the Industrial Enterprise*. MIT Press, Cambridge, MA.

Coch, L. and French, J. R. P. (1948). Overcoming resistance to change. *Human Relations, 1*: 512-32.

Cohen, M. D., March, J. G., and Olsen, J. P. (1972). A garbage can model of organizational choice. *Administrative Science Quarterly, 17*: 1-25.

Collins, P. D. and Hull, F. (1986). Technology and span of control: Woodward revisited. *Journal of Management Studies 23*: 143-64.

Connolly, T., Conlon, E. J., and Deutsch, S. J. (1980). Organizational effectiveness: a multiple-constituency approach. *Academy of Management Review, 5*: 211-17.

DiMaggio, P .J. and Powell, W. W. (1983). The iron cage revisited: Institutional isomorphism and collective rationality in organizational fields. *American Sociological Review, 48*: 147-60.

Duncan, R. B. (1972). Characteristics of perceived environments and perceived environmental uncertainty. *Administrative Science Quarterly, 17*: 313-27.

Duncan, R. B. (1979). What is the right organization structure? Decision tree analysis provides the answer. *Organizational Dynamics, Winter*: 59-80.

Fayol, H. (1916). *Administration Industrielle et Generale*. Dunod, Paris.

Follett, M. P. (1949). *Freedom and Coordination*. Management Publications Trust, London.

Fried, B. J. and Rundall, T. G. (1994). Managing groups and teams. In S. M. Shortell and A. D. Kaluzny, *Health Care Management: Organization Design and Behavior, 3rd ed.* Delmar, Albany, NY.

Fried, B. J. and Worthington, C. (1995). The multiconstituency approach to organizational performance assessment: a Canadian mental health system application. *Community Mental Health Journal 31(1)*: 11-24.

Fried, B. J., Johnsen, M. C., Calloway, M. O., Starrett, B. E., and Morrissey, J. P. An empirical assessment of rural community support networks for individuals with severe mental disorders. *Community Mental Health Journal*, in press.

Friedlander, F. and Pickle, H. (1968). Components of effectiveness in small organizations. *Administrative Science Quarterly 13*: 289-304.

Galbraith, J. R. (1973). *Designing Complex Organizations*. Addison-Wesley, Reading, MA.

Galbraith, J. R. (1977). *Organization Design*. Addison-Wesley, Reading, MA.

Hage, J. and Aiken, M. (1967). Relationship of centralization to other structural properties. *Administrative Science Quarterly 12*: 72-91.

Hannan, M. T. and Freeman, J. (1984). Structural inertia and organizational change. *American Sociological Review 49*: 149-64.

Hersey, P. and Blanchard, K. H. (1988). *Management and Organizational Behavior*. Prentice-Hall, Englewood Cliffs, NJ.

Hesterly, W. S., Liebeskind, J., and Zenger, T. R. (1990). Organizational economics: an impending revolution in organization theory? *Academy of Management Review 15*: 402-20.

House, R., Rousseau, D. M., and Thomas-Hunt, M. (1995). The Meso Paradigm: a framework for the integration of micro and macro organizational behavior. *Research in Organizational Behavior, 17*: 71-114.

Katz, D. and Kahn, R. L. (1978). *The Social Psychology of Organizations, 2nd ed.* Wiley, New York.

Lawrence, P. and Lorsch, J. (1967). *The Organization and Its Environment.* Harvard University Press, Cambridge, MA.

Leatt, P. and Schneck, R. (1984). Criteria for grouping nursing subunits in hospitals. *Academy of Management Journal, 27*: 150-65.

Levine, S. and White, P. E. (1961). Exchange as a conceptual framework for the study of interorganizational relationships. *Administrative Science Quarterly, 5*: 583-601.

Longest, Jr., B .B. (1990). Interorganizational linkages in the health care sector. *Health Care Management Review, 15(1)*: 17-28.

March, J. G. and Simon, H. A. (1958). *Organizations.* Wiley, New York.

Maslow, A. H. (1970). *Motivation and Personality, 2nd ed.* Harper and Row, New York.

Mayo, E. (1945). *The Social Problems of an Industrial Civilization.* Graduate School of Business Administration, Harvard University, Boston.

McGregor, D. (1960). *The Human Side of Enterprise.* McGraw-Hill, New York.

McNeese-Smith, D. (1996). Increasing employee productivity, job satisfaction, and organizational commitment. *Hospital and Health Services Administration 41(2)*: 160-75.

Miles, R. E. and Snow, C. C. (1978). *Organization Strategy, Structure, and Process.* McGraw-Hill, New York.

Mintzberg, H. (1993). *Structure in Fives: Designing Effective Organizations.* Prentice-Hall, Englewood Cliffs, NJ.

Morrissey J. P. (1992). An interorganizational network approach to evaluating children's mental health service systems. In L. Bickman and D.J. Rog, eds., *Evaluating Mental Health Services for Children.* Jossey-Bass, San Francisco.

Nadler, D. and Tushman, M. (1988). *Strategic Organization Design.* Scott Foresman, Glenview, IL.

Nutt, P. C. (1986). Tactics of implementation. *Academy of Management Journal, 29(2)*: 230-61.

Nutt, P .C. (1996). Views of implementation approaches by top managers in health service organizations. *Hospital and Health Services Administration, 41(2)*: 176-96

Perrow, C. (1961). The analysis of goals in complex organizations. *American Sociological Review, 26*: 854-66.

Pfeffer, J. (1991). Organizational theory and structural perspectives on management. *Journal of Management, 17(4)*: 789-803.

Pfeffer, J. and Salancik, G. R. (1978). *The External Control of Organizations: A Resource Dependence Perspective.* Harper and Row, New York.

Provan, K. G. (1984). Interorganizational cooperation and decision making in a consortium multihospital system. *Academy of Management Review, 9*: 494-504.

Pugh, D. S., Hickson, D. J., Hinings, C. R., and Turner, C. (1969). The context of organizational structures. *Administrative Science Quarterly, 14*: 91-114.

Schermerhorn, Jr., J. R. (1993). *Management for Productivity, Fourth Edition.* John Wiley and Sons, New York.

Scott, W. R. (1978), Theoretical perspectives. In M.W. Meyer, *Environments and Organizations.* Jossey-Bass, San Francisco: 21-8.

Scott, W. R. (1981). *Organizations: Rational, Natural, and Open Systems, 2nd ed.* Prentice-Hall, Englewood Cliffs, NJ.

Shortell, S. M. (1991). *Effective Hospital-Physician Relationships.* Health Administration Press, Ann Arbor, MI.

Shortell, S. M., Morrison, E. M., and Friedman, B. (1990). *Strategic Choices for America's Hospitals: Managing Change in Turbulent Times.* Jossey-Bass, San Francisco.

Sofaer, S. and Myrtle, R. C. (1991). Interorganizational theory and research: Implications for health care management, policy, and research. *Medical Care Review, 48:* 371-409.

Starkweather, D. B. (1981). *Hospital Mergers in the Making.* Health Administration Press, Ann Arbor, MI.

Taylor, F. W. (1911). *The Principles of Scientific Management.* Harper and Row, New York.

Terreberry, S. (1968). The evolution of organizational environments. *Administrative Science Quarterly, 12:* 590-613.

Thompson, J. D. (1967). *Organizations in Action.* McGraw-Hill, New York.

Tsui, A. S. (1990). A multiple-constituency model of effectiveness: An empirical examination at the human resource subunit level. *Administrative Science Quarterly, 35:* 458-83.

Vroom, V. H. and Jago, A. G. (1988). *The New Leadership: Managing Participation in Organizations.* Prentice-Hall, Englewood Cliffs, NJ.

Wallace, P. E. (1996). Managing Diversity: A Senior Management Perspective. *Hospital and Health Services Administration, 41(1):* 91-104.

Weber, M. (1947). *The Theory of Social and Economic Organizations,* ed., Talcott Parsons, trans. A.M. Henderson and Talcott Parsons. Free Press, New York.

Williamson, O. E. (1975). *Markets and Hierarchies: Analysis and Antitrust Implications.* Free Press, New York.

Woodward, J. (1965). *Industrial Organization: Theory and Practice.* Oxford University Press, London.

Yuchtman, E., and Seashore, S. (1967). A system resource approach to organizational effectiveness. *American Sociological Review, 32:* 891-903.

Zuckerman H. S. and D'Aunno, T. A. (1990). Hospital alliances: cooperative strategy in a competitive environment. *Health Care Management Review, 15(2):* 21-30.

Zuckerman H. and Kaluzny, A. D. (1991). The management of strategic alliances in health services. *Frontiers of Health Services Management 7(5):* 3-23.

43.

GOVERNING HOSPITALS, MEDICAL GROUPS AND SYSTEMS

Grant T. Savage, *Texas Tech University, Lubbock, TX*

Rosemary L. Taylor, *Texas Tech University Health Sciences Center, Lubbock, TX*

Governance has been defined as "the making or not making of important decisions and the related distribution of authority and legitimacy to make decisions" (Kovner, 1990, p. 4). Another definition of governance is "the fulfillment of responsible ownership on behalf of the community" (Umbdenstock, Hageman and Amundson, 1990, p. 484). From a stakeholder perspective (Blair and Fottler, 1990), these definitions suggest that the two major governance problems facing health care organizations are (1) the coordination of internal stakeholder interests and (2) the meeting of social responsibilities to a growing number of external stakeholders.

I. STAKEHOLDERS AND THE GOVERNANCE OF HEALTH CARE ORGANIZATIONS

All health care organizations have stakeholders (Blair and Fottler, 1990). A growing body of literature focuses on identifying key organizational stakeholders and analyzing ways to manage them (Mason and Mitroff, 1981; Mitroff, 1983; Freeman, 1984; MacMillan and Jones, 1986; Näsi, 1995). One aspect of this academic interest involves linking stakeholder and strategic management (Freeman, 1984; Gray, 1989; Roberts and King, 1989; Blair and Fottler, 1990; Savage, Nix, Blair and Whitehead, 1991). Broadly speaking, stakeholders are those individuals, groups, or organizations who have a contractual, ethical, financial, and/or political interest (stake) in the decisions and actions of a particular organization. Stakeholders attempt to affect those actions in order to influence the direction of the organization so that it is consistent with meeting the needs and priorities (i.e., stakes) of the stakeholders.

An organization does not choose its own stakeholders. Instead, stakeholders, by necessity, choose to have particular stakes in the organization's decisions. A stakeholder's view of an organization and the supportive or threatening position it has on an organization's decisions are contingent upon the specific issue at hand. In other words, for each strategic decision, organizations typically face a diverse set of stakeholders with varied, and frequently conflicting, interests and goals. Balancing these competing interests is the basic problem of administration (Pfeffer and Salancik, 1978), and the ability to satisfy changing stakeholder preferences over time is arguably one way to assess organizational effectiveness (Zammuto, 1982).

A. External and Internal Stakeholders

Some stakeholders are internal to the organization (e.g., employees), some are on the interface between the organization and its environment (e.g., the board of directors, accreditation agencies), and some of them are external (e.g., suppliers, competitors). Stakeholders vary in their significance for, and potential to impact on, the strategic management process. On one hand, external stakeholders typically fall into three categories (Blair and Fottler, 1990): (1) those who provide inputs into the organization; (2) those who are competitors with the organization; and (3) those who have a special interest in the functioning of the organization. Directors and health care executives typically try to manage external stakeholders based on such criteria as the amount of mutual dependence between the stakeholder and the organization, the relative power of each party, the norms within the community, and the mission of the health care organization. On the other hand, internal stakeholders are those that operate almost entirely within the generally accepted "bounds" of the organization and typically include managers, health care professionals, and non-professional staff. Both directors and executives attempt to manage these internal stakeholders by providing sufficient inducements to gain continual contributions from these stakeholders (Blair and Fottler, 1990).

B. Strategic Implications of Stakeholders on Board Governance

Health care organizations do not face just one or a few stakeholders. Rather, health care directors and executives must learn to manage a portfolio of stakeholders. It is vital that the leaders of health care organizations see the strategic implications of these stakeholder portfolios. This strategic importance that stakeholders have on health care organizations must be understood by their governing boards. Each governing board faces the challenge of creating consistency and effectiveness in its relationships with stakeholders.

Figure 1 is a highly simplified stakeholder map of a health care organization. It shows only some of the complex array of organizations and other stakeholders that can influence a health care provider organization. Both day-to-day operations and strategic planning depend on the configuration of relationships the health care organization has with these stakeholders.

The health care organization is shown in the bolded rectangle in the center of Figure 1. The health care organization's stakeholders are shown in the two concentric circles. For simplicity, we have not cluttered the health care organization stakeholder map with every specific stakeholder. These unidentified stakeholders are, however,

Figure 1 - Health Care Stakeholders of an IDS/N

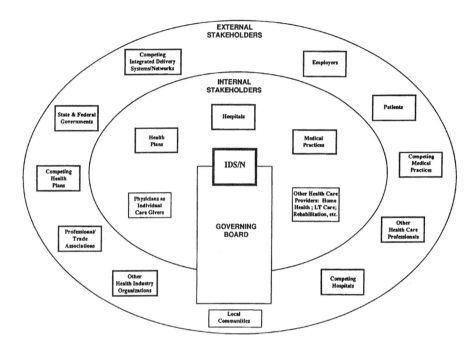

explicitly recognized as being crucial to health care organizations. The inner circle represents internal stakeholders of the health care organization. These include the health care professionals—e.g., physicians, nurses, pharmacists, dietitians, technicians—whose interests must be integrated in order for the organization to provide effective care. In addition, other employees—e.g., clerks, custodians, maintenance workers—are also acknowledged as being key internal stakeholders.

The outside concentric circle shows a select few of the many external stakeholders of an health care organization. These include patients, competing provider organizations (hospitals, medical groups), state and federal governments (as payers and regulators), employers and employer coalitions, and other health care organizations, such as pharmaceutical firms and medical equipment suppliers.

The rectangular box which transcends the health care organization and the internal and external stakeholders represents the governing board of the health care organization. This board, as depicted in Figure 1, is more than just an internal or external stakeholder. It is the glue that binds the health care organization together. A central thesis of this chapter is that the governing board must transcend all the different levels of stakeholders and must meet the primary needs of these myriad stakeholders. In articulating this theme, we believe the intricacies of governance can be better understood by examining governing boards in the past and looking at where governing boards will be headed in the future.

II. TRADITIONAL CONCERNS ABOUT HEALTH CARE GOVERNING BOARDS

During the nineteenth century, almost all health care organization governing boards were for community hospitals. A hospital governing board's value was in its ability to provide funding (Johnson, 1994). The hospital board was a place for citizens of the community who had wealth and influence (Ward, 1990), with trustees holding a special and powerful place in the organization and in the community (Coile, 1994). They saw their trusteeship as a civic obligation which was fulfilled by governing the hospital to serve the needs of the sick, the poor, and the community as a whole (Stoeckle and Reiser, 1992). Members of the board had authority over the hospital administration and staff. As such, they were directly involved in the detailed operation of hospitals, even making some decisions which would be considered to be strictly medical today (Mason, 1987).

   Due to the increasing complexity and legality of administrative and clinical functions during the twentieth century, the governing board's authority was superseded by physicians and administrative managers (Pointer and Ewell, 1995). However, court rulings in the 1970s found the hospital governing board to be legally accountable for the fiscal management and quality of services (Molinari, et. al., 1993). Because of both legal mandates and functional necessity, boards once again play a major part in health systems and hospitals, a part that is much more important and challenging than in the past (Pointer and Ewell, 1995).

III. FUNDAMENTALS OF GOVERNANCE

Effective health care organizations, according to Umbdenstock, Hageman and Amundson (1990), should have governing boards with the following foci:

- • A common working definition of governance,
- • A clearly defined mission with specific goals and objectives,
- • A well-planned decision-making process,
- • A board structure that is tailored to the priorities at hand, and
- • An information, reporting, and communication system that keeps priorities clearly in focus.

   While a common working definition of governance certainly is a point of contention for relationships between the board, the executive team of the health care organization, and its stakeholders, we submit that governance should encompass coordination of the legitimate interests of internal stakeholders with concern for the economic and social needs of external stakeholders. Based on this understanding of governance, we next discuss how the board's efficacy is affected by four key elements and processes: (1) mission statement; (2) decision-making process; (3) structure and function; and (4) information, reporting, and communication system.

A. Mission Statement

To function effectively, clear definitions of authority and accountability have to be established for the board, the top management team, the medical staff, and other health care professionals. Decisions can only be made and implemented properly if the behaviors of all areas of a health care organization (e.g., hospital, medical group, or health care system) are discussed and accepted in advance, making it possible for the board, top managers, and medical staff to know who is responsible for what.

In order to do this, there must be a statement of values or mission. Although very few boards actually have a shared mission (Axelrod, et al., 1994), it should be what focuses the organization on actions, defines the strategies that will help achieve goals, and creates discipline throughout the organization (Umbdenstock, Hageman and Amundson, 1990). A mission statement should envision what an organization can and should do; the goal should be to have everyone (including the board, managers, medical staff, employees, and community) understand and accept the mission statement (Mason, 1987).

B. Decision-Making Process

Routine, annual functions that must take place should be identified so meetings can be planned in advance. Planning relates not only to setting a calendar of meeting dates but also to making the schedule agree with the level of work that needs to be done. Committees should be set up in such a manner that they will have enough time to thoroughly research the area of concern in order to make the best recommendation to the board as a whole. Also, educational sessions need to be planned so that members can be brought up to date on issues and have an understanding of a subject before a key decision must be made. A governing board must constantly evaluate itself on how well its decision-making process is working, including whether plans were accomplished or if unplanned modifications were necessary (Umbdenstock et al., 1990).

C. Board Structure and Function

Traditionally, considerations about the board's structure and function focus on its size, composition (inside or outside directors), members' qualifications, members' continuing education, and members' compensation.

1. Board Size

Hospital boards were composed of an average of 20 in the early 1980s (Coile, 1991). Today, however, the trend is toward smaller boards, with the average board having approximately 14 members (Coile, 1991; Kovner, 1990; Pointer and Ewell, 1994). Smaller boards sometimes lead to more commitment on the part of each board member and to a more timely decision-making process. Smaller boards also tend to make riskier decisions, perhaps because fewer members and interests have to be taken into account when making decisions (Kovner, 1990).

2. Board Composition

A controversial way to assure the quality of governing boards is the recent move towards corporate and away from community boards. Also known as philanthropic boards, most community boards are large, consisting of members with diverse experience. They have few, if any, inside directors and very little management participation. In contrast, corporate boards are smal, and do not emphasize geographical representation or the representation of stakeholders. Rather, they include members who have health care backgrounds, experience in strategic planning, and other complex business skills and abilities (Axelrod et al., 1994). They also include inside directors such as physicians and top managers. Proponents of corporate boards argue that these few outside directors (i.e., business people) and many inside directors (i.e., physician leaders and top executives) make more effective decisions than do community boards.

3. Member Qualifications

The average age of most board members is 51 to 70 (Kovner, 1990; Coile, 1991). The qualifications of board members are, however, in a state of change. Traditionally, board members reflect the community they serve and help to form the public conscience for the health care organization. Each person brings a unique perspective to the board (Hodges, 1993). Many trustees have joined boards because they want to contribute their experience and expertise to the community (Zimmerman, 1991). Usually they are business and professional leaders in a hospital's service area (Rosenthal, Doemland and Parisella, 1991), with 37% having business backgrounds (Coile, 1991). However, most governing board members do not have health care training and experience (Rosenthal et al., 1991), and they have much to learn to be able to adequately govern such complex organizations. There is much evidence that other knowledge, skills and talents are needed on boards today (Hash, 1989), including administration, financial management, marketing, fund raising, regulatory oversight, and acute medical and long-term care (Rosenthal et al., 1991). The majority of board members also have never had actual board experience, so they need to be trained in the practices of governance itself (Selbst, 1994). One solution to solving this problem is by requiring continuing education for board members.

4. Continuing Education

Orientation and education programs can increase board effectiveness. In fact, hospital governing boards are presently held to such a high standard of accountability that board education is a very important part of hospital governance. Three things have brought about this need for board education in hospitals: (1) the Accreditation Manual for Hospitals recommends continuing education for the board, (2) legal decisions which have held the board accountable require that the board be aware of internal and external hospital activities, and (3) environmental changes such as increased competition, quality assurance and cost containment require that directors be capable of making the necessary decisions and policies (Molinari et al., 1992).

5. *Compensation*

In addition to including those who are more qualified on boards, some argue that these members would generate better performance if they were compensated. Others are opposed to this concept, indicating that in the corporate world there are many paid board members who are not necessarily more effective (Axelrod et al., 1994). The majority of governing board members are not compensated, with smaller, investor-owned hospitals being more likely to compensate their board members (Coile, 1991). It is also thought that compensation must be tied to accountability in order to generate better performance. The crucial question with regard to the compensation of board members is whether an organization will get the best people available to really commit the necessary time and energy without compensation (Axelrod et al., 1994).

D. Information, Reporting, and Communication System

The focus on information, reporting and communication systems should be on quality, not quantity. Most governing boards receive so much information before board meetings that they cannot review it thoroughly. Improving the quality of information would include summary reports on priority issues and general developments, study sessions in advance of upcoming key decisions, more graphics, and retreats to assess the board's performance (Umbdenstock, Hageman, and Amundson, 1990).

IV. GOVERNANCE OF MEDICAL GROUPS

Especially in the Midwest, medical groups have had a distinguished history of successful practice and have been governed in a variety of ways (Madison, 1990). Depending upon whether they are a simple partnership, for-profit corporation, or not-for-profit entity, medical groups will tend to be governed in one of four basic patterns: (1) executive/managing partner, (2) democratic association, (3) executive board/committee, or (4) joint policy board with a physician management company. As Zinober (1991) notes, each of these patterns has its positive and negative aspects and will work more-or-less well under different conditions. In addition, during the past decade, medical practices have tried various governance mechanisms to create loose- to tightly-coupled alliances with other physician groups. In the following discussion, independent and quasi-independent group practice governance structures are briefly reviewed.

A. Independent Practice Governance Structures

Independent medical groups typically adopt one of three forms of governance: executive/managing partner, democratic association, or executive board/committee.

1. *Executive/Managing Partner*

For many small groups set up as partnerships, the selection of an executive or managing partner is the most expedient way to operate. This physician partner serves as a general manager and chief executive for the medical group, making all key decisions for the practice. While this physician executive may be assisted by other physicians or administrators, both policy and strategic decisions typically are made by this one individual in consultation with the other physician partners. Such governance arrangements allow the medical group to be as agile and entrepreneurial as the talent of the executive partner permits. The downside to this power is most apparent when the executive partner fails to adequately heed the interests of the other physician partners or stumbles in the marketplace because of overconfidence and a lack of business acumen.

2. Democratic Association

The democratic model also has appeal for some medical group partnerships or incorporated group practices. In this model, each physician partner or member participates in policy formulation and strategic decision making. As the size of the group increases, however, this form of governance becomes unwieldy unless the medical group has established a strong culture of democratic participation, has invested in physician leadership education, and has developed a separate administrative structure and staff for addressing all but the most critical strategic and policy concerns. In any size group, effective and shared physician leadership is essential for this form of governance. Typically, these leadership roles are informally enacted by physicians in small groups, while medium and large groups will have formally elected leadership roles such as president or chief executive, which are filled by physician members.

3. Executive Board/Committee

Larger group practices, either for legal reasons and/or operational efficiency, often adopt an executive board or committee model of governance, constituted by physicians and sometimes outside members. Note that the for-profit/not-for-profit status of the medical group has an important impact, with not-for-profit practices tending to have more community-oriented boards and for-profit practices tending to have more corporate-oriented boards. Multiple specialty groups will often have the specialties represented through a set number of board seats, with rotating elections. Regardless of whether the group is a single-specialty or multi-specialty, selection of the chairman of the board can occur in at least three ways. This selection may be based on a vote from all group practice members, on a vote from board members, or on rotation (e.g., every six months) among existing board members.

B. Quasi-Independent Practice Governance Structures

Increasingly, some medical groups—especially those that have been newly formed for negotiating leverage with managed care organizations, or are well-established and seeking capital, information system or management expertise—outsource some or most of the management of their practices (Mitka, 1996). While the types of physician management contracts vary widely, those contracts that allow the external partner to exercise tight fiscal and operational controls often abdicate considerable governance responsibilities to the physician management company (Zinober, 1991). However, medical groups can maintain considerable physician autonomy either by creating a joint policy board with representatives of the physician management company (Mitka, 1996) or by carefully circumscribing the policy responsibilities of both parties in the management contract agreement (Zinober, 1991). Note that these types of arrangements with a physician management company do not involve the purchase of the medical group's assets. Once that step is taken, the medical group has entered into the practical equivalent (if not legal equivalent) of an employee–employer relationship. Indeed, to avoid this entanglement and to gain strength through larger numbers, many medical groups have sought alliances with other group practices, with hospitals, or with integrated delivery systems/networks. Similar, if not more severe challenges face rural health care organizations.

V. GOVERNANCE IN A RURAL ENVIRONMENT

During 1990, more than 23% of the people in the United States lived in rural communities, representing approximately 60 million people (O'Hagan, 1991). In addition, half of all community hospitals and one fourth of all community hospital beds in the United States are located in rural areas (Moscovice et al., 1991). Rural hospitals, in particular, are often the first or second largest employer in a rural community. As such, they are also a major part of the infrastructure of a small rural community, providing a competitive edge over communities without a hospital (Berry and Seavey, 1994). Moreover, the involvement of physicians in governance has an overall positive effect on rural hospitals, adding administrative depth to the board. Rural physicians also have more incentive to participate in governance and policy making since they have few alternative sources of inpatient care (Kralewski, 1993).

A. The Rural Environment

Although rural communities may seem tranquil, this impression often is deceptive. Their small size facilitates greater informality, and this atmosphere often creates an impression of consensus when there is actually dissension over central issues (Straub and Walzer, 1992). Some rural communities are known to have relational discord among various parties (including difficulties between administrators and trustees or between trustees and community "agitators") that adversely affect local services. While these problems are not unique to rural health care, they can have a great impact on rural communities (Burke et al., 1994). There are few resources that board members or community leaders can access, and because the rural culture encourages "going it alone," some boards will not seek outside help.

Many rural hospitals were constructed as social enterprises to serve the "public interest" with funds provided by the Hill-Burton program (Hospital Survey and Construction Act of 1946). Later, the retrospective reimbursement system initially established in the Medicare program, provided payments that helped fund health care and capital improvements in rural areas. However, changes to prospective reimbursement, prospective approval of procedures by other third party payors, and the reliance on competition to help alleviate the health care cost problems have led to changes in the ground rules for success (Berry and Seavey, 1994). Rural hospitals now face pressures such as cost containment and demands for capital and the acquisition of new technology (Moscovice et al., 1991). As a result of this turbulent environment, rural hospitals are struggling to survive (Bell and Bell, 1991).

B. Challenges to Effective Rural Governance

The fundamentals of governance should apply to rural areas just as they apply to other health care organizations. Most rural health care governing boards are composed of those who, like trustees in larger institutions, have been appointed to or elected to boards because of their desire to contribute to the community.

Because of the current environment, the need for local leadership is critical for health care in rural communities (Moscovice, 1989). A survey of physicians' perspectives on the causes of rural hospital closure from 1980 to 1988 showed inadequate hospital board leadership and planning to be one of the major causes (Pirani, Hart and Rosenblatt, 1993). Many leaders of rural health perceive that the weak link in rural health is the governing board. Amundson (1993) lists some of the following reasons for these views:

- Many still do not use strategic planning in order to focus on key goals and threats,
- Many boards do not know that a body of knowledge of board responsibilities and functions even exists, much less practice them,
- The conduct of meetings is inefficient and unfocused, not based on institutional issues they must face,
- There is little, if any, systematic and effective feedback to the chief operating officer (CEO) or to the board itself.

Several factors might cause these problems, but the primary reason is that most small, rural areas do not have a large pool of talented, business-oriented citizens to fill board memberships (Alexander, 1990). There are not many volunteers in these areas who have had an opportunity to manage or govern an organization as complex as a hospital or a network of clinics, nursing homes, and home health care providers. This low level of first-hand experience in health care policy and governance makes it hard for management to focus the board's attention on basic responsibilities; also, much time must be spent educating the board, leaving less time for the board to do its work (Umbdenstock, Hageman, and Amundson, 1990). As discussed previously, many of these same problems are also weaknesses of larger, urban governing boards. Clearly, more emphasis should be placed on educating and training board members. Indeed, those rural health care organizations that have remained stable and strong usually are characterized by a high-quality local leadership, a willingness to face community weaknesses, an acceptance of outside help, and a tendency to develop regional partnerships and linkages (Amundson, 1993; Burke et al., 1994).

C. Affiliations and Networks

Even though some rural (and urban) health care organizations would like to deny it, many experts now believe the future of the independent, free-standing community hospital is limited unless the hospital joins other hospitals in a network or forges some other type of affiliation (Blair, Fottler, Paolino, and Rotarius, 1995). Specifically, health care industry experts predict that by 1999 only 5% of all hospitals will be free-standing (Rotarius, Paolino, McMurrough, Fottler and Blair, 1995). The independent hospital does not have the size or economic strength to become a substantial player in a managed care environment (Shortell et al., 1994). However, if the hospital joins a network that is large enough to create significant bargaining power with managed care organizations and other third-party payers, the chances for survival are better for all members of the network (Johnson, 1994). The other alternative, creating an integrated health delivery system, also has been a successful way for rural hospitals to survive (Gamm et al., 1996).

By 1990, over one-third of all rural hospitals had entered into alliances of some type with multihospital systems, being either owned, leased or contract managed by the systems (Christianson et al., 1990). As Brown and McCool (1994) note, these alliances benefit rural hospitals because of several advantages of scale:

- economy—the ability to achieve lower input costs;
- efficiency—the ability to select inputs and organize the work to achieve lower output costs; and
- opportunity—the ability to generate new ideas and attract new business because of the strength of existing services.

Rural health care organizations belonging to loosely coupled networks also benefit from managerial expertise provided by other members of the network (Gamm et al., 1996). Not surprisingly, the urban hospital systems see these alliances as opportunities to increase tertiary referrals and market penetration and consider this the return for their investments (Savage et al., 1992).

Nonetheless, the primary difficulty rural health care organizations have to joining an affiliation or network is a fear of loss of control. Because of the strong linkages between local governing boards, medical staffs, and hospitals in rural areas, giving up even a small amount of autonomy to outsiders can cause many internal power conflicts. These community stakeholders are more oriented to competitive strategies and are very hesitant to support strategies that reduce the autonomy and visibility of their hospital. This local resistance is especially important for rural hospitals to consider since they are usually a major player in the local economy (Kralewski et al., 1993).

VI. INTEGRATED SYSTEMS BRING CHANGES IN GOVERNANCE

Cost containment pressures from managed care organizations (Shortell, Gillies and Anderson, 1994), current and proposed changes in Medicare and Medicaid funding (Savage and Purtell, 1995; Savage, Purtell, Friedman, Cochran and Moorman, 1996) and the development of network alliances and integrated health care delivery systems are among the key challenges of this decade (Blair, Fottler, Paolino and Rotarius, 1995). Innovative governance structures that are responsive to internal and external stakeholder needs are extraordinarily important as health care organizations join together to form integrated delivery systems/networks (IDS/Ns). As previously discussed, the recent growth of affiliations and alliances between rural and urban hospitals illustrates some of the ramifications of these changes. Generally, these changes have had the effect of making the health care environments in which governing boards must function more uncertain, more complex, and more challenging.

To adapt to this new situation, new strategies and structures have been devised. These structures, which include horizontal and vertical integration, joint ventures, and IDS/Ns, have made governance and decision making even more difficult (Alexander and Zuckerman, 1989). IDS/Ns are complex, multi-faceted organizations which are growing in importance in the turbulent health care industry (Rotarius, Paolino, McMurrough, Fottler, and Blair, 1995). They typically have organization structures which vertically integrate medical group practices, physicians, hospitals, and health plans, such as managed care organizations, in order to provide a coordinated continuum of health services for a defined population. This health care organization often is willing to be held clinically and financially accountable for the outcomes and health status of the population served (Shortell, Gillies, Anderson, Mitchell, and Morgan, 1993). A key principle of IDS/Ns is the alignment of incentives to encourage cooperation rather than adversarial relationships between physicians, hospitals and health plans (Coddington, Moore, and Fischer, 1993; 1994).

As soon as a health care organization enters into an IDS/Ns for the delivery or financing of a continuum of health services (including prevention, primary and acute care, long-term care, and rehabilitation), the governing body is accountable to a larger population for a longer period with an ever-increasing emphasis on cost-effectiveness (Conrad, 1990). The major responsibilities of the governing board do not change materially, but even a greater amount of time must be spent to assure quality decision making, with the emphasis being on risk taking and a more bottom-line, results-oriented approach (Alexander and Zuckerman, 1989; Coile, 1994). At the same time, the future success of an IDS/N also brings new scrutiny to its provision of health care to the community. Many IDS/Ns have the potential to become monopolies or oligopolies. As Thomas Weil (1996) has suggested, under these circumstances "utility regulation" of health care organizations and health plans is a distinct possibility. External stakeholders, in this case, may press for socially responsible outcomes from the IDS/N via regulation. Hence, effective governance that balances internal with external stakeholders' interests is even more important in IDS/Ns than it has been in the past.

Although the concept and practice of vertical integration across the continuum of care was articulated in the mid-1960s (Toomey, 1996), many of the IDS/Ns formed in the past few years are not yet well understood. In fact, there are still only a few systems that might be considered completely integrated (Devers, Shortell, Gillies, Anderson, Mitchell, and Erickson, 1994; Zuckerman, 1995). Currently, most efforts at integration consist of stand-alone hospitals, large medical groups, insurance companies, or multihospital systems seeking to align themselves through contracts, joint ventures, or other loosely coupled means (Blair, Fottler, Paolino, and Rotarius, 1995). According to Zuckerman (1995), some of the many barriers to integration include:

- Lack of trust among key constituencies
- Insufficient understanding about the changing environment and issues affecting health care organizations
- Emphasis on institutions and autonomy
- Lack of a system perspective
- Ambiguity about roles, responsibilities, relationships, and accountabilities
- Resistance to change.

As entities overcome these barriers and affiliate with each other and with other types of organizations to become true integrated health care delivery systems, they will have to change continuously. In addition, this multitude of changes and the complex issues that must be faced in making these changes will demand that new governance forms be created along the way (Pointer, Alexander, and Zuckerman, 1995). The structure and form of governance is usually put into place after handling what seem to be the more immediate problems and issues that come from integration. However, if it is not considered in advance, governance could be an obstruction that will block chances of a successful integration. In other words, true integration among the various component entities (hospital, medical group, health plan, etc.) is achieved through governance (Carver, 1991).

VII. ISSUES AND CHALLENGES OF IDS/N GOVERNANCE

The governance challenges facing IDS/Ns include understanding the role of key players, ensuring that each of the dimensions of governance fit the organizational needs of the IDS/N and adapting existing governance models to satisfy the needs of IDS/N stakeholders.

A. Key IDS/N Players

An IDS/N is, by definition, a coming-together of two of the three major health care policy issues: cost and access (the third issue relates to quality). When we discuss the delivery (i.e., access) and financing (i.e., cost) of health care being combined into a loosely-coupled network of health care organizations or into a tightly-coupled, fully integrated delivery system (Blair, Fottler, Paolino, and Rotarius, 1995), we are referring to the coming-together of the providers (hospitals and medical practices) and payers (traditionally, insurance organizations) such as managed care. In other words, an IDS/N must contain, at a minimum, hospitals, medical practices, and health plans. Indeed, surveys from 1994 and 1995 show that approximately 80% of health care experts believe both medical practices and hospitals will belong to IDS/Ns by 1999 (Rotarius, Paolino, McMurrough, Fottler, and Blair, 1995).

B. Governance Dimensions

All governance models, whether community, corporate, or some other variant, are affected by four dimensions which have identified by Pointer, Alexander, and Zuckerman (1995) as control, structure, composition, and functioning. An understanding of these four dimensions allows for an organization to effectively face IDS/N governance issues and challenges. Three such issues include the levels of governance, system complexity and functions of governance, and board composition (Pointer et al., 1995). The levels of governance issue addresses the need to determine how many layers of governing boards are needed to effectively govern an IDS/N. Similarly, the system complexity and governance functions issue addresses determining which roles and the relative authority the system board and the boards of the individual system entities should have in developing and maintaining the IDS/N. Lastly, the issue of board composition involves determining the board structure and function of governing boards. The way in which these four dimensions affect the traditional forms of governance vis-à-vis IDS/Ns is discussed below.

1. Control

Whether an IDS/N is centralized and governed by a single board, or whether it is decentralized with subordinate boards is the primary concern of the dimension of control. There are advantages and disadvantages to both centralization and decentralization. A decentralized system makes it possible to place certain decision making functions at a level where they can be governed by persons who are familiar with local circumstances (Pointer et al., 1995).

The presence, however, of both centralized and decentralized governing boards within one system can make it more difficult to facilitate overall governance of an IDS/N. Decisions can be made much more quickly in a single, centralized board simply because time is saved in meetings and reviews, as less people are involved in the process. This ability to make quick decisions is critical to health care organizations because the current high level of competition in the health care industry environment is so competitive that rapidity of movement is a necessity (Arnwine, 1991). A decentralized form of governance might lead subordinate boards to approve activities that help individual strategic business units (SBUs) but hurt the IDS/N as a whole via suboptimization (Pointer et al., 1995). Still, even with these problems, there are many who argue that local, subordinate boards are necessary to ensure an attitude of caring towards local communities (Axelrod, et. al., 1994). One way an IDS/N can help to ensure local communities of their concern is to establish advisory boards for the various components of a IDS/N. While advisory boards do not assume any ultimate responsibility for the IDS/N (Pointer et al., 1995), they do help to assure a certain degree of community voice to the various local components (Toomey and Toomey, 1993). Other pros and cons of a centralized system over a decentralized system are discussed by Greene (1991).

2. Structure

The "structure" dimension of IDS/N governance pertains to how the various boards relate to each other; in other words, it outlines which parts of the system or network are governed by which boards. Broadly considered, a governance board could be established for each geographic market/region, each strategic business group (for example, hospitals, medical groups, and rehabilitation), or each organizational entity (Pointer et al., 1995). This structure dimension implicitly covers the concept of structural integration between diverse organizations. The continuum of degree of structural integration ranges from minimal integration to partial to full (Cox [1991] refers to these degrees of integration as the monolithic dimension, plural dimension, and multicultural dimension, respectively). Both the corporate and community governance models would tend to have a minimal degree of structural integration.

3. Composition

How IDS/N board members are selected is the focus of the "composition" dimension. For IDS/Ns, the key issue is whether boards are composed of representative or non-representative members. Members of representative boards are usually chosen because of the management positions they hold in either the IDS/N or one of its SBUs, while members of non-representative boards do not have a direct relationship with any of the IDS/N's SBUs but will often be drawn from key external stakeholders such as banks, large businesses, etc.

4. Functioning

What the board does and how the IDS/N and subordinate boards share these activities and responsibilities are the dual foci of the "functioning" dimension. In other words, governance requires fulfilling responsibilities (what matters the board should be involved in) and performing roles (how the board should govern). The responsibilities and roles of the governing board include:
- formulating organizational ends, such as the mission and vision,
- ensuring high levels of executive management performance,
- ensuring quality of patient care,
- ensuring financial health of the organization, and
- assuming responsibility for itself (for its efficient and effective performance).

Roles include:
- formulating policy to guide decision making and action,
- making decisions, either by retaining authority with respect to its responsibilities or by delegating this authority to others, and
- performing oversight by monitoring decisions and actions to make sure they are in compliance with policies.

Where there is centralized control, the IDS/N board must take care of each of the duties listed above. Where there is decentralized control, there should be some mechanism for subdividing and coordinating board duties within the IDS/N. That is, each duty must either be assigned to the IDS/N board, shared by the IDS/N board and subordinate boards, or delegated to the subordinate boards (Pointer et al., 1995).

C. Modifying Existing Health Care Governance Models

Existing health care organizations exhibit particular patterns of governance, depending on a variety of factors. Two such governance forms span a governance continuum from community governance at one end to corporate governance at the other end. As discussed previously, community governing boards are typically rather large boards which tend to be dominated by outside directors. These members have diverse business experiences and tend to be from higher socioeconomic backgrounds (Coile, 1994). In fact, community board members are often on the board in order to emphasize geographical representation or representation of specific constituents. Because community boards have few, if any, inside directors, the problems of coordinating the interests of internal stakeholders is handled poorly. Hence, for IDS/Ns choosing governance structures with few, if any inside directors, we suggest adding inside directors either as voting or ex officio (non-voting) members (see Figure 2).

Corporate governance boards tend to be smaller than community boards and are typically dominated by inside directors. Corporate boards differ from community boards in other ways, too. The members of corporate boards of health care organizations tend to have health care industry backgrounds, along with experience in strategic planning and other complex business knowledge, skills and abilities (Axelrod, et. al, 1994). For IDS/Ns choosing governance structures with few, if any outside directors, the establishment of advisory committees or community task forces are essential to help to keep the IDS/N informed on issues of importance to various external stakeholders (see Figure 2).

VIII. AN INTEGRATIVE MODEL OF IDS/N GOVERNANCE

Clearly, the existing literature on health care organization governance focuses on the two opposite-end governance structures of community vs. corporate form (Weiner & Alexander, 1993). Corporate governance structures typically take a great interest in the day-to-day coordination of internal stakeholders, creating operational efficiencies and cost savings. Community governance structures, on the other hand, generally excel at being responsible to external stakeholders. In order to capitalize on the benefits that each of these ideal governance types has to offer, we suggest the creation of a two-tiered governance model. A union-management variation of this model has been a feature of large corporations in Germany since 1946 (Demb and Neubauer, 1992), while a two-layer model has been used extensively in Norway in order to address internal and external stakeholder interests (Huse, 1995).

Figure 2 - Basic Governance Models and Their Modification for Integrated Delivery System/Networks

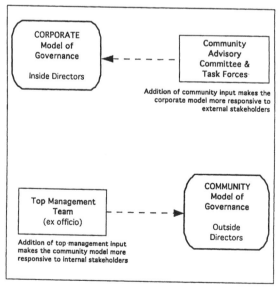

A. The Two-Tiered Governance Model

The basic two-tiered model is shown in Figure 3. The overarching board would be made up of members from the top management team, plus outside directors such as business and community leaders within the IDS/N's principal service areas. These overarching board members would address strategic issues.

The facilitating board would be composed of representative, inside directors from each of the individual components (hospitals, medical groups, health plans, etc.) within the IDS/N. These facilitating board members would primarily address operational issues vis-à-vis coordination of internal component stakeholders.

As Figure 3 shows, the two-tiered governance model also includes an interlocking inside directorate. These interlocking board members would be drawn from a subset of directors sitting on both the overarching and the facilitating boards. This would allow for dialogue and integration between the boards and should enhance a broad understanding of the IDS/N's role in the community, as well as its unique competencies.

B. The Four Governance Dimensions and the Two-Tiered Model

The two-tiered governance structure provides a means for both coordinating across SBUs (and, thereby, satisfying internal IDS/N stakeholders), while also creating overall corporate policies and strategies which should satisfy external IDS/N stakeholders and are socially responsible. This integrative flexibility is explicated by considering the governance dimensions of control, structure, composition, and functioning.

1. Control

The first-tier of the two-tier model is the overarching board (see Figure 3). This board has somewhat-centralized characteristics. The IDS/N using a two-tier governance model must present a coherent and consistent image to the external stakehold-

Figure 3 - A Two-Tiered Governance Model for Integrated Delivery Systems/Networks

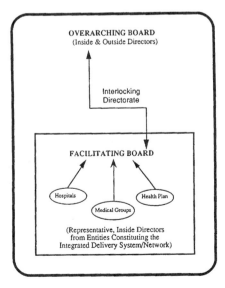

ers. For example, the IDS/N may negotiate with suppliers of medical equipment for all the IDS/N components and must present a united front to the suppliers. This is accomplished through a centralized mode of governance. The facilitating board, however, allows for representation by the IDS/N components in a more decentralized manner (see Figure 3).

2. Structure

The two-tier model creates the potential for full structural integration (Cox, 1991). The interlocking inside directorate between the overarching and facilitating boards has the potential to bring the needs and stakes of both internal and external IDS/N stakeholders in line with one another. This point is reflected in the two-tier model's composition.

3. Composition

Members of the facilitating board within the two-tier model of governance form a representative board, while the overarching board members form a non-representative board. The overarching board would typically consist of inside directors, including the top management team, and representatives of the most powerful external stakeholders. In a fully integrated delivery system, the top-level administrators of the component organizations would be considered part of the top management team. However, in a loosely-coupled integrated delivery network where there is not much vertical integration within the IDS/N, key members of the component organizations' board of directors should be included in the IDS/N's overarching board..

The IDS/N facilitating board would typically be composed of managerial representatives from the various operating units within the IDS/N. In addition, members would also represent physicians and the different professional and technical employee groups, such as nurses and other clinical technicians. These types of members of the facilitating board should be able to express and represent the stakes and interests of the internal stakeholders to the overarching board

4. Functioning

In a two-tiered model of governance, the assignment of duties could be both centralized and differentiated. As noted earlier, the overarching board is responsible for making decisions about corporate strategy and establishing IDS/N-wide policies, while the facilitating board is responsible for making operational decisions that involve coordination among IDS/N components. This differentiation among the boards allows for faster decision making at the operational level since the facilitating board is not weighed down by having to also handle strategic issues such as the IDS/N's competitive positioning vis-à-vis other health care providers. Moreover, because the facilitating board is representational and would typically include physicians and other health care professionals dealing with front-line care issues, it should allow the IDS/N to be more responsive to internal stakeholders and to be more efficient in its operations (Molinari et al., 1993).

VIII. SUMMARY

The three ideal types of governance structures complement each other. As we have previously noted, the community board needs an infusion of inside directors to ensure that the internal stakeholders are kept satisfied and organizational efficiencies are achieved. In turn, the corporate board should establish advisory committees or community task forces in order to understand the needs and stakes of the various external stakeholders and accomplish socially responsible outcomes. The proposed governance model, the two-tiered structure with its facilitating board, its overarching board, and its interlocking directorate, should be complete regarding meeting both internal and external stakeholder needs. However, it may be the most cumbersome of the models to actually practice.

The four governance dimensions of control, structure, composition, and functioning are very important issues for all health care governing boards and community leaders. Whether the final determination of a health care delivery network is to have centralized control with local advisory boards or decentralized control with local subordinate boards, community leaders will certainly want to retain a voice in what happens to health care locally. Fortunately, participation in governance does not have to be focused on board membership alone. Community involvement can occur through task forces, forums, councils, and memberships on board committees in an effort to obtain (and allow) local input on governance issues (Pointer et al., 1995b).

Governance in health care organizations is, indeed, difficult to assess. Health care organizations have grown increasingly complex, and the traditional forms and practices of governance (even at their best) are no longer adequate to manage issues that must be dealt with today. New standards for governance are being continually developed in attempts to cope with the changing health care environment (see Figure 2). These changes in both the environment and governance will have significant effects on health care in the future, as medical groups, hospitals, and hospital systems will have to modify their current governance structures or adopt new structures—such as the two-tier model (see Figure 3)—in order to form and manage integrated delivery systems or networks.

REFERENCES

Alexander, J. A. (1990). Governance for whom? The dilemmas of change and effectiveness in hospital boards. *Frontiers of Health Services Management*, 6: 38-41, 46.

Alexander, J. A., and Zuckerman, H. S. (Fall 1989). Health care governance: are we keeping pace? *The Journal of Health Administration Education*, 7: 760-777.

Amundson, B. (1993). Myth and reality in the rural health service crisis: facing up to community responsibilities. *The Journal of Rural Health*, 9: 176-187.

Arnwine, D. L., (1991). Systems require visionaries [interview by Donald E. L. Johnson]. *Health Care Strategic Management*, 9: 8-12.

Axelrod, N., Gappmayer, M., Leech, J., Lewis, C., McManis, G., Orlikoff, J. E. and Prybil, L. (1994). The age of denial - as health care enters a new era, will traditional governance survive? *Hospitals & Health Networks*, 68: 60-66.

Bader, B. S. (1991). What governing boards expect from physician executives. *Physician Executive*, 17: 8-13.

Bell, T. L., and Bell, S. L. (1991). Hospital-sponsored rural health clinics: An effective diversification alternative for rural hospitals. *The Journal of Rural Health*, 7: 30-38.

Berry, D. E., and Seavey, J. W. (1994). Assuring access to rural health services: The case for revitalizing small rural hospitals. *Health Care Management Review, 19:* 32-42.

Blair, J. D. and Myron D. Fottler. (1990). *Challenges in Health Care Management: Strategic Perspectives for Managing Key Stakeholders.* Jossey-Bass Publishers, San Francisco, CA.

Blair, J. D., Fottler, M. D., Paolino, A. R., and Rotarius, T. M. (1995). *Medical Group Practices Face the Uncertain Future: Challenges, Opportunities and Strategies.* Center for Research in Ambulatory Health Care Administration, Englewood, CO.

Blair, J. D., Fottler, M. D., and Whitehead, C. J. (Jan/Feb., 1996). Diagnosing the stakeholder bottom line for medical group practices: Key stakeholders' potential to threaten and/or cooperate. *Medical Group Management Journal.*

Blair, J. D., Fottler, M. D., Lazarus, S. S., Paolino, A. R. and Rotarius, T.M. (1995). Strategic stakeholder management: First round results from 'Facing the uncertain future'. *Medical Group Management Journal, 42:* 16-21. (Cover Article).

Brown, M. and McCool, B., (1994). HCMR perspective: Collaboration, competition, and communication—a field experience on the road to reform. *Health Care Management Review, 19:* 74-83.

Burke, G. C., Savage, G. T., Baird, K. C., Durden, V. L. and Pascasio, R. A. (1994). Stakeholder impact on two rural Texas hospital closures. *Texas Journal of Rural Health, 13:* 5-13.

Carver, J. (1991). *Boards that Make a Difference: A New Design for Leadership in Nonprofit and Public Organizations.* Jossey-Bass, San Francisco.

Christianson, J., Moscovice, I., Johnson, J., Kralewski, J. and Grogan, C. (1990). Evaluating Rural Hospital Consortia. *Health Affairs, 10:* 136-147.

Coddington, D. C., Moore, K. D. and Fischer, E. A. (1994). *Integrated Health Care: Reorganizing the Physician, Hospital and Health Plan Relationship* Center for Research in Ambulatory Health Administration, Englewood, CO.

Coddington, D. C., Moore, K. D. and Fischer, E. A. (November/December 1993). Integrated health care systems: The key characteristics. *Medical Group Management Journal.*

Coile, R. C., Jr. (January/February 1996). Management teams for the 21st century. *Healthcare Executive,* 10-13.

Coile, R. C., Jr. (1991). The new governance: Five most critical trustee functions in the 1990s. *Hospital Strategy Report, 3:* 1-8.

Coile, R. C., Jr. (1994). *The New Governance: Strategies for an Era of Health Reform.* Health Administration Press, Ann Arbor, MI.

Conrad, D. A. (1990). Editorial. *Frontiers of Health Services Management, 6:* 1-2.

Cox, T. H. (1991). The multicultural organization. *Academy of Management Executive, 5:* 34-47.

Demb, A. and Neubauer, F. F. (1992). *The Corporate Board: Confronting the Paradoxes.* Oxford University Press, Oxford.

Devers, K. J., Shortell, S. M., Gillies, R. R., Anderson, D. A., Mitchell, J. B., and Erickson, K. L (1994). Implementing organized delivery systems: An integration scorecard. *Health Care Manage Review, 19:* 7-20.

Dymond, S., Nix, T. W., Rotarius, T. M., and Savage, G. T. (1995). Why do key integrated delivery stakeholders really matter? Assessing control, coalitions, resources, and power. *Medical Group Management Journal, 42:* 26-38.

Freeman, R. E. (1984). *Strategic Management: A Stakeholder Approach.* Pitman Publishing, Marshfield, MA.

Gamm, L. D., Cathy, K. S. Brannon, D., and Fennell, M. L. (1996). Linkage strategies of rural hospitals—independent hospital, local health system, and/or externally linked facility. *Hospital & Health Services Administration, 41:* 236-54.

Gorey, T. M. (February). Physician-hospital organizations: prospects and pitfalls. *Bulletin of the American College of Surgeons, 80,* 13-17.

Gray, B. (1989). *Collaborating: Finding common ground for multiparty problems.* Jossey-Bass Publishers, San Francisco.

Greene, J. (1991). Hospital, system boards adjust to changing roles. *Modern Healthcare, 21:* 22-28.

Hash, M. M., (1989). Board composition and the community. *Trustee, 42:* 21.

Hodges, E. N., III. (1993). The fine line between governance and administration. *Trustee, 46:* 28.

Huse, M. (ed.). (1995). *Stakeholder Perspectives on Corporate Governance: A Sample of Scandinavian Contributions,* Nordland Research Institutes, Bodø, Norway.

Johnson, R. L. (1994). HCMR perspective: The purpose of hospital governance. *Health Care Management Review, 19:* 81-88.

Kovner, A. R. (1990). Improving hospital board effectiveness: An update. *Frontiers of Health Services Management, 6:* 3-27.

Korenchuk, K. M. (July-August). Once the choice is made: a close look at the joint venture option. *Medical Group Management Journal, 38:* 24-28, 30, 33.

Kralewski, J. E., Moscovice, I. S., Johnson, J. A. Christianson, J. B. and Chan, B. (Fall 1993). Organizational and administrative factors influencing the adoption of consortia programs by rural hospitals. *Hospital & Health Services Administration, 38:* 307-328.

Kurtz, M. E. (September/October). A discussion of group practice governance issues. *Medical Group Management Journal, 39:* 46, 48, 50-55.

MacMillan, I. C. and Jones, P. C. (1986). *Strategy formulation: Power and politics* (2nd ed.), West, St. Paul, MN.

Madison, D. L. (1990). Notes on the history of group practice: The tradition of the dispensary. *Medical Group Management Journal, 37:* 54.

Mason, L. F. (1987). Hospital management and governance: vision, values, and leadership. *National Forum on Hospital and Health Affairs,* 6-13.

Mason, R. O., and Mitroff, I. I. (1981). *Challenging Strategic Planning Assumptions.* Wiley, New York, NY.

Mitka, M. (May/June 1996). A closer look at physician management companies: Why they're strong and getting stronger. *Healthcare Executive,* 8-11.

Mitroff, I. I. (1983). *Stakeholders of the Organizational Mind.* Jossey-Bass, San Francisco.

Molinari, C., Morlock, L., Alexander, J., and Lyles, C. A. (Summer 1992). Hospital board effectiveness: Relationships between board training and hospital financial viability. *Health Care Management Review, 17:* 43-49.

Molinari, C., Morlock, L., Alexander, J., and Lyles, C. A. (August 1993). Hospital board effectiveness: Relationships between governing board composition and hospital financial viability. *Health Services Research, 28:* 3357-377.

Moscovice, I. (July 1989). Strategies for promoting a viable rural health care system. *The Journal of Rural Health, 5:* 216-230.

Moscovice, I., Johnson, J., Finch, M., Grogan, C. and Kralewski, J. (Fall 1991). The structure and characteristics of rural hospital consortia. *The Journal of Rural Health, 7:* 575-587.

Näsi, J (Ed.). (1995). *Understanding Stakeholder Thinking.* LSR-Publications, Helsinki.

O'Hagan, J. (Spring 1991). Small-town attitudes can be big-city problems. *Perspectives in Healthcare Risk Management, 11:* 8-11.

Paolino, A. R., Greaves, J. M., Blair, J.D., Fottler, M. D., and Rotarius, T. M. (September/October, 1995). Medical practice and physician executives face the uncertain future: strategic stakeholder management. *Medical Group Management Journal, 42:* 36-43, 76-78.

Pirani, M. J., L. Hart, G., and Rosenblatt, R. A. (Nov.-Dec. 1993). Physician perspectives on the causes of rural hospital closure 1980-1988. *Journal of the American Board of Family Practice, 6:* 556-561.

Pointer, D. D., and Ewell, C. M., (5 June 1994). Governance 100 survey: membership makeup of hospital boards hasn't changed much—yet. *Hospitals & Health Networks, 68,* 76.

Pointer, D. D. and Ewell, C. M. (Fall 1995). Really governing: What type of work should boards be doing? *The Journal of the Foundation of The American College of Healthcare Executives, 40:* 315-331.

Pointer, D. D., Alexander, J. A., and Zuckerman, H. S. (Spring 1995a). Loosening the gordian knot of governance in integrated health care delivery systems. *Frontiers of Health Services Management*, 11: 3-37.

Pointer, D. D., Alexander, J. A., and Zuckerman, H. S. (Spring 1995b). Loosening the gordian knot of governance in integrated health care delivery systems. [Reply]. *Frontiers of Health Services Management*, 11: 51-52.

Roberts, N. C. and King, P. J. (Winter 1989). The stakeholder audit goes public. *Organizational Dynamics.* 17: 63-79.

Rosenthal, T. C., Doemland, M., and Parisella J. S. (Winter 1991). An assessment of rural hospital trustees' health care knowledge base. *The Journal of Rural Health.* 7: 13-22.

Rotarius, T. M., Paolino, A. R., McMurrough, B. M., Fottler, M. D., and Blair, J. D. (July/August 1995). *Integrated Delivery Systems/Networks in the Uncertain Future, 42*: 22-31.

Savage, G T., Blair J. D., Benson M. J., and Hale, B. (Winter 1992). Urban-rural hospital affiliations: Assessing control, fit, and stakeholder issues strategically. *Health Care Management Review, 17*: 35-49.

Savage, G. T., Nix, T. W., Whitehead,C. J., and Blair J. D. (1991). Strategies for assessing and managing stakeholders. *Academy of Management Executive, 5*: 61-75.

Savage, G. T., and Purtell, D. (1995). Transforming health insurance: Problems and promises with state reforms. 1995 *Southern Management Association Proceeding.* M. Schnake, editor. Valdosta State College: Southern Management Association.

Savage, G. T., Purtell, D, Friedman, L.H., Cochran, C.E., and Moorman, J. (August 1996). *Transforming health care insurance: problems and promises with state reforms.* Health Care Administration Division, Academy of Management. Cincinnati, OH.

Selbst, P. (June 1994). Shedding light on board practices. *Trustee, 47*: 22-23.

Shortell, S. M., Gillies, Robin R., and Anderson, D. A. (Winter 1994). The new world of managed care: Creating organized delivery systems. *Health Affairs, 13*: 46-64.

Shortell, S. M., Gillies, R., Anderson, D., Mitchell, J., and Morgan, J. (Winter 1993). Creating organized delivery systems: The barriers and facilitators. *Hospital & Health Services Administration*, 38.

Stoeckle, J. D., and Reiser S. J. (1 March 1992). The corporate organization of hospital work: Balancing Professional and Administrative Responsibilities. *Annals of Internal Medicine, 116*: 407-413.

Straub, L. A. & Walzer, N. (1992). *Rural Health Care - Innovation in a Changing Environment.* Connecticut: Praeger.

Toomey, R.E. Governance and Management in Healthcare. *The collected papers of Robert E. Toomey.* Spartanburg, SC: The Reprint Company, 1996.

Toomey, R. E., and Toomey, R K. (Winter 1993). The role of governing boards in multihospital systems. *Health Care Management Review, 18*: 21-30.

Umbdenstock, R. J., Hageman, W. M., and Amundson, B. (Winter 1990):. The five critical areas for effective governance of not-for-profit hospitals. *Hospital & Health Services Administration, 35*: 481-492.

Ward, R. D. (April 1990). A job description for hospital trustees. *Michigan Hospitals, 26*: 50-53.

Weil, T. P. (Summer 1996). How health networks and HMOs could result in public utility regulation. *Hospital & Health Services Administration, 41*: 266-80.

Weiner, B. J. and Alexander J. A. (1993). Corporate and philanthropic models of hospital governance: A taxonomic evaluation. *Health Services Research, 28*: 325-355.

Zammuto, R. F. (1982). *Assessing Organizational effectiveness.* State University of New York Press, Albany.

Zimmerman, J. (1991). Nipping board problems in the bud. *Michigan Hospitals, 27*: 39-40.

Zinober, J. W. (1991). A physician's guide to practice governance. *Medical Group Management Journal, 38*: 54-56, 59-60.

Zuckerman, H. (12 October 1995). Lecture. *The John Aure Buesseler, M.D., Health Organization Management Distinguished Lecture Program, Lubbock*, TX.

44.
PROJECT MANAGEMENT

John R. Adams, *Western Carolina University, Cullowhee, NC*

Reagan McLaurin, *Western Carolina University, Cullowhee, NC*

David Snyder, *Medical University of South Carolina, Charleston, SC*

Health care administrators are routinely required to complete projects through the use of interdisciplinary teams. These projects might include the revision of a patient classification system (Schifiliti and Morin, 1989), the integration of project management and quality improvement approaches to make changes in the delivery of care to dialysis patients (Heard, 1994), improvement in medication delivery systems (Day et al., 1994; Donnells, McDonald, and Trimble, 1995), and the development of critical pathways as a means of streamlining the provision of quality care (Heacock and Brobst, 1994).

A discussion of project management must begin with some basic definitions. A project is a temporary endeavor that creates a unique product or service (PMI, 1996). Project management is the coordination of funding, planning, management, and support of a new initiative or the modification of an existing strategic initiative (Belinger, 1995). The application of knowledge, skills, tools, and techniques to complete projects involves balancing demands among scope, time, cost quality, and stakeholders' needs and expectations (PMI, 1996).

The emergence of project management in health care organizations is the result of administrators and administrative team members seeking to optimize performance by involving all those who have a stake in the results of the project. Unfortunately, health administrators without any formal introduction to project management ideas and concepts are often asked to participate in, sometimes even lead, these special project work teams (Berry, 1994). Without proper preparation, the chances for success in any of these project is greatly diminished.

I. PROJECT MANAGEMENT CONCEPTS

A. Temporary Organization

A project has several important general characteristics:
- It is a job large and complex enough to require the integrated efforts of several individuals to organize and complete;
- It is a task that is only performed once;
- It is an activity important to those sponsoring and paying for its completion.

Establishing such a project concentrates management's attention. The work must be completed with the quality required, in the time available, and within the allocated budget. Since an integrated effort is required and the work has not been accomplished before, a temporary organization devoted to accomplishing the task must be developed. This organization is made up of all those who are necessary to accomplish the work; it is led by an individual named the project manager.

For very large projects, the organization can be quite formal and might last for an extended period of time. The addition of a new wing to the hospital, for example, may involve a core project team of twenty or thirty people, including representatives from the hospital, the architectural firm, and the construction contractor. Such a project team may work for several years, starting with a few people who generate the funding and develop the design of the addition, expanding to include those involved in its construction, finishing with those who equip and move into the completed facilities. Such a team usually has a formal organizational structure with job descriptions, a published organizational chart, and standardized operating procedures. Individuals and organizations drop out as their contribution is completed; the organization itself disappears when the addition is completed and integrated into the hospital's organization.

Smaller projects can be less formal and last for a much shorter period of time; in fact, they may not even be called projects. For example, a task force may be established to investigate a promising new operating procedure. Charged with providing a recommendation concerning its adoption by the hospital, this group will have no formal organization structure or job descriptions. It is likely to complete the work in a few days or weeks. It may involve only a few interested individuals representing the departments that would be involved in the new procedures.

Regardless of its formal label, this type of task is a project. The task force leader fills the role of project manager. The temporary project organization is tied to the task to be performed and is tailored to include only those individuals and skills necessary to accomplish the job. Upon completion, the organization is no longer needed and disappears. The temporary organization (project team) should therefore be a prime example of efficiency since it carries no surplus baggage and includes even essential units only for the period in which their contribution is needed.

B. Project Management Life Cycle

Most models of the project management process are based on a concept known as the project life cycle. This approach calls for the project to be broken into phases based upon the type of work being performed and the type of individuals needed to perform the work. One example of a typical project life cycle chart is shown in Figure 1. In this

Figure 1 - Typical Project Life Cycle Chart.

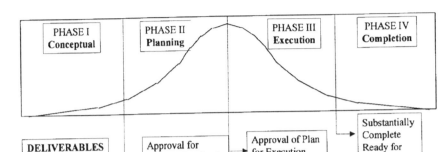

model the life cycle is divided into four phases with clearly defined outcomes marking the transition from one to another.

In the first phase, management above the level of the project manager conceives of a project, evaluates it with respect to other possible projects, and commits to proceeding. This commitment is generally associated with the appointment of the project manager and marks both the delivery of the results expected from this phase (deliverable) and entry into the planning phase of the project.

Phase 2 involves the development of the detailed project plan and the project's managerial team. Formal acceptance and approval of the plan by the project's accountable administrator (sponsor) marks the transition to Phase 3 and the initiation of physical work to accomplish the project. Phase 3 may involve laboratorians, risk managers, safety officers, review coordinators, physicians, administrators, or other health professionals with expertise needed to accomplish the particular project.

The transition to the completion phase traditionally occurs when the outcome of the project is ready for evaluation or some form of demonstration to confirm that it is complete and ready to be accepted. The project ends with the formal acceptance by the accountable administrator of the outcome produced by the project team (or by the project's early termination if it is determined that the outcome is no longer required and the project should be abandoned).

C. Project Management Process

Models of project management attempt to relate the project's phases to the processes being implemented to accomplish that work. All projects involve specific actions: initiating, planning, executing, controlling and closing. These actions are defined as process groups. More detailed processes that occur in managing projects are classified as either core processes or facilitating processes based on how they are related to the conduct of the project. The basic model is shown in Figure 2 (adapted from PMI, 1996).

Facilitating processes are shown outside the flow of the core processes; they can be integrated into the project's work flow as needed based on the particular characteristics of the project. Facilitating processes include those activities that are frequently

Figure 2 - Basic Model of Project Management Process.

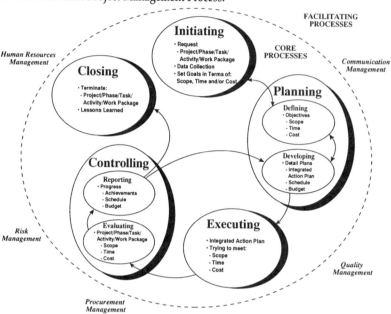

provided as a service to the project by the ongoing processes of the organization, at least for those projects that are conducted within large organizations and tend to be implemented as needed depending on the specific characteristics of the product being developed by the project. Facilitating processes are drawn from the project management knowledge areas of quality management, human resource management, communications management, risk management, and procurement management. In organizations that lack some of the required support or in stand-alone projects, facilitating processes must be developed and/or provided by the project.

On the other hand, core processes must be conducted in approximately the same sequence on any project; they provide the feedback necessary to modify the plan and even the objectives. Core processes include those activities that must be accomplished uniquely for each project. The detailed project plan will include the work breakdown structure, the logic flow and schedule of activities, and the budget. Core processes are drawn from the project management knowledge areas of scope management, time management, cost management, and the integration of these knowledge areas into a single project plan, at least within the descriptions shown as the planning process group.

Work on a project begins with the Initiating Process Group. Senior management defines the basic requirements and requests that a project be initiated. Senior management might include managers above the project manager in an organization, sponsors of the project, future owners of the product produced by the project, or any combination of these. The project manager looks to senior management for guidance and direction. The goals of the project are defined in terms of the scope of the work to be accomplished, the time available to complete it, and the money or resources senior management will commit to the project

Similar to the typical definition of the conceptual phase of the project life cycle, the transition to the Planning Process Group (or planning phase) would generally be accomplished by establishing a project charter and objective, and by appointing a project manager. Planning takes place at two different levels within the Planning Process Group. First, the project manager interacts with senior management to define the project objective in more detail; to specify the priorities among the scope, time, and budget aspects of the project; and to determine the appropriate levels of decision-making authority within the project. In particular, the project manager must develop at least a general understanding of what decisions are within his or her prerogative and when senior management wishes to be involved in making decisions relevant to conducting the project.

Second, the project team develops an integrated project plan to include the project's action plan or workflow, the schedule, the budget, and the interaction among them. This is where the fourth core process is drawn from the project integration management knowledge area and brought into the model. More specifically, the project management process requires that planning, executing and controlling be accomplished as an integration of the scope, time, and cost project management knowledge areas. The feedback arrows in the model indicate that the project manager coordinates the integrated project plan developed by the team with senior management for approval before the project proceeds to the executing phase or before the executing processes are implemented.

The Executing Process Group implements the planned activities according to the approved schedule and budget. The work of the project, consuming both resources and time, is actually performed here. In the project world, we must recognize that the project plan, no matter how carefully designed and well developed, is actually based on a complex structure of estimates or guesses concerning durations and costs. No project manager would assume that all these guesses will prove to be correct. Instead, the project manager must implement a series of checks and balances designed to identify when the project is deviating from the approved plan and to provide the information needed to take action concerning any significant deviations found. This series of checks and balances are commonly known as the Controlling Process Group.

The Controlling Process Group, unlike the other four process groups, does not have an equivalent phase in the project life cycle model. Rather, the control process, missing from the project management life cycle concept, provides the feedback that allows and requires project revision. This lack in the project life cycle models makes the life cycle inappropriate as a model of the project management process.

Two aspects of controlling must be recognized. Periodically during the conduct of the project, personnel must evaluate the progress being made and document the time that has been consumed, the money that has been spent, and the work that has actually been accomplished. On small projects, the process may be informal. On large projects, however, it tends to become very formal, consuming considerable time and effort. Progress must be reported in terms of specific activities, documenting the status of each activity being conducted at that point in time. If a given activity is complete, then the associated work proceeds to the Closing Process Group to be terminated. In all other cases, variances from the plan concerning the scope of work accomplished, the time consumed, and/or the money spent to date are used as a basis for revising the project plan.

The closed loop from the Planning Process Group through the Executing Process Group and the Controlling Process Group back to the Planning Process Group demonstrates how feedback is used in managing projects to revise both the integrated plan and the basic objectives as necessary throughout the project life cycle. All projects are completed one activity at a time. Schedules and resources may need to be revised any time an activity's actual accomplishments vary from what was planned. Controlling processes identify these variances and report them so that necessary adjustments can be made in the project plan. If an activity is accomplished late, other activities may have to be delayed and resources reallocated to minimize the impact of delay. If the impact is small or can be managed by a minor adjustment in schedule, budget, or resource allocation, then the adjustments to the plan can usually be accomplished within the project. If the impact is large, however, or if a significant opportunity develops that had not been considered during definition of the project's scope, the project manager may need to prepare documentation and make proposals that could modify the overall objectives of the project. In such a case, the project manager must consult with senior management to determine the appropriate course of action that would best serve those for whom the project is being conducted. This latter situation is reflected by the double-headed arrows leading back from planning to the Initiating Process Group.

Finally, the project is completed when the objectives (as revised during the project, to include the possibility of simply terminating the project completely) have been met. In the Closing Process Group, termination processes such as closing out contracts, paying contractors, reassigning responsibilities for the project's product and personnel, and documenting lessons learned are implemented.

II. PROJECT MANAGEMENT TOOLS

A. Project Team Building

Project teams are goal-oriented groups that function during the life of the project. They differ from traditional group or team approaches. (See Table 1.)

It is evident from this comparison of traditional work groups and project teams that many advantages emerge from the use of project teams. Project teams have a clearly defined goal to challenge the team members—a challenge that leads to increased commitment. Project team members may use their own initiative to help plan and participate in the project, encouraging creativity and innovation. Open communication channels make it possible for all project team members to obtain needed information to perform their own tasks better and to contribute to problem-solving within the project. Individual project team members perceive personal recognition for their own skills, abilities, and knowledge. In summary, project teams have emerged into a unique vehicle by which to bring change to the organization.

In order to build a highly efficient, functioning project team, the following steps are recommended. First, a clearly established team identity needs to be defined. Who are the members of the team? A team review of the expertise and motivations of individual team members should be conducted.

Second, a team purpose and a plan for achieving that purpose should be established. Questions such as the following will need to be answered: What is the purpose of the team? What tasks have to be accomplished? What are the resource requirements and the time constraints of the project? In this step, the organizational

Table 1 - Comparison of Project and Traditional Work Teams

<u>Characteristic</u>	<u>Comparison</u>
Long-term goals	Traditional work groups are task oriented performing functions that keep departments functioning over an indefinite period of time. Project teams are goal oriented performing functions that are directed to the completion of the project in a fast and efficient manner within certain time constraints.
Power and Authority	Traditional work groups use formal authority. Project teams use cooperation and collaboration as a team, with persuasion by the project manager.
Organization	Traditional work groups are segregated into department-specific tasks, characterized by little turnover, established administrative procedures, and a dominant culture. Project teams are composed of continually changing members of the team. As skills and knowledge are needed, individuals are brought into the project team. If the need no longer exists, individuals drop out of the project team. This creates the need for fluid administrative procedures and an evolutionary culture.
Training of personnel	Traditional work groups have formalized training and development. Project teams use individuals for their specific skills, abilities, and knowledge as needed in the phase of the project.
Creativity/Flexibility	Traditional work groups have limited creativity within defined organizational roles. Project teams have unlimited creativity focused on the development of the team and completion of the project.
Reward	Traditional work groups are rewarded for standardized performance as set by the organization. Project teams are rewarded based upon personal performance as an expert in a particular field. There is opportunity for self-enhancement and development.
Communication	In traditional work groups, communication is vertical and formal within the organizational structure. Project teams use informal means and techniques of communication that cut across departmental and organizational barriers.
Longevity	Traditional work groups tend to be of an indefinite duration leading to a slow, tedious change process. Project teams utilize the five phase life cycle of groups: storming, forming, norming, performing, and terminating.

support for the project and its relative value to the organization should be made clear to the project team. A common language for the project is created.

Third, individual project team member roles are defined. All project team member should know why they were selected. Their individual contributions should be defined, expectations made clear.

Fourth, the agendas involved in the project, both surface and hidden, should be understood. All individuals possess certain needs and will seek to meet those needs. Project team members will ask what benefits are to be derived from the project and what they need to do to influence the group to meet their needs. What special relationships do they wish to develop within the project team? Is involvement in this project likely to be detrimental to their careers? Who should they avoid in this project team? Project team members must have an understanding of project roles and a commitment to role achievement. Project managers need to be aware of the surface agendas and hidden agendas. They should be on the watch for conflict between the two. If a member possesses a hidden agenda that creates a conflict within the project team, the problem must be solved. As groups mature and trust is built, hidden agendas are often reduced.

Sixth, an effective performance system must be established. Specific rewards for good performance must be communicated to the project team members, consequences for poor performance established. Project team members need to understand how this project enhances their career.

Seventh, creating and maintaining effective working relationships is key to high performance project teams. Patterns of communication need to be established as do methods of conflict resolution. All must be accepted by the project team. Conflict is inevitable. Project managers need to know the difference between positive and negative conflict and step in to resolve the latter. Finally, the project team needs to know when the project has reached completion and whether or not it was successful.

B. Work Breakdown Structure

Developing the work breakdown structure (WBS) is the first, most important step in creating the detailed plan needed to complete the project in an organized and structured manner. The WBS is a complete, structured list of the tasks that will have to be performed in order to complete the project. The process used to obtain this list is to first identify the major task (objective) to be performed (accomplished) by the project and then to break down that task into its major components. Each part is then broken down into its components. The process continues until, at the lowest level of detail defined, each item of work is considered to be manageable and can be reasonably estimated in terms of both the amount of time it should take and the resources it should consume while being completed. This list provides the data that will be used as a basis for all other planning. The WBS actually defines the scope of the project at a level of detail sufficient to allow the project schedule and budget to be determined.

A portion of a WBS for an Operations-Human Resources project is shown in Figure 3. The second column in this figure, labeled "Task Name," provides the relevant example. A numbering system has been imposed on the WBS to help keep track of the activities to be completed. Typically, items at successively higher levels of detail have successively higher decimal designations. Various nomenclatures have been

Figure 3 - Portion of a WBS for an Operations-Human Resources Project.

ID	Task Name	Duration	Start	Finish
27	1.09 Collect Data	30d	4/4/95	5/16/95
28	1.10 Analyze Data	7d	5/16/95	5/25/95
29	1.11 Present Results to	1h	5/25/95	5/25/95
30	**2.0 Plan Development**	**15d**	**5/25/95**	**6/15/95**
31	2.01 Set Plan Objectives/	1d	5/25/95	5/26/95
32	2.02 Confirm Objectives/	3d	5/26/95	5/31/95
33	2.03 Develop Plan Detail	4d	5/31/95	6/6/95
34	2.04 Create Model	3d	6/6/95	6/9/95
35	2.05 Computer Analysis	2d	6/9/95	6/13/95
36	2.06 Model Evaluation an	1d	6/13/95	6/14/95
37	2.07 Package Model for	1d	6/14/95	6/15/95
38	3.0 Present Plan	8h	6/15/95	6/16/95
39	4.0 Evaluate Feedback	1d	6/16/95	6/19/95
40	5.0 Modify Plan & Finalize	1d	6/19/95	6/20/95
41	**6.0 Design Computer Tracki**	**12.5d**	**6/20/95**	**7/6/95**
42	6.01 Create Database	1d	6/20/95	6/21/95
43	**6.02 Create Spreadshe**	**1d**	**6/21/95**	**6/22/95**
44	6.02.01 Idebtufy Re	1d	6/21/95	6/22/95
45	6.02.02 ID Data So	1d	6/21/95	6/22/95
46	6.02.03 ID Fields &	1d	6/21/95	6/22/95
47	6.02.04 Build Form	1d	6/21/95	6/22/95
48	6.02.05 Test Sprea	1d	6/21/95	6/22/95
49	6.03 Create Reports	4h	6/22/95	6/22/95
50	Distribute System Plan f	7d	6/23/95	7/3/95
51	Modify Tracking System	3d	7/4/95	7/6/95
52	**Plan Implementation**	**291d**	**7/7/95**	**8/16/96**

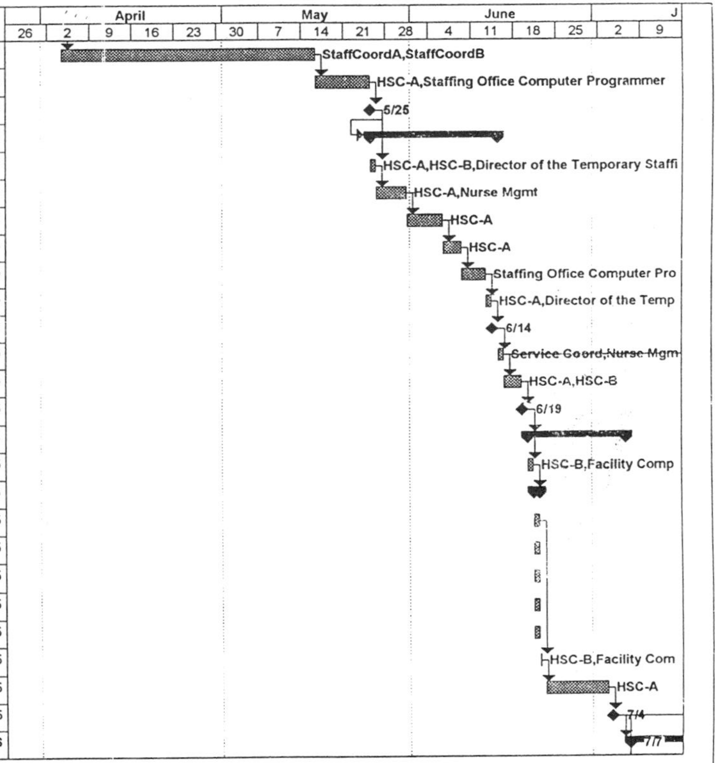

Project: Operations - Human Resource
Date: 4/24/97

Task — Progress — Milestone — Summary — Rolled Up Task — Rolled Up Milestone — Rolled Up Progress developed for these successive levels of detail, but projects can generally be broken down through the task, sub-task, activity, and work package levels, depending on the magnitude and complexity of the project. The larger and more complex the project, the more levels involved in the work breakdown structure.

C. Logic Flow Analysis

After the WBS is developed, the next step is to determine the logical flow of work that will be used to complete the project. The best technical approach to accomplishing the work is the starting point. However, the basic logic flow used to develop the initial plan may change many times as the project is implemented through its life cycle, due in many cases to non-technical issues that arise as the project progresses. For example, new rules or regulations may be developed that affect the way the project can be conducted. Personnel with unique expertise may be unavailable for a period of time because some other work in the organization with higher priority may need them. Any moderately sized project is complex enough to guarantee changes before completion. The best technical logic flow simply gives us a good starting point for managing the project, a baseline from which we can deviate as we adjust to the pressures of actually accomplishing the work.

D. Developing the Project Schedule

Once the workflow has been established, the expected duration of each activity must be entered into the network. To do this, one must have at least some idea of the resources necessary for particular activities. In general, the more qualified resources that can be applied to a particular activity, the shorter period of time it will take to complete the activity.

Figure 3 shows some of the resources that will be used in completing the activities in an Operations-Human Resources project. Given these resources, the amount of time available for each activity to be completed must be defined independently of all other activities. When these estimates are entered into the computer, the effect of each activity taking the amount of time estimated is automatically calculated by the software and the critical path is defined. The critical path is the longest path through the network allowing for no extra or slack time, the path that determines the shortest period of time in which the project can be completed under the given constraints.

In Figure 4, the subnetwork consisting of activities 2, 3, 4, and 5 demonstrates a critical path of activities 2, 4, and 5, which together will require 183.75 days as shown by the summary activity "Create a Database." The higher level activity represents the subordinate network. The starting and ending dates as well as the estimated duration for each activity are shown in the lower section of the activity block. Other items of relevance to the project plan can also be shown in this block.

E. Developing the Project Budget

All projects must be completed within the amount of money allocated. Figure 5 shows another view of the WBS that was shown in Figure 3. This time the estimated dollar costs for each activity is shown in a column matching the date that the resource

Figure 4 - Subnetwork of Activities.

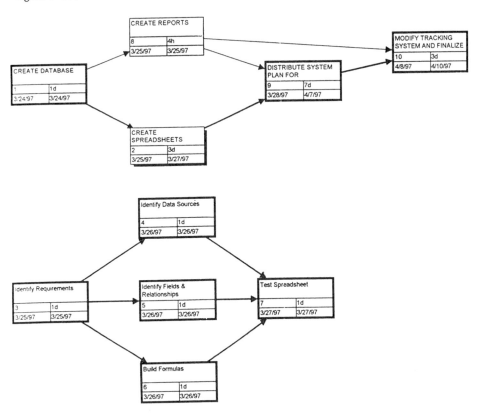

will be consumed. The costs for the "Track Pool Assignment" activity, some $9,706.44, represents the sum of the costs for the eleven subordinate activities shown on the chart. The Gantt chart on the right shows when these activities will be conducted and approximately when funds will be required. As the project progresses, additional columns of information show the amount of money spent to date and the funds remaining for each detailed activity and for each summary activity all the way to the project level. Cash flow can be projected for the duration of the project, and anticipated project costs can be developed based upon the budgetary performance of the project to date. This insight into budget can be extremely valuable to any manager attempting to take best advantage of the cash flow projections of the sponsoring company.

III. SUMMARY

This chapter has described a way of managing project work that can provide a much higher probability of success in completing the project within an appropriate period of time and within the targeted budget. There is no secret to project management. Adequately managing a project simply involves several steps:

Figure 5 - Another View of the WBS Shown in Figure 3.

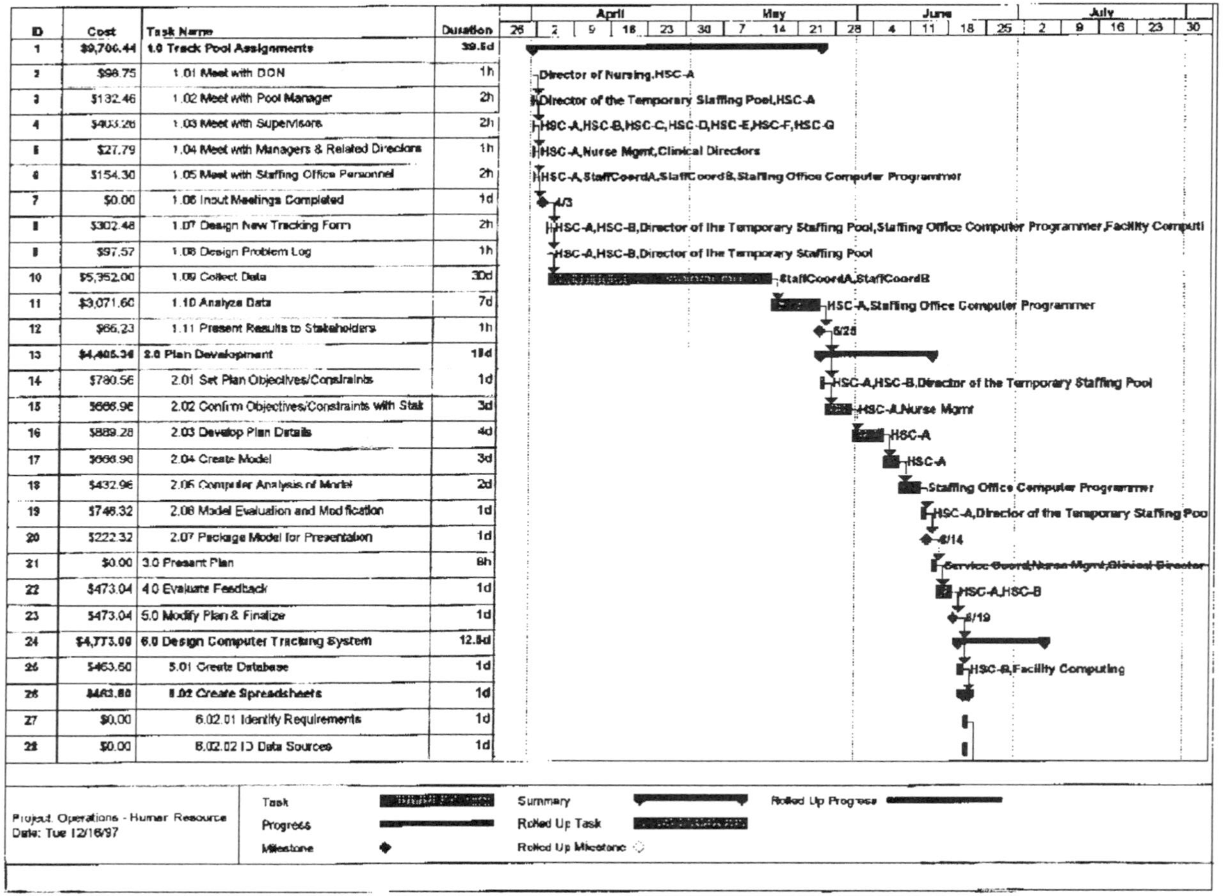

ID	Cost	Task Name	Duration
1	$9,706.44	1.0 Track Pool Assignments	39.6d
2	$98.75	1.01 Meet with DON	1h
3	$132.46	1.02 Meet with Pool Manager	2h
4	$403.26	1.03 Meet with Supervisors	2h
5	$27.79	1.04 Meet with Managers & Related Directors	1h
6	$154.30	1.05 Meet with Staffing Office Personnel	2h
7	$0.00	1.06 Input Meetings Compiled	1d
8	$302.48	1.07 Design New Tracking Form	2h
9	$97.57	1.08 Design Problem Log	1h
10	$5,352.00	1.09 Collect Data	30d
11	$3,071.60	1.10 Analyze Data	7d
12	$66.23	1.11 Present Results to Stakeholders	1h
13	$4,465.34	2.0 Plan Development	11d
14	$790.56	2.01 Set Plan Objectives/Constraints	1d
15	$696.96	2.02 Confirm Objectives/Constraints with Stat	3d
16	$589.28	2.03 Develop Plan Details	4d
17	$568.98	2.04 Create Model	3d
18	$432.96	2.05 Computer Analysis of Model	2d
19	$746.32	2.06 Model Evaluation and Modification	1d
20	$222.32	2.07 Package Model for Presentation	1d
21	$0.00	3.0 Present Plan	8h
22	$473.04	4.0 Evaluate Feedback	1d
23	$473.04	5.0 Modify Plan & Finalize	1d
24	$4,773.00	6.0 Design Computer Tracking System	12.8d
25	$463.50	5.01 Create Database	1d
26	$463.60	1.02 Create Spreadsheets	1d
27	$0.00	6.02.01 Identify Requirements	1d
28	$0.00	8.02.02.01 Data Sources	1d

Project: Operations - Human Resource
Date: Tue 12/16/97

Task   Progress   Milestone   Summary   Rolled Up Task   Rolled Up Milestone   Rolled Up Progress

- Creating a project team encompassing all the skills necessary to accomplish the project;
- Developing a detailed project plan showing the work to be accomplished, the sequencing of that work, the resources required, and the anticipated budget for each task;
- Managing that plan by collecting detailed information and letting the computer provide a detailed analysis about how the project is progressing.

While this process sounds simple, it does require a great deal of discipline and support from senior management, especially in an organization that is used to hierarchical direction and functional distribution of responsibilities.

REFERENCES

Belinger, T. C. (1995). *Successful project management*, (pp. 12-16). American Management Association, Watertown, MA.

Berry, R. (1994). Project Management for nurses. *Journal of Intravenous Nursing, 17*: 28-34.

Day, G., Hindmarsh, J., Hojna, C., and Ventimiglia, N. (1994). Improving medication administration through an enhanced occurrence reporting system. *Journal of Nursing Care Quality, 9*: 51-56.

Donnels, M., McDonald, B., and Trimble, J. (1995). Improving care through a medication administration process action team. *Journal of Nursing Care Quality, 9*: 38-44.

Frame, J. D. (1995). *Managing project in organizations* (pp. 7-16). Jossey-Bass, San Francisco, CA.

Heard, K. (1994). Improving patient outcomes in a dialysis unit: An integrated approach to CQI. *Journal of Nursing Care Quality, 9*: 44-50.

Heacock, D., and Brobst, R. (1994). A multidisciplinary approach to critical path development: A valuable CQI tool. *Journal of Nursing Care Quality, 8*: 38-41.

Lewis, J. P. (1995). *Fundamentals of project management.*, (pp. 7-8). American Management Association, New York, NY.

PMI Standards Committee. (1996). *A guide to the project management body of knowledge*, (Chapters 2 and 3. pp. 11, 27-33). Project Management Institute: Upper Darby, PA.

Schifiliti, C. and Morin, T.A. (1989). A project management approach to nursing documentation. *Nursing Management, 20*: 72A-72H.

45.
THE PHYSICIAN EXECUTIVE

Howard P. Greenwald, *University of Southern California, Sacramento, CA*

Jo Ann Ott and Eugene S. Schneller, *Arizona State University, Tempe, AZ*

Mary L. Richardson, *University of Washington, Seattle, WA*

The emergence of physician-executives as a new class of decision-makers in the United States health care system represents both opportunity and challenge. The technical expertise of physicians and their high credibility in clinical matters give weight to the belief that these professionals should occupy an increasing percentage of management posts in health service delivery organizations. But the movement of physicians into management reflects neither predominant trends in the history of medicine in the United States nor the core capabilities of medical doctors. This chapter draws on available research findings, less formal information from the management literature, and observations of several physicians in positions providing strategic perspectives on the physician-executive. On this basis, the work to follow examines the physician-executive in social and historical context, defines the physician-executive role in terms of generic and physician-specific management functions, assesses the preparation of physicians today for management roles, and raises questions about the value which physician-executives may add to health care in the United States. Acknowledging incomplete information, this chapter proposes models to promote training and utilization of physician-executives in a manner consistent with the needs of both providers and consumers of health care.

The executive role, characterized by explicit and formal management responsibilities, serves as the focus of this chapter. Executive roles of this kind differ markedly from leadership positions traditionally occupied by physicians. Physicians have historically exercised leadership by acting as monitors, helping assess the work of others to ensure conformity to professional norms, or as representatives, carrying positions formulated by colleagues to boards and governing bodies of which they are constituents. The physician-executive departs from these roles by assuming responsibility for hiring other medical staff members, orienting them to organizational roles, assigning work, evaluating performance, and, when necessary, arranging for dismissal (Leatt 1994). While still a colleague to other physicians in an important sense, the physician-executive has responsibility for representing the provider organization's interests to other physicians.

I. THE EMERGENCE OF PHYSICIAN-EXECUTIVES: SOCIAL AND HISTORICAL CONTEXT

Rapid and fundamental changes in the financing and organization of health care in the United States during the 1980s and 1990s have provided the major impetus for development of physician-executives. Medicine has diverged from the loosely-integrated array of highly independent, free professionals, and small enterprises it long comprised. Observers such as Starr (1984) have characterized this change as corporatization and bureaucratization. While some (Freidson, 1985) believe that the medical profession as a corporate body maintains its autonomy and dominance over medical work, others (McKinlay 1982; McKinlay and Stoekle, 1988) argue that physicians now face "deprofessionalization" and even "proletarianization." Both a desire to protect individual autonomy and to take positive leadership in development of the new system has led increasing numbers of physicians to enter executive roles.

The integrated delivery system (IDS), a prime example of the organizational changes referenced above, serves as an important illustrative context for the movement of physicians into management. The IDS — which includes increasingly familiar entities such as "vertically integrated" and "managed care" health plans — is a coordinated system of individuals and organizations providing services under central financing arrangements and administrative structures. In the IDS, the treatment outcomes and financial well-being of each individual and organizational unit depend directly on the orientation and performance of others. Outcomes of the work of individual physicians become more observable and accessible to other physicians and non-physicians alike. In part due to competitive pressures, IDSs have increasingly engaged in processes designed to demonstrate, maintain and improve quality as indicated by outcome measures available to larger publics than ever before. These mandates require collaborative efforts such as Total Quality Management (TQM) and Continuous Quality Improvement (CQI), which necessarily involve mutual scrutiny and collaboration among physicians to a degree unparalled in the past.

Although true deprofessionalization appears unlikely, these developments radically change the relationship among physicians and between the physician and the provider organization (Gray, 1986). The IDS's operations require collaboration among teams of managers and clinicians working across professional and institutional boundaries, thus challenging conventional jurisdictions and alignments of power, authority, and status in health care organizations (Lammert, 1978; Abbott, 1988). Attenuation of traditional boundaries and jurisdictions raises the possibility that some physicians may lose the ability to function as independent authorities in medical matters and as clear patient advocates.

Within this changed environment, physicians appear likely to view participation in management as essential for maintaining personal satisfaction and goals. An important formulation by Hirschman (1970) provides a framework for interpreting current phenomena and projecting future trends. Hirschman proposes "voice" and "exit" as alternative options for action by individuals to dissatisfaction with organizations that no longer meet their needs, have deteriorated in performance, or have developed in directions perceived as unsatisfactory. Whereas the individual reduces or ceases participation under the exit option, he or she seeks mechanisms for working toward favorable organizational change under the voice alternative. Until recently, physicians almost always registered their dissatisfaction with health care delivery organizations through the mechanism of exit. A physician dissatisfied with a particular hospital, for example, could easily admit his or her patients to another hospital at which he or she maintained privileges. Eventually, however, most physicians in the United States seem likely to become employees of IDSs, contractors to individual IDSs or hospitals, or bound to a greater or lesser degree to other large, centrally managed provider organizations, making options for exit increasingly scarce. Development of voice, then, attains crucial importance for the physician as a mechanism for exercising influence in the organization. Participation in management offers an increasingly attractive opportunity for putting the voice option into effect.

The interest of physicians in management doubtlessly reflects a desire to maintain professional dominance but may be viewed more broadly as an effort to preserve basic norms and values in the practice of medicine. Linkage of traditional commitments with emerging system needs within the physician-executive role may be its strongest asset. An analysis by Wolinsky (1993) suggests that the physician-executive may have a significance well beyond day-to-day management of service delivery. He writes that only renewal of public trust in medicine as a fiduciary agency committed to social well-being, including significantly greater stewardship of the limited resources available for the provision of health care, can ensure continued autonomy and professional dominance. The physician-executive may symbolize commitment of the medical profession to values and goals shared by the vast majority of Americans.

II. THE PHYSICIAN-EXECUTIVE ROLE

A. The Physician-Executive Versus Traditional Leadership

Physicians who have held formal leadership positions have nearly always done so in hospitals, large multispecialty practices, and university medical centers. Ruelas and Leatt (1985) identify the most familiar associated titles as:

- Department Head: a "clinician-manager" with responsibilities in specialty areas;
- Chief of Medical Staff: a physician selected by the medical staff to represent their interests before managers and governing bodies and to chair major groups and committees;
- Medical Director: a hospital staff employee reporting to management on the status and operation of medical services.

Of these positions, the role of Medical Director most closely approaches that of a true manager. While the Chief of Medical Staff represents physicians in the "house of management," the Medical Director is a member of the management team responsible

to other executives. In contrast, traditional physician leaders have emphasized collegial relationships and focused on clinical matters (Warner, 1985; Berwick and Coltin,
1986; Linton and Peachey, 1989; Berkwick, 1989; Weiss, et al. 1990; Liu, 1992). The representative and monitoring functions exercised by traditional medical leaders omit the
imperative content and independent vision associated with true executive roles.

Researchers and commentators on distinctions between traditional physician leaders and physician-executives have emphasized differences between managers and clinicians in perspective and style of decision making. Characterizing executive functions
as "organization and accomplishment of work by others," Forkosh (1982) identifies differences between clinical leadership and management in several key areas:

- Handling problems: The clinician reacts, whereas the manager is proactive
  (anticipating, planning, designing, innovating);
- Relations with patients: The clinician relates on a one-to-one basis, the manager
  to groups rather than individuals;
- Discharge of authority: The clinician exercises personal authority over the
  patient, whereas the manager delegates authority to improve efficiency;
- Types and criteria for rewards: The clinician receives immediate and personal
  rewards, while the manager receives delayed and vicarious rewards.

Others have contrasted the clinical and managerial approaches to problem-solving
as reactive versus proactive (McEachern 1991) and patient versus system-oriented
(Shortell et al., 1985; Trentalance 1990). Shortell (1991) highlights differences between
clinicians and managers regarding basis of professional knowledge (social and management science versus biomedical science), criteria for decision making (qualitative
versus quantitative information tightly linking cause and effect), and assessment of
resources (limited versus unlimited to maximize quality of care). Among physicians
who enter management, Kralewski and Wingert (1994) stress a change in concern with
individual patients to "an emphasis on populations and cost-effective ways of organizing services for those populations."

Distinctions in outlook between clinicians and managers appear to stem in part
from differences in values and personality traits. Focusing on personality differences
between physicians and managers, Ottensmeyer and Key (1991) cite valuation of
autonomy versus teamwork, crisis mentality versus long-range orientation, and conflict avoidance versus conflict management. Colligan and Berglund (1985) write that
the physician's traits emphasize autonomy, ego, and orientation toward immediate
and personal rewards, while the manager's traits predispose him or her toward team
efforts in pursuit of relatively subjective, vague, long-term rewards for the organization. Porter and Royer (1987) add that the manager's criteria for success are often
vague and outcomes too ambiguous for the scientifically-trained physician. Conflicts
between clinicians and managers appear to be recreated within physicians themselves
who move from one field to the other in the form of reluctance to abandon clinical
medicine as a primary career focus (Lloyd, 1982).

The distinctions specified above do not imply that the emerging physician-executive will merely exchange his or her clinical orientation for a generic management outlook. Rather, the capacity to span the boundary between historically distinct outlooks
and sets of activities may come to define the physician-executive's unique function.

Conflict between management structures and professionals, particularly where these professionals are physicians, is a well-known phenomenon (Freidson, 1975). The feeling among physicians that increasingly visible management structures signify decreasing professional discretion and independence constitutes an essential source of conflict (Burgoyne and Lorbiecki, 1993). Acknowledging, accommodating, and resolving such conflict appears likely to become an essential requirement for productive provider organizations, implying permanent need for executives capable of balancing clinical and management imperatives.

Management of conflicts among individuals and groups with differing orientations and interests is vital to the cojoint system of authority (Scott, 1982) envisioned for the future of health care in the United States. In such a system, physician and non-physician managers collaborate directly in making key decisions. Several researchers (Landgarten, 1981; Olazagasti, 1990) emphasize that the presence of diverse stakeholders necessarily expose the physician-executive to conflict, underscoring the importance among his or her functions of bringing about reconciliation. Kissick (1989) characterizes people in top leadership positions as "prime ministers," leading multiple constituencies with diverse agendas.

B. Emerging Roles

When asked for examples of physician-executives today, the strategic observers described holders of such positions at aggressive, growing group practices, major hospitals (Mayo Clinic, Boston University Hospital, Long Island Jewish) and very large HMOs. These included paid medical directors and senior partners in large partnerships. The generation of physician-executives currently nearing retirement includes pioneers gifted with multiple talents and a powerful sense of vision. The editor and elder statesman cited Harvard's Eugene Braunwald as illustrative of the ideal physician-executive:

> He is a great CEO. He exudes the qualities that generate respect
> from colleagues. He is very outstanding professionally as a
> researcher and teacher and is on anyone's list of outstanding cardiol-
> ogists. He has it all. He is a step ahead of the rest of the world and
> sets big, broad targets. He knows more than anyone else but has a
> nose for talent, spots good people, and delegates.

As physician-executives become a more familiar part of the health care system, they will doubtlessly perform functions requiring less extraordinary gifts. Several specialized executive roles are already identifiable. Technically-oriented physician-executives, "data-driven physician-experts" concerned with strategic decisionmaking through large-scale outcome and epidemiological data, are joining those with more traditional organizational skills. Physician-entrepreneurs have become highly visible, identifying and acting on business opportunities offered by new technology, raising capital, and arranging mergers and acquisitions of health care practices (Anundsen 1988; Anders, 1993). Only physician-executives in top management may require a broad combination of capabilities.

C. Current Status

Much research suggests that the physician-executive role is currently in an early stage of development (Cohn, 1986). Witt Associates (1988) has reported that the percentage of hospitals surveyed having or seeking a Vice President for Medical Affairs — individuals resembling the Medical Director described above but with additional authority to hire, reward, and discipline medical staff—grew from 53 to 92 between 1979 and 1988. According to a survey reported by Kindig and Lastiri-Quiros (1989), however, the average physician-manager spent only 65% of his or her time in that role. Others writing in the 1980s reported that physician-managers often maintained their private practices. Executives outside medicine nearly always hold their responsibilities as full-time jobs.

Surveys of self-designated physician-executives suggest not only that actual numbers of physician-executives today are low but that recent growth has been slow. According to Betson and Petroja (1989), the number of physicians in positions similar to those described by Ruelas and Leatt grew from 11,715 in 1968 to 14,399 in 1986, an increase small in comparison with those of most health professions during a comparable period. As indicated above, moreover, most traditional physician leaders are not true executives. A strategic observer occupying a high-level executive position in a California-based not-for-profit hospital system estimated that physicians playing senior executive roles today number only 35-40 nationwide. Major impacts of physician-executives in health care delivery may have to await substantial increases in holders of such positions.

III. TALENTS, SKILLS AND PHYSICIAN-EXECUTIVE CAREERS

Developing policies and procedures to ensure that physician-executives in the coming years achieve maximum effectiveness in their roles requires an understanding of the needed personal and technical capabilities, as well as mechanisms through which these are acquired and used as the basis for career progression. Acknowledging that the physician-executive role is still in a developmental stage, it is important to note that mechanisms and career pathways that have heretofore prepared and placed physicians in leadership positions appear obsolete. The value physician-executives contribute to health care delivery will depend on future transformations in these areas.

A. Skills and Personality Features

Observation of the tasks now most frequently engaged in by physician-executives provides insights into the essential skills and knowledge required in such roles. According to Betson and Pedroja (1989), major physician-executive tasks include (in order of importance) policy management, program management, and resource management. Based on a survey of physician-managers, Kindig and Lastiri-Quiros (1989) detected 33 frequently-encountered tasks including governance, general internal management, clinical internal management, management of physicians, and external and environmental relationships. The physicians surveyed attributed greatest importance to general internal management and clinical management.

Consistent with a key element of the physician-executive role described above, research highlights the ability to facilitate communication and cooperation as a basic qualification (Brady and Carpenter, 1986). This is consistent with Fitzgerald and Sturt's (1992) finding that members of clinical executives in the United Kingdom, where they have long played a central role in management, serve as liaison to people and communicators to decision makers and exercise direct management functions themselves in strategic planning, resource allocation, standard determination, and outcome assessment. A survey of physician-executives by Ottensmeyer and Key (1991) identifies communication skills (particularly spoken) as the most important qualifications for such positions, enabling their occupants to exercise the vital function of conflict resolution.

The majority of personal qualities specified in the literature seem identical with those desirable in any manager. Ottensmeyer and Key (1991) indicate as crucial qualities for success communicativeness, willingness to take a stand, ability to influence others, flexibility, skill at committee work, comfort with bureaucracy, orientation toward people, confidence, and team spirit. McCall (1989) adds qualities of "temperament" such as ability to deal with ambiguity and uncertainty and to admit and learn from mistakes.

Several items in the literature imply or specify a more cohesive set of characteristics of special significance to the physician-executive's success. All these characteristics contribute to the physician-executive's ability to play his or her central role in the health care delivery organization, characterized by Schneller (1991) as maintaining clinical integrity by integrating clinical data into management practice.

Perhaps the most important distinguishing characteristic of physician-executives is the need to maintain credibility among practicing physicians (HCMR 1984; Barrable 1988). Authority in his or her field of practice supports the physician-executive's ability to communicate with clinicians and increases his or her credibility as a manager. Closely associated with this is the physician-executive's need to project the image that he or she had not fled clinical practice to enter management, but has chosen management in order to favorably influence the practice behavior of his or her peers (Ottensmeyer and Key, 1991). According to the Chief of Staff in a large medical practice,

> The physician-manager stands to lose his physician constituency if
> he is not first and foremost a strong clinician who in some fashion
> stays current...I don't see this person as a classic line manager but
> rather as a cheerleader, someone who can help other physicians
> adjust to the new medical reality of managed care....This person
> needs to be fully engaged in developing clinical pathways, measur-
> ing quality, and developing practice profiles ...

Development and maintenance of capabilities in clinical medicine appear to remain a requirement for physician-executives at this time. Their importance is underscored by the belief among many of today's clinicians reported by the strategic observer identified above that physicians choose management careers because they do not enjoy or have failed at medicine.

B. Development of the Physician-Executive

Today, a physician's pathway to executive status almost always begins in clinical medicine. Lloyd (1982), for example, reports that three out of four medical directors are recruited from among members of a hospital medical staff. The literature suggests specific pathways through which clinicians become executives. Jensen (1986), for example, traces the executive's development to the point of becoming a "centered" manager, with a balanced view of complex delivery systems. But while it is possible to discern definite career patterns, development of skills, knowledge, and concrete capabilities appears to have traditionally taken place in an unstandardized and perhaps even accidental way.

According to the Dean for Curricular Affairs of a California medical school, the career path of a contemporary developed in a manner supportive of these generalizations:

> (The physician) entered management through circumstance, original-
> ly coming to the school to do pulmonary medicine. He was asked to
> serve on some small committees and later on larger committees. As
> time went on, he was chosen as Chief of Staff and then offered a full-
> time management position.

Citing his own experience, the Dean noted:

> My own career has been exactly the same way — someone asked if I
> could serve. People feel it is a duty to be of service.

Formal education in management plays a role in the development of today's physician-manager, but its value and importance appear uncertain. A significant percentage of today's physician-executives have undergone at least some formal training. In a study of Canadian physician-managers, Barrable (1988) reports that 38% had taken administrative courses. Based on a survey of members of the American Academy of Medical Directors, Betson and Pedroja (1989) report that 83% had some "management education," 78% through continuing education programs. Kindig and Lastiri-Quiros (1989) report that 13% of physicians in the United States who identify administration as their primary activity held graduate degrees in administration. Kindig and Lastiri-Quiros also report that 83.6% of these physicians felt that management coursework was required or advisable.

Several observers have questioned the value of formal management training for the potential physician-executive. Chester and Wood (1988) characterize the results of training physicians on their attitudes towards management and the economic impacts of patient care as difficult to judge. Betson (1986) reports that of the physician-managers in her survey who had received at least some management education, only 61% felt that this education was helpful in preparing them for their positions. Barrable (1988) reports that 44% of the Chiefs of Staff he studied claimed that administrative training would not result in improvements in their performance. Ottensmeyer and Key (1991) report that a group of HMO consultants with experience as medical directors rated the value of formal management training as very low, these informants indicating that they had acquired their skills through on-the-job training. Negative comments by physician-managers may reflect dissatisfaction with existing procedures and programs rather than principled disbelief in such education. Fitzgerald and Sturt (1992) write that physicians prefer "action learning" based on concrete problems, a feature often absent from management education curricula.

IV. FUNCTIONAL CONTRIBUTIONS OF THE PHYSICIAN-EXECUTIVE

Perhaps the best argument in favor of potential contributions by physician-executives to health care organizations rests on their special sensitivity to clinical appropriateness. The essential variability of clinical practice (Eddy, 1990) suggests clinical training as a necessity for appreciation of this critical element in quality of care. It is further arguable that only a physician has sufficient understanding of the unstandardizable aspects of medical care to exercise authority over practitioners.

Well-executed studies support this argument. Shortell, Morrison, and Friedman (1990) reports that significant physician participation in management decision making characterizes the nation's most successful hospitals. Several studies indicate that traditional forms of physician participation in management yield benefits for the organization (Burns et al.,1989; Shortell, 1991). Shortell and LoGerfo (1981) highlight the impact of physician participation in organizational decision making on quality, reporting, for example, a relationship between physician presence on hospital boards and low mortality rates in specific surgical procedures. Other researchers present evidence suggesting that physician participation in specific management areas add value in health care delivery. These include policy-making related to medical affairs (Betson, 1986); hospital strategic planning and governance (Kovner and Chin, 1985); cost control (Heyssel, 1984); information systems, communication, and networking (Friedman and Martin, 1988).

Several authors, however, question whether inclusion of physicians in management (as distinct from their participation through advisement) actually helps control costs. Brown (1989) has suggested that physicians may seek management training to change the institution's performance to conform more closely with their traditional values and desires. These have not always proven cost-effective in American health care. Prehn's (1993) comment that there is little research about the factors that build an effective team of physician and non physician managers raises further issues about the potential contributions of physician-executives to the delivery organization as a whole. The physician-executive's unusual combination of capabilities lend themselves to areas such as QA and strategic planning, but are less clearly valuable in top leadership positions such as external relations, marketing, risk management, and finance.

Perhaps the greatest area of doubt surrounding the physician-executive concerns his or her attachment to the physician versus the management role. At one extreme, the physician-executive may "go native," becoming indistinguishable from the manager with no clinical education. Under this scenario, the patient could lose an important traditional advocate. Alternatively, the physician-executive may use his or her management position to act upon pre-existing clinical orientations. Based on this possibility, Larkin (1988) draws negative implications for the functional contributions physician-executives might make to core management objectives. He writes:

Because physicians traditionally approach hospital resources with a clinical orientation, they use their operational or policymaking power to gain more resources for patient treatment with little regard for cost containment.

V. DISCUSSION

A. Unanswered Questions

Several unanswered questions deserve special attention. First, research on physician-executives has typically focused on their functioning in the hospital rather than the IDS, which is rapidly becoming the predominant health care delivery organization in the United States. Second, little systematically-collected data now exist on the actual number of physicians who function as true executives, the positions they hold, and the career paths they have followed. Third, no definitive information exists on the most useful curricular elements in educational programs for physician-executives or the best methods for their delivery. Most important, research has yet to determine the managerial functions for which medical training actually increases an individual's capabilities and the degree to which physician-executives add value to a health care delivery organization.

Despite an incomplete understanding, planners and policymakers must take action now to prepare the coming generation of physician-executives for roles in which they are truly needed. To lay the foundation for such action, this chapter concludes with models for improving the process through which physician-executives are recruited, prepared, and organized.

B. Educating the Future Physician-Executive

Future physician-executives will require greater range and depth in management expertise than their predecessors and hence more formal management education. A model of management education for physicians should account for variation in career paths and specific functions. At least in the foreseeable future, many (perhaps a majority) of physician-executives will enter such roles in the traditional manner, having functioned primarily as clinicians in the early part of their careers. At the same time, it seems likely that a new breed of physicians will specialize in management throughout their professional lives. Some of the specific management roles identified above may require lifetime commitments, others may be best pursued after years of exclusive involvement with patient care.

Several innovative programs to develop physician-executives have focused on early training, an approach recommended by Ruelas and Leatt (1985). As early as 1977, Polvnick, Fry, and Rubin argued for formal management training programs for physicians and field tested related elements at Massachusetts Institute of Technology (MIT). One such program at the University of Arizona (Cordes et al., 1989) has incorporated teaching of managerial skills into its residency programs in selected medical specialties. Subjects covered include budgeting, fiscal control, political and regulatory processes, personnel, planning and organization, and computer techniques. Residents take courses during the academic year. They may take rotations which provide opportunities to observe and participate in administrative activities.

Practicing physicians seeking to enter management have often looked toward general training programs, such as the Master of Public Health (MPH) with a specialty in administration, Master in Health Administration (MHA) or the Master of Business Administration (MBA). Innovative programs, however, have attempted to integrate the physician's work organization with executive recruitment and training. Bloom (1990) recommends that medical directors should work with in-house staff members who show leadership potential to develop their management skills. In-house training through advanced instructional techniques appears likely to increase. Anundsen (1988), for example, discusses the option of bringing in outside experts and training potential physician-executives with the aid of computers.

Specialized programs and modules adapted to the needs of physicians at different stages in management careers and levels of management functioning will increase the effectiveness of formal management education. Ruelas and Leatt (1985) suggest that top executives primarily require conceptual training followed by interpersonal skills; middle-level executives primarily require technical management skills; first-line managers require primarily interpersonal skills followed by conceptual and technical training. The best training programs will emerge from an improved understanding of actual pathways leading to management roles emphasizing specific sets of skills. At this time, however, it appears reasonable to expect growth in increasingly distinct physician-executive pathways, initiated in early versus mid to late career. Integration of management education with undergraduate medical curricula and clinical residency training is clearly compatible with the first pathway, more traditional part-time and executive education with the second.

Potential functional contributions by physician-executives appear greatest in quality assurance, relationships with practicing clinicians, and adjustment of clinical practice to organizational objectives. Recent survey results indicate wide agreement between physicians and non-physician managers about assigning these responsibilities to physician-executives (Dunham et al.). These tasks represent some of the greatest challenges facing the IDS today. Greater participation of physicians in other areas of management such as marketing, finance, and chief executive functioning appears of less certain benefit. Outside the executive clinical directorate, physician-executives and executives without medical training appear likely to occupy many of the same management positions according to the interests, talents, and capacities of individuals, and the needs of each provider organization.

ACKNOWLEDGMENT

We are grateful to the Center for Health Management Research at Arizona State University and to the Network for Healthcare Mangement for supporting the research on which this chapter is based.

REFERENCES

Abbott A. (1988). *Systems of Professions.* University of Chicago Press, Chicago.

Anders G. McDonald's methods come to medicine as chains acquire physicians' practices. *Wall St. Journal. August 24, 1993*: Sec. B, pg. 1.

Anundsen K. (Jan-Feb 1988). The rewards of innovation. *Healthcare Forum Journal.* 31(1): 20-1, 24-5.

Barrable, W. (Winter 1988). A profile and educational framework for physician managers in a teaching hospital. *The Journal of Health Administration Education,* 6(1): 23-38.

Berwick, D. M. (1989). Continuous improvement as an ideal in health care. *The New England Journal of Medicine, 320:* 53-6.

Berwick, D.M., and Coltin, K.L. (Mar 21, 1986). Feedback reduces test use in a health maintenance organization. *The Journal of the American Medical Association.* 255(11): 1450-54.

Betson, C.L. (1986). *Managing the Medical Enterprise: A study of physician managers.* UMI Research Press, Ann Arbor, MI.

Betson, C., and Pedroja, A. T. (Fall 1989). Physician Managers: A description of their job in hospitals. *Hospital & Health Services Administration,* 34(3): 353-369.

Bloom, D.M. (Jan-Feb 1990). The chief of staff and the medical director. *Physician Executive,* 21-2.

Brady, T. F., and Carpenter, C. R. (Sept/Oct 1986). Defining the management role of the department medical director. *Hospital & Health Services Administration,* 31(5): 69-85.

Brown, G. D. (Fall 1989). Physician executives, or management training for physicians. *The Journal of Health Administration Education,* 7(4): 694-701.

Burgoyne, J., and Lorbiecki, A. (Nov 1993). Clinicians into management: the experience in context. *Health Services Management Research,* 6(4): 248-259.

Burns, L., Andersen, R., and Shortell, S. M. (Oct 1989). Impact of corporate structures on physician inclusion and participation. *Medical Care,* 27: 967-982.

Chester, T. E., Wood, J. (1988). *Journal of Health Administration Education,* 6: 515-525.

Cohn, R. E. (Nov/Dec 1986). The medical director-the untapped potential of the position. *Hospital & Health Services Administration,* 31(6): 51-61.

Colligan, R. D., and Berglund, E. (1985). Changing roles of physicians, nurses, and administrators. *Medical Group Management,* 32: 38-42.

Cordes, D. H., Rea, D. F., Vuturo, A., and Rea, J. (Nov 1988). Management roles for physicians: training residents for the reality. *Journal of Occupational Medicine* 30(11): 863-867.

Dunham, N. C., Kindig, D.A., and Schulz, R. The value of the physician executive role to organizational effectiveness and performance. *Medical Care Review,* Forthcoming.

Eddy, D. M. (Jan 12, 1990). The Challenge. *The Journal of the American Medical Association,* 263(2): 287-290.

Fitzgerald, L., and Sturt, J. (July 1992). Clinicians into management: On the change agenda or not? *Health Services Management Research,* 5(2): 137-146.

Forkosh, D.S. (May 1982). Good doctors aren't always good managers. *The Hospital Medical Staff,* 11(5): 2-5.

Freidson, E. *(1985).* The reorganization of the medical profession. *Medical Care Review,* 42: 11-35.

Fredison, E. (1975). *Doctoring Together.* University of Chicago Press, Chicago.

Friedman, B., and Martin, J. (1988). The physician as a locus of authority, responsibility, and operational control of medical systems. *Journal of Medical Systems, 12:* 389-396.

Gray, B. H. (1986). The changing nature of physician influence in medical institutions. In *For-Profit Enterprise in Health Care.* National Academy Press, Washington, D.C.: 171-181.

HCMR (Health Care Management Review). (Fall, 1984). HCMR interviews physician administration leaders. *Health Care Management Review,* 9: 81-91.

Heyssel, R. M. (1984). Decentralized management in a teaching hospital: ten years at Johns Hopkins. *New England Journal of Medicine,* 310: 1477-1480.

Hirschman, A. O. (1970). *Exit, Voice, and Loyalty: Responses to Decline in Firms, Organizations, and States.* Harvard University Press, Cambridge.

Jensen, A. T. (Sept-Oct 1986). Physician executive leadership. *Medical Group Management, 33*(5): 20-27.

Kindig, D. A., and Lastiri-Quiros, S. (Winter 1989). The changing managerial role of physician executives. *The Journal of Health Administration Education, 7*(1): 33-46.

Kirkman-Liff, B., Schneller, E. (Spring 1992). The resource management initiative in the English National Health Service. *Health Care Management Review, 17*(2): 59-70.

Kissick, W. L. (Fall, 1989). Health care management according to Ben Franklin. *Journal of Health Administration Education, 7*(4): 723-733.

Kovner, A. R., and Chin, M. J. (Nov-Dec 1985). Physician leadership in hospital strategic decision making. *Hospital and Health Services Administration, 30*(6): 64-79.

Kralewski, J., and Wingert, T. (Mar 1994). The emerging role of the physician in administration. *Physician Executive, 20*(3): 3-7.

Lammert, H. (Jul-Sept 1978). Power, authority and status in health systems: a Marxian-based conflict analysis. *The Journal of Applied Behavioral Science, 14*(3): 321-333.

Landgarten, S. (May 1981). Skilled medical director can turn conflict into collaboration. *The Hospital Medical Staff, 10*(5): 2-9.

Larkin, H. (1988). Do physician managers save money? *Trustee, 41*(6): 18.

Leatt, P. (1994). Physicians in health care management. 1. Physicians as managers: roles and future challenges. *Canadian Medical Association Journal, 150*(2): 171-176.

Linton, A., and Peachey, D. (Sept 15, 1990). The roles of physician-executives in hospitals: a framework for management education. *Canadian Medical Association Journal, 143*(6): 485-490.

Liu, P. (Sep-Oct 1992). Physician executives: where they are and what they do. *Physician Executive, 18*(5): 30-4.

Lloyd, J. S. (March 1982). Hiring a medical director. *The Hospital Medical Staff, 11*(3): 17-22.

McCall, M. W. (Nov-Dec 1989). Secrets of management success. *Physician Executive, 15*(6):10-2.

McEachern, J. E., Makens, E. K., Buchanan, E. D., and Schiff, L. (Mar 1991). Quality Improvement: An imperative for medical care. *Journal of Occupational Medicine, 33*(3): 364-71.

McKinlay, J. (1982). Toward the proletarianization of physicians. In: *Professionals as Workers: Mental Labor in Advanced Capitalism.* G.K. Hall, Boston.

McKinlay, J., and Stoekle, J. (1988). Corporatization and the social transformation of doctoring. *International Journal of Health Services, 18*: 191-205.

Olazagasti, R. A. (Mar-Apr 1990). Chief of staff and medical director: Conflict or cooperation? *Physician Executive,* 33-35.

Ottensmeyer, D. J., and Key, M. K. (Spring 1991). Lessons learned hiring HMO medical directors. *Health Care Management Review, 16*(2): 21-30.

Phren, R. A. (Spring 1993). Variables in effective CEO-medical director relations. *Hospital Topics, 71*(2): 25-28.

Plovnick, M. S., Fry, R. E., and Rubin, I. M. (Jun 1977). A management development course for physicians. *Journal of Medical Education, 52*(6): 518-20.

Porter, R. E., and Royer, T. (1987). Physician managers — a challenge for training and teaching. *MGMA Journal, Nov-Dec*: 42-47.

Ruelas, E., and Leatt, P. (Spring, 1985). The roles of physician-executives in hospitals: a framework for management education. *Journal of Health Administration Education, 3*(2): 151-169.

Schneller, E. S. (Spring 1991). The leadership and executive potential of physicians in an era of managed care systems. *Hospital & Health Services Administration, 36*(1): 43-55.

Scott, W. (Fall, 1982). Managing professional work: three models of control for health organizations. *Health Services Research. 17*(3): 213-40.

Shortell, S. M. (1991). *Effective Hospital-Physician Relationships.* Health Administration press Perspectives, Ann Arbor, MI.

Shortell, S. M., Morrisey, M. A., and Conrad, D. A. (Dec 1985). Economic regulation and hospital behavior: The effects on medical staff organization and hospital-physician relationships. *Health Services Research, 20*(5): 597-628.

Shortell, S. M., Morrison, E. M., and Friedman, B. (1990). *Strategic Choices for American Hospitals.* Jossey-Bass, San Francisco.

Shortell, S. M., and LoGerfo, J. P. (Oct 1991). Hospital medical staff organization and quality of care: Results for myocardial infarction and appendectomy. *Medical Care, 19*: 1041-1055.

Starr, P. (1984). *The Social Transformation of American Medicine.* Basic Books, New York.

Trentalance, A. E. (1990). Physician managers can play key financial management role. *Physician Executive, Jan-Feb*: 23-6.

Warner, A. M. (1985). Education for roles and responsibilities in quality assurance: physician leadership. *Quality Review Bulletin, 11*: 111-114.

Weiss, R., Charney, E., Baumgardner, R. A., German, P. S., Mellits, E. D., Skinner, E. A., and Williamson, J. W. (May 1990). Changing patient management: what influences the practicing pediatrician? *Pediatrics, 85*(5): 791-5.

Witt Associates, Inc. (1988). Vice President of Medical Affairs: Report of a Survey. Witt Associates, Inc., Oak Brook, IL.

Wolinsky, F. D. (1993). The professional dominance, deprofessionalization, proletarianization, and corporatization perspectives: an overview and synthesis. In: F.W. Hafferty and J.B. McKinlay: *The Changing Medical Profession.* Oxford, New York: 11-24.

46.

INFORMATION TECHNOLOGY TO ASSURE QUALITY CARE AT REASONABLE COST

Judith J. Kirchhoff, *Long Island University, Brooklyn, NY*

It is widely accepted that quality in health care is "the degree to which health services for individuals and populations increase the likelihood of desired health outcomes and are consistent with current professional knowledge" (JCAHO, 1993, p. 59). Some authors place additional constraints on the definition of quality: "Quality of care is the production of improved health and satisfaction of a population within the constraints of existing technology, resources and consumer circumstances" (Palmer, 1995, p. 27). Palmer adds satisfaction to improved health and resources and consumer circumstances as qualifiers to achievement of improved health. Both sources accept that quality is a judgment made on the basis of perspective and interest, that is, quality is relative.

It also is widely accepted that judgments of health care quality must be based upon the performance of health care providers. Performance is what health care providers do, their inputs and processes and what they achieve--their results (JCAHO, 1993). Performance is the empirical basis for judgments about quality, regardless of how one defines the term quality. To be a basis for quality judgments, performance must be measured, and the measurements must be disseminated to those who need to make judgments.

Those who need to make judgments include key participants of the health care industry, its stakeholders. Stakeholders include the community, payers, consumers, providers, regulators, and accreditors. In the organizational arrangements comprising the health care industry, some stakeholders possess performance information about health services, and others need it but have little, and always second hand, access to it. For example, patients need to select primary physicians, but they have neither the technical knowledge of medicine (Eastaugh, 1992) nor access to performance information about physician practice patterns (AHA, 1991) whose variations of which are known to raise many questions about costs and quality (Chassin, et al., 1992).

In addition to the consensus about the subjectiveness of quality judgments and the need for performance data to support valid judgments, there is widespread concern about the rate of growth of health care expenditures and of health care as a percentage of Gross Domestic Product (GDP) (Knickman and Thorpe, 1995). That concern is exhibited in efforts to contain costs. "Costs" are used to describe many aspects of the use of money in health care (Gapenski, 1993), from charges billed by hospitals to negotiated payments between payers and providers; from the resources used to produce service capacity to expense allocations from non-direct services to direct services; from resources expended per unit to aggregated expenditures; from payer premiums to payment mechanisms like DRGs or capitation rates to tax burdens. The reason is that the third party payer system in health care places "costs" in different positions depending upon the participant. Payments to providers are costs to the payers and revenues to providers. Provider costs yield expenditures which are referred to as the "costs" of health care to society, costs distributed between public and private sectors. Thus, costs refer to the monetary value of what they define and are measures of health care industry activity.

Cost containment, on the other hand, means reducing one's total or particular liability (Eastaugh, 1992) by means ranging from limiting covered services to pre-setting prices; from setting global budgets to excluding high risk individuals and groups from coverage; from negotiating discounts and volume rate contracts to developing health maintenance organizations (HMOs). As the literature of cost containment rises to a crescendo in praise of "managed care competition" (Wolford, Brown and McCool, 1994) as health care's economic salvation, its singular voice drowns out the parade of thousands of independent service providers into fewer and fewer provider organizations. The shift to fewer provider organizations leads eventually to vertical integration and oligopoly (Williamson, 1975), with increasing closure of access channels to data about performance and costs needed to make quality judgments. Vertical integration and oligopoly may contain costs in the short run, but if this change reduces the availability of health services data, society's goal of improved quality through better quality judgments will not be met.

The purpose of this chapter is to propose that effective use of information technology can assure public access to health services data for quality judgments without adding unnecessary costs to the delivery system. The proposed solution also makes consolidation into vertical integrated and oligopolistic hierarchy less attractive because it lowers transaction costs between and among independent entities by facilitating timely data exchange.

The proposed solution connects fragmented elements of the health care industry into a coherent system through information technology called electronic data interchange (EDI). EDI refers to the transmission and processing of data among computers without human interaction (HINT, 1995). EDI is not a computer system but rather a concept for using the existing electronic environment to re-engineer communications processes among partners involved in recurrent exchange transactions. The absence of human interaction speeds up transactions and reduces errors, lowering labor costs and errors, thus increasing efficiency (HINT, 1995). In the proposed EDI environment, all participants share data they hold and receive data they need at minimal cost and interference with data use by others.

Development of the solution begins with a brief description of the forces driving the health care industry toward closure of data access channels, that is, toward hierarchy. This is followed by a scenario focusing on a typical transaction between patient and physician with all participants cooperating to create a seamless system using the potential of EDI to speed data from originator to user. The scenario reveals four necessary conditions for information technology to be a solution to information impactedness:

- the need to specify where relevant data originate and where they need to go;
- computerization;
- standardization of computer transactions; and
- rules of access and exchange in an appropriate policy environment.

Each of the conditions is addressed, with focus on the current status and what will facilitate progress toward implementation of the scenario.

I. FROM COMPETITION TO INFORMATION

Market competition in the health care industry is likely to lead to hierarchy and then oligopoly, a market characterized by competition among a few large scale organizations. Williamson (1975) explains that this transition occurs when the transaction costs of recurrent exchanges in an industry (like health care) rise to the point that an organization decides to bypass the market and resort to hierarchy. Costs rise when human conditions of bounded rationality (in Simon's sense) and opportunism combine with environmental conditions of uncertainty and small numbers to produce information impactedness (Williamson, 1975). Opportunism refers to using knowledge, unfairly if necessary, to gain advantage in exchanges. Small numbers refers to the diminishing number of contractors that occurs as contractors gain knowledge during the contract period that gives them an advantage at re-contracting time. Information impactedness refers to the situations in which information is known to some and is very costly for others to obtain (Williamson, 1975).

Markets lead to hierarchies when the resourceful coopt market transactions into managerial decisions by acquiring control through long-term contracts or ownership of the knowledge source(s) (Williamson, 1975). Contracts or ownership, but primarily ownership, reduces both uncertainty and opportunism by transforming market decisions into managerial ones and precluding access to knowledge for others (Williamson, 1975). Those who remain outside become information impacted.

Elsewhere, Williamson's logic has been applied to the health care industry to show that we can expect the industry to develop into an oligopoly of the bureaucratic form that Williamson describes (Kirchhoff, 1995). The current demand for "market competition" is already stimulating health care industry consolidation, often into vertically integrated health maintenance organizations (HMOs) or product-line mergers (e.g., hospitals and physician groups). Merged organizations are likely candidates for future vertical integration.

For example, a physician group may buy a hospital, lab, and other ancillary services to gain control over a comprehensive array of services. In some cases, a large employer may purchase such a vertically integrated system to control health care delivery to its employees.

Insurer sponsored preferred provider organizations (PPOs), governed by contingent claims contracts, produce information impactedness for insurers. Insurers can gain knowledge advantages and preclude physician opportunism by creating geographically dispersed, vertically integrated hierarchies with physician employees. Similar processes are likely for other arrangements currently in operation (Conrad and Dowling, 1994).

The progression from competition to hierarchy and oligopoly that Williamson predicts is not desirable for the health care industry because proprietary administrative decision making denies access to the participants who most need performance and cost data to make judgments of quality: the community, employers, employees, patients, and their families.

Historically, health care data were held by physicians and hospitals in discrete and disconnected files. Information was inaccessible and costly for industry participants to obtain except where laws required reporting of specific conditions (e.g., death, infectious disease, child abuse or neglect). Indemnity insurers had access to large amounts of utilization data but used it for actuarial analyses to assure their profitability (Eastaugh, 1992). Widespread public access to industry data did not occur until the federal government became a major payer with the advent of Medicare and Medicaid. Establishment of a national Medicare data base using claims of health services delivered to those over age 65 lowered the costs of obtaining data, and the use of computers expanded society's ability to analyze data, thereby increasing the availability of information about the health services delivery and costs.

The result has been a proliferating literature about health services quality, costs and delivery dynamics, information prompting the questions that put health care quality and costs on the political agenda and, in part, led to the Clinton Administration attempt to enact universal health care coverage through managed competition (Enthoven and Kronick, 1992).   The failure of the Clinton Plan as public policy does not, however, signal the demise of health care as an issue. It means that the emphasis has shifted from universal coverage to cost containment through contracting, consolidation and, in time, vertical integration.

Access to data about health services may disappear in the transition to a few large, vertically integrated, proprietary corporations controlling costs and outcomes through administrative decisions. Indeed, one group of major employers is concerned enough about the absence of access to data that they have joined to create a Foundation for Accountability to push for access to data collected by health maintenance organizations (Noble, 1995). In its baseline report, the foundation asserted that, while HMOs had demonstrated their ability to reduce the overall costs of health care, they were not gathering and providing enough information about the quality of care to enable employers (who purchase care) and consumers to make good decisions about the plans. One health care economist is even more blunt: "Consumerism should extend beyond simple price disclosure activities to include expanded information on quality and availability of care. The libertarian conservatives in the Bush administration should be supportive of any efforts designed to promote informational equality between providers and patients. Improved information equality is a necessary condition for stimulating competitive markets (Eastaugh, 1993).

One might argue that access to publicly funded patient data, the basis for current knowledge development, will remain. That is not likely in the current anti-government environment. Private HMO enrollment of Medicare and Medicaid eligible patients and replacement of fees-for-service by capitated rates will reduce government incentives to maintain centralized data bases. What we know about health services decisions will be what health care provider organizations choose to report, what government mandates them to report, or what is revealed in lawsuits.

Thoughtful consideration of health-related issues now exclusively in the private sector and subject to administrative control, like tobacco or breast implants, suggests that voluntary reporting will be inadequate. Consider, for example, whether smoking would be so prevalent and socially costly if proprietary information about the known addictive effects of nicotine (NYT, 1995) had been public during the last five decades. Consider also whether women would have had breast implants if they had been informed of the potential toxicity of many silicones and the limited testing of the one used for implants (Cowley, 1995). The path to market competition in the health care industry leads eventually to information impactedness for many interested participants.

We must not conclude from this discussion that the markets to hierarchies cycle should be avoided because it may already be too late for that. Rather, what we must avoid is the condition of information impactedness for interested participants.

II. A SCENARIO OF THE HEALTH CARE SERVICE DELIVERY SYSTEM

Consider the following scenario. A patient walks into a physician's office to keep a medical appointment. The patient presents an identification card to the receptionist, who swipes the card's magnetic strip through a machine and waits a few seconds. Swiping the card sends a message across computer lines to verify that the patient's medical care coverage is active and identifies the carrier to be billed for today's office visit. If the patient has been seen before and has a record of encounters with the physician, the swipe also causes a screen to appear on the physician's computer, showing patient information, which the receptionist checks with the patient, making any appropriate changes and filling in the date of today's encounter, an office visit. The receptionist invites the patient to be seated.

The nurse calls the patient and takes her into an examining room where the nurse types the patient's name into the computer; the encounter document screen appears on the examining room's computer with the receptionist entered information current and verified. The nurse takes the patient's weight, height, and vital signs and enters them into the computer. The nurse asks the patient for her symptoms and enters them on the screen in the appropriate place. The doctor will be in shortly, the nurse assures the patient, then asks the patient to prepare for examination and leaves, closing the door.

A few moments later, the physician enters the room, reviews information on the computer screen, and asks the patient about her symptoms, typing notes about them as she speaks. The physician asks a few questions, typing the patient's answers. Rising, the physician walks to the sink, washes her hands, and turns to examine the patient. Following the examination, the physician returns to the computer terminal and enters additional information as she talks to the patient. "I believe you have a strep infection," the physician says. "I am going to take a throat culture and send it to the lab for analysis. That takes 24 hours, but I want you on antibiotics right away."

"What is your pharmacy?" The physician asks the patient, who names the pharmacy and provides its location. The doctor types that information into the computer, along with the prescriptions and a code. She cautions the patient to be sure to take all the antibiotics, reminding the patient that the antibiotics will not work unless the entire prescription is finished. Then the physician takes the throat culture, places it into an envelope, marks it, and puts it into a box marked "Lab Pickup." The physician returns to the computer and types in a labwork order on the patient's chart, then tells the patient to stop at the receptionist's office to schedule a followup appointment in ten days; this also is noted on the patient's chart in the computer. (In three days, the laboratory culture results will be sent to the patient's medical record, with a message to the physician to note the results.) The physician closes the patient's file and leaves the examining room so the patient can prepare to leave. The episode of care is suspended until the followup visit.

A. The Role of Computers in the Care Transaction

While the above interpersonal care transaction takes place, the computer is busy providing support. When the receptionist swipes the patient's identification card, thereby calling up an encounter screen with basic patient information already entered, the physician's computer network sends the previous encounter record to an archive of that patient's history of encounters with the physician and initiates the new encounter form, drawing the patient's identifying data elements from storage so that they need not be re-entered manually but can be updated manually. Also included on the screen from the patient's historical record are the patient's allergies, chronic diseases, current medications, and special conditions.

When the nurse enters on the encounter form the patient's height, weight, temperature, and vital signs, items falling outside normal ranges cause a message to appear at the bottom of the computer screen indicating the direction and intensity of the variance. For example, if the patient has a temperature of 99.8, the message for temperature would show +1.2, indicating that the temperature is 1.2 degrees above normal. The computer also indicates whether the values entered are "normal" for this patient based on the patient's history with the physician and other historical information. When the nurse enters patient symptoms, the computer sends a signal about whether those symptoms have been experienced by this patient previously and when.

The physician begins her entries on the computer by entering a secret code, a signal to the computer that what follows is the official legal record of the encounter. The physician's signout is her handwritten signature at the end of the encounter document. When the physician signs the encounter form, ending the care transaction, the computer performs several tasks for the physician.

From the diagnostic information in the physician's encounter notes, the computer generates an information sheet for the patient, informing her of the particulars of her condition and what she, as the patient, needs to do to ensure proper and timely recovery. The information sheet, with the patient's name at the top, is delivered to the nurse, who places the sheet in an envelope to be given to the patient before she leaves.

The computer also recognizes the particular diagnosis in this case as a reportable contagious disease and generates and sends electronically a report to the state health department, which signals its receipt and proper disposition. The health department computer enters the report into a "suspected strep throat" file pending receipt of the laboratory test, which the computer processes as noted above.

Finally, from the diagnosis entries, the computer generates a claim and releases it, again on the electronic network, to the patient's payer. The payer's computer verifies the legitimacy of the claim, checks elements on the claim, signals for a payer representative to contact the physician's office about any questionable data, reverifies the corrected claim and issues a payment voucher. If the claim involves coordination of benefits, the computer transmits claim information and accomplishes coordination electronically.

The payment voucher includes an electronic funds transfer to the physician's bank account and verification messages. The message to the physician's computer is that payment (specified amount) has been deposited in the bank. The message to the patient is an explanation of benefits received. In the case of capitated payments systems, the transaction above is the same, except that the payment step is excluded. "Claims" will continue in the form of "encounter reports" in a capitated system because the payer will collect data for tracking costs and monitoring utilization.

From the laboratory information, the computer electronically contacts the laboratory, indicating that a pickup is needed. The laboratory computer receives the pickup order, identifies the physician, notes the office location, and signals the appropriate driver. The laboratory computer also sends a message to its technicians to prepare for the test, thus alerting technicians to the workload they can expect. Once the test has been completed, the laboratory reports results electronically to the physician's office and to the state health department, confirming or negating the physician's diagnosis.

Since the health department information system has logged physician diagnosis as a suspected strep throat infection, confirmation causes the health department's computer to update its infectious disease report. Negations are logged into the particular physician's incorrect diagnosis file, to be reported periodically to the physician and, if mandated by law, to relevant entities such as the physician's employer, licenser or organization accreditor.

A researcher at a distant state university, doing a research study on strep throat infections, receives an e-mail message that new patient data have been added to his data base, in what fields the data appear, and the identity of the physician in the event followup is required. Only patient demographic data are known to the researcher, but the researcher's computer has properly filed the incoming data as a second episode of strep throat for this patient rather than the first episode for an entirely new patient.

From the prescription information that the physician enters into the encounter notes, the computer contacts the specified pharmacy's computer electronically, submits appropriate security codes and the medications needed for the patient to the pharmacy's computer, which signals the pharmacist that prescriptions need to be filled and for whom. The pharmacist fills the prescriptions and enters confirming data into the patient's record in his computer. Once the patient picks up the prescription, the pharmacist commands the computer to issue a claim to the patient's health care coverage carrier. The carrier's computer receives the claim, verifies the patient as eligible for payment, checks prescription claim data, authorizes payment, triggers the accounting department to issue payment, and forwards payment to the pharmacy's bank account. The pharmacy's computer also adds these prescriptions to the day's sales records and reorders the sold medications to restock inventory. If the law requires, the pharmacy's computer also files a report with the appropriate local, state, or federal agency. When the patient arrives at the pharmacy, the prescription is ready for pickup.

B. Interpreting the Data Flow in the Transaction

Except at a very few points in the above scenario, computers handle all of the "paperwork" associated with the health care transaction between patient and physician. It is important to notice certain things about the scenario, however. All participants in the system use computers. The physician does not collect data on paper for someone else to enter later but actually records the event as it happens. Data items are entered once and automatically appear as necessary in subsequent transactions.

Data entry into the computer at the physician's office initiates immediate transmission to computers of those who need it to perform associated tasks. Data flow from those who initiate it to those who need it. The computers receive relevant information, understand it, and initiate appropriate actions. Each participant performs a task, signals the physician that patient data have been used and with what result, adds relevant data where necessary and transmits to others in the system, all without disturbing the physician or interfering with her continued use. No apparent breach of security or confidentiality occurs.

As a result of the electronic network and its configuration, the computers reduce labor needs and greatly shorten the time lags between the many support tasks that accompany the health services transaction. The health care transaction is complete, fully documented and compensated, all in the same day--a process that can take anywhere from a few days to a month or more in the real world. More importantly, official monitoring agencies (e.g., health department) and other authorized users (e.g., accreditors and researchers) receive current, accurate, and timely data almost immediately after the data are entered into the patient's record at the physician's office. Lags between data collection and reporting of results for many studies and empirical description of the health care system's delivery of service patterns can be reduced from years to months, perhaps even weeks. Additionally, trends are based on data from large numbers of patients, often whole populations rather than small samples.

C. Conditions for Data Flow Among Participants

If a system of EDI like the one described in the scenario above were operational, then, theoretically, each participant in the health care industry would have access to complete, current, accurate, and valid information upon which to make decisions, and most of the work of making data available to them and completing routine transactions would be done by computers. Indeed, the scenario describes how data can flow among stakeholders in the health care industry, but it assumes important conditions have been met. We need to consider those conditions, asking whether they are likely to be met. If they are not likely to be met, then the scenario is a pleasant fantasy but will never be reality.

Four important conditions can be identified from the above interpretation of the scenario:

- it needs to be clear where data originate and where they need to go;
- all participants use computers to document their activities;
- all computers understand messages received and can react appropriately;
- access routes are specified, data security and patient confidentiality are intact, and the public has access to pertinent data. That is, information is not impacted.

These conditions are addressed in the following sections.

III. FROM ORIGINATOR TO USER: HEALTH CARE INDUSTRY NETWORK

Identifying where data originate and where data need to go requires identification of relevant participants and understanding of how information impactedness affects each participant, that is, considering what information each participant holds and what information each participant needs to participate effectively. Once this is known, the types of transactions among participants can be specified.

A. Computer Communications Technologies

Certainly, if the scenario described earlier is to become reality, health industry stakeholders must use computers for documenting activities and transmitting and receiving data to and from other stakeholders. Computers can be used for single, self-contained tasks or can be designed to work with other computers to share data and tasks. The key to transmitting and receiving data is computer communications technology (HINT, 1995).

Computer communications technology is required for inter-computer communications, that is, transmission of data. As the nature of computers evolved, communications technologies evolved also, from direct connections between a mainframe and its distributed terminals, to local (LAN) or wide (WAN) area networks of independent computers, and then to national and global networks like the Internet and World Wide Web (HINT, 1995). All of these variants are in use in the health care industry.

B. Terminal Model Computer System

For example, one 300-bed community hospital offering general medical and surgical care, outpatient care, diagnostics, emergency services, intensive care services, and preventive services in a mid-sized New Jersey community recently installed a large mainframe computer system to integrate all administrative and clinical functions throughout the hospital with the exceptions of magnetic resource imaging (MRI) and x-ray (HINT, 1995). A mainframe system is called a "terminal network" (HINT, 1995). It uses a single language and related protocols to eliminate transmission problems. However, a terminal network cannot communicate with unconnected independent computers without installation of a translator described below (HINT 1995).

Table 1 - Health Care Industry Participants in Data Exchange				
Participant	**Goal**	**Role**	**Have Data**	**Need Data**
Community Interpreters Distributors	TR RT, TR	Disseminate Report		Availability Efficiency Effectiveness Respect/Care Safe/Timely Continuity Health Status
Payers Insurers and HMOs Governments	TR	User, Source Broker Broker	Members Service Use MD Diagnosis Acturial	Efficiency Effectiveness Comparisons
Consumers Employers Taxpayers Insureds Patients	 TR TR TR RT	Source, User Purchaser Purchaser Choice Supplier Participant Recipient Output	 Employees Values Values Judgements Characteristics Lifestyle	Efficiency Actuarial Service Use Efficiency Efficiency Appropriate Available Safe/Timely Respect/Care Effective
Providers Administrators Physicians	 TR RT	Source, User Attract Payers Listen Examine Diagnose Prescribe/treat Follow-up MD Orders	 Costs, Expenses Staffing Capacity Incidents Knowledge Patient Data Medical Need Resource Use Satisfaction Assessments Pt Use/Result	Comparisons Standards Technology Efficacy Effectiveness Patient history Referrals Outcome
Regulators Federal State	TR	Source Define Enforce	 Rules Reports	 Compliance Data
Accreditors JCAHO NCQA	RT Evaluate	Source Set Standards Survey Rankings	 Standards Evaluations	 Provider Data Patient Data

C. Two Hospital Computer Network

Another New Jersey provider, a two-hospital system, has installed a computer system consisting of two local area networks (LAN) connected by a computer capable of translating transmissions of one (or many) LAN language and protocol to another (HINT, 1995). The goal of this system is to establish a case management system that connects all major clinical and administrative functions in each hospital with each other such that everything from admissions and physician orders entry to billing and results reporting can be accomplished through computer commands. If the scenario above had occurred in a hospital setting, this system, when operational, would accomplish all of the communications noted there, except for claims processing through payers. That is, the system is inter-facility but intra-organizational. It does, however, have the capacity to become inter-organizational (HINT, 1995).

The linkage of different LANs using routers is the mechanism for many operational administrative computing applications in the health care industry. Most of these link providers and payers to facilitate claims processing (HINT, 1995). Providers participating in these inter-organizational networks include hospitals, PPOs and IPAs; payers include indemnity insurers, HMOs, Blue Cross and Blue Shield of New Jersey, the Health Care Financing Administration (HCFA), and independent claims processing firms acting on behalf of providers. For example, HCFA accepts electronic filing of Medicare claims from hospitals and physicians offices on a standardized form. In 1992, HCFA received more than 75% of hospital claims and 44% of other claims electronically (HINT, 1995).

D. Inter-Organizational EDI Network

An inter-organizational example of networking is a New York City university teaching hospital long heralded for providing care in a medically underserved community (Hendrickson, et al., 1992). The hospital complex consists of several independent institutions offering inpatient, outpatient, mental health care, and many other specialties, conducting research, training physicians and other health professionals, providing undergraduate and graduate education in medical and health professions, running a major health sciences library, and reaching out to the community. Before the network could be launched, all participants had to agree to common rules for transmitting data, data ownership, confidentiality and integrity, access to sensitive information like student records, payroll information, and clinical data. Anyone familiar with processes for gaining consensus recognizes what a task this was.

The operational network permits authorized users access to seven functions ranging from core services like network, e-mail, and basic communications to specialized services (Hendrickson, et al., 1992). Among the information services are clinical information such as medical records, orders, nursing documentation; administrative information like space and facilities, directories, grants management, personnel, word processing, desktop publishing; scholarly information services including library holdings, electronic textbooks, natural language processing; clinical research services such as epidemiology, research databases, statistical packages; basic medical research like biomedical research tools, super-computing and graphics; medical informatics research providing operations support and access to decision making, knowledge base, workstations, human interface, and education.

In this comprehensive local network, data are entered only once but used to develop information in many ways (HINT, 1995). The system's large mainframe core is used to integrate communications among its many disparate user groups and serves to link the entire network to the Internet, thereby providing all users national communications capability.

E. Community-Wide Application of EDI Technology

An even broader application of electronic data interchange is the Community Health Management Information System (CHMIS) initiated and supported by the John A Hartford Foundation (HINT, 1995). According to the Hartford Foundation, "Information is the key to reforming our health care system. Information allows consumers to reward those physicians, hospitals and health plans that offer the best quality at the best price. It can ease the administrative log jam created by government regulation and claims processing in the fee-for-service environment. And for patients it can mean better informed, timely, higher quality treatment and care. Williamson, no doubt, would agree, calling the situation that prompted the Hartford Foundation a condition of "information impactedness."

To address information impactedness, the Hartford Foundation designed and funded CHMIS to perform three operating functions: facilitate reduction of paperwork by linking health care participants in a transactions system; provide a secured database of medical histories, performance, and costs; provide a network where data can be transmitted almost instantaneously (HINT, 1995). Clearly, the Hartford Foundation's vision and its operationalization as CHMIS provides the inspiration for the scenario presented earlier.

CHMIS originally consisted of a communications network, standard transactions flowing on the network and a data repository of network information. The data repository has been dropped as unnecessary under the assumption that participant computers will store their own portions of the data, which can be accessed electronically by authorized users without disturbing its repository. The Hartford Foundation has funded its model as pilot projects in Iowa, Minnesota, New York, Ohio, Memphis, Vermont, and Washington State. Each site has taken a different approach to implementation (HINT, 1995) but most combine private sector initiatives with state laws to provide a framework for ensuring widespread participation and appropriate standards and resolving issues of data ownership, confidentiality, access, and use.

F. Health Care EDI Technology Exists

This brief review of the use of computers and networks in the health care industry makes it clear that the technology exists to make the scenario described earlier a reality and there are scattered efforts to implement aspects of the scenario. However, computer use appears to be limited in health care organizations and not widespread between and among health care providers. For example, a recent survey in New Jersey (HINT, 1995) found pharmacists (89%) to be most likely to use computers to maintain patient records and to process claims with payers. All surveyed pharmacies filed some claims electronically; 43% file all claims electronically.

Among the other groups sampled, 63% of payers, 62% of physicians and 47% of laboratories process claims manually. A majority of hospitals surveyed (59%) use computers, but only 12% of patient medical information is recorded using computers, and no hospital electronically files all claims. Fewer laboratories (40%) and physicians (33%) use computers. If New Jersey is typical, and it likely is typical (HINT, 1995), the health care industry currently is slow to adopt computers and uses them for self-contained tasks.

One group analyzing the health care industry argues that the complexity of health care services delivery and the information the industry generates is the cause of slow adoption and limited use (HINT, 1995). For example, the delivery system consists of thousands of independent providers serving millions of individual patients in a variety of settings (e.g., inpatient, outpatient, laboratory, radiology, therapies, pharmacy).

Administratively, payments nationally involve over 3,000 payers using 450 claims forms and patients generating nearly five billion claims per year (WEDI, 1993). Simplifying this complexity to take advantage of the potential for using information technology to eliminate information impactedness is the challenge, particularly when WEDI's national survey of 2200 health care industry providers indicates that respondents perceive no common basis for electronic communication among participants in the health care sector (WEDI, 1992). Enlightenment is required.

IV. STANDARDIZATION OR TRANSLATION

Computers cannot transfer data to other computers without a means of interpreting incoming data that arrives in an unknown format (HINT, 1995). Mainframe computers use a single language and formatting system that is used in all the terminals attached to them. Computer networks either share a common language and formatting system or are connected through computers that translate from one computer's language and format to another's. The distinguishing feature of the more elaborate networks used today is their ability to allow dissimilar computers to communicate directly with other computers through unique addresses and standardized formats.

Replacing the central processor and distributed terminals or tightly controlled networks are "clients," "servers," and "routers". Clients enter, edit, and display data on their individual machines. Clients operate at the "applications" level, frequently unaware that multiple levels of standardized communications are required to support the transmission of the application to other computers. Servers store files, print commands and messages (for example, e-mail) to busy addressees, and schedule access when addressees become free to receive. Routers are translators that receive signals from one LAN and convert them into data bits that can be forwarded to one or more other LANs. Once in a LAN, the common language and protocols of the LAN permit transfer among its computers. Routers also segment LANs to increase efficiency and provide "firewall" services, which blocks unauthorized computers (HINT, 1995).

The broadest potential for transmission and exchange of data lies with the Internet, which interconnects multiple network providers who allow users to connect to one network and send data to and receive data from any part of the Internet. The communication protocol for the Internet is standardized. Exchange of data among network-connected computers is controlled by a set of rules, a network protocol specifying how messages are prepared and transmitted electronically (HINT, 1995). The protocol must be understood by both sending and receiving computers so the messages being sent are understood. For example, the protocol identified as Transmission Control Protocol/Internet Protocol (TCP/IP - Comer, 1991) is becoming the de facto standard for network communication, embraced by many hardware vendors.

This brief and incomplete description of the technology for transmitting data shows that a key to broad use of information technology is standardization. In the health care industry, complexity and the perceived absence of a common basis for communication create high barriers to standardization of clinical and administrative data formats and vocabulary (HINT, 1995). Data format standards allow identification of a message's component parts, for example, separation of words from a string of letters without spaces between. Sender and receiver can store data in any format they choose, but data must be transmitted in a shared format. Vocabulary standards ensure a receiving computer understands what a sending computer conveys. For example, a medical diagnosis sent by ICD-9-M code is not understood by a system that knows only DSM-IIIR codes, even if the data format is the same.

A. Vocabulary Standards

Currently there are seven distinct sets of medical terminology and no translation device, or router (HINT, 1995). The American Dental Association (ADA) publishes professionally accepted codes for dental procedures and nomenclature. The American Medical Association (AMA) publishes the Current Procedural Terminology (CPT-4) Manual, a listing of descriptive terms and identifying codes for reporting medical services and procedures performed by physicians. The American Psychiatric Association (APA) publishes the Diagnostic and Statistical Manual of Mental Disorders (DSM-III-R). The Health Care Financing Administration (HCFA) publishes several documents containing health care codes. They are: HCFA Common Procedural Coding System for grouping procedures; HCFA Code List to document providers; Electronic Media Claims National Standard Format, a variety of codes indicating the place where service was rendered. These documents are the basis for submitting claims using UB-92 electronic claims standards.

The Health Insurance Association of America (HIAA) publishes the National Healthcare Claim Payment Advice Committee Bulletins identifying reason codes payers use to make adjustments to claims. HIAA also publishes a series of bulletins describing codes for electronic standards used by the insurance industry. The National Center for Health Statistics publishes the International Classification of Diseases, 9th Revision, Clinical Modification (ICD-9-CM), which classifies morbidity and mortality information for statistical purposes and indexing hospital records by disease and operations.

The National Uniform Billing Committee (NUBC) publishes the National Uniform Billing Data Element Specifications, which include: revenue codes (UB-82 and UB-92); admission source and type codes identifying who recommended and priority of the admission; claim frequency, type of medical facility and patient status codes. The U.S. Government Printing Office publishes the Health Insurance Manual 15 (HM 15), which contains Diagnostic Related Groups (DRG) classification numbers. The National Library of Medicine seeks to create a Unified Medical Language System (HINT, 1995).

In addition to medical vocabulary, the clinical communications system will need to deliver lab and radiology reports, patient information, referral and admissions information, clinical graphics and digitized voice file. Signficant efforts exist in each of these areas as well. For example, experiments and pilot projects in the transmission of medical images via EDI are underway (HINT, 1995).

Minimum data sets for service providers also exist. For example, the National Institute of Mental Health developed a minimum data set for mental health service providers containing patient, organization, care event, staff, and financial information (MHSIP, 1989). HCFA's Health Standards and Quality Bureau (HSQB) developed under contract a minimum data set for nursing home assessment of patient case mix (MDS+ 1992). Minimum or common data sets like those mentioned are not required for EDI because EDI permits users to select what is relevant from available data elements. However, standardized definitions are necessary, and standardized data sets contain widely accepted common definitions. Thus, they can be used to facilitate EDI development.

B. Data Format Standardization

Several data format standardization efforts for the health care industry are underway. However, for example, with 450 different claims forms carrying similar data in different places on the form, it is not surprising that data format standards are elusive. A Health Information Standards Planning Panel (HISPP) was developed in 1992 under the auspices of the American National Standards Institute (ANSI) to coordinate the many health care industry standardization efforts in progress. The role of the planning panel is to facilitate evolution toward a unified set of non-redundant, non-conflicting standards compatible with the seven level Open Systems Interconnect (OSI) communications model--the basis for the Internet (HINT, 1995). The OSI communications model is a highly technical, seven level process for organizing the protocols for transforming data constructs into electrical signals. Of the seven levels, all are transparent (invisible) to the user. The user will be aware, however, of Level 7, the applications level. An example of which would be "claims transmission." Standardization activities now underway are directed toward Levels 7 and 6, the latter of which is called "Presentation". The presentation level translates data from the applications syntax to a transfer syntax expressed in a binary form that can be understood at the next lower level. The lowest levels deal with physical connections and standardized information units (packets) and related issues.

C. Performance and Accountability

Key contributors to the standardization processes described above are the accrediting agencies. One of these is JCAHO which sets performance standards for health care providers and accredits them (Brooks, 1995). A similar organization, the National Committee for Quality Assurance (NCQA), accredits health maintenance organizations (Goldfield and Nash, 1995). These organizations are critical to development of EDI because, through their accrediting processes, they define performance measures that become indicators for data collection. Entered into data bases, these data eventually will be transmitted electronically from collectors to users. By focusing organization attention on common measures, JCAHO and NCQA reduce the thousands of potential measures to manageable numbers for standardization efforts.

Further, survey methods of accreditors (and state licensing agencies in their licensing activities) cause health care professionals and provider organizations to focus on their performance relative to measured elements of health services delivery, making these elements more likely to be institutionalized in the service delivery culture. If accrediting measuring processes are indicative of quality health services delivery, performance data relative to those measures are exactly those that should be available on a health care industry EDI system.

This information on the standardization element of the health care industry can be viewed either as evidence of the degree of complexity that makes the task of standardization so daunting or as evidence of the enormous energy that can be brought to bear on the quest for reduction of information impactedness. Progress toward standardization required to achieve widespread use of EDI can be facilitated by government legislation. Steps in that direction have been taken in the administrative simplification provisions of the 1996 Health Insurance Portability and Accountability Act, which requires that the secretary of DHHS adopt standards for the exchange of administrative health data, including a universal patient identifier by the end of 1998.

V. SECURITY OF ACCESS AND CONTROL

Health care data cannot be available to anyone and everyone. Only those who have good reason should be able to enter, transmit, or manipulate health care data. Security and access controls are essential components of EDI or any computer system. Three items are associated with security: physical security of the information, authentication of those who seek entry, and access control over who may read, update, and replace data. Proper security in the computer system respects the constitutional right of patient privacy by protecting the confidentiality of patient records (HINT, 1995). Proper security also assures the integrity of data by allowing access only to authorized users. Finally, proper security assures availability or continued access to authorized users. A good example of a well-functioning secure EDI system is the automated teller machine (ATM) in widespread use today. One's bank card and PIN provide access, and once access is gained, allows the user to deposit, query or withdraw. However, one cannot change previous entries or gain access to the bank's computer files with the ATM card.

Authentication of patients presenting themselves for episodes of care is one necessary function of an EDI network. In the scenario, the patient's card was swiped to initiate the episode by confirming that the patient had coverage. Realistically, however, a person other than the authorized card holder may receive services by using the "authentic" card of someone else. A PIN number can be helpful, but the intent to defraud makes the PIN number useless as a security device. Concern about fraudulent use of patient identification cards has led to evaluation of other ways to ensure that the patient served is the patient with coverage. These include several adaptations of card technologies as well as alternatives to cards. Alternatives include computerized biometric identification using the patient's personal characteristices as identifiers.

Biometrics include fingerprints, voice characteristics, retinal configurations, iris shapes, facial images, and DNA (HINT, 1995).

A. Privacy and Confidentiality

Confidentiality of patient records is particularly important because confidentiality is perceived as a major obstacle to health care industry EDI development by both the general public and health care industry participants (HINT, 1995). The issue of confidentiality of patient records is addressed in state laws, which vary greatly in their requirements (HINT, 1995). This adds another complexity to those already noted in previous sections. There is, however, model health information legislation language developed by the American Health Information Management Association (HINT, 1995) to meet constitutional requirements for the protection of rights and permit computerized data flow among health care industry participants.

VI. THE POTENTIAL AND THE PROMISE

This broad discussion of the potential role of information technology began with the recognition that the debate about costs and quality in the health care industry has put health care service delivery on a path toward consolidation and closure. With closure, the danger of losing information that supports necessary judgments about quality of service delivery exists. Using Williamson's explanation of the process of consolidation and vertical integration, information impactedness is relieved for some in consolidation. However, in the case of health care, it will be exacerbated for key participants, primarily the community, payers, and consumers. The chapter describes the use of information technology as a method of overcoming information impactedness for all participants in the health care industry. Specifically, using EDI, data can be entered once and travel from its entry point to users' computers immediately without human intervention and without interfering with the source's use of the data. Thus, EDI can reduce information impactedness and increase productivity at the same time. A typical health care transaction scenario establishes the potential for EDI. From the scenario, four conditions are identified and addressed to explain what is necessary to accomplish EDI in the health care industry.

First, a health care system-wide EDI architecture is necessary. The architecture specifies who contributes what data, and who needs what data. The architecture is defined in terms of key participants identified as the community, payers, consumers, providers, regulators, and accreditors. Within each participant group, roles help to identify what data are contributed, and the group's goals are used to identify what data are needed by the participant. Generally, data originate from patients and enter the health care system in patient transactions with providers. Thus, providers are key points of data entry.

In functional tasks, providers transmit data to payers, regulators, and repositories, like state health departments, but have no incentive to transmit to the community or consumers. The community, consumers, and payers identified as purchasers (employers and taxpayers) are important net users of data but are the least likely to gain access if services are delivered by hierarchies. EDI can overcome the absence of incentives because it becomes relatively costless to transmit the data once the EDI capability is present.

Second, computers of all kinds are used in the health care industry, primarily for functional tasks within organizations. The beginnings of inter-organizational computer transactions are apparent (i.e. multi-hospital systems and provider-payer claims transactions). A few broad-based, multi-organization, multi-function EDI environments exist in demonstration projects or as fully operating systems, like the New York City university hospital example. The examples show EDI development requires tremendous amounts of cooperation and coordination prior to initiation of communications. Political, legal, professional, organizational, functional, and individual concerns must be accommodated in the system design and operation.

Third, a widely cited reason for the health care industry's slowness in adopting EDI arrangements is the complexity of the service delivery environment, from physicians practicing alone to community hospitals offering a wide variety of services, and from radiology labs developing x-rays to pharmacies dispensing pills. The commonalities lie in billing for the services, but even there, 450 separate insurers require similar data to be presented in 450 different formats. The hope for EDI lies in scattered efforts to standardize reporting forms, medical and organizational terminology. The existence of minimum data sets with common definitions and standards applied by licensers and accreditors may also assist standardization efforts by providing shared foundations for discussion.

Finally, accommodation of political, legal, professional, organizational, functional, and individual concerns requires rules of access and exchange in the EDI network. Important are physical security of the data, authentication of users at each point of access, and confidentiality safeguards to protect individual rights of privacy, particularly for patients who are the primary sources of data elements. Technical and legal aspects of protecting data are well-developed, but political and organizational issues need to be resolved by network participants.

One way to begin resolving these issues is to visualize what an EDI system can accomplish for the health care industry in the hope that clear expression and identification of participants and their interactions in such an environment will stimulate the desire to achieve the visualization. Achievement of the visualization safeguards access to needed information for participants who need to judge health care services quality-- that is, the community and payers (specifically employers and taxpayers, and consumers).

It is clear from the brief review of examples of computerization, standardization and access and control issues that some have visualized elements of the system and implemented those elements using the technologies capable of expanding to a complete EDI network. Those efforts, as they evolve to more complex systems involving more participants, may provide a framework for a comprehensive health care EDI network. However, concern about consolidation of health services delivery into proprietary, oligopolistic hierarchies that portend closure of access to data needed for quality judgements should move us to action. Action involves putting an EDI infrastructure on the federal public policy agenda and urging Congress and the President to facilitate its development by coordinated effort on the four conditions discussed herein.

REFERENCES

American Hospital Association. (1991). *Practice pattern analysis: a tool for continuous improvement of patient quality care.* American Hospital Association, Chicago.

Brooks, D. C. (1995). The Joint Commission on Accreditation of Healthcare Organizations. In Goldfield, N. and Nash, D. B. (Eds.). *Providing quality care: future challenges.* Health Administration Press, Ann Arbor, MI: 145-162.

Carey, R. G., and Seibert, J. H. (1993). A patient survey system to measure quality improvement. *Medical care. 31(9):* 834-45.

Chassin, M. R., Kosecoff, J., Park, R. E., Winslow, C. M., Kahn, K. L., Merrick, N. J., Keesey, J., Fink, A., Solomon, D. H., and Brook, R. H. (1992). Does inappropriate use explain geographic variations in the use of health care services? A study of three procedures. In Kindig, D. A. and Sullivan, R. B. (Eds.). *Understanding universal health programs: issues and options.* Health Administration Press, Ann Arbor, MI.

Conrad, D. A. and Dowling, W. L. (1994). Vertical integration in health care services: theory and managerial implications. In Brown, M. (Ed.). *Managed care: strategies, networks and management.* Aspen, Gaithersburg, MD.

Cowley, G. (1995). Silicone: juries vs. science. *Newsweek. November 13.*

Daft, R. L. (1989). *Organization theory and design.* West Publishing, St Paul, MN.

Eastaugh, S. R. (1992). *Health economics: efficiency, quality and equity.* Auburn House, Westport, CT.

Enthoven, A. C. and Kronick, R. (1992). Universal health insurance through incentives reform. In Kindig, D. A. and Sullivan, R. B. (Eds.). *Understanding universal health programs: issues and options.* Health Administration Press, Ann Arbor, MI.

Gapenski, L. C. (1994). *Understanding health care financial management.* Health Administration Press, Ann Arbor MI.

Health Information Networks and Technologies (HINT). (1995). *Electronic network solutions for rising healthcare costs.* New Jersey Institute of Technology, Newark, NJ.

Hendrickson, G. R. K., Anderson, P. D., Clayton, J. C., Hripcsak, G. M., Johnson, S. B., McCormack, M., Sengupta, S., Shea, S., Sideli, R., and Roderer, N. (1992). The integrated academic information system at Columbia-Presbyterian Medical Center. *M. D. computing 9(1):* 35-42.

Joint Commission on the Accreditation of Healthcare Organizations (JCAHO). (1993). *The measurement mandate, on the road to performance improvement in health care.* JCAHO, Oakbrook Terrace, IL.

Kirchhoff, J. (1995, July). Achieving health policy goals without organizing the system into a straightjacket. Paper presented at the American Society for Public Administration National Meeting. San Antonio, TX.

Knickman, J. R. and Thorpe, K. E. (1995). Financing for health care. In Kovner, A. R. (Ed.). *Jonas's health care delivery in the United States. 5th ed.,* Springer Publishing, New York: 267-293.

Noble, H. B. (1995). Linking technology and health care groups to find best cure. *The New York Times. September 24:* A32.

Palmer, R. H. (1993). Considerations in defining quality of health care. In Palmer, H. R., Donabedian, A. and Povar, G. J. (Eds.). *Striving for quality in health care, an inquiry into policy and practice.* Health Administration Press, Ann Arbor, MI: 3-54.

Rosen, B. M., Goldsmith, H. F., and Jackson, D. J. (1982). A study of differing social areas and use of psychiatric services: a model for needs assessment and planning. In Bell, R. A., Goldsmith, H. F., Lin, E., Hirzel, S. S. (Eds.), *Social indicators for human service systems.* University of Louisville, Lousiville, KY: 40-62.

Workgroup for Electronic Data Interchange (WEDI). (1993). Workgroup for electronic data interchange report. Travelers Insurance Company and Blue Cross and Blue Shield Association, Chicago.

Workgroup for Electronic Data Interchange (WEDI). (1992). Workgroup for electronic data interchange report. Travelers Insurance Company and Blue Cross and Blue Shield Association, Chicago.

Williamson, O. E. (1975). *Markets and hierarchies: analysis and antitrust implications.* The Free Press, New York.

Wolford, G. R., Brown, M. and McCool, B. J. (1994). Getting to go in managed care. In Brown, M. (Ed.). *Managed care: strategies, networks and management.* Aspen, Gaithersburg, MD.

47.
ACCESSING ONLINE HEALTH RESOURCES

Genie N. L. Stowers, *San Francisco State University, San Francisco, CA*

Today the health administrator, practitioner, researcher, and student have vast resources available on a wide variety of health-related topics. Using the Internet, cutting edge, up-to-date information can be accessed quickly and cheaply. This chapter will discuss today's online information tools, examples of the kind of health information available online, and how the health professional can best access these tools.

I. WHAT IS THE INTERNET?

The Internet is a vast, decentralized network or networks comprised of a myriad of regional nets and computers communicating at high speeds. Due to its origins as a military communications system designed to sustain itself during and after attacks, it operates in a decentralized fashion, which has vast implications for Internet communications. No one owns or operates the Internet. Instead, anyone can own and operate Internet nodes and can charge for access to the Internet. Communications and information provision thus becomes free-wheeling, quick, and wide-spread. This design has created important implications for using the Internet as an information resource or communications venue (Eddings, 1994; SAMS, 1994).

Internet tools and computer-mediated communications (like email and computer conferencing) allow the creation of a "virtual" space among geographically dispersed users communicating with one another on a host machine or over regional computer networks. In this sense, the communications are not taking place in real-time or in real space; they are occurring "out there" in "virtual" space. William Gibson, in his novel *Neuromancer* (1984), coined the term "cyberspace"; this term is often used interchangeably with virtual space to indicate interactions online.

A growing number of health administrators and policy analysts in the United States, Canada, and around the world are benefiting from the resources available online. In fact, the health community has taken advantage of the Internet far more effectively than most. Administrators use online resources for research purposes, to improve communications, to provide services, to promote discussion, and to create communities around issues of interest like health policy and health administration. The next section describes some of the tools being used for these purposes.

A. Computer-Mediated Communication Tools

Many Internet or online tools are being used to enhance researcher, administrator, and patient access to health, medical, and other professional information. These tools include electronic mail (email), listservs (electronic mailing lists), gophers, World Wide Web (WWW) sites, web conferencing, UseNet newsgroups, IRC (Internet Relay Chat) and file transfer protocol (ftp). In many communities, some tools are used together in comprehensive packages called community networks, or freenets.

1. Electronic Mail

The most basic Internet tool is electronic mail (email). Email can be defined as "a personal message system that sends text messages to a person's (or a group's) computerized 'in-basket.' Messages are sent, stored, and read using terminals or personal computers" (Boone, 1993, p. 364). (See Figure 1 for an example of email.) After the message is sent, it travels along the computer networks of the Internet, guided by the email address heading the message, until it arrives at its destination. It then resides in the email "inbox" of the addressee until read (SAMS, 1994).

Figure 1 - Example of Email Message

From: Email Address **(typically name@computer name.com or .gov. or .edu)**
Date: Thu, 15 Feb 1996 10:23:00 EST   **Date and Time Automatically Attached**
To: Email Address of Recipient   **Email Address of Recipient**
Subject: 12 hour clinicals   **Subject of Email Message**

Typically Informal Message—this message concerns nursing education...
I agree with you. While I can see the advantages of longer/fewer clinical days with census problems, etc., I already spend 9-10 hours a day in clincal two days a week. No wonder I live for the golf season!!!
Have a good one!

The Recipient Can Then Return the Message with This Original Message Intact—to Keep the "thread" of the Conversation Going...

Due to its informality and the rapidity of possible response, email is commonly used to enhance and increase communication among policy networks and organization administrators and managers. Today, many organizations have intra-office email available on Local Area Networks (LANs) or on Wide Area Networks (WANs) within their offices or organizations and, through the Internet for their interoffice and world-wide administrative and policy communications.

2. Listservs

Listservs are electronic mailing lists which become "virtual" policy, administrative, or issue networks operating on the Internet across the country or around the world. Participants subscribe to a list, chosen from thousands of topics. When messages are sent to the list, subscribers receive them as email messages. Participants may respond to the listserv address; the software then automatically sends the message to everyone subscribed to that particular electronic mailing list. Today, listservs are used as tools to gather information, develop virtual communities with those of like interests (Rheingold, 1993), and to keep informed about particular topics.

In the health field, hundreds of listservs exist on a variety of topics from Nursing Education (NRSINGED) to the more general health listserv (HEALTH-L). Comments and discussions on these listservs range from questions on a difficult diagnosis to questions from health educators on how best to structure clinical sessions. Users may search for listservs of interest to them by using gophers' list searching facilities (discussed later) or by accessing hard copy information in their field.[1]

3. World Wide Web (WWW)

The World Wide Web (WWW) is a hypermedia system, allowing information to be provided via text, graphics, sound, video, animation, and other multimedia types. This information is combined in a series of computer files which, presented through Windows- or MacIntosh-based software known as a "browser," is seen as a World Wide Web "home page" or starting point. In addition to seeing the multimedia or hypermedia effects listed above, users may connect to other web pages through "hyperlinks"; moving from one page to another is called "surfing the Web." Today, users may also exchange messages, carry on conversations and ongoing discussions through Web-based computer conferencing systems, and order goods and services over the Web. Although the World Wide Web really only began its popularity in 1993 with the release of the Mosaic browsing software, it has now surpassed electronic mail as the most commonly used Internet tool.

To access a World Wide Web page, the user enters a Web site's address, or Uniform Resource Locator (URL), in the space on the browser titled URL or the icon labeled Open. The format of the URLs is:

http://www.computersite.type of computer system/File Name/File Name/FileName

For instance, the URL of the Virtual Hospital is:
http://indy.radiology.uiowa.edu/VirtualHospital.html

The http designation means hypertext transfer protocol, the rules and standards regulating how files are transferred across the World Wide Web. In the example given, the home page is located at the Radiology Department of the University of Iowa on the computer named indy. The name of the file containing the information shown is Virtual Hospital.html. The designation html means the file is written in Hyper Text Markup Language, the simple programming language used to create World Wide Web pages; seeing that designation at the end of a file name, the browser knows the file is a Web page.

The "home pages" or Web sites created for each organization (Figure 2) have grown more and more creative over time, providing a visual picture of the user's site, information about the organization, and linkages to other sites or to graphics, video, or sound. Figure 2 illustrates the Web page for University of Iowa's Virtual Hospital. The user selects hyperlinks by moving the cursor around the page. When the cursor image changes to that of a hand with pointing finger, the user selects that area, which represents the linkage to another Web page. The graphic image in the Virtual Hospital is known as an image map—it is "clickable" in that the user may select areas of the graphic such as Welcome to the Virtual Hospital, For Patients, For HealthCare Providers, or Beyond the Virtual Hospital. The user may also click to select the underlined text (typically appearing in blue on the Web page) to connect to other Web pages, other sections of a Web page, or to other Web sites. For instance, when the user clicks on either the image stating For Healthcare Providers or the underlined text, another Web page lists linkages to multimedia textbooks, teaching files including appropriate graphics of x-rays and other materials, and assorted publications. Connections may also be made to the home pages of the sponsors of the Virtual Hospital. Under the Welcome to the Virtual Hospital section, the user may also find a linkage to What's New, one of the best places to start on any quest for information on the World Wide Web.

Figure 2 - Example of World Wide Web Page - University of Iowa's Virtual Hospital

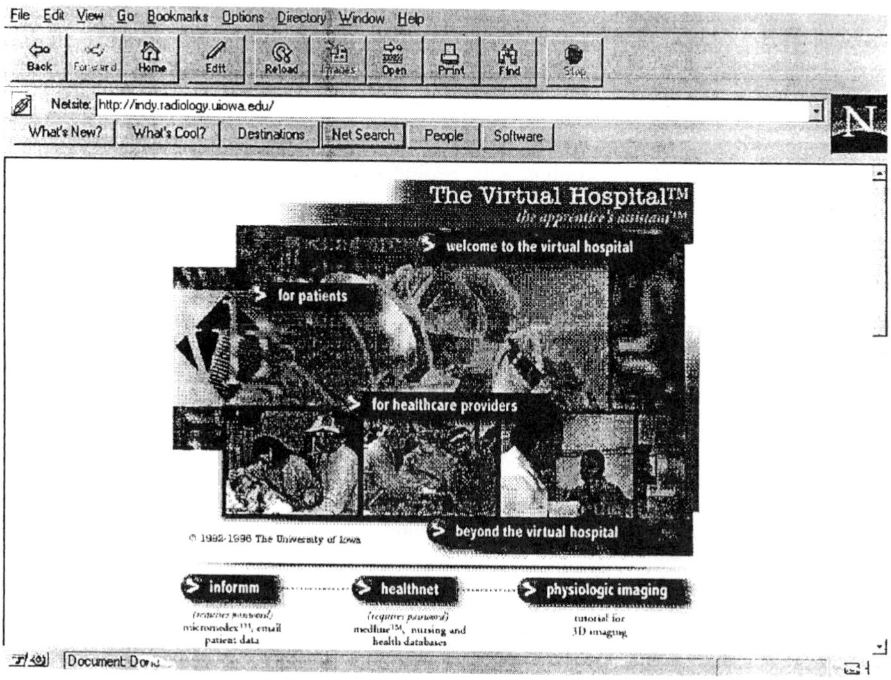

Table 1 - Top Government Health Sites on the World Wide Web

World Wide Web Site Name	World Wide Web Address	Highlights of the Site
U.S. Centers for Disease Control (CDC)	http://www.cdc.gov/	Morbidity & Mortality Weekly Reports; Data and Statistics; Grant Funding Opportunities
U.S. National Institutes of Health	http://www.nih.gov/	Health Surveillance Grants and Contracts Listings; Connections to Institutes and Offices; Connections to CancerNet Gopher with CancerLit Citations and Abstracts
U.S. Health Care Financing Agency	http://www.hcfa.gov	Medicare and Medicaid Press Releases; Speeches; Testimony; Statistics and Data; Reports; Research and Demonstration Projects
U.S. Department of Health and Human Services	http://www.os.dhhs.gov /progorg/progorg.html	
National Health Information Center	http://nhic-nt.health.org/	Health Information Resource Database

Table 1 presents a listing of selected top government health administration Web sites and their addresses. These sites are excellent resources for health administrators, allowing instant access to everything from the U.S. Centers for Disease Control's Morbidity and Mortality Weekly Reports and Data/Statistics to current policy information from the U.S. Health Care Financing Agencies on Medicare and Medicaid (testimony, press releases, speeches, statistics, and data).

Table 2 lists elected non-governmental health sites on the World Wide Web. The Virtual Hospital, already described above, is one of the most interesting of these. It provides online access to health information and teaching resources. Similar to the Virtual Hospital with its multimedia teaching files is the Virtual Nursing College, containing the Online Journal of Nursing, Healing Workshops, and linkages to other resources. Two other sites— the Wellness Web (The Patient's Network) and Medical Resources on the Internet from the University of Tennessee also contain many linkages to general medical resources. Newly available are online medical periodicals such as the New England Journal of Medicine Online, the National Library of Medicine, and the Mayo Online Health Magazine. Of more specific interest is the Robert Wood Johnson Foundation homepage and the OncoLink page (which provided the first live online coverage of the American Society for Clinical Oncologists Annual Meeting). Finally, the Genome Database provides a searchable database to allow the public access to information on the Genome mapping process.

Table 2 - Top Health Sites on the World Wide Web

World Wide Web Site Name	World Wide Web Address	Highlights of the Site
Virtual Hospital	http://indy.radiology. uiowa.edu/	HealthNet (requires password); Multimedia Teaching cases with images of X-rays available; Many Other Resources Available
Virtual Nursing College	http://www.langara. bc.ca/vnc	Online Journal of Nursing; Healing Workshop; linkages to other resources
Wellness Web— The Patient's Network	http://www.wellweb.com/	Health Care Internet Alert; Linkages to 10 Best Health Sites' Smokers' Clinic; Elders Watch
Medical Resources on the Internet- U. Tennessee	http://planetree1. utmem.edu/NetResources/ NetResources.html	Linkages to many other Health-related resources
National Library of Medicine	http://www.nlm.nih.gov/	Features searchable medical databases
New England Journal of Medicine	http://www.nejm.org/	Can access abstracts of current and past NEJM articles and order full text copies of articles
Mayo Online Health Magazine	http://healthnet.ivi.com /hnet/common/ html/pubs.htm	Mayo Clinic Health Letter, including Hot Topics and Ask The Physician
Robert Wood Johnson Foundation	http://www.rwjf.org /main.html	American Health Line - Daily Executive Briefing; Grant Information; online search capabilities
OncoLink	http://cancer.med. upenn.edu/	A First- Providing Live Coverage of the American Society of Clinical Oncologists; linkages to other sites

Table 2 - Continued

World Wide Web Site Name	World Wide Web Address	Highlights of the Site
Diseases, Disorders, & Related Topics	http://www.mic.ki.se/other.html	Karolinska Institute (Stockholm, Sweden) listings of Online Resources of Multitude of Diseases and Disorders; Includes Virtual Lectures and searchable Family Practice Handbook
Internet Mental Health	http://www.mentalhealth.com/	Listings of Disorders and Medications
Food & Nutrition	http://www.nalusda.gov/answers/info_centers/fnic/fnic-etexts.html	Sponsored by the USDA, contains linkages to information on food safety, preservation, labeling, and nutrition
Acupuncture	http://www.acupuncture.com/	information on acupuncture, Chinese medicine, and links to other alternative medicine pages
The Genome Database	http://gdbwww.gdb.org/	Searchable database to allow public access to information on Genome mapping

Of great importance when faced with the ever-changing information are tools which allow the user to search the Web. Search "engines" like WebCrawler, Lycos, and Yahoo are among the tools emerging everyday. To search, the user enters a phrase, the software searches its database, and the screen lists the sites with that phrase in the title. Search engines like WebCrawler accomplish this task by sending "infobots," or files, to search out new Web sites and gather their address information. This search capacity is critical as information on the Web constantly changes.

Using a system called Lynx, the user who does not possess the hardware and software requirements needed to access images can instead access the World Wide Web in text-only format. It is important to note, however, that most Web page developers do not test their pages for coherence and ease of reading in a text-based format and the value added by graphics and other media is often lost.

Figure 3 - Example of Gopher System

San Francisco State University Gopher System

Internet Gopher Information Client v2.0.16

WHO gopher

    1. About The World Health Organization (WHO).../
    2. About This Gopher and WHO's World-Wide Web Server.../
—> 3. WHO's Major Programmes.../   **select option 3 by typing 3 or cursoring to**
    4. WHOSIS (WHO Statistical Information System).../   **option 3 and pressing**
    5. Outbreaks.../   **Return**
    6. News; Press Releases & Resolutions of UN agencies, etc.../
    7. E-mail Directories and Telecomm Catalogues.../
    8. WHO's Web Server.../
    9. Other Gopher & Information Servers.../

after selecting option 3 from first menu, the WHO's Major Programmes submenu appears

WHO's Major Programmes...

    1. Communicable Diseases (CDS).../
    2. Action Programme on Essential Drugs (DAP).../
    3. Drug Management and Policies (DMP).../
    4. Food and Nutrition (FNU).../   **the user may then select**
    5. Global Programme on AIDS (GPA).../   **another submenu option**
    6. Global Programme for Vaccines and Immunization (GPV).../ **then select a file**
    7. Library and Health Literature Services (HLT).../   **to be emailed to**
    8. Development of Human Resources for Health (HRH).../   **them or saved**
    9. Human Reproduction Programme (HRP).../
    10. WHOSIS - The WHO Statistical Information System (HST).../
    11. Office of Information (INF).../
    12. Noncommunicable Diseases (NCD).../
    13. Programme for the Promotion of Chemical Safety (PCS).../
    14. Programme for the Promotion of Environmental Health (PEH).../
    15. Programme on Substance Abuse (PSA).../
    16. Strengthening of Health Services (SHS).../
    17. Task Force on Health Economics (TFHE).../
    18. Tropical Diseases Research (TDR).../

Press ? for Help, q to Quit, u to go up a menu Page: 1/2

4 . Gopher

A gopher is an older text- and menu-based information retrieval tool which resides on various computers on the networks (see Figure 3). (Gophers are so named due to their origins at the University of Minnesota, where the mascot is a gopher.) Users may access gophers from other computer systems without accounts on those systems. They may also connect to distant gophers from their home computer system. Thus, within seconds a user may access a gopher to obtain information about services, health information, upcoming conferences, and online library catalogues (SAMS, 1994).

As can be seen from Figure 3, the user may easily access this text-based information by typing in an option number from the hierarchical menu system, then selecting another option from a submenu. Information or full files may be downloaded or emailed to the user's home machine. Furthermore, gophers worldwide may be searched (by key word) utilizing search software known as Veronica, available on most gopher systems. Gophers may also be accessed through the more visually interesting World Wide Web by typing in the address of the gopher, then clicking on file folders representing each menu option.

Today, gopher usage is diminishing with the incredible growth and versatility of the graphical and multimedia-based Web. Because they do not allow interactive communication and because of their text-only format, gophers are more limited in their usefulness; in fact, many administrators are discontinuing their gopher sites or are not keeping their information current. Still, gophers remain important sources of information when site administrators keep up-to-date information residing in them.

5. File Transfer Protocol (ftp)

File Transfer Protocol, or ftp (also sometimes called anonymous ftp), still one of the most commonly used Internet tools, is gradually being supplanted by the file retrieval abilities of the World Wide Web. Ftp is a tool used to access files from other sites and bring them to the user's home computer. As such, it is an enormous research and information retrieval tool that can be utilized without an account on the computer hosting the target files. With it, the user has quick access to millions of files that previously might have been unattainable. Organizations can post files containing information useful to citizens in a host computer's archive; users may then access this information without cost. Ftp sites thus may become a useful way for organizations to provide access to grant or permit application information, to provide access to forms, to post proposed policies, to distribute teaching files or notes.

6. UseNet groups

UseNet groups are discussion groups on a variety of topics. Users participate via a type of software called a newsreader. They select the desired topic by choosing the relevant newsgroup. Currently over 30,000 newsgroups operate across the country and even across the world; more are being created every day. Messages from each selected newsgroup can be regularly read and replied to.

7. *Internet Relay Chat (IRC)*

Internet Relay Chat (IRC) is a process of so-called "real-time" conversation between two individuals who are both online at the same time. This can be accomplished via a host computer system and two email accounts. It should not be confused with the newer phenomena of chat rooms online services like American Online, CompuServe, Delphi, and Prodigy provide. While these chat rooms provide instantaneous communications with whomever else happens to be "present" in the chat room, this is not the same as IRC, for which one does not have to subscribe to an online service.

8. *Community Networks or Freenets*

Community networks are local public access computer networks which are springing up around the country and around the world. While the public sector is often involved in their creation (particularly public libraries), they are as often a creation of local universities or coalitions of groups. These computer networks will often provide health policy and administration information along with other valuable information about a community.

Free-Net ®[2] community computer systems represent, in effect, a new application in computing. " A multi-user computer is established at a central location in a given area and the machine is connected to the telephone system through a series of devices called modems. Running on the machine is a computer program that provides its users with everything from electronic mail services to information about health care, education, technology, government, recreation, or just about anything else the host operators would like to place on the machine" (National Public Telecomputing Network, Undated A).

"Anyone in the community with access to a home, office, or school computer and a modem can contact the system 24 hours a day. They simply dial a central phone number, make connection, and series of menus appear on the screen which allows them to select the information or communication services they would like. All of it is free and all of it can easily be accomplished by a first-time user" (National Public Telecomputing Network, Undated A). Many community networks operate today with software that allows the network to provide information about community resources but also to facilitate communication and discussion about issues.

II. ACCESSING THE INTERNET

To access the Internet, a user requires several items—software for communicating with a remote computer and for viewing Internet resources, a connection to some computer providing Internet service, and computer facilities adequate for providing an interface between the user and the Internet. At an office or university, some of these requirements are met by the Local Area Network (LAN) or Wide Area Network (WAN), which connects all the computers and provides software to all. In these cases, the Internet service is arranged by system administrators and is provided through a "hard-wired" connection or cables so that service is very fast and relatively trouble-free.

At home, the connection between the user and the Internet is typically provided through telephone hookup. The user must select an Internet Service Provider (ISP)—NetCom is a large provider, one of a multitude of regional and local providers—or an online service provider (like American Online, CompuServe, Delphi, or Prodigy) to provide the actual connection to the Internet. Then the user must connect to that service, typically by telephone. The home computer connects to a telephone line through a device called a modem, and the modem calls into a phone number provided by the Internet Service Provider.

In order to access the World Wide Web, the home user must have a modem capable of transmitting data at a rate of at least 9,600 bps (bits per second), but this connection will still be slow; faster modems with speeds of 14,400, 28,800 bps and higher, as they are developed and put on the market, are recommended. In addition, ISDN (Integrated Services Digital Network) service is just becoming available for home use; ISDN provides a much faster service and is eventually intended to transfer not just data but also video and sound into the home[3] (Derfler and Freed, 1993).

To make the connection to the Internet from home, communications software which works in conjunction with the modem is also required. This software often allows easy downloading or printing of Internet information as well as providing such other features as fax capabilities. Online services provide the necessary software bundled with their marketing offer and diskettes. Specific software required to access the Internet includes a Web browser, ftp, gopher, and newsgroup reader. This software is typically provided on the Local Area Network, by an online service provider, or in a bundled set of software available at the local computer store. Assistance in installing and using this software or hardware is typically available at the local computer store, university, or private training company.

CONCLUSION

Setting up an Internet connection and learning to use online resources opens the health administrator, practitioner, or student to a rapidly changing world of cutting edge information and worldwide communications. This essay provides an important introduction to the riches of this new world. However, the software, hardware, and resources are always changing. Nothing compares to personal experience. Users should seek out news articles, magazines, and professional communications to keep informed of the latest resources available in the health field.

ENDNOTES

1. See Lent, 1995 and Maxwell, 1995 for examples of these listservs.

2. Freenet® is a trademark of the National Public Telecomputing Network; community networks are called freenets when they are registered with the NPTN.

3. To date, there have been numerous problems with the installation of this technology in the home but these problems will undoubtedly be resolved.

REFERENCES

Boone, M. E. (1993). *Leadership and the Computer*, Prima Publishing, Rocklin, CA.

Derfler, F., Jr. and Freed, L. (1993). *How Networks Work*, Ziff-Davis Publications, Emeryville, CA.

Eddings, J. (1994). *How the Internet Works*, Ziff-Davis Publications, Emeryville, CA.

Gibson, W. (1984). *Neuromancer*, Ace Books, New York.

Lent, M. (1995). *Government On-Line*. Harper Perennial, New York.

Maxwell, B. (1995). Washington Online: How to Access the Federal Government on the Internet , *Congressional Quarterly*, Washington, D.C.

Miller, T. J. (1994). Community Computing and Free-Nets. *The Internet Unleashed*, SAMS Publishing/Prentice-Hall Computer Publishing, Indianapolis, IN.

National Public Telecomputing Network. (Undated A). Community Computing and National Public Telecomputing Network: The Concept of Community Computing. *File: concept.community.computer from ftp archive nptn.org*

Rheingold, H. (1993). *The Virtual Community: Homesteading on the Electronic Frontier*, Addison-Wesley, Reading, MA.

SAMS Publisher (Ed.) (1994). *Internet Unleashed*, SAMS Publishing/Prentice-Hall Computer Publishing, Indianapolis, IN.

48.

IMPROVING ACCESS THROUGH COMMUNITY PARTNERSHIPS: A CASE STUDY

Leiyu Shi, *University of South Carolina, Columbia, SC*

Michel E. Samuels, *University of South Carolina, Columbia, SC*

Brian C. Martin, *East Tennessee State University, Johnson City, TN*

Thomas E. Brown, *Richland Memorial Hospital, Columbia, SC*

Providing adequate access to primary care is a critical concern in many communities, particularly those with a disproportional share of poor and minority populations (Health Resources and Services Administration, 1990; Pepper Commission, 1990). Such access is often lacking for Medicaid recipients and for the working poor who are uninsured or underinsured and not eligible for public welfare (Holahan et al., 1991). The number of persons without adequate health care coverage continues to increase as employers reduce their contributions, limit coverage, or raise deductibles in their employees' health insurance policies. Underserved poor and minority populations suffer significantly higher rates of premature morbidity, disability, and mortality than the rest of the US population (Health Resources and Services Administration, 1990; Levine et al., 1994). The overall health status of the population would improve only after significant progress is made in decreasing the gap in the health status of the underserved poor and minorities. The urgency of ensuring access to health care is also emphasized through one of the three goals stated in Healthy People 2000 (U.S. Public Health Service, 1990): all Americans will have access to preventive services.

One proactive way to improve access to primary care and community services is through a community partnership approach where community leaders, providers, and residents become partners in community organizing, needs assessment, services restructuring, and evaluation (Levine et al., 1994; Barker et al., 1994; Farley, 1993; Young, 1994). Figure 1 presents such an approach based on our experience in community health development and incorporating aspects of community analysis models by Levine et al. (1994), Barker et al. (1994), and Stoner et al. (1992), and health planning models by Green and Kreuter (1991) and Dignan and Carr (1987). This partnership model enables the community to express its needs and contribute to its well-being by

Figure 1 - Community partnership model.

Community Organizing	Community Needs Assessment	Community Restructuring	Community Based Evaluation
Tools:			
• Form ad-hoc committee	• Available community data	• Distribute findings	• Community health status indicators
• Build coalition	• Provider study	• Community-wide program planning	• Patient/client surveys
• Identify funding sources	• Patient/client study	• Seek funding	• Provider surveys
	• Consensus meetings	• Implement interventions	• Outcome measures
Objectives:			
• Broad based participation	• Problems identification	• Informed agency and community policy makers	• Program monitoring
• Ownership of community based programs	• Problems prioritizing		• Timely feedback
• Concerted efforts	• Targeted outcomes	• Determine strategies and timelines	• Desired outcomes
		• Integrated health and human services systems	• Program adjustments
		• More effective and efficient service provisions	

restructuring health and human services. It focuses on community-oriented primary care that includes appraisal of community health needs, planning of services, and evaluation of the effects of care as well as provision of health and human services (Hubbell et al., 1989; Kark, 1981; Mullan, 1982).

In this model, the first stage is community organizing through such activities as the formation of an ad hoc committee with community representation, coalition building, and the identification of funding sources. The objective is to build broad-based participation including decision makers, providers, and residents. Community-wide participation will ensure ownership of community-based programs, which will promote concerted efforts from multiple sectors.

In the second stage, community needs assessment, community-wide data are identified and collected from a variety of sources, including available data bases, provider and patient/client focus groups, interviews, surveys, and consensus building meetings. The objectives are to identify and diagnose community problems, prioritize them based on their critical nature and complications, and determine desired outcomes.

In the third stage, community restructuring, findings of the needs assessment are distributed to all stakeholders so that agency and community policy makers become informed. Community-wide program planning is conducted to specify the strategies and timelines of implementing change. Funding sources are sought to assist in the implementation of interventions. Formal interventions are then implemented with the objectives of improving the integration of health and human services and enhancing the effectiveness and efficiency of service provisions.

In the fourth and final stage, community-based evaluation is conducted through assessing community health status indicators, conducting patient/client and provider surveys, and measuring clinical and service outcomes. The objectives are to monitor

program implementation, provide timely feedback, assess to which extent desired outcomes have been realized, and make program adjustments.

This chapter reports the application of this community partnership model in
Richland County, the third largest county in South Carolina. This study was undertak-
en for the purpose of developing a plan to reduce barriers and improve access to
health and human services for low income persons in the community. Richland
County is one of the poorest counties in one of the poorest states of the country and
provides an ideal setting to implement community-based interventions. The Richland
experience can be adapted in many similar communities with access to primary care
problems. Indeed, whatever emerges from national health care reform, it would be
inadequate if it did not address the severe access problems faced by many inner-city
and rural communities with a large proportion of low income persons.

I. THE RICHLAND COMMUNITY

With a population of nearly 290,000, Richland County is the third largest county in
South Carolina. It is also one of the poorest, with pockets of low-income and homeless
individuals and families. About 14% of individuals and 10% of families are below the
poverty line, and an average of $1.7 million is given every month to about 8,300 house-
holds and 9,600 recipients of AFDC (Aid to Families with Dependent Children) and
food stamps. Table 1 compares the socio-demographic and health characteristics of
Richland County and those of the US in 1990. Richland County had a considerably
higher proportion of minorities than the national average (44% versus 20%). Median
household income was over $1,200 less in Richland County than the national average
($28,848 versus $30,056), and there were more families with children below the poverty
line than the national average (14.4% versus 12.6%). The violent crime rate was significantly higher in Richland than the national average (977 versus 732 per 100,000 population). The health status of Richland County residents was also below the national
average. Infant mortality was 12.3 per 1,000 live births in Richland compared with the
national average of 10.

Due to lack of insurance and a severe problem in access to primary care, the emergency room became an expensive outlet for many people to receive medical treatment
for non-urgent conditions. Among Richland County emergency room users in 1993,
nearly 75% were black, over 50% were unemployed, and two-thirds had either
Medicaid coverage or no insurance at all.

Over the years, both medical and social services were fragmented, expensive, and
often unsatisfactory to both recipients and providers. Patients and clients had to fill
out numerous and often repetitive forms. The verification stage was also lengthy and
often invaded into the private lives of individuals. Services provided by different
organizations were not coordinated. Patients and clients often received duplicating
services at one time and no services at another time. The time spent waiting to be
served was often lengthy. Providers were overworked and turnover rates were very
high. Both clients and providers complained about the status quo of health and
human service delivery for low income families and individuals.

Table 1 - Socio-demographic and Health Characteristics in Richland County, South Carolina, and United States, 1990

	Richland County	United States
Elderly population (65+)	9.3%	12.6%
Minority population	43.9%	19.7%
Median household income	$28,848	$30,056
Per capita income	$13,243	$14,420
Families below poverty line	10.1%	10.0%
Persons below poverty line	13.8%	13.1%
Families with children below poverty	14.4%	12.6%
Households with no telephone	5.3%	5.2%
Total births to teenage mothers	16.8%*	12.5%
Low birth weight births (<2500 grams) to total live births	10.3%	–
Infant mortality per 1,000 live births	12.3	10.0
Population receiving public aid (AFDC and SSI)	5.8%*	6.5%
Households receiving food stamps	7.6%*	8.7%
Violent crime rate per 100,000 population	977*	732

Source: South Carolina State Budget and Control Board Division of Research and Statistical Services, South Carolina Statistical Abstract, 1993. Columbia, SC: Division of Research and Statistical Services, 1994.
*South Carolina state average.

II. COMMUNITY ORGANIZING

To improve access to primary care and reduce service fragmentation, leading health care providers and human services organizations in the community formed the Richland County Health and Human Services Coalition (RCHHSC). The participating organizations included the community teaching hospital (an umbrella organization), the county health department, the county department of social services, community health centers, health maintenance organization (HMO), family planning clinic, shelters, voluntary, and citizen organizations. With the exception of the HMO, all organizations had as their mission to serve the indigent. Leadership in the coalition was provided by the first founding organizations: the community teaching hospital, the county health department, the county department of social services, a community health center, and the HMO.

Two standing committees were formed under RCHHSC. Executive directors from the founding organizations formed an executive committee, which served as the board to the Coalition. The board reviewed all recommendations from member organizations and gave final approval. The board met about once a month. The second committee was called the program committee and comprised of one or two mid-level administrators from each member organization. Members of this committee met at least once a month to discuss community-wide concerns, clarify identified problems, and initiate community-based problem solving. The committee enabled organizations to actively participate in program development and implementation and to provide support for community-wide activities (e.g., sharing data on patients/clients, sharing resources). Two members served as liaisons between the board and the program committee, making sure the agendas of the two committees were well coordinated and consistent.

In a period of competition and concern for market share in health care, the RCHH-SC has been unique in its collaborative approach. Each organization looked beyond its own needs to develop a community-wide vision. Participants established respectful working relationships, overcoming the territoriality inherent in a competitive health care system. Trust and cooperation evolved from a common commitment to serve the poor and disadvantaged.

III. COMMUNITY NEEDS ASSESSMENT

A community needs assessment was conducted using a variety of methods, including analyzing existing data, conducting focus groups with major community providers, interviewing patients and clients, and conducting focus groups with patient/client representatives. Core funding for these efforts was provided by a variety of sources, most notably, the Duke Endowment through its assistance in developing an integrated primary care program for Medicaid and other low-income persons. In this section, we describe the process of needs assessment and summarize major features and findings related to each step.

A. Existing Data

The principal advantage of using existing data is economy, achieved through money, time, and personnel saved in data collection and management ((Jacob, 1984; Singleton et al., 1993). Health related existing data include collections of documents containing mainly factual information compiled in a variety of ways (eg., directly from patients/clients, or indirectly from employers, doctors, and agencies acting as informants) and used by health services organizations to record the development and implementation of decisions and activities that are central to their functions. Existing data also afford the opportunity to study trends and change over a long period of time.

The principal weakness of using existing data is the extent of compatibility between available data and the research question. Available data such as surveys, records, and documents must be found rather than created to the researcher's specification. Once identified, the value of available data will depend on the degree of match between the research questions and the data that happen to be available. Accessibility to available data may pose a challenge to investigators. Some data sets extracted from government records are routinely released for public use. In other cases, access may need to be negotiated or there may be constraints on access due to confidentiality and ethical concerns (e.g., HIV/AIDS). Another limitation of existing data, particularly administrative records not collected for research purposes, is that records are frequently incomplete.

Table 2 - Patient Visits and Demographic Characteristics, Richland County, 1993

SEX	Emergency Freq.	%	Inpatient Freq.	%	Outpatient Freq.	%	Clinics Freq.	%	Dental Freq.	%
female	29,406	53.63%	14,475	58.23%	51,808	66.14%	53,850	73.86%	4,365	63.37%
male	25,427	46.37%	10,383	41.77%	26,518	33.86%	19,060	26.14%	2,523	36.63%
total	54,833	100.00%	24,858	100.00%	78,326	100.00%	72,910	100.00%	6,888	100.00%
AGE										
0-5	9,156	16.70%	5,024	20.21%	5,382	6.87%	8,500	11.66%	6	0.09%
6-10	3,585	6.54%	641	2.58%	2,880	3.68%	3,097	4.25%	97	1.41%
11-18	4,695	8.56%	1,095	4.41%	3,800	4.85%	4,322	5.93%	553	8.03%
19-44	27,210	49.62%	8,085	32.52%	24,544	31.34%	33,156	45.48%	4,164	60.45%
45-64	7,015	12.79%	4,767	19.18%	22,662	28.93%	13,851	19.00%	1,681	24.40%
65+	3,172	5.78%	5,246	21.10%	19,058	24.33%	9,984	13.69%	387	5.62%
Total	54,833	100.00%	24,858	100.00%	78,326	100.00%	72,910	100.00%	6,888	100.00%
RACE										
Black	38,462	70.14%	12,034	48.41%	29,629	37.83%	45,423	62.30%	2,386	34.64%
White	15,343	27.98%	11,214	45.11%	43,912	56.06%	22,203	30.45%	3,437	49.90%
Other	538	0.98%	1,420	5.71%	4,396	5.61%	4,653	6.38%	1,026	14.90%
Hispanic	338	0.62%	99	0.40%	169	0.22%	428	0.59%	9	0.13%
Oriental	142	0.26%	84	0.34%	211	0.27%	196	0.27%	26	0.38%
Indian	10	0.02%	7	0.03%	9	0.01%	7	0.01%	4	0.06%
Total	54,833	100.00%	24,858	100.00%	78,326	100.00%	72,910	100.00%	6,888	100.00%
EMPLOYMENT										
Employed	17,244	31.45%	6,663	26.80%	26,416	33.73%	17,509	24.01%	5,564	80.78%
Unemployed	22,827	41.63%	8,290	33.35%	15,309	19.55%	31,478	43.17%	250	3.63%
Unspecified	11,729	21.39%	5,114	20.57%	19,383	24.75%	15,548	21.32%	788	11.44%
Retired	3,033	5.53%	4,791	19.27%	17,218	21.98%	8,375	11.49%	286	4.15%
Total	54,833	100.00%	24,858	100.00%	78,326	100.00%	72,910	100.00%	6,888	100.00%
PAYER SOURCES										
Self-pay	17,161	31.30%	552	2.22%	4,320	5.52%	9,348	12.82%	689	10.00%
Medicaid	16,130	29.42%	4,630	18.63%	10,584	13.51%	28,568	39.18%	58	0.84%
Medicare	4,660	8.50%	6,274	25.24%	19,111	24.40%	11,264	15.45%	123	1.79%
Other	16,882	30.79%	13,402	53.91%	44,311	56.57%	23,730	32.55%	6,018	87.37%
Total	54,833	100.00%	24,858	100.00%	78,326	100.00%	72,910	100.00%	6,888	100.00%

Note: The other category includes all third-party insurance, charity, VA, and Champus programs.

The existing data we gathered were mainly published information available in the public domain and private administrative records and materials provided by collaborating community organizations. Examples of public information included the numerous volumes of official statistics such as vital statistics from birth, death, marriage, and divorce certificates, and population demographics from census data. The variables in birth records included demographic information about the newborn child and information about the parents (e.g., names of mother and father, address, age, and occupation). Death records contained data on biographic information of the deceased, cause of death, length of illness, whether injuries were accidental, homicidal, or self-inflicted, and the time and place of death. These data made possible research ranging from a study of fertility patterns in the county to epidemiological investigation about the incidence and prevalence of disease based on the Health Promotion 2000 goals set for Richland County. The census data provided detailed information about the characteristics of the population of the state, county, neighborhood tracts, and blocks, including data on the age, gender, race, and marital status of each person.

Examples of private administrative records were records kept by health and human services agencies. Examples included health and human services records, insurance membership and payment records, organizational accounts and personnel records, and agency revenues and expenditures. We requested each agency to provide its administrative records regarding both total and unduplicated patients/clients by sex, age distributions, race, occupation, employment status, county, zip codes, insurance or payment sources, and primary discharge (diagnosis) codes.

Table 2 summarizes the demographic characteristics of patients in 1993 based on patient visits. The data were extracted from the hospital's management information system. Overall, there were more female visits than male visits in all hospital settings, particularly in clinics (74% female vs. 26% male) and outpatient (66% female vs. 34% male) settings. This finding is consistent with the literature that females are more likely to utilize health care services than males (National Center for Health Statistics, 1993). The significant difference in sex distributions across care settings indicates that females were more likely than males to seek preventive, primary care services. This finding is also consistent with the literature on health seeking behavior.

In terms of age, there were wide differences across hospital settings. In the inpatient setting, the elderly (age 65+) accounted for 21% of the visits and the very young (age 0-5; presumably related to childbirth) accounted for another 20%. In the emergency department, most patients (over 81%) fell into the young and middle age categories (under 45). In the primary care clinics of outpatients setting, patients of young-to old-age categories (age 19+) were somewhat evenly distributed and accounted for most of the visits (85% and 78% respectively).

In terms of race, there were more black than white inpatients (48% vs. 45%). This is consistent with the national distributions: there are 96.3 black patients discharged per 1,000 population versus 88.6 white patients discharged per 1,000 population (National Center for Health Statistics, 1993). In addition, there is a higher proportion of black population in South Carolina than the national average. Minority patients accounted for most of the emergency (over 70%) and clinic (62%) visits. White patients had more outpatient (56% vs. 38%) and dental (50% vs. 35%) visits than black patients. Nationally white patients, on average, have more physician visits than black patients (2.9 vs. 2.1 visits per year) (National Center for Health Statistics, 1993).

In terms of employment, except for the dental clinic, the hospital was frequented by a high proportion of the unemployed patient population, ranging from 20% in outpatient, 33% in inpatient, 42% in emergency department, to 43% in clinics. Since those who are unemployed are usually poor, these findings indicate that the hospital has indeed provided care to a large segment of the poor population in the community.

In terms of payer status, the emergency department was predominantly visited by those who had no insurance (31%) or were covered by Medicaid (29%). Primary care clinics also served a large segment of the uninsured (13%) or Medicaid recipients (39%). Both inpatient and outpatient settings displayed more even distribution across insurance categories. As expected, a high proportion of the inpatients, over 25%, were Medicare beneficiaries. Among private insurance, commercial insurance played a significant role across all hospital settings, particularly in inpatient (14%), outpatient (19%), and dental (22%).

812   *Shi, Samuels, Martin, and Brown*

Figure 2 - Agency and services matrix

Programs/Services	Hospital	Clinics	DSS	CHD	CHC
Clinical Health Services					
Pediatric	x	x		x	x
Adult	x	x		x	x
Rehabilitative				x	
Family Planning		x		x	
OB/GYN		x		x	
STDs		x		x	
WIC		x		x	x
Vital Records				x	
Community Health Services					
Home Health			x	x	
Personal Care				x	
Health Promotion				x	
HIV/AIDS Education				x	
Environmental Health Services					
Waste/Waste Water				x	
Rabies Control				x	
Vector Control				x	
General Sanitation				x	
Economic Services					
AFDC			x		
Food Stamp Program			x		
Work Support					
Medicaid			x		
Optional State Support			x		
Human Services					
Abuse & Neglect Program			x		
Child Protective Services			x		
Adult Protective Services			x		
Sexual Abuse		x	x		
Volunteer Services			x		

DSS = Department of Social Services, CHD = County Health Department, CHC = Community Health Centers.

Examples of health and human services provided by member organizations are included in Figure 2. These services included clinical health services (pediatric, adult, rehabilitative, family planning, obstetrics/gynecology or OB/GYN, sexually transmitted diseases (STDs), women, infant, and children (WIC), vital records), community health services (home health, personal care, health promotion, HIV/AIDS, education), environmental health services (waste, waste water, rabies control, vector control, general sanitation), economic services (AFDC, food stamp program, work support, Medicaid, optional state support), and human services (abuse and neglect programs, child protective services, adult protective services, sexual abuse, volunteer services). Detailed literature was provided by each agency for its services and programs.

B. Provider Focus Groups

A focus group study is an interview with a small group of people on a specific topic (Patton, 1990; Grady and Wallston, 1988). A focus group typically consists of 6 to 12 people who are brought together in a room to engage in a guided discussion of some topic for a lengthy period of time, typically several hours. Participants are selected on the basis of relevancy to the topic under study, although they are not likely to be chosen through rigorous, probability sampling methods. The purpose of the focus group is to explore a topic rather than describe or explain it in any definitive sense. Participants listen to one another's comments as well as voice their own responses. Typically, more than one focus group is convened in a given study since there is a danger that a single group of 6 to 12 people would be too atypical to offer any generalizable insights. The principal advantages of focus group are its flexibility, high face validity, and low cost. It can be highly enjoyable to most participants. The principal weaknesses of focus group are its limited generalizability, the danger of the process to be dominated by one or two participants, and the difficulty to analyze focus group results.

Separate focus groups were conducted with representatives from each of the major health and human services agencies in the community. Each focus group lasted for half a day. A detailed focus group guide was used which included participants' profiles, questions concerning agency's services/programs, and questions concerning services in the Richland community. Participants' demographic variables were age, sex, race, agency name, agency position, years in such position, education level, and profession (e.g., physician, nurse, social worker, clerk, etc.). In questions regarding agency's services/programs, participants were asked to identify all programs/services, service objectives, funding, staffing, clients, information system, and problems related to each of these elements. In questions concerning services in the Richland community, participants were asked to assess community needs, identify current community-wide services/programs that address those needs, identify problems and deficiencies of current community services/programs, make recommendations to improve current community services/programs, and choose a course of action to implement the recommendations.

Upon the completion of individual focus groups, a joint focus group was conducted with representatives of all major agencies who participated in the individual focus groups. Participants were asked to discuss and prioritize the problems identified. The top ten problems identified, ranked in descending order of reported frequency, were: lack of a common computer-based information system covering all agencies, thus causing problems of referral, follow-up, and excessive paperwork; lack of adequate transportation system; lack of funding for prescription drugs; complex eligibility requirements; high staff turnover and low pay; non-compliance versus different priorities of clients; lack of dental services; lack of adequate linkage with mental health services; lack of emergency shelter for children; and fragmented information systems within provider organizations.

Based on a series of focus groups, the program committee identified a list of access barriers facing the Richland community, including individuals not having adequate amount of health insurance or possessing adequate resources to purchase health services, complicated Medicaid eligibility requirement, fragmented and poorly coordinated human and health services, pockets of families not being eligible for Medicaid assistance, increased use of emergency department for primary care, limited number of private physicians who accept Medicaid patients, and inadequate attention to prevention resulting in a crisis approach to health care. Committee members were unsure of the magnitude of these problems or whether additional problems existed. Existing data collected about the community were unable to address these issues. Therefore, they requested that a thorough community-wide needs assessment be conducted prior to any community-wide interventions.

C. Patient/Client Survey

Results of the agency focus groups represented the providers' perceptions of the problems facing the community. Providers, understandably, have perceptions about a community's needs and how to address those needs. These perceptions, however, may not be consistent with the concerns of community residents. In order to find out the perspectives of the patients/clients, we conducted a large-scale survey with a representative sample of the patient/client population.

The face-to-face interview method was used as a means of data collection because we expected most of the respondents to have little education, and therefore would be unable to comprehend the questionnaire instrument by themselves. Trained interviewers were able to answer common queries by respondents, while administering the questionnaire instrument. The use of the interview survey was also expected to improve both response and completion rates.

The questionnaire instrument used for the interview survey was developed after an extensive review of the literature related to access to care, access barriers, health beliefs, minority health, community health, primary care, and patient satisfaction. The draft instrument was then circulated to administrators of the organizations where the interviews would be conducted, community leaders, medical and social services providers, and university research scholars. The revised instrument was then pretested with patients from the hospital's clinics. Further revisions were made based on the pretest results so that the instrument became population sensitive, reflecting the concerns and language of the poor and underserved.

The final version of the interview questionnaire consisted of seven parts: about this interview; access to care by patient or client; access barriers by patient or client; health beliefs by patient, client, or caretakers; reason for current visit by patient or client; demographic characteristics of patient or client; and emergency department patients. The interview questionnaire may be requested from the authors.

In recruiting interviewers, we targeted middle-age African American women because preliminary trials indicated they were most likely to gain rapport from the patients, most of whom were minority women themselves. We also recruited some white men and women as interviewers. All interviewers underwent training offered by the investigators and were closely monitored during the initial days of the interview. Any questions from the interviewers were immediately directed to the investigators who provided timely assistance and instructions that were consistent across research settings.

A two-stage, stratified sampling method was used to select interview participants. In the first stage, we selected health and human services facilities based on their representativeness. In the second stage, we selected strata believed to represent different patient/client populations of each organization. The strata used were different days of the week, morning and afternoon, and, for emergency department, evening time.

Patients were then selected from each stratum for each agency. Specifically, a research coordinator who was either a nurse, social worker, or clerk for the agency was taught to approach all eligible patients or clients who were not being treated. After agreeing to participate in the interview, patients were directed to the interviewers who conducted the interview in a private setting. Depending on the number of services received, the amount of information given, and the experience of the interviewers, the interview lasted between 15 and 40 minutes. A total of 804 patients/clients were interviewed.

Table 3 summarizes respondents' access barriers by provider settings. Twenty-nine percent of the respondents indicated having delays in seeking medical care. Among the factors identified as related to such a delay, 56% thought the problems were not as serious as they were, 42% indicated high cost as a factor, and 34% referred to lack of insurance coverage. Other factors included lack of time (20%), difficulty in getting transportation (17%), difficulty in getting an appointment (13%), and lack of knowledge about providers (12%). The Department of Social Services (DSS) respondents were more likely to delay seeking medical care than respondents from all other settings.

Fifteen percent of the respondents indicated having delays in seeking social services. Among the factors identified as related to such a delay, 36% attributed it to long waiting, 33% blamed unfriendly staff, and 25% referred to lack of knowledge about services. Other factors included lack of time (23%), problems not thought to be serious (20%), difficulty in getting transportation (19%), difficulty in getting appointment (15%), and complicated eligibility requirement (12%). As with medical care, DSS respondents were more likely to delay seeking social services than respondents from all other settings.

Table 4 summarizes barriers to medical care and social services by provider settings. The listed factors to which respondents were asked to designate as "no problem", "some problem", or "great problem", included the following: getting information about providers, making appointment to see providers, transportation, waiting time during the visit, getting good treatment or service, providers' attitudes, ability to pay for treatment or service, and ability to pay for medicine. Most respondents indicated no problem for the listed factors. In particular, respondents had no problem with making an appointment to see providers (80%). Most believed that they received good treatment or service (80%).

Respondents had the greatest problem with waiting time during the visit (54% including 19% who identified this as a great problem), followed by ability to pay for

Table 3 - Respondents' Access Barriers by Provider Setting

	TOTAL	ED	Clinics	DSS	CHD	CHC
Delay in medical care*						
Yes	227 (29%)	48 (25%)	53 (40%)	33 (23%)	34 (30%)	59 (28%)
No	566 (71%)	145 (75%)	81 (60%)	110 (77%)	80 (70%)	150 (72%)
Factors related to delay						
Problems not thought to be serious***	126 (56%)	24 (50%)	35 (66%)	20 (61%)	13 (38%)	34 (58%)
Lack of knowledge about providers***	26 (12%)	4 (8%)	7 (13%)	9 (27%)	1 (3%)	5 (9%)
Difficulty in getting transportation***	39 (17%)	6 (13%)	9 (17%)	10 (30%)	3 (9%)	11 (19%)
Cost too much***	96 (42%)	18 (38%)	24 (45%)	19 (58%)	14 (41%)	21 (36%)
Lack of time	46 (20%)	6 (13%)	18 (34%)	4 (12%)	7 (21%)	11 (19%)
Difficulty in getting appointment***	29 (13%)	2 (4%)	7 (13%)	8 (24%)	2 (6%)	10 (17%)
Lack of insurance coverage***	77 (34%)	7 (15%)	18 (34%)	19 (58%)	17 (50%)	16 (27%)
Other***	34 (15%)	13 (27%)	4 (8%)	2 (6%)	4 (12%)	11 (19%)
Delay in social services*						
Yes	103 (15%)	14 (8%)	25 (25%)	22 (15%)	17 (18%)	25 (13%)
No	588 (85%)	151 (92%)	76 (75%)	120 (85%)	77 (82%)	164 (87%)
Factors related to delay						
Problems not thought to be serious***	21 (20%)	1 (7%)	1 (4%)	13 (59%)	1 (6%)	5 (20%)
Lack of knowledge about services***	26 (25%)	5 (36%)	3 (12%)	12 (55%)	2 (12%)	4 (16%)
Difficulty in getting transportation***	19 (19%)	5 (36%)	1 (4%)	8 (36%)	1 (6%)	4 (16%)
Long waiting***	37 (36%)	5 (36%)	6 (24%)	13 (59%)	5 (29%)	8 (32%)
Lack of time	24 (23%)	5 (36%)	3 (12%)	2 (9%)	4 (24%)	10 (40%)
Difficulty in getting appointment***	15 (15%)	1 (7%)	2 (8%)	6 (27%)	4 (24%)	2 (8%)
Complicated eligibility requirement***	13 (13%)	0 (0%)	3 (12%)	5 (23%)	3 (18%)	2 (8%)
Unfriendly staff***	34 (33%)	3 (21%)	3 (12%)	10 (46%)	6 (35%)	12 (48%)
Other***	18 (18%)	5 (36%)	3 (12%)	4 (18%)	0 (0%)	6 (24%)

*** *Differences among settings statistically significant at a=.01; ** at a=.05; * at a=.10.*
Note: Multiple answers are permitted in identifying access barriers.
ED = Richland Hospital Emergency Department; Clinics = Richland Hospital Outpatient Clinics; DSS = Department of Social Services; CHD = County Health Department; CHC = community health center.

Table 4 - Barriers to Medical Care and Social Services by Provider Setting

	TOTAL	ED	Clinics	DSS	CHD	CHC
Getting information about providers*						
No problem	607 (77%)	157 (82%)	107 (81%)	100 (71%)	87 (77%)	156 (75%)
Some problem	146 (19%)	29 (15%)	20 (15%)	36 (26%)	24 (21%)	37 (18%)
Great problem	32 (4%)	5 (3%)	6 (5%)	5 (4%)	2 (2%)	14 (7%)
Making appointment to see providers*						
No problem	627 (80%)	151 (79%)	107 (81%)	101 (72%)	98 (87%)	170 (82%)
Some problem	133 (17%)	30 (16%)	23 (17%)	34 (24%)	15 (13%)	31 (15%)
Great problem	25 (3%)	10 (5%)	3 (2%)	6 (4%)	0 (0%)	6 (3%)
Transportation***						
No problem	541 (69%)	132 (69%)	103 (77%)	74 (53%)	92 (81%)	140 (68%)
Some problem	167 (21%)	40 (21%)	22 (17%)	38 (27%)	15 (13%)	52 (25%)
Great problem	77 (10%)	19 (10%)	8 (6%)	29 (21%)	6 (5%)	15 (7%)
Waiting time during the visit***						
No problem	359 (46%)	54 (28%)	65 (49%)	80 (57%)	45 (40%)	115 (56%)
Some problem	276 (35%)	65 (34%)	44 (33%)	38 (27%)	60 (53%)	69 (33%)
Great problem	149 (19%)	71 (37%)	24 (18%)	23 (16%)	8 (7%)	23 (11%)
Getting good treatment/service***						
No problem	628 (80%)	156 (83%)	119 (90%)	93 (66%)	92 (81%)	168 (82%)
Some problem	127 (16%)	24 (13%)	10 (8%)	38 (27%)	19 (17%)	36 (18%)
Great problem	27 (4%)	9 (5%)	4 (3%)	10 (7%)	2 (2%)	2 (1%)
Providers' attitudes***						
No problem	626 (80%)	147 (77%)	118 (89%)	97 (69%)	94 (83%)	170 (83%)
Some problem	129 (17%)	37 (20%)	11 (8%)	34 (24%)	16 (14%)	31 (15%)
Great problem	27 (4%)	6 (3%)	4 (3%)	9 (6%)	3 (3%)	5 (2%)
Ability to pay for treatment/service***						
No problem	505 (65%)	103 (54%)	96 (75%)	78 (56%)	81 (72%)	147 (71%)
Some problem	159 (20%)	60 (31%)	24 (19%)	24 (17%)	20 (18%)	31 (15%)
Great problem	114 (15%)	28 (15%)	8 (6%)	38 (27%)	12 (11%)	28 (14%)
Ability to pay for medicine***						
No problem	479 (62%)	99 (52%)	85 (65%)	76 (54%)	81 (72%)	138 (68%)
Some problem	181 (23%)	64 (34%)	35 (27%)	23 (16%)	21 (19%)	38 (19%)
Great problem	119 (15%)	28 (15%)	11 (8%)	41 (29%)	11 (10%)	28 (14%)

*** *Differences among settings statistically significant at a=.01;* ** *at a=.05;* * *at a=.10.*
ED = Richland Hospital Emergency Department; Clinics = Richland Hospital Outpatient Clinics; DSS = Department of Social Services; CHD = County Health Department; CHC = community health center.

medicine (38%, including 15% who identified this as a great problem), and ability to pay for treatment or service (35%, including 15% who identified this as a great problem). Emergency Department respondents had the greatest problem with waiting time during appointment (71%, including 37% who identified this as a great problem), ability to pay for medicine (49%, including 15% who identified this as a great problem), and ability to pay for treatment or service (46%, including 15% who identified this as a great problem). DSS respondents had the greatest problem with transportation (27%, including 21% who identified this as a great problem).

D. Patient/Client Focus Groups

A patient/client focus group was conducted to gain a better understanding of perceptions and needs. Patients/clients were selected from each agency that participated in the patient/client survey. The intent was to find out the causes of the problems identified in the patient/client survey and to verify that problems and potential solutions identified by providers were accurate from the perspectives of patients and clients.

The results of the focus group confirmed most of the findings from the patient/client interviews. In particular, focus group participants were critical about waiting time during the visit, lack of awareness of services (e.g., lack of information about the program), complex and sometimes humiliating eligibility process, excessive and duplicating paperwork, restrictions by Medicaid to pay for certain services, lack of ability to pay for prescription drugs, transportation problem, and lack of ability to pay for treatment or service by those not qualified for Medicaid. Unlike interviews, focus group participants were also critical of providers' attitudes toward people covered by Medicaid or without insurance. There was a general perception that very few private sector doctors would accept Medicaid patients. Participants noted that providers behaved differently toward people with Medicaid than those with private insurance.

E. Community Diagnosis

Information collected from the above sources provided input for community diagnosis. The following summarizes the major problems identified by all sources:

1. Insufficient and inadequate community-wide data base in Richland County. Data on patients' or clients' demographics and service use patterns are either missing or inadequate. Data are not collected in a format required for cross-agency and national comparisons. Data are not stored in a manner accessible for analysis within agencies or by researchers. The lack of a common data base was thought to contribute to excessive paper work, inefficient work patterns, lack of awareness of community-wide services, and inadequate follow-ups or referrals.
2. Limited knowledge of existing community-wide health and human services which contributes to inadequate level of utilization of existing community services by low-income people.
3. Insufficient community resources for low-income patients/clients in selected service areas, particularly primary care and human services. There is a shortage of primary care physicians in the community in general and those who accept Medicaid patients in particular.

4. Negative attitudes and beliefs regarding service delivery (intimidation with application process, eligibility requirements, waiting time for appointments, transportation arrangements, child care service needs).
5. Lack of integration of existing community-wide health and human services.

III. COMMUNITY RESTRUCTURING

The ultimate goal of restructuring Richland County health and human services is to design an integrated, community-based, prevention-oriented health and human services system. Inappropriate utilization of emergency rooms will be reduced and patients will be diverted to ambulatory clinics and community programs where they can receive more appropriate, better coordinated, and more efficient services. The community-wide needs assessment enabled agencies to promote the strengths and overcome the weaknesses of current services provision, and to address the most critical concerns of patients and clients. The following summarizes the major steps taken by Richland community in its restructuring process.

A. Distribute Findings

Findings of the needs assessment were shared with all participating organizations one month after data collection. Presentations were made to each major participating organization at their request. Written reports that provided summary and analysis of study results were mailed to participating organizations as well as those interested in the study. Through these avenues, policy makers were informed about organizations' concerns related to health care access and were equipped to make decisions to improve the situation based on needs assessment. Individual organizations also used findings to plan changes in service delivery, improve access to care, and reduce barriers.

1. Establish Richland Community Health Partners

Upon the completion of needs assessment, the ad hoc coalition (RCHHSC) renamed itself as the Richland Community Health Partners (RCHP). RCHP's goal is to improve community health status in Richland County through the development and implementation of an integrated health and human services delivery system. Its specific strategies included the following (Richland Community Health Partners, 1995):
- Focusing on Richland County populations with the poorest health status;
- Developing a multi-organizational, cooperative network of public and private health and human service providers and private medical providers;
- Establishing a community health information network which links all participating providers and facilitates coordination and integration of services;
- Maximizing the effectiveness of existing funding sources through coordination and integration of services;
- Developing a managed care organization which targets low income persons receiving health care coverage through Medicaid and the Medicare beneficiaries who enroll in the Social HMO II demonstration; and

• Developing innovative alternatives for enhancing health and human service system effectiveness and for the financing and delivery of these services.

2. Establish a Community-wide Information Network

Since many of the problems (e.g., excessive paper work, inefficient work patterns, lack of awareness of community-wide services, and inadequate follow-ups or referrals) were related to the lack of a community-wide information system, RCHP decided to start with the development of a case management information system to be used by participating organizations as well as inter-agency units. RCHP is in the process of implementing a community-based information system. Such a system would record and maintain community-wide vital statistics, health care utilization data, practitioner registries, disease and injury registries, disease, injury, and behavioral risk factor surveillance systems, and periodic surveys such as the needs assessment surveys recently completed. In addition, the system will be logically integrated, in which information collected once at one agency can serve multiple purposes for many other agencies.

Such a system has the potential to overcome many of the problems experienced today such as problems with fragmentation, lack of standardization, episodic data collection, and the fact that data for public health purposes are often collected separately and redundantly from encounter data in the medical treatment system. These problems have exacerbated the burden and costs of collecting data, limited the linkability and usefulness of the data that are collected, and resulted in critical data gaps or unnecessary duplications.

RCHP planners recognize that realizing the potential of a community-based information system would require: a standardized multipurpose nomenclature for all health concepts, uniform standards for electronic data transmission, unique identifiers for all units of interests (including individuals, providers, worksite, etc.) a secure environment for transmitting and linking data, strong privacy protections, and appropriate data sharing policies. In addition, much of the current workforce needs to be trained in terms of information technology. Professionals who are unfamiliar with information technology are unlikely to take full advantage of technology that is available to them, or to contribute innovative ideas for applying the information infrastructure to population-based health.

B. Promote Community Awareness

Another intervention implemented is to promote community-wide awareness of existing health and human services targeted at the poor and underserved population. Awareness is enhanced at both the individual and organization levels. For individuals, promotional efforts implemented include: pamphlets in provider and community areas; pamphlet mailouts to households; signs at bus stop benches; billboards; health fairs/screenings; booths at community events (e.g., Mayfest); membership cards; and monthly newsletters. For organizations, promotion efforts include: utilization of the information system, particularly by smaller agencies, as a means of referring clients for appropriate services; use of outreach workers (e.g., former AFDC mothers); one-on-one marketing efforts by leaders of participating agencies; and booths at business events (e.g., Business Expo). RCHP is considering a contract with the CDC-funded Prevention Center at the School of Public Health, University of South Carolina to assist with development of community-wide health promotion programs and services.

IV. COMMUNITY BASED EVALUATION

RCHP has included an evaluation mechanism to assess the cost effectiveness of all programs. Outcome analysis over time will look at health status in regard to morbidity and mortality patterns, as well as functional status at the community level, including educational attainment, occupational status, and community indicators of healthful living, such as safe environment. These data are collected from both existing records and periodic community surveys. A case-control design is planned to see whether patients/clients in the intervention group (those receiving the integrated services) receive more effective and efficient services than those in the control (those in nearby community not yet receiving the integrated services). Measures of effectiveness include health, social, and economic indicators, as well as patient and provider satisfaction. Measures of efficiency include before-after and case-control comparisons of costs.

V. DISCUSSION

We believe the Richland project will make both theoretical and practical contributions to health policy and health services. From a theoretical standpoint, the project will improve our understanding of the social and economic determinants of health particularly with regard to the poor and underserved population. From a practical viewpoint, the project has both local and national significance. Locally, the project helps organize the community to identify and solve its problems based primarily on community resources, improve the effectiveness and efficiency of service delivery, address the most critical yet unmet needs of patients or clients, and provide the infrastructure for continual problem solving and service improvement. Nationally, the project offers a conceptual model for collaborative practice and methodology of integrating community-wide health and human services and restructuring the delivery of health care with principal emphasis on prevention and primary care services and correspondingly reduced reliance on inpatient treatment .

The Richland experience demonstrates one approach to community participation and collaboration. The social, economic, and political forces shaping the health of the community should be identified and recruited in a broad-based community coalition or partnership. Establishing a mutually beneficial partnership is essential for a productive relationship among agencies in a racial/ethnic minority community. Respect is developed and collaboration enhanced as each partner acknowledges other partners' contributions to community improvement. Community involvement also promotes community-based ownership of programs and interventions, and hence improves their implementation (Lillie-Blanton and Hoffman, 1995).

The Richland experience indicates the importance of community-wide needs assessment prior to program development and intervention. A community-wide needs assessment that provides inputs to population based planning and services delivery is critical in an era of managed care and capitated payment for a defined number of enrolled lives (Shortell et al., 1995). In addition to analysis of existing data on population demographics and disease trends, community needs assessment includes primary data collection, information on prevention and health promotion services, and interviews and focus groups with residents and community leaders. The goal is to develop a community health data base that can be used to manage populations of patients and community members over time.

Focus groups and key informants help in identifying critical questions that can be asked using a more structured format such as mail surveys or face-to-face interviews in a larger sample population. If original data are to be collected using the survey method, researchers must develop or use survey instruments that are population sensitive, i.e., instruments that reflect a knowledge of the culture and norms of the population group under study. This includes sensitivity not only to race/ethnicity but to such population characteristics as age, social class, language, reading level, and religious customs. Researchers may use questionnaire items that have been validated using the racial/ethnic population that is predominant in the community, if such items are available for the questions of interest. Respect for the culture and customs of the community when conducting fieldwork is essential for accurate results and efficient use of resources (Lillie-Blanton and Hoffman, 1995).

After data are collected and analyzed, the collaborating agencies and community groups should be involved in efforts to interpret and assess the implications of the findings. Agencies benefited from this collaborative community project by obtaining data for program planning, recognizing limitations in current agency data bases, developing effective working relationships with key members of other agencies, becoming aware of each others' organizational issues, and sharing resources to meet common community goals. Project data also provide substantive rationale for seeking external funds for necessary services. Participation of students in such projects provides valuable learning experiences.

The Richland experience, the community partnership approach, is consistent with many of the implications of several major national reports, such as The Future of Public Health by the Institute of Medicine (Remington et al., 1988), Healthy America: Practitioners for 2005 by the Pew Health Professions Commission (Shugars et al., 1991), Health Professions Education for the Future: Schools in Service to the Nation by the Pew Health Professions Commission (The Pew Health Professions Commission, 1993), and Healthy People 2000, issued by the U.S. Department of Health and Human Services (U.S. Public Health Service, 1990). It is an optimal way to address the needs of the poor and underserved population (Ginzberg, 1995).

REFERENCES

Barker, J., Bayne, T., Higgs, Z., Jenkin, S., Murphy, D., and Synoground, G. (1994). Community analysis: A collaborative community practice project. *Public Health Nursing* (11): 113-118.

Dignan, M., and Carr, P. (1987). Program Planning for Health Education and Health Promotion. Philadelphia: Lea and Febiger.

Farley, S. (1993). The community as partner in primary health care. *Nursing and Health Care* (14): 244-249.

Ginzberg, E. (1995). Hospitals: From center to periphery. *Inquiry*, 32: 11-13.

Grady, K.E., and Wallston, B.S. (1988). *Research in Health Care Settings*. Newbury Park, CA: Sage Publications.

Green, L., and Kreuter, M. (1991). Health Promotion Planning: An Educational and Environmental Approach. Mountain View, CA: Mayfield.

Health Resources and Services Administration. (1990). *Health Status of the Disadvantaged: Chartbook 1990*. (DHHS Publication no. HRSA-HRS-P-DV 90-1). Washington, DC: U.S. Government Printing Office.

Holahan, J., Moon, M., Welch, W., and Zreckerman, S. (1991). Balancing Access, Costs, and Politics: The American Context for Health System Reform (Report no. 91-6). Washington, DC: Urban Institute Press.

Hubbell, F., Waitzkin, H., Mishra, S., and Dombrink, J. (1989). Evaluating health-care needs of the poor: A community-oriented approach. *The American Journal of Medicine* (87): 127-131.

Jacob, H. (1984). Using Published Data. Beverly Hills, CA: Sage.

Kark, S. (1981). *The Practice of Community-Oriented Primary Health Care*. New York: Appleton-Century-Crofts.

Levine, D., Becker, D., Bone, L., Hill, M, Tuggle, M, and Zeger, S. (1994). Community-academic health center partnerships for underserved minority populations. *JAMA* (272): 309-311.

Lillie-Blanton, M., and Hoffman, S. (1995). Conducting an assessment of health needs and resources in a racial/ethnic minority community. *Health Services Research*, (30): 225-236.

Mullan, F. (1982). Community-oriented primary care: An agenda for the '80s. New England *Journal of Medicine*, (307): 1076-1078.

National Center for Health Statistics. (1992). *Health United States 1992*. Hyattsville, MD: Public Health Service.

Patton, M.Q. (1990). *Qualitative Evaluation and Research Methods* (2nd ed.). Newbury Park, CA: Sage.

Pepper Commission. (1990). *U.S. Bipartisan Committee on Comprehensive Health Care: A Call for Action*. Washington, DC: U.S. Government Printing Office.

The Pew Health Professions Commission. (1993). Health Professions Education for the Future: Schools in Service to the Nation: Report of the Pew Health Professions Commission. The Pew Health Professions Commission. Durham, NC.

Remington, R., Axelrode, D., and Bingham, E. (1988). *The Future of Public Health*. Washington, DC: Committee for the Study of the Future of Public Health, Division of Health Care Services, Institute of Medicine, National Academy Press; Institute of Medicine publication: 88-102.

Richland Community Health Partners. (1995). *Business Plan*. Richland Community Health Partners, Columbia, SC.

Shortell, S., Gillies, R., and Devers, K. (1995). Reinventing the American hospital. *The Milbank Quarterly*, (73): 131-160.

Shugars, D., O'Neil, E., Bader, J. (Eds.). (1991). Healthy America: Practitioners for 2005, an Agenda for Action for U.S. Health Professional Schools. Durham, NC: The Pew Health Professions Commission.

Singleton, R., Straits, B., and Straits, M. (1993). Chapter 12: Research using available data in R.A. Singleton. *Approaches to Social Research* (2nd ed.). New York: Oxford University Press.

Stoner, M., Magilvy, J., and Schultz, P. (1992). Community analysis in community health nursing practice: The GENESIS model. *Public Health Nursing* 9: 223-227.

U.S. Public Health Service. (1990). *Healthy People 2000: National Health Promotion and Disease Prevention Objectives*. (DHHS Publication no. PHS 91-50213). Washington, DC: U.S. Government Printing Office, 1990.

Young, K. (1994). An evaluative study of a community health service development. *Journal of Advanced Nursing*, 19: 58-65.

49.

MANAGED CARE AND NETWORKED INFORMATION SYSTEMS

Catherine M. Crawford, *National Health Information Center, Washington, DC*

The National Information Infrastructure (NII) crosses the traditional boundaries of the public and private sectors and can provide the framework within which joint efforts can occur. The private sector will have primary responsibility for the design, deployment and operation of the NII, since traditionally the private sector has had the research and development money for such efforts. But all levels of government can play a role in working with the private sector to ensure the effective development and deployment of the NII within managed care environments.

In response to the need for cooperation between the two sectors, especially in the managed care arena, a collaborative public and private sector White Paper was written at the request of the Health Information Applications Work Group (HIAWG), part of the Vice-President's Information Infrastructure Task Force (IITF). The report was to focus on managed care and the NII[1]. This chapter summarizes that report, which describes a unique set of circumstances that are changing the way health care is delivered in this county[2].

I. EMERGING SYSTEMS

Complex changes are occurring rapidly throughout the Nation and throughout the world as a result of merging technologies and applications. In recognition of these changes, the Federal government has placed high priority on working with the private sector in the development of an advanced National Information Infrastructure, or NII.

In 1993 the Information Infrastructure Task Force (IITF) formalized several Federal NII policy development mechanisms and enumerated the guiding principles and goals for policy development in its report The National Information Infrastructure (NII): Agenda for Action. Since that time, the NII has been fast becoming the basic framework upon which the raw material of the next century—information--will be transmitted, making it possible to transmit to and receive from potentially every individual within the U.S. and eventually throughout the world (IITF, 1994).

While a number of reports on the NII have dealt with the issues involved in health care and the NII (e.g., NIIAC, 1995; Patrick and Koss, 1995; Bashshur et al., 1995; Bashshur et al., 1994; Fitzmaurice, 1994; HIAWG, 1994; NIST, 1994a and 1994b), there is a particular need to explore the uses of the NII in a managed care environment.

A. Managed Care

Pressures on the budgets and bottom lines of businesses and government are now changing the delivery of health care on a level hardly imagined a few years ago. In 1993 we spent more than $844 billion for health care; close to $938 billion was spent in 1994 (Levit et al., 1994). It is estimated that in 1995 we spent $1.0 trillion in health care and by the year 2000 annual spending will reach $1.5 trillion (Burner and Waldo, 1995). As a result, players in the health care system are becoming more cost-conscious, competitive and market-based.

Managed care is defined as the use of financial incentives and management controls intended to direct patients to efficient providers, who are responsible for giving appropriate medical care in cost effective treatment settings (Boland, 1991). Forms of managed care organizations (MCOs) include, but are not restricted to, health maintenance organizations (HMOs), preferred provider organizations (PPOs) and point-of-service plans (POS) (ProPAC, 1995).

Managed care plans select providers to contract with the plan. Enrollees have a financial incentive to use participating providers that agree to furnish a broad range of services to them. Providers may be paid on a negotiated fee-for-service, capitated, per diem or salaried basis. Managed care plans may or may not be capitated. Capitation occurs when MCOs directly pay a fixed per month fee to primary care providers (PCPs) in advance of rendering services. If the costs of rendering the services exceeds the capitation dollars, then the PCP loses money. Conversely, if the cost is less, the PCP makes money.

Total MCO enrollment has been rising rapidly in the last 20 years, from 6 million persons in 1976 to 50 million persons in 1994 (GHAA, 1994). The MCO market saw double-digit growth in 1994, with an 11.5 percent increase over 1993 (Coile, 1995a). Projected MCO enrollment for the Year 2000 is expected to reach 100 million members, as traditional indemnity and government sponsored health plans (Medicare and Medicaid) convert enrollees to managed care (Coile, 1995b; Hegner, 1995).

Up until now, MCO enrollment has been concentrated in urban areas, with 87 percent of all members living in 57 cities. It is important to note that enrollment growth varies geographically. In 1994 growth rates were slowest in the West and much higher in other regions of the country. While many markets do not have the population density to support MCOs, low density does not necessarily preclude MCOs from gaining market share. Other barriers can impede market penetration. For example, busy primary care physicians may not want to take discounted managed care patients (Cochrane, 1994).

Some of the variation in enrollment is also related to market maturity. Maturity in this case does not refer to the length of time an MCO has been in a particular geographic market. Rather, it refers to the degree of penetration (MCO enrollment) within a geographic region. For example, Los Angeles has some of the oldest MCOs in the country, but it remains a viable and somewhat immature market because much of its population has yet to join an MCO (Appleby, 1995).

Immature managed care markets are typically dominated by fee-for-service and indemnity insurance plans. Transitional markets describe another variation in market maturity. The emphasis in these markets is to maximize the fee-for-service business, generate admissions and patient days, and maximize net revenues. In mature managed care markets, comprehensive networking among hospitals and providers dominate. MCOs have captured more than 20 percent of the market and capitation prevails. Physicians integrate group practices; hospitals combine. The emphasis is on wellness and keeping patients out of the hospital. Integrated health systems start developing, and measuring value and controlling utilization become the goals (Cochrane, 1995).

B.   Integrated Delivery Systems

Competition is the underlying incentive for creating a more organized health care delivery system. In response to highly competitive markets, provider organizations, practitioners and insurers are restructuring their relationships at an unprecedented rate to secure a position in a rapidly changing market (ProPAC, 1995). Managed care organizations (MCOs) are now spending millions of dollars integrating the provider side of care the hospitals, clinics, the personnel and other assets - to build integrated delivery systems. With continued development of the NII, it is expected that MCOs will continue to move towards an information base, investing in group practices and information technologies. MCOs may create a new set of health services that use networked information to integrate the consumer/patient side of health care.

There is evidence that much of this restructuring is occurring in mature markets and is in the form of vertically integrated health care networks. Physicians and hospitals are merging; insurers and providers are merging; physicians are joining one another to form new managed care organizations. These newer forms of integrated MCOs are one response to criticism that cost controls, procedures, and utilization review were overemphasized. They are intended to focus on quality improvement mechanisms, better patient outcomes, and better plan performance (Goff, 1995).

Historically, vertical integration has been defined as the linking of production functions of individual organizations that either precede or follow another organization's core business functions (Thompson, 1967). For example, a food distributor vertically integrates when it acquires the produce farms that grow the vegetables the food distributor buys and then ships to grocery stores. The distributor also vertically integrates when it buys the chain of grocery stores that sell the vegetables.

In health care, vertical integration can be broadly understood to include the integration of providers and health care facilities, as well as the financing and administrative functions of a managed care organization (Bushick, 1995). Other terms applied to integrated systems include "organized delivery systems," "integrated service networks," or "organized systems of care."

By and large, MCOs have traditionally controlled costs by controlling the demand for specialty, inpatient and emergency care via rigorous referral protocols and utilization reviews. They have also had the purchasing power to negotiate generous provider discounts for services they do offer and for those services they do not offer themselves (which could range all the way from primary care to transplants, trauma care, burn care, dialysis, etc.) (Bushick, 1995).

Capitated managed care environments are one response to reducing costs and are becoming a dominant force in the healthcare marketplace transforming health care services delivery (ProPAC, 1'1'35; GHAA, 1994). In 1980 about five percent of primary care physicians' payments were capitated. By 1990 that had almost doubled to nine percent (GHAA, 1994) and is expected to rise to 25 percent by the year 2000 (Weiner, 1994). An analysis of MCOs in 1994 showed that capitation is the dominant method of reimbursing primary care physicians, with approximately 63 percent of managed care enrollees in large markets, 46 percent in medium markets and 41 percent in small markets covered using capitation (InterStudy, 1995).

By folding coverage for both outpatient and inpatient care into one premium, MCOs have been able to reduce hospitalization utilization by shifting some services to less expensive ambulatory settings. While fee-for-service reimbursement rewards high volume, capitation does not; profits are earned with low visit volumes. Low volume moves the emphasis away from treating the sick to prevention and wellness. Traditional measures of profit, such as visits, patient days, hospital census and volumes of high-end services, now become indicators of cost. The new measures of success and profit include increasing enrollment and the delivery of appropriate value (Cochrane, 1994).

Integrated MCOs may increasingly adopt global capitation, a method in which both hospital and provider care are included in the monthly payment to an integrated health system (Cochrane, 1994). Global capitation requires information gathering and analysis from all aspects of care delivery. Such integrated systems coordinate care across a full spectrum of treatment settings including hospitals, outpatient-care sites and homes (Goff, 1995; Cochrane, 1995; Shortell et al., 1994; Cronin and Milgate, 1993).

"Virtual" MCOs are more recent responses to changing and highly competitive health care markets. It is expected that virtual organizations will build upon vertically integrated health care systems and contain group practices that contract with other providers to offer a full continuum of care to capitated MCOs (Crawford, 1996). All practices in a region will be connected electronically and ownership of every provider site is not required. Some of the companies that are attempting to build the first generation of virtual integrated systems include: Phycor Inc., Nashville, TN; Apogee of King of Prussia, PA; Physicians Reliance Network of Dallas; and Coastal Healthcare Group of Durham, NC (Burns, 1995).

This emerging health care system may do more than assist in the provision of medical services. It may become a new prototype for a broader approach to health called "TeleHealth"[3]. TeleHealth is the linkage of the NII and the health system. Using telecommunications, a broad array of health services to providers and consumers can be utilized. The services include medical care, but also place a new emphasis on wellness, prevention, shared decision making, and quality of care. In the long run, the most successful MCOs may be those able to optimize TeleHealth, leveraging networked information to promote wellness and prevention and provide appropriate and cost-effective longitudinal care to consumers (Crawford, 1996).

With the development of TeleHealth and integrated systems of managed care, four broad and basic issues are expected to dominate: networked information systems; consumer health education; and the need for privacy and confidentiality. These issues may impact on the success of MCOs to remain competitive; they may also impact on the health status of consumers, and the ability of other players in the health care system to assess change and ongoing needs. Furthermore, public policies related to these issues may need to be developed or changed.

II. NETWORKED INFORMATION SYSTEMS

We are entering the age of integrated information systems, distributed computer-based patient records (CPRs) and new imaging technologies which may dramatically affect how information is stored and transmitted. MCOs are uniquely poised to assess clinical data over time and to observe which clinical interventions result in the most desirable outcomes, over the shortest period of time, for the least cost. When this information is appended to other member information such as demographic data, health risk assessment data, prevention screening data, and lifestyle and disease-specific self-management data, we may begin to see the full potential for what a managed care environment can deliver.

In 1994 the health care industry spent $8.5 billion on computerized information systems, up 13 percent from the previous year. Some expect that information systems expenditures will have increased by more than 50 percent in 1995 (Miller, 1996). Developing and managing integrated information will become increasingly important as MCOs attempt to decrease costs and improve the health status of their members in order to compete in a highly competitive market (Burns, 1995; Goff, 1995; Cave, 1995; Bushick, 1995; WEDI, 1993).

Because capitated managed care environments are becoming a dominant force in the healthcare marketplace and because those environments are undergoing rapid change (ProPAC, 1995; GHAA, 1994), realizing the goal to develop integrated information systems within managed care may be akin to trying to hit a moving target. Health information systems will need to continue to adapt to the changing needs of an industry in rapid transition, grow in capacity, and handle the standards and reforms expected to eventually be effected by the Federal government and the States (Meszaros, 1994).

Therefore, the ability of MCOs to weather environmental demands and to perform key tasks may well depend upon the development and implementation of information systems that are digitized, flexible and integrated. And as a result, the islands of information and fragmented information processes that currently exist within MCOs may need to become highly integrated.

A. Islands of Information

In general, MCOs today comprise four separate information subsystems, or islands of information. Typically, these islands are not digitally interconnected or integrated, and thus have very little direct and immediate impact on one another. These include the administrative, financial, clinical and demographic subsystems.

All health care environments require enrollment forms, medical records and fund transmittals. Many additional types of information must be managed due to the "gate-keeper" focus of managed care. However, these information exchanges are not yet electronically linked in most MCOs. Moreover, each information exchange may be paper-based and the information within one exchange may not be fully compatible for coordination with information from another exchange. For example, MCO processes require enrollment data, capitated physician encounter/visit documentation, prescription information and specialist referral authorizations. As a result, it is estimated that a typical small MCO can receive as many as 2,000 paper documents in a single day; a larger MCO may receive as many as 20,000 documents in a single day (Troy, 1995). These documents, upon receipt, must then be routed, analyzed and stored. However, some MCOs have begun the complex process of automating these subsystems (Edlin, 1993).

For the most part today, patient data in clinical settings are still recorded in a paper medical record. If the patient record is needed for use outside of its institutional home, such as accompanying the patient from a hospital to a physician's office, it must be faxed or mailed in advance, or even provided to the patient to carry to the next care site. One industry expert has claimed that, "Right now, the taxi driver in Boston has access to everybody's record" because medical charts are often transported from one facility to another via taxicab (Appleby, 1996). This picture is changing however.

B.   Integrating Information with the CPR

As a result of the need to contain costs and the shift in focus on the quality, outcomes and value of care provided to members (Miller, 1996; Meszaros, 1995), the MCO industry is beginning to rethink how information collected can be optimally integrated and utilized. Increasingly, MCOs are placing networked, integrated information systems at the very center of integrated managed care (Bushick, 1995; O'Leary et al., 1995; Fitzmaurice, 1995).

The concept of the CPR has emerged as an organized means to acquire integrated and complete information on productivity and quality (NIST, 1994b). Major elements of that infrastructure may include patient-centered care facilitated by CPRs, continuity of care enhanced by sharing information across information networks, and outcomes measurement aided by the greater availability of health information (Blair, 1995). A report by the Institute of Medicine (Dick and Steen, 1991) defined the CPR as an electronic patient record that resides in a system designed to support users through availability of complete and accurate data, practitioner reminders and alerts, clinical decision support systems, shared (provider/patient) decision support systems, links to bodies of medical knowledge, and other aids.

CPR systems may significantly expand upon the paper-based medical record concept to incorporate the islands of information and the fragmented gatekeeper exchanges captured by providers and patients during the delivery of direct patient care in any setting. They may also incorporate critical paths, literature citations, and other resource data, as well as information that provides consumer health information for health care decision making and education.

The primary barriers to implementing integrated information systems include: the general lack of data standards, costs; certain State requirements; and security and privacy issues (GAO, 1994; GAO, 1993; GAO, 1991). These problems are tightly interwoven. For example, in today's fragmented information environment, the lack of standards necessitates building multiple systems to address the diversity of data received and sent. This problem is costly for MCOs and providers. Distributed CPRs may enhance the ability of MCOs to make critical information exchanges; data repositories may enhance analysis of health status, health outcomes and cost of care across populations. But such connections will require standardized formats and technologies to facilitate the exchange of information between MCOs and their designated connecting points (McKenna, 1994). For these reasons, many MCOs, government agencies and policy makers are recommending wide-scale adoption of EDI among health care constituents when benefits exceed the costs (WEDI, 1994; WEDI, 1993).

In addition, the development of large electronic files that contain medical history and health status information over the life of an individual may create uncertainties regarding the security and privacy of health information. For example, who is the ultimate owner of the CPR? Who is responsible for the privacy and security of information in a data repository?

III. CONSUMER HEALTH EDUCATION

Consumers currently have available to them enormous amounts of health information. Consumer health information is any material that enables individuals to understand their health and make health-related decisions for themselves or their families (Patrick and Koss, 1995). Consumer health education (CHE), on the other hand, is more than information-acquisition. It includes information and the processes of communicating information in ways that promote and enhance individual health, self-care, shared decision making, patient education and rehabilitation. CHE encompasses the knowledge and skills needed by consumers to effectively obtain medical care for themselves and their families to prevent disease and injury and to promote health (Kemper el al., 1995).

Improving the overall health status of member populations may become critical to MCOS as they try to achieve greater efficiencies in a highly competitive market. By assuring that consumers are well-informed and have access to a full range of education services, from personal health promotion or lifestyle enhancement programs to options for long term care, MCOs are increasingly enlisting consumers as partners by emphasizing preventive measures, such as routine screening and primary care (Zablocki, 1995; Whitmore and Gabel, 1995; Brown, 1995).

A. Improving Outcomes

Hundreds of research studies conducted over the years demonstrate that telling patients what to do yields no better than a thirty percent success rate (Haynes et al., 1987). Alternatively, involving patients in the process of making therapeutic (or diagnostic or management) choices, on the other hand, is much more likely to result in better outcomes as well as lower costs (Wagner et al., 1995; Kasper et al., 1992; Greenfield et al., 1988). Recognizing that decisions made by consumers on their own behalf or on behalf of their families have significant implications for the outcomes and costs of care, some MCOs are beginning to view their members as active self-providers of preventive care and vital partners in the treatment of acute illness and the management of chronic disease. As a result, CHE is increasingly viewed as a vital component of managed care, from information that assists MCO members to select a primary care provider to educational programs that help individuals parent children, self-manage diabetes, or even affect life style behavior to promote health (Zablocki, 1995).

B.   Reducing Costs

Evidence supports the cost-saving benefits of prevention, the primary demand management intervention for morbidity. For example, it's been estimated that current methods for preventing infectious disease could save $1.3 billion in direct medical costs and prevent 80,000 deaths annually (Bennett et al., 1987). Additional evidence indicates that self-care interventions are effective in decreasing demand for medical services, especially since perceived need is the primary basis upon which consumers make decisions to seek medical care (e.g., Fries et al., 1994; Fries et al., 1993; Mayo et al., 1990; White, 1988; Vickery et al., 1983; Levine and Britten, 1973; Miller and Goldstein, 1972). Furthermore, studies of self-care programs in corporate settings, retirement groups and managed care populations have reported program benefits outweigh program costs (Vickery el al., 1983). The findings of other studies examining the impact of selfcare on patient preference imply costs savings because fully informed patients who are allowed to express a preference will often choose options that are less risky and less expensive (Gardner and Sneiderman, 1990; Options and Choices, Inc., 1992).

Emerging integrated systems of managed care, with the aid of the NII, may help to foster the use of CHE since such systems are beginning to place an emphasis on wellness and on the role of consumers (Bushick, 1995). Emerging CHE services may include: conducting individualized, confidential risk assessments; conferring with experts on the latest medical research; accessing the most up-to-date information on treatment and medication; and utilizing customized tools to explore personal health care options.

At present, however, the extent of consumer education provided to members of MCOs is uneven. The changes occurring in information technology, particularly the rapid development of the NII and the new media, hold great promise. Furthermore, the old forms of media, including television, radio, phone, print and photographs, are being changed into new forms that are digitized, computerized and connected over networks and the NII. These changes present an historic shift from passive, closed and producer-driven media to interactive (or smart), seamlessly connected and user-driven media (Harris, 1995). For example, health information, once confined to the written or spoken word, is becoming available through a number of different kinds of media, from video to computer CD. The impact of the new media on CHE interventions could be substantial (Harris, 1995; Harris and Crawford, 1996).

A recent report by the Institute of Medicine (1993) supports the need for broad public health and health education initiatives that help people understand how to take care of their health. Even today, most health-related decisions made by patients and the well population are made outside of a medical setting. Therefore, their ability to choose appropriate self-care depends on the degree to which they are well-informed, which may depend to some extent on their ability to access information and educational processes on the NII.

C. Access Is Key

While the development of the NII may provide greater access to health information, education and services, new barriers to access may also result. Historically, health access problems have had to do with the ability to gain entry to a health service. Does the patient have access to public transportation to get to the clinic in a downtown neighborhood? Is there a medical clinic in a rural farming community? How will a patient in a remote are of the country receive care from specialists who reside and practice in urban areas?

Another completely different set of access questions arise with the emergence of the NII. Many MCOs may offer CHE services through closed systems on the NII (services made available only to enrollees). How will these CHE services differ from others generally available on the NII? Will access to CHE services on the NII be available to every MCO member in his/her home? If not, can an individual get access at retail outlets, supermarkets, libraries, schools? How do these points of access differ from having access at home? Do costs impact on access? Does lack of access to CHE services persist in communities that have historically lacked access to the health care system in general and thus create a double-barrier to health care? How is a link made to the individual's CPR?

D. Costs

Costs of computers, processing technologies, the communications infrastructure and the educational resources themselves have a significant effect on access to technologies by MCOs and consumers. If these technologies are to be widely used, they must be cost-effective for MCOs. Continuing development of the NII to facilitate CHE requires a considerable investment of funding and technical expertise. However, in light of the current budget-cutting climate within government, it is increasingly clear that MCOs may have to join other private sector entities to create the needed information infrastructure. While each MCO has considerable need to use an advanced information infrastructure, individual MCOs cannot afford to build one (WEDI, 1993 and 1992), nor should they. Avoiding needless duplication of effort and building integrated systems are also important goals. While the development of the NII is expected to cost money, those costs can be balanced with the savings accrued as a result of reductions in administrative costs, more appropriate use of medical services, and improved health of the population.

E. Absence of a Trusted Source

Successful CHE requires that patients receive complete and unbiased information about the options available to them and the potential outcomes that might result (Kemper et al., 1995; Vickery and Fries, 1994; Kemper et al., 1985). Accuracy, reliability and timeliness are clearly prime determinants of the value of all health communication products and services. Currently, the Federal government is responsible for ensuring the integrity of its own information, which is in the public domain. In the future, the Federal government may still be responsible for quality assurance of its own content. But it is likely there may also be multiple sources of health information available about specific problems. How will the consumer know if only some or all of that information is credible? Will the consumer have at least one trusted source from which to obtain information that has been tested and substantiated?

The dissemination of medical information has long been an area in which protection of patients' well being was seen as a legitimate government interest. For most of this century, the Federal Trade Commission (FTC) has used its powers under the Federal Trade Commission Act to regulate advertisements for health care products. Also, during most of this century, under the 1938 Federal Food, Drug and Cosmetic Act,[4] and under earlier laws, the Food and Drug Administration (FDA) has regulated the labels and labeling for drugs and medical devices. Labeling has been defined broadly to include brochures, booklets, literature, mailing pieces, and virtually any materials descriptive of a product and disseminated by or on behalf of the manufacturer, packer or distributor of that product[5].

The merging of NII technology and integrated systems of managed care may improve upon the advantages and/or may accentuate the perverse incentives within each system regarding the provision of information. For example, some MCOs may have incentives to reduce overall clinical utilization. These same incentives may bias the CHE, informational, triage and telemedicine systems towards reducing the use of health services even when indicated or preferred by the patient. Moreover, within a competitive environment there may also be incentives for MCOs towards limiting the information that is made available to consumers (Pear, 1995; Lasalandra, 1995; Bass, 1995; Woolhandler and Himmelstein, 1995; Gold et al., 1995; Hillman et al., 1991).

IV. PRIVACY AND CONFIDENTIALITY

While it is generally assumed that medical records are confidential, that belief may be outdated (AHA, 1993; Lorenzi and Riley, 1995). The prospect of unauthorized disclosure of confidential data increases with the growth of computerized health records. Which world will dominate the future? Will we find ourselves in the midst of an Orwellian 1984? Or is there reason to be enthusiastic about the information possibilities? More specifically, will the storage and transmission of information electronically help managed care organizations (MCOs) provide care and hinder unauthorized efforts to gain access to our personal health information?

The transformations currently underway in the health care system and in the National Information Infrastructure (NII) will present new challenges and opportunities in patient information protection. The need to protect the privacy and confidentiality of private health information will become more pressing, even as the technological capability to protect such information will become more available. Furthermore, changing market incentives are encouraging integrated structures among MCOs that will require better and more sophisticated use of information (Blair, 1995; Bushick, 1995; CPRI, 1995a).

Reports of the Information Infrastructure Task Force (IITF, 1995a; IITF, 1995b) highlight the importance of safeguarding telecommunications-related personal information (TRPI). They focus on the privacy of personal information which can be linked to an individual or distinct group of individuals. Information privacy refers to an individual's claim to control that personal information and the terms under which it can be acquired, disclosed and used. The risks for consumers will likely increase as telecommunications services become more sophisticated and aggressive in use of TRPI. In all likelihood, "privacy concerns will likely grow as the NII becomes a pervasive, functioning reality" (IITF, 1995b, p. 3).

A. Confidentiality and Security

Confidentiality is the status accorded data or information indicating that it is sensitive for some reason (OTA, 1993). The information needs to be protected against theft or improper use and must be disseminated only to individuals or organizations authorized to have it. Confidentiality requires an understanding of privacy, which is the right of an individual to be left alone, to withdraw from the influence of the environment, to be secluded, not annoyed, and not intruded upon by extension of the right to be protected against physical or psychological invasion or against the misuse or abuse of something legally owned by an individual or normally considered by society to be personal property (CPRI, 1995b; OTA, 1993).

Confidentiality also requires that security measures be in place. Security refers to the protection of data or information from accidental or intentional disclosure to unauthorized persons and from unauthorized alteration. Security embodies both protections for confidentiality and data integrity. Techniques for security include: software and hardware features; physical measures such as locks, badges, etc.; and informed, security-conscious staff and professionals who adhere to the ethical tenets of confidentiality (CPRI, 1995b; OTA, 1993).

Within the context of the NII, confidentiality issues are related to the security built into the infrastructure to ensure at least the same level of confidentiality now afforded health care information retained primarily on paper. Although the degree of confidentiality currently afforded paper-based medical records is empirically unknown, perceptions vary widely. Many believe current health care information is quite secure and that their health care information is confidential. Others subscribe to the opposite extreme, believing that insurance companies, drug companies, employers and many others have very easy access to their health care information and that confidentiality of private health care information no longer exists today. Survey results about confidentiality of private information (both health care information and other information such as financial) indicate there is a growing concern regarding confidentiality of all private information (Harris-Equifax, 1993).

CPRs, especially those which are a part of the NII, may provide the opportunity for a significant increase in breach of confidentiality through harmful use by authorized users, as well as resultant harm through access by unauthorized users. Networked environments can increase the ability to quickly access significantly more data. There have been numerous security breaches with electronic mail systems on the Internet (Chin, 1996). The security of information on the Internet is variable and must be considered inadequate for passing private information. Alternatively, security on private networks (e.g., those built and maintained by an integrated delivery system or community health information network) can be maintained at a very high level. While use of the Internet in health care is increasing (e.g., anonymous chat groups on coping with chronic disease), MCOs that might refer patients to use the Internet may want to consider educating patients concerning security measures.

Computerization can allow significantly better access controls through measures to positively identify users, determine their authorization for access to specific data, and track their actual access. Messages can be sent to primary providers of access to data when desired. Controls, backup procedures and software to ensure data integrity are much better than in a paper record system. Reminders and alerts can be imposed when systems have been left unattended or when there are attempts to use the system in a manner inconsistent with the current user's authorization. Encryption techniques can further protect the data. Numerous other technical measures are available and being devised (Amatayakul, 1996; Meux, 1994).

Because of the level of legitimate concern and opportunity for more widespread breach of confidentiality, adequate NII protections need to be present for the stakeholders in health care to feel comfortable. Various organizations, including the Computer-based Patient Record Institute, are promoting uniform technological standards for systems operability in the health care environment (Blair, 1996; CPRI, 1996; CPRI, 1995b). Such standards promise to accelerate the development of distributed medical information systems generally, and may eventually enable patients' records to be accessed in real-time by authorized physicians both regionally and nationally.

SUMMARY

The recommendations provided below are derived from broad themes developed in the White Paper; specific recommendations are listed in the original report. The purpose of the recommendations is to foster the development of the NII within managed care environments so that all participants in the managed health care system can take advantage of its potential benefits.

1. Develop collaborative partnerships for the development and implementation of health applications using the NII.

2. Encourage rapid development and adoption of data content and quality standards so that appropriate information exchanges can be made among all participants in the managed health care system.

3. Fund the development and evaluation of computer-based patient records that contribute relevant information to designated participants in the managed health care system.

4. Reorient health data collection by public agencies to take account of the rich array of data collected by MCOs.

5. Promote confidentiality and security mechanisms in the form of Federal law, industry accepted standards and technological capability to protect private health information as it becomes increasingly important for managed health care.

ENDNOTES

1. A unique collaborative effort that eventually included more than 60 individuals from the private and public sectors was initiated. Interestingly the use of telecommunications made the process of engaging individuals from around the country possible. For example, the vast majority of participants "attended" bimonthly meetings in Washington, DC via phone conferences. Announcements and written materials were used using the fax, the Internet, the telephone and electronic mail.

2. Crawford, C. M. and Information and Applications Work Group on Managed Care, (1996). Managed Care and the NII: A Public/Private Perspective. Health Information Applications Work Group (HIAWG), Information Infrastructure Task Force (IITF), Washington, DC, Final Report, May.

3. This term typically defines telemedicine activities related to health care (e.g., Witherspoon et al., 1993). As defined by Crawford, TeleHealth encompasses a much broader scope of telecommunications activity, with telemedicine being one of many components.

4. 21 USC 321 et seq.

5. 21CRF202.1(1)(2).

REFERENCES

AHA. (1993). *Toward a National Health Information Infrastructure: Report of the Work Group on Computerization of Patient Records to the Secretary of the U.S. Department of Health and Human Services.* AHA Work group on Computerization of Patient Records. American Hospital Association, April.

Amataycakul, M. (1996). Privacy protections afforded by computer-based patient record systems. *Topics in Health Information Management.* Gaithersburg, MD: Aspen Publishers, Inc., 16(4), May.

Appleby, C. (1995). The measure of medical services. *Hospitals & Health Networks,* June 20: 26-34.

Appleby, C. (1996). The mouse that roared. *Hospitals & Health Networks,* February 20: 31-36.

Bashshur R., Puskin D., and Silva J. (1995). Conference Report: Second Invitational Consensus Conference on Telemedicine and the National Information Infrastructure. *Telemedicine Journal,* 1(4): 321-376.

Basllshur R., Scott, J., Silva, J., Neuberger, N. (Eds.). (1994). *Report of the Working Conference on Telemedicine Policy for the NII.* Health Information and Applications Working Group, Information Infrastructure Task Force Committee on Applications and Technology and The Senate/House Ad Hoc Steering Committee on Telemedicine and Health Care Informatics, August 7-9.

Bass, A. (1995). Focusing on managed care: Doctors' pay often tied to controlling costs, study finds. *The Boston Globe,* City edition. December 21, 1995: 32.

Bennett, V., Kolmberg S., Rogers M., Solomon S. (1987). Infectious and parasitic diseases. In R.W. Amler and H.B. Dull (Eds.). *Closing the Gap: The Burden of Unnecessary Illness.* New York: Oxford University Press: 102-163.

Blair, J. S. (1995). *Overview of Standards Related to the Emerging Health Care Information Infrastructure.* Schaumburg, IL: The Computer-based Patient Record Institute, Inc.

Boland, P. (1991). Market overview and delivery system dynamics. In P. Boland (Ed.), *Making Managed Healthcare Work: A Practical Guide to Strategies and Solutions*. New York: McGraw-Hill, Inc.

Brown, E. (1995). How cost effective are wellness programs? *Managed Healthcare, 5(1)*: 40-42.

Burner, S. Waldo, D. (1995). National Health Expenditure Projections, 1994-2005. *Health Care Financing* Review, *16(4)*: 221-242.

Burns, J. (1995). Group practice managers using technology to build. *Health Data Management*, October: 57-60.

Bushick, J. B. (1995). Creating an integrated health care system as a basis for managed care excellence: A health plan's perspective. *Managed Care Quarterly, 3(1)*: 1-10.

Cave D. G. (1995). Vertical integration models to prepare health systems for capitation. *Health Care Management Review, 20(1)*: 26-39.

Chin T. L. (1996). Moving records on the Internet. *Health Data Management*, April: 24-26.

Cochrane, J. D. (1995). California & Columbia/HCA mega-deals. *Integrated Healthcare Report, 1995*. Lake Arrowhead, CA, September: 10.

Cochrane, J.D. (1994). The dynamics of market reform. *Integrated Healthcare Report, 1995*. Lake Arrowhead, CA, April: 1-13.

Coile, R.C. (1995a). Managed care outlook, 1995-2000: Top 10 trends for the HMO insurance industry. *Health Trends, 7(5)*: 2.

Coile, R. C. (1995b). Future of HMOs and providers: Compete or consolidate'? *Health Trends, 7(5)*: 2.

CPRI, (1995a). *Description of the Computer-based Patient Record and Computer-based Patient Record System*. Work Group on CPR Description, High Level Description Project Team. Draft Version 1.0. Schaumburg, IL: Computer-based Patient Record Institute, May.

CPRI. (1995b). *Guidelines for Establishing Information, Security Policies at Organizations Using Computer-based Patient Records*. Schaumburg, IL: Computer-based Patient Record Institute, February.

Crawford, C. M. (1996). *TeleHealth. Expected Changes in Managed Care*. Concept Paper, February 1996.

Cronin, C. and Milgate, K. (1993). A *Vision of the Future Health Care System: Organized Systems of Care*. Washington, DC: Washington Business Group on Health, March.

DHHS. (1991). *Healthy People 2000*. U. S. Public Health Service. Department of Health and Human Services, Washington, DC: U.S. Government Printing Office.

Dick, R. and Steen, E. (Eds.) (1991). *The Computer-based Patient Record: An Essential Technology for Health Care*. Washington, DC: National Academy Press.

Edwin, M. (1993). Health care industry taking its time to establish electronic connection. *Managed Healthcare, 3(2)*: 1, 25-26.

Fitzmaurice, I. M. (1995). Computer-based patient records. J. D. Bronzino (Ed.). *The Biomedical Engineering Handbook*. Boca Raton, FLA: CRC Press, Inc.: 2623-2634.

Fitzmaurice JM, 1994. *Health Care and the NII, Putting the Information Infrastructure to Work. Report of the Information Infrastructure Task Force Committee on Applications and Technology, Gaithersburg, MD*: National Institute of Standards and Technology, U.S. Department of Commerce, Special Publication 857: 41-56.

Fries, J., Harrington, H., Edwards, R., Kent, L., Richardson, N. (1994). Randomized controlled trial of costs reductions from a health education program: The California Public Employees' Retirement System (PERS) study. *American Journal of Health Promotion, 8(3)*: 2 16-223.

Fries, J., Koop, C., Beadle, C., Cooper, P., Endland, M., Greaves, R., Sokolov, J., Wright, D. (1993). Reducing health care costs by reducing the need and demand for medical services. *The New England Journal of Medicine, 329*: 321-325.

GAO. (1994). *Health Care: Benefits and Barriers to Automated Medical Records. U. S.* General Accounting Office, Washington, D. C., GAO/T-AIMD-94-117.

GAO. (1993). *Automated Medical Records: Leadership Needed to Expedite Standards Development. U.S.* General Accounting Office, Washington, DC, GAO/IMTEC-93-17.

GAO. (1991). *Medical ADP Systems: Automated Medical Records Hold Promise to Improve Patient Care*. U.S. General Accounting Office, Washington, DC, GAO/B-240642, January.

Gardner, H., Sneideman, C. (1990). Ensuring value by supporting customer decision making. *Journal of Occupational Medicine*, 32: 1223-1228.

GHAA. (1994). *1994 National Directory of HA~IOs*. Wasllingtoll, DC: Group Health Association of America, June.

Goff, V. (1995). *Information Technology and Health Care Delivery*. Washillgton, DC: Washington Business Group on Health.

Gold, M., Hurley, R., Lake, T., Ensor, T., Berenson, R. (1995). A national survey of the arrangements managed care plans make with physicians. *The New England Journal of Medicine*, 333: 1678-1683.

Greenfield, S., Kaplan, S., Ware, J., Yano, E., Frank, H. (1988). Patients' participation in medical care: Effects on blood sugar control and quality of life in diabetes. *Journal of General Internal Medicine*, 3: 448-457.

Harris, L., and Crawford, C. (1996). The new media and smart health care consumers. *Healthcare Forum Journal*, January/February: 26-31.

Harris, L. (1995). Differences that make a difference. In L. Harris (Ed.). *Health and the New Media: Technologies Transforming Personal and Public Health*. Hillsdale, NJ: Lawrence Erlbaum Associates, Inc.: 3-18; url:http://Health.Dartmouth.edu/NewMedia.

Harris-Equifax. (1993). *Heath Information Privacy Survey 1993*. Louis Harris and Associates for Equifax. Atlanta: Equifax Inc.

Haynes, R., Wang, E., and Da Mota, G. (1987). A critical review of interventions to improve compliance with prescribed medications. *Patient Education and Counseling*, 10: 5-166.

Hegner, R. E. (1995). *Section 1115: Demonstrations or Strategy for Incremental Reform?* National Health Policy Forum Issue Briefs, 662: 1-10.

HIAWG. (1994). *Report of the Working Conference on Telemedicine Policy for the NII.* Health Information and Applications Working Group (HIAWG) of the Information Infrastructure Task Force Committee on Applications and Technology. Arlie House, Virginia, August.

Hillman A., Pauly, M., Kennan, K., and Martinek, C. (1991). HMO managers' views on financial incentives and quality. *Health Affairs, 19*(4): 207-219.

IITF. (1995a). *Privacy and the NII: Principles for Providing and Using Personal Information.* Report of the Information Infrastructure Task Force (IITF). National Telecommunications and Information Agency, U.S. Department of Commerce, Washington, DC, June.

IITF. (1995b). *Privacy and the NII: Safeguarding Telecommunications-Related Personal Information.* Report of the Information Infrastructure Task Force (IITF). National Telecommunications and Information Agency, U.S. Department of Commerce, Washington, DC, October.

IITF. (1994). *Global Information Infrastructure: Agenda for Action.* Report of the Information Infrastructure Task Force (IITF), U.S. Department of Commerce. Washington, DC: U.S. Government Printing Office, February.

IITF. (1993). *The National Information Infrastructure: Agenda for Action.* Information Infrastructure Task Force (IITF), White Paper, September 15.

Institute of Medicine. (1993). *Assessing Health Care Reform*. Washington, DC: National Academy Press.

InterStudy. (1994). *Competitive Edge,* 4,1. InterStudy: Minneapolis, MN.

Kasper, J., Mulley, A., Wennberg, J. (1992). Developing shared decision-making programs to improve the quality of health care. *Quarterly Review Board, 18*(6): 183-190.

Kemper, D. W. et al., (1995). *HealthWise Handbook,* (12th ed.) Boise, Idaho: Healthwise, Inc.

Kemper, D. W. et al.. (1985). *Pathways: A Success Guide for a Healthy Life.* Boise, Idaho: HealthWise, Inc.

Lasalandra, M. (1995). Doc: I was fired for HMO criticism. *The Boston Herald*, (2nd Ed.). December 21: 12.

Levine, P., and Britten, A. (1973). Supervised patient-management of hemophilia: A study of 45 patients with hemophilia A and B. *Annals of Internal Medicine*, 87: 195-201.

Levit, K., Sensenig, A., Cowan, C., Lazenby, H., McDonnell, P., Won, D., Sivarajan, L., Stiller, J., Donham, C., Stewart, M. (1994). National Health Expenditures, 1993. *Health Care Financing Review*, Fall: 247-294.

Lorenzi, N., and Riley, R. (1995). *Organizational Aspects of Health Informatics. Managing Technological Change.* NY: Springer-Verlag.

Mayo, P., Richman, J., and Harris, H. (1990). Results of a program to reduce admissions for adult asthma. *Annals of Internal Medicine, 112*: 861-871.

McKenna, J. F. (1994). Just scratching the surface: Quality, though deemed important lags quality price as priority. *Managed Healthcare, 4(4)*: 46-50.

Meszaros, E.C. (1994). A brave new world: Information systems help MCOs refine treatments, lower costs and stay on top of the market. *Managed Healthcare, 4(5)*: 26-27.

Meszaros, E.C. (1995). Information systems: Helping managed care become truly "managed." *Managed Healthcare, 5(1)*: 21-23.

Meux, E. (1994). Encrypting personal identifiers. *Health Services Research, 29(2)*, June.

Miller, J., (1996). Is "value" the new frontier? *Integrated Healthcare Report*, February: 1-11.

Miller, L. and Goldstein, J. (1972). More efficient care of diabetic patients in a county hospital setting. *The New England Journal of Medicine*, 286: 1388-1391.

NIIAC. (1995). *Common Ground: Fundamental Principles for the National Information Infrastructure.* First Report of the National Information Infrastructure Advisory Council (NIAAC), Washington. DC, March.

NIST. (1994a). *Putting the Information Infrastructure to Work: Report of the Information Infrastructure Task Force Committee on Applications and Technology.* National Institute of Standards and Technology, U.S. Department of Commerce. Washington, DC: U.S. Government Printing Office, May.

NIST. (1994b). *The Information Infrastructure: Reaching Society's Goals.* Report of the Information Infrastructure Task Force, Committee on Applications and Technology. National Institute of Standards and Technology (NIST), U.S. Department of Commerce, Washington, DC: U.S. Government Printing Office, September.

O'Leary, D., Nadzam, D., Loeb, J., and Jesse, W. (1995). Framework for Performance Measurement of Health Care Networks and Health Plans. *Managed Care Quarterly, 3(3)*: 48-53.

Options and Choices, Inc. (1992). *OPTIS Analysis Service Reports.* Cheyenlle, WY.

OTA. (1993). *Protecting Privacy in Computerized Medical Information.* Office of Technology Assessment, OTATCT-576. Washington, DC: U.S. Government Printing Office, September.

Patrick, K. and Koss, S. (1995). *Consumer Health Information White Paper.* Consumer Health Information Subgroup, Health Information and Applications Working Group, Information Infrastructure Task Force Committee on Applications and Technology, Washington, DC, Working Draft, May 15.

Pear, R. (1995). Doctors say HMOs limit what they can tell patients. *The New York Times*, Late Edition. December 21, 1995: Al.

ProPAC. (1995). *Medicare and the American Health Care .System.* Washington, DC: Prospective Payment Assessment Commission.

Shortell, S., Gillies, R., Anderson, A. (1994). The new works of managed care: Creating organized delivery *systems. Health Affairs, 13(5)*: 46-64.

Thompson, J. D. (1967). *Organizations in Action.* New York. NY: McGraw Hill.

Troy, T. N. (1995). The birth of a new age. *Managed Healthcare. 5(6): 25-28.*

Vickery, D., and Fries, J. (1994). *Take Care of Yourself: The Complete Guide to Medical Self-Care* (5th ed.). Reading, MA: Addison-Wesley Publishing Company.

Vockery, D., Kalem, H., Lowry, D., Constantine, M. Wright, E., and Loren, W. (1993). Effect of a self-care education program on medical visits. *Journal of the American Medical Association. 250*: 2952-2956.

Wagner, E., Barry, M., Barlow, W., and Fowler, F. (1995). The effect of a shared decision making program on rates of surgery for benign prostatic hyperplasia. *Medical Care, 33*(8): 765-77().

WEDI. (1994). *Workgroup for Electronic Data Interchange Report.* Workgroup for Electronic Data Interchange.

WEDI (1993). *Workgroup for Electronic Data Interchange Report.* Workgroup for Electronic Data Interchange.

Weiner, J. (1994). Forecasting the effects of health reform on US physician workforce requirements: Evidence from HMO staffing patterns. *Journal of the American Medical Association, 272*(3): 222-230.

White, P. (1988). Use of patient-controlled analgesia for management of acute pain. *Journal of the American Medical Association, 259*: 243-247.

Whitmore, H. and Gabel, J. (1995). Linking research to patient care. *HMO, 36*(5): 38-42.

Woolhander, S., and Himmelstein, D. (1995). Extreme risk -- The new corporate proposition for physicians (Editorials). *The New England Journal of Medicine, 333*(25): 1706-1709.

Zablocki, E. (1995). Keeping at-risk members healthy. *HMO. 36*(5): 73-76.

50.
HUMAN RESOURCES MANAGEMENT

Bruce J. Fried, *The University of North Carolina at Chapel Hill, Chapel Hill, NC*

The delivery of health services is fundamentally dependent upon people. Unlike any other industry, healthcare organizations require an extensive range of people, from individuals with little formal training and education to highly skilled professionals. These individuals are also organized into complex bureaucracies with many formal and informal linkages among individuals, groups and departments. The effectiveness of a healthcare organization depends in large part on the ability of the organization to motivate and obtain the commitment of its employees. It has been well demonstrated that sound human resources (HR) management practices contribute positively to productivity, financial viability, retention, and other factors vital to organizational performance (Huselid, 1994; Toketsky and Kornides, 1994).

Human resources management is not exclusively within the domain of the formal HR department. Anyone who manages at least one employee is in fact a manager of human resources, just as individuals manage finances, information, and other resources. A key issue is understanding the relationship between the formal HR department and managers elsewhere in the organization. What responsibilities are within the domain of the HR department and what should be devolved in departments? Clarifying the division of responsibilities is essential to ensure consistent human resource management practices. As will be discussed later, many HR departments have in fact divested themselves of certain HR functions, choosing instead to outsource them to external organizations.

In this chapter, discussion focuses on the formal HR department in healthcare organizations, with emphasis as well on the multiple roles of the HR department within the larger organization.

I. HUMAN RESOURCES MANAGEMENT HISTORY

The term "human resources management" is relatively new to the healthcare field and to organizations in general. Personnel departments traditionally provided such functions as recruitment, selection, training, and ensuring that employees were compensated for their work. Little attention was given to how these functions related to each other, and even less attention was given to how these functions fit in with the broader goals of the organization. At times, personnel departments were in fact viewed in an adversarial manner by senior managers and line managers. Increasingly, however, HR departments are becoming partners in the achievement of the organization's strategic goals. HR departments are also expected to understand and interpret a myriad of federal, state, and local regulations for the organization, and to ensure compliance throughout the organization. To function effectively, HR departments must also understand broad societal trends, such as the needs of dual wage earner families and equal employment issues, and how these trends affect HR policies and procedures. Finally, HR departments have been transformed from a technical support role with little need to understand the industry, to one which requires that human resources management practitioners understand the businesses in which the organization functions and the environmental trends that affect the organization. Today's hospital human resources department, for example, must understand the implications of managed care for the organization as a whole, as well as for HR management in particular.

The evolution of the human resources department has generally paralleled society's attitudes towards employees. During the nineteenth century, the concentration of workers in factories focused society's attention on the often deplorable working conditions found in these settings. In the 1880s, several states passed laws regulating hours of work for women and children, established minimum wages, and regulated working conditions affecting health and safety. Frederick Taylor's work at the Midvale Steel plant in Philadelphia initiated the era of scientific management, which among other things, required accurate employee performance standards based on objective time studies and other sources. These standards formed the basis for compensation and rewarding productive employees.

Around the turn of the century, many companies began participating in the industrial welfare movement. This consisted largely of voluntary employer efforts to improve working conditions, and more generally, to improve the general welfare of workers by a focus outside the work setting. Social secretaries were employed by organizations to help employees with finances, housing, health, recreation, education, and other concerns (Pround, 1916).

In the 1890s and early 1900s, contributions of early industrial psychologists began to influence the workplace. Efforts focused largely on the analysis of jobs in terms of their physical, mental, and emotional requirements, and the development of testing procedures for selecting workers. Industrial psychologists were also involved in efforts to assess the validity of selection tests, that is, the extent to which selection tests predict success on the job.

The era of industrial psychology led into the human relations movement, which emphasized the impact on productivity of group behavior and workers' attitudes. The famous experiments at the Western Electric Company's Hawthorne Plant in the 1920s demonstrated the importance of social interaction in the workplace. This led in turn to a great deal of research, much of it continuing to this day, on organizations as social systems.

The widespread emergence of labor unions had a profound effect on human resources management. The most important legislative event was the 1935 passage of the National Labor Relations Act (NLRA), which established the legal basis for labor management relations. The NLRA established employee rights to organize, join unions, and engage in collective bargaining. It also identified and recognized employer unfair labor practices, making it unlawful for an employer to interfere with an employee's right to join a union and engage in concerted union activities. More than any previous legislation, this Act promoted the widespread growth of labor unions in the U.S.

While the NLRA was largely pro-labor, the 1947 Labor-Management Relations Act (also known as the Taft-Hartley Act) established certain protections for management, most notably the identification of unfair labor practices on the labor side of the equation. Until 1974, healthcare organizations were largely excluded from labor-management relations. The 1974 healthcare amendments to the Labor-Management Relations Act extended coverage to nonprofit hospitals and enacted special provisions for the healthcare industry as to bargaining notice requirements and the right to picket or strike (Feldacker, 1990).

The growth of human resources management as a profession was stimulated greatly by passage of the Pendleton Act of 1883 which established the Civil Service Commission. This Act established the use of competitive examinations for admission into the public services, provided job security for public employees, and encouraged an unbiased approach to employee selection (French, 1994; Van Riper, 1958).

Throughout the early 1900s, personnel specialists, such as employment agents, pension administrators, and safety specialists, began to emerge. Today, the profession of human resources management has become highly professionalized. There are now several professional associations serving HR executives including the Society for Human Resources Management, the International Personnel Management Association, and the American Society for Training and Development. The American Society for Healthcare Human Resources Administration focuses specifically on human resources issues in the healthcare field.

II. ROLES AND FUNCTIONS OF THE HUMAN RESOURCES DEPARTMENT

Human resources management refers to the strategic and operational management of activities related to the performance of the human resources in an organization. The human resources management function is a shared set of activities carried out by the formal human resources department as well as by managers and supervisors throughout the organization (Shimko, 1990). Four trends that HR management must deal with have been identified:
- Linking HR strategy to the business strategy
- Automating HR Processes
- Outsourcing HR activities
- Measuring the return on investment of HR programs (McNerney, Sept., 1996).

The HR department assumes a number of roles in the organization. At the most basic level, the HR department is concerned with attracting applicants, retaining desirable employees, and motivating employees. In the current environment, retraining is also gaining increasing attention (Schuler and Huber, 1993). From these areas flow the standard roles of HR departments (Sherman, Bohlander and Snell, 1996). While each organization may organize these functions somewhat differently, these functions are generally present in all moderate to large size healthcare organizations.

- Human Resource Planning
- Job Design
- Job Analysis
- Compensation
- Employee Benefits
- Recruitment
- Training and Development
- Performance Appraisal
- Labor/Management Relations
- Legal/Regulatory Compliance

Senior management and the HR department may interact in a variety of ways. Each can act in isolation with little communication between the two. Alternatively, management can inform the HR department of its needs, and the department can respond accordingly. The HR department may provide advice regarding the implications of alternative business strategies. Finally, the HR department may be fully integrated into business planning decisions, along with such functions as finance, marketing, and information systems (Fottler et al., 1990; Buller, 1988). Fottler suggests that organizations may achieve a competitive advantage if its HR functions are fully integrated into the strategic plan. Thus, HR departments should fulfill not only traditional roles, but also strategic roles, ensuring that HR functions are aligned with the strategic plan of the organization.

Unfortunately, Fottler's study of ten healthcare organizations in the southeast and southwest United States revealed that none were integrating human resources into the strategic planning function. At best, two were using a "two-way approach," encouraging human resources to provide insight into various business strategies. Most, however, were only using a "one-way approach"; management communicated selected strategies to the HR department and expected the department to do what it could to help implement those strategies (Fottler et al., 1990).

III. STRATEGIC ROLE

What is the strategic role for HR departments? Fottler defines strategic human resource management as ensuring that qualified personnel are available to staff the portfolio of business units that will be operated by the organization. To manage human resources strategically, healthcare executives must understand the relationships that exist among the important organizational components and the human resources functions so that appropriate methods can be selected to accomplish the objectives in service delivery desired by the organization (Fottler, Hernandez and Joiner, 1988).

More than ever, today's healthcare organization is changing. Hospitals are no longer just providing acute care, but are now in the business of home care and managing physician offices. Today's healthcare organizations are diverse and represent a broad spectrum of health related services. If the HR function is integrated with the overall strategic direction of the organization, HR must also adapt its role to fit with the changing healthcare organization.

No longer can HR only be responsible for "personnel;" the department must now perform a strategic role in the organization (Fottler et al., 1990). While the operational role (e.g., ensuring that vacant positions are filled, administering employee benefits programs) certainly is a mainstay of human resources management, HR departments are increasingly concerned with strategic planning, identifying emergent legal issues and workforce trends, organizational downsizing and restructuring, advising on mergers and acquisitions, quality improvement, and developing compensation programs that are aligned with the strategic goals of the organization (Freedman, 1990). HR must eliminate non-value added work and achieve more efficient utilization of resources. They must add value to the business through lower costs, better service, and beneficial cultural changes (Young and Brockbank, 1995). Thus, HR departments must focus on bottom line concerns—survival, growth, profitability, competitiveness, and flexibility in adapting to changing conditions.

What are possible mechanisms through which the HR department can affect strategic or bottom line concerns of the organization? First, HR departments may focus their efforts on improving productivity and quality. This has broad implications for all HR functions. It means, for example, developing compensation schemes that motivate performance, ensuring that employees are adequately trained, and facilitating quality improvement initiatives. Another area of focus may involve improving the quality of work life for employees. HR departments assume a key role in giving employees a voice in the organization (which contributes to quality improvement efforts) and facilitating communication throughout the organization. In certain respects, HR departments are in fact employee advocates; however, they may be also called upon to represent the organization, sometimes in an adversarial role with employees.

As healthcare organizations move towards the use of teams and continuous quality improvement approaches, HR departments may be increasingly concerned with the development of team—rather than individual—performance and rewards (Carroll, 1991). Total quality management initiatives have significant implications for HR. "Traditional HR policies conceived in command and control cultures have given way to new HR policies supportive of cultures characterized by employee commitment, cooperation, and communication. . . . The evolution from traditional HRM practices to 'new' HRM policies also illustrates the evolving role of HRM; from a support function to a leadership function in the enterprise. . . . Policies with respect to communication, job design, conditions of employment, training, evaluation systems, and reward systems must be congruent with TQM objectives" (Blackburn and Rosen, 1993).

The domain of the human resources function is also expanding into new areas of responsibility. These changes are occurring across all types of healthcare delivery organizations. Among these changes is a transformation in the relationship between professionals and the organization. Historically, physicians have been detached organizationally from healthcare entities such as hospitals. Through the "medical staff" structure, physicians have maintained separate reporting relationships, largely dependent on compliance with rules established by their peers, rather than compliance with overall organizational goals. Now, as physicians continue to be integrated into healthcare organizations, the human resources function has extended into areas previously designated for physicians and hospital boards, such as physician recruitment, appraisal, and compensation. HR departments will also have to contend with other "new" employees, such as multi-skilled healthcare professionals and physician extenders.

As integrated delivery systems continue to erode the formal boundaries between organizations (such that, for example, productivity and efficiency will be system-wide or "health plan-wide" and not just organizational concerns), human resources departments will need to assume system-wide as well as intraorganizational roles. These human resources challenges are not unlike those facing newly merged organizations, where there is typically a need to align disparate compensation policies, develop equitable outplacement services, and re-deploy staff given a new mission and organizational structure. Further, as organizations continue to coalesce into healthcare systems and alliances, human resources departments will assume responsibility for bridging differences in organizational cultures and resolving historical conflicts among organizations and between organizations and professional groups. This will perhaps be most pronounced as public health departments, managed care organizations, hospitals, and other organizations forge alliances. While these alliances may be strategically mutually beneficial, differences in culture will need to be understood and managed.

At the same time that HR departments are expanding their roles, they also must demonstrate their value to the organization. In an era of increasing cost containment, healthcare organizations are being forced to eliminate functions that do not add value to the organization. Traditionally, HR departments have been viewed as cost centers; now they must define their function as one that leads to value-added service (e.g., appropriately training appraisers results in improved employee performance which in turn, results in achievement of the organization's strategic goals). "As important, in the heat of organizational efforts to implement a total quality culture, the HR professional must look internally at the HR function itself and determine to what extent that unit is employing the same TQM techniques and ideas being pursued by the remainder of the organization. For instance, can the HR function determine how satisfied internal and external customers are with its products and services? To what extent have cross-functional or autonomous work teams been formed within HR as a way of reducing cycle time and increasing the quality of service provided? Has the function made any efforts to benchmark its important activities against accepted "best practices"? To what extent is the HR function designed for continuous learning and continuous improvement? Efforts at helping others develop their quality cultures should not preclude similar efforts directed at the HR function" (Blackburn and Rosen, 1993). When HR departments implement TQM principles, they become partners in organization-wide TQM efforts (Blackburn and Rosen, 1995). They must be cognizant of the need to consider readiness for change and to be certain the changes in philosophy and practice "fit" the particular organization within which they are operating (Haddock, et al., 1995).

As a result of these changes, some healthcare organizations have begun to reengineer their HR functions. In many instances, this implies some degree of outsourcing. Others are shifting functions from a centralized HR department to line managers. Although the functional lines between line managers and central HR vary by organization, traditional roles will be explored throughout this chapter. As the HR department expands its own role to the strategic level, more "personnel" functions may be shifted to individual line managers.

A. Human Resources Planning

Human resource planning is concerned with issues of supply of and demand for personnel. Specifically, it is concerned with projecting staffing needs and monitoring the use of staff against pre-established budgets. The HR department may be involved in maintaining personnel inventories and participating in succession planning. The human resources planning function may also involve modeling career paths for current and future employees. Effective human resources planning requires a clear understanding of relevant labor markets, as well as local, regional and national trends. This frequently involves close communication with suppliers (e.g., training programs) and health professional organizations (e.g., nursing associations). This is frequently accomplished collaboratively with the relevant professional group.

To ensure that the organization has the resources it needs to achieve its strategic plan, the HR department must forecast the organization's future human resources needs based on objectives identified in the strategic plan. The HR department also works with line managers to assess the supply that exists within the organization. Then external environmental factors that may affect labor supply, such as migration patterns, economic forecasts, number of professionals graduating, and government regulations, must be identified and assessed as to their impact on the ability of the organization to meet its forecasted needs. The net result of these assessments (future need, existing supply, future availability) equals either a surplus of human resources, a deficit of required resources, or status quo. If the organization is projected to experience a surplus, HR must develop strategies to manage the surplus: downsize, attrition, early retirement, layoffs. If the organization is projected to experience a deficit, the HR department must develop specific recruitment and/or retraining strategies to overcome the deficit. Thus, planning is the initial HR function that drives many others.

B. Job Design

Job design is concerned with structuring jobs to improve organizational efficiency and employee job satisfaction. It should facilitate the achievement of organizational objectives and the performance of the work the job was established to accomplish (Sherman, Bohlander and Snell, 1996). Job design involves four components:
- The organization's objectives to be achieved through job
- Human capability of performing job
- Quality-of-life considerations within the job
- Efficiency of the job

In some cases, these components may be in direct conflict with each other. For example, the most efficient process for performing the job may not provide sufficient quality-of-life considerations. The process of job design seeks to maximize each of these components to achieve a balance of overall organizational efficiency and employee satisfaction.

Workforce restructuring is an area key to current efforts at improved quality and efficiency. Specifically, individuals working in the job design area will need to consider:

- teaming aspects of jobs, or how jobs fit together to promote patient-focused care;
- flexibility and breadth of duties in job design;
- a re-configuration of traditional career tracks and progress through the organization; and
- the impact of new technology on work and job design.

As the structure of many healthcare organizations is changing, so are the jobs performed by those organizations. There is currently a trend in healthcare organizations towards increased use of multi-skilled workers. Among the most important concerns facing healthcare organizations of the future will be the need for increased productivity. Individuals with multiple sets of skills will be able to move more freely about the clinically integrated health system to perform a variety of functions, adding flexibility to the workforce and increasing overall productivity. Notwithstanding current professional licensure regulations and accreditation policies which may inhibit flexibility in staffing, organizations are likely to place a high priority on designing work around such individuals (e.g., radiology technologists who also perform basic nursing functions).

New types of healthcare organizations will also generate new jobs, such as health information specialists to provide health education, health promotion, and wellness services. Health information specialists will also serve as a link (and in some cases, buffer), between the medical community and consumers, and may, in fact, assume increasing responsibility for integrating illness and wellness services in vertically integrated health systems. Certainly, as the locus of health services continues to shift from the hospital to facilities and programs providing preventive and primary care services, health information specialists will assume key roles in the healthcare system. Other new jobs may include those of advance practice nurses, physician assistants, and other nonphysicians who will provide primary care services as well as alternative therapies.

C. Job Analysis

Job analysis forms the basis for many other HR functions. Job analysis is concerned with determining the actual tasks and duties of a specific job. Operationally, job analysis is used to develop job descriptions (work to be performed) and job specifications (skills and education required to perform the job). Strategically, HR managers may use job analysis to determine recruitment needs, develop performance standards, and construct needed training and development programs, for the purpose of improving overall organizational performance.

The process of job analysis involves gathering information about jobs and translating that information into a job description and job specifications. Information may be gathered through a variety of techniques, including observation, interviews, questionnaire, or a combination of these techniques. The job analyst may obtain this information directly from the employee, supervisors, or in the case of observation, from first-hand knowledge.

While future job analysis will still be concerned with the behaviors and skills required for a particular job, healthcare organizations are increasingly concerned with the relationships among jobs and how they fit together to form patient-focused care teams. Healthcare organizations are placing increasing emphasis on delivery of "seamless care," and moving from a highly compartmentalized, vertical organization to a horizontal, integrated one, aligned with the manner in which patients move through the organization.

Future healthcare organizations will also find themselves needing to be increasingly flexible in the manner in which human resources are deployed. Organizations will move more towards flexible job descriptions, providing individuals with greater breadth of responsibilities. Professional standards for a multi-skilled worker may be quite different from those established by traditional licensing bodies. Moving towards these types of arrangements requires substantial training, development of an environment fostering strong professional relationships, and new performance management systems.

D. Compensation

Compensation policies set out to meet a variety of objectives: to recruit and retain high-quality employees; to compensate employees at prevailing market wages and salaries while adhering to legal constraints; to maintain internal equity while being externally competitive; and to induce and reward improved performance. There are three traditional forms of compensation: pay (salary or hourly wage), incentive (bonus or commission), and benefits (vacation, health insurance, retirement). The basis for determining compensation is another issue that must be addressed by HR. Traditionally, healthcare workers have been paid based on time, either an hourly wage or an established salary. Other bases for compensation include productivity (piecework) in which employees are paid for each unit that is produced or skill-based pay in which employees are paid for the skills they possess.

Strategically, one HR function is to target the percentage of expenses that will be spent on labor costs. On the one hand, healthcare organizations are seeking to contain costs, and with labor costs accounting for the highest proportion of healthcare budgets, the most obvious method of cost reduction is staff reduction or greater flexibility in the use of staff (including the increasing of a variety of contingent workers, such as part-time and contract workers). Concurrent with this relatively insecure employment relationship, organizations are seeking to enlist loyalty, commitment, and higher levels of productivity from their employees. How they achieve these two seemingly opposing objectives is in the domain of the organization's reward system.

In addition to determining the amount of financial resources that can be allocated to compensation, the HR department must also develop a compensation philosophy that meets the organization's overall goals and HR strategies. The major challenge facing compensation systems in healthcare organizations is in ensuring that the system rewards the right things, namely, activities associated with achieving the strategic objectives of the organization (Milkovich and Newman, 1990). Traditionally, there has been a weak link between the reward system and organizational priorities.

Compensation systems are typically based on qualifications (based mainly on experience and education) and longevity in the organization. The need for increased productivity is forcing organizations to become more precise in their expectations of employees with respect to their performance and skill levels. A number of modifications to existing compensation systems are being tested, including skills- or knowledge-based pay, performance-based pay, value-added executive compensation, and flexible benefit plans.

Under a highly competitive system, healthcare organizations will be held increasingly accountable for the cost and quality of their services. System performance will be evaluated on criteria associated with these two elements. Congruent with this trend is the need for compensation systems to be designed more around skills, competencies, and performance and less around formal job descriptions. Under a skills-based pay structure, employees are paid for the range, depth, and types of skills that they are capable of using. Individuals are therefore paid at a rate based on their knowledge and skills, not on length of service, job title, or formal education. Pay increases are achieved when employees demonstrate an expansion in their skill base. The advantages of such an approach are clear: employees have incentives to improve; the organization achieves increased flexibility; employee self-esteem is enhanced; and there is often a higher level of employee commitment (Ledford, 1991; Tosi and Tosi, 1986). There are, however, several obstacles to be overcome in implementing skills-based pay. Wage rates and training costs may increase, and employees may be dissatisfied with the ambiguity in work roles that this implies. In addition, attention needs to be given to internal equity concerns and developing the mechanics of skills-based pay—developing skill blocks, defining progression paths, formulating time requirements in a particular skill block, and establishing certification tests.

Competency-based pay is based on competencies, behaviors, and knowledge the organization finds necessary for its success in addition to skills (Gribb and O'Donnell, 1995). Competencies added as a consideration to objectives-based compensation systems that often exist can help determine pay positioning relative to the market (Vogeley and Schaeffer, 1995).

Performance-based pay systems and discretionary bonuses have received considerable attention in various sectors of the economy. Essentially, performance-based pay is a method of variably paying individuals such that at least part of their pay is at risk, or linked to their performance. In developing a performance-based pay system, healthcare organizations need to ensure that:

- the outcomes valued (and thus compensated for) are those that will continue to have value in the long-term;
- by rewarding one outcome the organization is not compromising other equally or more important outcomes (e.g., compromising quality for productivity);
- outcomes worth rewarding are measurable in a valid and meaningful way; and
- rewarded outcomes are under the control of the job incumbent (or team).

While healthcare organizations typically adhere to a philosophy of teamwork, compensation systems are rarely aligned with this concept. The problems associated with team-based reward systems are well-documented (e.g., social loafing, dysfunctional competition among teams), and many organizations are reluctant to deviate from generally well-accepted individual incentive programs. Some current thinking on teams holds that jobs can enhance efficiency and employee satisfaction (Campion and Higgs, 1995). Given intense competitive pressures, variable group compensation plans will become increasingly common. The plans will likely target improvements in quality, profits, service, and cost reductions. IBM, for example, has moved to a variable pay system, in which each employee's compensation is influenced by IBM's overall corporate pay position as compared to its competitors, the individual's contribution to their unit's performance, and the unit's actual business performance (Blackburn and Rosen, 1993).

Flexibility will be the most critical part of compensation systems. Compensation systems, particularly in large organizations, however, tend to be rigid and difficult to change. Job evaluation systems are typically built around the concept of "compensable factors" and assigning job points for such job factors as experience, training requirements, work environment, and responsibility. Factoring in performance outcomes is typically a messy and controversial endeavor, and is particularly difficult when group rewards are included as a component of the compensation scheme. Such arrangements are particularly difficult to implement in unionized organizations. However, there is evidence that many healthcare organizations are modifying rigid compensation systems and adopting such approaches as broadbanding which, in general, removes some restrictions to pay flexibility and places greater responsibility on line managers to define compensation levels.

Operationally, HR is responsible for actually developing the compensation system, conducting wage surveys to maintain the competitiveness of the organization's compensation system, and to develop pay structures and policies.

E. Employee Benefits

Employee benefits are an indirect form of compensation offered to employees and sometimes family members. Some employee benefits are mandated: social security, unemployment, and workers compensation; others are not legally mandated but are increasingly expected by employees: health insurance, paid time off, life insurance, retirement, pensions, and employee assistance programs. Like the compensation system, HR managers must strategically determine the total amount the company will expend in the form of benefits, ensure that the benefits package meets the organization's goals and achieves HR strategies, and determine which benefits are offered to which employees. Operationally, the HR department must develop (and in many instances negotiate) the benefit packages, communicate benefits to employees and answer questions regarding the package, assist employees with accessing benefits, and manage the cost of the benefit package.

F. Recruitment

The recruitment function involves finding appropriately qualified applicants to fill jobs within the organization. Recruiting is the fundamental action step to implementing HR objectives. Organizations may recruit internally (from existing employees within the organization) or externally (from those outside the organization). Recruiting from within is generally viewed as having a positive impact on employee morale, because it rewards employees for their performance and encourages other employees. However, too much internal recruitment can stifle an organization, limiting "fresh" ideas that may be brought by an outsider. Outside recruitment may be necessary if special skills or education are required that existing employees do not have. In addition, outside recruitment for high level managerial positions may be essential to ensure that the organization changes and adapts to maintain its future viability.

The HR department's strategic recruitment responsibilities include establishing recruitment objectives based on HR planning, establishing recruitment techniques and policies, (Is the organization required to recruit internally before initiating any external recruiting?), and evaluating the success of various recruitment techniques.

Healthcare organizations can no longer use the kind of recruitment and retention incentives (e.g., promises of career progress and continued employment) that were available in the past. In the current environment, organizations need to explore alternative recruitment strategies. First, it is important for healthcare organizations to establish recruitment plans that are sufficiently robust to accommodate cycles of shortage and surplus. For many years, for example, hospitals have responded to periodic nurse shortages through extraordinary recruitment efforts (usually a combination of financial and scheduling incentives). While one can empathize with the hospital recruiter and the short-staffed director of nursing, these efforts often resulted in internal inequities (between, for example, longer term nurses and new employees) and dissatisfaction when these incentives are removed.

Today's recruitment and retention strategies often involve enhancing the quality and flexibility of working life. Considerable experience has been gained with quality enhancing strategies, such as flextime, job sharing, work sharing, compressed work weeks, and telecommuting. These strategies, if well designed, are quite compatible with an orientation towards productivity outcomes and quality. Generally, these innovations have been initiated by employees most typically to accommodate family responsibilities. Progressive organizations, however, have initiated flexibility in work scheduling as a recruitment and retention tool (Goddard, 1987).

Demographic changes in the workforce will also demand different recruitment strategies. The increase in women and minorities, for example, will require that organizations change their strategies rather than simply increasing current efforts to overcome shortages (D'Aunno, 1996). Operationally, HR may actually conduct recruitment efforts and write copy for recruitment ads. In some organizations, these operational functions may be performed by line managers are who better able to judge the skill and competency level of prospective employees.

G. Training and Development

The purpose of training and development is to ensure that the organization achieves its strategies by having personnel who have the skills and knowledge required to achieve these strategies. Strategically, the HR department must determine what training is required to achieve the organization's strategies, based on the skill and knowledge level of existing employees. In addition, HR should be involved in promoting career development for existing employees, driven by the future needs of the organization. HR must be mindful of the fact that as HR and its focuses change, so do HR career paths (McNerney, March, 1996).

Traditional career tracks in healthcare organizations typically begin with entry-level direct service positions. Individuals then progress to positions of increasing responsibility, through middle management, and ultimately, for some individuals, to senior management positions. In fact, promises of career progression have traditionally played an important role in recruitment, retention, and employee commitment and motivation. As has happened in other industries, this career scenario has been upset by pressures for increased productivity and dramatic reductions in middle management. For a number of reasons, healthcare organizations can no longer present to prospective employees a well-developed career track within the organization. First, the future structure of healthcare organization is uncertain as many move into alliances, mergers, and other interorganizational configurations. Second, the nature of clinical career tracks is changing because of the changing nature of clinical positions. What is the "natural" career track, for example, of a multi-skilled individual with competencies in drawing blood, providing genetic counseling, designing and delivering health promotion programs, and taking patients' vital signs? Finally, a key stepping-stone for many careers, the middle manager role, is undergoing continued assault because of perceived duplication and inefficiency, particularly among organizations who are practicing TQM principles. These organizations are usually flatter, which limits opportunities for promotion.

> "Career development in TQM organizations must de-emphasize promotions as symbols of corporate achievement. . . . In years to come, we might expect a much greater emphasis on career development strategies such as job rotation, liaison assignments, and task force leadership" (Blackburn and Rosen, 1993).

Nursing has taken a number of steps to address career progress issues by instituting an alternative to the managerial career route. Clinical nurse specialist roles provide a nonmanagement avenue for advancement within the organization while allowing the nurse to maintain a clinical focus and increase earnings. Changing organizational structures will need to address career tracks in even more innovative ways.

Future training and development activities within the organization will need to focus to a greater extent on better fitting individuals to organizational needs. It will no longer be the case that the skills of well-trained registered nurses will necessarily match the needs of the organization. Efficient training initiatives will be required to provide individuals with requisite skills within a particular organization. In many cases, this will involve a broadening of individuals' skills base (including cross-training), while in other instances, individuals may require training in a particular programmatic area or set of procedures. The formal training and development function will need to be linked with management at the most senior levels of the organization to ensure that training programs are supportive of current and future organizational strategies.

Operationally, the HR department is usually involved in conducting employee orientation, providing specific on-the-job training sessions, and coordinating off-site training for all employees. Particularly in healthcare organizations, these functions may be performed by line managers with better clinical knowledge of the training needs of individual employees.

H. Appraisal

Performance appraisal involves comparing how well an employee does his/her job with required standards for performance of that job, communicating that information to the employee, and developing a plan for improvement with the employee. Appraisal has two roles in an organization: administrative (providing information for other HR functions such as compensation, promotion, and termination) and development (providing the individual employee with specific information to improve their performance and achieve higher goals). Strategically, these functions allow HR to match current capacity with the future needs of the organization and to translate organizational strategies into performance standards for employees. As previously discussed, personnel employed by healthcare organizations are changing. HR departments must develop appraisal systems for new types of employees, such as physicians and multi-skilled workers. In addition, just as compensation systems must reward desired behaviors, the organization's appraisal system must also evaluate those qualities and skills necessary to achieving the organization's objectives. For example, some TQM companies, in the tradition of Deming, are moving from retrospective performance review practices to performance planning for the future (Blackburn and Rosen, 1993).

Operationally, the HR department should develop the appraisal system and policies, including the methods for performance appraisal and who is responsible for conducting appraisals. Although organizations frequently assume that a manager knows how to conduct an appraisal, many have never received actual training. Thus, HR departments should routinely train and retrain managers in conducting appraisals. HR departments are also sometimes responsible for monitoring and scheduling the timing of appraisals, although line managers may also perform this function, particularly in larger organizations.

Many healthcare organizations are modifying their performance appraisal systems to incorporate customer service goals. One approach is the use of 360-degree feedback, in which employees receive feedback from co-workers, subordinates, internal customers, external customers (clients or patients), as well as the formal supervisor. It is rare that such information is used to determine compensation, because of possible legal and ethical problems, but the approach holds great potential for improving individual performance while also improving quality and service. 360-degree feedback can be used in both traditional structures and team-based work groups. It is a useful

Figure 1 - Reasons for Unionization in American Hospitals ASHHRA/Omni 8th Semi-Annual Labor Activity Report

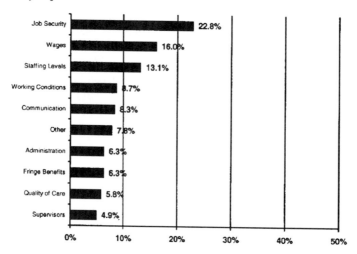

tool for providing insight into the organization as a whole and aids in defining competencies (Hoffman, 1995). A competency-based approach to HR may be used to supplement processes such as reengineering and TQM (Kochanski and Ruse, 1996). A resource-based view suggests HR systems can contribute to competitive advantage by developing competencies (Lado and Wilson, 1994).

I. Employee and Labor/Management Relations

The employee and labor/management relations role of HR within an organization involves a variety of issues, including employee health and safety, employee rights, employee grievance, employee discipline, and union/management relations. In unionized organizations, the labor-management function is often carved out because of the attention demanded in such settings. From a strategic perspective, HR departments must monitor legislative actions involving all of the issues outlined above. In the past ten to fifteen years, so many labor laws have been passed at both the state and federal level, this HR function has become increasingly complex and challenging. Because of the significant implications of many of these issues, the HR department must also ascertain their impact on the organization's ability to achieve its strategic objectives.

Given the continued pressure for unionization among healthcare organizations, HR managers must develop proactive strategies to deal with unionization issues. Recently published statistics from the National Labor Relations Board indicate that unions win 62.7 percent of healthcare elections, compared to an average of 50.1 percent for all industries. According to a survey conducted by the American Society for Healthcare Human Resources Administration (ASHHRA), job security is the primary organizing issue, as illustrated in Figure 1.

This survey also shows that all categories of healthcare employees are targeted by union organizers, with Registered Nurses targeted most frequently (Figure 2).

Figure 2. - Personnel Targeted for Unionization in American Hospitals, 1995. ASHHRA/Omni 8th Semi-Annual Labor Activity Report

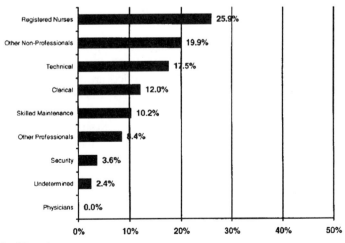

Operationally, HR departments provide a variety of labor/management relations functions, including developing health/safety programs (conducting health and wellness programs, providing physical examinations, overseeing treatment services and drug testing, ensuring compliance with the Occupational Safety and Health Administration (OSHA), conducting safety campaigns and inspections, giving awards, conducting accident investigations, overseeing security) working with union organizations, overseeing collective bargaining, instituting labor/management cooperative programs, training managers about employee rights, developing grievance procedures and policies, monitoring grievances, resolving grievances between managers and employees, developing disciplinary polices and processes. Most importantly, HR must coordinate all of these HR functions and other organization-wide HR policies to ensure consistency throughout the organization.

J. Legal/Regulatory Issues

As alluded to earlier, HR departments have numerous legal and regulatory issues that must be constantly monitored. HR departments must be familiar with the actions of agencies such as the Occupational Safety and Health Administration, the Equal Employment Opportunity Commission, the Office of Federal Contract Compliance Programs, the Immigration and Naturalization Services, and the various state and city equal employment commissions and human or civil rights commissions (Miner, 1988). In addition, the HR department is responsible for ensuring that the organization in its entirety is in compliance with all of these requirements. Communication regarding legal compliance becomes even more important in an organization that is decentralizing traditional HR functions of hiring, appraisal, and termination to line managers. All of these functions are subject to laws and regulations related to equal employment, discrimination, and affirmative action.

IV. CONCLUSION

In summary, healthcare organizations are undergoing tremendous change. Organizations are changing structurally, forming alliances with very different organizations; organizational strategies that require systemwide changes are emerging, including total quality management, continuous quality improvement, reengineering, patient-focused care; employees of healthcare organizations are changing as the services provided the organization and the way those services are delivered continue to change. The role of the human resource function must also change with the organization. Human resources must be integrated into the strategic planning and management of the organization. Human resources must function to support the organization's goals, just as finance and marketing have for years. In addition to expanding its responsibility to strategic functions, the human resource department must also expand its roles to encompass new types of healthcare employees: physicians, physician extenders, and multi-skilled healthcare workers. Finally, human resources must continue its traditional functions, while also aligning these functions with the organization's strategic objectives.

REFERENCES

Blackburn, R., and Rosen, B. (1995). Does HRM walk the TQM talk? *HRMagazine, July:* 69-72

Blackburn, R., and Rosen, B. (1993). Total quality and human resources management: lessons learned from Baldridge Award-winning companies. *Academy of Management Executive, 7(3):* 49-65.

Buller, P. F. (1988). Successful partnerships: HR and strategic planning at eight top firms. *Organizational Dynamics, 17(Autumn):* 27-43.

Carroll, S. J. (1991). New HRM roles, responsibilities, and structures. In R.S. Schuler, ed. *Managing HR in the Information Age.* SHRM/BNA Books, Washington, D.C.

Campion, M. A. and Higgs, A. C. (1995). Design work teams to increase productivity and satisfaction. *HRMagazine,* 101-7,

Feldacker, B. S. (1990). *Labor Guide to Labor Law,* Third Edition. Prentice Hall, Englewood Cliffs, NJ.

Fottler, M. D., Phillips, R. L., Blair, J. D. and Duran, C. (1990). Achieving competitive advantage through strategic human resource management. *Hospital and Health Services Administration, 35(3):* 341-63.

Fottler, M. D., Hernandez, S. R., and Joiner, C. L., eds. (1988). *Strategic Management of Human Resources in Health Services Organizations.* John Wiley and Sons, New York.

Freedman, A. (1990). *The Changing Human Resource Function.* The Conference Board, New York.

French, W. (1994). *Human Resources Management,* Third Edition. Houghton Mifflin, Boston, MA.

Goddard, R. W. (1988). How to harness America's gray power. *Personnel Journal, May:* 100-5.

Gribb, G., and O'Donnell, S. (1995). Pay plans that reward employee achievement. *HRMagazine July:* 49-50.

Haddock, C., Nosky, C., Fargason, C., Crayton Jr.,A. , and Kurz, R S. (1995). The impact of CQI on human resources management. *Hospital and Health Services Administration: Special CQI Issue, 40(1):* 138-53.

Hoffman, R. (1995). Ten reasons you should be using 360-degree feedback. *HRMagazine, April:* 82-5.

Huselid, M. A. (1995). Documenting the HR's effect on company performance. *HRMagazine 39(1):* 79-85.

Kochanski, J. T. and Ruse, D. H. (1996). Designing a competency-based human resources organization. *Human Resource Management, 35(1):* 19-33.

Lado, A. A. and Wilson, M. C. (1994). Human resource systems and sustained competitive advantage: a competency-based perspective. *Academy of Management Review, 19(4):* 699-727.

Ledford, G. E. (1991). Three case studies on skill-based pay: an overview. *Compensation and Benefits Review, (March-April):* 11-23.

McNerney, D. J., ed. (1996). Career development: as HR changes, so do HR career paths. *Human Resources Forum, (March):* 2.

McNerney, D. J., ed. (1996). HR management: four trends to reckon with. *Human Resources Forum (September).*

Milkovich, G. T., and Newman, J. M. (1990). *Compensation.* BPI/Irwin, Homewood, IL.

Miner, M. G. (1989). Legal concerns facing human resource managers: an overview. In *Readings in Personnel and Human Resource Management,* Third Edition, (R.S. Schuler, S.A. Youngblood, and V.L. Huber, eds.) West Publishing, St. Paul.

Pround, E. D. (1916). *Welfare Work.* G. Bell and Sons, London.

Schuler, R. S. and Huber, V. L. (1993). *Personnel and Human Resource Management,* Fifth Edition. West, Minneapolis/St. Paul.

Sherman, A., Bohlander, G., and Snell, S. (1996). *Managing Human Resources,* Tenth Edition. South-Western College Publishing, Cincinnati.

Shimko, B. W. (1990). All managers are HR managers. *HRMagazine, (January):* 67-70,

Tokesky, G .C., and Kornides, J. F. (1994). Strategic HR management is vital. *Personnel Journal,* 73(12): 115-17.

Tosi, H., and Tosi, L. (1986). What managers need to know about knowledge-based pay. *Organizational Dynamics, (Winter)*: 52-64.

Van Riper, P. P. (1958). *History of the United States Civil Service.* Row, Peterson, Evanston, IL.

Vogeley, E. G., and Schaeffer, L. J. (1995). Link employee pay to competencies and objectives. *HRMagazine, (October)*: 75-81.

Young, A., and Brockbank, W. (1995). Reengineering HR through information technology. *Human Resource Planning, 18(2)*: 25-37

51.
JOB ANALYSIS

Myron D. Fottler, *University of Alabama at Birmingham, Birmingham, AL*

M. Elizabeth Woodard, *University of Alabama at Birmingham, Birmingham, AL*

The present chapter will review the fundamental foundation or cornerstone of human resource management - job analysis. More specifically, it will examine the nature and uses of job analysis, reasons for its use, the job analysis process, data collection methods, legal constraints, and strategic aspects of job analysis in a health care environment.

I. NATURE OF JOB ANALYSIS

The ultimate purpose of job analysis is to improve overall performance and productivity in the organization. It is often referred to as the cornerstone of the human resource management (HRM) process because the information generated serves many HRM functions.

Job analysis is the systematic process of gathering and analyzing information about jobs by determining the job's duties, tasks, and/or activities. Job analysis was once thought to be so insignificant, that it was left to be conducted by lower-level personnel technicians (Prien, 1977). Today, the significance of an accurate and up to date job analysis to effective HRM has gained recognition and the level of expertise required to conduct such analyses is being raised (Gatewood and Feild, 1990).

Before an individual can be hired to perform a job or the pay level for the job established, the requirements of the job must be identified. Before the performance of the employees can be evaluated, what the employee should be doing must be identified. A prerequisite for a manager to perform these functions is that he or she be aware of the knowledge, skills, and abilities (KSAs) necessary to perform the job.

Knowledge is defined as the degree to which a job holder is required to know special technical material. **Skills** are defined as adequate performance on tasks requiring the use of tools or equipment. Finally, **abilities** refer to the physical and mental capacities needed to perform tasks not requiring the use of tools or equipment.

There must be a thorough understanding of the domain of each job before any of the human resource functions can be performed. Human resource professionals achieve this understanding through the use of job analysis, which is a means of collecting information about various aspects of the job. Results of the job analysis serve as a foundation for most of the human resource functions.

The job analysis process results in written job description and job specifications. A job description is a written form that identifies the essential functions of a job and provides specific information concerning the duties, responsibilities and working conditions contained in the job. The job description also describes the job's function in relation to the organization as a whole. Such descriptions should identify the whats, whys, wheres, and hows of a job. Since there is no standard format for job descriptions, they tend to differ from organization to organization.

In general terms, the major items contained in a job description are:

- **Identification:** Job title, job number and classification (exempt or non-exempt), and department. It may also include reporting relationships and number of employees holding the job.

- **Job Summary:** A general summary of the major components of the job and how it differs from other positions.

- **Duties and Responsibilities:** Clear and concise statements of the essential and non-essential functions of the job. May also include the percentage of time devoted to each task, working conditions and potential hazards, and supervisory or reporting functions.

- **Job specifications:** Most job descriptions also include the specification information including specific knowledge, skills, and abilities required to perform the job as well as educational and experience criteria.

A detailed job description for a staff nurse position at a large Southeastern hospital is shown in Figure 1.

Figure 1 - An Example of a Combined Job Description/Job Specification.

(Used with permission of St. Vincents' Hospital) Reproduced by permission. Strategic Management of Human Resources in Health Services Organizations by Myron D. Fottler, S. Robert Hernandez, and Charles L. Joiner. Delmar Publishers, Albany, New York, Copyright 1995.

ST. VINCENT'S HOSPITAL
Birmingham, Alabama

CRITERIA BASED JOB DESCRIPTION AND PERFORMANCE STANDARDS

JOB TITLE   Staff Nurse
DEPARTMENT   Nursing-Labor and Delivery

DATE 8/17/92   JOB CODE 2339   FLSA STATUS Nonexempt
DEPARTMENT APPROVAL: _____
PERSONNEL APPROVAL: _____
ADMINISTRATIVE APPROVAL   _____

JOB SUMMARY

Assesses, prescribes, delegates, coordinates, and evaluates the nursing care provided. Ensures provision of quality care for selected groups of patients through utilization of nursing process, established standards of care, and policies and procedures.

SUPERVISION

SUPERVISED BY: Unit Manager, indirectly by Charge Nurse
SUPERVISES: No one
LEADS/GUIDES: Unit Associates/Ancillary Associates in the delivery of direct patient care

JOB SPECIFICATIONS

EDUCATION
- Required: Graduate of an accredited school of professional nursing
- Desired:
EXPERIENCE
- Required:
- Desired:
LICENSES, CERTIFICATIONS, AND/OR REGISTRATIONS: Current R.N. license in the State of Alabama; BCLS and certifications specific to areas of clinical specialty preferred.
EQUIPMENT/TOOLS/WORK AIDS: PCA infusors, infusion pumps and other medical equipment, computer terminal and printer, facsimile machine, photocopier, and patient charts.
SPECIALIZED KNOWLEDGE AND SKILLS: Ability to work with female patients of child-bearing age and new-born patients in all specialty and subspecialty categories, both urgent and nonurgent in nature.
PERSONAL TRAITS, QUALITIES, AND APTITUDES: Must be able to: 1) perform a variety of duties often changing from one task to another of a different nature without loss of efficiency or composure; 2) accept responsibility for the direction, control, and planning of an activity; 3) make evaluations and decisions based on measurable or verifiable criteria; 4) work independently; 5) recognize the rights and responsibilities of patient confidentiality; 6) convey empathy and compassion to those experiencing pain or grief; 7) relate to others in a manner that creates a sense of teamwork and cooperation; and 8) communicate effectively with people from every socioeconomic background.
WORKING CONDITIONS: Inside environment, protected from the weather but not necessarily temperature changes. Subject to frequent exposure to infection, contagious disease, combative patients, and potentially hazardous materials and equipment. Variable noise levels. Also subject to rapid pace, multiple stimuli, unpredictable environment, and critical situations.
PHYSICAL DEMANDS/TRAITS: Must be able to: 1) perceive the nature of sounds by the ear; 2) express or exchange ideas by means of the spoken word; 3) perceive characteristics of objects through the eyes; 4) extend arms and hands in any direction; 5) seize, hold, grasp, turn, or otherwise work with hands; 6) pick, pinch, or otherwise work with the fingers; 7) perceive such attributes of objects or materials as size, shape, temperature, or texture; and 8) stoop, kneel, crouch, and crawl. Must be able to lift 50 pounds maximum with frequent lifting, carrying, pushing, and pulling of objects weighing up to 25 pounds. Continuous walking and standing. Must be able to identify, match, and distinguish colors. Rare lifting of greater than 100 pounds.

Figure 1 - Continued

JOB RESPONSIBILITIES AND PERFORMANCE STANDARDS

Assigned
Weight

10%   1. UTILIZES THE NURSING PROCESS (i.e., ASSESSMENT, PLANNING, IMPLEMENTATION, AND EVAL-
UATION) IN THE PROVISION OF PATIENT CARE IN ACCORDANCE WITH THE STANDARDS OF CARE AND POLI-
CIES AS WRITTEN

Assessment

- Admission assessment includes at least the following:
  - Patient identification
  - Current medical history
  - Current obstetrical history
  - Reason for admission
  - Relevant physical, psychological, and sociological status
  Allergies
  Drug use
  Disabilities
  Impairment
  Surgical Consent Form
  Medical Consent Form
  Pediatrician's Consent Form
- Assessments performed in accordance with the patient care standard. S-2-7010-VI:
  - Admission physical assessment
  - Affected system each shift
  - Labor patients:
  Maternal temperature q 4 hours
  Maternal pulse q 4 hours
  Maternal blood pressure q 1 hour
  Pitocin order
  Vaginal exam prior to Pitocin
  Epidural level of anesthesia hourly
  FHR q 30 minutes during 1st stage
  FHR q 15 minutes during 2nd stage

10%   - Plan of care
  - Conceptualized plan of care is developed for each patient:
  Identify one nursing diagnosis pertinent to this patient's care.
  Identify one nursing intervention related to this diagnosis.
  Identify to whom this plan of care should be communicated.
  - Nursing intervention(s) relative to the identified nursing diagnosis is documented
  - Written plan of care is initiated on patients whose stay in Labor and Delivery exceeds 24 hours (Exception: patients
  in labor).
  - Plan of care mutually developed with patient and/or SO.
  - Written plan of care updated in response to changes in patient care needs.
  - Plan of care consistent with medical plan of care.
  - All components of the written plan of care are included:
  Date
  Problem number
  Nursing diagnosis
  Nursing orders
  Patient goal(s)
  Projected goals state are:
  - Patient goals stated are:
  Realistic
  Measurable
  - Patient's response to care given is documented
  - Changes in patient's condition are documented

10%   2. DETERMINES CONDITION OF PATIENTS AND CLASSIFIES APPROPRIATELY
  - Appropriate acuity level determined based on care provided to the patient/SO.

Figure 1 - Continued
- All asterisk (*) items have narrative documentation.

5% 3. DEMONSTRATES KNOWLEDGE OF DISCHARGE PLANNING REHABILITATIVE MEASURES AND COMMUNITY RESOURCES BY MAKING APPROPRIATE AND TIMELY REFERRALS
- Initial assessment of discharge needs is accomplished through a complete patient family history on admission.

5% 4. DEMONSTRATES KNOWLEDGE AND UNDERSTANDING OF TEACHING/LEARNING PROCESS AND IMPLEMENTS PATIENT TEACHING TO MEET LEARNING NEEDS OF PATIENT AND/OR SIGNIFICANT OTHER
- Patient and/or significant other are involved in the identification of learning needs for short-term teaching/counseling during labor.
- Patient teaching during labor is evidenced by anticipatory guidance relative to all procedures and events.

5% 5. ASSUMES RESPONSIBILITY FOR ASSIGNING, DIRECTING, AND PROVIDING CARE FOR GROUPS OF PATIENTS
- Demonstrates necessary skills and knowledge to make appropriate assignments and considers the following factors when making patient care assignments:
  • The patient's status
  • The environment in which nursing care is provided
  • The competence of the nursing staff members who are to provide the care
  • The degree of supervision required by and available to the associates
  • The complexity of the assessment required by the patient
  • The type of technology employed in providing nursing care
  • Relevant infection control and safety issues
- Demonstrates the necessary skills and knowledge to provide care for patients in accordance with the Nursing Department and unit specific required skills and competencies.
- Compassionately gives personal patient care to provide comfort and well-being to the patient, acknowledging psychological needs.
- Delegates aspects of care to other nursing staff members as appropriate.
- Appropriately documents and communicates pertinent observations and care provided.

10% 6. ADMINISTERS MEDICATIONS, INTRAVASCULAR FLUIDS, AND TREATMENTS IN ACCORDANCE WITH HOSPITAL STANDARDS AND FEDERAL REGULATIONS
- Demonstrates or obtains knowledge of drugs and fluids to be administered.
- Accurately administers medications and intravascular fluids as ordered and scheduled.
- Accurately and completely documents administration and patient's response to drugs and intravascular fluids.
- Demonstrates ability and appropriate technical skills and procedures in accordance with physician's orders and nursing policies and procedures:
  • Procedures and treatments performed in a timely manner
  • Makes adequate preparation for performance of procedures and/or treatments
- Completes appropriate documentation.

10% 7. MAINTAINS EFFECTIVE COMMUNICATION WITH SUPERVISORS, HOSPITAL ASSOCIATES, MEDICAL STAFF, PATIENTS, FAMILIES, AND VISITORS
- Enhances cohesiveness of unit staff group through effective interpersonal communication.
- Communicates with all persons involved in a patient's care in a manner that facilitates timely meeting of stated goals.
- Utilizes approved lines of authority and channels of communication in sharing concerns.
- Actively participates in a minimum of four (4) interdepartmental meetings annually.
- Interacts effectively with patients, families, and/or significant others.
- Supports problem-solving approach to both unit and patient needs.
- Follows through on problems that may compromise patient care by using the appropriate chain-of-command.
- Gives a thorough concise change of shift report.

5% 8. RESPONDS APPROPRIATELY TO ENVIRONMENTAL AND SAFETY HAZARDS AND FUNCTIONS EFFECTIVELY IN EMERGENCY SITUATIONS
- Recognizes, takes action, and reports unsafe acts or situations involving patients, visitors, or staff.
- Responds promptly and appropriately to environmental and safety hazards.
- Promptly removes unsafe equipment from patient care areas and notifies the appropriate department.
- Functions promptly and effectively in codes, emergencies, or other stressful patient situations.
- Identifies high-risk patients and monitors accordingly.
- Complies with hospital and departmental policies and procedures concerning infection control.
- Demonstrates correct and safe technique in the use of equipment according to specific product

Figure 1 - Continued

information and policy and procedure manuals.
- Maintains a clean, neat, and safe environment for patients, visitors, and staff according to hospital and unit policies.

5%   9. UTILIZES HOSPITAL SYSTEMS EFFECTIVELY TO ENSURE ECONOMICAL USE OF EQUIPMENT AND SUPPLIES
- Effectively utilizes unit dose, classification, pneumatic tube, beepers, emergency checks, and services of other hospital departments.
- Demonstrates appropriate economical use of supplies and equipment.
- Ensures appropriate handling of charges.
- Accurately utilizes the computer system.
- Correctly initiates and discontinues daily charges when indicated.
- Ensures the supplies and equipment necessary for patient care are stored in an organized and efficient manner.
- Follows appropriate procedure for obtaining and returning or cleaning and/or disposing of equipment and supplies.

5%   10. DEMONSTRATES THROUGH ACTIONS THE ACCEPTANCE OF LEGAL AND ETHICAL RESPONSIBILITIES OF THE PROFESSIONAL NURSE
- Documents effectively, accurately, and in a timely manner, the patient's medical record according to hospital and department standards and policies.
- Adheres to drug handling regulations.
- Exhibits knowledge of reportable incidents appropriate documentations, and follow-up.
- Maintains current State R.N. license.
- Protects patients' rights to privacy and confidentiality.
- Demonstrates professional responsibility for nonprofessional group members.
- Accurately transcribes or verifies accuracy of physician orders.

5%   11. ASSUMES RESPONSIBILITY FOR KEEPING SKILLS CURRENT AND KNOWLEDGE UPDATED THROUGH STAFF DEVELOPMENT AND CONTINUING EDUCATION PROGRAMS
- Actively seeks learning experiences.
- Appropriately verbalizes learning needs.
- Attends a minimum of eight (8) hours or eight classes of relevant continuing education/staff development programs annually.
- Maintains current Educational Profile.

10%   12. COMPLETES A VOLUME OF WORK THAT ENSURES OPTIMUM PRODUCTIVITY WHILE MAINTAINING QUALITY PATIENT CARE
- Completes care of assigned patients in a timely manner.
- Assists other associates in completing their assignment in a timely manner.
- Supports cost-effective methods for improving patient care.
- Willingly accepts adjustment of posted schedule to meet unit emergencies and patient care needs as requested.
- Demonstrates an ongoing awareness of and participation in, the Quality Review (QR) program.
- Is alert to potential QR problems and actively participates in solving such problems.
- Responds with improved performance to results obtained from QR monitors.
- Does not incur excessive unscheduled overtime.

5%   13. PARTICIPATES IN ASSIGNED COMMITTEES, CONFERENCES, PROJECTS, STAFF DEVELOPMENT PROGRAMS, AND STAFF MEETINGS
- Attends and actively contributes to assigned committees, projects, and so forth.
- Assists immediate supervisor in the orientation and performance evaluation of associates.
- Actively supports departmental projects.
- Effectively implements approved departmental changes.
- Adapts to changes in a positive, professional manner.
- Attends staff meeting or reads and signs all minutes of staff meetings not attended.

The associate is expected to perform this job in a manner consistent with the values, mission, and philosophy of St. Vincent's Hospital and the Daughters of Charity National Health System.

This job description is meant to be only a representative summary of the major duties and responsibilities performed by incumbents of this job. The incumbents may be requested to perform job-related tasks other than those stated in this description.

A job specification lists the minimum acceptable qualifications required to adequately perform the job. Information generally found in a job specification falls into three categories:

- general qualification requirements including experience and training;
- educational requirements, including high school, university, and/or vocational education;
- knowledge, skills, and abilities.

A job specification should only include such qualifications, including physical demands, that directly relate to the acceptable performance of the job. Requirements that are not directly related to performing the job, especially unnecessary educational requirements, discriminate against minorities and are prohibited by equal employment opportunity laws (Griggs, W. S. et al. v. Duke Power Company, 1971). The specification should also include the required knowledge, skills, and abilities including specific licensure or certification requirements as well as mental and physical requirements necessary for satisfactory performance of the job.

II. WHY ANALYZE JOBS?

Job descriptions should be maintained and updated whenever the job content, performance requirements, or qualifications change. In today's turbulent health care environment, such changes should be frequent. With updated information, communication among managers, employees, applicants, and the human resource department is greatly simplified. When a vacancy occurs, the human resource department is notified by means of a requisition, and recruitment for an applicant who meets the requirements begins. In a similar manner, the description allows clear communication in the areas of human resource management including human resource planning, selection, performance appraisal, compensation, training, and career development.

Some of the uses of the job analysis include:

- **HR Planning:** Job analyses are used to develop job categories. They are also used in productivity assessments and organizational restructuring efforts.
- **Recruitment:** Used to describe and advertise job openings and new positions whether recruited internally or externally.
- **Training Program:** Used in the determination of training needs by identifying the activities that employees ought to be able to competently perform.
- **Job Related Interviews and Selection:** Job analysis can benefit a trained interviewer by identifying those requirements necessary for success on the job thus allowing the recruiter to assess the applicant's qualifications, and by allowing the applicant to decide if they are really interested in the position.
- **Performance Evaluation:** Used to identify performance standards by which employees will be evaluated.
- **Compensation:** Job analysis is used to evaluate job worth and to aid in developing a wage structure.

- **Equal Employment Opportunity (EEO):** Job analysis can also be helpful in determining what tasks are job related thus satisfying EEO requirements.

When writing job descriptions, employers must be as succinct and precise as possible. Direct and simple wording with verbs should be used in describing job duties.

III. JOB ANALYSIS PROCESS

Figure 2 outlines the elements of the job analysis process and the functions for which it is used. The human resources department typically has primary responsibility for conducting the job analysis. However, sometimes the individual charged with responsibility for the particular position has primary responsibility. Although job analysts are typically responsible for the job analysis program, they usually enlist the cooperation of the employees and the supervisor in the department in which positions are being analyzed. These supervisors and employees are the source of much of the job information generated through the process.

Figure 2 - The Elements and Functions of the Job Analysis System.

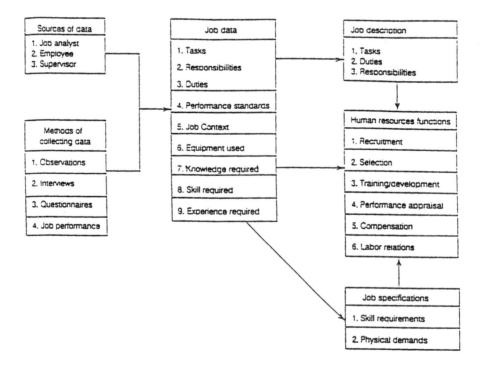

The process of implementing a job analysis for a given position or group of positions is described by the following six steps:

A. Determine the Purpose of the Job Analysis

The purpose of conducting a job analysis should be explicit and tied to the organization's overall business strategy in order to increase the effectiveness of the job analysis program. With the rapid growth and downsizing efforts of organizations, job content may have changed (Fottler, 1994).

B. Identify Jobs and Review Existing Documentation

Part of the identification phase is to review existing documentation, such as existing job descriptions, organization charts, previous job analysis information, and other industry related sources.

C. Explain the Process to Managers and Employees

A critical step in conducting the job analysis is to explain the process to management, employees and other concerned people such as union stewards. Items to be covered should include the purpose of the job analysis, who is conducting it, the steps involved and an associated timetable, how managers and employees will participate, and to whom questions should be directed should they arise.

D. Conduct the Job Analyses

The next step is to gather the job analysis information. The methods utilized in this process will be discussed later in this chapter. As the information is received and reviewed for completeness, follow-up interviews may need to be scheduled for clarification.

E. Prepare Job Descriptions and Specifications

All information gathered in the job analysis process should be sorted, evaluated, and used when drafting the job's descriptions and specifications. Once the drafts are completed, they should be discussed with the appropriate managers and employees. Following the review, all necessary changes should be made and final job descriptions and specifications completed. Upon completion, the manager should provide feedback to the current job holders, especially if their duties have changed as a result of the analysis.

F. Maintain and Update Job Descriptions and Specifications

Once job descriptions and specifications have been completed and reviewed with the appropriate individuals, a system should be developed to ensure that they continue to be current representations of the work being done. Failure to keep the job descriptions and specifications current will result in the costly undertaking of another job analysis in a few years. Because organizations are constantly evolving and changing, jobs rarely remain the same for long periods of time.

IV. DATA COLLECTION METHODS

Rather than describing reality, job analysis frequently reports perceptions of what the individuals plan to do or what managers think the individuals ought to do. Four methods that can be used to gather information required for the job analysis are: observations, interviews, questionnaires, and structured analysis. None of these methods is superior for all situations and each has advantages and disadvantages.

A. Observation

Observation may be continuous or based on sampling. Observers (a manager, job analyst, or industrial engineer) may watch an individual perform the job and then make brief descriptions of the tasks and duties performed. Using observers to gather information may have an unrealistic outcome in that employees may behave differently when being observed. The employees may make their jobs appear more difficult than they really are. The use of observation is limited in at least two ways. First, the job may not have a complete and easily observable job cycle. Observations may not be as useful in situations where "knowledge work" is necessary as opposed to physical work. Second, some managers may not be properly trained to assess what they see.

Video tapes or films of workers performing their jobs may be more beneficial than direct observation. One study, however, found that there was no difference in using a high performer or a low performer for the job analysis observation (Conley and Sackett, 1987). The high and low performers as well as the supervisors rated the jobs similarly in terms of knowledge, skills and abilities required to perform the job.

Work sampling observations do not require attention to every detail of the work cycle. Instead, a manager can determine the pace and content of a job through the random sampling of certain actions rather than through continuous observation and timing of all actions. Work sampling is most useful in repetitive and routine job tasks.

Job holders may be asked to keep a log of their activities (a type of diary) during a period of time. These diaries are usually filled out at specific times (e.g., every half-hour or hour, or at the completion of a task) and maintained over a specific length of time.

B. Interviews

Job analysis information can be obtained by interviewing the job holder as well as the job supervisor. Information from these interviews is of particular interest when evaluating professional and technical jobs that involve thinking and problem solving.

In an effort to fully understand the job, the interviewer must interview both the employee and the supervisor. A useful question to ask the job incumbent (in an effort to describe the knowledge, skills, and abilities needed for the job) is to describe what would be needed by a new employee who would be replacing them.

Group interviews can also be used to gather job analysis information. Group members are usually experienced job holders and/or supervisors. This process usually involves a member of the HR department to act as a mediator. Although this is an expensive assessment tool because of the number of people involved, it does bring together, at one time, a large group of experienced, well informed, individuals. This method is best used to analyze hard-to-define jobs.

C. Questionnaire

The most convenient and widely used form of obtaining job analysis information is the questionnaire. Although a questionnaire developed for a certain organization tends to have a high initial cost, it does have the advantage of probing in great detail into various aspects of work unique to the organization.

An open-ended questionnaire asks the employee/supervisor to answer specific questions about their jobs. The major advantage to this form of questionnaire method is that information on a wide variety of positions may be gathered in a short period of time and rather inexpensively. At the same time, this method may not be the most useful because it assumes that employees can analyze and communicate information about their jobs. Research shows that job analysis outcomes are influenced by the employees chosen to participate in them (Mullins and Kimbrough, 1988).

A checklist is sometimes used. A checklist differs from an open ended questionnaire in that it offers a simplified way for employees to give information. The major drawback of this format is its construction which can be a complicated, time intensive process.

D. Structured Analysis

Several job analysis methods are built on the questionnaire approach. Most managers would prefer methods of data collection that do not require a lot of work and up-front costs especially if job content is constantly changing. One option would be to utilize one of the existing structured questionnaires.

One of the best-known job analysis questionnaires is the position analysis questionnaire (PAQ) developed by Ernest J. McCormick and his colleagues at Purdue University (McCormick, 1972). The PAQ uses degree of importance as its measure. Some users caution that the PAQ has a high reading comprehension level and complex instructions, which make it difficult for some employees to complete the questionnaire without assistance (Ash and Edgell, 1975). The PAQ is a checklist of 195 job elements that measure six major categories of each job (McCormick, 1972):
- **Information input:** Where and how does the worker get information to perform the job?
- **Mental Process:** What levels of reasoning are necessary on the job?
- **Work Output:** What physical activities are performed?
- **Relationships with Others:** What relationships are required to perform the job?
- **Job Context:** What working conditions and social contexts are involved?
- **Other:** What activities, conditions, or characteristics other than those described above are relevant to the job?

Individuals completing the PAQ use multiple choice alternatives to describe the job of each of the 195 elements. This information can then be further analyzed to classify the job into other job dimensions, and it allows for a comparison of jobs across occupational groups. Although its complexity may deter many potential users, the PAQ is easily quantified and can be used to conduct validity studies on selection on selection tests (Campion, 1989).

The functional job analysis (FJA) method is another comprehensive approach to job analysis. Through observation, FJA considers: (1) the goals of the organization, (2) what a worker does to achieve those goals, (3) the level and orientation of what workers do, (4) performance standards, and (5) content of training. The distinctive feature of FJA is that it analyzes jobs with respect to three components: data, people, and things (Fine, 1986).

Identification of the level of data, people, and things is used to identify and compare important elements of jobs in a standardized data source provided by the U.S. Department of Labor's *Dictionary of Occupational Titles* (DOT), (1991). First published in 1939, the DOT has been updated in 1949, 1965, 1977, and 1991. The Department of Labor frequently issues supplements to the DOT to describe new occupations resulting from new technology and to update occupations that have changed. Over 20,000 occupations are described in the DOT and each has a unique job title and occupational code. Each occupational definition in the DOT consists of six basic parts that always appear in the same order:

- the occupational code number;
- the occupational title;
- the industry designation;
- alternative titles, if any;
- the body of the definition; and
- undefined related titles, if any.

As computer technology has expanded, efforts have been made to develop a computerized job analysis systems. The first characteristic of Computerized Job Analysis (CJA) is that task statements are used that relate to all jobs. Second, individual employees indicate if and to what degree each task statement is present in their jobs.

A CJA system has banks of job duty statements that relate to each of the task and scope statements of the questionnaires, and the job questionnaire data is input into the computer using optical scan forms. The data from employees are then used to develop behaviorally specific job descriptions. A benefit of these CJA systems is that because they are behaviorally based, they can identify the specific skills and abilities required in the job. Some of the skill-based approaches also define the proficiency levels of each job, so that performance appraisals can be made more job specific (Lundquist and Jones, 1992).

Because managerial jobs are different in character from jobs with clearly observable procedures and routines, some specialized methods have evolved for their analyses. One of the most well known was developed at Control Data Corporation and is labeled the *Management Position Description Questionnaire* (MPDQ). The MPDQ, composed of over 200 statements, examines a variety of managerial dimensions, including supervising and making decisions (Tornow and Pinto, 1976). A more recent approach can be found in the *Executive Checklist* (EXCEL), developed by Lozada-Larsen and Parker (1991). This is a self-administered test covering approximately 250 statements on planning and decision making, product research and development and sales, among others. If appropriate, these two methods can be supplemented with interviews.

V. LEGAL CONSTRAINTS

According to Grant (1988), there are several problems frequently associated with job descriptions. When poorly written and seldom updated, they provide little guidance for the job holder. They may violate the law by containing specifications that are not job performance related. They may also be written in a vague, unspecific manner. Finally, they may limit the scope of activities of the job holder in an everchanging environment. All of these limitations may be problematic in terms of the possibility for legal challenge.

Since job analysis serves as the basis for all of the human resource functions, job analysis is faced with several legal constraints. Prior to 1971, job specifications, used as a basis for employee selection decisions, bore little resemblance to the duties actually performed under the job description. The Supreme Court, in Griggs v. Duke Power (1971), forced employers to show that the job specifications used in the selection process specifically relate to the job's duties.

The validity of selection decisions has been successfully challenged in cases where job analyses have not been performed (*Albemarle Paper Company v. Moody (422 U.S. 405)* 1975). The court has ruled that a company,. in order to prevent discrimination, should have written promotion standards (*Rowe v. General Motors (325 U.S. 305)* 1972). In *U.S. v. City of Chicago* [573 F. 2nd 416 (7th Cir.)] (1978), the court ruled that these promotion standards should also describe the position for which the individual is being considered for promotion. In both of these cases, the standards can be determined through the job analysis process (Nobile, 1991).

The passage of the Americans with Disabilities Act (ADA) dramatically increased the legal importance of the objective of job analysis, description, and specification. The ADA mandates that organizations identify the *essential functions* of jobs. According to *Equal Employment for Individuals with Disabilities*, the ADA indicates that:

> essential functions means "the fundamental job duties of the employment position that an individual with the disability holds or desires." The term "essential functions" does not involve the marginal functions of the positions.

After identifying the essential job functions, and employer must be prepared to make reasonable accommodations. Once again, the principle job duties and KSAs must be evaluated. A major result of the passage of ADA is increased emphasis by employers on the development and maintenance of current and accurate job descriptions (Vacarro, 1992).

VI. STRATEGIC ASPECTS OF JOB ANALYSIS

As the external environment and business strategies change in the turbulent health care environment of the late 1990s, so too must human resources practices and job analysis information. A failure of the job analysis information to keep pace with the other environmental and strategic changes will result in poorer individual and organizational performance.

The dynamic nature of today's health care organization brings into question the very logic of job analysis. More specifically, it must be assumed that the job analyzed today will consist of the same set of duties and functions tomorrow. This may not be the case in health care organizations by design or otherwise as the environment forces various types of corporate and job restructuring. Thus, one could be recruiting, selecting, and training based on job requirements that are obsolete. For example, computerization and downsizing may substantially alter the nature of jobs and personal employee characteristics needed to successfully meet the new job requirements.

If health care executives have a clear view of how jobs are going to be restructured in the future, then a *future-oriented* job analysis may be undertaken. This approach requires health care executives to identify future duties and tasks for those jobs that are expected to change. The extent to which skills required of the present duties and tasks overlapped or contributed to the future duties and tasks would be a key judgement are for executives. Those judgements might determine the weights placed on various aspects of present performance and could form the basis for retention decisions in a downsizing situation.

In these times of intense competitive pressure, total quality management, continuous quality improvement, and flexibility, a future-oriented job analysis can offer a solution when organized and anticipated change is going to take place. However, it is unclear what approach should be taken by an organization which desires to be more flexible but cannot plan for or anticipate the exact nature of future changes.

A second approach to the dynamic health care environment under the above conditions is *generic job analysis*. The traditional job analysis approach serves to constrain desired change and flexibility by compartmentalizing and specifically defining presumably static job characteristics. It impedes shifting decision-making downward in the organization, cross-training employees, and getting employees involved in quality improvement efforts (Blayney, 1992). Reducing the number of job titles and developing fewer but more generic job descriptions can provide needed flexibility to manage unanticipated change.

For example, Nissan Motor Company has only one job description for hourly wage production employees. This description is generic and gives the organization the opportunity to use employees as needed. Cross-training and multiple job assignments can occur. The company rejects explicit and specific job descriptions because they are static and prevent innovation and continuous improvement. Another approach to generic job analysis is to focus on understanding the personal characteristics important for performance in an innovative and continuous improvement environment. The focus here is not on specific duties and tasks, but on the personal qualities necessary to function in a continuous improvement culture such as flexibility, innovativeness, and the ability to work as a team member. These personal characteristics should be an important part of the job specification since they are consistently important even through duties and tasks may be in flux.

Both future-oriented and generic job analysis offer promise in terms of managing health care organizations in a dynamic environment. However they also pose certain challenges. First, health care executives may not be able to make accurate judgements about the requirements of future jobs (even when the likely changes are known). Second, how will employees react to generic job descriptions? They may experience role conflict and role ambiguity. Third, future-oriented and generic job analysis may or may not meet the legal requirements for job descriptions and job specifications described earlier in this chapter.

All of the job analysis methods discussed provide viable alternatives for the manager. However, the choice of a particular method is often based on the manager's familiarity with it. Given that job analysis provides managers with clear job descriptions and specifications, it is possible to determine what jobs are the most critical for a particular organizational strategy or objective. For example, if management decides it needs to downsize the organization in order to remain competitive, the information provided by the job analysis should prove invaluable in helping the organization determine which jobs to retain, change, or eliminate. Obviously, those positions which relate to attainment of the strategic objectives are most likely to be retained. Similarly, an organization with a growth strategy can use this information to identify positions which need expansion or development based on their relevance to the areas of growth (Butler, Ferris, and Napier, 1991).

VII. SUMMARY

Job analysis is the collection of information relevant to the preparation of job descriptions and job specifications. An overall written summary of the task requirements for a particular job is called a job description and an overall written summary of the personal requirements an individual must possess in order to successfully perform the job is called a job specification. Job analysis information developed in the form of job descriptions and job specifications provides the basic foundation for all human resources management functions.

Some combinations of available job analysis methods (observation, interviews, questionnaires, and structured analysis) should be used since all have advantages and disadvantages. Key considerations regarding the choice of methods should be the fit between the method and the purpose, cost, practicality, and an overall judgement concerning the appropriateness of the methods for the situation in question. The primary purpose for conducting the job analysis should be clearly specified to ensure all relevant information is collected. In addition, time and cost constraints should be specified before choosing one or more of the available data collection methods.

Health care executives in the human resources area should follow the following steps when conducting a job analysis: (1) determine the purpose; (2) identify jobs to be analyzed; (3) explain the process to employees; (4) collect job analysis information; (5) process the information into job descriptions and job specifications; and (6) review and update frequently.

The particular method of job analysis should be chosen after an analysis of the purpose, types of information required, expected of desired degree of employee involvement, level of detail desired, business strategy of the organization, and the consequent human resource functions to be emphasized. Certain human resource activities (such as recruitment of training) may require different job analysis information than others. Thus the organization might need to use different methods of gathering the information.

Job descriptions and job specifications as derived from job analysis must not only be done, but the process must be valid, accurate, and job related. Otherwise, the health care organization may face legal repercussions, particularly in the areas of employee selection, promotion, and compensation. The *Uniform Guidelines* of 1978 and associated court cases provide guidelines for avoiding charges of discrimination in the development of job analysis data.

Finally, in today's rapidly changing health care environment, health care executives should consider the potential advantages of future oriented job analysis (when change is more predictable) and generic job analysis (when change is less predictable). Both are relatively new concepts which may have legal or practical limitations which need to be considered before they are fully adopted.

REFERENCES

Ash, R. A. and Edgell, S. L. (1975). A note on the readability of the position analysis questionnaire (PAQ). *Journal of Applied Psychology, 60*: 765-66.
Albemarle Paper Company v. Moody. (1975). 422 U.S. 405.
Blayney, K. D. (Ed.). (1992). *Healing hands: Customizing your health team for institutional survival.* W. K. Kellogg Foundation, Battle Creek, MI.
Butler, J. H., Ferris, G. R., and Napier, N. K. (1991). *Strategy and Human Resources Management.* South-western, Cincinnati, OH.
Campion, M. (1989). Ability requirements implications of job design: an interdisciplinary perspective. *Personnel Psychology, 42*, 9.
Conley, P. R. and Sackett, P. R. (1987). The effects of using high- v. low-performing job incumbents as sources of job-analysis information. *Journal of Applied Psychology, 72*: 434-37.
Dictionary of Occupational Titles, 5th edition. (1991) Department of Labor, Washington, D.C.
Equal Employment for Individuals with Disabilities. (1991). *Federal Register, 56* (144): 35735.
Fine, S. A. (1986). Job analysis. In Ronald Berk (Eds.), *Performance Assessment.* Johns Hopkins University Press, Baltimore, MD.
Fottler, M. D. (1994). Job analysis. In Fottler, M. D., Hernandez, S. R., and Joiner, C. L. (Eds.), *Strategic Management of Human Resources in Health Services Organizations,* 2nd edition. Delmar Publishers, Albany, NY: 249-264.
Gatewood, R. D., and Feild, H. S. Jr. (1990). *Human Resource Selection.* Dryden, Chicago.
Grant, P. C. (1988). Why job descriptions don't work. *Personnel Journal, 67*: 53-59.
Griggs, W. S. et al. v. Duke Power Company. (1971). 401 U. S. 424.
Lozada-Larsen, S. R. and Parker, S. B. (1991). The executive checklist (EXCEL): A common-metric questionnaire for analyzing supervisory, managerial, and executive jobs. Presented to the sixth annual conference of the society for industrial and organizational psychology, St. Louis, Missouri, April 1991.
Lundquist, K. K. and Jones, D. P. (1992). Skill-based analysis. *Technical and Skills Training,* February-March: 1-5.

McCormick, E. J. (1972). A study of job characteristics and job dimensions as based on position analysis questionnaires. *Journal of Applied Psychology, 57*: 347-68.

Mullins, W. and Kimbrough, W. (1988). Group composition as a determinant of job analysis outcomes. *Journal of Applied Psychology, 73*: 657-64.

Nobile, R. J. (1991). The law of performance appraisals. *Personnel, 35*: 1.

Prien, E. P. (1977). Development of a clerical position description questionnaire. *Personnel Psychology, 30*: 167-174.

Rowe v. General Motors. (1972). 325 U.S. 305.

Tornow, W. W. and Pinto, P. R. (1976). The development of a managerial job taxonomy: A system for describing, classifying, and evaluating executive positions. *Journal of Applied Psychology, 61*: 410-18.

U.S. v. City of Chicago. (1978). 573 F. 2nd 416 (7th Cir.).

Vacarro, P. (1992). Review job descriptions. *Human Resource Executive*, 20.

52.
DEVELOPING LEARNING ORGANIZATIONS

Lauren Jones, *Organizational Learning Group, Mt. Pleasant, SC*

Imagine this scenario: You have had a wonderfully relaxing weekend with your family, but something has been hanging over your head--something quite similar to the Sword of Damocles (Lee, 1996). This week you begin evaluations of all employees who report to you. You have tried putting off the evaluations, but your VP issued an edict: Effective November 1, 1998, all performance evaluations must be up to date and in the personnel files. Normally you run through the evaluation forms and circle "Satisfactory" on each employee's evaluation. Then, to prove that you know the employee, you illustrate one particular incident that requires improvement. Sound familiar? If so, perhaps the Organizational Learning Group's experience will help you.[1]

I. THE LEARNING CYCLE

Before the Organizational Learning Group begins looking at how to create a constantly improving work environment, we must assess the kind of learning organization that already exists. To make collective assessment, we must know the basis of the continuum--the learning cycle. (See Figure 1.) In most health care organizations, questions are viewed as problems, and there is usually a knee-jerk response to fix problems, thereby obviating two very important parts of this cycle: hypothesis and reflection.

Often in health care we have discouraged any employee from asking questions (Coffey et al., 1993). Questions could mean "Why are you challenging me or my authority?" "If you're asking that, you must not know the answer, and more importantly, why don't you know the answer?" Often the responses to questions also

Figure 1 - The Learning Cycle

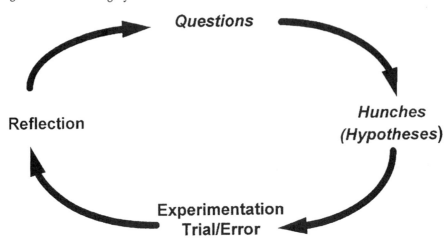

decrease the likelihood of more questioning. "We've always done it that way; we tried that five years ago, and it didn't work." "You're new; you just don't understand our system yet." Perhaps the questioning segment of the circle can best be summarized by Roshi: "In the beginner's mind, there are many possibilities; in the expert's mind, there are few"(Roshi, 1984). How many of us perceive ourselves as experts? How does it affect our problem solving? Often when we think we are experts, our risk taking and openness as well as the multiplicity of solutions are severely limited. If we are in power positions, this thinking severely limits others as well.

The next part of the cycle is hypothesizing. This data-gathering phase responds to the questions generated. In essence, the questions may be "Why? I wonder if this is why?" Data is gathered to either prove or disprove the hypotheses. In many health care organizations, we tend to think we know the answer to a problem (often a question): "It's their department; we have known it for years." We tend to fix blame; not the problem. Recently a registered nurse in a very large health care organization was relating a complaint about the number of late admissions they were getting. Late admissions, particularly mid-afternoon, adversely affect the staffing and shift change. When he was asked the exact number of the late admissions, he responded, "A lot!" It's quite hard to develop a reliable benchmark with those kind of data. Many employees have gotten into this habit of broad, abstract terms because they feel powerless in the system and do not believe they have the ability to change things.

The bottom of the learning cycle reflects the area of trial/error and experimentation. This stage of the process implies multiple solutions, not one. Often a singular solution is implemented and may not work very well. Therefore, we revert to the old way. It's difficult to be immediately successful without properly setting the stage for success. Often implementation questions are ignored: "What would we need to communicate, do, or prepare to make these proposed solutions work?"

The last part of the learning cycle is reflection. Reflection is taking a step out of "business as usual" to evaluate, discuss, refine and expand one's insight--personally and professionally (Argyris, 1991). "Is this working? What am I doing?" Most executives value reflection time. Retreats, meetings off-site, and strategic planning meetings

Figure 2 - Learning Organization Continuum

"ARE WE ALLOWED?"	VERBAL COMMITMENT	MOMENTUM BUILDING	FLUID LEADERS	SYNTHESIS
INFORMATION CONTENT PRINCIPLES PARAMETERS WHY? WHAT'S IN IT FOR ME? WHAT'S EXPECTED? STAYING AT THIS LEVEL RESULTS IN HAMSTRUNG EMPLOYEES WHO ARE AFRAID OF LOSING THEIR JOBS.	EDUCATING OTHERS MANAGERS & EXECS COMMUNICATE EXPECTATIONS SOME RISK-TAKING LITTLE OR NO DISCOMFORT BECAUSE THERE ARE FEW CHALLENGES TO AUTHORITY EXECUTIVES BEGIN VISIONING PROCESS AND DEVELOPMENT OF ORGANIZATIONAL VALUES AND BEHAVIORS THAT EXPRESS VALUES (PERFORMANCE EXPECTATIONS) TEAM FORMATION TEAMS WORKING ON "SAFE" PROJECTS	ACUTELY AWARE OF "FISH BOWL" EXISTENCE STRUGGLING WITH "LETTING GO" AND ROLE MODELING REVERTS TO PREDICTABLE BEHAVIORS IN CRISES ASKING FOR HELP (COACHING) COLLECTIVE INFORMATION BEGINS TO CONSISTENTLY FLOW TOP-DOWN DIFFERENTIATES AMONG COMMAND-CONSULTATIVE-CONSENSUS DECISIONS POINT OF NO RETURN	COACHING VERSUS MANAGING ASKING MORE QUESTIONS THAN GIVING ANSWERS COMFORTABLE WITH MISTAKES (OWN & OTHERS) INFORMATION FLOWS RELATIVELY FREELY TOP-DOWN-TOP LEARNING TOGETHER ORGANIZATIONALLY FOCUSED VERSUS DIVISION/DEPARTMENT FOCUSED BUDGETS ARE BASED ON ORGANIZATIONAL NEEDS AND DATA; ALLOWING NEGOTIATION AMONG PROCESS OWNERS	FORM CHANGES FROM PYRAMIDAL TO MATRIX AND FOLLOWS FUNCTION OPEN HORIZONTAL AND VERTICAL COMMUNICATION LINES CREATION OF A LEARNING ORGANIZATION WHERE EMPLOYEES ARE CONSTANTLY DEVELOPING NEW SERVICES TO MEET CUSTOMER NEEDS IN THIS ORGANIZATION *OR* ARE GROWING TO MAKE THEMSELVES MARKETABLE TO SUBSEQUENT ORGANIZATIONS
QUESTIONS	HYPOTHESES	TRIAL & ERROR	REFLECTION	

are all practiced by this group. However, all employees need reflection time. That does not imply that all employees should be sent to Hawaii to think. However, there should be opportunities within any organization to think about what is being done. In most of our organizations, the doing has been valued, not the thinking. More time spent thinking can positively affect the doing.

We have developed this learning cycle, so useful to many health care organizations, into specific collective behaviors that reflect each phase of the cycle. We call it the Learning Organization Continuum; anyone is able to use this Continuum to determine where an organization falls and perhaps discuss how to move to the next stage. It's important to translate ideas into behaviors (Senge, 1990). As most educators know, learning doesn't occur without a behavioral change. Historically, many leaders in health care organizations have talked about change, but their behaviors have not changed. The avoidance of specifying behaviors has resulted in intellectualizations and ambiguity in performance evaluations.

With the learning cycle as the framework for learning organizations, we can be more specific with regard to individual behaviors. Looking at individual behaviors allows management to determine the types of employees they have and where these employees might be on the learning cycle (see Figure 6). We developed this individual survey because many hierarchical organizations have created vastly different levels of employees. For instance, in health care organizations physicians may need help with reflection while line employees may be afraid to question the system. How often do we hear comments such as the following: "The company owes me." "It's not my job." "Why should I care? Nobody else does." "I'm just here for the paycheck." These familiar comments are those of what Bardwick (1989) refers to as an "entitled employee." Entitled employees are those who begin to take their jobs and performance for granted. They put themselves on automatic pilot, show up physically for work, and just do. Thinking seems to have gone out of their skills repertoire. These are the folks who often say they are not paid to think--that's the job of someone above them in the hierarchy.

How did the hierarchy evolve? Typically, connecting the boxes on an organizational chart produces a structure that may resemble Figure 3. This structure was the result of a functional organization, developed by specific functions--admitting, lab, nursing, pharmacy. The functional orientation worked well until organizations became more complex and customers began to move horizontally rather than vertically through our organizations.

Interestingly, employees were often promoted within their own functional area (silo) because of particular technical skills (Kaeter, 1993). Unfortunately, they were promoted to positions that no longer required those skills. These newly appointed managers, trying to be conscientious, refined and honed their own areas (silos) sometimes to the exclusion of other areas (silos). This self-absorption with their own functional areas often created silos that rarely interacted with each other. Again, not a problem if customers were only impacted by one silo, but the complexity of today's organizations emphasizes collaboration and the resultant horizontal communication.

This same hierarchy promoted competition among silos. However, some silos reacted to the competitive drive by turning inward, becoming more isolated and keeping a low profile. That low profile often resulted in little risk taking and an emphasis on status quo. Most leaders will readily identify that not taking risks to stay competitive produces mediocrity--mediocrity that encourages and abets entitled employees.

Let's illustrate the development of entitled employees by using a specific example. A new, eager employee bounces onto the work scene excited and full of questions and ideas. He/she is clearly giving the job 100%. After a year or so (sometimes less), this employee looks around and sees longer term employees getting by on 70% effort. When he questions these employees, he often hears, "You'll never change anything

Figure 3 - Traditional Organizational Structure

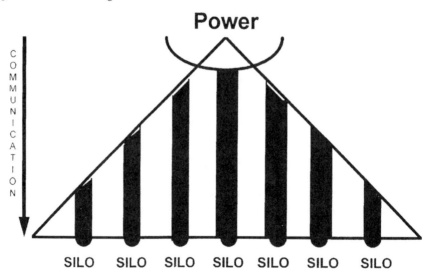

here; it's been this way forever"; "We've always done it this way"; "So and so wants it this way."   He also observes these same employees are not being disciplined or challenged to improve. More likely than not, they continue to get their raises just like he does. It doesn't take long for this employee to figure out that getting by is O.K., so he begins functioning at 70%. Voilà, we have another entitled employee on our hands with the consequences compounded daily as the cost of poor quality.

For our purposes in this chapter, we are going to divide entitled employees into two categories: the cocooned (isolated) employee and the skeptical (chrysalis) employee. The cocooned employee is one who shows up year after year, performing minimally and eschewing new ideas or change. These employees have seen it all and heard it all. They are also eager to share with new employees not only their observations, but their strategies for "beating the system."

Very often in describing the isolated employee, managers might say, "He's very skilled, but has a lousy attitude," or "She does her job well, but when she's in a bad mood, look out." Isolated employees don't expect change--neither in their outlook nor in the work environment. These are folks who've been taught that work is indeed a four-letter word and should be endured not enjoyed. The cocooned employee is sometimes the long-term employee who says, "You never wanted my opinion before, why now?" "I'm not paid to think; that's why managers get paid the big bucks."

The second type of entitled employee is the chrysalis or skeptical employee. These employees stand on the sidelines wondering whether to get involved in any organizational change. They are not big risk takers; rather they are individuals who have learned that it is best to keep a low profile. Yet when presented with clear-cut expectations and some help in achieving the expectations, they will quickly come on board and become involved in the work process. The chrysalis often wonders whether to get involved and may even ask, "What's in it for me?" These skeptical employees move between being accepted by the cocoons on the one hand and by those promoting organizational change and employee involvement on the other.

Before we discuss the causes of entitled employees and the strategies to decrease the number of entitled employees in an organization, we need to explore the environment that grows entitled employees. Besides the pyramidal hierarchy described earlier, a number of other situations create entitled employees and impending death for an organization:

- Tenured employees who are not challenged to expand their skills;
- Unclear expectations;
- Lack of organizational vision;
- Few rewards/recognition for improving performance;
- Inordinate numbers of policies and procedures;
- Controlling middle managers;
- No coaching for improvement; and
- Few consequences for mediocre or substandard performance.

II. TENURED EMPLOYEES

Some employees assume they are not expected to grow with an organization once they are hired. They've tapped out at a certain level and don't expect to exceed that level. Often, when presented with a challenge and some help in meeting the challenge, these employees can flourish and become a tremendous role model for their peers. Today's leader must ask, "What will get an employee's attention?" This question is especially relevant for the entitled employees who are quite used to business as usual since they are comfortable with performing at a level that goes unchallenged. Bardwick, despite Total Quality Management expert's advice to drive out fear in an organization, contends that a little fear is necessary to jar entitled employees out of their stupor. Her idea of fear is to communicate the organization's expectations clearly and to have explicit consequences for not meeting the expectations.

Unfortunately, some managers have promoted entitlement by giving high ratings in performance evaluations. Employees then begin to expect outstanding ratings for standard performance.

III. UNCLEAR EXPECTATIONS

Have leaders clearly stated their expectations to employees? Recently, an employee was told that his negative attitude was not conducive to a learning organization. The incredulous employee, who had been with the organization for 20 years, remarked, "I didn't think that my attitude bothered anyone. No one else complained!" To carry this example further, all this employee's previous managers knew he had a negative attitude, but noted that he performed his job O.K.

If employees are negative, can they really perform their jobs O.K.? Most leaders agree that how we perform our job is as important as what job we are performing. But Kelley and Caplan (1993) question whether employees are aware of these performance expectations.

IV. LACK OF ORGANIZATIONAL VISION

Do employees know the big picture of the organization? Are they aware of the direction the organization is taking? The vision can challenge all employees to stretch their imaginations. As the Cheshire cat observed, "If you don't know where you're going, any road will take you there."

It's not enough to have a vision. It takes developing an organizational theme to ensure consistent behaviors. What values or guiding principles will move the organization toward the vision? And to ensure integration, what behaviors would express the organizational values? The behaviors become the performance expectations that leaders can use to coach for improvement and growth.

V. FEW REWARDS / RECOGNITION FOR IMPROVING PERFORMANCE

Some leaders say, "Of course, you're doing a good job; if you weren't, I'd tell you," or "You get paid, don't you?" These leaders need to take a look at their systems for rewards and recognition as well as their attitude toward these systems (Carr, 1993). When asked, most employees initially comment that they don't need recognition for their work. Usually, once the stoicism fades, people admit that it would be nice to hear they're doing a good job. Most of us want to be appreciated in a visible way--not always monetarily--for organizational contributions. Verbal recognition has been rated very highly among employees as meaningful feedback. Unfortunately, leaders must value recognition and be willing to take the time to give appropriate feedback. Recent research indicates that performance evaluations are expensive. The Educational Testing Service in Princeton, NJ, estimated that approximately $1,500 per employee is spent conducting yearly performance evaluations (Editorial Contributors, 1996).

VI. NUMBERS OF POLICIES AND PROCEDURES

Has the organization developed a plethora of policies and procedures? Does this practice give the message that employees are not expected to think--just do? Policies and procedures are often developed for all employees when individual coaching would be appropriate. An example is the chronically late employee who dresses inappropriately for work. The consequence is the issuance of a blanket statement that insults 99% of the remaining employees, who were responsible enough to dress professionally and arrive on time.

The development of standardized processes does accomplish consistency, and it decreases the common causes of variation in a process. A true learning organization is composed of involved, un-entitled employees, and it looks towards employees when developing these standardized processes. Again the development of an organizational theme provides the broad parameters of where we are going and how we want to get there; thus, we ensure behavioral consistency among employees.

VII. CONTROLLING MIDDLE MANAGERS

In many organizations we take very bright employees who are technically competent and promote them to a position where those competencies are no longer needed. Most of these employees are excited about the promotion and take their new assignment very seriously--sometimes, to the exclusion of other middle managers (McVey, 1993).

Organizations frequently neglect to educate middle managers about their new roles; consequently, they become either controlling managers who believe they are solely responsible for thinking or laissez-faire managers who provide neither direction nor support. Couple this educational neglect with the lack of peer support, and managers often become protective of their silos and demand compliance from their employees. Most leaders will quickly admit that hierarchy is no longer a measure of who's important in an organization.

Often, peer and subordinate evaluations as well as heightened horizontal communication will provide insight into a manager's style and perhaps an opportunity to change behavior as will be described later. A well-defined organizational theme will also provide explicit behaviors (performance expectations) that express the organization's values in service to its vision.

VIII. NO COACHING FOR IMPROVEMENT

For our purposes, a coach, according to Jones (1990), is a person who cares about our dignity as a human being and our growth as a spiritual being. This person is usually a leader who strives to create a learning atmosphere which cultivates professional and personal growth. The shift from manager to leader is intended to differentiate between people who manage things and people who manage people.

Often, new coaches are overwhelmed as they become involved in the role change from manager to coach. Issues that were easily resolved through command decisions now are communicated to employees for consultation or consensus. The emphasis in today's workplace is on buy in and ownership, not compliance and reaction. Entitled employees may not be aware of the coaching role and, consequently, do not avail themselves of coaching skills.

The coach puts the burden of accountability and job performance squarely on the employee. The organizational theme (mission-vision-values-behavior) clearly spells out performance expectations so that employees must tell the coach what kind of help they need in meeting those expectations.

IX. FEW CONSEQUENCES FOR MEDIOCRE OR SUBSTANDARD PERFORMANCE

What happens in an organization when performance is mediocre or even substandard? Do the performers become invisible, no longer invited to key meetings? Do performers stay in their position, deemed unpromotable? The dearth of skilled human resources precludes keeping these people in the organization. It's important for the coach to determine whether the expectations were unclear, whether help for successfully meeting these expectations was unavailable, or whether employees are of the entitled, cocoon variety.

The first two reasons for low performance are easily remedied. The last may be a bit more elusive and time-consuming. Four important steps in first dealing with a cocooned employee are

• Determining whether they want to change;
• Finding out whether they understand the expectations;
• Asking whether they understand what is necessary to meet those expectations; and
• Helping them to change behavior to meet the expectations.

If there is no change in the cocooned employee, it's obvious that the job is not a fit, so moving the employee out of the department or organization will be necessary (Hart,

Figure 4 - Sample from Organizational Learning Group Survey

LEADERSHIP SKILLS ASSESSMENT

Participant Survey

Please complete the following survey as thoroughly as possible. Your responses will remain confidential. Thank you for your cooperation.

Position:_____

Please describe the specific skills you think you need to perform the above position and how you think they should be measured:

_____

The skills you think you have to perform the position and specific examples that illustrate these skills:

_____

The skills you think you should improve upon to perform the position:

_____

1995). Interestingly, most employees know who isn't pulling their weight and are usually not surprised when a cocooned employees are terminated. Sometimes the termination may even improve morale. As one employee related, "We were pleased to see something done about Joan. We didn't think management knew she hadn't been doing her job well for years."

When we have large numbers of cocooned employees, the above steps may need to be preceded by an organizational crisis. For example, leaders who present the financial picture along with data from competitors and future projections may create the urgency needed to change cocooned employees into skeptical or involved employees.

The bottom line on truly cocooned employees is not to invest a lot of time and effort in a hopeless case if that's the conclusion drawn after following the above steps. The wondering or skeptical employee could thrive on that effort and the already involved employees will continue to grow. The attention and spotlight needs to be on those who are meeting (skeptical employees) or exceeding (involved employees) performance expectations.

Since all employees will change their performances over time and may not be predictable, their leader must learn to coach and value coaching. (This is Number Seven of Deming's 14 Points (Rakich et al., 1992).) The latest term for this type of leadership is fluid leadership, and the implication is that leaders should have more questions than answers. Employees know their jobs, and the leader's job is to remove barriers to job performance.

But what kind of evaluations and coaching skills will help them accomplish this? Traditionally, in most organizations performance evaluations have been historical; in other words, they were based on last year's performance. Historical evaluations force leaders to watch for specific incidents. They do not encourage a long-term plan or employee involvement for determining next year's goals. Many of us have developed checklists that attempt to list all skills necessary for performing a particular job. Unfortunately, we are assuming that all employees are exactly alike and have the same skills. The Organizational Learning Group developed a performance evaluation that is based on defining the skills necessary for a particular job and, from several sources, determining which skills are strong and which skills need improvement. This tool is given to peers, subordinates (if appropriate), and people to whom the person being evaluated reports. Not surprising is a great deal of consensus among all groups in the areas of identifying the skills and the strengths, which provides positive reinforcement for these skills. The biggest discrepancy lay in the person being evaluated amplifying his or her weaknesses. This tool also has the advantage of providing guidelines for ongoing learning from collective as well as individual perspectives which provides continuing reinforcement.

Needless to say, it is more important to dynamic, fluid organizations that performance expectations be clearly described with individuals determining their professional goals within these guidelines. Helping employees achieve those goals requires something that has not been very valued in most health care organizations: coaching. Many leaders in health care organizations were promoted because they exhibited excellent clinical or technical skills. We took these folks and said, "Great job. Now we're going to put you in a management position where you'll never have to use those skills again!"

Few health care organizations are helping leaders grow. Perhaps as we discussed in the questioning phase of the learning cycle, we assume that we are all experts. But experts have few possibilities. They are finished products who don't need to learn and grow continuously.

How do leaders in health care organizations learn to be leaders? Typically, they learn through on-the-job training (Georges, 1996). They emulate behaviors they think should be leadership behaviors. Some practice a domineering, in-control philosophy emphasizing that leaders should have all the answers. Many of us have worked under leaders like that, and we assumed those were acceptable leadership behaviors.

Then how do we learn to coach? How do we learn to help our employees grow personally and professionally? Coaching of this type is a learnable skill. However, like the organizational theme of mission-vision-values-behaviors, we have to value the time it takes to elicit input and buy in and the time to make sure the process is ongoing.

Extremely effective leaders usually get where they are by being efficient, controlling, and dependable. We have been very content-oriented in health care, and it's difficult to start valuing things and changing behaviors that are more process-oriented (Geber, 1992). Coaching, like effective meetings, requires time. Getting to know all employees as individuals and understanding their learning needs require time. Helping them meet those needs also requires time. However, too much time is now wasted in doing other people's jobs for them, in hiring additional people because work is not getting completed, and in running interference with MDs because employees who aren't being treated with respect don't know how to respond.

Coaching is a process-focused skill and should be valued throughout the organization (Waldroop and Butler, 1996). (Again, we have historically valued the doing, not the thinking.) For example, one leader's doing might be to issue a definitive policy about arriving on time with severe consequences to lateness outlined. This type of policy development is easier than talking one-to-one with the employee who is con-

Figure 5 - Coaching

A Coach is someone who cares about your dignity as a human being and your growth as a spiritual being

COACHING SKILLS:

- Take what you do, not yourself, seriously.
- Active listening.
- Willingness to "unlearn."
- Willingness to confront with dignity.
- Valuing the time to coach.
- Being clear about "who owns the problem."
- Create the environment for self-evaluation.
- Willingness to support the employee's proposed solution or goals.
- Willingness to set follow-up date(s).

stantly late, but it would insult the other employees who are always on time. Confrontation is usually not a comfortable skill for health care employees (Schaef and Fassel, 1988). Because we don't confront well, passive-aggressive behavior has become paramount. As a result, we issue unit-, department- or organization-wide statements, and we confide in others how frustrated we are or we take our frustrations out on the family.

The coaching skill is learned through certain steps (See Figure 5). Each step in the process deserves careful consideration.

X. VALUING THE TIME TO COACH

Coaching requires a time commitment. The time is not cumulative; it's a process that may mean not spending any time with a particular employee daily, but still knowing that employee's goals and working with him/her over an extended period of time. Giving ongoing feedback is also a time-consuming, yet valued effort.

XI. WILLINGNESS TO CONFRONT WITH DIGNITY

Confronting is usually not comfortable. It is a skill not often practiced in health care organizations and therefore not often valued. Because so few health care employees are used to such confrontation, when it does happen, their response is negative. Again, the passive-aggressive behavior common to health care workers at all levels leads employees to resent any feedback and to wait until things build up and dump on employees. The latter is known as "gunny-sacking." Gunny-sacking is a technique that results in letting issues build without confronting. In essence, issues then become "the straw that breaks the camel's back."

Historically, evaluations have been conducted yearly, and they focus on general satisfactory feedback. When employees are doing OK, they begin to expect a satisfactory evaluation without feedback for improvement. Often, a great deal of resentment builds. Evaluations could become growth opportunities. This attitude assumes that we are all works in progress, capable of improving continuously. But most employees expect the usual satisfactory rating unless the leader is clear about the evaluation process and its purpose.

XII. CREATE THE ENVIRONMENT FOR SELF-EVALUATION

What is valued in an organization? If questions are not expected and valued, how can an environment that encourages open feedback be developed? Are all employees expected to be finished products when they arrive? Are they encouraged to develop their own behavioral contracts that they share with their peers and leader?

Unfortunately, most leaders will say that is the work environment they support, but their behaviors may indicate something very different. An old cartoon shows two dogs walking together. One dog says to the other, "You know, it's always 'sit, stay and heel,' never, 'think, innovate, and be yourself.'" What messages do we give about self-evaluation and professional growth? Often our lips say one thing, but our behaviors say something very different. Do leaders discuss their own behavioral contracts and ask for feedback on progress? Do people quickly become offended and defensive when feedback is given? What kind of learning environment has been developed? Are mistakes welcome? Or are mistakes documented and saved for the annual evaluation? Encouraging employees to learn and take risks puts much accountability on them.

A. Being Clear About Who Owns the Problem

Leaders often assume accountability for their employees; therefore, an important coaching skill is being clear about who owns the problem. Consider this scenario: an employee repeatedly arrives late to work. Other employees are aware of this tardiness, but no one has confronted the employee directly. Instead, concerned employees complain to management. Because many leaders are uncomfortable with confronting, elaborate policies and procedures are developed declaring that all employees must arrive at work on time. Usually that pronouncement works. If it doesn't, employees receive a negative yearly evaluation (after the fact). No one seems to notice that the pronouncement offends all the employees who show up on time!

So what happens if a manager assumes a leadership position and decides to talk with this employee? Let's say that the leader values time spent coaching and sets up a meeting to talk within an environment promoting self-evaluation. This leader is comfortable confronting with dignity. The employee begins by explaining that his car needs repair, and the following dialogue takes place:

Leader: "If it's just a repair day, why don't you take the bus?"
Employee: "It doesn't stop by my house."
Leader: "Well, couldn't you get a ride from someone you work with?"
Employee: "No one in my neighborhood works days."
Leader: "Well, I could probably pick you up so that you can drop your car off for repairs."
Employee: "I have to drop off my daughter at the Day Care Center."

Clearly, in the process of this conversation the coach is working harder than the employee. The tables need to be turned. To do so, the coach might say, "You know that the policy is to be here on time. What are you going to do to make that happen, and what can I do to help?" The coach is being supportive, but the employee owns the problem.

B. Willingness to Unlearn

Most of us are somewhat comfortable with the behaviors that have moved us forward (or upward) in organizations. We are also quite willing and able to learn new information. However, getting rid of old information and behaviors is difficult since learning or unlearning requires a behavioral change. Let's compare unlearning to writing with our nondominant hand: We have to think consciously about it, it takes longer, and we may have to explain it to communicate effectively. Unlearning requires risk taking and replacing old behaviors with new ones. On an intellectual level, this process may be pretty easy. However, on bad days, days out of our control, we tend to revert to old behaviors in a crisis (See Phase 3 on the Learning Organization Continuum, Figure 2). Leaders need to have coaches with whom to share a behavioral contract so that their behavior can be interrupted if necessary. If this is not possible, keeping a journal will often force the reflective part of the learning cycle described at the beginning of this chapter. Most executives don't take the time to process their day, week, month or year, and the reflection gets subverted. We will talk more about processing when we discuss specific performance evaluations.

C. Active Listening

Active listening is a skill that most executives have heard in Psych. 101 or in an MBA Program: really listening and feeding back what we hear so that we truly understand the communication received. This coaching skill requires time, but not as much as one thinks. Most employees in health care service organizations adopt a shorthand to communicate. Our language is based on abbreviations; departments and/or units develop their own language that prevents open communication and understanding with outsiders. For example, we recently had a nurse who was working in the emergency department on the weekend. A patient asked him a question he was unable to answer. The employee called the administrator-on-call and asked if the hospital was a PPO. He knew what NPO was, but he had no idea that PPO stood for a Preferred Provider Organization. We might find this amusing, but many of us assume we know what someone is trying to communicate so we finish their sentences for them or make a decision based on our assumption of what they needed. The behaviors just described take much more time to undo than spending one or two minutes allowing someone to finish a thought and then giving feedback to see if we understand. An old adage explains that we were all given two ears and one mouth so that we could listen twice as much as we talk!

D. Willingness to Support the Employee's Proposed Solutions or Goals

When we do talk, how can we support the employee? As leaders, are we truly supportive of that chronically late employee who decided that to make it to work on time, she will need to buy a new Mercedes? Is that a workable solution? Will we support the singular solution even if we don't believe it will work? Often, employees arrive at only one solution. The leader, as a coach, should force the employee to have other options and to conduct a fault analysis prior to implementation of the solutions. This analysis allows employees to shoot holes through their own solutions and to anticipate why these solutions may not be effective. Getting employees to do this kind of problem solving requires more than one meeting.

E. Willingness to Set Follow-up Date(s)

Because we are all so tremendously time limited and busy in health care, it is easy to meet with employees, assume things are resolved, and let them go on their way. Ongoing coaching requires regular meeting dates that may start weekly but are then moved to bi-monthly or monthly. Behavioral changes do not occur after one conversation, nor do they occur overnight. Coaches who realize that immediate change is impossible will coach employees regularly so that change can occur incrementally. Many coaches make appointments with employees, and those appointments become carved in stone; they are immutable because both the coach and employee value the coaching process.

F. Take What You Do, Not Yourself, Seriously

Since competitive, hard-driving professionals are in a leadership position, they often take themselves seriously. Unfortunately, they may have taken themselves seriously to the exclusion of others. If they don't feel totally responsible for their department/division/unit, they probably don't value employee involvement, risk taking (sometimes mistakes), and open communication. The role model they provide to employees' peers sets the stage for coaching to occur. If Dr. Jones insists on being called Dr. Jones and everyone else is known by first name, a barrier to communication and to coaching has been constructed. Taking oneself too seriously stifles creativity and does not allow the learning process to unfold. In the words of Charles DuBois: "The most important part is this: to sacrifice who you are for what you might become."

G. Coaching Summary

Coaching is to help employees improve. There are times, however, when coaching occurs to remove an employee. Measurable expectations have been established with the employee and with the understanding that the coach will help. We all know, though, that sometimes employees make decisions that indicate they choose not to be successful in that position or in that organization.

The role of the coach in performance evaluations has been explored; they are the ones who facilitate the accomplishment of the performance expectations of their employees. Not all managers or leaders know how to coach. Teaching that skill may require many sessions since managers have been used to controlling things and people (Geber, 1992).

XIII. TYPES OF PERFORMANCE EVALUATIONS

Does continued performance rely on evaluations that are historic or futuristic? Historic evaluations focus on what has already happened; things that might be too late to change or that employees have forgotten; therefore, the learning opportunity has passed. Employees may not value the same performance skills mandated by their supervisor. Most leaders would agree that people who are actually doing a job are the best judges of the skills necessary to perform that job successfully and to provide concrete feedback on the performance itself.

Despite that logic, most organizations have yearly performance evaluations based on historic data and occasional observations. The validity and reliability of these evaluations are doubtful. The late Dr. W. Edwards Deming, on numerous occasions, eschewed the traditional evaluation. He maintained that it did not positively affect performance or promote creativity--it merely added to the fear that exists in most organizations. Interestingly, his assertions were made prior to the massive downsizings now occurring in health care and other industries. Truly helpful evaluations would provide coaching opportunities for employees either to improve their performance or remove themselves from the organization.

If employees are to feel in control of their jobs, we must first have them define those jobs and establish the skills they need to perform. Not all employees, however, value the autonomy necessary to define their positions. When completing my dissertation in 1983, I used autonomy as an attribute of professionalism (Jones, 1983). Interestingly enough, of the 181 respondents to the questionnaire, roughly 50% believed in autonomy and 50% did not! These respondents were from all levels of health care, not just the staff level. This phenomenon has continued to be in evidence in subsequent health care organizations since that time. That's the reason not all employees value autonomy and embrace empowerment (Bell, 1991). Many employees quite enjoy having others above them on the organizational ladder make decisions. It removes their responsibilities but, unfortunately, not the "Monday-morning Quarterbacking" that still occurs.

Leaders/coaches can easily determine how employees view autonomy by asking them to define their jobs in measurable terms. The sighing, ceiling-focused employees typically will be very uncomfortable and will often either sabotage this process or try to convince the leader/coach that it simply will not work. For example, one employee told his leader/coach that he would rather have her do his evaluation: "I may not like it, but I can do something about it during appeal, and I don't have to think about what I did last year." This attitude may sound like it makes for an easy process, but woe to the leader/coach who does not continue to circle "satisfactory" or "above average."

Although recent research indicates that ongoing feedback to tenured nursing faculty (Suess, 1995) improves performance, many leaders/coaches would rather evaluate employees historically because the process is familiar and predictable. Again, we have a procedure that results in doing, not thinking. It really depends on how leaders/coaches view control empowerment and their employees. Another recent study could provide the basis for ongoing coaching research. The authors were investigating the effects of integrating tactics on improved performance (Gordon, 1996). Integrating tactics include enhancement of others: making people feel they are important. Interestingly, a recent publication describes significance as an essential gift of leaders in sharing spirit. Significance is making employees feel an integral part of an organizational community. Several years ago one CEO remarked when employee involvement in performance evaluations was recommended, "Are you suggesting the inmates run the asylum?" The incident is a prime example that not everyone thinks of empowerment (employee involvement) as the panacea to all organizational ills!

Leaders/coaches should evaluate tools they use to evaluate employee performance. Do these tools measure what they are supposed to measure? Again, employees who perform a particular job are in the best position to define the job and the skills necessary to perform the job (Yukl and Lepsinger, 1995). Even if the leaders themselves are satisfied with their current performance evaluation tools, they should ask whether employees agree. Do their peers have an opportunity to provide feedback performance? In the 360 evaluation tool previously mentioned (Figure 4), the leaders/coaches were asked to define the skills necessary for their position, the skills they believe they have, and the skills they believe they need to develop. These forms were given to employees who reported to the leader/coach and to the leader's peers and supervisors (Harris, 1992). This form was developed in 1987, and it has proven its reliability many times--particularly in the areas of educational needs. The person being evaluated consistently lists more needs than strengths. However, the other respondents consistently identify more leadership skills than the leader being evaluated. This form not only provides the basis for solid coaching sessions that highlight the extant skills, but also provides the basis for development of a measurable behavioral contract. From a more global perspective, this form provides educational needs that may affect many leaders.

Whatever the forms, standardized or other, that an organization uses for evaluations, each employee, not just leaders, should develop their own behavioral contracts--contracts that can be measured throughout the year (Parry, 1996). Again, such evaluation provides a basis for ongoing coaching and expansion of skills. Many employees (at all levels within the organization) can select internal coaches to assist with their behavioral contracts. It's helpful to have regular appointments with one's coach to discuss strategies and progress. For many employees, it is less stressful initially to select a coach of a non-reporting nature. These coaches are usually unbiased and can provide specific behavioral examples if they interact with the employee regularly.

For example, one employee recently identified his inability to speak openly in meetings and to become involved in decision-making opportunities. This particular employee chose a coach who was a peer. The peer was not a friend, but an employee who was exhibiting skills identified by the employee. They worked out strategies and interventions that the coach could provide during specific meetings. Strategies included asking the employee questions during the meeting and providing specific feedback after the meeting.

Many readers would argue that the form attached (see Figure 4) only emphasizes leadership skills. Leadership, however, occurs from the consumer's bedside to the boardroom: it's merely a matter of span of control. Therefore, these coaching sessions and behavioral contracts are not limited to the official leadership group (Haskell, 1993). The contracts also provide incremental growth in acquiring and refining leadership skills.

The use of standardized forms does not preclude the addition of behavioral contracts to the employee's evaluation dossier. Often, this provides a tailored plan for

Figure 6 - Sampling of an Organizational Survey (Written by Organizational Learning Group)

The purpose of this brief survey is to determine where you are on the Learning Organization Continuum in relationship to your colleagues. The collated responses will help you plan educational strategies to advance the collective learning within your organization.

Please indicate the level of your duties within your organization
_____ Sr. Management
_____ Middle Mgmt
_____ Physician
_____ Frontline

Please respond to the following questions using the scale below:

SD (Strongly Disagree) - An experience that rarely or never occurs
D   (Disagree) - An experience that occurs less than 50% of the time
N   (No Response) - You have no response to the question
A   (Agree) - An experience that occurs at least 50% of the time
SA (Strongly Agree) - An experience that occurs more than 50% of the time

STAGES OF ORGANIZATIONAL LEARNING
1. Questions in my organization mean:

	you're attacking your immediate supervisor	SD	D	N	A	SA
2	you are "rocking the boat"	SD	D	N	A	SA
3	you should know the answer	SD	D	N	A	SA

REFLECTION

10	we value "doing" in our organization, not "thinking"	SD	D	N	A	SA
11	we value "thinking" in our organization, not "doing"	SD	D	N	A	SA
12	we are supposed to solve problems but have no time	SD	D	N	A	SA

TRIAL/ERROR-EXPERIMENTATION

30	we are encouraged to come up with several solutions to an identified problem	SD	D	N	A	SA
31	in our organization, it's either this one new way or back to the old way	SD	D	N	A	SA
32	our team gets frustrated when our solution is not implemented	SD	D	N	A	SA

HYPOTHESES

44	we are encouraged to think about hunches	SD	D	N	A	SA
45	when a question arises we are encouraged to think about "why"	SD	D	N	A	SA
46	when a question arises we are expected to "fix it"--fast	SD	D	N	A	SA

professional growth which can be used as the basis for ongoing coaching sessions.

The final point to make about the suggested behavioral contracts or any performance evaluation forms already in use is that they should be consulted regularly, not the usual yearly evaluation time frame. We all need ongoing feedback and coaching; yearly is not the answer. Imagine communicating with your children yearly and expecting them to let that be the interaction that would allow them to grow as human beings. Impossible....

ENDNOTE

[1]   Organizational Learning Group, founded in 1992 by Lauren and Allen Jones, helps health care organizations create learning organizations. A learning organization, as discussed in this chapter, is one in which employees at all levels continue to grow and learn. Select consultants from across the United States work with particular organizations to help executives identify where their organization is on the Learning Organization Continuum and develop strategies to advance the organization along the continuum.

REFERENCES

Argyris, C. (1991). Teaching Smart People How to Learn. *Harvard Business Review, May-June*: 99-109.

Bolman, L. G., and Deal, T. E. (1995). *Leading With Soul*, Jossey-Bass, Inc., San Francisco, CA.

Carr, C. (1993). The Ingredients of Good Performance. *Training, August*: 51-54.

Coffey, R. Jones, L., Kowalkowski, A., and Browne, J. (1993). Asking Effective Questions: An Important Leadership Role to Support Quality Improvement. *Journal on Quality Improvement, Oct*: 454-464.

Editorial Contributors: Filipczak, B., Hequet, M., Lee, C., Picard, M., and Stamps, D. (1996). What Do You Do With An Egg-Sucking Dog? *Training, October*: 17-20.

Geber, B., (1992). From Manager Into Coach. *Training, February*: 25-31.

Georges, J. C. (1996). The Myth of Soft-Skills Training. *Training, January*: 48-54.

Gordon, R. A. (1996). Impact of Ingratiation on Judgments and Evaluations: A Meta-Analytic Investigation. *Journal of Personality and Social Psychology, July*: 54-70.

Harris, C. (1992). Work Redesign Calls for New Pay and Performance Plans. *Hospitals, October 5*: 56-60.

Hart, C. W. L. (1995). The Power of Internal Guarantees. *Harvard Business Review, January-February*: 64-73.

Haskell, J. R. (1993). Getting Employees to Take Charge of Their Careers. *Training and Development, February*: 51-54.

Jones, L. (1983). *Unpublished Dissertation*.

Kaeter, M. (1993). The Age of the Specialized Generalist. *Training, December*: 48-53.

Kelley, R., and Caplan, J. (1993). How Bell Labs Creates Star Performers. *Harvard Business Review, July-August*: 128-139.

Lee, C. (1996). Performance Appraisal - Can We 'Manage' Away The Curse? *Training, May*: 44-59.

McVey, C., Moore, L. E. (1993). Managing Mediocrity. *Nursing Management, June*.

Parry, S. B. (1996). The Quest for Competencies. *Training, July*: 48-56.

Rakich, J., Longest, B., and Darr, K. (1992). *Managing Health Services Organizations* (3rd ed.). Binghamton, New York: Maple Press.

Schaef, A. W., Fassel D. (1988). *The Addictive Organization,* Harper Collins, NY.

Senge, P. M. (1990). The Leader's New Work: Building Learning Organizations. *Sloan Management Review, Fall*: 7-23.

Suess, L. R. (1995). Attitudes of Nurse-Faculty Toward Post-Tenure Performance Evaluations. *Journal of Nursing Education, January*: 25-30.

Waldroop, J., Butler, T. (1996). The Executive as Coach. *Harvard Business Review, November-December*: 111-118.

Yukl, G., and Lepsinger, R. (1995). How to Get the Most Out of 360º Feedback. *Training, December*: 45-50.

53.
RECRUITMENT AND INTERVIEWING

J. Larry Tyler, *Tyler and Company, Atlanta, GA*

As an executive recruiter, I have learned that one of the most important things that a successful Healthcare Executive can do is to recruit good people to join his/her team. Regardless of all of the discussion about financial capital and physical assets, the main difference between outstanding organizations and those that merely get by is the caliber of the people working for the organization. Good people can make the difference in almost any environment. Therefore, one of the highest priorities for the organization has to be the recruitment of new employees.

I. READY ! FIRE ! AIM !

One of the most vexing problems in recruitment is the tendency of individuals to run ahead of themselves when recruiting new employees. When the new position is being contemplated, there is a tendency to hurriedly create a position, and immediately start recruiting new candidates. Only later, after having recognized that the organization does not have its act together, are the results of this manifested through delays in the hiring process.

It is very important the recruitment process have a definite beginning and a definite end. Once an existing position becomes vacant, the first thing that should be done is preparation of the job description. This is often done in conjunction with the staff of individuals in the Human Resources Department, who will meet with the line department in order to interview key people and help draft a job description. Although the Human Resources Department may assist in preparing the job description, the responsibility really is that of the hiring department. The job responsibilities of any given position are ever changing. It is quite possible that the job description for the position has not been updated in a number of years, and the significant parts of the job description have changed. An old job description could be the starting point for trying to develop a new one.

II. THE JOB DESCRIPTION

In general, job descriptions should have no more than twenty description statements, which reflect the responsibility and duties. Special care must be taken to make sure that the words used properly reflect the way the job is actually handled. For example, the phrase "assist with" might be substituted in cases where a position previously was "solely responsible for" an activity. Caution must be maintained to ensure that the job description encompasses all aspects of the position and also adequately describes the depth and breadth of the job. One should also attach an organizational chart so there is an visual understanding of the number of reporting relationships throughout the organization and how this position fits within the organization as a whole.

One of the challenges of preparing job descriptions in the new healthcare environment is that numerous relationships are matrixed, or are hard to explain by the historical means employed in job descriptions. We all are familiar with concepts of "straight-line" and "dotted-line" relationships. As I work with client organizations, I'm also now encountering both multiple dotted-line and straight-line relationships. As the health care field evolves from "command and control" structures, organizational charts have begun to look more dynamic, unusual and strange. Organizations now depict their structures as circles, semi-circles, and inverted pyramids. With the advent of three dimensional graphics software, it won't be long before we see three-dimensional organizational charts, which will probably look something like the structure of the atom. At any rate, an organizational chart communicates a tremendous amount of information to everyone dealing with the position, including the supervisor, peers, subordinates, and potential candidates. At the same time the job description is being put together, some attention must be placed on the preparation of goals to be achieved in the first 90 days, 180 days, and the first year of the position. Goals are important because they allow the candidate and the organization to understand priorities of the various accomplishments expected in the position. The establishment of goals tends to focus the new employee in the right direction, rather than waiting on the employee to discern direction through the actions of individuals around him/her or direct input from the boss. Once the list of goals are established, then they can be communicated to potential candidates.

In general, internal candidates should be identified first since their promotion is looked upon favorably by almost everyone. It says to the organization "Hey--this is a great place to work because here you can develop your career. You can move up in the organization, gain new responsibilities and earn additional compensation here." The downside of promoting from within is that if positions are always filled from within, you may limit the diversity of opinions and ideas that are generated. There could also be the possibility that promotion from within becomes so common and expected that people who are incompetent and unable to get jobs in other organizations are promoted into higher and higher positions. Dilbert, the cartoon character, says that people who are incompetent, hazardous, or unworthy of the position are moved into the level where they can not bother the organization; this level is called "management."

III. POSTING OF POSITIONS

Generally organizations post new positions, a formal process to inform member organization that a position is available. Public institutions are often required by law to make the posting public for a certain number of days and to interview all candidates that apply for the position regardless of their qualifications. One of the first decisions one has to make with regard to selecting internal candidates is whether the position is going to be kept open to internal candidates or if the organization will seek outside candidates. To my knowledge there are no rules of thumb as to how often one should interview external candidates, but certainly when the pace of change is very rapid, looking at external candidates for new positions seems to be an accepted mode. I believe that internal candidates should be treated the same as external candidates. One should interview them in the same way, check references, and keep them abreast of the process as one would with external candidates.

IV. RECRUITING

The ultimate high in recruiting new employees is to have an excellent selection of candidates from which to make your choice. The feeling of having interviewed a number of candidates for a given position knowing that any one of them could do the job well gives both the interviewer and his/her organization a wonderful feeling of confidence in their ability to attract good people. There are a number of ways to attract candidates in order to generate an adequate candidate flow. Several methods for attracting candidates require lead time; therefore, when constructing a recruiting plan, one should think about the quick ways of attracting candidates and ways that are more time consuming.

V. ADVERTISEMENTS

Advertisements may require significant lead time from publications. If an ad is going to run in a local paper, then only a day or two is needed in order to place the ad and have it run. However, if an ad is going to be placed in a national publication, it is likely that a 60-day lead time will be needed. Within healthcare there are many excellent publications where an advertisement can be placed. In addition to general healthcare publications such as Modern Healthcare, there are also numerous specialty publications which might appeal to a specific group of people; for example, financial recruiters will look at the ads in the back of Healthcare Financial Management Review or nurse executives might look at the Journal of America Organization of Nurses. Often, people in Human Resources feel a need to minimize the number of words in the ad in order to cut down on cost. I believe that the more you can say in an ad about a position, the better. The minimal amount of expenditures added is more than justified by increased responses to the ad.

Most people who answer ads have an expectation of some degree of privacy with regard to the correspondence. Those receiving the letters and resumes, should respond by sending correspondence to the candidates' homes rather than their places of work.

VI. PLACING ANNOUNCEMENTS

Announcements may be considered another form of advertising. There are numerous groups who run bulletins or maintain job listings accessible to their members. This gives the recruiting organization a tremendous amount of opportunity because generally this does not incur a fee. Announcements may come out periodically, or they might be placed on a home page on the Internet. It is a good idea to utilize any additional resources you might have within your organization, such as various professional societies of which your colleagues may be members. In most cases, this networking may result in a reduced rate for the ad.

VII. DIRECT MAIL

One of the seldom used but highly effective possibilities for recruiting is direct mail. Direct mail is used by Executive Search and Recruiting firms. Most often the direct mail piece is a letter, or an announcement of the opening with some description of the opportunity and contact information. Most often the solicitation letter does not directly recruit the individual, but merely announces that the opening exists and requests referrals for the position. Direct mail can be especially effective when there is a very small number of candidates. For example, programs in Health Administration seeking to find a member of the faculty may send a direct letter to all members of the Association of University Programs in Health Administration (AUPHA).

VIII. NETWORKING

Networking takes place among both colleagues and strangers. I usually begin the networking process by calling individuals whom I know and, in turn, will receive referrals to centers of influence or potential candidates, then calling those who have been recommended. This process is very time consuming because of the length of conversations spent with these sources, trying to develop rapport and then discussing the potential candidate. In addition, many calls will not be returned. However, for a very difficult assignment, networking may be the only technique that works very effectively. Networking efficiently, a recruiter will find herself being referred to the same people over and over again. This is a good indication that the networking is effective and comprehensive. Almost any search needs some networking in order to make sure there are no outstanding candidates over looked.

IX. CONTINGENCY SEARCH

Depending upon the circumstances, some organizations will turn directly to contingency search firms to fill an opening. These outside recruiters are called contingency firms because their fee is contingent upon whether or not a potential candidate is hired. Contingency agencies usually charge between 20 to 30 percent of the first year's salary. One of the advantages of using a contingency search firm is there is an immediate list of candidates. Typically the resume is faxed to a contact person within the organization. If appropriate a contingency recruiter will schedule an interview with the candidate, either over the telephone or face-to-face. Be aware that contingency agencies may obtain information about your position by questioning candidates who disclose with whom they interviewed. Once you list positions with one agency, the chances are very high you will receive calls from other recruiting agencies. Depending on the time you have available for a search, you may want to give an agency an exclusive listing for a short time to see how well it can develop candidates for your organization. The more agencies involved, the more candidates produced, with some agencies presenting the same candidate. When this happens, be prepared to resolve a fee dispute which may result between your organization and two or more contingency agencies. Generally, the contingency agency that is there first with the candidate's resume is the one which ends up receiving the placement fee, even if it has not contacted the candidate or done anything to screen the candidate. With contingency agencies, the employer must conduct referencing and degree verification.

X. RETAINED SEARCH

Retained search firms are paid during the course of the search. In addition to the fee charged, retained firms are paid for out-of-pocket expenses. These expenses include interviewing, traveling, and solicitation of candidates. Retained search firms are generally used for higher positions, beginning at about $80K. Organizations often employ them when searches involve a search committee, and the position is a significant role in the organization. A retained search begins with a site visit by the consultant to meet the hiring manager and the rest of the management team face-to-face. From the visit, a set of specifications called a "profile" emerges which defines the position, client and the candidate. Based upon the specifications agreed to, a search plan is executed and from three to five candidates are presented to the client 40 to 50 days later. Search firms should verify all degrees and should be responsible for checking all references, delivering them to the client, either verbally or written. Retained search firms will guarantee the candidate at least 1 year of employment.

After recruiting, the candidates then enter the screening process. Based upon the specifications, someone within the organization will review the resumes, dividing them into three stacks: one for people who are qualified for the position, one for those who are not, and one for those who should be given a second look. The "second look" stack is screened to separate between qualified and not qualified. (Note: sometimes it is helpful to bring someone else in to look over the resumes. This would normally be done between the hiring manager and Human Resources Department.) Those resumes in the unqualified stack should be sent a letter stating that their credentials were reviewed. One should always leave the door open for other possible situations, including candidates who were qualified but not hired. If someone is marginally qualified you may want to keep the door open for revisiting at a later date.

Only a small group of candidates who have potential to fill the position remains. Usually someone will contact the candidate from the organization and conduct a short phone interview to elicit more information. Candidates will not have had much information at this point about the opportunity. They should be sent the job description, organizational charts and any other recruiting information. This is especially important because candidates need to be encouraged.

XI. ARRANGING THE INTERVIEW SCHEDULE

On site interviews are extremely important to the hiring process. People can be hired without resumes, reference checks, and verifications, but they are never hired without interviews. When deciding on when to interview, it is best to bring the candidate in the night before so that the candidate is rested and able to be interviewed for an entire day. I recommend that the first interview be with the hiring manager, on a one on one basis. To conduct a proper interview, it usually takes about 1-1/2 to 2 hours. Other interviews will last probably 45 minutes to an hour with the rest of the management team and others with whom the candidate would interact. One decision is whether the person will interview with the potential subordinates, and, if so, during which round of interviews. Normally subordinate interviews are conducted in a group setting – e.g. during lunch, so people can ask questions and answers. The "down-side" to group interviewing is that no one gets one-on-one time with the candidate. Sometimes the interview team will include people from outside the organization. For example, a hospital hiring a new CEO might want input from a member of the community. If the organization has a joint venture with another group, it might want input from the other joint venture partner.

On the second round of interviews, the spouse usually accompanies the candidate. In this situation it is helpful to have other spouses meet with the candidate's spouse so that information may be exchanged.

XII. THE INTERVIEW

Initially, the interview usually involves "breaking the ice" which can be accomplished in several ways. From an organization's perspective it is important that the candidate be relaxed. (Most organizations have rejected stress interviewing as a negative process.) Helping the candidate to relax by finding common ground will facilitate the discussion process. If the interviewer has become familiar with the candidate from review of the resume, the conversation can open with some personal aspects. Once the interview progresses, there are several questions necessary to ask the candidate. Often interviewers are not sure about themselves, and don't know which questions to ask. Attached is a list of structured interview questions which may prove helpful.

The most important questions are "Can this person do the job?" "Does he/she want to do the job?"

After the candidate has interviewed with the interviewing team, it is important that some kind of decision be made. Generally, I found that it is best that the people doing the interview complete an evaluation form on each candidate. (See sample on pp. 910-911.) If enough people support the candidate, particularly the hiring manager, the candidate should be asked back for a second interview. There are no magic number of interviews, and some organizations will put a candidate through four and five interviews before he/she is hired. However, I believe that one can gather enough information after two interviews in order to make a decision. One interview tends to be not enough.

It has been my experience in dealing with candidates on the second interview the cards are shifted in the deck, and often the candidate who was in third place after the first interview is the first choice after the second interview. Reviewing the evaluation forms, certain things will arise which will elicit questions which can be asked on the second interview. For example, if enough people question the candidate's motivation then motivation should be explored deeper when the second interview comes around.

XIII. NEGOTIATING OFFERS

Negotiating offers with candidates was always the hardest part of the employment process for me, until I realized that I needed to be willing to negotiate a little bit all along. Whenever possible, I will often get salary parameters out of the way on the first interview. From a candidate's perspective, there are three things about which he/she has to make decisions: money, opportunity, and location. In most cases when someone is changing jobs, a 15 percent raise is the norm. This compensates a candidate for the risk incurred when changing jobs. But depending upon the circumstances, no raise or even a decrease may be appropriate. For example, if someone is forced to make a move because of a change in location, then perhaps a lateral salary will be appropriate. The location is the major component in which the spouse must be involved. On the second interview, in which the spouse accompanies the candidate, location issues are discussed directly with the spouse, and every effort is made to make sure the spouse has the opportunity to see the community and to investigate schools, housing and employment opportunities. It is appropriate for offers of employment be made in a letter form, and delivered to the candidate. Although letters are binding legal documents, they can be withdrawn in certain circumstances. Most offers of employment should be contingent upon a satisfactory reference check at the current place of employment in order to determine whether the candidate is in good status. Sometimes the hiring manager will conduct the reference check; sometimes Human Resources will do it. It is best handled by someone who has personal contact with an individual of the candidate's organization.

After one has checked the references and they are acceptable, then it is important to transition the candidate into the new position. Someone in the hiring organization should follow up, within a few days, with the candidate to make sure the candidate has resigned their present position. In the current healthcare environment, each individual within a management team is extremely important. Thus, the loss of a key management team member can be devastating to the organization; therefore, more organizations are making counter offers to convince the employee to reconsider his/her move. The hiring organization may have moved ahead with press releases and announcements of a new employee which have to be reconciled if the candidate does not accept; this can be extremely embarrassing.

STRUCTURED INTERVIEW FORMAT
Prepared by the staff of Tyler & Company

I. **Personal Background**
    A.   Tell me about your background.
    B.   Where are you from?
    C.   Outside interests?
    D.   Academic achievements?

II. **Work Experience**
    A.   Tell me about your work experience.
       1. What were your duties?
       2. What did you like or dislike about each job?
       3. Specific achievements (list).
       4. Why did you leave each job?
       5. What has been the biggest disappointment in your career?

III. **Personality and Interpersonal Skills**
    A.   How would you describe yourself as others (subordinates) see you?
    B.   Most important aspects of your life?
    C.   How do you get along with people?
    D.   What type of characteristics do you like in other people?
    E.   What type of people rub you the wrong way?
    F.   How do you react when someone criticizes your work?
    G.   How do you handle interpersonal disagreements?
    H.   Why did you choose this field of work?
    I.   What do you consider to be your strengths? Weaknesses?
    J.   Do you consider yourself organized? Creative? Careful? Disciplined?
       A hard worker? Why or why not?
    K.   What causes stress for you? How do you handle it?
    L.   How well do you express yourself before groups? In writing?
       Can you furnish examples of your reports?

IV. **Supervision and Management Style**
    A.   Describe your management style. (Or your selling, planning, etc. style)
    B.   What are the two most important points or considerations to
       remember when managing, dealing with, or handling people?
    C.   What do you consider to be the characteristics a good supervisor should have?
    D.   How could your last supervisor have been better? (Fair and consistent, respect
       and dignity).
    E.   How would you describe your relationship with other departments?
       Review by department.
    F.   What financial reports must you generate that help you manage your department?
    G.   When faced with a difficult management problem, whom do you
       consult for a resolution of the problem?
    H.   Rate yourself in the following areas: Planning? Organizing? Controlling? Motivating?

V. **Job Expectations**
    A.   Why are you leaving your present job?
       1. What are its negatives?
       2. Does your supervisor know you are looking for a change?
    B.   What are you looking for in a job?
       1. Ideal job?
       2. Future goals?
    C.   What appeals to you about our position?
    D.   What can you do for us?
    E.   Current salary?
    F.   Salary requirements?
    G.   Time frame for making a change?
    H.   Are you considering other job opportunities?
    I.   Geographical preference?
    J.   Have you discussed relocation with your family members? What was their response?

February 19, 1997

Name
Address

Dear Mr./Mrs.:

Thank you for your interest in the search we are conducting for an Executive Director - Medical Group Development at Holy Cross Hospital. We have reviewed your credentials and experience and find them impressive. However, we have identified other candidates whose backgrounds are more compatible with our client's needs. Please rest assured this bears no reflection on your own fine qualifications.

While this opportunity did not materialize for you, we do have other potential searches. Therefore, with your permission, we will retain your resume for future reference.

Again, thank you for your interest. If we can be of further assistance, please let us know.

Sincerely,

Consultant/RA
Title

???/scg

Tyler & Company

is pleased to announce an outstanding opportunity for
CHIEF INFORMATION OFFICER
XYZ Hospital

XYZ Hospital, the second largest hospital in Virginia, with 540 general acute
bed, 180 long-term beds, and 44 personal care beds is located in Norfolk. The
organization in addition operates two skilled and intermediate care facilities with
a third opening in 1999. Joining with 350 physicians, the hospital formed
Healthy Lives, a PHO. XYZ has also contracted to establish an HMO.

This key executive will give primary guidance in strategic planning and
operations for telecommunications, Records Management, and
Computer Services. A substantial part of the CIO's focus will be on
IDS development, not just on the hospital. The CIO has responsibility for 90
FTE's and an operating budget of $5.5M.

The ideal candidate will be an IS executive with 7-10 years senior
management experience from a moderate to an intense managed care
environment. A Bachelor's degree in MIS, Business Administration,
or Computer Science is required. A Master's degree is preferred.

Contact Person, Title
Company, Address
Fax, Phone

CANDIDATE EVALUATION

Candidate Name:
Position interviewed for: Title of search/position
Interviewed by:

Please rate the candidate in the following areas according to this scale.
1 = Poor, 2 = Fair, 3 = Acceptable, 4 = Very Good, 5 = Excellent

Ratings

❏   Appearance.
     Comments:

❏   Interviewing facility (i.e.: nervousness, body language, ability to "break the ice").
     Comments:

❏   Educational background.
     Comments:

❏   Ability to ask intelligent questions
     Comments:

❏   Ability to answer questions.
     Comments:

❏   Compatibility of management styles.
     Comments:

❏   How well do the candidate's accomplishments correspond with the
     position's needs?
     Comments:

Please rate the candidate according to the following requirements which were taken from the data sheet on this position.

Ratings

❏   A strategic visionary who clearly grasps the impact of current decisions on
     the future.
     Comments:

❏   Honesty, integrity.
     Comments:

❏   Politically astute, diplomatic.
     Comments:

❏   Possesses excellent interpersonal skills, friendly, open.
     Comments:

❏   Flexible.
     Comments:

❏   Innovative, creative, a risk taker.
     Comments:

❏ Possesses strong physician relations, open and direct physician communications.
Comments:

❏ Possesses superior communication skills, able to listen and understand, able to work with people at all levels.
Comments:

❏ A team builder, a mentor who is able to get staff to work together, a participative leader.
Comments:

❏ Energized by challenge, takes initiative, assertive, anticipates challenges and tenacious.
Comments:

❏ Financially astute.
Comments:

❏ Confident, sincere, able to deal with area business, civic, and healthcare executives on a peer basis.
Comments:

❏ Able to relate to a smaller community.
Comments:

❏ Possesses good negotiation skills.
Comments:

Perceived Strengths of this Candidate:

Perceived Weaknesses of this Candidate:

Overall Comments:

Recommendation:
  ❏ Hire
  ❏ Hire with Reservations Noted
  ❏ Do not Hire

PROGRAM OUTLINE

I. POTENTIAL DISCRIMINATION TROUBLE SPOTS

A. Forms of Prohibited Discrimination
    (1) Race
    (2) Sex
        -- equal pay
        -- comparable worth
        -- stereotype
        -- pregnancy
        -- sexual harassment
    (3) Religion
        -- reasonable accommodation
    (4) National Origin
    (5) Disability (ADA)
        -- reasonable accommodation
    (6) Age -- 40 (ADEA)
    (7) Retaliation

B. Search Firm or Employment Agency Can Along With Employer Be Liable For Discrimination

C. Cost to the Company of a Finding of Discrimination
    (1) Back pay
    (2) Front Pay
    (3) Injunction
    (4) Liquidated damages
    (5) Punitive and compensatory damages
    (6) Attorney's fees
    (7) Possible personal liability of supervisor/individual alleged to have discriminated

II. ADA - DISCUSSION OF DO'S AND DON'TS IN THE INTERVIEW/ APPLICATION PROCESS

III. DISCUSSION OF DEFAMATION AND INVASION OF PRIVACY

Source: Forrest W. Hunter, Alston and Bird, One Atlantic Center, 1201 West Peachtree Street, Atlanta, Georgia 30309-3424

PRINCIPAL LEGISLATION AFFECTING EMPLOYMENT PRACTICES

LAW	PURPOSE
CIVIL RIGHTS ACTS	Established the principal of equal rights and equal protection for black and white citizens of the United States.
FAIR LABOR STANDARDS ACT (1938)	Defines the workweek and established standards for minimum wages, overtime pay, equal pay, recordkeeping and child labor.
NATIONAL LABOR RELATIONS ACT (1947)	Protects employees' rights to engage in or refrain from concerted activity. (unionization)
EQUAL PAY ACT (1963)	Makes it unlawful to pay employees of one sex at a different rate than those of the other sex for equal work. Jobs are considered equal when they require equal skill, equal effort, equal responsibility, and similar working conditions in the same establishment.
TITLE VII OF THE CIVIL RIGHTS ACT OF 1964 AS AMENDED BY THE EQUAL ACT OF 1972	Prohibits discrimination in employment on the basis of race, color, sex, religion, and national origin.
	Defines covered areas of employment as recruiting, hiring, compensation, discharges, job assignments, training programs, promotions, and other terms and conditions of employment.
	Gives victims of discrimination right to be "made whole" through recovery of lost wages, reinstatement, employment, promotion, back pay, front pay, injunction against retaliation or punishment from defending company, and attorney's fees.
EXECUTIVE ORDER 11246 AS AMENDED BY EXECUTIVE ORDER 11375 (1968)	Requires government contractors and subcontractors to incorporate an equal employment opportunity clause in all contracts. This clause requires the contractor to be non-discriminatory and to engage in affirmative action.
	Requires employers with 50 or more employees and certain government contracts to prepare written affirmative action plans.

	Gives victims of discrimination right to be "made whole" through recovery of lost wages, reinstatement, employment, promotion, back pay, front pay, and injunction against retaliation or punishment from defending company.
AGE DISCRIMINATION IN EMPLOYMENT ACT (1967) AS AMENDED (1978 & 1986)	Prohibits discrimination in employment against applicants or employees aged 40 and older. Prohibits mandatory retirement at any age.
OCCUPATIONAL SAFETY AND HEALTH ACT (1970)	Establishes safety and health standards for employment environment.
	Requires records to be maintained on occupational-related injuries, illnesses, or deaths.
REHABILITATION ACT (1973)	Prohibits discrimination in employment because of physical or mental handicap.
	Requires employers with 50 or more employees and federal contracts of $50,000 or more to develop written AAPs covering handicapped employees.
	Emphasizes employers' responsibility to modify the work environment to reasonably accommodate handicapped individuals and to actively recruit the handicapped.
VIETNAM ERA VETERANS READJUSTMENT ASSISTANCE ACT (1974)	Requires government contractors to take affirmative action to employ and promote disabled veterans and veterans of the Vietnam era.
	Requires employers with 50 or more employees and $50,000 or more in government contracts to develop a written AAP.
	Emphasizes employers' responsibility to modify the work environment to reasonably accommodate disabled veterans and to actively recruit Vietnam veterans.
PREGNANCY DISCRIMINATION ACT (1978)	Prohibits discrimination in employment on the basis of pregnancy, childbirth, or related medical conditions.
	Requires employers to cease differentiating between maternity and medical leaves.

IMMIGRATION REFORM AND CONTROL ACT (1986)	Requires employers to verify employee's identity and authorization to work in the United States. Prohibits discrimination on the basis of national origin or citizenship status.
EMPLOYEE RETIREMENT INCOME SECURITY ACT (1974) as amended by COBRA (1986)	Regulates benefit plans and prohibits employment action intended to interfere with the attainment of benefits. Provides for benefit continuation after employee termination.
DRUG-FREE WORKPLACE ACT (1988)	Applies to federal contractor and federal grant recipients and requires certification regarding employers maintaining a drug-free workplace.
WORKER ADJUSTMENT AND RETRAINING NOTIFICATION ACT (1988) (WARN)	Plant Closing bill giving workers right to 60 days notice before plant closes.
EMPLOYEE POLYGRAPH PROTECTION ACT (1988)	Prohibits most employer use of polygraphs of employees
AMERICANS WITH DISABILITIES ACT (1990)	To protect the rights of employees and applicants with disabilities and to require that employers accommodate employees with disabilities.
CIVIL RIGHTS ACT OF 1991	Gives claimants under Title VII right to jury trial and right to seek punitive damages. Also-reverses several pro employer Supreme Court decisions.
FAMILY AND MEDICAL LEAVE ACT OF 1993	Gives employee right to up to 12 weeks' unpaid leave for birth or adoption or to care for ill spouse, child or parent, or for employee's own illness. Protects employee's health insurance coverage and job reinstatement rights.

EEOC GUIDELINES/PRE EMPLOYMENT INQUIRIES/ADA

A. Enforcement Guidance on Pre-Employment Inquiries Under the Americans With Disabilities Act Issued May 19, 1994.

B. Concerns the ADA's restrictions on an employer's use of disability-related inquiries and medical examinations.

C. ADA unique among federal civil rights laws in that it flatly prohibits certain inquiries and examinations at the pre-offer stage of the hiring process.

D. Rationale and Legal Framework
    1. Reflect the intent of Congress to prevent discrimination against individuals with hidden disabilities.
    2. In the past, applicants often asked about medical conditions at the time they submitted applications for employment. If rejected, would not know whether rejection was because of disclosure of disability, or because of non-medical criterion.
    3. Under ADA, employer may not ask about existence, nature, or severity of disability and may not conduct medical examinations until after it makes a conditional job offer to the applicant. Ensures that the applicant's hidden disability is not considered prior to the assessment of the applicant's non-medical qualifications.
    4. After conditional offer made, employer may require medical examinations and may make disability-related inquiries if it does so for all entering employees in the job category.
    5. Any medical information obtained must be kept confidential by the employer. Employer must collect and maintain information on separate forms and in separate medical files. May disclose information only to persons and entities specified in the ADA.

E. The following examples are inquiries which are not disability-related:
    1. Can you perform the functions of this job (essential and/or marginal), with or without reasonable accommodation?
    2. Please describe/demonstrate how you would perform these functions (essential and/or marginal).
    3. Do you have a cold? Have you ever tried Tylenol for fever? How did you break your leg?
    4. Can you meet the attendance requirements of this job? How many days did you take leave last year?
    5. Do you illegally use drugs? Have you used illegal drugs in the last two years?
    6. Do you have the required licenses to perform this job?

F. The following examples are disability-related inquiries:
    1. Do you have AIDS? Do you have asthma?
    2. Do you have a disability which would interfere with your ability to perform the job?
    3. How many days were you sick last year?
    4. Have you ever filed for workers' compensation? Have you ever been injured on the job?
    5. How much alcohol do you drink each week? Have you ever been treated for alcohol problems?
    6. Have you ever been treated for mental health problems?

G. Medical Examinations are procedures/tests that seek information about an individual's physical or mental impairment, or physical or psychological health. The following factors are used in determining whether any particular test is medical:
    1. whether the test is administered by a health care professional or trainee;
    2. whether the results of the test are interpreted by a health care professional or trainee;
    3. whether the test is designed to reveal an impairment or the state of an individual's physical or psychological health;
    4. whether the test is given for the purpose of revealing an impairment or the state of an individual's physical or psychological health;

5. whether the test is invasive (e.g., requires drawing of blood, urine, breath, etc.);
6. whether the test measures physical/psychological responses (as opposed to performance of a task);
7. whether the test is normally done in a medical setting; and
8. whether medical equipment/devices are used for the test.

H. The following are tests which generally are not medical:
   1. physical agility/physical fitness tests which do not include medical monitoring;
   2. certain psychological tests, such as tests which simply concern an individual's skills or tastes; and
   3. tests for illegal use of drugs.

I. It is important to note, however, that disability-related inquiries may not be asked as part of a pre-offer test, even if that test is not otherwise medical.

J. The following examples are tests which, depending on the test and application of the above-factors, might be medical:
   • certain psychological tests;
   • certain vision tests; and
   • certain alcohol tests.

DEFAMATION / INVASION OF PRIVACY

I. DEFAMATION

Generally, defamation is an untruthful statement which tends to injure a person's reputation in the community. The statement may be written (libel), spoken (slander) or be communicated by conduct. Many states have codified the elements and defenses of both libel and slander.

Elements of Libel and Slander

The definition of a defamatory statement, whether it be libel or slander, is an unprivileged, false, malicious statement, publicized to a person other than the plaintiff, which tends to create an unfavorable impression in the mind of a third party.

A. False Statement

To constitute defamation, a written or spoken statement must contain false words regarding an employee's character, behavior or reputation. Truth is an absolute defense. Some states have adopted the "innocent-construction" rule under which the court must interpret the allegedly defamatory statement to be innocent where such interpretation is reasonable.

> Examples: A court found that a supervisor who gave an employee a poor reference by stating that she "did not get along well with others" and "did not follow up on assignments" was not liable for defamation. The court reasoned that the statements were subject to innocent construction" as they could be construed as applying only to her performance in that particular organization. *Anderson v. Vanden Dorpel,* 1996 WL 189400 (m. 1996).

> A supervisor's request that an employee not return to company property until the conclusion of the investigation was not slanderous absent evidence that his words contained hurtful innuendo regarding the employee's character or behavior. *Lepard v. Robb,* 201 Ga. App. 41 (1991).

B. Malice

In order to prevail under a theory of libel or slander, a plaintiff is also required to show that the statement was malicious. Two types of malice may be shown. "Common-law malice" means a statement made with ill will and deliberately calculated to injure. "Actual malice" is present when a statement is made with knowledge of its untruthfulness, or a reckless disregard for whether it is truthful.

C. Publication

Generally, courts consider a statement to be "published" when it is communicated to any person other than the person defamed. In an employment context, some courts have held that the publication of allegedly defamatory information (e.g., facts regarding discipline or an internal investigation) will not occur if the communication is made only to agents of the employer who are in positions of authority.

> Examples: An employee evaluation form which was provided to management personnel was "published" for purposes of recovering for injury to reputation under Indiana's state constitution. *Bals v. Verduzco,* 600 N.E.2d 1353 (Ind. 1992).

> There was no publication of allegedly defamatory information on job applicant where the only communication of the challenged matter was between the former employer and the agent of a prospective employer, and the applicant had expressly authorized such communication. *Kenney v. Gilmore,* 19S Ga. App. 407 (1990).

D. Privilege

Communications which form the basis for a claim of defamation may be privileged, a defense which will avoid liability in most cases. To maintain a privilege, an employer generally must show good faith, an interest to be upheld, a statement limited in its scope to this purpose, a proper occasion, and publication in a proper manner and to proper parties. Overpublication or malice can defeat a claim of privilege.

Twenty-three states have enacted laws protecting employers who provide "good faith" job references.

> Examples: Information disclosed by job applicant's former employer to the agent of a prospective employer was protected by a statutory privilege, absent evidence of actual malice. *Kenney v. Gilmore, 195* Ga. App. 407 (1990).

> Reports prepared by the immediate supervisor of a corporate employee evaluating her performance and intended for use by personnel employees within the corporation were conditionally privileged. *Land v. Delta Airlines. Inc.,* 147 Ga. App. 738 (1978).

II. INVASION OF PRIVACY

The common law generally recognizes four distinct torts under the general title of invasion of privacy:

(1) Intrusion upon the plaintiff's seclusion or solitude, or into his private affairs; (2) Public disclosure of embarrassing private facts about the plaintiff; (3) Publicity which places the plaintiff in a false light in the public eye; and (4) Appropriation, for the defendant's advantage, of plaintiff's name or likeness.

A. Intrusion Upon Seclusion

Under category (1), the Plaintiff must allege a physical intrusion which is analogous to a trespass. The courts have defined the "unreasonable intrusion" aspect of invasion of privacy as involving a prying or intrusion, which would be offensive or objectionable to a reasonable person into a person's private concerns. Highly personal questions or demands by a person in authority may be regarded as an intrusion on psychological solitude or integrity, and therefore an invasion of privacy. However, the courts also recognize that there are certain inconveniences and annoyances which members of society must necessarily tolerate without the right of legal redress.

This aspect of invasion of privacy arises most commonly in the following situations:

(a) sexual harassment; (b) surveillance; (c) searches of desks/lockers; and (d) e-mail.

> Examples: Female employees who alleged that their supervisor told them to wear less clothes, to come to work without a bra, and to install a stick on their machines so that they could excite themselves during work stated a claim for invasion of privacy. *Busby v. Truswal Systems Corp.,* 551 So.2d 322 (Ala. 1989).

> Employee had no cause of action for intrusion into seclusion where his supervisor conducted surveillance of his house to discern whether he had a work-related disability. The court found that the employer was justified in investigating such matters. *Saldana v. Kelsey-Hayes Co.,* 443 N.W.2d 382 (Mich. App. 1989).

B. Public Disclosure of Private Facts

In order to prove a claim under this aspect of invasion of privacy, a plaintiff must show:
> (1) a public disclosure of facts;

    (2)   the facts disclosed to the public must be private, secluded or secret facts and not public ones; and

    (3)   the matter made public must be offensive to a reasonable man of ordinary sensibilities under the circumstances.

Examples:

Although sexual harassment plaintiff's employer disclosed that she was having sexual relations with her supervisor, plaintiff waived her right to bring an invasion of privacy action when she informed others of this fact herself. *Cummings v. Walsh Construction. Co.,* 561 F.Supp. 872 (S.D. Ga. 1983).

Employer who revealed to the plaintiff's co-workers that she had a mastectomy stated a claim for invasion of privacy where that disclosure caused embarrassment and distress. *Miller v. Motorola Inc.,* 560 N.E.2d 900 (Ill. App. 1990).

Drug and Alcohol Testing- Most states have enacted drug free work place acts which outline the requirements for drug and alcohol testing programs implemented by an employer. If, in implementing such a program, an employer complies with the requirements of the state statute, it is unlikely that a common law cause of action such as invasion of privacy would succeed. However, employers should be careful to assure that there is not a publication of test results to third parties who are not in positions of authority, and who do not need to know the results. Such conduct can lead to claims of invasion of privacy and/or defamation.

    Drug and alcohol programs should also expressly dispel any expectation of privacy with regard to their scope and implementation. The policy should clearly indicate that searches may extend to private belongings such as lockers and desks.

C. False Light

    To constitute an invasion of privacy by placing one in a false light in the public eye, there must be a publicity which is false, and which depicts the plaintiff as something or someone which he is not. Generally, the false publicity must be "highly offensive." However, the courts have stated that the hypersensitive individual will not be protected.

    This aspect of invasion of privacy will arise, in most cases, outside of the employment context, i.e.- with regard to media publications. However, employers should be aware that false light invasion of privacy can also arise in an employment situation where personal information about an employee is widely distributed or released. Such a situation may occur, for example, where a disparaging conversation is inadvertently broadcast over a company's intercom system.

D. Appropriation of Plaintiff's Name or Likeness

    This aspect of invasion of privacy occurs almost exclusively in commercial appropriation, where there is an appropriation, for the defendant's benefit, use or advantage, of the plaintiff's name or likeness. This usually arises where an individual's name or photograph is used in an advertisement to publicize or advertise the product or the publication.

54.
CONFLICT RESOLUTION[1]

Jeffrey T. Polzer, *University of Texas, Austin, TX*

Margaret A. Neale, *Stanford University, Stanford, CA*

The field of conflict management has grown dramatically in the last decade, reflected both by the amount of research conducted on this topic and the increased importance placed on teaching conflict management techniques. This increase in popularity, particularly concerning negotiation, has been fueled by several general environmental trends that are especially noticeable in the health services industry (Neale and Bazerman, 1991). First, the marketplace is growing increasingly global as firms face competition from foreign companies. For example, pharmaceutical firms such as Burroughs-Wellcome, Inc. increasingly find themselves conducting business in different countries as their current markets become more competitive. This increased diversity in potential business partners heightens the need for managers to be able to negotiate effectively with people who have different backgrounds, interests, and values.

Secondly, at the firm level, there has been a vast increase in corporate restructuring throughout the 1980s and into the 1990s. Managers in corporations that are going through structural transformations need negotiation skills to ensure their position within the new organization. At an individual level, the workforce is growing increasingly mobile. Many employees proactively manage their career paths, often within multiple organizations. Increased mobility demands better negotiation skills of those changing jobs and those employing these people.

Finally, the shift from a manufacturing-based to a service-based economy means that typical negotiations are likely to be more difficult, because desired outcomes are more ambiguous and therefore harder to specify in negotiated agreements (Neale and Bazerman, 1991). This ambiguity is clearly present in many areas of the health services field, increasing the importance of good negotiating skills as negotiations become more difficult.

We will explore negotiation in depth later in the chapter. Before we focus on ways to resolve conflict, though, we will discuss various types of conflict and some of the typical reasons conflict occurs in organizations.

I. THE CAUSES OF CONFLICT

A. The Role of Resource Scarcity

Conflict arises for many reasons and can be characterized in numerous ways. At a very basic level, most conflict occurs because of a fundamental problem inherent in every organization. Organizational members desire several types of resources, including power, money, information, advice, and praise (Homans, 1961). However, resource scarcity dictates that the members of an organization will not all be able to receive the level of resources they desire. Therefore, conflict arises between organizational members regarding the distribution of desired resources.

It is useful to distinguish conflict from competition because many people confuse the two concepts. While conflict is a typical result of resource scarcity, organizational members also compete for resources. However, conflict and competition are distinct concepts. In both cases, the goals of the parties are incompatible. In situations involving resources, this means that the parties cannot both acquire their desired level of resources. However, competition is characterized by parallel striving toward a goal that both parties cannot reach simultaneously, while conflict is characterized by mutual interference. Conflict occurs when a concern of one party is frustrated, or perceived to be frustrated, by another party (Thomas, 1976). Parties can compete and still remain relatively independent of each other. Conflict, on the other hand, requires some interaction or contact between the parties.

Conflict can also occur for reasons that are less tangible than resource acquisition. People may have conflicting perceptions, ideas, or beliefs as well as conflicting resource allocation goals. For example, one subordinate may perceive that another subordinate receives more praise, even when both subordinates actually receive the same objective amount of praise; two administrators may have different ideas about what an employee dress code policy should entail; and people may have different beliefs about the appropriateness of a certain medical treatment or procedure. A basic but important point to be drawn from these examples is that conflict always occurs because of the differences between people, even though these differences occur on a variety of dimensions.

B. Beneficial versus Detrimental Effects of Conflict

Because differences between people are unavoidable, conflict will always exist in organizations and groups. The question that must be addressed by successful managers is how to handle the conflicts that they will inevitably face. Should managers try to create a work environment in which there is as little conflict as possible or is some important purpose served by having certain levels of ambient conflict? This boils down to the question of whether conflict is good or bad, and therefore, whether it should be encouraged in work groups or discouraged and suppressed.

In trying to ascertain whether conflict is good or bad, functional or dysfunctional, something to be explored or suppressed, part of the puzzle may lie in differentiating various types of conflict. It may be that some types of conflict are important for successful organizational performance while other forms of conflict are associated with problematic organizational performance. In the next section, we will consider three different types of conflict—content conflict, emotional conflict, and administrative conflict—and their unique impact on organizational functioning.

C. Jehn's Typology of Conflict

Conflict within an organization can be characterized by type regardless of the level at which it occurs. Karen Jehn (1992) devised a typology that includes three types of conflict. Task content conflict, the first type, refers to disagreements about the actual task being performed by organizational members. The focus in this type of conflict is on differing opinions pertaining to the task, rather than the goals of the people involved. For example, everyone in a group medical practice may agree that the group should have a marketing campaign, but members may disagree about the content of the advertisements and whether advertising should be run on radio, television, or in newspapers.

Emotional conflict is an awareness of interpersonal incompatibilities among those working together on a task. It involves negative emotions and dislike of the other people involved in the conflict. The third type of conflict is administrative conflict and is defined as an awareness by the involved parties that there are controversies about how task accomplishment will proceed (Jehn, 1992). Disagreements about individual responsibilities and duties are examples of administrative conflict. For example, members of a group practice may disagree about who should decide what type of advertising to use or who should be responsible for working with an advertising agency.

In general, the research conducted by Jehn and others suggests that a moderate amount of task content conflict is critical to the effective functioning of groups. Groupthink, for example, is probably more likely to occur when there is an implicit avoidance of all conflict, but especially task content conflict. Administrative conflict and, to a greater extent, emotional conflict are likely to be the culprits when groups become dysfunctional or impaired because a high degree of conflict inhibits their ability to interact. All three of these types of conflict may occur between individuals, groups and individuals, or different groups as people perform the tasks that make up organizational life. These various levels at which conflict can occur are the focus of the next section.

II. LEVELS OF CONFLICT

It is useful to consider the level at which conflict occurs, along with the type of conflict, when trying to decide how to manage it. That is, conflict can occur within an individual (intrapersonal conflict), between individuals (interpersonal conflict), within a group (intragroup conflict), and between groups (intergroup conflict). The alternatives available for resolving the conflict may depend on the level in the organization at which it exists.

A. Individual Level

Individual conflict occurs when the locus of the dispute is the individual. Intrapersonal conflict may occur for a variety of reasons. People are often faced with a choice between two options that may vary in attractiveness. In characterizing conflict at this level, it is valuable to think about the relative attractiveness of each option. When two options are equally attractive, approach-approach conflict occurs within the person. This conflict results from the person's effort to differentiate between the two alternatives. For example, a health maintenance organization (HMO) executive may have two equally viable and attractive plans for expanding enrollment. It is difficult to choose either of the options because selecting one necessarily means the other must be turned down.

On the other side of the coin, avoidance-avoidance conflict occurs when a person has to choose between equally unattractive options. If a nursing home is trying to reduce costs, one of two good nurses may have to be laid off. The decision is made more difficult because the options are equally unattractive.

The most prevalent type of intrapersonal conflict is approach-avoidance conflict, which occurs when multiple options each have favorable and unfavorable features. Conflict that is initially approach-approach conflict often turns into approach-avoidance conflict when the person making the decision looks at the alternatives more critically in an attempt to differentiate them. Unattractive components of each option may be found that were overlooked initially, such as additional costs associated with each option for expanding HMO membership enrollment. A person may arrive at a different decision depending on which features of each option the person focuses. After the decision is made, postdecision regret frequently occurs, as the alternative that the person passed up looks increasingly better as more information is gathered about the chosen option.

B. Group Level

When most people think about conflict, the examples that first come to mind are at an interpersonal level, between two or more people. Conflict at this level typically occurs because of incompatible goals, ideas, feelings, beliefs, or behaviors, as illustrated by the examples in the first section of this chapter. This level of conflict is usually characterized by interdependence between the parties, whereby the choice of each party affects the outcome of the other party. The choice that is optimal for one party may result in a poor outcome for the other, leading to conflict. This is the most common level of conflict that comes to the surface in organizations.

Paralleling individual conflict, group conflict can occur between members of the same group (intragroup conflict) or between members of different groups (intergroup conflict). Intragroup conflict is similar in many ways to interpersonal conflict, with the former type being more complex because of the higher number of people involved. However, this is not the only difference. When a group is involved that has an identity above and beyond its individual members, several things can occur as a result of the influence of the group on its members. A formal definition of what we mean by a "group" may help to clarify the ideas that follow. In this context, a group is defined as an organized system of two or more individuals who are interrelated so that the system performs some function, has a standard set of role relationships among its members, and has a set of norms that regulate the function of the group and each of its members (Northcraft and Neale, 1990).

As this definition of a group implies, the interactions of the group members are influenced by their roles within the group and by the norms of the group. Members of the group may not always be amenable to these influences, leading to conflict between the individual member and the group. Conflict between the members of a group may result in decreased coordination, communication, and productivity (Deutsch, 1949). Intragroup conflict will come up again later in this chapter in the section on multi-party negotiations.

Intergroup conflict can have a profound impact on the perceptions and behaviors of people. When acting as a member of a group, people tend to divide others into an ingroup and an outgroup. The ingroup consists of all the other members of the salient group. The outgroup consists of those outside the boundaries of the ingroup. Some examples of the characteristics people frequently use to divide people into in- and out-groups include gender, race, religious preference, geographic location, organizational membership, departmental membership, and functional position within an organization. Most people are members of numerous groups based on demographic, organizational, or other demarcations. This creates abundant opportunities for intergroup conflict to arise. Intergroup conflict occurs whenever the disputants identify with or represent different groups that are relevant to the conflict during the conflict episode.

Intergroup conflict may have a variety of causes, many of which are the same as those that cause interpersonal conflict, such as resource scarcity, differing beliefs, or incompatible goals. The distinction is simply that the relevant unit from which the differences stem is the group rather than the individual. Intergroup conflict can have a variety of consequences both within and across the groups involved in the conflict. Within the groups, cohesiveness, task orientation, loyalty to the group, and acceptance of autocratic leadership may increase. Between the groups, distorted perceptions, negative stereotypes of outgroup members, and reduced communication may result. A mentality of "us versus them" often forms and grows stronger as the conflict escalates (Sherif, 1977). The strength of group affiliations as a contributing factor to conflict is often overlooked but should always be considered when trying to determine the causes of conflict.

III. MANAGING CONFLICT

It is clear that conflict is commonplace, and that for organizational members to function productively, they must manage conflict effectively. There are many strategies for managing conflict, including those that are planned as well as those that emerge as conflict is experienced. Some conflict management techniques apply to conflict on all levels, while others are relevant for a limited number of types and levels of conflict. In this section, we will briefly introduce the dual-concern model as a typology of conflict management techniques, focusing on four ways that people handle conflict—accommodation, pressing, avoidance, and negotiation.

Figure 1 - Dual Concern Model

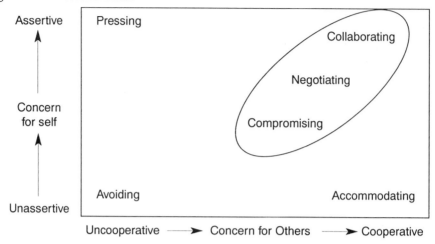

A. The Dual Concern Model

Kenneth Thomas has developed a two-dimensional model of conflict management techniques that reflects a concern for both an individual's own outcomes as well as an opponent's outcomes. Depending on these two dimensions of concern, a negotiator might prefer one of five different strategies for handling conflict. If concern for both self and other's outcomes are low, this model predicts that one might prefer an avoidance strategy. If concern for one's own outcome is high and concern for the other's outcome is low, then one should prefer a competing, or pressing, strategy. If concern for one's own outcome is low and concern for the other's outcome is high, then accommodation or capitulation is probably the preferred strategy. If concern for both one's own outcome and the other's outcome is high, then collaboration is the appropriate strategy. Finally, if one has intermediate concern for both one's own and the other's outcomes, then one is likely to prefer a compromise strategy. The Dual Concern Model is graphically represented in Figure 1.

If we think about how differing preferences for these five strategies might be expressed by an organizational actor in various situations, four different conflict management techniques can be identified. Accommodation, pressing, avoiding, and negotiation (incorporating compromise and collaboration) are described in greater detail in the following sections.

B. Accommodation

Capitulating to or accommodating the other party is one popular way to deal with conflict. Accommodation does not necessarily require any interaction among the parties and can simply entail giving the other side what they want. It is one of the least confrontational methods for dealing with conflict. Capitulation has the advantage of being efficient in that, by giving the other party what he wants, the conflict ends quickly. Other advantages are that the relationship between the parties may be preserved and that the other party may feel a sense of indebtedness, which may come into play in the future. The adage, it is better to give than to receive, seems to recommend accommodation, although it is not clear that this advice was meant for organizational members in an increasingly competitive environment. While capitulation may be recommended in some situations, people are unlikely to get what they want by relying on others accommodating them. They may rarely achieve outcomes that are good for them if they use capitulation too often. In most situations, there are better ways to manage conflict.

C. Pressing

When individuals have as their primary objective the achievement of their interests and are unconcerned about whether other parties get what they want (or even wish to "beat" the other side), they often rely on a series of strategies that are typically described as contentious. These strategies include a variety of tactics such as irrevocable commitments, threats or promises, and persuasive argumentation (Pruitt and Rubin, 1986).

Irrevocable commitments occur when one party credibly guarantees to continue behaving in a certain way that once begun will not be changed. An excellent example of an irrevocable commitment is the game of Chicken. Chicken involves two participants who are driving their cars at breakneck speed on a direct collision course with each other. The loser in this game is the one who first turns aside—the "chicken"—thereby avoiding a head-on collision and almost certain death for both players. In this game each side tries to convince the other that they are committed to their course of action—driving straight toward the other car. More generally, irrevocable commitments occur when two parties engage in a test of wills in which neither side is willing to concede. A typical example of the risk of such games and tactics can be seen in the escalation of losses and acrimony that can occur when couples divorce.

Irrevocable commitments are useful because they do not require agreement of the other party to work nor do they require that the committing party be of equal or greater power. In the case of irrevocable commitments, weakness can become strength. Consider Gandhi's power, stemming from his weakness in the face of the other party's strength, to compel the British to modify their policies in India.

Threats and promises are both meant to convey intention. The typical promise is designed to induce some particular behavior by describing what will happen if such an action occurs. For example, one might promise to trade future support on issue A for current support on issue B. Promises do not give information about what will happen if compliance does not occur. Threats, on the other hand, convey what will happen if the preferred behavior does not happen. As such, one might threaten to vote against my interests unless I vote for her interests. Threats and promises are designed to have the same effect, but the mechanism by which the effects come about are different. Promises rely on the benefits of compliance while threats work because of the costs of noncompliance. In fact, compared to promises, threats provide more information because they describe how an individual intends to behave in response to a broader variety of actions. Promises only tell me what you will do if I take one particular action. They tell me nothing about what you would do if I take no action or another action.

Compared to threats and promises, persuasive argumentation is a less controlling tactic, although one that requires considerable skill. Through per se, argumentation, I can influence you to give up something that you hold dear, change a situation you currently enjoy, or lower your aspirations. Consider the difficulty of persuading employees to work fewer hours rather than laying off other organizational members. When undertaking this tactic, one typically appeals to the unattractive alternatives that will ensue if the situation is left unchanged.

D. Avoidance

The most common response to conflict on any level is to avoid it. In many situations, people avoid conflict when both they and their organizations would benefit had they managed it more proactively. For example, issues involving quality of care are sometimes ignored because people fear the conflict associated with addressing them. However, avoidance does have its merits. If the issues involved in the conflict are trivial and the parties do not care much about their own outcome or the other party's outcome, avoidance may be the best strategy. The costs incurred by confronting the problem may be greater, at least in the short run, than the benefits that accrue from having the conflict resolved. Avoidance may also be the best way to deal with conflict when someone else can resolve the problem more effectively or when the problem would be better dealt with in the future after the involved parties have cooled down. If avoiding conflict becomes a habit, however, important issues, when they arise, may never get addressed.

E. Negotiation

Unlike other conflict resolution tactics, negotiation is a process through which multiple parties work together on the outcome. People negotiate every day although they do not always think of their activities as negotiations. This becomes clearer, however, when negotiation is defined as the process whereby two or more parties decide what each will give and take in an exchange between them (Rubin and Brown, 1975). This broad definition encompasses a preponderance of activities that people do every day, both within and outside organizations. Negotiations typically, but not always, involve some type of direct interaction between the parties, with the interaction being face to face, verbal, or written. The parties in a negotiation are interdependent in that they both desire something the other party has control over.

An interesting aspect of negotiation that distinguishes it from other forms of conflict resolution is the considerable amount of attention it has received in both applied and scholarly settings. One result of this trend is that we now know more about the behavior of negotiators and the structural factors that influence them than we did in the past. In the next section, we will provide a framework for thinking about negotiations that can be applied equally well to almost any negotiation situation, whether it involves a husband and wife or two nations. By analyzing the structure of a negotiation, negotiators should be able to improve their preparedness for, the process of, and the outcome of the negotiation.

IV. NEGOTIATION

A. Basic Concepts

A negotiator never has to negotiate; there are always alternatives to reaching an agreement through a negotiation. Many were discussed above, such as avoiding the situation or giving to the other party what they want. However, when a person in an interdependent situation (i.e., the person desires something the other party has control over and vice versa) does not reach a negotiated agreement with the other party, that person has to settle for another alternative regarding the desired resource controlled by the other party. For example, if a hospital is trying to hire a nurse but does not reach an agreement on an employment contract with a particular nurse, the hospital has to either accept the alternative of not having the position filled or choose the alternative of trying to hire another person for the job. From the nurse's point of view, if an agreement is not reached with the hospital, he will have to settle for another alternative, perhaps accepting a job with another hospital or continuing the job search.

Whether they have thought about them or not, the parties in a negotiation have alternatives that they will implement if the negotiation ends in an impasse. The negotiator will obviously choose her best alternative to an agreement if an impasse is reached, so this alternative will be our focus. Specifically, a negotiator's Best Alternative To a Negotiated Agreement (BATNA) is an important consideration because it is a source of power in the negotiation (Fisher and Ury, 1981). Being able to walk away from the negotiation if a satisfactory agreement does not appear to be forthcoming can be a valuable negotiating tool. Besides the opportunity to use this information strategically, it is also important to know when you actually should walk away. Knowing your best alternative allows a comparison to be made between the value of your best alternative and the value of various agreements that might be reached, which in turn allows you to know which agreements are desirable and which should be turned down.

A BATNA is put into action by determining a reservation price. A reservation price can be thought of as a bottom line, or the point at which you are indifferent between an impasse and an agreement (Raiffa, 1982). A reservation price should be stated in terms of whatever units are being negotiated. In many negotiations the units of exchange are dollars so that, for example, a negotiator might have a reservation price of $18,000 when buying a car (i.e., the buyer will pay no more than $18,000 for a car). A BATNA and a reservation price, although closely related, are distinct concepts. The connection between the two is that a reservation price should equal the value placed on your best alternative plus whatever transaction costs you will incur to enact your best alternative (White and Neale, in press). For example, the expenses that would be involved in hiring another nurse should be taken into consideration in determining a reservation price for a negotiation with a nurse candidate.

An aspiration level is what a negotiator would ideally like to achieve in the negotiation. It can also be referred to as a target or goal. An aspiration level should be challenging but attainable. A goal that is too challenging is not motivating because it is not within the realm of possibilities, while one that is too easy also loses its motivating potential once it is surpassed. Typically an aspiration level is stated in the same units as the reservation price (e.g., dollars).

Figure 2 - Bargaining Zones

The three concepts just discussed focus on one party rather than the constellation of parties involved in a negotiation. When the parties in a negotiation come together, additional structural features come into play. The most prominent feature is the bargaining zone The bargaining zone is found by combining the reservation prices of each negotiator and determining whether they overlap, and if so, the extent of the overlap. A positive bargaining zone occurs if a set of agreements exists that both parties prefer over impasse (Neale and Bazerman, 1991). It is easier to understand this concept with the aid of a diagram. Imagine that a nurse and a hospital are negotiating over the nurse's salary. The nurses reservation price is $30,000 and the hospital's reservation price is $35,000. This is outlined in Figure 2. The bargaining zone is the range of agreements between and including $30,000 and $35,000. If there is no overlap region between the reservation prices of the parties, then a negative bargaining zone exists. Because there are no agreements that are acceptable to both parties, no resolution is possible. It is important for a negotiator to gather information about the size of the bargaining zone during the course of the negotiation.

B. The Distributive Dimension of Negotiation

Of the two dimensions of negotiation, only the distributive dimension is necessarily part of every negotiation. The integrative dimension, on the other hand is never applied in many negotiations. Negotiation always involves the allocation, or distribution, of some set of resources. The distributive dimension is often referred to as that part of negotiation in which value is claimed In every negotiation, regardless of the amount of resources to be distributed, an integral task for the negotiators is to determine how much each party will take from the "pie" of resources. Single issue negotiations are the most common example of purely distributive negotiations. The amount of resources is fixed, and whatever one party gains is always at the expense of the other party. Resolving negotiations that are distributive often entails compromise by both parties, as each party concedes a little at a time in a reciprocal manner until they

Table 1- Claiming Value: Distributive Bargaining Strategies

1. Know your BATNA.
2. Determine your bottom line or reservation price.
3. Set a goal or aspiration level that is (a) significantly better than your bottom line and (b) optimistically realistic.
4. Think of what objective standards might be acceptable to the other party.
5. Plan your opening. An initial offer should not be too extreme, but it should prevent the other party from "anchoring" the negotiation.
6. Develop reciprocity. Avoid making unilateral concessions.

reach an agreement. Negotiators should consider several strategies that may help them claim as large a share of the resources as possible. These strategies are outlined in Table 1.

Many negotiators presume that all negotiations are purely distributive and that their task as negotiators is to get as much as they can from the fixed amount of resources to be divided. A common assumption is that the interests of the other party are diametrically opposed to their own interests, and therefore there is a direct conflict over the resources in question. This is called the "fixed-pie bias"(Bazerman, Magliozzi and Neale, 1985). Based on this assumption, they view negotiation as an adversarial process. The integrative dimension of negotiation is often overlooked because of this bias.

C. The Integrative Dimension of Negotiation

The most basic assumption underlying the integrative dimension of negotiation is that one party can gain without the other party necessarily having to lose. Another way to say this is that there are ways for the parties to mutually benefit. To do this, the parties need to take more of a problem-solving, cooperative approach rather than the contentious, competitive approach that typically characterizes purely distributive negotiations. In effect, the parties try to "expand the pie" of resources, or create value. A key element that should be present for a problem-solving orientation to work is trust between the parties. Trust is crucial because information sharing is at the heart of the negotiation process, and if information is not openly and accurately shared, albeit in a reciprocal manner, it is unlikely that integrative solutions can be found. Negotiating along the integrative dimension, or trying to find mutually beneficial solutions, can be difficult because it frequently requires finding creative or novel solutions that may not have been considered prior to the negotiation.

There are several ways to achieve integrative solutions. Most of them are based on differing interests underlying the conflict on the surface. Although this may sound strange because differences are the reason for the conflict, it is differences in preferences that allow integrative negotiation to occur.

There are many techniques for finding integrative solutions. Logrolling entails trading issues that are of differing importance to the two parties (Pruitt and Rubin, 1986). Cost cutting occurs when one party finds a way to make the concessions of the other party less costly. This is often accomplished by one party offering the conceding party some sort of compensation that is related to the issues being negotiated. Cost cutting differs from nonspecific compensation, in which the party that concedes is paid by the other party in some currency that is unrelated to the negotiated issues. Obtaining added resources may sometimes be possible so that both parties can meet their goals. Frequently, the time and effort spent negotiating over a given set of resources may instead be spent finding ways to increase the amount of available resources (Pruitt, 1983). By undertaking one or more of these strategies, the parties in a negotiation may both be better off than if they simply compromised on the issues.

There are many obvious and some not-so-obvious benefits of finding integrative solutions in negotiations. Increasing the amount of resources to be distributed may be necessary for both parties to be able to reach their reservation prices. In these cases, an impasse is likely unless some integrative solution is found. An obvious benefit to finding integrative agreements is that a party's outcomes may be increased because a larger amount of resources is available to be distributed.

Less obviously, a party may also benefit from the opponent receiving a higher outcome. An opponent's satisfaction with the negotiation should increase as the outcome gets better. This should have a positive effect on the relationship between the two parties and should make the agreement more stable. If the other party is required to implement a decision that was reached as part of the negotiated agreement, successful implementation is more likely if the opponent is happy with the outcome, rather than disgruntled. Of course, the importance a party places on an opponent's outcome may vary with the expectation or probability of future interaction or with the types of issues that are being negotiated (e.g., some issues may require implementation, while others may not). The point here is that most people think only of their own outcome when they determine whether they were successful in a negotiation when several benefits, however indirect, may accrue to them if the other party also achieves a good outcome. Several specific strategies for reaching integrative agreements are outlined in Table 2.

Table 2 - Creating Value: Integrative Bargaining Strategies

1. Know your BATNA. Try to ascertain the other side's BATNA.
2. Analyze your own and the other party's reservation prices to determine the bargaining zone.
3. Set priorities on your interests and those of the other party.
4. Construct multi-issue packages of offers that take into account differences between your own and the other party's priorities.

D. The Mixed-Motive Nature of Negotiation

When thinking about the distributive and integrative dimensions of negotiation, it is crucial to keep in mind the mixed-motive nature of negotiations. Creating value by finding integrative solutions requires primarily cooperative behavior, while claiming value along the distributive dimension of the negotiation requires primarily competitive behavior. Many people make the mistake of thinking they can segment a negotiation into integrative and distributive components so that, for example, the parties can first integratively expand the pie and then negotiate the distribution of the enlarged pie. In fact, it is very unlikely for these to happen sequentially. Instead, the processes of integration and distribution occur simultaneously.

Negotiators must simultaneously balance cooperative and competitive behavior, so that they enlarge the pie while they claim an acceptable share of the enlarged pie. It is this "fundamental tension between cooperation and competition" that is the heart of negotiation, and that makes negotiation both an art and a science The way that the value is created affects the way it is divided; the process of creating value is entwined with the process of claiming it (Lax and Sebbenius, 1986). This is especially true if the motives and behaviors of the other parties are unpredictable before the negotiation or are hard to read during the negotiation.

E. The Role of Information Sharing

Cooperative or competitive orientations are easy to talk about in general terms, but how do they manifest themselves in actual behavior during a negotiation? One of the core behavioral components of negotiation is information sharing. It is through the sharing of information that parties learn about their opponent's preferences on the issues, BATNA and reservation price, willingness to concede, interest in adding other issues to the negotiation, and in general, their opponent's overall orientation. Although the total amount of information that is shared during the negotiation is likely to affect the quality of the outcome reached by the parties, examining the subtleties of the parties' information sharing patterns may be more revealing. First, if one party shares much more information than the other party, the party that receives the greater amount of information may have an advantage because they may know more about how far the other party can be pushed or what the chances are of finding an integrative solution. For example, if only one party knows the other's reservation price, the party with this information knows the size of the bargaining zone while the other does not. This could have a profound impact on the outcome of the negotiation.

One clarification here is that sharing information is not the same as talking. One side may talk more than the other party but share a lesser amount of important information. If negotiation is viewed solely as a persuasive process, then the party that talks more may be expected to do more persuading, and thus achieve a better outcome. However, persuasion is typically not included in what we refer to as information sharing. Information that is relevant in this analysis concerns the interests of the party and thus the side that gives away less of this information may have an advantage.

Even if the amount of information shared by the parties is symmetric, the order in which it is shared may influence the outcomes of the parties. If one party gives away all of his information before the other party gives away any of her information, the party that delays sharing information may have an advantage, knowing more about the issues and the structure of the negotiation than the other party at an earlier point in the negotiation. Ideally, information should be shared in a reciprocal fashion so that one party gives away information incrementally while receiving equivalent amounts of information from the other party.

There are several strategies aimed at getting more information from the other party. Some of them, such as asking questions, are simple but often overlooked. These strategies include:
- building trust between the parties so that information is more likely to be shared

- asking questions
- giving away some information unilaterally in the hope that the other party will reciprocate
- making multiple offers simultaneously so the other party's interests can be inferred from the acceptability of each offer
- searching for post-settlement settlements (agreements that occur based on an extended search after an initial agreement is reached) (Raiffa, 1985)

Of course, the accuracy and specificity of information obtained by the other party is crucial. Discerning the accuracy of the information given by the other party is primarily a matter of trust, both on the part of the party giving information (trusting that the other party will not take advantage of true information) and on the part of the party receiving information (believing the information given by the other party).

F. Compatible Issues

There is one other type of issue we have not yet mentioned that is frequently overlooked when people think of negotiation. Compatible issues are those for which the parties have the same preferences. The parties have no conflict over these issues, perhaps making it seem odd that we include them in a chapter about conflict management. However, they are often included in negotiations because the negotiators do not know they have the same preferences on these issues and they make assumptions about the preferences of the other party.

Specifically, as mentioned earlier, many negotiators have a fixed-pie bias, meaning that they systematically assume their task in a negotiation is to split a fixed amount of resources (Bazerman, et al. 1985; Thompson, 1991). The incompatibility bias inhibits negotiators in a related way, as they assume that the other party's preferences on the issues are necessarily in direct conflict with their own preferences and that they have no common interests (Thompson, 1991). Because of these biases, issues that are included in a negotiation for which the negotiators want the same outcome are often not identified as compatible, and a substantial number of negotiators settle for an outcome on these issues other than the one they both want.

G. Multi-Party Negotiations

Most of the examples that are used to illustrate negotiations are dyadic, involving two parties. Although there are certainly many negotiations that involve only two parties, a substantial portion of negotiations involve three or more parties (which we refer to as multi-party). In health care, frequent examples involve negotiations among state or federal payment agencies, hospitals, and physicians. While many of the concepts of negotiation generalize from dyadic to multi-party negotiations, there are important differences between these types of negotiation.

The biggest difference is the increased complexity that occurs when parties are added to the negotiation. This complexity falls into two categories. First, interpersonal complexity increases as more people become involved in the interaction. For each person, there are more signals, gestures, and other types of communications from others to interpret. The second type of complexity involves the issues themselves. There are now multiple sets of preferences to be worked through rather than just two sets.

For example, regarding the same subset of issues, two parties may have compatible preferences, two other parties may have opposite preferences but place a different amount of importance on these issues, while the preferences of two other parties may be diametrically opposed. Sharing the information to determine these preferences becomes much more difficult with multiple parties, and even if perfect information is shared, it is still a complex task to determine an optimal solution that is acceptable to everyone.

The bargaining zone in a negotiation with multiple parties is defined as the set of agreements that exceed every party's reservation price. It can be very difficult to determine whether a bargaining zone exists, much less the size of the bargaining zone. Furthermore, there may be people involved in the negotiation who would prefer that no agreement be reached, so that their purpose at the negotiation table (whether disguised or not) is to impede the process of the negotiation. Building trust may be more difficult between multiple parties, especially if coalitions form within the group of negotiators.

Coalition formation can have a major effect on the negotiation process and outcome. Coalitions may be based on longstanding relationships outside of the negotiation, or they may form during the negotiation based on similarity of preferences. They may form either to try to reach a specific agreement or to try to block a specific type of agreement. What is best for the coalition may not be what is best for the entire group. Negotiators in a multi-party situation should think about who they would like to form a coalition with, who might like to form a coalition with them, and who is unlikely to want to include them in a coalition.

Proactive behavior may be especially helpful in building a coalition because it should be easier to form a coalition initially than to break up an existing coalition and reform another one. However, coalitions, especially those formed around specific preferences in the negotiation, are likely to be unstable. When considering that the typical reason for joining a coalition is to increase your own outcomes, it is not surprising that people readily switch allegiances when they get better offers from other potential coalition partners. As such, coalitions may shift repeatedly during the course of a negotiation.

Decision rules for reaching agreement may also be necessary in multi-party negotiations. Possible decision rules include unanimity, majority rule, or some other special rule detailing how many people must agree in order to reach a settlement. Some parties may also have veto power, which affects the power balance in the negotiation. These latter considerations may be influenced by the context within which the negotiation takes place. For example, if all the parties are working in the same organization (e.g., physicians employed by the same hospital), there may be hierarchical considerations, existing norms guiding the selection of a decision rule, or pressure from superiors to reach an agreement. Conversely, in a group negotiation in which the parties represent several different organizations (e.g., physicians having their own organizations), many of the parties may have more freedom to withdraw from the negotiation or force an impasse because they may have better alternatives with other sets of organizations. Also, few norms may exist if the negotiation itself is the first time the parties have been together in a group.

The above factors should be considered when preparing for and participating in a multi-party negotiation. If properly managed, the increased complexity inherent in this type of negotiation does not have to be an impediment and can in fact be used strategically if other parties are less prepared for or less able to cope with the complexity.

H. Fairness and Ethics in Negotiation

Negotiators often make claims about fairness to support their arguments. Fairness is not a unidimensional concept, however, and the application of different norms of fairness can lead to different outcomes. For this reason, it is important to think about which different norms of fairness can be applied in particular situations so that generalized claims for fairness are not used inappropriately. In a negotiation context, fairness will be discussed as it applies to the allocation of resources, which is the typical result of negotiation.

The most prevalent fairness in our society is equality, in which every party gets the same absolute amount of resources (Rawls, 1971). A second fairness norm that is used in most organizations to determine compensation is equity, whereby each person gets allocated an amount of resources proportional to his inputs (Adams, 1963; Homans, 1961). Defining what relevant inputs consist of and measuring these inputs can often lead to additional conflict, but once norms are in place in organizations regarding these issues, allocating resources equitably is often regarded as fair. Equity can be invoked in many negotiations other than organizational compensation situations as well. A third popular norm of fairness upon which allocations can be based is need, so that parties receive an amount of resources proportional to their need for them (Deutsch, 1975). As with inputs in the equity norm situation, determining the relative needs of each party can be tricky. Besides these three pure allocation norms of fairness, people may combine two or three of these norms to determine a fair allocation. Negotiators should consider which of these norms is applicable when they or one of their opponents claim that the negotiated outcome should be "fair."

Many people think of fairness and ethics in negotiation as somewhat entwined. Fairness may not always refer to the norm used for resource allocation, as discussed above, but instead may refer to the process by which people negotiate. For instance, people often say that if a negotiator is "unethical," she is not negotiating fairly. This triggers the same kind of problem that is triggered when determining fair allocations, in that people are not always in agreement about what constitutes ethical behavior. This is especially relevant for negotiation because there are many typical negotiating strategies, such as bluffing or avoiding an answer to a specific question, that fall in a gray area concerning the ethicality of such behavior. Furthermore, many people . believe that what is ethical is partially determined by context. For example, in some cultures bribes are an accepted way of doing business when negotiating. Others adhere to a more absolute form of ethicality, believing that actions are either ethical or unethical regardless of the situation

We are not going to state any rules about what is ethical or unethical. Instead, our purpose in discussing ethics is to increase the reader's awareness of several issues. First, however it is defined, unethical behavior is typically the result of self-interest (Murnighan, 1992). People act unethically because they benefit from it. When negotiating, regardless of your particular beliefs about ethics, it is important not to assume that the other party has the same beliefs you do or that they will behave (or restrict their behavior) in the same way you will. Also, unethical behavior can have consequences, especially regarding reputations, such that unethical behavior may help negotiators in the short run but may come back to haunt them in the long run. Negotiations can be full of ethical dilemmas. Thinking through and determining your own standards before you get into difficult situations is advised, as is being cautious, especially when making assumptions about the other party's ethical standards.

I. Preparing to Negotiate

Preparing for a negotiation often has as much to do with achieving a successful outcome as does the actual negotiation. But what exactly should a negotiator do to prepare for the negotiation? In this section, we offer several suggestions for how to increase the probability of a successful negotiation by preparing appropriately.

The least obvious, and perhaps most important, activity that should be worked on before the negotiation is to develop a BATNA, which was discussed earlier. If negotiators can develop a better and more certain alternative to a negotiated outcome, they will have more power in the negotiation and be likely to reach a better outcome. Determining a reservation price, based partially on the BATNA, is the next step to knowing in advance when you will be willing to walk away from the negotiation rather than reach agreement.

Concerning the negotiation more directly, a negotiator should think about what issues are likely to be included in the negotiation if they have not been specified in advance by either party. What additional issues could you bring to the negotiation? What issues might your opponent want to include? Whatever the set of issues includes, the negotiator should determine the importance of each issue relative to the other issues. This facilitates the process of comparing different offers made by the other party and trading low-priority issues for high-priority issues. Collecting information about the other party's alternatives and the importance that party places on each issue is a priority during a negotiation. It follows that negotiators can enhance their position if they can discover some or all of this information about their opponent before the negotiation. Sometimes this information can be gathered directly from the other negotiator prior to negotiating, while in other situations it may be learned from other sources.

Another important piece of information to gather is how many negotiators the other party will be bringing to the table. A negotiator should also determine before the negotiation how important the relationship with the other party is. What future effects are likely to be caused by reputations that are developed in this negotiation? How much is the other party likely to be concerned about the relationship? The extent to which the decisions that are reached during the negotiation need to be implemented by either party after the negotiation is an important factor related to the relationship between the parties. If you have to rely on the other party to implement part of the deal, it is obviously not good to have the other party unhappy with that agreement or with you. Determining the time constraints faced by each party can be useful, as the party who has the longer time before needing to reach an agreement has an advantage, if both parties know about the time constraints of the other.

Even the end of a negotiation should be prepared for. If negotiators do not reveal all of their information during the negotiation, they should think about whether they want to share any of this information after the negotiation. It is usually advisable to keep some information confidential even after the negotiation so the other party does not grow concerned about whether she received a good outcome in the negotiation. The better-prepared party in a negotiation is often the most successful during the negotiation. As in school, doing your homework before the negotiation is half the battle when it is time to take the test.

V. MANAGING CONFLICT THROUGH THIRD PARTY INTERVENTION

In many conflict situations, the disputants are unable to resolve the conflict. A third party that is not directly involved in the conflict can frequently intervene in one of several different ways to help resolve the conflict. There are many formal, institutional third parties that can be turned to outside of any particular organization. The court system in the United States is a very large example of a third party. Arbitrators are third parties that resolve differences between parties on many different issues, such as professional baseball salaries. The focus of this chapter, however, is on the manager's role as a third party in the day-to-day conflicts that occur in organizational life, rather than on formal third party systems. To the extent that conflict is disruptive in organizations and hampers productivity, managers can increase the effectiveness of their organizations by intervening in conflict situations. Of course, the time the manager spends trying to resolve the disputes of other people is a cost to the organization, which needs to be balanced with the benefit derived from decreased conflict.

A. Dispute Intervention Goals

After making the decision to intervene in a conflict, the manager has a wide range of third party intervention strategies to choose from. The particular role the manager plays in the dispute may depend on what he is trying to accomplish and on the constraints imposed by the situation. When intervening in a dispute between subordinates, a manager has a high level of authority making any type of intervention an option. This is not the case when a manager intervenes in a dispute between two peers. The amount of conflict between the parties may also influence the manager's selection of intervention strategies. The importance of the issues in dispute, the amount of time pressure faced by the manager, the relative power of the disputants, and the relationships between the parties and between the manager and the parties may all affect the manager's choice of intervention strategies (Neale and Bazerman, 1991). The manager may also be concerned with how satisfied the disputants will be with the resolution and their perceptions of fairness regarding the intervention.

B. Types of Intervention Strategies

The types of intervention strategies a manager can undertake can be usefully categorized along two dimensions—the control the third party has over the process of the dispute and the control the third party has over the outcome of the dispute. Suppose a medical group practice manager is trying to manage the conflict between primary care physicians and specialists involving sharing revenue generated by the group practice. The control the manager desires over the process and outcome is likely to be affected by the factors discussed in the preceding paragraph. When the manager desires high control over both the process and outcome of the dispute, she may act as an inquisitor. In this type of intervention, the manager gathers information on the dispute by asking questions of the physicians, rather than letting them present the information as they would like. The manager then makes a decision about the outcome of the dispute and communicates this to the physicians. As in the court system, a manager acts as a judge or arbitrator when he controls the outcome but not the process of the dispute. The parties are free to present their sides of the dispute as they wish, after which the manager makes the decisions necessary to end the dispute. Mediators have control over the process of the dispute but have no authority or do not use their authority, to control the outcome. Acting as mediator, the group practice manager may control the flow of information between the physicians' groups by separating them and acting as a go-between or may guide the discussion between them when they are together. The outcome, however, will ultimately be decided by the leaders of the respective physician groups.

The manager who chooses not to have high process or outcome control can choose from several options. The most efficient approach from the manager's perspective is to ignore the conflict and hope the disputants will resolve it by themselves. Managers can also delegate responsibility for getting the dispute resolved to someone else. Another option is to threaten the disputants to increase their motivation to resolve the conflict.

Managers have many options to choose from in determining which third party intervention strategies best fit their needs. It is possible that, for the same dispute situation, a manager may change intervention strategies if the previously chosen strategy does not work. When this happens, a manager will usually progress from strategies involving less control to strategies involving more control.

Although conflict is pervasive, it can be successfully managed through an understanding and application of various conflict management techniques and negotiation skills. By managing conflict more effectively, health services executives make important contributions to organizational effectiveness while improving the productivity and satisfaction of the people with whom they work.

VI. MANAGERIAL GUIDELINES

1. Managers need to analyze the amount and type of both beneficial and detrimental conflict that currently exists in their organization so that they can focus on eliminating the detrimental conflict.
2. Health care managers should evaluate the level at which conflict usually occurs in their organization. Are there strong group boundaries (e.g., between departments or functional areas) that contribute to conflict, or is most conflict at the individual level?
3. When managers are involved in conflict, they should think explicitly about how much concern they have for the other party, as well as how concerned they are about their own outcomes for the issues involved in the conflict. This should

help to determine what conflict management strategy will be most appropriate.

4. When negotiating, managers need to determine the exact issues that are currently being negotiated and identify any other issues that might be included in the negotiation. Also, the importance of each issue to both the manager and the other party should be compared to determine where mutually beneficial tradeoffs might occur.

5. Managers should think carefully about what ethical standards they feel comfortable with before they enter situations that involve ethical considerations.

6. Managers should not underestimate the importance of preparing for a negotiation. Failing to adequately prepare is probably the single biggest mistake made by negotiators.

7. If managers are going to intervene in a conflict as a third party, they need to consider how much control they want to have over both the process and the outcome of the dispute. Distinguishing between these types of control will facilitate effective intervention implementation.

ENDNOTE

1. Originally published in 1994 in *Health Care Management Organization Design and Behavior, Third Edition*. Reprinted with permission of the pubisher.

REFERENCES

Adams, J. S. (1963). Toward an understanding of inequity. *Journal of Abnormal and Social Psychology, 67*: 422-436.

Bazerman, M. H., Magliozzi, T. and Neale, M. A. (1985). The acquisition of an integrative response in a competitive market. *Organizational Behavior and Human Decision Processes. 35*: 294-313.

Deutsch, M. (1975). Equity, equality, and need: What determines which value will be used as the basis of distributive justice? *Journal of Social Issues. 31*: 137-149.

Deutsch, M. (1949). An experimental study of the effects of cooperation and competition upon group process. *Human Relations, 2*: 199-232.

Fisher, R. and Ury, W. (1981). *Getting to Yes*. Houghton-Mifflin: Boston, Mass.

Homans, G. (1961). *Social Behavior: Its Elementary Forms*. Harcourt, Brace: New York.

Jehn, K. A. (1992). The impact of intragroup conflict on effectiveness: A multimethod examination of the benefits and detriments of conflict. Unpublished dissertation: Northwestern University, Evanston, Ill.

Lax, D. and Sebenius, J. (1986). *The Manager as Negotiator*. Free Press: New York, NY.

Murnighan, J. K. (1992). *Bargaining Games*. William Morrow and Company, Inc.: New York, NY.

Neale, M. and Bazerman, M. (1991:2). *Cognition and Rationality in Negotiation*. Free Press: New York, NY.

Northcraft, G. and Neale, M. (1990). *Organizational Behavior: The Managerial Challenge*. Dryden Press: Homewood, Ill.

Pruitt, D. G. (1983). Achieving integrative agreement. In M. H. Bazerman and R. J. Lewicki, (Eds.), *Negotiating in Organizations*. Sage: Beverly Hills, CA.

Pruitt, D. G. and Rubin, J. Z. (1986). *Social Conflict*. Academic Press: New York, NY.

Raiffa, H. (1982). *The Art and Science of Negotiation*. Belknap: Cambridge, Mass.

Raiffa, H. (1985). Post settlement settlements. *Negotiation Journal*. 1: 9-12.

Rawls, J. (1971). A Theory of Justice. Harvard University Press: Cambridge, Mass.

Rubin, J. and Brown, B. (1975). The Social Psychology of Bargaining and Negotiation. Academic Press: New York, NY.

Sherif, M. (1977). *Intergroup Conflict and Cooperation*. University Book Exchange: Norman, OK.

Thomas, K. (1976). Conflict and conflict management. In: M. Dunnette (Ed.), *Handbook of Industrial and Organizational Psychology*. Rand-McNally: New York, NY.

Thompson L. L. (1991). Information exchange in negotiation. *Journal of Experimental Social Psychology*, 27(2): 161-179.

White, S. and Neale, M. The role of negotiation aspiration and settlement expectancies on bargaining outcomes. *Organizational Behavior and Human Decision Processes*, In press.

55.
MEDIATION

Anne Osborne Kilpatrick, *Medical University of South Carolina, Charleston, SC*

Jacquelyn K. Jones, *Medical University of South Carolina, Charleston, SC*

In the 1980s, the average employee, working only 40 hours per week, sleeping 8 hours per night with two weeks vacation per year, was estimated to spend 42% of waking hours in the workplace (Conti, 1985). During the 1980s and 1990s, economic constraints have forced employees to work longer hours, to work harder with fewer employees, and to function in an era of increasing stress, often with older equipment and fewer resources. Job insecurity has contributed to the existent stress in the workplace, and much of the trust traditionally experienced between employer and employee has eroded (Haas, 1991). Outcomes of this increasingly stressful environment have been reflected in reduced productivity, reports of higher burnout, increases in employee personnel actions and grievances, workaholism, strikes, and workplace violence (Nigro and Waugh, 1996; US Department of Justice, 1994). This latter consequence has seen tragedies in public and private organizations. The US Postal Service has experienced numerous violent deaths in recent years; in fact, the new phrase "going Postal" has been added to our vernacular to describe employees who assault coworkers and supervisors (Elders, 1993; Haggerty, 1993; Taylor, 1995).

The management of conflict and the nonviolent resolution of disputes in the workplace have been identified as a major responsibility for today's managers (Evans, 1992; Firth, 1991; Milite, 1992; Pulhamus, 1991; Rue and Byers, 1992). Traditionally, dispute resolution programs in the workplace have been tied to formal disciplinary processes with legalistic methods of appeal, attorney representation, and jury-like grievance protections. These adversarial relationships between employer and employee are patterned after the United States legal system's model of litigation, imposing a win-lose model of zero-sum employer power. This model presumes that any power given to an employee diminishes the power left to employer. In commenting on win/lose approaches an article published by George Truell Associates (1980) states, "[a]lthough these approaches may work at times, they leave 'debris' in the form of smoldering resentment, hurt feelings, damaged egos, and a strong desire by the loser to get even." In situations where continuity of a cooperative relationship is essential, use of the adversarial zero sum approach can be very destructive; it leads to alienation, mistrust, and hence lowered productivity. Consequently, another approach is needed—an approach which enables both parties to "win." Much of the personnel/human resources management literature and many human resources management texts describe the steps and processes by which the rights of employer, and secondarily the employee, may be protected to avoid possible future litigation (Byars and Rue, 1994; Fottler et al., 1994; Noe et al., 1994). All these texts devote only one or two sentences to a definition of alternative dispute processes while emphasizing other more formal dispute resolution mechanisms—generally applied through the judicial and administrative court systems.

Mediation programs, which focus on positive win-win outcomes for all participants, have emerged as a fairly recent addition to the methods of alternative dispute resolution (ADR) available to employers. This chapter reviews the background of mediation in the context of conflict management strategies, presents a case study of the establishment of one mediation program in a large public organization, and suggests factors to consider in the development of a mediation program. Additional areas for research are also presented.

I. DEFINING MEDIATION AND ALTERNATIVE DISPUTE

Alternative dispute resolution (ADR) is increasingly viewed as a desirable conflict management strategy in health care (Barton, 1991; Darr, 1988; Dunkin, 1991; Grant 1995; Kauffman, 1992; Sherman, 1991; and Stillwell, 1992). According to Darr (1988), ADR encompasses several extra-judicial means of formal problem solving, all with one common attribute: all are private, confidential, and the public has no access to information). Strategies included under this rubric include—from least formal to most formal—mediation, arbitration, and private adjudication. The latter form uses corporations comprised of retired judges in quasi-judicial surroundings and legally binding agreements. Mini-trials allow disputants to present cases through attorneys and again may identify empowered individuals to resolve the dispute.

Mediation is one method of ADR. Both arbitration and mediation use a trained neutral third party whose purpose is to bring the parties together so that they can devise a "best solution." In mediation, the emphasis is on problem solving and consensus. The neutral participant, or mediator, helps the parties seek and identify a solution that each can live with, rather than make a decision for the parties. This leads to constructive participation by all. The parties gain more control over the situation because they have equal input into crafting an agreement that addresses their needs and their interests. This approach encourages the parties to view a dispute as a problem to be solved, rather than a battle to be won. Parties meet face to face to resolve their differences. They are encouraged to clearly state their feelings and needs. Information is disclosed openly without fear of reprisal. Each party is committed to listening and understanding the other party's interests. The individuals actually affected are part of the process. They do not act through agents, such as lawyers. They characterize the problem together, and they educate each other concerning the issues. They generate, evaluate, and reach reasonable solutions together (Hanna, et al., 1993).

In the early 1980s, Kilpatrick (1983), in a multidisciplinary review of publications on conflict resolution, wrote: Mediation is a form of voluntary intervention in which the conflicting parties select a third party to mediate their dispute. Aided by the mediator, the parties work out certain agreements. They are not always legally bound by these agreements, but they are morally committed to resolving their differences. Mediation is being used with increasing frequency in new environments as an alternative to litigation.

More structured than mediation, arbitration is generally binding on both parties. Unlike mediation, in which the decision is made jointly by the conflicting parties, arbitration shifts the responsibility of the final decision to the third party arbitrator. Currently, arbitration is most frequently used in labor-management conflicts. It is being adopted increasingly by family courts and local domestic courts in the form of both voluntary and compulsory arbitration (Ibid, p. 3).

In the early 1980s, most applications of mediation were divorce mediation, where both parties had agreed to divorce but wanted an amicable settlement of property and/or custody issues and court-directed mediation, mostly in cases of juvenile vandalism, allowing for restoration of a victim's property, and simultaneously offering the opportunity for a victim to confront his assailant. The Mennonite Church, who published several popular reference and how-to documents, assisted in the implementation of some programs, including the Mennonite Conciliation Service and a victim-offender reconciliation service (Kraybill, 1981).

In 1971, Michigan established one of the earliest court-annexed arbitration programs and termed them mediations. Justification for these programs in the courts—to reduce court congestion and to speed case disposition—may be seen in the increased numbers of cases filed in US district courts: 35,000 in 1940, 180,000 in 1981, and 240,000 in 1987 (Rosati, 1990).

Several bills introduced into Congress to allow for ADR for the resolution of professional liability disputes are patterned after a program available to physicians in Michigan since 1976. The Michigan program allows for use of binding arbitration, but mediation has not been suggested as part of the program. The US Government Accounting Office also noted that few hospitals, providers and patients had participated, but that response was positive from those who had participated in the process (Watkins, 1991). More recently, mediation has been recommended as a way to address disputes and avoid litigation under the Americans with Disabilities Act (Blanck, 1995).

Mediation differs from other forms of ADR in the following ways: voluntary participation; commitment to problem-solving; equal playing field: management is participant, not host; clear rules of conduct; informal nature of meetings: face-to-face, usually without attorneys, tape recorders, stenographers, or materials/transcripts. At the beginning of the proceedings, confidentiality must be maintained. The mediator informs participants that he or she will not willingly testify in future legal battles and that notes will be destroyed at the end of mediation. At the beginning of the mediation, consensus, defined as agreement between two participants, should be established as a goal.

Advantages of mediation include high user satisfaction, high compliance by participants in implementing agreements, high settlement rates, speedier settlements, and lower costs (Kressel et al., in Brett, 1992). Others may include improvements in job satisfaction; reduced stress in the work environment; employees who perceive they are heard; feelings of safety and improved trust. Additionally, sexual harassment and other forms of harassment may be eliminated without resort to formal litigation and disciplinary procedures (Abreuzzi, 1992). Finally, long-term effectiveness in resolving conflicts in work relationships should increase (Phillips et al., 1992).

II. INNOVATIONS IN HEALTH CARE

Total Quality Management (TQM), Continuous Quality Improvement (CQI), patient focused care, self-directed work teams, guest relations, and facilitating cultural diversity all share a common premise: to be successful, these and other similar work place initiatives require employees at all levels in the organization to communicate effectively and to solve problems collaboratively.

For example, Baptist Memorial Hospital (BMH) of Memphis, Tennessee, introduced TQM into its organization in the late 1980s. A 1991 article published by Organizational Dynamics, Inc., explained that BMH identified communication and collaboration as two of the seven goals and principles for its total quality process. To achieve these goals, BMH developed a communications committee and incorporated the FADE (focus, analyze, develop and execute) problem solving process. BMH's approach has resulted in "a more harmonious and collaborative work environment and without question a more efficient hospital," according to Joseph H. Powell, President (1991, p. 14).

III. CASE STUDY OF MEDIATION PROGRAM

A Southern state-supported medical university, which includes an academic medical center, employs approximately 8,200 employees. Over half the employees work in the medical center. The employee population is 71.7% female and 30% African-American; the largest group of African-American females cluster in the lower-skill occupational categories.

This organization has experienced tremendous growth in the last few years— growth reflected in capital equipment, buildings, revenue, operating budget, and an increased number of employees. It seeks to become one of the South's premier health care facilities. However, until recently interpersonal relationships among employees were not clearly perceived as a key element to achieving this goal.

During the early 1990s, several important workplace initiatives were introduced including TQM/CQI, patient-focused care, and a reassessment of its guest relations program. As previously mentioned, these initiatives require the empowerment of all employees, from the bottom up, to be able to collaborate, communicate, and solve problems across cultural, professional, and departmental lines.

A. Justifying the Program: Assessment of Climate

A work environment assessment was conducted by the Human Resources Management Department prior to developing an ADR program. The review involved an analysis of three years of available data on exit interviews; the number, types of and reasons for disciplinary actions; the disciplinary appeal process; Equal Employment Opportunity (EEO) complaints; and individual departmental reviews that had been conducted by the university's employee relations staff. The assessment revealed that in spite of increased visibility and aggressiveness of the employee relations function, expanded training of supervisors, and improved policies and adjusted relationships with departments, some anticipated changes had not occurred. For some employees, this work environment was still hostile. Overall findings indicated that on the average, two employees per day received formal disciplinary action. The data indicated that the number of internal appeals of terminations and suspensions had remained the same—between 30 and 35 per year—for the last three years. The organization strongly asserted that its grievance appeals process was important as a check-and-balance process for management practices and that it provided employees an objective means for protecting their rights. However, in most cases this process required that someone win and someone else lose. In these formal dispute mechanisms, all too often nobody really wins regardless of the decision because some issues and emotions remain unresolved.

The use of the progressive disciplinary process had not decreased over the years. Management literature indicates that discipline is an important management tool for correcting behavior, communicating expectations and educating employees. But how many employees feel good after they have been disciplined? Too often, the employee continues to engage in counterproductive behavior, which simply becomes more clandestine. Another concern is that less enlightened managers would apply discipline to only specific segments of the employee population.

A review of the exit interview data indicated that some employees were voluntarily terminating their employment, not because of wages, workloads or schedules, but because they didn't feel a part of the team. Others believed their supervisors harbored feelings of hostility against them.

Over the previous three years, satisfaction surveys and personal interviews were conducted with approximately 525 employees from a variety of departments. A review of the surveys indicated that about 30% of the respondents identified as a problem lack of effective communication between them and their supervisors. The corresponding interviews revealed that employees were not informed of how decisions were made. The interviews also revealed that employees seldom received regular feedback from their supervisors regarding their performance. Too often employees had to wait until their annual appraisal reviews or until a problem arose before they knew if they were performing satisfactorily. The interviewees didn't feel that enough effort had been given to sharing information, eliciting their input and developing a sense of organizational harmony.

During the last few years a number of employees had expressed dissatisfaction that no appeal process assisted them with interpersonal issues that were not covered by the existing grievance process. Until recently, employees could only appeal Title VII acts of discrimination or certain disciplinary such as suspensions, terminations, reductions-in-force, and demotions.

Table 1 Characteristics of Mediation

- Support from top management
- Training of supervisors
- Well-trained mediators
- Formal dispute resolution structure supports mediation
- Training with emphasis on diversity and communication skills
- Role play and feedback
- Ethical issues
- Co-mediate where possible
- Continuous maintenance of skills
- Role clarification is ongoing

B. Implementation

The above data and additional information—the cost of appeals per fiscal year, the percentage of employees in various stages of progressive discipline, and estimates of the number of days missed from work because of unresolved disputes—were presented to the Vice President of Finance and Administration. It was agreed that unresolved conflict, even based on limited data, was expensive for the organization. Consultants with training in conflict resolution and cultural diversity were chosen. Two consultant groups combined their expertise to develop a comprehensive 40 hour training program.

Nineteen individuals were selected to be trained as certified mediators. The volunteers were outstanding employees who were willing and, with their managers' support, able to devote the time and energy to this endeavor. Additionally, they were representative of the demographics of the institution, racially, ethnically, functionally, and in age. The first 35 hours of training took place during five days (March 23-31, 1993). The final five hours were conducted in September, 1993.

The training included four major components: cultural diversity, communication, mediation skills development, and legal issues. Role plays, lectures, and case studies were used for instructional purposes. These volunteer mediators conducted their first mediation in the spring of 1993, with over 20 following in the first six months of the program.

The program has been publicized in the employee newspaper, departmental meetings, and individual mailings to all employees. Requests for mediation may be initiated by any individual involved in a dispute. During the first year, the number of mediations accompanied a reduction in grievances and employee disciplinary actions.

Findings which have emerged from the introduction of the mediation program include the following: Management must take ownership of the program. Leadership must support the mediation program, and believe that it will be positive for the organization in real costs as well as in less quantifiable ways. High visibility for the program within the institution is important. Employees and managers should know what the program is and how to participate. Managers and supervisors need to be educated about the program and should have as part of their own performance evaluations assessment of their support of mediation—both through supporting their own employ-

Table 2 Organizational Criteria for Successful Mediations

- Maintaining of the quality of the process (openness, active participation, cooperation, tolerance, flexibility)
- Impartiality with respect to the parties
- Servicing the interests of the parties through careful preparation, maintaining access to independent advice, if relevant, confidentiality, and sensitivity to cultural difference
- Maintaining of the conditions for promoting a constructive exchange (without violence, threats, or provocation)
- Ensuring voluntary participation through provision of maximum information on the nature of the process and preserving the freedom for any party to leave the mediation without loss or blame
- Encouraging parties to take control of their own conflict and its resolution as a major goal for the mediator
- Ensuring fairness as far as possible, by dealing with power discrepancies, giving the parties sufficient time to state their case, encouraging full sharing of information, and ensuring that each is fully cognizant of his or her own interests and legal rights
- Having concern for the viability of agreements (with regard to implementation and interpretation and, if necessary, checking with independent advisers)
- Offering follow-up mediation at the parties' choice
- Endeavoring to increase his or her expertise by taking advantage of training opportunities and maintaining links with others involved in mediation

ees to be trained and serve as mediators and through encouraging participation in the program when disputes arise. Documentation and record-keeping of all types of dispute resolution should be maintained.

DISCUSSION

Mediation is a relatively new phenomenon in the workplace. It offers significant advantages to the rapidly changing, highly-stressed health care organization. However, it will not be widely adopted until certain changes take place: employers must be convinced of the importance of the program; they must adequately fund the program; and supervisors must be at least partly be evaluated by how employees feel about their work environment.

In 1994, Evans wrote concerning the employee's role in quality health care delivery, "[E]ffective communication is an essential element in healthy employee relations. [A]ny organization attempting to participate with its workforce to achieve common goals must also empower that workforce to make decisions and take responsibility for outcomes" (p. 50). This organization has chosen to provide its employees with the tool of conflict resolution as one means of fostering effective communication and developing harmonious relationships for their and the institution's mutual benefit.

Success of the mediation program depends on certain variables which are outlined in Table 2. First, support from top management is crucial. Management must commit to recognizing and rewarding supervisors for applying non-adversarial managerial strategies. Next, training of supervisors should be expanded to adopt mediation as a part of acceptable, quality management. Mediators then must be thoroughly trained— mediators who have demonstrated organizational commitment and professionalism in their work. The training program for mediators should include an emphasis on diversity and communication skills. Adequate time should be allotted to repeated role play and feedback because techniques ensure confidence and competence. Ethical issues training should address how mediators may be able to protect rights of less powerful employees (Rahim et al., 1992). Where possible, co-mediation will ensure and improve feedback and increase confidence of new mediators. This is also a way to experiment with alternative types of mediation—e.g., dual-advocacy mediation (Phillips, et al., 1992). Continuous maintenance of skills is crucial. If mediators don't exercise their training, they may not continue to be competent. Role clarification must be maintained. It is most important that mediators constantly clarify their roles to themselves as well as to the participants. Possible role conflicts which may occur for mediators include the following:

- Human resources/employee relations roles vs. mediator roles. Human resources staff are part of management, and will always have a conflict when working with employees. This conflict will be present when Human Resources staff function as mediators in formal mediations. Their usual role of generalist and expert in human resources policy may cause them to be more directive than desired in facilitating a neutral function as mediator. One suggestion is to regularly practice questioning one's present role.
- Mediation vs. grievance: knowing when to end a mediation and to allow the formal grievance procedures to be applied is important. One indication is when the role authority imbalance between disputants has resulted in a shut down of communication.
- Mediator vs. OD consultant: in a group mediation, it is important to note when mediation has ended, and the participants are moving to an organizational planning or development stage. Mediators should attempt constantly to be aware of which role they have. One trainer suggested that different clothes be worn to distinguish the separate roles.

In conclusion, much still needs to be documented about the implementation of mediation. While many organizations are adopting these programs, little empirical research exists to date on the structural process itself, changes in organizational climate, length and strength of agreements made, and comparative cost savings from these programs. Most publications report descriptive information about improved workplace climates and encourage adoption of mediation programs; the case described herein reported positive outcomes. Future longitudinal studies of organizational effectiveness could assess the effectiveness of mediation programs over time. It is the belief of the authors that as people learn how to seek win-win solutions to disputes, the organization's climate and effectiveness will improve.

REFERENCES

Apruzzese, V. J. (1992). Selected recent developments in EEO law: The Civil Rights Act of 1991, Sexual Harassment, and the emerging role of ADR. *Labor Law Journal, Stetson Labor Conference,* (June), 325-339.

Blanck, P. D. (1995). Resolving disputes under the Americans with Disabilities Act. *SPINE,* 20(7): 853-859.

D'Alemberte, T. S. (1991). ABA officer: ADR has come into its own. *Arbitration Journal,* 46(March): 3-5.

Dunkin, A. (1991). Got a beef? Call a peacemaker. *Business Week, September 23,* 122-123.

Elders, Evans, K. (1993). Managing labor relations: A vital element in healthcare's quest for quality. *Carolina Health Services Review, 1*(1): 63-67.

Evans, S. (1992). Conflict can be positive. *HR Magazine,* (May): 49-51.

Haggerty, Hall, J., and Stong, R. (1993). Alternative dispute resolution and the Physician: The use of mediation to resolve hospital-medical staff conflicts. *The Medical Staff Counselor. 7(2),* 1-6.

Hanna, J., Ewing, and Rawl, R. (1993). Mediation training program for MUSC mediators. Columbia, SC.

Kauffman, N. (1992). Expedited arbitration and other innovations in alternative dispute resolution. *Labor Law Journal, June,* 382-387.

Kilpatrick, A.O. (1983). *Resolving Community Conflict: An Annotated Bibliography.* Herald Press: Institute for Community and Area Development.

Kraybill, R.S. (1981). *Repairing the breach: Ministering in Community Conflict.* Scottdale, PA:

Marshall, T. F. (1990). The power of mediation. *Mediation Quarterly 8,*(2, Winter).

Meyer, G. (1992). Practice conflict resolution safely on a PC. *HRM Magazine, February,* 30-36.

Milite, G. (1992). When the team becomes too human. *Supervisory Management. (May):* 9-10.

Milkovich, G. and Boudreau, J. (1991). Human Resources Management (6th ed.). Homewood, IL: Irwin Nigro and Waugh, (1996).

Phillips, D., Cooke, J. and Anderson, A. (1992). A surefire resolution to workplace conflicts. *Personnel Journal, (May),* 111-114.

Rahim, M., Garrett, J., and Buntzman, G. (1992). Ethics of managing interpersonal conflict. *Journal of Business Ethics, 11:* 423-432.

Rue, L. and Byars, L. (1992). Management: Skills and application, (2nd ed.). Homewood, IL: Irwin.

Savage, P. (1987). *Who cares wins: How to Unlock the Hidden Potential in People at Work.* New York: Mercury Books.

Scarpello, V. and Ledvinka, J. (1988). *Personnel/Human Resources Management: Environments and Functions.* Boston, MA: PWS Publishing Company.

Sherman, Mark R. (1991). Streamlined mediation: Alternative to litigating discharge disputes. *Arbitration Journal, (March):* 34-37.

Stillwell, S. (1992). Seven steps to resolving disputes through arbitration. *Business Credit,* (February): 22-23.

TQM drives exceptional performance at Baptist Memorial Hospital. (1991). Organizational Dynamics, Inc.

Truell, G. (1980). *A win/win approach.* (Handout) US Department of Justice, (1994)

Watkins, R.A. (1991). Malpractice arbitration: A new idea, an old alternative. *Michigan Medicine, (September):* 46-47.

56.
JOB SATISFACTION

John F. Newman, *Georgia State University, Atlanta, GA*
Gerald Eldridge, *Georgia State University, Atlanta, GA*

I. WHAT IS JOB SATISFACTION?

A. Definitions

"Job satisfaction" has been defined in various ways. Simply stated, it is the enjoyment and feeling of fulfillment employees receive through their line of work. According to New Webster's Dictionary, a "job" is "a specific piece of work, especially done for pay" or "an occupation as a steady source of livelihood." "Satisfaction," on the other hand, is defined as "a source or cause of pleasure, fulfillment, compensation, or gratification." Job satisfaction has also been explained as "a multifaceted construct that reflects an employee's feelings about a variety of both intrinsic and extrinsic job elements" (Schappe, 1996, p. 339). In addition, one might explain job satisfaction as "the extent to which rewards actually received meet or exceed the perceived equitable level of rewards" (Porter and Lawler, 1968, p. 10).

A variety of descriptive criteria may be used in defining job satisfaction. Among these are the following: Satisfaction with wages, equality of treatment from supervision, enjoyment of type of work, feeling of appreciation from supervision, attitude toward fringe benefits (such as pensions, vacations, holiday pay, insurance, sick leave), opportunity for promotion, job security, perception of company/environment (Fottler et al., 1995).

According to Gordon (1993), job satisfaction results when a job fulfills or facilitates the attainment of individual values and standards; dissatisfaction, on the other hand, occurs when the job is seen as blocking such attainment. Job satisfaction, desirable in and of itself, is an attitude managers should encourage.

In November, 1995, *Inc.* magazine in a partnership with the Gallup Organization, conducted a nationwide poll to determine how satisfied or happy Americans were in their jobs (Seglin, 1996). The results suggest that these important factors affect employees' job satisfaction and job performance: While at work, employees have the daily opportunity to do what they do best. A supervisor or coworker seems to care about them as people. While at work, employees' opinions seemed to matter. Over the course of the past year, employees were given opportunities for learning and development. Their organization's mission makes the employees feel that their jobs are important. Employees have the necessary equipment and materials to perform their jobs properly. Employees feel that their companies were "family friendly."

B. How Do the Definitions Relate?

It appears that the majority of adjectives describing the term "job satisfaction" are similar. Job satisfaction, by definition a broad concept, exists for every employee to some degree. Most descriptions of employee satisfaction include some form of recognition by coworkers and supervisors as well as the ability to learn and develop in their organizations. Interestingly, wage level and other forms of monetary compensation were typically not mentioned as critical components for happy employees.

While most definitions of job satisfaction are similar, no two people share the same values and expectations from their respective employment. In addition, these perceptions change over time. For example, within the health care industry, employees' ideas about job satisfaction continually evolve as regulatory agencies, technology, and patient preferences act and react to the dynamic health services environment (Atkins et al., 1996). An alternative definition of job satisfaction is that it is simply the absence of tension in the workplace (Gordon, 1993). Furthermore, some people view job satisfaction in terms of the absence of feeling bad—in other words, the absence of job dissatisfaction (Crow and Hartman, 1996).

II. ARE JOB SATISFACTION AND MOTIVATION CONNECTED?

Why do individuals behave differently at home and on the job? What motivates individuals to work harder and ultimately increase output? Are highly satisfied employees necessarily more productive or motivated than their less satisfied co-workers? For years managers and researchers have discussed and debated these issues. Various theories relate job satisfaction and motivation. The following section attempts to describe some of the major models which have been used to diagnose motivation in the workplace.

A. Maslow's Hierarchy of Needs

Abraham Maslow (1970) developed the concept of the hierarchy of needs, one of the most popular, well-known theories on motivation. Maslow's theory states that a person's motivation is based on a series of five needs, arranged in a pyramid-shaped hierarchy from the most basic at the lowest level ascending to the most complex. Physiological needs are the most rudimentary. Items here include the need for food, water, shelter, and sex. Safety and security are next on the hierarchy. A person's desire for physical safety and protection as well as job security are represented in this category. The next level in the hierarchy is belongingness needs and love. In this stage, an individual's desire for social relationships and affection are addressed both in and outside of the work environment. Esteem, the ensuing level, is the need to master work, hold a position of prestige, receive public recognition, demonstrate competence, and feel self-esteem. Finally, at the apex of the pyramid is self-actualization, the desire to grow or develop to full potential.

Organizations and managers should strive to meet unsatisfied needs. According to Maslow, the lowest unsatisfied need level becomes the most powerful or important need to the individual. The lower levels of needs do not necessarily motivate an individual. However, once lower-level needs are met, a person will act to satisfy needs at the next highest level. Motivation is increased at work when the esteem and self-actualization needs are being satisfied. The basis for the popularity of Maslow's theory stems from its apparent simplicity and logic and not because it has been justified by supporting research. Consequently, research has indicated that there are actually only two or three relevant categories of needs and that the order of their importance varies from one individual to another. In addition, Maslow's theory cannot be labeled as universal due to the variation in its sequencing of needs from country to country.

B. Herzberg's Two-Factor Theory

Frederick Herzberg's (1979) theory on motivation was another relatively simplistic model of job satisfaction. Herzberg's theory consists of two main segments: motivators and hygiene factors. Motivators describe features of a job's content including responsibility, autonomy, self-esteem, and self-actualization opportunities. Herzberg and his associates believed that these criteria, when maximized, motivate a person to work harder and ultimately improve job performance. On the other hand, hygiene factors—those that fulfill physiological, security, or social needs—satisfy an individual's lower-order needs, thus preventing dissatisfaction. Among those listed were physical working conditions, salary, company policies and practices, and benefits. Herzberg believed that in order for a person to want to work harder, hygiene factors had to be at an acceptable level. In essence, hygiene factors did not directly lead to increased performance levels.

Herzberg's theory has been widely criticized. Some criticize the classification of certain factors, specifically salary, as both a motivator and hygiene factor. Variations in individual's preferences and inherent differences in personalities are ignored in Herzberg's theory. As a result, it was believed that his theory may have overemphasized the importance of pleasure as a desired outcome.

C. Equity Theory

The equity theory evolved from what is known as social comparison theory (Adams, 1963). Because people lack objective measures of performance and appropriate attitudes, they have a tendency to compare and assess their performance and attitudes relative to others. The premise of equity theory is that people appraise their job performance and satisfaction by comparing their efforts and the benefits they derive from work to the efforts and benefits of a "comparison other." The problem with this analogy is that the comparison other may be unlike the worker. Moreover, equity theory states that workers are motivated in proportion to the perceived fairness of the rewards they receive for a certain level of effort or contribution. Perceptions of inequity may exist when in reality no actual inequity exists. Regardless, individuals will alter their actions based upon this perception.

The most important aspect in regard to equity theory is that perceptions, not facts, influence motivation. Employees will be motivated to reduce or eliminate perceived inequities. The people making comparisons will attempt to rectify the inequity by reassessing their perception of the circumstances creating the situation. The problem with this theory stems from its oversimplification of motivation and the fact that it does not address differences in people's needs, values, or personalities.

D. Expectancy Theory

Since the early 1970s, expectancy theory has been the most widely researched theory of motivation (Porter and Lawler, 1966). Expectancy theory incorporates many of the elements of other theories on motivation. In addition, it has received significant empirical support, integrates people's differing perspectives, and provides clear methods to increase employee motivation. The latest model of the Expectancy theory is depicted through the following formula: Motivation = [E à P] x [(P à O) (V)] E à P refers to a person's perception of whether his or her effort produces performance. P à O symbolizes the employee's belief that performance leads to outcomes. Among these outcomes are fatigue, pay, benefits, and job challenge. V stands for valence, the value assigned to the outcome. Values between 0 and 1 are assigned for E à P and P à O and a value in the range of -1 to 1 for V. As a result, differences in personalities and perceptions may be better accounted for. When the equation results in a negative value, low motivation potential is indicated for that particular job or task.

E. Does Job Satisfaction Produce Higher Levels of Organizational Commitment?

Organizational commitment refers to the psychological attachment of workers to their places of employment (Becker et al., 1996). Commitment to organizations is positively related to desirable outcomes such as job satisfaction and attendance, negatively related to absenteeism and turnover.

III. RELATION BETWEEN MANAGEMENT EFFECTIVENESS AND EMPLOYEE JOB SATISFACTION

A. How Can Managers Promote Job Satisfaction?

In a survey conducted by Half International, a California staffing services firm, 150 executives were asked to name the single most important reasons that employees would leave an organization (Boyd, 1995). Thirty-four percent of the respondents complained that recognition was limited and that they received little praise. One of the primary goals of a good manager is to assist workers in achieving effective performance while at the same time eliminating such obvious sources of job dissatisfaction as pay inequities, abusive supervision, favoritism, and poor communications (Crow and Hartman, 1995). Employees should be kept busy and productive and provided with a sense of accomplishment when their work is done. Interestingly, workers found even dull work to be less dissatisfying than idleness. Management should develop employee-relations philosophies that encourage employees to take responsibility for both the quality and quantity of their work and the satisfaction aspects of their jobs. Furthermore, expensive policies that promise to increase productivity by improving job satisfaction should be avoided (Crow and Hartman, 1995). In respect to studies that have revealed heredity or predisposition to job dissatisfaction, better decisions need to be made so as not to hire potentially dissatisfied employees. Finally, employers should develop systems of rewards for exceptional employees and attempt to focus on these persons. Usually, companies spend inordinate amounts of time trying to identify and improve "bad" employees.

There are a variety of simple, effective, and inexpensive ways to reward workers (Boyd, 1995). With respect to low-cost rewards, most managers are limited by their imaginations and not their budgets. Simple acts of recognition are especially beneficial because they do not create jealousy or competition between employees (Boyd, 1995). Several low-cost ways include the following: personal and public recognition, financial rewards tied to performance, responsibility for tasks/jobs not normally performed, and acting on employee suggestions for efficiency improvements (Boyd, 1995). In addition, recognition awards (Boyd, 1995) could be given for birthdays, service anniversary, performing special tasks, showing a positive attitude, or demonstrating ways in which the company can save money.

B. Do Satisfied Employees Benefit the Organization?

Pollack (1996) described four ways to keep employees happy. First, formal performance evaluations should be conducted regularly. They should be direct and in person—not written. Also, managers should provide informal feedback by talking to their employees and letting them know how they are performing. Second, workers should receive personal attention from management. Employees need to believe that their employers care about them in and outside of the office. Third, employee responsibilities should be expanded as soon as performance merits. Workers become restless when they perform jobs that have lost their challenge. Finally, supervisors should ask their employees for advice. They should seize every opportunity to make these individuals feel important and respected.

Most individuals realize that when they are frustrated or tense at work, they will not be able to focus on the job at hand. When employees face difficult situations, they will not be as effective as they might be (Seglin, 1996). Even minor sources of job dissatisfaction, like uncomfortable room temperature, can disturb a person enough to affect performance. According to Herzberg's two-factor theory, the presence of motivational factors such as recognition, achievement, responsibility, and opportunities for advancement cause increased satisfaction. The result, of course, is increased productivity (Seglin, 1996).

The adoption of quality frameworks, such as the Malcolm Baldridge National Quality Award, has led to an increase in the use of employee-related measures which set predetermined levels of job satisfaction, commitment, and morale. In a 1995 survey of the Times Top 500 companies, over two-thirds had at least one form of formal quality management program in effect (Anonymous, 1996). In addition, 85% of the companies surveyed felt that economic value had been added through these quality initiatives. However, only 35% reported employee satisfaction data to support this claim. Overall, the results of this survey revealed that 50% of the companies that reported using quality improvement frameworks indicated increases in employee satisfaction. Of this number, the majority of respondents felt at least "moderately" confident that economic value had been added through their employee-focused activities. On the other hand, job dissatisfaction and labor turnover are positively related (Van de Looij and Benders, 1995). Job dissatisfaction increases the probability that a worker will resign. A dissatisfied employee will probably—but not certainly—seek new employment depending on his or her perception of the opportunities at that time (Atkins et al., 1996).

IV. RELATION BETWEEN QUALITY AND JOB SATISFACTION

A. What Impact Does Job Satisfaction Have on Quality of Care?

The recent trend toward consolidation in the health care industry may be linked to decreasing employee satisfaction. Although reducing the number of employees, nurses for example, may save money in the short run, the bottom line may eventually suffer because employees are unable to meet patients' needs (Atkins, et al., 1966). Fewer employees in a health care organization lead to increased workloads and higher levels of job uncertainty. As a result, employee dissatisfaction may be increasing and at the same time reducing patients' quality of care perceptions. These negative perceptions may be affecting patients' desire to return to the facility for subsequent care and/or the inclination to refer friends for treatment. Logically, the profitability of an organization with unsatisfied workers will decline.

The health care industry should borrow from the research of other service industries. For example, the banking and retailing industries have long realized the correlation between satisfied employees and satisfied customers. Thus, these industries have realized the value of meeting the expectations of their internal and external customers (Atkins, et al., 1966). Similar to employee job satisfaction being an indicator of effective management, health care marketers use patient satisfaction ratings as the ultimate quality of care measure. Quality of care can be analyzed using patient satisfaction data because the patients' values and expectations define their interpersonal aspects of quality (Atkins, et al., 1966). Patient satisfaction is an important measure of how well the provider has met patient needs and expectations and is also a strong predictor of a patient's intent to return for future treatment.

B. How Is Quality Perceived in the Health Care Industry?

It is difficult to gauge quality in any service industry, especially health care, because service quality is a performance and not a product. Monitoring quality in the service industry is intangible. The performance is dependent on the actions of the individuals involved where the producer and customer may have differing perceptions of value. In addition, production and consumption occur simultaneously (Atkins, et al., 1966).

Defining and measuring health care quality are controversial, costly endeavors. Quality of care is a multidimensional concept; it can be viewed narrowly (clinical effectiveness, for example) or broadly (all the attributes of medical care that patients value). The difficulty with any multidimensional concept is weighting the disparate components. Even if individuals agree on the attributes of care that determine quality, they may disagree about the relative importance of each attribute (Custer, 1995).

Donabedian classified attempts to measure quality of care as evaluations of three main aspects: structure, process, and outcome (Custer, 1995). Structure refers to the attributes of care such as the caregiver's qualifications and the resources available at the site of care. Examining the process of care takes into account the provider's activities, the decisions made at each phase in an episode of illness, and the appropriateness of the treatment rendered. Outcome measures the impact of care on health status and patient satisfaction.

In other service industries, quality is similarly difficult to measure. Generally, though, a user of a service has a few characteristics or attributes in mind that serve as a basis for comparison among alternatives. Lack of one attribute may eliminate a specific service from consideration. Quality also may be perceived as a whole bundle of attributes where many lesser characteristics are superior to those of competitors, and quality is more difficult to measure for services than for manufactured goods (Murdick, et al., 1990). Customers assess service quality in terms of reliability, responsiveness, competence, access, courtesy, communication, credibility, security, understanding/knowing the customer, and other tangibles.

REFERENCES

Adams, S. (1963). Toward an understanding of inequity. *Journal of Abnormal and Social Psychology, 67(5)*, 422-436.

Anonymous. (1996). Increased employee satisfaction may add value. *IRS Employment Review, 620(Nov.)*, 3.

Atkins, M., Marshall, B., and Javalgi, R. (1966). Happy employees lead to loyal patients. *Journal of Health Care Marketing, 16(4)*, 14-23.

Becker, T., Billings, R. Eveleth, D, and Gilbert, N. (1966). Foci and bases of employee commitment: implications for job performance. *Academy of Management Journal, 39(2)*, 464-482.

Crow, S., and Hartman, S. (1995). Can't get no satisfaction. *Leadership & Organization Development Journal, 16(4)*, 34-38.

Custer, W. (1995). Measuring the quality of health care. Employee Benefit Research Institute Brief, 159.

Fottler, M., Hernandez, R., and Joiner, C. (Eds). (1995). *Strategic Management of Human Resources in Health Care Organizations*. Albany, NY: Delmar.

Gordon, J. (1993). *A Diagnostic Approach to Organizational Behavior (4th ed.)*. Needham Height, MA: Allyn and Bacon.

Herzberg, F., Mausner, B., and Synderman. (1959). *The Motivation to Work*. New York: John Wiley.

Malia, B. (1995). Motivating on a dime. *Incentive (Performance Supplement), 1995*, 62-65.

Maslow, A. (1970). *The Motivation to Work*. New York: Harper & Row.

Murdick, R., Render, and Russell. (1990). *Services Operations Management*. Needham Heights, MA: Allyn and Bacon.

Porter, L., and Lawler, E. (1968). *Managerial Attitudes and Performance*. Homewood, IL: Richard D. Irwin.

Pollack, T. (1996). A personal file of stimulating ideas, little-known facts and daily problem solvers. *Supervision, 57*(9), 21-23.

Schapp. S. (1996). Bridging the gap between procedural knowledge and positive employee attitudes. *Group & Organization Management, 21*(3), 337-364.

Seglin, J. (1966). The happiest workers in the world. *INC., 18,* 62-74.

Van de Looij, F., and Bender, J. (1995). Not just money: quality of working life as employment strategy. *Health Manpower Management, 21*(3), 27-33.

Weil, P. and Kimball, P. (1995). A model of voluntary turnover among hospital CEOs. *Hospital & Health Services Administration, 40*(3), 337-364.

57.
LEADERSHIP

Thomas W. Kent, *Charleston, SC*

It would seem basic to begin by establishing some definitions. Is there a difference between *management and leadership*? How will we use those words here? After a review of the literature one clearly finds that questions such as these are often ignored in discussions of leadership. Through the middle part of this century leadership was treated almost as an afterthought. Management was the key dynamic or issue to be understood. Leadership was a secondary factor, an ingredient of the management process.

I. THE STRUGGLE FOR A DEFINITION

The majority of theoretical and scientific work reflected this thinking. The Western Reserve studies of the late 1950s and early 1960s reflect this bias. (See for example Campbell, 1962; Campbell, et al., 1962; Otis, et al., 1962; Prien and Liske, 1962.) In these studies, researchers attempted to identify factors that contributed to managerial performance. They looked at leadership along with persuasiveness, creativity, and planning as contributors to managerial effectiveness. All these studies highlight the thinking that leadership was simply a subset of effective management.

During the 1970s leadership became a more important subject, but the confusion or lack of clarity about the differences between managing and leading remained. Vroom and Yetton (1973) seem to use the words interchangeably. In *Leadership and Decision-Making*, they state:

> One of the most persistent and controversial issues in the study of management is that of participation in decision-making by subordi-

nates. Traditional models of the managerial process have been auto-cratic in nature. The manager makes decisions on matters within his area of freedom, issues orders or directives to his subordinates, and monitors their performance to ensure conformity with these directives. (p. 10)

The title of their work would indicate that they are primarily interested in leadership, yet they seem to speak predominantly of management. Similarly, Campbell, et al. (1970) clearly demonstrate the confusion that arises as people discuss the concepts of managerial style and leadership style as if they were one and the same—or more commonly that leadership is a subfunction of managing.

This confusion has not been clarified by the various authors who have attempted to describe "leadership styles" as contingent upon certain situations or conditions. For example, Tannenbaum and Schmidt (1973) describe the manager's use of authority as one condition defining the continuum from "Boss-centered Leadership" to "Subordinate-Centered Leadership." They seem to say that use of authority as a manager defines his or her leadership style. Without a definition of terms, we are not sure if the authors are describing the manager's management style or leadership style.

A landmark article by Zaleznik (1977) highlighted the differences between managers and leaders. Zaleznik attempted to identify fundamental differences in the needs, attitudes, and behaviors of leaders vs. managers. However, little scientific data verifies these differences.

Kotter (1990) describes the cause of the confusion between leaders and managers as the tendency to associate leadership with position. That is, we expect leadership to come from those in the highest management positions. He distinguishes between management and leadership by pointing out that over the years we have come to think of good management as providing a measure of order and consistency to key dimensions like the quality and profitability of products. On the other hand, he points out that leadership does not generate consistency; it produces energy, movement, direction, motivation, and change. He distinguishes between management processes and leadership processes. Management processes include planning, budgeting, organizing, staffing, controlling, and problem solving. Leadership processes include establishing direction, aligning people, motivating and inspiring.

Van Eron (1995) echoes this belief:

> A leader is more concerned with change, and therefore focuses attention on a compelling vision of the future—one that also addresses the needs and values of constituents. Leaders rely primarily on their personal ability to influence others to shift or transform their thinking and, in the process of doing so, gain support for their visions.

A manager, on the other hand, focuses on maintaining the status quo of organizations by clarifying functions, roles, and tasks—in essence, managing the complexity often created by the leader. Managers work within the existing organizational culture, norms and beliefs, and relate to subordinates primarily by an exchange or a transaction. Managers rely more heavily on their position power to influence others rather than on their personal power. (p. 3)

Over the past 20 years, authors, theorists, and practitioners alike have come to see leadership as a phenomenon that deserves understanding for its own merit.

Table 1 - Differentiation and Definition of Leading and Managing in Terms of Their Respective Purposes, Products, and Processes.

MANAGING	LEADING
Purpose: To establish and accomplish goals through the efficient utilization of available resources.	**Purpose:** To create direction and the will to pursue it through the development of peoples' thinking and valuing.
Products: Goals, plans, resources, organized effort, and awareness of performance and progress toward goals.	**Products:** Sense of direction and common pursuit of that direction based on shared vision; increased energy and motivation for accomplishment; higher states of behavior in terms of values.
Processes: Planning, staffing, budgeting, organizing, controlling, and problem solving.	**Processes:** Creating vision, aligning people, motivating, inspiring.

Leadership goes beyond and is separate from managing—one does not need to be in a position of management in order to lead. Leadership has to do with the values of an organization or a culture. It both influences and is influenced by those values; it is worth understanding so we can comprehend it as a cultural influence. It transforms and develops people as a part of an organization, subculture, or society.

Based on what we have said thus far we can begin to differentiate between leading and managing in specific ways. Table 1 attempts to define leading and managing in specific terms.

The table first defines the purpose of each process, and why the process exists at all. In other words, why is managing important to us, and why is leading a necessary function? Purpose defines the mission or reason for the process.

Products are different from purpose. Products are the results of the process. Purpose supersedes product since we have to ask of every product we produce whether it serves the purpose of this process. A manufacturer of health care products, whose purpose or mission might be to create products that improve personal health and that generate profits for the company, has to assess its results in terms of that purpose.

Process describes the actions or interactions that must be carried out to generate a product or products. We will review much of the literature on leadership processes in later sections of this article.

II. WHAT IS LEADERSHIP?

In recent years studies have looked upon leadership as a process or dynamic that can change an organization and the people in the organization. Leadership is beyond an individual's management style, and it is much broader than a simple outcome of a person's management interactions with subordinates.

Burns (1978) differentiates between transformational and transactional leadership. Transactional leadership is an exchange of "favors" that occurs at the leader's bidding in order to accomplish the goals of the leader. The transactional leader says, "If you do this for me, I will do that for you." Or, "If you do not do this for me, I will withhold certain rights and privileges from you because I have the power to do that."

In contrast, Burns says that transformational leadership "occurs when one or more persons engage with others in such a way that leaders and followers raise one another to higher levels of motivation and morality." Transformational leaders "serve as an independent force in changing the makeup of the followers' motive base." Transforming leaders work from a set of values that are "forged and hardened" as they grow and mature from childhood to adulthood. Their behaviors create leadership through their influence on others' consciousness of purpose and value. That is, leaders engage others in a way that changes their thinking, regarding why they are doing what they are doing and regarding the importance of what they are doing. Leaders affect the consciousness of others regarding what is going on or what needs to go on and, thereby, change their motivations, their values, and their morality.

Bennis and Nanus (1985) define "transformative leadership" as "the capacity to translate intention into reality and sustain it." Effective transformative leadership "can move organizations from current to future states, create visions of potential opportunities for organizations, instill within employees commitment to change, and instill new cultures and strategies in organizations that mobilize and focus energy and resources."

Clearly, leadership is not a management oriented function employed to accomplish specific tasks. It is not personality based, and it does not change dramatically from one situation to another. It is not situationally determined, and leaders are not like chameleons who change their color (or leadership style) depending on task complexity or position power.

Rather, leadership is a process that raises the consciousness, motivations, aspirations, and values of both leaders and followers. As a result of this elevation in consciousness of the purpose or mission, leadership brings about sustained motivation and commitment, clarity of vision, opportunity and direction, and focused and mobilized energy and resources. Leadership can only be thought of as a process that invades or permeates every interaction between leader and subordinates with such impact that it alters their thinking at the deepest levels. As Bass (1985) says,

> What we see here is much more than the desire for superficial change in attitudes or for minor increments in the level of motivation which can be accomplished by transactional leadership. Unlike the transactional leader who indicates how current needs of followers can be fulfilled, the transformational leader sharply arouses or alters the strength of needs which may have lain dormant. (p. 17)

Bass, discussing leadership and organizational culture, further goes on to say,

> The transactional leader works within the organizational culture as it exists; the transformational leader changes the organizational culture. For Mitroff, Kilmann, and Saxton's (unpublished) conception of organizational culture, this means the transactional leader accepts

what can be talked about; the transformational leader changes what can be talked about. The transactional leader accepts group and self-identities as currently defined; the transformational leader changes them. Other aspects of the organizational culture which the transactional leader accepts and the transformational leader changes include: who rules and by what means; the work-group norms, as well as ultimate beliefs about religion, ideology, morality, ethics, space, time, and human nature. The transactional leader accepts and uses the rituals, stories, and role models belonging to the organizational culture to communicate its values; the transformational leader invents, introduces, and advances the cultural forms. The transformational leader changes the social warp and woof of reality (p. 24).

III. LEADERSHIP PROCESSES

Most authors agree that the stereotypes and myths associated with what makes great leaders are passé. As Bennis and Nanus (1985) indicate, a great leader can be introverted or extroverted, playful, or serious. Style and personality do not define successful leadership. What we can surmise from the literature is that every leader engages in certain processes. These processes are defined as interactions between leader and follower which develop in certain ways and which result in types of outcomes which are key to achieving the purposes of the leader and follower. Table 2 summarizes these leadership processes as defined by four authors or groups of authors.

Bass emphasizes several "qualities" that seem essential for an individual to engage in transformational leadership processes. The first he describes as charisma. Charisma, Bass explains, is made up of three ingredients:

- An enormous sense or consciousness of self-purpose which endows the leader with extraordinary self-determination, power and capability;
- Self-confidence in his or her position and capabilities to solve whatever problem must be faced—strength in knowing that one's values and ethics are clear and will provide the direction needed;
- Confidence in and optimistic expectations about their followers' performance.

The second essential quality is the ability to inspire emotionally. As Bass points out, the process for generating this inspiration will be different depending on the leader and on the followers. Not all leaders can be a Vince Lombardi or a Martin Luther King. The key is that the leader uses his or her own gifts to influence others to exert themselves beyond their own expectations and self-interests.

The third quality Bass calls "individualized consideration." To explain this, Bass uses the example of Andrew Carnegie who gave responsibility to employees at all levels in management to make the most of whatever talents they had. The quality includes both consideration of others as a consistently important aspect of leader-follower relations and the assignment of responsibilities up to the level that challenges a given individual.

This quality is defined by Greenleaf (1977) as the "Servant Leader." The leader as servant takes on a distinctly different mind-set, first asking whether each person's highest priority needs are being served. Notice both the attention to the individual as

Table 2 - Leadership Processes or Qualities

Bass (1985)	Conger (1989)	Kotter (1990)	Kent (1996)
Clarisma	Sensing opportunity and formulating a vision	Establishing Direction	Visioning
			Creating Possibilities
	Communicating a vision that inspires		Communicating for Meaning
Individual Consideration	Encouraging commitment in followers	Aligning People	Developing Stakeholders
Inspiration	Building trust through personal commitment	Motivating & Inspiring	Building Spirit and Will
	Empowering others to achieve the vision		
			Sustaining Focus

well as to that individual's set of needs. The Servant-Leader continually asks whether this person is growing, becoming healthier, wiser, freer, and more autonomous as a result of working on particular tasks. And does this approach foster new servant-leaders?

While a few unique processes are proposed by some of the authors in Table 2, there is general agreement about four of the processes: visioning, communicating for meaning, developing stakeholders, and building spirit and will.

IV. VISIONING

Bass is one of the few authors who does not mention vision. Most concur that creating a vision of the future is critical to leading others through transformational processes. Wall, et al. (1992) writes, "The new leader's role is much like a symphony conductor: ensuring that all the autonomous sections blend together harmoniously toward a single goal." They describe vision as the key ingredient to success in this new role. In traditional, top-down organizations, communications are too sluggish, and too removed from the action to be relevant, or motivating to people. In today's organizations, people need to understand the direction of the organization; they then need to have the tools, skills, and freedom necessary to achieve that direction. The vision is the vehicle for communicating that direction. It is the picture that tells a thousand words. It is the image that provides individuals with a sense of direction, hope, and meaning.

Kouzes and Posner (1995), who have researched and written extensively about the subject of leadership assert,

> Not only do constituents demand that leaders be credible, they also demand that leaders be forward looking: that they have a sense of direction, a vision for the future. Credibility is the foundation of leadership, but the capacity to paint an uplifting and ennobling picture of the future differentiates leaders from other credible sources (p. 31).

We define vision as a mental picture or map of where the organization is going, what it is to become, and how it will get there. The leader must have a clear sense of all three. More importantly, the leader must enable others to see this vision, reflect upon it, and modify or personalize it as appropriate. Individuals must be able to see themselves contributing to the accomplishment of this vision or it will have no relevance to them. Vision motivates and focuses performance. Without vision a person can only follow orders or procedures. When there is no vision, a manager attempting to change orders or procedures may meet resistance.

V. COMMUNICATING THROUGH MEANING

Table 2 indicates that all the authors believe in communicating as a way to inspire and motivate; such communication is a critical process in transformational leadership. Every interpersonal process involves communication. Specifically, we are talking about a communication process that Bennis and Nanus call "meaning through communication." Leaders are able to shift the thinking and understanding of others by developing, building, shifting, or extending the level of meaning people hold. Important subjects and ideas are not treated as facts or data to be communicated objectively and without dialogue. If people are to understand something and act upon it accurately, they must engage in dialogue about it. Leaders know this takes time, and usually the more important the subject, the longer it takes.

Leaders go beyond facts and data by drawing upon values, symbols, or symbolic gestures to communicate. Communication does not occur through words alone. The leader's actions can speak as loudly as his or her words.

The point here is that communicating meaning is not simply a matter of sharing facts and knowledge. More importantly it involves shifting or developing the thinking of people. It challenges old ways of viewing things. It causes change by bringing about a change in the way people think about their lives and work, thus inspiring and motivating people to achieve and excel.

VI. DEVELOPING STAKEHOLDERS

The word stakeholders defines a category of people who have an investment in the organization and its success. In many organizations the stake that employees feel becomes narrowly and personally defined over the years. For example, employees may feel that they are only in it for their paycheck.

The transformational leader attempts to raise the stakes for all who are involved in the organization. When suppliers are committed to their customers, they strive to find better ways of serving the customer and to help the customer find better ways of carrying out business. Committed employees work toward improving the methods and systems of the organization in order to help achieve its vision.

A sense of commitment, having a stake, and "buying-in" are products of this process. While overused, the words *involvement, empowerment,* and *self-management* begin to describe the process.

VII. BUILDING SPIRIT AND WILL

This leadership process has two inextricably bound components—spirit and will. Spirit describes the leader's state of being. One might think of it as the leader's emotional condition. For instance, is the leader hyperactive, distracted, calm, patient, angry, or nurturing? Perhaps Bass is describing a quality of spirit when he writes about "charisma." He defines charisma as consciousness of self-purpose which endows the leader with extraordinary self-determination, self-confidence in his or her capabilities, and confidence in their followers' performance.

Will is related to such qualities as the leader's persistence, perseverance, and steadfastness. This process is related to the heart and soul of the leader. It is the dynamic that creates trust among people and confidence within the organization. Trust is based on predictability, reliability, and knowledge of a person's values (which is based on behavioral experiences with that person). Leaders are unrelenting, unwavering, tirelessly steadfast, and therefore, predictable and trustworthy. This is similar to Conger's description of "building trust through personal commitment."

Leaders build confidence and energy within the organization by employing what Bennis and Nanus describe as the "deployment of self through positive self-regard." Leaders recognize and utilize their own and others' strengths. They nurture and develop the capabilities of others. They build rather than tear down. They reinforce rather than punish. They do require discipline and high standards of performance; however, they recognize that for people to excel and to go beyond previous performance, they must continually learn, stretch themselves, and on occasion, fail. Leaders recognize that people must be supported, trusted, nurtured, and respected. The process of building spirit and will may describe the quality of the leader's interactions and specific types of engagements with others. That is, the leader interacts with others in a way that builds trust, confidence, persistence, and motivation. This describes the quality of his or her interactions. He or she also engages others in order to build trust, confidence, persistence, and motivation. This describes the purpose of his or her interactions.

SUMMARY

When discussing leadership, the subject must be clarified and defined. Too often leadership with management are confused or used interchangeably. Both subjects, while worthy of discussion in and of themselves, are different from each other. Leadership is not a subservient process of management. Not all managers are leaders. Not all management positions call for leadership. Different processes are associated with each subject. Management processes include planning, budgeting, organizing, staffing, controlling, and problem solving. Leadership Processes include establishing direction, aligning people, and motivating and inspiring.

There appears to be consensus among authors that transformational leadership is not related to personality, organizational position, or other individual or sociological factors. Rather there are a number of processes or interactions that leaders engage in for the good of the purpose being pursued.

REFERENCES

Bass, B. M. (1985). *Leadership and Performance Beyond Expectations.* The Free Press, New York.

Bennis, W., and Nanus, B. (1985). *Leaders.* Harper & Row, Publishers, New York.

Burns, J. Mc. (1978). *Leadership.* Harper & Row, Publishers, New York.

Campbell, J. P., Dunnette, M. D., Lawler, III, E. E., and Weick, Jr., K. E. (1970). *Managerial Behavior, Performance, and Effectiveness.* McGraw-Hill. New York.

Campbell, J. T. (1962). Assessments of higher level personnel. I. Background and scope of the research. *Personnel Psychology, 15*: 57-62.

Campbell, J. T., Otis, J. L., Liske, R. E., and Prien, E. P. (1962). Assessments of higher level personnel. II. Validity of the overall assessment process. *Personnel Psychology, 15*: 63 - 74.

Dicken, C. F., and Black, J. D. (1965). Predictive validity of psychometric evaluations of supervisors. *Journal of Applied Psychology, 49*: 34-47.

Conger, J. A. (1989). *The Charismatic Leader.* Jossey-Bass Publishers, San Francisco.

Greenleaf, R. K. (1977). *Servant Leadership.* Paulist Press, New York.

Kent, T. W., Graber, D., and Johnson, J. A. (1996). Leadership in the Formation of New Health Care Environments. *The Health Care Supervisor, 15*(2): 27 - 34.

Kotter, J. P. (1990). *A Force for Change.* The Free Press, New York.

Kouzes, J. M., and Posner, B. Z. (1995). Leadership is Everyone's Business and Other Lessons from Over a Dozen Years of Leadership Research. *O. D. Practitioner, 27*(1): 25 - 33.

Otis, J. L., Campbell, J. T., and Prien, E. P. (1962). Assessment of higher level personnel. VII. The nature of assessments. *Personnel Psychology, 15*: 441- 446.

Prien, E. P., and Liske, R. E. (1962). Assessments of higher level personnel. III. Rating criteria: A comparative analysis of supervisor ratings and incumbent self ratings of job performance. *Personnel Psychology, 15*: 187 - 194.

Tannenbaum, R., and Schmidt, W. H. (1973). How to Choose a Leadership Pattern. *Harvard Business Review. May-June.*

Van Eron, A. M. (1995). Leading Today and into the Future. *O. D. Practitioner, 27*(1): 3 - 7.

Vroom, V. H., and Yetton, P. W. (1973). *Leadership and Decision-Making.* University of Pittsburgh Press, Pittsburgh.

Wall, B., Solum, R. S., and Sobol, M. R. (1992). *The Visionary Leader.* Prima Publishing.

Wheatley, M. J. (1994). *Leadership and the New Science.* Berrett-Koehler Publishers, Inc.

Zaleznik, A. (1977). Managers and Leaders: Are They Different? *Harvard Business Review, 55*(3): 67 - 78.

58.
FINANCIAL ACCOUNTING

James V. Salvo, Jr., *Medical University of South Carolina, Charleston, SC*

What is the general financial health of the local hospital, or nursing home, or any of a variety of other health care organizations (HCOs)? Is it good, average or poor? Board members and managers responsible for HCOs, vendors and lending institutions that extend them credit, owners that expect a return on their investment, citizens that rely on them for care, agencies that regulate them, and other "stakeholders" all have vested interests in the answer to this question. If "stakeholders" neglect to periodically ask this question, their risk of "awakening" one day to find their HCO in full, financial cardiac arrest increases. An unhealthy financial condition can result in the following:

1. Board members and managers are replaced by those more skilled in monitoring and managing the HCO's finances.
2. Creditors are paid late or not at all.
3. Owners lose their investments.
4. Citizens no longer receive the health care services they need.
5. The HCO dies (closes and goes out of business).

Cleverley (1992) warns that "decision makers tend to assume that, if the entity is breathing at the end of the year and is capable of publishing a financial statement, all must be well." This assumption is dangerous. An annual financial exam for signs of financial illness in an HCO is the same as an annual personal physical exam for physical illness. The main purpose of both exams is to provide warnings of actual or potential illness early enough to prevent or correct the unhealthy condition.

This chapter demonstrates how financial accounting determines the general financial health of HCOs. The following are described:

1. Asking the questions that, when answered, provide the information needed to determine the HCO's general financial health;

2. Annual financial accounting report(s) that contains the information needed to answer the questions;
3. "Basic" financial statements (balance sheet, income statement, statement of change in equity, statement of cash flows, and the related notes to these statements) contained in the annual financial report(s);
4. The language common to the basic financial statements;
5. Industry-wide financial ratios for comparable HCOs;
6. Key financial ratios of the HCO;
7. Comparing the HCO's key ratios internally and to industry ratios;
8. Answering the questions in Step 1; and
9. Determining the HCO's financial health.

The remainder of this chapter explains each step in detail and how to complete it.

I. DETERMINING GENERAL FINANCIAL HEALTH

Many different types of organizations provide health care directly to patients. Of these, hospitals received about 37% of every dollar spent on health care in 1993 (The Sourcebook, 1995). Because of hospitals' financial prominence in the health care industry, Mercy Hospital will be the fictitious organization whose financial health is determined in this chapter. It is an urban, non-profit, non-governmental hospital with 500 beds.

A. The Meaning of "General"

The word "general" is used in discussing financial health since the examination is of the HCO as a whole and does not address departments, centers, or programs within it. Additionally, the exam does not include micro financial analysis where an attempt is made to identify what is causing poor "general" financial health. For example, the HCO's basic financial statements may indicate a lack of sufficient cash to pay current liabilities (bills). This is a serious "general" financial health problem for the HCO. But what is the cause of the problem? It may be some problem in its billing department or elsewhere in its cash collection cycle that has extended the time between the delivery and receipt of the cash payment for services. Using various micro financial analyses may identify the cause of the problem and offer solutions. Some of these analyses are discussed in another chapter of this handbook. Determining an HCO's general financial health can alert stakeholders to financial problems of the organization as a whole but does not indicate root causes or solutions for problems.

B. Source of Financial Accounting Information

As discussed in more detail in Step 2, the annual financial report (AFR) contains the financial accounting information needed to determine the general financial health of a HCO. Usually it contains an audit opinion, the required basic financial statements and notes, and supplemental financial schedules. The main "product" of financial accounting is the basic financial statements. These statements are most often called the balance sheet, the income statement, the statement of cash flows, and the statement of changes in owners' equity. Other names used will be reviewed in Step 3. Regardless of their names, these statements contain information on assets, liabilities, revenues, expenses, and other accounts needed to determine the financial health of an HCO. Mercy Hospital's financial statements are found in Tables 1-4. If an audit is required of the HCO's financial statements, the annual financial report will also contain an external auditor's opinion concerning whether the financial statements are materially correct in reporting on the fiscal year's operations.

C. Ratio Analysis

Ratio analysis is the tool used to examine Mercy's financial statements. The information it provides will then be used to determine Mercy's general financial health. Ratio analysis involves establishing relationships between various accounts in the basic financial statements. These relationships or ratios are then compared to ratios from previous fiscal years of the HCO as well as to industry-wide ratios of similar HCOs. This chapter will focus on 11 common ratios in order to introduce the basic relationships that indicate financial health or illness. Comparing these 11 ratios internally for 5 or more years and to current industry-wide ratios should allow a stakeholder to answer the questions asked in Step 1 to form an opinion on the general financial health of the HCO.

D. Issues

An awareness of some important accounting issues increases the chances that the financial information used in ratio analysis will allow for a more accurate determination of a HCO's general financial health.

1. Timeliness of Information

For financial information to be useful in determining the financial health of the HCO, it must be timely. The annual financial report, which contains the information needed for the financial examination, is normally not published until 2 to 6 months after the end of the HCO's fiscal year. Ideally, stakeholders would like this information within two to six days after the end of the fiscal year. However, to expect audited financial statements to be ready this soon is unrealistic. Most HCO's that develop serious financial health problems do so over several years and not several months. So in most cases, the basic financial statements provide information in a timely enough manner to allow decision makers to identify problems and correct them before they become too large. Computing and interpreting the 11 financial ratios in this chapter is one important way of identifying serious financial problems and should be done each year as soon as possible after the financial statements are issued.

2. Type of Legal Entity

An HCO is classified according to the type of legal entity it is. Is it for-profit, non-profit, or governmental (state or local)? HCOs of the federal government are not considered for this chapter because they do not prepare annual financial reports in accordance with generally accepted accounting principles (GAAP). For all other HCOs specific rules, GAAPs, governing how the basic financial statements of each are prepared. Under the Financial Accounting Foundation (FAF), the Financial Accounting Standards Board (FASB) sets the rules or GAAP for non-profit and for-profit HCOs, and the Governmental Accounting Standards Board (GASB) sets GAAP for governmental (state and local) HCOs. Stakeholders need to be aware that the format and names of the basic financial statements can vary depending on the type of legal entity the HCO is. For example, the financial statement containing the assets, liabilities, and equity of the HCO is called the balance sheet by for-profit and governmental HCOs and the statement of position by non-profit HCOs. Also, FASB and GASB may differ on which of the financial statements an HCO must include in its annual financial report. In the past, a statement of cash flows was required by governmental and some non-profit HCOs but not by for-profit organizations. In addition, changes in GAAP occur annually and sometimes will affect the accounts included in the ratios. These changes, if not adjusted for, may make the ratio comparisons misleading. For example, several years ago a change in GAAP required that the account for bad debt write-offs be moved from the deductions from gross patient revenue account to an operating expense account on the income statement which significantly affected several financial ratios. Knowing how changes in GAAP affect the financial statements allows internal financial ratio comparisons to be done more consistently. Changes in GAAP are normally explained in the notes to the financial statements.

3. External Auditor's Opinion

A third issue is the external auditors' opinion on the basic financial statements. An unqualified (clean) opinion would say in part, "In our opinion, the financial statements referred to above present fairly, in all material aspects, the financial position of X Company"(Bailey and Miller, 1993). An unqualified or "clean" opinion, however, in no way means the HCO's financial health is good. It only tells users that the auditors consider the amounts contained in the financial statements to be accurate and complete enough to be reliable in making decisions. For example, net accounts receivable is usually the largest asset that most HCOs have on their balance sheets. To arrive at net accounts receivable, management must estimate, and the auditors must agree on, the amount of gross accounts receivable that will not be collected. Considerable differences of opinion can arise as to the how much will not be collected as a result of bad debts, contractual allowances, and other deductions. The final amount of net patient accounts receivable collected is seldom, if ever, the amount on the financial statement. It should, however, fall within the auditors' materiality limits and provide reliable information for decision making.

4. Integrated Delivery Systems

A fourth issue involves the increasing number of HCOs forming integrated delivery systems (IDS). An IDS may include a combination of any of a number of different HCOs such as hospitals, physician groups, long-term care facilities, and nursing homes. Goldstein (1995) defines an IDS "as a comprehensive continuum of health care services made available to a defined community within a geographic region through a financially integrated, centrally managed network of health care providers." Thus, the "financial reporting" HCO named on the cover of the AFR may have several of these separate legal HCOs "blended" into its financial statements. Financial ratios are affected when new HCOs become part of the "financial reporting" package. Unless adjustments are made, current year ratios may not be comparable with prior years. The notes to the financial statements should disclose any new HCOs whose financial statements have been "blended" with the those of the reporting HCO.

5. Seasonal Trends

A final issue concerns the accounts on the financial statements, like cash, that represent an amount at a point in time. For the audited annual financial statements this point in time is the end of the last day in the HCO's fiscal year. For various reasons the cash account at year end may vary from the end of other months during the year. Cash or other accounts that may have seasonal variations can cause some ratios to be above or below industry average at year end. Any accounts that are consistently higher or lower than average at certain times during the year should be identified.

II. THE NINE STEPS OF ASSESSMENT

The following 9 steps serve as a guide to help determine the general financial health of an organization. Based on the information developed in Steps 1-8, stakeholders should, in Step 9, be able to rate the HCO's health as either good, average, or poor and give a brief explanation supporting their rating.

A. The Questions - What to Ask (Step 1)

An ancient proverb states that the ability to ask questions is the greatest resource in learning the truth. If true, why don't more stakeholders ask the questions that would "lead them to the truth" about the HCO's general financial health? Is it a fear of hearing bad news, embarrassing executive management, appearing dumb, just not caring, or not knowing what questions to ask? Possibly, as mentioned earlier, it is the assumption that if the HCO can issue financial statements at year end, all must be well financially (Cleverley, 1992). This assumption by stakeholders can have serious effects on the HCO and the community it serves, which can range from failure of the HCO to accomplish key elements of its strategic plan to its closure. What then are the questions stakeholders should ask to "learn the truth?" The following five questions are suggested:
1. Does the HCO have enough cash to pay its current liabilities (bills) as they become due?
2. Will the HCO have enough cash to pay off it existing long-term debt as it becomes due?
3. How much total new debt can the HCO incur?
4. Will the HCO have sufficient net income to provide the cash needed to accomplish the objectives of its operational and strategic plans?

5. Does the HCO have adequate funds set aside for replacement or renovation of its plant (i.e., buildings, equipment, and land improvements)?

The remaining steps are designed to help answer these questions to determine the HCO's general financial health. While no previous accounting background is necessary, stakeholders should become familiar with the financial accounting reports, schedules, terms, and words. This will require an investment of time, but the benefits to both stakeholders and the HCO are worthwhile.

B. Annual Financial Report(s) (Step 2)

The annual financial report (AFR) contains three main parts: the auditors' opinion, the required basic financial statements and notes, and supplemental financial schedules. A comprehensive annual financial report (CAFR) will have two additional sections: an introductory section and a statistical section. The most important part of the introductory section is the CEO's transmittal letter which explains the key financial trends and programs of the HCO in non-technical terms. The statistical section of the CAFR usually shows financial trends for the previous ten years and may include financial accounting ratios. While all parts of the AFR or CAFR are important, the basic financial statements and notes has the information needed for the financial exam. These statements will be discussed in detail in Step 3.

AFRs can have a variety of names. They may be called the Annual Financial Report, the Comprehensive Annual Financial Report (CAFR), Financial Statements and Schedules, or some other name. A review of the AFRs of several local HCOs revealed the following names on their covers:

1. Financial Statements and Schedules (With Auditors' Report)
2. Audited Combined Financial Statements and Other Financial Information
3. Annual Financial Statements
4. Report on Financial Statements

Regardless of what the AFR is called, it will always contain the HCO's basic financial statements and notes. They are the part of the AFR that gives the results of the HCO's financial operations for the fiscal year. The cover of AFRs will include the name of the HCO that is the financial reporting entity and the period of time (almost always a fiscal year) covered. Normally they are issued once a year - somewhere between 2 to 5 months after the end of the fiscal year. The financial reporting entity may include more than one legal entity, and the notes to the financial statements should explain what separate legal entities make up the financial reporting entity. If management has external auditors prepare the AFR, the cover page will often include the name of the accounting firm that performed the audit.

For HCOs that make their AFRs available to the public, copies are usually located in the chief executive officer's (CEO's) office or the public relations department. Often AFRs can also be found in the CFO, controller, or business manager's office. Interested stakeholders can usually request the AFR by mail or pick them up directly. Seldom do HCOs charge for this service even when previous AFRs are requested. For governmental (local and state) HCOs, copies of AFRs should be available in local public libraries. Some for-profit HCOs make their AFRs available on the Internet. For example, Columbia HCA corporation has an extensive site on the Internet (World Wide Web) which includes its AFR for the past 3 years. For HCOs that don't make their AFRs available to external stakeholders, other documents, such as "official bond statements" or fund raising brochures, may contain financial statements. Official bond statements, however, are available only when bonds are publically issued. A bond is a legal document representing the amount of money the HCO has borrowed from the investing public.

Generally, 5 years of AFRs are needed for financial ratios to adequately reveal both favorable and unfavorable trends in the financial health of the HCO. If only the most recent AFR is available, only comparisons to similar industry HCOs' financial ratios can be made, however even this limited comparison should still provide some idea of the HCO's general financial health.

As mentioned earlier, for financial information to be useful it must be timely. In addition, it must be accurate and complete. AFRs audited by independent, external accountants give stakeholders more assurance that the data in the basic financial statements are "materially correct." Materiality means the accounts are accurate and complete enough to provide reliable information for decision makers. Usually some law, regulation, or policy requires an HCO to have an audit of its fiscal year financial operations.

C. Basic Financial Accounting Statements and Notes (Step 3)

The next step is to become familiar with the basic financial statements and notes found in the AFR. Depending on the type of HCO, the AFR will contain either three or four of the following financial statements:
1. balance sheet (or statement of financial position)
2. income statement (or statement of revenues and expenses or statement of activities)
3. statement of cash flows
4. statement of change in equity (or statement of changes in fund balance or statement of changes in net assets).

The name used is dependent on whether the HCO is for-profit, non-profit, or governmental (state or local). In this chapter the statements will be called the balance sheet, income statement, statement of cash flows, and statement of change in equity even though Mercy Hospital is a non-profit HCO.

Stakeholders of some HCOs must also become familiar with "fund" accounting. The financial statements of most governmental HCOs are divided into "funds" with each fund having some combination of the four statements listed above. Broyles (1982) explains the need for fund accounting by stating that

> Frequently, hospitals and other health facilities receive gifts or endowments whose use is limited by donor restrictions, such as the acquisition of fixed assets or for teaching or research, or as endowments to provide investment income. By accepting these gifts, the institution is legally obliged to adhere to those restrictions. To fulfill the fiduciary responsibility thus created, a separate set of accounting records for those accounts is established.

The fund that contains unrestricted assets should be used when determining the general financial health of HCOs that use fund accounting for annual financial reporting purposes. This fund is referred to as the "general" or "unrestricted" fund.

In addition, financial statements are prepared using two basis of accounting-- either an accrual or cash basis. An accrual basis recognizes an accounting transaction when goods or services are exchanged; cash basis recognizes accounting transactions only when cash is received or disbursed. The statement of cash flows reflects a HCO's annual financial operations on the cash basis of accounting and the other three statements reflect annual operations on the accrual basis.

1. Balance Sheet

The balance sheet (or statement of financial position) will be discussed first since it is the first financial statement in the AFR. Its heading includes the name of the HCO, the date the fiscal year ends, and the name of the statement. It has three main parts: assets, liabilities, and equity and is a snap shot of the assets, liabilities and fund balance of an HCO at a point in time. In the AFR this date is the close of business on the last day of the fiscal year. Table 1 gives the summarized balance sheets for Mercy Hospital June 30, 1992, through June 30, 1996:

Table 1 - Balance Sheets for Mercy Hospital (in millions)

Assets

	1996	1995	At June 30, 1994	1993	1992
Cash and cash equivalents	$ 0.4	$ 1.2	$ 3.9	$ 0.9	$ 4.9
Accounts Receivable:					
Patients (net)	45.7	35.6	33.6	24.2	22.6
Other	8.3	8.2	7.4	11.1	6.6
Inventories	2.9	2.7	2.6	2.1	1.5
Current Assets	57.3	47.7	47.5	38.3	35.6
Property, plan and equipment (net)	123.1	96.1	97.0	93.4	102.8
Assets restricted to replace buildings	2.0	2.0	1.0	3.0	8.0
Other	7.9	6.0	2.4		
	$190.3	$151.8	$47.9	$134.7	$146.4

Liabilities and Equity

	1996	1995	1994	1993	1992
Accounts payable	$ 12.6	$ 6.5	$ 5.7	$ 2.3	$ 2.0
Accrued salaries	2.0	1.4	1.2	1.1	1.1
Current Portion–bonds payable	4.2	4.6	3.0	1.5	1.5
Other	8.0	6.0	5.2	6.3	8.2
Current liabilities	26.8	18.5	15.1	11.2	12.8
Bonds payable (net of current portion)	78.6	64.8	69.3	66.3	67.8
	105.4	83.3	84.4	77.5	80.6
Equity	84.9	68.5	63.5	66.3	67.8
	$190.3	$151.8	$47.9	$134.7	$146.4

Mercy Hospital is the HCO whose financial health will be analyzed later in this chapter. The first part of the balance sheet list the HCO's assets. Assets are things the organization owns even though there may be payments yet to be made. Assets are listed in order of decreasing liquidity or the ease with which they can be converted to cash. Cash, therefore, is the first asset listed followed by those most easily converted to cash. Following assets are the liabilities--what the HCO owes and must be paid for either within a year after the balance sheet date (current liabilities) or at some time beyond one year (long-term liabilities). The HCO's assets minus its liabilities equals its equity (fund balance or net assets). The equity is the "book value" of the organization or what is left when liabilities are subtracted from assets. The "book value" of the HCO may be considerably different than its fair market value or what someone would pay for it. Any HCO interested in knowing what its fair market value is should seek the advice of experts that specialize in helping HCOs do this. The format of the balance sheet always presents assets equal to liabilities plus equity. This statement helps to answer questions about the HCO's ability to pay its bills currently and in the future.

2. Income Statement

The income statement (or statement of revenues and expenses or statement of activities) follows the balance sheet in the AFR. Table 2 gives the summarized income statements for Mercy Hospital for the fiscal years ended June 30, 1992 through June 30, 1996. This statement is always for a period of time, usually 1year. After the statement's heading, most begin with net patient services revenues and end with net

Table 2 - Income Statements for Mercy Hospital (in millions)

| | For the years ended June 30, | | | | |
	1996	1995	1994	1993	1992
Net patient service revenues	$218.3	$148.6	$133.0	$102.6	$91.1
Other operating revenues	2.3	13.1	2.3	2.1	1.7
Operating revenue	220.6	161.7	135.3	104.7	92.8
Operating expenses:					
Nursing services	91.5	72.0	58.5	49.4	42.6
Other professional services	69.2	52.8	46.6	44.2	36.0
General services	21.5	17.4	16.3	13.9	12.3
Administrative services	32.3	15.0	13.0	10.6	9.2
Depreciation	10.1	9.0	8.7	7.2	4.2
Interest	4.7	5.0	5.0	4.5	4.0
	229.3	171.2	148.1	129.8	108.3
Operating income (loss)	(8.7)	(9.5)	(12.8)	(25.1)	(15.5)
Non operating gains (losses)	25.1	14.5	19.1	16.5	12.5
Net income	$16.4	$5.0	$6.3	$(8.6	$(3.0)

income--the "bottom line" of the HCO. The statement has three main parts: net operating income or loss, non-operating gain or loss, and net income. Net operating income or loss is the difference between operating revenues and operating expenses. Operating revenues consist mostly of revenues that patients pay for the health care services they receive. Other operating revenues may result from cafeteria sales, gift shop sales, or other activities considered essential to daily operations. Gross patient service revenues less deductions from gross patient service revenues equals net patient service revenues. The notes to the financial statements (Table 5) usually contain details on the deductions from gross patient service revenues. The largest of these deductions is often contractual adjustments. Cleverley (1992) defines contractual adjustments as "the difference between rates billed to a third-party payer, such as Medicare, and the amount that will actually be paid by that third-party payer." Next operating expenses are subtracted from operating revenues to arrive at net operating income. Operating expenses may be by function (i.e., nursing services), by natural object (i.e., salaries, supplies), or by some combination of these two. Following net operating income are non operating gains and losses. These are revenues and expenses from activities that are considered incidental to the organizations daily operations. Gifts, donations, and interest income are examples of non-operating gains. In the third part of this statement, net operating income (loss) is added to net non-operating gain (loss) to arrive at the HCO's net income (loss) or "bottom line." This statement gives us an indication of the HCO's profitability and ability to maintain or expand its current level of services in the future.

3. Statement of Changes in Equity

The statement of changes in equity (or statement of changes in fund balance or net assets) gives detail information regarding net income (loss) or other transactions which increased or decreased the HCO's equity each year. Like the income statement it is also for a period of time--normally one year. Table 3 gives the summarized statements of changes in equity for Mercy Hospital for the years ended June 30, 1992 through June 30, 1996. In some years the only change will be from revenues either over or under expenses. At the end of each fiscal year, the amounts in the HCO's revenue and expense accounts are transferred to the equity account. As a result, the revenue and expense accounts begin each new fiscal year with zero balances. Equity may

Table 3 - Statements of Changes in Equity for Mercy Hospital (in millions)

| | For the years ended June 30, | | | | |
	1996	1995	1994	1993	1992
Balance at the beginning of the year	$68.5	$63.5	$57.2	$65.8	$68.8
Additions and deductions					
Net income	16.4	5.0	6.3	(8.6)	(3.0)
Bakance at the end of the year	$84.9	$68.5	$63.5	$57.2	$65.8

also increase or decrease from the sale of stock by a for-profit HCO or the transfer of funds to or from a parent or subsidiary HCO.

4. Statement of Cash Flows

The statement of cash flows, which some HCOs may not prepare, gives the cash inflows and outflows from operations, investing and financing activities. Operating,

Table 4 - Statements of Cash Flows for Mercy Hospital (in millions)

		For the years ended June 30,			
	1996	1995	1994	1993	1992
Cash flows from operations and gains (losses)					
Cash received from patients and third-parties	$208.1	$145.8	$126.7	$96.5	$92.0
Cash from other	0.2	9.4	0.0	1.5	1.2
Cash paid to employees and suppliers	(205.8)	(155.4)	(132.0)	(119.7)	(98.8)
Interest paid	(4.7)	(5.0)	(5.0)	(4.5)	(4.0)
Gifts and donations	25.1	14.5	19.1	16.5	12.5
Net cash provided (used)	22.9	9.3	8.8	(9.7)	2.9
Cash flow from investing activities					
Purchase of buildings and equipment`	(37.1)	(9.1)	(12.3)		(2.0)
Proceeds from sale of assets			2.0	7.2	
Net cash provided (used)	(37.1)	(9.1)	(10.3)	7.2	(2.0)
Cash flow from financing activities					
Principal; payment on long-term debt (bonds)	(4.5)	(2.9)	(2.5)	(1.5)	(1.0)
Proceeds from bond issue	17.9		7.0		
Net cash provided (used)	13.4	(2.9)	4.5	(1.5)	(1.0)
Net increase (decrease) in cash	(0.8)	(2.7)	3.0	(4.0)	(0.1)
Cash beginning of year	1.2	3.9	0.9	4.9	5.0
Cash end of year	$0.4	$1.2	$3.9	$0.9	$4.9
Reconciliation of net income to net cash provided by operations and gains/losses					
Net income	$16.4	$5.0	$6.3	$(8.6)	$(3.0)
Adjustments to reconcile net income to net cash provided by operations and gains (losses)					
Depreciation	10.1	9.0	8.7	7.2	4.2
Increase (decrease) in cash due to changes in assets and liabilities:					
Accounts receivable	(10.2)	(2.8)	(5.7)	(6.1)	0.9
Other assets	(2.1)	(3.7)	(2.9)	(0.6)	(0.5)
Accounts payable	2.6	0.8	3.4	0.3	0.0
Other liabilities	2.6	1.0	(1.0)	(1.89)	1.3
Net adjustment	6.5	4.3	2.5	(1.1)	5.9
Net cash provided by operations and gains (losses)	$22.9	$9.3	$8.8	$(9.7)	$2.9

Table 5 - Notes Common to the Financial Statements of Mercy Hospital

Note 1. Property, plant and equipment (in millions)

Property, plant and equipment consisted of the following at the end of each of the last 5 fiscal years. All buildings and equipment are depreciated using the straight-line method.

	At June 30,				
	1996	1995	1994	1993	1992
Major movable equipment	$66.6	$56.9	$56.9	$53.6	$54.0
Buildings	117.7	100.4	100.6	94.7	95.4
Land	10.5	9.0	9.0	8.5	8.5
	194.8	166.3	166.5	156.8	157.9
Less accumulated depreciation	71.7	70.2	69.5	63.4	55.2
Net property, plant and equipment	$123.1	$96.1	$97.0	$93.4	$102.7

Note 2. Patient service revenue (in millions)

Contractual adjustments related to Medicare and Medicaid and other allowances were deducted from gross patient service revenues to arrive at the following net patient service revenues:

	For the years ended June 30,				
	1996	1995	1994	1993	1992
Gross patient service revenue	$237.9	$203.9	$191.0	$161.8	$140.7
Less deductions:					
Contractual and other adjustments	54.7	55.3	58.0	59.2	49.6
Recoveries of accounts written off	(35.1)				
	19.6	55.3	58.0	59.2	49.6
Net patient service revenue	$218.3	$148.6	$133.0	$102.6	$91.1

investing, and financing are the three parts of this statement when prepared in accordance with FASB Statement 95.

GASB Statement 9 requires a slightly different format for governmental HCOs. Both GASB and FASB recommend this statement be prepared using the "direct" method because it shows details that will allow stakeholders to better identify the specific sources of cash receipts and cash disbursements. Cash flows from operating activities result from the daily operating activities of the HCO. Cash flows from investing activities mainly involve the purchase of land, buildings, and major pieces of equipment. Cash flows from financing activities are monies the HCO receives when it issues long term debt (i.e., bonds), and the monies it spends when it repays this debt. For example, the financing activities section of Mercy's cash flow statement (Table 4) shows how much principal it paid on long-term debt during the year. This statement is also for a period of time--normally 1 year-and helps an HCO see if it is producing enough cash from its operations to pay its bills and acquire or maintain the facilities that it needs. An HCO can be profitable on the income statement but be in serious financial trouble if it is not converting its revenues to cash. Or as Cleverley points out "more firms fail for a lack of ready cash than for any other reason" (1992, p. 445). Because the statement of cash flows is a relatively new requirement, industry ratios using its information have yet to be fully developed. Therefore, none of the 11 ratios in Step 5 use information directly from this statement.

5. Notes to the Financial Statements

The notes to the financial statements are an integral part of the financial statements. Table 5 gives two notes that are common to most financial statements. Notes provide information that is impractical or impossible for the financial statements to include. For example, the notes give information such as how much principal must be paid each year on long term debt, whether depreciation is computed using the straight-line or some accelerated method, the adequacy of the retirement plan's funding, contingent liabilities involving legal actions such as malpractice claims, and other helpful information. Also, when not included in the financial statements, the notes show gross patient service revenue, the specific deductions from this revenue, and the historical cost of property, plant, and equipment less the accumulated depreciation. Even though notes are sometimes difficult for even accountants to understand, they do provide valuable information.

D. Accounting Terms and Words -The Language (Step 4)

Learning the meaning of the various accounting terms and words found on financial statements is also important. This knowledge is needed to understand the information provided by the 11 financial ratios suggested. Table 6 lists, in alphabetical order, the accounting terms and words most commonly found in HCOs' financial statements and notes. A brief definition is given after each. This list is not all inclusive but does include all the words and terms that are necessary to complete the financial exam outlined in this chapter.

E. Industry-wide Financial Ratios (Step 5)

Publications containing industry-wide financial ratios of similar HCOs are needed. Ratios in these publications serve as standards or bench marks against which the HCO's internal ratios are compared. How the HCO's ratios compare to industry standards is important information in determining its general financial health. The following are selected publications that contain industry-wide financial ratios for hospitals and the organizations that publish them:

1. The Comparative Performance of U.S. Hospitals: The Sourcebook
   HCIA Inc. (Baltimore, MD) and Deloitte and Touche LLP (Chicago, IL)
   (800) 568-3282   (312) 946-3433
2. The 1996 Almanac of Hospital Financial and Operating Indicators
   The Center for Healthcare Industry Performance Studies
   (800) 859-2447

Moody's and Standards and Poor also produce financial ratios for HCOs. These publications are usually quite expensive. However, some large libraries and HCOs may have reference copies the public can use. For some of the newer types of HCOs (i.e., home health agencies, ambulatory surgery centers), no industry-wide financial ratios may be available. In this situation, only internal comparisons of ratios can be made, which can still provide valuable information if management has adopted some carefully considered internal ratio standards. Most of the financial ratios are 12 to 18 months old when published. However, this is still timely enough for them to be use-

Table 6 - Accounting Terms and Words with Definitions

ACCOUNTS PAYABLE = A promise to pay money for goods or services received.

ACCOUNTS RECEIVABLE = Legally enforceable claims on customers for prior services or goods.

ACCRUED SALARIES = Obligations that result from prior operations; a present right or enforceable demand by employees.

ACCUMULATED DEPRECIATION = The amount of depreciation taken on the assets to the date of the balance sheet.

ALLOWANCES = The amount of accounts receivable the HCO estimates won't be collected from third-party payers who don't pay the full charge or from patient bad debt.

ASSETS = The things you own. Your economic resources.

ASSETS WHOSE USE IS LIMITED = These are funds that boards of trustees restrict for the replacement of things such as buildings and equipment or to implement new programs. Also funds restricted by third parties, other than donors, may be classified in this account. For example, a third party may restrict part of the funds a HCO receives from a bond sale to protect investors against default.

BONDS PAYABLE = The amount of money the HCO has borrowed from the investing public. Any part that must be paid within one year of the balance sheet date is classified as a current liability. The remainder is classified as a non-current liability.

CASH = Examples are coins and currency on hand, checking and savings accounts, and cashier's checks.

CASH EQUIVALENTS = Certificates of deposit and other temporary marketable securities that can be converted to cash very easily.

CONSTRUCTION IN PROGRESS = The amount of money that has been expended on projects that are still not completed at the balance sheet date.

CONTRACTUAL ADJUSTMENT = Normally the largest of the "deductions from gross patient revenue," it is the difference between the HCO's full established charge and what it agrees to accept as payment from third parties such as Medicare and Medicaid.

CURRENT ASSETS = Assets to be exchanged for cash or consumed during the operating cycle of the entity.

CURRENT LIABILITIES = Obligations that are expected to require payment in cash during the coming year.

DEDUCTIONS FROM GROSS PATIENT REVENUE = The difference between the HCO's full established charge (price), and what it agrees to accept as payment from third parties, employees, or others.

DEFERRED REVENUES = Obligations for goods or services that the organization must deliver in return for an advance payment from a customer.

DEPRECIATION = The periodic allocation of the cost of a tangible long-lived asset over its useful life.

EQUITY (FUND BALANCE) = The difference between assets and the claim to those assets by third parties (liabilities).

GROSS PATIENT SERVICE REVENUE = The amount of revenue that results from the provision of health care services to patients before it is reduced by deductions such as contractual allowances. It represents the HCO's full established price charged for the services and goods provided.

INVENTORIES = Items to be used in the delivery of health care services.

LIABILITIES = What you owe others for goods and services received.

NET PATIENT SERVICE REVENUE = Gross patient service revenue less deductions.

NONCURRENT LIABILITIES = Obligations that will not require payment in cash for at least one year or more.

Table 6 - Continued

NON OPERATING GAINS (LOSSES) = Revenues generated from activities not considered to be part of the HCO's daily operations. Two examples are interest income from investments and unrestricted gifts.

OPERATING EXPENSES = The cost to provide goods and services needed for daily operations. They may be classified by function (nursing services) or natural object (salaries).

OPERATING INCOME = Operating revenues minus operating expenses.

OTHER ASSETS = This is a "catch-all" account for assets that can't be classified in any other category. Intangible assets such as goodwill are included in this account.

OTHER CURRENT LIABILITIES = This is a "catch-all" account for liabilities that can't be classified in any other category.

OTHER OPERATING REVENUE = Revenues from normal daily operations which are not directly related to patient care. Some examples are cafeteria sales, gift shop sales, and building or equipment rentals.

PREPAID EXPENSES = Expenditures already made for future goods or services. Two examples are insurance premiums and magazine subscriptions paid in advance of receiving the goods and services.

PROPERTY, PLANT, AND EQUIPMENT:
Buildings = a structure owned by the entity and used in the normal course of its operations.
Land = historical cost of the earth's surface
Land improvements = historical cost of improvements erected on it
Major moveable equipment = things that are usually stationary but capable of being moved, such as hospital beds and x-ray machines

Sources: Cleverley, 1992, Chapter 4, and Needles, Anderson, and Caldwell, 1990.

Table 7 - Eleven Industry-wide Financial Ratios (urban, 400-plus bed hospitals)

	1994 Percentiles		
Ratios	75th	50th	25th
1. Days cash on hand	147	75	30
2. Average payment period (in days)	80	60	48
3. Days of net patient revenue in net accounts receivable	81	69	57
4. Debt service coverage	7.3	4.3	2.5
5. Long term debt to capitalization	.35	.23	.15
6. Cash flow to total debt	.58	.42	.28
7. Total profit margin	8.8	5.6	2.3
8. Operating profit margin	7.3	4.4	1.2
9. Return on assets	7.5	4.7	2.2
10. Average age of plant	9.3	8.0	6.6
11. Replacement viability	NA	.35	NA

Sources: Ratios 1 - 10 The Comparative Performance of U.S. Hospitals: The Sourcebook, 1995 and Ratio 11 Cleverley, 1992, p. 156.

ful. Table 7 contains the eleven industry-wide financial ratios that will be used to help determine the financial health of Mercy Hospital.

F. Organization-specific Financial Ratios (Step 6)

This step involves calculating the 11 financial ratios listed in Table 7 for Mercy Hospital for its five most recent fiscal years. These ratios represent relationships between various accounts on a HCO's financial statements. Each has a numerator and a denominator. Table 8 shows these 11 ratios for Mercy Hospital for its fiscal years ended June 30, 1992 through June 30, 1996. All amounts used in the ratios are found in Mercy's financial statements and notes (Tables 1 through 5). Comparisons of Mercy Hospital's ratios to similar hospitals and for different years within its own operation should identify significant financial strengths and weaknesses. The 11 ratios are calculated based on criteria in *The Sourcebook* and Cleverley's *Essentials of Health Care Finance* (1992, Chapter 6). They are divided into four types: liquidity, capital structure, profitability, and other.

1. Liquidity Ratios

Because most entities fail due to a lack of cash (Cleverley, 1992), liquidity ratios will be computed first. They indicate whether there is sufficient cash to pay current liabilities (bills) when they become due. Current liabilities are those due within one year after the date on the balance sheet. The need for adequate cash to pay current liabilities seems obvious. HCOs, however, frequently fail to determine the adequacy of their cash supply by periodically computing the following three liquidity ratios: cash on hand, average payment period, and days of net patient revenue in net accounts receivable.

a. Days cash on hand

According to The Sourcebook, this ratio measures the number of days a hospital could operate if no further revenues were received (1995) and is calculated as:

$$\frac{\text{Cash} + \text{Temporary investments} + \text{Balance of depreciation fund}}{(\text{Total operating expenses} - \text{Depreciation}) \,/\, 365}$$

Mercy Hospital's balance sheet (Table 1) has the assets accounts of cash, temporary investments , and balance of depreciation fund needed for the numerator. At June 30, 1996, Mercy's cash is $400,000 (cash and cash equivalents). It has no temporary investments listed as a separate account. They may be included as cash equivalents. Cash equivalents are temporary investments maturing in 90 days or less from the date of purchase. The balance of the depreciation fund is normally the amount restricted for replacement of buildings and equipment. It often falls under the broad category of assets whose use is limited. Mercy has $2 million in its depreciation fund at June 30, 1996, and the account is called assets restricted to replace buildings. The notes to the financial statements usually give more details about this account. The amount of total operating expense and the depreciation expense account needed for the denominator is found on the income statement (Table 2). Mercy's total operating expense for the year ended June, 30, 1996, was $229.3 million and its depreciation expense was $10.1 million. Depreciation expense is a non cash expense and is subtracted from total operating expense to get a rough estimate of the amount of cash Mercy spent for daily operations during the year. This is divided by 365 to get an estimate of the average amount of daily cash disbursements for operations. The amount is $600,500 rounded to the nearest $100. Mercy's days cash on hand ratio at June 30, 1996 is 4.0 days.

$$\frac{\$400,000 + \$2,000,000}{(\$229,300,000 - \$10,100,000) \, / \, 365} \quad = \; 4.0 \text{ days}$$

At June 30, 1996, Mercy would be able to meet its average daily cash disbursement operating needs for 4 calendar days if all its cash receipts stopped. This ratio is included in Table 8 along with Mercy's ratios for the previous 4 years. This 1996 ratio helps determines Mercy's financial health when it is compared to some external industry standard and to the internal standard from the other 4 years. The larger this ratio normally the better.

b. Average payment period

This ratio measures the average amount of time that elapses before current liabilities are met (The Sourcebook, 1995). It has the following accounts in its numerator and denominator:

$$\frac{\text{Total Current Liabilities}}{(\text{Total Operating Expense} - \text{Depreciation}) \, / \, 365}$$

The balance sheet (Table 1) has the total current liabilities accounts needed for the numerator. At June 30, 1996, Mercy's total current liabilities were $26.8 million. The income statement (Table 2) has the expense accounts needed for the denominator. The denominator for this ratio is the same as the "days cash on hand" ratio. Mercy's average payment period ratio for year ended June 30, 1996, is 73.4 days.

$$\frac{\$26,800,000 = 44.6 \text{ days}}{(\$229,300,000 - \$10,100,000) \, / \, 365}$$

The higher this ratio the more money the HCO has in effect "borrowed" from its vendors. This limits the HCO's ability to delay payment to its vendors and in effect "borrow" more of their money. If days in the average payment period are low, then the HCO has the added safety of being able to delay payments to some vendors until it can correct any short term cash problem. This is an often overlooked source of cash, although an HCO may lose some discounts and incur some late payment fees.

c. *Days of net patient revenue in net patient accounts receivable*

This ratio is the number of days of net patient revenue that a hospital has due from its patient billings after all deductions (The Sourcebook, 1995). It has the following accounts in its numerator and denominator:

$$\frac{\text{Net patient accounts receivable}}{\text{Net patient revenue} \ / \ 365}$$

The balance sheet (Table 1) has the net patient accounts receivable account needed for the numerator. At June 30, 1996, net patient accounts receivable was $45.7 million. Net patient accounts receivable is gross patient accounts receivable reduced by contractual allowances, bad debts, courtesy discounts, and other estimated uncollectibles. The income statement (Table 2) has the net patient revenue account needed for the denominator. Net patient revenue is gross patient revenue reduced by deductions (i.e., contractual allowances) for the year. It is the amount the HCO estimates it will ultimately collect in cash from its gross patient revenue. For year ended June 30, 1996, this amount was $218.3 million. This is divided by 365 to get an estimate of the average daily amount of cash receipts received from patients ($598,082). Mercy's days of net patient revenue in net accounts receivable at June 30, 1996, is 76.4 days.

$$\frac{\$45.7 \text{ million}}{\$218.3 \text{ million} \ / \ 365} = 76.4 \text{ days}$$

Management should understand the importance of each of these 76.4 days. For each day Mercy could reduce its days of net patient revenue in net accounts receivable through collections, it would receive a one time cash inflow of $598,082. Five days would mean a $2,990,410 increase in the cash on its balance sheet. A large number of days is normally unfavorable because patients are, in effect, borrowing the HCO's cash. And the longer they hold it the higher the probability it will become bad debt, and the more interest income is lost. If "days" in net patient revenue are increasing, the HCO is "loaning" more of its cash to patients. When this condition exists, an assertive collection effort should be made to reduce the number of days.

2. Capital Structure Ratios

Three ratios provide information that helps determine if an HCO will have enough cash to pay its long-term debt, and how much additional debt it can safely assume. They include debt service coverage, long-term debt to capitalization, and cash flow to debt. HCOs with inadequate cash flow to pay the principal and interest on their long-term debt will almost certainly be unable to borrow enough to upgrade their existing buildings and equipment or start new programs. If this situation is not corrected, the HCO, at some time in the future, will go out of business. These ratios help management see unfavorable cash flow trends in time to develop solutions before the situation becomes "life threatening."

a. **Debt service coverage**

This ratio measures the ratio of a hospital's funds available for the payment of debt service to the same year's principal and interest payments (The Sourcebook, 1995). It has the following accounts in its numerator and denominator.

$$\frac{\text{Net income + Depreciation + Interest expense}}{\text{Debt service (principal and interest payments)}}$$

The income statement (Table 2) has the revenue and expense accounts needed for the numerator. For the year ended June 30, 1996, Mercy had net income of $16.4 million, depreciation expense of $10.1 million, and interest expense of $4.7 million. When depreciation (a non-cash expense) and interest expense are added to net income, this gives an estimate of the total cash in-flows from operations of the HCO that are available to meet its debt service (principal and interest) payments. The denominator of the ratio is the interest expense portion of debt service (Table 2) plus the principal part. The amount of long-term debt principal the HCO paid is found on the statement of cash flows (Table 4) or in the notes to the financial statements. Mercy's principal and interest payments for the year ended June 30, 1996 totaled $4.5 million and $4.7 million respectively. Its debt service coverage for the year was 3.4 times. The amounts in the ratio are in millions of dollars.

$$\frac{\$16.4 + \$10.1 + \$4.7}{\$4.7 + \$4.5} = 3.4$$

This means Mercy had enough cash flow from operations to pay its debt service 3.4 times during its year ended June 30, 1996.

b. Long-term debt to capitalization

According to The Sourcebook, this ratio measures the proportion of a hospital's total capitalization provided by debt (1995). It has the following accounts in its numerator and denominator:

$$\frac{\text{Long-term debt (non-current liabilities)}}{\text{Long-term debt + Equity (fund balance)}}$$

Capitalization is long-term debt plus equity (fund balance). This ratio shows how much of the HCO's capitalization was used to acquire assets from borrowing as compared to the amount acquired from equity. The balance sheet (Table 1) has the liability and equity accounts needed for the numerator and denominator. At June 30, 1996 Mercy had long-term debt (bonds payable) of $78.6 million and equity of $84.9 million. This ratio for 1996 is 48.1%. The amounts in the ratio are in millions of dollars:

$$\frac{\$78.6}{\$78.6 + \$84.9} = 48.1\%$$

This ratio shows that Mercy's capitalization was financed with about 48% from borrowed funds and about 52% from equity.

c. Cash flow to total debt

This ratio measures the proportion of a hospital's total debt obligations that could be met with available cash flow if demanded by creditors within 1 year (The Sourcebook, 1995). It has the following numerator and denominator.

$$\frac{\text{Net income} + \text{Depreciation} + \text{Interest expense}}{\text{Total liabilities (current and long-term)}}$$

The income statement (Table 2) has the revenue and expense accounts needed for the numerator. The numerator is the same as that for the debt service coverage ratio and represents the total cash flow from operating activities available to pay total liabilities if all came due at once. The balance sheet (Table 1) has the liability accounts (current and long-term) needed for the denominator. Mercy has only one long-term debt account---bonds payable. The notes to the financial statements should give the number of years the bonds are financed for. The cash flow to total debt ratio for 1996 is 29.6%. The amounts in the ratio are in millions of dollars.

$$\frac{\$16.4 + \$10.1 + \$4.7}{\$105.4} = 29.6\%$$

This ratio shows that one year of cash flow from operations could pay off about 30% of Mercy's total liabilities or debt.

3. Profitability Ratios

These ratios give users another way of looking at the HCO's ability to provide the cash it needs for daily operations, debt service payments, and investments in new and existing property, plant, and equipment. Ultimately an HCO must pay for all its assets and other costs of operations from the cash that results from net income. Three ratios are important in helping obtain information on profitability: operating profit margin, total profit margin, and return on assets. If adequate profitability ratios are not maintained, then ultimately there will be insufficient cash for the HCO to remain in business. These ratios should be studied carefully to understand how profitable the HCO is from operations and how significant non operating gains are to net income or the bottom line.

Many non-profits and governmental HCOs can look to foundations for endowment income, governmental bodies for appropriations, and donors for unrestricted gifts. Often the non-operating gain for non-profits make up a significant percentage of total net income. Mercy Hospital's non-operating gains are essential to its survival (Table 2). As long as the non operating gains are long term and recurring, there is less risk to the HCO. In many situations, however, the HCO has little control over the amount of non-operating gains (i.e., unrestricted gifts) it receives each year. The notes to the financial statements should give the amount of financial control the HCO has over these gains. For example, how much control does it have over the assets of a foundation created to receive gifts and donations on its behalf?

Careful consideration should be given to these ratios in the development of the HCO's plans. How much profit the HCO needs to accomplish its operational and strategic management objectives is a critical management decision.

a. Total profit margin

The Sourcebook states that this ratio is a measure of the overall profitability of a hospital and includes the contributions of philanthropy, endowment revenue, government grants, investment income, and other revenue and expense not related to patient care operations (1995). It has the following accounts in its numerator and denominator.

$$\frac{\text{Net income}}{\text{Total revenue (operating and non-operating)}}$$

The income statement (Table 2) has the revenue and income accounts needed for the numerator and the denominator. For the year ended June 30, 1996, Mercy had $16.4 million of net income and total revenue of $245.7 million $220.6 operating and $25.1 non-operating). Its total profit margin for 1996 was 6.7%.

$$\frac{\$16.4 \text{ million}}{\$245.7 \text{ million}} = 6.7\%$$

b. Operating profit margin

This ratio is a measure of a hospital's profitability with respect to its patient care services and operations (The Sourcebook, 1995). These are the activities the HCO has most control over. It has the following accounts in its numerator and denominator:

$$\frac{\text{Operating income (loss)}}{\text{Operating revenue}}$$

The income statement (Table 2) has the accounts needed for both the numerator and denominator. For the year ended June 30, 1996, Mercy had an operating loss of $8.7 million (operating expenses exceeded operating revenue) and operating revenues of $220.6 million. The operating profit margin for 1996 was a negative 3.9%.

$$\frac{(\$8.7) \text{ million}}{\$220.6 \text{ million}} = 3.9\%$$

This ratio shows that unless Mercy continues to receive significant non-operating revenue, it very likely could go out of in business in the near future. Also, it may need to reduce costs, increase prices, or take some other appropriate action to increase its operating profit.

c. Return on assets

This ratio is another measure of the overall profitability of a hospital, as it compares the amount of total revenue over total expenses (i.e., net income) generated in relation to the amount of assets controlled by the hospital (The Sourcebook, 1995, p. 140). It has the following accounts in its numerator and denominator:

$$\frac{\text{Operating income (loss)}}{\text{Total assets}}$$

The income statement (Table 2) has the accounts needed for the numerator. The balance sheet (Table 1) has the total assets. For 1996, Mercy had $16.4 million of net income and $190.3 million of total assets. This gives a return on total assets ratio of 8.6 percent.

$$\frac{\$16.4 \text{ million}}{\$190.3 \text{ million}} = 8.6\%$$

This ratio tells stakeholders that for every dollar of assets, Mercy is generating a profit of 8.6 cents. The return on assets ratio must be considered in relation to the profit margin ratios. The HCO may have a good total profit margin but an unsatisfactory return on its total assets. For example, a HCO with net income of $10 million, total revenue of $100 million, and total assets of $300 million would have a total profit margin of 10% and a return on assets of only 3.3%. On the other hand, if the HCO has net income of $10 million, total revenue of $300 million, and total assets of $100 million, its total profit margin would be 3.3%, and its return on assets would be 10%. This ratio gives information on how efficiently assets are being used. Without an adequate return on its assets, the HCO may not have enough total net income to remain competitive, even though it has a good total profit margin.

4. Other Ratios

The final two ratios to be computed for Mercy are classified as "other" ratios. They give a rough estimate of the accounting age of the plant (i.e., buildings, equipment, and land improvements) and information on whether there are sufficient funds on hand to pay for major renovations and replacements as they are needed. Generally the greater the age of the plant and equipment, the more funds that should be available for renovations and replacements. Additional funds may also be needed for new programs and facilities in order to maintain market share.

a. Average age of plant

This ratio measures the average accounting age of a hospital's capital assets, such as buildings, fixtures, and major moveable equipment (The Sourcebook, 1996). It has total accumulated depreciation and current years depreciation expense in its numerator and denominator.

Note 1 to Mercy's financial statements (Table 5) has its total accumulated depreciation. Sometimes it is found on the balance sheet. The income statement (Table 2) has the current depreciation expense needed for the denominator. At June 30, 1996, Mercy had $71.3 million of accumulated depreciation on its plant and $10.1 million in depreciation expense for the year ended. The average age of its plant is 7.1 years.

$$\frac{\$71.3 \text{ million}}{\$10.1 \text{ million}} = 7.1 \text{ years}$$

Again, this is a very rough estimate. Because most HCOs use straight line depreciation, this ratio should provide at least a meaningful comparison with like HCOs. Straight line depreciation is calculated by dividing the historical cost (less salvage value) of the asset by its estimated useful life (in years). Land is not depreciated.

b. Replacement viability

Has the HCO accumulated sufficient funds to replace or renovate its buildings, land improvements, and equipment when they wear out or must be replaced due to obsolescence? If little or no funds have been set aside for this and the HCO has a weak debt service coverage ratio, it may have difficulty borrowing the needed funds. Market share may be lost if it is unable to borrow sufficient funds to maintain its plant compared to other organizations. Cleverley (1992) uses the replacement viability ratio to determine financial health in this area. This ratio is used to measure the adequacy of current investments to meet replacement needs (Cleverley, 1992, p. 155). It has the following accounts in its numerator and denominator:

$$\frac{\text{Restricted plant fund balance + Unrestricted investments}}{\text{Price level adjusted accumulated depreciation } \times \text{ .50}}$$

The balance sheet (Table 1) has the accounts needed for the numerator. Unrestricted investments are normally funds "restricted" by the board to provide funds for the renovation or replacement of its plant. This account may be called funded depreciation. Because the board can remove the restrictions, these investments are considered part of the HCO's unrestricted equity. These accounts are often listed under the asset category of "assets whose use is limited." For Mercy the amount at June 30,1996 was $2 million. The restricted plant fund balance has only funds restricted by donors for a specific purpose. These funds must be accounted for in the restricted fund of HCOs that use fund accounting and must be spent in accordance with the donor's restriction. Mercy does not have a restricted fund. The denominator is computed by taking accumulated depreciation and adjusting it for an increase in price. This is an estimate of what the HCO thinks it should have accumulated currently toward meeting plant replacement needs. This price level adjusted depreciation is then multiplied by 50% because national averages show that HCOs pay for plant replacement with about 50% from debt and 50% from equity (Cleverley , 1992). Mercy's historical cost accumulated depreciation is $71.7 million at June 30, 1996. This is increased by 10% to reflect how inflation has affected the funds needed for replacement. Mercy's price level adjusted accumulated depreciation is therefore $71.7 million plus $7.2 million, or $78.9 million, at June 30, 1996. Its replacement viability ratio is .05 assuming Mercy's board plans to fund future renovations and replacements with 50% from debt and 50% from earnings.

$$\frac{\$2.0 \text{ million}}{\$78.9 \text{ million } \times \text{ .50}} = .05$$

This ratio shows that Mercy has only $2 million of the $39.5 million ($78.9 x .50) it needs if it plans to finance 50% of future replacements and renovations from equity.

G. Comparison of Financial Ratios (Step 7)

Table 8 compares 11 financial ratios for Mercy for fiscal year ended June 30, 1996 to ratios from its previous 4 fiscal years and to industry-wide financial ratios. The 5 year comparison of internal ratios should point out trends of improving, stable, or deteriorating financial health. Also, a comparison of Mercy's 1996 ratios to 1994 industry-wide ratios is another indicator of its financial health. Although the most current industry-wide ratios are about 18 months old, they still provide a good standard for comparison since they remain relatively stable within a 2 year period.

Table 8 - Ratio Comparisons - Mercy Hospital

Ratio	1994 Percentiles			Trends		Mercy's Ratios 1996 -1992				
	75	50	25	Ext.	Int.	96	95	94	93	92
1. Days cash on hand	147	75	30	U	↓	4	23	13	12	45
2. Average payment period	80	60	48	F	↓	45	42	40	33	45
3. Days of net patient revenue in net accounts receivable	81	69	57	U	↑	76	88	92	86	90
4. Debt service coverage	7.3	4.3	2.5	U	↑	3.4	2.4	2.7	.5	1.0
5. Cash flow to total debt	.35	.23	.15	F	↑	.30	.23	.24	.04	.06
6. Long term debt to capitalization	.58	.42	.28	U	↑	.48	.49	.52	.54	.51
7. Operating profit margin	7.3	4.4	1.2	U	↑	(.039)	(.057)	(.095)	(.240)	(.163)
8. Total profit margin	8.8	5.6	2.3	F	↑	.067	.028	.041	(.071)	(.028)
9. Return on total assets	.075	.047	.022	F	↑	.086	.033	.043	(.064)	(.020)
10. Average age of plant	9.3	8.0	6.6	F	↑	7.1	7.8	8.0	8.8	13.1
11. Replacement viability	NA	.35	NA	U	↓	.05	.05	.03	.09	.26

Sources: Ratios 1 - 10 (The Sourcebook, 1995), ratio 11 (Cleverley, 1992, p. 155)
Symbols: ↑ an improving internal trend
↓ a deteriorating internal trend
'F' Mercy's 1996 ratio compares favorably to the industry-wide ratio
'U' is unfavorably
( ) indicates a negative amount

Percentiles from *The Sourcebook* are for hospitals whose fiscal years ended sometime in 1994. Cleverley's ratio is from the *1990 Financial Analysis Service* of the Healthcare Financial Management Association.

The next step is to use the information provided by the ratio comparisons in Table 8 to answer some basic questions asked in Step 8 about Mercy's financial health.

H. Answers to the Questions (Step 8)

The ratio comparisons in Step 8 are the results of the financial exam performed on Mercy Hospital. Now these results, along with the financial statements and notes, must be used to answer five key questions about Mercy's general financial health. Answering these questions should allow stakeholders to determine Mercy's general financial health and give a brief explanation supporting their opinion.

1. Does the HCO Have Enough Cash to Pay its Current Liabilities (bills) as They Become Due?

Mercy Hospital has only 4 days of cash on hand of which most has been restricted for the replacement of buildings. Unless cash on hand is increased (peer hospitals' median was 75 days), Mercy will almost certainly have periods of time when it will not be able to pay its current liabilities when they become due. This may happen when a large third party payer such as Medicare delays its normal payments to the hospital, or when other "man-made" or natural events also cause a temporary decrease in cash receipts. Mercy has several short-term options for dealing with this critical lack of cash. First, its average payment period for its current liabilities (45 days) is good compared to the industry-wide median of 60 days. Therefore, when faced with a cash shortage, it could delay payments to some of its vendors by 10 to 15 days without causing them to stop accepting orders. This would, in effect, allow Mercy to "borrow" between 3 to 4 million dollars from its vendors ($600,000 average daily cash disbursements x 50% non-personal expense x 10 or 15 days). This is a "one-time" source of cash which the hospital has immediate control over. A second approach would be to try to reduce the number of days of net patient revenue in net accounts receivable. Mercy has 76 days of net patient revenue in net accounts receivable compared to the industry-wide median of 69 days. If, through a more assertive collection effort, it could reduce its "days" to the industry-wide median, this would provide a one-time cash inflow of about $4.2 million ($598,000 average daily net patient revenue x 7 days). A third approach would be to borrow the cash needed from a foundation established to benefit the hospital, (i.e., from a governmental body, a bank, or any other source allowed by policy, law, or regulation). HCOs operating with insufficient days cash on hand need to have an adequate line-of-credit established with a bank or similar lending institution.

While Mercy does have some options available to deal with its insufficient cash on hand, this is still a serious financial health condition. Mercy should prepare weekly, if not daily, cash forecasts to anticipate cash shortages while developing plans for improving its cash position in the longer term. How much cash on hand an HCO should have will vary based on a number of factors. For example, the more uncertainty there is about the amount of revenue it will receive from one of its main sources, the greater the number of days cash on hand it will want to have. Management should recommend, and the board should approve, internal standards for days cash on hand and other key financial ratios. This should be an activity that is part of both operational and strategic planning.

2. Will the HCO Have Enough Cash to Pay Off its Existing Long-term Debt as it Becomes Due?

Mercy's ability to pay its current liabilities when they become due is certainly questionable. Is this condition likely to be corrected in the future so that Mercy has enough cash to pay its long-term debts? Long term debts are the liabilities it must pay that become due in one year or more after the date on its balance sheet.

Mercy's debt service coverage ratios over the past 5 years provide some important information that helps answer this question. In 1992, it had exactly enough net cash flow from its operating activities to pay the principal and interest (debt service) on its debt that came due during the year. In 1993, its net cash flow from operations would pay only one-half of its debt service. Since then, its debt service coverage ratio has shown a significant increase. In 1996, Mercy had enough net cash flow from its operating activities to pay its debt service for the year 3.4 times. Unless Mercy has deferred a significant portion of its debt to future years, it should have sufficient cash to pay off its long-term debt as it becomes due. The notes to the financial statements normally disclose annual debt service payments for 5 years after the current fiscal year. This should alert stakeholders to any large amounts of deferred debt service. In addition to the notes, the cash flow to total debt ratio and long term debt to capitalization ratio are also helpful in determining if the HCO has deferred any significant amount of debt to future year.

Mercy's 1996 cash flow to total debt ratio of .30 is well above the industry-wide median of .23. If this ratio were well below the median, it could indicate a significant amount of long-term debt had been deferred. At the time additional long term debt was needed, a weak debt service coverage ratio may have encouraged management to structure the new debt so that payments in the early years were considerably lower than those in later years. Mercy's cash flow to total debt ratio of .30 indicates it could pay off all of its debt in just over 3 years if no interest was charged.

The long-term debt to capitalization ratio also helps determine Mercy's ability to pay its long term debt. At June 30, 1996, it shows that Mercy's capitalization was financed with about 48% from debt and 52% from equity. This is somewhat unfavorable when compared to the industry-wide average which shows 42% of capitalization is from long term debt and 58% from equity. If this ratio showed Mercy with 60-70% or more of its capitalization from long term debt, then a careful review of the annual debt service payments over the life of all outstanding long term debt should be made. Any significant increases in annual debt service in later years should be identified and an explanation obtained as to how the HCO plans to provide the funds necessary to meet the increased debt service payments. This ratio indicates Mercy has not borrowed too heavily to acquire its assets. They also indicate that Mercy Hospital will most probably be able to pay its long term debt service.

3. *How Much Total New Debt Can the HCO Incur?*

With a serious shortage of cash on hand and its debt service coverage below industry-wide standards, Mercy should not acquire new debt unless it is essential to maintain daily operations. Replacement of a heating and air conditioning unit to permit continued occupancy of the hospital or starting a new service essential to retaining market share are two examples where borrowing would be warranted. Otherwise, for the next 2 or 3 years, Mercy may want to increase its cash on hand to somewhere around the industry median of 75 days. This would mean an increase to about $40,000,000. Once this is achieved, and cash flows from operating activities adequately covers its debt service requirements, Mercy should be in a good position to incur more long-term debt if needed. Information from liquidity and capital structure ratios provide key information in helping determine how much, if any, new debt the HCO can incur. Management should carefully consider these ratios when preparing strategic plans. A key planning question is what percent of a HCO's assets should be acquired by borrowing and how much from equity should be acquired.

4. *Does the HCO Have Sufficient Net Income (excess of revenues over expenses) to Provide the Cash Needed to Accomplish the Objectives of Its Operational and Strategic Plans?*

Three ratios that help answer this question are total profit margin, operating profit margin, and return on total assets. Mercy must be sufficiently profitable to subsequently provide the cash needed to accomplish its operational and strategic plans. Both its total profit margin and operating profit margin ratios for 1996 show significant increases over these same ratios in 1992. In 1996, its total profit margin was 6.7% compared with the industry-wide median of 5.6%, while its 1996 operating profit margin was a negative 3.9% compared to an industry median of 4.4%. Generous non-operating revenue from gifts and donations (See Table 2) over the past 5 years have made up for negative operating profit margin ratios. While its operating profit margin was negative in each of the last 5 years, Table 2 shows it made dramatic improvements during this period. Note 2 (Table 5) to Mercy's financial statements helps explain this improvement. In 1992 for every dollar of gross patient charges, Mercy collected 65 cents. In 1996, it collected 92 cents on every dollar of gross patient charges. In other words, it had reduced deductions from gross patient revenues (mainly contractual allowances to Medicare and Medicaid), which dramatically increased its net patient revenue and net income. If Mercy can maintain its 1996 total profit margin into future years, the probability is high that it will collect sufficient cash to allow it to accomplish its plans. Two keys to maintaining its 1996 profitability are its non-operating revenues from gifts and donations and its deductions from gross patient revenues. Both of these areas are somewhat out of the direct control of the HCO, and as a result, do present some greater risks. Information from the return on total assets ratio is also needed to make sure the information from the profit margin ratios is not misleading. For example, Mercy's total profit margin of 6.7% could be based on one dollar of total revenues minus 92.3 cents of total expenses or net income of 6.7 cents. Only when its 6.7 cents of net income was divided by its $190.3 million in total assets would the complete answer on profitability be clear. This overstated example points out the need for this third profitability ratio. In 1996, Mercy's return on total assets ratio was 8.6% compared to the industry median of 4.7%. This ratio indicates there is a sufficient profit (net income) volume to provide the cash needed. If Mercy is able maintain these three ratios at 1996 levels, it should be profitable enough to generate the cash needed for its plans.

5. *Does the HCO Have Adequate Cash Set Aside for Replacement or Renovation of Its Plant?*

Even though in 1996 Mercy has much newer buildings and equipment (7.1 accounting years old) compared to 1992 (13.1 accounting years old), it still didn't have sufficient cash on hand to pay for future replacement and renovations of its plant. At June 30, 1996 it had only $2 million restricted for the replacement of its buildings (Table 1) on which $71.1 million in historical cost depreciation had accumulated (Table 5). If historical cost depreciation is increased by 10% to adjust for increases in prices, Mercy replacement viability ratio is 5% compared to an industry median of 35% (Table 8). A 5% replacement viability ratio means Mercy needs to have about $40 million in cash and investments currently on hand if it plans to pay for plant replacements and renovations with 50% from borrowing and 50% from equity. How to build up sufficient funds for renovation and replacement of its plant is an important policy issue for the board. Until this is done, Mercy may be unable to borrow sufficient funds for major unexpected emergencies.

I. Determine General Financial Health

Should Mercy's general financial health at June 30, 1996 be rated as good, average, or poor based on the information provided by the 11 financial ratios and the answers to the above questions? Poor health is usually the answer if most of the 11 ratios show unfavorable internal trends over a 5-10 year period, and the most recent year's ratios are below the industry-wide median for comparable HCOs. Under these conditions, the HCO often has insufficient cash-on-hand to pay its currents liabilities, has insufficient net cash flow to pay its long term debt (liabilities) when they become due, can incur no additional debt, is not profitable enough to generate the cash it needs for its plans, and has insufficient cash restricted for future replacement of its plant. Good health is normally the answer if conditions opposite to those of poor health exist. Mercy's general financial health is, most probably, average because its ratios show mixed internal trends and mixed comparisons to industry medians (Table 8). The following is the rationale to support this opinion.

Its ability to pay its current liabilities is poor since it has only 4 days of cash-on-hand, so there may be periods of time when it will be unable to pay its vendors in a timely manner. This weakness is somewhat offset by the fact that its average payment period is low, which means it can delay payments to vendors by an average of 10 to 15 days without causing them to stop shipping or accepting orders. It does have sufficient cash flow provided from its operating activities to pay its long-term debt as it becomes due. For 1996, its operating activities provided an estimated $26.5 million in cash flow ($16.4 million net income plus $10.1 million in depreciation expense), which allowed it to "cover" the principal and interest payments on its debt service of $9.2 million by 3.4 times. This left $17.3 million in cash which it used to help acquire new buildings (Table 4). In fact, over the past 5 years, Mercy has spent most of it cash provided from operating activities on its debt service and upgrading its buildings. During the past 5 years, Mercy spent over $50 million upgrading its buildings (Table 4). This has left it with insufficient cash-on-hand and in a position where it should not take on new debt until there is adequate cash-on-hand--maybe as much as $40 million. While overall its current cash position is weak, it has the profitability to improve this substantially in the near future. Because of its mix of favorable and unfavorable conditions, Mercy's financial health is determined to be average. Various stakeholders may arrive at different conclusions about its health. The important thing is that the financial exam is done periodically (at least annually) and the results evaluated. This almost certainly will point out some actual or potential problems that need to be addressed in order to prevent them from developing or becoming worse.

SUMMARY

In the past the general financial health of HCOs was seldom, if ever, examined even by its executive management and boards. The 11 financial ratios recommended in this chapter allow stakeholders to examine an HCO and determine whether its financial health is good, average, or poor. There are other financial ratios that can also provide valuable information about an HCO's financial health. It is important, however, to select a manageable number and learn how they help answer the important questions allowing those responsible to make more timely and informed decisions. Including financial ratios in the operational and strategic planning processes will also help decision makers in determining their unique standards. Individuals acquiring skills in determining the financial health of HCOs should improve their value to their organizations, increase the chances they will assume positions of greater responsibility, and help ensure that the community will continue to have access to quality health care at a reasonable price.

REFERENCES

Bailey, L. P. and Miller, M. A. (1993). *HBJ Miller Comprehensive GAAS Guide 1993,* Harcourt Brace Jovanovich, Publishers, New York: 10.05.

Broyles, R. W. (1982). *Hospital Accounting Practice (Volume I),* Aspen Systems Corporation, Rockville, MD: 40.

Cleverley, W. O. (1992). *Essentials of Health Care Finance,* Third Edition, Aspen Publishers, Inc., Gaithersburg, MD.

Goldstein, D. E. (1995). *Alliances: Strategies for Building Integrated Delivery Systems,* Aspen Publishers, Gaithersburg, MD.

Needles, B. E., Jr., Anderson, H. R., Caldwell, J. C. *Principles of Accounting,* Fourth Edition, Houghton Mifflin Company, Boston, Massachusetts: G-7.

The Comparative Performance of U.S. Hospitals: The Sourcebook. (1995). HCIA Inc. and Deloitte and Touche LLP, Baltimore, MD.

59.

MICRO-FINANCIAL ANALYSIS

Yvonne J. Kochanowski, *SteelEdge Business Consulting, Placerville, CA*

Americans view high quality healthcare as a right and an entitlement. Providers face shrinking financial resources with which to supply care. Employers cannot afford to cover rising healthcare premiums. Many individuals in American society use the hospital emergency room, one of the highest cost levels of care, as their sole access to the system. Government deep pockets cover less and less of the bills for the medically indigent. How should these extremes be balanced? When does care cost too much? How would the actual direct and indirect costs of providing a healthcare service or product be calculated? What does a healthcare manager need to know about cost accounting to make informed operations decisions?

This chapter presents a basic introduction to cost accounting for healthcare providers and furnishes a micro-view financial road map to follow within different types of organizations. The primary intent is to provide a meaningful understanding of cost-related financial management decisions facing healthcare operations professionals. Broad exposure to the concepts and techniques of healthcare financial analysis will encompass such topical areas as:

- Budgeting impacts, cost behaviors, cost allocation methodologies, and standard costs in a rapidly changing environment;
- Healthcare 'product' pricing, including cost reimbursement, fee for service, capitation and other emerging revenue models;
- Capital project analysis and allocation of scarce capital resources;
- Strategies and tactics to make more effective financial decisions; and
- Financial planning for the organization.

Future trends and their potential impacts on micro-financial analysis in the healthcare organization will also be considered.

I. BUDGETING BASICS

The financial side of healthcare has developed from a long tradition of powerful, influential players. From the 1929 birth of insurance in Baylor University Hospital's plan for schoolteachers to the government reimbursement triad of Medicare Parts A and B and Medicaid, healthcare has enjoyed a market in which the cost of care was inconsequential. Physicians and hospitals were reimbursed per procedure, thus increasing the flow of healthcare dollars. Technology offered great treatment advances with these higher intensity services echoed in higher costs of care. Further, the impact of for-profit chains increased competition. When fixed reimbursement rates and managed care entered the field, many organizations suddenly responded— they needed to know what it cost to provide services, since the payors' checks were no longer blank. Many organizations had little understanding about the true costs of care on a per-case or per-diagnosis basis, and estimates of costs were based on traditional accounting methods which did not adequately reflect how care was provided.

In many institutions, better operational and financial controls were brought about by the acceptance of financial risk for services to patients. As primary care physicians become partners in cost controls, they reduce utilization of services by approximately 30% (Beckman, 1995). Coupled with closer examination of the budget in other parts of the healthcare system, organizations have made great strides in reducing expenses. For most organizations, the first step in this cost control process is an examination of its budget.

A budget is the financial tactical plan for an organization. To be effective, it must accurately reflect best estimates about volume, the resources required to provide those services and products, and the costs of the resources. Aggregated costs tied to outcomes and tracking of productivity and volume provide the organization with a method to measure the effectiveness of its budget. The development of future adjustments to activities then assures that the organization continues to remain financially viable.

In earlier, less controlled times, healthcare costs were allocated and charges set based on the ability of the payor to cover provider charges. This practice, called cost shifting, meant that some payors covered a disproportionately large share of expenses because of their lack of purchasing power, while others with greater purchasing power or fixed charges were allocated amounts less than expenses for the actual services received. This differential pricing mechanism increased charges to one group because others were unable or unwilling to absorb actual costs. Cost shifting has been considered by some researchers as a destabilizing force in the insurance market (Dobson and Clark, 1992), separating ties between what a service or product costs and what is charged. Recent changes by the purchasers of healthcare have changed this direction. The current trend recognizes that costs overall must reflect actual performance, and payors should absorb expenses which accurately reflect the services and products provided.

A. Importance of Cost Data

When prospective payment mechanisms were implemented in hospitals in 1984, these institutions began to pay closer attention to the interrelationships between cost and volume. Standard cost information helped to provide the basis for pricing decision and to identify areas of inefficiency. As the level of sophistication improved, systems which measured individual units of service, applied weighted productivity values to the service, and measured acuity came into use. Today's detail depends on the statistical and accounting data sources available, the organization's ability to identify accurately the components of a unit of service, and access to resources that undertake time-consuming, costly calculations. However, the impact of better cost management on financial performance continues to result from a combination of such external factors as changes in payors, treatment methods, and volumes and internally controlled factors.

Internal factors which can be controlled within the organization have become the subject of serious interest. A recent study about the effects of Medicare prospective payment on the financial results of hospitals brought the following cost-related results:

> The striking difference between winners and losers was on the cost side. Losers had higher costs per case compared with winners, and despite these higher costs the losers had greater increases in costs over time. These higher costs ...were attributed to a host of factors, including weaker financial control and management systems, rudimentary utilization control practices, and less physician involvement in efforts to improve hospital financial performance (Bray, p. 49).

When cost containment was part of the culture of the institution, better monitoring and budgeting systems were in place. Greater focus on cost-related issues as a means of enhancing the mission of the organization and freeing assets for service expansion produced better financial results. Staffing levels, purchasing, and pricing all showed evidence of reasonable expectations of expenditures and better staff performance against realistic financial goals (Bray, 1994). The first step in a healthy control process is a plan.

B. Budget Basics from a Cost Accounting Perspective

A budget satisfies a number of objectives:

- Quantify policies and plans of the organization in writing,
- Provide a basis for evaluating financial performance,
- Use as a tool to control costs, and
- Raise cost awareness and bridge goals among all participants.

A traditional model for the budget process is represented in Figure 1.

Because a tactical plan depends on a vision for the future, the first step in the budget process is defining the organization's direction. Issues such as geographic coverage, participation in an integrated system, and clinical programs support the vision for the organization.

The next step in determining the global or organizational budget is to measure workload volume or activity. Tracking these statistics, the organization can assess its current productivity, long term trends of business, and future opportunities. Volume information derived from past history, projected changes in operations, and estimations are then assessed in measures of weighted output for levels of effort or intensity of productivity required.

Figure 1 - Budget Steps and Outputs

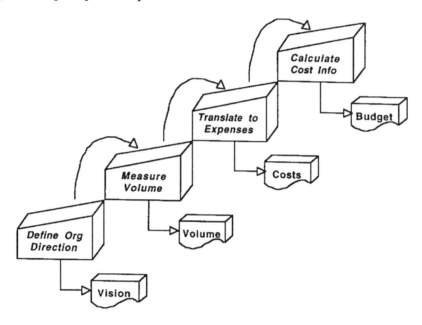

Sources of data include service logs, patient care schedules, delivery logs, number of prescriptions filled, visit logs, and time studies per care unit. The financial information system may also track information. If in-house data is not available, such as in the inception and projection of a new service line, industry averages and peer data can be used as an initial benchmark.

The organization must then translate volume into expenses using standards, actual charges or averages. Data can be generated from a number of sources:

- Direct costs can be identified to the unit of productivity; e.g., Pay Per Visit rate is $38 per specialty nursing unit of service.
- It can be calculated based on multiplying the weighted output by the cost unit; e.g., .75 hour of pharmacist service times $24 per hour = $18 for labor.
- Finally, it can be a more encompassing calculation from a representative period of business - usually at least three months. The total indirect costs are divided by the number of care units in the period (using the statistics developed through the studies); e.g., total vehicle operating costs are $205,000 divided by 8,000 deliveries for the period = $26 per delivery.

At this point, the manager has tools to calculate cost information for the organization. Multiplying the number of units of activity times the cost per unit will provide a budget figure for the organization or department. However, additional tools might provide more accurate and detailed information. This information is generated from a cost accounting system.

II. STANDARD COST ANALYSIS

Consider this:

> According to Modern Healthcare's 1994 Multi-unit Providers Survey, for-profit chains had an average operating margin of 9.9% in 1993, compared with a 5.8% margin for nonpublic, not-for-profit systems. The survey also showed for-profits surpasses not-for-profits on revenues, assets and total net income (Pallarito, p. 92).

Clearly, little margin is left to invest in new programs, purchase new equipment, or expand services if operating margins are not controlled. Understanding costs of operations provides vital information on how a more productive operating margin can be achieved.

Cost accounting is the assignment of usual or standard financial resources used to provide a care unit of service or output. Providers must gain an understanding of what it costs to supply care, so as to control expenses. Today's patients are sicker and require higher cost treatments, while the introduction of high tech methods of treatment directly impact costs. For example, in an acute setting, cost of care for an admission becomes a function of basic operating costs, the severity of the patient's illness, the patient's socio-demographics, the physician providing the care, and the payor regulating authorization for services. Each of these functions can be translated into a calculation in the standard cost equation.

A. Definitions of Standard Cost Accounting

Standard cost refers to the concept of usual costs--what the average care unit is expected to consume. This is a benchmark for the business, not an absolute. It can be reviewed in two ways—as a standard cost for a particular item, such as a bed day on a particular floor based on staffing and standard supplies used, or on an activity-based costing unit, such as the critical path of treatment for the patient. Cost accounting requires the manager to analyze how costs in the department's unique business relate to the volume of care units provided. Typically, the level of acceptance of cost accounting systems rises with the greater pressures felt from managed care and cost controls placed on the organization by external parties. Immediate control needs are usually faced by short-term cost cutting measures. Longer term repairs are required through more comprehensive systems.

Segments of the healthcare industry have reached varying levels of sophistication in their cost accounting processes. A four-stage approach to hospital cost accounting has been identified:

- In Stage 1, hospitals improve their overall cost-accounting systems.
- In Stage 2, they assess cost behavior in their departments.
- In Stage 3, they control overall costs, and
- In Stage 4, they design new cost-conscious administrative systems (Young and Pearlman, 1993).

Under this model, cost accounting for specific activities has been the norm. Rather than looking at all costs related to a diagnosis and discharge, costs are maintained on a single unit of activity within each department. While providing greater detail about costs and assisting managers in controlling costs, this method does little to address the widely varying needs of patients within a diagnostic group.

To increase sophistication in cost accounting, it is useful to consider "a costing system as one that determines or identifies costs at the procedure level regardless of the hospital's name for the system and gathers those costs on a regular basis" (Hill and Johns, 1994).

Under this definition, three general characteristics identify comprehensive systems — data sufficiently detailed to be examined in a number of ways (matrix data management), separation of fixed and variable cost measures, and accurate and useful information in decision making.

Other researchers stress the control aspects of costing systems. For example:

a hospital's cost accounting system should serve three purposes.
First, a properly designed cost accounting system should promote
cost efficiency within the hospital without sacrificing the institution's
product and service quality. Second, a hospital's cost accounting
system should allow the organization to maximize its resources
through product and service line management. Finally, today's hospital cost accounting system should highlight opportunities for continuous improvement of the hospital's operations (Ramsey, 1994, p.
385).

An activity-based approach emphasizes an analysis of inputs the activity consumes, outputs created, drivers or events which cause change, and appropriate methods of allocating overhead. Therefore this approach would be more appropriate in generating meaningful data.

Figure 2 - Cost Accounting Process

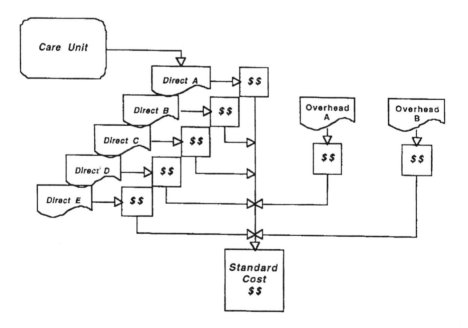

Despite the best efforts to make cost accounting a simplified process, the savvy manager must weigh the value of the data produced with the cost of gathering it. How is the cost of generating and tracking the data with the relative value of the information produced balanced? If the goal is a permanent commitment to the use of cost accounting, the expense of designing systems to capture necessary statistical and cost information and to use it as a basis for calculation is well worth the effort. However, for snapshot projects or one-time analyses, a shortcut or less detailed approach is adequate.

B. The Cost Accounting Process

The cost accounting process, captured in Figure 2, determines a standard cost for the service or product. Steps include:
- Specifying the care unit service or product;
- Working closely with clinical and financial staff to identify the resources used to produce the care unit;
- Valuing the resources normally used for the care unit in terms of what is paid for the resource;
- Identifying alternative methods or resources to reduce costs while maintaining quality;
- Defining line item expenses which tie directly to the care unit; and
- Allocating the major overhead categories which support care, but are not tied to a specific care unit.

Costs are identified within various classes or boundaries. Layers of cost per unit can be defined, and a single procedure or treatment for a diagnosis distilled into its component parts and their costs.

While a variety of cost accounting systems exist, many are not useful when comparing cost and charge information for enhanced operations management. Some practitioners believe that combining the varied information systems of an institution will enhance this processing capability. Data elements required for more accurate and meaningful cost information, necessary in today's market to be more competitive with the variety of third party payors, include information by department, procedure code and name, diagnosis code, date of service, physician, payor, and patient identifier. This information will be filtered through a screen which assigns a relative statistical value to the service to make it comparative to other procedures (Tselepsis, 1989). Understanding the concepts of cost will support the standard cost process.

C. Concepts of Cost

Four categories within which costs can be defined are
- Time period of costs,
- Behavior of the cost as it relates to the output or activity,
- Ability to trace cost to the item and
- Management responsibility for control.

Each is important to consider for a line item of cost in light of standard cost accounting function.

The time period under consideration is significant because costs vary over time and with different levels of activity. Comparing like periods of volume and cost will produce accurate information; comparing different periods may skew the results.

Standard costs for historical purposes should be based on historical data. Standard costs for future business planning should be based on future changes in operations. Further, historical costs are useful for projecting future costs, but applicable line items need to be adjusted for future conditions, given that they will not be identical to the past.

Cost behavior refers to what happens to total dollars by cost category:

- Variable - change as output or volume changes in a constant, proportional manner
(such as direct charge or on-call salaries, and supplies);
- Fixed - no change in response to a change in volume (depreciation, for example);
- Semi-fixed (step) - change with respect to changes in output, not proportional (supervisory salaries and space costs for examples); and
- Semi-variable - elements of both fixed and variable such as (utilities with base rates and usage charges).

When volume changes, due to cost behaviors, some costs calculated per care unit will change.

Traceability ties dollars to the specific care unit. Costs are defined as:

- Direct - specifically traceable to the object being assigned cost (clinical care salaries, employee benefits, supplies) and
- Indirect - not traceable to a given cost objective without resorting to allocation (supervision, overhead, depreciation, some costs from other departments).

As much of the cost as possible must be tied to the specific care unit. Costs which cannot be tied to a unit of service must be allocated to the unit in a standard cost methodology. Allocation, an arbitrary method of assignment, opens the calculations to fluctuations and variations based on the assumptions made.

The final cost category, controllability, refers to how much costs can be influenced by a department manager or designated responsibility center within a defined period. Internal costs controlled by the manager are distinguished from external costs which may be imposed outside the operating environment. Controllability is important to the manager because if costs are too high to be competitive, they can be adjusted for the operating reality.

D. Cost Allocation Methods

After costs have been identified to the extent possible, overhead costs will likely be allocated. Since all methods of allocation rely on a set of assumptions as the basis for distribution of costs, their results may sometimes be called into question as arbitrary and subjective. However, if assumptions are applied consistently and results are supportable, allocation is a justified method of tying cost to a unit of services or product.

The most common ways to allocate costs include:

- Weighting - allocating the cost based on its portion of a statistical base. For example, if the service area uses 42% of the activities of an overhead department, it would be allocated 42% of that department's

cost. This figure would then be divided by the number of units of
service to calculate the cost per unit.
- Step-down - the overhead department that receives the least amount of
service from other indirect departments and that provides the most
service to other departments allocates its costs first to all other
departments calculated on a statistical basis. This department is
then fully allocated. The next department with low service and high
provision would be allocated to the remaining departments, and so
on down the line until all overhead departments have been allocated
and only service departments remain. Overhead costs in each service department then would be allocated based on service units.

Again, it is important to tie a cost category or department to its utilizing service
units. If not all departments benefit from an overhead department's services, costs
should only be allocated to the customer departments. Likewise, if a particular line
item of overhead cost does not benefit all service units within the department, it
should be allocated only to those service units which benefit.

E. The Standard Cost Calculation

The standard cost process is a mechanical exercise of assumptions, statistics, and
calculations. The steps can be generalized as follows:
- Define assumptions.
- Identify financial period covered by data.
- Determine the volume of care units actual or planned for the period.
- Identify the unit being costed.
- Capture standard direct costs per care unit.
- Allocate indirect costs per care unit.
- Add costs per care unit to develop total standard cost.

The Standard Cost Worksheet represented in Figure 3 provides a format for calculating the cost per unit. Documentation of the calculation is vital to maintaining a history of the details behind the standard cost in preparation for the next stage in the
financial management process, variance analysis.

To complete the Worksheet or a similar form, a step-by-step process should be
followed:
- Note the care unit being costed and the date the information is generated.
- Identify and document assumptions which are made in the costing process.
- Note the financial period of data used in the calculation.
- List each direct cost item which ties to the production of the service or prod-
uct under "Direct Costs per Unit".
- Note each type of allocated cost item under the "Allocated Costs per Unit".

After basic data elements are captured, the worksheet is ready for calculations.
For each direct cost, the value of the cost item per unit is entered into the dollar column. The source of the data is noted next to the item. For example, if the direct cost
item is salary, the source may be payroll records (an average of all applicable positions)

Figure 3

STANDARD COST WORKSHEET

Care Unit _____   Date generated _____

Assumptions:

_____

_____

_____

_____

_____

Financial Period of Data: _____

Direct Costs per unit:	$$$	Source	
_____		_____	
_____		_____	
_____		_____	
_____		_____	
_____		_____	

TOTAL DIRECT _____   _____

Allocated Costs per unit:	$$$	Source	Method
_____		_____	_____
_____		_____	_____
_____		_____	_____
_____		_____	_____
_____		_____	_____

TOTAL ALLOCATED _____

TOTAL COST PER UNIT _____

and the amount of time per unit would be multiplied by the hourly rate. Benefits would be calculated as a percentage of salary dollars. Supplies could be set at actual cost per unit of service, with the dollars figured based on a log of supply usage, costs of those supplies, and units of care provided. The direct costs for each line item would be calculated, and a total of all direct costs noted on the worksheet.

Allocated costs are calculated using one of the methods described in Section B. For each overhead item, the source of data and the calculation method are noted on the worksheet. For example, an overhead department may be able to identify 23% of its activities to the product of this type of unit of care. To calculate the dollar value, 23% is multiplied by the total costs for the department, then divided by the total number of service units to which this overhead applies. Each line item is similarly and applicably calculated, and all allocated costs per unit are totaled. The total costs for direct and allocated items becomes the "Total Cost per Unit", the standard cost for that item.

This standard cost can be used as the basis for a number of comparative studies. For example, two treatment methods can be compared to determine which might be more cost effective given like patient outcomes. It can be used to compare operations between two sites of business. The standard cost, multiplied by the number of units anticipated for a period, can be used as the basis for the department budget. Finally, the standard cost can be used to measure and analyze why variances from expected expense totals may exist in actual operations.

F. Using Standard Costs as Building Blocks

In addition to providing per unit calculations, standard costs can be used as building blocks of care at the treatment or diagnosis level. For example, based on a critical path for a home infusion therapy treatment, various services and products may be used. Each individual unit can be costed, then aggregated for total costs of care. Figure 4 provides a diagram of these components.

All calculations, particularly those which will be used on an ongoing basis, can be designed into computer worksheets for ease of use. A set of assumptions and basic cost items, along with the various calculations and totals, can be designed into a spreadsheet program, thus allowing for regular updating and easier adjustments.

Figure 4 - Sample Cost Components

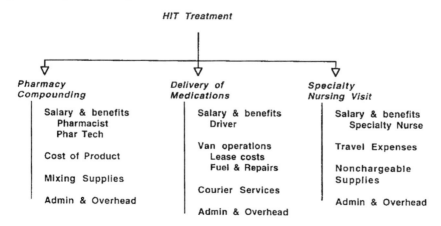

III. THE MEANING OF VARIANCES

Variances include both differences of costs and expenses from plan, and differences in the volume of units used or produced. Volume differences can be used to determine if overhead costs, those allocated based on the global expenses, will be adequately recovered within the actual volume realized. Under-recovery, having a lower volume than planned and not covering all overhead costs from the standard cost of services, can then be avoided by adjusting expenses before they negatively impact profit.

Variance analysis can be used to compare the organization's performance to a previous period, its budget for the period, external benchmarks, or competitor or peer standards. Further, a variance must be broken down into the components from which the difference is generated. For example, the total variance for a line time may be due to volume or price paid for the item. To this end, multiple step variance analysis is often useful.

A. Types of Variances

Variances measure the differences between the expected and the actual, and depending upon which variable is changed, an appropriate response for the variances can be identified. Following are three calculations which form the basis for standard variance analysis:
- Actual quantity x actual cost = actual cost (1)
- Actual quantity x standard cost = expected cost (2)
- Standard quantity x standard cost = budget (3)

The price variance indicates that the variance is due to a difference between the actual cost of the item and the standard or expected cost of the item. The price variance is the difference between the results of calculations 1 and 2: (1) - (2). This variance is useful in determining whether the purchasing agent overpaid or underpaid for the line item.

The quantity variance is the difference between calculations 2 and 3. It indicates that the actual quantity of units used differs from the standard or expected amount: (2) - (3). This productivity measure identifies the efficiency of the number of units needed to produce the service or product.

In cost recoveries which rely heavily on fixed costs absorption, the volume variance is a useful measure. It reflects differences between the expected and actual output, and it is calculated by taking the difference in volume and multiplying it by the standard fixed cost per unit: (budgeted - actual volume) x average fixed cost per unit.

For each type of variance, a notation of favorable or unfavorable result must be made. For example, if fewer units are required for a service, but a higher price per unit was paid, a combination of a favorable and unfavorable variance will result. It is therefore important to break each significant variable into its component parts to determine which activities need further management attention and adjustment.

B. Variance Analysis in Practice

In practice, variance analysis becomes a more meaningful exercise if the organization examines those items for which it knows itself to be at greatest risk. A variance
- Assumes the budget is accurate;

- Signals a problem;
- Suggests the cause and
- Monitors the correction.

To address a variance, it is important to 1) recognize a variance, 2) find the cause, and 3) correct and adjust. A selection of variance analysis theory is available for use in this process.

Classical statistical theory considers variances as a statistical calculation based on standard deviations of differences from the expected outcome. To use this method, a computer program or spreadsheet is necessary to make the multiple step calculations. A variance is considered in control if it is within limits, set within X number of standard deviations. However, this method is cumbersome for a large organization with lots of data. It also cannot measure the cost of finding the root cause of the variance and cannot evaluate the benefits of investigation.

Decision theory weighs the costs of investigation against the benefits which may be realized in future periods. In this method, the analyst sets ranges within which the variance is acceptable and makes subjective estimates of the probability of being out of control. Again, however, this method may prove to be less useful for an organization with multiple cost centers and many line items of data which need to be regularly analyzed.

Real life variance analysis is intuitive rather than statistical; its use develops managers who better interpret their financial reports and what they represent. It is based on an understanding of relationships between line items. In other words, if volume increases, logic demands that certain line items of expenses, those related to variable costs, also increase. This method relies on gut level input by the manager based on experience and tracking over time and thresholds of tolerance for ranges within which a variance is considered acceptable.

In real life variance analysis, the manager compares actual performance to the budget and/or to a prior period. Factors such as the volume in units, costs related to prices for the items, and efficiency standards are reviewed, and variances which required further study are highlighted. From this data, the manager can determine if adjustments to operations should be made. Some items may never be studied since the variance appears to be minor. However, if favorable and unfavorable variances are offsetting, some level of risk for inaction exists from these hidden variances.

IV. FACTORING IN RISK

Some costs are fixed, no matter what the volume of care units provided. Others are indirect, but would not be incurred were the service not provided. The impact of changes in volume on assumptions and costs must be considered. Additionally, researchers such as Gapenski and Langland-Orban (1995) stress that many of today's managed care contracts expose providers to considerable subjective risk. This risk can be minimized through more complete access to socio-demographics and health assessment data for the population to be covered. Understanding the costs of care to allow for reductions in cost as appropriate is also critical.

A. Minimizing Risk

To minimize risk in standard cost accounting, questions which expose potential areas of risk are helpful:
- Are the costs stated in consistent dollars?
- Are the costs and outputs consistent for the data period?
- Is the time period under consideration representative or stable in operations?
- Is the information system providing good, reliable cost data?
- Are the utilization rates typical of the organization's experience?
- What assumptions are high risk? Which three are most at risk?

By answering these questions, the manager can justify additional review of standard costs, further distinct costing units, and variance analysis to track performance against expectations.

B. The Role of Quality

Quality has a place in the cost discussion. Without quality outcomes, there would be little need for cost information, since the referral volume would slowly diminish and disappear and the organization would no longer be financially viable. The value to the organization and the rate of return on the investment in quality-related activities can be highlighted by examples.

Consider the use of preventive care. In a community wellness program, the key element is prevention of disease or injury which keeps patients from ever entering the facility or needing a physician. Therefore care cost is held down. Controlling costs of care in this very positive fashion translates into a contribution to the operating margin of the healthcare provider.

Similarly, the costs of appraising the situation appropriately can also improve quality and save costs. If members are given a health status assessment upon entering service, staff can monitor any conditions which may appear to be potential risks. A developing health problem hopefully can be caught in the early stages, before becoming a significant risk to the patient and a costlier treatment modality. Again, this translates into a positive bottom line impact under cost-controlled environments.

Cost data also supports clinical evaluations. In addition to forcing departments to examine productivity and cost management, evaluate services profitability and review the impact of managed care contracts, cost accounting systems assist clinical departments in their reviews of alternative treatments. In cases of like outcomes for the patient, clinical departments can now review the cost of one treatment as compared to another and make a decision with both medical and financial data available. This becomes particularly important in cases where the insurer does not pay for a portion of the treatment; the patient must then pay part of the cost or the provider absorbs the difference. Also, comparative costs assist in decisions when the outcomes from both treatments are identical but the costs are not, such as inpatient versus outpatient care, and the organization is capitated for the patient's care. Integration of financial analysis with standardized clinical paths can be beneficial to both patient and program.

V. GETTING PAID FOR SERVICES

Payment systems are fragmented and complex. The variety of payors reimbursing providers for health services and products use alternative tactics to reduce the costs of healthcare. Federal and state governments, the largest purchasers of healthcare services, use legislation and regulation to control ever-larger portions of the Gross National Product going to health. Their controls are exercised through utilization controls and authorizations for services, and through restructuring of the reimbursement models. Employers have used the market-based approach, purchasing from lower cost plans and encouraging employees to move their allegiance to managed care coverage. The fee setting process in response to these challenges
   • determines utilization for the patient population covered by the contract,
   • determines the discounts offered under various agreements,
   • calculates the acceptable full list price, or
   • calculates the minimum capitation rate acceptable.
   Knowing the standard cost per care unit is essential to determine the adequacy of reimbursement rates. Under capitated agreements, the manager will need to know total cost per care unit and expected volume — utilization of service or product by covered patient population.
   Recently, efforts at managed competition, single purchaser networks, and other trends have attempted to provide basic healthcare coverage while curbing spending through selective contracting and authorization structures. Further, "many advocates of medical cost containment have therefore sought to introduce regulatory incentives that shift economic risk from third party payors to hospital and physician providers" (Manheim, p. 56). Greater burden then falls on the provider to design accurate cost accounting mechanisms and set pricing policies for charges based on full disclosure of volume assumptions by the plans. Rate setting becomes an important offshoot of the costing process.

A. Pricing

For payors' pricing that the organization can control, charges and discounts should be based on actual costs of providing the service or product and some contribution to the ongoing growth of the company, frequently called profit. The price should equal the standard cost of the unit of service plus some flexibility for cost coverages, such as new program start-up or additional expansionary funding and strategic capital. To set an adequate price, all costs of the organization must be fully allocated.

A price can be set using the following formula:

$$\text{Price} = \frac{\text{Standard cost per unit + Cost coverage per unit}}{1 - \text{Weighted discounts offered}}$$

The weighted discount is the sum of individual discount times the percentage of unit volume for all payors. Figure 5 is a worksheet to calculate the price for a unit.

Figure 5

PRICING WORKSHEET

Care Unit _____ Date generated _____

Assumptions:

_____

_____

_____

_____

_____

Standard cost per care unit: _____ <A>

Cost coverages: $$$ Source

_____   _____

_____   _____

_____   _____

TOTAL COVERAGES   _____ <B>

Payor:	Planned Units	Discount % times Discount	Units/Total Units
_____	_____	_____
_____	_____	_____
_____	_____	_____
_____	_____	_____
_____	_____	_____

TOTAL UNITS   _____ <C>

TOTAL WEIGHTED DISCOUNT   _____ <D>

Price $_____ = $$\frac{<A>_____ + (<B>_____/<C>_____)}{1 - <D>_____}$$

SET PRICE AT $_____

To complete the Pricing Worksheet, the manager should:

- Complete the care unit, date generated, assumptions and standard cost per care unit;
- List items, dollar values and data sources for cost coverages;
- List each major payor, the planned units of service, and discounts which are contracted or anticipated, and multiplied to create the weighting factor (planned units divided by <C> times discount percentage);
- Complete the formula and calculate the price; and
- Note the price to be used in full charge fee schedules.

Clearly, the method is more complex if there are different types of service provided and a multitude of payors. In some cases, items of service accessed most often are the units to be priced with others based on a standard mark-up or recovery over standard cost of the item.

B. Capitation Rates

Capitation is a growing payment strategy. Under this pricing method the provider receives a set reimbursement each month for each plan member or covered life. Using this method, the provider must know

- Socio-demographics of the population covered under the contracted plan,
- Products and services which are specifically covered under the plan,
- Typical utilization patterns of the potential patient population, and
- The organization's cost of care for each potential service or product utilization.

Figure 6 provides a worksheet to calculate a capitated rate per covered life or member. These rates can vary further based on rate adjusted for age and sex (risk adjusted rate) and a set percentage of the capitation dollar.

Steps for completing the Capitation Worksheet include the following:

- Note the contract payor and period of coverage.
- List the expected service units or diagnoses of treatment, number of units anticipated, and costs per unit of service or treatment.
- Multiply the units times the cost to derive total costs to be covered.
- Note the number of lives under the plan.
- Calculate a break-even rate for the contract (divide total costs by number of lives).
- Divide the result by 12 to calculate a monthly rate.

A risk corridor is normally set to accommodate and absorb potential changes or shifts in operations during the contract period.

Figure 6

CAPITATION CALCULATION WORKSHEET

Contract payor source:_____

Period covered by contract:_____

Utilization of services annually and costs:

Service Unit	# of units annually (A)	Cost per Unit (B)	Cost times Units (A) × (B)
_____	_____	_____	_____
_____	_____	_____	_____
_____	_____	_____	_____
_____	_____	_____	_____
_____	_____	_____	_____
_____	_____	_____	_____
_____	_____	_____	_____
_____	_____	_____	_____

TOTAL COSTS TO BE COVERED: (C) _____

Number of lives covered under the plan: (D) _____

Calculated capitated break-even rate: Divide (C) by (D) (annual rate) _____

Monthly break-even rate: (divide annual by 12)   _____
(Per Member, Per Month or PMPM)

Risk corridor: (+ or - 10%)   _____ to _____

VI. DECISION MAKING AND PLANNING

Financial decision making involves consideration of the commitment of resources expressed in types of resources and the amount of capital expenditures required. A capital project provides benefits to the organization over a period normally considered to be longer term--over two or more years. The time period of the investment and the flow of costs are then considered.

To successfully consider all financial decisions in both the internal situation and external environment, the manager should consider community need, ongoing viable business requirements, influences of payor sources, and internal goals and objectives. This can be accomplished through a method of life cycle costing. This method for estimating the cost of a capital project reflects total costs, both operating and capital, over the project's estimated useful life. The benefits derived from this method include continued operations of the organization, reduction in costs or increase in profits to enhance and create financial value, and structure which meets community needs.

To enhance the capital project, we should consider the following questions:

- What problem is the project intended to solve?
- What is the goal or objective for this project?
- What alternatives are available to achieve that goal?
- What resources can be committed, both internally from the organization and externally through other resources or leveraging?
- What are the life cycle costs of implementing the project?
- What hard (cash) and soft (enhancement) benefits will be derived?
- How does proposed performance compare to history?
- What risks will the organization assume? Can they be mitigated or subjected to a probability analysis for control purposes?
- What feedback is the organization going to measure, and how will the information be gathered?

Within this structure, project evaluation and feasibility can be established. These tools commonly include the rate of return on a project, its contribution to attainment of objectives given resource constraints, a cost benefit analysis, and the criteria for evaluation. The feedback loop will include a method by which the organization can take corrective action, verify assumptions and modify data, and reflect on biases or estimation methods.

In integrated systems, the capital project issues are particularly important today. Valuation of start-up costs for an integrated system, additional capital needs for purchases of providers, shifting sources of capital, and limited benefits derived can further complicate the formation of these systems. For example, the financial stakes are important when physician recruitment and presalary practice costs are $50-75K in the first year, information system costs are incurred at a rate of $3-8M per year for a few years, and a healthcare plan needs $5M minimum to capitalize (Coddington et al., 1994).

The tools to make effective financial decisions focus on the following:

- Accounting data at the necessary level of detail,
- Adequate investment for replacement of assets,
- Increases in working capital,
- Retention of funds for future investment,
- Debt capacity plan,

- Portfolio analysis for community need and Return On Investment (ROI),
- Value of investments,
- Financial plan tied to management of business,
- Regular updates, and
- Formal approvals.

With these tools, the organization can build the bridge between two balance sheets, current and projected. By assessing the current position and trends, determining how to finance needs based on goals and objectives, and defining policy on the assumption of debt, its amount and structure, the organization can determine if its financial picture and future growth are realistic.

VII. FUTURE FINANCIAL TRENDS

Almost all of the healthcare trends the industry is experiencing today and into the future have cost control impacts. Costs of staffing, supplies, and other product and service inputs are rising. Provider mix is shifting between different levels of clinical background and certification. Treatment modalities are increasingly complex and higher priced. Technology is more sophisticated, more costly, and more vital to the massive amounts of data which need to be transmitted and managed. Societal needs are greater, resources fewer. Government has less funding available and the private sector offers less support.

Within this challenging time, healthcare managers feel the impact. With less dollars, people and technology healthcare managers must do more. Situations change rapidly, so organizations must remain responsive to the environments within which they operate. Information needs to be meaningful in format and content and finally, each manager must interpret their data and weigh options from their operational viewpoint.

According to Coile (1995), key trends for 1996-2000 include market-based reform, increasing competition and capitation, improving primary care, and integrating systems; increasing managed care impacts in areas where it is not prevalent today; conversion of Medicare and Medicaid programs to HMOs; smaller bottom lines or contributions to operating margin; increasing use of capitation; larger, more sophisticated (and more expensive) information systems networks; and more reorganizations through mergers and acquisitions, continued for-profit expansion, and staff-model integrated delivery systems. Within this framework, cost accounting, adequate standard cost detail, and variance and budgetary analysis will become more critical to the success of healthcare managers and the organizations they represent.

REFERENCES

Beckham, J. D. (1995). Follow the Money. *Healthcare Forum Journal, 38*(6): 36-44.

Bray, N., Carter, C., Dobson, A., Watt, J. M., and Shortell, S. (1994). An Examination of Winners and Losers Under Medicare's Prospective Payment System. *Health Care Management Review, 19*(1): 44-55.

Caltrider, J., Pattison, D., and Richardson, P. (1995). Can Cost Control and Quality Care Coexist? *Management Accounting, 77*(2): 38-42.

Canby, IV, J. B. (1995). Applying Activity-Based Costing to Healthcare Settings. *Healthcare Financial Management, 49*(2): 50-56.

Carpenter, C. E., Weitzel, L. C., Johnson, N. E., and Nash, D. B. (1994). Cost Accounting Supports Clinical Evaluations. *Healthcare Financial Management, 48*(4): 40-44.

Cleverly, W. O. (1992). *Essentials of Health Care Finance*. Aspen Publishers, Gaithersburg.

Cleverly, W. O. (1989). *Handbook of Health Care Accounting and Finance: Volumes 1 and 2*. 2nd ed. Aspen Publishers, Rockville.

Coddington, D. C., Moore, K. D., and Fischer, E. A. (1994). Costs and Benefits of Integrated Healthcare Systems. *Healthcare Financial Management, 48*(3): 21-29.

Coile, Jr., R. C. (1995). Assessing Healthcare Market Trends and Capital Needs. *Healthcare Financial Management, 49*(8): 60-65.

Dobson, A. and Clarke, R. L. (1992). Shifting No Solution to Problem of Increasing Costs. *Healthcare Financial Management, 46*(7): 25-32.

Dove, H. G., and Forthman, T. (1995). Helping Financial Analysts Communicate Variance Analysis. *Healthcare Financial Management, 49*(4): 52-54.

Gapenski, L. C., and Langland-Orban, B. (1995). Predicting Financial Risk Under Capitation. *Healthcare Financial Management, 49*(1): 38.

Gapenski, L. C. (1993). *Understanding Health Care Financial Management*. AUPHA Press/Health Administration Press, Ann Arbor.

Hill, N. T., and Johns, E. L. (1994). Adoption of Costing Systems by U.S. Hospitals. *Hospitals and Health Systems Administration, 39*(4): 521-537.

Manheim, L. M., and Feinglass, J. (1994). Hospital Cost Incentives in a Fragmented Health Care System. *Health Care Management Review, 19*(1): 56-63.

Meyer, J. W., and Feingold, M. G. (1995). Integrating Financial Modeling and Patient Care Reengineering. *Healthcare Financial Management, 49*(2): 33-40.

Pallarito, K. (1995). CFOs Take New Tack. *Modern Healthcare, 25*(1): 85-94.

Pauly, M. V. (1993). U.S. Health Care Costs: The Untold True Story. *Health Affairs, 12*(3): 152-159.

Ramsey, IV, R. H. (1994). Activity-Based Costing for Hospitals. *Hospitals and Health Systems Administration, 39*(3): 385-396.

Rezaee, Z. (1993). Examining the Effect of PPS on Cost Accounting Systems. *Healthcare Financial Management, 47*(3): 58-61.

Rosenstein, A. H. (1994). Cost-Effective Health Care: Tools for Improvement. *Health Care Management Review, 19*(2): 53-61.

Suver, J. D., Neumann, B. R., and Boles, K. E. (1992). *Management Accounting for Healthcare Organizations*. 3rd edition. Healthcare Financial Management Association/Pluribus Press, Chicago.

Tselepis, J. N. (1989). Refined Cost Accounting Produces Better Information. *Healthcare Financial Management, 43*(5): 27-34.

Waress, B. J., Pasternak, D. P., and Smith, H. L. (1994). Determining Costs Associated with Quality in Health Care Delivery. *Health Care Management Review, 19*(3): 52-63.

Young, D. W., and Pearlman, L. K. (1993). Managing the Stages of Hospital Cost Accounting. *Healthcare Financial Management, 47*(4): 58-80.

60.

EXECUTIVE BUDGET MANAGEMENT

Donna L. Gellatly, *Financial HealthCare Associates, Palos Hills, IL*

Many people may ask what comes first? Budgeting or actual financial statements? This question is similar to the one that asks "What comes first, the chicken or the egg?" In order to budget (estimate) future expenses, one must have some idea of what they will be. The best source of information is the historical data accumulated by the organization. However, what happens when this is the first operating period? Where there is no organizational history? One must make reasonable estimates based on whatever information is available. Some sources could be financial data from other similar facilities, national averages, or surveys.

Do you have to have a budget? It depends. Many physician medical practices operate without a formal budget. Fast growing organizations' budgets are out-of-date before budget data is entered into financial statement programs. However, there are many external health care organizations, which require budgets or forecasts of expenses and revenues. Under Public Law 92-603, Medicare certified health care organizations (e.g. hospitals, nursing homes, and home health agencies) must prepare an annual operating budget (of revenues and expenses) and a three year capital budget (of equipment purchases and major renovation expenditures). Among the questions asked by the Joint Commission on Accreditation of Health care Organizations are questions regarding forecasting of revenues and expenses, analysis of actual-vs.-budget variances, and the use of actual-versus-budget performance in management by objectives (MBO) performance evaluations. Of course, financing organizations, such as banks and the Small Business Administration, also will require budgeting/forecasting of operations before they will loan monies to health care organizations.

What is a budget? It is a formal plan of future operations expressed in quantitative terms. It serves as a basis for subsequent control of such operations. It is a written document in which the objectives of the health care facility are reflected in dollars and in various non-monetary statistical units.

The final master budget usually consists of pro forma (projected) statements of revenues and expenses, a balance sheet, statement of changes in financial position (cash flow), and supporting schedules. These statements are the results of a series of planning decisions made by each department and summarized at the institutional level. The major benefits of budgeting are the formalization of responsibility for planning, which provides definite expectations for judging subsequent performance.

Most organizations prepare only one budget per annum. This fixed budget is prepared under a single assumption as to anticipated statistical and financial activities. An example would be the preparation of the next year's budget assuming 300,000 days of patient care and 100,000 emergency room visits. However, to secure the fullest benefits from budgeting, an organization may wish to develop flexible (variable) budgets, which are really a series of "mini" fixed budgets prepared under various assumptions as to the possible levels of activity that may be actually experienced. An example of such a flexible budgeting technique would be to prepare the next year's budget assuming a range of 280,000 to 310,000 patient days of care at intervals of 5000 days, and from 80,000 to 110,000 emergency visits at intervals of 5000 visits.

In fast-growing organizations, it may be prudent to use the continuous form of budgeting. This could entail adding a future month or quarter as the month/quarter just ended is dropped. Continuous budgets are desirable because they compel managers to think specifically about the next 12 months and adjust for changes in utilization, costs, or reimbursement. Therefore, at all times, there would be 12 months of projected financial and statistical operations. Flexible budgeting and continuous budgeting can be accomplished by the use of software budgeting/financial statement programs, which are compatible with desktop personal computers. Smaller organizations or medical practices could use such software programs as PeachTree or QuickBooks, while larger organizations may use programs developed by Medicus Systems or Wheaton Systems.

What are the advantages and disadvantages of such methods? The advantages of a fixed budget include the fact that it is a simple and easy to understand method. It requires less time to prepare such a budget than other methods and would be a meaningful tool for measuring performance if actual results approximate budgeted projections. However, if the actual activity varies widely from budgeted activity, it becomes difficult to analyze variances caused by changes in volume, price, cost, or efficiency. Flexible budgeting allows for adjustments to reflect actual activity levels, which makes it easier to obtain meaningful variance analysis. Department managers may more readily accept the flexible budget process since it would factor out volume variances, which they cannot control. However, it requires more time and resources in the accounting and data systems departments to develop and update such programs. It will require additional accountant training to ensure that the flexible budget(s) are being prepared and utilized properly. It also requires the budget accountant to identify fixed costs (which do not change in relation to volume within a reasonable range) and variable costs that are subject to changes in direct proportion to volumes.

I. BUDGET MANAGEMENT

A good operating budget requires a sound organizational structure supported by a written organizational chart. At the very least, budgeting and financial reporting should adhere to the boxes (departments) shown on a facility's organizational chart. However, in many cases, it may not disclose enough data for decision making and for department management. For example, while the organizational chart may indicate a department named "Technical Services," it may in fact be the combination of several functions, including electrocardiology, electroencephalogy, and electromyography. At some future time, questions may arise as to what are the specific costs/revenues from one of these three functions. It is always easier to budget and report at the lowest or most detailed level and then total the three functions into a total departmental budget for Technical Services than it would be to after-the-fact attempt to allocate the revenues and expenses to each function. Specific identification of revenues and expenses can be accomplished by assigning unique cost-center department numbers from the facility's chart of accounts.

Long before budgeting is begun at the department level, the board of trustees and executive administration must agree on the overall facility (global) utilization forecasts and basic budgeting assumptions. The support of administration and management in the formal budgeting process is crucial to its success. The board of trustees usually appoints a budget committee to work with administration in determining the planning premises and approving the budget calendar. Perhaps the best way to prepare the budget calendar is to work backwards—after determining the final board meeting's agenda for approving the budget (Figure 1).

Questions to ask regarding the timelines included in the budget calendar (Figure 2) include:

- Have advanced notification, approval, or filing requirements of Blue Cross, state, and other rate setting agencies been incorporated in the schedule?
- Has work been spread over a period of time to avoid unnecessary interference with the normal operations of the facility? Check the holiday calendar, dates of JCAHO site visits, state Department of Public Health scheduled visits, and scheduled continuing education seminar dates for key physician administrators and executive administration.
- Has every activity been planned?
- Is the responsibility for each activity defined? Is the assignment appropriate for the activity?
- Is the time allotted to each activity reasonable in relation to the task being completed?
- Does the calendar provide an adequate interfacing with the board and/or budget committee?
- Has sufficient time been allotted for summarization and for rate determination or cost reductions? Will proposed revenue rate adjustments be presented to the Board prior to commencement of the budget year?

Figure 1

Prepared by: _____ date

Approved by: _____ date

GSU HOSPITAL BUDGET PLANNING WORKSHEET 1997

1996 Week Ending	Board/Budget Committee	Budget Director	Department Heads	Accounting Assistance
Dec. 13	Final approval			
Dec. 6	Approve operating budget	Pro forms statements, cash and capital budgets		Cash budget
Nov. 29		Complete operating budget, Cost-finding and contractual allowances		Summarize capital expenditures. Cost-finding.
Nov. 22		Complete expense budget		Summarize expense
Nov. 15	Revise capital expenditures and expenses	Complete revenue budget	Revise expense and capital expenditure budgets	Revenue budget
Nov. 1		Forms distributed to department heads		
Oct. 25	Approve forecast of units		Discuss units of service	
Oct. 11 Sept. 27				Accumulate units of service, capital expenditures, revenue and expense data
Sept. 20	Approve budget plans, calendar, goals and objectives	Send physician questionnaires		Assist with physician questionnaires
Sept. 13		Budget plans and calendar completed	Formulate goals and objectives	

Figure 2

GSU HOSPITAL BUDGET CALENDAR

Date	Participants/Responsibility	Activity
Sept. 6	Governing Board	Formulate overall goals and objectives.
Sept 13	Budget Director	Budget plan and calendar completed.
Sept 20	Budget Committee and Board	Approval of budget plan and calendar.
Sept. 27	Budget Director	Physician questionnaires sent. Begin accumulating statistics and expense data.
Oct. 11	Budget Director	Complete accumulation of statistics and expense data.
Oct. 18	Budget Director	Forecasts of units of service prepared and reviewed with appropriate department heads.
Oct. 25	Budget Committee	Approval of forecasts.
Nov. 1	Budget Director and Department Heads	Meeting on budget; forms distributed. Work begins on budget preparation.
Nov. 8	Budget Director and Department Heads	Expense and capital expenditure budgets completed.
Nov. 15	Budget Committee and Department Heads	Expense and capital expenditure budgets reviewed and revised.
Nov. 22	Budget Director	Expenses summarized and revenue budget completed.
Nov. 29	Budget Director	Cost-finding and contractual allowances completed, operating budget completed.
Dec. 6	Budget Committee	Operating budget approved.
Dec. 6	Budget Director	Capital expenditures and cash budgets completed, pro forma statements completed.
Dec. 13	Budget Committee and Board	Final approval of budget.

A departmental budget manual should be developed. It should include the objectives of the facility's budget program, definitions of authority and responsibilities, instructions in full detail, mechanics, and examples of completed schedules. A calendar of budgeting activity, time schedule for completion of each stage, and a discussion of the detailed procedures used in reviewing, revising, and approving the budget are also included in the manual.

Customized schedules of data and financial information should be prepared for each department. This customization should include the following information.
- Inflationary percentage increases for specific vendors (e.g. radiology film).
- Historical productivity for the department.
- Historical staffing mix (e.g. number of RN, LPN, Aides).
- Any Board approved changes in patient mix, service utilization, etc.
- Historical intensity of service utilization.
- Historical revenue per procedure annualized for any interim rate increases.

A. Budget Memo

The administrator of the institution normally attaches a budget memo to the budget forms that are transmitted to the assistant administrators and department managers. This budget memo sets the tone for the budget process. It includes guidelines (such as board-set limitations, e.g. cost containment to 105% of the current year's expenditures or a maximum capital request for the entire hospital of $4.0 million).

A sample budget memo may contain the following sections:
Preface
- Introductory comments
- Principal institutional goals
    - short-term
    - long-term
- Institutional objectives for the budget

Current Year Accomplishments
- Overall institutional accomplishments
- Special departmental accomplishments
- Overall institutional budget performance
- Specific departmental budget performance

Policy Directives
- Improvement objectives
- Activity forecasting
- Expense limitations
- Capital expenditure limitations
- Staffing limitations

Budget Process
- Budget calendar
- Overview of budget process

- Budget planning worksheet
- Responsibilities

Guidelines and Worksheet
- General economic outlook
- Departmental objectives
- Departmental service units worksheet

Worksheets
- Department staffing summary
- Salary budget
- Department activity and expense
- Capital expenditures
- Justification and documentation

Conclusion
- Call for cooperation
- Designation of person(s) to call for assistance
- Closing comments

What is the order of departmental budget preparation? Many institutions start with the capital budget request since it may require additional data or materials from outside sources. Examples of such data may be vendor quotes, site visits to existing equipment installations, comparisons of alternative available equipment, and contractor quotes on renovation of the physical plant to accept the installation of the new equipment. After the capital equipment budget is approved, the department manager then may begin completing the statistical budget, expense budget, and revenue budget. However, it is the Board of Trustees and the Finance Department, which ultimately decide on the amount of revenue increases.

What is the order of facility budget preparation? The Finance Department will perform, in order, the following tasks:
- Summarize the capital budgets.
- Summarize the expense budgets.
- Apply the surplus (profit) requirement.
- Determine cash flow requirements.
- Prepare the revenue budget based upon the four above requirements.
- Determine if the required revenue increases are realistic. If not, begin again by revising the expense budget or capital budget downwards.

II. STATISTICS BUDGET

Each department must have an appropriate statistical unit of measurement that can be used to forecast utilization and calculate revenues/costs per procedures. These individual department statistics are compared to the facility's global statistics such as admissions, patient days of care, and outpatient/emergency/clinic visits.

Global budget statistics may be based on historical trends, physician questionnaires, and/or internal and external factors. Historical trends reflecting increased/

decreased facility utilization may be forecasted for the next budget period. Physician questionnaires may be used to obtain further information as to potential changes in physician utilization patterns and plans to expand or retire from practice. Internal facility factors that may affect global utilization may be the planned addition or deletion of services, disruption from construction projects which may restrict admissions, the reorganization of service delivery from inpatient to outpatient, or restricted admissions of patients with certain types of illnesses due to decreased insurance reimbursement, lack of technological equipment, or qualified personnel.

External factors that may affect a facility's global utilization may be the unusual growth or decline in service area population or use rate, competitive facilities' plans to increase or delete services, economic fluctuations from rising/decreasing service area, and unemployment. Insurance coverage or changes in the health care delivery system may restrict admissions or services under managed care contracts.

Individual department statistics are compared to the facility's global statistics. Department statistics compared to global statistics allow for the calculation of the intensity of service. The intensity of service reflects the ratio of a department statistic to a facility statistic. An example may be the ratio of radiology procedures to facility utilization:

$$\frac{\text{Inpatient Radiology Procedures}}{\text{Admissions}} = \frac{125{,}000}{50{,}000} = 2.5 \text{ procedures per admission}$$

$$\frac{\text{Outpatient Radiology Procedures}}{\text{Emergency, Outpatient, \& Clinic Visits}} = \frac{20{,}000}{105{,}000} = 2 \text{ procedures per visit}$$

The above examples show that on the average, each inpatient receives 2.5 radiology procedures during their stay. On the average, one in five outpatients (20%) receive a radiology procedure.

It is extremely important that the statistic used for each department is the most appropriate statistic for that department. The most appropriate statistic for the Laundry Department may be pounds of laundry processed. However, pounds of laundry may be determined by weighing laundry when it is dry (clean) or wet (dirty). Whatever method is used, it must be reliable, auditable, and the accumulated statistics must be consistent.

Many of the statistics for the ancillary and nursing departments may be obtained from the billing system. As the charges are accumulated on the patients' bills, the statistics may be generated for each department. However, such systems do not have the ability to also accumulate spoiled tests or procedures, calibration, and quality control procedures and procedures that were done but not charged for. For this reason, most departments also keep records of monthly utilization. Non-revenue producing (support departments) keep their own internal records of statistics that are used in reporting and budgeting.

Medical departments such as radiology, laboratory, technical services (ECG, EMG, EEG) and physical therapy have developed relative value units. These relative value units (RVU) reflect the degree of difficulty in performing each individual procedure or test. The accumulation of these relative value units provides a better indicator of the time spent by each department.

Each department may react differently to facility utilization. Some departments may relate well to inpatient admissions. Others, which are dependent upon the number of day's stay, would react better to days of patient care. An example may be that pharmacy prescriptions relate better to patient days of care since each additional day would require additional medication. On the other hand, the number of surgical minutes may relate better to inpatient admissions, as the surgical procedure is contingent upon surgical admissions rather than the number of days that the patient is hospitalized.

III. EXPENSE BUDGET

Expenses are usually budgeted by natural classification within each department. Natural classifications of expenses include salaries and wages, medical supplies, office supplies, and other expenses such as books, dues and subscriptions, travel, interdepartmental transfers, and utilities. The number of line items budgeted is dependent upon the chart of accounts. Many institutions may summarize certain accounts for budget purposes while other institutions (which usually have computer assistance) may budget at each account level.

A. Salaries and Wages Expense

To budget salaries and wages for each department, one must list all personnel assigned to the department. Each employee's position must include the name of the current occupant, current salary, anniversary date, seniority increase to become effective on that anniversary date (if any), and the number of hours related to that salary (part-time or full-time) (Figure 3).

Based upon the statistics budget already prepared, the manager must determine the required staffing to service the projected utilization. To determine the amount of time it took to perform each procedure, a historical productivity analysis must be prepared.

$$\text{PRODUCTIVITY:} \quad \frac{\text{department statistics}}{\text{hours paid}} \quad = \quad \text{statistics per hour paid}$$

The department statistics include inpatient, outpatient, and overhead (quality control, calibration, and training) procedures done during a historical time period.

Once the productivity ratio is determined for the department, the results should be compared to similar institutions in the geographic area. Sources for these may be (C.H.I.P.S) The Center for Health Care Industry Performance Studies (formerly known as Monitrend) report(s) produced by local, state, or national alliances. C.H.I.P.S. has recently added a nursing home's report. These reports classify hospitals by bed size within each geographic area and may give some indication as to how well the hospital appears to operate as compared to other reporting institutions within the methodologies (primary care nursing), acuity (children's hospitals), and physical plant layout. Variances in actual to industry standards may be due to differences in staffing methodologies, e.g. primary care nursing, acuity of children's hospitals or physical plant.

After the decision is made regarding budgeted productivity, budgeted hours may

Figure 3 - GSU HOSPITAL NURSING UNIT - 7 EAST YEAR: 1997

SALARY BUDGET

BUDGET STATISTIC: 10,000 patient days

PREPARED BY: _____
APPROVALS:
   DIRECTOR: _____
   ASST. ADM.: _____
   ADM.: _____

		HOURS PAID	PROJECTED SALARY EXPENSE (A)
Unit Manager:			
	MacCormick	2,080	$50,000
Registered Nurses:			
	Porter	2,080	(C) 41,600
	Boyd	2,080	38,600
	Williams	2,080	38,000
	Albrecht	1,040	19,500
	Lyons	1,040	18,600
	Ringbauer	2,080	40,000
	Bunte	2,080	40,000
	Whittemore	1,040	18,000
	Massey	2,080	37,000
	Bell	1,040	18,600
	Miller	2,080	37,000
	Malec	2,080	39,000
	Rhee	1,040	18,700
	Brown-Smith	2,080	42,400
Vacation & Holiday Relief		2,016	16,300
		25,936	463,300
Licensed Practical Nurses:			
	Darcy	2,080	29,100
	Staub	2,080	29,600
	O'Neil	2,080	(C) 31,000
	Anderson	2,080	28,000
	Matteson	2,080	27,000
	Peterson	1,040	7,000
Vacation & Holiday Relief		720	9,500
		12,161	161,200
Unit Clerk:			
	Laken	2,080	(C) 14,800
	Toberman	2,080	13,000
Vacation & Holiday Relief		288	2,000
		4,448	29,800
Nursing Pool (B)		5,376	97,000
	TOTAL	50,000	$801,300

SUMMARY:

1997 Salary Request	$801,300
Less 1.5% turnover factor (D)	<12,000>
Adjusted total	789,300
Add cost of living/merit Adjustment factor	X 1.020
TOTAL SALARY REQUEST	**$805,100**

Hours Paid Summary:	Full-Time Equivalents
Full-Time Employees (17)	17.00
Part-Time Employees (6)	3.00
Relief (FTE)	1.46
Nursing Pool	2.58
TOTAL FTE	**24.04**
Hours per Patient Day (E)	5.00

NOTE A — Projected salary expense including regularly scheduled seniority increases.

B — Remaining required hours to be covered by in-house nursing pool.

C — These employees have reached the top of their salary scale; and therefore, no seniority increases have been calculated for fiscal year 1997.

D — Historical turnover for nursing division.

E — (FTE x 2,080) ÷ pt. days - (24.04 x 2,080) ÷ 10,000 = 5.00 hours
   paid hours = 52 weeks @ 40 hours per week

be calculated. If it is assumed that a nursing unit will average 5 paid hours of nursing care per patient day, and patient days are budgeted at 10,000 days of care for this unit, the budgeted paid hours would be 50,000 (5 hours x 10,000 patient days). These paid hours are then converted into full-time equivalent employees. Full-time equivalent (FTE) employees are determined by the number of hours paid per annum. If an employee is paid for 8 hours per calendar day, then the standard hours per FTE are assumed to be 2,080 hours (52 weeks x 40 hours per week). The budgeted 50,000 paid hours converts to 24.04 full-time equivalent employees (50,000 x 2,080).

The listing of employees currently assigned to the unit is compared to the budgeted need of 24.04 FTE. If the number of current employees is not sufficient to cover the budgeted staff, then additional full-time, part-time, over-time, or pool staff must be included in the list to complete the staff analysis. If current staff exceeds the necessary staffing for the coming budget year, management decisions must be made to transfer, lay-off, or otherwise reduce the staff to its budget goal.

Additional factors must be considered in determining total salary and wage expense. A factor for turnover of personnel must be made. As senior employees retire or leave the institution, they will be replaced with new employees who will normally receive a lower starting salary. This turnover factor may be based upon historical turnover rates, industry trends, and management plans for recruitment and retention. If a general cost of living or merit increase will be made available to all employees, then this factor must be added to the salary and wage expense budget, as well.

In order to promptly respond to abrupt changes in patient census, many institutions rely on a mixture of in-house nursing pools and outside nursing registries. These concepts allow the institution to directly vary the amount of nursing hours at a day's notice. If all of the nursing staff are full-time employees, it is difficult to react to a dynamic situation requiring material changes in staff complements.

B. Non-wage Expense Budget

The Non-wage Budget is composed of accounts that are not related to employee compensation. These expenses are usually supplies, dues and subscriptions, printing, postage, interdepartmental transfers from central service and pharmacy that are not charged to the patient, and other expenses (Figure 4).

These expenses should be classified into variable and non-variable categories. The variable expenses vary in direct proportion to the number of procedures/patient days that have been recorded. Non-variable expenses do not have this direct ratio but are incurred in operating the department whether the utilization is at 100% or at some point above or below it.

Variable non-wage expenses are budgeted based upon the historical cost per unit adjusted for some inflation factor. These inflation factors are usually given in the administrator's budget memo, which accompanies the budget forms to the Departments. Inflation factors may be obtained from the local hospital council, state hospital association, or national publications. Non-variable non-wage expenses are budgeted based upon historical cost adjusted for some inflation factor.

If there are substantial increases or decreases in utilization from one year to another, it is wise to prepare the budget based upon the concept of zero-based budgeting. This concept requires that the hospital manager re-evaluate all activities and costs to

Figure 4 - **GSU HOSPITAL NURSING UNIT - 7 EAST YEAR: 1997**

NON-WAGE BUDGET
BUDGET STATISTIC: 10,000 patient days

PREPARED BY:__________
APPROVALS:
DIRECTOR__________
ASST. ADM.;__________
ADM.:__________

	PROJECTED 1996 EXPENSES	PROJECTED 1996 PER UNIT	X	INFLATION FACTOR	=	BUDGETED 1997 PER UNIT	BUDGETED 1997 EXPENSES
Variable Expenses:							
Medical Supplies	$ 50,000	$ 5.00		1.06		$ 5.30	$ 53,000
Offices Supplies	20,000	2.00		1.05		2.10	21,000
Interdepartmental Transfers	10,000	1.00		1.06		1.06	10,600
Total	80,000	$ 8.00				$ 8.46	$ 84,600
Non-variable Expenses:							
Dues & Subscriptions	500			1.05			525
Travel	3,000			1.05			3,150
Total	3,500						3,675
TOTAL NON-WAGE EXPENSES	$ 83,500						$ 88,275
Statistic: Patient Days	10,000						10,000

NOTES: Projected 1996 expenses based upon eight months' actual expenses, four months' projected expenses.
Inflation factors based upon those factors given in Administrator's budget memo.

decide whether they should be eliminated, reduced, or funded. Appropriate funding levels are then determined by priorities and ranking established by administration according to the overall availability of funds. If new procedures are to be implemented in the budget year or new equipment, which will change the ratio of supplies and/or staffing, these adjustments must be made to the salary and non-wage budgets.

It is important to "flag" potential increases in staffing and/or non-wage expenses if a particular piece of medical equipment is approved for purchase. If the equipment were approved for purchase, then the hospital would incur additional expenses. If the equipment is removed from the approved budget, then these additional expenses (or reductions thereof) would be removed from the final budget.

IV. OTHER EXPENSES - CAPITAL RELATED EXPENSES

The total cost of capital assets is distributed over its estimated useful life in a systematic manner. This process is called depreciation. It is the estimated decline in value of the asset during the period.

The service life of a capital asset is the period of time it will be used in producing other assets or services. Predicting a capital asset's service life is sometimes difficult because of such factors as wear and tear and technological obsolescence. The Internal Revenue Service and the American Hospital Association have prepared "Estimated Depreciable Lives" lists which include many of the equipment categories used in health care facilities.

A. Depreciation

Depreciation expense may be calculated using the straight-line method, declining-balance method, sum-of-the-years' digits method, or units-of-production method. Each is acceptable and falls within the realm of generally accepted accounting principles. The Medicare and Medicaid programs require the straight-line method of depreciation. In rare cases, the Medicare/Medicaid programs allow 150% declining-balance depreciation on assets acquired before August 1, 1970 if the facility can demonstrate the need for cash flow. Some Blue Cross programs allow accelerated methods such as the 150% declining-balance method or the sum-of-the-years' digits method.

The straight-line method of depreciation is calculated as follows:
Cost - salvage value
Service life in years

The salvage value of a capital asset is the portion of its cost that is recovered at the end of its service life. It may be the trade-in value or scrap value. Normally no salvage value is assumed.

Capital assets are normally bought when needed and are sold or discarded when they are no longer usable or needed. Purchases and sales are not necessarily made at the beginning or at the end of the fiscal year. Therefore, depreciation must often be calculated for partial years. Normally, for routine replacement assets, 1/2 years' depreciation is taken in the year of acquisition. For those acquisitions that are of a substantial dollar value, the actual number of months in service is calculated.

B. Interest Expense

Another expense included in the budget is interest expense. Interest expense may be incurred from working capital loans, mortgages, bond issues or other liabilities. It is summarized from loan agreements, repayment tables, and principal and interest tables (called amortization tables). If a loan agreement requires interest payments based on a percentage of prime, then a prime rate must be assumed. The prime interest rate refers to the interest rate charged to the most credit-worthy customers.

C. Amortization

The third type of other expense is the amortization of other intangible assets. Amortization is the process of allocating financing cost associated with long-term debt to the periods during which the liability is outstanding. Another expense that is deferred is start-up costs. These costs are amortized (expensed) over a 60-month period.

D. Insurance

The fourth type of other expense is insurance expense. Insurance expense will include premiums or self-insurance deposits for malpractice (professional) liability, fire, and theft, business interruption, or other forms of insurance.

E. Other

Other expenses are normally budgeted at the global level rather than at the department level. They include expenses for legal and accounting services, contract services such as utilization review or executive recruitment, utility expenses, and employee benefit expenses. Trend analysis of these items, adjusted for anticipated changes in service volume and inflation, is a reasonable approach to projecting these needs for the next budget year.

Expenses applicable to grants or specific purposes should be budgeted as a separate line item. Its corresponding revenue should be included in other operating income. Have we forgotten anything? A master budget checklist should be maintained to assure that all expenses have been budgeted.

Among the expenses which should be verified by using the Budget Audit Checklist are the following:

- Salaries: Are all positions listed whether filled or vacant?
              Are cost-of-living, merit, and seniority increases budgeted?
              Are shift differential, overtime, standby and call, vested sick leave
                  pay-offs and vacation coverage by pool personnel budgeted?
              Are temporary personnel expenses for special projects and vacation
                  coverage budgeted?

- Supplies: Have amounts been budgeted for supplies related to new services or
                  procedures?
              Will there be any changes in charging for certain supplies?

- Other: Have amounts been budgeted for existing maintenance contracts and for new contracts for equipment currently under warranty?

   Have amounts been budgeted for yearly drapery/cubicle cleaning?

   Have amounts been budgeted for equipment rental/leasing contracts, copying cost, private telephone/fax lines, new telephone lines, pagers, and the main trunk line?

   Have amounts been budgeted for outside laboratories, management and consultant fees, legal and audit fees, and other purchased services?

   Have amounts been budgeted for all utilities, scavenger, sewer charges, and special assessments?

V. REVENUE BUDGET

Revenues are projected from statistics prepared in the Statistics Budget. Any increase or decrease in the budgeted statistics will directly affect the actual revenue of the facility. In addition to regular operating expenses, rates must be set to cover items such as (1) replacement of facilities, taking into account inflation and technological change factors; (2) working capital requirements; (3) all quasi-service costs (education, research, and free care), not otherwise reimbursed; (4) debt requirements; and (5) as much excess (profit) as necessary to provide for sound financial operations. Omitted in the above requirements is the most important requirement of all: to determine revenues to cover contractual allowances or discounts given to third-party payors.

Gross patient service revenue is generated from rendering patient services and supplies. Nursing and the "hotel" expenses for rendering patient care are charged as a daily room and board charge. These "hotel" expenses include the patient's room, meals, linen, and other type expenses. The nursing expenses include the direct cost of nursing and support care from floor nurses, department clerks, orderlies, and aides.

Ancillary departments such as surgery, radiology, laboratory, and physical therapy generate revenue based upon procedures undertaken or services rendered. These charges are segregated into revenues generated from inpatients and outpatients (emergency room, referred outpatients, and clinic patients).

Based upon each department's budgeted statistic, the budgeted revenue for the department may be calculated by using an average charge for the entire department. If computers are used, the revenue generated from each individual test or procedure by each department is accumulated.

The most important step to remember is to annualize all interim rate increases that were implemented in the previous (or current) fiscal year. For example, if GSU Hospital implemented increases for the last six months of the fiscal year, the annualized amount of the rates that were in effect for the 12 months must be calculated.

Other operating revenues are generated from services and supplies rendered incidental to providing care. These revenues include income from the parking lot, gift shop, papers, cafeteria charges, medical record transcription fees, income from vending machines, pay telephones, recovery of silver from x-ray, and all other sources of miscellaneous income. Included in other operating revenues are unrestricted contributions and donations received by the institution, general funding from governmental sources, and investment income from operating fund investments.

The Revenue Budget may be prepared as the first component of the budget process, thereby confining all increases in expenses and requirements to what the revenue budget will bear or prepared last so that rates may be increased to cover the anticipated expenses and requirements. In this era of cost-based or prospective-based reimbursement, managed care, and competition, it becomes difficult to continue to increase prices. The controlling factor has become cost containment.

If room and board charges are increased, a state or intermediary (such as the Blue Cross program in the state of Illinois) will require a 30 day notice before the program will honor price increases. Other states require state approval of all revenue rates on an annual basis.

A. Revenue Deductions

Normal deductions from revenue include contractual allowances or discounts to third-party payors, administrative discounts, write-offs for charity or free care, Hill-Burton program provisions for free care, and provisions for doubtful accounts (bad debts).

Contractual adjustments are based on an analysis of the reimbursement formula or payment formula for each payor. The difference between what is charged on the patient's bill and what is ultimately received from both the patient and third-party payor is the contractual discount.

Provisions for free care are based upon historical analysis, as well as Board policy decisions. Free care requirements under the Hill Burton Program are determined by the contractual agreement that the hospital entered into when it received Hill Burton funds for construction programs.

VI. CASH FLOW BUDGET

The cash flow budget is prepared from the completed budget statement of revenues and expenses, pro forma balance sheet, and capital equipment/asset requests. Expenses are estimated to be paid, revenues and contributions are estimated to be received, and capital asset acquisitions and debt repayments are assumed to be made on a monthly basis.

For those months in which outflow exceeds inflow, the facility must look to its internal resources (savings) or to short-term financing to cover its deficits. For short-term working capital deficits, it is feasible to incur short-term debt. Lines of credit should be established by the facility so that it may draw on its credit line when necessary and repay the balance when monies become available. The best time to establish a line of credit is before the need for money arises.

For long-term capital requirements, long-term debt may be arranged. Such financing vehicles may include leasing, mortgages, bond issues, or loans.

VII. CAPITAL BUDGET

The capital budget is composed of the anticipated purchases of equipment, build-ings and related equipment, land and improvements, and renovation of existing facili-ties. A capital item is defined by the Medicare program to be an expenditure of over $500 and a useful life of over one year. A capital asset, sometimes called a fixed asset or property, plant, and equipment asset, is not bought and sold in the ordinary course of business (Figure 5).

Cost is the basis for recording the acquisition of a plant asset. The cost of the capi-tal asset includes freight expense, installation, renovation of facilities to accommodate the equipment, and initial training and calibration expenses. This cost is offset by its salvage or trade-in value. Capital costs do not include regular staffing, supplies, or other non-wage costs once the equipment/project becomes operational.

Prospective review of capital expenditure projects to determine the need and appro-priateness of the expenditure may be required. This process, called certificate-of-need (CON) is handled in Illinois by the Illinois Health Facilities Planning Board (IHFPB). Before such assets may be purchased or ordered, approval must be received form the IHFPB. Otherwise, depreciation expense, related interest expense, and amortized financ-ing expense may not be reimbursed from third-party governmental programs.

During the capital budget process, departments are requested to submit their lists of desired purchases. Such requests, which sometimes become "Christmas Wish Lists", should be prioritized to reflect the urgency of the item. A suggested means of prioritizing these assets include:
1)   required for continued licensure or certification,
2)   needed to implement a cost reduction program,
3)   required to implement a newly approved program or objective,
4)   desired, but not necessary.

In each of the above scenarios, a justification must be prepared for each item. Justification may be based upon normal replacement of antiquated equipment, increased volumes justifying additional equipment, a new service being implemented, or a premature replacement due to cost reduction, technological obsolescence, improved patient care, etc.

As part of the evaluation process, mathematical methods to evaluate capital equipment requests will take into consideration the time value of money. Any good generic or health care specific accounting and finance textbook will explain the calcula-tions and assessment techniques.

At the time that each item is justified, an additional request for operational funds may be required if the equipment requires additional staff or supplies. It is extremely important that these operational costs be included. If the equipment is approved, the resulting additional operating costs must also be included in the proposed operating expense budget and the resultant revenues in the revenue budget. If equipment purchas-es will not be covered under warranty agreements, maintenance contract costs must be included in the operating budget (Figure 6). If the installation of equipment or the reno-vation of the facility will temporarily interfere with existing services, the effect of such interference must be quantified and the results included in the operating budget.

Medical equipment is usually approved through the equipment committee. The committee is normally composed of administrative personnel and medical staff. The

Figure 5

GSU HOSPITAL

CAPITAL ASSET REQUEST #_____
FOR THE THREE YEAR PERIOD: 1997 - 2000

Priority Class: _____
Replacement?   YES _____ NO _____
Date Needed: MONTH _____
                    YEAR _____

• Additional Operating Expenses?   YES _____ NO _____
• New Maintenance Contract ?   YES _____ NO _____

Name and Description: _____

Justification and Recommended Supplier of Vendor:
(Include payback or return on investment calculations.)
Attach additional information and vendor quotes if available.

# of Items _____
Unit Cost _____   X
Total Request _____   = $ _____
Less trade-in _____
NET REQUEST _____ $ _____
Source of Funding: _____

• Attach copy of budget to this form as well as to the operating budget request.

Replacement Information:
Name of item, including serial number: _____

Hospital Tag Number (Identification number): _____
Assigned to Department: _____
Currently located in Department: _____

Disposition of Item:

Trade-in _____
Sell _____
Retire & Store _____
Donate _____
Junk _____

APPROVALS:
Requested By: _____   Equipment Committee: _____   Asst. Administrator: _____
Chair of Department _____   Space Committee: _____   Administrator: _____

Figure 6

Department. _____

Dept. No. _____

GSU HOSPITAL

ADDITIONAL OPERATING EXPENSES TO BE INCURRED IF

CAPITAL ASSET REQUEST # _____ IS APPROVED FOR ACQUISITION

STAFFING (Job class, salary, scheduling)   # of FTE   _____

                                         SALARY REQUEST $ _____

SUPPLIES AND OTHER EXPENSES   SUPPLIES $ _____

                                    OTHER: Maint. Contract   _____

                                                    _____   _____

                                                    _____   _____

IMPACT ON OTHER DEPARTMENTS (if any) Initial construction or operation
 of the department.

STATISTICS BUDGET (number or procedures or additional procedures to be undertaken) Include a start-up schedule showing the monthly growth utilization.

REVENUE BUDGET (additional revenue to be generated)

determination of which vendor's equipment to purchase is decided by this committee.
Assets to be purchased during the budget year should be segregated according to source
of funding. Those assets to be funded out of operations or savings should be listed separately from those items that will be funded from long-term financing vehicles.

SUMMARY

    The final master budget presents management's estimates of the most probable
financial position, results of operations, and changes in financial position for the budget period. The budgets are based on assumptions made by management concerning
future events and circumstances. Unanticipated events or circumstances may occur
subsequent to the approval of the final budget. The budgets reflect management's
judgment, based on present circumstances, of the most likely set of conditions and its
most likely course of action. Some assumptions inevitably will not materialize and
unanticipated events and circumstances may occur. Actual results achieved during the
budget period will vary from the budget, and the variations may be material. The
achievement of any budget results is dependent upon future events, the occurrence of
which cannot be assured.

REFERENCES

Cleverley, W. O. (1997). *Essentials of Health Care Finance* (4th edition). Aspen Publishers, Inc., Gaithersburg, MD. ISBN 0-8342-0736-2.

Esmond, Jr., T. H. (1982). *Budgeting Procedures for Hospitals.* (1982 edition). American Hospital Association, Chicago. ISBN 0-939450-14-3.

Herkimer, Jr., A. G. (1988). *Understanding Health Care Budgeting.* Aspen Publishers, Inc., Gaithersburg, MD. ISBN 0-87189-772-5.

Kirk, R. (1988). *Heathcare Staffing & Budgeting, Practical Management Tools.* Aspen Publishers, Inc., Gaithersburg, MD. ISBN 0-87189-784-9.

61.
FLASH MANAGEMENT

Donna L. Gellatly, *Financial HealthCare Associates, Palos Hills, IL*

Mark S. Boyd, *Ovation Healthcare Research, Highland Park, IL*

Financial statements provide a historical perspective of a facility's operations. It may take 12 to 15 working days after month-end for the accounting department to provide the previous month's financial results for administrative review. In the interim, how does the administrator effectively manage the facility? One means is to provide a daily *Flash Report* (Figure 1) which reports the previous day's operations, and the month and year-to-date utilization and financial information. The *Flash Report* allows the administrator a snapshot view of the facility's daily progress.

The daily *Flash Report* is prepared by the general accounting department. Using information obtained from the overnight processing of census and utilization information, the generation of patient charges, and bank account information, this management information report can be prepared and be on the desk of key administrative personnel before 11:00 a.m. the next morning. Viewing these key facts on a daily basis will give administrators a progressive view of the facility's operations. Trends can be easily tracked as well as potential problems identified. Prudence dictates that the earlier a problem can be identified, the easier it is to cure.

Figure 1

GSU HOSPITAL
DAILY FLASH REPORT

DATE: 02/19/XY

	02/18/XY	02/01-02/18/XY	01/01-02/18/XY		
	DAY	MONTH-TO-DATE	YEAR-TO-DATE		

A.   CASH ACCOUNTS INFORMATION

Beginning Balance	$ 49,500	$ 17,000	$ 85,000		
Cash Deposit (+) (B)	22,000	1,450,000	5,142,000		
Line of Credit					
Draw-down (+)		150,000	250,000		
Repayment (-)		(50,000)	(100,000)		
Cash Disbursements (-)					
Payroll & Taxes	0	(1,019,000)	(4,090,000)		
Non-payroll	(12,500)	(489,000)	(1,228,000)		
Ending Balance	$ 59,000	$ 59,000	$ 59,000		

B.   DETAIL OF CASH DEPOSIT

				PAYOR MIX CASH FLOW	
				ACTUAL	BUDGET
Medicare	$ 9,000	$ 643,950	$ 2,283,000	44.40%	36.00%
Medicaid	0	131,500	468,000	9.10%	10.00%
Blue Cross	6,800	224,000	792,000	15.40%	7.00%
Commercial Insurance	4,000	65,000	231,000	4.50%	15.00%
Self-Pay	600	1,300	5,000	.10%	.10%
Other Third Party Payors	1,200	254,250	899,300	17.50%	30.00%
Sub-Total (C)	21,600	1,320,000	4,678,300	91.00%	98.10%
Cafeteria & Coffee Shop	400	26,000	92,600	1.80%	1.50%
Other Operating Income		3,850	15,400	.30%	.10%
Contributions		100,150	355,700	6.90%	.10%
Interest Income		0	0	.00%	.10%
Total Deposits (B)	$ 22,000	$ 1,450,000	$ 5,142,000	100.00%	100.00%
Actual Deposits as a Percentage of Budget:		92.00%	87.00%		100.00%

C.   ACCOUNTS RECEIVABLE INFORMATION

	Daily		Year-To-Date	
Charges Captured	$ 82,440	100.00%	$ 5,378,000	100.00%
Billing Amounts	84,100	102.00%	5,162,900	96.00%
Collection Amounts (C)	21,600	26.20%	4,678,300	87.00%

Billing and Collection Amounts as a percentage of Charges Captured.

Unapplied Amounts	$ 720		$ 21,500	(Net)
Unanswered Correspondence	46		46	(Net)

D.   UTILIZATION INFORMATION

				BUDGET YTD
Beds in Service	165	165	165	165
Admissions	27	513	1,357	1,489
Patient Days of Care	120	2,052	5,782	6,174
Discharges	24	527	1,377	1,506
Average Daily Census	120	114	118	126
Average Length of Stay (E)	5.00	3.89	4.20	4.10
Occupancy	72.70%	69.10%	71.51%	76.36%
Emergency Room Visits	30	570	1,960	2,020

E.   OTHER INFORMATION

Cash needed for 02/28/XY payroll	$ 1,020,000		
Accounts Receivable Balance	$ 8,780,400		
Days of Revenue in A/R	= 80 days	GOAL:	65 days
Outstanding Line of Credit Balance	$ 400,000	MAXIMUM LINE OF CREDIT:	$ 1,000,000
Average Length of Stay on Discharge Basis (E)			

Some information that should be included in the report is as follows:
*   beginning cash balances,
*   cash deposits,
*   line-of-credit transactions,
*   cash disbursements,
*   ending cash balances,
*   details of cash deposits,
*   accounts receivable information,
*   utilization information, and
*   other key financial information.

Cash is so important that a hospital or other business can operate at a loss as long as it does not run out of cash. A business must close even if it is operating at a profit if it has no cash. Bills are paid against cash and not net income (Beck, 1994). The control of cash is one of the most important responsibilities of administration. Delayed payroll checks and past-due vendor payments will cause employee unrest, and possible resignations. Vendors may be leery of advancing credit and may require cash on delivery or deposits before goods are shipped.

I. CASH ACCOUNTS INFORMATION

The Beginning Cash Balance is the sum of available cash funds from checking accounts, short-term investment accounts, and savings accounts. If long-term investment funds are available for operating use, the amount should be noted in the Other Information portion of the report as well as the maturity date(s) of these long-term available investments.

Cash Deposits are reported on a daily, month-to-date, and year-to-date basis. In addition, the Detail of Cash Deposit by payor source (Section B) is included in the report. This detail reveals where the cash came from. By including actual and budgeted payor mix cash flow information, this portion of the report can indicate where cash collection problems exist. In Figure 1, there appears to be problems in commercial insurance and other third-party payor collections. In both cases, actual cash collections are substantially lower than their respective budgeted percentages of collections. In total, monthly and year-to-date collections are also under budget.

When cash shortages exist, a facility, hopefully, will have a negotiated line of credit available that can be used to "draw-down" sources of temporary cash for operating use. These lines of credit allow the facility to obtain cash advances and to repay them as cash from operations, or when other financing funds become available. These agreements are usually negotiated on an annual basis, with interest rates based on a percentage of the prime interest rate. Excellent credit ratings could yield an annual interest rate at prime (8.25% at June 23, 1997). Lower credit arrangements may yield a rate of 1-2% over the prime rate. These lines are usually secured by the facility's accounts receivable and/or property, plant, and equipment. In all cases, the lending institution will require interim financial reports and may require periodic audits of the secured assets by their audit personnel.

Cash disbursements include payroll and the related payroll taxes, and non-payroll disbursements. Payroll related disbursements include the net amount of the payroll, and the employee payroll taxes withheld along with the employer's matching share of such payroll taxes as social security (FICA), Medicare, and state and federal unemployment taxes. Non-payroll disbursements include payments to suppliers, utility companies, and independent contractors. Additional important information such as the amount of cash needed for an upcoming payroll should be included in the Other Information section of the *Flash Report*. As the payroll disbursement date approaches, the Ending Balance of the cash accounts should equal or exceed the required disbursement. If a cash shortage exists, the facility will have to continue to draw-down on its available line of credit.

II. ACCOUNTS RECEIVABLE INFORMATION

The information in Section C-- Accounts Receivable Information indicates where the cash flow problem(s) reside. If Collection Amounts are less than Charges Captured, the accounts receivable balance increases. Billings should, on a year-to-date basis; nearly approximate charges captured (revenue earned during the same period). When Billing Amounts are under the amount of Charges Captured, the discharged, not-yet-billed accounts have increased. Immediate action should be taken to catch-up with this delayed billing. Section B will detail each individual payor class collection problems. When actual collections are below budgeted cash collections, immediate additional collection efforts should be undertaken for the payors whose actual collections are under the budgeted collections. Section E--Other Information also indicates collection problems: Days of revenue outstanding in accounts receivable are at 80 days. Current national averages are between 60-70 days. Immediate efforts to collect commercial insurance and other third-party payor bills should be undertaken.

If the Cash Application Clerk cannot identify the patient's account to apply payment, the bank deposit should still be made. The unidentified payor amount is then credited to an Unidentified Cash Payable general ledger account. This amount is a liability that either must be identified and applied to a specific patient's account or refunded to the payor if the payment does not belong to the facility. The unidentified payment should be investigated in a timely manner. If more information is needed, correspondence with the payor should be undertaken within seven days of payment receipt. The longer the unidentified payment account goes unreconciled, the harder it will be to determine the correct patient's account to which to apply payment. Some reasons that may cause unidentified payments are: maiden versus married names, hyphenated names, parent (insured) surname differs from the child's last name, and/or multiple outstanding accounts for the same patient.

One of the worst public relations problems an administrator may face is an irate patient/payor who continues to receive incorrect bills or delinquent letters after having attempted to contact or correspond with the facility. A preset day and time (at least once a week) should be set aside to answer correspondence and work on patient account problems. If further investigation is required, the business office should send a letter to the patient/payor noting the receipt of the contact/correspondence and state that the facility is in the process of reviewing the account. The patient/payor should be given the name and telephone number of the employee who will be responsible for reviewing the problem.

The daily Flash Report for GSU Hospital indicates 46 pieces of unanswered correspondence. This means that there are at least 46 upset patients with perhaps an equal number of third-party payors who are handling these patients' insurance claims. Immediate action should be taken to answer this correspondence.

III. UTILIZATION INFORMATION

The Utilization Information on the *Flash Report* details the daily, month-to-date, and year-to-date utilization information. While there may be minor fluctuations in occupancy and utilization on a daily basis, fluctuations should average-out as the year progresses. If variances continue to increase, the budget assumptions should be reviewed and revised, if necessary, to project a more realistic picture for the remainder of the year.

Information for the first 49 days indicates the average length of stay to be slightly above budget, while actual admissions and patient days to be below budget. In addition, emergency room visits are approximately 3% under budget.

Besides comparing the facility's actual to budget utilization data, the administrator should compare this year's utilization statistics to last year's utilization statistics and compare the facility's actual results to current utilization trends provided by such sources as the American Hospital Association, state associations and agencies, metropolitan healthcare councils, and state planning boards.

IV. OTHER INFORMATION

Other information included in this section of the *Flash Report* may be needed to fully understand the importance of the above sections' data. In this example, the administrator can review the following information:

- The facility needs to have at least $1,020,000 in the cash accounts before February 28th, to meet the next payroll distribution. If the cash can not be raised through the collection of patient accounts, the facility may have to draw-down on its available line of credit. As of today, February 18th, the facility has $600,000 remaining on its available line of credit (maximum line of credit of $1,000,000 less $400,000 already drawn-down and outstanding).
- The days of revenue in accounts receivable are 80 days. The business office's goal is 65 days of revenue in accounts receivable. The administrator should request a detailed plan of action with achievable interim goals be prepared by the Vice-President of Finance so that this problem can be resolved.
- If utilization ratios can be calculated using various data, the definition of each ratio should be defined.

By having and utilizing timely accurate data, the administrator and other key personnel can be aware of current operations and be able to make informed decisions.

REFERENCE

Beck, D. (1994). Cash is King. *Health Care Supervisor, 13* (1): 1-9.

62.
REGULATION IN THE ERA OF ACCOUNTABILITY

Frederick G. Jones, *Anderson Area Medical Center, Anderson, SC*
Dale S. Duncan, *Anderson Area Medical Center, Anderson, SC*

This chapter addresses the history of the health care regulation and accountability and reviews organizations involved in ensuring accountability among organizations. Future trends affecting health care performance measurement are also identified.

I. BACKGROUND AND HISTORY

In 1988, Arnold Relman, M.D. wrote that the United States had seen two revolutions in the medical care system since World War II. He predicted that we are now on the threshold of a third related to assessment and accountability. He described the first of these as beginning in the late 1940s and continuing through the 1960s, characterized as the era of expansion with a rapid growth in health care facilities and numbers of physicians, as well as new developments in science and technology. Fostered by legislation like the Hill-Burton Hospital Survey and Construction Act of 1946, the expansion encouraged construction of health care facilities by recognizing that voluntary hospitals needed capital support for renovation and expansion (Hosking, 1987). The number of hospitals and the resulting number of services grew and proliferated. No questions were raised at that time as to the necessity of all services provided by all hospitals. The industry was encouraged to grow and was reimbursed to accommodate that growth. With the passage of Medicare and Medicaid legislation in 1966, this expansion further accelerated.

These developments led inevitably to a second revolution from the 1970s through the 1980s when Relman refers to the revolt of the payers or the era of cost containment.

Considerable attention was paid during the 1980s to bringing the cost of the health care system under control. Legislature again played a significant role in the history of the industry, this time to control rather than to encourage. In 1972 Congress established the Professional Standards Review Organizations (PSROs) to oversee costs and the quality of health care provided by federally funded programs. In 1982 the Health Care Financing Administration Medical Peer Review policies established through the Peer Review Improvement Act (P.L. 97-248) and the Tax Equity & Fiscal Responsibility Act of 1982 (TEFRA) created both Title XI Part B of the Social Security Act and the Peer Review Organizations (PROs) (Bittle, 1987). This further increased the oversight of admissions and lengths of stay, as well as curbed utilization of inpatient services.

Perhaps the most important event with the most far-reaching effects occurred in 1983 with the advent of the Prospective Payment System (PPS) (Epstein, 1987). Diagnosis Related Groups (DRGs) and Diagnosis & Operative Procedure Codes would strive to provide a finite monetary amount for services provided rather than fee for services. All of these events helped to create the modern health care delivery system by imposing licensure, certification, and other professional standards on a health care system that until then had been remarkably unregulated (Paris, 1987).

II. STATE REGULATION

While policy is passed on a federal level, the actual process of control is operationalized on the state level. The Peer Review Organizations, for example, operate from a state level while enforcing federal mandates. The states' Departments of Health & Environmental Control (DHEC) also wield control and oversight functions.

DHEC grants licensure to health care organizations. Yearly, licensure surveys are held with utilization of the Conditions of Participation or standards that pertain to structure, process, and governance. Safety, infection control, and medical staff functions are reviewed to determine compliance with state regulations. State DHECs have the authority to remove licensures or to issue sanctions, but usually attempts are made to allow organizations the opportunity to correct any deficiencies. Surveyors review the laboratory functions to determine compliance with federal regulations such as Clinical Laboratory Improvement Act (CLIA). The College of Pathology (CAP) reviews laboratories, and its stamp of approval usually bestows status as far as other regulatory agencies are concerned.

DHEC responds to complaints from consumers through surprise on-site inspections. Consumers might bring accusations such as premature discharge or inappropriate transfers. The surveyors will review for policies and procedures that support the processes of care. Validated complaints could result in monetary fines or sanctions, such as exclusion from Medicare or Medicaid.

In addition to licensure regulations, health care organizations must be cognizant of and compliant with standards promulgated by the state peer review organizations responsible for Medicaid and Medicare recipients. Medicaid recipients are those who fall below the current poverty levels. Both inpatient and outpatient services are covered, provided certain criteria are met. The same applies to the Medicare or elderly population. On the national level, the Health Care Finance Administration (HCFA) delegates review responsibilities to the states who, through cooperative projects, review medical records of inpatients to determine adequacy of care. Pre-certification, continued stay, and admission criteria must be met, or the costs are not covered by the payer. Often conflicts arise between the health care providers and the payers when the best interest of the patient is at odds with rules and regulations. Hospitals employ utilization review functions to oversee the care of patients covered by state and federal funds. Staff work with the medical personnel in determining what services are required and when the patients no longer require inpatient services.

Hospital Issued Notices (HINs) indicate that inpatient services are no longer required, that coverage has been denied, and the patient is now responsible for payment. Hospitals can be placed in precarious situations when no funds are generated. The patient remains in the hospital, and there is no place that the patient can be safely discharged. A frequent example would be patients awaiting nursing home placement when none can be found, and the patients cannot take care of themselves. The hospital remains responsible.

While change has been seen from these cost-control activities—a shift from inpatient to outpatient care and much more emphasis on the ambulatory setting—many believe the change is not enough.

"The revolution failed," says Herzlinger (1989) of the Harvard Business School. The failure "was almost entirely that of management, not of strategy" (Herzlinger, 1989). She attributes a large measure of the reason for failure to the entrepreneurial "fixation" on marketing and finance. Very little thought was given to how these new enterprises would be run, and so often they were run badly. Hertzlinger also accused some of the new companies of creative accounting to hide the truth of their individual failures. While they were concentrating on financing marketing, the entrepreneurs failed to improve the "quality and efficiency of health care in key areas (Herzlinger, 1989). She further believes that the next stage of the revolution in the health care system will be more successful. Beckham's rebuttal of Hertzlinger suggests that health care executives should be more aggressive in telling their story (1990).

Relman predicts that we will enter a new era as a strong new consensus on the need for assessment, and accountability seems to be building. He predicts that we need to know much more about the relative cost, safety, and effectiveness of all that physicians do or employ in the diagnosis, treatment, and prevention of disease. Armed with these facts, physicians will be in a much stronger position to advise their patients in determining the use of medical resources; payers will be better able to decide what to pay for, and the public will have a better understanding of what is available and what they want. Relman states that this theme was sounded by Ellwood when he called for a national program of "outcomes management": a system linking medical management decisions to new, systematic information about outcomes (Ellwood, 1988). Epstein responded in the New England Journal of Medicine with a sounding board entitled "The outcomes movement: Will it get us where we want to go?" In this paper, the outcomes movement was acknowledged to be well under way and the call for increased assessment and accountability to be healthy. Caution was called for in these efforts, so that our progress does not undermine a healthy evolution and allow revolutionary zeal to lead us to carry a good thing too fast and too far (Epstein, 1990).

Certainly, in subsequent years, accountability has become a major health care issue. Another major piece of legislature sought to control the quality of health care by increasing physician scrutiny. The Health Care Quality Improvement Act of 1986 was passed to prevent physicians from moving from state to state without a paper trail of malpractice claims and actions taken by hospitals and other health care entities. The Act created the National Practitioner Data Bank with rules and regulations posted in the Federal Register. Under this law, hospitals and other health care entities had to report certain physician behavior to the Data Bank; also incorporated was a mandatory querying function for physicians and other health care providers prior to the granting of their privileges. Malpractice insurance providers, for example, report sums of money paid on physicians for malpractice claims. Hospitals report revocation, suspension, or removal of privileges. Any health care organization considering the granting of privileges to a health care provider has access to information in the Data Bank. Health care entities which do not query the Data Bank prior to granting privileges are presumed to know the contents in the Data Bank in the event of legal action brought against it by the physician's activities. Additional fines are put into place; however, the greatest threat comes from exemption from the protection afforded peer review activities by the Act. This protection is afforded as long as organizations and physicians in the peer review activities have acted in a reasonable manner without malice in the belief of furthering patient care.

Since 1996, the Data Bank has a track record of operations, and we, as users of the process, have begun to see more data reported. While a health care entity does not have to wait until the results are known, delaying the credentialing decision is nevertheless prudent.

Emanuel and Emanuel (1996), note that accountability entails the procedures and processes by which one party justifies and takes responsibility for its activities. The concept of accountability contains three essential components:

- The loci of accountability—health care consists of many different parties that can be held accountable or hold others accountable;
- The domains of accountability—in health care, parties can be held accountable for many activities; professional competence, legal and ethical conduct, financial performance, adequacy of access, public health promotion, and community benefit; and
- The procedures of accountability--including formal and informal procedures for evaluating compliance with domains and for disseminating the evaluation responses by the accountable parties.

The Emanuals characterize and compare three dominant models of accountability: (1) the professional model in which the individual physician and patient participate in shared decision-making, and physicians are held accountable to professional colleagues and to patients; (2) the economic model in which the market is brought to bear in health care, and accountability is mediated through consumer choice of providers; and (3) the political model in which physicians and patients interact as citizen members within the community, and in which physicians are accountable to a governing board elected from the members of the community, such as a board of a hospital or managed care plan. The authors argue that no single model of accountability is appropriate to health care. Instead, they advocate a stratified model in which the professional model guides the physician-patient relationship, the political model operates within managed care plans and other integrated health delivery networks, and the economic and political models operate in the relations between managed care plans and such groups as employers, government, and professional organizations.

As the United States health care delivery system changes to managed care medicine, Robert Brook asks whether quality will remain on the agenda as health system reform proceeds (Brook, et al., 1996). In this special communication in the JAMA, Brook suggests that we can no longer focus on macro-level issues such as the benefits of the single payer or on whether a medical market can function efficiently. More specifically, as the increase in health care resources is curtailed, how will the trade-off between cost and quality be affected? The article presents eight critical questions that should be considered by everyone involved in changing health care systems—questions that illustrate the importance of maintaining quality of care concerns in the policy agenda. The rest of the article provides information on what happens to quality when the system is changed and on how quality can be measured and maintained on the policy agenda. Finally, actions are suggested that physicians might pursue in order to ensure that quality remains a central value of the new American solution to the health care crisis of the 1990s.

Accountability is becoming the key word in health care. For example, health plans are being held accountable by employers and consumers, while physicians and other providers are being held accountable by health plans and patients. Purchasers of health care are increasingly seeking assurances of value for their health care dollar. Although the cost of care remains a prime consideration, large employers, government purchasers, and consumer groups are also demanding high quality medical services. This purchaser-driven quest for accountability has spawned report cards, satisfaction surveys, consumer guides and publications, performance standards, and planned ratings. These tools are being developed by an equally diverse variety of accreditation bodies, employers, business coalitions, trade groups, physicians, HMOs—practically anyone who wants to claim the title "quality expert." Cognizant of widespread variation in diagnosis, treatment, outcomes, and consumer services, purchasers are no longer content with promises of good care from health care organizations; rather, they are seeking a window into the "black box" of health care delivery.

Health care purchasing coalitions typically hold health plans accountable by collecting and evaluating data from the health delivery organizations regarding their price, quality and service; examining the reports of accreditation organizations which rate health care plans; and surveying employees regarding their satisfaction with various plans. In order to respond to purchaser demands for accountability, many health care organizations are hastening to obtain some type of accreditation. From the perspective of employers and health plans, accreditation represents rigorous, objective application of uniform standards to compare planned performance across a broad range of areas. Accreditation is offered by several independent, nonprofit organizations and is based on satisfaction of various performance measures.

III. ORGANIZATIONS AND ACCOUNTABILITY

A. Joint Commission on Accreditation of Health Care Organizations

In 1910, Ernest Codman identified the need for every hospital to follow every patient it treats long enough to determine whether or not the treatment was successful and to determine whether the desired result was achieved. If not, the hospital should discover how to prevent similar results in the future. From this beginning, the American College of Surgeons would form a standardization program (Affeldt, 1987) resulting in today's Joint Commission on Accreditation of Health Care Organizations (JCAHO). While JCAHO standards are voluntary, organizations have traditionally desired accreditation as a measure of certain standards. Federal law allows ready states to "deem" JCAHO-accredited hospitals eligible to receive Medicare and Medicaid payments without any additional state licensure inspection. Currently, 26 states automatically grant a license to any JCAHO-accredited hospital while nine others consider the JCAHO's findings in licensure decisions.

Comparative data with peer entities on a local, state, and global level are used to identify opportunities for improvement. Changes in the processes of care can then be made by analyzing the process in a statistically-based method. While critics of JCAHO expound the conflict of interest between the dual role as "de facto regulator and industry promotional body," this body has been a major player in the way hospitals and now other health care organizations do business.

The Joint Commission on Accreditation of Health Care Organizations, perhaps the best known, was established in 1951 by several professional medical societies. Its board includes representatives from the American College of Physicians, American Hospital Association, American Medical Association, American College of Surgeons, and the American Dental Association, as well as consumer and nursing groups. JCAHO has traditionally accredited providers of care including hospitals, outpatient centers, nursing homes, clinical laboratories, mental health centers, and home health agencies. In the 1980s, the organization briefly entered the HMO accreditation field only to withdraw until 1994 when it began rating health care networks. JCAHO characterizes these groups as entities that provide health services to a defined population, offer comprehensive or specialty services, and retain a central structure which coordinates care provided by a network. According to JCAHO, health care networks include HMOs, PPOs, integrated delivery networks, and specialty networks.

The organization's mission is to improve "the quality of care provided to the public through the provision of health care accreditation and related services that support performance improvements in health care organizations." It evaluates health care networks in eight areas: rights, responsibilities, and ethics; continuum of care; education and communication; health promotion and disease prevention; leadership; management of human resources; management of information; and improving network performance. The precise character of JCAHO assessment survey is determined by the type of network being evaluated. The four levels of accreditation are "with commendation; with recommendations; provisional; or non-accredited." JCAHO accredits approximately 5,300 hospitals and over 9,000 other health care organizations. A mix of process-oriented and outcomes-related indicators support internal comparisons of performance over time and also comparisons with similar organizations.

B. National Committee for Quality Assurance

In contrast, purchasers of health care are increasingly seeking accreditation from the National Committee for Quality Assurance (NCQA). This organization based in Washington, DC was founded in 1979 by Group Health Association of America and the American Managed Care Review Association. The group became an independent, nonprofit organization in 1990. Its board of directors includes representatives from employers, consumer groups, organized medicine, health plans, and organized labor, as well as quality experts and government regulators. NCQA primarily accredits HMOs, although PPOs and point of service plans, physician hospital organizations, and provider sponsored organizations, may also qualify for review so long as they have provided comprehensive inpatient and outpatient care through an organized delivery system for at least 18 months and used defined administrative procedures.

NCQA characterized its mission as "providing information that enables purchasers and consumers of managed care to distinguish among plans based on quality thereby allowing them to make more informed decisions. NCQA accreditation evaluates how well a health plan manages all parts of its delivery system—both providers (e.g. physicians, hospitals, clinics) and administrative services—in order to continuously improve health care for its members" (1996).

NCQA reviews six aspects of health plan practice: quality improvement, credentialing and medical affairs, member rights and responsibilities, preventive care services, utilization management, and medical records. NCQA awards full three years, standard one year, and provisional accreditation depending on the degree to which health plans satisfy performance criteria. As of January 1996, NCQA reported that 35% of those plans evaluated received the full accreditation, 40% received one year accreditation, 11% obtained provisional status, and 14% were denied accreditation. NCQA receives approximately 500 requests per month for its accreditation status list which provides general health plan ratings.

C. Utilization Review and Accreditation Commission

The Utilization Review and Accreditation Commission (URAC) was formed in 1980 by the American Managed Care Review Association and the AMA. Initially, the organization set out to improve consistency, efficiency and quality of utilization review programs and to facilitate interactions between the U.R. industry and health care providers, payers and purchasers. Its board of directors consist of representatives from provider, managed care, regulatory, commercial and consumer groups. URAC entered the field of managed care planned accreditation in October 1995 through its purchase of the American Accreditation Program, Inc. (AAPI), which evaluated PPOs as an affiliate of the American Association of Preferred Provider Organizations. URAC is now marketing itself as an accreditor of many different types of managed care organizations, especially PPOs, but also HMOs, PHOs, PSOs, and other forms of integrated delivery systems.

D. Accreditation Association for Ambulatory Care

The Accreditation Association for Ambulatory Care (AAHC) was part of the JCAHO until 1979 when it broke away as an independent entity. Its board includes representatives from 13 health care organizations. Its mission is "to assist ambulatory health care organizations in improving the quality of care they provide to patients. . . by setting standards, measuring performance, providing consultation and education where needed, and ultimately by awarding accreditation to those organizations that are found to be in compliance with its standards. " AAHC traditionally accredits ambulatory care centers, medical group practices, and clinics. However, because these providers are contracting with managed care plans, AAHC's impact on managed care has been increasing to the point where it has begun accrediting other HMO affiliated providers including surgery centers and even a few HMOs.

IV. PERFORMANCE MEASURES

A. Capitalized Performance Measures

While purchasers are driving the general trend toward health plan accountability, they are also demanding that the plans be held accountable in specific terms through use of substantive criteria broadly known as performance measures. These measures assess a broad range of areas including patient satisfaction, financial performance, and outcomes associated with specific procedures or medical conditions. Several performance measurement systems have emerged, including NCQA's Healthplan for Employer Data and Information Set (HEDIS), Foundation for Accountabilities (FAcct) Guidebook for Performance Measurement, and Agency for Health Care Policy and Research (AHCPR)/Harvard University's Computer Oriented Needs Quality Measurement Evaluation System (CONQUEST). The use of performance measures raises several issues. Methods of data collection and reporting affects the degree to which various quality standards are satisfied. Moreover, the priorities held by those who develop performance measures are reflected in the areas which those measures seek to evaluate as well as in the relative weight given to different measures in the set. The performance measures provide an objective means of assessing health care plan quality; their only objective is the reasoning which underlies their development and application. The better known sets of performance measures are HEDIS, FAcct's Guidebook for Performance Measurement, and CONQUEST.

B. Measuring Accountability—HEDIS

NCQA's HEDIS system is recognized as the most commonly used set of quality measures. HEDIS 1.0 was devised in 1989 in an attempt to simplify and standardize the quality data which employers sought from health plans. NCQA adapted the system, released two updates, and expects to release HEDIS 3.0 by early 1997. In its present form, HEDIS uses numerous statistical measures to assess health plan performance in five basic areas:
- Clinical quality, including preventive, prenatal, acute, chronic, and behavioral health care;
- Access to care and patient satisfaction;
- Membership in utilization, focusing on enrollment, disenrollment, and utilization of health services;
- Financial performance, including liquidity, efficiency, compliance, and medical loss ratio; and
- Planned management, including such aspects as network coordination and information systems.

Approximately 330 health plans use the current version of HEDIS as a vehicle to report standardized indicators.

Performance data must be considered in the process of physician reappointment. Specifically, the standards require that data related to member satisfaction, utilization, member complaints, and quality reviews be incorporated in the recredentialing process of primary care providers. The selection of indicators, as well as the validity and reliability of data become a significant challenge, especially if physicians feel threatened. The data should be used to improve both performance and clinical care. HEDIS 3.0 includes eight major areas of performance: effectiveness of care, access to care, member satisfaction, informed health care choices, health plan descriptive information, cost of care, health plan stability, and use of services.

C. Other Organizational Initiatives

The Foundation for Accountability, an alliance of public and private health care purchasers and consumer organizations formed by Paul Elwood, MD, President of the Jackson Hole Group, hopes to establish national health care standards as well. "Responsible Choices," a 1995 proposal, outlined the formation of a health accountability system. This system included a public-private collaborative body— the Health Accountability Foundation (HAF)—modeled on the Financial Accounting Standards Board. In 1995, the Foundation for Accountability (FAcct), a nonprofit foundation based in Portland, Oregon, was created to encourage public discussion about the best ways to monitor and improve the quality of health care. FAcct guiding principles are as follows:
- Health systems and providers must be accountable to the American public,
- Accountability must be expressed in terms of consumers and patients' experiences of care and service, and the outcomes they ultimately achieve.

The National Account Consortium (NAC), comprising nine Blue Cross and Blue Shield plans covering 20 million lives, has proposed nationwide criteria for health insurers and medical practitioners. The consortium is standardizing operation, procedures, utilization review rules, and marketing strategies.

JCAHO is currently evaluating nearly 150 measurement systems and expects to choose the best ones by the fall of 1997. In April 1996, the Agency for Health care Policy Research (AHCPR) released Conquest 1.0, a computer tool that links a database of performance measures with a database of clinical conditions, allowing users to collect and assess clinical performance measures with great specificity. Conquest is available to the public free of charge on the Internet.

V. PERFORMANCE MEASURES: THE NEXT GENERATION

Physicians are being affected by the accountability trend. As purchasers place increased demands on health plans, the plans in turn impose pressures on physicians. For example, physicians with several managed care contracts may be required to comply with the accreditation requirements of all these plans, a requirement that could be a great administrative burden. Further, they may need to provide medical record data within a specified, standardized format to help plans satisfy clinical performance measures. The NCQA is taking applications for a new round of certification surveys covering services that verify physician credentials on behalf of managed care organizations. Certification will stand as sufficient evidence for NCQA accreditors and eliminate the need for each plan to cover the same ground. A physician's application for membership in the HMO must contain attested statements about "lack of present illegal drug use; history of loss of license and/or felony convictions; and history of loss or limitation of privileges or disciplinary action." Furthermore, an HMO must show it has a mechanism for reporting provider suspensions or termination to the appropriate authorities as well as an appeals process. The AMA may soon bestow an "AMA seal of approval" on doctors, especially those working in managed care. The AMA Physician Performance Assessment Program will include clinical and nonclinical evaluations. CME, also part of the new assessment program, will link the educational offering to the topic under review.

For physicians, accountability could be a difficult goal. According to Nash (1995), "The problem is that medical school training and its culture fly in the face of market place accountability." Physicians are trained to make decisions without consulting anybody else first. Nash recommends that the medical community must retool physicians for the market place—teach them how to practice decisively with full awareness that there are limits to the financial resources of the purchasers. The majority of physicians and providers have not routinely questioned the value of the procedures they perform nor is benchmarking widely used.

Brennan and Berwick conclude that most health care regulation today is anachronistic. They review the JCAHO, medical licensure boards, certificate of need, rate setting, utilization review, PROs, and laws regulating a variety of areas and others; most such regulatory efforts are viewed as relatively ineffective, even counterproductive. They may be captured by the regulators, seek to regulate physicians without accounting for the systems in which they work, or use structural measures without regard to their relation to outcomes. Uniformly, they fail to account for two overriding trends. First, the rise of managed care and integration of health care delivery, the most important regulatory issues for the future, will be tradeoffs between cost and quality. Second is the development of industrial quality management science emphasizing consumer focus, statistics, and coaching. Brennan and Berwick reject the idea that market incentives by themselves will improve health care adequately. Rather, in order to make health care regulation more effective, they propose the idea of responsive regulation, flexible regulation tailored specifically to those regulated and which actively promote the outlook, and the tools of quality improvement. Recommendations include the following:

- establish safe havens for major innovations;
- encourage the progression of managed care (and rational consolidation in general);
- transform malpractice liability to a no fault approach and enterprise liability; and
- increase exchange of information on improvements and innovations.

The current health care debate has focused on the classic triad of cost, access, and quality. Although there has been a substantial debate over cost and a growing debate over access, discourse on the question of quality has been, until recently, quite minimal.

SUMMARY

As perpetual students and current players in the health care arena, the authors attest to the increasing demands that accountability brings to the playing field. What other industries have known for many years, this industry is now learning—the ability to measure its performance in many dimensions. Many tools are available to us, and we need to be able to utilize the tools; more importantly we must use performance data to affect change. As one JCAHO surveyor so eloquently stated, "[I]t is not good enough to say how hard we have flapped our wings, we need to be able to say how far we flew" (AMHS, 1996).

REFERENCES

Affeldt, J. E. (1987). Voluntary accreditation of hospitals. In: L. F. Wolper, J. J. Pena (Eds.).
    Health Care Administration Principles and Practices Rockville:. Aspen Publishers, Inc.: 232-233.

Beckham, J. D. (1990). In defense of health care management. *Journal of Health care Forum,*
    (July/Aug): 65-67.

Bittle, L. J. (1987). Quality assurance. In: L. F. Wolper, J. J. Pena (Eds.). *Health Care*
    Administration Principles and Practices (pp. 131). Rockville: Aspen Publishers, Inc.

Brook, R., Kamberg, C., and McGlynn, E. A. (1996). Health system reform and quality. *JAMA,*
    276: 476-480.

Changing roles and changing standards. (1996, February 21-23). *AMHS/ Premier/ SunHealth:*
    Charlotte, NC.

Ellwood, P. M. (1988). Outcomes management: a technology of patient experience. *NEJM, 318:*
    1549-56.

Emanuel, E. and Emanuel, L. (1996). What is accountability in health care? *Ann Intern Med, 124:*
    229-239.

Epstein, A. M. (1990). The outcomes movement - will it get us where we want to go. *NEJM, 323:*
    266-269.

Epstein, J. D. (1987). Legal structure of hospitals. In: L. F. Wolper and J. J. Pena (Eds.) *Health*
    Care Administration Principles and Practices, (p. 46). Rockville: Aspen Publishers, Inc.

Herzlinger, R. E. (1989). The failed revolution in health care - the role of management. *Harvard*
    Business Review..

Hosking, J. E. (1987). Planning health care facilities and managing the development process. In:
    L. F. Wolper, and J. J. Pena (Eds.). *Health Care Administration Principles and Practices.* (p. 21).
    Rockville: Aspen Publishers, Inc.

Nash, D. B. (1995). Editorial: accountability in health care. *Journal of Outcome Management,* (2): 4.

Paris, M. (1987). The medical staff. In: L. F. Wolper, and J. J. Pena (Eds.). *Health Care*
    Administration Principles and Practices. (p. 289). *Rockville:* Aspen Publishers, Inc.

Relman, A. S. (1988). Assessment and accountability - the third revolution in medical care.
    NEJM , 319: 1220-1222.

63.

DEVELOPING HIGH-INVOLVEMENT ORGANIZATIONS FOR THE FUTURE

David R. Graber, *Medical University of South Carolina, Charleston, SC*
Arnold D. Kaluzny, *Research University of North Carolina at Chapel Hill, Chapel Hill, NC*

I. CASE

Ms. Connie Livingston is a 31-year-old woman living with breast cancer. Her cancer was diagnosed several years ago and, following a lumpectomy and adjuvant therapy, she was doing quite well--well enough to plan a future involving marriage.

The wedding was planned and the date was set. A license was obtained, guests were invited, and the endless details, usually associated with such events, were slowly coming into place. Unfortunately, shortly before the wedding, Ms. Livingston developed a pulmonary embolism and was rushed to a university hospital located in an adjacent state. After being admitted to the emergency room, the attending oncologist was called, and arrangements were made to transfer her to the oncology unit. Her condition was critical and was deteriorating rapidly. Fearing the worst, Connie, and her fiancé Jim Smith, requested that the marriage be conducted in the university hospital chapel. They insisted that this be a "legal marriage," not just a ceremony.

The legal marriage required a marriage license (issued in the county where the marriage took place) and new blood tests and certification. It also required the scheduling and coordinating of a group of people, both within and outside the hospital who just minutes earlier had no idea who Connie Livingston or Jim Smith were, and time was running out. The administrator-in-charge contacted the county registrar to obtain a marriage license and the state laboratory for certification of the required blood test. What typically is done in weeks was now occurring in minutes. Physicians, nurses, and hospital managers also played key roles in coordinating and expediting the wedding. Timing was critical; any one of these individuals could have created a delay ending the effort. Instead, "things did happen." The wedding occurred--a wish fulfilled--and three hours later Mrs. Livingston-Smith died.

A tragedy? Yes! A lost life? Yes! But this is the reality of healthcare--a reality that every day provides an opportunity to demonstrate what people can accomplish given the challenge. The objective of this chapter is to examine some of the critical current and future challenges facing health care managers within rapidly changing healthcare environments. Some are structural, based on informal and formal contracts held between the healthcare organization, its staff and clinicians. Others involve processes and cultural conditions, all of which affect the success or failure of the organization. This chapter analyzes these factors and their influence and provides some guidelines to assure that, even in a restructured healthcare environment, it is possible to "make things happen."

II. THE HEALTH CARE ENVIRONMENT: DISTINGUISHING CHARACTERISTICS

Health care, increasingly defined as an economic good, possesses unique characteristics that require recognition. The culture of healthcare organizations and issues involving organizational power and employee participation within these organizations must be well understood in order to build an effective and motivated workforce.

A. Culture

Hospitals have distinctly fractionated cultures in addition to having a general institutional culture. This is primarily a product of physician/management differences or clinician/non-clinician differences. Other less apparent but nonetheless important subcultures involve the distinct motivational and working conditions of a hospital laundry department (Smith and Kaluzny, 1986), and the unique culture observed in the humor, teamwork, and bonding of operating room staff (Cushman, 1984).

The clinician/management dichotomy pervades not only hospitals, but virtually all healthcare organizations. The clinician's primary ethical obligation is to the patient, not to the organization (Summers, 1989). Clinicians tend to think in terms of a sense of duty towards patients that is more important than other considerations. Shortell (1992), for example, identifies a number of specific cultural differences between physicians and health care executives. Physician training mainly focuses on scientific subjects. Medical students and residents are exposed primarily to other health care professionals in training. Their focus is narrow, typically on individual patients, and the time frame of action is generally short run to meet the immediate needs of patients. Physicians believe that resources should be readily available to maximize the quality of care essential for their own patients. In contrast, health care executives receive training primarily in the social and management sciences and have relatively little exposure to health care professionals when training. Their focus is broad, not on individual patients, but on all patients in the organization and the community. Managers' time frame of action is middle to long run, and considerable emphasis is placed on positioning the organization for the future. Obtaining and allocating resources to provide the best quality of care is viewed as problematic, and compromises are seen as unavoidable.

The world view of physicians and managers is clearly asynchronous. There are also differences between other health professionals (e.g., nurses, physical therapists) and health care managers. However, none of the above differences have been as critical to organizational loyalty, motivation, and cohesion as the fact that physicians have not usually been employees of the hospital or health care organization during the twentieth century. In fact, physicians as suppliers of revenue (patients) to hospitals, traditionally could more logically be considered customers than employees. However, as will be discussed later, this relationship is rapidly changing with the proliferation of health maintenance organizations and physician-hospital organizations.

Many organizations, especially large ones, will have subcultures based on location, department, membership in informal groups, and professional membership or identification. However, the mix of cultures and dual sources of power in hospitals have contributed to an innate resistance to management control and organizational initiatives.

B. Power

Closely connected to manager/physician cultural and value differences are issues of power and control in hospitals and health networks. Physicians have traditionally worked in autonomous professional organizations where, "organizational officials delegate to the group of professional [participants] responsibility for defining and implementing the goals, for setting performance standards, and for seeing to it that standards are maintained" (Scott, 1982). Examples of the autonomous model for physicians have included general hospitals, psychiatric hospitals, and medical clinics. As largely autonomous professionals, physicians have been allowed to discipline and control each other with minimal interference from management or regulators.

Access to critical resources (Salancik and Pfeffer, 1977) or control over critical tasks (Crozier, 1964) are often described as sources of intra-organizational power. In the early twentieth century, charitable and local contributions constituted the major revenue source for American hospitals. During this period, the influence of trustees and hospital board members (who made contributions) was paramount (Smith and Kaluzny, 1986). With the development of insurance coverage, charitable contributions became less important. By the 1930s, the advances of medical science had considerably increased the prestige of physicians. This and their control over a critical resource (patients) led to their becoming a dominant force in many healthcare organizations.

The advent of Medicaid and Medicare (and consequent third party payments) and the capital needs of hospitals have tended to enhance administrative influence and moderate physician power. However, administrator and physician influence is largely asserted within separate spheres or through a dual hierarchy of control (Harris, 1977). Although this dual hierarchy has operated more or less effectively, it has not been conducive to manager/physician collaboration or joint participation in decision-making, but more to negotiation, compromise, and, occasionally, confrontation. In addition to internal individuals and groups, it is important to note that considerable power resides in external entities (e.g., government agencies, JCAHO), which are very influential in prompting actions and programs by healthcare administrators and clinicians.

Health care providers are generally, like physicians, members of professional groups with licensure requirements. Many of these groups have been impeded in moving vertically or horizontally on the organizational ladder, as licensure requirements or professional certification act to restrict the availability of many positions. Although these groups may have strong professional identities (e.g., Registered Nurses, technologists), their members have generally been employees of the health care organization. Salaried professionals generally practice in heteronomous professional organizations, where professional participants are clearly subordinated to the administrative framework (Scott, 1982). In the heteronomous model, healthcare professionals, such as nurses, are more constrained by bureaucratic and management controls than in autonomous structures.

In recent years, the growth of health maintenance organizations (with salaried physicians), and pressures for greater efficiency and accountability in health care have combined to increase the prevalence of the heteronomous model. This has effectively shifted more authority and influence to healthcare managers, particularly in managed care settings.

C. Employee Participation

Cultural, power, and status distinctions influence communication and participation in all businesses, including healthcare organizations. Until recently, the dual hierarchy of control in hospitals tended to minimize management influence in patient care issues. Similarly, in relatively stable periods in recent decades, physician input (into management decisions) was often considered unnecessary and was not solicited.

The devolution of some decision-making authority was aided by two developments in the 1980s and 1990s: Total Quality Management and interdisciplinary teams. In the 1980s, Total Quality Management (TQM) was adopted as a continuous quality improvement process in many health care organizations. A basic tenet of TQM is that decision-making teams are expected to identify and develop solutions to problems within their assigned domains. TQM has thus served to empower many staff members.

The use of teams in corporate America has been highly discussed and lauded in recent years. Many health care organizations are also adopting team approaches, more typically for patient care decisions and coordination than for operational decisions. One rather thorny obstacle has been educating physicians to share authority and decision-making responsibility in team settings. Correspondingly, lower-status team members have needed encouragement to participate. However, in many settings these problems have been successfully surmounted; thusly, both TQM and interdisciplinary teams have helped to democratize the health care environment.

III. THE DEMISE OF TWENTIETH CENTURY HEALTHCARE

The very nature and orientation of health care was in the midst of a rapid metamorphosis in the last decade of the twentieth century. The growth of managed care plans and capitation reduced (in many areas) the patient supply for specialist physicians, and correspondingly reduced their incomes.

Under managed care, a new complex of incentives and expectations has arisen, and this has altered both the authority and culture of physicians. The "traditional boundaries and relationships...built to insulate physicians from the business aspects of organized health care...are being breached" (Nurkin, 1995). As colorfully expressed by Jeff Goldsmith, "The old reimbursement system and the moral and economic contract that physicians had with their patients are being blown to smithereens" (Montague, 1994). As discussed previously, much of the power of physicians has been grounded in their capacity to bring revenue (patients) to the hospital. More and more, however, the customer to be cultivated is not the patient, or the doctor--it is the insurance companies or administrative groups that bring in the contracts for care of large, insured populations.

Closely connected to the growth of managed care plans has been the formation of integrated delivery systems (IDS) - groups of providers positioning themselves for managed care. Prior or attendant to the formation of an IDS, are often significant staff layoffs, or as it is often termed "right sizing," principally of nurses and middle managers. For better or worse, healthcare executives realized that considerable reductions in expenses could be achieved through substituting unlicensed staff for more costly licensed nurses. Consequently, the nursing shortages of the late 1980s were unexpectedly followed (in the mid-1990s) with widespread layoffs (Kent, 1995).

Personnel reductions or "right sizing" are one facet of a larger, philosophical and structural shift in health care: substituting lower level, and less expensive, institutions and providers for more expensive ones. Thus, patients previously cared for in acute hospitals receive care in rehabilitation facilities, nursing home subacute units, or by home health agencies. Residential care and assisted living settings replace nursing homes. Nursing assistants replace nurses, and primary care physicians replace specialists. This process has not been smooth or unimpeded, but has been inexorable, due to the growing ascendancy of cost considerations.

The importance of costs by the mid-1990s, relegated health care quality and access concerns to be comparatively inconsequential considerations, at least in legislative policy debates. In recent years, healthcare executives appear to be possessed of a survival instinct that demands rapid changes, personnel cuts, and coalition and network building. Thus, organizational restructuring and an emphasis on cost reductions have tended to de-emphasize human considerations.

IV. MANAGING HUMAN RESOURCES IN A CHANGING ENVIRONMENT

Health care is changing! What has not changed is the fact that health care remains labor-intensive, requiring well-trained and well-motivated personnel that function effectively, beyond simply managing crises. Unfortunately, recent developments in many health care organizations - restructuring, layoffs, and uncertainty about professional status - have seriously eroded the loyalty and trust of many health care professionals. This has put at risk their ability to meet unexpected and non-routine challenges, which by definition characterize healthcare organizations.

A. Health Care Restructuring and Employee Morale

The re-engineering and restructuring that was endemic in corporate America in the 1980s spilled over to health care organizations and became widespread in the late 1980s and the 1990s. In this period, a significant number of senior American workers and managers were laid off from their positions. These developments gave many Americans ample time to reconsider and reframe their expectations of corporate loyalty and lifetime employment. Consequently, Americans are now more likely to view corporations as far more motivated by survival and bottom-line concerns than employee concerns.

Healthcare managers have often intensified the inevitable pains of restructuring through excessive managerial secrecy. Pompa (1982), for example, cites eight reasons a manager will purposefully not divulge an imminent reduction in force.

1) Productivity will drop because people will be so upset they won't concentrate on work.
2) There could be sabotage to company assets.
3) The wrong people will begin looking for work, rather than waiting to see who is let go.
4) That his/her own productivity will be hampered by people continuously asking him/her for updated information.
5) That his/her people will tell others and create wider morale problems.
6) The company's downsizing plans will leak to the press and damage the company's competitive situation.
7) Giving out information early will only upset the staff needlessly.
8) Finally, he/she fears anger and even violence directed toward himself/herself.

These are very real issues, and managers thereby often feel caught on the horns of a dilemma. However, managerial secrecy in these instances is indicative of a self-serving organizational orientation and a certain callousness towards staff. Staff are not permitted to know critical details about the company's plans, are not given the opportunity to assess their potential for continuing employment, and most (once terminated) will be unemployed for longer periods than they would have been if they were informed earlier. Thus their ability to take care of themselves and their families is restricted.

Restructuring, acquisitions, and mergers have been identified as having negative effects on survivors, as well as the casualties. In a study by Petchers and Associates (1988) of the effects of a hospital merger, 77% of the respondents stated it had been a stressful experience. Loss of relationships, loss of a sense of belonging, and demotions were widespread experiences. A study of 20 companies with significant merger activity identified five common characteristics among surviving managers: anxiety and uncertainty, helplessness and rejection, divided loyalties, withdrawal and avoidance, and conflicts over new values (Fulmer and Gilkey, 1992). These individual characteristics can readily pervade the workplace, leading to 'organizational depression' and lack of trust (Jones and Arana, 1995).

Loss of trust often results in declines in information flow, deterioration of morale, ambiguous verbal messages, and negative outside signals, such as customer complaints (Bartolome, 1989). Organizational depression in healthcare organizations may be indicated by increased incident reports, increased attrition, withdrawal and demotivation among many who remain, and increased absenteeism (Jones and Arana, 1995).

The fundamental structure of hospitals and many other health care organizations, as well as cultural factors and power balances, mitigate against organizational participation and cohesion. In addition to existing structural factors, the restructuring of healthcare organizations has generally not been beneficial for healthcare employee relations. Layoffs and restructuring are difficult for all involved. However, even under such difficult challenges, it is possible to maintain employee morale and participation.

B. The High-Involvement Health Care Organization

Honest and open communication with staff (Veninga, 1990; Marks and Mirvis, 1986), and moving quickly to establish a new organizational culture (Harris et al., 1992; Veninga, 1990), are often cited as approaches to assure successful mergers and reduce the pain of layoffs. Although these may be important steps, the assumption is often made that management has already decided the nature of the restructuring and the anticipated layoffs; the next step is to heal organizational wounds and establish a new culture.

Healthcare executives who seek to exclude lower-level staff and managers may be subject to a command-and-control orientation. On the other hand, they may believe that employees are incapable of making objective decisions when they involve issues relating to their own continuing employment. However, many healthcare organizations have formed planning teams and transition teams for cost-cutting or restructuring purposes with substantial employee representation (Olm, 1986; Burns, 1993). Using such task forces for critical decisions and open communication are key features of high-involvement organizations (Lawler, 1993). When such steps are taken, management demonstrates a commitment to staff participation, a willingness to share power, and also some measure of philosophical consistency.

During periods of organizational restructuring, healthcare executives must also avoid some of the more egregious errors that are clear signals of hypocrisy and insensitivity. In the experience of one of the authors, high-level hospital managers were given substantial pay increases within a few months after layoffs of hundreds of hospital employees. This contributed to widespread cynicism and feelings of resentment. Terms like retooling, reengineering, change management, downsizing, and employee repositioning, purposefully do not express the human costs involved. Telling staff that downsizing was carried out so staff could work smarter implies that current and previous staff members were dumb workers. Staff may accept the necessity of staff reductions but resent attempts to glorify the process (O'Neill and Lenn, 1995). As euphemisms are intended to conceal, their use suggests insincerity, and thus they often backfire or illuminate the unexpressed attitudes of management.

Restructuring healthcare organizations always have the opportunity to retrain staff, help pay tuition or other educational expenses for career changes, and assist departing staff in finding other positions. All too often the programs that are implemented are woefully inadequate and ineffective (Ross, 1989). However, if executives feel no obligation to departing workers, they obviously never cared for them at all.

Although concern for employees, and employee participation and empowerment, are professed by virtually all organizations (i.e., espoused values), in times of crisis or rapid change, the real or actual organizational values become evident (Graber, 1995). In such instances, a high-involvement organization with deeply-held values will, consistent with those values, implement substantial programs to assist departing staff members.

C. Preparing for the Future

Opportunities for more effective and comprehensive management/staff relations will arise, as physicians increasingly become employees of health care organizations. As employees, physicians will no longer be autonomous and independent of management control. This may, indeed, be abhorrent to many physicians. However, physicians should continue to be elite and highly-regarded health professionals on the basis of their skills and training. In a sense, the high regard of individuals for physician skills has worked against the democratization of the health care workplace. However, with physician employees, management will have greater opportunities to develop and cultivate a unified workforce, instead of dealing with a structurally fractionated one. Moreover, given the professional and cultural differences between clinicians and non-clinical staff, it will continue to be important to develop specialized approaches to improve communication with clinicians. For example, although some physicians may read the employee newsletter, special topic mini-seminars may be more relevant and helpful to them (Ross, 1989).

In managed care settings, physicians will have greater opportunities to assume management responsibilities, simply by virtue of being employees. Greater use of physician-managers and clinician-managers has been often described as an expected future development (Coile, 1994; Smallwood and Wilson, 1992). Clinician-managers (who are trained in both management and clinical disciplines) are much more likely to understand the perspectives and issues of both management and clinical staff. As such, they possess great potential to reconcile the concerns and ideas arising from disparate, intra-organizational cultures. However, organizational leaders should be aware that physician- and other clinician-managers will be more likely to take an ethics-based position in decisions concerning the allocation of resources (Lemieux-Charles and Hall, 1997). Organizations may benefit by better integrating the clinicians' perspectives into their analytical and philosophical perspectives, rather than seeking to transform clinician-managers into analytical businessmen. Compared to traditional managers, clinician-managers will be better prepared to assist the organization in developing clinical performance benchmarks and clinical practice guidelines and in conducting technology assessments. Such skills will be critical to the success of high-involvement managed care systems that take advantage of the scientific and clinical knowledge of the clinician-manager.

Although clinician-managers should increase in the coming years, the actual extent of their spread is uncertain. Working against the growth of clinician managers is, to some degree, the greater prevalence of leaner healthcare organizations with fewer management positions. It is also questionable how many clinicians will wish to undergo the rigors of both management and clinical education.

Interdisciplinary teams, multiskilled practitioners, and the greater use of different mixes of health care professionals may move decision-making (on both care and management issues) to lower levels in the hierarchy. Staff involvement efforts will be incomplete if they focus only on physicians and other highly-paid health professionals. Nursing assistants who are empathic, alert to patient and family member psychosocial needs, and who are reasonably aware of available clinical and human resources, can make an incalculable contribution to their healthcare organizations. To effectively employ and utilize this wealth of human resources, managers will need to discard a narrow focus on their more prestigious employees.

Similarly, a greater emphasis on wellness and prevention may tend to empower non-physician staff who are likely to be entrusted with these responsibilities. If these activities are important to organizational success, and these staff members clearly contribute to the financial well-being of their organizations, their stature and influence will inevitably increase. Management can be proactive, instead of reactive, by studying the contribution of wellness and prevention activities to customer health, using this information for strategic planning, and centralizing and institutionalizing wellness and prevention activities.

SUMMARY

Although changes in healthcare delivery may contribute to organizational cohesion and morale, it is ultimately the managers of each health care organization that will have the greatest impact. Executives can retain a great deal of staff respect, even during major restructuring, through open communication and employee participation. However, these efforts are likely to fail if they are superficial and employed primarily as techniques to control dissent. Success is more likely if the efforts reflect established organizational values and a genuine concern for people within the organization. Such consistency is a key contributor to individual and organizational trust.

Through consistency and caring, management invests in a good will bank where credits accumulate. In tough times, the reserve of credits can be spent and will help the organization weather the crisis (Ross, 1989). However, if management has neglected this investment, during periods of turmoil or change, employee ill-will and distrust will quickly surface.

Human concern is a very practical organizational investment. Without this leaders will find it difficult to be what Bennis calls, "pragmatic dreamers - men and women whose ability to get things done is often grounded in a vision that includes altruism" (Bennis, 1996).

It is not only special cases, such as Ms. Livingston's, but in the daily operation of the healthcare organization, where good will, teamwork and the coordination of staff and managers are critical. Healthcare organizations are repositories of considerable human ability, intelligence, skill, and caring. As described in the case of Ms. Livingston, with proper motivation and leadership, these qualities are evoked. Such high involvement from all staff members is actuated when people believe they have a contribution to make, and that contribution is valued. This will occur when people are well-trained and increasingly cross-trained. It will also only occur if the feeling of egalitarianism, the sense that everyone can make a significant contribution to the organization, is instilled in all staff members.

In the early 2000s and beyond, healthcare managers can take a number of steps to realize their human potential. Many of the organizational theories and models that provide a solid foundation for creative managers have been demonstrated to be effective in research studies and real-world applications. The use of teams, greater egalitarianism, open communication, and shared power can be cultivated, whatever the organizational starting point or current conditions may be.

REFERENCES

Bartolome, F. (1989). Nobody Trusts the Boss Completely - Now What? *Harvard Business Review, March-April* : 135-142.

Bennis, W., and Nanus, B. (1985). *Leaders: The Strategies for Taking Charge.*. HarperCollins, New York.

Bennis, W. (1996). The Leader as Storyteller. *Harvard Business Review. January/February*: 154-160.

Burns, J. (1993). Placing Layoffs in Pretty Packages. *Modern Healthcare, February*: 28-30.

Coile, R. (1994). Transformation of American Healthcare in the Post-Reform Era. *Healthcare Forum Journal. July/August*: 9-11.

Cushman (Producer). (1984). *Hospital Corporate Cultures [Film]*. Los Angeles, California: Hospital Satellite Network.

Crozier, M. (1964). *The Bureaucratic Phenomena*. University of Chicago Press, Chicago, IL.

Fulmer, R. M., and Gilkey, R. (1988). Blending Corporate Families: Management and Organization Development in a Postmerger Environment. *The Academy of Management Executive, 2*: 275-283.

Graber, D. (1995). An Organizational Typology of Environmental Agencies and Businesses, *Proceedings of the American Public Health Association*. San Diego, CA.

Harris, C., Hicks, L .L., and Kelly, B. J. (1992). Physician-hospital Networking: Avoiding a shotgun wedding. *Health Care Management Review, 17(4)*: 17-28.

Harris, J. E. (1977). The Internal Organization of Hospitals: Some Economic Implications. *Bell Journal of Economics, 8*: 467-82.

Jones, L., and Arana, G. (1995) *When the New Way of Doing Business Sets In: Recognizing and Fighting Organizational Depression*. Unpublished manuscript.

Kent, C. (1995). Nurse Layoffs and Hospitals: Changing the Course of Care. *Medicine and Health Perspectives, March 13*.

Lawler, E. (1993). Creating the High-Involvement Organization. *Organizing for the Future (E. Lawler, J. Galbraith, eds.)* Jossey-Bass, San Francisco.

Lemieux-Charles, L., and Hall, M. (1997). When Resources are Scarce: The Impact of Organizational Practices on Clinician-Managers. *Health Care Management Review, 22(1)*: 58-69.

Marks, M. L., and Mirvis, P. H. (1986). The Merger Syndrome. *Psychology Today, October*: 36-42.

Montague, J. (1994). Old Traditions, New Realities. *Hospitals and Health Networks, December 5*: 22-31.

Nurkin, H. A. (1995). The Creation of a Multiorganizational Health Care Alliance: The Charlotte-Mecklenburg Hospital Authority. In *Partners for the Dance* (A.D. Kaluzny, Zuckerman, H. S., Ricketts, T. C., eds.) , Health Administration Press, Ann Arbor, MI.

Olm, P. (1986). *Staff Needs Met During Merger. March-April*: 3-4.

O'Neill, H. M., and Lenn, J. (1995). Voices of Survivors: Words that Downsizing CEOs Should Hear. *Academy of Management Executive. 9(4)*: 23-34.

Petchers, M. K., Swanker, S. , and Singer, M. I. (1988). The Hospital Merger: Its Effects on Employees. *Health Care Management Review. 13(4)*: 9-14.

Pompa, V. (1992). Managerial Secrecey: An Ethical Examination. *Journal of Business Ethics*. 11: 147-156.

Ross, A. (June 27, 1989). *The Anguish of Downsizing*. Presentation at the Medical Group Management Association, Kauai, Hawaii.

Salancik, G. R., and Pfeffer, J. (1977). Who Gets Power and How They Hold on To It: A Strategic Contingency Model of Power. *Organizational Dynamics, Winter*.

Scott, W. R. (1982). Managing Professional Work: Three Models of Control for Health Organizations. *Health Services Research, 17*(3): 212-219.

Shortell, S. (1992). *Effective Hospital-Physician Relationships*. Health Administration Press, Ann Arbor, MI.

Smallwood, K. G., and Wilson, N. (1992). Physician-Executives Past, Present, and Future. *Southern Medical Journal. 85*(8): 840-844.

Smith, D. B., and Kaluzny, A. D. (1986). *The White Labyrinth*. Health Administration Press, Ann Arbor, MI.

Summers, J. (1989). Clinicians and Managers: Different Ethical Approaches to Honoring Commitments. *Journal of Healthcare Material Management. May/June*: 62-63.

Veninga, R. L. (1990). Strategies for Managing the Merger. *Hospital Topics. 68*(4): 11-16.

64.
VALUES, HEALTH CARE, AND POLICYMAKING

Thomas M. Wilson, *Auburn University at Montgomery, Montgomery, AL*

Interest in American health care policy has grown enormously in the past 25 years. Two reasons among many stand out. One is the tremendous rise in public expenditures for medical care. The second is the expanding scope of public policy, especially at the national level of our government. Almost every facet of the health care system of the United States is affected by the formulation and implementation of public policy. Increasing attention to this state of affairs has occurred among the public at large, journalists, and analysts working within the traditional confines of the university. In their own way all have been attempting to understand a very complex process.

Some fundamental questions need to be asked. How should health care policy in the United States be analyzed and evaluated? Is there a way to do it? Which approach should be chosen? For academic analysts, are the concepts and methods of a particular discipline preferred over those of another discipline? Does it matter as long as we believe that our understanding is somehow advanced?

The well-known health economist, Victor Fuchs, is aware of these issues. He writes that, "Today, health policy looms as the proverbial five-hundred-pound gorilla of American politics, frightening in size, baffling in complexity, and compelling in urgency" (Fuchs, 1993). Fuchs believes that not only economics, but "all forms of analysis" have an important limitation. Fuchs states that, "It arises from the fact that policy implies choice, and choices depend on values as well as analysis." He goes on to observe that, "Conflicts over values are particularly stark in the health policy arena. By what criteria should a health care system be judged" (Fuchs, 1993, p. 4).

Three other prominent economists, Henry Aaron, Thomas Mann, and Timothy Taylor, have written recently that, "A particular gulf separates scholarly and popular discussions of many social issues." They note that, "Social scientists--especially economists--evaluate public policies and institutions by examining incentives and behavioral responses. These scholars usually take values, habits, and social norms as given-- beyond analysis and the reach of public policy" (Aaron, Mann, and Taylor 1994, p.1). One very obvious difficulty is that many analysts may try to avoid matters of taste, values, and preferences, but the public does not, and policymakers cannot.

Conflict over values pervades all components of the health care system and, there- fore, has consequences for public policy. Jeanne Liedtka maintains that not enough attention has been paid to value conflict in health care institutions, where one finds enduring subcultures, shifting balances of power, overlapping decision boundaries, and different value systems. She argues that:

> More so than in any other sector of our economy, these characteris- tics can be found in American health care, where the value systems of physicians, nurses, and administrators appear to be increasingly at odds with each other, where administrative involvement in clini- cal decision-making grows more evident daily, and where the deci- sions to be made on a routine basis evoke the most fundamental val- ues that a society holds. The results of this conflict continue to be both extraordinarily painful for caregivers and patients, and expen- sive for American society as a whole (Liedtka 1991, p. 4).

All of this suggests that the analysis and evaluation of health care policy must take into account, in some way, the fact that health care policy is not "value-free." Policies are choices. They are choices between or among competing values. These val- ues are often deeply held by individuals and groups, and conflict over values is com- mon and can be serious. This appears to be especially true of health care, which involves questions of life and death. While the purpose of public policy analysis is not to resolve, or even attempt to resolve these profound problems, it may be advanced through a recognition of the basic issues.

This raises a number of important questions. What are values? Can an American system of values toward health care be specified? Are values stable or changing? How are values linked to policymaking? Can values be modified by policy? Should they?

I. AMERICAN VALUES AND HEALTH CARE

Innumerable observers have commented on, written about, analyzed, or puzzled over American national character, or culture, and how it is unique or differs from those of other nations. Americans themselves, it is generally acknowledged, view their nation, its values, and its institutions as unique, special, different, or unprecedented. In fact, "American exceptionalism," the perception that the United States stands apart from the rest of the world, is itself viewed as a defining element of American culture. It is not surprising that a number of writers believe that Americans hold different and distinct, values about health care.

In *Medicine and Culture: Varieties of Treatment in the United States, England, West Germany, and France* (1988), Lynn Payer makes the argument that in four nations with high levels of economic and scientific development, historical ties to one another, and a common base of medical theory and information, medicine is not practiced the same way. Diagnoses and therapies often differ quite strikingly. She asks, "How can medicine, which is commonly supposed to be a science, particularly in the United States, be so different in four countries whose peoples are so similar genetically? The answer is that while medicine benefits from a certain amount of scientific input, culture intervenes at every step of the way" (p. 26). Payer persuasively argues that the delivery of health care is not simply a rational scientific enterprise, but a process unavoidably influenced by cultural values which vary from one society to another. Payer writes that, "American medicine is aggressive. From birth--which is more likely to be cesarean than anywhere in Europe--to death in hospital, from invasive examination to prophylactic surgery, American doctors want to do something, preferably as much as possible" (p. 124). Payer adds that:

> This medical aggressiveness reflects an aggressiveness of the American character that has often been attributed to the effect the vast frontier had on the people (mostly Europeans) who came to settle it. The once seemingly limitless lands gave rise to a spirit that anything was possible if only the natural environment, with its extremes of weather, poisonous flora and fauna, and the sometimes unfriendly native Americans, could be conquered. Disease also could be conquered, but only by aggressively ferreting it out diagnostically and just as aggressively treating it, preferably by taking something out rather than adding something to increase the resistance. Disease might even be prevented by cleansing the environment of hostile elements (p. 127).

Another value, according to Payer, is that, "Americans not only want to do something, they want to do it fast, and if they cannot, they often become frustrated" (p. 137). Consequently, Americans are not very good at treating chronic diseases." They place a lower value on rehabilitation, and have a bias against conditions regarded as incurable or resistant to treatment.

Third, Payer believes, "The American regards himself as naturally healthy" (p. 139). Americans, therefore, demand an explanation, a diagnosis, and a reason for the assault upon their bodies. This leads to a penchant for tests and an expectation that the problem be identified and eliminated, and the quicker the better.

Fourth, Payer maintains that Americans do not see themselves as responsible or culpable for their illnesses. The result is a tendency to look for the origins of disease in infectious agents or environmental conditions. She states that, "In America, the presence of a virus (or of bacteria) is emphasized with little play given to host resistance" (p. 143). Americans are prescribed antibiotics more than western Europeans, and in cases many European physicians consider not serious. On the positive side, Americans have made many contributions to a scientific understanding and control of infectious disease.

Fifth, Payer writes that Americans have a nearly obsessive compulsion for cleanliness. She maintains that, "The American penchant for cleanliness undoubtedly has health benefits, and there is no doubt that certain diseases are less common here than in dirtier countries. But the practices also have some negative effects on health. Besides the fact that diseases acquired early in life can actually act as a sort of natural vaccination...too much cleaning zeal can directly cause medical problems" (p. 145). She cites as examples--ear infections and vaginal ulcers resulting from excessive efforts to keep orifices clean, and hysterectomies and circumcisions performed for reasons of hygiene.

Finally, Payer argues that Americans often regard the human body as a machine (in reality or metaphorically) and thus capable of being repaired, "tuned-up," or having parts replaced. She believes that it is this aspect of our culture that leads to an exceptionally high number of bypass surgeries in the United States compared to Western Europe. Payer also believes that this "mechanistic" point of view extends even to psychiatry. The consequence is that American medicine is being drained of any appreciation or understanding of the spiritual dimensions of life and death, of health and illness. We neglect emotional needs and try to keep people alive when the situation is sometimes hopeless and act contrary to the wishes of patients and their families. Payer concludes her examination of American values and their consequences by writing that, "our medicine is not the inevitable result of medical progress but of choices--conscious or not--that arise from our own cultural biases. Perhaps, if we come to know these biases better, our choices will reflect less the memory of a frontier past and more our needs as inhabitants of a complex modern society" (p. 152).

Other studies have also attempted to identify and describe values that Americans hold, in regard to the health care system of the United States. One of these studies is by Reinhard Priester, which appeared in the spring 1992 issue of *Health Affairs*. Priester writes that six major values have shaped the health care system of the United States in the post-World War II period. According to Priester these are:

1 **Professional autonomy.** This encompasses clinical autonomy and professional regulatory autonomy.

2 **Patient autonomy.** This includes the right of a patient to make an informed decision and the right to refuse care.

3 **Consumer sovereignty.** Individuals have the right to choose their physicians and their insurance plans.

4 **Patient advocacy.** Priester maintains that, "Patient advocacy connotes a mix of values, including caring, service, benevolence, fidelity, and effacement of self-interests." It also means disregarding the problem of costs in making clinical decisions.

5 **High-quality care.** This includes care provided in facilities and institutions, and care broadly affecting quality of life.

6. **Access to care.** Priester maintains that Americans believe people should have access to care but do not agree whether this means universal access (more people) or comprehensiveness (more services).

Priester adds that:

> These six values have been shaped by the values of our broader society, among them faith in individualism, distrust of government and preference for private solutions to social problems, belief in American exceptionalism, a standard of abundance as the normal state of affairs, the power of technology, and the uniquely American frontier orientation. Although these values are not universally adhered to throughout the United States, they do form part of the ethos of many elements of our society--including the health care system (p. 87).

A small number of other studies claim that Americans hold distinctive values about health care and the health care system and assert that these values contrast with those held by Western Europeans. Rodwin (1987) maintains, as did Louis Hartz earlier (1955), that the values of classical liberalism have profoundly shaped American culture and thus the health care system of the United States. Rodwin writes that classical liberalism "has colored American perceptions of equity, of the proper role for government, and of citizenship. These perceptions represent a range of American values and popular opinions which distinguishes the United States from Western Europe and Canada" (p.121).

A study by Lockhart (1981) a decade and a half ago is one of the few empirical efforts to examine differences between Americans and Western Europeans in regard to values, health care, and policymaking. Lockhart's hypothesis was that the political structures of Western democracies are too much alike to account for differences in social policies. Drawing on an earlier study by Anthony King (1973), Lockhart hypothesized that "the ideas of political elites must be the determining factors" in explaining cross-national differences in specific social policies.

To test his hypothesis, Lockhart interviewed 15 health policy elites in each of three nations: the United States, the United Kingdom, and West Germany. The interview questions were directed at personal perceptions of how the respondent "fit into the health policy formulation process, the criteria on which a desirable national health policy should be built, the reasons why the respondent found these criteria particularly important, and the perceived consequences of various existing national policies" (p. 99).

Lockhart found that there were differences among the three groups of health policy elites. The British spoke of health care as a "field of social cooperation to which many contribute in order to improve the quality of life" (p. 101). The British further saw health policy as closely tied to other areas of social policy, such as housing and employment, and put strong emphasis on cooperation to meet human needs and improve the delivery of health care.

Lockhart identified four values held by the German policy elites. The first was "equality of access to health care, regardless of social class or geographic location." The second was "economic efficiency, which manifests itself in a preference for a decentralized and partially private system of health care provision." The third was "individual liberty in the sense of personal autonomy, which applies to health care providers and consumers." The fourth was economic security of individuals and households (p. 107).

Unlike the British, the Americans were sharply divided in their views. According to Lockhart, they fell into two groups. The majority group believed that the values "underlying economic efficiency (often initially expressed as 'economic theory' or private enterprise), and social continuity." On the other hand, "respondents in the minority group appeal to equality and economic security. They perceive that health care is a right of citizenship, and access should be based solely on medical need" (pp. 103-104). The values of American health policy elites do appear to be different from those in Great Britain and Germany. Moreover, Lockhart concluded in his study that "the substance of health policy in each nation is generally consistent with the ideas of its health policy elites" (p. 109). This suggests support for King's thesis, but Lockhart was cautious on this point. He suggested that it is possible that elites create policy consistent with their ideas, but it is also possible that elites "derive their ideas from what already exists in a society" (p. 109).

Lockhart's research was carried out 16 years ago and consisted of a very small sample. Prudence is therefore advisable in generalizing from the results, but the study is a rare example of an empirical investigation that indicates a difference between the values held by Americans and Europeans in regard to health care and health care policymaking. Lockhart's conclusions are fairly consistent with other writers who maintain that Americans value a limited role for government in providing and regulating health care, an efficient private sector, and a tolerance of difference levels or tiers of care.

II. VALUES, OPINIONS, AND POLICYMAKING

What other empirical data exist that indicate the values the American people hold about health care and health care policymaking? One possible source is opinion polls. Opinion polling has, of course, become commonplace in the United States and is carried out frequently on a truly staggering variety of subjects or topics.

Pollsters have been asking American citizens questions about health care matters at least since 1936 (Erskine, p. 128) and many public opinion organizations now conduct surveys and gather data. Some of the better known organizations include the Gallup Poll, the Roper Poll, Louis Harris and Associates, and the National Opinion Research Center at the University of Chicago. Interest groups such as the American Association of Retired Persons (AARP), the American Medical Association (AMA), and the Health Insurance Association of America (HIAA) also conduct or sponsor surveys on health care topics. Major news media such as *The New York Times, USA Today,* and the Cable News Network (CNN) also periodically sponsor polls.

A. Values and Opinions

The polling and opinion expert, Daniel Yankelovich, writes that:

> Values are notoriously difficult to define, let alone measure, and it can be confusing when measures of values are mixed interchangeably with measures of opinions, attitudes, beliefs, motivations, and other subjective states of mind and feelings. In the literature values are usually defined as the most stable and enduring of these predispositions, opinions as the most superficial and volatile, with attitudes falling somewhere between the two (pp. 28-29).

Yankelovich thus refers to values in terms similar to those used by Milton Rokeach. As noted earlier, Rokeach says that one of the fundamental characteristics of values is that they are enduring and have some measure of stability. Although Yankelovich and Rokeach maintain that one of the defining characteristics of values is that they are enduring, each writer recognizes that values can and do change. Rokeach writes that, "If values were completely stable, individual and social change would be impossible. If values were completely unstable, continuity of human personality and society would be impossible" (pp. 5-6).

Yankelovich approaches the problem from a different perspective. He believes that in relating values to public policy, the distinction among values, opinions, attitudes, and beliefs "may be more confusing than helpful" (p. 28). He goes on to state that:

> For one thing they do not always hold up under careful scrutiny.
> According to the convention, opinions are supposed to be easy
> to change, values very difficult to change. In practice,
> however, one will sometimes find rock solid opinions (on the
> death penalty, for example) that resist change and fundamental
> values (on the sacredness of human life, for example) that yield
> to change (p.28).

Yankelovich further argues that, "For most public policy purposes, it is not too important whether cultural changes involve values in the narrow sense of the word, or attitudes, opinions, and beliefs, or a blend of all. What is important is that cultural change
has taken place and thus affects public policy" (p. 28).

Finally, Yankelovich conceives of value change in a way that researchers on public
policy probably should heed. He believes that the pattern of change is "not linear but
dialectic." The most typical pattern of change starts with a swing to the opposite
extreme, which is then followed by a series of multidirectional movements as people
struggle to adapt their new values to more traditional ones and to changing circumstances" (p.28). He rejects the analogies of backlashes and pendulums. When people's
values change they do not go back to an earlier pattern. Yankelovich believes that,
"The most frequent pattern is one in which people vacillate between old and new values, trying to hold onto both until the new pattern grows so uncomfortable that they
have to choose one or the other or evolve some sort of compromise. Unfortunately,
these patterns cannot be measured along elegant, unidirectional trend lines" (pp.28-29).
It would appear, however, that Rokeach has a stricter view of values. Recall that
Rokeach argues that values are "prescriptive or proscriptive" beliefs; they are beliefs
about the correct way to behave. Moreover, they are beliefs about an "end-state of
existence." Further, values are preferences for a mode of behavior or end-state of existence over an opposite or contrary mode or end-state. Finally, Rokeach insists values
have a moral component. Values have an "ought" character that is meant to guide
behavior, not just our own behavior but that of others as well.

The vast literature on public opinion and health care offers no clear solutions to
this issue. No research has tried to distinguish among values, opinions, and attitudes
about health care. There are, however, some recurring themes that may suggest what
"deeper" values are held as opposed to more transient or "superficial" attitudes or
opinions. Two stand out above all others: (1) the appropriate role and scope of government, and (2) medical care for the poor.

1. The Role and Scope of Government

The central concept of the American constitutional system, established in the late
eighteenth century, is limited government. The powers of the national government
were especially limited and continued to be restricted well into the twentieth century.
Freedom of the individual and a limited role for government became defining characteristics of American political culture. Lawrence Jacobs has studied public opinion and
health care in the United States and Great Britain. He writes that, "Americans' understandings [sic] of the state and health care before 1800 diverged from those in Britain.
Although the public in both countries was strongly attracted to the democratic proce-

dures associated with a representative state, most Americans found government involvement in social welfare provision inconceivable" (Jacobs, 1993 p. 42).

The reasons Jacobs offers are rather complex. Briefly, he believes they stem from the American view of government as "impersonal" procedures and from the history of medicine in the United States. In the first case, Americans did not see government as having a purpose to provide medical care. In the latter case, organized medicine developed more slowly than in Britain, and therefore Americans relied on self-help and unorthodox treatments.

It is a well-known fact that in the United States government throughout the nineteenth century played a limited role in providing health care and in regulating it. Significantly, Jacobs maintains that this is what the public wanted. He writes that although some "special programs" were developed in the aftermath of the Civil War, the "absence of widespread public acceptance of state social welfare presented a stubborn barrier to generalizing these arrangements to the entire country" (Jacobs, 1993, p. 52).

Jacobs further maintains that throughout the 1920s, 1930s, and 1940s, state-sponsored medical care was much more limited in America than in Great Britain because of popular resistance. In fact, Jacobs argues that Franklin Roosevelt had a clearer understanding of the depth of popular opposition to an expanded government role in health care than Harry Truman did. Jacobs writes that, "The public's enduring uneasiness with state provisions led Roosevelt and his administration to omit health insurance from their draft of the Social Security Act; Truman's insensitivity to public understandings contributed to congressional defeat of his proposals for compulsory insurance for the entire country" (Jacobs, 1993, p. 54).

By the time of the inauguration of John Kennedy as president, public opinion polling had become commonplace in the United States. The issue of providing health care to the poor and to elderly retirees had also reemerged as a significant item on the political agenda. Jacobs writes that private polls taken for Kennedy and published data indicated broad public support for a federally-sponsored health care plan for the elderly that would be tied to the Social Security system. This support continued after Kennedy's assassination. Jacobs argues that in large measure public support for Medicare was based on favorable experience with Social Security. Although the public did not clearly understand the details of the Medicare proposal, approval of the general principles was high. Consequently, opposition from interest groups resulted in concessions to their demands but not the defeat of Medicare. The passage of Medicare in 1965 was a significant expansion of the role of national government in providing health care services, but it was relatively limited compared to the comprehensive and universal system established in Great Britain. While interest groups played a role in the details, Jacobs indicates a central reason for more modest role of government in the United States; it was what people wanted (Jacobs, 1993).

The Medicare and Medicaid programs did not, of course, create a compulsory universal national health care system comparable to those in Western Europe. A decade after their adoption, the issue of what to do about those persons who had no private insurance and were not covered by either of the two federal programs was a major item on the nation's political agenda. Rapidly rising expenditures for health care had also begun to attract the attention of policymakers. The Nixon Administration and the Congress made major efforts at developing legislative proposals aimed at solving these problems. Did this signal an increase in public support for more government activism?

Examinations by Erskine (1975), Shapiro and Young (1986), and Page and Shapiro (1992) of numerous polls indicate public support for the general principle of universal health insurance and an active role for government, but nevertheless a limited role. In their study of American public opinion and policy preferences from the 1930s to the early 1990s, Page and Shapiro write that many surveys found majority support for the concept of national health insurance (NHI). They also write:

> But this does not mean that people want the federal government
> to provide it. When NHI was contrasted with 'the present system
> of private insurance and health plans' in nine Roper surveys from
> 1973 through 1983, opinion was much more evenly split with
> support dropping to the 43%-53% range. Much the same is
> true of the seven-point scale used by SRC/CPS and Market
> Opinion Research, which compared support for a government
> insurance plan with expenses paid by individuals and through
> private insurance like Blue Cross.' When the government or taxes
> are explicitly mentioned, support is generally lower though it still
> outweighs the opposition by a bit. On a five point NORC-GSS
> scale, only 50% of respondents in 1975 put themselves on the
> side of the government in Washington helping people pay medical
> bills, in contrast to people taking care of themselves (Page
> and Shapiro, 1992, pp. 30-31).

The Shapiro and Young (1986) review of published and unpublished data arrived at essentially the same conclusion. The authors looked at polling results from the 1970s and early 1980s and found the public compassionate and altruistic toward all citizens, not just the needy, in regard to health care. The authors found support for the idea of national health insurance, "but this has not necessarily been support for governmentally provided insurance or health services." Shapiro and Young concluded that the public wants the federal government "to guide private and public efforts to provide and pay for medical care" (p. 419).

During the administrations of Ronald Reagan and George Bush, the explosive increase in expenditures for health care and the persistent problem of the uninsured dominated all other health policy issues. Public opinion polls seemed to measure considerable popular discomfort with the American system of health care and possibly a willingness to overhaul it dramatically. For instance, a 1989 study of public opinion and health care in the United States, Canada, and the United Kingdom based on a survey by Louis Harris and Associates found Americans were the most dissatisfied with their health care system. Only 10% of Americans said that their system on the whole worked well as opposed to 56% of Canadian respondents and 27% of the British interviewees. Similarly, 29% of Americans answered that the system needed to be completely rebuilt, while only 5% of Canadians and 17% of the British perceived that such dramatic change was necessary (Blendon and Taylor, 1989).

A 1990 follow-up study of ten industrialized nations by Blendon and others found dissatisfaction very high among Americans. Compared to the United States, only in Italy did a higher percentage of respondents agree with the statement that their health care system needed to be completely rebuilt (Blendon et al., 1990).

The irony, or "contradiction" in the view of some observers, was not that Americans were dissatisfied on the whole with their personal physicians or medical care. Several studies indicated that one of the major sources of discontent was the cost of medical care (Rochefort and Boyer, 1988; Gabel, Cohen, and Fink, 1989; Jajich-Toth and Roper, 1990; Blendon, 1988). The "cost issue" to Americans was not health care spending as a percentage of GDP that was receiving so much attention among policy-makers and analysts. In fact, all during the 1970s and 1980s a majority of respondents sampled by the National Opinion Research Center (NORC) consistently agreed that as a nation we were spending too little on "improving and protecting the nation's health" (Wood 1990, p. 732, emphasis added). Other studies arrived at essentially the same conclusion (Blendon, 1988). The issue to Americans was their own out-of-pocket costs, the cost of their insurance, and concern about loss of insurance or huge medical bills they may not be able to pay.

In the elections of 1992, health care received the greatest attention in decades as a public policy issue. Bill Clinton made reform of health care financing and insurance one of his major campaign themes and promised immediate action. Following his election and inauguration as president the White House, Clinton began developing a plan to reform the health care system of the United States. The president's wife, Hillary Rodham Clinton, was put in charge of the effort.

As the plan was being developed, the Clinton victory and results of opinion polls indicated to some analysts that the American people were ready to accept a more active federal role in regulating and providing health care. In 1993, Theda Skocpol of Harvard University wrote that, "the time seems ripe for national health care reform" (Skocpol, 1993, p. 531). She added that, "At last it has become politically feasible to do something through government about these problems" (p. 533). In a review of many different polls, Jacobs, Shapiro, and Shulman (1993) stated that, "The data clearly show the public's dissatisfaction with the nation's health care system and its readiness for government activism" (p. 395). The authors did note, however, that the American people were "ambivalent" about what the government's role should be (p. 395).

In a study of public opinion and health care published in *JAMA, The Journal of the American Medical Association*, Blendon, Hyams, and Benson (1993) found a "gap between expert and public views on health care reform." While experts were concerned about such issues as aggregate spending, economic growth, and budget deficits, the public was concerned about such things as waste, loss of insurance, and the prices of particular medical goods and services. The authors saw a problem for reform because of this divergence of views, but one they thought could be overcome.

The Clinton health care plan was finally submitted to Congress. The plan was lengthy and complex, and it soon stalled. In November 1994, the Democrats lost control of both houses of Congress, and the Clinton reform plan was abandoned. What happened? Had the American people changed their minds? Were the polls and experts wrong?

Clearly there is considerable room for analysis, but two papers in *Health Affairs* examine public opinion and the failure of the Clinton plan. Blendon, Brodie, and Benson (1995) examine polling data from 28 surveys gathered during 1993 and 1994. They find that between September 1993 and April 1994, support for the Clinton plan fell in virtually every sector of American society. Moreover, the authors write that while the public supported the concept of reform "Americans held overwhelmingly negative views about government." They add that:

> Similarly, while the Clinton planners were developing long lists of proposed new government health regulations, 65% of Americans told pollsters that the federal government controlled too much of their daily lives, and 69% agreed that when something is run by the government it is usually inefficient or wasteful. Eighty percent said that the value they get from taxes paid to the federal government was only fair or poor, and 60% favored a smaller government with fewer services
> (pp. 12-13).

In his review of public opinion data, Daniel Yankelovich (1995) finds similar patterns. He writes that during 1993 and 1994, there was a "disconnect" between the nation's "leadership class" and the American people. The Clinton health care plan was a product of the former. It was conceived by members of the former group and argued among its members. The American people were never included in the debate, and by "July 1994, nine months after the announcement, the public's favorable endorsement of the plan had eroded from 57% to 37%" (p. 11). Yankelovich believes the plan failed for three main reasons. First, the public feared it meant increased costs to average citizens. Second, the public feared what seemed to be major and comprehensive change. The third reason is "growing antigovernment sentiment," which Yankelovich states has intensified since 1992 (p.16).

In summary, opinion data do not resolve the issue entirely, but they suggest that in the area of health policy the American people see a role for active government, but at the same time, a restricted and limited one. They are not willing to turn over all decision-making to government or to approve a government-run health care system, such as those in many other industrial societies. The value of limited government appears to be still strong, even if its exact meaning is unclear.

2. Medical Care for the Poor

Care of the sick poor is in no sense a recent issue or concern. It is a problem that dates back many centuries. It is one that faces almost every society. How should the sick poor be cared for? Who should do it? Who should pay? These are a few of the recurring questions.

Treatment of the sick who are unable to pay for their care in some way affects our deepest values, such as charity and sacrifice. Consequently, by looking at public opinion and medical care for the poor, we may obtain some insight into the values of the American people rather than more ephemeral attitudes. Moreover, we may receive some indication of stability (or lack of stability) of these values and their ramifications for health care policymaking.

Obviously, we have no polling data for most of the history of the United States. We do know, however, that throughout much of this history care of the sick poor was the responsibility of individuals and families, charitable organizations, and to some extent, local government. Gradually, state governments began taking a more active role, and only recently did the national government become a major participant.

Looking at the last 60 years, we have a somewhat clearer picture of what people think. In 1975 Erskine reviewed polling data from 1936 to 1974 data on the issue of health insurance. She found that, "about three-quarters favored government action on the needy when it was on the pollsters' agenda from 1936 to 1944" (p. 128).

Other studies of opinion polls support the conclusion that, on the whole, the American people are concerned about the poor who need medical care, and believe that government should do something to help them. As cited above, the Shapiro and Young (1986) examination of polls taken during the 1960s, 1970s, and early 1980s concluded that the public was "motivated by compassion and altruism," especially toward the "truly needy" (pp. 418-419).

In a paper published in *The New England Journal of Medicine*, Blendon and Donelan (1990) studied "several hundred opinion surveys on health care issues that were conducted by 25 survey organizations between 1938 and 1990, using various methods and instruments." Blendon and Donelan write that:

> Americans see universal access to health care as an important
> concern, but it is not as important to them as other issues are,
> or as it is to citizens of several European nations. For many
> years, public-opinion surveys have indicated that a majority of
> Americans (75 to 82%) believe government should
> provide the resources necessary for medical care to be
> available to everyone who needs it. However...they do not
> feel as strongly about this issue as do citizens of some
> European countries (p. 209).

Blendon and Donelan further write that Americans feel conflict about "health and welfare programs that aid the poor" (p. 211). The implication is that the American people are supportive of government programs and spending that are specifically aimed at health or medical care. If these actions are perceived as welfare, support is much lower.

These kinds of findings may be reflecting, and perhaps not very clearly, the values many Americans hold about the sick, the poor, and welfare. It has been argued by some (e.g. Olasky, 1992) that in an earlier historical time, especially the eighteenth and nineteenth centuries, only the worthy poor should receive help. Furthermore, private individuals and voluntary associations were the preferred agents of assistance. The sick poor were worthy, at least until they were able to help themselves. Those poor who were capable of work were expected to do so, and moral improvement was the most important goal. Fundamentally, these were theistic values, rooted in Christianity.

In the decades following World War II, the ways in which American society comes to the aid of the sick and poor have changed dramatically. The values underlying contemporary efforts also appear to have been altered. Moral judgments of aid recipients are condemned by policy elites and intellectuals, as well as efforts to provide moral guidance. It may be, however, that many ordinary Americans retain something of the "old" value system that opinion polls do not adequately measure or describe. Thus, the American people may have a different view of compassion than those in the "leadership class."

This may also help explain what seems to be a contradiction in opinion polls. Polls on the one hand indicate popular support increasing spending on health care, and support for the concept of universal health insurance. On the other hand, polling data suggest an unwillingness to raise taxes, ration care, or establish a national health care system run by the federal government (Gabel, Cohen, and Fink, 1989; Jajich-Toth and Roper, 1990). It may be, however, that Americans want to help the sick poor, but not if this means a decline in the quality of their own care, increased taxes, or if such assistance is given to those who could help themselves. At the same time Americans are uncertain how this can be accomplished.

While the Clinton health care plan was being debated, a study led by Robert Blendon concluded that a moral commitment to the uninsured remains a core public value (Blendon et al., 1994). The chief problem seems to be a lack of consensus about who should help the poor when they need medical care and how this is to be done. Major fissures exist between policymakers and voters (Yankelovich, 1995) and between races (Blendon et al., 1995). For these reasons the issue of medical care for the poor is not likely to be resolved anytime soon.

B. Values, Politics, and Reform of the Health Care System

If the American health care system is changed in any dramatic way through the political process, it is clear that values will be central to the effort. It is unrealistic to expect that a purely "technical" or value-free solution can be found. Indeed, even to state that the system ought to be overhauled or reformed implies a value judgment. Furthermore, all sorts of questions arise. On what values should reform be based? Should reform be consistent with American values? Should these values be changed or modified? How should value conflict be resolved?

Some advocates of reform recognize that values are central to the whole undertaking. Uwe Reinhardt, an economist at Princeton University, believes that certain traditional American political values are an obstacle to reform. One of these is the separation of powers at the national level that creates political "fiefdoms." Reinhardt also states that other American values such as "vanity" and "national ego" are blocking reform. He asserts that Americans believe the system is egalitarian when it is not and that if the "best" or "perfect" legislation cannot be adopted "we won't do anything" (*Medical Economics*, 1992).

Other observers suggest that the reform movement in health care is hamstrung by confusion and conflict over values that define goods. In the fall of 1993, *Hospital Ethics*, a publication of the American Hospital Association, reviewed a number of articles that have tried to sort out the moral and ethical assumptions underlying reform proposals but found no consensus or agreement.

There have been attempts to make explicit the values that should guide reform of the delivery and financing of health care in the United States. Dougherty (1992) proposes six "key" values: three intrinsic values and three instrumental values. Essentially, the latter are the means of obtaining the former. Dougherty argues that the most important intrinsic values are: (1) respect for the dignity of persons, (2) caring in therapeutic relationships, and (3) protection of the least well-off. The instrumental values are: (1) service to the common good, (2) containment of health care costs, and (3) simplicity in the system of health care provision.

Priester (1992) has developed what he calls a "master list of potential values, which can be pared down to 11 values to guide the restructuring and reform of our health care system" (p.92). Similar to Dougherty, Priester distinguishes between what he calls "essential values" and instrumental values. Priester proposes five essential values: (1) fair access, (2) quality, (3) efficiency, (4) respect for patients, and (5) patient advocacy. His six instrumental values are: (1) personal responsibility, (2) social solidarity, (3) social advocacy, (4) provider autonomy, (5) consumer sovereignty, and (6) personal security.

In a rather complex proposal, David Hadorn (1991) of The RAND Corporation suggests that "public values" replace the present system of allocating services according to the preferences of individual patients. He proposes the development of a preference-for-outcome approach. He argues that the expected benefits of treatments and procedures can now reasonably be defined. Average population preferences should then be used to evaluate outcomes and establish priorities. Through this method the marginal and often expensive benefits that individuals receive when their preferences are supreme would no longer be paramount.

The importance of values seemed to be recognized by the Clinton Administration when it began drafting its sweeping health care proposal, although how values were to be decided upon and what role they would play was evidently less than clear (O'Connell, 1994). An Ethics Working Group of the White House Health Care Task Force was chosen and given the responsibility of writing a "preamble" to reform legislation that would "articulate the central values and principles underlying health care reform and connect those values and principles to central religious and moral traditions in the country" (Daniels, 1994, p. 425). A series of "principles and values" was eventually drawn up, but they were not ranked and they were never put to a formal vote (O'Connell, 1994). Discussions of these values and principles may be found in articles written by some of the members of the Ethics Working Group (Daniels, 1994; O'Connell, 1994; Brock and Daniels, 1994).

In 1993 the White House Domestic Policy Council released a summary or "blueprint" of the Clinton proposal, entitled *The President's Health Security Plan* (White House, 1993). One of the opening sections of the plan was called "Ethical Foundations of Health Reform." It contained 14 "values and principles" that would "anchor health reform in shared moral traditions." These values and principles were:

1. Universal access
2. Comprehensive benefits
3. Choice
4. Equality of care
5. Fair distribution of costs
6. Personal responsibility
7. Inter-generational justice
8. Wise allocation of resources
9. Effectiveness
10. Quality
11. Effective management
12. Professional integrity and responsibility
13. Fair procedures
14. Local responsibility

When the Clinton health care proposal was submitted to Congress, however, it contained no mention of these values and principles.

The Clinton plan never garnered broad bipartisan support in Congress or strong popular support. The 1994 mid-term elections ended any attempts to adopt it into law. If the plan had been based on a "shared moral tradition", what happened? Why had the president been unsuccessful in the passage of a bill by a Congress controlled in 1993 by members of his own party?

Lawrence J. O'Connell (1994), who had served on the Ethics Working Group, writes that, "While it would be uplifting to think that a shared moral vision was at the root of health care reform...there is little evidence to confirm such a claim" (p. 421). O'Connell adds that:

> Any careful reading of the American people reveals a morally conflicted society. A recent unpublished survey of basic values among varying socio-economic groups in the United States with reference to health care underscores our tattered moral fabric. The results from three broad categories tell the story: affluent, well educated; high school educated, working class; and less well educated, poor. The affluent, well educated value universal health care coverage but they do not want to pay more in taxes to provide it. The high school educated working class wants relief from the costs of health care, but feels that the health system is controlled by elitists, on the one hand, and exploited by the 'deadbeats' on Medicaid, on the other hand. The less well educated poor place high value on universal health care coverage, and they were the only ones who even included community as a value in their list of values (p. 421).

In summary, there have been some attempts among policy elites to formulate explicitly a set of values that would provide guidance and a foundation for reform of the American health care system. It appears that this enterprise has so far been a failure. Any major overhaul of the American health care system will inevitably produce conflict and compromise. These would likely be reduced if there were a consensus, or at least greater agreement, on values. Such a situation does not appear to be imminent. Furthermore, it seems that recent reform attempts have been at odds with the traditional, and still strong, values of the majority of the American people. Future reform movements will need to consider this complex matter thoughtfully.

SUMMARY

Social scientists for many years have tended to shy away from explicit discussions of values in their research. One reason is no doubt the desire to be objective and dispassionate, and to follow what are seen as the norms and standards of science. As Aaron, Mann, and Taylor (1994) put it, one consequence is that, "Traditional analyses of public policies take human motivations as given" (p. 10). They further argue that this traditional framework is incomplete. People do respond to incentives, but this does not occur in a vacuum. Our responses are profoundly shaped by our values which we begin to acquire in infancy and evolve gradually throughout our lives. Similarly, Rokeach (1973) argues that our behavior and our attitudes are the "consequents" of our values (p. 326).

The reasons for paying more attention to the relationship between values and health care policymaking seem clear enough. We now spend more money on health care than national defense. The role of government in providing, financing, and regulating health care has increased enormously in only three decades. Health care touches our deepest emotions and raises some of the thorniest moral questions. Nevertheless, a better understanding of values, health care, and policymaking must overcome a number of obstacles.

First, the meaning and measurement of values must be clarified and improved. To use the term "value" synonymously with attitudes, opinions, preferences, likes, dislikes, situations, and conditions does more than create confusion. It trivializes the meaning of values, or it says nothing at all. How are "cynicism" and "lack of self-blame" core "values" of the American people (Blendon et al. 1994)? These may be regrettable states of affairs (assuming they are true), but they are not core values. A value is a "conception of the preferable," such as charity, kindness, or humility. This does not mean that there are no undesirable values, or harmful values; it does mean, however that "value" is used sometimes as the motivation for behavior and sometimes for behavior itself.

Measuring values is another obstacle. Public opinion polls have become a prominent feature of American politics. In a democratic society public opinion is obviously important. But is a poll of that opinion a desirable and reliable guide to policymaking? Do polls measure values or something else? Do polls really predict what people want and how they will behave? ·Do those being polled have the knowledge, information, and judgment to choose between competing and highly technical policy proposals? Marc Berk (1994) has argued persuasively in *Health Affairs* that we have unrealistic expectations of polling. The public, he says, is capable of "articulating its concerns; it is less able to articulate solutions" (p. 300).

A third problem concerns the relationship between values and reform of the health care system. Has reform remained elusive due to a lack of consensus on values, value conflict, or because the American people have "wrong" values? Is it the job of researchers to describe and analyze, or to develop the "right" values? It is doubtful that anyone would argue that all values have equal merit and could provide the basis of public policy. It is difficult, if not impossible, for researchers to remain always neutral. When researchers advocate particular policies, however, they join the political fray. They may win or lose. They may see their ideas put to uses not intended or have consequences unforeseen. They should at least be aware of the stakes involved.

REFERENCES

Aaron, H. J., Mann, T. E., and Taylor, T. (1994). *Values and Public Policy.* The Brookings Institution, Washington, D.C.

American values: Are they blocking health-system reform? (1992). *Medical Economics, November* 2, 126-148 [Interview].

Blackburn, S. (1994). *The Oxford Dictionary of Philosophy*. Oxford University Press, Oxford and New York.

Blendon, R. J., Brodie, M., and Benson, J. (1995). What happened to Americans' support for the Clinton health plan? *Health Affairs*, 14: 7-23.

Blendon, R .J., Scheck, A. C., Donelan, K., Hill, C. A., Smith, M., Beatrice, D., and Altman, D. (1995). How White and African Americans view their health and social problems. *JAMA*, 273: 341-346.

Blendon, R. J., Marttila, J., Benson, J. M., Shelter, M. C., Connolly, F. J., and Kiley T. (1994). The beliefs and values shaping today's health reform debate. *Health Affairs*, 13(I): 274-2284.

Blendon, R. J., Hyams, T. S., and Benson, J. M. (1993). Bridging the gap between expert and public views on health care reform. *JAMA*, 269: 2573-2578.

Blendon, R. J., Leitman, R., Morrison, I. and Donelan, K. (1990). Satisfaction with health systems in ten nations. *Health Affairs*, 9: 185-192.

Blendon, R. J. and Donelan, K. (1990). The public and the emerging debate over national health insurance. *The New England Journal of Medicine*, 323: 208-212.

Blendon, R. J. and Taylor, H. (1989). Views on health care: Public opinion in three nations. *Health Affairs*, 8: 149-157.

Blendon, R. J. (1988). The public's view of the future of health care. *JAMA*, 259: 3587-3593.

Brock, D. W. and Daniels, N. (1994). Ethical foundations of the Clinton administration's proposed health care system. *JAMA*, 271: 1189-1196.

Daniels, N. (1994). The articulation of values and principles involved in health care reform. *The Journal of Medicine and Philosophy*, 19: 425-433.

Dougherty, C. J. (1992). Ethical values at stake in health care reform. *JAMA*, 268: 2409-2412.

Edwards, P. (1967). *The Encyclopedia of Philosophy*. The Macmillan Company & The Free Press, New York.

Erskine, H. (1975). The polls: Health insurance. *Public Opinion Quarterly*, 39: 128-143.

Fuchs, V. R. (1993). *The Future of Health Policy*. Harvard University Press, Cambridge.

Gabel, J., Cohen, H., and Fink, S. (1989). Americans' views on health care: Foolish inconsistencies? *Health Affairs*, 8: 103-118.

Hadorn, D. C. (1991). The role of public values in setting health care priorities. *Social Science and Medicine*. 7: 773-781.

Hartz, L. (1955). *The Liberal Tradition in America*. Harcourt Brace, New York.

Jacobs, L. R. (1993). *The Health of Nations: Public Opinion and the Making of American and British Health Policy*. Cornell University Press, Ithaca.

Jacobs, L. R., Shapiro, R. Y., and Shulman, E. C. (1993). Poll trends: Medical care in the United States. *Public Opinion Quarterly*, 57: 394-427.

Jajich-Toth, C. and Roper, B. W. (1990). Americans' views on health: A study in contradictions. *Health Affairs*, 9: 149-157.

King, A. (1973). Ideas, institutions, and the policies of governments: A comparative analysis. *British Journal of Political Science*, 2: 291-313.

Liedtka, J. M. (1991). When values collide: Value conflict in American health care. *Business & Professional Ethics Journal*, 10: 3-28.

Lockhart, C. (1981). Values and policy conceptions of health policy elites in the United States, the United Kingdom, and The Federal Republic of Germany. *Journal of Health Politics, Policy and Law*, 6: 98-119.

Morone, J.A. (1990). American political culture and the search for lessons from abroad. *Journal of Health Politics, Policy and Law*, 15: 129-143.

O'Connell, L. J. (1994). Ethicists and health care reform: An indecent proposal? *The Journal of Medicine and Philosophy*, 19: 425-433.

Olasky, M.. (1992). *The Tragedy of American Compassion*. Regnery, Washington, D.C.

Page, B. I. and Shapiro, R. Y. (1992). *The Rational Public: Fifty Years of Trends in England, West Germany, and France*. Henry Holt, New York.

Payer, L. (1988). *Medicine & Culture: Varieties of Treatment in the United States, England, West Germany, and France.* Henry Holt, New York.

Priester, R. (1992). A values framework for health system reform. *Health Affairs, 11:* 84-107.

Rochefort, D. A. and Boyer, C. A. (1988). Use of public opinion data in public administration: Health care polls. *Public Administration Review, 48:* 649-660.

Rodwin, V. G. (1987). American exceptionalism in the health sector: The advantages of "backwardness" in learning from abroad. *Medical Care Review, 44:* 119-154.

Rokeach, M. (1973). *The Nature of Human Values.* The Free Press, New York.

Searching for values that define goods in health care. (1993). *Hospital Ethics, 9:* 1-5.

Shapiro, R. Y. and Young, J. T. (1986). The polls: Medical care in the United States. *Public Opinion Quarterly, 50:* 418-428.

Skocpol, T. (1993). Is the time finally ripe? Health insurance reforms in the 1990s. *Journal of Health Politics, Policy and Law, 18:* 531-549.

White House Domestic Policy Council. (1993). *The President's Health Security Plan.* Times Books, New York.

Wood, F. W. (1990). *An American Profile-Opinions and Behavior, 1972-1989.* Gale Research Inc., Detroit.

Yankelovich, D. (1995). The debate that wasn't: The public and the Clinton plan. *Health Affairs, 14:* 7-23.

Yankelovich, D. (1994). How changes in the economy are reshaping American Values. In *Values and Public Policy,* (H. J. Aaron, E. E. Mann, and J. Taylor, eds.). The Brookings Institution, Washington, D.C.

65.

HEALTH CARE IN THE NEW MILLENNIUM: IMPLICATIONS FOR EXECUTIVES AND MANAGERS[1]

Anne Osborne Kilpatrick, *Medical University of South Carolina, Charleston, SC*

Patricia W. Holsclaw, *Medical University of South Carolina, Charleston, SC*

Our nation's health care system has experienced tremendous upheavals since the turn of the previous century. Provision of care (including availability), payment mechanisms, education and training, and methods of delivery (including structure), have all been influenced by changes in funding and methods of leadership and management at the national, state, and local levels. Additionally, the public/private/non-profit debates have enveloped hospitals and health care provision for the last two decades. Efforts to make the provision of health care more "businesslike", efficient, cost-effective, and hence competitive, have resulted in a proliferation of hospitals, skyrocketing increases in technology and its subsequent costs, and the evolution of "managed care." One consequence of this activity is the growing number of uninsured and medically indigent patients. The largest group of whom are children. Because of changes in demographics, the growth of the aging population and resultant expansion of chronic illnesses, as well as growing disparity between the wealthy and the poor, health care and its administration are among the most turbulent occupations in today's workplace. Challenges for educators and practitioners will include understanding these changes and providing educational and skills training programs to address the ever evolving and complex health care system.

This chapter presents an overview of the characteristics of our health care environment, the emerging issues affecting delivery systems, characteristics of the evolving health care system, competing tensions affecting administrators and educators, and competencies needed by and challenges facing policy leaders and implementers for the future.

The delivery of health care during the past century has fundamentally changed and evolved as a result of responding to various economic, domestic and international crises — resulting primarily from wars and conflicts, technological advancements, and financial constraints. Physicians and other health professionals, while conscientiously and sincerely attempting to treat and alleviate illness and suffering, have labored without the benefit of an organized and efficient universal health care system. Competing tensions within and throughout the various levels of health care delivery, changing demographics, economic stresses, and the aging of the American population have strained the ability of the system to deliver meaningful affordable results and universal access in spite of progressive and monumental research and development. Indeed, as a consequence of the ongoing shrinking of the health care dollar, the number of uninsured, underserved, and medically indigent patients is growing.

Systematic reinvention and health care reform leading to universal national health care delivery was investigated by the Clinton Administration during the first half of their administration, but was subsequently rejected by Congress. However, dynamic changes have occurred in spite of that rejection. These changes are reflected in the emergence of mega-health care systems crossing traditional geographic boundaries; mergers, acquisitions and affiliations; financial and organizational threats to the Medicare and Medicaid programs; rapid and steady growth in managed care penetration, and various new designs for health education. All these confirm the necessity for new vision, new models for health and medical education and practice, and systems integration. The delivery of health care is people oriented— i.e., human resources drive the success or failure of care. Health professionals practicing in the 21st century must be more health- rather than illness-oriented. The patient, their families, environmental stresses, and resource constraints will affect decisions and plans for prevention, treatment, and follow up care.

Implications for administrators and policy makers include, of necessity, careful considerations regarding systematic standards of care; control over costs, prices and income; up-to-date and sophisticated integration of information systems; development and implementation of health care technology and treatment modalities; continuous quality improvement; careful consideration of the patient and their community; and excellence in training and development of the professional work force.

I. HEALTH CARE TRENDS

Understanding and responding to the various tensions, conflicts, and opportunities emerging during this time of transition necessitates a clear vision of the trends which drive change. Skyrocketing increases in the costs of the health care system have resulted in public demands to become 'leaner and meaner', more businesslike, and thereby possibly more successful in providing health care to more people. These forces have influenced health care delivery for the past several decades. In 1994, the National Association of Academic Medical Centers identified factors affecting the environment of the new health care workforce (Larson, Osterweis, and Rubin, Eds., 1994).

A. Efficiency and Effectiveness Through Coordinated Care

Emergence of sophisticated high technology information systems has led to more efficient and effective delivery through coordinated care. Coordination of care, which involves integration of services over a continuum of time and information, will increase the capacity of the health care delivery system to expand from focusing solely on the individual to include community and population based efforts (Ibid, 1994).

B. Diversity and Aging in the Population

Increasing recognition of the diversity in our population and the "graying" of America are leading to greater understanding of the cultural forces which move people to seek health care, and a shift from acute to chronic illness as the driving characteristics in health care needs. Health professionals will increasingly include a larger proportion of minority applicants in the pool of the medical workforce. Health profession educators and health professionals in general will need to be sensitive to this growing segment of society. Emergence of long term and skilled nursing facilities as a response to chronic and long term care needs will continue to pressure health care delivery leading to a shift from cure to care as population needs change. A growing burden on young persons to provide and finance these needs may profoundly affect the balance of care and availability to care (The Pew Health Professions Commission, 1991).

C. Tensions in the Expansion of Science and Technology

In addition to the impressive benefits which the amazing growth of diagnostic and therapeutic and information technologies have brought to the American forefront, Americans are increasingly calling for balancing these dimensions with quality of life issues, consumer choice, risk-benefit decisions, and access to care. The need for personalization of care and integration of the thoughtful use of technology coupled with the caring quality of the human element, will continue to affect the transitions evident in the training and development of health professionals —both administrative and clinical (Ibid, 1991). Additionally, health care practitioners of the future must learn to utilize these advancements, which leads to the need for continuous professional growth and development (Osterweis, Marian, et al., 1996).

D. Consumer Empowerment

Traditional roles of providers and consumers of health care have evolved in the past few decades as well resulting in the empowerment of the consumer in assuming more responsibility and control over his/her health. Expectations on both sides have increased, necessitating a reassessment of options, obligations, and interdependence on outcomes of care. Confusing the issue is the continuing imbalance of provider access, cost coverage, and complexity of service mix (Clay, In process). Consumer knowledge and expectations are leading to increased demands for accountability and quality. Coupled with the shift from illness to wellness as the motivating factor for health care service, previous perceptions and decisions surrounding delivery are evaporating to be replaced by a more informed and involved consumer population.

E. Values that Shape Health Care

A growing dissatisfaction in the delivery of health care in America has produced growing tension between providers, payers, and consumers of medical services. We are one of only two industrialized countries in the world that does not guarantee financial access to health care for all its citizens. The resulting social and ethical inequities challenge providers of health care — clinical as well as management — to seek continuous improvement. The numbers of those who are without health insurance or who are underinsured continues to grow as downsizing, rightsizing and cost containment drive the economic engine of our society. Health care and medical services have traditionally been controlled and delivered at the discretion of clinical providers. The emergence of managed care and capitation as the basis for coverage is causing a fundamental rethinking of the importance of respecting the core rights of the individual while maintaining a perspective for the common good. A disproportionately low number of physicians deciding to serve rural and indigent populations remains another difficulty to be balanced between costs, discretion, and access to services. Considerations of quality of life, cost, and resource constriction must be examined and included in managerial decisions regarding education and practice.

II. TRENDS AMONG HEALTH CARE DELIVERY SYSTEMS

The 1991 Pew Commission Report identified eight trends which were predicted to shape the delivery of health care. Some of these are described in this section, along with some which have emerged in the five years since publication of that report.

A. Increased Organizational Complexity and Diversity

The provision of health care has been traditionally directed by independent practice physicians serving individual patients in hospitals or on an outpatient basis, paid by fee-for-service. Increasingly, health care organizations will change from hospitals to comprehensive systems of care, associations of physician groups, and capitated groups of patients.

B. The Spread of the Corporate Paradigm in Health Care

Another trend is the tendency to merge health care organizations into collaborative networks, or to be acquired by larger corporations, a characteristic reflected in portions of the commercial sector. In the past two years, hundreds of networks, affiliations and mergers have transformed the health care landscape into one unrecognizable a decade ago.

C. Shift from Professional Values to Managerial Values

Physicians were traditionally the "captains of the health care team." (Fuchs, 1974). Major focuses today in the control of health care delivery today are toward economy, cost-effectiveness, and practices. Hence, effective health care management may supersede the leadership of decision-making by physicians.

D. Shift from Inpatient to Outpatient Care

Increasing emphasis on prevention and controlling costs of care through implementation of rigorous practice guidelines are reducing lengths of stay, expanding use of alternative treatment modalities, and enlarging the types of care provided.

E. Emphasis on Primary Care

Long advocated by health planners, education and prevention, as well as regular checkups, have been proven to reduce costs and increase efficacy. Early diagnosis and treatment of illness also create more positive outcomes.

F. The Changing Nature of Long-Term Care

A growing industry in our country is the development of affordable and high quality continuing care to the elderly. As our population's longevity grows as a percent of the total population, not only will demand increase, but insistence upon alternatives and emphasis on quality will also affect this sector of the health care system.

G. Growing Acceptance of Mental Health Services

The increasing stresses of today's society, our focus on comprehensive health, the connection between mental and physical health, as well as tensions resulting from economic and social stressors in our society, have highlighted the need for increasing access to and provision of mental health services.

H. Health Care Personnel

According to the Department of Labor, the health care industry is the largest employer and continues to grow in numbers and types of personnel (Pew, 1991). However, geographic distributions and levels of specialization have not necessarily reflected a fit with community needs; nor have costs of care or access been positively affected by the doubling of physicians between 1960 and 1990 (Ibid). Changes in education and training of health support personnel in the 1990s and the movement to primary/outpatient care will continue to influence the demand for nurses, physician extenders, multi-skilled health providers, and primary care physicians.

I. Continued Mergers, Acquisitions, Affiliations and HMO Penetration

As employers continue to demand economical health care coverage for their employees, and as pressure to reduce costs continues, and particularly as long as the opportunities to make financial gains in health care exist, the result will be these new and larger organizational configurations and the growing penetration of HMOs and other managed care structures. According to the 1995 Pew Commission Report, "within another decade 80-90% of the insured population of the US will receive its care through one of these [integrated care that combine primary, specialty and hospital services] systems," (p.v).

III. COMPETING TENSIONS IN HEALTH CARE

Because of the trends in our economy and the turbulence in the way we deliver health care, there are a number of competing tensions which affect delivery, and hence education of health professionals.

A. Cost Containment vs. Quality

For the past two decades, health care costs have increased exponentially. Efforts to contain costs have resulted in DRGs (diagnostic related groups) and recently managed care and capitation. However, many fear that the push to be cost-effective will harm quality, and that insurance companies will become decision-makers on medical issues. However, the process initiatives created to address quality improvements in health care organizations may also result in containing costs. Additionally, the development of "best practices" and universally established standards of care may be mechanisms to guide health care practitioners in treatment modalities.

B. Competition vs. Regulation

One of the theories of the 1980s was that competition was the way to reduce health care costs. If we only had competition in hospitals and among providers, costs would go down. It was proven to be false, and costs continued to climb. As a result, many communities have too many hospital beds and low occupancy rates, too many of certain specialties, and not enough primary care providers. One result has been the proliferation of networks and affiliations, described previously. Meanwhile, however, these failed attempts to reduce health care costs have also resulted in a negative impact on public hospitals and thus the provision of indigent care (Roberts, 1998). Community health planning, which exists in few communities today, was an attempt in the 1970s and 1980s to recommend, but not necessarily regulate, facilities and new technologies for those communities. The only real regulation left is for DRGs, payments for certain diagnoses at standard rates of pay and days of stay.

C. Competition and Collaboration

While competition was rewarded in the 1980s and early 1990s, collaboration among competitors has emerged as we enter the new millennium. Affiliations, lease agreements, and networks are vehicles that health care organizations are operating to survive the turbulent health care environment. The tremendous growth of investor-owned corporations and their acquisitions of public and community hospitals in the 1990s — e.g., Columbia-HCA and Humana — reflect the tension resulting from both these values.

D. Restrictions on Access vs. Increased Access

Capitation —complete primary health care coverage of individuals for a predetermined set fee and time period — and managed care are vehicles which are designed to control costs by restricting access to higher cost treatment modalities through selecting gatekeepers: primary care physicians who are responsible for the overall care of families enrolled in their employer's plan.

However, one goal of the Clinton Health Care Plan was universal access, an issue which has challenged the American population throughout the entire evolution of modern health care (White House Domestic Policy Council, 1993). With the lack of passage of a national plan, this problem has not been addressed with a national or thus consistent perspective. While some states have developed programs to serve uninsured and underinsured persons in addition to existing federally subsidized Medicaid programs, the number of uninsured and underinsured persons in the United States continues to grow. Reports in the early and mid-1990s indicated that most of the uninsured are poor or near poor, and many are children (Clay, In progress). While minorities have traditionally experienced less access to care (Ibid.), immigrants — legal and illegal — may face a total lack of access to services if state legislation and national welfare reform are implemented in their present forms. Proposition 187, which passed by a large margin in California in 1995, proposed that children of illegal aliens would not be eligible for public services. National welfare reform, signed into law by President Clinton in 1996, has only begun to be implemented by social and health organizations, and thus the effects are not yet known.

IV. QUALITY ASSURANCE VS. TOTAL QUALITY MANAGEMENT AND CONTINUOUS QUALITY IMPROVEMENT

The Joint Commission for Accreditation of Health Care Organizations has begun enforcing guidelines requiring continuous quality and process improvements (CQI) be established and implemented in health care organizations. Full implementation began in 1996, although hospitals were given a number of years to prepare. The use of strategic planning, CQI teams, the focus on quality rather than blame, and establishment of benchmarks to evaluate effectiveness will continue to be an important component of accreditation.

A. Laissez-Faire to Growing Accountability

While health care organizations have always had some degree of accountability for service provision and management, until the establishment of Medicare DRGs, cost-based reimbursement from insurance companies and individuals was the norm for most medical services. With the advent of DRGs and the growth in managed care and capitation, health care providers are held increasingly accountable to regulators and payers for services provided and charged. Increasingly, outcomes assessment is considered an important part of health implementation (Barr, In progress).

B. Specialization vs. Generalization

One of the most challenging tensions in health care is that between specialization and generalization. Two different groups are affected by these tensions. Among physicians, there has been a growing trend to specialize, reinforced by the tremendous costs of medical education and the high income potential of many specialties and subspecialties. Technology has also contributed to specialization. However, under managed care, future demand is for primary care physicians, and many specialists may have to retrain in order to be employed.

In the allied health field, many activities previously performed by nurses have evolved into allied health professions with their own certification and licensure processes, including physical and occupational therapists, phlebotomist, respiratory therapists, etc. At the same time, an effort to address cost constraints and increase human resources has resulted in a trend toward "patient-focused care", using "multi-skilled" health providers. These persons are trained for a relatively brief period of time, learning skills for bedside patient care, and frequently for a specific type of unit. Although problems are emerging, many organizations are experimenting with these providers.

C. Centralization to Decentralization

The expansion of the corporate movement in health care has generated tensions which reinforce "economies of scale" through centralization of certain processes, including human resources policy development and benefits, while decentralizing other services such as compensation rates. Some of the new affiliations have afforded resources to the member organizations which allow for improved services by smaller members.

D. Education and Training

Lifelong learning will be necessary to function successfully in the new health care environment. However, continuous training will also be of increasing importance, in order to maintain a universally adopted organizational focus and commitment from employees, as well as an excellent workforce.

E. Tactical (short term) Focus and Strategic (long term) Focus

The tendency of the 1980s was to emphasize short time spans, with rapid decisions and often long-term consequences. For example, during that period many reductions in force resulted in eliminating the employees who were essential to the accomplishment of the organization's mission. Although decision and goal projections will probably never return to the "three or five year plan" of the past, the importance of a well planned strategic mission, vision, values, and objectives philosophy is increasingly understood to be necessary for success. Flexibility within a stable and universally accepted organizational framework strengthens and cements a successful paradigm. Increasingly, particularly with the Joint Commission's focus on organizational mission and goals, a longer term focus and strategy are being emphasized.

F. Growth Management vs. Rightsizing, Downsizing, etc.

The emphasis on managing growth will continue as a priority for health care organizations. However, with strategic planning based on an organizational mission as a focus, strategic planning and program development should result in more realistic resource allocations. "Humanizing the downsizing process" has evolved into what could be called "proactive growth management for the future."

G. Networks vs. Vertical Integration/Solo, etc.

The establishment of new types of relationships among health care providers is a major change and one which requires new skills. In the past, solo practices and perhaps vertically integrated health care organizations could compete for patients and patient groups. However, networks among competing hospitals afford the opportunity to collaborate, to share limited resources, and thereby to increase the output for all members. These relationships result in new "lenses" and associations for the members.

H. Hierarchies vs. Webs, and Dependence to Interdependence

Traditional organization charts are based on hierarchies of power and authority associated with roles. One possible change is to create "webs" where relationships rather than roles dictate structure (Helgeson, 1995). Teams are a primary future method for accomplishing many major goals in health care. Networks also afford the opportunity for increasing interdependence among members.

V. LEADERSHIP CHALLENGES/AND RECOMMENDATIONS

Health care leaders of the new millennium will face many changes and challenges: the growing number of elderly, "very old" persons, the increasing gap between "haves and have nots," tensions among diverse groups in our population, the influx of persons from other nations, and continuing exponential changes in technology. Accompanying these changes are resource debates and conflicts over how to provide care, who should provide that care, and even more fundamentally, the question "Is access to health care a right or a privilege?" In order to manage these changes and the people affected by them, increased skills and competencies will be needed. Recommendations from the 1993 Report of the Pew Health Commission serve as a framework to describe and discuss some of these competencies (Pew, 1993).

A. Build [one's profession] from a Foundation of Values

Schools of public policy and health administration traditionally are very values-explicit: a focus on public service, acceptance of responsibilities resulting from that commission, and a commitment to the provision of services based on quality, efficiency, and effectiveness. These values should be part of the socialization process of any educational curriculum, one which should also provide individuals with opportunities to test their values and beliefs.

B. Concentrate on Core Educational Activities

A standardized curriculum which provides tools for administrators in human resources management, finance, methodologies, administration, and management, as well as leadership, would be of benefit to leaders.

C. Redefine Political and Economic Relationships

Health care leaders need competency in negotiating, as they must work with divergent groups for the good of the entire community.

D. Focus on the Health Needs of the Community, Including an Expanding Community Leadership Role

As a health care leader, a major activity focus should center around improvement of the health status of the entire community, not just current clients or patients. The healthy communities movement, sponsored by the Healthcare Forum, has provided models and a vehicle to share successful ways to improve contributors to health status, including safety, housing, crime, education and access.

Strengthen Leadership Tools for Change, including[2]:
* Leading in a racially and culturally diverse society;
* Emphasize and practice life-long learning;
* Practice ethical and moral decision-making (i.e., continuously question and explore potential consequences of decisions made);
* Develop personal leadership and supervisory skills;
* Financial management;
* Professional responsibility/clear code of ethics;
* Negotiating skills (win-win rather than win-lose);
* Dispute resolution;
* Staying technologically current;
* Sensitivity to community and change;
* Learn and maintain strategic planning and reinvention/re-engineering competencies.

SUMMARY

These are exciting times. Health care leaders will face the need to do more with less but will have many tools to assist them. Educational institutions and professional associations will serve as resources, repositories of instruction, socialization, research and training, and networks for affiliating and sharing. The "orientation" of the US health care system will move more toward an emphasis on prevention, education, and management, and less on expensive treatment modalities. Regulation of costs and charges will increase as there is increased performance accountability and capitation of populations (Pew, 1995). Challenges to administrators and policymakers will be to maintain clear values, integrity and focus, as well as to accept a leadership responsibility for improving community health status. This means developing a broader definition of health, which includes supporting universal access to the health care system, and building healthy communities.

ENDNOTES

1. Originally published in Public Administration Review, Winter 1997. Reprinted with permission of publisher.

2. Based on, but not limited to, recommendations from Pew Commission's 1991 Report, Healthy America: Practitioners for 2005.

REFERENCES

Allison, F., Jr. (1993). Public Hospitals - Past, Present and Future. *Perspectives in Biology and Medicine,* 36(4): 596-610.

Baker, D. W., Stevens, C. D., and Brook, R. H. (1991). Patients Who Leave a Public Hospital Emergency Department Without Being Seen By a Physician. Causes and Consequences. *JAMA,* 266(8), 1123-5.

Barnard, C. (1966). *The Functions of the Executive.* Harvard University Press. Cambridge, MA.

Coile, R. C. (1990). *The New Medicine: Reshaping Medical Practice and Health Care Management.* Aspen Publishers, Rockville, MD.

Duncan, W. J., Ginter, P. M., and Swayne, L. E. (1995). *Strategic Management of Health Care Organizations.* Second Edition. Blackwell Business: Cambridge.

Evans, R. G. (1995). The Healthy Populations or Healthy Institutions: The Dilemma of Health Care Management. *The Journal of Health Administration Education.* 13(3): 453-472.

Fuchs, V. R. (1974). *Who Shall Live?* Basic Books, New York.

Greenspan, B., and Dubey, D. (1993). Patients and Communities. *Health Management Quarterly.* Third quarter: 24-28.

Helgeson, S. (1995). *The Web of Inclusion: A New Architecture for Building Great Organizations.* Currency/Doubleday, New York.

Johnson, R. B. (1993). Health Care Reform: What It Might Mean To Urban Public Hospitals. *Journal of Health Care for the Poor and Underserved.* 4(3): 172-6.

Kilpatrick, A. O., and Holsclaw, P. W. (1996). Health Care In the New Millennium: Implications for Executives and Managers. *Public Administration Quarterly,* 20(3): 365-380.

Kilpatrick, A. O. and Beasley, L. W. (1995). Urban Public Hospitals: Evolution, Challenges, and Opportunities in an Era of Health Reform. *Journal ofHealth and Human Services Administration,* 18(2): 143-162.

Kilpatrick, A. O. (1993). *The Future of the Department of Veterans Affairs Health Care System and Public Hospitals Quovadis?* Paper presented at the Annual Meeting of the American Public Health Association, San Francisco, October 24-28, 1993.

Kilpatrick, A. O., Mirvis, D. M.and Magnetti, S. M. (1992). Anticipating Change: Effects of Uncertainty on VA Leadership. *Journal of Health and Human Resource Administration* 14(3): 327-339.

Larson, P. F., Osterweis, M. and Rubin, E. R., Eds. (1994). *Health Workforce Issues for the 21st Century.* Association of Academic Health Centers, Washington, DC.

Osterweis, M., McLaughlin, C. J., Manasse, Jr., H. R., and C. L. Hopper. (1996). *The U.S. Health Workforce: Power, Politics, and Policy.* Association of Academic Health Centers: Washington, DC.

The Pew Health Professions Commission. (1995). *Critical Challenges: Revitalizing the Health Professions for the Twenty-First Century.* The Pew Health Professions Commission: Durham, NC.

The Pew Health Professions Commission. (1991). *Healthy America: Practitioners for 2005. An Agenda for Action for U.S. Professional Schools.* The Pew Health Professions Commission, Durham, NC.

Reddy, A. C., and Campbell, D. P. (1993). Positioning hospitals: A model for regional hospitals. *Journal of Health Care Marketing. Winter:* 40-44.

Rohrer, J. E. (1987). The Political Development of The Hill-Burton Program: A Case Study in Distributive Policy. *Journal of Health Politics, Policy and Law.* 12(1): 137-175.

Salit, S. A., and Marcos L.R. (1991). Have General Hospitals Become Chronic Care Institutions for the Mentally Ill? *American Journal of Psychiatry,* 148(7): 892-7.

Shea, D. G., and Mucha, L. (1995). Employment Trends And The Traditional Baccalaureate Health Administration Student. *The Journal of Health Administration Education.* 13(3): 401-419.

Shortell, S. M., and Reinhardt, U.E., Eds. (1992). *Improving Health Policy and Management: Nine Critical Research Issues for the 1990's.* Health Administration Press, Ann Arbor, MI.

The White House Domestic Policy Council. (1993). *The President's Health Security Plan: The Clinton Blueprint.* Times Books, New York.

Wright, R. A. (1993). Community-Oriented Primary Care. The Cornerstone Of Health Care Reform. *JAMA,* 269(19): 2544-7.

GLOSSARY

Andrea W. White, *Medical University of South Carolina, Charleston, SC*

ABBREVIATIONS, ACRONYMS AND TERMS COMMONLY ASSOCIATED WITH HEALTHCARE DELIVERY

ACP	American College of Physicians
ACS	American College of Surgeons
ADLs	Activities of Daily Living (see meaning)
AFDC	Aid to Families with Dependent Children (see meaning)
AHA	American Hospital Association
ALOS	Average length of stay
AMA	American Medical Association

Activities of Daily Living: Activities performed by an individual in the course of daily living such as bathing, brushing teeth, dressing, cooking, and walking.

Aid to Families with Children: Federal government program which provides cash payments, or welfare, to qualified low-income families; in most instances AFDC families are automatically eligible for Medicaid.

Ambulatory Care: Care provided to the noninstitutionalized patient; can include care provided in physicians' offices, emergency rooms, clinics, neighborhood health centers, school health clinics, etc.

Ancillary Services: Patient care services such as clinical laboratory, radiology, or anesthesiology.

Block Grants: A type of federal formula grant which permits the federal government to distribute money to states according to a formula established by law; the block grant can be used for broadly stated purposes. Many block grants are distributed for health purposes.

Blue Cross/Blue Shield: Nonprofit community-based health care plans that insure against hospital and medical costs.

CDC	Center for Disease Control
CHAMPUS	Civilian Health and Medical Program of the Uniformed Services (see meaning)
CHINS	Community Health Information Networks (see meaning)
CON	Certificate of Need (see meaning)
CPR	Computer-Based Patient Record (see meaning)
CQI	Continuous Quality Improvement (see meaning)

Capitation: A reimbursement system commonly used in managed care; a pre-arranged dollar amount paid to a provider, usually on a monthly basis, to cover the costs of any health care needed by one enrolled individual. The amount is paid whether or not the patient is seen during the month. The provider is responsible for delivering or arranging for delivery all services required by the enrollee as specified by the negotiated contract.

Case Management: Use of experienced health professionals, often nurses, social workers, or physicians who work with patients, providers, and insurers to coordinate all of a patient's appropriate health services to achieve the optimum patient outcome in a cost-effective manner.

Case Mix: A measurement of the relative frequency and intensity of a hospital's admissions and services. Can be based on patient diagnoses, severities of illness, and utilization of service.

Categorical Grants: A type of federal formula grant provided to distribute money to states; money may not be used for general purposes by the state but is earmarked for and must be used for a particular type of activity, such as cancer control.

Certificate of Need: A regulatory, cost-containment approach which requires hospitals or other health care providers seeking to substantially expand their facilities or scope of services to obtain prior approval from a government-endorsed entity. Its intent is to provide a systematic mechanism for assessing whether requests meet community needs and objectives.

Civilian Health and Medical Program of the Uniformed Services: An extensive health insurance plan which is a special subsystem of military medicine that provides medical coverage for health services for dependents of active military personnel. Allows dependents to purchase health services from private practitioners and nonmilitary health facilities.

Clinical Practice Guidelines: Systematically developed recommendations about appropriate healthcare interventions for specific clinical situations to aid physicians and patients in clinical decision making.

Coinsurance: A type of cost-sharing arrangement in which the insured patient pays a percentage of the charges for services rendered. An example is 20% of a $60.00 office visit. Co-insurance generally applies after patient has first met the deductible.

Community Health Information Networks: "Regional electronic networks that link all health care players in the area, including hospitals, doctor's offices, outpatient clinics, home health agencies, insurers, and employers " (Appleby, 1995).

Computer-based Patient Record: "An electronic patient record that resides in a system specifically designed to support users by providing accessibility to complete and accurate data, alerts, reminders, clinical decision support systems, links to medical knowledge, and other aids" (IOM, 1991).

Continuous Quality Improvement: A philosophy of quality management which builds on traditional quality assurance techniques, but which focuses on processes and meeting expectations of both internal and external customers. Presumes that all processes can be improved.

Copayment: A type of cost-sharing arrangement in which the insured patient pays a flat amount for a specified service at the time the service is rendered. An example is $10.00 per office visit. Also known as copay.

Critical Pathways: The optimal sequence and timing for intervention by health care practitioners for a particular diagnosis or process.

DHHS	Department of Health and Human Services
DRGs	Diagnosis Related Groups (see meaning)

Deductible: The amount of money the insured patient must first pay out-of-pocket each year before the insurance plan begins to make payments for covered benefits.

Diagnosis Related Groups: A classification system for inpatient hospital services used as a prospective reimbursement mechanism to hospitals for covered services. The classification is based on expected uses of hospital resources. It is determined by principal and secondary diagnoses, surgical procedures, age, sex, and presence of complications. There are currently 495 DRGs, but the number is continually revised.

EDI	Electronic Data Interchange (see meaning)
EPO	Exclusive Provider Organization (see meaning)

Electronic Data Interchange: A computer to computer exchange of information from one organization to another.

Encounter: A face-to-face contact between a patient and a provider in ambulatory care.

Episode of Care: One or more medical services received by an individual during a period of relative continuous care in relation to a particular illness.

Exclusive Provider Organization: A type of managed care organization in which patient must receive care from participating providers to be covered; more restrictive than a PPO, thus reducing consumer choice.

FDA	Food and Drug Administration
FFS	Fee-for-Service (see meaning)
FI	Fiscal Intermediary (see meaning)

Fee-for-service: The traditional reimbursement system in which a physician receives payment for service rendered.

Fiscal Intermediary: Fiscal agent such as Blue Cross or other commercial insurance companies contracted by Medicare that reviews, processes, and pays claims of Medicare patients.

Gatekeeper: A primary care physician for a managed care organization who serves as the patient's first contact for either treatment or referral.

Group Model HMO: A type of HMO which contracts with a group of physicians (partnership, association, or professional corporation) to provide or arrange for health services for an enrolled population. Compensation is based on negotiated rate.

HCFA	Health Care Financing Administration (see meaning)
HEDIS	Health Plan Employer Data and Information Set (see meaning)
HIS	Health Information Systems (see meaning)
HMO	Health Maintenance Organization (see meaning)

Health Care Financing Administration: The federal agency which administers Medicare and oversees states' administration of Medicaid.

Health Information System: A broad term used to refer to a health care organization's financial/administrative information system and its clinical information system.

Health Maintenance Organization: An entity that provides or arranges for enrolled members specified health services for a fixed, prepaid premium. There are four basic types of HMOs: staff model, group model, IPA, or PPO (see individual meanings).

Health Plan Employer Data and Information Set: A core set of performance measures to enable employers and purchasers to assess the value of a managed care organization's health plan. Measures and assesses quality of care, patient access and satisfaction, membership stability, utilization of resources, and financial information.

Hill-Burton Act: Program enacted in 1946 which provided federal grants for construction and renovation of community hospitals.

Home Health Agencies: A facility or program licensed by the state to provide health services within the home.

Hospice Care: A facility or program licensed by the state to provide palliative and supporting care for terminally ill patients and their families.

Hospital Alliance: A formal affiliation of two or more hospitals or hospital systems which allows them to retain their autonomy, but improves their economic advantage, such as permitting group purchasing or shared product development.

ICD-9-CM: International Classification of Diseases, 9th Revision, Clinical Modification. A universal classification system for grouping illnesses. Also used for hospital disease indexing.

ICF	Intermediate Care Facilities (see meaning)
IOM	Institute of Medicine
IPA	Independent Practice Association (see meaning)
IS	Information Systems

Independent Practice Association: A type of HMO in which the plan contracts with physicians to provide health care services for its enrolled population for a negotiated fee. The fee may be fee-for-service, a capitated fee, or a discounted fee schedule. Physicians may also continue providing services for patients outside the HMO.

Indicators: Structure, process, and outcome criteria which permit assessment of the quality of health care.

Inpatient: A patient who has been admitted into a hospital and has been receiving services for at least 24 hours.

Integrated Delivery System: A group of physicians and other health care practitioners, hospitals, and other health care entities who agree to provide all required services to a defined community or population.

Intermediate Care Facilities: A facility which provides care for a patient which is more than what could be provided for in the home, but less than what is provided in hospitals or skilled nursing facilities.

JCAHO: Joint Commission on Accreditation of Healthcare Organizations (see meaning)

Joint Commission for Healthcare Organizations: Organization responsible for accrediting hospitals and other health care organizations; also responsible for developing and revising quality standards.

LOS	Length of stay
LTC	Long term care (see meaning)

Long Term Care: Assistance and care for individuals who are unable to perform normal activities of daily living. May be provided to a patient with a temporary disability or care provided for patients with chronic disabilities. The goal is to help a patient be as independent as possible. Long-term care may be provided in a variety of settings such as a nursing facility, a rehabilitation center, or a psychiatric facility.

MCO	Managed care organization (see meaning)

Malpractice: The improper, injurious, or negligent treatment of a patient.

Managed Care Organization: A generic term that encompasses any type of health care entity which attempts to provide quality patient care in a cost-effective manner. It may include prepaid capitation or managed fee-for-service health care.

Medicaid: A federal program administered and operated by participating states which provide comprehensive health care services for eligible low income persons. The program's costs are shared by state and federal governments.

Medicare Part A: A federal entitlement health insurance program for people 65 and older and some other eligible persons; pays for hospitalizations.

Medicare Part B: Supplementary Medical Insurance offered by federal government which helps pay for physician charges, physician-ordered supplies, outpatient charges, etc. Patient must pay deductible and monthly premium.

"Medigap": Also known as Medicare Supplement Policy. A policy which can be purchased by eligible Medicare insured persons guaranteeing that a health plan will pay a policyholder's deductible and copayment and other specified services not covered by Medicare.

Multihospital system: Two or more hospitals which are owned, leased, or managed by the same corporation or institution to improve economies of scale and to offer a wider spectrum of care

| NCQA | National Committee for Quality Assurance (see meaning) |
| NIH | National Institute of Health |

National Committee for Quality Assurance: Organization which accredits managed care organizations and is responsible for revising HEDIS.

| OBRA | Omnibus Budget and Reconciliation Act |
| OSHA | Occupational Safety and Health Act |

Outcomes: Any consequence of health care, but particularly changes in health status, changes in knowledge or behavior that will affect health status, and patient satisfaction.

Outcomes Assessment: Evaluating the effectiveness of medical interventions on patient outcomes for specific clinical conditions.

Outliers: Refers in health care to a hospital stay that is unusually long in length of stay (day outlier) or unusually expensive in costs (cost outlier); results in extra payment for the hospital above the standard DRG rate. Can also refer to physician provider groups that use an abnormally high or low volume of resources.

Outpatient clinic: A hospital facility which provides primary and/or specialty care services to individuals not admitted as inpatients.

Outpatients: An individual who receives health care services without being admitted to a hospital.

PHO	Physician-Hospital Organizations (see meaning)
PHS	Public Health Service
POS	Point-of-service (see meaning)
PPO	Preferred Provider Organization (see meaning)
PPS	Prospective Payment System (see meaning)
PRO	Peer Review Organization (see meaning)
PSRO	Professional Standards Review Organization (see meaning)

Peer Review Organization: An entity established by TEFRA in 1982 which is contracted by HCFA to perform utilization-oriented activities including review of the necessity and appropriateness of admissions, transfers, and discharges and review of the quality of care provided to Medicare beneficiaries.

Physician-Hospital Organization: A legal entity established by one or more hospitals and physician practice groups to offer health care services to a purchaser, such as an industry or insurance company for a contracted payment.

Point-of-service: A type of health maintenance organization which permits the enrollee to obtain care outside of the network of providers of the HMO but at a slightly higher amount for the service.

Preferred Provider Organization: A type of managed care organization in which providers render services to enrollees and are paid fee-for-service, but at discounted fees. Financial incentive is provided to the enrollee to use the network providers, although enrollees may use out-of-network providers for higher out-of-pocket fees.

Primary care: "The provision of integrated, accessible, health care services by clinicians who are accountable for addressing a large majority of personal health care needs, developing a sustained partnership with patients, and practicing in the context of family and community" (Institute of Medicine, 1994, p.16).

Professional Standards Review Organization: An entity established in 1972 to review the quality and appropriateness of care provided to Medicare patients. Its goal was to contain costs, but it was not effective and was disbanded. It was replaced by PROs.

Prospective Payment System: A system of reimbursement which pays a specified amount for health services based on a formula, often using DRGs. This system reimburses health care providers on the specified rate rather than on actual costs incurred. It is an attempt to place the hospital at financial risk and therefore eliminate unnecessary procedures.

Provider: A physician, hospital, health care facility, or any individual or group of individuals who provide a health care service

QA   Quality Assurance; Quality Assessment (see meanings)

Quality Assessment: The measurement of quality at a given point in time with no attempt to improve quality.

Quality Assurance: A formal set of activities and mechanisms to review, measure and evaluate patient care to make certain it meets or is improved to an acceptable level.

RBRVS   Resource-Based Relative Value Scale (see meaning)

Resource-Based Relative Value Scale: A reimbursement mechanism for physicians introduced by HCFA based primarily on time and resources expended while treating Medicare patients.

Risk Management: A program which initiates activities intended to identify areas of risk and potential loss, seeks to reduce or eliminate that risk, and plans for loss funding and risk financing.

SNF   Skilled Nursing Facility (see meaning)
SSI   Supplemental Security Income (see meaning)

Secondary Care: Specialized medical care provided in hospitals or outpatient settings that requires more complex equipment and the services of a specialist.

Social Security Act of 1935: Established grants-in-aid from the federal government to states, some of which were to aid state and local health departments and to provide maternal and child health services.

Staff Model HMO: A type of HMO which employs physicians to provide services for enrolled patients. Payment is given to HMO which pays physicians salaries and bonuses through incentive programs.

Supplemental Security Income: Federal income support for the aged, the blind, and the disabled who meet eligibility requirements. Qualifies recipients to also receive Medicaid.

TEFRA Tax Equity and Fiscal Responsibility Act of 1982 which converted Medicare reimbursement from a cost-based system to a prospective payment system based on DRGs.

    TQM   Total Quality Management

Tertiary Care: Specialized medical care rendered in inpatient settings by specialists using sophisticated technology. Includes the most complex services such as transplantation, burn treatment, and open heart surgery.

Third-party Payment: Reimbursement for health care service paid by an insurance carrier or government but not by the patient.

Title V- Maternal and Child Health: Federal grants given to states to promote the health of mothers and children, first granted in 1935 and then expanded in 1965.

Title XVIII of Social Security Act: Amendment to Social Security Act Enacting Medicare.

Title XIX of Social Security Act: Amendment to Social Security Act Enacting Medicaid.

    UCDS   Uniform Clinical Data Set (see meaning)
    UHDDS   Uniform Hospital Discharge Data Set (see meaning)
    UR   Utilization Review (see meaning)

Uniform Clinical Data Set: A database which provides detailed clinical information on Medicare discharged patients allowing HCFA to select patient cases for quality improvement review. Between 200 and 350 data elements are captured for each record.

Uniform Hospital Discharge Data Set: The minimum common core of data which is required to be collected on individual hospital discharges for Medicare and Medicaid patients by the Department of Health and Human Services. A minimum of fourteen data elements are collected.

VA Health Care System: Veterans Administration Health Care System which provides care for retired, disabled, and other deserving veterans of previous military service.

    WIC   Women and Infant Care (see meaning)

Women and Infant Care: A diet supplement program supported by the US Department of Agriculture.

Workers' Compensation: Provides two benefits for employees injured on the job: cash payment for a portion of wages lost by disability and payment for all or part of necessary medical care.

REFERENCES

Appleby, C. (1995). The trouble with CHINs. *Hospitals and Health Networks, 69* (9): 43.

Graham, N. O. (1995). *Quality in Health Care: Theory, Application, and Evolution.* Gaithersburg, MD: Aspen Publishers.

Huffman, E.K. (1994). *Health Information Management* (10th Edition). Berwyn, IL: Physicians' Record Company.

Institute of Medicine. (1991). *The Computer-Based Patient Record: An Essential Technology for Health Care.* Washington DC: National Academy Press.

Institute of Medicine. (1994). *Defining Primary Care: An Interim Report.* Washington, DC: National Academy Press.

The United Health Care Corporation. (1994). *The Managed Care Resource: The Language of Managed Care and Organized Health Care Systems.* Minnetonka, MN: The United Health Care Corporation.

Williams, S. and Torrens, P. (1993). *Introduction to Health Services* (4th Ed). Albany, NY: Delmar Publishers.

Wolper, L. (1995). *Health Care Administration: Principles, Practices, Structure, and Delivery.* (2nd Ed.). Gaithersburg, MD: Aspen Publishers.

INDEX